BUREAU OF JUSTICE STATISTICS
SOURCEBOOK
OF CRIMINAL JUSTICE STATISTICS - 2003

Edited by

Ann L. Pastore
Kathleen Maguire

Assistant Editors

Jamie L. Flexon
Charles S. Lanier
Thomas P. LeBel
Richard L. Legault
Jack K. Reed
Lisa N. Sacco

Editorial Assistants

Marcy O'Connor
Carol Jordan

The Hindelang Criminal Justice Research Center
University at Albany
State University of New York
Albany, New York 12222

This project is supported by Agreement No. 2005-BJ-R-005 awarded to The Hindelang Criminal Justice Research Center, Albany, New York, by the U.S. Department of Justice and is currently supported by the Bureau of Justice Statistics, U.S. Department of Justice, under the Justice System Improvement Act of 1979. The project, entitled "Utilization of Criminal Justice Statistics," is directed by Kathleen Maguire and Ann L. Pastore, and is monitored for the Bureau of Justice Statistics by Rhonda Keith. Points of view or opinions stated in this document are those of the editors and do not necessarily represent the official position or policies of the U.S. Department of Justice.

The Bureau of Justice Statistics authorizes any persons to reproduce, publish, translate, or otherwise use all or any part of the copyrighted material in this publication, with the exception of those items indicating that they are copyrighted by or reprinted by permission of any source other than The Hindelang Criminal Justice Research Center.

Copyright 2005 by The Hindelang Criminal Justice Research Center

U.S. Department of Justice
Office of Justice Programs
Bureau of Justice Statistics
NCJ 208756

U.S. DEPARTMENT OF JUSTICE

Bureau of Justice Statistics

Lawrence A. Greenfeld
Director

SUGGESTED CITATION

Ann L. Pastore and Kathleen Maguire, eds., *Sourcebook of Criminal Justice Statistics 2003*. U.S. Department of Justice, Bureau of Justice Statistics. Washington, DC: USGPO, 2005.

Library of Congress Cataloging in Publication Data

United States. Department of Justice, Bureau of Justice Statistics.
    Sourcebook of Criminal Justice Statistics 2003, by Ann L. Pastore (and others).

"NCJ 208756"
    1. Criminal statistics--United States. 2. Criminal justice, administration of--United States--Statistics. 3. Corrections--United States--Statistics.
    I. Author. II. Title.

Foreword

Sourcebook's original goal was to be the most comprehensive single source of quality criminal justice statistical information in the United States. This volume - number 31 - and the Sourcebook website continue to fulfill that goal. Yet, while guiding principals stay constant, technology moves on. In 1973, printing Sourcebook was the only option. The revolution in the delivery of information brought about by the Internet was not even imagined.

In 2003 BJS commissioned the first prospective study of Sourcebook in its 30-year history. This study took 18 months to look at Sourcebook's users, mission, and future. (You can read the executive summary of the study findings at the end of this volume.) BJS learned that the functions of a statistical compendium remain valid. However, for Sourcebook to preserve its success in a world dominated by the Internet, its essentials must be based on electronic technology and good human-computer interaction. In assessing the usability of the Sourcebook website, which now largely displays the printed volume online, the study concluded that many of the features of the printed document did not work well on the web. In addition, users demand new capacities that only the web can provide.

Based on study findings, the excellent staff at the Hindelang Criminal Justice Research Center have drawn a blueprint of improvements to the Sourcebook website. To bring the Sourcebook into the 21st century, they need to focus all of their resources on these improvements. While this volume will be the last printed edition, the Sourcebook will continue to be the most comprehensive single source of quality criminal justice statistical information in the United States via a vastly improved website designed to meet the needs of current and future users.

The focus of the new design will be to make finding information easier. A new search engine, enhanced searching features, and an improved index are priorities. Trend tables, freed from the confines of the printed page, will cover as much data as are available. More links to original data and documents will open to users all the details for evaluating and understanding information. Unlike the restriction to current tables on the existing site, the new site will add tables from past editions. In the future Sourcebook will apply new technologies to speed the release of data, no longer lagging behind the original sources.

I want to thank all of the people who participated in the Sourcebook study and the recent BJS customer survey. We have heard what you want and are taking steps to make that happen. We are very excited about the prospects. As the delivery mechanism changes to benefit our customers, the Sourcebook will continue to provide quality statistics.

Lawrence A. Greenfeld
Director
Bureau of Justice Statistics

Visit the *Sourcebook* World Wide Website

http://www.albany.edu/sourcebook/

For your information

This is the 31st annual *Sourcebook of Criminal Justice Statistics*. As in past editions, nationwide data of interest to the criminal justice community are brought together in a single volume.

The objective of *Sourcebook* is to compile information from a variety of sources and to make it accessible to a wide audience. Over the course of *Sourcebook*'s history, technological developments have changed the manner in which statistical data were collected, stored, and analyzed. Over the more recent past, technological advances have changed how information is disseminated and how users research their areas of interest.

To better serve our users, a move to an all-electronic *Sourcebook* is being made and print editions will no longer be produced. The current website is being redesigned to make data retrieval easier and to include features that are not possible to include in a print edition because of the constraints of the page and the length of such documents. For example, individual data tables over time will be included, enhanced searching features will make finding relevant information easier, and more links to original data and documents will be provided.

At the same time, readers should be assured that the tables presented in this and past editions will be reflected on the website. Users will still be able to find the tables they require, plus additional useful references. Our hope is that the expanded *Sourcebook* website will improve and broaden our ability to meet the needs of current and future users.

Statistical information about crime and criminal justice in the United States is published by hundreds of public and private agencies, academic institutions, research organizations, public opinion polling firms, and other groups. All levels of government collect and disseminate such data.

In order to be included in *Sourcebook*, the data must meet two standards. First, the information must be national in scope or of nationwide relevance. Nearly all the data presented are nationwide in scope and, where possible, they are displayed by regions, States, and cities to increase their value for local decision-makers and for comparative analyses. Data available for limited groups of cities, States, or jurisdictions are included if they pertain to a topic of major concern. Second, the data must be methodologically sound with respect to sampling procedures, data collection methods, estimation procedures, and reliability of the information.

Organization of the Sourcebook

This book is divided into six sections:

1 Characteristics of the criminal justice systems presents data on the number and types of criminal justice agencies and employees, criminal justice expenditures, and workload of agency personnel. It also includes tables that summarize, State by State, the statutory, regulatory, or administrative characteristics and practices of selected criminal justice agencies.

2 Public attitudes toward crime and criminal justice-related topics presents the results of nationwide public opinion polls on such matters as fear of victimization, the death penalty, gun control, drug use, and ratings of law enforcement and judicial system performance.

3 Nature and distribution of known offenses presents data from several indicators of the extent of illegal activities. They include surveys of individuals and households that may have been victims of crime, self-report data on drug use or participation in other illegal activities, and law enforcement agency counts of offenses reported to them.

4 Characteristics and distribution of persons arrested includes tabulations of arrestees by age, sex, race, and area; proportions of known crimes cleared by arrests; and counts of illegal goods and assets seized.

5 Judicial processing of defendants presents data on the number of adults and juveniles processed through the courts and on the characteristics, dispositions, and sentences of defendants.

6 Persons under correctional supervision presents data about persons on probation and parole, persons in local jails, population counts in State and Federal prisons, and characteristics of State and Federal prisoners. The section also includes data on offenders executed and offenders currently under sentence of death.

Annotated sources and list of publishers

Publications from which tables have been selected for presentation in *Sourcebook* are described in annotations that precede the appendices. The annotations include standard bibliographic information, periodicity of publication, dates of tabular information appearing in the publication (many sources, even some annual reports, contain data for a number of years), a brief summary of the publication's contents, and a list of *Sourcebook* tables taken from the sources. Addresses of the publishers follow the annotations.

Explanatory appendices

For sources that use complex survey methods or that require a long list of definitions of terms, explanatory text is presented in the *Sourcebook*. These appendices add information or clarify the data presented, but readers should consult the original sources for more detailed explanations.

Reliability of the data

Data in this book are no more reliable or complete than the sources from which they are taken. Responsibility for the quality of data is borne by the original source; responsibility for its selection and presentation rests with the *Sourcebook* staff.

Reporting periods

The aim for each edition of the *Sourcebook* is to combine the most recent data available with earlier data to show trends. Unfortunately, many reports are based on data already several years old at the time of publication.

It is sometimes impossible or inappropriate to compare data from different sources. For example, data in one source may be expressed only in fiscal years whereas those in another are expressed only in calendar years. It is best to check a table's explanatory note to verify the precise periods covered by data presented. Readers should exercise caution when combining or comparing data from different sources or in examining data from the same source over time.

Table preparation

Updating. For tables from annual data collections, such as the FBI's ***Crime in the United States*** and BJS's ***Criminal Victimization in the United States***, updating involves replacing older with newer data, taking care to note any changes in methodology or reporting procedures that should be brought to the reader's attention.

For tables from nonannual and special publications (such as surveys, research reports, and public opinion polls), updating and expansion involves searches for new or more recent data. Sometimes, data from previous editions of the *Sourcebook* are retained, either alone or along with more recent data.

Bodies of tables. The bodies of most *Sourcebook* tables appear exactly as in the original sources. This presentation is consistent with the *Sourcebook*'s main function--to bring together data from diverse sources for presentation as originally published, rather than to transform or recompute the original data.

However, the *Sourcebook* staff has:
(a) <u>constructed</u> some tables based on printed narrative or machine-readable data from the source; and
(b) <u>adapted</u> some tables with only nonsubstantive changes from the source.

Notes. *Sourcebook* tables carry three types of explanatory and cautionary notes:

(1) Notes that follow tables and begin with "Note:" are written by the *Sourcebook* staff from information in the original source.

(2) Some are brief notes in parentheses "( )" just above the table body. Most of these notes repeat information from the source table, but a few are added by the *Sourcebook* staff.

(3) Some are footnotes reprinted as they appeared in the original source. Most of these footnotes are keyed to specific table entries or to variables that require explanation.

A note on definitions of terms

Because the *Sourcebook* includes data from so many sources, similar or identical terms sometimes have different meanings when used in different sources. For example, the precise meaning of terms such as "case," "caseload," "rate," and "race/ethnicity," differs among sources. To clarify the meaning of terms as they are used by various sources, definitions are provided in notes on tables and in appendices to which table notes refer.

However, in a compilation such as this it is impossible to provide an exhaustive list of definitions and explanations for each table that will satisfy the needs of all readers. Users with strong interest in particular tables are advised to consult the original source for a fuller explanation of data collection procedures, data exclusions, definitions of terms, and other details.

Cross-references to last year's edition

The table list (which follows the table of contents) indicates whether last year's edition contained exactly the same table or an equivalent table with data from an earlier year.

Your input requested

Your critical comments and suggested changes will help us to improve future editions of the *Sourcebook*.

Please tell us about appropriate sources of criminal justice statistics you believe we have overlooked. Of special interest are sources of data--preferably, but not necessarily, national in scope--that have not been drawn upon for this edition.

It would help us to know for what purposes you have used the *Sourcebook* and how much it has helped in achieving those purposes.

A special page for your comments and suggestions appears at the end of the book, just after the index. Please use this self-mailer to give us the benefit of your comments and suggestions for a more useful *Sourcebook*.

Guide to symbols used in tables

The following symbols have been used uniformly, unless otherwise noted in specific tables:

0	Represents the quantity zero or rounds to less than half the unit of measurement shown.
NA	Data not separately enumerated, tabulated, or otherwise available.
X	Figure not applicable because column heading, stub line, or other contingencies make an entry impossible or meaningless.
B	Not computed because the base figure is too small from which to generate a derived figure that meets statistical standards for reliability or figure does not otherwise meet standards of precision set by the Source.
( )	Figure in parentheses is the base on which percentages or other statistics in the table column or row have been calculated. A lower case letter in parentheses in a table cell is a footnote entry.
--	No entry in original source; reason not differentiated in original source.
Y	Indicates that the relevant attribute is present.

Where a different symbol meaning is used in order to maintain clarity within the context of a given table, this is noted for that particular table.

Acknowledgments

Sourcebook has always been the result of the efforts of many people and this 31st edition is no different. The individuals who worked with us this year are thanked below. In addition, we would like to extend our gratitude, once again, to the more than 65 people that have been part of the project since the first edition, the many staffers at the Bureau of Justice Statistics with whom we have worked through the years, as well as the countless contributors who make it possible for us to present the array of criminal justice statistics included in each edition.

First, we would like to recognize the staff of the Utilization of Criminal Justice Statistics Project and the Hindelang Criminal Justice Research Center.

Marcy O'Connor, senior Editorial Assistant, has responsibilities that range from ordering sources to organizing requests for permission to reprint to checking revisions on final copies. She also maintains our library of source materials. Her dedication and willingness to help out with all aspects of production make her an indispensable member of our staff. Carol Jordan, longtime Editorial Assistant, retired from *Sourcebook* this year. We thank her for her good work and wish her the best as she enjoys her new freedom. We miss her, but are certain that she will maintain a connection to the project (and continue to share her travel photos with us).

The Utilization Project continues to benefit enormously from the bright and talented graduate students here at the School of Criminal Justice. Our research team for this edition has been Charlie Lanier, Jack Reed, Jamie Flexon, Rik Legault, Tom LeBel, and Lisa Sacco. It is our pleasure and good fortune to work along side these talented and dedicated individuals.

Congratulations to our most senior researcher, Charlie Lanier, who after many years of service to the *Sourcebook* project completed his doctoral degree in May 2004. Charlie has moved on to pursue a research career but his first post-graduate position is with the Hindelang Center and the School of Criminal Justice so he continues to be a frequent visitor and good friend to the project.

We are grateful for the support of Arleen deGonzague, Administrative Associate, and Andrea Downey, secretary, at the Hindelang Center. Through their quiet hard work and diligence they handle countless administrative tasks. For this, and for the problems they solve that we don't even know about, they have our appreciation.

Thanks go to our sponsoring agency, the Bureau of Justice Statistics and, specifically, to Rhonda Keith, Tom Hester, and Marianne Zawitz for their ongoing assistance and guidance.

The *Sourcebook* staff relies on many individuals in State and Federal justice agencies, research centers, universities, and other organizations who produce criminal justice statistical information. These people assist us in many ways, including advising us of new sources of criminal justice data, providing prepublication copies of materials, and answering questions from our editorial team about terminology and data collection procedures. The importance their cooperation cannot be overstated.

This year, the following individuals were particularly helpful and we acknowledge their generous assistance: Gwendolyn Coleman and William R. Burchill Jr., Administrative Office of the United States Courts; Lloyd Johnston, Jerald Bachman, Patrick O'Malley, Ginger Maggio, and Adam Burke, the Monitoring the Future Project; Allan Sobol and David Richert, American Judicature Society; Lydia Saad, The Gallup Organization, Inc.; Vivian Faden, National Institute on Alcohol Abuse and Alcoholism; Sue Allison, Federal Bureau of Prisons; Patrick R. Gartin and Philip A. Jessar, Drug Enforcement Administration; Janie Pitcock, PRIDE Surveys; Bonnie Hughes, Harris Interactive, Inc.; Janice Windau, Bureau of Labor Statistics; Susan M. Kuzma, Office of the Pardon Attorney; Edgar N. Brown, Witness Immunity Unit; and Emily C. Spadoni, Office of the Solicitor General.

Finally, we wish to thank the many *Sourcebook* users for their support. All inquiries, suggestions, and comments are welcome; please fill out the evaluation form at the end of this book or contact the Editors at the Hindelang Criminal Justice Research Center, State University of New York, University at Albany, 135 Western Avenue, Albany, New York 12222, (518) 442-5608; or e-mail us at: asksb@albany.edu.

Contents

For your information iii

Guide to symbols used in tables iv

Acknowledgments v

Table list viii

Section 1
Characteristics of the criminal justice systems 1

Expenditures for criminal justice activities 2
Corrections expenditures 12
Federal budget authorities for criminal justice activities 15
Federal drug control funding 17
Edward Byrne Law Enforcement Assistance funds 19
Employment and payroll for criminal justice activities 20
State and local police employees and agencies 36
Police agencies in each State 43
Local police departments and sheriffs' offices 47
Local police and sheriffs, race, ethnicity, and sex 48
Local police and sheriffs' offices, education and training requirements 49
Local police and sheriffs' offices, budgets and salaries 50
Local police and sheriffs' offices, sidearms and nonlethal weapons authorized 51
Community policing 52
School resource officers 52
Police departments in large cities 53
Female and minority police officers 53
State law enforcement agencies 56
Tribal law enforcement agencies 59
Employment, payroll, and personnel expenditures for law enforcement 60
Salaries for police officers and other law enforcement personnel 64
Federal law enforcement officers and agencies 69
Drug Enforcement Administration, budget and staff 72
U.S. Marshals Service, workload, budget, and staff 73
U.S. attorneys, personnel and work hours 74
Appropriations, salaries, and personnel for the Federal judiciary 74
Characteristics of Presidential appointees to Federal courts 75
Criminal cases filed per judgeship in U.S. District Courts 77
Duties performed by magistrate judges in U.S. District Courts 79
Prosecutors in State courts 80

Salaries and selection process for State court judges 82
Utilization of petit and grand jurors in U.S. District Courts 88
Jury fees in State and Federal courts 89
Investigative reports by Federal probation officers 90
Jails and jail staff 91
State, Federal, and private correctional facilities and staff 95
Private jails and correctional facilities 96
Federal Bureau of Prisons facilities and staff 97
Education programs in prisons and jails 100
Background checks for firearm transfers 101
Statutory provisions related to alcohol use and driving 102

Section 2
Public attitudes toward crime and criminal justice-related topics 105

Most important problems for country, government, and teenagers 106
Problems and fear in schools 109
Drug testing and locker searches in schools 111
Public confidence in institutions 112
Confidence in the criminal justice system 113
Confidence in the police 113
Confidence in the U.S. Supreme Court 115
Confidence in the government to protect citizens from terrorism 119
Ethics of various occupations, lawyers, and police 119
Police, performance and fairness 121
Police use of force, brutality 122
Racial profiling 126
Increased law enforcement powers 126
Approaches to lowering the crime rate 126
Fear of terrorism 127
Terrorism and civil liberties 127
Perceptions of crime and safety in neighborhoods and at home 127
Responses to concern about crime 132
Level of spending for the problems of crime and drugs 133
Progress coping with drugs 138
Fairness of criminal justice system 139
Rehabilitation 139
Severity of local courts 140
Treatment of juveniles who commit violent crime 143
Penalty for murder 143
Death penalty 144
Death penalty as a deterrent 148
Gun ownership and use 149
Gun control policies 151
Legalization of marijuana 157
High school seniors' attitudes:
    Selected social problems 161
    Performance of selected institutions 163
    Performance of the police 164
    Performance of the courts and justice system 165
Perceptions of the harmfulness of drug and alcohol use 167

Students' perceptions of availability of drugs 173
Students disapproving of drug use 174
High school seniors' attitudes toward legalization of marijuana 177
College freshmen attitudes:
    Legalization of marijuana 178
    Abortion 178
    The courts 179
    Capital punishment 179
    Homosexual relations 181
    Gun control 181
Doctor-assisted suicide 181
Pornography 182
Homosexual relations 184
Abortion 185
Environment 186

Section 3
Nature and distribution of known offenses 187

Personal and property victimization 188
Violent and personal victimization 191
Victim-offender relationship in violent victimization 196
Weapon use in personal victimization 198
Self-protective measures employed by victims 199
Rate of property victimizations 200
Households experiencing crime 203
Characteristics of lone-offender victimizations 204
Characteristics of multiple-offender victimizations 205
Reporting and not reporting victimization to police 207
High school seniors:
    Victimization experiences 211
    Victimization experiences at school 217
    Self-reported delinquency 222
    Involvement in traffic violations 232
    Involvement in traffic violations while under the influence of drugs 234
    Involvement in traffic accidents 236
Students:
    Reporting problem behaviors and delinquency 238
    Delinquency and victimization experiences at school 240
    Self-reported drug and alcohol use 244
College students' and young adults' self-reported drug and alcohol use 253
College students' experiences of binge drinking, violence, and harassment 258
Drug and alcohol use in the U.S. population 262
Drug and alcohol use among military personnel 264
Drug abuse-related emergency department episodes 267
Alcohol use and frequency of use 270
Alcohol and drugs as family problems 272
Drinking and driving 274
Fatalities in alcohol-related motor vehicle crashes 275
Offenses known to police 278

Violent and property crime in U.S. cities 290
Average loss incurred for selected offenses 297
Bias-motivated (hate) crimes 297
Offenses in Federal parks 300
Murders 301
Murder offenders and victims 303
Murder and other violence by intimate partners 311
Murders resulting from Sept. 11, 2001 terrorist attacks 312
Sniper attacks 313
Workplace violence 314
Suicide 316
Robberies 318
Aggravated assaults 319
Burglaries 319
Larceny-thefts 320
Motor vehicle thefts 321
Bank fraud and embezzlement investigations 321
Violations of Federal bank robbery statutes 322
Law enforcement officers killed and assaulted 324
Arson: fires, deaths, and property loss 335
Bombing incidents 337
Terrorist incidents 340
Criminal acts related to air transportation 342

Section 4
Characteristics and distribution of persons arrested 343

Number and rate of arrests, national estimates 344
Arrests in each State 348
Offense charged 353
Age of persons arrested 354
Sex of persons arrested 356
Race of persons arrested 358
Arrests in cities 361
Arrests in suburban areas 365
Arrests in rural counties 369
Arrest rates for violent crimes 373
Arrest rates for property crimes 374
Offenses cleared by arrest 375
Clearances from arrest of persons under 18 years of age 379
Juveniles taken into police custody 382
Alcohol-related arrests 383
Drug-related arrests 385
Drug and alcohol use by adult male arrestees 386
Arrests for Federal offenses 388
Drug seizures by Federal agencies 390
Seizures of marijuana operations and illegal drug laboratories 391
Arrests and assets seized by the Drug Enforcement Administration 392
Drug and property seizures by the U.S. Customs Service 394
Value of asset forfeitures by U.S. attorneys 396
Deportable aliens located and removed 396

Section 5
Judicial processing of defendants 399

Requests for immunity by Federal prosecutors 400
Court-authorized interception of wire, oral, or electronic communications 400
Grand jury proceedings and cases filed and disposed of by U.S. attorneys 403
Cases filed, terminated, and pending in U.S. District Courts 405
Defendants detained by U.S. District Courts 412
Pretrial release and detention of defendants in U.S. District Courts 414
Defendants prosecuted, convicted, and sentenced in U.S. District Courts 418
Type and length of sentences imposed in U.S. District Courts 420
Application of U.S. Sentencing Commission guidelines 432
Citizens and non-citizens sentenced under U.S. Sentencing Commission guidelines 439
Departures from U.S. Sentencing Commission guidelines 440
Dispositions and sentences of drug law violators in U.S. District Courts 441
Convictions resulting from arrests by the Drug Enforcement Administration 444
Antitrust cases filed in U.S. District Courts 444
Length of time to disposition of cases in U.S. District Courts 445
Felony cases and convictions in State courts 449
Type of sentences imposed by State courts 451
Sentence lengths imposed by State courts 451
Felons sentenced to additional penalties by State courts 452
Length of time to sentencing in State courts 453
Felony defendants in large counties 453
Pretrial processing of felony defendants in large counties 455
Conviction and sentencing of felony defendants in large counties 457
Characteristics of juvenile offenders and case outcomes 459
Prisoner petitions filed in U.S. District Courts 461
Appeals filed, terminated, and pending in U.S. Courts of Appeals 462
Activities of the U.S. Supreme Court 464
Cases filed, disposed, and pending in the U.S. Supreme Court 465
Writ of certiorari petitions to the U.S. Supreme Court 466
Cases argued in the U.S. Supreme Court 467
Executive clemency applications 468
Arrests and convictions handled by the U.S. Postal Inspection Service 469
Prosecutions and convictions for violations of immigration and nationality laws 470
Immigration offenders processed 472
Abuse of public office cases 473
Courts-martial cases of the U.S. armed forces 474

Section 6
Persons under correctional supervision 477

Adults under correctional supervision 478
Adults on probation 480
Federal offenders under community supervision 481
Persons under supervision of the Federal Probation System 482
Federal probationers terminating supervision 484
Juveniles in residential custody facilities 485
Adults in prison and jail, trends 488
Jail inmates, number and confinement status 489
Jail inmates, characteristics 493
Jail inmates, offenses 494
Jail inmates, drug and alcohol use 496
Jail inmates with HIV 499
AIDS-related and other deaths among jail inmates 499
Prison population growth 500
Prisoners in State, Federal, and private correctional facilities 502
Prisoners in private facilities and local jails 504
Characteristics of prisoners 505
Prisoners possessing firearms during offense 506
Prisoners under age 18 507
Female prisoners 508
Noncitizens in State and Federal prisons 509
Time served by State prisoners 510
Educational attainment and participation in education programs for prisoners, jail inmates, and probationers 511
Recidivism of State prisoners 513
Number and characteristics of Federal prisoners 517
Federal prisoners serving time for drug offenses 519
Time served by Federal prisoners 520
Immigration offenders in Federal prison 522
Bureau of Immigration and Customs Enforcement detainees 522
Persons in drug and alcoholism treatment facilities 523
State sex offender registries 524
Military correctional facilities 525
Adults on parole 525
Offenders returning to Federal prison 527
Discharges from Federal supervised release and parole 528
Mental health treatment in prisons 530
Prisoners with HIV/AIDS 532
Deaths and AIDS-related deaths among sentenced prisoners 533
Trend data for murders, death sentences, and executions 535
Prisoners under sentence of death 535

Hispanic and female prisoners under sentence of death 538
State and Federal prisoners executed 539
Methods of execution in States 543

Annotated list of sources 545

Addresses of publishers 561

Appendices 563

    1   Justice Expenditure and Employment Data Survey methodology and definitions of terms 564

    2   *The Municipal Year Book 2004* Definitions of terms and survey response rates 569

    3   *Crime in the United States* Definitions of terms 571

    4   Census of Jails, Annual Survey of Jails, and Survey of Inmates in Local Jails Methodology and survey sampling procedures 574

    5   Public opinion survey sampling procedures 576

    6   Monitoring the Future Survey methodology and definitions of terms 581

    7   National Survey on Drug Use and Health Survey methodology 587

    8   National Crime Victimization Survey Survey methodology and definitions of terms 589

    9   Drug Abuse Warning Network Methodology, estimation procedures, and data limitations 593

    10 Arrestee Drug Abuse Monitoring Methodology and survey sampling information 595

    11 Federal Justice Statistics Program Methodology and definitions of terms 597

    12 National Judicial Reporting Program Survey sampling procedures and definitions of terms 601

    13 State Court Processing Statistics Methodology, definitions of terms, and crimes within offense categories 603

    14 Juvenile Court Statistics Methodology, definitions of terms, and offenses within categories 605

    15 *Correctional Populations in the United States* Survey methodology, definitions of terms, and jurisdictional explanatory notes 608

Index 611

Evaluation form 635

Positioning *Sourcebook of Criminal Justice Statistics* for the 21st Century
Executive Summary 637

Table list

For users who wish to compare data in this edition with that in the *2002 Sourcebook*, the numbers for equivalent tables in the *2002 Sourcebook* are shown in parentheses. Table numbers marked with an asterisk (*) contain identical data in the 2002 and 2003 editions; these tables have been repeated from 2002 to 2003, with possible changes in titles and notation for accuracy and consistency within this edition. The table numbers within parentheses and without asterisks are those for which the most recent data are presented in (generally) the same format as in the 2002 edition. Tables for which dashes (--) appear have no comparable table in the 2002 edition.

Tables

Section 1
Characteristics of the criminal justice systems 1

1.1 Justice system direct and intergovernmental expenditures, by level of government, United States, fiscal years 1982-2001 (1.1) 2

1.2 Justice system direct and intergovernmental expenditures, by type of activity and level of government, United States, fiscal years 1980-99 (1.2*) 3

1.3 Justice system direct and intergovernmental expenditures, by level of government and type of activity, United States, fiscal year 2000 (1.3) 4

1.4 Justice system direct and intergovernmental expenditures, by level of government and type of activity, United States, fiscal year 2001 (--) 5

1.5 Justice system direct expenditures, by level of government, United States, fiscal years 1982-2001 (1.4) 5

1.6 Direct expenditures for State and local justice system activities, by type of activity and level of government, fiscal year 2000 (1.5) 6

1.7 Justice system per capita expenditures, by type of activity, United States, fiscal years 1980-99, and 2001 (1.6) 11

1.8 State and local justice system per capita expenditures, by type of activity and State, fiscal year 2000 (1.7) 11

1.9 Direct expenditures for correctional activities of State governments and percent distribution, by type of activity, United States, fiscal years 1980-99 (1.8*) 12

1.10 Direct expenditures for correctional activities of State governments, by type of activity and State, fiscal year 2000 (1.9) 13

1.11 Direct expenditures for correctional activities of State governments, by type of activity and State, fiscal year 2001 (--) 14

1.12 Federal criminal justice budget authorities, fiscal years 2003 (actual) and 2004-2009 (estimated) (1.10) 15

1.13 Allocation of Office of Justice Programs' funds, by type of budget activity, fiscal years 1990-2001 (1.11*) 16

1.14 Federal drug control budget, by function, fiscal years 1996-2005 (1.12) 17

1.15 Federal drug control funding, by agency, fiscal years 2003 (final), 2004 (enacted), and 2005 (requested) (1.13) 18

1.16 Allocation of Edward Byrne Memorial State and Local Law Enforcement Assistance Program funds, by jurisdiction, fiscal years 2001, 2002, and 2003 (1.14) 19

1.17 Justice system employment and payroll, by level of government and type of activity, United States, March 2001 (1.15) 20

1.18 Justice system payroll, by level of government, United States, October 1982-95, and March 1997-99 and 2001 (1.16) 21

1.19 State and local justice system payroll, by type of activity and level of government, March 2001 (1.17) 22

1.20 Justice system employment, by level of government, United States, October 1982-95, and March 1997-99 and 2001 (1.18) 27

1.21 Justice system employment, by type of activity and level of government, United States, October 1980-95 and March 1997-99 (1.19*) 28

1.22 State and local justice system full-time equivalent employment, by type of activity and level of government, March 2001 (1.20) 30

1.23 Rate (per 10,000 population) of State and local justice system full-time equivalent employment, by type of activity and State, March 2000 (1.21) 35

1.24 Rate (per 10,000 population) of State and local justice system full-time equivalent employment, by type of activity and State, March 2001 (--) 35

1.25 State and local sworn police full-time equivalent employment and percent of total police employment, by level of government, United States, October 1980-95 and March 1997-99 (1.22*) 36

1.26 State and local police protection full-time equivalent employment and payroll, by type of employee and level of government, March 2000 (1.23*) 37

1.27 State and local law enforcement agencies and employees, by type of agency, United States, 2000 (1.24*) 42

1.28 State and local law enforcement agencies and full-time employees, by State, 2000 (1.25*) 43

1.29 Local police departments and full-time employees, by State, 2000 (1.26*) 44

1.30 Sheriffs' offices and full-time employees, by State, 2000 (1.27*) 45

1.31 State law enforcement agency full-time employees, by State, 2000 (1.28*) 46

1.32 State and local law enforcement agencies with special jurisdictions and full-time employees, by State, 2000 (1.29*) 47

1.33 Local police departments and full-time personnel, by size of population served, United States, 2000 (1.30*) 47

1.34 Sheriffs' offices and full-time personnel, by size of population served, United States, 2000 (1.31*) 47

1.35 Full-time sworn officers assigned to respond to citizen calls for service in local police departments, by size of population served, United States, 2000 (1.32*) 48

1.36 Full-time sworn officers assigned to respond to citizen calls for service in sheriffs' offices, by size of population served, United States, 2000 (1.33*) 48

1.37 Race, ethnicity, and sex of full-time sworn personnel in local police departments, by size of population served, United States, 2000 (1.34*) 48

1.38 Race, ethnicity, and sex of full-time sworn personnel in sheriffs' offices, by size of population served, United States, 2000 (1.35*) 48

1.39 Minimum educational requirements for new officer recruits in local police departments, by size of population served, United States, 2000 (1.36*) 49

1.40 Minimum educational requirements for new officer recruits in sheriffs' offices, by size of population served, United States, 2000 (1.37*) 49

1.41 Training requirements for new officer recruits in local police departments, by size of population served, United States, 2000 (1.38*) 49

1.42 Training requirements for new officer recruits in sheriffs' offices, by size of population served, United States, 2000 (1.39*) 49

1.43 Average operating budget of local police departments, by size of population served, United States, fiscal year 2000 (1.40*) 50

1.44 Average operating budget of sheriffs' offices, by size of population served, United States, fiscal year 2000 (1.41*) 50

1.45 Average base minimum and maximum annual salaries for selected positions in local police departments, by size of population served, United States, 2000 (1.42*) 50

1.46 Average base minimum and maximum annual salaries for selected positions in sheriffs' offices, by size of population served, United States, 2000 (1.43*) 50

1.47 Semiautomatic sidearms authorized for use by sworn personnel in local police departments, by size of population served, United States, 2000 (1.44*) 51

1.48 Semiautomatic sidearms authorized for use by sworn personnel in sheriffs' offices, by size of population served, United States, 2000 (1.45*) 51

1.49 Nonlethal weapons authorized for use by sworn personnel in local police departments, by size of population served, United States, 2000 (1.46*) 51

1.50 Nonlethal weapons authorized for use by sworn personnel in sheriffs' offices, by size of population served, United States, 2000 (1.47*) 51

1.51 Full-time community policing officers in local police departments, by size of population served, United States, 2000 (1.48*) 52

1.52 Full-time community policing officers in sheriffs' offices, by size of population served, United States, 2000 (1.49*) 52

1.53 Full-time school resource officers in local police departments, by size of population served, United States, 2000 (1.50*) 52

1.54 Full-time school resource officers in sheriffs' offices, by size of population served, United States, 2000 (1.51*) 52

1.55 Full-time employees and sworn personnel in large city police departments, by size of population served, United States, 1990 and 2000 (1.52*) 53

1.56 Female and minority full-time sworn personnel in large city police departments, by size of population served, United States, 1990 and 2000 (1.53*) 53

1.57 Number and rate (per 100,000 residents) of full-time employees and sworn personnel in large city police departments, by size of population served and city, United States, 1990 and 2000 (1.54*) 54

1.58 Female and minority full-time sworn personnel and ratio of minority officers to minority residents in large city police departments, by size of population served and city, United States, 1990 and 2000 (1.55*) 55

1.59 Full-time personnel, sworn officers, officers assigned to respond to calls, officers per 100,000 residents, and percent change in full-time personnel in State law enforcement agencies, by agency, 2000 (1.56) 56

1.60 Sex, race, and ethnicity of full-time sworn personnel in State law enforcement agencies, by agency, 2000 (--) 57

1.61 Starting salaries in State law enforcement agencies, by agency, 2000 (--) 58

1.62 Operating expenditures of State law enforcement agencies by agency, 2000 (--) 58

1.63 Number and rate (per 1,000 residents and per 100 square miles) of full-time sworn personnel, service population, and reservation land area in the 20 largest tribally operated law enforcement agencies, United States, 2000 (1.57*) 59

1.64 Mean number of full-time paid personnel of police departments in cities with populations of 10,000 or more, by population group, geographic division, and metro status, United States, 2003 (1.58) 60

1.65 Mean and per capita police department personnel expenditures in cities with populations of 10,000 or more, by population group, geographic division, and metro status, United States, 2003 (1.59) 60

1.66 Number and rate (per 1,000 inhabitants) of full-time law enforcement employees, by geographic division and population group, on Oct. 31, 2002 (1.60) 61

1.67 Number and rate (per 1,000 inhabitants) of full-time law enforcement officers, by geographic division and population group, on Oct. 31, 2002 (1.61) 62

1.68 Full-time law enforcement employees, by sex and population group, on Oct. 31, 2002 (1.62) 63

1.69 Entrance and maximum salaries, and mean number of years to reach maximum salary, for police officers in cities with populations of 10,000 or more, by population group, geographic division, and metro status, United States, as of Jan. 1, 2003 (1.63) 64

1.70 Mean and median salaries of city chief law enforcement officials, by city population, region, city type, and form of government, United States, July-November 2003 (1.64) 65

1.71 Mean and median salaries of county chief law enforcement officials, by county population, region, metro status, and form of government, United States, July-November 2003 (1.65) 67

1.72 Federal agencies employing 100 or more full-time officers authorized to carry firearms and make arrests, June 2002 (1.66*) 69

1.73 Federal offices of inspector general employing full-time officers authorized to carry firearms and make arrests, June 2002 (1.67*) 69

1.74 Federal officers authorized to carry firearms and make arrests in selected large agencies, by primary State of employment, June 2002 (1.68*) 70

1.75 Characteristics of full-time Federal officers authorized to carry firearms and make arrests in agencies employing 500 or more full-time officers, by agency, June 2002 (1.69*) 71

1.76 Budget and staff of the Drug Enforcement Administration, fiscal years 1972-2005 (1.70) 72

1.77 Workload of the U.S. Marshals Service, by type of activity, fiscal years 1985-2000 (1.71*) 73

1.78 Budget and staff of the U.S. Marshals Service, fiscal years 1954-2000 (1.72*) 74

1.79 Personnel and court-related work hours of U.S. attorneys' offices, United States, 1989-2002 (1.73) 74

1.80 Annual salaries of Federal judges, by judicial office, as of Jan. 1, 2004 (1.74) 74

1.81 Characteristics of Presidential appointees to U.S. Courts of Appeals judgeships, by Presidential administration, 1963-2002 (1.75*) 75

1.82 Characteristics of Presidential appointees to U.S. District Court judgeships, by Presidential administration, 1963-2002 (1.76*) 76

1.83 Felony criminal cases filed per judgeship in U.S. District Courts, by circuit and district, 1983-2003 (1.77) 77

1.84 Duties performed by magistrate judges in U.S. District Courts, 1990, 1997-2003 (1.78) 79

1.85 Personnel in prosecutors' offices, United States, 2001 (1.79*) 80

1.86 Budget for prosecutorial functions in full- and part-time prosecutors' offices, by size of population served, United States, 2001 (1.80*) 80

1.87 Length of service and annual salary of chief prosecutors in full- and part-time prosecutors' offices, by size of population served, United States, 2001 (1.81*) 80

1.88 DNA evidence used by full- and part-time prosecutors' offices, by size of population served, United States, 2001 (1.82*) 80

1.89 Prosecutors' offices serving districts with populations less than 250,000, by size of population served and selected characteristics, United States, 2001 (1.83*) 81

1.90 Salaries of judges of highest, appellate, and general trial courts, by type of court and jurisdiction, as of Oct. 1, 2003 (1.86) 82

1.91 Method of selection and length of initial and retention terms of the highest appellate court justices, by State, as of June 2004 (1.87) 83

1.92 Method of selection and length of initial and retention terms of intermediate appellate court judges in 39 States, as of June 2004 (1.88) 85

1.93 Method of selection and length of initial and retention terms of general jurisdiction court judges, by State and name of court, as of June 2004 (1.89) 86

1.94 Grand jury and grand juror utilization in U.S. District Courts, fiscal years 1988-2003 (1.90) 88

1.95 Petit juror utilization in U.S. District Courts, 1977-2003 (1.91) 88

1.96 Jury fees in State and Federal courts, by jurisdiction, as of June 2003 (1.92*) 89

1.97 Investigative reports by Federal probation officers, by type of investigation, 1980-2003 (1.93) 90

1.98 Number of jails, rated capacity, percent of capacity occupied, and number of inmates per employee, by region and jurisdiction, June 30, 1999 (1.94*) 91

1.99 Jail staff, by occupational category, region, and jurisdiction, June 30, 1999 (1.95*) 92

1.100 Jail staff and correctional officers, by sex, region, and jurisdiction, June 30, 1999 (1.96*) 93

1.101 Jail staff and correctional officers, by race, Hispanic origin, region, and jurisdiction, June 30, 1999 (1.97*) 94

1.102 Federal, State, and private adult correctional facilities, by facility characteristics, United States, 1995 and 2000 (1.98*) 95

1.103 Federal and State adult correctional facilities, by type of facility and facility function, United States, June 30, 2000 (1.99*) 95

1.104 Employees of Federal, State, and private adult correctional facilities, by type of employee and selected characteristics, United States, 1995 and 2000 (1.100*) 96

1.105 Privately operated jails, by selected characteristics, United States, June 30, 1999 (1.101*) 96

1.106 Federal Bureau of Prisons facilities, by selected characteristics, as of Sept. 30, 2003 (1.104) 97

1.107 Characteristics of Federal Bureau of Prisons staff, by race and ethnicity, January 2004 (1.105) 99

1.108 Characteristics of Federal Bureau of Prisons correctional officers, by race and ethnicity, January 2004 (1.106) 99

1.109 Education programs in State, Federal, and private prisons, and in local jails, by type of program, United States, 1995, 1999, 2000 (1.107*) 100

1.110 Estimated number of applications and rejections for firearm transfers, United States, 1999-2003 (1.108) 101

1.111 Reasons for rejection of firearm transfer applications, United States, 1999-2003 (1.109) 101

1.112 Statutory provisions related to alcohol use and driving, by State, as of Jan. 1, 2002 (1.110*) 102

1.113 Statutory provisions requiring blood alcohol concentration tests for victims of fatal traffic accidents, by jurisdiction, as of Jan. 1, 2002 (1.111*) 104

Section 2
Public attitudes toward crime and criminal justice-related topics 105

2.1 Attitudes toward the most important problem facing the country, United States, 1984-2004 (2.1) 106

2.2 Attitudes toward important issues for the government to address, United States, 1993-2004 (2.2) 107

2.3 Teenagers' attitudes toward the most important problem facing people their age, United States, selected years 1999-2004 (2.3) 108

2.4 Attitudes toward the biggest problems facing public schools, by school status, United States, 1988-2003 (2.8) 109

2.5 Students' perceptions of safety at school, by grade level of respondent, 2002-2003 (--) 110

2.6 Students age 12 to 18 reporting fear of school-related victimization, by student characteristics, United States, 1995, 1999, and 2001 (2.9) 110

2.7 Teenagers' perceptions of drug testing and locker searches in their schools, United States, 2003 (--) 111

2.8 Parents' perceptions of safety, drug testing, and locker searches at schools, United States, 2003 (--) 111

2.9 Reported confidence in selected institutions, United States, 1979-2004 (2.10) 112

2.10 Reported confidence in selected institutions, United States, selected years 1979-2004 (2.11) 112

2.11 Reported confidence in the criminal justice system, by demographic characteristics, United States, 2004 (2.12) 113

2.12 Reported confidence in the police, by demographic characteristics, United States, 2004 (2.13) 113

2.13 Reported confidence in the police to protect from violent crime, United States, selected years 1981-2003 (2.14) 115

2.14 Reported confidence in the U.S. Supreme Court, by demographic characteristics, United States, 2004 (2.15) 115

2.15 Reported confidence in the U.S. Supreme Court, by demographic characteristics, United States, selected years 1984-2002 (2.16*) 116

2.16 Reported confidence in the U.S. Government to protect citizens from terrorist attack, United States, 2002, 2003, and 2004 (2.17) 119

2.17 Respondents' ratings of the honesty and ethical standards of various occupations, by type of occupation, United States, 2003 (2.18) 119

2.18 Respondents' ratings of the honesty and ethical standards of lawyers, United States, selected years 1976-2003 (2.19) 119

2.19 Respondents' ratings of the honesty and ethical standards of lawyers, by demographic characteristics, United States, 2003 (2.20) 120

2.20 Respondents' ratings of the honesty and ethical standards of police, United States, selected years 1977-2003 (2.21) 120

2.21 Respondents' ratings of the honesty and ethical standards of police, by demographic characteristics, United States, 2003 (2.22) 121

2.22 Respondents' ratings of performance of police in own community, United States, 2000 and 2002 (2.23*) 121

2.23 Attitudes toward a police officer striking an adult male citizen, by demographic characteristics, United States, selected years 1973-2002 (2.26*) 122

2.24 Attitudes toward a police officer striking a citizen under certain circumstances, United States, selected years 1973-2002 (2.27*) 124

2.25 Attitudes toward a police officer striking a citizen under certain circumstances, by demographic characteristics, United States, 2002 (2.28*) 125

2.26 Respondents' attitudes toward racial profiling, by race and ethnicity, United States, 2004 (--) 126

2.27 Respondents favoring increased law enforcement powers, United States, 2001-2004 (2.29) 126

2.28 Attitudes toward approaches to lowering the crime rate in the United States, United States, selected years 1989-2003 (--) 126

2.29 Respondents reporting fear that they or someone in their family will become a victim of terrorism, United States, 2002, 2003, and 2004 (2.30) 127

Table list xi

2.30 Respondents reporting how worried they are that there will soon be another terrorist attack in the United States, United States, 2001, 2002, and 2003 (--) 127

2.31 Respondents reporting whether they think it will be necessary to give up some civil liberties to curb terrorism in the United States, United States, selected years 1996-2003 (--) 127

2.32 Attitudes toward requiring all citizens to carry a national identity card to curb terrorism in the United States, United States, 2001, 2002, and 2003 (--) 127

2.33 Attitudes toward level of crime in the United States, United States, selected years 1989-2003 (2.31) 127

2.34 Attitudes toward level of crime in the United States, by demographic characteristics, United States, 2003 (2.32) 128

2.35 Attitudes toward level of crime in own area, United States, selected years 1972-2003 (2.33) 128

2.36 Attitudes toward level of crime in own area, by demographic characteristics, United States, 2003 (2.34) 129

2.37 Respondents reporting fear of walking alone at night, United States, selected years 1965-2003 (2.35) 129

2.38 Respondents reporting whether they feel afraid to walk alone at night in their own neighborhood, by demographic characteristics, United States, selected years 1973-2002 (2.36*) 130

2.39 Respondents reporting concern about crime victimization, by sex and race, United States, 2003 (2.37) 132

2.40 Respondents reporting whether they engaged in selected behaviors because of concern over crime, by sex and race, United States, 2003 (2.38) 132

2.41 Respondents indicating too little is spent on selected problems in this country, United States, selected years 1973-2002 (2.40*) 133

2.42 Attitudes toward the level of spending to halt the rising crime rate, by demographic characteristics, United States, selected years 1985-2002 (2.41*) 134

2.43 Attitudes toward the level of spending to deal with drug addiction, by demographic characteristics, United States, selected years 1985-2002 (2.42*) 136

2.44 Respondents' perceptions of the Nation's progress in coping with illegal drugs, United States, selected years 1972-2003 (--) 138

2.45 Respondents reporting whether they think the criminal justice system is fair in its treatment of people accused of committing crime, by demographic characteristics, United States, 2003 (--) 139

2.46 Attitudes toward whether the criminal justice system should try to rehabilitate criminals, United States, 2002 and 2003 (--) 139

2.47 Attitudes toward severity of courts in own area, by demographic characteristics, United States, selected years 1985-2002 (2.43*) 140

2.48 Attitudes toward the treatment of juveniles who commit violent crimes, by demographic characteristics, United States, 2003 (--) 143

2.49 Attitudes toward the penalty for murder, United States, selected years 1985-2004 (2.44) 143

2.50 Attitudes toward the death penalty for persons convicted of murder, by demographic characteristics, United States, selected years 1980-2002 (2.48*) 144

2.51 Attitudes toward the death penalty for persons convicted of murder, United States, selected years 1953-2003 (2.49) 146

2.52 Attitudes toward the death penalty for persons convicted of murder, by demographic characteristics, United States, 2003 (2.50) 146

2.53 Attitudes toward the death penalty for murder for selected groups, United States, 2002 (2.51*) 146

2.54 Attitudes toward fairness of the application of the death penalty, by demographic characteristics, United States, 2004 (2.52) 147

2.55 Reported reasons for favoring the death penalty for persons convicted of murder, United States, 1991, 2000, 2001, and 2003 (2.53*) 147

2.56 Reported reasons for opposing the death penalty for persons convicted of murder, United States, 1991 and 2003 (2.54*) 147

2.57 Respondents reporting whether they believe the death penalty acts as a deterrent to murder, United States, 1985, 1986, 1991, and 2004 (--) 148

2.58 Respondents reporting whether they believe the death penalty acts as a deterrent to murder, by demographic characteristics, United States, 2004 (--) 148

2.59 Respondents reporting having a gun in their home, United States, selected years 1959-2003 (2.56) 149

2.60 Respondents reporting having a gun in their home, by demographic characteristics, United States, 2003 (2.57) 149

2.61 Respondents reporting a firearm in their home, by demographic characteristics, United States, selected years 1973-2002 (2.58*) 150

2.62 Respondents reporting a firearm in their home, by type of firearm and demographic characteristics, United States, 2002 (2.59*) 151

2.63 Attitudes toward laws covering the sale of firearms, United States, selected years 1990-2003 (2.60) 151

2.64 Attitudes toward laws covering the sale of firearms, by demographic characteristics, United States, 2003 (2.61) 153

2.65 Attitudes toward a law restricting the possession of handguns, United States, selected years 1959-2003 (2.62) 153

2.66 Attitudes toward a law requiring a police permit prior to gun purchase, by demographic characteristics, United States, selected years 1976-2002 (2.65*) 154

2.67 Attitudes toward legalization of the use of marijuana, United States, selected years 1969-2003 (2.66) 157

2.68 Attitudes toward legalization of the use of marijuana, by demographic characteristics, United States, selected years 1976-2002 (2.67*) 158

2.69 Respondents' attitudes toward making marijuana legally available for doctors to prescribe, by demographic characteristics, United States, 2003 (--) 160

2.70 High school seniors reporting that they worry about selected social problems, United States, 1991-2003 (2.68) 161

2.71 High school seniors reporting that they worry about crime and violence, by sex, race, region, college plans, and illicit drug use, United States, 1991-2003 (2.69) 162

2.72 High school seniors reporting positive attitudes toward the performance of selected institutions, United States, 1991-2003 (2.70) 163

2.73 High school seniors reporting positive attitudes toward the performance of the police and other law enforcement agencies, by sex, race, region, college plans, and illicit drug use, United States, 1991-2003 (2.71) 164

2.74 High school seniors reporting positive attitudes toward the performance of the U.S. Supreme Court, by sex, race, region, college plans, and illicit drug use, United States, 1991-2003 (2.72) 165

2.75 High school seniors reporting positive attitudes toward the performance of the courts and the justice system in general, by sex, race, region, college plans, and illicit drug use, United States, 1991-2003 (2.73) 166

2.76 Students' perceptions of the harmfulness of alcohol and drug use, by grade level of respondent, 2002-2003 (2.74) 167

2.77 Teenagers' perceptions of the harmfulness of alcohol and drug use, United States, 2002 and 2003 (2.75) 167

2.78 Teenagers' perceptions of someone their age smoking, getting drunk, and using drugs, United States, 2004 (--) 167

2.79 High school seniors' perceptions of the harmfulness of drug use, alcohol use, and cigarette smoking, by type of drug and frequency of use, United States, 1980, 1990, and 1993-2003 (2.76) 168

2.80 Eighth and tenth graders' perceptions of the harmfulness of drug use, alcohol use, and cigarette smoking, by type of drug and frequency of use, United States, 1991, 1995, and 2000-2003 (2.77) 169

2.81 Young adults' perceptions of the harmfulness of drug use, alcohol use, and cigarette smoking, by type of drug, frequency of use, and age group, United States, 1991-2003 (2.78) 170

2.82 Respondents' perceptions of the harmfulness of selected drug use behaviors, by age group, United States, 2002 and 2003 (2.79) 172

2.83 High school seniors' perceptions of availability of drugs, by type of drug, United States, 1980, 1990, and 1993-2003 (2.80) 173

2.84 Eighth and tenth graders' perceptions of availability of drugs, by type of drug, United States, 1992, 1995, and 2000-2003 (2.81) 173

2.85 High school seniors disapproving of drug use, alcohol use, and cigarette smoking, by type of drug and frequency of use, United States, 1980, 1990, and 1993-2003 (2.82) 174

2.86 Eighth and tenth graders disapproving of drug use, alcohol use, and cigarette smoking, by type of drug and frequency of use, United States, 1991, 1995, and 2000-2003 (2.83) 175

2.87 High school seniors favoring prohibition of drug use, alcohol use, and cigarette smoking, by type of drug and place of use, United States, 1975-2003 (2.84) 176

2.88 High school seniors' attitudes toward the legalization of marijuana use, United States, 1975-2003 (2.85) 177

2.89 High school seniors' attitudes toward legalization of the sale of marijuana if the use of marijuana were legal, United States, 1975-2003 (2.86) 177

2.90 College freshmen reporting that marijuana should be legalized, by sex, United States, 1969-2003 (2.87) 178

2.91 College freshmen reporting that abortion should be legal, by sex, United States, 1977-2003 (2.88) 178

2.92 College freshmen reporting there is too much concern in the courts for the rights of criminals, by sex, United States, 1969-83 and 1987-2003 (2.89) 179

2.93 College freshmen reporting that the death penalty should be abolished, by sex, United States, 1969, 1970, 1971, and 1978-2003 (2.90) 179

2.94 College freshmen reporting that homosexual relationships should be legally prohibited, by sex, United States, 1976-2003 (2.91) 181

2.95 College freshmen reporting that the Federal Government should do more to control the sale of handguns, by sex, United States, 1989-2003 (2.93) 181

2.96 Attitudes toward legalization of doctor-assisted suicide, United States, selected years 1996-2004 (2.94) 181

2.97 Attitudes toward laws regulating the distribution of pornography, by demographic characteristics, United States, selected years 1987-2002 (2.97*) 182

2.98 Attitudes toward the legality of homosexual relations, United States, selected years 1977-2004 (2.98) 184

2.99 Attitudes toward the legality of homosexual relations, by demographic characteristics, United States, 2004 (2.99) 184

2.100 Attitudes toward the legality of abortion, United States, selected years 1975-2004 (2.100) 185

2.101 Attitudes toward the legality of abortion, by demographic characteristics, United States, 2004 (2.101) 185

2.102 Attitudes toward whether there should be stricter laws and regulations to protect the environment, United States, selected years 1992-2003 (--) 186

Section 3
Nature and distribution of known offenses 187

3.1 Estimated average number, rate, and percent change in rate of personal and property victimization, by type of crime, United States, 2000-01 and 2002-03 (3.1) 188

3.2 Estimated number and rate of violent and property victimization, by type of crime, United States, 2002 and 2003 (3.2) 189

3.3 Estimated rate of criminal victimization and percent change in rate, by type of crime, United States, 1993, 1994, 1999-2003 (3.3) 190

3.4 Estimated rate (per 1,000 persons age 12 and older) of personal victimization, by type of crime and selected characteristics of victim, United States, 2003 (3.4) 191

3.5 Estimated number and rate (per 1,000 persons age 12 and older) of personal victimization, by type of crime and sex of victim, United States, 2002 (3.5) 192

3.6 Estimated rate (per 1,000 persons in each age group) of personal victimization, by type of crime and age of victim, United States, 2002 (3.7) 192

3.7 Estimated rate (per 1,000 persons in each age group) of personal victimization, by sex and age of victim, and type of crime, United States, 2002 (3.8) 193

3.8 Estimated number and rate (per 1,000 persons age 12 and older) of personal victimization, by type of crime and race of victim, United States, 2002 (3.9) 193

3.9 Estimated number and rate (per 1,000 persons age 12 and older) of personal victimization, by type of crime and ethnicity of victim, United States, 2002 (3.10) 194

3.10 Estimated number and rate (per 1,000 persons age 12 and older) of personal victimization, by type of crime, and sex and race of victim, United States, 2002 (3.13) 194

3.11 Estimated rate (per 1,000 persons in each age group) of personal victimization, by race and age of victim, and type of crime, United States, 2002 (3.14) 195

Table list xiii

3.12 Estimated rate (per 1,000 persons age 12 and older) of personal victimization, by type of crime and annual household income of victim, United States, 2002 (3.15) 195

3.13 Estimated rate (per 1,000 persons age 12 and older) of personal victimization, by type of crime, size of population, and locality of residence, United States, 2002 (3.16) 196

3.14 Estimated number and percent distribution of violent victimization incidents, by type of crime and victim-offender relationship, United States, 2002 (3.17) 196

3.15 Estimated percent distribution of violent victimization, by type of crime and victim-offender relationship, United States, 2002 (3.18) 197

3.16 Victim-offender relationship in violent victimization, by type of crime and sex of victim, United States, 2003 (3.19) 197

3.17 Estimated percent distribution of violent victimization incidents, by type of crime, victim-offender relationship, and type of weapon used, United States, 2002 (3.20) 198

3.18 Estimated percent of violent victimizations in which victim took self-protective measures, by type of crime and victim-offender relationship, United States, 2002 (3.21) 199

3.19 Estimated percent distribution of self-protective measures employed by victims of violent crime, by sex and race of victim, United States, 2002 (3.22) 199

3.20 Estimated percent distribution of violent victimizations in which self-protective measures were employed, by person taking measure, type of crime, and outcome of measure, United States, 2002 (3.23) 200

3.21 Estimated rate (per 1,000 households) of property victimization, by type of crime and characteristics of household, United States, 2003 (3.24) 200

3.22 Estimated number and rate (per 1,000 households) of property victimization, by type of crime and race of head of household, United States, 2002 (3.25) 201

3.23 Estimated number and rate (per 1,000 households) of property victimization, by type of crime and ethnicity of head of household, United States, 2002 (3.26) 201

3.24 Estimated rate (per 1,000 households) of property victimization, by type of crime and annual household income, United States, 2002 (3.27) 202

3.25 Estimated rate (per 1,000 households) of property victimization, by type of crime, size of population, and locality of residence, United States, 2002 (3.28) 202

3.26 Estimated rate (per 1,000 households) of property victimization, by locality of residence, race of head of household, and type of crime, United States, 2002 (3.29) 203

3.27 Estimated percent distribution of households experiencing crime, by type of crime, United States, 1994-2000, 2002, and 2003 (3.30) 203

3.28 Estimated percent distribution of violent victimizations by lone offenders, by type of crime and perceived age of offender, United States, 2002 (3.31) 204

3.29 Estimated percent distribution of violent victimizations by lone offenders, by type of crime and perceived race of offender, United States, 2002 (3.32) 204

3.30 Estimated percent distribution of violent victimizations by multiple offenders, by type of crime and perceived age of offenders, United States, 2002 (3.33) 205

3.31 Estimated percent distribution of violent victimizations by multiple offenders, by type of crime and perceived race of offenders, United States, 2002 (3.34) 205

3.32 Estimated percent distribution of personal and property incidents, by type of crime and place of occurrence, United States, 2002 (3.35) 206

3.33 Estimated percent distribution of personal and property victimization, by type of crime and whether or not reported to police, United States, 2002 (3.36) 207

3.34 Estimated percent distribution of reasons for reporting personal and property victimizations to police, by type of crime, United States, 2002 (3.37) 208

3.35 Estimated percent distribution of reasons for not reporting personal and property victimizations to police, by type of crime, United States, 2002 (3.38) 208

3.36 Estimated percent of violent victimizations reported to police, by selected victim and household characteristics, 1992-2000 (aggregate) (3.39*) 209

3.37 High school seniors reporting victimization experiences in last 12 months, by type of victimization, United States, 1991-2003 (3.40) 211

3.38 High school seniors reporting victimization experiences in last 12 months, by type of victimization and sex, United States, 1991-2003 (3.41) 212

3.39 High school seniors reporting victimization experiences in last 12 months, by type of victimization and race, United States, 1991-2003 (3.42) 214

3.40 High school seniors reporting victimization experiences at school in last 12 months, by type of victimization, United States, 1991-2003 (3.43) 217

3.41 High school seniors reporting victimization experiences at school in last 12 months, by type of victimization and sex, United States, 1991-2003 (3.44) 218

3.42 High school seniors reporting victimization experiences at school in last 12 months, by type of victimization and race, United States, 1991-2003 (3.45) 220

3.43 High school seniors reporting involvement in selected delinquent activities in last 12 months, United States, 1991-2003 (3.46) 222

3.44 High school seniors reporting involvement in selected delinquent activities in last 12 months, by sex, United States, 1991-2003 (3.47) 224

3.45 High school seniors reporting involvement in selected delinquent activities in last 12 months, by race, United States, 1991-2003 (3.48) 228

3.46 High school seniors reporting receiving traffic ticket or warning for a moving violation in last 12 months, United States, 1991-2003 (3.49) 232

3.47 High school seniors reporting receiving traffic ticket or warning for a moving violation in last 12 months, by sex, United States, 1991-2003 (3.50) 232

3.48 High school seniors reporting receiving traffic ticket or warning for a moving violation in last 12 months, by race, United States, 1991-2003 (3.51) 232

3.49 High school seniors reporting receiving traffic ticket or warning for a moving violation in last 12 months while under the influence of alcohol or drugs, by type of drug, United States, 1991-2003 (3.52) 234

3.50 High school seniors reporting receiving traffic ticket or warning for a moving violation in last 12 months while under the influence of alcohol or drugs, by type of drug and sex, United States, 1991-2003 (3.53) 234

3.51 High school seniors reporting receiving traffic ticket or warning for a moving violation in last 12 months while under the influence of alcohol or drugs, by type of drug and race, United States, 1991-2003 (3.54) 236

3.52 High school seniors reporting involvement in driving accidents in last 12 months, United States, 1991-2003 (3.55) 236

3.53 High school seniors reporting involvement in driving accidents while under the influence of alcohol or drugs in last 12 months, by type of drug, United States, 1991-2003 (3.56) 237

3.54 Students reporting problem behaviors, by grade level of respondent, 2002-2003 (3.57) 238

3.55 High school students reporting involvement in delinquent and risk-related behaviors, and drug, alcohol, and cigarette use, United States, selected years, 1991-2003 (3.58) 239

3.56 High school students reporting involvement in delinquent and risk-related behaviors, by sex, race, ethnicity, and grade level, United States, 2003 (3.59) 240

3.57 High school students reporting victimization experiences and involvement in delinquent activities on school property, by sex, race, ethnicity, and grade level, United States, 2003 (--) 240

3.58 Students reporting involvement in delinquent activities at school, by grade level of respondent, 2002-2003 (3.60) 241

3.59 Students reporting victimization experiences at school, by grade level of respondent, 2002-2003 (3.61) 241

3.60 Number and rate (per 1,000 students) of nonfatal violent crimes against students age 12 to 18 occurring at school, by type of crime and student characteristics, United States, 1995, 1999-2001 (3.62) 242

3.61 Students age 12 to 18 reporting victimization, bullying, hate-related behavior, and gangs at school, by student characteristics, United States, 2001 (3.63) 243

3.62 High school students reporting drug, alcohol, and cigarette use, by sex, race, ethnicity, and grade level, United States, 2003 (3.64) 244

3.63 Students reporting use of alcohol and drugs, by grade level of respondent and frequency of use, 2002-2003 (3.65) 245

3.64 Reported alcohol use and most recent use among students, by sex, college plans, region, and population density, United States, 2003 (3.66) 245

3.65 Reported use of any illicit drug and most recent use among students, by sex, college plans, region, and population density, United States, 2003 (3.67) 246

3.66 Reported use of any illicit drug in last 12 months among students, by sex, race, ethnicity, and college plans, United States, 1991-2003 and 1975-2003 (--) 247

3.67 Reported use of any illicit drug other than marijuana in last 12 months among students, by sex, race, ethnicity, and college plans, United States, 1991-2003 and 1975-2003 (--) 248

3.68 Reported drug and alcohol use in last 12 months among high school seniors, by type of drug, United States, 1991-2003 (3.68) 249

3.69 Reported drug use, alcohol use, and cigarette use in last 30 days among high school seniors, by type of drug, United States, 1991-2003 (3.69) 250

3.70 Reported drug use and most recent use among students, by type of drug and grade level, United States, 1991-2003 (3.70) 251

3.71 Reported drug use, alcohol use, and cigarette use in last 12 months among college students, by type of drug, United States, 1988-2003 (3.71) 253

3.72 Reported drug use, alcohol use, and cigarette use in last 30 days among college students, by type of drug, United States, 1988-2003 (3.72) 254

3.73 Reported daily use in last 30 days of drugs, alcohol, and cigarettes among college students, by type of drug, United States, 1988-2003 (3.73) 254

3.74 Reported drug use, alcohol use, and cigarette use in last 12 months among young adults, by type of drug, United States, 1988-2003 (3.74) 255

3.75 Reported drug use, alcohol use, and cigarette use in last 30 days among young adults, by type of drug, United States, 1988-2003 (3.75) 256

3.76 Reported daily use within last 30 days of drugs, alcohol, and cigarettes among young adults, by type of drug, United States, 1988-2003 (3.76) 257

3.77 Reported drinking behaviors among college students, by sex, United States, 1993, 1997, 1999, and 2001 (3.77*) 258

3.78 Prevalence of binge drinking among college students, by selected characteristics, United States, 1993, 1997, 1999, and 2001 (3.78*) 258

3.79 Drinking behaviors among college students reporting alcohol consumption in past year, by sex, United States, 1993, 1997, 1999, and 2001 (3.79*) 259

3.80 Alcohol-related problems among college students, United States, 1993, 1997, 1999, and 2001 (3.80*) 259

3.81 Binge drinking among underage and legal age college students, by living arrangement, United States, 2001 (3.81*) 259

3.82 Alcohol-related effects experienced by underage college students, by living arrangement, United States, 2001 (3.82*) 260

3.83 College students and underage college students reporting alcohol use, by frequency of use, United States, 1998-2002 (3.83) 260

3.84 College students reporting drug use, by type of drug, United States, 1998-2002 (3.84) 261

3.85 College students reporting experiences of violence or harassment and involvement of alcohol or drugs before the experience, United States, 1995-2002 (3.85) 261

3.86 Estimated prevalence of drug use during lifetime, by type of drug and age group, United States, 2002 and 2003 (3.86) 262

3.87 Estimated prevalence of drug use during the last 12 months, by type of drug and age group, United States, 2002 and 2003 (3.87) 263

3.88 Estimated prevalence of drug use during the last 30 days, by type of drug and age group, United States, 2002 and 2003 (3.88) 263

3.89 Prevalence of any illicit drug use among military personnel, by branch of service and recency of use, United States, selected years 1980-2002 (--) 264

3.90 Prevalence of illicit drug use among military personnel, by branch of service, type of drug, and recency of use, United States, 2002 (--) 265

3.91 Prevalence of heavy alcohol use in the past 30 days among military personnel, by branch of service, United States, selected years 1980-2002 (--) 266

3.92 Drug abuse-related emergency department episodes, by patient and episode characteristics, United States, 1994-2002 (3.90*) 267

Table list xv

3.93 Type of drug mentioned in drug abuse-related emergency department episodes, by patient and episode characteristics, United States, 1999-2002 (3.91*) 268

3.94 Type and rate (per 100,000 population) of drug mentioned in drug abuse-related emergency department episodes, by patient characteristics, United States, 1999-2002 (3.92*) 269

3.95 Reported alcohol use, by sex, United States, selected years 1939-2004 (3.93) 270

3.96 Reported alcohol use, by demographic characteristics, United States, 2004 (3.94) 271

3.97 Respondents reporting whether they drink more than they should, by demographic characteristics, United States, 2004 (3.95) 271

3.98 Alcohol use and underage alcohol use in the last 30 days, by age group, level of use, and demographic characteristics, United States, 2002 and 2003 (3.96) 272

3.99 Respondents reporting whether drinking has ever been a source of family trouble, United States, selected years 1947-2004 (3.97) 272

3.100 Respondents reporting whether drinking has ever been a source of family trouble, by demographic characteristics, United States, 2004 (3.98) 273

3.101 Respondents reporting whether drug abuse has ever been a source of family trouble, by demographic characteristics, United States, 2003 (--) 273

3.102 Respondents reporting having driven a vehicle under the influence of alcohol or drugs during the last 12 months, by demographic characteristics, United States, 2002 and 2003 (3.99) 274

3.103 Total fatalities and fatalities in alcohol-related motor vehicle crashes, by highest blood alcohol concentration level in the crash, United States, 1982-2002 (3.100) 275

3.104 Blood alcohol concentration level of motor vehicle drivers involved in fatal crashes, by age, United States, 1990-2002 (3.101) 276

3.105 Total fatalities and fatalities in alcohol-related motor vehicle crashes, by highest blood alcohol concentration level in the crash and jurisdiction, 2002 (3.102) 277

3.106 Estimated number and rate (per 100,000 inhabitants) of offenses known to police, by offense, United States, 1960-2002 (3.103) 278

3.107 Estimated number and rate (per 100,000 inhabitants) of offenses known to police, by offense and extent of urbanization, 2002 (3.104) 279

3.108 Estimated number and rate (per 100,000 inhabitants) of offenses known to police, by offense, jurisdiction, and extent of urbanization, 2002 (3.105) 280

3.109 Offenses known to police, by offense and size of place, 2001 and 2002 (3.106) 288

3.110 Offenses known to police in cities over 100,000 population, 2001 and 2002 (3.110) 290

3.111 Number of offenses known to police and average loss incurred, by selected offenses and type of target, United States, 2002 (3.112) 297

3.112 Bias-motivated (hate) crimes known to police, by offense, United States, 2002 (3.113) 297

3.113 Bias motivations in hate crimes known to police, United States, 2002 (3.114) 298

3.114 Race of suspected offender in bias-motivated (hate) crimes known to police, by type of bias motivation, United States, 2002 (3.115) 299

3.115 Offenses in Federal parks known to park rangers and park police, by offense, 1975-2002 (3.116*) 300

3.116 Offenses in Federal parks known to park rangers and park police, and reported by other law enforcement agencies, by offense, 2002 (3.117*) 301

3.117 Percent distribution of murders and nonnegligent manslaughters known to police, by type of weapon used, United States, 1964-2002 (3.118) 301

3.118 Percent distribution of murders and nonnegligent manslaughters known to police, by type of weapon used and region, 2002 (3.119) 303

3.119 Murders and nonnegligent manslaughters known to police, by type of weapon used and age of victim, United States, 2002 (3.120) 303

3.120 Murders and nonnegligent manslaughters known to police, by victim-offender relationship and circumstances of the offense, United States, 2002 (3.121) 304

3.121 Percent distribution of murders and nonnegligent manslaughters known to police, by age of victim, United States, 1964, 1974, 1984, 1989-2002 (3.122) 306

3.122 Percent distribution of murders and nonnegligent manslaughters known to police, by sex of victim, United States, 1964-2002 (3.123) 307

3.123 Percent distribution of murders and nonnegligent manslaughters known to police, by race of victim, United States, 1964-2002 (3.124) 307

3.124 Murders and nonnegligent manslaughters known to police, by sex, race, and age of victim, United States, 2002 (3.125) 308

3.125 Rate (per 100,000 persons in each group) of murder and nonnegligent manslaughter victimization, by age, sex, and race of victim, United States, 1976-2002 (3.126) 308

3.126 Rate (per 100,000 persons in each group) of murder and nonnegligent manslaughter victimization, by age, sex, and race of victim, United States, 1976-2002 (3.127) 309

3.127 Estimated rate (per 100,000 persons in each group) of offenders committing murder and nonnegligent manslaughter, by age, sex, and race of offender, United States, 1976-2002 (3.128) 309

3.128 Estimated rate (per 100,000 persons in each group) of offenders committing murder and nonnegligent manslaughter, by age, sex, and race of offender, United States, 1976-2002 (3.129) 310

3.129 Murders and nonnegligent manslaughters known to police, by race and sex of victim and offender, United States, 2002 (3.130) 310

3.130 Percent distribution of U.S. population, and murder and nonnegligent manslaughter victims and offenders, by age, sex, and race, United States, 1976-2002 (3.131) 311

3.131 Murders and nonnegligent manslaughters by intimates of the victims, by sex and race of victim, and victim-offender relationship, United States, 1976-2002 (3.132) 311

3.132 Estimated rate (per 1,000 persons age 12 and older) of nonfatal intimate partner violence and percent change in rate, by sex of victim, 1993-2001 (3.133*) 312

3.133 Murder and nonnegligent manslaughters resulting from the Sept. 11, 2001 terrorist attacks, by sex and race of victim, and location (3.134*) 312

3.134 Sniper-attack murder incidents, victims, and offenders, by type of firearm, 1982-2001 (--) 313

3.135 Workplace homicides, by victim characteristics, type of event, and selected occupation and industry, United States, 1992-2002 (3.135) 314

3.136 Suicide rate (per 100,000 persons in each age group), by age, United States, 1980, 1985, 1990-2002 (3.139) 316

3.137 Suicide rate (per 100,000 persons in each age group), by age, sex, and race, United States, 2002 (3.140) 316

3.138 Suicide rate (per 100,000 persons in each age group) for persons 15 to 24 years of age, by age and sex, United States, 1950, 1960, 1970, 1980, 1990, 1993-2002 (3.141) 317

3.139 Firearm suicide rate (per 100,000 persons in each age group), by age, United States, 1980, 1985, 1990-2002 (3.142) 317

3.140 Percent distribution of robberies known to police, by type of weapon used, United States, 1974-2002 (3.143) 318

3.141 Percent distribution of robberies known to police, by type of weapon used and region, 2002 (3.144) 318

3.142 Percent distribution of robberies known to police, by place of occurrence, United States, 1973-2002 (3.145) 318

3.143 Percent distribution of aggravated assaults known to police, by type of weapon used, United States, 1964-2002 (3.146) 319

3.144 Percent distribution of aggravated assaults known to police, by type of weapon used and region, 2002 (3.147) 319

3.145 Percent distribution of burglaries known to police, by place and time of occurrence, United States, 1976-2002 (3.148) 319

3.146 Percent distribution of larceny-thefts known to police, by type of target, United States, 1973-2002 (3.149) 320

3.147 Motor vehicle registrations and thefts, United States, 1980-2002 (3.150) 321

3.148 Financial institution fraud and failure matters handled by the U.S. Department of Justice, United States, 1986-2003 (3.151) 321

3.149 Violations of the Federal Bank Robbery and Incidental Crimes Statute, by type of violation, United States, 1985-2002 (3.152) 322

3.150 Violations of the Federal Bank Robbery and Incidental Crimes Statute, by type of violation and jurisdiction, 1999-2002 (3.153) 323

3.151 Injuries, deaths, and hostages taken during violations of the Federal Bank Robbery and Incidental Crimes Statute, by type of victim, United States, 1999-2002 (3.154) 324

3.152 Assaults on Federal officers, by department and agency, 1991-2002 (3.155) 324

3.153 Assaults on Federal officers, by extent of injury and type of weapon used, 1977-2002 (3.156) 325

3.154 Law enforcement officers killed, United States, 1972-2002 (3.157) 327

3.155 Law enforcement officers feloniously killed, by circumstances at scene of incident, United States, 1979-2002 (3.158) 328

3.156 Law enforcement officers feloniously killed, by circumstances at scene of incident and type of assignment, United States, 1993-2002 (aggregate) (3.159) 329

3.157 Law enforcement officers feloniously killed, by circumstances at scene of incident and type of assignment, United States, 2002 (3.160) 330

3.158 Percent distribution of law enforcement officers feloniously killed, by selected characteristics of officers, United States, 1984-2002 (3.161) 330

3.159 Law enforcement officers feloniously killed in Sept. 11, 2001 terrorist attacks, by selected characteristics of officers (3.162*) 331

3.160 Persons identified in the felonious killing of law enforcement officers, by demographic characteristics and prior record, United States, 1993-2002 (aggregate) and 2002 (3.163) 331

3.161 Persons identified in the felonious killing of law enforcement officers, by type of disposition, United States, 1991-2000 (aggregate) (3.164) 331

3.162 Law enforcement officers accidentally killed, by circumstances at scene of incident, United States, 1980-2002 (3.165) 332

3.163 Law enforcement officers assaulted, by circumstances at scene of incident and type of weapon, United States, 2002 (3.166) 333

3.164 Law enforcement officers assaulted, by circumstances at scene of incident and type of assignment, United States, 2002 (3.167) 334

3.165 Assaults on law enforcement officers and percent sustaining personal injury, by type of weapon used, 1980-2002 (3.168) 335

3.166 Estimated number of structure fires and intentionally set structure fires, and resulting civilian fire deaths and value of property damage, United States, 2002 (3.169) 335

3.167 Estimated number of intentionally set structure fires, and resulting civilian fire deaths and value of property damage, United States, 1977-2002 (3.170) 335

3.168 Arson offenses and average value of property damage, by type of target, 2002 (3.171) 336

3.169 Arson of structures and percent not in use, by type of structure, 2002 (3.172) 336

3.170 Bombing incidents known to police, by type of incident and device, value of property damage, and outcome of incident, United States, 1973-99 (3.173) 337

3.171 Bombing incidents known to police, by type of target and device, and value of property damage, United States, 1999 (3.174) 338

3.172 Bombing incidents known to police, by type of incident and device, and region and jurisdiction, 1999 (3.175) 339

3.173 Terrorist incidents and preventions, United States, 1980-2001 (3.176) 340

3.174 Terrorist incidents, by type of incident and region, United States, 1980-2001 (aggregate) (3.177) 340

3.175 U.S. citizen casualties resulting from international terrorism, by type of casualty, 1981-2003 (3.178) 341

3.176 Terrorist attacks against the United States internationally, by type of event, 1994-2003 (3.179) 341

3.177 Results of airline passenger screening, United States, 1977-2000 (3.180) 342

Section 4
Characteristics and distribution of persons arrested 343

4.1 Estimated number of arrests, by offense charged, United States, 2002 (4.1) 344

Table list xvii

4.2 Arrest rates (per 100,000 inhabitants), by offense, 1971-2002 (4.2) 345

4.3 Number and rate (per 100,000 inhabitants) of arrests, by offense charged and size of place, 2002 (4.3) 346

4.4 Percent distribution of total U.S. population and persons arrested for all offenses, by age group, United States, 2002 (4.4) 347

4.5 Arrests, by offense charged, age group, and State, 2002 (4.5) 348

4.6 Arrests, by offense charged and age group, United States, 1993 and 2002 (4.6) 353

4.7 Arrests, by offense charged and age, United States, 2002 (4.7) 354

4.8 Arrests, by offense charged and sex, United States, 2002 (4.8) 356

4.9 Arrests, by offense charged, sex, and age group, United States, 2001 and 2002 (4.9) 357

4.10 Arrests, by offense charged, age group, and race, United States, 2002 (4.10) 358

4.11 Arrests in cities, by offense charged and sex, 2002 (4.11) 361

4.12 Arrests in cities, by offense charged, age group, and race, 2002 (4.12) 362

4.13 Arrests in suburban areas, by offense charged and sex, 2002 (4.13) 365

4.14 Arrests in suburban areas, by offense charged, age group, and race, 2002 (4.14) 366

4.15 Arrests in rural counties, by offense charged and sex, 2002 (4.15) 369

4.16 Arrests in rural counties, by offense charged, age group, and race, 2002 (4.16) 370

4.17 Arrest rates (per 100,000 inhabitants) for violent crimes, by offense charged and region, 1971-2002 (4.17) 373

4.18 Arrest rates (per 100,000 inhabitants) for property crimes, by offense charged and region, 1971-2002 (4.18) 374

4.19 Offenses known to police and percent cleared by arrest, by offense and population group, 2002 (4.19) 375

4.20 Offenses known to police and percent cleared by arrest, by type of offense, United States, 1971-2002 (4.20) 377

4.21 Percent of offenses known to police that were cleared by arrest, by extent of urbanization and type of offense, 1972-2002 (4.21) 378

4.22 Number of offenses known to police that were cleared by arrest and percent of clearances from arrest of persons under 18 years of age, by offense and population group, 2002 (4.22) 379

4.23 Percent of offenses known to police that were cleared by arrest of persons under 18 years of age, by type of offense, United States, 1972-2002 (4.23) 381

4.24 Arsons cleared by arrest and clearances by arrest of persons under 18 years of age, by type of target, United States, 2002 (4.24) 381

4.25 Juveniles taken into police custody, by method of disposition and population group, 2002 (4.25) 382

4.26 Percent distribution of juveniles taken into police custody, by method of disposition, United States, 1972-2002 (4.26) 383

4.27 Arrests for alcohol-related offenses and driving under the influence, United States, 1970-2002 (4.27) 383

4.28 Arrests for alcohol-related offenses, by offense and State, 2002 (4.28) 384

4.29 Percent distribution of arrests for drug abuse violations, by type of drug, United States, 1982-2002 (4.29) 385

4.30 Drug use by adult male arrestees in 43 U.S. cities and counties, by type of drug, 2000-2003 (4.30) 386

4.31 Adult male arrestees in 39 U.S. cities and counties reporting receiving drug or alcohol treatment ever and in past year, by type of treatment, 2003 (4.31) 387

4.32 Adult male arrestees in 43 U.S. cities and counties reporting binge drinking in past 30 days, 2000-2003 (4.32) 387

4.33 Persons arrested for Federal offenses, by offense, United States, fiscal year 2001 (4.33) 388

4.34 Persons arrested for Federal offenses, by Federal agency, United States, fiscal year 2001 (4.34) 389

4.35 Characteristics of persons arrested by Federal agencies, by offense, United States, fiscal year 2001 (4.35) 389

4.36 Federal drug seizures, by type of drug, fiscal years 1989-2003 (4.36) 390

4.37 Drug removals from the domestic market by the Drug Enforcement Administration, by type of drug, fiscal years 1978-2003 (4.37) 390

4.38 Number of marijuana plants eradicated and seized, arrests made, weapons seized, and value of assets seized, under the Drug Enforcement Administration's Domestic Cannabis Eradication/Suppression Program, by State, 2003 (4.38) 391

4.39 Seizures of illegal drug laboratories by the Drug Enforcement Administration, by type of drug manufactured, United States, fiscal years 1975-2003 (4.39) 392

4.40 Arrests by the Drug Enforcement Administration, by type of drug, fiscal years 1992-2003 (4.40) 392

4.41 Characteristics of persons arrested by the Drug Enforcement Administration, by type of drug, United States, fiscal year 2001 (4.41) 393

4.42 Asset seizures by the Drug Enforcement Administration, by type and value of asset seized, fiscal years 1992-2003 (4.42) 393

4.43 Drug seizures by the U.S. Customs Service, by type and amount of drugs seized, fiscal years 1975-2001 (4.43*) 394

4.44 Property seizures by the U.S. Customs Service, by type and value of property seized, fiscal years 1979-2001 (4.44*) 395

4.45 Value of asset forfeiture recoveries by U.S. attorneys, United States, 1989-2002 (4.45) 396

4.46 Deportable aliens located by the Bureau of Customs and Border Protection and the Bureau of Immigration and Customs Enforcement, and aliens removed from the United States, by type of removal, fiscal years 1961-2003 (4.46) 396

4.47 Aliens formally removed from the United States for violation of immigration laws, by reason for removal, fiscal years 1991-2003 (4.47) 397

Section 5
Judicial processing of defendants 399

5.1 Requests for immunity by Federal prosecutors to the U.S. Attorney General and witnesses involved in these requests, by origin of request, fiscal years 1973-2003 (5.1) 400

5.2 Court-authorized orders for interception of wire, oral, or electronic communications, United States, 1969-2003 (5.2) 400

5.3 Court-authorized orders for interception of wire, oral, or electronic communications, by most serious offense under investigation, United States, 2003 (5.3) 401

5.4 Court-authorized orders for interception of wire, oral, or electronic communications, by jurisdiction, 1997-2003 (5.4) 401

5.5 Arrests and convictions resulting from court-authorized orders for interception of wire, oral, or electronic communications, United States, 1987-2003 (5.5) 402

5.6 Grand jury proceedings and criminal cases filed and terminated by U.S. attorneys, United States, fiscal years 1980-2002 (5.6) 403

5.7 Criminal cases filed and disposed of and number of defendants handled by U.S. attorneys, by offense type, United States, fiscal year 2002 (5.7) 404

5.8 Criminal cases commenced, terminated, and pending, and judgeships authorized in U.S. District Courts, 1982-2003 (5.8) 405

5.9 Criminal cases filed, terminated, and pending in U.S. District Courts, 1955-2003 (5.9) 406

5.10 Criminal cases filed in U.S. District Courts, by offense, fiscal years 1990, 1994-2003 (5.10) 407

5.11 Criminal cases filed, terminated, and pending in U.S. District Courts, by type of offense, circuit, and district, fiscal year 2003 (5.11) 408

5.12 Defendants detained by U.S. District Courts, by circuit and district, fiscal year 2003 (5.12) 412

5.13 Federal defendants released or detained prior to trial in U.S. District Courts, by offense, United States, fiscal year 2001 (5.13) 414

5.14 Federal pretrial detention hearings and defendants ordered detained in U.S. District Courts, by characteristics, United States, fiscal year 2001 (5.14) 416

5.15 Federal defendants released or detained prior to trial in U.S. District Courts, by characteristics, United States, fiscal year 2001 (5.15) 416

5.16 Behavior of Federal defendants released prior to trial in U.S. District Courts, by offense, type of release, and characteristics, United States, fiscal year 2001 (5.16) 417

5.17 Disposition of cases terminated in U.S. District Courts, by offense, United States, fiscal year 2001 (5.17) 418

5.18 Federal defendants convicted in U.S. District Courts, by offense and characteristics, United States, fiscal year 2001 (5.18) 419

5.19 Sentences imposed in cases terminated in U.S. District Courts, by offense, United States, fiscal year 2001 (5.19) 420

5.20 Federal offenders sentenced to incarceration in U.S. District Courts, by offense and characteristics, United States, fiscal year 2001 (5.20) 421

5.21 Mean and median length of sentences imposed on Federal offenders sentenced to incarceration in U.S. District Courts, by offense and characteristics, United States, fiscal year 2001 (5.21) 422

5.22 Defendants disposed of in U.S. District Courts, by type of disposition, 1945-2003 (5.22) 423

5.23 Defendants sentenced in U.S. District Courts, by type and length of sentence, 1945-2003 (5.23) 424

5.24 Defendants disposed of in U.S. District Courts, by offense and type of disposition, fiscal year 2003 (5.24) 426

5.25 Defendants sentenced in U.S. District Courts, by offense, and type and length of sentence, fiscal year 2003 (5.25) 428

5.26 Offenders sentenced in U.S. District Courts under the U.S. Sentencing Commission guidelines, by primary offense, sex, race, and ethnicity, fiscal year 2002 (5.26) 432

5.27 Offenders sentenced in U.S. District Courts under the U.S. Sentencing Commission guidelines, by primary offense and age, fiscal year 2002 (5.27) 433

5.28 Offenders sentenced in U.S. District Courts under the U.S. Sentencing Commission guidelines, by primary offense and education level, fiscal year 2002 (5.28) 434

5.29 Sentences imposed in U.S. District Courts under the U.S. Sentencing Commission guidelines, by primary offense and type of sentence, fiscal year 2002 (5.29) 435

5.30 Length of sentences to imprisonment imposed in U.S. District Courts for U.S. Sentencing Commission guideline cases, by type of offense, fiscal years 1997-2002 (5.30) 436

5.31 Length of sentences to imprisonment imposed in U.S. District Courts for U.S. Sentencing Commission guideline cases, by primary offense, fiscal year 2002 (5.31) 436

5.32 Fines and restitution ordered in U.S. District Courts for U.S. Sentencing Commission guideline cases, by primary offense, fiscal year 2002 (5.32) 437

5.33 Fines and restitution ordered for organizations sentenced in U.S. District Courts for U.S. Sentencing Commission guideline cases, by primary offense, fiscal year 2002 (5.33) 438

5.34 Mode of conviction in U.S. District Courts for U.S. Sentencing Commission guideline cases, by primary offense, fiscal year 2002 (5.34) 439

5.35 U.S. citizens and non-U.S. citizens sentenced in U.S. District Courts under the U.S. Sentencing Commission guidelines, by primary offense, fiscal year 2002 (5.35) 439

5.36 Sentences within and departing from U.S. Sentencing Commission guidelines in U.S. District Courts, by primary offense, fiscal year 2002 (5.36) 440

5.37 Defendants charged with violation of drug laws in U.S. District Courts, by type of disposition, 1945-2003 (5.37) 441

5.38 Defendants sentenced for violation of drug laws in U.S. District Courts, by type and length of sentence, 1945-2003 (5.38) 442

5.39 Drug offenders sentenced in U.S. District Courts under the U.S. Sentencing Commission guidelines, by offender characteristics, mode of conviction, and drug offense, fiscal year 2002 (5.39) 443

5.40 Convictions resulting from arrests by the Drug Enforcement Administration, by type of drug, fiscal years 1992-2003 (5.40) 444

5.41 Antitrust cases filed in U.S. District Courts, by type of case, 1975-2003 (5.41) 444

5.42 Length of civil and criminal trials completed in U.S. District Courts, by circuit and district, fiscal year 2003 (5.42) 445

5.43 Median amount of time from filing to disposition of criminal defendants in U.S. District Courts, by method of disposition, and circuit and district, fiscal year 2003 (5.43) 447

5.44 Felony convictions in State courts, by offense, United States, 2000 (5.44*) 449

5.45 Characteristics of felony offenders convicted in State courts, by offense, United States, 2000 (5.45*) 450

5.46 Felony convictions in State courts, by offense and method of conviction, United States, 2000 (5.46*) 450

5.47 Felony sentences imposed by State courts, by offense, United States, 2000 (5.47*) 451

5.48 Mean and median maximum length of felony sentences imposed by State courts, by offense, United States, 2000 (5.48*) 451

5.49 Felons sentenced to additional penalties by State courts, by offense and type of penalty, United States, 2000 (5.49*) 452

5.50 Time between arrest and sentencing for felons convicted in State courts, by offense, United States, 2000 (5.50*) 453

5.51 Arrest offense of felony defendants in the 75 largest counties, United States, 2000 (5.51) 453

5.52 Characteristics of felony defendants in the 75 largest counties, by arrest charge, United States, 2000 (5.52) 454

5.53 Prior felony convictions of felony defendants in the 75 largest counties, by arrest charge, United States, 2000 (5.53) 454

5.54 Felony defendants released before or detained until case disposition in the 75 largest counties, by arrest charge, United States, 2000 (5.54) 455

5.55 Type of pretrial release or detention of felony defendants in the 75 largest counties, by arrest charge, United States, 2000 (5.55) 455

5.56 Released felony defendants charged with misconduct and rearrested in the 75 largest counties, by arrest charge, United States, 2000 (5.56) 456

5.57 Adjudication outcome for felony defendants in the 75 largest counties, by arrest charge, United States, 2000 (5.57) 457

5.58 Conviction offense of felony defendants in the 75 largest counties, United States, 2000 (5.58) 457

5.59 Type of sentence received by convicted defendants in the 75 largest counties, by conviction offense, United States, 2000 (5.59) 458

5.60 Length of prison sentence received by felony defendants in the 75 largest counties, by conviction offense, United States, 2000 (5.60) 458

5.61 Characteristics of juvenile offenders in cases disposed by juvenile courts, by type of offense, United States, 2000 (5.61*) 459

5.62 Type of offense in cases disposed by juvenile courts, by characteristics of juvenile offenders, United States, 2000 (5.62*) 459

5.63 Juvenile court case outcomes, by characteristics of juvenile offenders and type of offense, United States, 2000 (5.63*) 460

5.64 Juvenile court case outcomes, by type of offense and race of juvenile offender, United States, 2000 (5.64*) 460

5.65 Petitions filed in U.S. District Courts by Federal and State prisoners, by type of petition, 1977-2003 (5.65) 461

5.66 Appeals commenced, terminated, and pending, and judgeships authorized in U.S. Courts of Appeals, 1982-2003 (5.67) 462

5.67 Appeals from U.S. District Courts filed in U.S. Courts of Appeals, by nature of suit or offense, 1980, 1985, 1990-2003 (5.68) 463

5.68 Activities of the U.S. Supreme Court, at conclusion of the October term, 1976-2002 (5.69) 464

5.69 Cases filed, disposed of, and pending in the U.S. Supreme Court, by method of filing, at conclusion of the October term, 1976-2002 (5.70) 465

5.70 Petitions for review on writ of certiorari to the U.S. Supreme Court filed, terminated, and pending, by circuit and nature of proceeding, fiscal year 2003 (5.71) 466

5.71 U.S. Supreme Court cases argued and decided on merits, at conclusion of the October term, 1982-2002 (5.72) 467

5.72 Executive clemency applications for Federal offenses received, disposed of, and pending in the Office of the U.S. Pardon Attorney, fiscal years 1953-2003 (5.73) 468

5.73 Arrests and convictions handled by the U.S. Postal Inspection Service, fiscal years 1981-2003 (5.74) 469

5.74 Arrests and convictions handled by the U.S. Postal Inspection Service, by type of offense, fiscal year 2003 (5.75) 469

5.75 Prosecutions for violations of U.S. immigration and naturalization laws, by type of case and disposition, and aggregate fines and imprisonment imposed, fiscal years 1990, 1993-2003 (5.76) 470

5.76 Convictions for violations of U.S. immigration and naturalization laws, by offense, fiscal years 1990-2003 (5.77) 471

5.77 Immigration offenders investigated, charged in U.S. District Courts, and admitted to Federal prison, United States, 1985-2000 (5.78*) 472

5.78 Nationality of suspects in matters referred to U.S. attorneys for immigration offenses, United States, 2000 (5.79*) 472

5.79 Persons indicted, awaiting trial on December 31, and convicted of offenses involving abuse of public office, by level of government, 1973-2002 (5.80) 473

5.80 U.S. Army personnel tried in general, special, and summary courts-martial, and discharges approved, by conviction status, United States, fiscal years 1997-2003 (5.81) 474

5.81 U.S. Navy and Marine Corps personnel tried in general, special, and summary courts-martial, and discharges approved, by conviction status, United States, fiscal years 1997-2003 (5.82) 474

5.82 U.S. Air Force personnel tried in general, special, and summary courts-martial, and discharges approved, by conviction status, United States, fiscal years 1997-2003 (5.83) 475

5.83 U.S. Coast Guard personnel tried in general, special, and summary courts-martial, and discharges approved, by conviction status, United States, fiscal years 1997-2003 (5.84) 475

Section 6
Persons under correctional supervision 477

6.1 Adults on probation, in jail or prison, and on parole, United States, 1980-2003 (6.1) 478

6.2 Adults under correctional supervision, by type of supervision, region, and jurisdiction, 2003 (6.2) 479

6.3 Adults on probation under State and Federal jurisdiction, by region and jurisdiction, 2003 (6.3) 480

6.4 Federal offenders under community supervision, by offense, United States, fiscal year 2001 (6.4) 481

6.5 Persons received for supervision by the Federal Probation System, by type of supervision, 1975-2003 (6.5) 482

6.6 Movement of persons under supervision of the Federal Probation System, fiscal year 2003 (6.6) 483

6.7 Persons under supervision of the Federal Probation System and authorized probation officers, United States, 1975-2003 (6.7) 483

6.8 Federal probation terminations, by outcome and offense, United States, fiscal year 2001 (6.8) 484

6.9 Number and rate (per 100,000 juveniles age 10 through upper age of jurisdiction) of juveniles in public and private residential custody facilities, by State, 1997, 1999, and 2001 (--) 485

6.10 Juveniles in public and private residential custody facilities, by race, ethnicity, and offense, United States, on Oct. 24, 2001 (6.9) 486

6.11 Juveniles in public and private residential custody facilities, by age and sex, United States, on Oct. 24, 2001 (6.10) 486

6.12 Juveniles in public and private residential custody facilities, by sex, race, ethnicity, and State, on Oct. 24, 2001 (6.11) 487

6.13 Number and rate (per 100,000 residents) of persons in State and Federal prisons and local jails, United States, 1985, 1990-2003 (6.12) 488

6.14 Number of jail inmates, average daily population, and rated capacity, by legal status and sex, United States, 1983-2003 (6.13) 489

6.15 Persons under jail supervision, by confinement status and type of program, United States, 1995-2003 (6.14) 490

6.16 Jail inmates, by confinement status, region, and jurisdiction, June 30, 1999 (6.15*) 491

6.17 Jail inmates, by sex, race, Hispanic origin, and conviction status, United States, 1990-2003 (6.16) 492

6.18 Characteristics of jail inmates, by conviction status, United States, 1983, 1989, 1996, and 2002 (--) 493

6.19 Most serious current offense of jail inmates, by conviction status, United States, 1983, 1989, 1996, and 2002 (--) 494

6.20 Most serious current offense of jail inmates, by sex, race, and Hispanic origin, United States, 2002 (--) 495

6.21 Percent of jail inmates reporting drug use, by type of drug and frequency of use, United States, 1996 and 2002 (--) 496

6.22 Percent of jail inmates reporting alcohol use, by sex, race, Hispanic origin, and most serious offense, United States, 1996 and 2002 (--) 496

6.23 Family background of jail inmates while growing up, United States, 1996 and 2002 (--) 496

6.24 Jail inmates, by sex, race, Hispanic origin, region, and jurisdiction, June 30, 1999 (6.17*) 497

6.25 Jails and jail inmates in Indian country, by selected characteristics, United States, midyear 1998-2002 (6.19) 498

6.26 Jail inmates known to be positive for the human immunodeficiency virus (HIV), by region and State, June 30, 1993 and 1999 (6.20*) 499

6.27 Deaths and AIDS-related deaths among local jail inmates, by region and State, July 1, 1998 to June 30, 1999 (6.21*) 499

6.28 Number and rate (per 100,000 resident population in each group) of sentenced prisoners under jurisdiction of State and Federal correctional authorities on December 31, by sex, United States, 1925-2003 (6.22) 500

6.29 Rate (per 100,000 resident population) of sentenced prisoners under jurisdiction of State and Federal correctional authorities on December 31, by region and jurisdiction, 1980, 1984-2003 (6.23) 501

6.30 Prisoners under jurisdiction of State and Federal correctional authorities, by region and jurisdiction, Dec. 31, 2002 and 2003 (6.24) 502

6.31 Prisoners in Federal, State, and private adult correctional facilities, by type of facility and sex of prisoner, United States, June 30, 1995 and 2000 (6.25*) 503

6.32 State and Federal prisoners housed in private facilities and local jails, by jurisdiction, on Dec. 31, 2002 and 2003 (6.26) 504

6.33 Rate (per 100,000 U.S. resident population in each group) of sentenced prisoners under jurisdiction of State and Federal correctional authorities, by sex, race, Hispanic origin, and age group, United States, 2003 (6.27) 505

6.34 Prisoners in Federal, State, and private adult correctional facilities, by race and Hispanic origin of prisoner, and region, United States, June 30, 2000 (6.28*) 505

6.35 State and Federal prisoners reporting prior possession of firearms, by type of firearm, United States, 1997 (6.29*) 506

6.36 State and Federal prisoners reporting possession of firearms during current offense, by type of offense, United States, 1991 and 1997 (6.30*) 506

6.37 State and Federal prisoners reporting possession of firearms during current offense, by offense, United States, 1997 (6.31*) 506

6.38 Source of firearms possessed by State prisoners during current offense, United States, 1991 and 1997 (6.32*) 506

6.39 Prisoners under age 18 in State prisons, by sex, United States, midyear 1990, 1995, and 1999-2003 (--) 507

6.40 Prisoners under age 18 in State and private adult correctional facilities, by type of facility, security level, and region, United States, June 30, 2000 (6.33*) 507

6.41 Female prisoners under jurisdiction of State and Federal correctional authorities, by region and jurisdiction, on Dec. 31, 1990, 1995, 2000-2003 (6.34) 508

6.42 Noncitizens in State and Federal prisons, United States, at midyear 1998-2003 (--) 509

6.43 Mean maximum sentence, mean time served, and percent of sentence served for violent offenders, by State, 1993, 1996, and 1999 (6.37*) 510

6.44 Mean sentence length and mean time served for first releases from State prison, by offense, United States, 1990 and 1999 (6.38*) 511

6.45 Educational attainment for those in State and Federal prisons, in local jails, on probation, and in the general population, United States, selected years (6.39*) 511

6.46 Participation in education programs for those in State and Federal prisons, in local jails, and on probation, by type of program, United States, selected years (6.40*) 512

6.47 Characteristics of prisoners released in 1994 from prisons in 15 States (6.41*) 513

6.48 Recidivism rates of prisoners released in 1994 from prisons in 15 States, by amount of time after release recidivism occurred and outcome (6.42*) 513

6.49 Recidivism rates of prisoners released in 1994 from prisons in 15 States, by selected prisoner characteristics (6.43*) 514

6.50 Recidivism rates of prisoners released in 1994 from prisons in 15 States, by most serious offense for which released (6.44*) 515

6.51 Rearrest rates of prisoners released in 1994 from prisons in 15 States, by most serious offense for which released and charge at rearrest (6.45*) 516

Table list xxi

6.52 Recidivism rates of State prisoners released in 1983 and 1994, by offense type (6.46*) 516

6.53 Characteristics of Federal prisoners, United States, yearend 1995, 1999-2003 (6.47) 517

6.54 Characteristics of Federal prisoners, by type of facility, United States, yearend 2003 (6.49) 518

6.55 Security level of facilities housing Federal prisoners, by sex and race of prisoner, United States, yearend 2002 (6.51*) 518

6.56 Type of commitment offense among Federal prisoners, by sex and race of prisoner, United States, yearend 2003 (6.53) 519

6.57 Federal prison population, and number and percent sentenced for drug offenses, United States, 1970-2004 (6.54) 519

6.58 Time served to first release by Federal prisoners, by offense, United States, fiscal year 2001 (6.55) 520

6.59 Mean time served to first release by Federal prisoners, by offense and characteristics, United States, fiscal year 2001 (6.56) 521

6.60 Immigration offenders in Federal prison and average time to be served, United States, 1985-2000 (6.57*) 522

6.61 Detainees under Bureau of Immigration and Customs Enforcement (ICE) jurisdiction, by type of facility, Dec. 31, 1995, 2000-2003 (6.58) 522

6.62 Drug and alcoholism treatment facilities and clients in treatment, by type of care received and jurisdiction, on Mar. 29, 2002 (6.59) 523

6.63 Offenders in State sex offender registries, by State, 1998 and 2001 (6.60*) 524

6.64 Prisoners under jurisdiction of U.S. military authorities, by branch of service, Dec. 31, 1996-2003 (6.61) 525

6.65 Rate (per 100,000 adult residents) of adults on parole, United States, 1981-2003 (6.62) 525

6.66 Adults on parole under State and Federal jurisdiction, by region and jurisdiction, 2003 (6.63) 526

6.67 Percent of State parole discharges successfully completing supervision, by method of release from prison, United States, 1990-99 (6.65*) 527

6.68 Offenders returning to Federal prison within 3 years of release, United States, 1986-97 (6.67*) 527

6.69 Offenders returning to Federal prison within 3 years of release, by demographic characteristics, conviction offense, and type of release, United States, 1986-97 (aggregate) (6.68*) 527

6.70 Federal supervised release terminations, by outcome and offense, United States, fiscal year 2001 (6.69) 528

6.71 Federal parole terminations, by outcome and offense, United States, fiscal year 2001 (6.70) 529

6.72 State correctional facilities providing mental health screening and treatment, by region and State, June 30, 2000 (6.71*) 530

6.73 Prisoners receiving mental health treatment in State correctional facilities, by region and State, June 30, 2000 (6.72*) 531

6.74 State and Federal prisoners known to be positive for the human immunodeficiency virus (HIV) and confirmed AIDS cases, by region and jurisdiction, 1995-2001 (6.73) 532

6.75 State and Federal prisoners known to be positive for the human immunodeficiency virus (HIV), by sex, region, and jurisdiction, 2001 (6.74) 533

6.76 Number and rate (per 100,000 prisoners) of deaths among State and Federal prisoners, by cause of death, United States, 2001 (--) 533

6.77 Number and rate (per 100,000 prisoners) of AIDS-related deaths among State and Federal prisoners, United States, 1991-2001 (--) 533

6.78 Number and rate (per 100,000 prisoners) of deaths and AIDS-related deaths among State prisoners, by region and State, 1995 and 2001 (6.75) 534

6.79 Number of murders and nonnegligent manslaughters, persons under death sentence, executions, and other death sentence dispositions, United States, 1972-2003 (6.76) 535

6.80 Prisoners under sentence of death, by race, ethnicity, and jurisdiction, on Apr. 1, 2004 (6.77) 535

6.81 Prisoners under sentence of death, by demographic characteristics, prior felony conviction history, and legal status, United States, on Dec. 31, 1996-2003 (6.78) 536

6.82 Prisoners under sentence of death, by race, region, and jurisdiction, on Dec. 31, 2002 and 2003 (6.79) 537

6.83 Hispanic and female prisoners under sentence of death, by State, 2002 and 2003 (6.80) 538

6.84 Prisoners executed, by jurisdiction, 1930-Dec. 31, 2003 (aggregate) (6.81) 539

6.85 Prisoners executed under civil authority, by region and jurisdiction, 1930-2003 (6.82) 540

6.86 Prisoners executed under civil authority, by race and offense, United States, 1930-98 (6.83) 542

6.87 Methods of execution in States authorizing the death penalty, by State, 2003 (6.84) 543

Section 1

Characteristics of the criminal justice systems

The administrative aspects of law enforcement, judicial, and correctional systems are featured in this section. Financial, budgetary, and employment data for local, State, and Federal levels provide both detailed information and a glimpse of the complex organizational and structural components of various agencies within the criminal justice systems. In addition, selected statutory provisions regarding alcohol use and driving are included.

The section begins with data from surveys of justice system governmental employment and financial expenditures, prepared for the Bureau of Justice Statistics (BJS) by the U.S. Census Bureau. These tables provide extensive information on criminal justice system total and per capita expenditures at the Federal, State, and local levels relating to police protection, judicial and legal services, and correctional activities. In addition, budgetary figures are shown for Federal criminal justice agencies, including Federal funding for drug control programs and the Edward Byrne law enforcement assistance program. The number of persons employed by police departments, judicial and correctional systems, as well as related payroll data are presented for Federal, State, and local levels of government and for each individual State.

The second portion of the section contains information on law enforcement agencies and police personnel from two BJS-sponsored programs: the 2000 Census of State and Local Law Enforcement Agencies and the 2000 Law Enforcement Management and Administrative Statistics (LEMAS) survey. Tables from the 2000 census program display by-State listings of the number of agencies and employees for State, local, sheriffs, and special police agencies. The LEMAS survey tables provide aggregate-level data for local law enforcement agencies and sheriffs' offices. These include statistics on a variety of topics such as the number of agencies and employees, the number of officers assigned to respond to calls for service, demographics of sworn officers, educational and training requirements, salaries and operating budgets, firearms and nonlethal weapons authorized by police and sheriffs' departments, and presence of community policing and school resource units. New this year are tables presenting data on demographics, salaries, and operating expenditures for State law enforcement agencies. Tables showing the proportion of female and minority officers employed in large law enforcement agencies and a table listing police departments operated by Indian tribes also are featured.

Next, surveys conducted by the International City/County Management Association provide aggregate-level data on police salaries, employment, and administrative expenditures for several levels of municipal government, including per capita and average expenditures for police department personnel. This section also includes counts of full-time police employees and officers, collected through the FBI's Uniform Crime Reporting Program. The following set of tables lists Federal agencies with law enforcement authority and characteristics of officers employed by these agencies, including staff and budget information for the Drug Enforcement Administration. Trend data on workload, staffing, and budget are presented for the U.S. Marshals Service.

The next segment of the section addresses the courts and the judiciary. Information on judges in Federal courts includes current salaries and detailed demographic data on appointees to Federal district and appellate court judgeships, dating back to President Johnson's administration. Workload data for the Federal judiciary include a 21-year trend on the number of criminal cases filed in each judicial district as well as trend data on duties performed by Federal magistrate judges. The BJS-sponsored National Survey of Prosecutors provides information on budgets and personnel of prosecutors' offices as well as on the utilization of DNA evidence in felony cases processed in State courts. Next are tables showing salaries, term lengths, and selection and retention processes for those holding judicial office in each State. Other tables in this segment include data on jury utilization, juror fee schedules, and trend data for various types of investigative reports filed by Federal probation officers.

Concluding this section is information focusing on incarceration. Included are data on the number of jail facilities, jail capacities and occupation levels, and the number and characteristics of jail personnel. Featured in this edition are results from the BJS-sponsored 2000 Census of State and Federal Correctional Facilities, including selected characteristics of Federal, State, and private correctional facilities in the United States. Following this are tables focusing on Federal prisons, including demographic characteristics of correctional officers and staff, and the number and location of facilities operated by the Federal Bureau of Prisons. A table reporting on educational programs in State, Federal, and private prisons, as well as local jails, also is included here. Next, information is presented from BJS' Firearm Inquiry Statistics program on applications and rejections for firearms transfers. The final tables in the section describe State statutes on alcohol use and driving, and blood alcohol concentration tests in fatal automobile accidents.

Table 1.1

Justice system direct and intergovernmental expenditures

By level of government, United States, fiscal years 1982-2001[a]

(Dollar amounts in millions)

Fiscal year	Total all governments	Federal	Total State and local	State	Local[b] Total	Counties	Municipalities
1982	$35,842	$4,458	$31,573	$11,602	$20,968	$8,636	$12,455
1983	39,680	4,944	34,836	12,785	23,186	9,792	13,550
1984	43,943	5,868	38,156	14,213	25,154	10,617	14,696
1985	48,563	6,416	42,284	16,252	27,462	11,610	16,011
1986	53,500	6,595	47,070	18,556	30,178	13,031	17,346
1987	58,871	7,496	51,640	20,157	33,265	14,530	18,973
1988	65,231	8,851	56,767	22,837	36,098	15,884	20,449
1989	70,949	9,674	61,745	25,269	38,825	17,503	21,579
1990	79,434	12,798	69,215	28,345	43,559	19,644	24,244
1991	87,567	15,231	75,461	31,484	47,075	21,913	25,599
1992	93,777	17,423	80,248	33,755	50,115	23,820	26,771
1993	97,542	18,591	83,113	34,227	52,562	24,625	28,321
1994	103,471	19,084	88,845	37,161	55,517	26,071	29,909
1995	112,868	22,651	96,127	41,196	58,933	27,917	31,581
1996	120,194	23,344	102,714	43,803	62,970	29,805	33,782
1997	129,793	27,065	109,269	46,444	67,083	31,778	35,869
1998	135,899[c]	22,834[c]	116,534	49,454	70,831	33,916	37,586
1999	146,556[c]	27,392[c]	124,408	57,186	74,830	35,547	39,995
2000	155,722[c]	27,820[c]	NA	58,165	78,995	NA	NA
2001	167,113[c]	30,443[c]	NA	63,372	83,377	NA	NA

Note: These data were collected from government documents and from the annual surveys of government finances and employment conducted by the U.S. Census Bureau. Justice data are extracted from these sources by the Census Bureau for the U.S. Department of Justice, Bureau of Justice Statistics. The Federal Government, all State governments, and a sample of county, municipal, and township governments were included in the surveys. Since not all local governments were included in the surveys, these data are subject to sampling variation. Duplicative transactions between levels of government are excluded from the total for all governments, the State and local total, and the local total. Such intergovernmental expenditure consists of payments from one government to another and eventually will show up as a direct expenditure of a recipient government. The fiscal year for the Federal Government begins October 1 and ends September 30; see Appendix 1 for fiscal year beginning and end dates for States and local jurisdictions. Some data have been revised by the Source and may differ from previous editions of SOURCEBOOK. For survey methodology and definitions of terms, see Appendix 1.

[a] Detail may not add to total because of rounding.
[b] Data for local governments are estimates subject to sampling variation.
[c] Beginning in 1998, expenditure data for the Federal Government are taken directly from the *Budget of the United States Government* rather than from U.S. Census Bureau compilations. Therefore, the "total all governments" and "Federal" categories are not directly comparable to prior years.

Source: U.S. Department of Justice, Bureau of Justice Statistics, *Trends in Justice Expenditure and Employment*, NCJ 178268, Table 1 [Online]. Available: http://www.ojp.usdoj.gov/bjs/data/eetrnd01.wk1 [Mar. 27, 2002]; and *Justice Expenditure and Employment in the United States, 2001*, Bulletin NCJ 202792 (Washington, DC: U.S. Department of Justice, May 2004), p. 2, Table 1. Table adapted by SOURCEBOOK staff.

Table 1.2

Justice system direct and intergovernmental expenditures

By type of activity and level of government, United States, fiscal years 1980-99[a]

(Dollar amounts in thousands)

Level of government and fiscal year	Total justice system	Police protection	Judicial and legal	Corrections	Level of government and fiscal year	Total justice system	Police protection	Judicial and legal	Corrections
All governments					**State**				
1980	NA	$15,163,029	NA	$6,900,751	1980	$9,256,443	$2,194,349	$2,051,108	$4,547,667
1981	NA	16,822,094	NA	7,868,822	1981	10,372,682	2,479,905	2,332,434	5,179,448
1982	$35,841,916	19,022,184	$7,770,785	9,048,947	1982	11,601,780	2,833,370	2,748,364	6,020,046
1983	39,680,167	20,648,200	8,620,604	10,411,363	1983	12,785,244	2,963,067	2,949,598	6,872,579
1984	43,942,690	22,685,766	9,463,180	11,793,744	1984	14,212,842	3,173,297	3,271,076	7,768,469
1985	48,563,068	24,399,355	10,628,816	13,534,897	1985	16,252,377	3,468,821	3,635,984	9,147,572
1986	53,499,805	26,254,993	11,485,446	15,759,366	1986	18,555,723	3,749,413	4,004,720	10,801,590
1987	58,871,348	28,767,553	12,555,026	17,548,769	1987	20,157,123	4,066,692	4,339,306	11,691,125
1988	65,230,542	30,960,824	13,970,563	20,299,155	1988	22,836,919	4,531,184	4,885,843	13,419,892
1989	70,949,468	32,794,182	15,588,664	22,566,622	1989	25,268,915	4,780,353	5,441,743	15,046,819
1990	79,433,959	35,923,479	17,356,826	26,153,654	1990	28,345,066	5,163,475	5,970,895	17,210,696
1991	87,566,819	38,971,240	19,298,379	29,297,200	1991	31,484,371	5,507,249	6,754,491	19,222,631
1992	93,776,852	41,326,531	20,988,888	31,461,433	1992	33,755,092	5,592,791	7,722,882	20,439,419
1993	97,541,826	44,036,756	21,558,403	31,946,667	1993	34,227,194	5,603,484	7,820,251	20,803,459
1994	103,470,564	46,004,536	22,601,706	34,864,322	1994	37,161,391	6,000,330	8,026,326	23,134,735
1995	112,868,448	48,644,529	24,471,689	39,752,230	1995	41,196,021	6,451,364	8,675,619	26,069,038
1996	120,194,175	53,007,425	26,157,907	41,028,843	1996	39,903,049	6,499,224	8,109,714	25,294,111
1997	129,793,452	57,753,530	28,528,774	43,511,148	1997	42,353,331	6,669,520	8,566,938	27,116,873
1998[b]	135,899,453	60,828,213	29,901,380	45,169,860	1998	49,453,806	7,996,298	10,858,191	30,599,317
1999[b]	146,555,501	65,364,070	32,184,560	49,006,871	1999	57,186,495	9,631,583	12,874,850	34,680,062
Federal					**Local, total**[c]				
1980	NA	1,941,000	NA	408,000	1980	NA	11,398,808	NA	2,277,257
1981	NA	2,118,000	NA	436,000	1981	NA	12,678,955	NA	2,636,064
1982	4,458,000	2,527,000	1,390,000	541,000	1982	20,967,562	14,172,313	3,784,285	3,010,964
1983	4,844,000	2,815,000	1,523,000	606,000	1983	23,186,040	15,276,352	4,361,362	3,548,326
1984	5,868,000	3,396,000	1,785,000	687,000	1984	25,154,172	16,515,727	4,627,473	4,010,972
1985	6,416,000	3,495,000	2,129,000	792,000	1985	27,461,643	17,847,016	5,090,344	4,524,283
1986	6,595,000	3,643,000	2,090,000	862,000	1986	30,178,432	19,355,599	5,690,544	5,132,289
1987	7,496,000	4,231,000	2,271,000	994,000	1987	33,265,315	21,089,053	6,229,510	5,946,752
1988	8,851,000	4,954,000	2,639,000	1,258,000	1988	36,097,549	22,370,517	6,826,419	6,900,613
1989	9,674,000	5,307,000	2,949,000	1,418,000	1989	38,825,015	23,671,582	7,682,188	7,471,245
1990	12,798,000	5,666,000	5,398,000	1,734,000	1990	43,558,671	26,097,219	8,675,732	8,785,720
1991	15,231,000	6,725,000	6,384,000	2,122,000	1991	47,075,424	28,017,151	9,418,374	9,639,899
1992	17,423,000	7,400,000	7,377,000	2,646,000	1992	50,115,498	29,658,955	10,052,330	10,404,213
1993	18,591,000	8,069,000	7,832,000	2,690,000	1993	52,561,979	31,733,159	10,282,702	10,546,118
1994	19,084,000	8,059,000	8,184,000	2,841,000	1994	55,517,277	33,364,901	11,022,716	11,129,660
1995	22,651,000	9,298,000	9,184,000	4,169,000	1995	58,932,933	35,364,493	11,673,851	11,894,589
1996	23,344,000	10,115,000	9,459,000	3,766,000	1996	62,811,126	38,227,201	12,355,193	12,228,732
1997	27,065,000	12,518,000	10,651,000	3,896,000	1997	66,916,121	40,974,010	13,078,836	12,863,275
1998[b]	22,833,998	12,207,611	7,461,582	3,164,805	1998	70,831,438	43,311,939	13,559,129	13,960,370
1999[b]	27,392,000	14,796,726	8,515,167	4,080,107	1999	74,829,679	45,592,589	14,141,549	15,095,541
Total State and local					**Counties**[c]				
					1980	NA	2,669,497	NA	1,777,763
1980	NA	13,424,029	NA	6,515,689	1981	NA	3,091,038	NA	2,066,269
1981	NA	14,918,094	NA	7,458,133	1982	8,635,936	3,486,823	2,805,312	2,343,801
1982	31,572,916	16,656,184	6,380,785	8,535,947	1983	9,791,530	3,754,693	3,238,571	2,798,266
1983	34,836,167	17,903,200	7,097,604	9,835,363	1984	10,616,787	4,051,074	3,401,793	3,163,920
1984	38,155,690	19,330,766	7,678,180	11,146,744	1985	11,609,827	4,400,716	3,736,030	3,473,081
1985	42,284,068	20,969,355	8,499,816	12,814,897	1986	13,031,109	4,801,572	4,209,092	4,020,445
1986	47,069,805	22,712,993	9,395,446	14,961,366	1987	14,530,194	5,254,562	4,611,863	4,663,773
1987	51,640,348	24,731,553	10,284,026	16,624,769	1988	15,883,574	5,574,280	5,047,003	5,262,291
1988	56,766,542	26,303,824	11,331,563	19,131,155	1989	17,503,442	6,099,265	5,692,464	5,711,713
1989	61,745,468	27,842,182	12,639,664	21,263,622	1990	19,644,273	6,669,385	6,416,194	6,558,694
1990	69,214,959	30,579,479	14,075,826	24,559,654	1991	21,913,042	7,386,260	7,074,386	7,452,396
1991	75,460,819	32,801,240	15,303,379	27,356,200	1992	23,820,019	8,012,151	7,521,219	8,286,649
1992	80,247,852	34,623,531	16,573,888	29,050,433	1993	24,624,542	8,520,472	7,697,938	8,406,132
1993	83,112,826	36,691,756	16,896,403	29,524,667	1994	26,070,804	8,955,664	8,275,007	8,840,133
1994	88,844,564	38,686,536	17,880,706	32,227,322	1995	27,917,010	9,499,807	8,804,229	9,612,974
1995	96,127,448	41,096,529	19,162,689	35,868,230	1996	29,610,765	10,425,771	9,358,446	9,826,548
1996	102,714,175	44,726,425	20,464,907	37,522,843	1997	31,576,448	11,328,607	9,928,998	10,318,843
1997	109,269,452	47,643,530	21,645,774	39,980,148	1998	33,916,286	12,235,307	10,326,936	11,354,043
1998	116,534,453	50,475,213	25,573,380	42,485,860	1999	35,118,293	12,457,018	10,540,476	12,120,799
1999	124,407,501	53,400,070	25,299,560	45,707,871					

See notes at end of table.

Table 1.2

Justice system direct and intergovernmental expenditures

By type of activity and level of government, United States, fiscal years 1980-99[a]--Continued

(Dollar amounts in thousands)

Level of government and fiscal year	Total justice system	Police protection	Judicial and legal	Corrections
Municipalities[c]				
1980	NA	$8,791,989	NA	$527,060
1981	NA	9,678,462	NA	602,148
1982	$12,455,487	10,765,207	$981,963	708,317
1983	13,550,117	11,630,815	1,130,261	789,041
1984	14,696,313	12,565,350	1,235,073	895,890
1985	16,011,251	13,549,507	1,367,982	1,093,762
1986	17,346,101	14,685,842	1,495,968	1,164,291
1987	18,973,049	16,005,162	1,626,223	1,341,664
1988	20,449,324	16,964,757	1,788,158	1,696,409
1989	21,579,228	17,756,525	2,003,083	1,819,620
1990	24,244,122	19,674,855	2,274,164	2,295,103
1991	25,599,404	20,972,085	2,358,669	2,268,650
1992	26,770,919	22,034,381	2,546,171	2,190,367
1993	28,321,497	23,506,869	2,595,607	2,219,021
1994	29,908,762	24,766,007	2,765,164	2,377,591
1995	31,580,565	26,328,895	2,886,803	2,364,867
1996	33,200,361	27,801,430	2,996,747	2,402,184
1997	35,339,673	29,645,403	3,149,838	2,544,432
1998	37,585,662	31,627,623	3,249,087	2,708,952
1999	39,324,285	33,133,214	3,373,785	2,817,286

Note: See Note, table 1.1. Duplicative transactions between levels of government are excluded from the total for all governments, the State and local total, and the local total. Such intergovernmental expenditure consists of payments from one government to another and eventually will show up as a direct expenditure of a recipient government. The State government total for 1980 and 1981 includes a residual "other" category not displayed separately. Some data have been revised by the Source and may differ from previous editions of SOURCEBOOK. For survey methodology and definitions of terms, see Appendix 1.

[a] Detail may not add to total because of rounding.
[b] Beginning in 1998, expenditure data for the Federal government are taken directly from the *Budget of the United States Government* rather than from U.S. Census Bureau compilations. Therefore, the "all governments" and "Federal" categories are not directly comparable to prior years.
[c] Data for local governments are estimates subject to sampling variation.

Source: U.S. Department of Justice, Bureau of Justice Statistics, *Trends in Justice Expenditure and Employment*, NCJ 178272, Table 5 [Online]. Available: http://www.ojp.usdoj.gov/bjs/data/eetrnd05.wk1 [Mar. 27, 2002].

Table 1.3

Justice system direct and intergovernmental expenditures

By level of government and type of activity, United States, fiscal year 2000

Activity	Total all governments	Federal Government	State governments	Local governments[a]	Federal	State	Local[a]
Total justice system[b]	$155,721,690	$27,820,000	$58,166,467	$78,995,330	X	X	X
Direct expenditure	155,721,690	22,086,000	53,991,300	78,644,390	14.8%	34.7%	50.5%
Intergovernmental expenditure	X	4,734,000	4,175,167	350,940	X	X	X
Police protection[b]	68,911,071	14,002,473	9,787,596	48,219,165	X	X	X
Direct expenditure	68,911,071	12,113,000	8,580,703	48,217,368	17.6	12.5	70.0
Intergovernmental expenditure	X	2,483,884	1,206,893	1,797	X	X	X
Judicial and legal[b]	34,298,180	8,496,556	13,249,668	14,842,083	X	X	X
Direct expenditure	34,298,180	7,266,000	12,370,672	14,661,508	21.2	36.1	42.7
Intergovernmental expenditure	X	1,489,961	878,996	180,575	X	X	X
Corrections[b]	52,512,439	4,230,971	35,129,203	15,934,082	X	X	X
Direct expenditure	52,512,439	3,707,000	33,039,925	15,765,514	7.1	62.9	30.0
Intergovernmental expenditure	X	760,155	2,089,278	168,568	X	X	X

Note: See Note, table 1.1. For survey methodology and definitions of terms, see Appendix 1.

[a] Data for local governments are estimates subject to sampling variation.
[b] The total category for each criminal justice activity, and for the total justice system, excludes duplicative intergovernmental expenditure amounts. This was done to avoid the artificial inflation that would result if an intergovernmental expenditure of a government were tabulated and then counted again when the recipient government(s) expended that amount. The intergovernmental expenditure categories are not totaled for this reason.

Source: U.S. Department of Justice, Bureau of Justice Statistics, *2000 Justice Expenditure and Employment Extracts*, NCJ 194802, Table 1 [Online]. Available: http://www.ojp.usdoj.gov/bjs/pub/sheets/cjee00.zip, file cjee0001.wk1 [Aug. 6, 2004].

Table 1.4

Justice system direct and intergovernmental expenditures

By level of government and type of activity, United States, fiscal year 2001

Activity	Total all governments	Federal Government	State governments	Local governments[a]	Federal	State	Local[a]
Total justice system[b]	$167,112,887	$30,443,000	$63,372,304	$83,377,152	X	X	X
Direct expenditure	167,112,887	25,285,000	58,820,452	83,007,435	15.1%	35.2%	49.7%
Intergovernmental expenditure	X	5,158,000	4,551,852	369,717	X	X	X
Police protection[b]	72,405,970	15,013,811	10,496,730	50,717,839	X	X	X
Direct expenditure	72,405,970	12,470,000	9,219,650	50,716,320	17.2	12.7	70.0
Intergovernmental expenditure	X	2,543,811	1,277,808	1,519	X	X	X
Judicial and legal[b]	37,751,380	10,230,341	14,443,708	15,938,498	X	X	X
Direct expenditure	37,751,380	8,497,000	13,522,531	15,731,849	22.5	35.8	41.7
Intergovernmental expenditure	X	1,733,341	921,177	206,649	X	X	X
Corrections[b]	56,955,537	5,198,848	38,431,866	16,720,815	X	X	X
Direct expenditure	56,955,537	4,318,000	36,078,271	16,559,266	7.6	63.3	29.1
Intergovernmental expenditure	X	880,848	2,353,595	161,549	X	X	X

Note: See Note, table 1.1. For survey methodology and definitions of terms, see Appendix 1.

[a]Data for local governments are estimates subject to sampling variation.
[b]The total category for each criminal justice activity, and for the total justice system, excludes duplicative intergovernmental expenditure amounts. This was done to avoid the artificial inflation that would result if an intergovernmental expenditure of a government were tabulated and then counted again when the recipient government(s) expended that amount. The intergovernmental expenditure categories are not totaled for this reason.

Source: U.S. Department of Justice, Bureau of Justice Statistics, *2001 Justice Expenditure and Employment Extracts*, NCJ 202792, Table 1 [Online]. Available: http://www.ojp.usdoj.gov/bjs/pub/sheets/cjee01.zip, file cjee0101.wk1 [Aug. 6, 2004].

Table 1.5

Justice system direct expenditures

By level of government, United States, fiscal years 1982-2001[a]

(Dollar amounts in millions)

Fiscal year	Total all governments	Federal	Total State and local	State	Local[b] Total	Counties	Municipalities
1982	$35,842	$4,269	$31,573	$10,651	$20,922	$8,556	$12,366
1983	39,680	4,844	34,836	11,709	23,127	9,705	13,422
1984	43,943	5,787	38,156	13,081	25,075	10,518	14,557
1985	48,563	6,279	42,284	14,903	27,381	11,517	15,864
1986	53,500	6,430	47,070	16,978	30,092	12,935	17,157
1987	58,871	7,231	51,640	18,465	33,175	14,429	18,746
1988	65,231	8,464	56,767	20,880	35,887	15,778	20,108
1989	70,949	9,204	61,745	23,009	38,736	17,399	21,337
1990	79,434	10,219	69,215	25,764	43,451	19,510	23,941
1991	87,567	12,106	75,461	28,493	46,968	21,761	25,207
1992	93,777	13,529	80,248	30,271	49,977	23,672	26,305
1993	97,542	14,429	83,113	30,696	52,417	24,469	27,948
1994	103,471	14,626	88,845	33,495	55,349	25,856	29,493
1995	112,868	16,741	96,127	37,360	58,768	27,733	31,035
1996	120,194	17,480	102,714	39,903	62,811	29,611	33,200
1997	129,793	20,524	109,269	42,353	66,916	31,576	35,340
1998	135,899[c]	19,365[c]	116,534	45,995	70,539	33,571	36,968
1999	146,556[c]	22,148[c]	124,408	49,965	74,443	35,118	39,324
2000	155,722[c]	23,086[c]	NA	53,991	78,644	NA	NA
2001	167,113[c]	25,285[c]	NA	58,820	83,007	NA	NA

Note: See Note, table 1.1. For survey methodology and definitions of terms, see Appendix 1.

[a]Detail may not add to total because of rounding.
[b]Data for local governments are estimates subject to sampling variation.
[c]Beginning in 1998, expenditure data for the Federal Government are taken directly from the *Budget of the United States Government* rather than from U.S. Census Bureau compilations. Therefore, the "total all governments" and "Federal" categories are not directly comparable to prior years.

Source: U.S. Department of Justice, Bureau of Justice Statistics, *Trends in Justice Expenditure and Employment*, NCJ 178269, Table 2 [Online]. Available: http://www.ojp.usdoj.gov/bjs/data/eetrnd02.wk1 [Mar. 27, 2002]; and *Justice Expenditure and Employment in the United States, 2001*, Bulletin NCJ 202792 (Washington, DC: U.S. Department of Justice, May 2004), p. 2, Table 1. Table adapted by SOURCEBOOK staff.

Table 1.6

Direct expenditures for State and local justice system activities

By type of activity and level of government, fiscal year 2000

(Dollar amounts in thousands)

State and level of government[a]	Total direct expenditure[b]	Total justice system Amount[c]	Percent of total direct expenditure[c]	Police protection Amount	Percent of total justice system	Judicial and legal Amount	Percent of total justice system	Corrections Amount	Percent of total justice system
States-local, total	$1,742,913,626	$132,635,690	7.6%	$56,798,071	42.8%	$27,032,180	20.4%	$48,805,439	36.8%
State	757,027,323	53,991,300	7.1	8,580,703	15.9	12,370,672	22.9	33,039,925	61.2
Local, total	985,886,303	78,644,390	8.0	48,217,368	61.3	14,661,508	18.6	15,765,514	20.0
Counties	220,348,039	37,508,487	17.0	13,401,035	35.7	11,180,512	29.8	12,926,940	34.5
Municipalities	345,348,693	41,135,903	11.9	34,816,333	84.6	3,480,996	8.5	2,838,574	6.9
Alabama	25,319,135	1,321,833	5.2	655,951	49.6	261,598	19.8	404,284	30.6
State	11,964,239	537,086	4.5	92,171	17.2	172,010	32.0	272,905	50.8
Local, total	13,354,896	784,747	5.9	563,780	71.8	89,588	11.4	131,379	16.7
Counties	1,620,602	314,950	19.4	142,927	45.4	57,169	18.2	114,854	36.5
Municipalities	4,034,255	469,797	11.6	420,853	89.6	32,419	6.9	16,525	3.5
Alaska	8,515,351	481,705	5.7	176,972	36.7	129,744	26.9	174,989	36.3
State	5,584,192	341,390	6.1	49,669	14.5	118,097	34.6	173,624	50.9
Local, total	2,931,159	140,315	4.8	127,303	90.7	11,647	8.3	1,365	1.0
Boroughs	1,046,772	18,560	1.8	14,577	78.5	3,983	21.5	0	X
Municipalities	1,758,777	121,755	6.9	112,726	92.6	7,664	6.3	1,365	1.1
Arizona	27,293,135	2,662,075	9.8	1,096,134	41.2	610,941	22.9	955,000	35.9
State	10,375,264	949,183	9.1	144,730	15.2	144,230	15.2	660,223	69.6
Local, total	16,917,871	1,712,892	10.1	951,404	55.5	466,711	27.2	294,777	17.2
Counties	2,985,658	826,520	27.7	171,803	20.8	359,965	43.6	294,752	35.7
Municipalities	5,558,173	886,372	15.9	779,601	88.0	106,746	12.0	25	(d)
Arkansas	12,243,360	835,961	6.8	351,795	42.1	156,396	18.7	327,770	39.2
State	6,863,930	439,922	6.4	73,131	16.6	100,394	22.8	266,397	60.6
Local, total	5,379,430	396,039	7.4	278,664	70.4	56,002	14.1	61,373	15.5
Counties	740,932	170,602	23.0	70,760	41.5	38,702	22.7	61,140	35.8
Municipalities	1,785,454	225,437	12.6	207,904	92.2	17,300	7.7	233	0.1
California	234,115,548	22,128,975	9.5	8,703,685	39.3	6,254,902	28.3	7,170,388	32.4
State	84,383,256	7,586,898	9.0	1,051,106	13.9	2,417,422	31.9	4,118,370	54.3
Local, total	149,732,292	14,542,077	9.7	7,652,579	52.6	3,837,480	26.4	3,052,018	21.0
Counties	42,031,231	8,725,755	20.8	2,392,950	27.4	3,381,649	38.8	2,951,156	33.8
Municipalities	40,695,966	5,816,322	14.3	5,259,629	90.4	455,831	7.8	100,862	1.7
Colorado	26,169,571	1,979,115	7.6	830,063	41.9	328,713	16.6	820,339	41.4
State	10,226,930	856,645	8.4	77,172	9.0	180,271	21.0	599,202	69.9
Local, total	15,942,641	1,122,470	7.0	752,891	67.1	148,442	13.2	221,137	19.7
Counties	2,148,853	455,489	21.2	218,574	48.0	72,367	15.9	164,548	36.1
Municipalities	5,576,612	666,981	12.0	534,317	80.1	76,075	11.4	56,589	8.5
Connecticut	24,011,246	1,665,917	6.9	681,914	40.9	430,098	25.8	553,905	33.2
State	13,360,650	1,091,359	8.2	140,006	12.8	397,448	36.4	553,905	50.8
Local, total	10,650,596	574,558	5.4	541,908	94.3	32,650	5.7	0	X
Municipalities	9,723,886	574,558	5.9	541,908	94.3	32,650	5.7	0	X
Delaware	5,152,073	485,081	9.4	166,302	34.3	90,703	18.7	228,076	47.0
State	3,354,648	374,694	11.2	62,991	16.8	83,627	22.3	228,076	60.9
Local, total	1,797,425	110,387	6.1	103,311	93.6	7,076	6.4	0	X
Counties	292,521	48,734	16.7	41,928	86.0	6,806	14.0	0	X
Municipalities	359,843	61,653	17.1	61,383	99.6	270	0.4	0	X
District of Columbia	6,526,972	680,407	10.4	329,503	48.4	46,400	6.8	304,504	44.8
Local, total	6,526,972	680,407	10.4	329,503	48.4	46,400	6.8	304,504	44.8
Municipality	5,483,415	680,407	12.4	329,503	48.4	46,400	6.8	304,504	44.8
Florida	84,300,913	8,407,384	10.0	3,738,392	44.5	1,396,319	16.6	3,272,673	38.9
State	31,134,485	3,261,293	10.5	367,398	11.3	676,783	20.8	2,217,112	68.0
Local, total	53,166,428	5,146,091	9.7	3,370,994	65.5	719,536	14.0	1,055,561	20.5
Counties	16,238,727	3,467,007	21.4	1,811,422	52.2	643,780	18.6	1,011,805	29.2
Municipalities	11,533,309	1,679,084	14.6	1,559,572	92.9	75,756	4.5	43,756	2.6

See notes at end of table.

Table 1.6

Direct expenditures for State and local justice system activities

By type of activity and level of government, fiscal year 2000--Continued

(Dollar amounts in thousands)

State and level of government[a]	Total direct expenditure[b]	Total justice system Amount[c]	Percent of total direct expenditure[c]	Police protection Amount	Percent of total justice system	Judicial and legal Amount	Percent of total justice system	Corrections Amount	Percent of total justice system
Georgia	$43,516,518	$3,179,612	7.3%	$1,279,240	40.2%	$524,875	16.5%	$1,375,497	43.3%
State	17,633,200	1,279,918	7.3	193,087	15.1	118,094	9.2	968,737	75.7
Local, total	25,883,318	1,899,694	7.3	1,086,153	57.2	406,781	21.4	406,760	21.4
Counties	5,569,900	1,226,338	22.0	546,932	44.6	344,561	28.1	334,845	27.3
Municipalities	5,303,718	673,356	12.7	539,221	80.1	62,220	9.2	71,915	10.7
Hawaii	8,239,002	556,441	6.8	221,899	39.9	179,920	32.3	154,622	27.8
State	6,446,707	306,450	4.8	4,258	1.4	147,570	48.2	154,622	50.5
Local, total	1,792,295	249,991	13.9	217,641	87.1	32,350	12.9	0	X
Counties	497,173	78,771	15.8	65,101	82.6	13,670	17.4	0	X
Municipalities	1,277,997	171,220	13.4	152,540	89.1	18,680	10.9	0	X
Idaho	6,404,069	500,098	7.8	207,380	41.5	101,617	20.3	191,101	38.2
State	3,214,864	238,743	7.4	37,329	15.6	52,688	22.1	148,726	62.3
Local, total	3,189,205	261,355	8.2	170,051	65.1	48,929	18.7	42,375	16.2
Counties	688,357	163,156	23.7	79,038	48.4	41,764	25.6	42,354	26.0
Municipalities	635,628	98,199	15.4	91,013	92.7	7,165	7.3	21	(d)
Illinois	74,724,368	5,777,158	7.7	3,053,337	52.9	961,250	16.6	1,762,571	30.5
State	29,132,804	1,880,969	6.5	335,718	17.8	267,766	14.2	1,277,485	67.9
Local, total	45,591,564	3,896,189	8.5	2,717,619	69.8	693,484	17.8	485,086	12.5
Counties	4,910,146	1,442,754	29.4	336,676	23.3	621,088	43.0	484,990	33.6
Municipalities	14,485,636	2,453,435	16.9	2,380,943	97.0	72,396	3.0	96	(d)
Indiana	31,245,691	1,894,617	6.1	842,818	44.5	324,887	17.1	726,912	38.4
State	13,553,658	831,589	6.1	198,399	23.9	96,465	11.6	536,725	64.5
Local, total	17,692,033	1,063,029	6.0	644,419	60.6	228,422	21.5	190,187	17.9
Counties	3,727,023	479,181	12.9	153,910	32.1	170,586	35.6	154,685	32.3
Municipalities	5,551,845	583,847	10.5	490,509	84.0	57,836	9.9	35,502	6.1
Iowa	17,238,851	977,082	5.7	426,865	43.7	252,649	25.9	297,568	30.5
State	8,241,231	501,429	6.1	80,403	16.0	196,662	39.2	224,364	44.7
Local, total	8,997,620	475,653	5.3	346,462	72.8	55,987	11.8	73,204	15.4
Counties	1,713,395	220,793	12.9	101,639	46.0	46,488	21.1	72,666	32.9
Municipalities	3,013,771	254,860	8.5	244,823	96.1	9,499	3.7	538	0.2
Kansas	14,418,887	985,103	6.8	429,773	43.6	206,075	20.9	349,255	35.5
State	6,270,525	451,373	7.2	53,008	11.7	125,523	27.8	272,842	60.4
Local, total	8,148,362	533,730	6.6	376,765	70.6	80,552	15.1	76,413	14.3
Counties	1,496,815	252,438	16.9	118,989	47.1	58,245	23.1	75,204	29.8
Municipalities	2,639,675	281,292	10.7	257,776	91.6	22,307	7.9	1,209	0.4
Kentucky	21,473,123	1,388,829	6.5	488,139	35.1	290,125	20.9	610,565	44.0
State	12,402,221	793,810	6.4	161,148	20.3	238,440	30.0	394,222	49.7
Local, total	9,070,902	595,019	6.6	326,991	55.0	51,685	8.7	216,343	36.4
Counties	1,828,418	270,989	14.8	80,514	29.7	33,681	12.4	156,794	57.9
Municipalities	2,516,312	324,030	12.9	246,477	76.1	18,004	5.6	59,549	18.4
Louisiana	25,018,335	1,967,772	7.9	829,333	42.1	358,594	18.2	779,845	39.6
State	12,832,100	725,572	5.7	194,802	26.8	133,962	18.5	396,808	54.7
Local, total	12,186,235	1,242,200	10.2	634,531	51.1	224,632	18.1	383,037	30.8
Parishes	3,588,177	701,121	19.5	257,744	36.8	132,643	18.9	310,734	44.3
Municipalities	3,486,751	541,079	15.5	376,787	69.6	91,989	17.0	72,303	13.4
Maine	7,643,277	355,751	4.7	163,824	46.1	68,623	19.3	123,304	34.7
State	4,535,685	195,979	4.3	45,389	23.2	58,708	30.0	91,882	46.9
Local, total	3,107,592	159,772	5.1	118,435	74.1	9,915	6.2	31,422	19.7
Counties	88,895	55,202	62.1	17,556	31.8	6,963	12.6	30,683	55.6
Municipalities	1,935,175	104,570	5.4	100,879	96.5	2,952	2.8	739	0.7
Maryland	30,598,125	2,713,505	8.9	1,120,192	41.3	489,411	18.0	1,103,902	40.7
State	15,014,334	1,429,328	9.5	234,208	16.4	301,214	21.1	893,906	62.5
Local, total	15,583,791	1,284,177	8.2	885,984	69.0	188,197	14.7	209,996	16.4
Counties	12,247,739	907,387	7.4	551,300	60.8	146,091	16.1	209,996	23.1
Municipalities	2,988,421	376,790	12.6	334,684	88.8	42,106	11.2	0	X

See notes at end of table.

Table 1.6

Direct expenditures for State and local justice system activities

By type of activity and level of government, fiscal year 2000--Continued

(Dollar amounts in thousands)

State and level of government[a]	Total direct expenditure[b]	Total justice system Amount[c]	Percent of total direct expenditure[c]	Police protection Amount	Percent of total justice system	Judicial and legal Amount	Percent of total justice system	Corrections Amount	Percent of total justice system
Massachusetts	$44,180,713	$2,901,028	6.6%	$1,478,778	51.0%	$627,664	21.6%	$794,586	27.4%
State	23,237,473	1,572,327	6.8	391,383	24.9	575,788	36.6	605,156	38.5
Local, total	20,943,240	1,328,701	6.3	1,087,395	81.8	51,876	3.9	189,430	14.3
Counties	291,895	108,384	37.1	3,570	3.3	1,020	0.9	103,794	95.8
Municipalities	17,018,647	1,220,317	7.2	1,083,825	88.8	50,856	4.2	85,636	7.0
Michigan	61,443,616	4,550,728	7.4	1,792,535	39.4	905,473	19.9	1,852,720	40.7
State	25,547,864	1,907,977	7.5	283,956	14.9	141,075	7.4	1,482,946	77.7
Local, total	35,895,752	2,642,751	7.4	1,508,579	57.1	764,398	28.9	369,774	14.0
Counties	7,353,455	1,230,970	16.7	286,062	23.2	580,698	47.2	364,210	29.6
Municipalities	12,550,534	1,411,781	11.2	1,222,517	86.6	183,700	13.0	5,564	0.4
Minnesota	35,423,651	1,907,219	5.4	873,741	45.8	442,395	23.2	591,083	31.0
State	15,715,933	596,353	3.8	123,456	20.7	180,202	30.2	292,695	49.1
Local, total	19,707,718	1,310,866	6.7	750,285	57.2	262,193	20.0	298,388	22.8
Counties	4,182,091	800,074	19.1	263,389	32.9	238,892	29.9	297,793	37.2
Municipalities	6,246,565	510,792	8.2	486,896	95.3	23,301	4.6	595	0.1
Mississippi	15,378,511	850,076	5.5	403,888	47.5	154,349	18.2	291,839	34.3
State	7,724,155	372,371	4.8	67,018	18.0	63,405	17.0	241,948	65.0
Local, total	7,654,356	477,705	6.2	336,870	70.5	90,944	19.0	49,891	10.4
Counties	1,973,011	255,736	13.0	128,969	50.4	79,483	31.1	47,284	18.5
Municipalities	1,998,385	221,969	11.1	207,901	93.7	11,461	5.2	2,607	1.2
Missouri	27,950,969	1,916,548	6.9	885,498	46.2	358,717	18.7	672,333	35.1
State	12,764,365	817,052	6.4	124,571	15.2	178,646	21.9	513,835	62.9
Local, total	15,186,604	1,099,496	7.2	760,927	69.2	180,071	16.4	158,498	14.4
Counties	1,490,775	375,531	25.2	150,860	40.2	115,049	30.6	109,622	29.2
Municipalities	4,844,712	723,965	14.9	610,067	84.3	65,022	9.0	48,876	6.8
Montana	4,983,156	326,155	6.5	135,806	41.6	65,616	20.1	124,733	38.2
State	2,957,657	152,793	5.2	24,718	16.2	23,932	15.7	104,143	68.2
Local, total	2,025,499	173,362	8.6	111,088	64.1	41,684	24.0	20,590	11.9
Counties	402,060	111,260	27.7	57,352	51.5	33,725	30.3	20,183	18.1
Municipalities	429,166	62,102	14.5	53,736	86.5	7,959	12.8	407	0.7
Nebraska	10,820,079	562,621	5.2	235,245	41.8	95,919	17.0	231,457	41.1
State	4,186,571	261,369	6.2	48,731	18.6	40,010	15.3	172,628	66.0
Local, total	6,633,508	301,252	4.5	186,514	61.9	55,909	18.6	58,829	19.5
Counties	764,868	158,386	20.7	52,578	33.2	51,085	32.3	54,723	34.6
Municipalities	1,447,864	142,866	9.9	133,936	93.7	4,824	3.4	4,106	2.9
Nevada	11,223,671	1,258,843	11.2	539,187	42.8	248,163	19.7	471,493	37.5
State	3,796,937	318,405	8.4	57,902	18.2	42,937	13.5	217,566	68.3
Local, total	7,426,734	940,438	12.7	481,285	51.2	205,226	21.8	253,927	27.0
Counties	3,108,826	716,221	23.0	335,292	46.8	167,206	23.3	213,723	29.8
Municipalities	1,229,530	224,217	18.2	145,993	65.1	38,020	17.0	40,204	17.9
New Hampshire	6,222,433	394,551	6.3	187,070	47.4	92,297	23.4	115,184	29.2
State	3,312,805	199,551	6.0	38,402	19.2	76,205	38.2	84,944	42.6
Local, total	2,909,628	195,000	6.7	148,668	76.2	16,092	8.3	30,240	15.5
Counties	198,879	49,738	25.0	11,420	23.0	8,078	16.2	30,240	60.8
Municipalities	1,421,391	145,262	10.2	137,248	94.5	8,014	5.5	0	X
New Jersey	54,511,830	4,659,648	8.5	2,231,315	47.9	948,078	20.3	1,480,255	31.8
State	26,143,680	1,993,660	7.6	401,894	20.2	541,489	27.2	1,050,277	52.7
Local, total	28,368,150	2,665,988	9.4	1,829,421	68.6	406,589	15.3	429,978	16.1
Counties	5,540,532	841,441	15.2	156,264	18.6	257,855	30.6	427,322	50.8
Municipalities	9,933,167	1,824,547	18.4	1,673,157	91.7	148,734	8.2	2,656	0.1
New Mexico	11,194,843	864,578	7.7	382,185	44.2	166,974	19.3	315,419	36.5
State	6,253,225	442,509	7.1	77,574	17.5	148,213	33.5	216,722	49.0
Local, total	4,941,618	422,069	8.5	304,611	72.2	18,761	4.4	98,697	23.4
Counties	739,282	149,002	20.2	84,408	56.6	5,490	3.7	59,104	39.7
Municipalities	1,772,141	273,067	15.4	220,203	80.6	13,271	4.9	39,593	14.5

See notes at end of table.

Table 1.6

Direct expenditures for State and local justice system activities

By type of activity and level of government, fiscal year 2000--Continued

(Dollar amounts in thousands)

State and level of government[a]	Total direct expenditure[b]	Total justice system Amount[c]	Percent of total direct expenditure[c]	Police protection Amount	Percent of total justice system	Judicial and legal Amount	Percent of total justice system	Corrections Amount	Percent of total justice system
New York	$171,232,216	$12,371,653	7.2%	$5,716,952	46.2%	$2,262,471	18.3%	$4,392,230	35.5%
State	65,651,806	4,126,686	6.3	421,887	10.2	1,406,602	34.1	2,298,197	55.7
Local, total	105,580,410	8,244,967	7.8	5,295,065	64.2	855,869	10.4	2,094,033	25.4
Counties	14,198,451	2,314,254	16.3	1,177,465	50.9	290,369	12.5	846,420	36.6
Municipalities	65,945,675	5,930,713	9.0	4,117,600	69.4	565,500	9.5	1,247,613	21.0
North Carolina	46,134,556	3,010,205	6.5	1,381,315	45.9	470,322	15.6	1,158,568	38.5
State	20,314,037	1,663,902	8.2	350,889	21.1	407,349	24.5	905,664	54.4
Local, total	25,820,519	1,346,303	5.2	1,030,426	76.5	62,973	4.7	252,904	18.8
Counties	17,295,355	650,647	3.8	345,309	53.1	52,434	8.1	252,904	38.9
Municipalities	6,070,026	695,656	11.5	685,117	98.5	10,539	1.5	0	X
North Dakota	4,040,996	164,036	4.1	68,182	41.6	55,424	33.8	40,430	24.6
State	2,265,856	68,863	3.0	12,125	17.6	27,882	40.5	28,856	41.9
Local, total	1,775,140	95,173	5.4	56,057	58.9	27,542	28.9	11,574	12.2
Counties	283,717	55,457	19.5	18,799	33.9	25,243	45.5	11,415	20.6
Municipalities	582,154	39,716	6.8	37,258	93.8	2,299	5.8	159	0.4
Ohio	68,417,151	5,220,319	7.6	2,124,836	40.7	1,158,075	22.2	1,937,408	37.1
State	31,698,486	1,912,370	6.0	224,802	11.8	200,893	10.5	1,486,675	77.7
Local, total	36,718,665	3,307,949	9.0	1,900,034	57.4	957,182	28.9	450,733	13.6
Counties	9,198,446	1,589,148	17.3	443,687	27.9	730,469	46.0	414,992	26.1
Municipalities	10,342,096	1,718,801	16.6	1,456,347	84.7	226,713	13.2	35,741	2.1
Oklahoma	15,920,483	1,222,839	7.7	518,334	42.4	193,183	15.8	511,322	41.8
State	7,540,303	678,922	9.0	75,487	11.1	141,232	20.8	462,203	68.1
Local, total	8,380,180	543,917	6.5	442,847	81.4	51,951	9.6	49,119	9.0
Counties	899,533	124,005	13.8	49,538	39.9	25,421	20.5	49,046	39.6
Municipalities	3,426,768	419,912	12.3	393,309	93.7	26,530	6.3	73	(d)
Oregon	24,086,300	1,799,118	7.5	695,999	38.7	355,807	19.8	747,312	41.5
State	11,856,279	854,926	7.2	130,473	15.3	256,091	30.0	468,362	54.8
Local, total	12,230,021	944,192	7.7	565,526	59.9	99,716	10.6	278,950	29.5
Counties	2,375,330	562,832	23.7	203,867	36.2	80,859	14.4	278,106	49.4
Municipalities	2,958,503	381,360	12.9	361,659	94.8	18,857	4.9	844	0.2
Pennsylvania	75,466,693	5,510,353	7.3	2,220,991	40.3	1,067,391	19.4	2,221,971	40.3
State	36,311,954	2,509,003	6.9	776,384	30.9	318,979	12.7	1,413,640	56.3
Local, total	39,154,739	3,001,350	7.7	1,444,607	48.1	748,412	24.9	808,331	26.9
Counties	5,780,892	1,131,110	19.6	86,375	7.6	483,447	42.7	561,288	49.6
Municipalities	10,405,821	1,870,240	18.0	1,358,232	72.6	264,965	14.2	247,043	13.2
Rhode Island	6,406,396	455,578	7.1	211,195	46.4	105,158	23.1	139,225	30.6
State	3,970,456	270,911	6.8	36,159	13.3	95,527	35.3	139,225	51.4
Local, total	2,435,940	184,667	7.6	175,036	94.8	9,631	5.2	0	X
Municipalities	2,209,212	184,667	8.4	175,036	94.8	9,631	5.2	0	X
South Carolina	23,436,064	1,391,012	5.9	653,266	47.0	179,225	12.9	558,521	40.2
State	12,430,612	692,338	5.6	203,125	29.3	52,999	7.7	436,214	63.0
Local, total	11,005,452	698,674	6.3	450,141	64.4	126,226	18.1	122,307	17.5
Counties	2,662,556	441,335	16.6	212,118	48.1	108,927	24.7	120,290	27.3
Municipalities	1,669,307	257,339	15.4	238,023	92.5	17,299	6.7	2,017	0.8
South Dakota	3,760,194	208,732	5.6	88,020	42.2	39,631	19.0	81,081	38.8
State	1,954,972	102,325	5.2	17,543	17.1	22,467	22.0	62,315	60.9
Local, total	1,805,222	106,407	5.9	70,477	66.2	17,164	16.1	18,766	17.6
Counties	232,041	59,563	25.7	24,791	41.6	16,120	27.1	18,652	31.3
Municipalities	585,018	46,844	8.0	45,686	97.5	1,044	2.2	114	0.2
Tennessee	32,009,918	1,943,166	6.1	940,212	48.4	398,928	20.5	604,026	31.1
State	12,489,034	651,053	5.2	111,798	17.2	188,409	28.9	350,846	53.9
Local, total	19,520,884	1,292,113	6.6	828,414	64.1	210,519	16.3	253,180	19.6
Counties	7,294,182	579,534	7.9	222,664	38.4	150,160	25.9	206,710	35.7
Municipalities	10,850,039	712,579	6.6	605,750	85.0	60,359	8.5	46,470	6.5

See notes at end of table.

Table 1.6

Direct expenditures for State and local justice system activities

By type of activity and level of government, fiscal year 2000--Continued

(Dollar amounts in thousands)

State and level of government[a]	Total direct expenditure[b]	Total justice system Amount[c]	Percent of total direct expenditure[c]	Police protection Amount	Percent of total justice system	Judicial and legal Amount	Percent of total justice system	Corrections Amount	Percent of total justice system
Texas	$109,634,090	$8,314,329	7.6%	$3,204,048	38.5%	$1,354,638	16.3%	$3,755,643	45.2%
State	44,193,991	3,425,892	7.8	337,990	9.9	410,654	12.0	2,677,248	78.1
Local, total	65,440,099	4,888,437	7.5	2,866,058	58.6	943,984	19.3	1,078,395	22.1
Counties	8,919,975	2,421,782	27.2	640,495	26.4	764,808	31.6	1,016,479	42.0
Municipalities	18,281,668	2,466,655	13.5	2,225,563	90.2	179,176	7.3	61,916	2.5
Utah	13,043,870	934,625	7.2	380,972	40.8	202,238	21.6	351,415	37.6
State	6,614,065	450,937	6.8	74,401	16.5	131,164	29.1	245,372	54.4
Local, total	6,429,805	483,688	7.5	306,571	63.4	71,074	14.7	106,043	21.9
Counties	914,979	270,765	29.6	111,328	41.1	53,394	19.7	106,043	39.2
Municipalities	1,736,101	212,923	12.3	195,243	91.7	17,680	8.3	0	X
Vermont	3,756,032	183,612	4.9	77,900	42.4	39,408	21.5	66,304	36.1
State	2,287,784	140,298	6.1	37,127	26.5	37,044	26.4	66,127	47.1
Local, total	1,468,248	43,314	3.0	40,773	94.1	2,364	5.5	177	0.4
Counties	4,607	1,968	42.7	844	42.9	948	48.2	176	8.9
Municipalities	492,037	41,346	8.4	39,929	96.6	1,416	3.4	1	(d)
Virginia	38,092,058	2,934,733	7.7	1,175,518	40.1	513,080	17.5	1,246,135	42.5
State	17,181,613	1,308,431	7.6	210,428	16.1	238,570	18.2	859,433	65.7
Local, total	20,910,445	1,626,302	7.8	965,090	59.3	274,510	16.9	386,702	23.8
Counties	11,073,750	842,086	7.6	478,470	56.8	158,233	18.8	205,383	24.4
Municipalities	8,270,516	784,216	9.5	486,620	62.1	116,277	14.8	181,319	23.1
Washington	41,785,842	2,530,340	6.1	1,007,208	39.8	469,759	18.6	1,053,373	41.6
State	19,531,080	955,645	4.9	153,174	16.0	71,194	7.4	731,277	76.5
Local, total	22,254,762	1,574,695	7.1	854,034	54.2	398,565	25.3	322,096	20.5
Counties	3,950,472	879,448	22.3	273,025	31.0	302,954	34.4	303,469	34.5
Municipalities	5,430,308	695,247	12.8	581,009	83.6	95,611	13.8	18,627	2.7
West Virginia	9,990,456	462,998	4.6	171,146	37.0	107,720	23.3	184,132	39.8
State	6,192,166	281,767	4.6	52,445	18.6	73,132	26.0	156,190	55.4
Local, total	3,798,290	181,231	4.8	118,701	65.5	34,588	19.1	27,942	15.4
Counties	582,614	94,237	16.2	36,563	38.8	29,761	31.6	27,913	29.6
Municipalities	762,133	86,994	11.4	82,138	94.4	4,827	5.5	29	(d)
Wisconsin	34,457,512	2,594,282	7.5	1,124,272	43.3	440,190	17.0	1,029,820	39.7
State	14,662,959	1,065,901	7.3	99,418	9.3	220,426	20.7	746,057	70.0
Local, total	19,794,553	1,528,381	7.7	1,024,854	67.1	219,764	14.4	283,763	18.6
Counties	4,747,142	797,587	16.8	340,379	42.7	173,680	21.8	283,528	35.5
Municipalities	5,673,509	730,794	12.9	684,475	93.7	46,084	6.3	235	(d)
Wyoming	3,741,777	247,344	6.6	98,946	40.0	50,047	20.2	98,351	39.8
State	1,714,282	123,133	7.2	19,320	15.7	30,782	25.0	73,031	59.3
Local, total	2,027,495	124,211	6.1	79,626	64.1	19,265	15.5	25,320	20.4
Counties	426,989	70,239	16.4	30,814	43.9	14,503	20.6	24,922	35.5
Municipalities	421,081	53,972	12.8	48,812	90.4	4,762	8.8	398	0.7

Note: See Note, table 1.1. For survey methodology and definitions of terms, see Appendix 1.

[a]Data for local governments are estimates subject to sampling variation.
[b]Includes outlays of States and all types of local governments including independent school districts and special districts, which are not displayed separately. The "local, total" categories, which include these districts, will not equal the sum of the "counties" and "municipalities" categories.

[c]Justice system expenditure of independent school districts and special districts (primarily for special police forces) are not available.
[d]Less than 0.05%.

Source: U.S. Department of Justice, Bureau of Justice Statistics, *2000 Justice Expenditure and Employment Extracts*, NCJ 194802, Table 3 [Online]. Available: http://www.ojp.usdoj.gov/bjs/pub/sheets/cjee00.zip, file cjee0003.wk1 [Aug. 6, 2004].

Table 1.7
Justice system per capita expenditures

By type of activity, United States, fiscal years 1980-99, and 2001[a]

Fiscal year	July 1 population (in thousands)[b]	Total justice system	Police protection	Judicial and legal	Corrections
1980	227,225	NA	$66.73	NA	$30.37
1981	229,466	NA	73.31	NA	34.29
1982	226,548	$157.52	83.96	$34.30	39.25
1983	233,792	169.72	88.32	36.87	44.53
1984	235,825	186.34	96.20	40.13	50.01
1985	237,924	204.11	102.55	44.67	56.89
1986	240,133	222.79	109.34	47.83	65.63
1987	243,000	241.90	118.23	51.52	72.15
1988	244,499	266.79	126.63	57.14	83.02
1989	246,819	287.46	132.87	63.16	91.43
1990	249,402	318.50	144.04	69.59	104.87
1991	252,131	347.31	154.57	76.54	116.20
1992	245,807	381.51	168.13	85.39	127.99
1993	257,783	378.39	170.83	83.63	123.93
1994	260,341	397.44	176.71	86.82	133.92
1995	262,755	429.56	185.13	93.14	151.29
1996	264,741	454.01	200.22	98.81	154.98
1997	267,784	484.69	215.67	106.54	162.49
1998	269,773	503.75	225.48	110.84	167.44
1999	281,375	520.85	232.30	114.38	174.17
2001	285,094	586.16	253.97	132.42	199.78

Note: See Note, table 1.1. Some data have been revised by the Source and may differ from previous editions of SOURCEBOOK. For survey methodology and definitions of terms, see Appendix 1.

[a]Detail may not add to total because of rounding.
[b]Population figures are for July 1 of each year from the U.S. Census Bureau, Current Population Reports. They are consistent with the 1980 and 1990 decennial enumerations. They do not include adjustments for census coverage errors. They may differ from population data taken from previous *Justice Expenditure and Employment Extracts* reports because those tables were developed when only preliminary estimates were available.

Source: U.S. Department of Justice, Bureau of Justice Statistics, *Trends in Justice Expenditure and Employment*, NCJ 178278, Table 11 [Online]. Available: http://www.ojp.usdoj.gov/bjs/data/eetrnd11.wk1 [Mar. 27, 2002]; and *Justice Expenditure and Employment in the United States, 2001*, Bulletin NCJ 202792 (Washington, DC: U.S. Department of Justice, May 2004), p. 8. Table adapted by SOURCEBOOK staff.

Table 1.8
State and local justice system per capita expenditures

By type of activity and State, fiscal year 2000[a]

State[c]	Estimated population 2000[b] (in thousands)	Total justice system	Police protection	Judicial and legal	Corrections
Total	281,418	$471.31	$201.83	$96.06	$173.43
Alabama	4,447	297.24	147.50	58.83	90.91
Alaska	627	768.27	282.25	206.93	279.09
Arizona	5,131	518.82	213.63	119.07	186.12
Arkansas	2,673	312.74	131.61	58.51	122.62
California	33,872	653.31	256.96	184.66	211.69
Colorado	4,301	460.15	192.99	76.43	190.73
Connecticut	3,406	489.11	200.21	126.28	162.63
Delaware	784	618.73	212.12	115.69	290.91
District of Columbia	572	1,189.52	576.05	81.12	532.35
Florida	15,982	526.05	233.91	87.37	204.77
Georgia	8,186	388.42	156.27	64.12	168.03
Hawaii	1,212	459.11	183.08	148.45	127.58
Idaho	1,294	386.47	160.26	78.53	147.68
Illinois	12,419	465.19	245.86	77.40	141.93
Indiana	6,080	311.61	138.62	53.44	119.56
Iowa	2,926	333.93	145.89	86.35	101.70
Kansas	2,688	366.48	159.89	76.66	129.93
Kentucky	4,042	343.60	120.77	71.78	151.06
Louisiana	4,469	440.32	185.57	80.24	174.50
Maine	1,275	279.02	128.49	53.82	96.71
Maryland	5,296	512.37	211.52	92.41	208.44
Massachusetts	6,349	456.93	232.92	98.86	125.15
Michigan	9,938	457.91	180.37	91.11	186.43
Minnesota	4,919	387.72	177.63	89.94	120.16
Mississippi	2,845	298.80	141.96	54.25	102.58
Missouri	5,595	342.55	158.27	64.11	120.17
Montana	902	361.59	150.56	72.75	138.28
Nebraska	1,711	328.83	137.49	56.06	135.28
Nevada	1,998	630.05	269.86	124.21	235.98
New Hampshire	1,236	319.22	151.35	74.67	93.19
New Jersey	8,414	553.80	265.19	112.68	175.93
New Mexico	1,819	475.30	210.11	91.79	173.40
New York	18,976	651.96	301.27	119.23	231.46
North Carolina	8,049	373.98	171.61	58.43	143.94
North Dakota	642	255.51	106.20	86.33	62.98
Ohio	11,353	459.82	187.16	102.01	170.65
Oklahoma	3,451	354.34	150.20	55.98	148.17
Oregon	3,421	525.90	203.45	104.01	218.45
Pennsylvania	12,281	448.69	180.85	86.91	180.93
Rhode Island	1,048	434.71	201.52	100.34	132.85
South Carolina	4,012	346.71	162.83	44.67	139.21
South Dakota	755	276.47	116.58	52.49	107.39
Tennessee	5,689	341.57	165.27	70.12	106.17
Texas	20,852	398.73	153.66	64.96	180.11
Utah	2,233	418.55	170.61	90.57	157.37
Vermont	609	301.50	127.91	64.71	108.87
Virginia	7,079	414.57	166.06	72.48	176.03
Washington	5,894	429.31	170.89	79.70	178.72
West Virginia	1,808	256.08	94.66	59.58	101.84
Wisconsin	5,364	483.65	209.60	82.06	191.99
Wyoming	494	500.70	200.30	101.31	199.09

Note: See Note, table 1.1. For survey methodology and definitions of terms, see Appendix 1.

[a]Detail may not add to total because of rounding.
[b]Population figures are from the U.S. Census Bureau, Current Population Reports, Series P-25, No. 1045, July 2000.
[c]Local government portion of these data are estimates subject to sampling variation.

Source: U.S. Department of Justice, Bureau of Justice Statistics, *2000 Justice Expenditure and Employment Extracts*, NCJ 194802, Table 8 [Online]. Available: http://www.ojp.usdoj.gov/bjs/pub/sheets/cjee00.zip, file cjee0008.wk1 [Aug. 6, 2004].

Table 1.9

Direct expenditures for correctional activities of State governments and percent distribution

By type of activity, United States, fiscal years 1980-99[a]

(Dollar amounts in thousands)

Fiscal year	Total corrections direct expenditure	Institutions Total	Institutions Direct current	Institutions Capital outlay Construction	Institutions Capital outlay Other	Other corrections Total	Other corrections Direct current	Other corrections Capital outlay
1980	$4,257,509	$3,410,933	$2,869,492	$482,652	$58,789	$846,576	$824,439	$22,137
1981	4,843,857	3,886,234	3,276,441	533,419	76,374	957,623	927,529	30,094
1982	5,559,792	4,480,490	3,848,893	544,300	87,297	1,079,302	1,038,299	41,003
1983	6,323,240	5,135,550	4,488,027	557,237	90,286	1,187,690	1,122,558	65,132
1984	7,178,011	5,913,323	5,114,702	695,198	103,423	1,264,688	1,213,602	51,086
1985	8,336,040	6,927,619	5,932,686	858,856	136,077	1,408,421	1,335,947	72,474
1986	9,877,577	8,246,279	6,708,440	1,342,807	195,032	1,631,298	1,558,933	72,365
1987	10,732,880	8,843,089	7,587,706	1,077,207	178,176	1,889,791	1,722,418	167,373
1988	12,403,648	10,364,051	8,648,292	1,486,461	229,298	2,039,597	1,926,136	113,461
1989	13,854,499	11,617,138	9,661,969	1,724,021	231,148	2,237,361	2,099,149	138,212
1990	15,842,063	13,321,228	11,145,405	1,921,846	253,977	2,520,835	2,301,633	219,202
1991	17,789,540	14,995,912	12,497,915	2,235,632	262,365	2,793,628	2,591,245	202,383
1992	18,750,826	15,657,098	13,599,703	1,813,405	243,990	3,093,728	2,874,716	219,012
1993	19,091,342	15,965,881	14,239,710	1,479,871	246,300	3,125,461	2,999,462	125,999
1994	21,266,053	17,741,937	15,776,174	1,695,718	270,045	3,524,116	3,319,462	204,654
1995	24,091,069	20,095,376	17,674,884	2,080,678	339,814	3,995,693	3,662,847	332,846
1996	25,294,111	20,893,235	19,035,102	1,524,590	333,543	4,400,876	4,156,806	244,070
1997	27,116,873	22,289,014	20,614,214	1,336,567	338,233	4,827,859	4,500,849	327,010
1998	28,678,929	23,603,913	21,533,991	1,513,967	555,955	5,075,016	4,750,843	324,173
1999	30,769,783	25,243,574	23,014,267	1,755,025	474,282	5,526,212	5,240,325	285,887

Percent distribution								
1980	100%	80.1%	67.4%	11.3%	1.4%	19.9%	19.4%	0.5%
1981	100	80.2	67.6	11.0	1.6	19.8	19.1	0.6
1982	100	80.6	69.2	9.8	1.6	19.4	18.7	0.7
1983	100	81.2	71.0	8.8	1.4	18.8	17.8	1.0
1984	100	82.4	71.3	9.7	1.4	17.6	16.9	0.7
1985	100	83.1	71.2	10.3	1.6	16.9	16.0	0.9
1986	100	83.5	67.9	13.6	2.0	16.5	15.8	0.7
1987	100	82.4	70.7	10.0	1.7	17.6	16.0	1.6
1988	100	83.6	69.7	12.0	1.8	16.4	15.5	0.9
1989	100	83.9	69.7	12.4	1.7	16.1	15.2	1.0
1990	100	84.1	70.4	12.1	1.6	15.9	14.5	1.4
1991	100	84.3	70.3	12.6	1.5	15.7	14.6	1.1
1992	100	83.5	72.5	9.7	1.3	16.5	15.3	1.2
1993	100	83.6	74.6	7.8	1.3	16.4	15.7	0.7
1994	100	83.4	74.2	8.0	1.3	16.6	15.6	1.0
1995	100	83.4	73.4	8.6	1.4	16.6	15.2	1.4
1996	100	82.6	75.3	6.0	1.3	17.4	16.4	1.0
1997	100	82.2	76.0	4.9	1.2	17.8	16.6	1.2
1998	100	82.3	75.1	5.3	1.9	17.7	16.6	1.1
1999	100	82.0	74.8	5.7	1.5	18.0	17.0	0.9

Note: See Note, table 1.1. Some data have been revised by the Source and may differ from previous editions of SOURCEBOOK. For survey methodology and definitions of terms, see Appendix 1.

[a]Detail may not add to total because of rounding.

Source: U.S. Department of Justice, Bureau of Justice Statistics, *Trends in Justice Expenditure and Employment*, NCJ 178277, Table 10 [Online]. Available: http://www.ojp.usdoj.gov/bjs/data/eetrnd10.wk1 [Mar. 27, 2002].

Table 1.10

Direct expenditures for correctional activities of State governments

By type of activity and State, fiscal year 2000

(Dollar amounts in thousands)

State	Total corrections direct expenditure	Institutions Total	Institutions Direct current	Capital outlay Construction	Capital outlay Other	Percent of total corrections direct expenditure	Other corrections Total	Other corrections Direct current	Other corrections Capital outlay	Percent of total corrections direct expenditure
Total	$33,039,925	$26,758,605	$24,642,499	$1,761,633	$354,473	81.0%	$6,281,320	$5,890,466	$390,854	19.0%
Alabama	272,905	203,603	201,772	782	1,049	74.6	69,302	68,922	380	25.4
Alaska	173,624	151,137	149,050	1,273	814	87.0	22,487	22,093	394	13.0
Arizona	660,223	560,308	530,424	12,496	17,388	84.9	99,915	94,562	5,353	15.1
Arkansas	266,397	194,557	178,912	11,540	4,105	73.0	71,840	69,510	2,330	27.0
California	4,118,370	3,498,261	3,378,716	95,736	23,809	84.9	620,109	602,593	17,516	15.1
Colorado	599,202	447,913	342,946	97,942	7,025	74.8	151,289	147,232	4,057	25.2
Connecticut	553,905	496,953	481,758	10,885	4,310	89.7	56,952	56,320	632	10.3
Delaware	228,076	160,200	159,528	0	672	70.2	67,876	61,367	6,509	29.8
Florida	2,217,112	1,504,961	1,451,714	32,217	21,030	67.9	712,151	659,301	52,850	32.1
Georgia	968,737	690,725	675,750	6,716	8,259	71.3	278,012	267,456	10,556	28.7
Hawaii	154,622	138,409	135,812	1,781	816	89.5	16,213	16,090	123	10.5
Idaho	148,726	131,905	117,444	12,244	2,217	88.7	16,821	16,450	371	11.3
Illinois	1,277,485	1,071,355	900,231	154,508	16,616	83.9	206,130	193,224	12,906	16.1
Indiana	536,725	493,606	449,064	29,874	14,668	92.0	43,119	41,578	1,541	8.0
Iowa	224,364	213,391	210,006	691	2,694	95.1	10,973	10,517	456	4.9
Kansas	272,842	261,924	243,198	14,166	4,560	96.0	10,918	10,797	121	4.0
Kentucky	394,222	270,481	256,264	8,342	5,875	68.6	123,741	120,279	3,462	31.4
Louisiana	396,808	323,523	303,703	15,427	4,393	81.5	73,285	71,685	1,600	18.5
Maine	91,882	62,622	62,324	56	242	68.2	29,260	25,529	3,731	31.8
Maryland	893,906	500,097	482,443	16,180	1,474	55.9	393,809	366,348	27,461	44.1
Massachusetts	605,156	494,506	478,109	9,196	7,201	81.7	110,650	87,816	22,834	18.3
Michigan	1,482,946	1,382,025	1,284,682	77,843	19,500	93.2	100,921	98,818	2,103	6.8
Minnesota	292,695	207,581	199,925	2,417	5,239	70.9	85,114	79,656	5,458	29.1
Mississippi	241,948	215,864	207,504	6,038	2,322	89.2	26,084	25,522	562	10.8
Missouri	513,835	431,921	348,714	74,213	8,994	84.1	81,914	81,375	539	15.9
Montana	104,143	59,588	49,731	9,286	571	57.2	44,555	43,931	624	42.8
Nebraska	172,628	68,031	67,764	44	223	39.4	104,597	57,451	47,146	60.6
Nevada	217,566	186,694	151,108	34,570	1,016	85.8	30,872	30,239	633	14.2
New Hampshire	84,944	70,792	54,135	14,606	2,051	83.3	14,152	13,667	485	16.7
New Jersey	1,050,277	761,289	747,502	5,066	8,721	72.5	288,988	282,134	6,854	27.5
New Mexico	216,722	154,351	151,805	1,426	1,120	71.2	62,371	61,914	457	28.8
New York	2,298,197	1,939,695	1,606,012	313,612	20,071	84.4	358,502	345,539	12,963	15.6
North Carolina	905,664	738,897	721,512	9,446	7,939	81.6	166,767	151,232	15,535	18.4
North Dakota	28,856	23,646	22,402	928	316	81.9	5,210	5,210	0	18.1
Ohio	1,486,675	1,192,624	1,043,094	136,714	12,816	80.2	294,051	245,535	48,516	19.8
Oklahoma	462,203	199,284	194,168	1,926	3,190	43.1	262,919	252,333	10,586	56.9
Oregon	468,362	305,043	253,692	51,348	3	65.1	163,319	147,458	15,861	34.9
Pennsylvania	1,413,640	1,336,344	1,150,345	171,437	14,562	94.5	77,296	77,296	0	5.5
Rhode Island	139,225	128,914	124,964	3,120	830	92.6	10,311	10,206	105	7.4
South Carolina	436,214	385,668	361,999	17,773	5,896	88.4	50,546	48,428	2,118	11.6
South Dakota	62,315	38,155	37,780	0	375	61.2	24,160	23,063	1,097	38.8
Tennessee	350,846	295,054	274,464	18,376	2,214	84.1	55,792	54,810	982	15.9
Texas	2,677,248	2,382,548	2,269,087	59,205	54,256	89.0	294,700	290,613	4,087	11.0
Utah	245,372	162,014	159,956	46	2,012	66.0	83,358	82,348	1,010	34.0
Vermont	66,127	64,910	63,525	1,385	0	98.2	1,217	1,217	0	1.8
Virginia	859,433	821,304	807,807	307	13,190	95.6	38,129	35,639	2,490	4.4
Washington	731,277	544,114	427,835	107,780	8,499	74.4	187,163	185,935	1,228	25.6
West Virginia	156,190	145,541	108,701	32,344	4,496	93.2	10,649	10,641	8	6.8
Wisconsin	746,057	589,135	530,376	54,259	4,500	79.0	156,922	122,991	33,931	21.0
Wyoming	73,031	57,142	32,742	24,066	334	78.2	15,889	15,596	293	21.8

Note: See Note, table 1.1. For survey methodology and definitions of terms, see Appendix 1.

Source: U.S. Department of Justice, Bureau of Justice Statistics, *2000 Justice Expenditure and Employment Extracts*, NCJ 194802, Table 10 [Online]. Available: http://www.ojp.usdoj.gov/bjs/pub/sheets/cjee00.zip, file cjee0010.wk1 [Aug. 6, 2004].

Table 1.11

Direct expenditures for correctional activities of State governments

By type of activity and State, fiscal year 2001

(Dollar amounts in thousands)

		Institutions					Other corrections			
	Total corrections direct		Direct	Capital outlay		Percent of total corrections direct		Direct	Capital	Percent of total corrections direct
State	expenditure	Total	current	Construction	Other	expenditure	Total	current	outlay	expenditure
Total	$35,810,946	$29,197,575	$27,299,513	$1,574,245	$323,817	81.5%	$6,613,371	$6,286,927	$326,444	18.5%
Alabama	303,759	223,405	220,992	747	1,666	73.5	80,354	79,917	437	26.5
Alaska	172,610	151,751	149,962	880	909	87.9	20,859	20,504	355	12.1
Arizona	668,430	564,104	554,429	2,611	7,064	84.4	104,326	101,874	2,452	15.6
Arkansas	277,123	199,447	189,916	6,947	2,584	72.0	77,676	75,552	2,124	28.0
California	5,054,750	4,400,783	4,249,809	123,810	27,164	87.1	653,967	636,922	17,045	12.9
Colorado	616,452	448,392	388,437	55,514	4,441	72.7	168,060	165,127	2,933	27.3
Connecticut	602,756	536,029	506,861	25,085	4,083	88.9	66,727	63,729	2,998	11.1
Delaware	247,987	183,243	182,179	373	691	73.9	64,744	59,922	4,822	26.1
Florida	2,247,882	1,636,655	1,574,240	43,865	18,550	72.8	611,227	562,844	48,383	27.2
Georgia	970,854	687,564	655,696	22,924	8,944	70.8	283,290	270,490	12,800	29.2
Hawaii	148,607	130,645	127,553	1,806	1,286	87.9	17,962	17,845	117	12.1
Idaho	157,329	138,760	130,962	5,537	2,261	88.2	18,569	18,009	560	11.8
Illinois	1,318,078	1,107,386	938,181	160,307	8,898	84.0	210,692	200,170	10,522	16.0
Indiana	593,836	540,465	504,972	20,106	15,387	91.0	53,371	51,760	1,611	9.0
Iowa	234,677	225,344	222,645	1,252	1,447	96.0	9,333	9,317	16	4.0
Kansas	285,126	263,234	250,223	9,954	3,057	92.3	21,892	21,833	59	7.7
Kentucky	439,299	288,911	262,100	23,895	2,916	65.8	150,388	143,448	6,940	34.2
Louisiana	442,129	358,724	334,267	14,104	10,353	81.1	83,405	81,270	2,135	18.9
Maine	94,514	68,642	68,377	83	182	72.6	25,872	25,787	85	27.4
Maryland	964,027	537,342	516,369	18,259	2,714	55.7	426,685	391,612	35,073	44.3
Massachusetts	860,947	543,052	522,606	13,216	7,230	63.1	317,895	296,560	21,335	36.9
Michigan	1,613,781	1,506,299	1,397,408	87,702	21,189	93.3	107,482	105,243	2,239	6.7
Minnesota	310,036	220,285	212,306	1,268	6,711	71.1	89,751	85,729	4,022	28.9
Mississippi	259,960	217,200	213,491	1,671	2,038	83.6	42,760	40,894	1,866	16.4
Missouri	591,675	509,378	423,520	82,295	3,563	86.1	82,297	81,979	318	13.9
Montana	106,955	61,472	53,444	7,515	513	57.5	45,483	45,458	25	42.5
Nebraska	175,676	98,001	74,170	23,458	373	55.8	77,675	73,013	4,662	44.2
Nevada	234,640	198,683	176,321	19,989	2,373	84.7	35,957	35,692	265	15.3
New Hampshire	83,064	65,225	62,288	1,734	1,203	78.5	17,839	16,811	1,028	21.5
New Jersey	1,128,053	815,975	790,852	18,077	7,046	72.3	312,078	299,085	12,993	27.7
New Mexico	223,023	159,297	157,434	1,585	278	71.4	63,726	63,591	135	28.6
New York	2,423,600	2,103,112	1,844,427	234,953	23,732	86.8	320,488	306,640	13,848	13.2
North Carolina	934,544	779,713	757,229	17,428	5,056	83.4	154,831	151,975	2,856	16.6
North Dakota	35,463	29,597	25,370	3,701	526	83.5	5,866	5,866	0	16.5
Ohio	1,436,123	1,138,702	1,065,673	60,812	12,217	79.3	297,421	254,726	42,695	20.7
Oklahoma	474,183	206,710	197,957	5,297	3,456	43.6	267,473	262,530	4,943	56.4
Oregon	470,779	319,745	279,300	40,102	343	67.9	151,034	140,538	10,496	32.1
Pennsylvania	1,499,532	1,413,514	1,209,253	204,261	0	94.3	86,018	86,018	0	5.7
Rhode Island	151,172	140,120	137,203	2,153	764	92.7	11,052	10,929	123	7.3
South Carolina	480,354	429,483	388,677	38,180	2,626	89.4	50,871	50,391	480	10.6
South Dakota	65,592	39,601	38,939	334	328	60.4	25,991	25,744	247	39.6
Tennessee	374,225	313,443	305,279	7,426	738	83.8	60,782	59,706	1,076	16.2
Texas	2,975,833	2,708,800	2,627,826	17,634	63,340	91.0	267,033	265,759	1,274	9.0
Utah	265,689	178,476	176,790	238	1,448	67.2	87,213	86,667	546	32.8
Vermont	71,988	62,937	62,163	0	774	87.4	9,051	8,807	244	12.6
Virginia	954,658	910,846	891,123	1,026	18,697	95.4	43,812	39,849	3,963	4.6
Washington	728,945	508,930	438,747	65,439	4,744	69.8	220,015	216,787	3,228	30.2
West Virginia	122,009	112,208	110,395	512	1,301	92.0	9,801	9,801	0	8.0
Wisconsin	838,646	653,207	582,293	66,314	4,600	77.9	185,439	145,626	39,813	22.1
Wyoming	79,576	62,738	48,859	11,866	2,013	78.8	16,838	16,581	257	21.2

Note: See Note, table 1.1. For survey methodology and definitions of terms, see Appendix 1.

Source: U.S. Department of Justice, Bureau of Justice Statistics, *2001 Justice Expenditure and Employment Extracts*, NCJ 202792, Table 10 [Online]. Available: http://www.ojp.usdoj.gov/bjs/pub/sheets/cjee01.zip, file cjee0110.wk1 [Aug. 6, 2004].

Table 1.12

Federal criminal justice budget authorities

Fiscal years 2003 (actual) and 2004-2009 (estimated)[a]

(In millions of dollars)

Type of program	2003 actual	Estimated 2004	2005	2006	2007	2008	2009
Total	$39,689	$42,719	$41,958	$42,202	$43,573	$44,904	$47,189
Discretionary, total	35,741	36,993	38,146	39,304	40,602	41,918	44,188
Federal law enforcement activities, total	18,776	19,495	20,082	20,710	21,381	22,088	22,837
Criminal investigations[b]	6,213	6,253	6,433	6,632	6,844	7,070	7,309
Bureau of Alcohol, Tobacco, Firearms and Explosives	801	827	852	889	923	958	996
Border and transportation security directorate activities[c]	8,602	9,618	9,690	9,971	10,279	10,605	10,951
Equal Employment Opportunity Commission	322	325	337	351	363	377	392
Tax law, criminal investigations[d]	458	445	466	485	507	529	551
U.S. Secret Service	1,065	1,134	1,176	1,218	1,263	1,309	1,359
Other law enforcement activities	1,315	893	1,128	1,164	1,202	1,240	1,279
Federal litigative and judicial activities, total	7,978	8,208	8,544	8,836	9,199	9,526	10,747
Civil and criminal prosecution and representation	3,004	3,033	3,192	3,307	3,484	3,612	4,637
Representation of indigents in civil cases	337	335	339	344	350	357	364
Federal judicial and other litigative activities	4,637	4,840	5,013	5,185	5,365	5,557	5,746
Correctional activities[e]	5,259	5,564	5,743	5,923	6,116	6,322	6,540
Criminal justice assistance, total	3,728	3,726	3,777	3,835	3,906	3,982	4,064
High-intensity drug trafficking areas program	195	223	226	229	233	238	242
Law enforcement assistance, community policing, and other justice programs	3,533	3,503	3,551	3,606	3,673	3,744	3,822
Mandatory, total	3,948	5,726	3,812	2,898	2,971	2,986	3,001
Federal law enforcement activities, total	-583	-315	493	1,077	1,125	1,114	1,102
Border and transportation security directorate activities[c]	2,301	2,708	2,873	2,881	2,913	2,946	2,980
Immigration fees	-1,981	-2,079	-2,240	-2,265	-2,293	-2,341	-2,391
Customs fees	-1,326	-1,396	-591	-6	-6	-7	-7
Treasury forfeiture fund	253	251	251	251	251	251	251
Other mandatory law enforcement programs	170	201	200	216	260	265	269
Federal litigative and judicial activities, total	1,186	1,213	1,271	1,207	1,231	1,256	1,282
Federal forfeiture fund	530	489	500	448	458	468	478
Federal judicial officers' salaries and expenses and other mandatory programs	656	724	771	759	773	788	804
Correctional activities	-3	-3	-3	-3	-3	-3	-3
Criminal justice assistance, total	3,348	4,831	2,051	617	618	619	620
Crime victims' fund	592	608	1,606	567	567	567	567
September 11 victims' compensation	2,700	4,174	396	0	0	0	0
Public safety officers' benefits	56	49	49	50	51	52	53

Note: These data are from the budget submitted by the President to Congress in 2004. The "budget authority" (actual or estimated) is the authority becoming available during the year to enter into financial obligations that will result in immediate or future outlays of Government funds. Spending is divided into two categories: discretionary spending and mandatory (direct) spending. Discretionary spending is controlled through the annual appropriations process and includes items such as funding for salaries and other operating expenses of Government agencies. Mandatory spending is controlled by authorizing legislation; the major entitlement programs such as Social Security, Medicare and Medicaid payments, unemployment insurance benefits, and farm price supports are examples of mandatory spending because payments for these programs are authorized in permanent laws. (Source, *Analytical Perspectives, Fiscal Year 2005*, pp. 392, 393.) The negative figures appearing in the table represent Governmental receipts and collections such as court fines, customs duties, certain licensing fees, and various other collections from the public. These figures are deducted from the gross budget authority.

[a]Detail may not add to total because of rounding.
[b]Includes Drug Enforcement Administration, Federal Bureau of Investigation, Department of Homeland Security, Financial Crimes Enforcement Network, and interagency crime and drug enforcement programs.
[c]Department of Homeland Security.
[d]Internal Revenue Service.
[e]Federal prison system and detention trustee program.

Source: Executive Office of the President, Office of Management and Budget, *The Budget of the United States Government, Fiscal Year 2005*, [CD-ROM] (Washington, DC: USGPO, 2004), Table 24-12. Table adapted by SOURCEBOOK staff.

Table 1.13

Allocation of Office of Justice Programs' funds

By type of budget activity, fiscal years 1990-2001[a]

(In thousands of dollars)

Type of budget activity	1990[b]	1991[b]	1992	1993	1994	1995	1996	1997	1998[c]	1999[c]	2000[c]	2001[d]
Total	$762,358	$845,021	$865,689	$997,023	$848,960	$1,267,660	$2,702,011	$3,251,347	$3,733,066	$3,743,045	$3,919,611	$4,175,721
Executive direction and control	24,240	25,169	26,641[e]	27,219	29,600	31,702	28,696	30,579	35,039	38,103	44,103	47,728
Research, evaluation, and demonstration programs	22,766	23,929	23,739	22,995	22,500	27,000	30,000	30,000	41,148	46,148	43,448	69,846
Justice statistical programs	20,879	22,095	22,095	21,373	20,943	21,379	21,379	21,379	21,529	25,029	25,505	28,991
State and local assistance programs												
Alcohol and crime in Indian country	NA	NA	NA	NA	NA	NA	NA	NA	NA	NA	NA	4,989
Anti-drug abuse formula (Byrne grants)	395,101	423,000	423,000	423,000	358,000	450,000	475,000	500,000	505,000	505,000	500,000	498,900
Anti-drug abuse discretionary	49,636	66,994	73,500	223,000[f]	116,500	62,000	60,000	60,000	46,500	47,000	52,000	78,377
Counterterrorism	NA	NA	NA	NA	NA	NA	NA	17,000	19,000	0	152,000	220,494
Criminal records upgrade	NA	NA	NA	NA	0	100,000	25,000	50,000	45,000	45,000	0	0
DNA identification State grants	NA	NA	NA	NA	NA	NA	1,000	3,000	12,500	15,000	0	0
Drug courts	NA	NA	NA	NA	NA	11,900	0	30,000	30,000	40,000	40,000	49,890
Family support	NA	NA	NA	NA	NA	NA	1,000	1,000	1,000	1,500	1,500	1,497
Indian tribal courts program	NA	NA	NA	NA	NA	NA	NA	NA	NA	5,000	5,000	7,982
Law enforcement block grants	NA	NA	NA	NA	NA	NA	503,000	523,000	523,000	523,000	497,885[g]	521,849
Motor vehicle theft prevention	NA	NA	NA	NA	NA	NA	500	750	750	1,300	1,300	1,297
Public Safety Officers' Benefits Program	24,818	26,075	27,144	28,524	30,821	29,717	30,608	32,276	33,003	31,809	32,541	35,619
Regional Information Sharing System[h]	13,402	14,000	14,500	14,491	14,491	14,500	14,500	14,500	20,000	20,000	20,000	24,945
State and local correctional facilities grants	NA	NA	NA	NA	0	24,500	617,500	670,000	720,500	720,500	653,533[g]	684,990
State criminal alien assistance program	NA	NA	NA	NA	NA	130,000	300,000	330,000	420,000	420,000	420,000	399,120
State prison drug treatment	NA	NA	NA	NA	NA	NA	27,000	30,000	63,000	63,000	63,000	62,861
Telemarketing fraud prevention	NA	NA	NA	NA	NA	NA	NA	2,000	2,500	2,000	2,000	1,996
Televised testimony of child abuse victims	NA	NA	1,000	0	0	0	50	550	1,000	1,000	1,000	998
Weed and Seed program	NA	NA	NA	NA	NA	NA	NA	0	33,500	33,500	33,500	33,925
White Collar Crime Information Center[i]	NA	NA	NA	NA	0	1,400	3,850	3,850	5,350	7,350	9,250	9,230
Juvenile justice programs												
Block grants	NA	NA	NA	NA	NA	NA	NA	0	250,000	250,000	237,994[g]	249,450
Child abuse investigation and prosecution	NA	NA	1,500	1,500	3,000	4,500	4,500	4,500	7,000	7,000	7,000	8,481
Court appointed special advocates	NA	NA	NA	NA	4,500	6,000	6,000	6,000	7,000	9,000	10,000	11,475
Judicial child abuse training	NA	NA	500	500	500	750	750	1,000	2,000	2,000	2,000	1,996
Juvenile justice discretionary programs	21,044	22,796	22,823[e]	23,372[e]	44,640	70,600	70,600	80,100	130,850	193,394	196,910	207,452
Juvenile justice formula grants	48,361	49,255	49,735[e]	50,078	58,310	68,600	68,600	85,100	95,100	77,556	76,540	76,372
Missing Alzheimer's program	NA	NA	NA	NA	NA	NA	900	900	900	900	900	898
Missing children	3,971	7,971	8,471	8,471	6,621	6,721	5,971	5,971	12,256	17,168	19,952	22,997
Violence against women programs												
Encouraging arrest policies	NA	NA	NA	NA	NA	NA	28,000	33,000	59,000	34,000	34,000	33,925
Law enforcement and prosecution grants	NA	NA	NA	NA	NA	26,000	130,000	145,000	172,000	206,750	206,750	209,717
Rural domestic violence and child abuse enforcement	NA	NA	NA	NA	NA	NA	7,000	8,000	25,000	25,000	25,000	24,945
Violence against women training programs	NA	NA	NA	NA	NA	NA	1,000	1,000	2,000	5,000	5,000	4,989
Crime Victims Fund[j]	123,250	126,750	127,968	150,000	138,534	178,891	227,707	528,942	362,891	324,038	500,000[k]	537,500[l]
Programs previously funded by OJP[m]												
Emergency assistance[n]	9,927	0	1,000	0	0	0	0	0	0	0	0	0
High intensity drug trafficking areas[o]	NA	32,024	37,110	0	0	0	0	0	0	0	0	0
Mariel Cuban[p]	4,963	4,963	4,963	2,500	0	0	0	0	0	0	0	0
Other Crime Bill programs	NA	NA	NA	NA	NA	1,500	11,900	1,950	27,750	0	0	0

See notes on next page.

Table 1.13

Allocation of Office of Justice Programs' funds

By type of budget activity, fiscal years 1990-2001[a]--Continued

Note: The Office of Justice Programs (OJP) is comprised of five program bureaus, six program offices, and a number of administrative support offices. The mission of OJP is to provide Federal leadership in developing the Nation's capacity to prevent and control crime, administer justice, and assist crime victims. OJP develops, operates, and evaluates a wide range of innovative criminal and juvenile justice programs (including research and statistical programs) through partnerships with other Federal, State, and local agencies as well as national and community-based organizations. Some data have been revised by the Source and may differ from previous editions of SOURCEBOOK.

[a]Detail may not add to total because of rounding.
[b]Includes effect of Gramm-Rudman-Hollings reductions.
[c]Appropriations.
[d]Includes rescission per Public Law 106-554.
[e]Reflects the total program level, which includes unused carryover earmarked by Congress for addition to appropriated amount.
[f]Includes $150 million supplemental appropriation for the Police Hiring Program.
[g]Includes rescission per Public Law 106-113.
[h]A program to aid State and local law enforcement agencies in the exchange of intelligence information.
[i]This previously was part of the Regional Information Sharing System.
[j]Represents amount deposited in previous year.
[k]Collections totaled $985.2 million, however, an obligation limitation of $500 million was placed on total collections.
[l]Collections totaled $777 million, however, an obligation limitation of $537.5 million was placed on total availability.
[m]Previously funded OJP programs may still be operational for either of the following reasons: (1) the program may be operating on funds appropriated in prior fiscal years; (2) the program may be subsumed under another program that is currently funded.
[n]A program authorized to provide funds, equipment, intelligence information, and/or personnel to a requesting State in the event of a law enforcement emergency.
[o]Funds transferred from the Office of National Drug Control Policy.
[p]Refers to an appropriation to be allocated to States housing Mariel Cuban refugees in State correctional facilities.

Source: Table provided to SOURCEBOOK staff by the U.S. Department of Justice, Office of Justice Programs.

Table 1.14

Federal drug control budget

By function, fiscal years 1996-2005[a]

(In millions of dollars)

		Function							
						Supply reduction			
		Demand reduction		Domestic law enforcement		International		Interdiction	
Fiscal year	Total	Amount	Percent	Amount	Percent	Amount	Percent	Amount	Percent
1996	$6,274.1	$3,299.7	52.6%	$1,624.1	25.9%	$243.6	3.9%	$1,106.7	17.6%
1997	7,531.2	3,755.6	49.9	1,836.3	24.4	389.9	5.2	1,549.3	20.6
1998	7,628.0	3,819.9	50.1	1,937.5	25.4	464.0	6.1	1,406.5	18.4
1999	9,209.1	4,206.6	45.7	2,100.6	22.8	746.3	8.1	2,155.6	23.4
2000	10,151.5	4,389.7	43.2	2,238.3	22.0	1,619.2	15.9	1,904.4	18.8
2001	9,823.8	4,848.3	49.4	2,462.8	25.1	617.3	6.3	1,895.3	19.3
2002	10,891.9	5,098.9	46.8	2,794.7	25.7	1,084.5	10.0	1,913.7	17.6
2003	11,397.0	5,190.3	45.5	2,954.1	25.9	1,105.1	9.7	2,147.5	18.8
2004	12,082.3	5,377.3	44.5	3,080.5	25.5	1,133.9	9.4	2,490.6	20.6
2005	12,648.6	5,694.9	45.0	3,201.1	25.3	1,149.9	9.1	2,602.7	20.6

Note: "Demand reduction" refers to programs and research related to drug abuse treatment and prevention that are designed to reduce the demand for drugs. "Supply reduction" refers to a wide scope of law enforcement-related activities designed to reduce the supply of drugs.

The fiscal year 2005 national drug control budget reflects a restatement of reporting for 1996-2004 to reflect the removal of the Byrne Grant program. The Byrne program funding was removed from the drug control budget because States have discretion to use the funds in any of 29 specified purpose areas, many of which are not drug related (e.g., crime victim assistance). The effect of this restatement removes approximately $400 to $500 million per year from the Federal drug control budget. Also, the restatement includes the addition of the National Highway Traffic Safety Administration's Drug Impaired Driving program, which trains law enforcement officers and prosecutors in detecting and prosecuting drug-impaired drivers. (Source, pp. 4, 5.) Data for years prior to 2005 have been recalculated by the Source to reflect these changes and therefore will differ from previous editions of SOURCEBOOK.

[a]The data presented represent the following types of budget authority: 1996-1999, "actual"; 2000-2003, "final" budget authority enacted in the prior year; 2004, current year "enacted"; and 2005, "requested" for the budget year under formulation. Percents may not add to 100 because of rounding.

Source: Executive Office of the President, Office of National Drug Control Policy, *National Drug Control Strategy: FY 2005 Budget Summary* (Washington, DC: Executive Office of the President, 2004), p. 8. Table adapted by SOURCEBOOK staff.

Table 1.15

Federal drug control funding

By agency, fiscal years 2003 (final), 2004 (enacted), and 2005 (requested)[a]

(In millions of dollars)

Agency	2003 final	2004 enacted	2005 requested
Total Federal program	$11,397.0	$12,082.3	$12,648.6
Supply reduction	6,206.7	6,705.0	6953.7
Percent	54.5%	55.5%	55.0%
Demand reduction	$5,190.3	$5,377.3	$5,694.9
Percent	45.5%	44.5%	45.0%
Department of Defense	$905.9	$908.6	$852.7
Department of Education	644.0	624.5	611.0
Department of Health and Human Services	3,315.2	3,479.5	3,656.8
National Institute on Drug Abuse	960.9	990.8	1,019.1
Substance Abuse and Mental Health Services Administration	2,354.3	2,488.7	2,637.7
Department of Homeland Security	2,040.0	2,382.9	2,519.4
Immigration and Customs Enforcement	518.0	538.7	575.8
Customs and Border Protection	873.9	1,070.5	1,121.4
U.S. Coast Guard	648.1	773.7	822.3
Department of Justice	2,429.8	2,482.7	2,749.9
Bureau of Prisons	43.2	47.7	49.3
Drug Enforcement Administration	1,639.8	1,703.0	1,815.7
Interagency Crime and Drug Enforcement	477.2	550.6	580.6
Office of Justice Programs	269.6	181.3	304.3
Office of National Drug Control Policy	520.6	522.2	511.0
Operations	26.3	27.8	27.6
High intensity drug trafficking areas	226.0	225.0	208.4
Counterdrug Technology Assessment Center	46.5	41.8	40.0
Other Federal drug control programs	221.8	227.6	235.0
Department of State			
Bureau of International Narcotics and Law Enforcement Affairs	874.3	914.4	921.6
Department of Veterans Affairs			
Veterans Health Administration	663.7	765.3	822.8
Other Presidential priorities[b]	3.4	2.2	3.5

Note: See Note, table 1.14.

[a]Detail may not add to total because of rounding.
[b]Includes the Small Business Administration's Drug Free Workplace grants and the National Highway Traffic Safety Administration's Drug Impaired Driving program.

Source: Executive Office of the President, Office of National Drug Control Policy, *National Drug Control Strategy: FY 2005 Budget Summary* (Washington, DC: Executive Office of the President, 2004), pp. 6, 7. Table adapted by SOURCEBOOK staff.

Table 1.16

Allocation of Edward Byrne Memorial State and Local Law Enforcement Assistance Program funds

By jurisdiction, fiscal years 2001, 2002, and 2003

Jurisdiction	Funds allocated 2001	Funds allocated 2002	Percent to be passed through to local jurisdictions 2001, 2002	Funds allocated 2003	Percent to be passed through to local jurisdictions 2003	Jurisdiction	Funds allocated 2001	Funds allocated 2002	Percent to be passed through to local jurisdictions 2001, 2002	Funds allocated 2003	Percent to be passed through to local jurisdictions 2003
Alabama	$7,911,369	$7,763,473	50.95%	$7,659,952	60.10%	New Hampshire	$3,101,368	$3,052,472	51.46%	$3,087,951	54.68%
Alaska	2,218,368	2,158,472	21.97	2,189,951	24.14	New Jersey	13,639,369	13,584,474	57.67	13,500,953	59.23
Arizona	8,531,369	8,766,474	61.04	9,039,952	61.86	New Mexico	3,919,369	3,907,473	42.23	3,870,589	49.29
Arkansas	4,610,200	5,670,673	54.87	5,130,952	52.84	New York	28,900,369	29,080,474	63.29	28,542,953	65.16
California	51,592,369	50,933,474	63.15	51,258,953	67.34	North Carolina	12,892,369	13,048,474	41.36	13,116,953	42.41
Colorado	7,435,369	7,549,473	58.82	7,687,952	59.56	North Dakota	2,240,368	2,181,472	56.16	2,175,951	58.68
Connecticut	6,260,369	6,235,473	36.96	6,198,952	38.25	Ohio	18,365,369	17,895,474	64.42	17,487,589	64.06
Delaware	2,422,368	2,388,472	26.87	2,422,951	27.15	Oklahoma	6,375,369	6,301,473	45.41	6,245,952	45.79
District of Columbia	2,065,368	2,078,472	100.00	2,085,951	100.00	Oregon	6,312,369	6,258,473	46.98	6,285,952	49.95
Florida	24,216,369	24,687,474	61.56	25,063,953	64.85	Pennsylvania	19,485,369	19,257,474	64.83	18,831,953	56.04
Georgia	13,100,369	13,249,474	53.39	13,458,353	59.56	Rhode Island	2,782,368	2,777,472	41.76	2,795,951	41.05
Hawaii	3,077,368	3,016,472	46.45	3,044,951	49.53	South Carolina	7,176,369	7,125,473	42.53	7,119,952	47.05
Idaho	3,178,368	3,137,473	52.41	3,181,951	57.74	South Dakota	2,391,368	2,346,472	47.16	2,356,951	53.80
Illinois	19,688,369	19,460,474	64.51	19,209,953	65.51	Tennessee	9,602,369	9,586,474	48.78	9,524,952	60.11
Indiana	10,299,369	10,160,474	56.78	10,039,953	59.29	Texas	31,705,369	31,831,474	65.60	32,275,953	60.42
Iowa	5,633,369	5,532,473	40.79	5,453,952	48.19	Utah	4,511,369	4,515,473	49.76	4,569,952	52.34
Kansas	5,306,369	5,183,473	47.49	5,138,952	57.09	Vermont	2,153,368	2,344,472	25.11	2,150,951	29.32
Kentucky	7,290,369	7,169,373	32.30	7,098,952	38.50	Virginia	11,711,369	11,624,474	30.04	12,814,953	35.11
Louisiana	7,914,369	7,795,473	51.92	7,653,952	54.04	Washington	10,016,369	9,886,474	60.25	9,911,953	63.72
Maine	3,180,368	3,109,473	41.59	3,115,951	52.03	West Virginia	4,021,369	3,892,473	47.93	3,837,951	50.13
Maryland	9,128,369	9,009,474	44.47	9,042,952	43.52	Wisconsin	9,248,369	9,108,474	61.98	9,018,952	61.51
Massachusetts	8,474,400	11,591,053	34.52	10,400,364	36.52	Wyoming	2,006,368	1,963,472	54.95	1,982,951	61.59
Michigan	16,251,369	15,820,474	53.10	15,579,953	57.83						
Minnesota	8,527,369	8,456,473	70.29	8,418,952	65.72	Puerto Rico	7,182,369	6,826,473	0.00	6,765,952	0.00
Mississippi	5,480,369	5,412,472	52.52	5,360,952	56.93	Virgin Islands	1,459,368[a]	1,398,472	0.00	1,427,951	0.00
Missouri	10,538,869	9,448,474	58.22	9,347,952	58.53	Guam	1,336,068	1,443,752	0.00	1,471,363	0.00
Montana	2,618,369	2,562,472	58.56	2,590,884	52.56	American Samoa	875,221	953,222	0.00	944,424	0.00
Nebraska	3,807,368	3,749,473	60.36	3,734,951	62.12	Northern Marianas	488,521	470,076	0.00	479,474	0.00
Nevada	4,024,369	4,170,473	62.01	4,366,952	72.11						

Note: The U.S. Department of Justice, Bureau of Justice Assistance (BJA), through the Edward Byrne Memorial State and Local Law Enforcement Assistance Program, provides funds to State and local jurisdictions for the purposes of crime prevention and control, and improving criminal justice systems. Emphasis is placed on violent and drug-related crime, serious offenders, and the enforcement of State and local laws that establish offenses similar to those in the Federal Controlled Substances Act. Grants may provide support for personnel, equipment, training, technical assistance, and information systems for more widespread apprehension, prosecution, adjudication, detention, and rehabilitation of persons who violate such laws, and assistance to the victims of such crimes (other than compensation).

BJA makes program funds available through two types of grant programs: discretionary and formula. Discretionary funds are awarded directly to public and private agencies and private nonprofit organizations; formula funds are awarded to the States, which then make subawards to State and local units of government as well as to agencies and organizations. The above data reflect awards under the formula grant program and the minimum percentage that is required to be passed to local jurisdictions. (Source, *2002*, pp. 1, 3.) The exceptions are Puerto Rico, the Virgin Islands, Guam, American Samoa, and the Northern Marianas; in these jurisdictions Byrne formula awards are retained and managed at the "State" level.

[a] Anticipated award amount.

Source: U.S. Department of Justice, Bureau of Justice Assistance, *Edward Byrne Memorial State and Local Law Enforcement Assistance: Fact Sheet, Fiscal Year 2001*, p. 3; *Program Brief, Fiscal Year 2002*, p. 6 (Washington, DC: U.S. Department of Justice); and U.S. Department of Justice, Bureau of Justice Assistance [Online]. Available: http://www.ojp.usdoj.gov/BJA/html/FY2003BYRNE.pdf [Mar. 2, 2004]; http://www.ojp.usdoj.gov/BJA/html/03ByrnePassthrough.PDF [Mar. 2, 2004]. Table adapted by SOURCEBOOK staff.

Table 1.17

Justice system employment and payroll

By level of government and type of activity, United States, March 2001

Activity	Total all governments	Federal Government	State governments	Local governments[a]	Federal	State	Local[a]
Total justice system							
Total employees	2,295,423	197,263	741,007	1,357,153	8.6%	32.3%	59.1%
Full-time employees	NA	NA	714,516	1,196,978	NA	37.4	62.6
Full-time equivalent employment	NA	NA	730,340	1,257,384	NA	36.7	63.3
March payrolls	$8,149,988	1,035,280	2,513,012	4,601,696	12.7	30.8	56.5
Police protection							
Total employees	1,060,219	106,337	104,657	849,225	10.0	9.9	80.1
Full-time employees	NA	NA	101,976	742,214	NA	12.1	87.9
Full-time equivalent employment	NA	NA	103,141	781,526	NA	11.7	88.3
March payrolls	$4,003,488	580,678	406,577	3,016,234	14.5	10.2	75.3
Judicial and legal							
Total employees	488,143	57,953	162,982	267,208	11.9	33.4	54.7
Full-time employees	NA	NA	153,068	230,228	NA	39.9	60.1
Full-time equivalent employment	NA	NA	158,794	243,529	NA	39.5	60.5
March payrolls	$1,797,699	317,590	638,783	841,326	17.7	35.5	46.8
Corrections							
Total employees	747,061	32,973	473,368	240,720	4.4	63.4	32.2
Full-time employees	NA	NA	459,472	224,536	NA	67.2	32.8
Full-time equivalent employment	NA	NA	468,405	232,329	NA	66.8	33.2
March payrolls	$2,348,801	137,012	1,467,651	744,137	5.8	62.5	31.7

Note: See Note, table 1.1. The Federal budget source provides only "total employees" data for the Federal Government; that figure is included in the denominator used to compute the percent distribution of full-time employees and full-time equivalent employment for State and local governments. For survey methodology and definitions of terms, see Appendix 1.

Source: U.S. Department of Justice, Bureau of Justice Statistics, *2001 Justice Expenditure and Employment Extracts*, NCJ 202792, Table 2 [Online]. Available: http://www.ojp.usdoj.gov/bjs/pub/sheets/cjee01.zip, file cjee0102.wk1 [Aug. 6, 2004].

[a] Data for local governments are estimates subject to sampling variation.

Table 1.18

Justice system payroll

By level of government, United States, October 1982-95, and March 1997-99 and 2001[a]

(Payroll amounts in thousands)

One-month payroll period	Total all governments	Federal	Total State and local	State	Local[b] Total	Counties	Munici- palities
1982	$2,064,748	$209,433	$1,855,315	$577,808	$1,277,507	$472,129	$805,378
1983	2,285,595	256,930	2,028,665	639,616	1,389,049	513,129	875,920
1984	2,535,148	293,283	2,241,865	726,281	1,515,585	574,862	940,722
1985	2,767,277	298,106	2,469,171	812,136	1,657,035	640,502	1,016,533
1986	2,975,373	309,960	2,665,413	893,910	1,771,503	694,777	1,076,727
1987	3,248,834	347,102	2,901,732	995,531	1,906,201	746,986	1,159,215
1988	3,546,099	386,207	3,159,892	1,090,309	2,069,583	843,441	1,226,142
1989	3,862,304	418,184	3,444,120	1,207,762	2,236,358	926,432	1,309,926
1990	4,214,625	467,007	3,747,618	1,317,489	2,430,129	1,025,336	1,404,793
1991	4,534,954	537,074	3,997,880	1,391,992	2,605,888	1,109,816	1,496,073
1992	4,788,918	588,000	4,200,918	1,440,336	2,760,582	1,179,389	1,581,193
1993	4,985,971	592,593	4,393,378	1,523,042	2,870,366	1,227,871	1,642,465
1994	5,399,260	656,454	4,742,806	1,632,246	3,110,560	1,343,227	1,767,333
1995	5,812,706	720,212	5,092,494	1,776,638	3,315,856	1,426,094	1,889,761
1997	6,251,789	760,640	5,491,149	1,956,789	3,534,360	1,525,982	2,008,378
1998	6,650,770	853,026	5,797,744	2,051,111	3,746,633	1,626,790	2,119,843
1999	7,166,302	912,949	6,253,353	2,211,799	4,041,554	1,775,370	2,266,184
2001	8,150,000	1,035,000	NA	2,513,000	4,602,000	NA	NA

Note: See Note, table 1.1. The U.S. Census Bureau changed the reference month for employment and payroll data from October to March after the 1995 data collection. Data for 1995 and previous years refer to the month of October. No data were collected during the period of transition, consequently, there are no 1996 employment and payroll data. Beginning in 1997, employment and payroll data are for the month of March. Some data have been revised by the Source and may differ from previous editions of SOURCE-BOOK. For survey methodology and definitions of terms, see Appendix 1.

[a]Detail may not add to total because of rounding.
[b]Data for local governments are estimates subject to sampling variation.

Source: U.S. Department of Justice, Bureau of Justice Statistics, *Trends in Justice Expenditure and Employment*, NCJ 178271, Table 4 [Online]. Available: http://www.ojp.usdoj.gov/bjs/data/eetrnd04.wk1 [Mar. 27, 2002]; and *Justice Expenditure and Employment in the United States, 2001*, Bulletin NCJ 202792 (Washington, DC: U.S. Department of Justice, May 2004), p. 5, Table 4. Table adapted by SOURCEBOOK staff.

Table 1.19

State and local justice system payroll

By type of activity and level of government, March 2001[a]

(Payroll amounts in thousands)

State and level of government[b]	Total March payrolls[c]	Total justice system March payrolls[d]	Percent of total March payrolls[d]	Police protection March payrolls	Percent of total justice system March payrolls	Judicial and legal March payrolls	Percent of total justice system March payrolls	Corrections March payrolls	Percent of total justice system March payrolls
States-local, total	$49,252,853	$7,114,708	14.4%	$3,422,811	48.1%	$1,480,109	20.8%	$2,211,788	31.1%
State	14,136,252	2,513,012	17.8	406,577	16.2	638,783	25.4	1,467,651	58.4
Local, total	35,116,601	4,601,696	13.1	3,016,234	65.5	841,326	18.3	744,137	16.2
Counties	7,414,410	2,032,164	27.4	776,785	38.2	651,666	32.1	603,714	29.7
Municipalities	10,130,844	2,569,532	25.4	2,239,449	87.2	189,660	7.4	140,423	5.5
Alabama	714,397	73,818	10.3	36,589	49.6	16,862	22.8	20,367	27.6
State	255,083	30,047	11.8	4,199	14.0	11,926	39.7	13,922	46.3
Local, total	459,314	43,772	9.5	32,390	74.0	4,936	11.3	6,445	14.7
Counties	47,372	14,804	31.3	6,491	43.8	2,824	19.1	5,490	37.1
Municipalities	100,453	28,967	28.8	25,900	89.4	2,113	7.3	955	3.3
Alaska	185,781	20,314	10.9	7,727	38.0	5,605	27.6	6,982	34.4
State	89,577	13,811	15.4	2,108	15.3	5,068	36.7	6,636	48.0
Local, total	96,204	6,503	6.8	5,619	86.4	537	8.3	347	5.3
Boroughs	36,747	451	1.2	261	57.9	140	31.1	49	10.9
Municipalities	57,800	6,053	10.5	5,358	88.5	397	6.6	298	4.9
Arizona	742,241	132,968	17.9	61,975	46.6	33,000	24.8	37,994	28.6
State	199,304	39,981	20.1	6,861	17.2	5,948	14.9	27,173	68.0
Local, total	542,937	92,987	17.1	55,114	59.3	27,052	29.1	10,821	11.6
Counties	89,579	44,751	50.0	13,018	29.1	20,927	46.8	10,806	24.1
Municipalities	140,490	48,236	34.3	42,096	87.3	6,125	12.7	15	(e)
Arkansas	361,381	38,423	10.6	19,279	50.2	7,214	18.8	11,930	31.1
State	144,287	16,439	11.4	3,264	19.9	4,226	25.7	8,950	54.4
Local, total	217,094	21,984	10.1	16,015	72.8	2,988	13.6	2,981	13.6
Counties	23,367	8,037	34.4	3,484	43.3	1,652	20.6	2,901	36.1
Municipalities	46,940	13,947	29.7	12,531	89.8	1,336	9.6	80	0.6
California	7,178,514	1,114,171	15.5	515,760	46.3	251,310	22.6	347,101	31.2
State	1,687,261	297,627	17.6	62,740	21.1	21,373	7.2	213,514	71.7
Local, total	5,491,253	816,545	14.9	453,020	55.5	229,937	28.2	133,587	16.4
Counties	1,394,126	485,069	34.8	152,289	31.4	206,372	42.5	126,407	26.1
Municipalities	1,096,876	331,476	30.2	300,731	90.7	23,565	7.1	7,180	2.2
Colorado	765,069	108,151	14.1	52,125	48.2	21,928	20.3	34,098	31.5
State	254,903	41,473	16.3	5,320	12.8	13,577	32.7	22,577	54.4
Local, total	510,166	66,677	13.1	46,805	70.2	8,351	12.5	11,522	17.3
Counties	73,188	23,621	32.3	12,160	51.5	3,675	15.6	7,786	33.0
Municipalities	150,032	43,057	28.7	34,645	80.5	4,676	10.9	3,735	8.7
Connecticut	684,129	99,189	14.5	47,705	48.1	19,546	19.7	31,938	32.2
State	262,586	58,433	22.3	7,892	13.5	18,603	31.8	31,938	54.7
Local, total	421,543	40,756	9.7	39,813	97.7	943	2.3	0	X
Municipalities	394,832	40,756	10.3	39,813	97.7	943	2.3	0	X
Delaware	145,650	21,227	14.6	8,786	41.4	5,034	23.7	7,406	34.9
State	79,809	15,757	19.7	3,641	23.1	4,709	29.9	7,406	47.0
Local, total	65,841	5,470	8.3	5,144	94.0	326	6.0	0	X
Counties	6,860	2,077	30.3	1,860	89.6	217	10.4	0	X
Municipalities	8,532	3,393	39.8	3,284	96.8	109	3.2	0	X
District of Columbia	174,548	29,934	17.1	20,035	66.9	1,952	6.5	7,948	26.6
Local, total	174,548	29,934	17.1	20,035	66.9	1,952	6.5	7,948	26.6
Municipality	135,686	29,934	22.1	20,035	66.9	1,952	6.5	7,948	26.6
Florida	2,326,520	431,438	18.5	207,086	48.0	103,022	23.9	121,330	28.1
State	576,895	150,712	26.1	13,388	8.9	61,269	40.7	76,055	50.5
Local, total	1,749,625	280,726	16.0	193,698	69.0	41,753	14.9	45,276	16.1
Counties	454,828	179,740	39.5	97,654	54.3	38,346	21.3	43,740	24.3
Municipalities	333,082	100,986	30.3	96,045	95.1	3,407	3.4	1,535	1.5

See notes at end of table.

Table 1.19

State and local justice system payroll

By type of activity and level of government, March 2001[a]--Continued

(Payroll amounts in thousands)

		Total justice system		Police protection		Judicial and legal		Corrections	
State and level of government[b]	Total March payrolls[c]	March payrolls[d]	Percent of total March payrolls[d]	March payrolls	Percent of total justice system March payrolls	March payrolls	Percent of total justice system March payrolls	March payrolls	Percent of total justice system March payrolls
Georgia	$1,247,412	$165,154	13.2%	$68,479	41.5%	$31,038	18.8%	$65,638	39.7%
State	354,269	61,046	17.2	6,940	11.4	6,746	11.1	47,359	77.6
Local, total	893,143	104,109	11.7	61,539	59.1	24,291	23.3	18,279	17.6
Counties	150,888	64,301	42.6	28,619	44.5	20,676	32.2	15,006	23.3
Municipalities	110,567	39,807	36.0	32,919	82.7	3,615	9.1	3,273	8.2
Hawaii	207,801	30,878	14.9	14,398	46.6	9,544	30.9	6,936	22.5
State	160,375	14,397	9.0	0	X	7,461	51.8	6,936	48.2
Local, total	47,426	16,482	34.8	14,398	87.4	2,084	12.6	0	X
Counties	16,360	5,477	33.5	4,589	83.8	887	16.2	0	X
Municipalities	30,713	11,005	35.8	9,809	89.1	1,196	10.9	0	X
Idaho	197,283	23,839	12.1	11,482	48.2	5,266	22.1	7,091	29.7
State	66,320	8,379	12.6	1,726	20.6	2,187	26.1	4,466	53.3
Local, total	130,963	15,460	11.8	9,756	63.1	3,080	19.9	2,624	17.0
Counties	26,865	9,874	36.8	4,508	45.7	2,741	27.8	2,624	26.6
Municipalities	20,215	5,586	27.6	5,248	93.9	338	6.1	0	X
Illinois	2,041,738	324,370	15.9	175,120	54.0	63,883	19.7	85,368	26.3
State	439,777	89,456	20.3	18,034	20.2	18,265	20.4	53,157	59.4
Local, total	1,601,961	234,914	14.7	157,086	66.9	45,617	19.4	32,211	13.7
Counties	202,648	94,169	46.5	19,810	21.0	42,253	44.9	32,105	34.1
Municipalities	395,449	140,744	35.6	137,275	97.5	3,364	2.4	105	0.1
Indiana	902,665	106,156	11.8	51,394	48.4	18,583	17.5	36,179	34.1
State	260,036	38,765	14.9	7,499	19.3	6,399	16.5	24,868	64.2
Local, total	642,628	67,391	10.5	43,895	65.1	12,185	18.1	11,311	16.8
Counties	116,586	29,351	25.2	10,251	34.9	8,848	30.1	10,252	34.9
Municipalities	135,263	38,039	28.1	33,644	88.4	3,337	8.8	1,059	2.8
Iowa	508,651	48,576	9.5	22,929	47.2	11,952	24.6	13,695	28.2
State	192,799	23,924	12.4	3,726	15.6	9,245	38.6	10,953	45.8
Local, total	315,853	24,652	7.8	19,204	77.9	2,707	11.0	2,742	11.1
Counties	60,437	11,327	18.7	6,297	55.6	2,332	20.6	2,698	23.8
Municipalities	64,072	13,325	20.8	12,906	96.9	375	2.8	44	0.3
Kansas	457,926	52,908	11.6	26,993	51.0	11,055	20.9	14,859	28.1
State	132,937	19,119	14.4	3,293	17.2	6,592	34.5	9,234	48.3
Local, total	324,989	33,789	10.4	23,701	70.1	4,464	13.2	5,625	16.6
Counties	56,178	14,537	25.9	6,823	46.9	2,673	18.4	5,042	34.7
Municipalities	69,855	19,252	27.6	16,878	87.7	1,791	9.3	583	3.0
Kentucky	584,260	63,160	10.8	29,982	47.5	17,342	27.5	15,836	25.1
State	232,828	31,043	13.3	7,360	23.7	14,315	46.1	9,368	30.2
Local, total	351,431	32,117	9.1	22,622	70.4	3,027	9.4	6,468	20.1
Counties	50,925	17,082	33.5	8,819	51.6	2,673	15.6	5,590	32.7
Municipalities	58,373	15,036	25.8	13,803	91.8	354	2.4	878	5.8
Louisiana	691,281	98,985	14.3	42,321	42.8	20,630	20.8	36,034	36.4
State	261,984	33,032	12.6	4,799	14.5	6,829	20.7	21,405	64.8
Local, total	429,297	65,953	15.4	37,522	56.9	13,801	20.9	14,630	22.2
Parishes	110,546	32,581	29.5	15,622	47.9	9,301	28.5	7,659	23.5
Municipalities	84,892	33,372	39.3	21,901	65.6	4,500	13.5	6,971	20.9
Maine	198,888	18,478	9.3	10,013	54.2	3,187	17.2	5,279	28.6
State	66,753	8,293	12.4	1,715	20.7	2,576	31.1	4,003	48.3
Local, total	132,135	10,185	7.7	8,298	81.5	611	6.0	1,276	12.5
Counties	4,179	3,298	78.9	1,519	46.1	525	15.9	1,254	38.0
Municipalities	79,693	6,887	8.6	6,779	98.4	86	1.3	22	0.3
Maryland	984,197	144,647	14.7	70,212	48.5	25,158	17.4	49,277	34.1
State	325,846	64,650	19.8	11,037	17.1	14,386	22.3	39,227	60.7
Local, total	658,351	79,996	12.2	59,175	74.0	10,772	13.5	10,050	12.6
Counties	533,935	55,321	10.4	37,472	67.7	7,799	14.1	10,050	18.2
Municipalities	118,579	24,676	20.8	21,703	88.0	2,972	12.0	0	X

See notes at end of table.

Table 1.19

State and local justice system payroll

By type of activity and level of government, March 2001[a]--Continued

(Payroll amounts in thousands)

		Total justice system		Police protection		Judicial and legal		Corrections	
State and level of government[b]	Total March payrolls[c]	March payrolls[d]	Percent of total March payrolls[d]	March payrolls	Percent of total justice system March payrolls	March payrolls	Percent of total justice system March payrolls	March payrolls	Percent of total justice system March payrolls
Massachusetts	$1,173,964	$183,305	15.6%	$103,066	56.2%	$42,549	23.2%	$37,690	20.6%
State	366,406	95,496	26.1	26,829	28.1	41,348	43.3	27,319	28.6
Local, total	807,558	87,809	10.9	76,238	86.8	1,201	1.4	10,370	11.8
Counties	8,190	5,914	72.2	122	2.1	0	X	5,792	97.9
Municipalities	684,160	81,895	12.0	76,115	92.9	1,201	1.5	4,578	5.6
Michigan	1,712,502	232,170	13.6	99,250	42.7	44,897	19.3	88,023	37.9
State	523,523	93,874	17.9	13,708	14.6	9,669	10.3	70,498	75.1
Local, total	1,188,980	138,296	11.6	85,543	61.9	35,228	25.5	17,525	12.7
Counties	166,320	64,059	38.5	18,720	29.2	28,212	44.0	17,127	26.7
Municipalities	325,139	74,237	22.8	66,822	90.0	7,016	9.5	398	0.5
Minnesota	932,562	98,421	10.6	46,162	46.9	23,568	23.9	28,691	29.2
State	280,520	27,801	9.9	4,125	14.8	10,205	36.7	13,471	48.5
Local, total	652,043	70,619	10.8	42,037	59.5	13,363	18.9	15,220	21.6
Counties	142,271	40,599	28.5	13,185	32.5	12,194	30.0	15,220	37.5
Municipalities	125,408	30,020	23.9	28,851	96.1	1,169	3.9	0	X
Mississippi	437,090	41,397	9.5	21,089	50.9	7,976	19.3	12,332	29.8
State	152,293	15,541	10.2	3,389	21.8	3,259	21.0	8,893	57.2
Local, total	284,797	25,856	9.1	17,700	68.5	4,718	18.2	3,439	13.3
Counties	63,063	12,263	19.4	5,233	42.7	3,697	30.1	3,333	27.2
Municipalities	54,171	13,593	25.1	12,467	91.7	1,021	7.5	106	0.8
Missouri	812,853	104,947	12.9	52,572	50.1	22,816	21.7	29,558	28.2
State	249,750	43,931	17.6	7,112	16.2	12,281	28.0	24,539	55.9
Local, total	563,103	61,015	10.8	45,460	74.5	10,535	17.3	5,020	8.2
Counties	49,121	19,724	40.2	9,924	50.3	6,019	30.5	3,780	19.2
Municipalities	129,456	41,291	31.9	35,535	86.1	4,516	10.9	1,240	3.0
Montana	137,959	13,212	9.6	6,321	47.8	2,937	22.2	3,954	29.9
State	54,360	4,894	9.0	1,203	24.6	875	17.9	2,816	57.5
Local, total	83,600	8,318	10.0	5,118	61.5	2,062	24.8	1,138	13.7
Counties	13,897	5,118	36.8	2,377	46.4	1,658	32.4	1,082	21.2
Municipalities	11,575	3,201	27.7	2,741	85.6	404	12.6	56	1.7
Nebraska	305,326	27,765	9.1	14,684	52.9	5,559	20.0	7,522	27.1
State	88,988	9,611	10.8	2,116	22.0	2,450	25.5	5,045	52.5
Local, total	216,338	18,154	8.4	12,568	69.2	3,110	17.1	2,477	13.6
Counties	30,628	8,794	28.7	3,582	40.7	2,735	31.1	2,477	28.2
Municipalities	37,646	9,360	24.9	8,985	96.0	374	4.0	0	X
Nevada	316,508	64,350	20.3	30,027	46.7	13,652	21.2	20,672	32.1
State	78,404	17,327	22.1	3,265	18.8	2,903	16.8	11,160	64.4
Local, total	238,104	47,023	19.7	26,762	56.9	10,749	22.9	9,512	20.2
Counties	86,939	34,700	39.9	19,180	55.3	8,411	24.2	7,109	20.5
Municipalities	42,011	12,323	29.3	7,582	61.5	2,338	19.0	2,403	19.5
New Hampshire	187,449	22,092	11.8	12.668	57.3	3,965	17.9	5,459	24.7
State	58,136	8,661	14.9	1,567	18.1	3,102	35.8	3,991	46.1
Local, total	129,313	13,431	10.4	11,101	82.6	862	6.4	1,468	10.9
Counties	8,789	2,831	32.2	685	24.2	678	23.9	1,468	51.9
Municipalities	55,764	10,601	19.0	10,416	98.3	184	1.7	0	X
New Jersey	1,844,228	324,887	17.6	167,671	51.6	89,197	27.5	68,020	20.9
State	565,108	117,639	20.8	19,973	17.0	56,940	48.4	40,727	34.6
Local, total	1,279,120	207,248	16.2	147,698	71.3	32,257	15.6	27,293	13.2
Counties	215,771	58,787	27.2	10,334	17.6	21,263	36.2	27,190	46.3
Municipalities	400,079	148,461	37.1	137,364	92.5	10,994	7.4	103	0.1
New Mexico	311,482	40,976	13.2	17,003	41.5	9,688	23.6	14,285	34.9
State	131,721	20,981	15.9	2,253	10.7	8,508	40.6	10,220	48.7
Local, total	179,761	19,995	11.1	14,750	73.8	1,180	5.9	4,065	20.3
Counties	18,174	6,366	35.0	3,749	58.9	250	3.9	2,367	37.2
Municipalities	47,322	13,629	28.8	11,001	80.7	929	6.8	1,698	12.5

See notes at end of table.

Table 1.19

State and local justice system payroll

By type of activity and level of government, March 2001[a]--Continued

(Payroll amounts in thousands)

State and level of government[b]	Total March payrolls[c]	Total justice system March payrolls[d]	Percent of total March payrolls[d]	Police protection March payrolls	Percent of total justice system March payrolls	Judicial and legal March payrolls	Percent of total justice system March payrolls	Corrections March payrolls	Percent of total justice system March payrolls
New York	$4,583,732	$851,284	18.6%	$453,238	53.2%	$145,175	17.1%	$252,871	29.7%
State	1,009,548	264,598	26.2	28,673	10.8	94,032	35.5	141,893	53.6
Local, total	3,574,185	586,687	16.4	424,565	72.4	51,143	8.7	110,978	18.9
Counties	400,586	120,720	30.1	65,063	53.9	17,053	14.1	38,604	32.0
Municipalities	2,092,700	465,966	22.3	359,502	77.2	34,090	7.3	72,374	15.5
North Carolina	1,287,980	155,041	12.0	68,697	44.3	23,388	15.1	62,955	40.6
State	389,468	86,221	22.1	12,020	13.9	21,178	24.6	53,024	61.5
Local, total	898,513	68,819	7.7	56,677	82.4	2,211	3.2	9,932	14.4
Counties	733,675	29,716	4.1	17,913	60.3	1,872	6.3	9,932	33.4
Municipalities	135,228	39,103	28.9	38,764	99.1	339	0.9	0	X
North Dakota	103,884	8,443	8.1	4,191	49.6	2,344	27.8	1,908	22.6
State	43,484	3,404	7.8	631	18.5	1,402	41.2	1,371	40.3
Local, total	60,400	5,039	8.3	3,560	70.6	941	18.7	538	10.7
Counties	8,502	2,461	28.9	1,104	44.9	823	33.4	534	21.7
Municipalities	10,137	2,578	25.4	2,455	95.3	119	4.6	4	0.1
Ohio	1,875,652	263,943	14.1	118,967	45.1	60,676	23.0	84,299	31.9
State	457,395	83,540	18.3	9,548	11.4	11,556	13.8	62,435	74.7
Local, total	1,418,256	180,403	12.7	109,419	60.7	49,120	27.2	21,864	12.1
Counties	272,467	77,509	28.4	21,422	27.6	35,688	46.0	20,399	26.3
Municipalities	314,577	102,894	32.7	87,997	85.5	13,432	13.1	1,465	1.4
Oklahoma	498,940	60,237	12.1	29,998	49.8	13,064	21.7	17,175	28.5
State	182,895	30,476	16.7	5,737	18.8	9,488	31.1	15,250	50.0
Local, total	316,044	29,761	9.4	24,261	81.5	3,576	12.0	1,925	6.5
Counties	36,385	7,732	21.3	4,060	52.5	1,879	24.3	1,793	23.2
Municipalities	82,434	22,029	26.7	20,201	91.7	1,697	7.7	131	0.6
Oregon	579,457	80,708	13.9	35,137	43.5	17,016	21.1	28,556	35.4
State	173,842	32,114	18.5	5,200	16.2	10,847	33.8	16,067	50.0
Local, total	405,615	48,595	12.0	29,936	61.6	6,169	12.7	12,489	25.7
Counties	70,409	27,029	38.4	9,449	35.0	5,091	18.8	12,489	46.2
Municipalities	75,811	21,566	28.4	20,488	95.0	1,078	5.0	0	X
Pennsylvania	1,788,361	265,988	14.9	124,586	46.8	54,694	20.6	86,709	32.6
State	537,955	90,077	16.7	24,055	26.7	14,581	16.2	51,441	57.1
Local, total	1,250,405	175,911	14.1	100,531	57.1	40,113	22.8	35,268	20.0
Counties	149,288	61,171	41.0	6,924	11.3	27,557	45.0	26,690	43.6
Municipalities	257,996	114,740	44.5	93,607	81.6	12,556	10.9	8,578	7.5
Rhode Island	206,135	26,314	12.8	14,001	53.2	4,706	17.9	7,607	28.9
State	74,295	13,458	18.1	1,471	10.9	4,380	32.5	7,607	56.5
Local, total	131,840	12,856	9.8	12,530	97.5	326	2.5	0	X
Municipalities	123,758	12,856	10.4	12,530	97.5	326	2.5	0	X
South Carolina	619,197	73,213	11.8	36,391	49.7	9,861	13.5	26,961	36.8
State	227,286	33,693	14.8	9,084	27.0	2,851	8.5	21,758	64.6
Local, total	391,912	39,520	10.1	27,307	69.1	7,011	17.7	5,203	13.2
Counties	63,436	23,595	37.2	12,511	53.0	5,998	25.4	5,086	21.6
Municipalities	48,633	15,926	32.7	14,796	92.9	1,012	6.4	117	0.7
South Dakota	100,036	10,251	10.2	4,777	46.6	2,379	23.2	3,095	30.2
State	35,857	4,672	13.0	905	19.4	1,644	35.2	2,123	45.4
Local, total	64,179	5,579	8.7	3,872	69.4	735	13.2	972	17.4
Counties	7,828	2,917	37.3	1,316	45.1	655	22.5	946	32.4
Municipalities	14,658	2,662	18.2	2,556	96.0	80	3.0	26	1.0
Tennessee	804,326	94,566	11.8	50,305	53.2	17,731	18.8	26,530	28.1
State	232,593	29,125	12.5	5,349	18.4	7,953	27.3	15,824	54.3
Local, total	571,733	65,441	11.4	44,956	68.7	9,779	14.9	10,706	16.4
Counties	297,937	27,929	9.4	11,983	42.9	6,796	24.3	9,151	32.8
Municipalities	252,993	37,512	14.8	32,974	87.9	2,983	8.0	1,555	4.1

See notes at end of table.

Table 1.19

State and local justice system payroll

By type of activity and level of government, March 2001[a]--Continued

(Payroll amounts in thousands)

State and level of government[b]	Total March payrolls[c]	Total justice system March payrolls[d]	Percent of total March payrolls[d]	Police protection March payrolls	Percent of total justice system March payrolls	Judicial and legal March payrolls	Percent of total justice system March payrolls	Corrections March payrolls	Percent of total justice system March payrolls
Texas	$3,306,228	$437,798	13.2%	$192,514	44.0%	$77,194	17.6%	$168,090	38.4%
State	827,698	140,443	17.0	12,280	8.7	19,813	14.1	108,350	77.1
Local, total	2,478,531	297,355	12.0	180,234	60.6	57,380	19.3	59,740	20.1
Counties	318,618	142,280	44.7	37,439	26.3	45,214	31.8	59,628	41.9
Municipalities	507,931	155,075	30.5	142,795	92.1	12,167	7.8	112	0.1
Utah	354,852	40,836	11.5	17,831	43.7	9,563	23.4	13,443	32.9
State	149,534	17,435	11.7	2,674	15.3	5,591	32.1	9,170	52.6
Local, total	205,318	23,401	11.4	15,157	64.8	3,971	17.0	4,273	18.3
Counties	30,059	12,254	40.8	5,548	45.3	2,433	19.9	4,273	34.9
Municipalities	42,190	11,147	26.4	9,609	86.2	1,538	13.8	0	X
Vermont	104,250	9,820	9.4	4,391	44.7	2,333	23.8	3,096	31.5
State	44,603	7,350	16.5	2,040	27.8	2,214	30.1	3,096	42.1
Local, total	59,647	2,470	4.1	2,350	95.2	119	4.8	0	X
Counties	211	157	74.1	64	41.1	92	58.9	0	X
Municipalities	12,521	2,313	18.5	2,286	98.8	27	1.2	0	X
Virginia	1,175,419	154,079	13.1	65,113	42.3	27,681	18.0	61,286	39.8
State	385,896	64,529	16.7	9,911	15.4	13,804	21.4	40,814	63.2
Local, total	789,523	89,551	11.3	55,202	61.6	13,877	15.5	20,472	22.9
Counties	461,959	47,137	10.2	27,754	58.9	9,001	19.1	10,382	22.0
Municipalities	293,064	42,414	14.5	27,448	64.7	4,876	11.5	10,090	23.8
Washington	1,101,974	133,869	12.1	61,637	46.0	32,292	24.1	39,939	29.8
State	386,885	42,166	10.9	8,867	21.0	8,112	19.2	25,187	59.7
Local, total	715,089	91,703	12.8	52,770	57.5	24,181	26.4	14,753	16.1
Counties	140,421	51,050	36.4	17,449	34.2	19,556	38.3	14,046	27.5
Municipalities	152,811	40,653	26.6	35,321	86.9	4,625	11.4	707	1.7
West Virginia	251,072	18,069	7.2	9,035	50.0	5,783	32.0	3,250	18.0
State	95,838	9,448	9.9	2,917	30.9	3,799	40.2	2,731	28.9
Local, total	155,234	8,621	5.6	6,118	71.0	1,984	23.0	519	6.0
Counties	15,005	4,468	29.8	2,158	48.3	1,790	40.1	519	11.6
Municipalities	20,945	4,153	19.8	3,960	95.3	193	4.7	0	X
Wisconsin	933,965	119,752	12.8	56,298	47.0	21,986	18.4	41,469	34.6
State	257,605	43,948	17.1	3,529	8.0	10,882	24.8	29,536	67.2
Local, total	676,361	75,805	11.2	52,768	69.6	11,104	14.6	11,933	15.7
Counties	134,803	35,966	26.7	14,522	40.4	9,512	26.4	11,933	33.2
Municipalities	137,352	39,839	29.0	38,246	96.0	1,592	4.0	0	X
Wyoming	105,136	10,189	9.7	4,803	47.1	2,329	22.9	3,057	30.0
State	30,742	4,176	13.6	606	14.5	1,418	33.9	2,152	51.5
Local, total	74,395	6,013	8.1	4,197	69.8	911	15.2	904	15.0
Counties	14,045	3,053	21.7	1,469	48.1	679	22.2	904	29.6
Municipalities	9,982	2,961	29.7	2,728	92.2	232	7.8	0	X

Note: See Notes, tables 1.1 and 1.18. For survey methodology and definitions of terms, see Appendix 1.

[a] March payroll data may not sum to total because of rounding.
[b] Data for local governments are estimates subject to sampling variation.
[c] Includes payrolls of States and all types of local governments including independent school districts and special districts, which are not displayed separately. The "local, total" categories, which include these districts, will not equal the sum of the "counties" and "municipalities" categories.
[d] Justice system payrolls of independent school districts and special districts (primarily for special police forces) are not available.
[e] Less than 0.05%.

Source: U.S. Department of Justice, Bureau of Justice Statistics, *2001 Justice Expenditure and Employment Extracts*, NCJ 202792, Table 6 [Online]. Available: http://www.ojp.usdoj.gov/bjs/pub/sheets/cjee01.zip, file cjee0106.wk1 [Aug. 6, 2004].

Table 1.20

Justice system employment

By level of government, United States, October 1982-95, and March 1997-99 and 2001[a]

One-month payroll period	Total all governments	Federal	Total State and local	State	Local[b] Total	Counties	Munici-palities
1982	1,270,342	94,555	1,175,787	341,010	834,777	319,690	515,087
1983	1,313,831	103,842	1,209,989	358,528	851,461	331,071	520,390
1984	1,373,354	106,926	1,266,428	387,398	879,030	351,175	527,855
1985	1,422,718	110,653	1,312,065	407,792	904,273	368,500	535,773
1986	1,464,070	112,375	1,351,695	425,292	926,403	382,711	543,692
1987	1,524,976	121,321	1,403,655	451,633	952,022	396,743	555,279
1988	1,583,713	130,446	1,453,267	478,885	974,382	416,955	557,427
1989	1,636,895	134,546	1,502,349	505,143	997,206	432,748	564,458
1990	1,710,413	139,799	1,570,614	528,677	1,041,937	462,130	579,807
1991	1,760,563	150,098	1,610,465	542,650	1,067,815	480,003	587,812
1992	1,797,704	162,202	1,635,502	548,139	1,087,363	492,993	594,370
1993	1,825,953	161,786	1,664,167	570,934	1,093,233	495,557	597,676
1994	1,901,773	161,058	1,740,715	599,452	1,141,263	524,908	616,355
1995	1,983,797	167,115	1,816,632	634,692	1,181,940	543,272	638,668
1997	2,078,192	176,739	1,901,453	690,807	1,210,646	556,669	653,977
1998	2,133,240	185,140	1,948,100	705,512	1,242,588	575,661	666,927
1999	2,189,477	191,169	1,998,308	704,902	1,293,406	606,645	686,761
2001	2,295,423	197,263	NA	741,007	1,357,153	NA	NA

Note: See Notes, tables 1.1 and 1.18. Some data have been revised by the Source and may differ from previous editions of SOURCEBOOK. For survey methodology and definitions of terms, see Appendix 1.

[a] Detail may not add to total because of rounding.
[b] Data for local governments are estimates subject to sampling variation.

Source: U.S. Department of Justice, Bureau of Justice Statistics, *Trends in Justice Expenditure and Employment*, NCJ 178270, Table 3 [Online]. Available: http://www.ojp.usdoj.gov/bjs/data/eetrnd03.wk1 [Mar. 27, 2002]; and *Justice Expenditure and Employment in the United States, 2001*, Bulletin NCJ 202792 (Washington, DC: U.S. Department of Justice, May 2004), p. 5, Table 4. Table adapted by SOURCEBOOK staff.

Table 1.21

Justice system employment

By type of activity and level of government, United States, October 1980-95 and March 1997-99[a]

Level of government and one-month payroll period	Total justice system	Police protection	Judicial and legal	Corrections	Level of government and one-month payroll period	Total justice system	Police protection	Judicial and legal	Corrections
All governments					**State**				
1980	NA	714,660	NA	270,647	1980	292,588	75,896	53,022	163,670
1981	NA	716,600	NA	280,593	1981	302,245	76,477	55,455	170,313
1982	1,270,342	723,923	247,697	298,722	1982	341,010	77,538	79,825	183,647
1983	1,313,831	733,070	261,436	319,325	1983	358,528	77,387	83,546	197,595
1984	1,373,354	746,974	277,578	348,802	1984	387,398	83,539	88,869	214,990
1985	1,422,718	757,000	293,025	372,693	1985	407,792	83,603	93,543	230,646
1986	1,464,070	771,917	300,126	392,027	1986	425,292	85,158	96,934	243,200
1987	1,524,976	792,831	312,331	419,814	1987	451,633	87,571	100,108	263,954
1988	1,583,713	804,658	323,641	455,414	1988	478,885	90,300	102,901	285,684
1989	1,636,895	811,528	336,872	488,495	1989	505,143	90,648	107,620	306,875
1990	1,710,413	825,417	350,761	534,235	1990	528,677	89,302	110,093	329,282
1991	1,760,563	837,038	362,178	561,347	1991	542,650	87,011	111,823	343,816
1992	1,797,704	857,593	373,611	566,500	1992	548,139	86,606	113,548	347,985
1993	1,825,953	865,002	375,266	585,685	1993	570,934	86,613	117,264	367,057
1994	1,901,773	890,384	390,731	620,658	1994	599,452	87,270	123,088	389,094
1995	1,983,747	926,086	401,444	656,217	1995	634,692	91,252	130,169	413,271
1997	2,078,192	950,877	419,072	708,243	1997	690,807	93,945	138,674	458,188
1998	2,133,240	976,394	433,493	723,353	1998	705,512	94,628	143,650	467,234
1999	2,189,477	1,017,922	454,982	716,573	1999	704,902	99,686	148,463	456,753
Federal					**Local, total**[b]				
1980	NA	55,505	NA	9,636	1980	NA	582,292	NA	97,052
1981	NA	56,472	NA	9,925	1981	NA	584,618	NA	100,644
1982	94,555	55,922	28,588	10,045	1982	834,777	590,463	139,284	105,030
1983	103,842	63,898	29,834	10,110	1983	851,461	591,785	148,056	111,620
1984	106,926	65,173	31,216	10,537	1984	879,030	598,262	157,493	123,275
1985	110,653	66,024	33,168	11,461	1985	904,273	607,373	166,314	130,586
1986	112,375	66,735	33,584	12,056	1986	926,403	620,024	169,608	136,771
1987	121,321	72,793	35,668	12,860	1987	952,022	632,467	176,555	143,000
1988	130,446	78,755	37,808	13,883	1988	974,382	635,603	182,932	155,847
1989	134,546	78,702	39,733	16,111	1989	997,206	642,178	189,519	165,509
1990	139,799	77,608	43,285	18,906	1990	1,041,937	658,507	197,383	186,047
1991	150,098	81,798	46,824	21,476	1991	1,067,815	668,229	203,531	196,055
1992	162,202	87,616	50,768	23,818	1992	1,087,363	683,371	209,295	194,697
1993	161,786	86,229	50,722	24,835	1993	1,093,233	692,160	207,280	193,793
1994	161,058	84,048	50,872	26,138	1994	1,141,263	719,066	216,771	205,426
1995	167,115	86,087	52,535	28,493	1995	1,181,940	748,747	218,740	214,453
1997	176,739	94,294	52,636	29,809	1997	1,210,646	762,638	227,762	220,246
1998	185,140	100,257	54,447	30,436	1998	1,242,588	781,509	235,396	225,683
1999	191,169	104,096	56,099	30,974	1999	1,293,406	814,140	250,420	228,846
Total State and local					**Counties**[b]				
1980	NA	658,188	NA	260,722	1980	NA	131,645	NA	77,451
1981	NA	661,095	NA	270,957	1981	NA	135,919	NA	80,006
1982	1,175,787	668,001	219,109	288,677	1982	319,690	137,082	98,291	84,317
1983	1,209,989	669,172	231,602	309,215	1983	331,071	137,893	104,034	89,144
1984	1,266,428	681,801	246,362	338,265	1984	351,175	139,417	113,688	98,070
1985	1,312,065	690,976	259,857	361,232	1985	368,500	142,785	120,627	105,088
1986	1,351,695	705,182	266,542	379,971	1986	382,711	148,493	123,640	110,578
1987	1,403,655	720,038	276,663	406,954	1987	396,743	153,704	128,106	114,933
1988	1,453,267	725,903	285,833	441,531	1988	416,955	156,598	134,703	125,654
1989	1,502,349	732,826	297,139	472,384	1989	432,748	159,143	141,011	132,594
1990	1,570,614	747,809	307,476	515,329	1990	462,130	164,717	146,691	150,722
1991	1,610,465	755,240	315,354	539,871	1991	480,003	168,979	151,864	159,160
1992	1,635,502	769,977	322,843	542,682	1992	492,993	178,534	156,593	157,866
1993	1,664,167	778,773	324,544	560,850	1993	495,557	182,765	155,471	157,321
1994	1,740,715	806,336	339,859	594,520	1994	524,908	192,481	162,446	169,981
1995	1,816,632	839,999	348,909	627,724	1995	543,272	199,492	163,939	179,841
1997	1,901,453	856,583	366,436	678,434	1997	556,669	203,022	170,757	182,890
1998	1,948,100	876,137	379,046	692,917	1998	575,661	207,470	178,124	190,067
1999	1,998,308	913,826	398,883	685,599	1999	606,645	223,281	190,418	192,946

See notes at end of table.

Table 1.21

Justice system employment

By type of activity and level of government, United States, October 1980-95 and March 1997-99[a]--Continued

Level of government and one-month payroll period	Total justice system	Police protection	Judicial and legal	Corrections
Municipalities[b]				
1980	NA	450,647	NA	19,601
1981	NA	448,699	NA	20,638
1982	515,087	453,381	40,993	20,713
1983	520,390	453,892	44,022	22,476
1984	527,855	458,845	43,805	25,205
1985	535,773	464,588	45,687	25,498
1986	543,692	471,531	45,968	26,193
1987	555,279	478,763	48,449	28,067
1988	557,427	479,005	48,229	30,193
1989	564,458	483,035	48,508	32,915
1990	579,807	493,790	50,692	35,325
1991	587,812	499,250	51,667	36,895
1992	594,370	504,837	52,702	36,831
1993	597,676	509,395	51,809	36,472
1994	616,355	526,585	54,325	35,445
1995	638,668	549,255	54,801	34,612
1997	653,977	559,616	57,005	37,356
1998	666,927	574,039	57,272	35,616
1999	686,761	590,859	60,002	35,900

Note: See Notes, tables 1.1 and 1.18. Some data have been revised by the Source and may differ from previous editions of SOURCEBOOK. For survey methodology and definitions of terms, see Appendix 1.

[a] Detail may not add to total because of rounding.
[b] Data for local governments are estimates subject to sampling variation.

Source: U.S. Department of Justice, Bureau of Justice Statistics, *Trends in Justice Expenditure and Employment*, NCJ 178274, Table 7 [Online]. Available: http://www.ojp.usdoj.gov/bjs/data/eetrnd07.wk1 [Mar. 27, 2002].

Table 1.22

State and local justice system full-time equivalent employment

By type of activity and level of government, March 2001

State and level of government[a]	Total full-time equivalent employment[b]	Total justice system Number[c]	Percent of total full-time equivalent employment[c]	Police protection Number	Percent of total justice full-time equivalent employment	Judicial and legal Number	Percent of total justice full-time equivalent employment	Corrections Number	Percent of total justice full-time equivalent employment
States-local, total	15,372,855	1,987,724	12.9%	884,667	44.5%	402,323	20.2%	700,734	35.3%
State	4,173,400	730,340	17.5	103,141	14.1	158,794	21.7	468,405	64.1
Local, total	11,199,455	1,257,384	11.2	781,526	62.2	243,529	19.4	232,329	18.5
Counties	2,438,787	613,977	25.2	224,120	36.5	192,051	31.3	197,806	32.2
Municipalities	2,901,580	643,407	22.2	557,406	86.6	51,478	8.0	34,523	5.4
Alabama	268,438	25,599	9.5	12,861	50.2	5,378	21.0	7,360	28.8
State	84,308	9,378	11.1	1,333	14.2	3,461	36.9	4,584	48.9
Local, total	184,130	16,221	8.8	11,528	71.1	1,917	11.8	2,776	17.1
Counties	19,654	6,179	31.4	2,447	39.6	1,270	20.6	2,462	39.8
Municipalities	38,982	10,042	25.8	9,081	90.4	647	6.4	314	3.1
Alaska	49,183	4,809	9.8	1,640	34.1	1,386	28.8	1,783	37.1
State	23,937	3,359	14.0	451	13.4	1,234	36.7	1,674	49.8
Local, total	25,246	1,450	5.7	1,189	82.0	152	10.5	109	7.5
Boroughs	9,872	96	1.0	60	62.5	26	27.1	10	10.4
Municipalities	15,259	1,354	8.9	1,129	83.4	126	9.3	99	7.3
Arizona	251,737	40,125	15.9	16,606	41.4	9,873	24.6	13,646	34.0
State	65,185	12,865	19.7	1,874	14.6	1,417	11.0	9,574	74.4
Local, total	186,552	27,260	14.6	14,732	54.0	8,456	31.0	4,072	14.9
Counties	31,803	14,922	46.9	4,136	27.7	6,723	45.1	4,063	27.2
Municipalities	40,113	12,338	30.8	10,596	85.9	1,733	14.0	9	0.1
Arkansas	150,958	16,501	10.9	7,900	47.9	2,755	16.7	5,846	35.4
State	51,230	6,671	13.0	1,178	17.7	1,263	18.9	4,230	63.4
Local, total	99,728	9,830	9.9	6,722	68.4	1,492	15.2	1,616	16.4
Counties	12,553	4,194	33.4	1,754	41.8	866	20.6	1,574	37.5
Municipalities	20,227	5,636	27.9	4,968	88.1	626	11.1	42	0.7
California	1,735,139	233,652	13.5	100,079	42.8	53,238	22.8	80,335	34.4
State	372,678	65,649	17.6	12,958	19.7	3,795	5.8	48,896	74.5
Local, total	1,362,461	168,003	12.3	87,121	51.9	49,443	29.4	31,439	18.7
Counties	344,437	106,546	30.9	31,061	29.2	45,484	42.7	30,001	28.2
Municipalities	236,880	61,457	25.9	56,060	91.2	3,959	6.4	1,438	2.3
Colorado	234,033	27,690	11.8	12,401	44.8	5,591	20.2	9,698	35.0
State	67,328	11,216	16.7	1,176	10.5	3,546	31.6	6,494	57.9
Local, total	166,705	16,474	9.9	11,225	68.1	2,045	12.4	3,204	19.4
Counties	23,553	6,566	27.9	3,336	50.8	908	13.8	2,322	35.4
Municipalities	40,904	9,908	24.2	7,889	79.6	1,137	11.5	882	8.9
Connecticut	181,974	23,896	13.1	10,703	44.8	4,491	18.8	8,702	36.4
State	66,200	14,799	22.4	1,812	12.2	4,285	29.0	8,702	58.8
Local, total	115,774	9,097	7.9	8,891	97.7	206	2.3	0	X
Municipalities	107,720	9,097	8.4	8,891	97.7	206	2.3	0	X
Delaware	45,758	6,444	14.1	2,431	37.7	1,559	24.2	2,454	38.1
State	24,324	4,811	19.8	897	18.6	1,460	30.3	2,454	51.0
Local, total	21,434	1,633	7.6	1,534	93.9	99	6.1	0	X
Counties	2,371	625	26.4	554	88.6	71	11.4	0	X
Municipalities	2,767	1,008	36.4	980	97.2	28	2.8	0	X
District of Columbia	44,518	6,810	15.3	4,349	63.9	435	6.4	2,026	29.8
Local, total	44,518	6,810	15.3	4,349	63.9	435	6.4	2,026	29.8
Municipality	35,838	6,810	19.0	4,349	63.9	435	6.4	2,026	29.8
Florida	803,100	133,104	16.6	57,580	43.3	31,983	24.0	43,541	32.7
State	187,552	50,227	26.8	4,230	8.4	17,973	35.8	28,024	55.8
Local, total	615,548	82,877	13.5	53,350	64.4	14,010	16.9	15,517	18.7
Counties	145,898	56,598	38.8	28,537	50.4	13,177	23.3	14,884	26.3
Municipalities	100,746	26,279	26.1	24,813	94.4	833	3.2	633	2.4

See notes at end of table.

Table 1.22

State and local justice system full-time equivalent employment

By type of activity and level of government, March 2001--Continued

State and level of government[a]	Total full-time equivalent employment[b]	Total justice system Number[c]	Percent of total full-time equivalent employment[c]	Police protection Number	Percent of total justice full-time equivalent employment	Judicial and legal Number	Percent of total justice full-time equivalent employment	Corrections Number	Percent of total justice full-time equivalent employment
Georgia	459,215	62,294	13.6%	25,420	40.8%	9,963	16.0%	26,911	43.2%
State	121,180	23,781	19.6	2,302	9.7	1,467	6.2	20,012	84.2
Local, total	338,035	38,513	11.4	23,118	60.0	8,496	22.1	6,899	17.9
Counties	58,182	24,147	41.5	11,005	45.6	7,317	30.3	5,825	24.1
Municipalities	42,806	14,366	33.6	12,113	84.3	1,179	8.2	1,074	7.5
Hawaii	69,230	8,861	12.8	3,631	41.0	2,767	31.2	2,463	27.8
State	54,890	4,681	8.5	0	X	2,218	47.4	2,463	52.6
Local, total	14,340	4,180	29.1	3,631	86.9	549	13.1	0	X
Counties	5,085	1,348	26.5	1,114	82.6	234	17.4	0	X
Municipalities	9,139	2,832	31.0	2,517	88.9	315	11.1	0	X
Idaho	76,080	8,298	10.9	3,834	46.2	1,648	19.9	2,816	33.9
State	23,215	2,622	11.3	488	18.6	463	17.7	1,671	63.7
Local, total	52,865	5,676	10.7	3,346	58.9	1,185	20.9	1,145	20.2
Counties	10,571	3,983	37.7	1,743	43.8	1,095	27.5	1,145	28.7
Municipalities	7,020	1,693	24.1	1,603	94.7	90	5.3	0	X
Illinois	616,123	87,202	14.2	44,230	50.7	17,535	20.1	25,437	29.2
State	129,842	23,265	17.9	4,292	18.4	3,198	13.7	15,775	67.8
Local, total	486,281	63,937	13.1	39,938	62.5	14,337	22.4	9,662	15.1
Counties	62,898	28,863	45.9	5,607	19.4	13,629	47.2	9,627	33.4
Municipalities	106,108	35,074	33.1	34,331	97.9	708	2.0	35	0.1
Indiana	324,386	36,542	11.3	16,687	45.7	6,423	17.6	13,432	36.8
State	86,609	11,654	13.5	2,052	17.6	1,312	11.3	8,290	71.1
Local, total	237,777	24,888	10.5	14,635	58.8	5,111	20.5	5,142	20.7
Counties	48,581	12,429	25.6	3,841	30.9	3,887	31.3	4,701	37.8
Municipalities	46,550	12,459	26.8	10,794	86.6	1,224	9.8	441	3.5
Iowa	176,075	15,073	8.6	7,224	47.9	3,290	21.8	4,559	30.2
State	54,718	6,958	12.7	1,038	14.9	2,471	35.5	3,449	49.6
Local, total	121,357	8,115	6.7	6,186	76.2	819	10.1	1,110	13.7
Counties	23,833	4,004	16.8	2,170	54.2	740	18.5	1,094	27.3
Municipalities	22,025	4,111	18.7	4,016	97.7	79	1.9	16	0.4
Kansas	170,770	18,229	10.7	8,820	48.4	3,567	19.6	5,842	32.0
State	44,053	6,794	15.4	1,060	15.6	2,094	30.8	3,640	53.6
Local, total	126,717	11,435	9.0	7,760	67.9	1,473	12.9	2,202	19.3
Counties	22,780	5,428	23.8	2,500	46.1	938	17.3	1,990	36.7
Municipalities	23,734	6,007	25.3	5,260	87.6	535	8.9	212	3.5
Kentucky	227,566	23,118	10.2	10,233	44.3	6,054	26.2	6,831	29.5
State	76,906	10,765	14.0	2,221	20.6	4,747	44.1	3,797	35.3
Local, total	150,660	12,353	8.2	8,012	64.9	1,307	10.6	3,034	24.6
Counties	22,402	7,213	32.2	3,339	46.3	1,183	16.4	2,691	37.3
Municipalities	21,727	5,140	23.7	4,673	90.9	124	2.4	343	6.7
Louisiana	280,141	38,222	13.6	16,253	42.5	8,027	21.0	13,942	36.5
State	93,919	11,046	11.8	1,463	13.2	1,729	15.7	7,854	71.1
Local, total	186,222	27,176	14.6	14,790	54.4	6,298	23.2	6,088	22.4
Parishes	45,100	14,532	32.2	6,548	45.1	4,144	28.5	3,840	26.4
Municipalities	35,389	12,644	35.7	8,242	65.2	2,154	17.0	2,248	17.8
Maine	74,495	6,174	8.3	3,377	54.7	943	15.3	1,854	30.0
State	21,544	2,420	11.2	516	21.3	672	27.8	1,232	50.9
Local, total	52,951	3,754	7.1	2,861	76.2	271	7.2	622	16.6
Counties	1,917	1,445	75.4	581	40.2	253	17.5	611	42.3
Municipalities	31,479	2,309	7.3	2,280	98.7	18	0.8	11	0.5
Maryland	279,006	38,635	13.8	16,892	43.7	7,119	18.4	14,624	37.9
State	91,288	18,396	20.2	2,406	13.1	4,175	22.7	11,815	64.2
Local, total	187,718	20,239	10.8	14,486	71.6	2,944	14.5	2,809	13.9
Counties	149,545	13,530	9.0	8,597	63.5	2,124	15.7	2,809	20.8
Municipalities	35,977	6,709	18.6	5,889	87.8	820	12.2	0	X

See notes at end of table.

Table 1.22

State and local justice system full-time equivalent employment

By type of activity and level of government, March 2001--Continued

State and level of government[a]	Total full-time equivalent employment[b]	Total justice system Number[c]	Percent of total full-time equivalent employment[c]	Police protection Number	Percent of total justice full-time equivalent employment	Judicial and legal Number	Percent of total justice full-time equivalent employment	Corrections Number	Percent of total justice full-time equivalent employment
Massachusetts	332,556	44,858	13.5%	24,466	54.5%	10,492	23.4%	9,900	22.1%
State	95,259	23,066	24.2	5,701	24.7	10,212	44.3	7,153	31.0
Local, total	237,297	21,792	9.2	18,765	86.1	280	1.3	2,747	12.6
Counties	2,507	1,634	65.2	46	2.8	0	X	1,588	97.2
Municipalities	200,437	20,158	10.1	18,719	92.9	280	1.4	1,159	5.7
Michigan	499,481	62,681	12.5	26,140	41.7	12,099	19.3	24,442	39.0
State	141,375	24,260	17.2	3,277	13.5	2,022	8.3	18,961	78.2
Local, total	358,106	38,421	10.7	22,863	59.5	10,077	26.2	5,481	14.3
Counties	53,540	18,805	35.1	5,384	28.6	8,071	42.9	5,350	28.4
Municipalities	92,214	19,616	21.3	17,479	89.1	2,006	10.2	131	0.7
Minnesota	280,481	24,941	8.9	11,164	44.8	5,721	22.9	8,056	32.3
State	75,588	7,073	9.4	942	13.3	2,382	33.7	3,749	53.0
Local, total	204,893	17,868	8.7	10,222	57.2	3,339	18.7	4,307	24.1
Counties	42,495	11,020	25.9	3,629	32.9	3,084	28.0	4,307	39.1
Municipalities	35,669	6,848	19.2	6,593	96.3	255	3.7	0	X
Mississippi	192,946	17,921	9.3	8,771	48.9	2,741	15.3	6,409	35.8
State	56,781	6,250	11.0	1,286	20.6	656	10.5	4,308	68.9
Local, total	136,165	11,671	8.6	7,485	64.1	2,085	17.9	2,101	18.0
Counties	30,063	6,238	20.7	2,467	39.5	1,725	27.7	2,046	32.8
Municipalities	22,849	5,433	23.8	5,018	92.4	360	6.6	55	1.0
Missouri	305,550	38,653	12.7	17,371	44.9	7,546	19.5	13,736	35.5
State	92,563	17,898	19.3	2,390	13.4	3,907	21.8	11,601	64.8
Local, total	212,987	20,755	9.7	14,981	72.2	3,639	17.5	2,135	10.3
Counties	20,419	7,802	38.2	3,942	50.5	2,182	28.0	1,678	21.5
Municipalities	43,982	12,953	29.5	11,039	85.2	1,457	11.2	457	3.5
Montana	53,304	4,943	9.3	2,265	45.8	1,014	20.5	1,664	33.7
State	19,389	1,711	8.8	404	23.6	201	11.7	1,106	64.6
Local, total	33,915	3,232	9.5	1,861	57.6	813	25.2	558	17.3
Counties	6,373	2,128	33.4	919	43.2	673	31.6	536	25.2
Municipalities	4,233	1,104	26.1	942	85.3	140	12.7	22	2.0
Nebraska	112,068	9,433	8.4	4,595	48.7	1,778	18.8	3,060	32.4
State	32,707	3,373	10.3	687	20.4	675	20.0	2,011	59.6
Local, total	79,361	6,060	7.6	3,908	64.5	1,103	18.2	1,049	17.3
Counties	12,650	3,390	26.8	1,324	39.1	1,017	30.0	1,049	30.9
Municipalities	12,466	2,670	21.4	2,584	96.8	86	3.2	0	X
Nevada	87,072	15,146	17.4	6,632	43.8	3,199	21.1	5,315	35.1
State	23,156	4,540	19.6	745	16.4	628	13.8	3,167	69.8
Local, total	63,916	10,606	16.6	5,887	55.5	2,571	24.2	2,148	20.3
Counties	21,342	7,984	37.4	4,244	53.2	2,056	25.8	1,684	21.1
Municipalities	9,810	2,622	26.7	1,643	62.7	515	19.6	464	17.7
New Hampshire	65,366	6,857	10.5	3,869	56.4	1,171	17.1	1,817	26.5
State	18,920	2,662	14.1	432	16.2	914	34.3	1,316	49.4
Local, total	46,446	4,195	9.0	3,437	81.9	257	6.1	501	11.9
Counties	3,507	956	27.3	239	25.0	216	22.6	501	52.4
Municipalities	18,858	3,239	17.2	3,198	98.7	41	1.3	0	X
New Jersey	459,064	72,771	15.9	34,971	48.1	21,513	29.6	16,287	22.4
State	136,892	27,804	20.3	3,910	14.1	14,060	50.6	9,834	35.4
Local, total	322,172	44,967	14.0	31,061	69.1	7,453	16.6	6,453	14.4
Counties	59,765	13,273	22.2	2,531	19.1	4,341	32.7	6,401	48.2
Municipalities	99,620	31,694	31.8	28,530	90.0	3,112	9.8	52	0.2
New Mexico	120,516	14,221	11.8	5,642	39.7	3,143	22.1	5,436	38.2
State	47,839	7,229	15.1	633	8.8	2,746	38.0	3,850	53.3
Local, total	72,677	6,992	9.6	5,009	71.6	397	5.7	1,586	22.7
Counties	7,702	2,539	33.0	1,384	54.5	90	3.5	1,065	41.9
Municipalities	17,559	4,453	25.4	3,625	81.4	307	6.9	521	11.7

See notes at end of table.

Table 1.22

State and local justice system full-time equivalent employment

By type of activity and level of government, March 2001--Continued

State and level of government[a]	Total full-time equivalent employment[b]	Total justice system Number[c]	Percent of total full-time equivalent employment[c]	Police protection Number	Percent of total justice full-time equivalent employment	Judicial and legal Number	Percent of total justice full-time equivalent employment	Corrections Number	Percent of total justice full-time equivalent employment
New York	1,178,185	179,321	15.2%	86,454	48.2%	30,438	17.0%	62,429	34.8%
State	252,099	61,484	24.4	5,976	9.7	18,989	30.9	36,519	59.4
Local, total	926,086	117,837	12.7	80,478	68.3	11,449	9.7	25,910	22.0
Counties	115,470	28,251	24.5	12,761	45.2	3,934	13.9	11,556	40.9
Municipalities	518,371	89,586	17.3	67,717	75.6	7,515	8.4	14,354	16.0
North Carolina	463,088	54,206	11.7	23,397	43.2	6,506	12.0	24,303	44.8
State	129,691	29,558	22.8	3,346	11.3	5,804	19.6	20,408	69.0
Local, total	333,397	24,648	7.4	20,051	81.3	702	2.8	3,895	15.8
Counties	273,701	11,543	4.2	7,005	60.7	643	5.6	3,895	33.7
Municipalities	49,209	13,105	26.6	13,046	99.5	59	0.5	0	X
North Dakota	38,200	3,084	8.1	1,500	48.6	766	24.8	818	26.5
State	15,898	1,198	7.5	225	18.8	398	33.2	575	48.0
Local, total	22,302	1,886	8.5	1,275	67.6	368	19.5	243	12.9
Counties	3,835	1,043	27.2	471	45.2	331	31.7	241	23.1
Municipalities	3,396	843	24.8	804	95.4	37	4.4	2	0.2
Ohio	607,466	81,753	13.5	34,102	41.7	20,324	24.9	27,327	33.4
State	139,368	24,150	17.3	2,701	11.2	2,827	11.7	18,622	77.1
Local, total	468,098	57,603	12.3	31,401	54.5	17,497	30.4	8,705	15.1
Counties	101,297	28,648	28.3	7,416	25.9	13,020	45.4	8,212	28.7
Municipalities	94,826	28,955	30.5	23,985	82.8	4,477	15.5	493	1.7
Oklahoma	199,806	22,086	11.1	11,037	50.0	4,091	18.5	6,958	31.5
State	64,704	10,355	16.0	1,819	17.6	2,590	25.0	5,946	57.4
Local, total	135,102	11,731	8.7	9,218	78.6	1,501	12.8	1,012	8.6
Counties	17,942	4,117	22.9	2,217	53.8	952	23.1	948	23.0
Municipalities	31,068	7,614	24.5	7,001	91.9	549	7.2	64	0.8
Oregon	179,195	22,279	12.4	8,704	39.1	5,011	22.5	8,564	38.4
State	54,173	9,500	17.5	1,432	15.1	3,212	33.8	4,856	51.1
Local, total	125,022	12,779	10.2	7,272	56.9	1,799	14.1	3,708	29.0
Counties	21,558	7,756	36.0	2,542	32.8	1,506	19.4	3,708	47.8
Municipalities	19,773	5,023	25.4	4,730	94.2	293	5.8	0	X
Pennsylvania	540,326	77,998	14.4	31,938	40.9	17,917	23.0	28,143	36.1
State	153,818	24,372	15.8	5,709	23.4	2,846	11.7	15,817	64.9
Local, total	386,508	53,626	13.9	26,229	48.9	15,071	28.1	12,326	23.0
Counties	61,743	23,969	38.8	2,500	10.4	11,351	47.4	10,118	42.2
Municipalities	75,765	29,657	39.1	23,729	80.0	3,720	12.5	2,208	7.4
Rhode Island	57,016	6,598	11.6	3,489	52.9	1,257	19.1	1,852	28.1
State	20,145	3,302	16.4	305	9.2	1,145	34.7	1,852	56.1
Local, total	36,871	3,296	8.9	3,184	96.6	112	3.4	0	X
Municipalities	34,074	3,296	9.7	3,184	96.6	112	3.4	0	X
South Carolina	237,382	28,514	12.0	13,737	48.2	3,523	12.4	11,254	39.5
State	81,219	13,157	16.2	3,351	25.5	700	5.3	9,106	69.2
Local, total	156,163	15,357	9.8	10,386	67.6	2,823	18.4	2,148	14.0
Counties	26,630	9,348	35.1	4,822	51.6	2,434	26.0	2,092	22.4
Municipalities	18,947	6,009	31.7	5,564	92.6	389	6.5	56	0.9
South Dakota	40,744	3,795	9.3	1,703	44.9	762	20.1	1,330	35.0
State	13,269	1,669	12.6	281	16.8	519	31.1	869	52.1
Local, total	27,475	2,126	7.7	1,422	66.9	243	11.4	461	21.7
Counties	3,648	1,236	33.9	565	45.7	223	18.0	448	36.2
Municipalities	5,380	890	16.5	857	96.3	20	2.2	13	1.5
Tennessee	303,725	35,554	11.7	18,711	52.6	5,597	15.7	11,246	31.6
State	82,681	10,513	12.7	1,921	18.3	1,991	18.9	6,601	62.8
Local, total	221,044	25,041	11.3	16,790	67.1	3,606	14.4	4,645	18.5
Counties	124,897	11,519	9.2	4,984	43.3	2,533	22.0	4,002	34.7
Municipalities	89,025	13,522	15.2	11,806	87.3	1,073	7.9	643	4.8

See notes at end of table.

Table 1.22

State and local justice system full-time equivalent employment

By type of activity and level of government, March 2001--Continued

State and level of government[a]	Total full-time equivalent employment[b]	Total justice system Number[c]	Percent of total full-time equivalent employment[c]	Police protection Number	Percent of total justice full-time equivalent employment	Judicial and legal Number	Percent of total justice full-time equivalent employment	Corrections Number	Percent of total justice full-time equivalent employment
Texas	1,209,402	153,628	12.7%	59,604	38.8%	24,191	15.7%	69,833	45.5%
State	268,637	55,617	20.7	3,655	6.6	5,178	9.3	46,784	84.1
Local, total	940,765	98,011	10.4	55,949	57.1	19,013	19.4	23,049	23.5
Counties	119,483	51,991	43.5	14,064	27.1	14,921	28.7	23,006	44.2
Municipalities	168,364	46,020	27.3	41,885	91.0	4,092	8.9	43	0.1
Utah	125,971	12,871	10.2	5,541	43.1	2,704	21.0	4,626	35.9
State	52,070	5,479	10.5	763	13.9	1,606	29.3	3,110	56.8
Local, total	73,901	7,392	10.0	4,778	64.6	1,098	14.9	1,516	20.5
Counties	10,252	3,898	38.0	1,726	44.3	656	16.8	1,516	38.9
Municipalities	13,507	3,494	25.9	3,052	87.3	442	12.7	0	X
Vermont	36,969	2,913	7.9	1,259	43.2	656	22.5	998	34.3
State	13,666	2,093	15.3	489	23.4	606	29.0	998	47.7
Local, total	23,303	820	3.5	770	93.9	50	6.1	0	X
Counties	94	72	76.6	29	40.3	43	59.7	0	X
Municipalities	4,730	748	15.8	741	99.1	7	0.9	0	X
Virginia	397,418	49,197	12.4	19,202	39.0	7,413	15.1	22,582	45.9
State	123,521	21,697	17.6	2,678	12.3	3,457	15.9	15,562	71.7
Local, total	273,897	27,500	10.0	16,524	60.1	3,956	14.4	7,020	25.5
Counties	157,782	13,801	8.7	8,021	58.1	2,535	18.4	3,245	23.5
Municipalities	104,582	13,699	13.1	8,503	62.1	1,421	10.4	3,775	27.6
Washington	306,774	34,145	11.1	14,162	41.5	8,076	23.7	11,907	34.9
State	111,132	11,676	10.5	2,160	18.5	1,776	15.2	7,740	66.3
Local, total	195,642	22,469	11.5	12,002	53.4	6,300	28.0	4,167	18.5
Counties	38,074	13,233	34.8	4,126	31.2	5,128	38.8	3,979	30.1
Municipalities	37,407	9,236	24.7	7,876	85.3	1,172	12.7	188	2.0
West Virginia	96,531	7,517	7.8	3,720	49.5	2,167	28.8	1,630	21.7
State	35,348	3,652	10.3	1,038	28.4	1,287	35.2	1,327	36.3
Local, total	61,183	3,865	6.3	2,682	69.4	880	22.8	303	7.8
Counties	7,568	2,120	28.0	1,008	47.5	809	38.2	303	14.3
Municipalities	9,495	1,745	18.4	1,674	95.9	71	4.1	0	X
Wisconsin	288,027	34,931	12.1	15,731	45.0	5,752	16.5	13,448	38.5
State	69,428	12,145	17.5	949	7.8	2,068	17.0	9,128	75.2
Local, total	218,599	22,786	10.4	14,782	64.9	3,684	16.2	4,320	19.0
Counties	47,849	11,852	24.8	4,269	36.0	3,263	27.5	4,320	36.4
Municipalities	41,071	10,934	26.6	10,513	96.1	421	3.9	0	X
Wyoming	40,301	3,631	9.0	1,639	45.1	730	20.1	1,262	34.8
State	11,158	1,500	13.4	189	12.6	412	27.5	899	59.9
Local, total	29,143	2,131	7.3	1,450	68.0	318	14.9	363	17.0
Counties	5,566	1,163	20.9	555	47.7	245	21.1	363	31.2
Municipalities	3,503	968	27.6	895	92.5	73	7.5	0	X

Note: See Notes, tables 1.1 and 1.18. For survey methodology and definitions of terms, see Appendix 1.

[a]Data for local governments are estimates subject to sampling variation.
[b]Includes employment of States and all types of local governments including independent school districts and special districts, which are not displayed separately. The "local, total" categories, which include these districts, will not equal the sum of the "counties" and "municipalities" categories.

[c]Justice system employment of independent school districts and special districts (primarily for special police forces) are not available.

Source: U.S. Department of Justice, Bureau of Justice Statistics, *2001 Justice Expenditure and Employment Extracts*, NCJ 202792, Table 5 [Online]. Available: http://www.ojp.usdoj.gov/bjs/pub/sheets/cjee01.zip, file cjee0105.wk1 [Aug. 6, 2004]. Table adapted by SOURCEBOOK staff.

Table 1.23

Rate (per 10,000 population) of State and local justice system full-time equivalent employment

By type of activity and State, March 2000[a]

State[b]	Total justice system	Police protection Total	Police protection Sworn only	Judicial and legal	Corrections
Total	69.0	30.8	23.2	13.8	24.3
Alabama	56.9	29.5	22.9	11.4	16.0
Alaska	74.8	26.0	18.0	21.6	27.3
Arizona	76.7	31.5	23.9	18.8	26.4
Arkansas	56.8	29.4	22.2	7.3	20.0
California	66.9	28.6	19.1	15.3	23.0
Colorado	62.5	28.0	20.4	12.6	21.9
Connecticut	70.4	31.3	24.3	12.7	26.4
Delaware	81.0	30.3	21.5	19.8	30.9
District of Columbia	126.5	77.9	62.7	7.2	41.3
Florida	79.8	34.5	22.9	18.6	26.7
Georgia	73.5	29.6	23.6	11.4	32.5
Hawaii	71.8	29.8	23.0	22.2	19.8
Idaho	56.9	25.9	18.5	10.8	20.3
Illinois	69.8	35.5	27.6	14.1	20.3
Indiana	54.6	26.0	18.8	10.1	18.5
Iowa	51.0	24.8	18.4	11.1	15.1
Kansas	70.3	33.4	25.0	14.1	22.8
Kentucky	55.3	24.2	17.7	14.6	16.5
Louisiana	81.9	35.9	26.8	16.0	30.0
Maine	44.9	24.4	19.5	6.7	13.9
Maryland	71.5	31.4	23.8	13.0	27.1
Massachusetts	70.5	37.6	30.7	16.5	16.3
Michigan	61.9	26.0	20.2	12.0	23.9
Minnesota	49.3	21.6	15.9	11.7	16.0
Mississippi	62.5	30.3	21.7	10.2	22.0
Missouri	68.5	30.5	21.6	13.3	24.7
Montana	53.7	24.6	16.6	11.2	17.9
Nebraska	54.4	26.3	19.2	10.6	17.5
Nevada	73.6	33.8	20.1	17.1	22.7
New Hampshire	57.8	34.2	27.6	9.5	14.1
New Jersey	83.1	39.7	29.3	24.5	18.9
New Mexico	77.5	29.8	21.6	17.5	30.2
New York	93.5	45.5	39.2	15.7	32.3
North Carolina	65.4	28.6	22.6	8.3	28.4
North Dakota	47.0	22.4	17.3	12.1	12.5
Ohio	70.5	29.5	22.6	17.8	23.2
Oklahoma	64.4	32.0	23.8	11.7	20.7
Oregon	63.0	25.2	18.0	13.9	23.8
Pennsylvania	61.0	25.6	21.0	14.0	21.4
Rhode Island	61.3	32.0	23.2	11.9	17.4
South Carolina	70.9	33.9	25.1	8.7	28.3
South Dakota	50.5	22.5	16.8	10.1	17.9
Tennessee	60.4	31.7	24.3	9.8	18.9
Texas	72.3	28.2	20.9	10.9	33.1
Utah	55.2	24.2	16.7	11.8	19.2
Vermont	48.2	21.4	15.3	10.6	16.2
Virginia	67.9	26.5	20.4	10.1	31.3
Washington	58.1	24.0	16.8	13.1	21.0
West Virginia	41.6	20.8	16.4	11.9	8.8
Wisconsin	63.4	29.1	21.9	10.4	24.0
Wyoming	70.8	34.3	23.1	14.1	22.4

Note: See Notes, tables 1.1 and 1.18. For survey methodology and definitions of terms, see Appendix 1.

[a]Detail may not add to total because of rounding.
[b]Local government portion of these data are estimates subject to sampling variation.

Source: U.S. Department of Justice, Bureau of Justice Statistics, *2000 Justice Expenditure and Employment Extracts*, NCJ 194802, Table 8 [Online]. Available: http://www.ojp.usdoj.gov/bjs/pub/sheets/cjee00.zip, file cjee0008.wk1 [Aug. 6, 2004].

Table 1.24

Rate (per 10,000 population) of State and local justice system full-time equivalent employment

By type of activity and State, March 2001[a]

State[b]	Total justice system	Police protection Total	Police protection Sworn only	Judicial and legal	Corrections
Total	69.7	31.0	23.2	14.1	24.6
Alabama	57.3	28.8	22.0	12.0	16.5
Alaska	75.9	25.9	16.0	21.9	28.1
Arizona	75.6	31.3	23.6	18.6	25.7
Arkansas	61.2	29.3	22.0	10.2	21.7
California	67.5	28.9	19.4	15.4	23.2
Colorado	62.5	28.0	20.2	12.6	21.9
Connecticut	69.6	31.2	24.1	13.1	25.3
Delaware	80.9	30.5	21.3	19.6	30.8
District of Columbia	118.6	75.8	61.6	7.6	35.3
Florida	81.3	35.2	22.5	19.5	26.6
Georgia	74.1	30.2	23.7	11.9	32.0
Hawaii	72.2	29.6	22.9	22.6	20.1
Idaho	62.8	29.0	20.9	12.5	21.3
Illinois	69.7	35.3	27.6	14.0	20.3
Indiana	59.6	27.2	19.7	10.5	21.9
Iowa	51.4	24.6	17.8	11.2	15.5
Kansas	67.5	32.6	23.9	13.2	21.6
Kentucky	56.8	25.1	18.5	14.9	16.8
Louisiana	85.5	36.4	27.6	18.0	31.2
Maine	48.1	26.3	19.4	7.3	14.4
Maryland	71.7	31.4	23.6	13.2	27.2
Massachusetts	70.1	38.2	31.6	16.4	15.5
Michigan	62.6	26.1	20.3	12.1	24.4
Minnesota	50.0	22.4	16.0	11.5	16.2
Mississippi	62.7	30.7	21.5	9.6	22.4
Missouri	68.6	30.8	22.0	13.4	24.4
Montana	54.6	25.0	16.9	11.2	18.4
Nebraska	54.8	26.7	19.9	10.3	17.8
Nevada	72.2	31.6	19.2	15.2	25.3
New Hampshire	54.5	30.7	24.6	9.3	14.4
New Jersey	85.5	41.1	30.1	25.3	19.1
New Mexico	77.7	30.8	22.1	17.2	29.7
New York	94.0	45.3	38.9	15.9	32.7
North Carolina	66.1	28.5	22.5	7.9	29.6
North Dakota	48.4	23.5	18.3	12.0	12.8
Ohio	71.8	29.9	22.9	17.8	24.0
Oklahoma	63.6	31.8	23.1	11.8	20.1
Oregon	64.1	25.1	17.9	14.4	24.7
Pennsylvania	63.4	26.0	21.5	14.6	22.9
Rhode Island	62.2	32.9	23.7	11.9	17.5
South Carolina	70.2	33.8	25.0	8.7	27.7
South Dakota	50.1	22.5	16.6	10.1	17.5
Tennessee	61.8	32.5	24.4	9.7	19.6
Texas	71.9	27.9	20.7	11.3	32.7
Utah	56.5	24.3	17.0	11.9	20.3
Vermont	47.5	20.5	14.6	10.7	16.3
Virginia	68.4	26.7	20.4	10.3	31.4
Washington	57.0	23.6	16.7	13.5	19.9
West Virginia	41.7	20.7	16.3	12.0	9.1
Wisconsin	64.6	29.1	21.9	10.6	24.9
Wyoming	73.5	33.2	23.2	14.8	25.5

Note: See Notes, tables 1.1 and 1.18. For survey methodology and definitions of terms, see Appendix 1.

[a]Detail may not add to total because of rounding.
[b]Local government portion of these data are estimates subject to sampling variation.

Source: U.S. Department of Justice, Bureau of Justice Statistics, *2001 Justice Expenditure and Employment Extracts*, NCJ 202792, Table 8 [Online]. Available: http://www.ojp.usdoj.gov/bjs/pub/sheets/cjee01.zip, file cjee0108.wk1 [Aug. 6, 2004].

Table 1.25

State and local sworn police full-time equivalent employment and percent of total police employment

By level of government, United States, October 1980-95 and March 1997-99

One-month payroll period	Total State and local sworn police employees	State	Local[a] Total	Counties	Munici- palities
1980	461,810	50,672	411,138	94,533	316,605
1981	464,141	51,177	412,964	96,326	316,638
1982	470,909	49,865	421,044	97,829	323,215
1983	472,459	50,965	421,494	98,695	322,799
1984	475,124	51,155	423,969	99,045	324,924
1985	481,146	51,761	429,385	100,916	328,469
1986	491,276	52,754	438,522	104,643	333,879
1987	501,440	53,542	447,898	107,811	340,087
1988	509,619	54,978	454,641	111,306	343,335
1989	513,242	56,084	457,158	113,479	343,679
1990	525,075	56,729	468,346	116,836	351,510
1991	531,706	56,294	475,412	119,383	356,029
1992	538,510	55,104	483,406	123,851	359,555
1993	546,047	54,283	491,764	127,234	364,530
1994	560,509	56,981	507,783	138,817	373,221
1995	584,925	54,704	530,221	139,078	391,143
1997	602,718	56,023	546,695	142,330	404,365
1998	616,377	55,224	561,153	145,472	415,681
1999	638,066	58,917	578,909	153,075	425,834

Percent sworn of total police employees

1980	78.1%	67.3%	79.7%	77.4%	80.4%
1981	78.0	67.5	79.5	76.9	80.4
1982	77.8	65.0	79.7	77.3	80.5
1983	78.1	66.3	79.8	77.5	80.5
1984	77.7	65.4	79.5	76.9	80.4
1985	77.6	66.2	79.3	76.3	80.2
1986	76.3	66.1	77.7	75.2	78.5
1987	76.0	64.5	77.7	74.4	78.7
1988	76.0	64.1	77.8	75.0	78.7
1989	75.8	64.5	77.4	75.0	78.3
1990	75.6	64.4	77.3	74.8	78.1
1991	75.7	65.1	77.2	74.4	78.2
1992	75.3	64.1	76.9	73.2	78.3
1993	75.3	63.2	77.0	73.3	78.3
1994	74.9	62.1	76.8	74.1	77.9
1995	75.1	61.1	76.9	73.7	78.2
1997	75.5	60.7	77.4	73.7	78.7
1998	75.4	59.3	77.4	74.0	78.7
1999	75.2	60.2	77.2	72.4	79.1

Note: See Notes, tables 1.1 and 1.18. The formula for computing full-time equivalent employment changed in 1986; see Appendix 1 for more information. Some data have been revised by the Source and may differ from previous editions of SOURCEBOOK. For survey methodology and definitions of terms, see Appendix 1.

[a]Data for local governments are estimates subject to sampling variation.

Source: U.S. Department of Justice, Bureau of Justice Statistics, *Trends in Justice Expenditure and Employment*, NCJ 178276, Table 9 [Online]. Available: http://www.ojp.usdoj.gov/bjs/data/eetrnd09.wk1 [Mar. 27, 2002].

Table 1.26

State and local police protection full-time equivalent employment and payroll

By type of employee and level of government, March 2000[a]

(Payroll amounts in thousands)

		Sworn			Nonsworn		
State and level of government[b]	Total police protection full-time equivalent employment	Number	Percent of total police protection full-time equivalent	March payrolls	Number	Percent of total police protection full-time equivalent	March payrolls
States-local, total	867,368	651,618	75.1%	$2,616,329	215,750	24.9%	$608,610
State	101,265	61,282	60.5	256,512	39,983	39.5	123,119
Local, total	766,103	590,336	77.1	2,359,818	175,767	22.9	485,492
Counties	216,694	154,951	71.5	559,544	61,743	28.5	170,537
Municipalities	549,409	435,385	79.2	1,800,274	114,024	20.8	314,955
Alabama	13,123	10,188	77.6	28,201	2,935	22.4	5,844
State	1,353	745	55.1	2,711	608	44.9	1,456
Local, total	11,770	9,443	80.2	25,491	2,327	19.8	4,388
Counties	2,418	1,986	82.1	5,504	432	17.9	774
Municipalities	9,352	7,457	79.7	19,987	1,895	20.3	3,614
Alaska	1,628	1,127	69.2	5,474	501	30.8	2,051
State	440	310	70.5	1,625	130	29.5	413
Local, total	1,188	817	68.8	3,849	371	31.2	1,638
Boroughs	81	8	9.9	117	73	90.1	283
Municipalities	1,107	809	73.1	3,732	298	26.9	1,356
Arizona	16,141	12,258	75.9	46,999	3,883	24.1	12,027
State	1,902	1,066	56.0	4,139	836	44.0	2,579
Local, total	14,239	11,192	78.6	42,860	3,047	21.4	9,448
Counties	4,067	3,790	93.2	12,510	277	6.8	852
Municipalities	10,172	7,402	72.8	30,350	2,770	27.2	8,595
Arkansas	7,871	5,938	75.4	14,454	1,933	24.6	3,701
State	1,151	590	51.3	1,843	561	48.7	1,321
Local, total	6,720	5,348	79.6	12,611	1,372	20.4	2,380
Counties	1,784	1,365	76.5	2,797	419	23.5	581
Municipalities	4,936	3,983	80.7	9,814	953	19.3	1,799
California	96,858	64,675	66.8	361,959	32,183	33.2	115,438
State	12,843	7,343	57.2	40,999	5,500	42.8	18,316
Local, total	84,015	57,332	68.2	320,959	26,683	31.8	97,122
Counties	29,840	19,594	65.7	101,726	10,246	34.3	39,069
Municipalities	54,175	37,738	69.7	219,233	16,437	30.3	58,053
Colorado	12,042	8,783	72.9	39,471	3,259	27.1	9,760
State	1,144	706	61.7	3,364	438	38.3	1,719
Local, total	10,898	8,077	74.1	36,107	2,821	25.9	8,041
Counties	3,169	2,377	75.0	8,970	792	25.0	1,926
Municipalities	7,729	5,700	73.7	27,137	2,029	26.3	6,114
Connecticut	10,644	8,267	77.7	38,482	2,377	22.3	6,775
State	1,724	1,054	61.1	5,116	670	38.9	2,392
Local, total	8,920	7,213	80.9	33,366	1,707	19.1	4,382
Municipalities	8,920	7,213	80.9	33,366	1,707	19.1	4,382
Delaware	2,378	1,683	70.8	6,875	695	29.2	1,768
State	900	591	65.7	2,747	309	34.3	842
Local, total	1,478	1,092	73.9	4,128	386	26.1	926
Counties	507	324	63.9	1,397	183	36.1	492
Municipalities	971	768	79.1	2,731	203	20.9	433
District of Columbia	4,458	3,585	80.4	17,276	873	19.6	2,776
Local, total	4,458	3,585	80.4	17,276	873	19.6	2,776
Municipality	4,458	3,585	80.4	17,276	873	19.6	2,776
Florida	55,163	36,655	66.4	142,461	18,508	33.6	46,879
State	4,468	2,618	58.6	7,659	1,850	41.4	4,151
Local, total	50,695	34,037	67.1	134,802	16,658	32.9	42,728
Counties	25,570	15,791	61.8	61,414	9,779	38.2	25,729
Municipalities	25,125	18,246	72.6	73,388	6,879	27.4	16,999

See notes at end of table.

Table 1.26

State and local police protection full-time equivalent employment and payroll

By type of employee and level of government, March 2000[a]--Continued

(Payroll amounts in thousands)

State and level of government[b]	Total police protection full-time equivalent employment	Sworn Number	Sworn Percent of total police protection full-time equivalent	Sworn March payrolls	Nonsworn Number	Nonsworn Percent of total police protection full-time equivalent	Nonsworn March payrolls
Georgia	24,261	19,350	79.8%	$53,783	4,911	20.2%	$11,204
State	2,210	1,192	53.9	3,962	1,018	46.1	2,723
Local, total	22,051	18,158	82.3	49,821	3,893	17.7	8,481
Counties	10,009	7,813	78.1	21,978	2,196	21.9	5,185
Municipalities	12,042	10,345	85.9	27,843	1,697	14.1	3,296
Hawaii	3,612	2,788	77.2	11,311	824	22.8	2,323
State	0	X	X	X	X	X	X
Local, total	3,612	2,788	77.2	11,311	824	22.8	2,323
Counties	1,110	822	74.1	3,319	288	25.9	770
Municipalities	2,502	1,966	78.6	7,992	536	21.4	1,553
Idaho	3,346	2,391	71.5	7,519	955	28.5	2,150
State	468	255	54.5	964	213	45.5	609
Local, total	2,878	2,136	74.2	6,556	742	25.8	1,540
Counties	1,325	902	68.1	2,355	423	31.9	799
Municipalities	1,553	1,234	79.5	4,201	319	20.5	741
Illinois	44,094	34,302	77.8	139,520	9,792	22.2	31,114
State	4,074	2,195	53.9	11,236	1,879	46.1	6,705
Local, total	40,020	32,107	80.2	128,283	7,913	19.8	24,410
Counties	5,725	4,082	71.3	14,995	1,643	28.7	3,889
Municipalities	34,295	28,025	81.7	113,289	6,270	18.3	20,521
Indiana	15,779	11,440	72.5	37,165	4,339	27.5	8,965
State	1,971	1,264	64.1	4,257	707	35.9	1,356
Local, total	13,808	10,176	73.7	32,908	3,632	26.3	7,609
Counties	3,824	2,460	64.3	7,059	1,364	35.7	2,707
Municipalities	9,984	7,716	77.3	25,850	2,268	22.7	4,902
Iowa	7,251	5,378	74.2	17,596	1,873	25.8	4,588
State	995	668	67.1	2,613	327	32.9	1,076
Local, total	6,256	4,710	75.3	14,982	1,546	24.7	3,512
Counties	2,195	1,421	64.7	4,580	774	35.3	1,750
Municipalities	4,061	3,289	81.0	10,402	772	19.0	1,762
Kansas	8,984	6,716	74.8	21,516	2,268	25.2	5,299
State	992	615	62.0	2,042	377	38.0	853
Local, total	7,992	6,101	76.3	19,474	1,891	23.7	4,446
Counties	2,760	2,012	72.9	5,933	748	27.1	1,554
Municipalities	5,232	4,089	78.2	13,542	1,143	21.8	2,892
Kentucky	9,784	7,144	73.0	21,263	2,640	27.0	6,357
State	2,070	963	46.5	3,578	1,107	53.5	3,162
Local, total	7,714	6,181	80.1	17,685	1,533	19.9	3,195
Counties	3,088	2,552	82.6	6,753	536	17.4	1,160
Municipalities	4,626	3,629	78.4	10,932	997	21.6	2,036
Louisiana	16,058	11,961	74.5	30,344	4,097	25.5	8,593
State	1,650	979	59.3	3,486	671	40.7	1,520
Local, total	14,408	10,982	76.2	26,857	3,426	23.8	7,073
Parishes	6,496	4,682	72.1	10,982	1,814	27.9	4,007
Municipalities	7,912	6,300	79.6	15,875	1,612	20.4	3,066
Maine	3,109	2,481	79.8	7,658	628	20.2	1,350
State	383	325	84.9	1,209	58	15.1	126
Local, total	2,726	2,156	79.1	6,448	570	20.9	1,224
Counties	539	414	76.8	1,072	125	23.2	266
Municipalities	2,187	1,742	79.7	5,376	445	20.3	957
Maryland	16,628	12,580	75.7	52,139	4,048	24.3	13,302
State	2,411	1,616	67.0	8,053	795	33.0	2,245
Local, total	14,217	10,964	77.1	44,086	3,253	22.9	11,057
Counties	8,509	6,439	75.7	27,862	2,070	24.3	7,629
Municipalities	5,708	4,525	79.3	16,224	1,183	20.7	3,428

See notes at end of table.

Table 1.26

State and local police protection full-time equivalent employment and payroll

By type of employee and level of government, March 2000[a]--Continued

(Payroll amounts in thousands)

		Sworn			Nonsworn		
State and level of government[b]	Total police protection full-time equivalent employment	Number	Percent of total police protection full-time equivalent	March payrolls	Number	Percent of total police protection full-time equivalent	March payrolls
Massachusetts	23,868	19,516	81.8%	$84,274	4,352	18.2%	$10,739
State	5,469	4,624	84.5	18,103	845	15.5	2,102
Local, total	18,399	14,892	80.9	66,171	3,507	19.1	8,637
Counties	27	14	51.9	40	13	48.1	38
Municipalities	18,372	14,878	81.0	66,130	3,494	19.0	8,599
Michigan	25,813	20,033	77.6	77,525	5,780	22.4	15,958
State	3,213	2,139	66.6	9,581	1,074	33.4	3,719
Local, total	22,600	17,894	79.2	67,944	4,706	20.8	12,239
Counties	5,211	3,944	75.7	14,416	1,267	24.3	3,591
Municipalities	17,389	13,950	80.2	53,528	3,439	19.8	8,648
Minnesota	10,636	7,840	73.7	34,239	2,796	26.3	8,251
State	938	541	57.7	2,672	397	42.3	1,322
Local, total	9,698	7,299	75.3	31,567	2,399	24.7	6,929
Counties	3,245	2,246	69.2	8,572	999	30.8	2,722
Municipalities	6,453	5,053	78.3	22,995	1,400	21.7	4,207
Mississippi	8,627	6,163	71.4	14,995	2,464	28.6	4,744
State	1,182	666	56.3	1,935	516	43.7	1,255
Local, total	7,445	5,497	73.8	13,061	1,948	26.2	3,488
Counties	2,308	1,535	66.5	3,424	773	33.5	1,280
Municipalities	5,137	3,962	77.1	9,637	1,175	22.9	2,208
Missouri	17,084	12,109	70.9	37,645	4,975	29.1	12,056
State	2,247	1,162	51.7	3,919	1,085	48.3	2,691
Local, total	14,837	10,947	73.8	33,726	3,890	26.2	9,364
Counties	3,941	2,710	68.8	6,987	1,231	31.2	2,610
Municipalities	10,896	8,237	75.6	26,739	2,659	24.4	6,754
Montana	2,216	1,495	67.5	4,412	721	32.5	1,595
State	404	189	46.8	545	215	53.2	615
Local, total	1,812	1,306	72.1	3,867	506	27.9	980
Counties	927	618	66.7	1,766	309	33.3	566
Municipalities	885	688	77.7	2,101	197	22.3	414
Nebraska	4,495	3,278	72.9	10,975	1,217	27.1	2,807
State	682	470	68.9	1,626	212	31.1	538
Local, total	3,813	2,808	73.6	9,349	1,005	26.4	2,269
Counties	1,311	853	65.1	2,348	458	34.9	1,040
Municipalities	2,502	1,955	78.1	7,001	547	21.9	1,229
Nevada	6,751	4,022	59.6	18,504	2,729	40.4	8,910
State	859	465	54.1	1,692	394	45.9	1,243
Local, total	5,892	3,557	60.4	16,812	2,335	39.6	7,666
Counties	4,240	2,441	57.6	11,936	1,799	42.4	6,091
Municipalities	1,652	1,116	67.6	4,876	536	32.4	1,575
New Hampshire	4,227	3,411	80.7	10,635	816	19.3	1,902
State	429	303	70.6	1,175	126	29.4	348
Local, total	3,798	3,108	81.8	9,460	690	18.2	1,554
Counties	230	152	66.1	463	78	33.9	182
Municipalities	3,568	2,956	82.8	8,997	612	17.2	1,372
New Jersey	33,441	24,624	73.6	123,046	8,817	26.4	30,689
State	3,731	1,132	30.3	3,462	2,599	69.7	15,756
Local, total	29,710	23,492	79.1	119,584	6,218	20.9	14,933
Counties	2,492	1,831	73.5	7,394	661	26.5	2,104
Municipalities	27,218	21,661	79.6	112,190	5,557	20.4	12,830
New Mexico	5,417	3,927	72.5	12,163	1,490	27.5	3,282
State	633	462	73.0	1,617	171	27.0	602
Local, total	4,784	3,465	72.4	10,545	1,319	27.6	2,680
Counties	1,373	1,021	74.4	2,960	352	25.6	716
Municipalities	3,411	2,444	71.7	7,586	967	28.3	1,964

See notes at end of table.

Table 1.26

State and local police protection full-time equivalent employment and payroll

By type of employee and level of government, March 2000[a]--Continued

(Payroll amounts in thousands)

State and level of government[b]	Total police protection full-time equivalent employment	Sworn Number	Sworn Percent of total police protection full-time equivalent	Sworn March payrolls	Nonsworn Number	Nonsworn Percent of total police protection full-time equivalent	Nonsworn March payrolls
New York	86,256	74,309	86.1%	$389,702	11,947	13.9%	$44,861
State	5,659	4,064	71.8	21,969	1,595	28.2	4,729
Local, total	80,597	70,245	87.2	367,734	10,352	12.8	40,132
Counties	12,555	9,864	78.6	51,915	2,691	21.4	9,111
Municipalities	68,042	60,381	88.7	315,819	7,661	11.3	31,021
North Carolina	23,053	18,157	78.8	53,659	4,896	21.2	11,866
State	3,361	2,287	68.0	8,383	1,074	32.0	3,031
Local, total	19,692	15,870	80.6	45,277	3,822	19.4	8,836
Counties	6,854	5,367	78.3	13,929	1,487	21.7	3,280
Municipalities	12,838	10,503	81.8	31,348	2,335	18.2	5,555
North Dakota	1,440	1,108	76.9	3,146	332	23.1	697
State	220	125	56.8	382	95	43.2	216
Local, total	1,220	983	80.6	2,764	237	19.4	482
Counties	471	365	77.5	895	106	22.5	180
Municipalities	749	618	82.5	1,869	131	17.5	302
Ohio	33,476	25,651	76.6	93,194	7,825	23.4	20,131
State	2,597	1,391	53.6	6,076	1,206	46.4	3,448
Local, total	30,879	24,260	78.6	87,119	6,619	21.4	16,683
Counties	7,003	4,774	68.2	14,091	2,229	31.8	5,673
Municipalities	23,876	19,486	81.6	73,027	4,390	18.4	11,010
Oklahoma	11,048	8,207	74.3	23,571	2,841	25.7	5,426
State	1,790	966	54.0	3,242	824	46.0	1,881
Local, total	9,258	7,241	78.2	20,329	2,017	21.8	3,545
Counties	2,472	1,875	75.8	3,313	597	24.2	890
Municipalities	6,786	5,366	79.1	17,016	1,420	20.9	2,655
Oregon	8,627	6,148	71.3	25,236	2,479	28.7	7,562
State	1,423	895	62.9	3,483	528	37.1	1,471
Local, total	7,204	5,253	72.9	21,752	1,951	27.1	6,091
Counties	2,582	1,833	71.0	7,147	749	29.0	2,153
Municipalities	4,622	3,420	74.0	14,605	1,202	26.0	3,938
Pennsylvania	31,447	25,820	82.1	100,344	5,627	17.9	17,154
State	5,638	4,399	78.0	17,948	1,239	22.0	4,838
Local, total	25,809	21,421	83.0	82,396	4,388	17.0	12,316
Counties	2,359	1,431	60.7	3,664	928	39.3	2,329
Municipalities	23,450	19,990	85.2	78,732	3,460	14.8	9,987
Rhode Island	3,358	2,432	72.4	9,991	926	27.6	2,748
State	304	197	64.8	1,001	107	35.2	332
Local, total	3,054	2,235	73.2	8,990	819	26.8	2,416
Municipalities	3,054	2,235	73.2	8,990	819	26.8	2,416
South Carolina	13,598	10,055	73.9	27,381	3,543	26.1	7,464
State	3,305	1,495	45.2	4,596	1,810	54.8	4,000
Local, total	10,293	8,560	83.2	22,785	1,733	16.8	3,464
Counties	4,767	3,922	82.3	9,951	845	17.7	1,759
Municipalities	5,526	4,638	83.9	12,834	888	16.1	1,704
South Dakota	1,700	1,271	74.8	3,642	429	25.2	897
State	278	181	65.1	596	97	34.9	223
Local, total	1,422	1,090	76.7	3,047	332	23.3	674
Counties	571	396	69.4	1,015	175	30.6	319
Municipalities	851	694	81.6	2,032	157	18.4	356
Tennessee	18,057	13,805	76.5	38,849	4,252	23.5	9,463
State	1,846	1,103	59.8	3,629	743	40.2	1,618
Local, total	16,211	12,702	78.4	35,219	3,509	21.6	7,844
Counties	4,916	3,847	78.3	9,378	1,069	21.7	2,014
Municipalities	11,295	8,855	78.4	25,841	2,440	21.6	5,830

See notes at end of table.

Table 1.26

State and local police protection full-time equivalent employment and payroll

By type of employee and level of government, March 2000[a]--Continued

(Payroll amounts in thousands)

		Sworn			Nonsworn		
State and level of government[b]	Total police protection full-time equivalent employment	Number	Percent of total police protection full-time equivalent	March payrolls	Number	Percent of total police protection full-time equivalent	March payrolls
Texas	58,854	43,629	74.1%	$148,167	15,225	25.9%	$34,671
State	3,633	2,009	55.3	7,946	1,624	44.7	4,195
Local, total	55,221	41,620	75.4	140,221	13,601	24.6	30,476
Counties	15,015	11,271	75.1	31,203	3,744	24.9	8,448
Municipalities	40,206	30,349	75.5	109,018	9,857	24.5	22,029
Utah	5,400	3,735	69.2	12,578	1,665	30.8	4,215
State	782	404	51.7	1,373	378	48.3	1,133
Local, total	4,618	3,331	72.1	11,204	1,287	27.9	3,083
Counties	1,658	1,158	69.8	3,579	500	30.2	1,154
Municipalities	2,960	2,173	73.4	7,626	787	26.6	1,929
Vermont	1,302	932	71.6	3,359	370	28.4	994
State	509	327	64.2	1,487	182	35.8	569
Local, total	793	605	76.3	1,871	188	23.7	426
Counties	32	5	15.6	13	27	84.4	46
Municipalities	761	600	78.8	1,858	161	21.2	379
Virginia	18,750	14,467	77.2	51,441	4,283	22.8	10,709
State	2,603	1,793	68.9	7,427	810	31.1	2,103
Local, total	16,147	12,674	78.5	44,013	3,473	21.5	8,606
Counties	7,631	5,863	76.8	21,784	1,768	23.2	4,694
Municipalities	8,516	6,811	80.0	22,229	1,705	20.0	3,913
Washington	14,137	9,923	70.2	47,037	4,214	29.8	14,332
State	2,220	1,004	45.2	4,426	1,216	54.8	3,903
Local, total	11,917	8,919	74.8	42,611	2,998	25.2	10,429
Counties	3,923	2,860	72.9	13,323	1,063	27.1	3,970
Municipalities	7,994	6,059	75.8	29,288	1,935	24.2	6,459
West Virginia	3,767	2,965	78.7	7,549	802	21.3	1,320
State	1,067	679	63.6	2,239	388	36.4	670
Local, total	2,700	2,286	84.7	5,310	414	15.3	650
Counties	991	834	84.2	1,803	157	15.8	243
Municipalities	1,709	1,452	85.0	3,507	257	15.0	407
Wisconsin	15,616	11,753	75.3	44,147	3,863	24.7	9,486
State	904	606	67.0	2,002	298	33.0	776
Local, total	14,712	11,147	75.8	42,144	3,565	24.2	8,709
Counties	3,956	2,712	68.6	9,893	1,244	31.4	3,259
Municipalities	10,756	8,435	78.4	32,251	2,321	21.6	5,451
Wyoming	1,695	1,143	67.4	3,458	552	32.6	1,416
State	190	109	57.4	374	81	42.6	228
Local, total	1,505	1,034	68.7	3,084	471	31.3	1,188
Counties	617	375	60.8	1,018	242	39.2	651
Municipalities	888	659	74.2	2,066	229	25.8	537

Note: See Notes, tables 1.1 and 1.18. For survey methodology and definitions of terms, see Appendix 1.

[a]March payroll data may not sum to equal March police protection payrolls presented in table 1.19 because of rounding.
[b]Data for local governments are estimates subject to sampling variation.

Source: U.S. Department of Justice, Bureau of Justice Statistics, *2000 Justice Expenditure and Employment Extracts*, NCJ 194802, Table 7 [Online]. Available: http://www.ojp.usdoj.gov/bjs/pub/sheets/cjee00.zip, file cjee0007.wk1 [Sept. 9, 2003]. Table adapted by SOURCEBOOK staff.

Table 1.27

State and local law enforcement agencies and employees

By type of agency, United States, 2000

		Number of employees					
	Number of	Full-time			Part-time		
Type of agency	agencies	Total	Sworn	Nonsworn	Total	Sworn	Nonsworn
Total	17,784	1,019,496	708,022	311,474	99,731	42,803	56,928
Local police	12,666	565,915	440,920	124,995	62,110	27,323	34,787
Sheriff	3,070	293,823	164,711	129,112	22,737	10,300	12,437
Primary State	49	87,028	56,348	30,680	817	95	722
Special jurisdiction	1,376	69,650	43,413	26,237	13,583	4,667	8,916
Texas constable	623	3,080	2,630	450	484	418	66

Note: These data are from the 2000 Census of State and Local Law Enforcement Agencies. The data were collected for the U.S. Department of Justice, Bureau of Justice Statistics and the Office of Community Oriented Policing Services by the U.S. Census Bureau. The 2000 Census included all State and local agencies employing at least one full-time sworn officer (or the equivalent in part-time officers) with general arrest powers. The pay period that included June 30, 2000 was the reference date for all data. The final database includes responses from 12,666 general purpose local police departments, 3,070 sheriffs' offices, 49 primary State police departments, 1,376 special jurisdiction police agencies, and the 623 county constable offices in Texas. Hawaii does not have a State police agency; the Hawaii Department of Public Safety primarily provides court support services.

A local police department was defined as a general purpose police department operated by a municipal, county, tribal, or regional (multijurisdiction) government. A State police department was defined as the general purpose police agency operated by the State. Included among special police agencies are both State and local agencies policing special geographic jurisdictions such as airports, parks, transit systems, public schools, colleges and universities, and public housing. Also included are agencies with special enforcement responsibilities such as those pertaining to natural resource conservation or alcoholic beverage control and special investigative units such as those operated by prosecutors' offices. Texas constables are elected officials who are responsible for providing services for the justice, county, and district courts. About half of constable offices also performed law enforcement functions. Of the approximately 760 county constable offices in Texas, 623 employed sworn personnel as of June 2000.

Source: U.S. Department of Justice, Bureau of Justice Statistics, *Census of State and Local Law Enforcement Agencies, 2000*, Bulletin NCJ 194066 (Washington, DC: U.S. Department of Justice, October 2002), p. 2.

Table 1.28

State and local law enforcement agencies and full-time employees

By State, 2000

| | | \multicolumn{6}{c}{Full-time employees} |
| | | Total | | Sworn personnel | | Responding to calls[a] | |
State	Number of agencies	Number	Per 100,000 residents	Number	Per 100,000 residents	Number	Per 100,000 residents
United States, total	17,784	1,019,496	362	708,022	252	425,427	151
Alabama	424	16,062	361	10,655	240	7,287	164
Alaska	95	2,151	343	1,348	215	1,031	164
Arizona	135	20,595	401	11,533	225	6,889	134
Arkansas	356	9,207	344	6,157	230	4,066	152
California	517	115,906	342	73,662	217	40,349	119
Colorado	248	15,237	354	10,309	240	5,815	135
Connecticut	125	10,277	302	8,327	245	5,143	151
Delaware	43	2,257	288	1,774	226	1,151	147
District of Columbia	3	4,914	859	3,963	693	2,041	357
Florida	383	68,165	427	39,452	247	24,264	152
Georgia	561	31,282	382	21,173	259	12,393	151
Hawaii	7	3,731	308	2,914	241	1,722	142
Idaho	122	4,522	349	2,749	212	1,732	134
Illinois	886	52,769	425	39,847	321	23,728	191
Indiana	495	17,969	296	11,900	196	7,249	119
Iowa	400	7,600	260	5,333	182	3,769	129
Kansas	353	10,343	385	6,563	244	4,265	159
Kentucky	382	9,589	237	7,144	177	4,800	119
Louisiana	343	23,573	527	18,548	415	7,639	171
Maine	139	3,638	285	2,367	186	1,721	135
Maryland	146	20,272	383	15,221	287	9,024	170
Massachusetts	351	23,593	372	18,082	285	11,784	186
Michigan	565	29,654	298	21,673	218	13,456	135
Minnesota	460	12,677	258	8,606	175	5,748	117
Mississippi	333	10,163	357	6,562	231	4,416	155
Missouri	586	20,459	366	13,630	244	8,749	156
Montana	126	2,958	328	1,760	195	1,344	149
Nebraska	237	4,776	279	3,486	204	2,296	134
Nevada	62	7,918	396	5,252	263	2,959	148
New Hampshire	195	3,268	264	2,542	206	1,736	140
New Jersey	551	37,387	444	29,062	345	16,343	194
New Mexico	135	6,324	348	4,456	245	2,792	153
New York	517	94,863	500	72,853	384	45,462	240
North Carolina	491	26,101	324	18,903	235	11,070	138
North Dakota	129	1,755	273	1,293	201	944	147
Ohio	845	36,863	325	25,082	221	15,689	138
Oklahoma	449	11,376	330	7,622	221	5,129	149
Oregon	178	10,683	312	6,496	190	3,573	104
Pennsylvania	1,166	33,427	272	26,373	215	17,648	144
Rhode Island	51	3,390	323	2,688	256	1,636	156
South Carolina	258	13,046	325	9,741	243	5,973	149
South Dakota	170	2,468	327	1,708	226	1,201	159
Tennessee	367	22,148	389	14,494	255	9,296	163
Texas	1,800	80,535	386	51,478	247	28,831	138
Utah	129	6,346	284	4,179	187	2,545	114
Vermont	65	1,459	240	1,034	170	796	131
Virginia	327	25,842	365	20,254	286	9,900	140
Washington	256	15,513	263	9,910	168	6,367	108
West Virginia	229	4,148	229	3,150	174	2,387	132
Wisconsin	512	18,010	336	13,237	247	8,290	155
Wyoming	81	2,287	463	1,477	299	989	200

Note: See Note, table 1.27.

[a]Uniformed sworn officers whose regular duties included responding to citizen calls for service.

Source: U.S. Department of Justice. Bureau of Justice Statistics, *Census of State and Local Law Enforcement Agencies, 2000*, Bulletin NCJ 194066 (Washington, DC: U.S. Department of Justice, October 2002), p. 4.

Table 1.29

Local police departments and full-time employees

By State, 2000

		\multicolumn{4}{c}{Full-time employees}		
		\multicolumn{2}{c}{Total}	\multicolumn{2}{c}{Sworn personnel}	\multicolumn{2}{c}{Responding to calls[a]}
State	Number of agencies	Number	Per 100,000 residents	Number	Per 100,000 residents	Number	Per 100,000 residents
---	---	---	---	---	---	---	---
United States, total	12,666	565,915	201	440,920	157	290,297	103
Alabama	324	9,456	213	7,089	159	5,093	115
Alaska	87	1,357	216	899	143	692	110
Arizona	93	11,569	225	8,159	159	4,593	90
Arkansas	258	4,677	175	3,675	137	2,507	94
California	341	52,541	155	37,674	111	22,291	66
Colorado	167	8,205	191	6,028	140	3,551	83
Connecticut	106	7,890	232	6,592	194	4,343	128
Delaware	33	1,142	146	992	127	748	95
District of Columbia	1	4,468	781	3,612	631	1,851	324
Florida	287	29,922	187	21,035	132	12,835	80
Georgia	356	13,918	170	10,992	134	7,680	94
Hawaii	4	3,346	276	2,605	215	1,606	133
Idaho	74	1,634	126	1,279	99	858	66
Illinois	729	34,382	277	27,452	221	20,145	162
Indiana	379	8,779	144	7,016	115	4,631	76
Iowa	292	3,875	132	3,175	108	2,332	80
Kansas	227	5,254	195	3,870	144	2,614	97
Kentucky	245	5,763	143	4,518	112	3,372	83
Louisiana	246	7,866	176	6,339	142	4,020	90
Maine	115	1,920	151	1,503	118	1,137	89
Maryland	77	11,998	227	9,680	183	5,922	112
Massachusetts	308	16,718	263	13,826	218	9,550	150
Michigan	450	16,727	168	14,044	141	9,185	92
Minnesota	358	6,651	135	5,347	109	3,871	79
Mississippi	217	5,016	176	3,764	132	2,707	95
Missouri	449	12,294	220	9,372	168	6,407	115
Montana	62	983	109	765	85	581	64
Nebraska	141	2,556	149	2,040	119	1,481	87
Nevada	28	4,753	238	3,216	161	1,740	87
New Hampshire	181	2,562	207	2,031	164	1,428	116
New Jersey	484	25,114	298	21,046	250	14,304	170
New Mexico	89	3,651	201	2,539	140	1,602	88
New York	393	74,737	394	58,588	309	37,839	199
North Carolina	357	12,717	158	10,473	130	6,848	85
North Dakota	69	844	131	681	106	526	82
Ohio	712	21,086	186	16,956	149	11,391	100
Oklahoma	340	6,746	195	5,246	152	3,661	106
Oregon	135	4,726	138	3,465	101	2,218	65
Pennsylvania	1,015	21,545	175	18,913	154	13,497	110
Rhode Island	39	2,745	262	2,153	205	1,366	130
South Carolina	186	5,399	135	4,383	109	2,770	69
South Dakota	100	1,184	157	896	119	624	83
Tennessee	248	10,919	192	8,408	148	5,843	103
Texas	737	40,321	193	30,525	146	19,379	93
Utah	83	2,798	125	2,181	98	1,375	62
Vermont	48	735	121	571	94	465	76
Virginia	165	12,439	176	9,604	136	5,922	84
Washington	204	7,837	133	5,766	98	3,679	62
West Virginia	158	1,604	89	1,404	78	1,109	61
Wisconsin	417	9,639	180	7,879	147	5,615	105
Wyoming	52	907	184	654	132	493	100

Note: See Note, table 1.27.

[a]Uniformed sworn officers whose regular duties included responding to citizen calls for service.

Source: U.S. Department of Justice, Bureau of Justice Statistics, *Census of State and Local Law Enforcement Agencies, 2000*, Bulletin NCJ 194066 (Washington, DC: U.S. Department of Justice, October 2002), p. 7.

Table 1.30

Sheriffs' offices and full-time employees

By State, 2000

		Full-time employees				
		Total		Sworn personnel		Responding to calls[a]
State	Number of agencies	Number	Per 100,000 residents	Number	Per 100,000 residents	Number	Per 100,000 residents
---	---	---	---	---	---	---	---
United States, total	3,070	293,823	104	164,711	59	65,552	23
Alabama	67	4,379	98	2,210	50	1,182	27
Arizona	15	5,490	107	1,764	35	1,187	23
Arkansas	75	2,882	108	1,285	48	741	28
California	58	45,706	135	25,361	75	9,033	27
Colorado	62	5,229	122	3,072	71	1,319	31
Connecticut	4	358	11	336	10	0	X
Delaware	3	31	4	20	3	0	X
Florida	65	33,303	208	14,770	92	8,294	52
Georgia	158	12,990	159	7,703	94	2,921	36
Idaho	44	2,217	171	1,024	79	567	44
Illinois	102	13,051	105	9,073	73	1,875	15
Indiana	92	6,388	105	2,883	47	1,504	25
Iowa	99	2,805	96	1,458	50	808	28
Kansas	104	3,627	135	1,803	67	864	32
Kentucky	120	1,677	41	1,406	35	766	19
Louisiana	64	12,745	285	10,329	231	2,329	52
Maine	16	947	74	309	24	185	15
Maryland	24	2,696	51	1,711	32	657	12
Massachusetts	10	3,219	51	1,208	19	37	1
Michigan	83	8,351	84	4,641	47	2,327	23
Minnesota	87	4,704	96	2,287	46	1,103	22
Mississippi	82	3,291	116	1,698	60	978	34
Missouri	114	3,756	67	2,423	43	1,121	20
Montana	55	1,458	162	629	70	458	51
Nebraska	92	1,465	86	901	53	544	32
Nevada	16	1,444	72	1,008	50	464	23
New Hampshire	10	219	18	120	10	34	3
New Jersey	21	4,206	50	3,200	38	168	2
New Mexico	32	1,392	77	1,038	57	692	38
New York	57	10,208	54	6,018	32	2,085	11
North Carolina	100	10,457	130	6,140	76	2,469	31
North Dakota	53	550	86	384	60	264	41
Ohio	88	10,199	90	5,366	47	2,146	19
Oklahoma	77	2,415	70	1,092	32	608	18
Oregon	36	4,437	130	2,113	62	896	26
Pennsylvania	65	1,719	14	1,428	12	150	1
Rhode Island	5	163	16	159	15	0	X
South Carolina	46	5,439	136	3,569	89	1,798	45
South Dakota	64	679	90	388	51	240	32
Tennessee	94	8,126	143	4,242	75	1,954	34
Texas	254	23,621	113	11,133	53	4,095	20
Utah	29	2,728	122	1,311	59	742	33
Vermont	14	143	23	104	17	41	7
Virginia	125	8,914	126	7,382	104	1,687	24
Washington	39	5,028	85	2,753	47	1,667	28
West Virginia	55	1,220	67	814	45	546	30
Wisconsin	72	6,782	126	4,069	76	1,705	32
Wyoming	23	969	196	576	117	301	61

Note: See Note, table 1.27. No sheriffs' offices operated in Alaska, District of Columbia, and Hawaii.

[a] Uniformed sworn officers whose regular duties included responding to citizen calls for service.

Source: U.S. Department of Justice, Bureau of Justice Statistics, *Census of State and Local Law Enforcement Agencies, 2000*, Bulletin NCJ 194066 (Washington, DC: U.S. Department of Justice, October 2002), p. 10. Table adapted by SOURCEBOOK staff.

Table 1.31

State law enforcement agency full-time employees

By State, 2000

| | \multicolumn{6}{c}{Full-time employees} | | | | | |
State	\multicolumn{2}{c}{Total}	\multicolumn{2}{c}{Sworn personnel}	\multicolumn{2}{c}{Responding to calls[a]}
	Number	Per 100,000 residents	Number	Per 100,000 residents	Number	Per 100,000 residents
United States, total	87,028	31	56,348	20	39,240	14
Alabama	1,201	27	628	14	461	10
Alaska	409	65	232	37	155	25
Arizona	1,872	36	1,050	20	735	14
Arkansas	913	34	559	21	330	12
California	9,706	29	6,678	20	6,460	19
Colorado	909	21	654	15	500	12
Connecticut	1,692	50	1,135	33	585	17
Delaware	827	106	580	74	280	36
Florida	2,138	13	1,658	10	1,539	10
Georgia	1,785	22	786	10	650	8
Idaho	510	39	292	23	191	15
Illinois	3,792	31	2,089	17	915	7
Indiana	1,941	32	1,278	21	570	9
Iowa	599	20	455	16	452	15
Kansas	694	26	457	17	454	17
Kentucky	1,670	41	937	23	481	12
Louisiana	1,438	32	934	21	542	12
Maine	495	39	325	25	225	18
Maryland	2,328	44	1,575	30	893	17
Massachusetts	2,590	41	2,221	35	1,543	24
Michigan	3,189	32	2,102	21	1,310	13
Minnesota	791	16	548	11	469	10
Mississippi	1,031	36	532	19	332	12
Missouri	2,170	39	1,080	19	650	12
Montana	280	31	205	23	175	19
Nebraska	640	37	462	27	205	12
Nevada	597	30	414	21	389	19
New Hampshire	389	31	315	25	214	17
New Jersey	3,682	44	2,569	31	1,238	15
New Mexico	649	36	525	29	350	19
New York	4,948	26	4,112	22	2,400	13
North Carolina	1,810	22	1,416	18	1,133	14
North Dakota	193	30	126	20	90	14
Ohio	2,552	22	1,382	12	1,151	10
Oklahoma	1,420	41	782	23	555	16
Oregon	1,409	41	826	24	377	11
Pennsylvania	5,694	46	4,152	34	2,854	23
Rhode Island	268	26	221	21	185	18
South Carolina	1,220	30	977	24	791	20
South Dakota	233	31	153	20	111	15
Tennessee	1,715	30	899	16	800	14
Texas	7,025	34	3,119	15	2,130	10
Utah	441	20	397	18	256	11
Vermont	513	84	304	50	239	39
Virginia	2,511	35	1,883	27	1,226	17
Washington	2,145	36	987	17	689	12
West Virginia	1,044	58	681	38	502	28
Wisconsin	665	12	508	9	340	6
Wyoming	295	60	148	30	118	24

Note: See Note, table 1.27. Hawaii does not operate a State law enforcement agency.

[a] Uniformed sworn officers whose regular duties included responding to citizen calls for service.

Source: U.S. Department of Justice, Bureau of Justice Statistics, *Census of State and Local Law Enforcement Agencies, 2000*, Bulletin NCJ 194066 (Washington, DC: U.S. Department of Justice, October 2002), p. 11. Table adapted by SOURCEBOOK staff.

Table 1.32
State and local law enforcement agencies with special jurisdictions and full-time employees

By State, 2000

State	Number of agencies	Total Number	Total Per 100,000 residents	Sworn personnel Number	Sworn personnel Per 100,000 residents
United States, total	1,376	69,650	25	43,413	15
Alabama	32	1,026	23	728	16
Alaska	7	385	61	217	35
Arizona	26	1,664	32	560	11
Arkansas	22	735	27	638	24
California	117	7,953	24	3,949	12
Colorado	18	894	21	555	13
Connecticut	14	337	10	264	8
Delaware	6	257	33	182	23
District of Columbia	2	446	78	351	61
Florida	30	2,802	18	1,989	12
Georgia	46	2,589	32	1,692	21
Hawaii	3	385	32	309	26
Idaho	3	161	12	154	12
Illinois	54	1,544	12	1,233	10
Indiana	23	861	14	723	12
Iowa	8	321	11	245	8
Kansas	21	768	29	433	16
Kentucky	16	479	12	283	7
Louisiana	32	1,524	34	946	21
Maine	7	276	22	230	18
Maryland	44	3,250	61	2,255	43
Massachusetts	32	1,066	17	827	13
Michigan	31	1,387	14	886	9
Minnesota	14	531	11	424	9
Mississippi	33	825	29	568	20
Missouri	22	2,239	40	755	13
Montana	8	237	26	161	18
Nebraska	3	115	7	83	5
Nevada	17	1,124	56	614	31
New Hampshire	3	98	8	76	6
New Jersey	45	4,385	52	2,247	27
New Mexico	13	632	35	354	19
New York	66	4,970	26	4,135	22
North Carolina	33	1,117	14	874	11
North Dakota	6	168	26	102	16
Ohio	44	3,026	27	1,378	12
Oklahoma	31	795	23	502	15
Oregon	6	111	3	92	3
Pennsylvania	85	4,469	36	1,880	15
Rhode Island	6	214	20	155	15
South Carolina	25	988	25	812	20
South Dakota	5	372	49	271	36
Tennessee	24	1,388	24	945	17
Texas	185	6,488	31	4,071	20
Utah	16	379	17	290	13
Vermont	2	68	11	55	9
Virginia	36	1,978	28	1,385	20
Washington	12	503	9	404	7
West Virginia	15	280	15	251	14
Wisconsin	22	924	17	781	15
Wyoming	5	116	23	99	23

Note: See Note, table 1.27.

Source: U.S. Department of Justice, Bureau of Justice Statistics, *Census of State and Local Law Enforcement Agencies, 2000*, Bulletin NCJ 194066 (Washington, DC: U.S. Department of Justice, October 2002), p. 13.

Table 1.33
Local police departments and full-time personnel

By size of population served, United States, 2000[a]

Population served	Agencies Number	Agencies Percent	Full-time sworn personnel Number	Full-time sworn personnel Percent	Full-time civilian personnel Number	Full-time civilian personnel Percent
All sizes	12,666	100%	440,920	100%	124,995	100%
1,000,000 or more	15	0.1	96,675	21.9	28,330	22.7
500,000 to 999,999	38	0.3	46,017	10.4	13,093	10.5
250,000 to 499,999	41	0.3	31,845	7.2	11,443	9.2
100,000 to 249,999	182	1.4	49,906	11.3	16,626	13.3
50,000 to 99,999	388	3.1	47,314	10.7	14,093	11.3
25,000 to 49,999	771	6.1	48,224	10.9	13,311	10.6
10,000 to 24,999	1,826	14.4	56,237	12.8	14,712	11.8
2,500 to 9,999	4,108	32.4	46,695	10.6	11,014	8.8
Less than 2,500	5,297	41.8	18,007	4.1	2,373	1.9

Note: These data are from the 2000 Law Enforcement Management and Administrative Statistics (LEMAS) survey and were collected for the U.S. Department of Justice, Bureau of Justice Statistics and the Office of Community Oriented Policing Services by the U.S. Census Bureau. The LEMAS survey collects data from a nationally representative sample of publicly funded State and local law enforcement agencies in the United States. A total of 881 State and local law enforcement agencies with 100 or more sworn officers were included in the survey. For agencies with fewer than 100 sworn officers, a nationally representative sample was drawn. A stratified random sample based on type of agency (local police or sheriff), size of population served, and number of sworn personnel was used. A total of 2,985 agencies responded to the survey yielding a 97.4% response rate. The final database includes responses from 1,975 local police departments, 961 sheriffs' offices, and the 49 primary State police agencies. Hawaii does not have a State police agency. These data, however, exclude State and local law enforcement agencies that serve special jurisdictional areas or have limited enforcement responsibilities. Data from agencies with fewer than 100 sworn personnel were derived from a sample and therefore are subject to sampling variation. The reference date for the survey was June 30, 2000.

A "local police" department was defined as a general purpose police department operated by a municipal, county, tribal, or regional (multijurisdiction) government. "Sheriffs" offices included were those operated by county or independent city governments. A "State police" department was defined as the general purpose police agency operated by the State. "Sworn" employees are those with general arrest powers.

[a]Detail may not add to total because of rounding.

Source: U.S. Department of Justice, Bureau of Justice Statistics, *Local Police Departments 2000*, NCJ 196002 (Washington, DC: U.S. Department of Justice, 2003), p. 3, Table 3.

Table 1.34
Sheriffs' offices and full-time personnel

By size of population served, United States, 2000[a]

Population served	Agencies Number	Agencies Percent	Full-time sworn personnel Number	Full-time sworn personnel Percent	Full-time civilian personnel Number	Full-time civilian personnel Percent
All sizes	3,070	100%	164,711	100%	129,112	100%
1,000,000 or more	39	1.3	35,287	21.4	28,900	22.4
500,000 to 999,999	66	2.1	22,604	13.7	20,823	16.1
250,000 to 499,999	113	3.7	22,838	13.9	20,195	15.6
100,000 to 249,999	285	9.3	30,561	18.6	21,740	16.8
50,000 to 99,999	383	12.5	19,618	11.9	13,406	10.4
25,000 to 49,999	640	20.8	17,404	10.6	11,893	9.2
10,000 to 24,999	876	28.5	12,306	7.5	9,056	7.0
Less than 10,000	668	21.8	4,093	2.5	3,099	2.4

Note: See Note, table 1.33.

[a]Detail may not add to total because of rounding.

Source: U.S. Department of Justice, Bureau of Justice Statistics, *Sheriffs' Offices 2000*, NCJ 196534 (Washington, DC: U.S. Department of Justice, 2003), p. 3, Table 3.

Table 1.35

Full-time sworn officers assigned to respond to citizen calls for service in local police departments

By size of population served, United States, 2000

Population served	Full-time sworn officers assigned to respond to citizen calls for service[a] Number	Percent
All sizes	300,431	68%
1,000,000 or more	60,802	63
500,000 to 999,999	28,334	62
250,000 to 499,999	18,505	58
100,000 to 249,999	30,586	61
50,000 to 99,999	29,412	62
25,000 to 49,999	33,115	69
10,000 to 24,999	42,546	76
2,500 to 9,999	40,041	86
Less than 2,500	17,090	95

Note: See Note, table 1.33.

[a]Includes all uniformed officers whose regularly assigned duties included responding to citizen calls for service.

Source: U.S. Department of Justice, Bureau of Justice Statistics, *Local Police Departments 2000*, NCJ 196002 (Washington, DC: U.S. Department of Justice, 2003), p. 3, Table 5.

Table 1.36

Full-time sworn officers assigned to respond to citizen calls for service in sheriffs' offices

By size of population served, United States, 2000

Population served	Full-time sworn officers assigned to respond to citizen calls for service[a] Number	Percent
All sizes	66,075	40%
1,000,000 or more	10,490	30
500,000 to 999,999	6,683	30
250,000 to 499,999	8,331	36
100,000 to 249,999	11,655	38
50,000 to 99,999	9,252	47
25,000 to 49,999	9,138	56
10,000 to 24,999	7,462	61
Less than 10,000	3,064	75

Note: See Note, table 1.33.

[a]Includes all uniformed officers whose regularly assigned duties included responding to citizen calls for service.

Source: U.S. Department of Justice, Bureau of Justice Statistics, *Sheriffs' Offices 2000*, NCJ 196534 (Washington, DC: U.S. Department of Justice, 2003), p. 3, Table 5.

Table 1.37

Race, ethnicity, and sex of full-time sworn personnel in local police departments

By size of population served, United States, 2000[a]

Population served	Total Total	Total Male	Total Female	White Total	White Male	White Female	Black Total	Black Male	Black Female	Hispanic Total	Hispanic Male	Hispanic Female	Other[b] Total	Other[b] Male	Other[b] Female
All sizes	100%	89.4%	10.6%	77.4%	70.9%	6.5%	11.7%	9.0%	2.7%	8.3%	7.2%	1.1%	2.7%	2.4%	0.3%
1,000,000 or more	100	83.5	16.5	63.5	55.7	7.8	16.1	11.0	5.1	17.3	14.2	3.1	3.1	2.6	0.4
500,000 to 999,999	100	84.5	15.5	62.4	54.7	7.7	25.2	18.6	6.5	6.8	6.0	0.8	5.6	5.1	0.5
250,000 to 499,999	100	85.8	14.2	67.9	59.1	8.8	19.0	15.0	4.0	10.7	9.5	1.1	2.4	2.2	0.3
100,000 to 249,999	100	89.3	10.7	76.2	68.7	7.5	12.2	10.1	2.1	8.0	7.2	0.7	3.7	3.3	0.4
50,000 to 99,999	100	91.8	8.2	85.2	78.8	6.4	7.3	6.1	1.1	5.7	5.2	0.5	1.8	1.7	0.1
25,000 to 49,999	100	93.0	7.0	87.8	82.1	5.7	6.1	5.2	0.8	4.6	4.2	0.4	1.5	1.4	0.1
10,000 to 24,999	100	94.3	5.7	90.6	85.8	4.8	4.6	4.1	0.5	3.4	3.2	0.2	1.4	1.2	0.2
2,500 to 9,999	100	94.5	5.5	90.1	85.5	4.6	4.5	4.1	0.4	3.9	3.5	0.4	1.5	1.4	0.1
Less than 2,500	100	96.1	3.9	87.9	84.7	3.2	5.8	5.5	0.3	3.1	3.0	0.1	3.2	2.9	0.3

Note: See Note, table 1.33.

[a]Percents may not add to total because of rounding.
[b]Includes Asians, Native Hawaiians or other Pacific Islanders, American Indians, Alaska Natives, and any other race.

Source: U.S. Department of Justice, Bureau of Justice Statistics, *Local Police Departments 2000*, NCJ 196002 (Washington, DC: U.S. Department of Justice, 2003), p. 4, Table 7.

Table 1.38

Race, ethnicity, and sex of full-time sworn personnel in sheriffs' offices

By size of population served, United States, 2000[a]

Population served	Total Total	Total Male	Total Female	White Total	White Male	White Female	Black Total	Black Male	Black Female	Hispanic Total	Hispanic Male	Hispanic Female	Other[b] Total	Other[b] Male	Other[b] Female
All sizes	100%	87.5%	12.5%	82.9%	73.7%	9.1%	9.4%	7.0%	2.3%	6.1%	5.3%	0.8%	1.6%	1.4%	0.2%
1,000,000 or more	100	86.3	13.7	69.5	61.2	8.3	11.9	9.0	2.9	15.4	13.2	2.2	3.2	2.9	0.4
500,000 to 999,999	100	86.2	13.8	78.0	68.4	9.6	11.2	8.3	2.9	8.4	7.4	1.1	2.3	2.1	0.3
250,000 to 499,999	100	86.7	13.3	83.4	73.7	9.7	9.9	7.2	2.7	5.4	4.6	0.8	1.3	1.2	0.2
100,000 to 249,999	100	86.4	13.6	85.9	75.7	10.2	10.2	7.3	2.9	3.1	2.7	0.4	0.8	0.7	0.1
50,000 to 99,999	100	88.4	11.6	92.5	82.3	10.2	5.2	4.0	1.3	1.0	0.9	0.1	1.3	1.2	0.1
25,000 to 49,999	100	89.5	10.5	88.2	80.0	8.3	8.1	6.4	1.7	2.9	2.5	0.5	0.7	0.6	0.1
10,000 to 24,999	100	91.6	8.4	89.1	82.5	6.6	7.7	6.3	1.4	2.4	2.1	0.3	0.8	0.7	0.1
Less than 10,000	100	92.9	7.1	94.0	87.2	6.9	1.3	1.3	0.0	3.0	3.0	0.0	1.7	1.4	0.2

Note: See Note, table 1.33.

[a]Percents may not add to total because of rounding.
[b]Includes Asians, Native Hawaiians or other Pacific Islanders, American Indians, Alaska Natives, and any other race.

Source: U.S. Department of Justice, Bureau of Justice Statistics, *Sheriffs' Offices 2000*, NCJ 196534 (Washington, DC: U.S. Department of Justice, 2003), p. 4, Table 7.

Table 1.39

Minimum educational requirements for new officer recruits in local police departments

By size of population served, United States, 2000[a]

Population served	Total with requirements	Percent of agencies requiring a minimum of:			
		High school diploma	Some college[b]	2-year college degree	4-year college degree
All sizes	98%	83%	6%	8%	1%
1,000,000 or more	100	67	33	0	0
500,000 to 999,999	100	71	18	6	6
250,000 to 499,999	98	65	18	10	5
100,000 to 249,999	99	71	18	9	2
50,000 to 99,999	99	65	17	16	1
25,000 to 49,999	99	73	11	13	2
10,000 to 24,999	99	78	8	12	1
2,500 to 9,999	99	85	4	9	1
Less than 2,500	97	86	4	6	(c)

Note: See Note, table 1.33.

[a]Percents may not add to total because of rounding.
[b]Nondegree requirements.
[c]Less than 0.5%.

Source: U.S. Department of Justice, Bureau of Justice Statistics, *Local Police Departments 2000*, NCJ 196002 (Washington, DC: U.S. Department of Justice, 2003), p. 6, Table 10.

Table 1.40

Minimum educational requirements for new officer recruits in sheriffs' offices

By size of population served, United States, 2000[a]

Population served	Total with requirements	Percent of agencies requiring a minimum of:			
		High school diploma	Some college[b]	2-year college degree	4-year college degree
All sizes	97%	86%	5%	6%	(c)
1,000,000 or more	87	71	12	3	0%
500,000 to 999,999	100	87	9	3	2
250,000 to 499,999	98	86	4	9	0
100,000 to 249,999	96	79	7	10	0
50,000 to 99,999	98	77	12	9	0
25,000 to 49,999	98	86	4	7	1
10,000 to 24,999	97	89	3	5	0
Less than 10,000	95	91	1	3	0

Note: See Note, table 1.33.

[a]Percents may not add to total because of rounding.
[b]Nondegree requirements.
[c]Less than 0.5%.

Source: U.S. Department of Justice, Bureau of Justice Statistics, *Sheriffs' Offices 2000*, NCJ 196534 (Washington, DC: U.S. Department of Justice, 2003), p. 6, Table 10.

Table 1.41

Training requirements for new officer recruits in local police departments

By size of population served, United States, 2000

Population served	Average number of hours required[a]					
	Academy			Field		
	Total	State-mandated	Other required	Total	State-mandated	Other required
All sizes	637	514	123	417	228	189
1,000,000 or more	1,051	564	487	534	189	345
500,000 to 999,999	950	586	364	784	425	359
250,000 to 499,999	991	577	414	659	336	323
100,000 to 249,999	853	601	252	757	425	322
50,000 to 99,999	790	604	186	689	414	275
25,000 to 49,999	763	586	177	680	334	346
10,000 to 24,999	751	574	177	537	297	240
2,500 to 9,999	611	514	97	389	235	154
Less than 2,500	532	469	63	244	153	91

Note: See Note, table 1.33.

[a]Computations of average number of training hours required exclude departments not requiring training.

Source: U.S. Department of Justice, Bureau of Justice Statistics, *Local Police Departments 2000*, NCJ 196002 (Washington, DC: U.S. Department of Justice, 2003), p. 6, Table 11.

Table 1.42

Training requirements for new officer recruits in sheriffs' offices

By size of population served, United States, 2000

Population served	Average number of hours required[a]					
	Academy			Field		
	Total	State-mandated	Other required	Total	State-mandated	Other required
All sizes	603	493	110	449	178	271
1,000,000 or more	712	490	222	651	305	346
500,000 to 999,999	828	578	250	622	237	385
250,000 to 499,999	644	515	129	751	336	415
100,000 to 249,999	797	557	240	634	208	426
50,000 to 99,999	643	494	149	501	161	340
25,000 to 49,999	552	488	64	482	243	239
10,000 to 24,999	526	477	49	346	138	208
Less than 10,000	537	477	60	247	110	137

Note: See Note, table 1.33.

[a]Computations of average number of training hours required exclude departments not requiring training.

Source: U.S. Department of Justice, Bureau of Justice Statistics, *Sheriffs' Offices 2000*, NCJ 196534 (Washington, DC: U.S. Department of Justice, 2003), p. 6, Table 11.

Table 1.43
Average operating budget of local police departments

By size of population served, United States, fiscal year 2000

Population served	Total (in thousands)	Per agency	Per sworn officer	Per employee	Per resident
All sizes	$36,692,534	$2,896,000	$80,600	$61,400	$179
1,000,000 or more	8,287,504	552,500,000	85,700	64,300	262
500,000 to 999,999	4,167,422	122,571,000	90,500	69,400	180
250,000 to 499,999	3,065,187	76,630,000	96,100	69,800	216
100,000 to 249,999	4,562,209	26,525,000	92,300	67,500	175
50,000 to 99,999	4,194,379	11,009,000	88,700	66,700	159
25,000 to 49,999	4,106,538	5,278,000	83,500	63,800	152
10,000 to 24,999	4,258,348	2,297,000	72,100	55,300	146
2,500 to 9,999	3,005,089	744,000	58,800	47,100	142
Less than 2,500	1,045,859	195,000	42,300	35,800	156

Note: See Note, table 1.33. Data are for the fiscal year ending June 30, 2000, or the most recent fiscal year completed prior to that date. Figures do not include capital expenditures such as equipment purchases or construction costs. Computations of per officer and per employee averages include both full-time and part-time employees, with a weight of 0.5 assigned to part-time employees. Total and per agency figures are rounded to the nearest $1,000; per officer and per employee figures to the nearest $100.

Source: U.S. Department of Justice, Bureau of Justice Statistics, *Local Police Departments 2000*, NCJ 196002 (Washington, DC: U.S. Department of Justice, 2003), p. 7, Table 13.

Table 1.44
Average operating budget of sheriffs' offices

By size of population served, United States, fiscal year 2000

Population served	Total (in thousands)	Per agency	Per sworn officer	Per employee	Per resident
All sizes	$17,694,933	$5,764,000	$107,900	$59,000	$65
1,000,000 or more	4,796,269	122,981,000	160,100	83,100	65
500,000 to 999,999	3,081,806	46,694,000	134,800	67,500	65
250,000 to 499,999	2,779,279	24,595,000	118,200	62,400	70
100,000 to 249,999	2,859,762	10,034,000	91,700	51,400	65
50,000 to 99,999	1,584,233	4,136,000	76,500	46,900	59
25,000 to 49,999	1,350,461	2,110,000	70,100	41,500	58
10,000 to 24,999	967,781	1,105,000	77,700	42,900	67
Less than 10,000	275,343	412,000	66,900	3,700	74

Note: See Notes, tables 1.33 and 1.43.

Source: U.S. Department of Justice, Bureau of Justice Statistics, *Sheriffs' Offices 2000*, NCJ 196534 (Washington, DC: U.S. Department of Justice, 2003), p. 7, Table 13.

Table 1.45
Average base minimum and maximum annual salaries for selected positions in local police departments

By size of population served, United States, 2000

Average base starting salary[a]

Population served	Entry-level officer Minimum	Entry-level officer Maximum	Sergeant or equivalent Minimum	Sergeant or equivalent Maximum	Chief Minimum	Chief Maximum
All sizes	$25,500	$30,300	$35,100	$39,600	$43,700	$49,200
1,000,000 or more	33,900	51,300	53,700	65,300	104,400	136,400
500,000 to 999,999	33,400	47,500	50,000	59,000	99,600	116,000
250,000 to 499,999	34,200	48,400	49,000	59,400	85,000	111,600
100,000 to 249,999	34,700	46,800	49,100	58,900	84,400	104,300
50,000 to 99,999	34,100	44,300	49,800	57,300	78,300	92,700
25,000 to 49,999	32,800	42,500	46,700	54,000	70,100	82,200
10,000 to 24,999	29,700	36,600	41,800	46,700	58,000	65,800
2,500 to 9,999	25,900	30,900	34,200	38,200	43,300	48,700
Less than 2,500	20,900	22,900	26,000	29,200	30,200	32,600

Note: See Note, table 1.33. Salary figures have been rounded to the nearest $100.

[a]Computations of average salary exclude agencies with no full-time employees in that position.

Source: U.S. Department of Justice, Bureau of Justice Statistics, *Local Police Departments 2000*, NCJ 196002 (Washington, DC: U.S. Department of Justice, 2003), p. 8, Table 14.

Table 1.46
Average base minimum and maximum annual salaries for selected positions in sheriffs' offices

By size of population served, United States, 2000

Average base starting salary[a]

Population served	Entry-level deputy Minimum	Entry-level deputy Maximum	Sergeant or equivalent Minimum	Sergeant or equivalent Maximum	Sheriff Minimum	Sheriff Maximum
All sizes	$23,700	$27,900	$30,500	$34,800	$49,400	$51,900
1,000,000 or more	32,900	46,100	45,500	54,600	99,300	105,400
500,000 to 999,999	31,300	43,200	45,200	55,500	89,400	96,800
250,000 to 499,999	28,500	40,300	39,200	50,300	80,300	85,300
100,000 to 249,999	26,700	35,400	35,100	43,600	65,600	70,800
50,000 to 99,999	24,900	30,600	31,100	36,700	55,900	58,800
25,000 to 49,999	23,600	27,600	29,600	33,700	50,000	52,000
10,000 to 24,999	22,200	24,400	29,100	31,800	43,500	45,200
Less than 10,000	21,700	23,100	25,900	27,100	33,800	35,000

Note: See Notes, tables 1.33 and 1.45.

[a]Computations of average salary exclude agencies with no full-time employees in that position.

Source: U.S. Department of Justice, Bureau of Justice Statistics, *Sheriffs' Offices 2000*, NCJ 196534 (Washington, DC: U.S. Department of Justice, 2003), p. 8.

Table 1.47
Semiautomatic sidearms authorized for use by sworn personnel in local police departments

By size of population served, United States, 2000

	Percent of agencies authorizing semiautomatic sidearms[a]					
Population served	Any type	.40 caliber	9mm	.45 caliber	.380 caliber	10mm
All sizes	98%	75%	67%	54%	38%	30%
1,000,000 or more	100	54	73	40	27	13
500,000 to 999,999	94	68	83	50	50	21
250,000 to 499,999	100	60	80	53	43	20
100,000 to 249,999	99	68	81	61	57	32
50,000 to 99,999	100	72	74	54	53	31
25,000 to 49,999	100	76	69	53	46	30
10,000 to 24,999	100	74	61	46	38	26
2,500 to 9,999	98	78	64	54	36	31
Less than 2,500	96	75	71	57	36	30

Note: See Note, table 1.33.

[a]Some departments authorized more than one type of sidearm.

Source: U.S. Department of Justice, Bureau of Justice Statistics, *Local Police Departments 2000*, NCJ 196002 (Washington, DC: U.S. Department of Justice, 2003), p. 18, Table 37.

Table 1.48
Semiautomatic sidearms authorized for use by sworn personnel in sheriffs' offices

By size of population served, United States, 2000

	Percent of agencies authorizing semiautomatic sidearms					
Population served	Any type	.40 caliber	9mm	.45 caliber	.380 caliber	10mm
All sizes	97%	73%	65%	59%	38%	32%
1,000,000 or more	97	56	76	69	53	22
500,000 to 999,999	96	63	67	52	30	24
250,000 to 499,999	97	73	78	62	53	42
100,000 to 249,999	99	75	74	63	54	41
50,000 to 99,999	98	82	68	56	43	37
25,000 to 49,999	99	81	61	62	41	33
10,000 to 24,999	96	72	65	57	32	31
Less than 10,000	98	64	60	60	31	27

Note: See Note, table 1.33.

Source: U.S. Department of Justice, Bureau of Justice Statistics, *Sheriffs' Offices 2000*, NCJ 196534 (Washington, DC: U.S. Department of Justice, 2003), p. 18, Table 37.

Table 1.49
Nonlethal weapons authorized for use by sworn personnel in local police departments

By size of population served, United States, 2000

Percent of agencies authorizing:

	Chemical agents--personal use				Batons				Other weapons/actions						
Population served	Any type listed in survey	Pepper spray	CS	Tear gas	Any type listed in survey	Collap-sible	PR-24	Tradi-tional	Flash/bang grenade	Soft projectile	Electrical devices[a]	Choke/carotid hold[b]	Rubber bullet	Black-jack	Capture net
All sizes	91%	91%	4%	3%	88%	73%	40%	38%	13%	9%	7%	7%	3%	3%	1%
1,000,000 or more	87	87	0	0	100	80	53	67	40	33	40	40	7	0	0
500,000 to 999,999	88	88	9	0	91	77	41	59	41	23	15	18	6	0	3
250,000 to 499,999	88	85	5	0	100	78	45	55	58	25	28	33	13	5	3
100,000 to 249,999	96	95	2	1	98	84	42	53	63	41	21	28	12	2	3
50,000 to 99,999	97	96	4	3	97	83	42	50	58	33	17	19	10	1	2
25,000 to 49,999	95	94	4	3	99	82	51	39	41	23	12	13	9	1	3
10,000 to 24,999	98	97	3	2	95	76	42	33	23	14	8	5	4	2	(c)
2,500 to 9,999	92	92	3	2	91	79	41	41	8	5	5	7	3	2	0
Less than 2,500	87	86	5	5	82	65	36	36	3	4	6	4	2	3	1

Note: See Note, table 1.33.

[a]Includes hand-held direct contact devices (such as stun gun) and hand-held stand-off devices (such as taser).
[b]Includes neck restraints.
[c]Less than 0.5%.

Source: U.S. Department of Justice, Bureau of Justice Statistics, *Local Police Departments 2000*, NCJ 196002 (Washington, DC: U.S. Department of Justice, 2003), p. 19, Table 39.

Table 1.50
Nonlethal weapons authorized for use by sworn personnel in sheriffs' offices

By size of population served, United States, 2000

Percent of agencies authorizing:

	Chemical agents--personal use				Batons				Other weapons/actions						
Population served	Any type listed in survey	Pepper spray	CS	Tear gas	Any type listed in survey	Collap-sible	PR-24	Tradi-tional	Flash/bang grenade	Soft projectile	Electrical devices[a]	Choke/carotid hold[b]	Rubber bullet	Black-jack	Capture net
All sizes	89%	88%	4%	4%	84%	73%	34%	32%	23%	10%	10%	8%	5%	2%	(c)
1,000,000 or more	85	85	0	3	88	65	25	54	44	22	32	25	12	6	3%
500,000 to 999,999	93	90	9	3	90	78	34	29	44	18	15	15	3	0	0
250,000 to 499,999	84	84	1	0	88	80	49	38	48	28	22	13	11	0	1
100,000 to 249,999	93	91	5	3	89	76	33	37	43	17	14	9	12	2	(c)
50,000 to 99,999	93	93	5	3	90	85	38	41	38	11	9	3	4	1	0
25,000 to 49,999	93	92	6	5	86	76	38	32	30	13	8	5	6	1	0
10,000 to 24,999	86	85	3	3	82	73	31	28	11	4	10	8	2	2	1
Less than 10,000	84	84	3	6	77	62	30	30	6	9	6	8	9	4	3	0

Note: See Note, table 1.33.

[a]Includes hand-held direct contact devices (such as stun gun) and hand-held stand-off devices (such as taser).
[b]Includes neck restraints.
[c]Less than 0.5%.

Source: U.S. Department of Justice, Bureau of Justice Statistics, *Sheriffs' Offices 2000*, NCJ 196534 (Washington, DC: U.S. Department of Justice, 2003), p. 19, Table 39.

Table 1.51
Full-time community policing officers in local police departments

By size of population served, United States, 2000

	Full-time community policing officers		
Population served	Percent of agencies using	Number of officers	Average number of officers[a]
All sizes	66%	102,598	12
1,000,000 or more	100	33,214	2,208
500,000 to 999,999	85	8,617	297
250,000 to 499,999	95	6,866	180
150,000 to 249,999	94	8,580	53
50,000 to 149,999	93	7,167	20
25,000 to 49,999	83	7,854	12
10,000 to 24,999	72	9,184	7
2,500 to 9,999	63	12,745	5
Less than 2,500	60	8,370	3

Note: See Note, table 1.33. Community policing promotes organizational strategies to address the causes and reduce the fear of crime and social disorder through problem solving tactics and community partnerships. A fundamental shift from traditional reactive policing, community policing stresses the prevention of crime before it occurs. The implementation of a community policing plan supports and empowers front-line officers, decentralizes command, and encourages innovative problem solving (Source, p. 14). In some jurisdictions these officers may be known as community relations officers, community resource officers, or named for the community policing approach they employ (Source, p. 15).

[a]Excludes agencies that did not employ any full-time community policing officers.

Source: U.S. Department of Justice, Bureau of Justice Statistics, *Local Police Departments 2000*, NCJ 196002 (Washington, DC: U.S. Department of Justice, 2003), p. 15, Table 32.

Table 1.52
Full-time community policing officers in sheriffs' offices

By size of population served, United States, 2000

	Full-time community policing officers		
Population served	Percent of agencies using	Number of officers	Average number of officers[a]
All sizes	62%	16,545	9
1,000,000 or more	65	3,502	161
500,000 to 999,999	73	1,156	23
250,000 to 499,999	73	2,225	26
100,000 to 249,999	72	2,025	10
50,000 to 99,999	68	1,747	7
25,000 to 49,999	59	2,087	6
10,000 to 24,999	54	2,190	5
Less than 10,000	63	1,614	4

Note: See Notes, tables 1.33 and 1.51.

[a]Excludes agencies that did not employ any full-time sworn community policing officers.

Source: U.S. Department of Justice, Bureau of Justice Statistics, *Sheriffs' Offices 2000*, NCJ 196534 (Washington, DC: U.S. Department of Justice, 2003), p. 15, Table 32.

Table 1.53
Full-time school resource officers in local police departments

By size of population served, United States, 2000

	Full-time school resource officers		
Population served	Percent of agencies using	Number of officers	Average number of officers[a]
All sizes	44%	13,760	2
1,000,000 or more	73	942	85
500,000 to 999,999	67	603	26
250,000 to 499,999	85	497	15
100,000 to 249,999	85	1,193	8
50,000 to 99,999	86	1,380	4
25,000 to 49,999	82	1,757	3
10,000 to 24,999	66	2,127	2
2,500 to 9,999	45	3,095	2
Less than 2,500	25	2,167	2

Note: See Note, table 1.33.

[a]Excludes agencies that did not employ any full-time sworn school resource officers.

Source: U.S. Department of Justice, Bureau of Justice Statistics, *Local Police Departments 2000*, NCJ 196002 (Washington, DC: U.S. Department of Justice, 2003), p. 15, Table 33.

Table 1.54
Full-time school resource officers in sheriffs' offices

By size of population served, United States, 2000

	Full-time school resource officers		
Population served	Percent of agencies using	Number of officers	Average number of officers[a]
All sizes	48%	5,311	4
1,000,000 or more	59	872	44
500,000 to 999,999	66	418	9
250,000 to 499,999	70	607	8
100,000 to 249,999	63	951	5
50,000 to 99,999	62	712	3
25,000 to 49,999	52	805	2
10,000 to 24,999	40	603	2
Less than 10,000	33	344	2

Note: See Note, table 1.33.

[a]Excludes agencies that did not employ any full-time sworn school resource officers.

Source: U.S. Department of Justice, Bureau of Justice Statistics, *Sheriffs' Offices 2000*, NCJ 196534 (Washington, DC: U.S. Department of Justice, 2003), p. 15, Table 33.

Table 1.55

Full-time employees and sworn personnel in large city police departments

By size of population served, United States, 1990 and 2000

	Full-time employees						Full-time sworn personnel					
	Per agency		Per 100,000 residents		Per 10 square miles		Per agency		Per 100,000 residents		Per 10 square miles	
Population served	1990	2000	1990	2000	1990	2000	1990	2000	1990	2000	1990	2000
Total	2,691	3,220	370	404	85	101	2,101	2,465	289	310	66	78
1,000,000 or more	9,047	11,267	422	470	82	102	7,113	8,717	331	364	65	79
500,000 to 999,999	2,113	2,349	348	355	80	89	1,647	1,810	271	274	63	69
350,000 to 499,999	1,113	1,334	289	317	86	103	841	972	219	231	65	75
250,000 to 349,999	932	1,068	305	343	133	153	730	796	239	256	105	114

Note: See Note, table 1.33. These data are from the 1990 and 2000 Law Enforcement Management and Administrative Statistics (LEMAS) surveys sponsored by the U.S. Department of Justice, Bureau of Justice Statistics. Population data are from the U.S. Census Bureau decennial censuses. These data include the 62 cities that had a population of at least 250,000 in both the 1990 and 2000 decennial censuses. In most cases, the data represent a city and the local police department that serves it.

Source: U.S. Department of Justice, Bureau of Justice Statistics, *Police Departments in Large Cities, 1990-2000*, Special Report NCJ 175703 (Washington, DC: U.S. Department of Justice, May 2002), p. 2, Tables 1 and 2. Table adapted by SOURCEBOOK staff.

Table 1.56

Female and minority full-time sworn personnel in large city police departments

By size of population served, United States, 1990 and 2000

	Percent of full-time sworn personnel who were:											
	Female		Any minority		Black, non-Hispanic		Hispanic, any race		Asian/Pacific Islander		American Indian	
Population served	1990	2000	1990	2000	1990	2000	1990	2000	1990	2000	1990	2000
Total	12.1%	16.3%	29.8%	38.1%	18.4%	20.1%	9.2%	14.1%	2.0%	2.8%	0.3%	0.4%
1,000,000 or more	12.3	16.8	27.6	37.6	15.1	16.9	11.4	17.5	0.9	2.1	0.2	0.3
500,000 to 999,999	12.6	16.1	35.8	41.1	25.2	27.0	5.0	7.7	5.3	5.3	0.3	0.5
350,000 to 499,999	10.9	14.4	30.7	36.4	18.9	20.4	10.2	12.7	1.0	2.1	0.6	1.0
250,000 to 349,999	10.5	15.8	24.0	32.7	17.4	20.9	6.2	10.4	0.3	0.7	0.2	0.4

Note: See Notes, tables 1.33 and 1.55.

Source: U.S. Department of Justice, Bureau of Justice Statistics, *Police Departments in Large Cities, 1990-2000*, Special Report NCJ 175703 (Washington, DC: U.S. Department of Justice, May 2002), p. 3, Table 3. Table adapted by SOURCEBOOK staff.

Table 1.57

Number and rate (per 100,000 residents) of full-time employees and sworn personnel in large city police departments

By size of population served and city, United States, 1990 and 2000

Population served and city	Full-time employees Total number 1990	2000	Percent change	Per 100,000 residents 1990	2000	Percent change	Full-time sworn personnel Total number 1990	2000	Percent change	Per 100,000 residents 1990	2000	Percent change
1,000,000 or more												
New York (NY)	39,398	53,029	34.6%	538	662	23.1%	31,236	40,435	29.4%	427	505	18.4%
Los Angeles (CA)	10,695	12,409	13.2	315	336	6.8	8,295	9,341	12.6	238	253	6.2
Chicago (IL)	14,909	16,466	10.4	536	569	6.2	11,837	13,466	13.8	425	465	9.4
Houston (TX)	5,579	7,440	33.4	342	381	11.3	4,104	5,343	30.2	252	273	8.7
Philadelphia (PA)	7,354	7,928	7.8	464	522	12.6	6,523	7,024	7.7	411	463	12.5
Phoenix (AZ)	2,584	3,394	31.3	263	257	-2.2	1,949	2,626	34.7	198	199	0.3
San Diego (CA)	2,498	2,746	9.9	225	224	-0.2	1,816	2,022	11.3	164	165	1.1
Dallas (TX)	3,487	3,586	2.8	346	302	-12.9	2,635	2,862	8.6	262	241	-8.0
San Antonio (TX)	1,912	2,387	24.8	204	209	2.1	1,576	1,882	19.4	168	164	-2.4
Las Vegas (NV)	1,782	3,286	84.4	289	322	11.4	1,162	2,168	86.6	189	213	12.7
500,000 to 999,999												
Detroit (MI)	5,203	4,804	-7.7	506	505	-0.2	4,595	4,154	-9.6	447	437	-2.3
San Jose (CA)	1,465	1,812	23.7	187	202	8.1	1,110	1,408	26.8	142	157	10.9
Honolulu (HI)	2,220	2,270	2.3	265	259	-2.4	1,781	1,792	0.6	213	205	-4.0
San Francisco (CA)	2,566	2,520	-1.8	354	324	-8.5	1,777	2,227	25.3	245	287	16.8
Indianapolis (IN)	2,113	2,402	13.7	299	313	4.5	1,436	1,592	10.9	203	207	1.9
Jacksonville (FL)	2,080	2,541	22.2	327	345	5.5	1,181	1,530	29.6	186	208	11.9
Columbus (OH)	1,724	2,144	24.4	272	301	10.6	1,381	1,744	26.3	218	245	12.3
Austin (TX)	1,082	1,656	53.0	232	252	8.5	795	1,144	43.9	171	174	2.1
Baltimore (MD)	3,414	3,649	6.9	464	560	20.8	2,861	3,034	6.0	389	466	19.9
Memphis (TN)	2,092	2,791	33.4	343	429	25.3	1,382	1,904	37.8	226	293	29.3
Charlotte (NC)	1,201	1,864	55.2	261	298	14.1	930	1,442	55.1	202	231	14.0
Milwaukee (WI)	2,274	2,472	8.7	362	414	14.4	1,866	1,998	7.1	297	335	12.7
Boston (MA)	2,741	3,046	11.1	477	517	8.3	2,053	2,164	5.4	357	367	2.7
Washington (DC)	5,259	4,468	-15.0	867	781	-9.9	4,506	3,612	-19.8	742	631	-15.0
Nashville (TN)	1,319	1,693	28.4	258	297	15.0	1,020	1,249	22.5	200	219	9.8
El Paso (TX)	928	1,351	45.6	180	240	33.1	738	1,057	43.2	143	188	30.9
Seattle (WA)	1,775	1,918	8.1	344	340	-1.0	1,271	1,261	-0.8	246	224	-9.1
Denver (CO)	1,558	1,802	15.7	333	325	-2.5	1,318	1,489	13.0	282	268	-4.8
Fort Worth (TX)	1,255	1,510	20.3	280	282	0.7	950	1,196	25.9	212	224	5.4
Portland (OR)	955	1,347	41.0	218	255	16.6	769	1,007	30.9	176	190	8.2
Oklahoma City (OK)	1,158	1,269	9.6	260	251	-3.7	863	1,011	17.1	194	200	2.9
350,000 to 499,999												
Tucson (AZ)	989	1,253	26.7	244	257	5.5	745	928	24.6	184	191	3.8
New Orleans (LA)	1,686	2,050	21.6	339	423	24.7	1,397	1,664	19.1	281	343	22.1
Cleveland (OH)	2,060	2,386	15.8	407	499	22.4	1,761	1,822	3.5	348	381	9.3
Long Beach (CA)	968	1,363	40.8	225	295	31.0	643	881	37.0	150	191	27.5
Albuquerque (NM)	1,184	1,236	4.4	308	276	-10.5	808	859	6.3	210	191	-8.8
Kansas City (MO)	1,718	1,848	7.6	395	419	6.0	1,148	1,253	9.1	264	284	7.6
Fresno (CA)	657	1,011	53.9	185	236	27.5	429	683	59.2	121	160	31.9
Virginia Beach (VA)	796	881	10.7	203	207	2.3	597	721	20.8	152	170	11.6
Atlanta (GA)	1,916	1,984	3.5	486	476	-2.0	1,560	1,474	-5.5	396	354	-10.6
Sacramento (CA)	866	1,008	16.4	234	248	5.6	599	650	8.5	162	160	-1.5
Oakland (CA)	944	1,088	15.3	254	272	7.4	616	710	15.3	165	178	7.4
Mesa (AZ)	582	1,132	94.5	202	286	41.4	384	717	86.7	133	181	35.7
Tulsa (OK)	881	977	10.9	240	249	3.6	702	819	16.7	191	208	9.0
Omaha (NE)	741	933	25.9	221	239	8.4	594	750	26.3	177	192	8.7
Minneapolis (MN)	912	1,163	27.5	248	304	22.8	806	902	11.9	219	236	7.7
Miami (FL)	1,436	1,487	3.6	401	410	2.4	1,110	1,110	0.0	310	306	-1.1
Colorado Springs (CO)	591	873	47.7	210	242	15.1	406	586	44.3	144	162	12.4
250,000 to 349,999												
St. Louis (MO)	2,244	2,078	-7.4	566	597	5.5	1,544	1,489	-3.6	389	428	9.9
Wichita (KS)	578	1,097	89.8	190	319	67.6	423	609	44.0	139	177	27.1
Santa Ana (CA)	563	704	25.0	192	208	8.7	382	404	5.8	130	120	-8.1
Pittsburgh (PA)	1,239	1,315	6.1	335	393	17.3	1,153	1,036	-10.1	312	310	-0.7
Arlington (TX)	462	643	39.2	177	193	9.4	356	485	36.2	136	146	7.1
Cincinnati (OH)	1,166	1,321	13.3	320	399	24.5	938	1,030	9.8	258	311	20.7
Anaheim (CA)	493	588	19.3	185	179	-3.1	344	397	15.4	129	121	-6.3
Toledo (OH)	737	810	9.9	221	258	16.7	683	690	1.0	205	220	7.2
Tampa (FL)	1,083	1,229	13.5	387	405	4.7	824	939	14.0	294	309	5.2
Buffalo (NY)	1,177	1,135	-3.6	359	388	8.1	1,032	928	-10.1	315	317	0.8
St. Paul (MN)	718	798	11.1	264	278	5.4	532	576	8.3	195	201	2.6
Corpus Christi (TX)	514	592	15.2	200	213	6.9	367	407	10.9	143	147	2.9
Newark (NJ)	1,260	1,635	29.8	458	598	30.6	1,013	1,466	44.7	368	536	45.6
Louisville (KY)	812	1,009	24.3	302	394	30.5	630	689	9.4	234	269	14.8

Note: See Notes, tables 1.33 and 1.55.

Source: U.S. Department of Justice, Bureau of Justice Statistics, *Police Departments in Large Cities, 1990-2000*, Special Report NCJ 175703 (Washington, DC: U.S. Department of Justice, May 2002), p. 10.

Table 1.58

Female and minority full-time sworn personnel and ratio of minority officers to minority residents in large city police departments

By size of population served and city, United States, 1990 and 2000

	Female		Any minority			Black or African American			Hispanic or Latino		
	Percent of sworn personnel		Percent of sworn personnel		Officer-to-resident ratio, 2000[a]	Percent of sworn personnel		Officer-to-resident ratio, 2000[a]	Percent of sworn personnel		Officer-to-resident ratio, 2000[a]
Population served and city	1990	2000	1990	2000		1990	2000		1990	2000	
1,000,000 or more											
New York (NY)	12.3%	15.5%	25.5%	34.7%	0.53	12.6%	13.3%	0.50	12.1%	17.8%	0.66
Los Angeles (CA)	12.5	18.4	37.5	53.9	0.77	13.4	13.6	1.21	21.0	33.1	0.71
Chicago (IL)	13.0	21.3	30.4	40.3	0.59	23.6	25.9	0.70	6.3	12.7	0.49
Houston (TX)	9.6	12.4	26.3	39.7	0.57	14.4	19.4	0.77	11.4	17.9	0.48
Philadelphia (PA)	14.7	24.2	26.5	41.1	0.71	23.2	34.5	0.80	2.8	5.6	0.66
Phoenix (AZ)	8.1	15.0	15.5	17.9	0.40	3.6	3.9	0.76	11.0	12.0	0.35
San Diego (CA)	12.7	14.5	24.0	30.7	0.61	7.7	8.7	1.10	11.4	15.9	0.63
Dallas (TX)	13.3	15.8	22.7	36.8	0.56	15.5	21.4	0.83	6.2	13.5	0.38
San Antonio (TX)	5.7	6.0	43.9	48.0	0.70	5.8	5.8	0.85	37.9	41.7	0.71
Las Vegas (NV)	10.2	10.9	13.4	19.3	0.48	7.5	9.3	1.02	3.7	7.3	0.33
500,000 to 999,999											
Detroit (MI)	20.0	25.3	53.4	66.2	0.74	51.8	62.9	0.77	1.3	3.0	0.60
San Jose (CA)	6.8	8.6	29.6	36.6	0.57	3.8	5.6	1.60	19.3	22.7	0.75
Honolulu (HI)	8.3	10.3	80.4	82.5	1.03	0.8	1.6	0.67	1.1	1.7	0.39
San Francisco (CA)	11.1	15.5	29.9	40.1	0.71	8.8	9.7	1.24	10.1	13.5	0.96
Indianapolis (IN)	13.9	13.4	16.5	17.9	0.58	15.8	16.6	0.69	0.7	0.7	0.18
Jacksonville (FL)	5.0	11.0	18.9	22.6	0.60	17.5	19.5	0.67	1.1	1.2	0.29
Columbus (OH)	12.1	14.0	14.3	15.5	0.47	14.3	14.4	0.59	0.0	0.3	0.12
Austin (TX)	11.3	11.8	24.9	28.8	0.61	9.8	10.8	1.07	14.7	16.6	0.54
Baltimore (MD)	10.9	15.7	27.7	41.5	0.60	26.5	38.6	0.60	0.5	1.6	0.94
Memphis (TN)	14.6	16.2	32.2	47.8	0.72	32.1	45.7	0.74	0.0	1.9	0.63
Charlotte (NC)	15.5	13.9	20.6	20.5	0.52	20.3	17.9	0.64	0.3	1.5	0.23
Milwaukee (WI)	8.6	16.3	17.5	33.4	0.61	11.8	21.2	0.57	4.4	9.6	0.80
Boston (MA)	8.4	13.0	25.9	31.7	0.63	20.5	24.1	0.95	4.8	6.0	0.42
Washington (DC)	18.5	24.1	67.8	72.4	1.00	64.4	66.4	1.11	2.6	5.0	0.63
Nashville (TN)	7.8	21.9	13.0	21.5	0.60	12.5	19.3	0.72	0.5	1.1	0.23
El Paso (TX)	6.4	9.0	63.8	76.3	0.93	2.2	2.2	0.71	60.7	72.1	0.94
Seattle (WA)	10.2	14.4	16.1	24.3	0.76	6.5	9.9	1.18	2.4	4.6	0.87
Denver (CO)	9.4	11.1	23.7	30.7	0.64	6.8	10.0	0.90	16.2	19.1	0.60
Fort Worth (TX)	12.4	16.8	19.4	25.0	0.46	10.7	12.0	0.59	8.1	11.9	0.40
Portland (OR)	11.7	16.6	7.6	10.4	0.42	3.1	3.3	0.50	2.0	2.4	0.35
Oklahoma City (OK)	10.8	11.3	11.0	12.9	0.37	7.3	7.6	0.49	1.0	2.4	0.24
350,000 to 499,999											
Tucson (AZ)	12.2	15.7	24.4	26.7	0.58	3.1	3.4	0.79	20.0	20.7	0.58
New Orleans (LA)	12.0	14.5	40.1	54.0	0.74	39.4	51.4	0.76	0.6	1.9	0.61
Cleveland (OH)	12.8	16.9	27.9	33.5	0.55	24.6	27.0	0.53	3.3	5.9	0.81
Long Beach (CA)	8.7	10.6	17.3	32.7	0.49	5.3	6.5	0.44	10.1	18.5	0.52
Albuquerque (NM)	11.3	11.4	42.0	39.7	0.79	2.4	2.0	0.65	37.9	36.3	0.91
Kansas City (MO)	11.7	14.9	15.5	16.9	0.40	12.9	12.1	0.39	2.3	3.8	0.55
Fresno (CA)	6.1	10.7	30.1	38.1	0.61	7.7	6.3	0.75	20.3	26.8	0.67
Virginia Beach (VA)	9.5	10.4	11.2	14.4	0.47	8.0	9.6	0.51	1.5	1.7	0.40
Atlanta (GA)	12.9	16.6	54.1	59.2	0.86	52.5	57.1	0.93	1.6	1.3	0.29
Sacramento (CA)	9.7	13.7	25.7	29.4	0.49	6.3	6.5	0.42	11.9	11.5	0.53
Oakland (CA)	7.0	10.1	44.6	54.5	0.71	25.3	25.9	0.73	10.7	16.2	0.74
Mesa (AZ)	8.9	10.2	8.0	19.7	0.74	1.0	2.6	1.04	6.0	14.8	0.75
Tulsa (OK)	11.1	14.0	13.8	21.4	0.65	9.1	10.9	0.70	0.4	1.6	0.22
Omaha (NE)	8.2	19.7	14.0	18.1	0.74	10.8	11.1	0.83	2.7	5.5	0.73
Minneapolis (MN)	10.5	15.7	8.4	15.7	0.42	3.2	6.2	0.34	2.1	3.4	0.45
Miami (FL)	12.1	17.6	64.7	81.4	0.92	19.9	27.2	1.22	44.5	53.6	0.81
Colorado Springs (CO)	7.1	12.5	14.3	18.6	0.75	4.9	5.5	0.83	8.4	10.6	0.88
250,000 to 349,999											
St. Louis (MO)	7.1	13.3	26.8	33.8	0.61	26.3	31.9	0.62	0.5	1.1	0.55
Wichita (KS)	5.9	10.7	7.8	17.9	0.68	4.7	9.2	0.81	2.8	5.3	0.55
Santa Ana (CA)	3.9	10.4	29.6	42.1	0.76	2.4	1.2	0.71	24.6	36.9	0.48
Pittsburgh (PA)	22.8	24.6	24.6	24.9	0.80	24.3	24.9	0.92	0.2	0.0	0.00
Arlington (TX)	8.1	14.8	12.9	30.5	0.85	6.7	12.0	0.88	6.2	12.6	0.69
Cincinnati (OH)	10.1	19.6	17.2	30.0	0.65	16.5	28.7	0.67	0.3	0.0	0.00
Anaheim (CA)	6.4	10.3	15.4	23.7	0.49	2.3	2.0	0.74	10.2	17.6	0.38
Toledo (OH)	13.9	21.0	21.2	26.2	0.86	17.0	19.1	0.81	4.1	6.8	1.24
Tampa (FL)	15.5	15.4	23.7	27.2	0.57	11.8	12.4	0.48	11.3	12.9	0.67
Buffalo (NY)	12.9	20.9	25.7	31.9	0.68	19.2	23.5	0.63	6.0	8.1	1.07
St. Paul (MN)	7.1	16.1	9.2	13.4	0.41	4.9	6.6	0.56	2.3	3.3	0.42
Corpus Christi (TX)	6.0	6.6	46.0	45.0	1.07	4.1	3.2	0.68	41.1	41.3	0.76
Newark (NJ)	3.0	11.9	42.0	64.3	0.83	31.3	36.8	0.69	10.7	27.5	0.93
Louisville (KY)	11.1	16.3	16.5	17.7	0.48	16.5	16.8	0.51	0.0	0.21	

Note: See Notes, tables 1.33 and 1.55.

[a] The officer-to-resident ratios used to measure minority representation were calculated by dividing the percent of an agency's full-time sworn personnel who were members of a racial or ethnic group by the percentage in the population served who belong to that group. In some instances, this resulted in a value greater than 1 (that is, the group was over-represented).

Source: U.S. Department of Justice, Bureau of Justice Statistics, *Police Departments in Large Cities, 1990-2000*, Special Report NCJ 175703 (Washington, DC: U.S. Department of Justice, May 2002), p. 11.

Table 1.59

Full-time personnel, sworn officers, officers assigned to respond to calls, officers per 100,000 residents, and percent change in full-time personnel in State law enforcement agencies

By agency, 2000

Agency	Full-time personnel Total	Sworn officers Number	Sworn officers Percent	Officers assigned to respond to calls Number	Officers assigned to respond to calls Percent	State population[a]	Officers per 100,000 residents[b]	Percent change Total	Percent change Sworn	Percent change Civilian
Alabama Department of Public Safety	1,201	628	52%	437	70%	4,447,100	14	1%	8%	-6%
Alaska State Troopers	409	232	57	155	67	626,932	37	-9	-20	12
Arizona Department of Public Safety	1,872	1,050	56	782	74	5,130,632	20	12	10	14
Arkansas State Police	913	559	61	330	59	2,673,400	21	28	7	86
California Highway Patrol	9,706	6,678	69	6,046	91	33,871,648	20	6	7	4
Colorado State Patrol	909	654	72	500	76	4,301,261	15	13	13	12
Connecticut State Police	1,692	1,135	67	585	52	3,405,565	33	9	11	6
Delaware State Police	827	580	70	280	48	783,600	74	9	7	12
Florida Highway Patrol	2,138	1,658	78	1,539	93	15,982,378	10	-3	-5	3
Georgia State Patrol	1,785	786	44	650	83	8,186,453	10	-38	-10	-50
Idaho State Police	510	292	57	258	88	1,293,953	23	94	52	207
Illinois State Police	3,792	2,089	55	939	45	12,419,293	17	6	5	7
Indiana State Police	1,941	1,278	66	570	45	6,080,485	21	3	6	-2
Iowa State Patrol	599	455	76	443	97	2,926,324	16	28	5	311
Kansas Highway Patrol	694	457	66	457	100	2,688,418	17	-8	-17	17
Kentucky State Police	1,670	937	56	481	51	4,041,769	23	-1	-5	5
Louisiana State Police	1,438	934	65	542	58	4,468,976	21	17	7	43
Maine State Police	495	325	66	225	69	1,274,923	25	4	-4	24
Maryland State Police	2,328	1,575	68	1,575	100	5,296,486	30	-4	-3	-6
Massachusetts State Police	2,590	2,221	86	2,221	100	6,349,097	35	-10	-13	15
Michigan State Police	3,189	2,102	66	1,310	62	9,938,444	21	2	-3	12
Minnesota State Patrol	791	548	69	469	86	4,919,479	11	13	13	11
Mississippi Highway Safety Patrol	1,031	532	52	332	62	2,844,658	19	32	-1	102
Missouri State Highway Patrol	2,170	1,080	50	753	70	5,595,211	21	4	8	0
Montana Highway Patrol	280	205	73	175	85	902,195	23	1	-3	15
Nebraska State Patrol	640	462	72	382	83	1,711,263	27	0	0	2
Nevada Highway Patrol	597	414	69	414	100	1,998,257	21	14	10	22
New Hampshire State Police	389	315	81	237	75	1,235,786	25	17	29	-16
New Jersey State Police	3,682	2,569	70	1,297	50	8,414,350	21	1	-5	18
New Mexico State Police	649	525	81	350	67	1,819,046	29	-22	21	-68
New York State Police	4,948	4,112	83	2,439	59	18,976,457	22	6	4	21
North Carolina State Highway Patrol	1,810	1,416	78	1,133	80	8,049,313	18	3	3	6
North Dakota Highway Patrol	193	126	65	92	73	642,200	20	4	5	2
Ohio State Highway Patrol	2,552	1,382	54	1,151	83	11,353,140	12	7	-1	17
Oklahoma Highway Patrol	1,420	782	55	555	71	3,450,654	23	6	3	10
Oregon State Police	1,409	826	59	450	54	3,421,399	24	13	0	39
Pennsylvania State Police	5,694	4,152	73	2,854	69	12,281,054	34	7	1	30
Rhode Island State Police	268	221	82	148	67	1,048,319	21	14	15	9
South Carolina Highway Patrol	1,220	977	80	977	100	4,012,012	24	11	10	15
South Dakota Highway Patrol	233	153	66	0	0	754,844	20	2	-1	8
Tennessee Department of Safety	1,715	899	52	800	89	5,689,283	16	10	17	3
Texas Department of Public Safety	7,025	3,119	44	1,880	60	20,851,820	15	4	9	1
Utah Highway Patrol	441	397	90	257	65	2,233,169	18	10	12	-6
Vermont State Police	513	304	59	239	79	608,827	50	15	5	35
Virginia State Police	2,511	1,883	75	1,464	78	7,078,515	27	12	13	7
Washington State Patrol	2,145	987	46	689	70	5,894,121	17	4	9	0
West Virginia State Police	1,044	681	65	502	74	1,808,344	38	15	14	15
Wisconsin State Patrol	665	508	76	340	67	5,363,675	9	-2	2	-14
Wyoming Highway Patrol	295	148	50	133	90	493,782	30	-2	-2	-2

Note: See Note, table 1.33. Personnel data are for the pay period that included June 30, 2000.

[a] Population data are based on U.S. Census Bureau figures for Apr. 1, 2000.
[b] Figures for number of officers per 100,000 residents are based on all full-time sworn personnel only.

Source: U.S. Department of Justice, Bureau of Justice Statistics, *Law Enforcement Management and Administrative Statistics, 2000: Data for Individual State and Local Agencies with 100 or More Officers*, NCJ 203350 (Washington, DC: U.S. Department of Justice, 2004), p. 241.

Table 1.60
Sex, race, and ethnicity of full-time sworn personnel in State law enforcement agencies

By agency, 2000[a]

Agency	Percent of full-time sworn personnel Female	Percent of full-time sworn personnel Male	White, non-Hispanic	Black, non-Hispanic	American Indian, Alaska Native	Asian	Hawaiian, Pacific Islander	Hispanic, any race	Other race
Alabama Department of Public Safety	3%	97%	72%	28%	0%	0%	0%	0%	0%
Alaska State Troopers	8	92	78	6	9	3	0	4	0
Arizona Department of Public Safety	8	92	82	1	2	1	0	14	0
Arkansas State Police	6	94	84	15	0	0	0	1	0
California Highway Patrol	9	91	76	4	0	3	0	15	0
Colorado State Patrol	5	95	89	1	1	1	0	8	0
Connecticut State Police	7	93	86	7	1	0	0	6	0
Delaware State Police	10	90	87	9	1	1	0	2	0
Florida Highway Patrol	10	90	75	14	0	1	0	10	0
Georgia State Patrol	3	97	84	15	0	0	0	1	0
Idaho State Police	5	95	95	0	1	0	0	4	0
Illinois State Police	9	91	80	13	0	1	0	6	0
Indiana State Police	5	95	91	7	0	0	0	1	0
Iowa State Patrol	3	97	97	1	0	0	0	2	0
Kansas Highway Patrol	3	97	95	3	1	0	0	2	0
Kentucky State Police	3	97	96	3	0	1	0	0	0
Louisiana State Police	3	97	85	14	1	0	0	0	0
Maine State Police	5	95	99	0	0	0	0	0	0
Maryland State Police	10	90	79	19	0	1	0	2	0
Massachusetts State Police	9	91	89	11	0	0	0	0	0
Michigan State Police	12	88	84	10	2	0	0	4	0
Minnesota State Patrol	8	92	97	1	1	0	0	1	0
Mississippi Highway Safety Patrol	2	99	69	31	0	0	0	0	0
Missouri State Highway Patrol	4	96	90	6	2	0	1	1	0
Montana Highway Patrol	7	93	99	0	1	0	0	0	0
Nebraska State Patrol	3	97	97	1	0	0	0	2	0
Nevada Highway Patrol	6	94	89	3	0	3	0	5	0
New Hampshire State Police	9	91	99	0	0	0	0	0	0
New Jersey State Police	3	97	85	8	1	1	0	5	0
New Mexico State Police	3	97	56	0	3	0	0	40	0
New York State Police	8	92	83	10	0	0	0	7	0
North Carolina State Highway Patrol	2	98	83	15	2	0	0	0	0
North Dakota Highway Patrol	6	94	98	0	1	0	0	2	0
Ohio State Highway Patrol	9	91	84	11	0	0	0	3	2
Oklahoma Highway Patrol	4	96	83	6	9	0	0	2	0
Oregon State Police	9	91	92	1	2	2	0	3	0
Pennsylvania State Police	4	96	88	9	0	1	0	2	0
Rhode Island State Police	8	92	95	5	0	0	0	0	0
South Carolina Highway Patrol	3	97	85	14	0	0	0	1	0
South Dakota Highway Patrol	1	99	97	1	2	0	0	0	0
Tennessee Department of Safety	5	95	89	10	0	0	0	0	1
Texas Department of Public Safety	5	95	66	11	1	0	0	22	0
Utah Highway Patrol	4	96	95	0	1	2	0	2	0
Vermont State Police	7	93	99	1	0	0	0	0	0
Virginia State Police	4	96	92	7	0	0	0	1	1
Washington State Patrol	7	93	89	4	2	3	0	2	0
West Virginia State Police	3	98	97	2	0	0	0	1	0
Wisconsin State Patrol	14	86	92	3	2	1	0	2	0
Wyoming Highway Patrol	2	98	99	1	0	0	0	0	0

Note: See Notes, tables 1.33 and 1.59.

[a]Percents may not add to 100 because of rounding.

Source: U.S. Department of Justice, Bureau of Justice Statistics, *Law Enforcement Management and Administrative Statistics, 2000: Data for Individual State and Local Agencies with 100 or More Officers*, NCJ 203350 (Washington, DC: U.S. Department of Justice, 2004), p. 243. Table adapted by SOURCEBOOK staff.

Table 1.61

Starting salaries in State law enforcement agencies

By agency, 2000

Agency	Chief or sheriff	Sergeant	Entry-level officer
Alabama Department of Public Safety	$72,659	$31,366	$25,776
Alaska State Troopers	70,200	62,944	45,696
Arizona Department of Public Safety	117,300	50,718	34,646
Arkansas State Police	79,520	28,289	23,443
California Highway Patrol	117,960	51,804	42,600
Colorado State Patrol	75,288	42,720	32,760
Connecticut State Police	107,682	55,322	31,243
Delaware State Police	106,664	54,375	36,546
Florida Highway Patrol	56,484	26,084	21,063
Georgia State Patrol	111,774	35,034	27,570
Idaho State Police	78,000	46,000	32,600
Illinois State Police	106,000	58,136	35,700
Indiana State Police	78,258	33,758	28,804
Iowa State Patrol	72,904	40,331	33,883
Kansas Highway Patrol	77,251	34,860	26,020
Kentucky State Police	91,000	41,000	29,000
Louisiana State Police	81,120	27,900	22,716
Maine State Police	70,200	31,125	25,600
Maryland State Police	116,000	41,661	33,682
Massachusetts State Police	109,937	50,789	37,552
Michigan State Police	114,000	50,718	29,670
Minnesota State Patrol	78,258	52,158	38,252
Mississippi Highway Safety Patrol	70,000	30,446	23,976
Missouri State Highway Patrol	50,472	38,628	27,792
Montana Highway Patrol	40,000	31,000	23,000
Nebraska State Patrol	68,865	36,608	28,488
Nevada Highway Patrol	54,413	36,393	33,387
New Hampshire State Police	57,725	40,591	30,410
New Jersey State Police	104,202	51,393	39,255
New Mexico State Police	68,865	43,785	30,000
New York State Police	127,000	60,850	33,921
North Carolina State Highway Patrol	92,211	50,329	25,844
North Dakota Highway Patrol	68,865	37,644	28,560
Ohio State Highway Patrol	60,611	38,821	32,328
Oklahoma Highway Patrol	79,214	49,206	25,000
Oregon State Police	74,160	45,204	35,160
Pennsylvania State Police	102,777	56,604	39,671
Rhode Island State Police	116,419	48,000	32,000
South Carolina Highway Patrol	56,963	31,625	21,359
South Dakota Highway Patrol	58,656	33,904	27,872
Tennessee Department of Safety	56,496	32,160	26,280
Texas Department of Public Safety	78,258	43,400	29,000
Utah Highway Patrol	64,750	37,627	25,730
Vermont State Police	67,529	42,953	31,109
Virginia State Police	118,730	40,406	30,329
Washington State Patrol	106,090	58,296	37,872
West Virginia State Police	70,000	40,124	28,556
Wisconsin State Patrol	87,500	49,800	33,450
Wyoming Highway Patrol	61,200	38,400	27,672

Note: See Note, table 1.33.

Source: U.S. Department of Justice, Bureau of Justice Statistics, *Law Enforcement Management and Administrative Statistics, 2000: Data for Individual State and Local Agencies with 100 or More Officers*, NCJ 203350 (Washington, DC: U.S. Department of Justice, 2004), p. 246. Table adapted by SOURCEBOOK staff.

Table 1.62

Operating expenditures of State law enforcement agencies

By agency, 2000

Agency	Total	Per employee	Per officer	Per resident
Alabama Department of Public Safety	$87,377,852	$72,754	$139,137	$20
Alaska State Troopers	54,674,300	133,678	235,665	87
Arizona Department of Public Safety	123,655,000	66,055	117,767	24
Arkansas State Police	58,486,323	64,060	104,627	22
California Highway Patrol	917,355,000	94,054	137,370	27
Colorado State Patrol	66,223,000	72,733	101,258	15
Connecticut State Police	116,645,912	68,940	102,772	34
Delaware State Police	67,895,100	81,214	117,061	87
Florida Highway Patrol	141,237,296	66,060	85,185	9
Georgia State Patrol	112,846,027	62,849	143,570	14
Idaho State Police	47,000,000	90,385	160,959	36
Illinois State Police	373,040,400	98,376	178,574	30
Indiana State Police	105,917,669	54,569	82,878	17
Iowa State Patrol	36,047,438	59,681	79,225	12
Kansas Highway Patrol	24,720,000	35,517	54,092	9
Kentucky State Police	125,000,000	74,850	133,404	31
Louisiana State Police	126,863,639	88,222	135,828	28
Maine State Police	41,000,000	82,828	126,154	32
Maryland State Police	250,681,088	107,681	159,163	47
Massachusetts State Police	223,577,991	86,324	100,665	35
Michigan State Police	268,719,900	84,265	127,840	27
Minnesota State Patrol	60,226,000	76,139	109,901	12
Mississippi Highway Safety Patrol	49,200,000	47,721	92,481	17
Missouri State Highway Patrol	151,951,352	68,370	140,696	27
Montana Highway Patrol	17,000,000	59,649	82,927	19
Nebraska State Patrol	33,000,000	51,563	71,429	19
Nevada Highway Patrol	51,465,459	86,207	124,313	26
New Hampshire State Police	31,000,000	75,887	95,827	25
New Jersey State Police	203,087,000	55,157	79,053	24
New Mexico State Police	40,000,000	61,633	76,190	22
New York State Police	395,060,000	79,044	96,075	21
North Carolina State Highway Patrol	134,000,000	74,033	94,633	17
North Dakota Highway Patrol	12,000,000	62,176	95,238	19
Ohio State Highway Patrol	202,000,000	79,154	146,165	18
Oklahoma Highway Patrol	86,148,417	59,971	110,164	25
Oregon State Police	190,000,000	134,847	230,024	56
Pennsylvania State Police	511,795,000	89,883	123,265	42
Rhode Island State Police	37,724,490	140,763	170,699	36
South Carolina Highway Patrol	55,910,979	45,829	57,227	14
South Dakota Highway Patrol	13,300,000	56,596	86,928	18
Tennessee Department of Safety	139,538,000	81,363	155,215	25
Texas Department of Public Safety	350,560,935	49,902	112,395	17
Utah Highway Patrol	34,800,000	78,202	87,657	16
Vermont State Police	30,000,000	54,348	87,464	49
Virginia State Police	198,236,160	75,389	105,277	28
Washington State Patrol	157,193,811	73,284	159,264	27
West Virginia State Police	73,526,273	69,528	107,968	41
Wisconsin State Patrol	49,113,600	73,634	96,680	9
Wyoming Highway Patrol	15,800,000	53,469	106,757	32

Note: See Note, table 1.33. Budget data are for the calendar or fiscal year that included June 30, 2000. Capital expenditures such as equipment purchases and construction costs are not included. Computation of per employee expenditure includes all agency employees with a weight of .5 assigned to part-time employees. Computation of per officer expenditure includes all sworn agency employees with a weight of .5 assigned to part-time officers. Computation of per resident expenditure is based on State population. In some cases, data are estimates provided by the agency.

Source: U.S. Department of Justice, Bureau of Justice Statistics, *Law Enforcement Management and Administrative Statistics, 2000: Data for Individual State and Local Agencies with 100 or More Officers*, NCJ 2u3350 (Washington, DC: U.S. Department of Justice, 2004), p. 245. Table adapted by SOURCEBOOK staff.

Table 1.63

Number and rate (per 1,000 residents and per 100 square miles) of full-time sworn personnel, service population, and reservation land area in the 20 largest tribally operated law enforcement agencies

United States, 2000

Agency name and location of administrative headquarters	Full-time sworn personnel Total	Per 1,000 residents	Per 100 square miles	Bureau of Indian Affairs service population, 1999[a]	Reservation land area (square miles)
Navajo Nation Department of Law Enforcement (AZ)	321	2	1	169,617	22,174
Tohono O'Odham Tribal Police Department (AZ)	76	4	2	16,981	4,453
Seminole Department of Law Enforcement (FL)	67	26	(b)	2,626	(b)
Gila River Indian Community Law Enforcement (AZ)	58	4	10	15,084	584
Oglala Sioux Tribal Police Department (SD)[c]	58	1	2	40,873	3,159
Cheyenne River Tribal Police Department (SD)	53	5	1	10,589	4,260
Salt River Tribal Police Department (AZ)	51	8	63	6,655	81
Choctaw Law Enforcement Services (MS)	38	5	152	6,949	25
Saginaw Chippewa Tribal Police Department (MI)	37	36	17	1,026	218
White Mountain Apache Tribal Police Department (AZ)	36	3	1	13,161	2,628
Rosebud Sioux Tribal Law Enforcement (SD)	35	2	3	19,440	1,388
Oneida Indian Nation Police (NY)	33	17	(b)	1,893	(b)
Warm Springs Tribal Police Department (OR)	33	9	3	3,837	1,011
Colorado River Tribal Police Department (AZ)	32	16	9	1,942	361
Assiniboine and Sioux (Ft. Peck) Tribal Police (MT)	31	4	1	6,933	3,289
Yakima Tribal Police Department (WA)[d]	31	2	1	15,968	2,153
Cherokee Police Department (NC)	30	4	36	7,456	83
Miccosukee Tribal Police Department (FL)	30	51	23	589	128
Turtle Mountain Band of Chippewa Indians Police Department (ND)	26	2	38	11,116	68
San Carlos Tribal Police Department (AZ)	25	2	1	10,834	2,911

Note: See Note, table 1.27. Land area data are from the U.S. Census Bureau 2000 Census and include reservation land only.

[a] The service population is the total number of enrolled tribal members and members from other tribes who live on or near the reservation and are eligible to use the tribe's Bureau of Indian Affairs-funded services. The service population probably underestimates the population served by tribally operated law enforcement agencies because many agencies serve non-Indian residents and other persons using roads, stores, casinos, and other public places on tribal land.
[b] Reservation land consists of less than 1 square mile.
[c] Personnel data for this agency are from the 1996 Census of State and Local Law Enforcement Agencies.
[d] Personnel data for this agency are from the 1999 Law Enforcement Management and Administrative Statistics (LEMAS) survey.

Source: U.S. Department of Justice, Bureau of Justice Statistics, *Tribal Law Enforcement, 2000*, Fact Sheet NCJ 197936 (Washington, DC: U.S. Department of Justice, January 2003), p. 2, Table 4. Table adapted by SOURCEBOOK staff.

Table 1.64

Mean number of full-time paid personnel of police departments in cities with populations of 10,000 or more

By population group, geographic division, and metro status, United States, 2003

	All police personnel[a]			Uniformed sworn personnel		
	Number of cities reporting	Mean	Per 1,000 population	Number of cities reporting	Mean	Per 1,000 population
Total, all cities	1,474	132	2.53	1,441	101	1.95
Population group						
Over 1,000,000	6	5,478	3.16	6	4,279	2.49
500,000 to 1,000,000	7	1,920	3.18	7	1,407	2.34
250,000 to 499,999	19	1,068	2.89	18	817	2.20
100,000 to 249,999	90	369	2.50	90	270	1.82
50,000 to 99,999	193	162	2.39	189	121	1.78
25,000 to 49,999	354	86	2.47	351	64	1.83
10,000 to 24,999	805	41	2.58	780	32	2.04
Geographic division						
New England	110	63	2.27	102	54	1.89
Mid-Atlantic	168	114	2.11	156	103	1.84
East North Central	289	87	2.34	289	69	1.84
West North Central	143	95	2.18	138	68	1.72
South Atlantic	215	142	3.50	214	106	2.67
East South Central	60	144	3.35	57	106	2.58
West South Central	168	150	2.70	169	118	2.00
Mountain	97	214	2.77	93	146	1.85
Pacific Coast	224	198	2.08	223	142	1.48
Metro status						
Central	269	423	2.75	266	323	2.10
Suburban	890	72	2.40	867	54	1.84
Independent	315	52	2.71	308	40	2.11

Note: These data were collected through a mail survey conducted by the International City/County Management Association in January 2003. Of the 3,215 municipalities surveyed, 1,645 returned the questionnaires for a response rate of 51%. The term "cities" refers to cities, villages, towns, townships, and boroughs. For definitions of terms, a list of States in regions, and detail of survey response rates, see Appendix 2.

[a]Includes uniformed and civilian/nonuniformed personnel.

Source: Evelina R. Moulder, "Police and Fire Personnel, Salaries, and Expenditures for 2003," in *The Municipal Year Book 2004* (Washington, DC: International City/County Management Association, 2004), p. 124 and p. 125, Table 3/3. Table adapted by SOURCEBOOK staff. Reprinted by permission.

Table 1.65

Mean and per capita police department personnel expenditures in cities with populations of 10,000 or more

By population group, geographic division, and metro status, United States, 2003

	Number of cities reporting	Expenditures for police department personnel[a]	
		Mean expenditure	Per capita expenditure
Total, all cities	993	$8,009,679	$154.89
Population group			
Over 1,000,000	4	331,809,762	244.76
500,000 to 1,000,000	2	150,608,191	250.45
250,000 to 499,999	10	68,476,377	188.65
100,000 to 249,999	64	25,153,769	166.35
50,000 to 99,999	130	11,257,358	163.04
25,000 to 49,999	249	5,081,479	146.35
10,000 to 24,999	534	2,437,841	153.86
Geographic division			
New England	45	3,872,015	167.39
Mid-Atlantic	94	11,600,310	166.56
East North Central	158	5,744,321	162.56
West North Central	125	5,505,043	120.24
South Atlantic	184	7,128,261	190.08
East South Central	46	7,809,448	143.17
West South Central	145	6,956,330	124.48
Mountain	72	15,112,004	144.35
Pacific Coast	124	10,690,662	160.52
Metro status			
Central	195	22,903,008	163.36
Suburban	562	5,147,802	161.24
Independent	236	2,518,900	132.78

Note: See Note, table 1.64. For definitions of terms, a list of States in regions, and detail of survey response rates, see Appendix 2.

[a]Personnel expenditures include salaries and wages for all department personnel (civilian and uniformed), as well as contributions for Social Security; employee retirement programs; and health, hospitalization, disability, and life insurance programs.

Source: Evelina R. Moulder, "Police and Fire Personnel, Salaries, and Expenditures for 2003," in *The Municipal Year Book 2004* (Washington, DC: International City/County Management Association, 2004), p. 130, Table 3/12. Table adapted by SOURCEBOOK staff. Reprinted by permission.

Table 1.66

Number and rate (per 1,000 inhabitants) of full-time law enforcement employees[a]

By geographic division and population group, on Oct. 31, 2002

(2002 estimated population)

Geographic region and division	Total (10,653 cities; population 182,456,027)	Group I (70 cities, 250,000 and over; population 52,879,728)	Group II (162 cities, 100,000 to 249,999; population 24,457,039)	Group III (389 cities, 50,000 to 99,999; population 26,808,264)	Group IV (760 cities, 25,000 to 49,999; population 26,374,112)	Group V (1,763 cities, 10,000 to 24,999; population 27,930,903)	Group VI (7,509 cities, under 10,000; population 24,005,981)
Total cities: 10,653 cities; population 182,456,027:							
Number of employees	558,892	205,573	61,739	62,203	61,343	68,513	99,521
Average number of employees per 1,000 inhabitants	3.1	3.9	2.5	2.3	2.3	2.5	4.1
Northeast: 2,325 cities; population 42,246,114:							
Number of employees	147,425	67,114	9,530	14,657	18,533	19,439	18,152
Average number of employees per 1,000 inhabitants	3.5	6.2	3.5	2.5	2.4	2.2	2.9
New England: 758 cities; population 12,313,029:							
Number of employees	32,668	2,771	4,785	5,904	6,782	7,061	5,365
Average number of employees per 1,000 inhabitants	2.7	4.6	3.6	2.4	2.3	2.2	2.9
Middle Atlantic: 1,567 cities; population 29,933,085:							
Number of employees	114,757	64,343	4,745	8,753	11,751	12,378	12,787
Average number of employees per 1,000 inhabitants	3.8	6.3	3.4	2.6	2.4	2.1	3.0
Midwest: 3,150 cities; population 44,086,006:							
Number of employees	123,219	39,035	10,372	14,069	16,067	19,597	24,079
Average number of employees per 1,000 inhabitants	2.8	4.2	2.4	2.1	2.1	2.3	3.2
East North Central: 1,991 cities; population 31,512,235:							
Number of employees	91,525	31,322	7,334	10,367	12,012	14,769	15,721
Average number of employees per 1,000 inhabitants	2.9	4.4	2.5	2.2	2.1	2.3	3.3
West North Central: 1,159 cities; population 12,573,771:							
Number of employees	31,694	7,713	3,038	3,702	4,055	4,828	8,358
Average number of employees per 1,000 inhabitants	2.5	3.5	2.2	1.8	2.0	2.2	3.1
South: 3,811 cities; population 51,582,556:							
Number of employees	179,869	51,682	24,250	19,352	17,038	22,440	45,107
Average number of employees per 1,000 inhabitants	3.5	3.4	2.9	2.8	2.8	3.1	5.8
South Atlantic: 1,660 cities; population 20,995,073:							
Number of employees	83,945	21,293	12,207	11,094	7,654	10,254	21,443
Average number of employees per 1,000 inhabitants	4.0	4.5	3.0	3.1	3.0	3.3	7.1
East South Central: 941 cities; population 8,764,850:							
Number of employees	32,425	6,860	4,348	2,045	3,551	5,480	10,141
Average number of employees per 1,000 inhabitants	3.7	3.4	3.5	3.3	2.9	3.1	5.2
West South Central: 1,210 cities; population 21,822,633:							
Number of employees	63,499	23,529	7,695	6,213	5,833	6,706	13,523
Average number of employees per 1,000 inhabitants	2.9	2.8	2.4	2.3	2.5	2.7	4.9
West: 1,367 cities; population 44,541,351:							
Number of employees	108,379	47,742	17,587	14,125	9,705	7,037	12,183
Average number of employees per 1,000 inhabitants	2.4	2.7	2.0	1.9	2.0	2.2	4.6
Mountain: 593 cities; population 13,392,422:							
Number of employees	35,833	14,733	5,979	3,552	2,968	2,915	5,686
Average number of employees per 1,000 inhabitants	2.7	2.8	2.2	2.1	2.3	2.5	4.3
Pacific: 774 cities; population 31,148,929:							
Number of employees	72,546	33,009	11,608	10,573	6,737	4,122	6,497
Average number of employees per 1,000 inhabitants	2.3	2.7	1.9	1.9	1.9	2.1	4.8
Suburban areas:[b] 6,528 agencies; population 108,747,307:							
Number of employees	418,093	X	X	X	X	X	X
Average number of employees per 1,000 inhabitants	3.8	X	X	X	X	X	X
County:[c] 3,328 agencies; population 88,784,510:							
Number of employees	398,610	X	X	X	X	X	X
Average number of employees per 1,000 inhabitants	4.5	X	X	X	X	X	X

Note: These data are collected annually by the FBI Uniform Crime Reporting Program. "Full-time law enforcement employees" includes both law enforcement officers and civilian employees. Law enforcement officers include all "full-time, sworn personnel with full arrest powers." This excludes persons performing guard or protection duties (e.g., school crossing guards) who are not paid from police funds. "Civilian employees" includes persons such as clerks, radio dispatchers, meter attendants, stenographers, and mechanics. Persons not paid from police funds are excluded. Employees on leave with pay also are excluded. (U.S. Department of Justice, Federal Bureau of Investigation, *Uniform Crime Reporting Handbook* (Washington, DC: USGPO, 1984), pp. 71, 72.) These data are for employees who were on the payroll on Oct. 31, 2002. For a list of States in geographic divisions, see Appendix 3.

[a]Includes civilians.
[b]Includes law enforcement agencies in cities with less than 50,000 inhabitants and county law enforcement agencies that are within a Metropolitan Statistical Area; excludes all metropolitan agencies associated with a central city. The agencies associated with suburban areas also will appear in other groups within this table.
[c]Includes both suburban and rural counties.

Source: U.S. Department of Justice, Federal Bureau of Investigation, *Crime in the United States, 2002* (Washington, DC: USGPO, 2003), p. 324.

Characteristics of the criminal justice systems

Table 1.67

Number and rate (per 1,000 inhabitants) of full-time law enforcement officers

By geographic division and population group, on Oct. 31, 2002

(2002 estimated population)

Geographic region and division	Total (10,653 cities; population 182,456,027)	Group I (70 cities, 250,000 and over; population 52,879,728)	Group II (162 cities, 100,000 to 249,999; population 24,457,039)	Group III (389 cities, 50,000 to 99,999; population 26,808,264)	Group IV (760 cities, 25,000 to 49,999; population 26,374,112)	Group V (1,763 cities, 10,000 to 24,999; population 27,930,903)	Group VI (7,509 cities, under 10,000; population 24,005,981)
Total cities: 10,653 cities; population 182,456,027:							
Number of officers	428,365	154,116	46,124	47,762	47,960	54,413	77,990
Average number of officers per 1,000 inhabitants	2.3	2.9	1.9	1.8	1.8	1.9	3.2
Northeast: 2,325 cities; population 42,246,114:							
Number of officers	115,849	48,746	7,814	12,278	15,479	16,305	15,227
Average number of officers per 1,000 inhabitants	2.7	4.5	2.8	2.1	2.0	1.8	2.5
New England: 758 cities; population 12,313,029:							
Number of officers	26,633	2,143	3,855	5,042	5,661	5,750	4,182
Average number of officers per 1,000 inhabitants	2.2	3.6	2.9	2.1	1.9	1.8	2.3
Middle Atlantic: 1,567 cities; population 29,933,085:							
Number of officers	89,216	46,603	3,959	7,236	9,818	10,555	11,045
Average number of officers per 1,000 inhabitants	3.0	4.6	2.8	2.2	2.0	1.8	2.5
Midwest: 3,150 cities; population 44,086,006:							
Number of officers	98,902	32,032	8,314	10,986	12,508	15,467	19,595
Average number of officers per 1,000 inhabitants	2.2	3.4	1.9	1.6	1.6	1.8	2.6
East North Central: 1,991 cities; population 31,512,235:							
Number of officers	74,325	26,552	5,930	8,079	9,365	11,664	12,735
Average number of officers per 1,000 inhabitants	2.4	3.7	2.0	1.7	1.7	1.8	2.7
West North Central: 1,159 cities; population 12,573,771:							
Number of officers	24,577	5,480	2,384	2,907	3,143	3,803	6,860
Average number of officers per 1,000 inhabitants	2.0	2.5	1.7	1.4	1.5	1.8	2.5
South: 3,811 cities; population 51,582,556:							
Number of officers	136,446	39,058	17,964	14,721	13,045	17,400	34,258
Average number of officers per 1,000 inhabitants	2.6	2.6	2.1	2.1	2.2	2.4	4.4
South Atlantic: 1,660 cities; population 20,995,073:							
Number of officers	63,780	15,791	9,093	8,399	5,907	8,012	16,578
Average number of officers per 1,000 inhabitants	3.0	3.3	2.3	2.3	2.3	2.6	5.5
East South Central: 941 cities; population 8,764,850:							
Number of officers	24,583	4,914	3,124	1,563	2,798	4,253	7,931
Average number of officers per 1,000 inhabitants	2.8	2.5	2.5	2.5	2.3	2.4	4.1
West South Central: 1,210 cities; population 21,822,633:							
Number of officers	48,083	18,353	5,747	4,759	4,340	5,135	9,749
Average number of officers per 1,000 inhabitants	2.2	2.2	1.8	1.8	1.9	2.1	3.5
West: 1,367 cities; population 44,541,351:							
Number of officers	77,168	34,280	12,032	9,777	6,928	5,241	8,910
Average number of officers per 1,000 inhabitants	1.7	2.0	1.3	1.3	1.4	1.7	3.3
Mountain: 593 cities; population 13,392,422:							
Number of officers	25,099	9,989	4,129	2,535	2,122	2,159	4,165
Average number of officers per 1,000 inhabitants	1.9	1.9	1.5	1.5	1.7	1.9	3.1
Pacific: 774 cities; population 31,148,929:							
Number of officers	52,069	24,291	7,903	7,242	4,806	3,082	4,745
Average number of officers per 1,000 inhabitants	1.7	2.0	1.3	1.3	1.3	1.5	3.5
Suburban areas:[a] 6,528 agencies; population 108,747,307:							
Number of officers	275,584	X	X	X	X	X	X
Average number of officers per 1,000 inhabitants	2.5	X	X	X	X	X	X
County:[b] 3,328 agencies; population 88,784,510:							
Number of officers	237,190	X	X	X	X	X	X
Average number of officers per 1,000 inhabitants	2.7	X	X	X	X	X	X

Note: See Note, table 1.66. For a list of States in geographic divisions, see Appendix 3.

Source: U.S. Department of Justice, Federal Bureau of Investigation, *Crime in the United States, 2002* (Washington, DC: USGPO, 2003), p. 325.

[a] Includes law enforcement agencies in cities with less than 50,000 inhabitants and county law enforcement agencies that are within a Metropolitan Statistical Area; excludes all metropolitan agencies associated with a central city. The agencies associated with suburban areas also will appear in other groups within this table.
[b] Includes both suburban and rural counties.

Table 1.68

Full-time law enforcement employees

By sex and population group, on Oct. 31, 2002

(2002 estimated population)

Population group	Total police employees Total	Total police employees Percent male	Total police employees Percent female	Police officers (sworn) Total	Police officers (sworn) Percent male	Police officers (sworn) Percent female	Civilian employees Total	Civilian employees Percent male	Civilian employees Percent female
Total agencies: 13,981 agencies; population 271,240,537	957,502	73.2%	26.8%	665,555	88.7%	11.3%	291,947	37.9%	62.1%
Total cities: 10,653 cities; population 182,456,027	558,892	75.1	24.9	428,365	88.7	11.3	130,527	30.2	69.8
Group I 70 cities, 250,000 and over; population 52,879,728	205,573	70.5	29.5	154,116	83.5	16.5	51,457	31.8	68.2
10 cities, 1,000,000 and over; population 24,628,265	112,183	69.6	30.4	83,925	82.5	17.5	28,258	31.4	68.6
22 cities, 500,000 to 999,999; population 14,767,287	52,626	72.6	27.4	40,101	84.0	16.0	12,525	36.1	63.9
38 cities, 250,000 to 499,999; population 13,430,176	40,764	70.4	29.6	30,090	85.6	14.4	10,674	27.8	72.2
Group II 162 cities, 100,000 to 249,999; population 24,457,039	61,739	73.2	26.8	46,124	89.0	11.0	15,615	26.4	73.6
Group III 389 cities, 50,000 to 99,999; population 26,808,264	62,203	76.3	23.7	47,762	91.3	8.7	14,441	26.9	73.1
Group IV 760 cities, 25,000 to 49,999; population 26,374,112	61,343	78.0	22.0	47,960	92.2	7.8	13,383	27.3	72.7
Group V 1,763 cities, 10,000 to 24,999; population 27,930,903	68,513	79.4	20.6	54,413	93.1	6.9	14,100	26.5	73.5
Group VI 7,509 cities, under 10,000; population 24,005,981	99,521	79.9	20.1	77,990	92.1	7.9	21,531	35.8	64.2
Suburban counties 964 agencies; population 57,536,474	268,044	69.8	30.2	158,104	86.9	13.1	109,940	45.3	54.7
Rural counties 2,364 agencies; population 31,248,036	130,566	72.1	27.9	79,086	92.1	7.9	51,480	41.5	58.5
Suburban areas[a] 6,528 agencies; population 108,747,307	418,093	73.3	26.7	275,584	89.2	10.8	142,509	42.5	57.5

Note: See Note, table 1.66.

Source: U.S. Department of Justice, Federal Bureau of Investigation, *Crime in the United States, 2002* (Washington, DC: USGPO, 2003), p. 328.

[a]Includes law enforcement agencies in cities with less than 50,000 inhabitants and county law enforcement agencies that are within a Metropolitan Statistical Area; excludes all metropolitan agencies associated with a central city. The agencies associated with suburban areas also will appear in other groups within this table.

Table 1.69

Entrance and maximum salaries, and mean number of years to reach maximum salary, for police officers in cities with populations of 10,000 or more

By population group, geographic division, and metro status, United States, as of Jan. 1, 2003

	\multicolumn{5}{c}{Entrance salary}	\multicolumn{5}{c}{Maximum salary}	\multicolumn{2}{c}{Number of years to reach maximum}
	Number of cities reporting	Mean	First quartile	Median	Third quartile	Number of cities reporting	Mean	First quartile	Median	Third quartile	Number of cities reporting	Mean
Total, all cities	1,458	$35,162	$29,348	$34,738	$39,776	1,419	$48,733	$40,662	$48,024	$56,043	1,195	7
Population group												
Over 1,000,000	6	37,991	35,064	36,552	38,896	6	55,317	47,894	55,556	59,341	4	9
500,000 to 1,000,000	7	38,763	33,037	37,608	40,763	6	64,746	57,444	59,138	72,988	5	8
250,000 to 499,999	20	40,270	34,860	38,658	41,000	20	54,714	51,025	52,140	59,055	18	9
100,000 to 249,999	94	39,448	31,528	38,680	44,078	92	55,554	47,093	56,260	60,848	80	8
50,000 to 99,999	187	38,317	32,256	37,585	43,218	183	52,371	44,408	52,800	59,574	158	7
25,000 to 49,999	357	36,069	30,330	35,859	39,978	347	49,633	42,185	48,540	56,114	292	7
10,000 to 24,999	787	33,305	27,804	32,993	38,206	765	46,301	38,100	45,905	53,560	638	7
Geographic division												
New England	108	35,803	32,954	35,960	38,439	106	44,853	40,442	44,110	47,975	100	6
Mid-Atlantic	167	36,801	31,732	36,492	40,320	165	59,598	49,837	58,878	68,775	166	6
East North Central	291	36,674	33,030	36,941	40,288	285	49,177	42,512	50,148	55,450	272	6
West North Central	140	32,517	27,629	32,706	37,106	137	44,671	37,740	45,799	52,856	114	7
South Atlantic	215	29,518	26,098	28,929	32,354	205	45,107	38,959	44,075	50,398	103	12
East South Central	58	26,289	23,678	25,250	28,232	54	36,497	29,652	34,526	39,560	42	10
West South Central	167	29,838	24,888	29,120	35,201	159	39,658	31,813	37,877	48,179	127	8
Mountain	95	33,878	30,296	34,200	38,400	93	47,753	43,128	46,980	55,152	73	9
Pacific Coast	217	45,880	38,847	45,144	50,000	215	57,976	51,295	58,092	63,050	198	5
Metro status												
Central	271	34,494	28,894	33,526	38,718	264	48,207	41,728	47,247	54,058	213	8
Suburban	876	37,367	31,902	37,135	41,496	852	52,296	45,236	52,168	58,625	734	6
Independent	311	29,533	25,184	28,644	33,998	303	39,174	33,690	38,635	44,432	248	8

Note: See Note, table 1.64. The "entrance salary" refers to the annual salary paid during the first 12 months of employment with the department as a sworn police officer (excluding uniform allowance, holiday pay, hazard pay, or other additional compensation). The "maximum salary" refers to the highest annual salary paid to uniformed personnel who do not hold any promotional rank (excluding uniform allowance, holiday pay, hazard pay, or any other additional compensation). The mean is calculated by dividing the total number of salaries into the total amount paid in salaries. The median is the salary that marks the point below which and above which 50% of all the salaries fall. When there is an even number of observations, the mean of the two middle observations is reported. The first quartile salary is the salary below which 25% of all salaries fall; the third quartile salary is the salary below which 75% of all salaries fall. For definitions of terms, a list of States in regions, and detail of survey response rates, see Appendix 2.

Source: Evelina R. Moulder, "Police and Fire Personnel, Salaries, and Expenditures for 2003," in *The Municipal Year Book 2004* (Washington, DC: International City/County Management Association, 2004), p. 126, Table 3/5. Reprinted by permission.

Table 1.70

Mean and median salaries of city chief law enforcement officials

By city population, region, city type, and form of government, United States, July-November 2003

	Number of cities	Salary levels Mean	Salary levels Median		Number of cities	Salary levels Mean	Salary levels Median
All cities, total	3,413	$68,212	$63,128	50,000 to 99,999, total	211	$101,873	$97,864
Region				*Region*			
Northeast	680	77,307	75,280	Northeast	29	103,564	99,119
North Central	1,148	62,587	59,608	North Central	58	90,246	91,953
South	1,081	59,779	54,720	South	66	92,284	91,312
West	504	86,840	79,151	West	58	123,565	130,179
City type				*City type*			
Central	308	96,500	92,407	Central	114	94,288	91,726
Suburban	1,893	73,900	70,928	Suburban	94	111,505	106,612
Independent	1,212	52,140	49,978	Independent	3	88,280	90,147
Form of government				*Form of government*			
Mayor-council	1,320	61,076	55,000	Mayor-council	58	90,134	86,217
Council-manager	1,910	72,847	67,535	Council-manager	149	106,417	100,000
Commission	44	62,763	58,124				
Town meeting	110	71,292	71,272	25,000 to 49,999, total	397	90,628	87,525
Representative town meeting	29	84,327	83,902	*Region*			
				Northeast	94	94,502	89,210
Over 1,000,000, total	3	139,764	135,593	North Central	123	83,828	84,662
City type				South	99	81,902	80,616
Central	3	139,764	135,593	West	81	107,124	104,541
				City type			
500,000 to 1,000,000, total	9	139,672	139,578	Central	81	83,165	80,163
				Suburban	252	96,295	93,186
Region				Independent	64	77,758	75,191
South	5	145,667	141,484	*Form of government*			
City type				Mayor-council	106	83,240	79,493
Central	9	139,672	139,578	Council-manager	277	93,039	89,924
				Town meeting	4	97,256	94,431
Form of government				Representative town meeting	9	97,185	93,891
Mayor-council	7	139,151	132,130				
				10,000 to 24,999, total	853	74,977	72,418
250,000 to 499,999, total	16	132,706	127,507	*Region*			
Region				Northeast	221	84,398	81,383
South	5	136,609	129,251	North Central	282	71,584	71,152
West	8	138,735	141,320	South	259	66,514	63,877
City type				West	91	86,703	82,056
Central	15	133,558	129,251	*City type*			
				Central	20	73,841	64,613
Form of government				Suburban	575	80,460	78,645
Mayor-council	6	136,442	141,393	Independent	258	62,847	63,074
Council-manager	10	130,464	124,587	*Form of government*			
				Mayor-council	271	70,055	68,000
100,000 to 249,999, total	96	115,457	112,033	Council-manager	516	76,811	73,191
Region				Commission	17	63,009	66,192
Northeast	11	116,223	106,584	Town meeting	39	86,369	84,574
North Central	18	99,018	101,317	Representative town meeting	10	89,668	93,737
South	33	106,967	107,641				
West	34	132,152	136,209	5,000 to 9,999, total	815	59,893	57,678
City type				*Region*			
Central	65	108,208	107,302	Northeast	177	69,823	62,858
Suburban	31	130,657	129,297	North Central	267	58,512	57,100
				South	255	50,467	49,428
Form of government				West	116	68,639	66,767
Mayor-council	28	102,074	100,331	*City type*			
Council-manager	65	121,661	118,292	Suburban	435	66,013	63,285
				Independent	380	52,887	51,982
				Form of government			
				Mayor-council	335	57,793	54,834
				Council-manager	428	60,866	59,053
				Commission	12	58,365	54,162
				Town meeting	37	68,689	63,704
				Representative town meeting	3	53,041	52,000

See notes at end of table.

Table 1.70

Mean and median salaries of city chief law enforcement officials

By city population, region, city type, and form of government, United States, July-November 2003--Continued

	Number of cities	Salary levels Mean	Salary levels Median
2,500 to 4,999, total	717	$48,022	$46,000
Region			
Northeast	118	55,491	50,300
North Central	283	47,624	46,616
South	246	42,836	41,874
West	70	55,266	52,192
City type			
Suburban	312	54,524	51,531
Independent	404	43,004	41,886
Form of government			
Mayor-council	379	46,893	44,200
Council-manager	300	49,019	46,729
Commission	10	45,541	38,105
Town meeting	25	54,003	50,923
Representative town meeting	3	49,326	48,339
Under 2,500, total	296	44,762	41,597
Region			
Northeast	28	55,693	47,112
North Central	113	42,237	40,000
South	111	41,327	40,055
West	44	52,957	46,826
City type			
Suburban	193	46,543	42,445
Independent	103	41,426	39,936
Form of government			
Mayor-council	129	43,913	40,000
Council-manager	161	45,586	43,260
Town meeting	5	38,629	35,443

Note: These data are from a survey of local government officials conducted by the International City/County Management Association beginning in July 2003. Of the 8,050 cities surveyed, 4,172 returned the questionnaires for a response rate of 52%. The mean salary level is calculated by dividing the total number of salaries into the total amount paid in salaries. The median salary level is the salary that marks the point below which and above which 50% of all salaries fall. When there is an even number of observations, the mean of the two middle observations is reported. Classifications having less than three cities reporting are excluded by the Source because meaningful statistics cannot be computed. Therefore, the number reporting in subcategories does not always add to the total reporting. The term "cities" refers to cities, villages, towns, townships, and boroughs. For definitions of terms, a list of States in regions, and detail of survey response rates, see Appendix 2.

Source: Evelina R. Moulder, "Salaries of Municipal Officials, 2003," in *The Municipal Year Book 2004* (Washington, DC: International City/County Management Association, 2004), pp. 81-101. Table adapted by SOURCEBOOK staff. Reprinted by permission.

Table 1.71

Mean and median salaries of county chief law enforcement officials

By county population, region, metro status, and form of government, United States, July-November 2003

	Number of counties	Mean	Median		Number of counties	Mean	Median
All counties, total	990	$60,592	$55,420	**50,000 to 99,999, total**	129	$69,936	$69,256
Region				*Region*			
Northeast	46	68,425	60,430	Northeast	8	74,878	69,225
North Central	420	54,186	50,000	North Central	43	71,568	71,712
South	353	63,972	60,447	South	65	68,701	68,490
West	171	67,240	60,000	West	13	67,669	65,100
County type				*County type*			
Metro	285	85,626	80,801	Metro	64	71,491	71,906
Nonmetro	705	50,471	48,481	Nonmetro	65	68,405	66,000
Form of government				*Form of government*			
Commission	616	50,346	47,611	Commission	61	64,224	64,865
Council-manager/administrator	193	82,571	75,000	Council-manager/administrator	36	75,869	74,802
Council-elected executive	181	72,024	68,273	Council-elected executive	32	74,150	73,040
Population over 1,000,000, total	11	141,025	125,443	**25,000 to 49,999, total**	201	59,270	59,295
Region				*Region*			
South	3	120,477	118,625	Northeast	11	45,064	38,583
West	4	182,917	169,315	North Central	85	56,850	54,997
				South	75	61,785	62,103
County type				West	30	65,047	62,666
Metro	11	141,025	125,443				
				County type			
Form of government				Metro	29	63,630	59,804
Council-manager/administrator	6	160,334	158,639	Nonmetro	172	58,534	57,431
Council-elected executive	3	114,629	120,284				
				Form of government			
				Commission	128	55,306	54,075
				Council-manager/administrator	42	68,107	65,546
500,000 to 1,000,000, total	27	106,717	107,414	Council-elected executive	31	63,661	61,388
Region							
Northeast	3	115,429	120,225	**10,000 to 24,999, total**	245	50,485	48,369
North Central	9	90,334	98,797	*Region*			
South	10	119,520	115,371	North Central	117	48,422	47,770
West	5	105,373	95,004	South	95	49,955	50,019
				West	31	59,825	57,000
County type							
Metro	27	106,717	107,414	*County type*			
				Metro	15	64,289	61,910
Form of government				Nonmetro	230	49,585	48,037
Commission	7	107,072	100,000				
Council-manager/administrator	12	113,304	111,621	*Form of government*			
Council-elected executive	8	96,526	104,876	Commission	182	48,004	46,829
				Council-manager/administrator	26	60,399	61,579
250,000 to 499,999, total	39	103,902	99,000	Council-elected executive	37	55,725	53,323
Region							
Northeast	5	92,943	85,113	**5,000 to 9,999, total**	126	40,769	38,477
North Central	10	95,516	97,448	*Region*			
South	14	109,570	107,420	North Central	70	38,196	37,636
West	10	109,834	102,816	South	29	42,223	38,249
				West	26	45,724	41,964
County type							
Metro	39	103,902	99,000	*County type*			
				Nonmetro	125	40,839	38,655
Form of government							
Commission	10	86,521	85,311	*Form of government*			
Council-manager/administrator	16	117,000	113,272	Commission	107	40,370	38,800
Council-elected executive	13	101,152	97,199	Council-manager/administrator	5	42,752	38,249
				Council-elected executive	14	43,110	37,920
100,000 to 249,999, total	114	84,460	80,737				
Region				**2,500 to 4,999, total**	59	35,229	32,508
Northeast	13	64,550	60,613				
North Central	35	81,434	77,937	*Region*			
South	43	88,751	88,858	North Central	35	33,228	32,028
West	23	92,298	83,460	South	11	33,304	31,419
				West	12	43,160	37,204
County type							
Metro	99	85,875	82,010	*County type*			
Nonmetro	15	75,121	74,877	Nonmetro	59	35,229	32,508
Form of government				*Form of government*			
Commission	26	72,267	73,830	Commission	57	35,290	32,508
Council-manager/administrator	47	89,848	90,114				
Council-elected executive	41	86,017	82,346				

See notes at end of table.

Table 1.71

Mean and median salaries of county chief law enforcement officials

By county population, region, metro status, and form of government, United States, July-November 2003--Continued

	Number of counties	Salary levels Mean	Salary levels Median
Under 2,500, total	39	$34,701	$34,000
Region			
North Central	14	34,879	32,912
South	8	29,897	29,160
West	17	36,815	34,940
County type			
Nonmetro	39	34,701	34,000
Form of government			
Commission	36	33,601	31,905
Council-manager/administrator	3	47,900	42,000

Note: These data are from a survey of local government officials conducted by the International City/County Management Association beginning in July 2003. Of the 3,040 counties surveyed, 1,116 returned the questionnaires for a response rate of 37%. Classifications having less than three counties reporting are excluded by the Source because meaningful statistics cannot be computed. Consequently, the number reporting in subcategories does not always add to the total reporting. The mean is calculated by dividing the total number of salaries into the total amount paid in salaries. The median is the salary that marks the point below which and above which 50% of all the salaries fall. When there is an even number of observations, the mean of the two middle observations is reported. For definitions of terms, a list of States in regions, and detail of survey response rates, see Appendix 2.

Source: Evelina R. Moulder, "Salaries of County Officials, 2003," in *The Municipal Year Book 2004* (Washington, DC: International City/County Management Association, 2004), pp. 104-122. Table adapted by SOURCEBOOK staff. Reprinted by permission.

Table 1.72

Federal agencies employing 100 or more full-time officers authorized to carry firearms and make arrests

June 2002

Agency	Number of full-time officers[a]
Immigration and Naturalization Service	19,101
Federal Bureau of Prisons	14,305
U.S. Customs Service	11,634
Federal Bureau of Investigation	11,248
U.S. Secret Service	4,256
Administrative Office of the United States Courts[b]	4,050
Drug Enforcement Administration	4,020
U.S. Postal Inspection Service	3,135
Internal Revenue Service, Criminal Investigation Division	2,855
U.S. Marshals Service	2,646
Bureau of Alcohol, Tobacco and Firearms	2,335
National Park Service[c]	2,139
Veterans Health Administration	1,605
U.S. Capitol Police	1,225
U.S. Fish and Wildlife Service, Division of Law Enforcement	772
General Services Administration, Federal Protective Service	744
U.S.D.A. Forest Service, Law Enforcement and Investigations	658
Bureau of Diplomatic Security, Diplomatic Security Service	592
U.S. Mint	375
Bureau of Indian Affairs	334
Amtrak	327
Pentagon Force Protection Agency	327
Bureau of Land Management	235
Environmental Protection Agency	220
Department of Energy, Transportation Safeguards Division	212
Tennessee Valley Authority	197
Bureau of Engraving and Printing	195
Food and Drug Administration	162
National Marine Fisheries Service	137
Library of Congress	127

Note: These data were provided by Federal agencies in response to a survey conducted by the U.S. Department of Justice, Bureau of Justice Statistics. The survey was conducted prior to the enactment of legislation creating the Department of Homeland Security. The data include all supervisory and nonsupervisory personnel with Federal arrest authority who were authorized (but not necessarily required) to carry firearms in the performance of their official duties. The data presented exclude law enforcement personnel in the U.S. Armed Forces.

[a]Excludes employees based in U.S. Territories or foreign countries.
[b]Includes all Federal probation officers employed in Federal judicial districts that allow officers to carry firearms.
[c]Includes 1,549 Park Rangers commissioned as law enforcement officers and 590 U.S. Park Police officers.

Source: U.S. Department of Justice, Bureau of Justice Statistics, *Federal Law Enforcement Officers, 2002*, Bulletin NCJ 199995 (Washington, DC: U.S. Department of Justice, August 2003), pp. 2, 4. Table adapted by SOURCEBOOK staff.

Table 1.73

Federal offices of inspector general employing full-time officers authorized to carry firearms and make arrests

June 2002

Agency	Number of full-time officers
Total	2,860
Department of Health and Human Services	436
Department of the Treasury, Tax Administration	358
Department of Defense	321
Social Security Administration	270
Department of Housing and Urban Development	211
Department of Agriculture	201
Department of Justice	141
Department of Labor	137
Department of Veterans Affairs	103
Department of Transportation	96
Department of Education	64
Department of the Treasury	60
General Services Administration	53
Environmental Protection Agency	51
National Aeronautics and Space Administration	50
Federal Emergency Management Agency	48
Department of the Interior	47
Department of Energy	46
Federal Deposit Insurance Corporation	38
Small Business Administration	35
Department of State	16
Department of Commerce	14
Office of Personnel Management	14
Nuclear Regulatory Commission	13
U.S. Railroad Retirement Board	12
Agency for International Development	10
Amtrak	10
Government Printing Office	8

Note: See Note, table 1.72. Offices of inspector general investigate criminal violations and prevent and detect fraud, waste, and abuse related to Federal programs, operations, and employees (Source, p. 6).

Source: U.S. Department of Justice, Bureau of Justice Statistics, *Federal Law Enforcement Officers, 2002*, Bulletin NCJ 199995 (Washington, DC: U.S. Department of Justice, August 2003), p. 6, Table 3.

Table 1.74

Federal officers authorized to carry firearms and make arrests in selected large agencies

By primary State of employment, June 2002

State	Immigration and Naturalization Service	U.S. Customs Service	Federal Bureau of Investigation	Drug Enforcement Administration	U.S. Postal Inspection Service	Internal Revenue Service	U.S. Marshals Service	Bureau of Alcohol, Tobacco and Firearms
United States, total	19,101	11,634	11,248	4,020	3,175	2,855	2,646	2,335
Alabama	12	45	121	24	30	30	53	6
Alaska	39	59	30	8	6	10	12	32
Arizona	2,387	630	213	122	30	44	61	52
Arkansas	22	5	61	15	8	14	29	12
California	4,568	1,842	1,307	514	385	342	194	185
Colorado	96	41	128	68	50	40	27	36
Connecticut	23	21	98	21	39	33	24	11
Delaware	8	8	0	5	4	9	8	10
District of Columbia	168	282	1,359	78	219	94	166	190
Florida	816	1,373	631	374	142	205	168	144
Georgia	207	246	232	94	20	187	100	100
Hawaii	174	130	87	12	5	25	17	6
Idaho	45	14	0	7	103	12	14	7
Illinois	274	267	488	122	114	141	79	116
Indiana	10	22	90	28	21	45	38	32
Iowa	23	1	0	12	13	10	23	8
Kansas	15	2	0	33	2	9	20	6
Kentucky	22	46	71	20	11	28	38	50
Louisiana	165	159	152	77	46	32	64	49
Maine	120	115	0	10	47	3	14	11
Maryland	77	108	199	42	81	52	33	54
Massachusetts	137	158	238	89	82	66	43	58
Michigan	264	374	221	93	56	82	55	84
Minnesota	120	98	112	16	53	36	28	20
Mississippi	17	24	67	16	4	26	29	22
Missouri	86	35	198	59	80	57	56	58
Montana	73	82	0	7	1	11	16	9
Nebraska	44	0	66	10	8	10	15	9
Nevada	53	18	102	30	10	40	31	20
New Hampshire	9	3	0	12	6	5	10	6
New Jersey	275	464	329	91	177	85	46	39
New Mexico	595	117	93	38	4	8	33	11
New York	1,158	1,204	1,240	350	549	260	210	107
North Carolina	40	57	111	30	31	49	58	82
North Dakota	45	84	0	6	0	6	13	6
Ohio	54	61	235	42	92	94	59	66
Oklahoma	10	18	120	24	9	29	43	22
Oregon	59	35	91	33	14	26	28	15
Pennsylvania	144	139	419	113	225	124	89	83
Rhode Island	15	5	0	11	7	9	12	9
South Carolina	66	65	67	27	9	19	36	32
South Dakota	7	1	0	5	1	6	18	6
Tennessee	39	57	153	36	51	39	53	50
Texas	5,898	2,355	838	549	197	231	217	179
Utah	30	9	164	20	7	18	18	11
Vermont	147	129	820	6	0	0	11	9
Virginia	119	228	136	499	47	58	130	109
Washington	309	379	15	79	53	38	42	39
West Virginia	5	1	146	13	9	17	34	30
Wisconsin	6	18	0	24	18	36	19	19
Wyoming	6	0	0	6	2	5	12	8
U.S. Territories, total	306	343	150	91	41	13	46	24
Puerto Rico	197	293	150	75	40	13	28	16
U.S. Virgin Islands	42	47	0	10	0	0	10	2
Guam	67	0	0	6	1	0	6	6
Other	0	3	0	0	0	0	2	0

Note: See Note, table 1.72.

Source: U.S. Department of Justice, Bureau of Justice Statistics, *Federal Law Enforcement Officers, 2002*, Bulletin NCJ 199995 (Washington, DC: U.S. Department of Justice, August 2003), Appendix table A.

Table 1.75

Characteristics of full-time Federal officers authorized to carry firearms and make arrests in agencies employing 500 or more full-time officers

By agency, June 2002[a]

Agency	Number of full-time officers[b]	Sex Male	Sex Female	Total minority	Black, non-Hispanic	Hispanic or Latino, any race	Asian/Pacific Islander	American Indian
Immigration and Naturalization Service	19,407	87.9%	12.1%	46.7%	5.0%	38.1%	2.7%	0.5%
Federal Bureau of Prisons	14,457	86.4	13.6	40.0	24.9	12.3	1.5	1.4
U.S. Customs Service	11,977	81.4	18.6	36.4	6.9	24.7	3.7	0.8
Federal Bureau of Investigation	11,398	82.0	18.0	16.8	6.1	7.3	3.0	0.4
U.S. Secret Service	4,266	90.3	9.7	20.3	11.9	5.6	1.9	0.8
Drug Enforcement Administration	4,111	91.4	8.6	17.7	7.9	7.3	2.0	0.5
U.S. Postal Inspection Service	3,175	82.3	17.7	37.2	23.2	9.4	4.2	0.4
Internal Revenue Service	2,868	72.0	28.0	22.1	9.8	7.1	4.4	0.9
U.S. Marshals Service	2,692	88.4	11.6	17.6	7.1	7.6	2.1	0.6
Bureau of Alcohol, Tobacco and Firearms	2,362	87.1	12.9	19.8	9.2	7.4	1.9	1.1
National Park Service	2,148	84.8	15.2	12.8	5.1	4.1	2.1	1.6
Ranger Activities Division	1,558	83.1	16.9	9.9	2.1	3.9	1.9	2.1
U.S. Park Police	590	89.3	10.7	20.7	13.1	4.7	2.7	0.2
Veterans Health Administration	1,649	91.4	8.6	40.8	28.3	9.8	1.3	1.2
U.S. Capitol Police	1,225	81.2	18.8	33.0	29.0	2.8	1.0	0.2
U.S. Fish and Wildlife Service	728	88.9	11.1	12.0	1.8	6.0	0.4	3.6
General Services Administration, Federal Protective Service	709	90.7	9.3	40.3	30.4	8.5	1.1	0.4
U.S.D.A. Forest Service	611	78.1	21.9	18.8	3.6	6.5	1.5	7.1
Bureau of Diplomatic Security	592	90.4	9.6	16.7	7.3	4.9	3.7	0.8

Note: See Note, table 1.72 Data on sex and race/ethnicity of officers were not provided by the Administrative Office of the United States Courts.

[a] Detail may not add to total because of rounding.
[b] Includes employees in U.S. Territories.

Source: U.S. Department of Justice, Bureau of Justice Statistics, *Federal Law Enforcement Officers, 2002*, Bulletin NCJ 199995 (Washington, DC: U.S. Department of Justice, August 2003), p. 7.

Table 1.76

Budget and staff of the Drug Enforcement Administration

Fiscal years 1972-2005

Fiscal year	Annual budget (in millions of dollars)	Staff positions Total	Special agents	Support staff
1972	$65.2	2,775	1,470	1,305
1973	74.9	2,898	1,470	1,428
1974	116.2	4,075	2,231	1,844
1975	140.9	4,286	2,135	2,151
1976	161.1	4,337	2,141	2,196
1977	172.8	4,439	2,141	2,298
1978	192.3	4,440	2,054	2,386
1979	200.4	4,288	1,984	2,304
1980	206.7	4,149	1,941	2,208
1981	219.5	4,167	1,964	2,203
1982	244.1	4,013	1,896	2,117
1983	283.9	4,013	1,896	2,117
1984	326.6	4,093	1,963	2,130
1985	362.4	4,936	2,234	2,702
1986	393.5	4,925	2,440	2,485
1987	773.6	5,710	2,879	2,831
1988	522.9	5,740	2,899	2,841
1989	597.9	5,926	2,969	2,957
1990	653.5	6,274	3,191	3,083
1991	875.0	7,096	3,615	3,481
1992	910.0	7,264	3,696	3,568
1993	921.0	7,266	3,518	3,748
1994	970.0	7,049	3,611	3,438
1995	1,001.0	7,389	3,889	3,500
1996	1,050.0	7,369	3,708	3,661
1997	1,238.0	7,872	3,969	3,903
1998	1,384.0	8,452	4,214	4,238
1999	1,477.0	9,046	4,527	4,519
2000	1,586.6	9,141	4,566	4,575
2001	1,697.4	9,209	4,601	4,608
2002	1,799.5	9,388	4,625	4,763
2003	1,891.9	9,725	4,841	4,884
2004[a]	2,014.9	10,565	5,194	5,371
2005[b]	2,150.9	10,907	5,305	5,602

Note: Some data have been revised by the Source and may differ from previous editions of SOURCEBOOK.

[a] Enacted level.
[b] President's budget.

Source: U.S. Department of Justice, Drug Enforcement Administration [Online]. Available: http://www.usdoj.gov/dea/agency/staffing.htm [Sept. 30, 2004]. Table adapted by SOURCEBOOK staff.

Table 1.77

Workload of the U.S. Marshals Service

By type of activity, fiscal years 1985-2000

	Type of activity							
Fiscal year	Prisoners received	Prisoner productions	Prisoners in custody	Inter-district prisoner trips	Felony warrants Received	Felony warrants Closed	Process served	Seized properties received
1985	82,245	235,471	6,428	8,972	9,471	NA	318,242	5,279
1986	88,502	190,885	7,329	9,539	10,494	NA	280,745	8,973
1987	81,069	213,336	7,262	9,644	10,778	NA	278,125	13,948
1988	82,144	226,997	8,857	9,935	12,209	NA	255,222	21,809
1989	87,784	275,172	11,740	11,593	20,019	NA	302,882	25,363
1990	88,285	316,371	13,390	12,395	18,362	NA	319,863	41,708
1991	90,825	351,720	16,233	12,196	18,543	NA	316,185	38,644
1992	95,806	388,782	19,474	14,153	20,336	NA	262,807	37,498
1993	94,373	387,117	19,641	14,880	19,950	NA	233,288	38,737
1994	92,372	354,881	19,297	9,310	18,286	NA	210,427	35,983
1995	94,498	347,741	20,652	8,661	19,198	18,598	168,131	30,211
1996	98,935	377,649	23,228	9,290	18,742	18,466	214,434	29,122
1997	108,546	403,500	25,263	9,149	23,578	21,224	191,110	43,248
1998	122,774	451,752	28,692	NA	24,523	23,171	204,961	44,207
1999	129,344	486,223	32,119	NA	25,818	25,701	241,160	50,173
2000	138,464	516,854	34,528	NA	27,923	25,894	255,630	48,970

Note: The U.S. Marshals Service (USMS) is a law enforcement agency performing duties for the Executive Branch of the Federal Government. The agency executes all warrants issued by the Federal courts, conducts fugitive investigations, and maintains custody of all Federal pretrial detainees. In addition, the USMS is responsible for prisoner processing and detention, transportation and production of prisoners, protection of Federal judiciary, Federal witness security, the execution of court orders, and management of related Federal Government seizures. Further responsibilities include escorting missile convoys, suppressing prisoner disturbances in Federal prisons, and arresting dangerous fugitives.

"Prisoners received" is the number of prisoners taken into USMS custody. "Prisoner productions" is the number of prisoners presented for appearance at all judicial proceedings, meetings with attorneys, transported for medical care, transferred between sub-offices, and transferred between detention facilities. "Prisoners in custody" is the number of prisoners remanded into USMS custody at month end, averaged over a 12-month period. "Inter-district prisoner trips" is the total number of trips assigned to each district. These trips include movements by commercial airlines, chartered aircraft, and various modes of ground transportation. "Felony warrants received" includes felony warrants issued by Federal courts for escape, bond default, probation or parole violations, DEA fugitive warrants, and warrants generated by other Federal agencies without arrest powers. "Felony warrants closed" is the number of USMS arrests plus the number of arrests by other agencies, and dismissals in felony cases. "Process served" is the number of Federal or private court orders attempted or successfully served by the USMS in person or by mail. "Seized properties received" is the number of properties that were administratively seized by the USMS or seized by other Federal agencies and referred to the USMS for custody and disposal, as well as properties seized pursuant to judicial forfeiture actions. Judicial forfeiture actions are those in which the property is seized, held for custody, and disposed of by the USMS. These properties include real property, personal property, vehicles, jewelry, and cash, etc. (Source *2000*, pp. 107, 108.)

Source: U.S. Department of Justice, U.S. Marshals Service, *The FY 1996 Report to the U.S. Marshals* (Washington, DC: U.S. Department of Justice, 1997), pp. 115-124; and U.S. Department of Justice, U.S. Marshals Service, *FY 2000 Annual Report of the United States Marshals Service* (Washington, DC: U.S. Department of Justice, 2001), pp. 9, 124, 125. Table constructed by SOURCEBOOK staff.

Table 1.78
Budget and staff of the U.S. Marshals Service

Fiscal years 1954-2000

Fiscal year	Annual budget (in millions of dollars)	Staff positions
1954	$6.6	963
1955	6.8	996
1956	7.8	1,026
1957	8.0	1,014
1958	6.9	1,036
1959	9.7	1,034
1960	9.4	1,003
1961	10.2	992
1962	10.5	1,031
1963	11.6	1,053
1964	11.9	1,066
1965	12.7	1,078
1966	13.0	1,088
1967	13.8	1,095
1968	14.8	1,104
1969	16.3	1,130
1970	20.5	1,248
1971	26.8	1,917
1972	35.1	1,935
1973	38.1	1,967
1974	46.0	2,002
1975	53.3	2,049
1976	56.8	2,076
1977	63.8	2,136
1978	74.1	2,245
1979	77.9	2,328
1980	96.6	2,772
1981	103.6	2,177
1982	106.6	2,068
1983	113.6	2,132
1984	123.3	2,132
1985	139.9	2,579
1986	146.2	2,624
1987	164.4	2,724
1988	186.7	2,864
1989	205.1	2,947
1990	246.3	3,250
1991	291.3	3,515
1992	328.2	3,686
1993	338.9	3,682
1994	341.0	3,645
1995	396.6	3,854
1996	448.2	3,990
1997	483.5	4,165
1998	498.1	4,269
1999	501.9	4,210
2000	540.5	4,070

Note: See Note, table 1.77.

Source: U.S. Department of Justice, U.S. Marshals Service, *The FY 1996 Report to the U.S. Marshals* (Washington, DC: U.S. Department of Justice, 1997), pp. 109, 110; U.S. Department of Justice, U.S. Marshals Service, *FY 2000 Annual Report of the United States Marshals Service* (Washington, DC: U.S. Department of Justice, 2001), p. 126; and data provided by the U.S. Department of Justice, U.S. Marshals Service. Table constructed by SOURCEBOOK staff.

Table 1.79
Personnel and court-related work hours of U.S. attorneys' offices

United States, 1989-2002

	Personnel[a]		Court-related attorney work hours[b] (in thousands)
	Attorneys	Support staff	
1989	2,632	3,088	947
1990	3,005	3,609	1,045
1991	3,689	4,018	1,175
1992	4,178	4,474	1,241
1993	4,155	4,444	1,285
1994	4,064	4,620	1,127
1995	4,365	4,476	1,098
1996	4,530	4,553	1,083
1997	4,536	4,449	1,048
1998	4,686	4,674	1,026
1999	4,872	5,089	997
2000	4,938	5,239	927
2001	5,152	5,250	916
2002	5,304	5,384	930

Note: The U.S. attorney is the highest ranking law enforcement official in each of the 94 Federal judicial districts. Each U.S. attorney, under the direction of the U.S. Attorney General, is responsible for establishing law enforcement priorities, and for carrying out the prosecution and litigation activities within their respective districts. Each U.S. attorney also is the chief litigator representing the United States in civil judicial proceedings in the district. U.S. attorneys direct and supervise the work of the assistant U.S. attorneys and staff of the district's offices.

[a]These data represent full-time equivalent employees.
[b]Total hours U.S. attorneys devoted to court-related activities including criminal and civil trials, special hearings, grand jury proceedings, witness preparation, and court travel time.

Source: U.S. Department of Justice, Executive Office for United States Attorneys, *United States Attorneys' Annual Statistical Report: Fiscal Year 1998* (Washington, DC: USGPO, 1999), pp. 2, 3; and U.S. Department of Justice, Executive Office for United States Attorneys, *United States Attorneys' Annual Statistical Report: Fiscal Year 2002* (Washington, DC: U.S. Department of Justice, 2004), pp. 3, 4. Table adapted by SOURCEBOOK staff.

Table 1.80
Annual salaries of Federal judges

By judicial office, as of Jan. 1, 2004

Judicial office	Annual salary
Chief Justice of the United States	$203,000
Associate Justices of the Supreme Court of the United States	194,300
United States Circuit Judges	167,600
United States District Judges	158,100
Judges, United States Court of International Trade	158,100
Judges, United States Court of Federal Claims	158,100
United States Bankruptcy Judges	145,452
United States Magistrate Judges (full-time)	145,452

Source: Table provided to SOURCEBOOK staff by the Administrative Office of the United States Courts.

Table 1.81

Characteristics of Presidential appointees to U.S. Courts of Appeals judgeships

By Presidential administration, 1963-2002[a]

	President Johnson's appointees 1963-68[b] (N=40)	President Nixon's appointees 1969-74 (N=45)	President Ford's appointees 1974-76 (N=12)	President Carter's appointees 1977-80 (N=56)	President Reagan's appointees 1981-88 (N=78)	President George H.W. Bush's appointees 1989-92 (N=37)	President Clinton's appointees 1993-2000 (N=61)	President George W. Bush's appointees 2001-2002 (N=16)
Sex								
Male	97.5%	100%	100%	80.4%	94.9%	81.1%	67.2%	81.2%
Female	2.5	0	0	19.6	5.1	18.9	32.8	18.8
Race, ethnicity								
White	95.0	97.8	100	78.6	97.4	89.2	73.8	81.2
Black	5.0	0	0	16.1	1.3	5.4	13.1	18.8
Hispanic	0	0	0	3.6	1.3	5.4	11.5	0
Asian	0	2.2	0	1.8	0	0	1.6	0
Education, undergraduate								
Public-supported	32.5	40.0	50.0	30.4	24.4	29.7	44.3	43.8
Private (not Ivy League)	40.0	35.6	41.7	51.8	51.3	59.5	34.4	37.5
Ivy League	17.5	20.0	8.3	17.9	24.4	10.8	21.3	18.8
None indicated	10.0	4.4	0	0	0	0	0	0
Education, law school								
Public-supported	40.0	37.8	50.0	39.3	41.0	32.4	39.3	50.0
Private (not Ivy League)	32.5	26.7	25.0	19.6	35.9	37.8	31.1	25.0
Ivy League	27.5	35.6	25.0	41.1	23.1	29.7	29.5	25.0
Occupation at nomination or appointment								
Politics or government	10.0	4.4	8.3	5.4	6.4	10.8	6.6	6.2
Judiciary	57.5	53.3	75.0	46.4	55.1	59.5	52.5	50.0
Law firm, large	5.0	4.4	8.3	10.7	14.1	16.2	18.0	6.2
Law firm, medium	17.5	22.2	8.3	16.1	9.0	10.8	13.1	12.5
Law firm, small	7.5	6.7	0	5.4	1.3	0	1.6	6.2
Professor of law	2.5	2.2	0	14.3	12.8	2.7	8.2	12.5
Other	0	6.7	0	1.8	1.3	0	0	6.2
Occupational experience								
Judicial	65.0	57.8	75.0	53.6	60.3	62.2	59.0	68.8
Prosecutorial	47.5	46.7	25.0	30.4	28.2	29.7	37.7	25.0
Other	20.0	17.8	25.0	39.3	34.6	32.4	29.5	25.0
Political party								
Democrat	95.0	6.7	8.3	82.1	0	2.7	85.2	12.5
Republican	5.0	93.3	91.7	7.1	96.2	89.2	6.6	81.2
Independent or none	0	0	0	10.7	2.6	8.1	8.2	6.2
Other	0	0	0	0	1.3	0	0	0
American Bar Association rating								
Exceptionally well/well qualified	75.0	73.3	58.3	75.0	59.0	64.9	78.7	68.8
Qualified	20.0	26.7	33.3	25.0	41.0	35.1	21.3	31.2
Not qualified	2.5	0	8.3	0	0	0	0	0

Note: These data were compiled from a variety of sources. Primarily used were questionnaires completed by judicial nominees for the U.S. Senate Judiciary Committee, transcripts of the confirmation hearings conducted by the Committee, and personal interviews. In addition, an investigation was made of various biographical directories including *The American Bench* (Sacramento: R.B. Forster), *Martindale-Hubbell Law Directory* (Summit, NJ: Martindale-Hubbell, Inc.), national and regional editions of *Who's Who*, *The Judicial Staff Directory*, and local newspaper articles.

Law firms are categorized according to the number of partners/associates: 25 or more associates for a large firm, 5 to 24 associates for a medium firm, and 4 or less for a small firm. Percent subtotals for occupational experience sum to more than 100 because some appointees have had both judicial and prosecutorial experience.

The American Bar Association's (ABA) ratings are assigned to candidates after investigation and evaluation by the ABA's Standing Committee on Federal Judiciary, which considers prospective Federal judicial nominees only upon referral by the U.S. Attorney General or at the request of the U.S. Senate. The ABA's Committee evaluation is directed primarily to professional qualifications--competence, integrity, and judicial temperament. Factors including intellectual capacity, judgment, writing and analytical ability, industry, knowledge of the law, and professional experience are assessed. Prior to President George H.W. Bush's administration, the ABA's Standing Committee on Federal Judiciary utilized four ratings: exceptionally well qualified, well qualified, qualified, and not qualified. Starting with that administration, the ABA Standing Committee on Federal Judiciary dropped its "exceptionally well qualified" rating and "well qualified" became the highest rating. Nominees who previously would have been rated "exceptionally well qualified" and nominees who would have been rated "well qualified" now receive the same rating. The "exceptionally well qualified" and "well qualified" categories have been combined for all administrations' appointees, and therefore figures prior to President George H.W. Bush's administration may differ from previous editions of SOURCEBOOK. Some data have been revised by the Source and may differ from previous editions of SOURCEBOOK.

[a]Percents may not add to 100 because of rounding.
[b]No ABA rating was requested for one Johnson appointee.

Source: Sheldon Goldman, "Reagan's Judicial Legacy: Completing the Puzzle and Summing Up," *Judicature* 72 (April-May 1989), pp. 323, 324, Table 3; and Sheldon Goldman et al., "W. Bush Remaking the Judiciary: Like Father Like Son?," *Judicature* 86 (May-June 2003), p. 308. Table adapted by SOURCEBOOK staff. Reprinted by permission.

Table 1.82

Characteristics of Presidential appointees to U.S. District Court judgeships

By Presidential administration, 1963-2002[a]

	President Johnson's appointees 1963-68 (N=122)	President Nixon's appointees 1969-74 (N=179)	President Ford's appointees 1974-76 (N=52)	President Carter's appointees 1977-80 (N=202)	President Reagan's appointees 1981-88 (N=290)	President George H.W. Bush's appointees 1989-92 (N=148)	President Clinton's appointees 1993-2000 (N=305)	President George W. Bush's appointees 2001-2002 (N=83)
Sex								
Male	98.4%	99.4%	98.1%	85.6%	91.7%	80.4%	71.5%	79.5%
Female	1.6	0.6	1.9	14.4	8.3	19.6	28.5	20.5
Race, ethnicity								
White	93.4	95.5	88.5	78.7	92.4	89.2	75.1	85.5
Black	4.1	3.4	5.8	13.9	2.1	6.8	17.4	7.2
Hispanic	2.5	1.1	1.9	6.9	4.8	4.0	5.9	7.2
Asian	0	0	3.9	0.5	0.7	0	1.3	0
Native American	NA	NA	NA	0	0	0	0.3	0
Education, undergraduate								
Public-supported	38.5	41.3	48.1	55.9	37.9	46.0	44.3	42.2
Private (not Ivy League)	31.1	38.5	34.6	34.2	48.6	39.9	42.0	51.8
Ivy League	16.4	19.6	17.3	9.9	13.4	14.2	13.8	6.0
None indicated	13.9	0.6	0	0	0	0	0	0
Education, law school								
Public-supported	40.2	41.9	44.2	52.0	44.8	52.7	39.7	53.0
Private (not Ivy League)	36.9	36.9	38.5	31.2	43.4	33.1	40.7	39.8
Ivy League	21.3	21.2	17.3	16.8	11.7	14.2	19.7	7.2
Occupation at nomination or appointment								
Politics or government	21.3	10.6	21.2	5.0	13.4	10.8	11.5	8.4
Judiciary	31.1	28.5	34.6	44.6	36.9	41.9	48.2	48.2
Law firm, large	2.4	11.2	9.6	13.9	17.9	25.7	16.1	24.1
Law firm, medium	18.9	27.9	25.0	19.3	19.0	14.9	13.4	9.6
Law firm, small	23.0	19.0	9.6	13.9	10.0	4.7	8.2	4.8
Professor of law	3.3	2.8	0	3.0	2.1	0.7	1.6	2.4
Other	0	0	0	0.5	0.7	1.4	1.0	2.4
Occupational experience								
Judicial	34.4	35.2	42.3	54.0	46.2	46.6	52.1	53.0
Prosecutorial	45.9	41.9	50.0	38.1	44.1	39.2	41.3	50.6
Other	33.6	36.3	30.8	31.2	28.6	31.8	28.9	22.9
Political party								
Democrat	94.3	7.3	21.2	91.1	4.8	6.1	87.5	7.2
Republican	5.7	92.7	78.8	4.5	91.7	88.5	6.2	83.1
Independent or none	0	0	0	4.5	3.4	5.4	5.9	9.6
Other	NA	NA	NA	0	0	0	0.3	0
American Bar Association rating								
Exceptionally well/well qualified	48.4	45.3	46.1	51.0	53.5	57.4	59.0	69.9
Qualified	49.2	54.8	53.8	47.5	46.6	42.6	40.0	28.9
Not qualified	2.5	0	0	1.5	0	0	1.0	1.2

Note: See Note, table 1.81. Percent subtotals for occupational experience sum to more than 100 because some appointees have had both judicial and prosecutorial experience. Some data have been revised by the Source and may differ from previous editions of SOURCEBOOK.

[a]Percents may not add to 100 because of rounding.

Source: Sheldon Goldman, "Reagan's Judicial Legacy: Completing the Puzzle and Summing Up," *Judicature* 72 (April-May 1989), pp. 320, 321, Table 1; and Sheldon Goldman et al., "W. Bush Remaking the Judiciary: Like Father Like Son?," *Judicature* 86 (May-June 2003), p. 304. Table adapted by SOURCEBOOK staff. Reprinted by permission.

Table 1.83
Felony criminal cases filed per judgeship in U.S. District Courts

By circuit and district, 1983-2003

Circuit and district	1983	1984	1985	1986	1987	1988	1989	1990	1991	1992	1993	1994	1995	1996	1997	1998	1999	2000	2001	2002	2003
First Circuit																					
Maine	41	47	42	63	70	60	55	55	52	46	40	35	38	48	44	45	53	57	55	66	62
Massachusetts	29	33	29	32	31	25	29	23	23	24	26	22	28	28	27	28	32	32	30	38	31
New Hampshire	22	12	14	20	18	18	22	49	24	26	26	36	36	45	49	47	50	49	45	58	71
Rhode Island	34	33	27	22	25	26	26	34	40	50	30	34	34	32	32	40	41	44	38	39	37
Puerto Rico	36	42	52	76	79	82	59	59	63	49	56	52	50	53	41	32	54	44	59	55	42
Second Circuit																					
Connecticut	45	39	28	32	32	36	36	37	35	27	35	26	23	26	27	27	29	27	27	36	37
New York:																					
North	40	35	32	36	43	38	43	49	55	47	47	52	51	46	50	60	56	70	63	67	69
East	45	47	46	56	59	56	64	83	78	82	80	78	72	70	72	71	67	71	78	89	87
South	26	27	39	38	33	31	33	27	35	33	37	30	39	36	41	41	48	42	37	48	47
West	62	63	48	51	55	47	55	50	71	77	83	76	68	70	78	66	77	99	91	93	107
Vermont	23	25	32	38	41	48	49	50	64	47	42	40	71	48	43	55	57	56	63	88	74
Third Circuit																					
Delaware	18	19	11	17	26	15	26	30	22	24	19	19	19	20	24	27	18	19	18	38	25
New Jersey	33	30	28	34	30	29	30	38	35	37	36	34	36	39	38	39	39	43	41	49	48
Pennsylvania:																					
East	22	23	24	29	23	29	26	29	25	28	23	20	25	26	26	29	32	32	30	30	31
Middle	34	35	37	37	38	37	37	60	39	44	48	42	48	51	46	46	52	57	60	54	56
West	18	18	26	25	30	24	24	22	26	28	31	28	24	24	24	25	24	29	27	34	37
Virgin Islands	150	117	127	121	166	137	174	202	118	118	185	104	100	85	70	77	89	118	85	132	121
Fourth Circuit																					
Maryland	44	44	55	48	47	36	38	38	37	36	36	36	38	40	43	42	46	51	50	50	52
North Carolina:																					
East	60	80	55	60	52	57	54	68	87	76	82	82	77	76	72	77	82	101	105	123	128
Middle	73	67	69	80	75	72	91	99	68	74	67	70	75	64	70	77	78	96	91	89	95
West	85	91	106	88	95	110	121	131	139	137	135	98	124	89	108	104	114	126	106	117	61
South Carolina	41	34	25	35	33	50	50	74	56	65	56	61	68	59	70	80	74	72	65	84	83
Virginia:																					
East	51	37	31	51	58	53	63	72	84	84	81	79	84	78	94	104	106	107	103	122	126
West	37	31	32	32	37	37	40	51	72	72	63	68	64	50	62	59	77	75	68	82	107
West Virginia:																					
North	61	54	62	51	80	95	127	88	47	77	35	40	35	35	42	36	48	41	41	65	62
South	36	29	29	47	53	69	53	87	66	68	69	32	43	37	40	41	44	43	46	50	54
Fifth Circuit																					
Louisiana:																					
East	32	26	27	27	31	29	29	31	32	33	25	20	20	20	20	21	25	25	24	26	27
Middle	36	31	39	41	28	27	23	28	31	25	42	24	47	44	54	48	63	57	63	40	83
West	31	29	28	26	23	34	25	30	32	25	29	26	24	29	24	24	21	20	24	39	47
Mississippi:																					
North	33	24	19	28	37	31	42	45	32	44	60	44	36	37	40	32	35	44	39	46	41
South	47	44	26	30	44	36	34	47	40	38	42	38	29	30	35	38	42	55	52	56	61
Texas:																					
North	66	57	61	66	65	61	70	68	54	74	62	59	60	56	60	69	76	77	68	64	78
East	38	37	28	22	27	27	46	40	36	44	57	47	48	53	56	52	68	68	66	70	77
South	117	111	109	112	132	131	160	170	88	77	63	64	67	81	94	161	177	201	218	220	254
West	129	121	109	101	107	126	177	168	113	123	110	101	115	158	219	314	377	404	373	361	324
Sixth Circuit																					
Kentucky:																					
East	28	29	27	41	39	34	40	45	51	55	57	68	68	69	68	88	89	94	75	68	71
West	50	58	45	45	48	35	35	37	44	42	47	35	35	39	34	46	50	47	60	54	52
Michigan:																					
East	36	39	29	34	41	34	33	41	42	45	48	40	38	40	40	41	39	33	33	40	45
West	40	36	34	37	34	35	42	39	37	34	44	42	44	57	49	60	60	71	78	81	82
Ohio:																					
North	41	40	27	33	37	37	46	38	37	40	45	38	39	36	34	46	40	42	50	48	42
South	39	43	41	44	44	60	62	60	51	53	46	41	36	36	35	51	43	43	41	46	48
Tennessee:																					
East	75	59	37	51	44	46	58	97	72	89	78	72	65	47	55	55	63	83	100	92	112
Middle	81	71	69	77	61	58	72	66	61	46	43	45	28	36	36	39	49	51	51	60	65
West	87	79	71	81	60	87	88	81	77	85	65	64	69	52	57	67	75	61	69	100	104
Seventh Circuit																					
Illinois:																					
North	39	39	27	26	28	32	32	31	31	30	26	23	21	20	20	20	26	30	28	39	38
South	80	70	43	46	52	61	44	52	38	51	58	42	54	46	37	71	68	74	54	46	75
Central	57	59	56	43	63	72	83	72	61	64	69	30	51	54	51	65	70	63	75	91	85
Indiana:																					
North	24	24	21	35	49	47	43	35	34	41	45	41	34	33	40	56	61	65	69	79	60
South	29	29	27	30	31	34	38	38	39	39	35	39	33	34	36	34	30	32	35	40	42
Wisconsin:																					
East	44	40	38	35	32	40	47	56	57	60	51	42	48	54	53	50	51	49	43	48	46
West	40	36	41	32	60	60	69	57	47	60	65	46	46	31	50	49	44	53	58	63	78

See notes at end of table.

Table 1.83

Felony criminal cases filed per judgeship in U.S. District Courts

By circuit and district, 1983-2003--Continued

Circuit and district	1983	1984	1985	1986	1987	1988	1989	1990	1991	1992	1993	1994	1995	1996	1997	1998	1999	2000	2001	2002	2003
Eighth Circuit																					
Arkansas:																					
East	48	37	34	38	54	35	42	63	44	51	38	49	49	56	44	52	40	36	42	37	49
West	48	49	32	25	24	28	23	32	32	43	45	51	30	40	31	49	41	53	45	56	59
Iowa:																					
North	39	34	47	40	55	71	94	61	48	57	69	52	67	101	78	74	91	135	158	181	215
South	33	31	33	37	34	42	39	45	41	37	30	36	57	53	51	83	93	97	77	94	103
Minnesota	39	39	38	41	42	35	45	42	45	38	44	40	34	35	43	46	42	48	46	47	54
Missouri:																					
East	61	45	45	45	47	45	48	41	33	39	39	40	48	40	52	60	61	71	68	81	89
West	37	41	46	50	60	49	45	50	42	50	53	48	53	48	44	57	61	82	86	89	110
Nebraska	32	26	31	59	43	40	52	59	46	50	47	50	50	58	66	89	91	109	118	141	175
North Dakota	46	49	48	44	46	61	83	74	78	75	66	76	71	93	76	92	88	84	79	87	108
South Dakota	67	49	63	60	70	68	65	79	77	61	70	81	84	123	122	137	130	107	114	105	121
Ninth Circuit																					
Alaska	42	45	24	19	37	38	26	25	28	54	32	29	26	21	34	56	52	56	52	39	54
Arizona	65	67	67	73	86	92	103	100	122	143	116	103	110	158	187	283	346	259	255	283	294
California:																					
North	44	43	48	38	44	41	37	39	28	28	32	28	32	41	45	29	47	57	50	42	47
East	60	57	58	53	49	71	81	64	65	61	67	67	86	89	105	106	107	126	116	119	123
Central	59	67	48	48	47	43	50	41	38	43	45	40	40	47	45	50	43	51	47	58	49
South	121	126	116	133	155	120	122	111	128	174	169	141	213	272	392	467	468	488	478	437	274
Hawaii	50	73	48	45	47	42	52	44	40	37	39	36	48	50	47	58	64	60	51	58	79
Idaho	64	43	56	51	70	54	36	43	35	43	33	36	41	47	42	56	49	62	71	107	124
Montana	80	82	54	58	55	63	71	74	76	74	76	64	73	81	92	72	83	90	106	111	125
Nevada	96	92	91	59	81	65	76	69	90	102	108	85	79	84	69	131	132	81	75	101	97
Oregon	34	37	39	70	60	78	78	79	88	87	80	81	99	103	92	116	123	126	111	114	128
Washington:																					
East	101	128	81	93	96	145	164	159	128	108	110	100	97	93	72	96	82	111	94	132	127
West	53	43	31	32	38	45	49	42	45	43	41	46	46	48	46	64	71	64	49	56	68
Guam	25	58	65	72	48	68	120	119	128	113	119	155	132	92	145	150	104	100	123	161	103
Northern Mariana Islands	9	1	3	2	2	16	11	4	13	15	15	16	18	30	25	45	49	37	23	23	25
Tenth Circuit																					
Colorado	46	38	36	33	40	39	47	44	45	50	52	43	59	71	56	56	56	72	61	79	87
Kansas	52	51	50	55	48	51	52	43	36	42	42	49	45	43	51	55	59	67	72	76	88
New Mexico	47	61	54	72	106	127	122	125	120	121	118	128	120	127	146	163	245	308	225	357	340
Oklahoma:																					
North	64	45	64	67	79	62	66	53	38	44	48	48	46	47	45	47	42	34	32	46	49
East	96	80	58	68	48	37	55	50	48	42	35	36	42	38	44	41	56	51	56	54	65
West	54	54	40	53	50	51	44	48	37	34	39	32	27	31	33	37	41	31	34	29	37
Utah	44	51	42	40	45	53	52	57	51	56	58	36	44	55	69	114	112	105	119	142	162
Wyoming	90	85	45	32	35	32	58	53	33	30	30	30	25	32	32	39	32	35	33	47	65
Eleventh Circuit																					
Alabama:																					
North	50	37	44	40	43	40	35	35	29	38	33	37	35	43	42	40	46	50	55	73	58
Middle	46	50	33	31	39	52	53	45	58	66	61	49	41	38	52	44	25	39	42	33	67
South	35	60	59	55	53	57	64	55	80	86	90	66	78	74	77	67	59	77	72	81	75
Florida:																					
North	28	48	64	60	80	76	77	70	49	63	69	71	57	55	70	72	72	58	56	55	76
Middle	46	47	44	69	71	75	83	84	79	82	84	67	72	79	97	113	103	79	72	68	82
South	91	90	91	87	89	98	85	95	86	73	64	71	89	94	84	87	93	105	108	103	90
Georgia:																					
North	34	28	35	44	42	48	46	28	35	42	45	40	45	44	51	45	55	60	62	56	60
Middle	57	53	40	42	43	38	70	64	40	58	44	47	46	46	58	63	40	52	56	53	63
South	38	35	34	45	59	49	48	47	51	56	49	41	45	36	47	50	49	52	66	71	74
District of Columbia	21	29	29	28	32	31	31	34	48	33	29	29	23	28	35	27	28	21	28	34	35

Note: The Federal courts are organized into 11 geographic circuits. Each circuit consists of a number of District Courts, which are the trial courts, and a Court of Appeals, which hears appeals taken from other courts. There is also a separate District Court and Court of Appeals for the District of Columbia. Prior to 1987, data are reported for the 12-month period ending June 30. Beginning in 1987, data are reported for the Federal fiscal year, which is the 12-month period ending September 30.

Source: Administrative Office of the United States Courts, *Federal Court Management Statistics 1985, 1991, 1997, 2000, 2001, 2003* (Washington, DC: Administrative Office of the United States Courts). Table constructed by SOURCEBOOK staff.

Table 1.84

Duties performed by magistrate judges in U.S. District Courts

1990, 1997-2003

Activity	1990	1997	1998	1999	2000	2001	2002	2003
Total	448,107	579,771	612,688	648,097	807,401	873,948	880,129	948,570
Trial jurisdiction cases	100,930	85,257	96,832	109,101	88,449	84,067	72,109	83,247
Class A misdemeanors	13,248	10,177	10,633	10,773	8,990	8,687	8,816	9,616
Petty offenses	87,682	75,080	86,199	98,328	79,459	75,380	63,293	73,631
Preliminary proceedings	157,987	217,616	241,031	259,153	264,997	286,299	293,002	315,455
Search warrants	20,672	29,563	30,371	32,607	29,824	31,571	29,929	32,539
Arrest warrants/summonses	18,972	23,116	26,252	28,749	26,880	29,891	30,541	31,291
Initial appearances	49,624	60,419	68,982	74,875	77,752	83,582	86,324	93,991
Preliminary examinations	7,145	13,049	14,436	16,059	16,589	18,067	19,279	20,062
Arraignments	34,311	41,559	45,524	48,132	49,740	54,687	54,339	57,977
Detention hearings	17,191	28,996	32,948	36,381	37,490	39,468	43,198	47,860
Bail reviews	7,858	10,018	10,250	10,833	10,741	11,557	11,052	11,397
Other[a]	2,214	10,896	12,268	11,517	15,981	17,476	18,340	20,338
Additional duties	171,127	236,964	234,974	235,803	405,661	450,639	461,848	490,617
Criminal	35,576	52,382	49,587	51,182	108,823	126,813	138,504	156,115
Motions[b]	26,509	27,329	24,071	24,623	67,099	78,450	85,693	98,299
Evidentiary hearings	2,256	1,788	1,998	2,302	1,990	1,985	1,899	2,041
Pretrial conferences[c]	3,488	5,737	5,763	5,793	10,965	12,024	13,532	14,620
Probation/supervised release	529	2,600	2,960	3,007	3,109	3,570	3,948	4,570
Guilty pleas	NA	NA	NA	NA	10,614	13,150	15,275	17,018
Other[d]	2,794	14,928	14,795	15,457	15,046	17,634	18,157	19,567
Civil	114,968	155,158	158,003	158,830	271,025	296,921	298,109	309,720
Settlement conferences	12,656	23,549	23,113	24,666	24,255	24,997	24,420	26,506
Other pretrial conferences[c]	32,545	40,999	40,107	39,265	49,724	50,776	55,371	55,632
Motions[b]	61,594	66,535	69,517	68,043	171,659	194,918	192,075	200,068
Evidentiary hearings	1,964	981	988	771	650	639	851	646
Social Security	5,112	4,553	5,261	6,132	5,516	5,514	6,654	6,472
Special masterships	1,097	963	886	753	734	677	504	550
Other[e]	NA	17,578	18,131	19,200	18,487	19,400	18,234	19,846
Prisoner litigation	20,583	29,424	27,384	25,791	25,813	26,905	25,235	24,782
State habeas corpus	6,078	8,046	9,261	9,692	10,125	10,180	9,503	9,482
Federal habeas corpus	2,339	3,778	4,024	3,406	3,469	4,256	4,441	3,837
Civil rights	12,166	16,480	13,151	11,922	11,419	11,403	10,531	10,766
Evidentiary hearings	NA	1,120	948	771	800	1,066	760	697
Civil consent	4,958	10,081	10,339	11,320	11,481	12,024	12,710	13,811
Without trial	3,950	8,318	8,791	9,822	10,181	10,945	11,751	13,044
Jury trial	495	964	892	850	750	590	472	479
Non-jury trial	513	799	656	648	550	489	487	288
Miscellaneous matters[f]	13,105	29,853	29,512	32,720	36,813	40,919	40,460	45,440

Note: The Federal Magistrates Act (28 U.S.C. 636(b)) provides the authority under which magistrate judges assist courts in the performance of "additional duties." This authority was both broadened and clarified by Public Law 94-577, Oct. 21, 1976, and by new procedural rules governing most habeas corpus proceedings in the district courts, effective Feb. 1, 1977. The changes make clear the ability of the parties of a civil case to consent to have the case referred to a magistrate for trial as a special matter; the changes also empower magistrates to conduct evidentiary hearings in prisoner petition cases. Additionally, the role of magistrates in providing pretrial assistance to district judges in both dispositive and non-dispositive matters has been clarified. A magistrate's authority to conduct arraignments following indictment in a criminal case is provided under Rule 10 of the Federal Rules of Criminal Procedure in 86 Districts. Data for 1990 are reported for the 12-month period ending June 30. Beginning in 1997, data are reported for the Federal fiscal year, which is the 12-month period ending September 30. Some data have been revised by the Source and will differ from previous editions of SOURCEBOOK.

[a]Data for 1990 include material witness hearings only; data for 1997-2003 include material witness hearings and attorney appointment hearings.
[b]Prior to 2000, data include contested motions only; beginning in 2000, data include both contested and uncontested motions.
[c]Prior to 2000, data do not include status conferences; beginning in 2000, data include status conferences.
[d]Data for 1990 include writs only; data for 1997-2003 include writs, mental competency hearings, and motion hearings.
[e]Beginning in 1997, data include fee applications, summary jury trials, and motion hearings.
[f]Prior to 2000, this category included seizure/inspection warrants and orders of entry, judgment debtor exams, extradition hearings, contempt proceedings, Criminal Justice Act fee applications, naturalization proceedings, grand jury returns, civil and criminal IRS enforcement proceedings, calendar calls, and voir dire. Beginning in 2000, civil and criminal other jury matters, and international prisoner transfer proceedings were added.

Source: Administrative Office of the United States Courts, *Judicial Business of the United States Courts: 2000 Annual Report of the Director*, pp. 66, 67; *2001 Annual Report of the Director*, pp. 62, 63; *2002 Annual Report of the Director*, pp. 61, 62; *2003 Annual Report of the Director*, pp. 58, 59 (Washington, DC: USGPO). Table adapted by SOURCEBOOK staff.

Table 1.85
Personnel in prosecutors' offices

United States, 2001[a]

	Percent of total personnel in prosecutors' offices
Number of personnel	79,436
Percent	100%
Chief prosecutor	3.0
Assistant prosecutors	30.5
Civil attorneys	2.4
Supervisory attorneys[b]	3.5
Managers[c]	1.8
Victim advocates	5.8
Legal services personnel[d]	5.2
Staff investigators[e]	9.4
Support staff[f]	34.9
Other	3.7

Note: The 2001 National Survey of Prosecutors (NSP), sponsored by the U.S. Department of Justice, Bureau of Justice Statistics, was a census of the 2,341 chief prosecutors in the United States that handled felony cases in State courts of general jurisdiction. In 2001, there were 2,341 prosecutorial districts in the Nation, each with one chief prosecutor. The National Opinion Research Center (NORC) conducted the data collection for the NSP in May and June 2001 through mailed questionnaires. After the initial mailings, an extensive followup was required to obtain a returned survey from each of the prosecutors' offices. Overall, 2,243 or 96% of the 2,341 prosecutors' offices nationwide responded to the 2001 NSP. Data from the remaining 98 prosecutors' offices were retrieved from a secondary source (such as via the Internet or by contacting a different county office), or imputed from existing data.

[a] Detail may not add to 100% because of rounding.
[b] Attorneys in managerial positions who litigate cases.
[c] Attorneys or nonattorneys in primarily managerial positions who do not litigate cases.
[d] Includes law clerks and paralegals.
[e] Includes investigators on contract.
[f] Includes administrative staff, clerical staff, computer personnel, and fiscal officers.

Source: U.S. Department of Justice, Bureau of Justice Statistics, *Prosecutors in State Courts, 2001*, Bulletin NCJ 193441 (Washington, DC: U.S. Department of Justice, May 2002), p. 2, Table 1.

Table 1.86
Budget for prosecutorial functions in full- and part-time prosecutors' offices

By size of population served, United States, 2001

	All offices	Large (1,000,000 or more)	Medium (250,000 to 999,999)	Small (under 250,000)	Part-time offices
Number of offices	2,341	34	194	1,581	532
Budget for prosecutorial functions (in thousands)					
Total	$4,680,000	$1,910,000	$1,580,000	$1,120,000	$78,788
Median	318	32,115	6,100	379	95
Mean	2,000	56,223	8,119	706	148
Minimum	6	7,200	200	6	7
Maximum	373,000	373,000	53,351	13,113	2,268
Percent of offices in which budget includes:					
Staff salaries	97.6%	100.0%	99.5%	97.6%	96.8%
Expert services	65.3	97.1	86.5	65.9	51.8
Investigator services	52.9	100.0	83.8	53.5	34.4
DNA testing	39.9	70.6	67.4	38.0	31.6
Child support enforcement	31.7	37.5	31.7	33.0	27.1
Interpreter services	29.8	73.5	66.9	27.8	17.2
Social services	15.4	38.7	31.1	14.7	9.5

Note: See Note, table 1.85. Data on total budget for prosecutorial functions were available for 2,221 prosecutors' offices and estimated for 130 prosecutors' offices. Data on percent of prosecutors' offices budget including staff salaries were available for 2,146 offices; expert services, 2,029 offices; investigator services, 1,984 offices; DNA testing, 1,939 offices; child support enforcement, 1,919 offices; and social services, 1,839 offices.

Source: U.S. Department of Justice, Bureau of Justice Statistics, *Prosecutors in State Courts, 2001*, Bulletin NCJ 193441 (Washington, DC: U.S. Department of Justice, May 2002), p. 4, Table 4.

Table 1.87
Length of service and annual salary of chief prosecutors in full- and part-time prosecutors' offices

By size of population served, United States, 2001

	All offices	Large (1,000,000 or more)	Medium (250,000 to 999,999)	Small (under 250,000)	Part-time offices
Median					
Length of service (in years)	6.8	6.5	8.4	6.7	6.7
Annual salary	$85,000	$136,700	$115,000	$90,000	$39,750
Percent					
Serving 4 years or less	31.9%	29.4%	25.5%	32.5%	32.8%
Serving 15 years or more	20.3	17.6	23.4	19.2	22.6
With annual salary over $100,000	28.6	97.1	77.0	30.0	0.2

Note: See Note, table 1.85. Data on length of service were available for 2,173 prosecutors' offices and annual salary for 2,121 offices.

Source: U.S. Department of Justice, Bureau of Justice Statistics, *Prosecutors in State Courts, 2001*, Bulletin NCJ 193441 (Washington, DC: U.S. Department of Justice, May 2002), p. 3, Table 3.

Table 1.88
DNA evidence used by full- and part-time prosecutors' offices

By size of population served, United States, 2001

	All offices	Large (1,000,000 or more)	Medium (250,000 to 999,999)	Small (under 250,000)	Part-time offices
Used during plea negotiations or felony trials	68.2%	100.0%	98.3%	73.1%	38.3%
Stage of case					
Plea negotiations	59.4	81.3	89.0	63.6	32.6
Trial	48.0	100.0	95.0	50.7	17.1
Forensic laboratory analyzing DNA					
FBI	7.8	28.1	22.8	6.8	3.7
State-operated	60.7	65.6	81.7	66.5	33.7
Local agency	4.8	81.3	21.7	2.4	0.4
Privately operated	21.6	68.8	53.3	20.6	9.1
Problems with use of DNA evidence					
Improper collection of evidence by police	6.5	21.9	16.9	6.4	1.8
Inconclusive DNA results	14.9	46.9	34.3	14.9	5.0
Excessive delay in getting DNA results from laboratory	33.3	71.9	65.2	34.4	14.7
Difficulty in getting DNA results admitted in court as evidence	1.3	3.1	3.4	1.3	0.2

Note: See Note, table 1.85. Data on the use of DNA anytime, during plea negotiations, and during felony trials were available for 2,140 prosecutors' offices. Data on the forensic laboratory analyzing DNA were available for 2,145 prosecutors' offices. Data on problems with the use of DNA were available for 2,125 prosecutors' offices.

Source: U.S. Department of Justice, Bureau of Justice Statistics, *Prosecutors in State Courts, 2001*, Bulletin NCJ 193441 (Washington, DC: U.S. Department of Justice, May 2002), p. 8, Table 10.

Table 1.89

Prosecutors' offices serving districts with populations less than 250,000

By size of population served and selected characteristics, United States, 2001

	\	Size of population served			
	All	100,000 to 249,999	50,000 to 99,999	20,000 to 49,999	Under 20,000
Number of offices	1,581	335	357	488	401
Total staff size, median[a]	10	31	15	8	4
Annual salary of chief prosecutor[b]					
Median	$90,000	$100,000	$93,000	$88,000	$66,000
Percent with salary $100,000 or more	30.0%	52.1%	31.4%	22.7%	18.7%
Budget for prosecutorial functions (in thousands)[c]					
Total	$1,120,000	$594,000	$252,000	$193,000	$78,064
Median	379	1,351	600	325	150
Mean	706	1,772	705	396	195
Felony cases closed in previous 12 months[d]					
Median number	288	1,200	400	214	75
Percent convicted	90.0%	86.7%	90.0%	90.0%	90.0%
Median jury trial verdicts	10	30	15	8	2

Note: See Note, table 1.85.

[a] Includes chief prosecutor.
[b] Data on annual salary were available for 1,453 prosecutors' offices.
[c] Data on budget functions were available for 1,496 prosecutors' offices and estimated for 85 prosecutors' offices.
[d] Data on number of felony cases closed were available for 1,389 prosecutors' offices and estimated for 192 prosecutors' offices, data on percent convicted were available for 1,345 offices, and data on felony jury verdicts were available for 1,412 offices.

Source: U.S. Department of Justice, Bureau of Justice Statistics, *State Court Prosecutors in Small Districts, 2001*, Special Report NCJ 196020 (Washington, DC: U.S. Department of Justice, January 2003), p. 2, Table 2; p. 3, Tables 3 and 4; p. 6, Table 8. Table adapted by SOURCEBOOK staff.

Table 1.90

Salaries of judges of highest, appellate, and general trial courts

By type of court and jurisdiction, as of Oct. 1, 2003

Jurisdiction	Highest court Salary	Highest court Rank	Intermediate appellate court Salary	Intermediate appellate court Rank	General trial court Salary	General trial court Rank
Alabama	$152,027	8	$151,027	4	$111,973	24
Alaska	117,900	31	111,384	27	109,032	28
Arizona	126,525	20	123,900	13	120,750	15
Arkansas	126,054	21	122,093	16	118,128	18
California	175,575	1	164,604	1	143,838	2
Colorado	113,637	37	109,137	32	104,637	35
Connecticut	138,404	13	129,988	10	125,000	10
Delaware	147,000	10	X	X	140,200	4
District of Columbia	164,000	3	X	X	154,700	1
Florida	153,750	6	141,963	8	133,250	8
Georgia	153,086	7	152,139	2	121,938	13
Hawaii	115,547	32	110,618	29	106,922	32
Idaho	102,125	47	101,125	37	95,718	45
Illinois	158,103	5	148,803	6	136,546	7
Indiana	115,000	34	110,000	31	90,000	48
Iowa	120,100	27	115,540	22	109,810	26
Kansas	114,769	35	110,794	28	100,255	39
Kentucky	124,415	23	119,380	17	114,348	20
Louisiana	118,301	30	112,041	26	105,780	34
Maine	104,929	44	X	X	98,377	41
Maryland	131,600	17	123,800	14	119,600	16
Massachusetts	126,943	19	117,467	19	112,777	23
Michigan	164,610	2	151,441	3	139,919	5
Minnesota	129,674	18	122,186	15	114,700	19
Mississippi	102,300	46	95,500	38	94,700	46
Missouri	123,000	25	115,000	24	108,000	30
Montana	95,493	50	X	X	88,164	50
Nebraska	119,276	29	113,312	25	110,330	25
Nevada	140,000	11	X	X	130,000	9
New Hampshire	113,266	38	X	X	106,187	33
New Jersey	158,500	4	150,000	5	141,000	3
New Mexico	96,283	49	91,469	39	86,896	51
New York	151,200	9	144,000	7	136,700	6
North Carolina	115,336	33	110,530	30	104,523	36
North Dakota	99,122	48	X	X	90,671	47
Ohio	125,500	22	117,000	20	107,600	31
Oklahoma	106,716	41	101,714	36	95,898	43
Oregon	105,200	42	102,800	35	95,800	44
Pennsylvania	139,585	12	135,213	9	121,225	14
Rhode Island	132,816	15	X	X	119,579	17
South Carolina	119,510	28	116,521	21	113,535	21
South Dakota	102,684	45	X	X	95,910	42
Tennessee	123,684	24	117,924	18	112,836	22
Texas	113,000	39	107,350	34	109,158	27
Utah	114,050	36	108,900	33	103,700	38
Vermont	109,771	40	X	X	104,355	37
Virginia	132,523	16	125,899	12	123,027	11
Washington	134,584	14	128,116	11	121,972	12
West Virginia	95,000	51	X	X	90,000	49
Wisconsin	122,418	26	115,490	23	108,950	29
Wyoming	105,000	43	X	X	100,000	40
National average	122,418	NA	117,000	NA	109,810	NA
Median	125,292	NA	121,697	NA	112,724	NA
Federal system	193,000	NA	165,500	NA	157,000	NA
Guam	128,000	NA	X	NA	100,000	NA
Northern Mariana Islands	126,000	NA	X	NA	120,000	NA
Puerto Rico	120,000	NA	90,000	NA	80,000	NA
Virgin Islands	NA	NA	X	NA	135,000	NA

Note: The salaries reported refer to associate justices of the highest courts, associate judges of intermediate appellate courts, and judges of general jurisdiction trial courts. Where possible, the data presented are actual salaries. In jurisdictions where some judges receive supplements, the salary figures are the most representative available: the base salary, the midpoint of a range between the lowest and highest supplemented salaries, or the median. National averages for the highest courts and general trial courts are based on figures for the 50 States and the District of Columbia. For intermediate appellate courts, the average is based on the 39 States that have such courts.

Source: National Center for State Courts, *Survey of Judicial Salaries*, Vol. 28, No. 2 (Williamsburg, VA: National Center for State Courts, 2004), p. 15. Table adapted by SOURCEBOOK staff. Reprinted by permission.

Table 1.91
Method of selection and length of initial and retention terms of the highest appellate court justices

By State, as of June 2004

State	Initial selection Method[a]	Initial selection Term	Retention Method	Retention Term (in years)
Alabama	Partisan election	6 years	Partisan election	6
Alaska	Nominating commission	Until next general election but not less than 3 years	Retention election	10
Arizona	Nominating commission	Until next general election but not less than 2 years	Retention election	6
Arkansas	Nonpartisan election	8 years	Nonpartisan election	8
California	Appointed by governor	12 years	Retention election	12
Colorado	Nominating commission	Until next general election but not less than 2 years	Retention election	10
Connecticut	Nominating commission	8 years	Commission reviews, governor renominates, legislature confirms	8
Delaware	Nominating commission	12 years	Competitive reapplication to commission, reappointment by governor, senate confirms	12
District of Columbia[b]	Nominating commission	15 years	Reappointment by judicial tenure commission or President	15
Florida	Nominating commission	Until next general election but not less than 1 year	Retention election	6
Georgia	Nonpartisan election	6 years	Nonpartisan election	6
Hawaii	Nominating commission	10 years	Reappointment by commission	10
Idaho	Nonpartisan election	6 years	Nonpartisan election	6
Illinois	Partisan election	10 years	Retention election	10
Indiana	Nominating commission	Until next general election but not less than 2 years	Retention election	10
Iowa	Nominating commission	Until next general election but not less than 1 year	Retention election	8
Kansas	Nominating commission	Until next general election but not less than 1 year	Retention election	6
Kentucky	Nonpartisan election	8 years	Nonpartisan election	8
Louisiana[c]	Partisan election	10 years	Partisan election	10
Maine	Appointed by governor	7 years	Reappointment by governor, legislature confirms	7
Maryland[d]	Nominating commission	Until next general election but not less than 1 year	Retention election	10
Massachusetts	Nominating commission	To age 70	X	X
Michigan[e]	Nonpartisan election	8 years	Nonpartisan election	8
Minnesota	Nonpartisan election	6 years	Nonpartisan election	6
Mississippi	Nonpartisan election	8 years	Nonpartisan election	8
Missouri	Nominating commission	Until next general election but not less than 1 year	Retention election	12
Montana	Nonpartisan election	8 years	Nonpartisan election, but if unopposed, retention election	8
Nebraska	Nominating commission	Until next general election but not less than 3 years	Retention election	6
Nevada	Nonpartisan election	6 years	Nonpartisan election	6
New Hampshire	Appointed by governor[f]	To age 70	X	X
New Jersey	Appointed by governor	7 years	Reappointment by governor, with senate consent	To age 70
New Mexico	Nominating commission	Until next general election	Partisan election the first time; after that, winner runs in retention election	8
New York[d]	Nominating commission	14 years	Competitive reapplication to commission, reappointment by governor, senate confirms	14
North Carolina	Nonpartisan election	8 years	Nonpartisan election	8
North Dakota	Nonpartisan election	10 years	Nonpartisan election	10
Ohio[g]	Nonpartisan election	6 years	Nonpartisan election	6
Oklahoma[h]	Nominating commission	Until next general election but not less than 1 year	Retention election	6
Oregon	Nonpartisan election	6 years	Nonpartisan election	6
Pennsylvania	Partisan election	10 years	Retention election	10
Rhode Island	Nominating commission	Life tenure	X	X
South Carolina	Nominating commission[i]	10 years	Reappointed by legislature	10
South Dakota	Nominating commission	Until next general election but not less than 3 years	Retention election	8
Tennessee	Nominating commission	Until the biennial general election but not less than 30 days	Retention election	8
Texas[h]	Partisan election	6 years	Partisan election	6
Utah	Nominating commission	Until next general election but not less than 3 years	Retention election	10
Vermont	Nominating commission	6 years	Retained by vote in general assembly	6
Virginia	Appointed by legislature	12 years	Reappointed by legislature	12
Washington	Nonpartisan election	6 years	Nonpartisan election	6
West Virginia	Partisan election	12 years	Partisan election	12
Wisconsin	Nonpartisan election	10 years	Nonpartisan election	10
Wyoming	Nominating commission	Until next general election but not less than 1 year	Retention election	8

See notes on next page.

Characteristics of the criminal justice systems 83

Table 1.91

Method of selection and length of initial and retention terms of the highest appellate court justices

By State, as of June 2004--Continued

Note: These data were compiled through a survey of State statutes; they were then verified by personnel of the American Judicature Society.

"Initial selection" is defined as the constitutional or statutory method by which judges are selected for a full term of office. "Retention" refers to the method used to select judges for subsequent terms of office. "Partisan election" refers to elections in which the judicial candidates' names appear on the ballot with their respective party labels; "nonpartisan election" refers to elections in which no party labels are attached to judicial candidates' names on the ballot. Caution should be used when interpreting partisan and nonpartisan designations as definitions may vary. "Retention election" refers to an election in which a judge runs unopposed on the ballot and the electorate votes solely on the question of the judge's continuation in office. In a retention election, the judge must win a majority of the vote in order to serve a full term, except in Illinois which requires 60% and New Mexico which requires 57%. "Nominating commission" is a merit selection procedure that refers to the nonpartisan body, composed of lawyers and nonlawyers, which actively recruits, screens, and nominates prospective judicial candidates to the executive for appointment. The nominating commission method of selection was established by executive order in Delaware, Maryland, and Massachusetts and by constitutional or statutory authority in all other jurisdictions. Readers should consult State Constitutions for special provisions and procedures related to issues of premature vacancy (e.g., death, resignation) and other circumstances.

[a] In States that use nominating commissions, selection requirements may vary. The governor may make the appointment solely, with senate confirmation, or with legislative confirmation.

[b] Initial appointment is made by the President of the United States and confirmed by the Senate. At expiration of term, judge's performance is reviewed by the commission. Those found "well qualified" are automatically reappointed. For those found "qualified," the President may nominate for an additional term, subject to Senate confirmation. If the President does not wish to reappoint the judge, the District of Columbia Nomination Commission compiles a new list of candidates.

[c] Although party affiliation of judicial candidates appears on ballots, judicial primaries are open and candidates generally do not solicit party support. This gives judicial elections a nonpartisan character.

[d] The highest State court is named the Court of Appeals.

[e] Party affiliations of judicial candidates are not listed on the general election ballot, so the election is technically nonpartisan. However, candidates are nominated at party conventions.

[f] Subject to approval of an elected five-member executive council.

[g] Party affiliations of judicial candidates are not listed on the general election ballot, so the election is technically nonpartisan. However, candidates run in partisan primary elections.

[h] Oklahoma and Texas have two courts of final jurisdiction: the supreme court, which has final civil jurisdiction; and the court of criminal appeals, which has final criminal jurisdiction. The selection process is the same for both.

[i] The Judicial Merit Selection Commission screens and then recommends a list of judicial candidates to the legislature. The legislature votes only on the list submitted by the commission. If all candidates on the list are rejected, the process begins again with the commission.

Source: American Judicature Society, *Judicial Selection in the United States: A Compendium of Provisions*, 2nd edition (Chicago: American Judicature Society, 1993); http://www.ajs.org/js/judicialselectioncharts.pdf [Jan. 25, 2005]; and data provided by the American Judicature Society. Reprinted by permission.

Table 1.92

Method of selection and length of initial and retention terms of intermediate appellate court judges in 39 States

As of June 2004

State	Initial selection Method[a]	Initial selection Term	Retention Method	Retention Term (in years)
Alabama[b]	Partisan election	6 years	Partisan election	6
Alaska	Nominating commission	Until next general election but not less than 3 years	Retention election	8
Arizona	Nominating commission	Until next general election but not less than 2 years	Retention election	6
Arkansas	Nonpartisan election	8 years	Nonpartisan election	8
California	Appointed by governor	12 years	Retention election	12
Colorado	Nominating commission	Until next general election but not less than 2 years	Retention election	8
Connecticut	Nominating commission	8 years	Commission reviews, governor renominates, legislature confirms	8
Florida	Nominating commission	Until next general election but not less than 1 year	Retention election	6
Georgia	Nonpartisan election	6 years	Nonpartisan election	6
Hawaii	Nominating commission	10 years	Reappointment by commission	10
Idaho	Nonpartisan election	6 years	Nonpartisan election	6
Illinois	Partisan election	10 years	Retention election	10
Indiana	Nominating commission	Until next general election but not less than 2 years	Retention election	10
Iowa	Nominating commission	Until next general election but not less than 1 year	Retention election	6
Kansas	Nominating commission	Until next general election but not less than 1 year	Retention election	4
Kentucky	Nonpartisan election	8 years	Nonpartisan election	8
Louisiana[c]	Partisan election	10 years	Partisan election	10
Maryland	Nominating commission	Until next general election but not less than 1 year	Retention election	10
Massachusetts	Nominating commission	To age 70	X	X
Michigan	Nonpartisan election	6 years	Nonpartisan election	6
Minnesota	Nonpartisan election	6 years	Nonpartisan election	6
Mississippi	Nonpartisan election	8 years	Nonpartisan election	8
Missouri	Nominating commission	Until next general election but not less than 1 year	Retention election	12
Nebraska	Nominating commission	Until next general election but not less than 3 years	Retention election	6
New Jersey	Appointed by governor	7 years	Reappointment by governor with senate consent	To age 70
New Mexico	Nominating commission	Until next general election	Partisan election the first time; after that, winner runs in retention election	8
New York	Nominating commission	5 years	Commission reviews, makes recommendation to governor, governor reappoints	5
North Carolina	Nonpartisan election	8 years	Nonpartisan election	8
Ohio[d]	Nonpartisan election	6 years	Nonpartisan election	6
Oklahoma	Nominating commission	Until next general election but not less than 1 year	Retention election	6
Oregon	Nonpartisan election	6 years	Nonpartisan election	6
Pennsylvania[e]	Partisan election	10 years	Retention election	10
South Carolina	Nominating commission[f]	6 years	Reappointed by legislature	6
Tennessee[b]	Nominating commission	Until the biennial general election but not less than 30 days	Retention election	8
Texas	Partisan election	6 years	Partisan election	6
Utah	Nominating commission	Until next general election but not less than 3 years	Retention election	6
Virginia	Appointed by legislature	8 years	Reappointed by legislature	8
Washington	Nonpartisan election	6 years	Nonpartisan election	6
Wisconsin	Nonpartisan election	6 years	Nonpartisan election	6

Note: See Note, table 1.91. States not listed do not have intermediate appellate courts.

[a]In States that use nominating commissions, selection requirements may vary. The governor makes the appointment solely, with senate confirmation, or with legislative confirmation.
[b]Alabama and Tennessee have two intermediate appellate courts: the court of civil appeals, which has civil jurisdiction, and the court of criminal appeals, which has criminal jurisdiction. The selection process is the same for both.
[c]Although party affiliation of judicial candidates appears on ballots, judicial primaries are open and candidates generally do not solicit party support. This gives judicial elections a nonpartisan character.
[d]Party affiliations of judicial candidates are not listed on the general election ballot, so the election is technically nonpartisan. However, candidates run in partisan primary elections.
[e]Pennsylvania has two intermediate appellate courts; the superior court and the commonwealth court. The selection process is the same for both.
[f]The Judicial Merit Selection Commission screens and then recommends a list of judicial candidates to the legislature. The legislature votes only on the list submitted by the commission. If all candidates on the list are rejected, the process begins again with the commission.

Source: American Judicature Society, *Judicial Selection in the United States: A Compendium of Provisions*, 2nd edition (Chicago: American Judicature Society, 1993); http://www.ajs.org/js/judicialselectioncharts.pdf [Jan. 25, 2005]; and data provided by the American Judicature Society. Reprinted by permission.

Table 1.93

Method of selection and length of initial and retention terms of general jurisdiction court judges

By State and name of court, as of June 2004

State/name of court(s)	Initial selection Method[a]	Initial selection Term	Retention Method	Retention Term (in years)
Alabama Circuit court	Partisan election	6 years	Partisan election	6
Alaska Superior court	Nominating commission	Until next general election but not less than 3 years	Retention election	6
Arizona Superior court[b]	Nominating commission	Until next general election but not less than 2 years	Retention election	4
Arkansas Circuit court	Nonpartisan election	6 years	Nonpartisan election	6
California Superior court	Nonpartisan election or gubernatorial appointment[c]	6 years	Nonpartisan election[d]	6
Colorado District court	Nominating commission	Until next general election but not less than 2 years	Retention election	6
Connecticut Superior court	Nominating commission	8 years	Commission reviews, governor renominates, legislature confirms	8
Delaware Superior court	Nominating commission	12 years	Competitive reapplication to commission, reappointment by governor, senate confirms	12
District of Columbia Superior court[e]	Nominating commission	15 years	Reappointment by judicial tenure commission or President	15
Florida Circuit court[f]	Nonpartisan election	6 years	Nonpartisan election	6
Georgia Superior court	Nonpartisan election	4 years	Nonpartisan election	4
Hawaii Circuit court	Nominating commission	10 years	Reappointment by commission	10
Idaho District court	Nonpartisan election	4 years	Nonpartisan election	4
Illinois Circuit court	Partisan election[g]	6 years	Retention election	6
Indiana Circuit court	Partisan election[h]	6 years	Partisan election[h]	6
Superior court	Partisan election[i]	6 years[j]	Partisan election[k]	6
Iowa District court	Nominating commission	Until next general election but not less than 1 year	Retention election	6
Kansas District court	Nominating commission, partisan election[l]	Until next general election	Retention election[m]	4
Kentucky Circuit court	Nonpartisan election	8 years	Nonpartisan election	8
Louisiana[n] District court	Partisan election	6 years	Partisan election	6
Maine Superior court	Appointed by governor	7 years	Reappointment by governor, legislature confirms	7
Maryland Circuit court	Nominating commission	Until next general election but not less than 1 year	Nonpartisan election	15
Massachusetts Trial Court of the Commonwealth	Nominating commission	To age 70	X	X
Michigan Circuit court	Nonpartisan election	6 years	Nonpartisan election	6
Minnesota District court	Nonpartisan election	6 years	Nonpartisan election	6
Mississippi Circuit court	Nonpartisan election	4 years	Nonpartisan election	4
Chancery court	Nonpartisan election	4 years	Nonpartisan election	4
Missouri Circuit court	Partisan election[o]	6 years[p]	Partisan election[q]	6
Montana District court	Nonpartisan election	6 years	Nonpartisan election, but if unopposed, retention election	6
Nebraska District court	Nominating commission	Until next general election but not less than 3 years	Retention election	6
Nevada District court	Nonpartisan election	6 years	Nonpartisan election	6
New Hampshire Superior court	Appointed by governor[r]	To age 70	X	X

See notes at end of table.

Table 1.93

Method of selection and length of initial and retention terms of general jurisdiction court judges

By State and name of court, as of June 2004--Continued

State/name of court(s)	Initial selection Method[a]	Term	Retention Method	Term (in years)
New Jersey Superior court	Appointed by governor	7 years	Reappointment by governor with senate consent	To age 70
New Mexico District court	Nominating commission	Until next general election	Partisan election the first time; after that, winner runs in retention election	6
New York Supreme court	Partisan election	14 years	Partisan election	14
County court	Partisan election	10 years	Partisan election	10
North Carolina Superior court	Nonpartisan election	8 years	Nonpartisan election	8
North Dakota District court	Nonpartisan election	6 years	Nonpartisan election	6
Ohio[s] Common Pleas court	Nonpartisan election	6 years	Nonpartisan election	6
Oklahoma District court	Nonpartisan election	4 years	Nonpartisan election	4
Oregon Circuit court	Nonpartisan election	6 years	Nonpartisan election	6
Pennsylvania Common Pleas court	Partisan election	10 years	Retention election	10
Rhode Island Superior court	Nominating commission	Life tenure	X	X
South Carolina Circuit court	Nominating commission[t]	6 years	Reappointed by legislature	6
South Dakota Circuit court	Nonpartisan election	8 years	Nonpartisan election	8
Tennessee Circuit court	Nominating commission	8 years	Partisan election	8
Texas District court	Partisan election	4 years	Partisan election	4
Utah District court	Nominating commission	Until next general election but not less than 3 years	Retention election	6
Vermont Superior court	Nominating commission	6 years	Retained by vote in general assembly	6
Virginia Circuit court	Appointed by legislature	8 years	Reappointed by legislature	8
Washington Superior court	Nonpartisan election	4 years	Nonpartisan election	4
West Virginia Circuit court	Partisan election	8 years	Partisan election	8
Wisconsin Circuit court	Nonpartisan election	6 years	Nonpartisan election	6
Wyoming District court	Nominating commission	Until next general election but not less than 1 year	Retention election	6

Note: See Note, table 1.91. Courts of general jurisdiction are defined as having unlimited civil and criminal jurisdiction (Larry C. Berkson, "Judicial Selection in the United States: A Special Report," *Judicature* 64 (October 1980) p. 178).

[a]In States that use nominating commissions, appointment procedures may vary. The governor may make the appointment solely, with senate confirmation, or with legislative confirmation.
[b]Counties with populations less than 250,000 select and retain superior court judges in nonpartisan elections for 4-year terms.
[c]Local electors can choose either nonpartisan elections or gubernatorial appointment.
[d]Judge must be elected to a full term on a nonpartisan ballot at the next general election. If the election is not contested, the incumbent's name does not appear on the ballot.
[e]Initial appointment is made by the President of the United States and confirmed by the Senate. At expiration of term, judge's performance is reviewed by the commission. Those found "well qualified" are automatically reappointed. For those found "qualified," the President may nominate for an additional term, subject to Senate confirmation. If the President does not wish to reappoint the judge, the District of Columbia Nomination Commission compiles a new list of candidates.
[f]Voters in each circuit may opt for merit selection and retention of circuit court judges.
[g]Circuit court associate judges are appointed by the circuit judges in each circuit for 4-year terms, as provided by supreme court rule.
[h]In Vanderburgh County initial selection and retention are by nonpartisan election.
[i]A nominating commission is used for the superior court judges of Lake and St. Joseph Counties. In Allen and Vanderburgh Counties the election is nonpartisan.
[j]In Lake and St. Joseph Counties each appointed judge serves until the next general election but not less than 2 years.
[k]Nonpartisan elections are used in Allen and Vanderburgh Counties. Retention elections are used in Lake and St. Joseph Counties.
[l]Seventeen of 31 districts use a nominating commission for district judge selection; the remaining 14 select district judges in partisan elections.

[m]Fourteen of 31 districts use partisan elections.
[n]Although party affiliation of judicial candidates appears on ballots, judicial primaries are open and candidates generally do not solicit party support. This gives judicial elections a nonpartisan character.
[o]Nominating commissions are used for selecting circuit court judges in Jackson, Clay, Platte, and St. Louis Counties.
[p]An associate circuit court judge's term is 4 years; also in counties that use nominating commissions, the appointed judge serves until the next general election but not less than 1 year.
[q]Retention elections are used in Jackson, Clay, Platte, and St. Louis Counties.
[r]Subject to approval by an elected five-member executive council.
[s]Party affiliations of judicial candidates are not listed on the general election ballot, so the election is technically nonpartisan. However, candidates run in partisan primary elections.
[t]The Judicial Merit Selection Commission screens and then recommends a list of judicial candidates to the legislature. The legislature votes on the list submitted by the commission. If all candidates on the list are rejected, the process begins again with the commission.

Source: American Judicature Society, *Judicial Selection in the United States: A Compendium of Provisions*, 2nd edition (Chicago: American Judicature Society, 1993); http://www.ajs.org/js/judicialselectioncharts.pdf [Jan. 25, 2005]; and data provided by the American Judicature Society. Reprinted by permission.

Characteristics of the criminal justice systems 87

Table 1.94

Grand jury and grand juror utilization in U.S. District Courts

Fiscal years 1988-2003

Fiscal year	Juries serving	Sessions convened	Jurors Total	Jurors Average per session	Hours Total	Hours Average per session	Proceedings filed by indictment Cases	Proceedings filed by indictment Defendants	Average defendants indicted per session
1988	736	10,668	209,168	19.6	57,362	5.4	23,243	38,214	3.6
1989	744	10,413	205,131	19.7	56,792	5.5	24,050	39,679	3.8
1990	742	10,065	198,863	19.8	53,978	5.4	24,779	40,817	4.1
1991	788	10,914	215,789	19.8	58,293	5.3	27,168	44,607	4.1
1992	836	11,571	228,784	19.8	61,806	5.3	28,559	47,164	4.1
1993	847	11,181	221,505	19.8	59,117	5.3	27,039	44,480	4.0
1994	854	10,674	211,647	19.8	55,789	5.2	23,869	40,238	3.8
1995	960	10,585	208,625	19.7	55,378	5.2	25,202	42,866	4.0
1996	1,160	10,121	199,844	19.7	52,911	5.2	26,728	45,267	4.5
1997	1,352	9,764	193,805	19.8	51,603	5.3	28,925	47,461	4.9
1998	924	10,344	205,043	19.8	55,460	5.4	34,424	54,525	5.3
1999	797	10,415	205,862	19.8	54,043	5.2	36,696	56,210	5.4
2000	850	10,230	202,816	19.8	53,899	5.3	39,469	59,472	5.8
2001	843	10,042	199,169	19.8	51,258	5.1	41,191	60,633	6.0
2002	846	9,873	197,182	20.0	50,013	5.1	45,041	65,237	6.6
2003	835	10,190	203,553	20.0	51,918	5.1	47,629	68,295	6.7

Note: Grand jurors hear evidence of criminal activity presented by the prosecution and determine whether the Government's evidence is sufficient to justify the bringing of formal charges. Some data have been revised by the Source and may differ from previous editions of SOURCEBOOK.

Source: Administrative Office of the United States Courts, *Annual Report of the Director, 1992*, p. 75; *1997*, p. 63 (Washington, DC: USGPO); and Administrative Office of the United States Courts, *Judicial Business of the United States Courts: 2002 Annual Report of the Director*, p. 60; *2003 Annual Report of the Director*, p. 57 (Washington, DC: USGPO). Table adapted by SOURCEBOOK staff.

Table 1.95

Petit juror utilization in U.S. District Courts

1977-2003[a]

	Total jurors available Total[b]	Total jurors available Selected or serving	Total jurors available Challenged	Total jurors available Not selected, serving, or challenged[c]	Jury trial days Total	Jury trial days Criminal	Jury trial days Civil	Juror Usage Index
1977	584,122	60.4%	15.5%	24.1%	29,875	56.7%	43.3%	19.6
1978	570,523	60.5	15.5	24.0	29,238	55.0	45.0	19.5
1979	565,617	59.2	16.2	24.6	28,851	52.6	47.4	19.6
1980	605,547	60.9	15.2	23.1	32,159	48.7	51.3	18.8
1981	648,929	61.1	15.4	23.4	35,596	44.7	55.3	18.2
1982	631,606	61.6	15.6	22.8	35,263	44.2	55.8	17.9
1983	640,577	64.6	16.0	19.4	37,589	44.0	56.0	17.0
1984	666,942	64.6	16.5	18.9	39,572	42.4	57.6	16.9
1985	676,140	65.4	16.9	17.7	40,289	42.7	57.3	16.8
1986	705,819	65.9	16.9	17.2	41,945	45.9	54.1	16.8
1987	732,039	66.7	17.3	16.0	44,511	42.9	57.1	16.5
1988	762,083	65.9	17.6	16.5	44,324	45.1	54.9	17.2
1989	814,322	64.5	18.0	17.5	45,403	53.2	46.8	17.9
1990	828,527	65.2	18.2	16.6	46,194	49.8	50.2	17.9
1991	855,175	64.4	18.6	17.0	46,563	53.2	46.8	18.4
1992	887,234	64.3	18.7	16.9	48,368	52.2	47.8	18.3
1993	861,160	64.3	18.9	16.8	46,646	52.8	47.2	18.5
1994	788,066	65.3	18.5	16.2	45,060	45.7	54.3	17.5
1995	774,978	63.4	18.7	15.9	43,219	49.0	51.0	17.9
1996	778,170	64.2	18.9	16.9	43,133	46.1	53.9	18.0
1997	749,613	64.8	19.2	16.0	41,903	44.8	55.2	17.9
1998	718,778	63.6	19.5	16.9	39,521	44.7	55.3	18.2
1999	690,981	62.8	19.6	17.6	37,970	45.6	54.4	18.2
2000	641,399	60.6	20.0	19.5	34,713	NA	NA	18.5
2001	616,515	59.2	19.8	20.9	32,595	NA	NA	18.9
2002	583,413	58.7	20.0	21.4	30,233	NA	NA	19.3
2003	603,785	58.0	20.1	21.9	30,506	NA	NA	19.8

Note: In this table, 1977 data are for 94 District Courts; 1978 through 1982 data are for 95 District Courts; and 1983 through 2003 data are for 94 District Courts. Data for 1977-87 are reported for the 12-month period ending June 30. Beginning in 1988, data are reported for the Federal fiscal year, which is the 12-month period ending September 30. Data for 1988-91 have been revised by the Source and may differ from previous editions of SOURCEBOOK.

Petit jurors determine questions of fact, in any civil or criminal action, through hearing the evidence presented at trial. The "Juror Usage Index" is the average number of jurors on hand for each jury trial day; it is calculated by dividing the total number of available jurors by the total number of jury trial days.

[a]Percents may not add to 100 because of rounding.
[b]Each juror is counted for each day serving, traveling, or waiting at the courthouse to serve.
[c]Includes jurors in travel status.

Source: Administrative Office of the United States Courts, *Annual Report of the Director, 1980*, p. 574; *1981*, p. 6; *1986*, p. 23; *1999*, p. 70 (Washington, DC: Administrative Office of the United States Courts); Administrative Office of the United States Courts, *Annual Report of the Director, 1991*, p. 98; *1996*, p. 69; *1997*, p. 62 (Washington, DC: USGPO); and Administrative Office of the United States Courts, *Judicial Business of the United States Courts: 2002 Annual Report of the Director*, p. 59; *2003 Annual Report of the Director*, p. 56 (Washington, DC: USGPO). Table adapted by SOURCEBOOK staff.

Table 1.96
Jury fees in State and Federal courts

By jurisdiction, as of June 2003

Jurisdiction	Juror fees per day	Jurisdiction	Juror fees per day
Federal	$40.00[a]	Missouri	$6.00
		Montana	12.00[p]
Alabama	10.00	Nebraska	35.00
Alaska	12.50[b,c]	Nevada	9.00[q]
Arizona	12.00[d]	New Hampshire	10.00[b]
Arkansas	5.00[e]		
California	15.00[f]	New Jersey	(r)
		New Mexico	(s)
Colorado	(g)	New York	(t)
Connecticut	(h)	North Carolina	12.00[u]
Delaware	20.00[i]	North Dakota	25.00
District of Columbia	30.00[j]		
Florida	(k)	Ohio	10.00[l,v]
		Oklahoma	12.50
Georgia	5.00[l]	Oregon	10.00
Hawaii	30.00	Pennsylvania	(w)
Idaho	10.00[b]	Rhode Island	15.00
Illinois	4.00[l]		
Indiana	15.00[m]	South Carolina	10.00
		South Dakota	10.00[x]
Iowa	10.00	Tennessee	10.00
Kansas	10.00	Texas	6.00[l,y]
Kentucky	12.50	Utah	(z)
Louisiana	12.00		
Maine	10.00	Vermont	30.00
		Virginia	30.00
Maryland	15.00[l,n]	Washington	10.00[l]
Massachusetts	(g)	West Virginia	40.00
Michigan	7.50[b]	Wisconsin	8.00[b,l]
Minnesota	30.00[o]	Wyoming	30.00[aa]
Mississippi	15.00		

Note: Daily juror fees are set by statute and do not include any mileage payments to jurors.

[a] May be raised to $50.00 per day after 30 days of service upon discretion of the judge.
[b] Half-day rate.
[c] Anchorage provides $5.00 half-day rate for the first day, then $12.50 per half-day thereafter.
[d] No fee for first day (discretionary); $12.00 per day thereafter.
[e] $20.00 per day while actually serving (sworn).
[f] No fee for first day; $15.00 per day thereafter.
[g] No fee for first 3 days; $50.00 per day thereafter. Expenses for unemployed available. Employers must pay employees for first 3 days while serving.
[h] No fee for first 5 days; $50.00 per day thereafter. Expenses for unemployed available. Employers must pay employees for first 5 days while serving.
[i] No fee for first day; $20.00 per day thereafter.
[j] No fee for first day; $30.00 per day thereafter.
[k] If employer pays salary or wages of person on jury duty, there is no fee paid for 3 days; then $30.00 per day thereafter. If individual is not employed or employer does not pay salary, fee is $15.00 per day for first 3 days; then $30.00 per day thereafter.
[l] Fees vary among counties.
[m] $40.00 per day while actually serving (sworn).
[n] Provided as an expense; not reported as income.
[o] Child care expenses available.
[p] $25.00 per day while actually serving (sworn).
[q] $15.00 per day while actually serving (sworn). $30.00 per day after 5 days of service. $9.00 per day if not sworn.
[r] $5.00 for first 3 days; $40.00 per day thereafter.
[s] $5.15 per hour, established by minimum wage law.
[t] If employer has more than 10 employees, must pay at least $40.00 per day for the first 3 days. After 3 days, the court must pay $40.00 per day. If juror is not employed or if employer has less than 10 employees, court must pay $40.00 per day from day 1.
[u] $30.00 per day after 5 days of service.
[v] County commission shall fix the compensation not to exceed $40.00. After 10 days of actual service, compensation to be one and a half times the daily rate--minimum of $15.00. Maximum may be set by county not to exceed twice the daily rate for service of less than 10 days.
[w] $9.00 for first 3 days; $25.00 per day thereafter.
[x] $50.00 maximum per day while actually serving (sworn).
[y] $30.00 maximum per day while actually serving (sworn).
[z] $18.50 for first day; $49.00 per day thereafter.
[aa] May be raised to $50.00 per day after 4 days of service upon discretion of the judge.

Source: Table provided to SOURCEBOOK staff by the National Center for State Courts, Center for Jury Studies.

Table 1.97

Investigative reports by Federal probation officers

By type of investigation, 1980-2003

	Presentence investigation[a]	Collateral investigation for another district	Alleged violation investigation (probation and parole)	Prerelease investigation for a Federal or military institution
1980	23,961	16,836	12,347	9,883
1981	24,957	18,502	12,584	8,097
1982	27,463	21,233	12,241	6,996
1983	30,323	23,135	12,436	6,958
1984	30,745	23,057	12,585	7,292
1985	32,669	25,055	13,289	6,955
1986	35,594	28,456	14,046	7,691
1987	37,300	30,120	15,316	8,620
1988	36,737	28,630	16,456	9,955
1989	38,563	29,363	16,781	10,643
1990	41,812	28,584	18,236	10,581
1991	44,226	32,240	21,082	11,393
1992	48,267	34,747	23,975	11,457
1993	48,871	34,311	24,107	12,939
1994	44,434	32,663	24,014	13,677
1995	43,151	33,293	26,629	15,425
1996	48,372	33,589	26,759	16,550
1997	52,174	34,961	29,847	18,362
1998	57,794	39,461	29,701	20,524
1999	61,207	43,088	28,349	22,251
2000	63,666	46,341	29,976	23,639
2001	63,028	48,377	31,298	25,287
2002	63,668	46,664	35,944	27,281
2003	67,744	51,109	38,569	27,489

Note: Persons under supervision of the Federal Probation System include persons placed on probation--either by U.S. District Courts, U.S. magistrate judges, or at the request of U.S. attorneys (deferred prosecution)--and Federal offenders released from confinement on parole or mandatory release. Prior to 1989, the data represent the 12-month period ending June 30. In 1989 and 1990, the reporting period was the 12-month period ending March 31. Beginning in 1991, data are reported for the Federal fiscal year, which is the 12-month period ending September 30. Some data have been revised by the Source and may differ from previous editions of SOURCEBOOK.

[a]Beginning in 1997, category includes postsentence investigations for institutions.

Source: Administrative Office of the United States Courts, *Annual Report of the Director, 1982*, p. 20; *1984*, p. 20; *1988*, p. 42; *1990*, p. 29, Table 18; *1992*, p. 87, Table 19; *1994*, p. 21; *1996*, p. 35 (Washington, DC: USGPO); Administrative Office of the United States Courts, *Annual Report of the Director, 1980*, p. 15, Table 18; *1986*, p. 45; *1998*, p. 40 (Washington, DC: Administrative Office of the United States Courts); and Administrative Office of the United States Courts, *Judicial Business of the United States Courts: 2000 Annual Report of the Director*, p. 33; *2002 Annual Report of the Director*, p. 31; *2003 Annual Report of the Director*, p. 27 (Washington, DC: USGPO). Table adapted by SOURCEBOOK staff.

Table 1.98

Number of jails, rated capacity, percent of capacity occupied, and number of inmates per employee

By region and jurisdiction, June 30, 1999

Region and jurisdiction	Number of jails	Rated capacity[a]	Percent of rated capacity occupied[b]	Number of inmates per employee[c] — Total staff	Number of inmates per employee[c] — Correctional officers
United States, total	3,376	660,361	93%	2.9	4.4
Federal	11	8,040	139	3.6	6.7
State	3,365	652,321	93	2.9	4.3
Northeast	227	97,794	93	2.2	2.9
Maine	15	1,220	91	1.4	1.8
Massachusetts	21	9,978	108	2.3	3.6
New Hampshire	10	1,812	88	2.9	3.8
New Jersey	24	15,349	110	3.0	3.7
New York	81	39,904	84	1.5	2.0
Pennsylvania	76	29,531	91	3.2	4.5
Midwest	977	108,261	90	2.5	4.2
Illinois	93	19,069	89	2.7	8.1
Indiana	93	12,553	102	2.7	5.9
Iowa	94	3,125	96	1.8	2.5
Kansas	97	5,565	79	2.1	3.1
Michigan	93	16,661	94	3.2	4.9
Minnesota	78	5,970	84	1.8	2.8
Missouri	129	8,924	78	2.1	3.2
Nebraska	65	2,728	80	1.8	2.6
North Dakota	23	918	64	1.7	2.2
Ohio	108	17,219	97	2.3	3.3
South Dakota	31	1,623	66	2.2	3.1
Wisconsin	73	13,906	90	3.5	4.8
South	1,623	308,234	92	3.3	4.6
Alabama	155	11,600	98	3.7	5.6
Arkansas	87	6,122	79	2.6	3.5
District of Columbia	1	1,378	120	2.4	2.8
Florida	108	55,493	92	3.3	4.6
Georgia	204	36,213	91	3.9	5.3
Kentucky	82	9,915	105	3.7	4.9
Louisiana	107	27,544	93	3.8	6.0
Maryland	29	11,821	93	2.6	3.6
Mississippi	102	9,778	91	3.8	5.9
North Carolina	104	15,456	86	2.9	4.3
Oklahoma	102	7,663	88	3.3	4.6
South Carolina	52	9,115	96	3.4	4.4
Tennessee	108	21,572	91	3.1	4.4
Texas	271	66,521	87	3.5	4.5
Virginia	82	15,514	118	2.4	3.3
West Virginia	29	2,529	99	3.1	4.3
West	538	138,032	96	3.3	5.7
Alaska	15	160	43	0.6	1.8
Arizona	28	12,629	82	3.3	4.7
California	145	75,088	103	3.8	7.2
Colorado	61	9,151	98	2.4	3.2
Idaho	41	3,203	88	3.3	5.7
Montana	42	1,791	85	2.0	3.2
Nevada	21	5,436	90	2.5	4.2
New Mexico	34	6,258	83	2.9	5.9
Oregon	41	7,210	87	2.6	3.8
Utah	26	5,904	68	3.1	7.3
Washington	62	10,004	105	3.6	5.1
Wyoming	22	1,198	84	2.4	3.4

Note: These data are from the 1999 Census of Jails conducted for the U.S. Department of Justice, Bureau of Justice Statistics by the U.S. Census Bureau. The 1999 census included all locally administered jails that held inmates beyond arraignment (usually more than 72 hours) and were staffed by municipal or county employees. Excluded from the census were physically separate temporary holding facilities, such as drunk tanks and police lockups, that do not hold persons after they are formally charged in court. Also excluded were Connecticut, Delaware, Hawaii, Rhode Island, and Vermont because these jurisdictions have State-operated integrated jail/prison systems. Alaska also was excluded for this reason, however, 15 independently operated jails in Alaska were included. For additional information on the Census of Jails, see Appendix 4.

[a] Rated capacity is the number of beds or inmates assigned by a rating official to facilities within each jurisdiction.
[b] The number of inmates divided by rated capacity times 100.
[c] Inmate-to-staff ratios were calculated by dividing the number of confined inmates by the number of employees on June 30, 1999.

Source: U.S. Department of Justice, Bureau of Justice Statistics, *Census of Jails, 1999*, NCJ 186633 (Washington, DC: U.S. Department of Justice, 2001), pp. 14, 28. Table adapted by SOURCEBOOK staff.

Table 1.99

Jail staff

By occupational category, region, and jurisdiction, June 30, 1999

Region and jurisdiction	Total staff	Administrative	Correctional officers	Clerical and maintenance	Educational	Professional and technical[a]	Other
National estimate[b]	210,600	14,600	151,200	25,400	2,100	11,500	5,800
State estimate[b]	207,600	14,400	149,600	25,300	2,100	10,700	5,500
United States, total	197,375	13,722	141,663	23,772	1,969	10,764	5,485
Federal	3,110	253	1,685	93	30	715	334
State	194,265	13,469	139,978	23,679	1,939	10,049	5,151
Northeast	40,899	1,819	31,269	3,995	579	2,270	967
Maine	800	55	608	70	18	38	11
Massachusetts	4,617	370	3,007	611	100	448	81
New Hampshire	546	47	420	29	10	36	4
New Jersey	5,538	143	4,559	484	24	276	52
New York	21,454	717	16,707	2,093	317	928	692
Pennsylvania	7,944	487	5,968	708	110	544	127
Midwest	32,821	2,741	23,190	4,281	320	1,585	704
Illinois	2,936	233	2,091	383	17	76	136
Indiana	3,443	440	2,155	563	46	141	98
Iowa	1,566	176	1,212	155	1	13	9
Kansas	1,950	262	1,430	222	4	28	4
Michigan	4,738	311	3,199	755	73	304	96
Minnesota	2,600	203	1,804	364	40	136	53
Missouri	3,047	259	2,152	409	19	131	77
Nebraska	1,141	109	858	111	5	28	30
North Dakota	344	30	266	13	7	20	8
Ohio	7,007	415	5,072	805	68	540	107
South Dakota	479	50	346	61	0	7	15
Wisconsin	3,570	253	2,605	440	40	161	71
South	82,245	5,019	62,227	8,878	507	3,398	2,216
Alabama	2,919	394	2,044	266	6	55	154
Arkansas	1,813	175	1,393	200	5	18	22
District of Columbia	696	9	589	75	3	20	0
Florida	15,618	481	11,186	2,432	98	860	561
Georgia	8,188	653	6,229	891	32	184	199
Kentucky	2,632	181	2,115	231	19	45	41
Louisiana	6,100	371	4,255	798	40	337	299
Maryland	4,284	221	3,007	548	50	433	25
Mississippi	2,015	186	1,496	207	20	61	45
North Carolina	3,717	263	3,077	223	12	85	57
Oklahoma	1,995	199	1,452	203	47	24	70
South Carolina	2,420	104	1,989	202	15	82	28
Tennessee	6,177	354	4,471	651	40	426	235
Texas	15,477	965	12,744	1,124	58	463	123
Virginia	7,457	414	5,595	759	59	284	346
West Virginia	737	49	585	68	3	21	11
West	38,300	3,890	23,292	6,525	533	2,796	1,264
Alaska	79	20	37	11	0	1	10
Arizona	3,118	152	2,191	447	25	275	28
California	20,217	2,737	10,679	3,808	436	1,746	811
Colorado	3,660	242	2,791	365	12	166	84
Idaho	786	91	493	161	3	23	15
Montana	639	65	479	64	2	16	13
Nevada	1,997	83	1,178	483	0	49	204
New Mexico	1,218	93	885	126	16	82	16
Oregon	2,431	130	1,638	379	8	235	41
Utah	854	87	553	142	18	45	9
Washington	2,880	145	2,074	496	11	128	26
Wyoming	421	45	294	43	2	30	7

Note: See Note, table 1.98. "Total staff" includes full-time, part-time, payroll, and nonpayroll staff, and excludes contract staff and community volunteers. A total of 228 reporting units were unable to provide data for occupational category. For additional information on the Census of Jails, see Appendix 4.

[a] Includes psychiatrists, psychologists, social workers, counselors, medical doctors, nurses, paramedics, chaplains, and legal specialists.
[b] National and State estimates were calculated by summing the item values from reporting units and then multiplying by a nonresponse adjustment factor. All estimates for type of staff were rounded to the nearest 100.

Source: U.S. Department of Justice, Bureau of Justice Statistics, *Census of Jails, 1999*, NCJ 186633 (Washington, DC: U.S. Department of Justice, 2001), p. 25.

Table 1.100

Jail staff and correctional officers

By sex, region, and jurisdiction, June 30, 1999

Region and jurisdiction	Total staff Total	Total staff Male	Total staff Female	Correctional officers Total	Correctional officers Male	Correctional officers Female
National estimate[a]	210,600	139,100	71,500	151,200	108,700	42,500
State estimate[a]	207,600	139,900	70,700	149,600	107,400	42,200
United States, total	197,375	130,401	66,974	141,663	101,859	39,804
Federal	3,110	2,318	792	1,685	1,408	277
State	194,265	128,083	66,182	139,978	100,451	39,527
Northeast	40,899	29,308	11,591	31,269	23,557	7,712
Maine	800	584	216	608	484	124
Massachusetts	4,617	3,716	901	3,007	2,743	264
New Hampshire	546	408	138	420	344	76
New Jersey	5,538	4,137	1,401	4,559	3,698	861
New York	21,454	14,910	6,544	16,707	11,876	4,831
Pennsylvania	7,944	5,553	2,391	5,968	4,412	1,556
Midwest	32,821	21,007	11,814	23,190	16,342	6,848
Illinois	2,936	2,026	910	2,091	1,565	526
Indiana	3,443	2,236	1,207	2,155	1,570	585
Iowa	1,566	944	622	1,212	750	462
Kansas	1,950	1,331	619	1,430	1,043	387
Michigan	4,738	3,016	1,722	3,199	2,360	839
Minnesota	2,600	1,561	1,039	1,804	1,217	587
Missouri	3,047	2,083	964	2,152	1,617	535
Nebraska	1,141	613	528	858	487	371
North Dakota	344	201	143	266	164	102
Ohio	7,007	4,601	2,406	5,072	3,696	1,376
South Dakota	479	289	190	346	213	133
Wisconsin	3,570	2,106	1,464	2,605	1,660	945
South	82,245	52,819	29,426	62,227	43,446	18,781
Alabama	2,919	1,940	979	2,044	1,431	613
Arkansas	1,813	1,180	633	1,393	944	449
District of Columbia	696	435	261	589	379	210
Florida	15,618	9,325	6,293	11,186	7,591	3,595
Georgia	8,188	5,385	2,803	6,229	4,432	1,797
Kentucky	2,632	1,660	972	2,115	1,439	676
Louisiana	6,100	4,025	2,075	4,255	3,132	1,123
Maryland	4,284	2,656	1,628	3,007	2,086	921
Mississippi	2,015	1,272	743	1,496	1,019	477
North Carolina	3,717	2,307	1,410	3,077	1,979	1,098
Oklahoma	1,995	1,299	696	1,452	1,021	431
South Carolina	2,420	1,461	959	1,989	1,279	710
Tennessee	6,177	3,834	2,343	4,471	2,952	1,519
Texas	15,477	10,476	5,001	12,744	9,182	3,562
Virginia	7,457	5,005	2,452	5,595	4,093	1,502
West Virginia	737	559	178	585	487	98
West	38,300	24,949	13,351	23,292	17,106	6,186
Alaska	79	54	25	37	24	13
Arizona	3,118	1,976	1,142	2,191	1,620	571
California	20,217	13,297	6,920	10,679	7,842	2,837
Colorado	3,660	2,424	1,236	2,791	2,064	727
Idaho	786	491	295	493	346	147
Montana	639	419	220	479	342	137
Nevada	1,997	1,231	766	1,178	865	313
New Mexico	1,218	737	481	885	586	299
Oregon	2,431	1,559	872	1,638	1,253	385
Utah	854	575	279	553	425	128
Washington	2,880	1,907	973	2,074	1,524	550
Wyoming	421	279	142	294	215	79

Note: See Notes, tables 1.98 and 1.99. A total of 228 reporting units were unable to provide data by sex. For additional information on the Census of Jails, see Appendix 4.

[a] National and State estimates were calculated by summing the item values from reporting units and then multiplying by a nonresponse adjustment factor. All estimates for type of staff were rounded to the nearest 100.

Source: U.S. Department of Justice, Bureau of Justice Statistics, **Census of Jails, 1999**, NCJ 186633 (Washington, DC: U.S. Department of Justice, 2001), p. 26.

Table 1.101

Jail staff and correctional officers

By race, Hispanic origin, region, and jurisdiction, June 30, 1999

Region and jurisdiction	All staff						Correctional officers					
	Total	White, non-Hispanic	Black, non-Hispanic	Hispanic	Other races[a]	Race not reported	Total	White, non-Hispanic	Black, non-Hispanic	Hispanic	Other races[a]	Race not reported
National estimate[b]	210,600	126,300	47,100	15,600	3,600	18,000	151,200	89,600	35,800	11,700	1,700	12,400
State estimate[b]	207,600	125,200	46,200	14,800	3,500	17,900	149,600	89,000	35,400	11,200	1,700	12,300
United States, total	197,375	118,353	44,171	14,585	3,409	16,861	141,663	83,920	33,583	10,994	1,611	11,555
Federal	3,110	1,217	908	770	147	68	1,685	602	454	563	61	5
State	194,265	117,136	43,263	13,815	3,262	16,793	139,978	83,318	33,129	10,431	1,550	11,550
Northeast	40,899	23,633	11,767	3,146	311	2,042	31,269	17,014	9,840	2,649	188	1,578
Maine	800	790	5	2	3	0	608	599	4	2	2	0
Massachusetts	4,617	4,031	331	180	34	41	3,007	2,614	240	132	21	0
New Hampshire	546	523	13	7	3	0	420	399	12	6	3	0
New Jersey	5,538	2,873	1,079	341	16	1,229	4,559	2,250	960	277	10	1,062
New York	21,454	9,974	8,434	2,360	224	462	16,707	7,276	6,978	2,021	129	303
Pennsylvania	7,944	5,442	1,905	256	31	310	5,968	3,876	1,645	211	23	213
Midwest	32,821	27,177	3,773	507	230	1,138	23,190	18,572	2,613	410	158	1,437
Illinois	2,936	2,544	214	53	17	108	2,091	1,768	179	45	5	94
Indiana	3,443	3,035	262	28	9	110	2,155	1,835	205	26	6	83
Iowa	1,566	1,395	29	22	6	114	1,212	1,048	23	22	7	112
Kansas	1,950	1,628	104	65	24	129	1,430	1,169	88	55	21	97
Michigan	4,738	3,654	944	100	40	0	3,199	2,484	617	76	22	0
Minnesota	2,600	2,465	70	32	33	0	1,804	1,701	58	18	27	0
Missouri	3,047	2,119	518	16	17	377	2,152	1,351	237	13	12	539
Nebraska	1,141	989	75	47	3	27	858	726	71	43	3	15
North Dakota	344	324	1	3	8	8	266	249	1	2	6	8
Ohio	7,007	5,480	1,190	83	22	232	5,072	3,642	879	67	13	471
South Dakota	479	454	3	1	21	0	346	325	3	1	17	0
Wisconsin	3,570	3,090	363	57	30	33	2,605	2,274	252	42	19	18
South	82,245	44,045	24,504	4,790	577	8,329	62,227	33,585	19,070	4,351	419	4,802
Alabama	2,919	1,708	1,002	7	13	189	2,044	1,031	680	3	7	323
Arkansas	1,813	1,249	232	5	2	325	1,393	918	203	6	4	262
District of Columbia	696	30	624	4	5	33	589	2	521	4	4	58
Florida	15,618	7,690	4,360	1,193	143	2,232	11,186	6,142	3,729	979	83	253
Georgia	8,188	4,187	3,166	71	18	746	6,229	3,020	2,544	62	14	589
Kentucky	2,632	2,102	418	11	8	93	2,115	1,623	312	9	1	170
Louisiana	6,100	3,384	2,551	60	32	73	4,255	1,822	1,035	22	4	1,372
Maryland	4,284	1,883	2,346	33	17	5	3,007	1,194	1,776	22	12	3
Mississippi	2,015	972	834	15	2	192	1,496	679	624	14	2	177
North Carolina	3,717	2,378	1,208	32	63	36	3,077	1,690	946	27	46	368
Oklahoma	1,995	1,599	181	28	141	46	1,452	1,108	172	25	117	30
South Carolina	2,420	1,053	1,237	15	7	108	1,989	852	1,073	14	5	45
Tennessee	6,177	3,657	2,319	24	9	168	4,471	2,617	1,751	16	8	79
Texas	15,477	7,149	1,796	3,181	39	3,312	12,744	7,234	2,099	3,052	57	302
Virginia	7,457	4,303	2,199	111	74	770	5,595	3,099	1,579	96	51	770
West Virginia	737	701	31	0	4	1	585	554	26	0	4	1
West	38,300	22,281	3,219	5,372	2,144	5,284	23,292	14,147	1,606	3,021	785	3,733
Alaska	79	56	3	0	17	3	37	22	2	0	10	3
Arizona	3,118	805	86	347	35	1,845	2,191	595	56	253	20	1,267
California	20,217	10,073	2,362	3,686	1,649	2,447	10,679	5,591	974	1,742	541	1,831
Colorado	3,660	2,592	196	516	46	310	2,791	2,006	159	396	31	199
Idaho	786	750	3	23	10	0	493	471	0	14	8	0
Montana	639	585	1	5	16	32	479	435	2	5	11	26
Nevada	1,997	1,619	215	101	51	11	1,178	937	145	62	30	4
New Mexico	1,218	535	30	502	120	31	885	365	29	418	50	23
Oregon	2,431	2,050	69	53	51	208	1,638	1,360	48	41	29	160
Utah	854	811	7	20	15	1	553	524	7	9	12	1
Washington	2,880	2,008	246	101	132	393	2,074	1,578	183	72	42	199
Wyoming	421	397	1	18	2	3	294	263	1	9	1	20

Note: See Notes, tables 1.98 and 1.99. For additional information on the Census of Jails, see Appendix 4.

Source: U.S. Department of Justice, Bureau of Justice Statistics, *Census of Jails, 1999*, NCJ 186633 (Washington, DC: U.S. Department of Justice, 2001), p. 27.

[a] Includes American Indians, Alaska Natives, Asians, Native Hawaiians, and other Pacific Islanders.
[b] National and State estimates were calculated using a ratio adjustment based on the total estimated staff by occupation to the reported number of inmates by race, and rounding the estimate to the nearest 100 whole number.

Table 1.102

Federal, State, and private adult correctional facilities

By facility characteristics, United States, 1995 and 2000

Facility characteristics	Total 1995	Total 2000	Federal 1995	Federal 2000	State 1995	State 2000	Private 1995	Private 2000
Number[a]	1,464	1,668	77	84	1,277	1,320	110	264
Confinement	1,160	1,208	75	84	1,056	1,023	29	101
Community-based	304	460	2	0	221	297	81	163
Rated capacity	975,719	1,278,471	64,500	83,113	891,826	1,090,225	19,294	105,133
Percent of capacity occupied	105%	102%	125%	134%	104%	101%	86%	89%
Security level								
Maximum[b]	298	332	9	11	286	317	3	4
Medium	463	522	25	29	432	428	6	65
Minimum or low	703	814	43	44	559	575	101	195
Size[c]								
Fewer than 100 inmates	325	357	2	0	239	225	84	132
100 to 249	290	289	2	2	279	244	9	43
250 to 749	349	360	20	10	317	304	12	46
750 to 1,499	345	421	41	49	299	339	5	33
1,500 to 2,499	100	176	10	22	90	144	0	10
2,500 or more	55	65	2	1	53	64	0	0

Note: These data are from the 2000 Census of State and Federal Adult Correctional Facilities sponsored by the U.S. Department of Justice, Bureau of Justice Statistics. Facilities were included in the census if they were staffed with Federal, State, local, or private employees; housed primarily State or Federal prisoners; were physically, functionally, and administratively separate from other facilities; and were operational on June 30, 2000. Also included were 264 private facilities under contract to State governments or the Federal Bureau of Prisons to house prisoners. Facilities included were prisons and prison farms; reception, diagnostic, and classification centers; road camps; forestry and conservation camps; youthful offender facilities (except those in California); vocational training facilities; drug and alcohol treatment facilities; and State-operated local detention facilities in Alaska, Connecticut, Delaware, Hawaii, Rhode Island, and Vermont. Excluded from the census were jails and other local regional detention facilities; private facilities not exclusively for State or Federal prisoners; facilities for the military, the Immigration and Naturalization Service, the Bureau of Indian Affairs, and the U.S. Marshals Service; and correctional hospital wards not operated by correctional authorities. The "private" facilities included in the census are those with 50% or more of their inmates held for State or Federal authorities. Private facilities with more than 50% of their inmates held for local authorities were classified as jails and excluded from the census.

Correctional facilities were classified as "community-based" if 50% or more of the residents were regularly permitted to leave, unaccompanied, to work or study. These included halfway houses, restitution centers, and prerelease, work release, and study centers. Facilities in which less than 50% of the prisoners regularly left the facility unaccompanied were classified as "confinement" institutions.

[a]The classification of Federal facilities changed between 1995 and 2000. The 1995 count was adjusted by the Source to reflect the administrative merging of 38 camp facilities with 36 confinement facilities and the reclassification of 12 facilities as private.
[b]Includes facilities with the security designations super maximum, close, and high.
[c]Based on average daily population, July 1, 1999 to June 30, 2000.

Source: U.S. Department of Justice, Bureau of Justice Statistics, *Census of State and Federal Correctional Facilities, 2000*, NCJ 198272 (Washington, DC: U.S. Department of Justice, 2003), p. iv.

Table 1.103

Federal and State adult correctional facilities

By type of facility and facility function, United States, June 30, 2000

Facility function	Confinement Total	Confinement Federal	Confinement State	Confinement Private	Community-based Total	Community-based State	Community-based Private
Total	1,208	84	1,023	101	460	297	163
General confinement	1,081	82	919	80	83	57	26
Boot camp	84	3	78	3	11	9	2
Reception, diagnosis, or classification	173	3	165	5	5	3	2
Medical treatment or hospitalization	142	7	132	3	1	1	0
Alcohol/drug treatment	200	16	164	20	49	22	27
Youthful offender confinement	36	0	35	1	0	0	0
Work release/pre-release	107	1	95	11	426	277	149
Returned to custody confinement	58	2	48	8	20	11	9
Other[a]	317	11	298	8	36	15	21

Note: See Note, table 1.102. Figures may add to more than the total number of facilities because some facilities have more than one function.

[a]Includes psychiatric, geriatric, pre-sentence, conservation camp, work camp, community service, protective custody, transfer, sex offender, public works, death row, and skilled nursing functions.

Source: U.S. Department of Justice, Bureau of Justice Statistics, *Census of State and Federal Correctional Facilities, 2000*, NCJ 198272 (Washington, DC: U.S. Department of Justice, 2003), p. 5, Table 8.

Table 1.104

Employees of Federal, State, and private adult correctional facilities

By type of employee and selected characteristics, United States, 1995 and 2000

	1995	2000
All staff	347,320	430,033
Custody/security staff	220,892	270,317
Type of operation		
Federal		
All staff	24,836	32,700
Custody/security staff	10,048	12,376
State		
All staff	317,236	372,976
Custody/security staff	207,647	243,352
Private		
All staff	5,248	24,357
Custody/security staff	3,197	14,589
Type of facility		
Confinement		
All staff	339,070	381,214
Custody/security staff	215,824	248,567
Community-based		
All staff	8,250	16,119
Custody/security staff	5,068	9,374
Number of inmates per employee		
All staff	2.9	3.0
Custody/security staff only	4.6	4.8
Sex		
Male	246,581	288,306
Female	100,659	141,727
Not reported	80	0
Race, Hispanic origin[a]		
White, non-Hispanic	232,382	272,436
Black, non-Hispanic	65,513	83,697
Hispanic	20,702	31,697
Other races[b]	6,576	7,890

Note: See Note, table 1.102.

[a]Payroll staff only. Excludes unknown race accounting for 0.3% of payroll staff in 1995 and 2.9% in 2000.
[b]Includes American Indians, Alaska Natives, Asians, and Pacific Islanders.

Source: U.S. Department of Justice, Bureau of Justice Statistics, *Census of State and Federal Correctional Facilities, 2000*, NCJ 198272 (Washington, DC: U.S. Department of Justice, 2003), p. vi.

Table 1.105

Privately operated jails

By selected characteristics, United States, June 30, 1999

Number of facilities	47
Sex of inmates housed	
Male only	15
Female only	2
Both male and female	30
Size of facilities	
Fewer than 50 inmates	13
59 to 99	5
100 to 249	6
250 to 499	12
500 to 999	9
1,000 to 1,499	2
Inmates under supervision	16,656
In custody	13,814
Non-confined persons	2,842
Total staff	4,178
Male	2,242
Female	1,936
Inmates per employee	3.3
Correctional officers only	2,617
Male	1,548
Female	1,069
Inmates per correctional officer	5.3

Note: See Note, table 1.98. These data include private jails operated under contract to local government authorities. For additional information on the Census of Jails, see Appendix 4.

Source: U.S. Department of Justice, Bureau of Justice Statistics, *Census of Jails, 1999*, NCJ 186633 (Washington, DC: U.S. Department of Justice, 2001), p. 6. Table adapted by SOURCEBOOK staff.

Table 1.106
Federal Bureau of Prisons facilities

By selected characteristics, as of Sept. 30, 2003

Facility/State	Year opened	Security level	Sex of prisoners	1-day population count	Number of staff	Adjacent minimum security camp 1-day population count[a]
United States Penitentiaries (USP)						
Allenwood (PA)	1993	High	Male	1,107	299	
Atlanta (GA)	1902	High/Administrative	Male	2,315	664	489
Atwater (CA)	2001	High	Male	1,415	376	130
Beaumont (TX)	1997	High	Male	1,408	(b)	477
Coleman (FL)	2001	High	Male	1,657	(b)	
Florence (CO)	1996	High	Male	932	(b)	
Leavenworth (KS)	1906	High	Male	1,867	514	529
Lee (VA)	2002	High	Male	1,263	395	119
Lewisburg (PA)	1932	High	Male	1,273	541	545[c]
Lompoc (CA)	1959	High	Male	1,437	(b)	321
Marion (IL)	1963	High	Male	425	363	397
Pollock (LA)	2001	High	Male	1,488	403	107
Terre Haute (IN)[d]	1940	High	Male	1,158	479	438
Federal Correctional Institutions (FCI)						
Allenwood Low (PA)	1993	Low	Male	1,360	233	
Allenwood Medium (PA)	1993	Medium	Male	1,401	295	
Ashland (KY)	1940	Low	Male	1,165	299	293
Bastrop (TX)	1979	Low	Male	1,281	264	161
Beaumont Low (TX)	1997	Low	Male	2,041	(b)	
Beaumont Medium (TX)	1999	Medium	Male	1,785	(b)	
Beckley (WV)	1995	Medium	Male	1,692	358	379
Big Spring (TX)	1979	Low	Male	1,660	266	161
Butner Low (NC)	1996	Low	Male	1,342	(b)	
Butner Medium (NC)	1976	Medium/Administrative	Male	754	(b)	326
Coleman Low (FL)	1996	Low	Male	2,092	(b)	
Coleman Medium (FL)[e]	1996	Medium	Male	1,719	(b)	486
Cumberland (MD)	1994	Medium	Male	1,177	312	309
Danbury (CT)	1940	Low	Female	1,086	261	233
Dublin (CA)[e]	1974	Low; Administrative[f]	Female; Male	1,231	276	205
Edgefield (SC)	1998	Medium	Male	1,437	378	490
El Reno (OK)	1933	Medium	Male	1,311	355	225
Elkton (OH)	1997	Low	Male	1,842	347	565[g]
Englewood (CO)	1940	Medium/Administrative	Male	920	341	111
Estill (SC)	1993	Medium	Male	1,211	306	283
Fairton (NJ)	1990	Medium	Male	1,365	337	99
Florence (CO)	1994	Medium	Male	1,310	(b)	458
Forrest City (AR)	1997	Low	Male	1,845	319	256
Fort Dix (NJ)	1993	Low	Male	4,001	622	431
Gilmer (WV)	2003	Medium	Male	775	NA	122
Greenville (IL)[e]	1994	Medium	Male	1,306	286	242
Jesup (GA)	1990	Medium	Male	1,097	342	718[g]
La Tuna (TX)[h]	1932	Low	Male	1,138	380	661[g]
Lompoc (CA)	1970	Low	Male	1,523	(b)	182[c]
Loretto (PA)	1984	Low	Male	1,128	229	141
Manchester (KY)	1992	Medium	Male	1,220	317	518
Marianna (FL)[e]	1988	Medium	Male	1,262	341	288
McKean (PA)	1989	Medium	Male	1,305	305	286
Memphis (TN)	1977	Medium	Male	1,240	337	306
Miami (FL)	NA	Medium	Male	1,141	280	260
Milan (MI)	1933	Low/Administrative	Male	1,472	366	
Morgantown (WV)	1969	Minimum	Male	1,147	187	
Oakdale (LA)	1986	Medium	Male	1,322	(b)	
Otisville (NY)	1980	Medium	Male	1,027	307	115
Oxford (WI)	1973	Medium	Male	962	310	172
Pekin (IL)[e]	1994	Medium	Male	1,312	301	275
Petersburg Low (VA)	1932	Low	Male	1,181	(b)	347
Petersburg Medium (VA)	2002	Medium	Male	1,694	(b)	
Phoenix (AZ)[e]	1985	Medium	Male	1,299	333	236
Ray Brook (NY)	1980	Medium	Male	1,244	269	
Safford (AZ)	1964	Low	Male	819	169	
Sandstone (MN)	1939	Low	Male	903	236	
Schuylkill (PA)	1991	Medium	Male	1,230	322	306
Seagoville (TX)	1945	Low/Administrative	Male	1,633	318	137
Sheridan (OR)	1989	Medium/Administrative	Male	1,548	370	502
Talladega (AL)	1979	Medium	Male	1,057	323	363
Tallahassee (FL)	Late 1930s	Low; Adminstrative[f]	Female; Male	1,332	304	
Terminal Island (CA)	1938	Medium	Male	1,144	298	
Texarkana (TX)	1940	Low	Male	1,301	295	322
Three Rivers (TX)	1990	Medium	Male	1,145	299	288
Tucson (AZ)	1982	Medium; Administrative[i]	Male; Both	846	226	
Victorville (CA)[e]	2000	Medium	Male	1,706	386	288
Waseca (MN)	1995	Low	Male	1,063	230	
Yazoo City (MS)	1997	Low	Male	1,912	289	132

See notes at end of table.

Table 1.106

Federal Bureau of Prisons facilities

By selected characteristics, as of Sept. 30, 2003--Continued

Facility/State	Year opened	Security level	Sex of prisoners	1-day population count	Number of staff	Adjacent minimum security camp 1-day population count[a]
Federal Prison Camps (FPC)						
Alderson (WV)	1927	Minimum	Female	1,015	172	
Allenwood (PA)	1952	Minimum	Male	302	55	
Bryan (TX)	1988	Minimum	Female	805	159	112[c]
Duluth (MN)	1983	Minimum	Male	864	100	
Eglin (FL)	1962	Minimum	Male	820	126	
Montgomery (AL)	NA	Minimum	Male	862	115	
Nellis (NV)	1990	Minimum	Male	638	84	
Pensacola (FL)	1988	Minimum	Male	562	82	
Seymour Johnson (NC)	1989	Minimum	Male	617	86	
Yankton (SD)	1988	Minimum	Male	706	108	
Metropolitan Correctional/ Detention Centers (MCC/MDC)						
Brooklyn (NY)	1996	Administrative	Both	2,617	520	
Chicago (IL)	1975	Administrative	Both	713	210	
Guaynabo (PR)	1993	Administrative	Both	1,073	259	
Los Angeles (CA)	1988	Administrative	Both	1,065	276	
New York (NY)	1975	Administrative	Both	896	270	
San Diego (CA)	1974	Administrative	Both	988	252	
Federal Medical Centers (FMC)						
Butner (NC)	2000	Administrative	Male	847	(b)	
Carswell (TX)	1995	Administrative	Female	1,145	423	239
Devens (MA)	1999	Administrative	Male	1,084	463	125
Fort Worth (TX)	1971	Administrative	Male	1,534	384	
Lexington (KY)[e]	1974	Administrative	Male	2,066	518	252
Rochester (MN)	1985	Administrative	Male	794	432	
Springfield (MO)	1933	Administrative	Male	1,188	637	
Federal Detention Centers (FDC)						
Honolulu (HI)	2001	Administrative	Both	539	212	
Houston (TX)	2000	Administrative	Both	1,012	250	
Miami (FL)	1976	Administrative	Both	1,579	295	
Oakdale (LA)	1990	Administrative	Male	814	(b)	116
Philadelphia (PA)	2000	Administrative	Both	1,047	278	
SeaTac (WA)	1997	Administrative	Both	883	239	
Federal Transfer Center (FTC)						
Oklahoma City (OK)	1996	Administrative	Both	1,470	295	
Administrative Maximum (ADX)						
Florence (CO)	1995	Administrative	Male	386	(b)	

Note: Administrative facilities are institutions with special missions, such as the detention of pretrial offenders, the treatment of prisoners with serious or chronic medical problems, or the containment of extremely dangerous, violent, or escape-prone prisoners. Administrative facilities are capable of holding prisoners in all security categories.

[a]These minimum security satellite camps are adjacent to the main facility. A blank indicates no camp facility. Except where noted, the sex of prisoners housed in the camp and main facility is the same.

[b]A number of institutions are components of Federal Correctional Complexes (FCCs). At FCCs, institutions with different missions and security levels are located in close proximity to one another. For FCCs, the Source provided the total number of staff for the entire complex with no breakdown by institution. The number of staff at each FCC is as follows: Beaumont, 885; Butner, 1,000; Coleman, 984; Florence, 974; Lompoc, 740; Oakdale, 541; and Petersburg, 574.

[c]Figure includes prisoners in an Intensive Confinement Center (ICC) adjacent to the main facility. ICCs include programs for minimum security, non-violent offenders with no significant history of prior incarceration.

[d]This facility operates a Special Confinement Unit for prisoners under Federal death sentence.

[e]The adjacent camp is a minimum security facility for females.

[f]This facility houses low security females and administrative security males.

[g]Figure includes prisoners housed in a low security satellite facility adjacent to or affiliated with the main institution.

[h]Located on the New Mexico-Texas border.

[i]This facility houses medium security males and administrative security males and females.

Source: U.S. Department of Justice, Federal Bureau of Prisons, *State of the Bureau 2003* (Washington, DC: U.S. Department of Justice, 2004), pp. 31-52. Table constructed by SOURCEBOOK staff.

Table 1.107

Characteristics of Federal Bureau of Prisons staff

By race and ethnicity, January 2004[a]

	Total		White		Black		Hispanic		Other[b]	
	Number	Percent	Number	Percent	Number	Percent	Number	Percent	Number	Percent
Total	34,167	100.0%	22,040	64.5%	7,161	21.0%	3,753	11.0%	1,213	3.6%
Sex										
Male	24,504	71.7	16,352	74.2	4,455	62.2	2,824	75.3	873	72.0
Female	9,663	28.3	5,688	25.8	2,706	37.8	929	24.7	340	28.0
Age										
18 to 24 years	511	1.5	322	1.5	113	1.6	64	1.7	12	1.0
25 to 29 years	2,937	8.6	1,949	8.8	539	7.5	372	9.9	77	6.4
30 to 34 years	6,365	18.6	4,027	18.3	1,393	19.5	743	19.8	202	16.7
35 to 39 years	8,682	25.4	5,414	24.6	2,031	28.4	970	25.9	267	22.0
40 to 44 years	7,678	22.5	4,826	21.9	1,734	24.2	845	22.5	273	22.5
45 to 49 years	5,457	16.0	3,781	17.2	935	13.1	532	14.2	209	17.2
50 to 55 years	2,122	6.2	1,429	6.5	386	5.4	194	5.2	113	9.3
56 years and older	415	1.2	292	1.3	30	0.4	33	0.9	60	5.0
Education[c]										
Less than high school	93	0.3	47	0.2	25	0.4	16	0.4	5	0.5
High school	12,916	38.5	8,252	37.9	2,781	39.3	1,531	42.3	352	32.4
Technical school	1,358	4.0	972	4.5	266	3.8	95	2.6	25	2.3
Some college	10,263	30.6	6,550	30.1	2,117	29.9	1,255	34.6	341	31.4
College degree	6,221	18.5	4,193	19.2	1,357	19.2	470	13.0	201	18.5
Some graduate school	693	2.1	460	2.1	142	2.0	64	1.8	27	2.5
Master's degree	1,474	4.4	954	4.4	340	4.8	111	3.1	69	6.4
Ph.D. degree	556	1.7	360	1.7	48	0.7	81	2.2	67	6.2

Note: These data refer to staff who are in current pay status and exclude staff who are on leave without pay. This table represents all Bureau of Prisons employees including correctional officers.

[a]Percents may not add to total because of rounding.
[b]Includes Asians and Native Americans as well as non-Hispanic employees in Puerto Rico.
[c]Data on education level were not available for 593 employees; therefore, figures reported for education do not add to total.

Source: Table adapted by SOURCEBOOK staff from table provided by the U.S. Department of Justice, Federal Bureau of Prisons.

Table 1.108

Characteristics of Federal Bureau of Prisons correctional officers

By race and ethnicity, January 2004[a]

	Total		White		Black		Hispanic		Other[b]	
	Number	Percent	Number	Percent	Number	Percent	Number	Percent	Number	Percent
Total	14,844	100.0%	8,988	60.6%	3,607	24.3%	1,842	12.4%	407	2.7%
Sex										
Male	12,836	86.5	8,147	90.6	2,713	75.2	1,615	87.7	361	88.7
Female	2,008	13.5	841	9.4	894	24.8	227	12.3	46	11.3
Age										
18 to 24 years	308	2.1	197	2.2	61	1.7	42	2.3	8	2.0
25 to 29 years	2,021	13.6	1,335	14.9	363	10.1	274	14.9	49	12.0
30 to 34 years	3,730	25.1	2,243	25.0	882	24.5	495	26.9	110	27.0
35 to 39 years	4,066	27.4	2,358	26.2	1,103	30.6	482	26.2	123	30.2
40 to 44 years	2,754	18.6	1,583	17.6	763	21.2	333	18.1	75	18.4
45 to 49 years	1,529	10.3	983	10.9	331	9.2	179	9.7	36	8.9
50 to 55 years	423	2.9	280	3.1	103	2.9	35	1.9	5	1.2
56 years and older	13	0.1	9	0.1	1	(c)	2	0.1	1	0.3
Education[d]										
Less than high school	41	0.3	18	0.2	11	0.3	9	0.5	3	0.7
High school	7,476	50.4	4,479	49.8	1,838	51.0	967	52.5	192	47.2
Technical school	454	3.1	285	3.2	116	3.2	45	2.4	8	2.0
Some college	4,783	32.2	2,882	32.1	1,104	30.6	649	35.2	148	36.4
College degree	1,877	12.6	1,207	13.4	464	12.9	155	8.4	51	12.5
Some graduate school	101	0.7	61	0.7	24	0.7	11	0.6	5	1.2
Master's degree	93	0.6	44	0.5	44	1.2	5	0.3	0	X
Ph.D. degree	2	(c)	1	(c)	1	(c)	0	X	0	X

Note: See Note, table 1.107.

[a]Percents may not add to total because of rounding.
[b]Includes Asians and Native Americans as well as non-Hispanic employees in Puerto Rico.
[c]Less than 0.05%.
[d]Data on education level were not available for 17 employees; therefore, figures reported for education do not add to total.

Source: Table adapted by SOURCEBOOK staff from table provided by the U.S. Department of Justice, Federal Bureau of Prisons.

Table 1.109

Education programs in State, Federal, and private prisons, and in local jails

By type of program, United States, 1995, 1999, 2000[a]

	Prisons						Local jails,
	State		Federal		Private		
Education program	1995	2000	1995	2000	1995	2000	1999
With an education program	88.0%	91.2%	100.0%	100.0%	71.8%	87.6%	60.3%
Basic adult education	76.0	80.4	92.0	97.4	40.0	61.6	24.7
Secondary education	80.3	83.6	100.0	98.7	51.8	70.7	54.8
College courses	31.4	26.7	68.8	80.5	18.2	27.3	3.4
Special education	33.4	39.6	34.8	59.7	27.3	21.9	10.8
Vocational training	54.5	55.7	73.2	93.5	25.5	44.2	6.5
Study release programs	9.3	7.7	5.4	6.5	32.7	28.9	9.3
Without an education program	12.0	8.8	0.0	0.0	28.2	12.4	39.7
Total number of facilities	1,278	1,307	(b)	(b)	110	242	2,819

Note: These data are from two U.S. Department of Justice, Bureau of Justice Statistics surveys. The data for prisons are from the Census of State and Federal Correctional Facilities conducted in 1995 and 2000. The data for local jails are from the Census of Jails conducted in 1999.

[a] Detail may not add to total because facilities may have more than one education program.
[b] Changed definitions prevent meaningful comparisons of the numbers of Federal facilities for 1995 and 2000.

Source: U.S. Department of Justice, Bureau of Justice Statistics, *Education and Correctional Populations*, Special Report NCJ 195670 (Washington, DC: U.S. Department of Justice, January 2003), p. 4, Table 3.

Table 1.110

Estimated number of applications and rejections for firearm transfers

United States, 1999-2003

	Applications		
	Received	Rejected	Percent rejected
1999	8,621,000	204,000	2.4%
2000	7,699,000	153,000	2.0
2001	7,958,000	151,000	1.9
2002	7,806,000	136,000	1.7
2003	7,831,000	126,000	1.6

Note: The Brady Handgun Violence Prevention Act (the Brady Act) mandates criminal history background checks on persons applying to purchase firearms from federally licensed firearm dealers (Federal Firearm Licensees or FFLs). The permanent provisions of the Brady Act became effective on Nov. 30, 1998. The act established the National Instant Criminal Background Check System (NICS) and requires a background check by the Federal Bureau of Investigation (FBI) or a State point of contact on all persons applying to receive a handgun or long gun from a FFL. When a background check produces evidence of factors that disqualify an applicant from owning a firearm, the application is rejected. The Bureau of Justice Statistics began the Firearm Inquiry Statistics (FIST) program in 1995 to collect information on background checks conducted by State and local agencies. These data combine FIST estimates of the number of checks and rejections done by State and local agencies and the FBI number of actual transactions and rejections reported by the NICS operations reports. Counts of applications received and rejected are rounded.

Source: U.S. Department of Justice, Bureau of Justice Statistics, ***Background Checks for Firearm Transfers, 2003***, Bulletin NCJ 204428 (Washington, DC: U.S. Department of Justice, September 2004), p. 2. Table adapted by SOURCEBOOK staff.

Table 1.111

Reasons for rejection of firearm transfer applications

United States, 1999-2003[a]

Reason for rejection	State and local agencies						FBI	
	1999	2000	2001	2002	2003	1999-2003	2003	1999-2003
Total	100%	100%	100%	100%	100%	100%	100%	100%
Felony indictment or conviction	72.5	57.6	57.7	51.8	44.8	58.1	38.6	54.5
Other criminal history	NA	NA	NA	NA	NA	NA	24.3	15.0
Domestic violence								
Misdemeanor conviction	9.0	8.9	10.6	10.4	11.7	10.0	12.2	13.3
Restraining order	2.1	3.3	3.7	3.5	3.8	3.2	5.0	4.4
State law prohibition	3.5	4.7	7.0	9.9	10.4	6.7	(b)	(b)
Fugitive	5.0	4.3	5.8	8.0	7.8	5.9	4.7	3.3
Illegal alien	0.2	0.2	0.4	0.8	1.1	0.5	2.4	1.1
Mental illness or disability	0.5	1.0	1.2	1.4	2.4	1.2	0.5	0.4
Drug addiction	1.0	0.7	1.0	1.3	1.8	1.1	8.0	5.8
Local law prohibition	0.2	0.2	0.5	0.9	1.2	0.6	X	X
Other[c]	6.0	19.2	12.1	12.0	14.9	12.8	4.3	2.1

Note: See Note, table 1.110.

[a] Percents may not add to 100 because of rounding or missing data.
[b] The FBI rejects applications based on State law prohibitors, but does not specify them under this category.
[c] Includes persons dishonorably discharged from the armed services, persons who have renounced their U.S. citizenship, and other unspecified persons.

Source: U.S. Department of Justice, Bureau of Justice Statistics, ***Background Checks for Firearm Transfers, 2003***, Bulletin NCJ 204428 (Washington, DC: U.S. Department of Justice, September 2004), p. 6. Table adapted by SOURCEBOOK staff.

Table 1.112

Statutory provisions related to alcohol use and driving

By State, as of Jan. 1, 2002

State	Preliminary breath test law	Administrative per se at:	Blood alcohol concentration levels as evidence in State courts — Illegal per se at:	Blood alcohol concentration levels as evidence in State courts — Presumption at:	Open container law	Anti-consumption law	Dram shop law
Alabama		0.08	0.08	0.08	S		S
Alaska	S	0.08	0.08	0.08	S[a]	S[a]	S
Arizona	S	0.08	0.08	0.08	S	S	S
Arkansas		0.08	0.08			S	(b,c)
California	S	0.08[d]	0.08	0.08	S	S	S[e]
Colorado	S	0.10	0.10	0.05, 0.10[f]		S	S
Connecticut		0.10	0.10[g]				S[h]
Delaware	S	0.10[i]	0.10	0.10[j]		S[a]	
District of Columbia	S	0.05[j]	0.08	0.05[j]	S	S	(b)
Florida	S	0.08	0.08	0.08[j]	S	S	S[k]
Georgia		0.08	0.08		S	S	S
Hawaii	S	0.08	0.08	0.08[l]	S	S	(b)
Idaho		0.08	0.08		S	S	S
Illinois	S	0.08	0.08	0.08	S	S[m]	S[h]
Indiana	S[n]	0.08	0.08	0.08[o]	S[p]	S[a]	S
Iowa	S	0.10	0.10		S	S	S
Kansas	S	0.08	0.08	0.08[j]	S	S	
Kentucky	S	(q)	0.08		S	S	S
Louisiana		0.10	0.10	0.10	S[a]	S[a]	S[r]
Maine		0.08	0.08		S	S	S[h]
Maryland	S	0.08	0.08	0.07[s]	S[m]	S[a]	
Massachusetts		0.08		0.08	S		(b)
Michigan	S		0.10	0.07, 0.10[f]	S	S	S
Minnesota	S	0.10	0.10		S	S	S
Mississippi	S	0.10	0.10				S
Missouri	S	0.08	0.08	0.08[j]		S[a]	S
Montana	S		0.10	0.10	S[t]	S[t]	S
Nebraska	S	0.08	0.08		S	S	
Nevada	S	0.10	0.10		S	S[a]	
New Hampshire	S	0.08	0.08	0.08[j]	S		S
New Jersey			0.10		S	S	S
New Mexico		0.08	0.08		S	S	S
New York	S	(q)	0.10	0.07, 0.10[u]	S	S	S
North Carolina	S	0.08	0.08		S	S	S[h,v]
North Dakota	S	0.10	0.10		S	S	S
Ohio		0.10	0.10		S	S	S
Oklahoma		0.08	0.08	0.05, 0.08[w]	S	S	(b)
Oregon		0.08	0.08	0.08[x]	S	S	S
Pennsylvania	S		0.10		S	S	S
Rhode Island	S		0.08		S		S
South Carolina		0.15	0.10	0.10[y]	S	S	(z)
South Dakota	S		0.10	0.10	S	S	
Tennessee			0.10	0.10, 0.08[aa]	S[a]	S[a]	S
Texas		0.08	0.08		S		S[m]
Utah		0.08	0.08		S	S	S[h]
Vermont	S	0.08	0.08	0.08[y]		S[a]	S
Virginia	S	0.08	0.08	0.08		S[a]	
Washington		0.08	0.08		S	S	(b,k)
West Virginia	S	0.10[ab]	0.10	0.10[o]		S	(b)
Wisconsin	S	0.10[ac]	0.10[ac]	0.10[ad]	S	S	S[e]
Wyoming		0.10	0.10		S[a]	S[a]	S[ae]

Note: These data were collected through a review of the statutory provisions of the 50 States, the District of Columbia, and Puerto Rico.

In the table, "S" indicates that such a provision is provided expressly by statute. A blank indicates that no statutory or case law provisions exist. "Preliminary breath test" laws refer to a breath test given by a law enforcement officer to a suspected drunk driver prior to an arrest for a drunk driving offense. These results are used, along with other evidence, by the officer to determine if there is probable cause to arrest the driver. "Administrative per se" laws allow State driver licensing agencies to either suspend or revoke a driver's license based on the specified blood alcohol concentration (BAC) or on other criteria related to alcohol or drug use and driving. Such action is independent of licensing action resulting from a criminal conviction for a drunk driving offense. The evidentiary weight given to BAC levels generally falls into one of two categories. "Illegal per se" laws make it a criminal offense to operate a motor vehicle at or above the specified alcohol concentration level in either the blood, breath, or urine. Under these laws, the specified level is considered conclusive evidence of intoxication in a court of law.

"Presumption" indicates that the specified level of alcohol concentration in a driver's blood, breath, or urine creates a presumption of intoxication in a court of law. Statutory provisions of several jurisdictions treat the 0.10 level as both presumptive and illegal per se evidence of driving under the influence. This appears to be the result of States having adopted one of the standards without amending statutes that had previously authorized the other standard. In such cases, the actual statutes should be consulted for clarification. "Open container law" refers to laws prohibiting the possession of open containers of alcoholic beverages in the passenger compartment of a motor vehicle. "Anti-consumption law" refers to laws prohibiting the consumption of alcoholic beverages in the passenger compartment of a motor vehicle. "Dram shop law" refers to laws that provide that a person who serves alcoholic beverages to an intoxicated individual may be liable for damages and injuries caused in a motor vehicle accident.

In all jurisdictions, use of a controlled substance or use of a controlled substance in conjunction with alcohol also constitutes the basis for a driving while intoxicated charge. Most jurisdictions have established more stringent BAC levels for operators of commercial motor vehicles, as well as juvenile motor vehicle operators. Statutes should be consulted for the full text and meaning of specific provisions.

Table 1.112

Statutory provisions related to alcohol use and driving

By State, as of Jan. 1, 2002--Continued

[a] Applies to drivers only.
[b] Adopted via case law decisions.
[c] Case law has been modified by statute.
[d] Applies only to persons age 21 and older.
[e] Applies only to the actions of intoxicated minors.
[f] The lower number is driving while impaired; the higher is driving while under the influence.
[g] 0.07 if the driver has a previous violation of driving under the influence at 0.10 or greater.
[h] This State has a statute that places a monetary limit on the amount of damages that can be awarded in dram shop liability actions.
[i] Constitutes conclusive evidence of a driving while intoxicated offense.
[j] Constitutes prima facie evidence of driving while under the influence.
[k] Applies only to the actions of intoxicated minors or persons known to be habitually addicted to alcohol.
[l] Competent evidence of driving while intoxicated.
[m] Limited application.
[n] Applies only to drunk driving offenses that are related to either an injury or death.
[o] Has both prima facie and presumptive evidence laws with blood alcohol concentration at this level.
[p] Provided the driver has an alcohol concentration of 0.04 or more.
[q] Alternative before driving while intoxicated criminal adjudication licensing action by the courts.
[r] The statute appears to have limited actions to those committed by minors.
[s] An alcohol concentration equal to or greater than 0.07 but less than 0.10 constitutes prima facie evidence of driving while under the influence.
[t] Appears to be limited to persons operating "common carriers."
[u] Constitutes prima facie evidence of impairment.
[v] Applies specifically to the actions of intoxicated minors, but the law does not foreclose developing case law as to other types of dram shop action.
[w] The lower number is driving while impaired; the higher is prima facie evidence of driving under the influence.
[x] Not less than 0.08 constitutes being under the influence of intoxicating liquor.
[y] This blood alcohol level is an inference of driving while intoxicated.
[z] Possible via case law. Applies to actions of intoxicated minors.
[aa] For a first offense, an alcohol concentration of 0.10 or more; for a subsequent offense, an alcohol concentration of 0.08 or more.
[ab] Or under the influence of alcohol.
[ac] First and second offense 0.10; third offense 0.08; subsequent offenses 0.02.
[ad] 0.10 is prima facie evidence for first and second offenses. 0.08 is prima facie evidence for third and subsequent offenses.
[ae] Liability limited to the actions of persons who are under 21 years old.

Source: U.S. Department of Transportation, National Highway Traffic Safety Administration, *Digest of State Alcohol-Highway Safety Related Legislation, Current as of January 1, 2002* (Washington, DC: U.S. Department of Transportation, 2002), pp. 2-1--2-4. Table adapted by SOURCEBOOK staff.

Table 1.113

Statutory provisions requiring blood alcohol concentration tests for victims of fatal traffic accidents

By jurisdiction, as of Jan. 1, 2002

Jurisdiction	Statutory requirement	Driver	Vehicle passenger	Pedestrian	Jurisdiction	Statutory requirement	Driver	Vehicle passenger	Pedestrian
Alabama	(a)				Montana				
Alaska					Nebraska	S	S^k		S^l
Arizona	S	S			Nevada	S	S	S	S
Arkansas	S	S^b	(c)	(c)	New Hampshire	S	S	S	S
California	S	S	S	S	New Jersey	S	S		S
Colorado	S	S		S^d	New Mexico	S^g	S^g	S^g	S^g
Connecticut	S	S		S	New York	S^m	S		S^f
Delaware					North Carolina				
District of Columbia					North Dakota	S	S	S	S
Florida					Ohio	S	S		
Georgia	(e)	(e)	(e)	(e)	Oklahoma				
Hawaii	(e)	(e)	(e)	(e)	Oregon	S	S^n	S^n	S^n
Idaho	S	S		S	Pennsylvania	S	S^o	S^p	S^o
Illinois	S	S		S^f	Puerto Rico	S	S		S
Indiana	S	S		S^d	Rhode Island				
Iowa					South Carolina	S	S		S^f
Kansas	S^g	S		S^h	South Dakota	S	S	S	S
Kentucky	(e)	(e)	(e)	(e)	Tennessee	(q)	(q)	(q)	(q)
Louisiana	S	S	S	S	Texas	S^l	S^r		
Maine					Utah	S	S		S^s
Maryland					Vermont				
Massachusetts	S^i	S^j			Virginia				
Michigan	S	S			Washington	S	S		S
Minnesota	S	S		S^f	West Virginia	S	S		S^s
Mississippi	S	S			Wisconsin	S	S		S^h
Missouri	S	S	S	S	Wyoming				

Note: See Note, table 1.112. In the table, "S" indicates that such a provision is provided expressly by statute. Statutes should be consulted for the full text and meaning of specific provisions.

[a] Not specifically provided for by statute. However, case law provides that the blood alcohol concentration test law provisions were deemed to apply to dead persons.
[b] Based on probable cause of a driving while intoxicated offense.
[c] Possible.
[d] If the deceased is 15 years of age or older.
[e] Possible; at request of coroner or police officer, the medical examiner may take a blood sample.
[f] If the deceased is 16 years of age or older.
[g] Test results may only be used for statistical purposes that do not reveal the identity of deceased individuals.
[h] If the deceased is 14 years of age or older.
[i] Limited.
[j] If driver dies within 4 hours of accident. However, the law only applies if, at the time of the accident, (1) the driver was the only occupant of the vehicle and (2) no other individuals were involved.
[k] If death occurs within 4 hours of accident.
[l] If the deceased is 16 years of age or older and death occurs within 4 hours of accident.
[m] No test shall be conducted if there is reason to believe that the deceased is of a religious faith that is opposed to such a test.
[n] If the deceased is over 13 years of age and death occurs within 5 hours of accident.
[o] If the deceased is over 15 years of age and death occurs within 4 hours of accident.
[p] Only if the driver of the vehicle cannot be determined.
[q] Discretionary.
[r] Discretionary; a justice of the peace may order a blood test if there is evidence that the deceased was driving while intoxicated.
[s] Adults only.

Source: U.S. Department of Transportation, National Highway Traffic Safety Administration, *Digest of State Alcohol-Highway Safety Related Legislation, Current as of January 1, 2002* (Washington, DC: U.S. Department of Transportation, 2002), pp. 3-1--3-549. Table adapted by SOURCEBOOK staff.

Section 2

Public attitudes toward crime and criminal justice-related topics

Each year numerous public opinion surveys in the United States focus on criminal justice topics. These surveys are conducted by polling and research organizations as part of general social surveys or specifically for public and private organizations. Other surveys are conducted by government agencies or commissions concerned with specific problems. Selected populations such as high school seniors, college students, or parents often are the focus of these efforts. Results from a wide variety of opinion polls, examining attitudes toward many criminal justice issues, are presented in this section.

Initially addressed are public perceptions of important problems and issues such as crime and violence, and problems facing teens. Featured in this series are questions focusing on school-related concerns including the problems faced by schools, students' perceptions of safety, fear of victimization at school, and parents' and teenagers' perceptions of drug testing and locker searches in school.

The next series of tables relates to the confidence people express in numerous institutions including the criminal justice system, as a whole, and in the police and the U.S. Supreme Court, specifically. Ratings of the honesty and ethical standards of lawyers and police are presented, as are various measures of police performance and behavior (e.g., racial profiling, officers striking a citizen, and increased law enforcement powers).

Perceptions of terrorism and the level of crime in the country and in the respondent's own area are the topics of the next set of tables. Questions about the public's fear of future terrorist attacks and measures that may be needed to curb terrorism are included. Respondents' feelings of safety walking alone at night and fears concerning specific types of victimization also are displayed in this section. Reports of whether respondents engaged in selected behaviors, such as buying a gun for protection, or carrying mace or pepper spray, because of their concern over crime are included. Several tables cover public attitudes concerning the fairness of the criminal justice system in its treatment of the accused and juveniles, and attitudes concerning measures to reduce the crime and drug problems (e.g., level of spending and the severity of courts).

The focus of the section then shifts to public attitudes toward capital punishment. There are many tables on perceptions about the death penalty generally and as a penalty for people convicted of murder. Also explored are attitudes toward the death penalty for selected groups such as women, the mentally retarded, and juveniles; rationales given by respondents for favoring and opposing the death penalty; and beliefs about the deterrent effect of the death penalty.

Many public opinion surveys have examined firearms and gun control issues, and the next series of tables presents attitudes on these topics. Tables report on the prevalence of gun ownership, including trend data spanning 4 decades, attitudes toward numerous gun control measures, and legislation covering the sale and possession of firearms.

Attitudes about the legalization of marijuana, both prescribed and general use, and the harmfulness of drug use have been examined among several populations, including the general public, teenagers, high school seniors, and young adults. This segment of the section presents a large number of tables drawn from the results of several student surveys including the Monitoring the Future Project and PRIDE Surveys. Included are students' attitudes about selected social problems, such as the availability and harmfulness of both alcohol and drug use. High school seniors are surveyed annually on their attitudes and beliefs about social problems, crime and violence, the performance of police and the courts, harmfulness of drug and alcohol use and cigarette smoking, perceptions of the availability of drugs, and the legalization of marijuana. Attitudes of eighth and tenth graders toward alcohol and drug use and cigarette smoking, and perceptions of the availability of drugs also are included. Data from annual surveys of college freshmen mirror many of the issues explored among high school students, and further ask about legalization of marijuana and abortion, the rights of criminal defendants, the death penalty, and gun control. The section concludes with presentations of public attitudes on doctor-assisted suicide, the distribution of pornography, environmental protection laws, and the legality of homosexual relations and abortion.

When available, survey results are displayed by demographic characteristics of respondents–age, sex, race, income, and occupation–enabling comparisons across social dimensions. Some questions have been asked repeatedly over time and, whenever possible, these trends are presented.

Readers should be aware that many factors, including slight differences in the wording of survey questions, may have significant effects on responses. In addition, the margin of error for survey results, presented in Appendix 5, may vary slightly between surveys. Thus, attention to the exact wording of questions and the appropriate estimate of error always should accompany comparisons.

Table 2.1
Attitudes toward the most important problem facing the country

United States, 1984-2004

Question: "What do you think is the most important problem facing this country today?"

	Feb. 10-13, 1984	Jan. 25-28, 1985	July 11-14, 1986	Apr. 10-13, 1987	Sept. 9-11, 1988	May 4-7, 1989	July 19-22, 1990	Mar. 7-10, 1991	Mar. 26-29, 1992	Jan. 8-11, 1993	Jan. 15-17, 1994	Jan. 16-18, 1995	May 9-12, 1996	Jan. 10-13, 1997	Apr. 17-19, 1998	May 23-24, 1999	Mar. 10-12, 2000	Jan. 10-14, 2001	Mar. 4-7, 2002	Feb. 3-6, 2003	June 3-6, 2004
High cost of living; inflation; taxes	10%	11%	4%	5%	2%	3%	2%	2%	8%	4%	4%	7%	11%	6%	7%	3%	13%	6%	2%	2%	3%
Unemployment; jobs	29	20	23	13	9	6	3	8	25	22	18	15	13	NA	5	4	2	4	8	10	13
International problems; foreign affairs	11	NA	NA	NA	4	4	NA	1	3	8	3	2	4	3	4	3	4	4	2	8	4
Crime; violence	4	4	3	3	2	6	1	2	5	9	37	27	25	23	20	17	13	9	1	2	2
Guns/gun control	NA	NA	NA	NA	NA	NA	NA	NA	NA	NA	NA	(a)	NA	NA	1	10	7	1	NA	NA	NA
Fear of war/nuclear war; international tensions	11	27	22	23	5	2	1	2	NA	NA	NA	(a)	NA	NA	NA	2	NA	(a)	12	35	27
Ethics, moral, family decline	7	2	3	5	1	5	2	2	5	7	8	6	14	9	16	18	15	13	7	4	6
Terrorism	NA	NA	NA	NA	NA	NA	NA	NA	NA	NA	NA	NA	NA	NA	NA	NA	NA	NA	22	10	13
Excessive government spending; Federal budget deficit	12	18	13	11	12	7	21	8	8	13	5	14	15	8	5	1	4	1	1	3	3
Dissatisfaction with government; poor leadership; corruption	2	NA	NA	5	NA	2	1	NA	8	5	6	5	12	7	8	5	11	9	4	2	5
Economy (general)	5	6	7	10	12	8	7	24	42	35	14	10	12	21	6	3	6	7	18	34	19
Poverty; hunger; homelessness	NA	6	6	5	7	10	7	10	15	15	11	10	7	10	10	7	5	4	4	3	3
Drugs; drug abuse	NA	2	8	11	11	27	18	11	8	6	9	6	10	17	12	5	5	7	3	2	1
National security	NA	NA	NA	NA	NA	NA	NA	NA	NA	NA	NA	NA	NA	NA	NA	NA	NA	NA	6	3	3
Trade deficit; trade relations	NA	NA	NA	NA	3	3	1	1	4	3	2	1	2	1	1	1	1	(a)	NA	NA	(a)
Education; quality of education	NA	NA	NA	NA	2	3	2	2	8	8	7	5	13	10	13	11	16	12	7	4	4
Immigration; illegal aliens	NA	NA	NA	NA	NA	NA	NA	NA	NA	NA	NA	NA	NA	NA	NA	NA	NA	NA	NA	1	2
Environment; pollution	NA	NA	NA	NA	4	5	2	3	3	1	1	3	1	2	2	2	2	2	2	1	1
AIDS	NA	NA	NA	NA	1	2	(a)	3	2	2	1	(a)	1	1	(a)	(a)	(a)	NA	NA	NA
Abortion	NA	NA	NA	NA	NA	(a)	NA	NA	NA	NA	1	0	1	1	(a)	2	1	(a)	1	1
Health care; cost of health care	NA	NA	NA	NA	NA	NA	NA	NA	12	18	20	12	10	7	6	5	8	7	6	5	6
No opinion; don't know	4	3	3	4	12	7	5	6	2	2	2	2	7	6	4	2	6	8	4	5	3

Note: Exact wording of response categories varies across surveys. Multiple responses are possible; the Source records up to three problems per respondent. Some problems mentioned by a small percentage of respondents are not included in the table. Sample sizes vary from year to year; the data for 2004 are based on telephone interviews with a randomly selected national sample of 1,000 adults, 18 years of age and older, conducted June 3-6, 2004. For a discussion of public opinion survey sampling procedures, see Appendix 5.

[a] Less than 0.5%.

Source: George H. Gallup, *The Gallup Report*, Report No. 226, p. 17; Report No. 235, pp. 20, 21; Report No. 252, pp. 28, 29; Report No. 260, pp. 6, 7; Report No. 277, pp. 6, 7; Report No. 285, pp. 4, 5; Report No. 290, p. 6 (Princeton, NJ: The Gallup Poll); George Gallup, Jr., *The Gallup Poll*, Mar. 14, 1991, pp. 2, 3; Apr. 3, 1992, pp. 1, 2; Jan. 30, 1997, p. 2 (Princeton, NJ: The Gallup Poll); George Gallup, Jr., *The Gallup Poll Monthly*, No. 298, p. 14; No. 340, p. 43; No. 352, p. 7; No. 396, p. 34 (Princeton, NJ: The Gallup Poll); The Gallup Organization, Inc., *The Gallup Poll* [Online]. Available:
http://www.gallup.com/poll/releases/pr990528.asp [July 20, 1999];
http://www.gallup.com/poll/releases/pr000331.asp [Mar. 31, 2000];
http://www.gallup.com/poll/releases/pr010205.asp [Feb. 5, 2001];
http://www.gallup.com/poll/releases/pr020320.asp [Mar. 27, 2002];
http://www.gallup.com/poll/releases/pr030213.asp [Feb. 19, 2003];
http://www.gallup.com/poll/ [June 28, 2004]; and data provided by The Gallup Organization, Inc. Table constructed by SOURCEBOOK staff. Reprinted by permission.

Table 2.2

Attitudes toward important issues for the government to address

United States, 1993-2004

Question: "What do you think are the two most important issues for the government to address?"

Issue	January 1993	February 1994	February 1995	April 1996	May 1997	January 1998	February 1999	August 2000	February 2001	April 2002	February 2003	February 2004
The economy (non-specific)	26%	12%	7%	14%	8%	9%	7%	5%	12%	15%	37%	31%
Health care (not Medicare)	31	45	25	16	10	11	12	15	10	8	8	16
Employment/jobs	19	14	10	9	5	3	4	4	2	4	5	16
The war[a]	X	X	X	X	X	X	X	X	X	8	38	13
Education	10	6	10	14	15	14	21	25	30	12	5	11
Homeland/domestic security/public safety[a]	X	X	X	X	X	X	X	X	X	4	6	8
Foreign policy (non-specific)	6	4	2	3	3	5	4	3	4	4	2	6
Iraq/Saddam Hussein	X	X	X	X	X	X	X	X	X	X	15	6
Federal surplus/deficit/budget	19	8	22	22	20	12	5	4	4	2	3	5
Taxes	7	6	12	11	14	16	12	13	23	8	4	5
Defense/military	X	2	1	1	2	2	2	4	5	2	2	5
Terrorism[a]	X	X	X	X	X	X	X	X	X	23	16	4
Domestic/social issues (non-specific)	10	4	4	4	2	3	2	2	2	3	1	4
National security[a]	X	X	X	X	X	X	2	2	2	4	6	4
Environment	3	1	1	1	3	2	3	3	3	3	1	4
Drugs	3	6	3	4	8	6	2	5	4	2	2	3
Abortion	9	3	3	4	2	2	2	6	4	1	1	3
Crime/violence	3	36	21	16	19	13	8	10	5	5	(b)	3
Family values (decline of)	(b)	(b)	2	2	2	1	2	1	1	1	(b)	2
Medicare[c]	X	X	X	3	4	5	5	6	4	3	2	2
Welfare	2	7	16	13	14	8	4	2	1	2	1	2
Social Security[c]	X	X	X	X	6	6	24	16	12	5	1	2
(Programs for) the poor/poverty	7	8	10	2	3	2	2	3	1	2	1	2
Homelessness[d]	X	X	X	3	4	4	3	3	3	2	1	1
Peace/world peace/nuclear arms	2	1	1	3	1	3	3	1	1	3	3	1
Immigration	(b)	(b)	2	2	2	1	(b)	1	1	1	(b)	1
Programs for the elderly (not Medicare/Social Security)	3	2	5	6	1	1	1	2	1	2	1	1
Gun control	(b)	3	2	1	1	1	1	4	1	1	(b)	1
Human/civil/women's rights	X	1	1	2	2	1	(b)	1	1	1	(b)	(b)

Note: The issues mentioned are spontaneous, unprompted replies by the respondents. The numbers indicate the percent of respondents who mentioned the item as one of the top two issues for the government to address. Some issues mentioned by a relatively small percentage of respondents have been omitted. Sample sizes vary from year to year; the data for 2004 are based on telephone interviews with a randomly selected national sample of 1,020 adults, 18 years of age and older, conducted Feb. 9-16, 2004. For a discussion of public opinion survey sampling procedures, see Appendix 5.

[a]Previously coded as "other."
[b]Less than 0.5%.
[c]Previously coded under "programs for the elderly."
[d]Previously coded under "programs for the poor."

Source: Harris Interactive Inc., *The Harris Poll* ® (New York: Harris Interactive Inc., Apr. 24, 2002, p. 8; Feb. 19, 2004, p. 11). Table adapted by SOURCEBOOK staff. © 2002, 2004, Harris Interactive Inc. All rights reserved. Reproduction prohibited without the express written permission of Harris Interactive.

Table 2.3

Teenagers' attitudes toward the most important problem facing people their age

United States, selected years 1999-2004[a]

Question: "What is the most important problem facing people your age--that is, the thing which concerns you the most?"

Problem	1999	2000	2002	2003	2004
Drugs	23%	21%	24%	19%	23%
Social pressures, fitting in	18	14	18	20	22
Crime and violence in school	13	5	2	2	4
Doing well in school	6	10	16	14	11
Other crime and violence	5	2	2	1	1
Sexual issues	3	3	4	4	4
Getting into college	2	4	4	5	4
Alcohol	NA	3	2	3	4
Tobacco	NA	2	3	1	2
Jobs/economic opportunity	1	1	1	1	1
Getting along with parents/ other problems at home	1	2	3	3	3
Lack of money	1	1	1	1	1
General lack of quality education	1	1	1	1	1
Declining moral standards/ immorality	1	1	2	3	2
Having a say/communications	NA	NA	1	1	2
Other	11	9	4	10	5
Don't know/refused	16	20	16	12	11

Note: These data are from telephone interviews of nationwide samples of teenagers, ages 12 to 17. The surveys were conducted for the National Center on Addiction and Substance Abuse at Columbia University. Randomly generated telephone numbers were pre-screened to determine if a teen in the appropriate age range resided there. Subsequent calls were made to conduct the actual interviews. For the 1999 survey, 2,000 teens were interviewed during May and June. For the 2000 survey, 1,000 teens were interviewed during October and November. For the 2002 survey, 1,000 teens were interviewed between December 2001 and February 2002. For the 2003 survey, 1,987 teens were interviewed between April and July. For the 2004 survey, 1,000 teens were interviewed in April and May.

[a] Percents may not add to 100 because of multiple responses.

Source: National Center on Addiction and Substance Abuse at Columbia University, *Back to School 1999 - The CASA National Survey of American Attitudes on Substance Abuse V: Teens and Their Parents* [Online], p. 30. Available: http://www.casacolumbia.org/usr_doc/17635.pdf [Dec. 9, 1999]; National Center on Addiction and Substance Abuse at Columbia University, *The CASA National Survey of American Attitudes on Substance Abuse VI: Teens* [Online], pp. 25, 26. Available: http://www.casacolumbia.org/usr_doc/52809.pdf [Mar. 30, 2001]; National Center on Addiction and Substance Abuse at Columbia University, *National Survey of American Attitudes on Substance Abuse VII: Teens, Parents and Siblings* [Online], pp. 29, 30. Available: http://www.casacolumbia.org/usr_doc/TeenSurvey2002.pdf [Jan. 15, 2003]; National Center on Addiction and Substance Abuse at Columbia University, *National Survey of American Attitudes on Substance Abuse VIII: Teens and Parents* [Online], pp. 39, 40. Available: http://www.casacolumbia.org/pdshopprov/files/2003_Teen_Survey_8_19_03.pdf [Mar. 1, 2004]; and National Center on Addiction and Substance Abuse at Columbia University, *National Survey of American Attitudes on Substance Abuse IX: Teen Dating Practices and Sexual Activity* [Online], pp. 38, 39. Available: http://www.casacolumbia.org/pdshopprov/files/august_2004_casa_teen_survey.pdf. [Aug. 31, 2004]. Table adapted by SOURCEBOOK staff. Reprinted by permission.

Table 2.4
Attitudes toward the biggest problems facing public schools

By school status, United States, 1988-2003

Question: "What do you think are the biggest problems with which the public schools of your community must deal?"

	Lack of financial support/ funding/money[a]	Lack of discipline/ more control[b]	Fighting/ violence/ gangs	Overcrowded schools/ large schools	Use of drugs/dope	Difficulty getting good teachers/ quality teachers
National						
1988	12%	19%	1%	6%	32%	11%
1989	13	19	NA	8	34	7
1990	13	19	2	7	38	7
1991	18	20	3	9	22	11
1992	22	17	9	9	22	5
1993	21	15	13	8	16	5
1994	13	18	18	7	11	3
1995	11	15	9	3	7	2
1996	13	15	14	8	16	3
1997	15	15	12	8	14	3
1998	12	14	15	8	10	5
1999	9	18	11	8	8	4
2000	18	15	11	12	9	4
2001	15	15	10	10	9	6
2002	23	17	9	17	13	8
2003	25	16	4	14	9	5
Respondents with no children in school						
1988	10	20	2	4	34	10
1989	11	20	NA	6	35	8
1990	18	19	2	6	40	6
1991	15	20	4	8	24	11
1992	20	18	9	6	26	4
1993	19	15	12	6	17	4
1994	12	18	19	5	11	4
1995	10	17	9	3	7	2
1996	14	16	14	6	17	3
1997	15	15	12	6	14	3
1998	13	15	14	5	10	6
1999	9	18	10	6	9	4
2000	17	17	11	10	10	4
2001	15	17	11	7	9	6
2002	23	18	9	14	14	8
2003	26	17	3	12	10	5
Respondents with children in public schools						
1988	17	15	1	10	30	11
1989	18	16	NA	11	30	6
1990	17	17	2	10	34	10
1991	26	18	4	11	17	11
1992	25	15	9	13	17	7
1993	24	15	14	11	14	7
1994	16	17	16	11	13	2
1995	12	11	8	5	7	3
1996	13	12	15	11	14	3
1997	14	12	12	10	14	4
1998	11	9	20	11	12	4
1999	9	15	12	12	6	5
2000	19	9	11	14	9	4
2001	17	10	9	15	10	6
2002	23	13	9	23	11	8
2003	24	13	5	16	7	5

Note: Sample sizes vary from year to year; the data for 2003 are based on telephone interviews with a randomly selected national sample of 1,011 adults, 18 years of age and older, conducted May 28-June 18, 2003. Some problems mentioned by a small percentage of respondents have been omitted. Some data have been revised by the Source and may differ from previous editions of SOURCEBOOK. For a discussion of public opinion survey sampling procedures, see Appendix 5.

[a]The response "funding/money" was added in 1998.
[b]The response "more control" was added in 1997.

Source: George Gallup, Jr., *The Gallup Report*, Report No. 276, p. 41; Report No. 288, p. 41 (Princeton, NJ: The Gallup Poll); Stanley M. Elam, "The 22nd Annual Gallup Poll of the Public's Attitudes Toward the Public Schools," *Phi Delta Kappan* (September 1990), pp. 53, 54; Stanley M. Elam, Lowell C. Rose, and Alec M. Gallup, "The 24th Annual Gallup/Phi Delta Kappa Poll of the Public's Attitudes Toward the Public Schools," *Phi Delta Kappan* (September 1992), p. 43; "The 26th Annual Phi Delta Kappa/Gallup Poll of the Public's Attitudes Toward the Public Schools," *Phi Delta Kappan* (September 1994), p. 43; "The 28th Annual Phi Delta Kappa/Gallup Poll of the Public's Attitudes Toward the Public Schools," *Phi Delta Kappan* (September 1996), p. 49; Lowell C. Rose and Alec M. Gallup, "The 30th Annual Phi Delta Kappa/Gallup Poll of the Public's Attitudes Toward the Public Schools," Phi Delta Kappa [Online]. Available: http://www.pdkintl.org/kappan/kp9809-3.htm [Jan. 5, 1999]; and Lowell C. Rose and Alec M. Gallup, "The 34th Annual Phi Delta Kappa/Gallup Poll of the Public's Attitudes Toward the Public Schools," *Phi Delta Kappan* (September 2002), p. 51; "The 35th Annual Phi Delta Kappa/Gallup Poll of the Public's Attitudes Toward the Public Schools," *Phi Delta Kappan* (September 2003), p. 50. Table adapted by SOURCEBOOK staff. Reprinted by permission.

Table 2.5
Students' perceptions of safety at school

By grade level of respondent, 2002-2003[a]

Question: "In my school, I feel safe..."

	Never	Seldom	Sometimes	Often	A lot
In the classroom	10.2%	5.0%	13.3%	20.0%	51.4%
Grades 6 to 8	9.7	5.2	13.4	18.0	53.6
Grades 9 to 12	10.7	4.8	13.1	22.0	49.3
12th grade	10.1	4.0	10.7	21.4	53.9
In the cafeteria	12.3	6.8	14.9	20.9	45.1
Grades 6 to 8	12.4	7.2	14.8	19.0	46.6
Grades 9 to 12	12.1	6.4	15.1	22.7	43.7
12th grade	11.0	5.5	13.2	21.3	49.0
In the halls	14.0	8.3	16.7	20.3	40.6
Grades 6 to 8	15.2	9.2	17.0	18.6	40.0
Grades 9 to 12	12.9	7.4	16.5	22.0	41.2
12th grade	11.3	6.0	13.6	21.5	47.6
In the bathroom	15.6	8.7	15.4	19.2	41.1
Grades 6 to 8	17.1	9.6	15.5	17.3	40.4
Grades 9 to 12	14.1	7.7	15.3	21.1	41.7
12th Grade	12.0	6.2	12.2	21.1	48.4
In the gym	12.4	6.2	13.7	20.1	47.6
Grades 6 to 8	12.7	6.7	13.8	17.9	49.0
Grades 9 to 12	12.0	5.8	13.6	22.3	46.2
12th grade	10.8	5.2	11.5	21.4	51.1
At school events	14.2	7.1	14.8	20.4	43.5
Grades 6 to 8	15.2	7.7	14.5	18.5	44.1
Grades 9 to 12	13.2	6.4	15.1	22.3	43.0
12th grade	11.7	5.3	13.6	21.8	47.5
On the playground	17.2	7.1	13.9	18.4	43.3
Grades 6 to 8	18.6	8.0	14.1	16.7	42.7
Grades 9 to 12	15.9	6.3	13.7	20.1	44.0
12th grade	13.9	5.4	11.8	19.7	49.1
In the parking lot	18.2	9.1	15.8	18.5	38.4
Grades 6 to 8	21.5	10.3	15.4	16.1	36.7
Grades 9 to 12	15.1	7.9	16.1	20.9	40.0
12th grade	12.8	6.7	14.1	21.0	45.3
In all school areas	14.0	7.3	16.8	20.2	41.6
Grades 6 to 8	14.9	7.9	17.2	18.3	41.7
Grades 9 to 12	13.2	6.7	16.5	22.1	41.5
12th grade	11.7	5.7	14.0	21.5	47.0

Note: These data are from a survey of 6th through 12th grade students conducted between August 2002 and June 2003 by PRIDE Surveys. Participating schools are sent the PRIDE questionnaire with explicit instructions for administering the anonymous, self-report survey. Schools that administer the PRIDE questionnaire do so voluntarily or in compliance with a school district or State request. For the 2002-2003 academic year, survey results are based on students from 24 States. The following States participated in the 2002-2003 PRIDE survey: Alabama, Arkansas, Colorado, Georgia, Illinois, Indiana, Kentucky, Louisiana, Massachusetts, Michigan, Mississippi, New Jersey, New Mexico, New York, North Carolina, Ohio, Oklahoma, Pennsylvania, Tennessee, Texas, Virginia, Washington, West Virginia, and Wisconsin. To prevent any one State from having a disproportionate influence on the summary results, random samples of students were drawn from those States where disproportionately large numbers of students were surveyed. Therefore, no State comprises more than 10% of the sample. The results presented are based on a sample consisting of 109,919 students drawn from the total number of students who completed the PRIDE questionnaire.

[a]Percents may not add to 100 because of rounding.

Source: PRIDE Surveys, "2002-2003 PRIDE Surveys National Summary, Grades 6 through 12," Bowling Green, KY: PRIDE Surveys, 2003. (Mimeographed.) P. 228; p. 229, Tables 8.185 and 8.186; pp. 230, 231. Table adapted by SOURCEBOOK staff. Reprinted by permission.

Table 2.6
Students age 12 to 18 reporting fear of school-related victimization

By student characteristics, United States, 1995, 1999, and 2001

Student characteristics	Fear of attack at school or going to and from school[a]			Avoidance of one or more places at school[b]		
	1995	1999	2001	1995	1999	2001
Total	11.8%	7.3%	6.4%	8.7%	4.6%	4.7%
Sex						
Male	10.8	6.5	6.4	8.8	4.6	4.7
Female	12.8	8.2	6.4	8.5	4.6	4.6
Race, ethnicity						
White, non-Hispanic	8.1	5.0	4.9	7.1	3.8	3.9
Black, non-Hispanic	20.3	13.5	8.9	12.1	6.7	6.6
Hispanic	20.9	11.7	10.6	12.9	6.2	5.5
Other, non-Hispanic	13.5	6.7	6.4	11.1	5.4	6.2
Grade						
6th	14.3	10.9	10.6	11.6	5.9	6.8
7th	15.3	9.5	9.2	11.8	6.1	6.2
8th	13.0	8.1	7.6	8.8	5.5	5.2
9th	11.6	7.1	5.5	9.5	5.3	5.0
10th	11.0	7.1	5.0	7.8	4.7	4.2
11th	8.9	4.8	4.8	6.9	2.5	2.8
12th	7.8	4.8	2.9	4.1	2.4	3.0
Community						
Urban	18.4	11.6	9.7	11.7	5.8	6.0
Suburban	9.8	6.2	4.8	7.9	4.7	4.3
Rural	8.6	4.8	6.0	7.0	3.0	3.9
Type of school						
Public	12.2	7.7	6.6	9.3	5.0	4.9
Private	7.3	3.6	4.6	2.2	1.6	2.0

Note: These data are from the School Crime Supplement (SCS) to the National Crime Victimization Survey (NCVS). The NCVS is a continuous survey of a representative sample of households in the United States conducted for the U.S. Department of Justice, Bureau of Justice Statistics by the U.S. Census Bureau. The SCS is an additional questionnaire fielded with the 1995, 1999, and 2001 NCVS and was administered to a nationally representative sample of students 12 to 18 years of age. Eligible respondents were asked the supplemental SCS questions only after completing the NCVS interview. Persons eligible for the SCS were those NCVS respondents who were enrolled in grades 6 through 12 at a school leading to a high school diploma and had attended school at any time during the 6 months preceding the interview. A total of 9,728 students participated in the 1995 SCS, 8,398 in the 1999 SCS, and 8,374 in the 2001 SCS. The data presented are survey estimates and therefore are subject to sampling variation.

Beginning with the 2001 data, two changes were made to the SCS. First, in 1995 and 1999, "at school" was defined as in the school building, on the school grounds, or on a school bus. In 2001, "at school" was defined as in the school building, on school property, on a school bus, or going to and from school. The 1995 and 1999 estimates for "fear of attack at school" have been recalculated by the Source to combine fear of attack at school and fear of attack going to and from school and are now consistent with the 2001 estimates. Second, in 1995 and 1999, students were asked if they avoided places or were fearful because they thought someone would "attack or harm" them. In 2001, the language was changed to "attack or threaten to attack" them.

[a]Includes students who reported that they sometimes or most of the time feared being victimized in this way.
[b]Includes the entrance into the school, any hallways or stairs in the school, parts of the school cafeteria, any school restrooms, and other places inside the school building.

Source: Jill F. DeVoe et al., *Indicators of School Crime and Safety: 2003*, NCES 2004-004/NCJ 201257 (Washington, DC: U.S. Departments of Education and Justice, 2003), pp. 84, 85. Table adapted by SOURCEBOOK staff.

Table 2.7

Teenagers' perceptions of drug testing and locker searches in their schools

United States, 2003

Question	Percent
"Are students in your school ever tested for the use of illegal drugs?"	
Yes	29%
No	64
Don't know/no response	7
"How effective do you think drug testing is at keeping kids your age from using illegal drugs?"	
Very effective	21
Somewhat effective	46
Not very effective	21
Not effective at all	9
Don't know/no response	3
"Are students' lockers regularly searched at your school?"	
Yes	35
No	62
Don't know/no response	3
"How effective do you think locker searches are at keeping teenagers from using illegal drugs?"	
Very effective	19
Somewhat effective	36
Not very effective	28
Not effective at all	13
Don't know/no response	4

Note: See Note, table 2.3.

Source: National Center on Addiction and Substance Abuse at Columbia University, *National Survey of American Attitudes on Substance Abuse VIII: Teens and Parents* [Online], pp. 43, 44. Available: http://www.casacolumbia.org/pdshopprov/files/2003_Teen_Survey_8_19_03.pdf [Mar. 1, 2004]. Table adapted by SOURCEBOOK staff. Reprinted by permission.

Table 2.8

Parents' perceptions of safety, drug testing, and locker searches at schools

United States, 2003[a]

Question	Percent
"How safe do you feel your teen's school is?"	
Very safe	44%
Fairly safe	51
Fairly unsafe	2
Very unsafe	1
Don't know/no response	1
"How effective do you think drug testing is at keeping kids from using illegal drugs?"	
Very effective	11
Somewhat effective	49
Not very effective	24
Not effective at all	10
Don't know/no response	5
"How effective do you think locker searches are at keeping teenagers from using illegal drugs?"	
Very effective	11
Somewhat effective	42
Not very effective	30
Not effective at all	14
Don't know/no response	3
"Do you favor or oppose school officials searching students' lockers?"	
Favor strongly	51
Favor not strongly	21
Oppose not strongly	11
Oppose strongly	11
Don't know/no response	6

Note: See Note, table 2.3. In 2003, 504 parents (or guardians) of teens also were surveyed. Of the 504 parent/guardian interviews, 403 were conducted with households in which a teen was interviewed (two-interview households).

[a]Percents may not add to 100 because of rounding.

Source: National Center on Addiction and Substance Abuse at Columbia University, *National Survey of American Attitudes on Substance Abuse VIII: Teens and Parents* [Online], pp. 55, 57, 58. Available: http://www.casacolumbia.org/pdshopprov/files/2003_Teen_Survey_8_19_03.pdf [Mar. 1, 2004]. Table adapted by SOURCEBOOK staff. Reprinted by permission.

Table 2.9

Reported confidence in selected institutions

United States, 1979-2004

Question: "As far as people in charge of running. . .are concerned, would you say you have a great deal of confidence, only some confidence, or hardly any confidence at all in them?"

(Percent reporting "a great deal of confidence")

	1979	1980	1981	1982	1983	1984	1985	1986	1987	1988	1989	1990	1991	1992	1993	1994	1995	1996	1997	1998	1999	2000	2001	2002	2003	2004
The military	29%	28%	28%	31%	35%	45%	32%	36%	35%	33%	32%	43%	47%	50%	57%	39%	43%	47%	37%	44%	54%	48%	44%	71%	62%	62%
Medicine	30	34	37	32	35	43	39	33	36	40	30	35	NA	29	22	23	26	29	29	38	39	44	32	29	31	32
The White House	15	18	28	20	23	42	30	19	23	17	20	21	21	16	23	18	13	15	15	20	22	21	21	50	40	31
Major educational institutions such as colleges and universities	33	36	34	30	36	40	35	34	36	34	32	35	21	25	23	25	27	30	27	37	37	36	35	33	31	37
The U.S. Supreme Court	28	27	29	25	33	35	28	32	30	32	28	32	23	30	26	31	32	31	28	37	42	34	35	41	34	29
Congress	18	18	16	13	20	28	16	21	20	15	16	12	9	10	12	8	10	10	11	12	12	15	18	22	20	13
Television news	37	29	24	24	24	28	23	27	29	28	25	27	20	22	23	20	16	21	18	26	23	20	24	24	21	17
Organized religion	20	22	22	20	22	24	21	22	16	22	16	17	16	20	NA	NA	NA	24	NA	20	25	27	26	25	23	19	27
Major companies	18	16	16	18	18	19	17	16	21	19	16	14	15	11	16	19	21	21	18	21	23	28	20	16	13	12
The press	28	19	16	14	19	18	16	19	19	18	18	18	14	13	15	13	11	14	11	14	15	13	13	16	15	15
Law firms	16	13	NA	NA	12	17	12	14	15	13	NA	NA	NA	11	11	8	9	11	7	11	10	12	10	13	12	10
Organized labor	10	14	12	8	10	12	13	11	11	13	10	14	NA	NA	NA	NA	8	NA	9	13	15	15	15	11	14	15
Executive branch of the Federal Government	17	17	24	NA	NA	NA	19	18	19	16	17	14	NA	13	15	12	9	12	12	17	17	18	20	33	26	23
Wall Street	NA	12	NA	NA	NA	NA	NA	NA	NA	NA	8	9	9	12	13	15	13	17	17	18	30	30	23	19	12	17

Note: Sample sizes vary from year to year; the data for 2004 are based on telephone interviews with a randomly selected national sample of 1,020 adults, 18 years of age and older, conducted Feb. 9-16, 2004. Some data have been revised by the Source and may differ from previous editions of SOURCEBOOK. For a discussion of public opinion survey sampling procedures, see Appendix 5.

Source: Harris Interactive Inc., *The Harris Poll* ® (New York: Harris Interactive Inc., Feb. 7, 2001, pp. 4-6; Mar. 10, 2004, p. 5). Table adapted by SOURCEBOOK staff. © 2001, 2004, Harris Interactive Inc. All rights reserved. Reproduction prohibited without the express written permission of Harris Interactive.

Table 2.10

Reported confidence in selected institutions

United States, selected years 1979-2004

Question: "I am going to read you a list of institutions in American society. Please tell me how much confidence you, yourself, have in each one--a great deal, quite a lot, some, or very little?"

(Percent saying "a great deal" or "quite a lot")

	1979	1981	1983	1985	1986	1987	1988	1989	1990	1991	1993	1994	1995	1996	1997	1998	1999	2000	2001	2002	2003	2004
Banks and banking	60%	46%	51%	51%	49%	51%	49%	42%	36%	30%	37%	35%	43%	44%	41%	40%	43%	46%	44%	47%	50%	53%
Big business	32	20	28	31	28	NA	25	NA	25	22	22	26	21	24	28	30	30	29	28	20	22	24
Church or organized religion	65	64	62	66	57	61	59	52	56	56	53	54	57	57	56	59	58	56	60	45	50	53
Congress	34	29	28	39	41	NA	35	32	24	18	18	18	21	20	22	28	26	24	26	29	29	30
Criminal justice system	NA	NA	NA	NA	NA	NA	NA	NA	NA	NA	17	15	20	19	19	24	23	24	NA	27	29	34
Health maintenance organizations, HMOs	NA	NA	NA	NA	NA	NA	NA	NA	NA	NA	NA	NA	NA	NA	NA	17	16	15	13	17	17	18
Medical system	NA	NA	NA	NA	NA	NA	NA	NA	NA	NA	34	36	41	42	38	40	40	40	38	44	44
Military	54	50	53	61	63	61	68	63	68	69	68	64	64	66	60	64	68	64	66	79	82	75
Newspapers	51	35	38	35	37	31	36	NA	39	32	31	29	30	32	35	33	33	37	36	35	33	30
Organized labor	36	28	26	28	29	26	26	NA	27	22	26	26	26	25	23	26	28	25	26	26	28	31
Police	NA	NA	NA	NA	NA	NA	NA	NA	NA	NA	52	54	58	60	59	58	57	54	57	59	61	64
Presidency	NA	NA	NA	NA	NA	NA	NA	NA	NA	50	43	38	45	39	49	53	49	42	48	58	55	52
Public schools	53	42	39	48	49	50	49	43	45	35	39	34	40	38	40	37	36	37	38	38	40	41
Television news	NA	NA	NA	NA	NA	NA	NA	NA	NA	NA	46	35	33	36	34	34	34	36	34	35	35	30
U.S. Supreme Court	45	46	42	56	54	52	56	46	47	39	44	42	44	45	50	50	49	47	50	50	47	46

Note: Sample sizes vary from year to year; the data for 2004 are based on telephone interviews with a randomly selected national sample of 1,002 adults, 18 years of age and older, conducted May 21-23, 2004. For a discussion of public opinion survey sampling procedures, see Appendix 5.

Source: The Gallup Organization, Inc., *The Gallup Poll* [Online]. Available: http://www.gallup.com/poll/ [June 1, 2004]. Reprinted by permission.

Table 2.11

Reported confidence in the criminal justice system

By demographic characteristics, United States, 2004

Question: "I am going to read you a list of institutions in American society. Please tell me how much confidence you, yourself, have in each one--a great deal, quite a lot, some, or very little: the criminal justice system?"

	Great deal/quite a lot	Some	Very little	None[a]
National	34%	42%	22%	1%
Sex				
Male	34	41	23	2
Female	34	42	22	1
Race				
White	36	41	21	1
Nonwhite	27	43	28	2
Black	25	40	32	3
Age				
18 to 29 years	41	32	26	1
30 to 49 years	33	45	20	2
50 to 64 years	32	45	21	1
50 years and older	32	44	22	1
65 years and older	32	43	23	1
Education				
College post graduate	39	45	13	2
College graduate	37	50	12	0
Some college	32	42	24	2
High school graduate or less	33	38	27	1
Income				
$75,000 and over	35	45	17	2
$50,000 to $74,999	39	46	14	1
$30,000 to $49,999	32	43	24	1
$20,000 to $29,999	31	35	33	0
Under $20,000	31	36	31	2
Community				
Urban area	33	41	25	1
Suburban area	35	42	21	1
Rural area	35	42	20	2
Region				
East	26	47	24	2
Midwest	40	37	22	1
South	36	40	23	(b)
West	36	43	19	2
Politics				
Republican	39	44	15	1
Democrat	34	42	22	1
Independent	30	38	29	2

Note: See Note, table 2.10. The "don't know/refused" category has been omitted; therefore percents may not sum to 100. For a discussion of public opinion survey sampling procedures, see Appendix 5.

[a]Response volunteered.
[b]Less than 0.5%.

Source: Table constructed by SOURCEBOOK staff from data provided by The Gallup Organization, Inc. Reprinted by permission.

Table 2.12

Reported confidence in the police

By demographic characteristics, United States, 2004

Question: "I am going to read you a list of institutions in American society. Please tell me how much confidence you, yourself, have in each one--a great deal, quite a lot, some, or very little: the police?"

	Great deal/quite a lot	Some	Very little	None[a]
National	64%	26%	10%	(b)
Sex				
Male	64	25	10	1%
Female	64	26	10	(b)
Race				
White	70	22	8	(b)
Nonwhite	43	39	17	1
Black	41	46	13	0
Age				
18 to 29 years	61	19	19	1
30 to 49 years	62	27	10	1
50 to 64 years	65	30	5	0
50 years and older	68	27	5	0
65 years and older	71	24	5	0
Education				
College post graduate	66	30	4	(b)
College graduate	72	22	5	0
Some college	61	28	11	(b)
High school graduate or less	64	23	12	1
Income				
$75,000 and over	69	25	5	1
$50,000 to $74,999	70	21	9	0
$30,000 to $49,999	60	30	9	1
$20,000 to $29,999	57	31	12	0
Under $20,000	60	19	21	0
Community				
Urban area	60	28	11	1
Suburban area	64	25	10	1
Rural area	69	24	7	0
Region				
East	62	24	14	(b)
Midwest	68	25	6	1
South	63	28	9	0
West	65	25	10	(b)
Politics				
Republican	79	17	4	0
Democrat	59	30	11	(b)
Independent	55	30	14	1

Note: See Note, table 2.10. The "don't know/refused" category has been omitted; therefore percents may not sum to 100. For a discussion of public opinion survey sampling procedures, see Appendix 5.

[a]Response volunteered.
[b]Less than 0.5%.

Source: Table constructed by SOURCEBOOK staff from data provided by The Gallup Organization, Inc. Reprinted by permission.

Page 114 intentionally blank.

Table 2.13
Reported confidence in the police to protect from violent crime

United States, selected years 1981-2003

Question: "How much confidence do you have in the ability of the police to protect you from violent crime--a great deal, quite a lot, not very much, or none at all?"

	A great deal	Quite a lot	Not very much	None at all	Don't know/ refused
1981	15%	34%	42%	8%	1%
1985	15	37	39	6	3
1989	14	34	42	8	2
1990	17	35	46	(a)	2
1993	14	31	45	9	1
1995	20	30	39	9	2
1998	19	36	37	8	(a)
1999	29	41	25	4	1
2000	20	42	31	6	1
2001	25	41	27	6	1
2002	19	39	31	9	2
2003	20	40	31	8	1

Note: Sample sizes vary from year to year; the data for 2003 are based on telephone interviews with a randomly selected national sample of 1,017 adults, 18 years of age and older, conducted Oct. 6-8, 2003. For a discussion of public opinion survey sampling procedures, see Appendix 5.

[a] Less than 0.5%.

Source: George Gallup, Jr. and Alec Gallup, *The Gallup Poll Monthly*, No. 397, p. 50; No. 420, p. 55 (Princeton, NJ: The Gallup Poll); and The Gallup Organization, Inc., *The Gallup Poll* [Online]. Available: http://www.gallup.com/poll/ [Jan. 9, 2003]; and data provided by The Gallup Organization, Inc. Table adapted by SOURCEBOOK staff. Reprinted by permission.

Table 2.14
Reported confidence in the U.S. Supreme Court

By demographic characteristics, United States, 2004

Question: "I am going to read you a list of institutions in American society. Please tell me how much confidence you, yourself, have in each one--a great deal, quite a lot, some, or very little: the U.S. Supreme Court?"

	Great deal/quite a lot	Some	Very little	None[a]
National	46%	37%	14%	2%
Sex				
Male	50	33	14	2
Female	44	40	14	1
Race				
White	47	37	13	2
Nonwhite	47	37	15	1
Black	41	41	18	0
Age				
18 to 29 years	50	39	10	1
30 to 49 years	48	37	13	2
50 to 64 years	45	40	10	3
50 years and older	43	37	16	2
65 years and older	40	33	22	1
Education				
College post graduate	60	28	9	2
College graduate	52	38	8	1
Some college	44	42	13	1
High school graduate or less	42	36	18	2
Income				
$75,000 and over	57	34	7	1
$50,000 to $74,999	52	37	10	1
$30,000 to $49,999	46	41	12	1
$20,000 to $29,999	33	39	24	2
Under $20,000	42	33	22	1
Community				
Urban area	45	39	14	1
Suburban area	49	35	13	2
Rural area	43	39	14	3
Region				
East	46	35	15	2
Midwest	44	40	12	3
South	44	39	15	1
West	54	33	12	(b)
Politics				
Republican	53	34	11	1
Democrat	47	38	14	1
Independent	41	40	15	3

Note: See Note, table 2.10. The "don't know/refused" category has been omitted; therefore percents may not sum to 100. For a discussion of public opinion survey sampling procedures, see Appendix 5.

[a] Response volunteered.
[b] Less than 0.5%.

Source: Table constructed by SOURCEBOOK staff from data provided by The Gallup Organization, Inc. Reprinted by permission.

Table 2.15

Reported confidence in the U.S. Supreme Court

By demographic characteristics, United States, selected years 1984-2002

Question: "I'm going to name some institutions in this country. As far as the people running these institutions (U.S. Supreme Court) are concerned, would you say you have a great deal of confidence, only some confidence, or hardly any confidence at all in them?"

	1984 A great deal	1984 Only some	1984 Hardly any	1986 A great deal	1986 Only some	1986 Hardly any	1987 A great deal	1987 Only some	1987 Hardly any	1988 A great deal	1988 Only some	1988 Hardly any	1989 A great deal	1989 Only some	1989 Hardly any	1990 A great deal	1990 Only some	1990 Hardly any
National	33%	51%	12%	30%	52%	14%	36%	50%	10%	35%	50%	11%	34%	50%	11%	35%	48%	13%
Sex																		
Male	40	44	15	36	47	15	41	46	11	39	47	10	38	47	12	36	48	13
Female	29	56	11	25	56	14	33	52	10	31	53	11	32	52	10	34	48	12
Race																		
White	35	50	13	31	53	13	38	47	11	36	49	11	36	49	11	37	47	12
Black/other	25	54	11	24	49	19	26	61	7	26	56	10	26	55	12	27	53	14
Age																		
18 to 20 years	29	52	19	47	42	10	62	24	10	57	37	7	44	47	3	39	48	4
21 to 29 years	45	42	11	38	48	10	41	51	6	43	45	8	40	50	8	38	47	10
30 to 49 years	30	56	12	30	55	14	36	52	9	34	55	8	34	54	9	36	47	14
50 years and older	30	51	13	24	52	17	32	48	13	30	50	14	31	46	15	32	50	12
Education[a]																		
College	40	50	8	37	52	9	44	49	6	40	51	8	42	50	7	44	47	9
High school graduate	30	52	15	26	56	15	32	51	12	32	51	13	29	52	14	29	48	17
Less than high school graduate	25	46	17	21	39	27	24	47	18	27	46	12	26	41	13	21	51	13
Income																		
$50,000 and over	NA	NA	NA	NA	NA	NA	NA	NA	NA	NA	NA	NA	NA	NA	NA	NA	NA	NA
$30,000 to $49,999	NA	NA	NA	NA	NA	NA	NA	NA	NA	NA	NA	NA	NA	NA	NA	NA	NA	NA
$20,000 to $29,999	NA	NA	NA	NA	NA	NA	NA	NA	NA	NA	NA	NA	NA	NA	NA	NA	NA	NA
Under $20,000	NA	NA	NA	NA	NA	NA	NA	NA	NA	NA	NA	NA	NA	NA	NA	NA	NA	NA
Occupation																		
Professional/business	40	49	9	36	52	11	47	45	7	38	52	9	43	51	5	42	48	10
Clerical/support	24	62	12	25	57	14	33	58	7	32	54	10	33	50	12	35	48	10
Manual/service	33	48	14	27	51	17	29	52	13	32	50	12	27	52	14	28	49	17
Farming/agriculture	45	40	15	36	39	15	35	40	22	33	33	33	31	19	31	35	53	12
Region																		
Northeast	32	51	13	32	52	13	43	48	7	35	53	9	37	45	9	39	43	13
Midwest	30	55	12	30	54	13	32	52	12	33	51	11	33	55	9	37	48	10
South	32	49	14	28	50	16	33	50	12	37	44	12	32	48	16	29	53	13
West	41	48	9	30	54	14	41	48	8	32	58	8	38	52	6	39	44	15
Religion																		
Protestant	33	52	11	28	52	15	35	50	11	35	48	12	30	54	12	33	50	13
Catholic	32	52	13	32	54	11	39	48	9	34	55	9	47	40	6	40	42	12
Jewish	45	45	10	37	55	8	55	35	5	39	61	0	35	41	18	67	33	0
None	36	43	17	33	47	19	33	53	10	38	52	7	28	54	12	34	44	16
Politics																		
Republican	42	47	10	33	51	14	42	48	6	42	49	7	40	52	6	41	48	9
Democrat	34	51	12	29	53	14	34	50	12	33	52	12	32	51	13	31	48	16
Independent	27	54	14	28	52	15	35	50	12	30	50	12	33	46	13	33	48	13

Note: Sample sizes vary from year to year; the data for 2002 are based on interviews with a randomly selected national sample of 2,765 adults, 18 years of age and older, conducted February to April, 2002. The "don't know" category has been omitted; therefore percents may not sum to 100. Readers interested in responses to this question for previous years should consult previous editions of SOURCEBOOK. For a discussion of public opinion survey sampling procedures, see Appendix 5.

Source: National Opinion Research Center, "General Social Surveys, 1972-2002," Storrs, CT: The Roper Center for Public Opinion Research, University of Connecticut. (Machine-readable data files.) Table constructed by SOURCEBOOK staff.

[a] Beginning in 1996, education categories were revised slightly and therefore are not directly comparable to data presented for prior years.

	1991			1993			1994			1996			1998			2000			2002	
	A great deal	Only some	Hardly any	A great deal	Only some	Hardly any	A great deal	Only some	Hardly any	A great deal	Only some	Hardly any	A great deal	Only some	Hardly any	A great deal	Only some	Hardly any	A great deal	Only some	Hardly any
	38%	48%	13%	31%	52%	13%	30%	50%	16%	28%	50%	17%	31%	50%	14%	32%	49%	13%	35%	50%	11%
	44	42	14	34	51	12	34	48	16	33	45	18	34	47	15	36	46	14	36	48	13
	33	52	12	28	52	14	27	52	17	24	54	16	28	52	13	29	52	12	34	52	10
	38	47	12	32	51	12	30	50	17	30	49	16	33	50	13	32	50	12	36	51	10
	34	48	14	20	55	20	29	50	15	23	53	18	24	50	18	30	46	14	32	45	18
	32	42	21	38	52	7	32	47	21	38	40	15	52	33	7	46	38	9	41	41	12
	50	41	7	32	55	13	37	51	11	30	46	19	35	47	15	43	42	10	44	42	12
	36	51	12	32	52	14	30	52	16	26	55	15	29	54	14	31	52	12	34	52	11
	33	48	15	28	50	14	27	48	19	29	46	17	30	48	14	27	50	15	33	51	11
	45	45	9	36	51	11	36	49	13	33	52	13	36	51	11	38	49	9	36	51	10
	32	49	16	24	54	17	26	52	20	24	51	20	26	55	15	25	53	16	36	50	11
	23	57	13	27	46	13	19	42	20	22	41	22	26	38	21	23	44	19	31	46	15
	NA	NA	NA	37	52	10	38	48	14	34	51	12	34	54	11	37	53	8	40	52	8
	NA	NA	NA	28	58	12	31	54	13	27	54	16	31	50	15	30	54	13	38	48	11
	NA	NA	NA	33	46	17	30	53	15	31	49	16	28	52	14	28	51	13	31	55	12
	NA	NA	NA	26	51	16	26	46	22	24	49	21	32	45	15	30	44	17	28	50	16
	42	47	10	36	52	9	37	48	14	34	50	12	36	53	9	38	50	9	38	50	10
	45	45	10	25	57	14	28	54	16	29	52	17	25	56	15	28	53	12	35	54	8
	32	50	15	29	49	17	26	52	17	24	49	20	30	45	18	27	47	18	31	51	14
	30	60	5	26	58	5	35	38	25	13	42	29	32	42	19	23	60	11	28	44	17
	44	39	14	32	50	12	35	47	14	31	49	13	31	54	11	34	47	12	29	55	11
	34	51	13	33	52	11	29	50	18	29	51	17	30	49	15	30	51	14	37	50	10
	37	48	13	25	55	16	27	51	18	26	49	18	30	47	17	31	50	13	39	47	11
	38	51	9	34	48	13	32	51	15	29	51	17	33	53	11	33	50	12	34	50	14
	35	48	15	29	52	14	28	51	17	25	51	18	29	51	15	30	50	14	38	46	12
	45	44	9	36	50	12	32	51	14	33	48	15	35	48	12	33	49	11	35	53	9
	48	43	10	30	50	15	42	46	12	48	44	4	41	47	9	43	45	12	25	50	20
	24	64	11	29	56	13	33	47	18	30	45	19	29	51	14	33	49	14	30	57	10
	46	43	11	33	54	11	32	49	16	32	51	15	33	50	15	31	51	13	43	48	8
	34	50	13	27	52	16	32	48	16	30	51	13	31	50	13	33	50	10	34	49	14
	34	50	14	32	50	13	27	53	17	24	49	21	30	50	15	32	49	14	32	52	12

Public attitudes toward crime and criminal justice-related topics 117

Table 2.16
Reported confidence in the U.S. Government to protect citizens from terrorist attack

United States, 2002, 2003, and 2004

Question: "How much confidence do you have in the U.S. government to protect its citizens from future terrorist attacks--a great deal, a fair amount, not very much, or none at all?"

	Great deal	Fair amount	Not very much	None at all
March 2002	24%	58%	15%	2%
May 2002	22	54	18	5
June 2002	27	49	17	5
September 2002	24	56	16	3
February 2003	29	53	14	4
August 2003	23	53	19	5
January 2004	31	50	15	4

Note: Sample sizes vary from year to year; the data for 2004 are based on telephone interviews with a randomly selected national sample of 1,029 adults, 18 years of age and older, conducted Jan. 2-5, 2004. The "don't know/refused" category has been omitted; therefore percents may not sum to 100. For a discussion of public opinion survey sampling procedures, see Appendix 5.

Source: The Gallup Organization, Inc., *The Gallup Poll* [Online]. Available: http://www.gallup.com/poll/ [Apr. 5, 2004]. Table adapted by SOURCEBOOK staff. Reprinted by permission.

Table 2.17
Respondents' ratings of the honesty and ethical standards of various occupations

By type of occupation, United States, 2003

Question: "Please tell me how you would rate the honesty and ethical standards of people in these different fields--very high, high, average, low, or very low: . . .?"

	Very high	High	Average	Low	Very low	Don't know/ refused
Nurses	25%	58%	16%	1%	(a)	(a)
Clergy	17	39	34	6	2%	2%
Druggist, pharmacists	17	50	29	2	1	1
Medical doctors	16	52	27	4	1	(a)
Veterinarians	16	52	27	2	(a)	3
Police	14	45	35	4	2	(a)
College teachers	12	47	33	5	1	2
Engineers	12	47	36	2	(a)	3
Dentists	11	50	34	3	1	1
Psychiatrists	8	30	44	11	2	5
Bankers	5	30	53	9	2	1
Chiropractors	5	26	49	13	2	5
Journalists	4	21	49	18	7	1
State governors	4	22	52	18	3	1
Congress members	3	14	52	25	5	1
Lawyers	3	13	47	25	11	1
Business executives	2	16	56	20	5	1
Car sales people	2	5	39	39	14	1
HMO managers	2	9	45	28	11	5
Insurance sales people	2	10	56	24	7	1
Senators	2	18	53	21	6	(a)
Stockbrokers	2	13	54	23	6	2
Advertising practitioners	1	11	48	29	7	4

Note: These data are based on telephone interviews with a randomly selected national sample of 1,004 adults, 18 years of age and older, conducted Nov. 14-16, 2003. For a discussion of public opinion survey sampling procedures, see Appendix 5.

[a]Less than 0.5%.

Source: The Gallup Organization, Inc., *The Gallup Poll* [Online]. Available: http://www.gallup.com/poll/ [June 8, 2004]. Table adapted by SOURCEBOOK staff. Reprinted by permission.

Table 2.18
Respondents' ratings of the honesty and ethical standards of lawyers

United States, selected years 1976-2003

Question: "Please tell me how you would rate the honesty and ethical standards of people in these different fields--very high, high, average, low, or very low: Lawyers?"

	Very high	High	Average	Low	Very low	Don't know/ refused
1976	6%	19%	48%	18%	8%	1%
1977	5	21	44	18	8	4
1981	4	21	41	19	8	7
1983	5	19	43	20	9	6
1985	6	21	40	21	9	3
1988	3	15	45	22	10	4
1990	4	18	43	23	9	4
1991	4	18	43	24	10	5
1992	3	15	43	25	11	3
1993	3	13	41	26	13	2
1994	3	14	36	27	15	1
1995	4	12	36	28	17	2
1996	3	14	39	29	14	3
1997	3	12	41	30	10	3
1999	1	12	45	28	13	1
2000	3	14	42	29	11	1
2001	4	14	50	23	8	1
2002	2	16	45	25	10	2
2003	3	13	47	25	11	1

Note: See Note, table 2.17. For a discussion of public opinion survey sampling procedures, see Appendix 5.

Source: George Gallup, Jr., *The Gallup Report*, Report No. 279, p. 18; *The Gallup Poll Monthly*, No. 293, p. 23; No. 322, p. 2; No. 334, p. 38; No. 387, p. 23; *The Gallup Poll*, May 22, 1991, p. 3; Nov. 10, 1995, p. 2; Jan. 2, 1997, p. 2 (Princeton, NJ: The Gallup Poll); The Gallup Organization, Inc., *The Gallup Poll* [Online]. Available: http://www.gallup.com/poll/releases/pr991116.asp [Mar. 22, 2000]; http://www.gallup.com/poll/releases/pr001127.asp [Apr. 18, 2001]; http://www.gallup.com/poll/topics/hnsty_ethcs.asp [Jan. 4, 2002]; http://www.gallup.com/poll/releases/pr021204.asp [Feb. 10, 2003]; http://www.gallup.com/poll/ [June 8, 2004]; and data provided by The Gallup Organization, Inc. Table adapted by SOURCEBOOK staff. Reprinted by permission.

Table 2.19

Respondents' ratings of the honesty and ethical standards of lawyers

By demographic characteristics, United States, 2003

Question: "Please tell me how you would rate the honesty and ethical standards of people in these different fields--very high, high, average, low, or very low: Lawyers?"

	Very high	High	Average	Low	Very low
National	3%	13%	47%	25%	11%
Sex					
Male	3	9	46	27	14
Female	3	15	49	24	7
Race					
White	3	12	45	27	12
Nonwhite	6	13	54	20	6
Black	7	14	61	15	3
Age					
18 to 29 years	10	12	56	17	5
30 to 49 years	2	15	45	26	11
50 to 64 years	1	8	46	29	16
50 years and older	2	10	45	28	13
65 years and older	2	14	45	26	10
Education					
College post graduate	4	14	50	22	10
College graduate	1	11	49	27	12
Some college	2	10	48	27	12
High school graduate or less	5	14	45	24	10
Income					
$75,000 and over	2	10	52	25	11
$50,000 to $74,999	2	13	43	27	14
$30,000 to $49,999	5	8	49	24	13
$20,000 to $29,999	2	14	54	26	4
Under $20,000	5	21	41	20	10
Community					
Urban area	4	14	47	23	12
Suburban area	3	13	45	27	10
Rural area	4	9	51	24	11
Region					
East	4	13	48	25	9
Midwest	3	15	48	22	10
South	3	11	49	27	8
West	3	10	42	27	17
Politics					
Republican	2	12	40	32	13
Democrat	6	12	52	23	5
Independent	2	13	50	22	13

Note: See Note, table 2.17. The "don't know/refused" category has been omitted; therefore percents may not sum to 100. For a discussion of public opinion survey sampling procedures, see Appendix 5.

Source: Table constructed by SOURCEBOOK staff from data provided by The Gallup Organization, Inc. Reprinted by permission.

Table 2.20

Respondents' ratings of the honesty and ethical standards of police

United States, selected years 1977-2003

Question: "Please tell me how you would rate the honesty and ethical standards of people in these different fields--very high, high, average, low, or very low: Policemen?"

	Very high	High	Average	Low	Very low
1977	8%	29%	50%	9%	3%
1981	8	36	41	9	4
1983	7	34	45	7	4
1985	10	37	41	7	3
1988	10	37	39	8	3
1990	9	40	41	7	2
1991	7	36	42	10	3
1992	8	34	42	10	4
1993	10	40	39	7	3
1994	9	37	41	9	3
1995	8	33	44	11	3
1996	10	39	38	8	3
1997	10	39	40	8	2
1999	9	43	38	8	2
2000	12	43	34	8	3
2001	23	45	26	5	1
2002	13	46	33	6	2
2003	14	45	35	4	2

Note: See Note, table 2.17. The "don't know/refused" category has been omitted; therefore percents may not sum to 100. For a discussion of public opinion survey sampling procedures, see Appendix 5.

Source: George Gallup, Jr., *The Gallup Report*, Report No. 279, p. 10; *The Gallup Poll Monthly*, No. 293, p. 23; No. 322, p. 2; No. 334, p. 38; No. 387, p. 23; *The Gallup Poll*, May 22, 1991, p. 3; Nov. 10, 1995, p. 2; Jan. 2, 1997, p. 2 (Princeton, NJ: The Gallup Poll); The Gallup Organization, Inc., *The Gallup Poll* [Online]. Available: http://www.gallup.com/poll/releases/pr991116.asp [Mar. 22, 2000]; http://www.gallup.com/poll/releases/pr001127.asp [Apr. 18, 2001]; http://www.gallup.com/poll/topics/hnsty_ethcs.asp [Jan. 4, 2002]; http://www.gallup.com/poll/releases/pr021204.asp [Feb. 10, 2003]; http://www.gallup.com/poll/ [June 8, 2004]; and data provided by The Gallup Organization, Inc. Table adapted by SOURCEBOOK staff. Reprinted by permission.

Table 2.21
Respondents' ratings of the honesty and ethical standards of police

By demographic characteristics, United States, 2003

Question: "Please tell me how you would rate the honesty and ethical standards of people in these different fields--very high, high, average, low, or very low: Policemen?"

	Very high	High	Average	Low	Very low
National	14%	45%	35%	4%	2%
Sex					
Male	18	38	38	4	2
Female	11	51	33	4	1
Race					
White	15	47	33	4	1
Nonwhite	9	34	46	7	3
Black	6	26	52	12	3
Age					
18 to 29 years	18	34	36	9	3
30 to 49 years	15	46	34	3	2
50 to 64 years	10	46	39	4	1
50 years and older	11	48	37	3	1
65 years and older	14	50	34	2	(a)
Education					
College post graduate	13	48	34	3	2
College graduate	11	50	32	5	2
Some college	16	44	36	3	1
High school graduate or less	15	41	37	5	2
Income					
$75,000 and over	13	49	34	2	2
$50,000 to $74,999	14	45	36	3	2
$30,000 to $49,999	16	39	39	4	2
$20,000 to $29,999	16	38	34	11	1
Under $20,000	13	50	32	4	1
Community					
Urban area	9	48	33	7	3
Suburban area	15	43	38	3	1
Rural area	19	42	33	4	2
Region					
East	15	46	34	4	1
Midwest	16	48	29	6	1
South	13	41	41	3	2
West	13	45	36	3	3
Politics					
Republican	18	50	29	2	1
Democrat	12	43	37	7	1
Independent	13	41	39	4	3

Note: See Note, table 2.17. The "don't know/refused" category has been omitted; therefore percents may not sum to 100. For a discussion of public opinion survey sampling procedures, see Appendix 5.

[a]Less than 0.5%.

Source: Table constructed by SOURCEBOOK staff from data provided by The Gallup Organization, Inc. Reprinted by permission.

Table 2.22
Respondents' ratings of performance of police in own community

United States, 2000 and 2002[a]

Question: "How would you rate the police in your community on the following--excellent, pretty good, only fair or poor?"

	Excellent	Pretty good	Only fair	Poor	Not sure/refused
Responding quickly to calls for help and assistance					
2000	31%	38%	17%	8%	6%
2002	30	38	18	10	5
Not using excessive force					
2000	33	39	14	7	8
2002	29	38	17	7	9
Being helpful and friendly					
2000	37	37	16	8	2
2002	35	38	16	8	3
Treating people fairly					
2000	24	43	19	10	4
2002	26	40	20	10	4
Preventing crime					
2000	21	48	20	9	1
2002	20	45	21	10	3
Solving crime					
2000	16	47	23	7	6
2002	16	45	24	9	6

Note: Sample sizes vary from year to year; the data for 2002 are based on telephone interviews with a randomly selected national sample of 1,021 adults, 18 years of age and older, conducted Feb. 13-19, 2002. For a discussion of public opinion survey sampling procedures, see Appendix 5.

[a]Percents may not add to 100 because of rounding.

Source: Harris Interactive Inc., *The Harris Poll* ® (New York: Harris Interactive Inc., Mar. 1, 2000, p. 3; Mar. 20, 2002, p. 3). Table adapted by SOURCEBOOK staff. © 2000, 2002, Harris Interactive Inc. All rights reserved. Reproduction prohibited without the express written permission of Harris Interactive.

Table 2.23

Attitudes toward a police officer striking an adult male citizen

By demographic characteristics, United States, selected years 1973-2002

Question: "Are there any situations you can imagine in which you would approve of a policeman striking an adult male citizen?"

	1973 Yes	1973 No	1975 Yes	1975 No	1976 Yes	1976 No	1978 Yes	1978 No	1980 Yes	1980 No	1983 Yes	1983 No	1984 Yes	1984 No	1986 Yes	1986 No	1987 Yes	1987 No
National	73%	25%	73%	23%	76%	20%	76%	20%	73%	24%	78%	20%	69%	28%	72%	25%	73%	23%
Sex																		
Male	75	22	77	20	81	17	82	16	80	18	83	15	75	23	80	17	80	17
Female	71	28	70	26	72	22	72	23	68	29	73	23	65	32	66	31	67	27
Race																		
White	77	21	77	20	79	18	80	17	76	21	80	17	73	25	76	22	76	20
Black/other	42	54	46	47	48	44	48	45	45	49	59	37	50	46	49	46	56	35
Age																		
18 to 20 years	55	45	70	27	78	20	67	30	71	29	78	22	71	27	60	38	71	29
21 to 29 years	76	22	75	22	78	20	79	19	76	23	81	17	72	26	74	25	73	24
30 to 49 years	76	23	79	18	79	17	79	18	79	20	81	17	75	24	78	21	77	19
50 years and older	70	26	68	27	73	23	73	21	66	28	72	24	62	34	65	30	68	26
Education[a]																		
College	84	14	86	13	85	13	85	12	82	17	87	11	79	20	85	14	83	14
High school graduate	72	27	71	26	76	20	76	21	73	24	75	23	67	31	67	31	70	26
Less than high school graduate	56	38	58	35	62	33	59	33	52	41	56	36	46	46	51	38	48	39
Income																		
$50,000 and over	NA	NA	NA	NA	NA	NA	NA	NA	NA	NA	NA	NA	NA	NA	NA	NA	NA	NA
$30,000 to $49,999	NA	NA	NA	NA	NA	NA	NA	NA	NA	NA	NA	NA	NA	NA	NA	NA	NA	NA
$20,000 to $29,999	NA	NA	NA	NA	NA	NA	NA	NA	NA	NA	NA	NA	NA	NA	NA	NA	NA	NA
Under $20,000	NA	NA	NA	NA	NA	NA	NA	NA	NA	NA	NA	NA	NA	NA	NA	NA	NA	NA
Occupation																		
Professional/business	83	16	84	14	84	14	86	11	83	15	85	13	76	22	83	15	86	12
Clerical/support	80	18	77	20	78	18	79	19	78	21	83	16	74	26	70	28	66	29
Manual/service	66	32	66	30	73	24	72	25	67	29	71	26	64	32	66	30	65	29
Farming/agriculture	69	22	63	27	70	28	79	8	70	24	92	3	61	29	63	34	78	15
Region																		
Northeast	68	31	74	24	75	22	74	25	74	24	77	20	65	34	68	28	71	26
Midwest	72	25	77	21	78	18	80	18	70	26	76	22	70	26	72	26	72	24
South	73	25	71	24	74	20	74	21	71	26	77	20	67	30	70	26	71	23
West	79	19	70	26	78	20	80	16	79	18	84	14	76	23	78	21	79	17
Religion																		
Protestant	74	24	73	22	77	19	75	21	74	22	78	19	70	27	73	24	74	22
Catholic	70	27	71	27	74	23	76	21	70	28	75	22	66	32	68	30	68	27
Jewish	71	26	91	4	70	30	72	24	81	16	83	12	67	26	76	18	80	15
None	69	30	76	23	82	16	85	13	70	26	80	18	74	25	76	22	75	21
Politics																		
Republican	76	22	76	19	79	17	76	20	78	20	86	13	74	24	78	19	82	16
Democrat	67	31	67	29	72	24	73	23	67	29	72	26	62	35	68	30	66	29
Independent	79	19	78	19	79	17	80	19	75	22	79	17	73	25	73	24	74	21

Note: See Note, table 2.15. The "don't know" category has been omitted; therefore percents may not sum to 100. For a discussion of public opinion survey sampling procedures, see Appendix 5.

[a] Beginning in 1996, education categories were revised slightly and therefore are not directly comparable to data presented for prior years.

Source: National Opinion Research Center, "General Social Surveys, 1972-2002," Storrs, CT: The Roper Center for Public Opinion Research, University of Connecticut. (Machine-readable data files.) Table constructed by SOURCEBOOK staff.

	1988		1989		1990		1991		1993		1994		1996		1998		2000		2002	
	Yes	No	Yes	No	Yes	No	Yes	No	Yes	No	Yes	No	Yes	No	Yes	No	Yes	No	Yes	No
	73%	23%	70%	24%	70%	25%	66%	30%	73%	22%	71%	26%	67%	29%	66%	30%	64%	33%	66%	27%
	77	20	77	18	77	19	71	27	81	16	80	18	75	21	74	23	74	24	72	22
	69	25	66	28	64	30	62	33	68	27	64	32	60	35	59	36	56	40	60	32
	77	19	74	21	73	22	70	26	77	19	76	22	71	25	71	26	70	27	71	22
	51	41	51	40	52	41	44	51	51	40	48	46	47	45	47	47	39	56	44	47
	74	26	69	31	59	36	53	42	69	28	56	38	50	46	52	43	62	38	47	41
	70	26	73	21	74	24	68	30	80	19	70	27	68	28	66	30	63	36	70	24
	79	18	74	20	74	23	72	27	75	22	76	22	70	26	68	28	67	30	66	28
	68	26	65	28	63	28	58	34	68	24	66	30	63	31	63	31	61	33	65	28
	78	19	78	17	78	19	73	24	79	18	79	19	74	23	71	27	72	26	73	22
	73	23	66	30	64	30	64	32	70	26	66	32	62	33	68	28	59	37	64	28
	50	36	53	34	48	33	36	54	55	33	52	40	52	39	47	44	48	46	45	43
	NA	NA	NA	NA	NA	NA	NA	NA	83	16	81	18	76	22	73	25	76	22	77	20
	NA	NA	NA	NA	NA	NA	NA	NA	74	23	80	18	71	27	72	24	68	29	66	28
	NA	NA	NA	NA	NA	NA	NA	NA	77	20	69	28	68	28	66	31	66	32	63	31
	NA	NA	NA	NA	NA	NA	NA	NA	65	29	60	35	57	37	55	39	50	46	56	35
	79	19	80	14	80	18	75	23	79	17	80	18	75	21	71	26	73	25	75	21
	77	19	70	26	73	24	66	30	74	22	67	30	60	36	67	28	60	37	59	34
	69	26	64	30	64	29	60	35	72	24	68	29	66	30	62	33	58	38	61	31
	62	25	75	12	50	38	55	35	47	47	70	20	58	37	68	29	69	29	61	28
	68	29	62	30	68	24	63	34	71	25	65	32	57	38	57	37	57	38	56	35
	70	24	79	19	69	26	66	30	67	27	71	26	69	27	68	29	65	32	64	27
	75	19	71	20	67	27	65	31	77	18	71	26	66	29	67	28	64	32	68	25
	77	20	66	29	76	20	70	26	76	20	78	20	76	21	68	29	69	27	74	23
	74	21	73	22	70	25	67	28	74	21	70	27	69	26	66	30	65	31	67	27
	66	29	66	28	67	27	62	34	67	27	71	25	62	35	62	34	59	36	65	26
	91	4	75	19	71	29	68	32	79	21	76	22	61	37	69	31	67	33	75	20
	78	20	68	25	74	19	65	34	78	21	77	22	70	26	70	24	71	27	67	26
	75	21	76	18	76	19	72	25	78	17	77	20	78	18	73	23	74	24	77	18
	69	26	69	26	64	30	58	37	65	29	66	30	60	36	60	36	56	40	61	34
	75	20	66	26	70	25	68	28	76	20	71	26	66	30	64	30	64	32	63	28

Public attitudes toward crime and criminal justice-related topics 123

Table 2.24

Attitudes toward a police officer striking a citizen under certain circumstances

United States, selected years 1973-2002

Question: "Would you approve of a policeman striking a citizen who..."

	Was attacking the policeman with his fists?		Was attempting to escape from custody?		Had said vulgar and obscene things to the policeman?		Was being questioned in a murder case?	
	Yes	No	Yes	No	Yes	No	Yes	No
1973	97%	3%	87%	12%	22%	76%	8%	90%
1975	98	2	86	11	19	77	8	90
1976	94	5	78	18	20	77	8	90
1978	93	6	75	22	18	80	8	89
1980	94	4	76	20	14	84	8	90
1983	92	7	75	21	15	83	9	89
1984	92	6	73	23	12	86	9	89
1986	94	5	72	24	14	85	9	90
1987	92	7	77	18	11	86	10	87
1988	92	6	76	19	12	86	8	89
1989	94	5	76	20	11	87	8	90
1990	92	6	74	21	12	84	11	86
1991	90	8	69	26	9	89	6	92
1993	92	6	73	23	7	91	7	90
1994	93	6	75	21	9	90	7	92
1996	91	7	68	27	7	92	5	94
1998	90	8	68	27	7	92	6	93
2000	90	8	67	28	6	92	6	93
2002	89	9	67	25	6	91	9	88

Note: See Note, table 2.15. In 1973 and 1975 these data were based on a subsample of respondents who answered "yes" or "don't know" to the question presented in table 2.23. Since 1976, all survey respondents were asked the above questions. The "don't know" category has been omitted; therefore percents may not sum to 100. For a discussion of public opinion survey sampling procedures, see Appendix 5.

Source: National Opinion Research Center, "General Social Surveys, 1972-2002," Storrs, CT: The Roper Center for Public Opinion Research, University of Connecticut. (Machine-readable data files.) Table constructed by SOURCEBOOK staff.

Table 2.25

Attitudes toward a police officer striking a citizen under certain circumstances

By demographic characteristics, United States, 2002

Question: "Would you approve of a policeman striking a citizen who..."

	Was attacking the policeman with his fists?		Was attempting to escape from custody?		Had said vulgar and obscene things to the policeman?		Was being questioned in a murder case?	
	Yes	No	Yes	No	Yes	No	Yes	No
National	89%	9%	67%	25%	6%	91%	9%	88%
Sex								
Male	92	7	70	23	6	92	8	90
Female	87	11	65	26	7	91	10	87
Race								
White	92	6	72	21	7	92	8	89
Black/other	76	20	50	39	6	90	11	85
Age								
18 to 20 years	82	18	71	29	0	100	18	82
21 to 29 years	86	12	67	24	6	92	8	90
30 to 49 years	89	9	65	28	5	94	6	92
50 years and older	90	8	69	21	9	88	12	84
Education								
College	89	9	72	20	4	94	6	92
High school graduate	89	10	66	29	8	90	12	85
Less than high school graduate	89	10	52	34	10	85	13	82
Income								
$50,000 and over	93	6	78	16	3	96	5	93
$30,000 to $49,999	92	7	71	23	6	93	8	91
$20,000 to $29,999	86	12	62	30	7	92	7	90
Under $20,000	83	14	57	35	10	86	16	80
Occupation								
Professional/business	92	7	76	17	4	95	6	92
Clerical/support	84	12	57	30	8	90	8	88
Manual/service	89	10	66	28	8	90	11	86
Farming/agriculture	94	6	44	39	6	89	11	83
Region								
Northeast	87	12	56	31	6	91	11	83
Midwest	89	10	68	24	7	90	10	87
South	91	6	70	22	8	91	9	88
West	87	12	73	24	4	94	4	96
Religion								
Protestant	89	8	67	24	7	90	9	87
Catholic	89	10	70	25	6	92	8	90
Jewish	95	5	85	5	5	90	10	90
None	87	12	66	27	6	93	9	88
Politics								
Republican	95	5	81	14	8	90	11	87
Democrat	86	11	62	28	6	92	8	89
Independent	88	10	63	28	6	91	8	89

Note: See Note, table 2.15. The "don't know" category has been omitted; therefore percents may not sum to 100. For a discussion of public opinion survey sampling procedures, see Appendix 5.

Source: National Opinion Research Center, "General Social Surveys, 1972-2002," Storrs, CT: The Roper Center for Public Opinion Research, University of Connecticut. (Machine-readable data files.) Table constructed by SOURCEBOOK staff.

Table 2.26
Respondents' attitudes toward racial profiling

By race and ethnicity, United States, 2004

Questions: "It has been reported that some police officers or security guards stop people of certain racial or ethnic groups because these officials believe that these groups are more likely than others to commit certain types of crimes. For each of the following situations, please say if you think this practice, known as 'racial profiling,' is widespread, or not? How about . . ."

"Do you think it is ever justified for police to use racial or ethnic profiling when . . . or is it never justified?"

(Percent responding yes, widespread or yes, justified)

	Yes, racial profiling is widespread	Yes, racial profiling is justified
When motorists are stopped on roads and highways		
Total	53%	31%
White	50	31
Black	67	23
Hispanic	63	30
When passengers are stopped at security checkpoints in airports		
Total	42	45
White	40	46
Black	48	32
Hispanic	54	40
When shoppers are questioned/ attempting to prevent theft in shopping malls or stores		
Total	49	25
White	45	24
Black	65	19
Hispanic	56	38

Note: These data are based on telephone interviews with a randomly selected national sample of 2,250 adults, 18 years of age and older, conducted June 9-30, 2004, including oversamples of black and Hispanic respondents that are weighted to reflect their proportions in the general population. For a discussion of public opinion survey sampling procedures, see Appendix 5.

Source: The Gallup Organization, Inc., *The Gallup Poll* [Online]. Available: http://www.gallup.com/poll/ [July 20, 2004]. Table adapted by SOURCEBOOK staff. Reprinted by permission.

Table 2.27
Respondents favoring increased law enforcement powers

United States, 2001-2004

Question: "Here are some increased powers of investigation that law enforcement agencies might use when dealing with people suspected of terrorist activity, which would also affect our civil liberties. For each, please say if you would favor or oppose it."

Percent responding "favor" to:	2001	2002	2003	2004
Expanded under-cover activities to penetrate groups under suspicion	93%	88%	81%	80%
Stronger document and physical security checks for travelers	93	89	84	84
Stronger document and physical security checks for access to government and private office buildings	92	89	82	85
Use of facial-recognition technology to scan for suspected terrorists at various locations and public events	86	81	77	80
Issuance of a secure I.D. technique for persons to access government and business computer systems, to avoid disruptions	84	78	75	76
Closer monitoring of banking and credit card transactions, to trace funding sources	81	72	67	64
Adoption of a national I.D. system for all U.S. citizens	68	59	64	56
Expanded camera surveillance on streets and in public places	63	58	61	61
Law enforcement monitoring of Internet discussions in chat rooms and other forums	63	55	54	50
Expanded government monitoring of cell phones and e-mail, to intercept communications	54	44	44	36

Note: Sample sizes vary from year to year; the data for 2004 are based on telephone interviews with a randomly selected national sample of 1,020 adults, 18 years of age and older, conducted Feb. 9-16, 2004. For a discussion of public opinion survey sampling procedures, see Appendix 5.

Source: Harris Interactive Inc., *The Harris Poll* ® (New York: Harris Interactive Inc., Mar. 5, 2004, pp. 3, 4). Table adapted by SOURCEBOOK staff. © 2004, Harris Interactive Inc. All rights reserved. Reproduction prohibited without the express written permission of Harris Interactive.

Table 2.28
Attitudes toward approaches to lowering the crime rate in the United States

United States, selected years 1989-2003[a]

Question: "Which of the following approaches to lowering the crime rate in the United States comes closer to your own view--do you think more money and effort should go to attacking the social and economic problems that lead to crime through better education and job training or more money and effort should go to deterring crime by improving law enforcement with more prisons, police, and judges?"

	Attack social problems	More law enforcement	Don't know/ refused
1989	61%	32%	7%
1990	57	36	2
March 1992	64	27	9
August 1992	67	25	8
February 1994	57	39	4
August 1994	51	42	7
2000	68	27	5
2003	69	29	2

Note: See Note, table 2.13. In years prior to 2000, the question wording was: "To lower the crime rate in the United States, some people think additional money and effort should go to attacking the social and economic problems that lead to crime through better education and job training. Others feel more money and effort should go to deterring crime by improving law enforcement with more prisons, police, and judges. Which comes closer to your view?" For a discussion of public opinion survey sampling procedures, see Appendix 5.

[a] Percents may not add to 100 because of rounding.

Source: The Gallup Organization, Inc., *The Gallup Poll* [Online]. Available: http://www.gallup.com/poll/ [Mar. 20, 2001]; and data provided by The Gallup Organization, Inc. Reprinted by permission.

Table 2.29
Respondents reporting fear that they or someone in their family will become a victim of terrorism

United States, 2002, 2003, and 2004

Question: "How worried are you that you or someone in your family will become a victim of terrorism--very worried, somewhat worried, not too worried, or not worried at all?"

	Very worried	Somewhat worried	Not too worried	Not worried at all
March 2002	12%	33%	32%	23%
April 2002	8	27	39	25
May 2002	9	31	37	22
September 2002	8	30	37	25
January 2003	8	31	36	25
February 2003	8	28	33	31
March 2003	8	30	38	24
August 2003	11	30	33	26
December 2003	9	28	38	25
January 2004	5	23	42	30
February 2004	10	30	36	24

Note: Sample sizes vary from year to year; the data for February 2004 are based on telephone interviews with a randomly selected national sample of 1,002 adults, 18 years of age and older, conducted Feb. 9-12, 2004. The "don't know/refused" category and a volunteered category that includes respondents who reported that they already know a victim have been omitted; therefore percents may not sum to 100. For a discussion of public opinion survey sampling procedures, see Appendix 5.

Source: The Gallup Organization, Inc., *The Gallup Poll* [Online]. Available: http://www.gallup.com/poll/ [Apr. 5, 2004]. Table adapted by SOURCEBOOK staff. Reprinted by permission.

Table 2.30
Respondents reporting how worried they are that there will soon be another terrorist attack in the United States

United States, 2001, 2002, and 2003

Question: "How worried are you that there will soon be another terrorist attack in the United States?"

	Very worried	Somewhat worried	Not too worried	Not at all worried
Early October 2001	28%	45%	15%	11%
Mid-October 2001	29	42	18	10
December 2001	13	39	27	19
January 2002	20	42	28	9
June 2002	32	44	17	7
August 2002	16	46	25	12
October 2002	20	46	22	11
December 2002	31	42	18	8
January 2003	18	50	23	8
February 2003	34	41	17	7
March 2003	22	42	20	14
August 2003	13	45	29	12

Note: Sample sizes vary from year to year; the data for August 2003 are based on telephone interviews with a randomly selected national sample of 2,528 adults, 18 years of age and older, conducted July 14-Aug. 5, 2003. The "don't know/refused" category has been omitted; therefore percents may not sum to 100. For a discussion of public opinion survey sampling procedures, see Appendix 5.

Source: The Pew Research Center for the People & the Press, *The 2004 Political Landscape: Evenly Divided and Increasingly Polarized* (Washington, DC: The Pew Research Center for the People & the Press, 2003), p. T-59. Table adapted by SOURCEBOOK staff. Reprinted by permission.

Table 2.31
Respondents reporting whether they think it will be necessary to give up some civil liberties to curb terrorism in the United States

United States, selected years 1996-2003

Question: "In order to curb terrorism in this country, do you think it will be necessary for the average person to give up some civil liberties, or not?"

	Yes, it will be necessary	No, it will not be necessary	Don't know/refused
1996	30%	65%	5%
1997	29	62	9
Mid-September 2001	55	35	10
January 2002	55	39	6
June 2002	49	45	6
2003	44	50	6

Note: See Note, table 2.30. For a discussion of public opinion survey sampling procedures, see Appendix 5.

Source: The Pew Research Center for the People & the Press, *The 2004 Political Landscape: Evenly Divided and Increasingly Polarized* (Washington, DC: The Pew Research Center for the People & the Press, 2003), p. T-59. Table adapted by SOURCEBOOK staff. Reprinted by permission.

Table 2.32
Attitudes toward requiring all citizens to carry a national identity card to curb terrorism in the United States

United States, 2001, 2002, and 2003

Question: "To curb terrorism, would you favor or oppose requiring that all citizens carry a national identity card at all times to show to a police officer on request?"

	Favor	Oppose	Don't know/refused
Mid-September 2001	70%	26%	4%
August 2002	59	38	3
August 2003	56	40	4

Note: See Note, table 2.30. For a discussion of public opinion survey sampling procedures, see Appendix 5.

Source: The Pew Research Center for the People & the Press, *The 2004 Political Landscape: Evenly Divided and Increasingly Polarized* (Washington, DC: The Pew Research Center for the People & the Press, 2003), p. T-59. Table adapted by SOURCEBOOK staff. Reprinted by permission.

Table 2.33
Attitudes toward level of crime in the United States

United States, selected years 1989-2003

Question: "Is there more crime in the U.S. than there was a year ago, or less?"

	More	Less	Same[a]	Don't know/refused
1989	84%	5%	5%	6%
1990	84	3	7	6
1992	89	3	4	4
1993	87	4	5	4
1996	71	15	8	6
1997	64	25	6	5
1998	52	35	8	5
2000	47	41	7	5
2001	41	43	10	6
2002	62	21	11	6
2003	60	25	11	4

Note: See Note, table 2.13. For a discussion of public opinion survey sampling procedures, see Appendix 5.

[a] Response volunteered.

Source: The Gallup Organization, Inc., *The Gallup Poll* [Online]. Available: http://www.gallup.com/poll/ [Jan. 9, 2003]; and data provided by The Gallup Organization, Inc. Table adapted by SOURCEBOOK staff. Reprinted by permission.

Table 2.34

Attitudes toward level of crime in the United States

By demographic characteristics, United States, 2003

Question: "Is there more crime in the U.S. than there was a year ago, or less?"

	More	Less	Same[a]	Don't know/ refused
National	60%	25%	11%	4%
Sex				
Male	52	32	12	4
Female	66	19	10	5
Race				
White	57	26	12	5
Nonwhite	70	21	6	3
Black	84	11	4	1
Age				
18 to 29 years	59	32	7	2
30 to 49 years	61	24	11	4
50 to 64 years	56	29	12	3
50 years and older	59	23	12	6
65 years and older	63	15	13	9
Education				
College post graduate	41	39	16	4
College graduate	52	31	13	4
Some college	55	27	13	5
High school graduate or less	73	17	6	4
Income				
$75,000 and over	43	39	13	5
$50,000 to $74,999	50	33	14	3
$30,000 to $49,999	67	22	7	4
$20,000 to $29,999	72	15	8	5
Under $20,000	69	13	13	5
Community				
Urban area	61	25	10	4
Suburban area	58	26	11	5
Rural area	61	24	12	3
Region				
East	62	23	11	4
Midwest	57	28	11	4
South	60	28	9	3
West	58	21	14	7
Politics				
Republican	47	35	12	6
Democrat	69	17	10	4
Independent	62	24	10	4

Note: See Note, table 2.13. For a discussion of public opinion survey sampling procedures, see Appendix 5.

[a]Response volunteered.

Source: Table constructed by SOURCEBOOK staff from data provided by The Gallup Organization, Inc. Reprinted by permission.

Table 2.35

Attitudes toward level of crime in own area

United States, selected years 1972-2003[a]

Question: "Is there more crime in your area than there was a year ago, or less?"

	More	Less	Same[b]	Don't know/ refused
1972	51%	10%	27%	12%
1975	50	12	29	9
1977	43	17	32	8
1981	54	8	29	9
1983	37	17	36	10
January 1989	47	21	27	5
June 1989	53	18	22	7
1990	51	18	24	8
1992	54	19	23	4
1996	46	24	25	5
1997	46	32	20	2
1998	31	48	16	5
2000	34	46	15	5
2001	26	52	18	4
2002	37	34	24	5
2003	40	39	19	2

Note: See Note, table 2.13. For a discussion of public opinion survey sampling procedures, see Appendix 5.

[a]Percents may not add to 100 because of rounding.
[b]Response volunteered.

Source: The Gallup Organization, Inc., *The Gallup Poll* [Online]. Available: http://www.gallup.com/poll/ [Jan. 9, 2003]; and data provided by The Gallup Organization, Inc. Table adapted by SOURCEBOOK staff. Reprinted by permission.

Table 2.36

Attitudes toward level of crime in own area

By demographic characteristics, United States, 2003

Question: "Is there more crime in your area than there was a year ago, or less?"

	More	Less	Same[a]	Don't know/ refused
National	40%	39%	19%	2%
Sex				
Male	34	44	20	2
Female	46	34	19	1
Race				
White	40	38	20	2
Nonwhite	42	41	15	2
Black	47	43	10	0
Age				
18 to 29 years	43	45	11	1
30 to 49 years	37	41	19	3
50 to 64 years	43	36	19	2
50 years and older	42	33	23	2
65 years and older	42	28	29	1
Education				
College post graduate	26	43	28	3
College graduate	32	42	25	1
Some college	39	39	19	3
High school graduate or less	49	35	15	1
Income				
$75,000 and over	25	48	24	3
$50,000 to $74,999	38	42	20	(b)
$30,000 to $49,999	44	39	15	2
$20,000 to $29,999	43	37	19	1
Under $20,000	52	26	21	1
Community				
Urban area	41	36	20	3
Suburban area	39	41	18	2
Rural area	42	37	21	(b)
Region				
East	44	33	21	2
Midwest	35	43	21	1
South	41	41	16	2
West	41	36	20	3
Politics				
Republican	33	45	20	2
Democrat	45	34	19	2
Independent	42	38	19	1

Note: See Note, table 2.13. For a discussion of public opinion survey sampling procedures, see Appendix 5.

[a]Response volunteered.
[b]Less than 0.5%.

Source: Table constructed by SOURCEBOOK staff from data provided by The Gallup Organization, Inc. Reprinted by permission.

Table 2.37

Respondents reporting fear of walking alone at night

United States, selected years 1965-2003

Question: "Is there any area near where you live--that is, within a mile--where you would be afraid to walk alone at night?"

	Yes	No
1965	34%	66%
1967	31	67
1968	35	62
1972	42	57
1975	45	55
1977	45	55
1979	42	58
1981	45	55
1982	48	52
1983	45	55
1989	43	57
1990	40	59
1992	44	56
1993	43	56
1994	39	60
1996	39	60
1997	38	61
2000	34	66
2001	30	69
2002	35	64
2003	36	64

Note: See Note, table 2.13. The "don't know/refused" category has been omitted; therefore, percents may not sum to 100. For a discussion of public opinion survey sampling procedures, see Appendix 5.

Source: The Gallup Organization, Inc., *The Gallup Poll* [Online]. Available: http://www.gallup.com/poll/ [Jan. 9, 2003]; and data provided by The Gallup Organization, Inc. Table adapted by SOURCEBOOK staff. Reprinted by permission.

Table 2.38

Respondents reporting whether they feel afraid to walk alone at night in their own neighborhood

By demographic characteristics, United States, selected years 1973-2002

Question: "Is there any area right around here--that is, within a mile--where you would be afraid to walk alone at night?"

	1973 Yes	1973 No	1974 Yes	1974 No	1976 Yes	1976 No	1977 Yes	1977 No	1980 Yes	1980 No	1982 Yes	1982 No	1984 Yes	1984 No	1985 Yes	1985 No	1987 Yes	1987 No
National	41%	59%	45%	55%	44%	56%	45%	54%	43%	56%	47%	53%	42%	57%	40%	59%	38%	51%
Sex																		
Male	20	80	24	76	23	77	23	76	21	79	28	72	19	81	21	78	17	83
Female	59	40	63	36	61	39	63	37	60	39	60	39	57	41	56	43	55	44
Race																		
White	39	61	43	57	44	56	43	57	42	58	45	55	39	60	38	62	36	63
Black/other	54	45	60	40	48	51	59	40	52	47	61	39	54	43	60	39	50	50
Age																		
18 to 20 years	33	67	43	55	45	55	45	55	45	54	28	72	27	73	24	76	38	62
21 to 29 years	40	59	44	56	40	60	39	60	41	59	47	52	39	59	40	59	40	59
30 to 49 years	40	60	40	59	40	60	41	59	39	60	43	57	37	62	35	64	34	66
50 years and older	43	57	50	50	49	51	51	48	47	52	50	49	49	49	46	53	43	56
Education[a]																		
College	35	64	42	57	36	64	41	58	42	58	49	50	40	59	36	63	38	62
High school graduate	44	55	44	55	47	52	46	53	44	55	46	54	42	57	41	58	39	61
Less than high school graduate	41	58	51	49	48	52	47	52	42	57	43	56	46	51	51	48	39	59
Income																		
$50,000 and over	NA	NA	NA	NA	NA	NA	NA	NA	NA	NA	NA	NA	NA	NA	NA	NA	NA	NA
$30,000 to $49,999	NA	NA	NA	NA	NA	NA	NA	NA	NA	NA	NA	NA	NA	NA	NA	NA	NA	NA
$20,000 to $29,999	NA	NA	NA	NA	NA	NA	NA	NA	NA	NA	NA	NA	NA	NA	NA	NA	NA	NA
Under $20,000	NA	NA	NA	NA	NA	NA	NA	NA	NA	NA	NA	NA	NA	NA	NA	NA	NA	NA
Occupation																		
Professional/business	38	62	39	60	40	60	40	60	42	58	50	50	40	59	36	63	37	63
Clerical/support	55	44	59	40	56	43	60	39	53	46	57	43	51	48	46	53	47	53
Manual/service	41	58	40	60	40	60	41	59	38	62	39	60	39	60	41	58	36	63
Farming/agriculture	26	72	28	72	14	84	17	83	15	82	8	92	13	87	19	81	18	82
Region																		
Northeast	47	52	47	53	54	46	53	47	47	53	46	54	44	55	44	55	34	66
Midwest	40	60	39	60	34	66	36	63	33	66	40	60	35	64	30	68	37	63
South	39	61	47	53	42	58	47	52	44	55	50	50	48	51	44	56	42	58
West	38	61	48	51	50	50	46	54	52	48	53	47	39	61	44	55	40	60
Religion																		
Protestant	41	59	43	56	43	57	45	55	43	56	45	54	44	55	41	58	37	63
Catholic	43	56	50	48	46	54	45	54	45	55	49	51	40	58	39	60	43	56
Jewish	44	56	50	50	63	37	60	40	50	50	81	19	59	41	53	47	47	53
None	32	68	38	62	43	57	40	59	38	62	40	60	22	77	36	64	36	64
Politics																		
Republican	35	65	48	52	42	57	44	56	41	57	43	57	42	56	36	63	35	65
Democrat	46	53	45	54	49	50	48	52	46	54	51	49	46	52	47	52	40	60
Independent	39	61	42	58	39	61	41	58	41	59	44	56	37	62	35	63	39	60

Note: See Note, table 2.15. The "don't know" category has been omitted; therefore percents may not sum to 100. For a discussion of public opinion survey sampling procedures, see Appendix 5.

Source: National Opinion Research Center, "General Social Surveys, 1972-2002," Storrs, CT: The Roper Center for Public Opinion Research, University of Connecticut. (Machine-readable data files.) Table constructed by SOURCEBOOK staff.

[a]Beginning in 1996, education categories were revised slightly and therefore are not directly comparable to data presented for prior years.

	1988		1989		1990		1991		1993		1994		1996		1998		2000		2002	
	Yes	No	Yes	No	Yes	No	Yes	No	Yes	No	Yes	No	Yes	No	Yes	No	Yes	No	Yes	No
	40%	59%	40%	60%	41%	58%	43%	56%	43%	57%	47%	52%	42%	57%	41%	57%	39%	60%	32%	67%
	16	83	19	80	19	81	24	76	26	73	30	69	26	74	26	74	23	76	19	81
	56	42	55	45	58	41	58	41	55	44	60	39	55	44	52	46	52	47	47	52
	39	60	38	62	39	60	41	59	40	60	45	54	40	59	40	59	38	61	30	70
	45	53	52	46	50	48	56	44	58	42	56	43	51	48	47	51	45	54	41	58
	27	73	47	53	43	57	52	48	31	66	44	56	45	55	45	55	40	58	41	59
	38	61	42	58	33	65	40	60	40	60	49	50	39	60	41	57	41	58	30	70
	32	67	33	67	38	62	39	61	38	62	43	57	40	59	39	60	36	63	27	72
	51	48	45	54	48	51	49	49	51	48	51	47	45	54	44	54	41	56	37	63
	36	62	40	60	39	60	43	56	42	58	45	54	40	59	42	57	38	61	31	69
	41	58	38	62	41	58	42	58	44	56	48	51	43	56	37	62	38	61	34	64
	51	49	45	55	51	48	50	50	45	55	53	47	44	54	46	51	44	54	32	67
	NA	NA	NA	NA	NA	NA	NA	NA	39	61	41	59	34	66	31	68	28	71	22	78
	NA	NA	NA	NA	NA	NA	NA	NA	37	63	42	58	42	58	38	62	34	66	32	68
	NA	NA	NA	NA	NA	NA	NA	NA	43	57	46	53	43	57	42	58	42	58	37	62
	NA	NA	NA	NA	NA	NA	NA	NA	51	49	54	45	48	50	51	46	50	48	41	57
	37	62	41	59	36	63	39	61	44	56	44	55	39	60	39	60	34	65	31	69
	54	46	49	51	56	42	51	48	43	57	58	41	51	47	54	44	54	45	46	54
	35	64	33	67	38	61	41	59	42	58	42	57	40	60	34	64	37	62	26	74
	18	82	20	80	28	72	24	76	24	76	36	64	27	70	36	64	31	69	25	69
	41	57	35	65	40	59	36	62	44	56	44	56	41	58	41	57	37	62	35	65
	33	66	39	61	36	64	42	57	34	66	39	60	39	60	35	64	34	64	23	77
	44	56	42	58	46	52	43	57	46	54	54	45	44	55	44	54	42	57	33	65
	43	57	41	59	41	58	51	49	48	52	46	53	42	57	44	56	42	57	38	62
	42	57	41	58	43	56	45	54	44	56	48	52	44	55	40	58	39	59	31	69
	38	60	38	62	38	61	36	63	41	59	45	54	36	63	43	56	41	58	35	65
	71	24	53	47	61	39	67	33	65	35	58	39	51	46	65	35	36	64	60	40
	22	77	34	66	32	64	39	61	33	66	41	58	34	65	40	58	35	64	30	70
	41	59	37	62	41	58	36	63	42	58	45	54	36	64	36	63	33	66	30	70
	44	56	46	54	47	52	48	51	48	51	51	49	51	48	46	53	43	56	39	61
	35	63	33	67	35	64	44	56	39	61	44	55	38	61	40	58	39	59	28	72

Table 2.39

Respondents reporting concern about crime victimization

By sex and race, United States, 2003

Question: "How often do you, yourself, worry about the following things--frequently, occasionally, rarely or never?"

(Percent responding "frequently" or "occasionally")

	Total	Sex		Race		
		Male	Female	White	Nonwhite[a]	Black
Your home being burglarized when you are not there	48%	42%	52%	47%	47%	54%
Having your car stolen or broken into	45	43	47	44	49	49
Being a victim of terrorism	38	31	44	36	42	41
Having a school-aged child of yours physically harmed while attending school	35	31	38	32	46	51
Your home being burglarized when you are there	30	23	35	28	34	40
Getting mugged	28	21	34	27	32	46
Being attacked while driving your car	26	22	30	26	28	30
Being sexually assaulted	23	5	39	21	26	35
Getting murdered	18	15	21	17	24	35
Being the victim of a hate crime	17	14	18	13	30	35
Being assaulted or killed by a co-worker or other employee where you work	9	9	9	7	14	21

Note: See Note, table 2.13. For a discussion of public opinion survey sampling procedures, see Appendix 5.

[a]Includes black respondents.

Source: Table constructed by SOURCEBOOK staff from data provided by The Gallup Organization, Inc. Reprinted by permission.

Table 2.40

Respondents reporting whether they engaged in selected behaviors because of concern over crime

By sex and race, United States, 2003

Question: "Next, I'm going to read some things people do because of their concern over crime. Please tell me which, if any, of these things you, yourself, do or have done."

	Total	Sex		Race		
		Male	Female	White	Nonwhite[a]	Black
Avoid going to certain places or neighborhoods you might otherwise want to go to	49%	43%	55%	47%	57%	62%
Keep a dog for protection	31	28	34	32	27	25
Bought a gun for protection of yourself or your home	27	32	22	26	32	36
Had a burglar alarm installed in your home	25	25	25	22	37	44
Carry mace or pepper spray	19	8	29	17	28	31
Carry a gun for defense	12	17	9	11	16	23

Note: See Note, table 2.13. For a discussion of public opinion survey sampling procedures, see Appendix 5.

[a]Includes black respondents.

Source: Table constructed by SOURCEBOOK staff from data provided by The Gallup Organization, Inc. Reprinted by permission.

Table 2.41
Respondents indicating too little is spent on selected problems in this country

United States, selected years 1973-2002

Question: "We are faced with many problems in this country, none of which can be solved easily or inexpensively. I'm going to name some of the problems, and for each one I'd like you to tell me whether you think we're spending too much money on it, too little money, or about the right amount. First (problem) are we spending too much, too little, or about the right amount on (problem)?"

(Percent responding "too little")

	Halting the rising crime rate	Dealing with drug addiction	Improving the Nation's education system	Improving the conditions of blacks	Welfare
1973	64%	65%	49%	32%	20%
1974	66	60	50	31	22
1975	65	55	49	27	23
1976	65	58	50	27	13
1977	65	55	48	25	12
1978	64	55	52	24	13
1981	69	59	52	24	13
1982	71	57	56	28	20
1983	67	60	60	29	21
1984	68	63	64	35	24
1985	63	62	60	31	18
1986	64	58	60	34	22
1987	68	65	62	35	21
1988	72	71	66	38	24
1989	73	71	69	36	24
1990	70	64	71	37	22
1991	65	58	67	34	22
1993	71	60	67	36	16
1994	75	60	71	31	13
1996	67	58	68	32	15
1998	61	58	70	34	16
2000	59	58	71	34	20
2002	56	57	73	31	21

Note: See Note, table 2.15. For a discussion of public opinion survey sampling procedures, see Appendix 5.

Source: National Opinion Research Center, "General Social Surveys, 1972-2002," Storrs, CT: The Roper Center for Public Opinion Research, University of Connecticut. (Machine-readable data files.) Table constructed by SOURCEBOOK staff.

Table 2.42

Attitudes toward the level of spending to halt the rising crime rate

By demographic characteristics, United States, selected years 1985-2002

Question: "We are faced with many problems in this country, none of which can be solved easily or inexpensively. I'm going to name some of these problems, and for each one I'd like you to tell me whether you think we're spending too much money on it, too little money, or about the right amount. First (halting the rising crime rate) are we spending too much, too little, or about the right amount on (halting the rising crime rate)?"

	1985 Too little	1985 About right	1985 Too much	1986 Too little	1986 About right	1986 Too much	1987 Too little	1987 About right	1987 Too much	1988 Too little	1988 About right	1988 Too much	1989 Too little	1989 About right	1989 Too much	1990 Too little	1990 About right	1990 Too much
National	63%	28%	5%	64%	27%	5%	68%	24%	4%	68%	23%	4%	72%	20%	5%	70%	22%	4%
Sex																		
Male	61	29	7	59	32	6	66	26	4	67	25	4	70	20	7	70	22	5
Female	66	26	4	67	24	4	70	22	4	69	22	4	74	19	3	70	22	3
Race																		
White	63	28	5	63	28	5	68	24	4	67	24	4	71	21	5	68	23	4
Black/other	62	26	9	68	20	4	70	23	5	73	19	6	81	13	3	78	14	6
Age																		
18 to 20 years	80	20	0	75	20	0	68	21	5	63	26	0	67	29	0	64	24	8
21 to 29 years	67	29	2	65	29	4	65	27	5	63	32	2	72	20	6	72	24	1
30 to 49 years	62	30	5	62	30	4	65	26	5	74	19	4	71	20	5	69	22	5
50 years and older	62	26	8	64	24	6	74	19	3	66	22	6	74	18	4	70	20	4
Education[a]																		
College	61	30	4	62	30	3	62	30	5	71	24	2	72	21	4	71	23	3
High school graduate	67	26	5	66	25	6	73	19	4	68	24	3	73	19	5	70	20	5
Less than high school graduate	52	30	15	60	24	6	74	19	3	61	17	12	73	16	6	58	29	6
Income																		
$50,000 and over	NA	NA	NA	NA	NA	NA	NA	NA	NA	NA	NA	NA	NA	NA	NA	NA	NA	NA
$30,000 to $49,999	NA	NA	NA	NA	NA	NA	NA	NA	NA	NA	NA	NA	NA	NA	NA	NA	NA	NA
$20,000 to $29,999	NA	NA	NA	NA	NA	NA	NA	NA	NA	NA	NA	NA	NA	NA	NA	NA	NA	NA
Under $20,000	NA	NA	NA	NA	NA	NA	NA	NA	NA	NA	NA	NA	NA	NA	NA	NA	NA	NA
Occupation																		
Professional/business	63	28	4	60	32	3	62	29	4	68	25	4	72	19	5	66	26	3
Clerical/support	68	23	5	68	23	5	61	36	3	66	25	5	80	18	0	74	19	2
Manual/service	62	28	7	65	23	7	75	16	5	70	22	2	70	22	6	70	20	6
Farming/agriculture	46	46	4	68	32	0	76	18	0	70	20	0	77	8	15	57	21	14
Region																		
Northeast	60	28	6	63	30	3	63	28	7	70	22	3	73	20	3	70	25	3
Midwest	62	29	6	63	27	4	73	20	3	63	28	3	70	24	4	63	28	2
South	67	24	4	66	22	7	68	22	4	72	20	5	76	16	4	75	16	5
West	60	32	6	62	33	3	67	27	4	67	24	5	69	20	8	69	18	7
Religion																		
Protestant	63	29	6	64	26	4	70	22	5	66	24	4	74	20	4	71	21	4
Catholic	66	24	5	66	27	3	66	30	2	72	21	3	72	21	5	67	25	4
Jewish	76	6	12	52	39	9	60	40	0	94	6	0	91	9	0	71	18	12
None	52	37	2	54	28	14	64	19	7	64	29	4	57	22	12	67	28	2
Politics																		
Republican	62	29	6	61	32	3	63	30	3	67	26	5	72	24	3	65	27	6
Democrat	66	27	4	70	23	4	74	19	4	72	21	4	80	12	5	70	23	2
Independent	61	29	6	59	29	6	64	26	6	67	22	3	63	25	7	76	17	4

Note: See Note, table 2.15. The "don't know" category has been omitted; therefore percents may not sum to 100. Readers interested in responses to this question for previous years should consult previous editions of SOURCEBOOK. For a discussion of public opinion survey sampling procedures, see Appendix 5.

Source: National Opinion Research Center, "General Social Surveys, 1972-2002," Storrs, CT: The Roper Center for Public Opinion Research, University of Connecticut. (Machine-readable data files.) Table constructed by SOURCEBOOK staff.

[a]Beginning in 1996, education categories were revised slightly and therefore are not directly comparable to data presented for prior years.

	1991			1993			1994			1996			1998			2000			2002	
Too little	About right	Too much	Too little	About right	Too much	Too little	About right	Too much	Too little	About right	Too much	Too little	About right	Too much	Too little	About right	Too much	Too little	About right	Too much
65%	27%	5%	71%	20%	5%	75%	16%	6%	67%	23%	7%	61%	28%	7%	59%	32%	5%	56%	35%	7%
58	33	6	65	26	7	72	19	7	64	26	8	57	31	10	55	36	7	50	38	9
69	23	4	76	16	4	78	14	6	70	21	6	64	26	5	62	29	4	60	32	4
63	29	4	70	22	4	74	16	7	65	24	8	59	30	7	57	34	6	54	36	7
75	17	6	76	15	8	80	14	3	76	19	4	70	22	6	67	25	4	64	29	4
56	44	0	67	24	0	82	15	3	76	13	5	67	24	7	54	40	2	37	56	4
63	26	6	78	17	4	84	12	3	71	24	4	62	32	4	59	35	3	51	41	7
61	32	5	71	22	5	74	19	6	69	23	7	59	29	8	61	31	5	58	33	6
71	22	4	67	21	6	72	15	8	62	24	8	62	27	7	56	33	7	56	34	7
58	32	6	72	23	4	74	18	6	66	25	7	57	32	7	56	36	5	50	41	7
70	25	3	73	17	6	77	14	6	71	21	5	65	25	6	64	28	5	64	28	5
70	15	9	58	25	9	72	14	8	66	19	8	68	22	8	62	27	6	60	27	9
NA	NA	NA	74	21	2	72	20	7	64	27	8	55	34	7	56	40	3	54	39	5
NA	NA	NA	75	19	4	76	17	6	67	24	7	60	29	8	63	28	8	53	37	9
NA	NA	NA	74	17	5	79	15	4	71	20	6	71	22	6	58	33	6	61	31	5
NA	NA	NA	68	21	6	76	13	6	69	22	6	64	26	6	60	30	4	57	32	8
58	32	7	68	25	5	73	20	5	64	26	8	57	31	8	54	39	4	52	40	7
69	26	2	76	16	4	77	12	7	69	23	7	65	30	4	63	29	4	58	34	5
66	26	5	72	19	5	78	13	6	71	20	5	63	26	8	62	28	7	58	32	8
76	18	6	53	20	27	48	31	17	57	24	10	69	23	8	64	24	4	65	22	4
67	30	2	72	21	3	76	17	4	64	27	7	58	34	5	58	34	5	58	35	5
67	27	4	71	22	2	76	18	3	70	23	4	60	28	8	59	31	6	53	36	7
66	24	7	71	17	7	74	14	8	68	20	8	66	24	7	64	29	4	60	33	6
56	31	5	68	24	6	75	16	7	66	23	8	55	31	8	50	39	8	51	38	9
66	25	5	70	20	5	75	16	6	67	23	7	65	27	6	62	29	6	57	35	5
66	30	3	76	20	2	79	14	6	68	23	6	62	30	6	62	32	4	58	33	7
56	33	6	77	18	0	75	18	4	67	26	0	58	38	0	41	48	7	43	52	5
58	36	4	65	24	10	69	22	9	61	26	9	50	33	11	47	41	8	49	38	10
62	30	6	68	25	3	70	19	8	63	24	10	56	34	8	59	32	7	51	40	8
71	24	3	75	18	5	79	14	4	68	24	4	67	22	6	60	31	5	61	31	6
62	27	6	71	18	6	76	16	5	69	22	7	61	30	5	58	34	5	54	36	6

Public attitudes toward crime and criminal justice-related topics 135

Table 2.43

Attitudes toward the level of spending to deal with drug addiction

By demographic characteristics, United States, selected years 1985-2002

Question: "We are faced with many problems in this country, none of which can be solved easily or inexpensively. I'm going to name some of these problems, and for each one I'd like you to tell me whether you think we're spending too much money on it, too little money, or about the right amount. First (dealing with drug addiction) are we spending too much, too little, or about the right amount on (dealing with drug addiction)?"

	1985 Too little	1985 About right	1985 Too much	1986 Too little	1986 About right	1986 Too much	1987 Too little	1987 About right	1987 Too much	1988 Too little	1988 About right	1988 Too much	1989 Too little	1989 About right	1989 Too much	1990 Too little	1990 About right	1990 Too much
National	62%	28%	5%	58%	32%	6%	65%	28%	4%	68%	24%	4%	71%	19%	6%	64%	26%	7%
Sex																		
Male	61	27	8	55	36	7	62	31	4	72	21	5	74	15	7	60	28	8
Female	62	30	2	60	29	5	68	26	4	66	27	3	68	22	6	67	24	5
Race																		
White	62	28	5	57	32	6	66	28	4	67	25	4	69	20	6	63	27	6
Black/other	59	30	9	66	27	5	60	28	6	75	20	5	80	11	6	68	20	7
Age																		
18 to 20 years	60	40	0	50	40	10	58	26	10	50	40	5	67	33	0	68	24	8
21 to 29 years	62	29	6	53	42	4	57	40	2	57	34	7	69	22	7	66	28	4
30 to 49 years	64	29	5	59	33	6	65	29	4	73	22	2	72	18	6	66	26	5
50 years and older	61	26	6	60	24	7	70	22	6	71	20	4	71	18	7	61	26	9
Education[a]																		
College	59	32	5	54	39	5	59	36	4	70	25	4	74	19	4	64	29	6
High school graduate	67	25	5	61	28	7	69	23	4	67	26	3	69	19	8	67	22	7
Less than high school graduate	49	31	11	58	23	7	71	19	5	68	17	8	65	20	12	50	28	13
Income																		
$50,000 and over	NA	NA	NA	NA	NA	NA	NA	NA	NA	NA	NA	NA	NA	NA	NA	NA	NA	NA
$30,000 to $49,999	NA	NA	NA	NA	NA	NA	NA	NA	NA	NA	NA	NA	NA	NA	NA	NA	NA	NA
$20,000 to $29,999	NA	NA	NA	NA	NA	NA	NA	NA	NA	NA	NA	NA	NA	NA	NA	NA	NA	NA
Under $20,000	NA	NA	NA	NA	NA	NA	NA	NA	NA	NA	NA	NA	NA	NA	NA	NA	NA	NA
Occupation																		
Professional/business	59	31	5	54	37	6	63	31	5	68	25	4	73	18	6	62	30	6
Clerical/support	61	32	3	62	30	2	61	34	5	64	29	3	67	23	4	68	26	3
Manual/service	64	25	7	60	28	8	67	26	4	72	22	4	71	18	7	63	24	9
Farming/agriculture	50	38	8	63	32	5	65	24	12	90	10	0	77	8	15	71	14	14
Region																		
Northeast	66	25	6	54	34	4	71	26	2	71	23	5	69	20	4	58	29	8
Midwest	61	29	5	61	30	5	61	32	4	68	27	2	73	18	6	63	28	7
South	62	26	6	58	30	8	66	26	5	66	24	4	71	18	7	71	23	4
West	59	35	4	58	34	7	62	30	6	70	21	6	70	21	7	61	25	9
Religion																		
Protestant	64	28	4	60	29	7	67	26	4	68	24	4	72	18	7	67	25	6
Catholic	62	29	6	55	37	4	64	32	3	71	24	3	69	23	3	58	30	8
Jewish	65	18	6	52	35	4	60	20	20	67	33	0	91	9	0	65	29	0
None	49	38	6	54	33	7	51	37	7	64	23	9	59	21	16	57	26	12
Politics																		
Republican	58	31	5	52	37	7	58	38	3	68	26	4	69	23	5	60	32	7
Democrat	64	27	5	62	29	6	74	20	4	70	24	4	80	12	5	64	25	6
Independent	63	27	6	58	30	6	57	32	6	67	24	4	61	26	9	69	22	6

Note: See Note, table 2.15. The "don't know" category has been omitted; therefore percents may not sum to 100. Readers interested in responses to this question for previous years should consult previous editions of SOURCEBOOK. For a discussion of public opinion survey sampling procedures, see Appendix 5.

Source: National Opinion Research Center, "General Social Surveys, 1972-2002," Storrs, CT: The Roper Center for Public Opinion Research, University of Connecticut. (Machine-readable data files.) Table constructed by SOURCEBOOK staff.

[a]Beginning in 1996, education categories were revised slightly and therefore are not directly comparable to data presented for prior years.

	1991			1993			1994			1996			1998			2000			2002	
Too little	About right	Too much	Too little	About right	Too much	Too little	About right	Too much	Too little	About right	Too much	Too little	About right	Too much	Too little	About right	Too much	Too little	About right	Too much
58%	32%	7%	60%	27%	8%	60%	26%	9%	58%	27%	11%	58%	28%	9%	59%	28%	8%	57%	30%	9%
48	41	8	55	32	9	57	28	11	58	26	12	56	28	12	57	29	10	54	31	13
64	26	7	64	23	7	62	25	7	58	27	10	60	28	7	60	27	7	60	30	6
54	34	8	58	29	8	57	28	10	55	29	12	56	29	10	57	29	9	55	31	10
72	19	4	73	19	7	73	17	5	71	18	8	66	23	6	63	24	6	65	26	6
69	31	0	62	33	5	58	33	6	66	26	3	42	44	9	58	26	9	52	41	7
57	34	7	61	32	4	66	28	3	60	31	6	53	33	8	56	32	9	52	35	9
58	32	8	60	28	8	58	30	8	57	28	13	62	25	10	60	29	8	55	34	9
56	30	8	60	24	10	60	20	12	58	23	12	58	28	9	58	25	9	62	24	10
52	36	8	56	32	8	55	32	9	55	30	12	58	28	10	54	32	9	52	34	11
60	31	7	65	23	6	66	22	7	61	26	10	56	30	8	64	21	8	66	25	6
72	16	6	58	18	18	56	17	15	64	19	10	62	23	11	61	26	7	61	26	10
NA	NA	NA	55	31	9	58	30	10	53	31	14	57	32	8	58	33	6	52	33	12
NA	NA	NA	62	28	7	56	32	8	57	30	11	58	30	10	61	26	8	53	35	8
NA	NA	NA	66	26	7	68	24	8	64	26	8	61	24	10	57	31	8	68	23	8
NA	NA	NA	62	25	8	62	21	9	61	24	9	60	26	9	63	22	9	59	28	9
53	34	11	54	34	9	55	30	10	53	29	14	55	32	9	52	34	8	54	32	10
61	28	6	66	20	9	61	28	7	58	26	13	61	26	9	62	24	7	59	30	8
56	34	7	64	25	7	65	22	8	62	25	8	58	26	11	63	24	9	59	28	10
53	35	0	50	36	14	52	38	7	48	19	14	77	15	8	44	28	24	56	35	9
56	34	7	67	21	8	61	25	8	57	28	12	59	30	8	60	29	8	58	28	11
57	35	6	58	30	6	59	31	7	61	25	10	59	27	8	61	26	8	58	32	6
64	25	8	61	26	10	62	23	10	57	26	12	68	20	12	58	27	8	57	31	10
48	38	8	55	32	6	56	28	9	58	28	10	53	23	16	56	31	10	55	29	12
60	29	6	60	26	8	62	25	8	60	26	10	55	31	10	60	27	8	60	30	8
55	36	6	60	30	10	58	28	9	60	26	10	59	28	10	61	25	10	59	32	7
48	28	22	54	27	9	64	29	7	59	26	11	60	28	9	48	44	7	43	38	14
42	42	1	56	31	10	53	29	13	52	28	15	58	25	8	55	30	7	53	28	16
51	37	10	50	34	12	54	31	9	49	32	16	54	34	10	54	32	10	52	32	14
66	23	6	70	23	4	67	22	7	68	22	7	64	25	7	62	27	8	63	28	7
55	35	6	58	27	8	58	28	9	57	27	11	57	27	10	58	27	8	56	32	8

Public attitudes toward crime and criminal justice-related topics 137

Table 2.44

Respondents' perceptions of the Nation's progress in coping with illegal drugs

United States, selected years 1972-2003[a]

Question: "Now, how much progress do you feel the nation has made over the last year or two in coping with the problem of illegal drugs--has it made much progress, made some progress, stood still, lost some ground, or lost much ground?"

	Made much progress	Made some progress	Stood still	Lost some ground	Lost much ground	Don't know/ refused
1972	3%	32%	20%	21%	20%	5%
1974	4	36	21	19	16	5
1976	2	25	29	25	15	4
1995	2	36	30	19	11	2
1996	3	28	22	24	22	1
1999	4	42	27	14	12	1
2000	6	41	23	17	12	1
2003	3	35	32	17	11	2

Note: See Note, table 2.13. For a discussion of public opinion survey sampling procedures, see Appendix 5.

[a] Percents may not add to 100 because of rounding.

Source: The Gallup Organization, Inc., *The Gallup Poll* [Online]. Available: http://www.gallup.com/poll/ [Apr. 2, 2001]; and data provided by The Gallup Organization, Inc. Reprinted by permission.

Table 2.45

Respondents reporting whether they think the criminal justice system is fair in its treatment of people accused of committing crime

By demographic characteristics, United States, 2003

Question: "In general, do you think the criminal justice system is very fair, somewhat fair, somewhat unfair, or very unfair in its treatment of people accused of committing crime?"

	Very fair	Somewhat fair	Somewhat unfair	Very unfair	Don't know/ refused
National	18%	48%	22%	10%	2%
Sex					
Male	20	48	18	12	2
Female	15	49	25	9	2
Race					
White	18	50	21	9	2
Nonwhite	17	43	24	15	1
Black	13	40	27	19	1
Age					
18 to 29 years	24	44	23	8	1
30 to 49 years	15	53	21	10	1
50 to 64 years	16	45	24	12	3
50 years and older	16	46	23	12	3
65 years and older	17	48	20	12	3
Education					
College post graduate	15	52	24	7	2
College graduate	21	53	20	6	(a)
Some college	16	50	23	10	1
High school graduate or less	18	45	21	13	3
Income					
$75,000 and over	19	51	23	6	1
$50,000 to $74,999	22	44	25	7	2
$30,000 to $49,999	15	49	24	11	1
$20,000 to $29,999	17	49	20	13	1
Under $20,000	15	53	14	17	1
Community					
Urban area	16	50	22	10	2
Suburban area	19	47	23	9	2
Rural area	18	49	19	13	1
Region					
East	22	49	23	5	1
Midwest	14	51	22	12	1
South	18	46	21	13	2
West	17	49	19	10	5
Politics					
Republican	21	55	16	6	2
Democrat	17	43	28	10	2
Independent	15	49	21	13	2

Note: See Note, table 2.13. For a discussion of public opinion survey sampling procedures, see Appendix 5.

[a]Less than 0.5%.

Source: Table constructed by SOURCEBOOK staff from data provided by The Gallup Organization, Inc. Reprinted by permission.

Table 2.46

Attitudes toward whether the criminal justice system should try to rehabilitate criminals

United States, 2002 and 2003

Question: "For each statement, please tell me if you completely agree with it, mostly agree with it, mostly disagree with it or completely disagree with it: The criminal justice system should try to rehabilitate criminals, not just punish them."

	Completely agree	Mostly agree	Mostly disagree	Completely disagree	Don't know
2002	26%	43%	16%	10%	5%
2003	29	43	14	11	3

Note: Sample sizes vary from year to year; the data for 2003 are based on telephone interviews with a randomly selected national sample of 1,284 adults, 18 years of age and older, conducted July 14-Aug. 5, 2003. For a discussion of public opinion survey sampling procedures, see Appendix 5.

Source: The Pew Research Center for the People & the Press, *The 2004 Political Landscape: Evenly Divided and Increasingly Polarized* (Washington, DC: The Pew Research Center for the People & the Press, 2003), p. T-49. Table adapted by SOURCEBOOK staff. Reprinted by permission.

Table 2.47

Attitudes toward severity of courts in own area

By demographic characteristics, United States, selected years 1985-2002

Question: "In general, do you think the courts in this area deal too harshly or not harshly enough with criminals?"

	1985 Too harshly	1985 Not harshly enough	1985 About right	1986 Too harshly	1986 Not harshly enough	1986 About right	1987 Too harshly	1987 Not harshly enough	1987 About right	1988 Too harshly	1988 Not harshly enough	1988 About right	1989 Too harshly	1989 Not harshly enough	1989 About right	1990 Too harshly	1990 Not harshly enough	1990 About right
National	3%	84%	9%	3%	85%	8%	3%	79%	12%	4%	82%	10%	3%	84%	9%	3%	83%	9%
Sex																		
Male	4	84	10	4	84	8	4	78	14	5	79	13	4	79	12	3	82	11
Female	3	85	8	3	86	8	3	80	11	3	84	8	1	87	6	4	83	8
Race																		
White	3	85	9	2	87	8	2	81	12	3	83	10	2	83	10	3	84	9
Black/other	5	80	8	9	77	9	7	70	14	8	73	11	4	87	3	8	77	8
Age																		
18 to 20 years	6	78	14	8	79	8	0	76	17	8	84	8	10	83	8	10	80	5
21 to 29 years	6	79	10	5	81	9	4	78	9	8	77	10	2	86	8	5	80	9
30 to 49 years	3	85	9	3	86	8	4	78	13	3	82	11	3	83	9	4	81	10
50 years and older	2	87	8	2	88	7	2	82	12	2	83	9	2	84	9	2	86	8
Education[a]																		
College	3	83	11	2	84	9	3	77	14	3	78	13	2	81	10	4	82	10
High school graduate	4	86	7	3	88	7	3	84	9	4	85	7	3	86	8	4	83	9
Less than high school graduate	4	81	10	4	81	9	5	71	18	3	82	8	3	82	8	3	86	6
Income																		
$50,000 and over	NA	NA	NA	NA	NA	NA	NA	NA	NA	NA	NA	NA	NA	NA	NA	NA	NA	NA
$30,000 to $49,999	NA	NA	NA	NA	NA	NA	NA	NA	NA	NA	NA	NA	NA	NA	NA	NA	NA	NA
$20,000 to $29,999	NA	NA	NA	NA	NA	NA	NA	NA	NA	NA	NA	NA	NA	NA	NA	NA	NA	NA
Under $20,000	NA	NA	NA	NA	NA	NA	NA	NA	NA	NA	NA	NA	NA	NA	NA	NA	NA	NA
Occupation																		
Professional/business	2	84	11	1	88	8	2	80	13	3	83	10	2	82	11	3	82	11
Clerical/support	2	90	6	4	88	7	2	81	12	3	84	9	1	87	7	4	84	8
Manual/service	5	83	8	4	83	9	5	78	11	4	81	10	4	84	8	3	84	8
Farming/agriculture	3	89	5	3	83	6	2	82	12	8	79	8	0	86	9	0	85	15
Region																		
Northeast	2	86	8	3	88	6	3	82	10	6	83	9	2	86	5	4	83	10
Midwest	3	85	9	3	87	7	4	80	10	4	80	11	3	81	12	4	80	10
South	4	82	11	4	82	10	4	78	14	3	83	10	3	86	8	3	85	8
West	4	84	8	3	85	8	3	79	14	5	80	8	3	80	11	4	82	9
Religion																		
Protestant	3	84	10	3	85	8	3	80	12	4	83	9	2	85	9	3	85	8
Catholic	3	87	8	2	88	6	2	81	12	3	86	9	3	83	9	4	84	8
Jewish	3	78	6	8	90	3	0	80	20	3	73	17	0	96	0	0	82	15
None	6	76	10	4	72	14	7	70	7	11	64	18	7	72	9	1	74	16
Politics																		
Republican	2	88	8	2	87	8	2	86	10	2	85	9	1	91	6	2	87	8
Democrat	3	84	10	3	88	6	4	78	13	5	80	10	3	83	10	4	82	9
Independent	5	82	8	3	82	10	4	76	12	4	80	11	4	77	10	5	80	10

Note: See Note, table 2.15. The "don't know" category has been omitted; therefore percents may not sum to 100. The "about right" response was volunteered. Readers interested in responses to this question for previous years should consult previous editions of SOURCEBOOK. For a discussion of public opinion survey sampling procedures, see Appendix 5.

Source: National Opinion Research Center, "General Social Surveys, 1972-2002," Storrs, CT: The Roper Center for Public Opinion Research, University of Connecticut. (Machine-readable data files.) Table constructed by SOURCEBOOK staff.

[a]Beginning in 1996, education categories were revised slightly and therefore are not directly comparable to data presented for prior years.

	1991			1993			1994			1996			1998			2000			2002	
	Not			Not			Not			Not			Not			Not			Not	
Too	harshly	About	Too	harshly	About	Too	harshly	About	Too	harshly	About	Too	harshly	About	Too	harshly	About	Too	harshly	About
harshly	enough	right	harshly	enough	right	harshly	enough	right	harshly	enough	right	harshly	enough	right	harshly	enough	right	harshly	enough	right
4%	80%	11%	3%	81%	10%	3%	85%	8%	5%	78%	11%	6%	74%	13%	8%	68%	16%	9%	67%	18%
5	78	12	5	81	10	3	83	9	5	78	11	7	72	15	8	67	18	12	64	19
3	81	11	2	82	10	2	87	6	4	78	10	6	76	12	7	70	14	7	70	16
3	80	12	2	82	10	2	86	8	3	79	11	4	75	13	6	70	16	8	69	18
10	76	8	9	76	11	5	82	8	11	72	10	12	71	12	14	64	14	16	60	16
3	70	20	16	74	7	7	70	14	11	75	5	12	65	14	15	60	14	14	48	34
8	77	9	2	86	8	4	81	9	6	76	10	10	71	11	10	65	14	12	68	15
4	80	11	4	81	9	2	87	7	5	79	11	7	75	12	8	68	16	9	70	16
3	81	12	2	81	11	2	86	7	3	78	11	4	76	15	5	70	16	8	66	19
4	78	12	3	80	11	2	84	10	5	76	12	6	72	15	8	66	17	9	65	20
5	82	9	4	84	8	4	87	6	3	82	9	5	78	12	7	73	13	8	72	16
2	78	17	5	78	9	3	86	6	6	77	9	9	74	11	9	69	14	12	67	15
NA	NA	NA	3	81	10	2	84	9	4	78	12	3	78	13	6	70	16	9	70	17
NA	NA	NA	2	85	10	2	87	8	4	82	10	5	76	13	6	72	14	8	70	18
NA	NA	NA	4	86	7	2	87	7	4	76	13	6	77	11	7	72	14	8	63	20
NA	NA	NA	5	78	11	4	84	7	6	76	10	10	70	13	11	64	14	13	66	16
3	78	11	2	80	12	2	83	10	3	78	11	5	74	14	8	66	18	8	66	18
3	80	12	3	83	8	2	88	6	5	81	9	5	78	11	5	71	16	7	72	15
5	82	11	5	82	9	3	86	6	5	77	11	7	75	13	9	71	13	10	67	18
0	89	8	3	94	3	5	81	10	4	81	8	7	76	16	4	70	15	20	52	16
4	83	8	2	82	11	3	86	6	6	76	12	5	76	13	8	63	18	6	70	16
3	78	12	4	79	11	2	84	8	5	75	13	6	74	13	6	74	13	8	67	19
5	82	10	4	84	8	2	86	8	4	81	9	7	76	11	7	70	16	9	70	17
4	73	16	4	80	10	3	84	9	4	77	11	6	69	17	9	65	16	14	60	19
4	81	10	3	82	9	2	87	7	4	80	10	6	76	12	6	72	14	8	69	19
2	80	13	3	82	9	3	85	7	5	79	11	5	77	12	7	70	15	9	74	12
0	81	9	0	81	12	2	79	10	3	76	9	0	72	18	13	57	18	12	60	16
8	72	14	3	77	14	3	76	12	8	70	10	10	62	20	12	56	21	13	58	17
2	82	11	3	85	8	2	88	7	4	84	10	3	81	12	4	78	12	2	77	18
5	79	12	4	79	12	3	85	8	5	75	13	7	75	13	10	66	17	11	65	18
5	79	10	4	81	9	3	84	8	5	76	9	8	71	14	8	66	16	11	64	17

Table 2.48

Attitudes toward the treatment of juveniles who commit violent crimes

By demographic characteristics, United States, 2003

Question: "In your view, how should juveniles between the ages of 14 and 17 who commit violent crimes be treated in the criminal justice system--should they be treated the same as adults, or should they be given more lenient treatment in a juvenile court?"

	Same as adults	More lenient treatment	Tougher[a]	Depends[a]	Don't know/ refused
National	59%	32%	(b)	8%	1%
Sex					
Male	64	29	1%	5	1
Female	55	34	(b)	10	1
Race					
White	59	32	(b)	8	1
Nonwhite	58	32	1	8	1
Black	54	36	0	9	1
Age					
18 to 29 years	62	34	1	3	0
30 to 49 years	57	31	(b)	11	1
50 to 64 years	65	27	(b)	6	2
50 years and older	59	31	1	7	2
65 years and older	52	36	1	8	3
Education					
College post graduate	42	49	0	9	(b)
College graduate	51	41	(b)	7	1
Some college	61	27	1	9	2
High school graduate or less	68	25	(b)	6	1
Income					
$75,000 and over	58	36	(b)	5	1
$50,000 to $74,999	54	35	1	9	1
$30,000 to $49,999	63	28	(b)	8	1
$20,000 to $29,999	59	31	1	8	1
Under $20,000	58	31	0	7	4
Community					
Urban area	62	29	0	8	1
Suburban area	57	34	1	7	1
Rural area	60	31	(b)	7	2
Region					
East	57	34	0	7	2
Midwest	51	37	1	10	1
South	66	25	1	7	1
West	59	34	0	6	1
Politics					
Republican	64	24	1	10	1
Democrat	55	35	(b)	9	1
Independent	59	35	0	5	1

Note: See Note, table 2.13. For a discussion of public opinion survey sampling procedures, see Appendix 5.

[a]Response volunteered.
[b]Less than 0.5%.

Source: Table constructed by SOURCEBOOK staff from data provided by The Gallup Organization, Inc. Reprinted by permission.

Table 2.49

Attitudes toward the penalty for murder

United States, selected years 1985-2004[a]

Question: "If you could choose between the following two approaches, which do you think is the better penalty for murder--the death penalty or life imprisonment, with absolutely no possibility of parole?"

	Death penalty	Life imprisonment without possibility of parole	Don't know/ refused[b]
1985	56%	34%	10%
1986	55	35	10
1991	53	35	11
1992	50	37	13
1993	59	29	12
1994	50	32	18
1997[c]	61	29	10
1999[c]	56	38	6
2000	52	37	11
2001[c]	54	42	4
2003	53	44	3
2004[c]	50	46	4

Note: Sample sizes vary from year to year; the data for 2004 are based on telephone interviews with a randomly selected national sample of 1,000 adults, 18 years of age and older, conducted May 2-4, 2004. For a discussion of public opinion survey sampling procedures, see Appendix 5.

[a]Percents may not add to 100 because of rounding.
[b]Includes volunteered responses such as "other," "neither," and "depends."
[c]Asked of a half sample.

Source: The Gallup Organization, Inc., *The Gallup Poll* [Online]. Available: http://www.gallup.com/poll/ [May 19, 2004]. Table adapted by SOURCEBOOK staff. Reprinted by permission.

Table 2.50

Attitudes toward the death penalty for persons convicted of murder

By demographic characteristics, United States, selected years 1980-2002

Question: "Do you favor or oppose the death penalty for persons convicted of murder?"

	1980 Favor	1980 Oppose	1982 Favor	1982 Oppose	1983 Favor	1983 Oppose	1984 Favor	1984 Oppose	1985 Favor	1985 Oppose	1986 Favor	1986 Oppose	1987 Favor	1987 Oppose	1988 Favor	1988 Oppose
National	67%	27%	74%	20%	73%	22%	70%	24%	76%	19%	71%	23%	70%	24%	71%	22%
Sex																
Male	75	21	80	16	80	16	77	19	80	17	79	17	73	22	77	18
Female	61	32	69	24	68	27	66	27	72	22	66	28	67	26	66	26
Race																
White	70	24	77	18	76	19	75	20	79	17	75	20	74	21	76	18
Black/other	40	51	51	42	49	44	46	46	53	35	49	43	46	43	46	44
Age																
18 to 20 years	70	27	68	26	64	29	68	27	69	29	68	24	64	36	61	35
21 to 29 years	66	31	74	20	74	22	76	19	75	20	72	23	69	27	73	24
30 to 49 years	69	26	74	21	76	19	70	24	76	18	70	27	74	21	72	21
50 years and older	66	25	74	20	71	25	67	26	76	20	74	20	66	26	70	22
Education[a]																
College	67	30	71	21	75	22	73	22	73	22	72	23	70	26	71	23
High school graduate	71	23	78	17	75	20	71	23	78	17	73	23	73	20	73	20
Less than high school graduate	56	33	64	26	61	29	59	33	72	21	64	26	54	38	59	27
Income																
$50,000 and over	NA	NA	NA	NA	NA	NA	NA	NA	NA	NA	NA	NA	NA	NA	NA	NA
$30,000 to $49,999	NA	NA	NA	NA	NA	NA	NA	NA	NA	NA	NA	NA	NA	NA	NA	NA
$20,000 to $29,999	NA	NA	NA	NA	NA	NA	NA	NA	NA	NA	NA	NA	NA	NA	NA	NA
Under $20,000	NA	NA	NA	NA	NA	NA	NA	NA	NA	NA	NA	NA	NA	NA	NA	NA
Occupation																
Professional/business	68	28	72	23	73	23	75	20	76	19	76	21	72	25	72	21
Clerical/support	69	26	79	17	78	18	71	23	76	19	70	25	74	19	72	21
Manual/service	68	26	73	21	71	23	69	25	76	19	69	25	68	24	71	24
Farming/agriculture	71	15	77	15	85	10	61	39	76	22	83	17	65	28	67	29
Region																
Northeast	68	26	74	22	70	25	74	20	74	21	70	26	72	23	66	26
Midwest	66	26	72	21	75	21	65	28	73	20	69	26	67	26	70	24
South	66	28	74	21	70	25	68	27	76	19	67	26	67	26	72	21
West	70	25	76	18	79	16	78	16	79	17	83	13	76	19	76	17
Religion																
Protestant	67	26	73	21	74	22	70	24	76	19	72	23	70	24	72	22
Catholic	71	23	76	20	72	22	72	23	78	19	69	26	70	24	73	21
Jewish	75	22	73	19	67	26	85	4	62	31	79	16	80	10	63	23
None	54	39	73	16	72	26	68	26	75	20	73	24	65	28	67	26
Politics																
Republican	77	18	79	16	85	13	80	16	83	13	80	15	83	14	81	12
Democrat	63	31	71	24	67	28	64	30	70	24	66	30	61	32	62	32
Independent	66	28	73	20	72	22	70	23	75	19	72	23	69	24	72	20

Note: See Note, table 2.15. The "don't know" category has been omitted; therefore percents may not sum to 100. Readers interested in responses to this question for previous years should consult previous editions of SOURCEBOOK. For a discussion of public opinion survey sampling procedures, see Appendix 5.

Source: National Opinion Research Center, "General Social Surveys, 1972-2002," Storrs, CT: The Roper Center for Public Opinion Research, University of Connecticut. (Machine-readable data files.) Table constructed by SOURCEBOOK staff.

[a]Beginning in 1996, education categories were revised slightly and therefore are not directly comparable to data presented for prior years.

	1989		1990		1991		1993		1994		1996		1998		2000		2002	
	Favor	Oppose	Favor	Oppose	Favor	Oppose	Favor	Oppose	Favor	Oppose	Favor	Oppose	Favor	Oppose	Favor	Oppose	Favor	Oppose
	74%	20%	74%	19%	72%	22%	72%	21%	74%	20%	71%	22%	68%	25%	63%	29%	66%	30%
	81	16	79	18	77	19	78	16	79	17	79	17	74	20	71	23	73	24
	69	24	71	21	67	25	67	24	71	22	65	25	63	28	57	33	59	35
	77	18	78	16	75	19	75	18	78	16	75	18	72	20	69	24	70	26
	57	36	58	36	53	37	54	38	56	34	54	35	49	42	42	48	50	45
	69	25	66	34	60	33	70	23	73	21	70	22	60	37	53	38	55	41
	71	24	79	16	74	23	69	26	72	21	72	22	69	25	66	28	68	30
	76	20	74	21	71	22	73	20	75	20	71	22	69	24	64	29	68	27
	74	19	74	18	71	21	73	20	75	18	71	21	66	25	62	28	63	32
	72	22	73	21	69	25	69	24	73	21	69	24	67	26	63	29	65	31
	77	18	77	18	74	20	75	18	77	17	76	17	71	21	65	28	69	28
	69	24	70	21	72	21	71	18	67	25	68	23	63	27	61	28	62	32
	NA	NA	NA	NA	NA	NA	73	22	77	18	75	20	72	21	69	25	70	27
	NA	NA	NA	NA	NA	NA	74	18	76	18	74	18	70	22	67	25	67	31
	NA	NA	NA	NA	NA	NA	81	14	75	19	72	24	68	24	66	28	62	35
	NA	NA	NA	NA	NA	NA	67	25	71	22	64	25	60	31	55	36	62	35
	75	19	72	20	67	25	70	23	75	20	70	22	68	25	63	30	65	31
	73	21	81	14	73	22	72	21	74	19	73	20	68	24	63	28	60	36
	74	21	74	22	75	20	74	19	75	19	72	21	68	24	65	27	70	26
	91	4	78	7	81	11	74	21	74	18	72	20	71	20	72	22	72	24
	72	19	75	20	71	23	65	26	70	24	66	26	62	28	55	35	58	37
	72	22	76	20	70	24	72	18	72	20	72	22	70	24	65	27	68	28
	75	21	72	20	71	22	75	19	76	19	72	20	69	23	64	27	69	26
	76	19	76	16	76	20	72	24	78	16	74	19	68	24	66	28	66	31
	75	20	75	19	72	22	74	20	75	18	72	20	68	24	64	27	67	28
	73	20	76	18	75	21	68	22	75	19	70	23	68	25	66	27	68	28
	87	13	74	15	53	34	70	21	72	26	63	28	72	20	57	36	48	52
	71	24	72	24	65	28	72	23	73	20	69	22	64	26	60	32	61	36
	82	14	83	12	84	13	81	13	84	12	85	12	77	17	75	19	79	17
	68	26	68	24	63	29	64	30	65	28	61	30	62	31	57	34	56	41
	73	21	74	21	69	23	71	20	76	17	70	21	67	23	62	30	66	28

Public attitudes toward crime and criminal justice-related topics 145

Table 2.51

Attitudes toward the death penalty for persons convicted of murder

United States, selected years 1953-2003[a]

Question: "Are you in favor of the death penalty for a person convicted of murder?"

	Yes, in favor	No, not in favor	Don't know/ refused[b]
1953	68%	25%	7%
1956	53	34	13
1957	47	34	18
1960	53	36	11
1965	45	43	12
1966	42	47	11
1967	54	38	8
1969	51	40	9
1971	49	40	11
March 1972	50	41	9
November 1972	57	32	11
1976	66	26	8
1978	62	27	11
1981	66	25	9
January 1985	72	20	8
November 1985	75	17	8
1986	70	22	8
1988	79	16	5
1991	76	18	6
1994	80	16	4
1995	77	13	10
1999	71	22	7
2000	66	28	6
2001	68	26	6
2002	70	25	5
May 2003	70	28	2
October 2003	64	32	4

Note: See Note, table 2.13. For a discussion of public opinion survey sampling procedures, see Appendix 5.

[a]Percents may not add to 100 because of rounding.
[b]May include other response categories such as "depends."

Source: The Gallup Organization, Inc., *The Gallup Poll* [Online]. Available: http://www.gallup.com/poll/ [June 11, 2003]; and data provided by The Gallup Organization, Inc. Table adapted by SOURCEBOOK staff. Reprinted by permission.

Table 2.52

Attitudes toward the death penalty for persons convicted of murder

By demographic characteristics, United States, 2003

Question: "Are you in favor of the death penalty for a person convicted of murder?"

	Yes, in favor	No, not in favor	Don't know/ refused
National	64%	32%	4%
Sex			
Male	70	26	4
Female	58	37	5
Race			
White	67	29	4
Nonwhite	52	42	6
Black	39	54	7
Age			
18 to 29 years	65	34	1
30 to 49 years	65	33	2
50 to 64 years	65	31	4
50 years and older	62	31	7
65 years and older	58	29	13
Education			
College post graduate	47	50	3
College graduate	65	33	2
Some college	68	28	4
High school graduate or less	67	28	5
Income			
$75,000 and over	64	36	0
$50,000 to $74,999	65	31	4
$30,000 to $49,999	72	25	3
$20,000 to $29,999	62	33	5
Under $20,000	52	39	9
Community			
Urban area	60	35	5
Suburban area	67	30	3
Rural area	64	31	5
Region			
East	53	44	3
Midwest	61	36	3
South	71	24	5
West	69	26	5
Politics			
Republican	84	14	2
Democrat	51	42	7
Independent	58	39	3

Note: See Note, table 2.13. For a discussion of public opinion survey sampling procedures, see Appendix 5.

Source: Table constructed by SOURCEBOOK staff from data provided by The Gallup Organization, Inc. Reprinted by permission.

Table 2.53

Attitudes toward the death penalty for murder for selected groups

United States, 2002

Question: "Do you favor or oppose the death penalty for. . .?"

	Favor	Oppose	Don't know/ refused
Women	68%	29%	3%
The mentally ill	19	75	6
The mentally retarded	13	82	5
Juveniles	26	69	5

Note: These data are based on telephone interviews with a randomly selected national sample of 1,012 adults, 18 years of age and older, conducted May 6-9, 2002. For a discussion of public opinion survey sampling procedures, see Appendix 5.

Source: The Gallup Organization, Inc., *The Gallup Poll* [Online]. Available: http://www.gallup.com/poll/releases/pr020520.asp [May 23, 2002]. Reprinted by permission.

Table 2.54
Attitudes toward fairness of the application of the death penalty

By demographic characteristics, United States, 2004

Question: "Generally speaking, do you believe the death penalty is applied fairly or unfairly in this country today?"

	Applied fairly	Applied unfairly	Don't know/ refused
National	55%	39%	6%
Sex			
Male	59	35	6
Female	51	42	7
Race			
White	59	35	6
Nonwhite	41	51	8
Black	32	58	10
Age			
18 to 29 years	61	35	4
30 to 49 years	56	40	4
50 to 64 years	53	41	6
50 years and older	52	40	8
65 years and older	52	38	10
Education			
College post graduate	43	50	7
College graduate	56	41	3
Some college	59	34	7
High school graduate or less	57	36	7
Income			
$75,000 and over	56	41	3
$50,000 to $74,999	64	32	4
$30,000 to $49,999	56	38	6
$20,000 to $29,999	59	39	2
Under $20,000	44	46	10
Community			
Urban area	42	50	8
Suburban area	58	36	6
Rural area	64	31	5
Region			
East	53	40	7
Midwest	52	41	7
South	64	30	6
West	48	46	6
Politics			
Republican	75	20	5
Democrat	42	51	7
Independent	50	44	6

Note: See Note, table 2.49. For a discussion of public opinion survey sampling procedures, see Appendix 5.

Source: Table constructed by SOURCEBOOK staff from data provided by The Gallup Organization, Inc. Reprinted by permission.

Table 2.55
Reported reasons for favoring the death penalty for persons convicted of murder

United States, 1991, 2000, 2001, and 2003

Question: "Why do you favor the death penalty for persons convicted of murder?"

Reason for favoring	1991	2000	2001	2003
An eye for an eye/they took a life/fits the crime	40%	40%	48%	37%
Save taxpayers money/cost associated with prison	12	12	20	11
Deterrent for potential crimes/set an example	8	8	10	11
Depends on the type of crime they commit	6	6	6	4
Fair punishment	6	6	1	3
They deserve it	5	5	6	13
They will repeat their crime/keep them from repeating it	4	4	6	7
Biblical reasons	3	3	3	5
Serve justice	2	3	1	4
Don't believe they can be rehabilitated	1	1	2	2
If there's no doubt the person committed the crime	NA	NA	2	3
Would help/benefit families of victims	NA	NA	1	2
Support/believe in death penalty	NA	NA	6	2
Life sentences don't always mean life in prison	NA	NA	2	1
Relieves prison overcrowding	NA	NA	2	1
Other	10	10	3	4
No opinion	3	3	1	2

Note: See Note, table 2.51. This question was asked only of the respondents who answered "yes, in favor" to the question presented in table 2.51. Percents may add to more than 100 because up to two responses were recorded from each respondent. For a discussion of public opinion survey sampling procedures, see Appendix 5.

Source: The Gallup Organization, Inc., *The Gallup Poll* [Online]. Available: http://www.gallup.com/poll/tb/religvalue/20030603c.asp [June 10, 2003]. Table adapted by SOURCEBOOK staff. Reprinted by permission.

Table 2.56
Reported reasons for opposing the death penalty for persons convicted of murder

United States, 1991 and 2003

Question: "Why do you oppose the death penalty for persons convicted of murder?"

Reason for opposing	1991	2003
Wrong to take a life	41%	46%
Punishment should be left to God/religious belief	17	13
Person may be wrongly convicted	11	25
Does not deter people from committing murder	7	4
Possibility of rehabilitation	6	5
Unfair application of death penalty	6	4
Need to pay/suffer longer/think about their crime	NA	5
Depends on the circumstances	NA	4
Other	16	3
No opinion	6	4

Note: See Notes, tables 2.51 and 2.55. This question was asked only of the respondents who answered "no, not in favor" to the question presented in table 2.51. For a discussion of public opinion survey sampling procedures, see Appendix 5.

Source: The Gallup Organization, Inc., *The Gallup Poll* [Online]. Available: http://www.gallup.com/poll/tb/religvalue/20030603c.asp [June 10, 2003]. Table adapted by SOURCEBOOK staff. Reprinted by permission.

Table 2.57

Respondents reporting whether they believe the death penalty acts as a deterrent to murder

United States, 1985, 1986, 1991, and 2004

Question: "Do you feel that the death penalty acts as a deterrent to the commitment of murder, that it lowers the murder rate, or not?"

	Yes, does	No, does not	Don't know/ refused
1985	62%	31%	7%
1986	61	32	7
1991	51	41	8
2004	35	62	3

Note: See Note, table 2.49. For a discussion of public opinion survey sampling procedures, see Appendix 5.

Source: The Gallup Organization, Inc., *The Gallup Poll* [Online]. Available: http://www.gallup.com/poll/ [May 19, 2004]. Table adapted by SOURCEBOOK staff. Reprinted by permission.

Table 2.58

Respondents reporting whether they believe the death penalty acts as a deterrent to murder

By demographic characteristics, United States, 2004

Question: "Do you feel that the death penalty acts as a deterrent to the commitment of murder, that it lowers the murder rate, or not?"

	Yes, does	No, does not	Don't know/ refused
National	35%	62%	3%
Sex			
Male	41	57	2
Female	31	65	4
Race			
White	37	61	2
Nonwhite	31	64	5
Black	15	80	5
Age			
18 to 29 years	33	65	2
30 to 49 years	34	65	1
50 to 64 years	37	61	2
50 years and older	40	56	4
65 years and older	43	51	6
Education			
College post graduate	31	65	4
College graduate	33	67	0
Some college	28	69	3
High school graduate or less	44	53	3
Income			
$75,000 and over	37	61	2
$50,000 to $74,999	31	68	1
$30,000 to $49,999	37	60	3
$20,000 to $29,999	43	55	2
Under $20,000	27	71	2
Community			
Urban area	32	65	3
Suburban area	35	62	3
Rural area	40	58	2
Region			
East	39	58	3
Midwest	36	60	4
South	35	62	3
West	31	67	2
Politics			
Republican	49	49	2
Democrat	25	71	4
Independent	34	64	2

Note: See Note, table 2.49. For a discussion of public opinion survey sampling procedures, see Appendix 5.

Source: Table constructed by SOURCEBOOK staff from data provided by The Gallup Organization, Inc. Reprinted by permission.

Table 2.59

Respondents reporting having a gun in their home

United States, selected years 1959-2003

Question: "Do you have a gun in your home?"

	Yes	No
1959	49%	51%
1965	48	52
1968	50	50
1972	43	55
1975	44	54
1980	45	53
1983	40	58
1985	44	55
1989	47	51
1990	47	52
1991	46	53
March 1993	48	51
October 1993	51	48
July 1996	38	60
November 1996	44	54
1997	42	57
1999	36	62
April 2000	42	57
August 2000	39	60
2001	40	59
2002	41	58
2003	43	56

Note: See Note, table 2.13. The "don't know/refused" category has been omitted; therefore percents may not sum to 100. For a discussion of public opinion survey sampling procedures, see Appendix 5.

Source: The Gallup Organization, Inc., *The Gallup Poll* [Online]. Available: http://www.gallup.com/poll/ [Jan. 13, 2003]; and data provided by The Gallup Organization, Inc. Table adapted by SOURCEBOOK staff. Reprinted by permission.

Table 2.60

Respondents reporting having a gun in their home

By demographic characteristics, United States, 2003

Question: "Do you have a gun in your home?"

	Yes	No
National	43%	56%
Sex		
Male	50	49
Female	37	62
Race		
White	44	55
Nonwhite	38	60
Black	43	56
Age		
18 to 29 years	31	69
30 to 49 years	46	52
50 to 64 years	53	46
50 years and older	46	53
65 years and older	36	62
Education		
College post graduate	29	69
College graduate	35	65
Some college	49	51
High school graduate or less	47	51
Income		
$75,000 and over	44	55
$50,000 to $74,999	48	51
$30,000 to $49,999	50	50
$20,000 to $29,999	34	64
Under $20,000	29	70
Community		
Urban area	39	60
Suburban area	37	62
Rural area	58	41
Region		
East	29	70
Midwest	47	52
South	53	46
West	40	58
Politics		
Republican	55	45
Democrat	33	65
Independent	41	58

Note: See Note, table 2.13. The "don't know/refused" category has been omitted; therefore percents may not sum to 100. For a discussion of public opinion survey sampling procedures, see Appendix 5.

Source: Table constructed by SOURCEBOOK staff from data provided by The Gallup Organization, Inc. Reprinted by permission.

Table 2.61

Respondents reporting a firearm in their home

By demographic characteristics, United States, selected years 1973-2002

Question: "Do you happen to have in your home (or garage) any guns or revolvers?"

(Percent reporting having any firearms)

	1973	1974	1976	1977	1980	1982	1984	1985	1987	1988	1989	1990	1991	1993	1994	1996	1998	2000	2002
National	47%	46%	47%	51%	48%	45%	45%	44%	46%	40%	46%	43%	40%	42%	41%	40%	35%	32%	34%
Sex																			
Male	53	51	52	55	56	54	53	54	51	50	55	53	50	53	50	47	43	42	43
Female	43	42	43	47	41	39	40	36	43	33	39	34	32	34	33	34	29	25	24
Race																			
White	49	48	58	53	50	48	48	46	49	43	50	45	42	45	44	44	40	37	38
Black/other	38	32	37	34	29	30	30	29	33	28	23	29	29	26	24	24	16	13	15
Age																			
18 to 20 years	50	34	38	54	48	51	44	39	43	33	35	40	22	48	42	35	20	23	24
21 to 29 years	43	48	45	45	48	41	37	40	35	34	33	34	36	38	34	32	23	24	31
30 to 49 years	51	49	52	55	50	51	48	48	51	42	48	46	40	44	41	39	37	32	29
50 years and older	46	44	44	49	46	44	49	44	47	42	50	42	42	42	43	47	39	38	41
Education[a]																			
College	45	42	44	45	41	39	42	40	43	37	41	37	34	38	38	38	31	33	33
High school graduate	50	48	50	54	51	51	48	49	50	43	51	47	46	46	44	46	43	36	34
Less than high school graduate	44	49	42	51	51	41	43	38	44	39	46	47	39	47	37	38	34	25	37
Income																			
$50,000 and over	NA	NA	NA	NA	NA	NA	NA	NA	NA	NA	NA	NA	NA	49	52	49	43	43	45
$30,000 to $49,999	NA	NA	NA	NA	NA	NA	NA	NA	NA	NA	NA	NA	NA	48	50	44	42	37	37
$20,000 to $29,999	NA	NA	NA	NA	NA	NA	NA	NA	NA	NA	NA	NA	NA	44	38	44	32	37	26
Under $20,000	NA	NA	NA	NA	NA	NA	NA	NA	NA	NA	NA	NA	NA	32	28	26	22	18	20
Occupation																			
Professional/business	48	45	46	48	45	42	42	40	45	39	46	38	35	38	38	39	35	32	32
Clerical/support	42	43	40	49	45	39	41	40	45	37	37	38	35	36	36	40	31	28	25
Manual/service	48	48	48	52	48	49	48	48	46	41	52	50	47	51	45	43	38	35	41
Farming/agriculture	83	79	62	66	81	77	84	78	75	82	87	83	56	68	67	67	72	44	38
Region																			
Northeast	22	27	29	32	27	32	32	28	31	25	32	30	28	29	26	24	22	18	20
Midwest	51	49	48	53	52	48	44	48	46	41	46	44	42	41	46	42	37	37	35
South	62	59	60	62	59	52	52	53	55	47	53	52	50	52	48	48	42	37	42
West	47	42	44	46	44	47	49	40	47	42	48	39	32	39	35	39	32	33	33
Religion																			
Protestant	56	52	53	57	56	52	52	50	52	46	53	48	46	47	46	46	42	37	40
Catholic	35	37	36	39	36	36	34	35	36	31	36	36	30	36	34	34	27	26	29
Jewish	14	7	26	17	6	11	22	9	25	0	18	6	10	9	18	11	12	19	7
None	32	40	43	50	39	37	36	44	39	41	36	34	31	37	32	35	26	32	33
Politics																			
Republican	53	49	50	56	53	50	56	47	51	46	50	48	42	51	49	49	46	46	47
Democrat	44	45	45	49	46	44	42	47	44	39	43	40	41	35	37	35	30	27	28
Independent	49	47	48	50	47	44	40	39	44	36	46	42	37	42	39	38	32	30	30

Note: See Note, table 2.15. For a discussion of public opinion survey sampling procedures, see Appendix 5.

Source: National Opinion Research Center, "General Social Surveys, 1972-2002," Storrs, CT: The Roper Center for Public Opinion Research, University of Connecticut. (Machine-readable data files.) Table constructed by SOURCEBOOK staff.

[a]Beginning in 1996, education categories were revised slightly and therefore are not directly comparable to data presented for prior years.

Table 2.62

Respondents reporting a firearm in their home

By type of firearm and demographic characteristics, United States, 2002

Question: "Do you happen to have in your home (or garage) any guns or revolvers?" If yes, "Is it a pistol, shotgun, rifle, or what?"

(Percent reporting having a firearm)

	Firearm in the home			
		Type of firearm[a]		
	Any type	Pistol	Shotgun	Rifle
National	34%	58%	63%	59%
Sex				
Male	43	60	68	63
Female	24	54	52	52
Race				
White	38	59	65	61
Black/other	15	46	38	38
Age				
18 to 20 years	24	50	75	75
21 to 29 years	31	52	58	52
30 to 49 years	29	52	57	60
50 years and older	41	64	68	60
Education				
College	33	63	63	57
High school graduate	34	61	68	67
Less than high school graduate	37	39	56	54
Income				
$50,000 and over	45	63	64	63
$30,000 to $49,999	37	71	64	63
$20,000 to $29,999	26	31	59	41
Under $20,000	20	42	58	54
Occupation				
Professional/business	32	60	68	56
Clerical/support	25	65	55	58
Manual/service	41	54	60	60
Farming/agriculture	38	50	67	83
Region				
Northeast	20	46	63	63
Midwest	35	54	67	54
South	42	62	61	58
West	33	61	61	65
Religion				
Protestant	40	60	66	61
Catholic	29	54	59	62
Jewish	7	100	0	100
None	33	60	62	49
Politics				
Republican	47	64	62	59
Democrat	28	55	65	58
Independent	30	54	62	58

Note: See Note, table 2.15. For a discussion of public opinion survey sampling procedures, see Appendix 5.

[a]Percents for pistol, shotgun, and rifle are based on the 34% subsample of respondents reporting that they have a gun in their home. Percents add to more than 100 because some respondents reported owning more than one type.

Source: National Opinion Research Center, "General Social Surveys, 1972-2002," Storrs, CT: The Roper Center for Public Opinion Research, University of Connecticut. (Machine-readable data files.) Table constructed by SOURCEBOOK staff.

Table 2.63

Attitudes toward laws covering the sale of firearms

United States, selected years 1990-2003

Question: "In general, do you feel that the laws covering the sale of firearms should be made more strict, less strict, or kept as they are now?"

	More strict	Less strict	Kept as they are now	Don't know/ refused
1990	78%	2%	17%	3%
1991	68	5	25	2
March 1993	70	4	24	2
December 1993	67	7	25	1
1995[a]	62	12	24	2
1999	60	9	29	2
2000	62	5	31	2
2001	53	8	38	1
2002	51	11	36	2
2003	55	9	36	(b)

Note: See Note, table 2.13. For a discussion of public opinion survey sampling procedures, see Appendix 5.

[a]Asked of a half sample.
[b]Less than 0.5%.

Source: The Gallup Organization, Inc., *The Gallup Poll* [Online]. Available: http://www.gallup.com/poll/ [Jan. 13, 2003]; and data provided by The Gallup Organization, Inc. Table adapted by SOURCEBOOK staff. Reprinted by permission.

Page 152 intentionally blank.

Table 2.64

Attitudes toward laws covering the sale of firearms

By demographic characteristics, United States, 2003

Question: "In general, do you feel that the laws covering the sale of firearms should be made more strict, less strict, or kept as they are now?"

	More strict	Less strict	Kept as they are now
National	55%	9%	36%
Sex			
Male	46	12	42
Female	63	6	30
Race			
White	52	10	38
Nonwhite	68	5	27
Black	73	4	23
Age			
18 to 29 years	55	9	36
30 to 49 years	54	7	39
50 to 64 years	54	12	34
50 years and older	57	10	32
65 years and older	62	6	30
Education			
College post graduate	68	6	25
College graduate	58	6	36
Some college	49	9	42
High school graduate or less	55	11	34
Income			
$75,000 and over	59	7	34
$50,000 to $74,999	50	11	39
$30,000 to $49,999	55	7	38
$20,000 to $29,999	57	10	33
Under $20,000	57	9	33
Community			
Urban area	58	8	33
Suburban area	57	7	36
Rural area	50	13	37
Region			
East	66	6	28
Midwest	52	10	38
South	54	10	36
West	51	8	40
Politics			
Republican	40	13	47
Democrat	71	3	25
Independent	55	9	36

Note: See Note, table 2.13. The "don't know/refused" category has been omitted; therefore percents may not sum to 100. For a discussion of public opinion survey sampling procedures, see Appendix 5.

Source: Table constructed by SOURCEBOOK staff from data provided by The Gallup Organization, Inc. Reprinted by permission.

Table 2.65

Attitudes toward a law restricting the possession of handguns

United States, selected years 1959-2003

Question: "Do you think there should or should not be a law that would ban the possession of handguns, except by the police and other authorized persons?"

	Should	Should not	Don't know/ refused
1959	60%	36%	4%
1965	49	44	7
1975	41	55	4
January 1980	31	65	4
December 1980	38	51	11
April 1981	39	58	3
June 1981	41	54	5
1987	42	50	8
1988	37	59	4
1990	41	55	4
1991	43	53	4
March 1993	42	54	4
December 1993	39	60	1
1999	34	64	2
2000	36	62	2
2002	32	65	3
2003	32	67	1

Note: See Note, table 2.13. For a discussion of public opinion survey sampling procedures, see Appendix 5.

Source: The Gallup Organization, Inc., *The Gallup Poll* [Online]. Available: http://www.gallup.com/poll/ [Jan. 13, 2003]; and data provided by The Gallup Organization, Inc. Reprinted by permission.

Table 2.66

Attitudes toward a law requiring a police permit prior to gun purchase

By demographic characteristics, United States, selected years 1976-2002

Question: "Would you favor or oppose a law which would require a person to obtain a police permit before he or she could buy a gun?"

	1976 Favor	1976 Oppose	1977 Favor	1977 Oppose	1980 Favor	1980 Oppose	1982 Favor	1982 Oppose	1984 Favor	1984 Oppose	1985 Favor	1985 Oppose	1987 Favor	1987 Oppose	1988 Favor	1988 Oppose
National	72%	27%	72%	26%	69%	29%	72%	26%	70%	27%	72%	26%	70%	28%	74%	24%
Sex																
Male	64	35	64	35	63	36	68	31	62	37	65	34	62	36	66	33
Female	78	20	78	19	74	23	75	23	76	20	78	20	76	22	79	17
Race																
White	71	27	70	28	68	30	71	27	69	29	72	27	69	29	74	24
Black/other	74	24	81	17	81	15	78	19	79	18	76	22	74	23	75	23
Age																
18 to 20 years	78	22	69	31	71	29	77	23	71	24	71	29	69	29	73	24
21 to 29 years	71	27	72	26	73	27	76	24	73	25	74	25	76	23	73	26
30 to 49 years	73	25	70	29	70	29	72	26	70	29	71	28	68	30	72	26
50 years and older	70	29	74	24	67	29	69	29	70	26	72	26	69	29	75	20
Education[a]																
College	71	27	74	25	70	29	76	23	74	25	75	24	74	25	76	22
High school graduate	72	27	70	28	69	29	71	27	68	30	71	28	67	31	74	24
Less than high school graduate	71	28	72	25	70	27	64	30	72	23	69	26	70	27	66	27
Income																
$50,000 and over	NA	NA	NA	NA	NA	NA	NA	NA	NA	NA	NA	NA	NA	NA	NA	NA
$30,000 to $49,999	NA	NA	NA	NA	NA	NA	NA	NA	NA	NA	NA	NA	NA	NA	NA	NA
$20,000 to $29,999	NA	NA	NA	NA	NA	NA	NA	NA	NA	NA	NA	NA	NA	NA	NA	NA
Under $20,000	NA	NA	NA	NA	NA	NA	NA	NA	NA	NA	NA	NA	NA	NA	NA	NA
Occupation																
Professional/business	74	25	76	23	70	28	75	23	71	27	75	24	74	24	77	21
Clerical/support	78	20	75	22	77	21	77	23	76	23	79	21	77	22	78	19
Manual/service	68	30	68	30	67	32	69	29	68	29	68	31	64	33	71	26
Farming/agriculture	56	44	66	31	53	47	36	60	48	48	43	57	48	50	24	65
Region																
Northeast	86	13	85	14	86	13	85	13	80	18	82	17	83	15	84	13
Midwest	72	27	67	31	71	27	73	24	70	25	73	25	68	31	76	22
South	63	35	69	28	64	34	62	36	66	31	67	32	66	31	69	28
West	68	30	68	31	60	38	69	30	67	32	71	29	67	31	68	28
Religion																
Protestant	67	31	67	30	64	34	68	30	66	31	68	30	67	31	72	26
Catholic	82	18	80	20	83	16	81	17	79	20	79	20	74	24	77	20
Jewish	89	11	89	9	88	12	89	5	93	7	94	6	85	10	100	0
None	68	28	73	26	71	28	72	28	78	22	74	26	77	20	73	25
Politics																
Republican	71	27	71	26	64	35	66	33	66	32	70	28	71	27	68	29
Democrat	74	25	73	26	74	25	75	24	75	23	74	25	70	29	79	19
Independent	69	29	71	28	68	29	72	26	70	28	72	27	70	28	73	24

Note: See Note, table 2.15. The "don't know" category has been omitted; therefore percents may not sum to 100. Readers interested in responses to this question for previous years should consult previous editions of SOURCEBOOK. For a discussion of public opinion survey sampling procedures, see Appendix 5.

Source: National Opinion Research Center, "General Social Surveys, 1972-2002," Storrs, CT: The Roper Center for Public Opinion Research, University of Connecticut. (Machine-readable data files.) Table constructed by SOURCEBOOK staff.

[a] Beginning in 1996, education categories were revised slightly and therefore are not directly comparable to data presented for prior years.

	1989		1990		1991		1993		1994		1996		1998		2000		2002	
	Favor	Oppose	Favor	Oppose	Favor	Oppose	Favor	Oppose	Favor	Oppose	Favor	Oppose	Favor	Oppose	Favor	Oppose	Favor	Oppose
	78%	21%	79%	20%	81%	18%	81%	17%	78%	20%	80%	18%	82%	16%	80%	18%	80%	19%
	69	30	72	27	74	25	73	26	70	29	73	25	76	22	71	27	75	24
	85	13	84	14	86	12	87	11	84	14	86	12	86	12	86	11	86	14
	77	21	77	21	81	18	80	18	77	22	80	19	80	18	78	20	78	21
	81	18	86	12	84	15	84	15	84	14	84	13	88	10	86	11	87	12
	66	34	91	9	70	30	83	17	85	15	69	29	82	16	79	21	76	24
	81	17	83	15	82	18	83	17	78	20	78	21	82	16	81	16	82	17
	74	25	76	23	82	17	82	17	77	22	83	15	82	16	80	17	80	20
	81	17	78	19	80	17	80	18	79	19	80	19	81	16	79	18	80	20
	80	19	81	18	85	14	84	15	79	19	83	16	84	14	79	19	78	21
	75	23	77	20	79	20	79	19	76	22	79	19	79	19	80	18	83	16
	82	17	73	22	70	24	76	20	78	18	76	20	80	17	82	16	80	19
	NA	NA	NA	NA	NA	NA	84	15	79	20	82	16	83	15	77	22	78	22
	NA	NA	NA	NA	NA	NA	83	16	74	25	82	17	81	18	79	19	82	18
	NA	NA	NA	NA	NA	NA	84	15	80	19	81	18	83	15	79	18	78	21
	NA	NA	NA	NA	NA	NA	79	20	80	18	78	19	84	14	83	14	82	18
	82	17	78	20	89	11	84	15	79	20	82	17	83	14	79	19	78	22
	80	16	84	15	84	15	89	10	85	14	83	16	84	14	86	12	85	15
	72	26	77	22	75	23	75	23	74	24	80	18	79	19	78	19	80	20
	73	27	56	39	72	28	72	24	56	38	53	43	80	20	61	36	94	6
	90	10	85	15	84	15	90	9	85	15	84	13	88	10	85	13	87	12
	80	19	78	20	81	17	82	16	78	21	84	14	79	18	78	20	79	20
	72	26	77	20	78	21	75	22	77	21	78	20	79	18	82	16	77	22
	74	24	75	24	85	15	82	17	74	25	77	21	82	17	73	23	78	22
	75	23	76	22	78	20	79	19	75	23	81	17	80	18	79	18	77	22
	84	16	84	14	84	15	84	14	84	15	83	15	85	12	82	15	84	15
	100	0	100	0	100	0	96	4	94	6	89	11	88	9	85	15	87	13
	70	26	76	23	87	13	80	20	76	22	72	26	80	17	77	20	78	22
	76	22	78	21	81	18	76	22	71	28	77	22	75	23	71	27	72	27
	84	15	83	15	82	16	86	13	85	14	86	12	86	13	86	12	88	12
	71	26	76	23	80	19	81	17	77	21	79	19	83	14	80	16	79	21

Public attitudes toward crime and criminal justice-related topics 155

Page 156 intentionally blank.

Table 2.67

Attitudes toward legalization of the use of marijuana

United States, selected years 1969-2003

Question: "Do you think the use of marijuana should be made legal, or not?"

	Yes, legal	No, illegal	Don't know/refused
1969	12%	84%	4%
1972	15	81	4
1973	16	78	6
1977	28	66	6
1979	25	70	5
1980	25	70	5
1985	23	73	4
1995	25	73	2
2000[a]	31	64	5
2001	34	62	4
2003[a]	34	64	2

Note: Sample sizes vary from year to year; the data for 2003 are based on telephone interviews with a randomly selected national sample of 1,004 adults, 18 years of age and older, conducted Nov. 10-12, 2003. For a discussion of public opinion survey sampling procedures, see Appendix 5.

[a] Asked of a half sample.

Source: The Gallup Organization, Inc., *The Gallup Poll* [Online]. Available: http://www.gallup.com/poll/ [June 28, 2004]. Table adapted by SOURCEBOOK staff. Reprinted by permission.

Table 2.68

Attitudes toward legalization of the use of marijuana

By demographic characteristics, United States, selected years 1976-2002

Question: "Do you think the use of marijuana should be made legal or not?"

	1976 Should	1976 Should not	1978 Should	1978 Should not	1980 Should	1980 Should not	1983 Should	1983 Should not	1984 Should	1984 Should not	1986 Should	1986 Should not	1987 Should	1987 Should not	1988 Should	1988 Should not
National	28%	69%	30%	67%	25%	72%	20%	76%	23%	73%	18%	80%	16%	81%	17%	79%
Sex																
Male	32	64	34	63	30	67	25	71	28	68	23	75	19	78	21	74
Female	24	73	26	71	21	76	16	80	19	77	14	84	14	83	14	82
Race																
White	27	70	29	68	25	72	19	77	23	73	18	81	17	80	17	80
Black/other	33	60	38	59	27	71	28	69	22	75	19	77	12	84	18	75
Age																
18 to 20 years	57	39	51	48	45	52	33	67	36	62	16	82	21	74	16	74
21 to 29 years	49	48	49	49	42	56	29	68	34	62	27	71	25	70	24	70
30 to 49 years	25	72	29	69	27	71	21	76	27	68	20	79	19	79	19	78
50 years and older	16	81	16	80	13	84	13	83	9	87	12	87	8	90	12	86
Education[a]																
College	40	56	42	55	35	61	23	74	29	66	22	75	21	75	20	75
High school graduate	26	70	27	70	23	75	21	76	21	75	17	82	13	84	16	80
Less than high school graduate	11	86	13	84	3	88	9	87	7	91	8	91	10	88	12	88
Income																
$50,000 and over	NA	NA	NA	NA	NA	NA	NA	NA	NA	NA	NA	NA	NA	NA	NA	NA
$30,000 to $49,999	NA	NA	NA	NA	NA	NA	NA	NA	NA	NA	NA	NA	NA	NA	NA	NA
$20,000 to $29,999	NA	NA	NA	NA	NA	NA	NA	NA	NA	NA	NA	NA	NA	NA	NA	NA
Under $20,000	NA	NA	NA	NA	NA	NA	NA	NA	NA	NA	NA	NA	NA	NA	NA	NA
Occupation																
Professional/business	36	60	37	60	30	66	22	75	27	68	20	79	20	77	16	80
Clerical/support	26	72	27	71	23	75	18	79	22	72	16	82	11	83	14	82
Manual/service	25	71	28	69	23	74	22	75	20	77	19	79	16	81	20	75
Farming/agriculture	8	92	16	80	12	79	8	82	3	94	9	91	2	95	6	94
Region																
Northeast	32	64	33	62	27	70	20	76	24	74	20	80	18	78	19	76
Midwest	25	72	26	72	20	77	18	79	23	72	16	82	14	83	18	78
South	22	74	27	72	20	78	17	80	20	76	14	84	13	85	12	86
West	37	61	38	59	38	57	30	66	26	70	25	73	23	72	23	72
Religion																
Protestant	22	74	24	74	20	77	17	80	20	76	15	83	13	85	13	84
Catholic	32	64	31	64	26	71	17	78	20	76	18	80	16	81	16	80
Jewish	37	63	62	38	28	62	33	54	48	48	40	60	40	55	52	44
None	54	39	64	33	60	36	54	44	44	50	37	60	42	51	38	55
Politics																
Republican	20	78	19	80	18	80	15	82	17	80	13	86	13	84	14	84
Democrat	26	71	29	67	24	73	20	77	21	75	18	80	15	82	18	78
Independent	34	62	37	60	30	66	24	72	28	68	21	76	19	76	20	75

Note: See Note, table 2.15. The "don't know" category has been omitted; therefore percents may not sum to 100. Readers interested in responses to this question for previous years should consult previous editions of SOURCEBOOK. For a discussion of public opinion survey sampling procedures, see Appendix 5.

Source: National Opinion Research Center, "General Social Surveys, 1972-2002," Storrs, CT: The Roper Center for Public Opinion Research, University of Connecticut. (Machine-readable data files.) Table constructed by SOURCEBOOK staff.

[a]Beginning in 1996, education categories were revised slightly and therefore are not directly comparable to data presented for prior years.

1989		1990		1991		1993		1994		1996		1998		2000		2002	
Should	Should not	Should	Should not	Should	Should not	Should	Should not	Should	Should not	Should	Should not	Should	Should not	Should	Should not	Should	Should not
16%	81%	16%	81%	18%	78%	22%	73%	23%	72%	26%	69%	28%	66%	32%	63%	34%	60%
20	76	19	79	23	74	27	68	27	69	30	66	34	60	36	58	38	55
14	84	14	82	14	81	19	76	20	75	22	72	22	71	28	66	30	63
18	80	17	80	18	78	22	73	23	73	26	69	28	65	33	61	36	58
10	85	13	82	16	76	20	75	24	71	22	70	24	70	25	68	24	66
19	75	22	78	21	79	24	69	50	50	38	60	34	64	41	56	59	35
21	76	19	76	25	73	25	70	24	71	30	66	34	59	41	54	41	51
19	78	19	79	22	74	27	67	26	70	28	67	30	63	34	60	38	54
11	86	12	85	10	86	15	81	17	78	19	75	21	73	24	70	24	70
20	77	18	79	21	74	25	70	26	69	27	68	32	62	33	62	37	56
15	82	16	81	16	81	19	76	22	74	24	71	23	70	31	62	29	63
9	88	12	87	8	88	19	80	10	84	22	72	22	72	27	67	31	65
NA	NA	NA	NA	NA	NA	23	72	24	70	25	70	27	68	31	64	35	59
NA	NA	NA	NA	NA	NA	22	72	21	76	25	71	29	67	36	58	33	61
NA	NA	NA	NA	NA	NA	27	69	20	77	27	68	32	61	34	60	33	59
NA	NA	NA	NA	NA	NA	23	73	27	69	29	66	26	68	29	65	36	56
20	77	21	77	19	76	24	71	26	69	26	68	31	64	35	60	36	58
10	88	9	87	16	80	19	75	18	79	23	71	23	72	26	67	27	67
17	80	16	80	17	79	24	71	24	72	26	69	28	65	31	62	34	59
25	75	6	88	15	80	5	90	15	82	26	71	42	45	34	63	33	56
14	80	12	84	18	77	24	70	19	75	26	67	28	65	34	58	29	62
14	84	16	81	13	83	19	77	19	76	23	74	27	66	32	63	38	57
14	83	12	84	15	81	19	77	22	74	24	70	22	72	26	68	27	67
26	72	29	71	30	66	28	64	32	64	31	64	37	58	39	57	45	48
13	86	12	85	16	80	18	78	19	77	19	74	21	73	26	69	26	69
16	80	15	84	15	82	21	75	21	74	29	68	27	66	28	64	30	62
35	65	33	60	36	59	30	60	42	49	37	54	56	44	48	48	50	50
40	49	44	51	40	52	47	45	46	49	42	54	48	44	53	42	60	32
14	85	11	86	16	80	14	84	15	82	20	77	19	77	26	70	24	72
16	81	18	79	16	80	28	68	24	73	24	69	29	65	31	63	34	59
19	76	18	78	21	75	23	69	29	64	30	64	31	62	35	58	39	53

Public attitudes toward crime and criminal justice-related topics 159

Table 2.69

Respondents' attitudes toward making marijuana legally available for doctors to prescribe

By demographic characteristics, United States, 2003

Question: "Would you favor or oppose making marijuana legally available for doctors to prescribe in order to reduce pain and suffering?"

	Favor	Oppose	Don't know/ refused
National	75%	22%	3%
Sex			
Male	76	21	3
Female	73	24	3
Race			
White	76	22	2
Nonwhite	70	24	6
Black	69	26	5
Age			
18 to 29 years	75	24	1
30 to 49 years	77	21	2
50 to 64 years	81	17	2
50 years and older	72	23	5
65 years and older	62	30	8
Education			
College post graduate	80	19	1
College graduate	84	14	2
Some college	76	22	2
High school graduate or less	68	27	5
Income			
$75,000 and over	81	19	(a)
$50,000 to $74,999	79	19	2
$30,000 to $49,999	79	18	3
$20,000 to $29,999	63	30	7
Under $20,000	68	27	5
Community			
Urban area	73	24	3
Suburban area	79	19	2
Rural area	67	28	5
Region			
East	75	21	4
Midwest	76	22	2
South	70	26	4
West	78	19	3
Politics			
Republican	68	28	4
Democrat	81	17	2
Independent	74	23	3

Note: See Note, table 2.67. For a discussion of public opinion survey sampling procedures, see Appendix 5.

[a] Less than 0.5%.

Source: Table constructed by SOURCEBOOK staff from data provided by The Gallup Organization, Inc. Reprinted by permission.

Table 2.70

High school seniors reporting that they worry about selected social problems

United States, 1991-2003

Question: "Of all the problems facing the nation today, how often do you worry about each of the following?"

(Percent responding "sometimes" or "often")

	Class of 1991 (N=2,595)	Class of 1992 (N=2,736)	Class of 1993 (N=2,807)	Class of 1994 (N=2,664)	Class of 1995 (N=2,646)	Class of 1996 (N=2,502)	Class of 1997 (N=2,651)	Class of 1998 (N=2,621)	Class of 1999 (N=2,348)	Class of 2000 (N=2,204)	Class of 2001 (N=2,222)	Class of 2002 (N=2,267)	Class of 2003 (N=2,531)
Crime and violence	88.1%	91.6%	90.8%	92.7%	90.2%	90.1%	86.5%	84.4%	81.8%	83.5%	81.0%	75.5%	68.9%
Drug abuse	79.5	77.8	75.5	76.7	72.6	71.0	71.1	65.3	62.7	60.9	61.1	56.9	52.6
Hunger and poverty	66.4	68.1	71.1	65.7	62.3	62.6	61.1	55.5	54.5	54.4	51.3	49.7	46.1
Chance of nuclear war	41.5	33.4	28.8	27.9	20.0	21.6	20.4	29.0	32.1	23.7	23.9	35.9	50.3
Economic problems	63.9	70.6	71.8	62.6	55.7	57.9	51.5	47.6	44.8	45.2	47.0	47.0	49.0
Pollution	72.1	71.9	72.8	66.5	63.6	62.9	61.6	57.1	49.8	53.3	49.6	44.2	37.8
Race relations	59.4	68.7	75.4	71.6	68.9	70.7	64.7	56.0	55.6	51.2	52.6	46.9	41.8
Energy shortages	38.2	35.2	29.8	23.8	17.9	19.2	19.4	18.3	20.8	22.0	31.2	22.6	19.4
Using open land for housing or industry	33.8	34.7	32.9	32.7	28.9	32.6	32.7	30.8	27.5	32.6	30.6	28.5	26.7
Population growth	30.6	35.2	38.9	35.4	34.9	37.4	38.2	34.8	31.7	36.3	36.7	28.3	24.4
Urban decay	21.7	25.8	25.3	25.6	23.0	25.1	22.1	18.8	17.2	20.5	20.3	15.6	14.4

Note: These data are from a series of nationwide surveys of high school seniors conducted by the Monitoring the Future Project at the University of Michigan's Institute for Social Research from 1975 through 2003. The survey design is a multistage random sample of high school seniors in public and private schools throughout the continental United States. All percentages reported are based on weighted cases; the Ns that are shown in the tables refer to the number of weighted cases.

Response categories were "never," "seldom," "sometimes," and "often." Readers interested in responses to this question for 1975 through 1990 should consult previous editions of SOURCEBOOK. For survey methodology and definitions of terms, see Appendix 6.

Source: Lloyd D. Johnston, Jerald G. Bachman, and Patrick M. O'Malley, *Monitoring the Future 1991*, pp. 188, 189; *1993*, pp. 190, 191; *1995*, pp. 191, 192; *1997*, pp. 187, 188; *1999*, pp. 186, 187 (Ann Arbor, MI: Institute for Social Research, University of Michigan); Jerald G. Bachman, Lloyd D. Johnston, and Patrick M. O'Malley, *Monitoring the Future 1992*, pp. 189, 190; *1994*, pp. 189, 190; *1996*, pp. 182, 183; *1998*, pp. 188, 189; *2000*, pp. 187, 188 (Ann Arbor, MI: Institute for Social Research, University of Michigan); and data provided by the Monitoring the Future Project, Survey Research Center, Lloyd D. Johnston, Jerald G. Bachman, and Patrick M. O'Malley, Principal Investigators. Table adapted by SOURCEBOOK staff. Reprinted by permission.

Table 2.71

High school seniors reporting that they worry about crime and violence

By sex, race, region, college plans, and illicit drug use, United States, 1991-2003

Question: "Of all the problems facing the nation today, how often do you worry about... crime and violence?"

(Percent responding "sometimes" or "often")

	Class of 1991 (N=2,595)	Class of 1992 (N=2,736)	Class of 1993 (N=2,807)	Class of 1994 (N=2,664)	Class of 1995 (N=2,646)	Class of 1996 (N=2,502)	Class of 1997 (N=2,651)	Class of 1998 (N=2,621)	Class of 1999 (N=2,348)	Class of 2000 (N=2,204)	Class of 2001 (N=2,222)	Class of 2002 (N=2,267)	Class of 2003 (N=2,531)
Total	88.1%	91.6%	90.8%	92.7%	90.2%	90.1%	86.5%	84.4%	81.8%	83.5%	81.0%	75.5%	68.9%
Sex													
Male	82.6	87.6	85.7	88.4	85.8	84.8	79.4	76.5	74.4	76.0	71.7	66.5	59.3
Female	93.6	95.7	95.6	96.5	95.1	95.4	93.7	91.7	89.5	90.2	90.1	83.1	77.9
Race													
White	86.6	90.5	89.4	92.9	90.0	89.5	84.5	83.5	80.8	82.6	78.7	73.4	64.7
Black	94.5	96.9	95.1	90.7	93.0	92.9	90.4	85.7	84.8	91.1	90.2	80.8	76.9
Region													
Northeast	86.0	92.0	90.6	91.0	91.7	89.4	83.2	83.1	85.4	82.2	79.8	70.8	69.2
North Central	88.8	87.6	90.2	93.2	86.7	87.4	85.1	80.7	80.0	84.6	79.4	75.0	65.4
South	88.4	93.8	91.2	93.3	91.3	91.1	88.7	87.0	81.1	85.8	83.6	79.2	70.6
West	89.0	93.0	91.4	92.4	92.2	93.4	88.2	85.4	82.0	79.3	80.7	74.6	69.7
College plans													
Yes	89.9	93.1	92.4	94.1	92.6	91.6	88.4	85.3	84.5	85.0	83.5	76.9	71.8
No	83.9	87.7	85.8	89.4	84.0	86.2	80.7	82.2	72.3	77.9	72.7	69.0	59.5
Lifetime illicit drug use													
None	90.7	92.9	91.9	94.1	91.8	90.5	89.1	86.8	84.3	85.4	82.3	77.1	69.1
Marijuana only	85.4	89.6	91.1	91.5	90.9	91.9	85.7	82.3	82.8	85.8	85.2	77.0	71.7
Few pills	86.6	89.4	90.7	95.6	92.6	91.0	88.3	84.6	84.3	79.1	83.1	77.8	67.4
More pills	84.8	90.6	87.4	89.5	84.1	87.4	81.0	83.3	75.6	79.9	73.8	69.7	66.7

Note: See Note, table 2.70. Data are given for those who identify themselves as white or Caucasian and those who identify themselves as black or African-American; data are not given for the other ethnic categories because each of these groups constitutes a small portion of the sample in any given year and therefore would yield unreliable estimates (Source, *2000*, p. 10). "College plans" distinguishes those seniors who expect to graduate from a 4-year college from those who expect to receive some college training or none. The four drug use categories are mutually exclusive and are based on an index of seriousness of involvement. The "pills" category indicates use of any of a number of drugs including some that usually are not taken in pill form. Respondents indicating the use of one or more of a number of illicit drugs (other than marijuana) but who had not used any one class of them on three or more occasions and did not use heroin at all fall into the "few pills" category. Respondents indicating such use on three or more occasions and who did not use heroin at all fall into the "more pills" category. Respondents reporting heroin use were included in a separate category that is not presented here due to the small number of respondents indicating such use. (Source, *2000*, pp. 9, 14.)

Response categories were "never," "seldom," "sometimes," and "often." Readers interested in responses to this question for 1975 through 1990 should consult previous editions of SOURCEBOOK. For survey methodology and definitions of terms, see Appendix 6.

Source: Lloyd D. Johnston, Jerald G. Bachman, and Patrick M. O'Malley, *Monitoring the Future 1991*, p. 188; *1993*, p. 190; *1995*, p. 191; *1997*, p. 187; *1999*, p. 186 (Ann Arbor, MI: Institute for Social Research, University of Michigan); Jerald G. Bachman, Lloyd D. Johnston, and Patrick M. O'Malley, *Monitoring the Future 1992*, p. 189; *1994*, p. 189; *1996*, p. 182; *1998*, p. 188; *2000*, p. 187 (Ann Arbor, MI: Institute for Social Research, University of Michigan); and data provided by the Monitoring the Future Project, Survey Research Center, Lloyd D. Johnston, Jerald G. Bachman, and Patrick M. O'Malley, Principal Investigators. Table adapted by SOURCEBOOK staff. Reprinted by permission.

Table 2.72

High school seniors reporting positive attitudes toward the performance of selected institutions

United States, 1991-2003

Question: "Now we'd like you to make some ratings of how good or bad a job you feel each of the following organizations is doing for the country as a whole. . ... How good or bad a job is being done for the country as a whole by. . .?"

(Percent responding "good" or "very good")

	Class of 1991 (N=2,582)	Class of 1992 (N=2,684)	Class of 1993 (N=2,773)	Class of 1994 (N=2,642)	Class of 1995 (N=2,658)	Class of 1996 (N=2,455)	Class of 1997 (N=2,648)	Class of 1998 (N=2,608)	Class of 1999 (N=2,357)	Class of 2000 (N=2,216)	Class of 2001 (N=2,201)	Class of 2002 (N=2,250)	Class of 2003 (N=2,523)
Large corporations	36.3%	31.8%	31.5%	34.6%	37.9%	36.3%	35.3%	43.0%	42.1%	43.0%	39.3%	38.4%	33.7%
Major labor unions	31.3	28.9	27.2	29.2	28.0	30.8	29.2	32.8	34.5	32.0	33.1	32.5	30.7
The Nation's colleges and universities	70.2	67.2	61.1	67.7	66.6	70.5	65.7	70.1	72.5	71.0	71.0	69.4	67.5
The Nation's public schools	33.6	32.5	29.0	27.2	31.8	30.6	30.0	32.2	34.1	34.7	34.5	37.7	36.0
Churches and religious organizations	49.2	50.3	46.9	50.3	50.2	49.0	48.3	52.6	52.4	50.1	52.1	48.8	48.1
The national news media (TV, magazines, news services)	51.1	47.9	40.5	37.9	33.1	34.5	34.8	36.1	39.8	37.6	38.8	43.0	45.6
The President and his administration	56.8	23.8	24.9	22.1	19.7	24.0	26.8	34.1	33.3	35.7	32.8	54.0	43.6
Congress--that is, the U.S. Senate and House of Representatives	38.3	15.9	16.6	18.8	20.6	18.1	21.7	28.7	29.9	31.4	33.0	42.2	36.4
The U.S. Supreme Court	44.1	35.7	31.0	31.0	29.8	30.4	30.5	36.6	38.9	38.2	37.1	41.5	38.6
All the courts and the justice system in general	31.2	23.4	21.1	19.3	20.6	21.2	22.4	25.7	29.4	28.9	30.7	32.9	31.7
The police and other law enforcement agencies	28.0	26.9	27.1	29.3	28.7	27.6	28.7	33.0	33.7	33.6	33.2	38.9	40.8
The U.S. military	80.6	62.2	57.0	54.3	54.8	55.6	52.9	56.7	59.4	55.5	55.7	70.1	74.9

Note: See Note, table 2.70. Response categories were "very poor," "poor," "fair," "good," "very good," and "no opinion." Readers interested in responses to this question for 1975 through 1990 should consult previous editions of SOURCEBOOK. For survey methodology and definitions of terms, see Appendix 6.

Source: Lloyd D. Johnston, Jerald G. Bachman, and Patrick M. O'Malley, *Monitoring the Future 1991*, pp. 136-138; *1993*, pp. 138-140; *1995*, pp. 139-141; *1997*, pp. 135-137; *1999*, pp. 136-138 (Ann Arbor, MI: Institute for Social Research, University of Michigan); Jerald G. Bachman, Lloyd D. Johnston, and Patrick M. O'Malley, *Monitoring the Future 1992*, pp. 137-139; *1994*, pp. 137-139; *1996*, pp. 132, 133; *1998*, pp. 135-137; *2000*, pp. 137-139 (Ann Arbor, MI: Institute for Social Research, University of Michigan); and data provided by the Monitoring the Future Project, Survey Research Center, Lloyd D. Johnston, Jerald G. Bachman, and Patrick M. O'Malley, Principal Investigators. Table adapted by SOURCEBOOK staff. Reprinted by permission.

Table 2.73

High school seniors reporting positive attitudes toward the performance of the police and other law enforcement agencies

By sex, race, region, college plans, and illicit drug use, United States, 1991-2003

Question: "Now we'd like you to make some ratings of how good or bad a job you feel each of the following organizations is doing for the country as a whole. . . . How good or bad a job is being done for the country as a whole by. . .the police and other law enforcement agencies?"

(Percent responding "good" or "very good")

	Class of 1991 (N=2,582)	Class of 1992 (N=2,684)	Class of 1993 (N=2,773)	Class of 1994 (N=2,642)	Class of 1995 (N=2,658)	Class of 1996 (N=2,455)	Class of 1997 (N=2,648)	Class of 1998 (N=2,608)	Class of 1999 (N=2,357)	Class of 2000 (N=2,216)	Class of 2001 (N=2,201)	Class of 2002 (N=2,250)	Class of 2003 (N=2,523)
Total	28.0%	26.9%	27.1%	29.3%	28.7%	27.6%	28.7%	33.0%	33.7%	33.6%	33.2%	38.9%	40.8%
Sex													
Male	29.3	27.4	30.1	30.2	29.1	28.6	30.3	33.9	36.3	35.7	33.8	37.1	39.9
Female	27.2	26.8	24.3	28.4	28.1	26.5	27.7	32.1	31.5	32.7	33.5	41.4	41.5
Race													
White	31.5	30.0	31.1	32.2	31.5	30.7	32.1	35.7	35.2	38.0	37.2	43.5	44.4
Black	11.0	12.4	9.2	16.9	16.8	14.6	16.3	22.5	25.4	16.6	20.0	23.7	26.4
Region													
Northeast	26.3	26.6	28.0	29.5	25.5	30.7	32.7	33.4	29.9	36.1	35.8	42.8	41.1
North Central	35.7	27.7	28.5	29.9	29.9	24.5	25.4	32.8	34.3	33.2	35.7	39.2	42.5
South	22.1	24.5	25.4	29.3	27.3	26.5	28.9	32.4	34.6	31.7	32.9	38.5	41.7
West	30.0	30.7	27.8	28.4	32.9	31.1	28.6	34.2	35.0	35.3	27.7	35.9	37.0
College plans													
Yes	28.5	25.8	26.9	29.5	28.9	27.8	29.3	33.0	34.5	34.1	34.9	40.2	40.0
No	28.7	31.0	27.3	29.7	29.4	28.1	26.6	32.2	32.4	33.5	29.0	36.0	43.1
Lifetime illicit drug use													
None	31.1	29.5	29.7	32.9	31.7	29.4	33.0	39.3	38.1	39.5	37.1	42.4	42.3
Marijuana only	27.0	23.5	24.0	25.8	26.3	25.5	27.7	30.2	33.4	29.6	32.0	41.1	40.4
Few pills	29.4	23.3	25.2	26.7	24.2	36.3	26.1	29.1	34.2	32.3	34.2	38.5	43.0
More pills	17.5	21.3	22.2	22.9	25.8	20.0	21.6	25.9	24.9	28.8	26.8	30.8	38.6

Note: See Notes, tables 2.70 and 2.71. Response categories were "very poor," "poor," "fair," "good," "very good," and "no opinion." Readers interested in responses to this question for 1975 through 1990 should consult previous editions of SOURCEBOOK. For survey methodology and definitions of terms, see Appendix 6.

Source: Lloyd D. Johnston, Jerald G. Bachman, and Patrick M. O'Malley, *Monitoring the Future 1991*, p. 138; *1993*, p. 140; *1995*, p. 141; *1997*, p. 136; *1999*, p. 137 (Ann Arbor, MI: Institute for Social Research, University of Michigan); Jerald G. Bachman, Lloyd D. Johnston, and Patrick M. O'Malley, *Monitoring the Future 1992*, p. 139; *1994*, p. 139; *1996*, p. 133; *1998*, p. 136; *2000*, p. 138 (Ann Arbor, MI: Institute for Social Research, University of Michigan); and data provided by the Monitoring the Future Project, Survey Research Center, Lloyd D. Johnston, Jerald G. Bachman, and Patrick M. O'Malley, Principal Investigators. Table adapted by SOURCEBOOK staff. Reprinted by permission.

Table 2.74

High school seniors reporting positive attitudes toward the performance of the U.S. Supreme Court

By sex, race, region, college plans, and illicit drug use, United States, 1991-2003

Question: "Now we'd like you to make some ratings of how good or bad a job you feel each of the following organizations is doing for the country as a whole. . . . How good or bad a job is being done for the country as a whole by. . .the U.S. Supreme Court?"

(Percent responding "good" or "very good")

	Class of 1991 (N=2,582)	Class of 1992 (N=2,684)	Class of 1993 (N=2,773)	Class of 1994 (N=2,642)	Class of 1995 (N=2,658)	Class of 1996 (N=2,455)	Class of 1997 (N=2,648)	Class of 1998 (N=2,608)	Class of 1999 (N=2,357)	Class of 2000 (N=2,216)	Class of 2001 (N=2,201)	Class of 2002 (N=2,250)	Class of 2003 (N=2,523)
Total	44.1%	35.7%	31.0%	31.0%	29.8%	30.4%	30.5%	36.6%	38.9%	38.2%	37.1%	41.5%	38.6%
Sex													
Male	46.2	39.7	34.5	32.6	35.0	35.6	33.3	39.7	43.9	41.9	40.3	42.4	40.8
Female	41.7	32.1	27.8	29.6	24.8	25.7	28.3	33.5	34.9	36.0	34.7	41.7	36.3
Race													
White	47.1	38.4	33.3	32.9	32.5	31.3	33.5	38.1	39.9	40.1	41.1	44.6	42.6
Black	29.9	27.8	23.8	22.9	21.9	27.5	22.3	31.2	32.8	31.0	26.1	31.2	22.0
Region													
Northeast	40.1	31.9	31.5	31.5	26.6	32.7	30.2	31.4	40.4	36.7	35.7	41.6	35.6
North Central	47.9	38.3	33.4	32.2	32.8	27.4	27.8	36.5	42.9	40.1	40.8	41.8	42.9
South	43.9	35.9	28.9	30.3	30.4	34.0	34.0	38.3	35.6	37.2	37.6	43.0	41.6
West	42.8	34.8	31.0	30.2	27.5	25.0	28.7	39.0	38.3	39.2	32.2	38.7	31.4
College plans													
Yes	47.5	37.8	34.0	33.6	30.9	31.6	32.1	38.1	40.2	40.9	39.5	44.3	37.7
No	36.3	31.6	23.3	24.7	27.1	25.9	26.7	31.7	35.7	30.7	30.4	33.2	41.6
Lifetime illicit drug use													
None	46.8	39.3	33.4	32.6	30.7	30.5	31.7	38.8	40.1	39.9	38.0	42.5	40.0
Marijuana only	41.6	31.3	29.6	30.0	29.6	33.1	30.7	33.6	39.4	38.0	36.8	39.9	36.7
Few pills	41.9	30.7	27.6	29.1	34.5	32.5	32.3	34.2	45.3	38.9	37.6	44.9	39.1
More pills	37.2	27.7	27.7	29.3	24.5	26.4	28.6	38.8	31.7	35.0	37.2	39.6	39.2

Note: See Notes, tables 2.70 and 2.71. Response categories were "very poor," "poor," "fair," "good," "very good," and "no opinion." Readers interested in responses to this question for 1975 through 1990 should consult previous editions of SOURCEBOOK. For survey methodology and definitions of terms, see Appendix 6.

Source: Lloyd D. Johnston, Jerald G. Bachman, and Patrick M. O'Malley, *Monitoring the Future 1991*, p. 137; *1993*, p. 139; *1995*, p. 140; *1997*, p. 136; *1999*, p. 137 (Ann Arbor, MI: Institute for Social Research, University of Michigan); Jerald G. Bachman, Lloyd D. Johnston, and Patrick M. O'Malley, *Monitoring the Future 1992*, p. 138; *1994*, p. 138; *1996*, p. 133; *1998*, p. 136; *2000*, p. 138 (Ann Arbor, MI: Institute for Social Research, University of Michigan); and data provided by the Monitoring the Future Project, Survey Research Center, Lloyd D. Johnston, Jerald G. Bachman, and Patrick M. O'Malley, Principal Investigators. Table adapted by SOURCEBOOK staff. Reprinted by permission.

Table 2.75

High school seniors reporting positive attitudes toward the performance of the courts and the justice system in general

By sex, race, region, college plans, and illicit drug use, United States, 1991-2003

Question: "Now we'd like you to make some ratings of how good or bad a job you feel each of the following organizations is doing for the country as a whole. . . . How good or bad a job is being done for the country as a whole by. . .all the courts and the justice system in general?"

(Percent responding "good" or "very good")

	Class of 1991 (N=2,582)	Class of 1992 (N=2,684)	Class of 1993 (N=2,773)	Class of 1994 (N=2,642)	Class of 1995 (N=2,658)	Class of 1996 (N=2,455)	Class of 1997 (N=2,648)	Class of 1998 (N=2,608)	Class of 1999 (N=2,357)	Class of 2000 (N=2,216)	Class of 2001 (N=2,201)	Class of 2002 (N=2,250)	Class of 2003 (N=2,523)
Total	31.2%	23.4%	21.1%	19.3%	20.6%	21.2%	22.4%	25.7%	29.4%	28.9%	30.7%	32.9%	31.7%
Sex													
Male	33.8	25.3	24.0	20.5	22.3	25.7	23.9	27.0	32.1	32.4	31.5	34.4	32.6
Female	28.8	21.5	18.7	18.2	18.6	16.8	20.9	24.4	27.2	26.3	30.4	32.1	31.2
Race													
White	32.5	24.6	22.4	20.5	21.4	21.5	23.5	26.1	29.7	29.5	33.1	34.8	35.5
Black	23.5	18.6	13.6	12.0	17.3	20.8	17.6	23.5	25.5	22.9	22.3	26.6	19.3
Region													
Northeast	31.0	18.1	19.7	18.5	17.6	20.4	23.5	23.3	30.5	29.3	31.1	34.1	29.9
North Central	34.4	24.5	22.6	19.0	23.2	19.5	21.5	26.3	32.3	26.7	32.7	31.2	36.9
South	28.0	24.5	20.8	19.5	20.0	25.2	23.5	26.5	27.3	29.4	30.6	36.6	32.6
West	32.7	24.8	20.6	20.4	20.6	16.3	20.0	26.1	28.0	30.3	28.0	27.9	26.1
College plans													
Yes	32.7	24.0	21.8	20.6	20.4	20.6	22.8	26.1	30.3	30.4	32.4	34.5	31.0
No	27.6	22.8	17.6	16.4	21.0	23.2	21.6	22.9	28.8	25.2	26.2	27.7	35.5
Lifetime illicit drug use													
None	34.3	25.8	23.0	21.0	20.9	19.4	24.1	28.5	31.0	31.6	31.5	33.2	33.9
Marijuana only	29.3	22.0	19.6	18.3	19.5	23.4	21.8	25.0	32.4	28.2	29.6	33.8	30.0
Few pills	27.0	15.4	18.5	16.8	25.2	29.1	19.7	21.0	33.7	32.1	33.9	36.7	31.8
More pills	25.2	19.6	16.9	17.9	18.4	19.7	20.7	25.8	20.4	24.7	29.1	29.1	29.4

Note: See Notes, tables 2.70 and 2.71. Response categories were "very poor," "poor," "fair," "good," "very good," and "no opinion." Readers interested in responses to this question for 1975 through 1990 should consult previous editions of SOURCEBOOK. For survey methodology and definitions of terms, see Appendix 6.

Source: Lloyd D. Johnston, Jerald G. Bachman, and Patrick M. O'Malley, *Monitoring the Future 1991*, p. 137; *1993*, p. 139; *1995*, p. 140; *1997*, p. 136; *1999*, p. 137 (Ann Arbor, MI: Institute for Social Research, University of Michigan); Jerald G. Bachman, Lloyd D. Johnston, and Patrick M. O'Malley, *Monitoring the Future 1992*, p. 138; *1994*, p. 138; *1996*, p. 133; *1998*, p. 136; *2000*, p. 138 (Ann Arbor, MI: Institute for Social Research, University of Michigan); and data provided by the Monitoring the Future Project, Survey Research Center, Lloyd D. Johnston, Jerald G. Bachman, and Patrick M. O'Malley, Principal Investigators. Table adapted by SOURCEBOOK staff. Reprinted by permission.

Table 2.76

Students' perceptions of the harmfulness of alcohol and drug use

By grade level of respondent, 2002-2003[a]

Question: "Do you feel that using. . .is harmful to your health?"

	No harm	Some harm	Harmful	Very harmful
Beer	10.3%	31.7%	27.8%	30.1%
Grades 6 to 8	8.8	27.3	29.2	34.7
Grades 9 to 12	11.8	36.1	26.4	25.6
12th grade	12.7	38.5	24.0	24.7
Wine coolers	22.9	37.0	19.5	20.7
Grades 6 to 8	20.2	33.9	21.8	24.1
Grades 9 to 12	25.5	39.9	17.2	17.3
12th grade	25.0	40.4	17.1	17.5
Liquor	7.9	22.9	31.4	37.8
Grades 6 to 8	6.5	18.7	31.6	43.3
Grades 9 to 12	9.3	27.0	31.2	32.5
12th grade	9.9	29.6	30.5	30.1
Marijuana	10.0	11.8	17.4	60.8
Grades 6 to 8	6.7	6.3	13.5	73.5
Grades 9 to 12	13.2	17.3	21.1	48.4
12th grade	15.0	21.0	22.9	41.0
Cocaine	3.4	2.7	10.7	83.2
Grades 6 to 8	3.2	2.2	9.7	85.0
Grades 9 to 12	3.5	3.3	11.7	81.5
12th grade	4.0	3.7	12.3	80.0
Inhalants	5.5	11.4	22.0	61.2
Grades 6 to 8	6.1	12.9	22.8	58.2
Grades 9 to 12	4.8	9.9	21.2	64.0
12th grade	4.9	8.3	19.5	67.3
Hallucinogens	4.0	5.1	17.1	73.8
Grades 6 to 8	4.0	5.4	18.2	72.3
Grades 9 to 12	3.9	4.8	15.9	75.3
12th grade	4.5	4.7	14.6	76.2
Heroin	3.4	3.1	12.0	81.5
Grades 6 to 8	3.5	3.5	13.1	79.9
Grades 9 to 12	3.4	2.7	10.9	83.1
12th grade	3.9	2.4	10.1	83.6
Steroids	4.4	9.3	24.4	61.9
Grades 6 to 8	4.7	9.6	24.3	61.5
Grades 9 to 12	4.1	9.0	24.6	62.3
12th grade	4.6	7.9	22.9	64.7
Ecstasy	4.1	5.1	15.4	75.5
Grades 6 to 8	4.0	4.9	15.4	75.7
Grades 9 to 12	4.2	5.2	15.4	75.3
12th grade	4.5	5.3	15.8	74.3

Note: See Note, table 2.5.

[a]Percents may not add to 100 because of rounding.

Source: PRIDE Surveys, "2002-2003 PRIDE Surveys National Summary, Grades 6 through 12," Bowling Green, KY: PRIDE Surveys, 2003. (Mimeographed.) P. 180; p. 181, Tables 8.56 and 8.57; p. 182, Tables 8.60 and 8.61; p. 183. Table adapted by SOURCEBOOK staff. Reprinted by permission.

Table 2.77

Teenagers' perceptions of the harmfulness of alcohol and drug use

United States, 2002 and 2003[a]

Question: "How harmful to the health of someone your age is the regular use of each of the following?"

	Very harmful	Fairly harmful	Not too harmful	Not harmful at all	Don't know/ no response
Cocaine					
2002	88%	4%	1%	2%	4%
2003	92	3	2	2	2
Ecstasy					
2002	78	6	2	3	12
2003	84	5	2	2	7
Marijuana					
2002	66	18	9	4	3
2003	75	14	6	3	1
Tobacco					
2002	65	23	6	3	3
2003	70	21	5	3	1
Alcohol					
2002	48	32	14	3	3
2003	49	35	13	2	1

Note: See Note, table 2.3.

[a]Percents may not add to 100 because of rounding.

Source: National Center on Addiction and Substance Abuse at Columbia University, *National Survey of American Attitudes on Substance Abuse VII: Teens, Parents and Siblings* [Online], pp. 36, 37. Available: http://www.casacolumbia.org/usr_doc/ TeenSurvey2002.pdf [Jan. 15, 2003]; and National Center on Addiction and Substance Abuse at Columbia University, *National Survey of American Attitudes on Substance Abuse VIII: Teens and Parents* [Online], p. 47. Available: http://www.casacolumbia.org/ pdshopprov/files/2003_Teen_Survey_8_19_03.pdf [Mar. 1, 2004]. Table adapted by SOURCEBOOK staff. Reprinted by permission.

Table 2.78

Teenagers' perceptions of someone their age smoking, getting drunk, and using drugs

United States, 2004[a]

Question: "Do you think. . .by a teen your age is more likely to make the teen seem cool, or more likely to make the teen seem like a loser?"

	Seem cool	Seem like a loser	Neither[b]	Don't know/ no response
Smoking cigarettes	9%	83%	7%	2%
Regularly getting drunk	11	83	6	1
The use of illegal drugs	8	86	5	1

Note: See Note, table 2.3.

[a]Percents may not add to 100 because of rounding.
[b]Response volunteered.

Source: National Center on Addiction and Substance Abuse at Columbia University, *National Survey of American Attitudes on Substance Abuse IX: Teen Dating Practices and Sexual Activity* [Online], p. 45. Available: http://www.casacolumbia.org/pdshopprov/ files/august_2004_casa_teen_survey.pdf [Aug. 31, 2004]. Table adapted by SOURCEBOOK staff. Reprinted by permission.

Table 2.79

High school seniors' perceptions of the harmfulness of drug use, alcohol use, and cigarette smoking

By type of drug and frequency of use, United States, 1980, 1990, and 1993-2003

Question: "How much do you think people risk harming themselves (physically or in other ways), if they. . .?"

(Percent responding "great risk"[a])

Type of drug and frequency of use	Class of 1980 (N=3,234)	Class of 1990 (N=2,553)	Class of 1993 (N=2,759)	Class of 1994 (N=2,591)	Class of 1995 (N=2,603)	Class of 1996 (N=2,449)	Class of 1997 (N=2,579)	Class of 1998 (N=2,564)	Class of 1999 (N=2,306)	Class of 2000 (N=2,130)	Class of 2001 (N=2,173)	Class of 2002 (N=2,198)	Class of 2003 (N=2,466)
Try marijuana once or twice	10.0%	23.1%	21.9%	19.5%	16.3%	15.6%	14.9%	16.7%	15.7%	13.7%	15.3%	16.1%	16.1%
Smoke marijuana occasionally	14.7	36.9	35.6	30.1	25.6	25.9	24.7	24.4	23.9	23.4	23.5	23.2	26.6
Smoke marijuana regularly	50.4	77.8	72.5	65.0	60.8	59.9	58.1	58.5	57.4	58.3	57.4	53.0	54.9
Try LSD once or twice	43.9	44.7	39.5	38.8	36.4	36.2	34.7	37.4	34.9	34.3	33.2	36.7	36.2
Take LSD regularly	83.0	84.5	79.4	79.1	78.1	77.8	76.6	76.5	76.1	75.9	74.1	73.9	72.3
Try PCP once or twice	NA	55.2	50.8	51.5	49.1	51.0	48.8	46.8	44.8	45.0	46.2	48.3	45.2
Try MDMA (ecstasy) once or twice	NA	NA	NA	NA	NA	NA	33.8	34.5	35.0	37.9	45.7	52.2	56.3
Try cocaine once or twice	31.3	59.4	57.6	57.2	53.7	54.2	53.6	54.6	52.1	51.1	50.7	51.2	51.0
Take cocaine occasionally	NA	73.9	73.3	73.7	70.8	72.1	72.4	70.1	70.1	69.5	69.9	68.3	69.1
Take cocaine regularly	69.2	91.1	90.1	89.3	87.9	88.3	87.1	86.3	85.8	86.2	84.1	84.5	83.0
Try crack once or twice	NA	64.3	57.6	58.4	54.6	56.0	54.0	52.2	48.2	48.4	49.4	50.8	47.3
Take crack occasionally	NA	80.4	73.9	73.8	72.8	71.4	70.3	68.7	67.3	65.8	65.4	65.6	64.0
Take crack regularly	NA	91.6	87.5	89.6	88.6	88.0	86.2	85.3	85.4	85.3	85.8	84.1	83.2
Try cocaine powder once or twice	NA	53.9	53.2	55.4	52.0	53.2	51.4	48.5	46.1	47.0	49.0	49.5	46.2
Take cocaine powder occasionally	NA	71.1	68.6	70.6	69.1	68.8	67.7	65.4	64.2	64.7	63.2	64.4	61.4
Take cocaine powder regularly	NA	90.2	87.0	88.6	87.8	86.8	86.0	84.1	84.6	85.5	84.4	84.2	82.3
Try heroin once or twice	52.1	55.4	50.7	52.8	50.9	52.5	56.7	57.8	56.0	54.2	55.6	56.0	58.0
Take heroin occasionally	70.9	76.6	72.0	72.1	71.0	74.8	76.3	76.9	77.3	74.6	75.9	76.6	78.5
Take heroin regularly	86.2	90.2	88.3	88.0	87.2	89.5	88.9	89.1	89.9	89.2	88.3	88.5	89.3
Try amphetamines once or twice	29.7	32.2	31.3	31.4	28.8	30.8	31.0	35.3	32.2	32.6	34.7	34.4	36.8
Take amphetamines regularly	69.1	71.2	69.9	67.0	65.9	66.8	66.0	67.7	66.4	66.3	67.1	64.8	65.6
Try crystal methamphetamine (ice) once or twice	NA	NA	57.5	58.3	54.4	55.3	54.4	52.7	51.2	51.3	52.7	53.8	51.2
Try barbiturates once or twice	30.9	32.4	29.2	29.9	26.3	29.1	26.9	29.0	26.1	25.0	25.7	26.2	27.9
Take barbiturates regularly	72.2	70.2	66.1	63.3	61.6	60.4	56.8	56.3	54.1	52.3	50.3	49.3	49.6
Try one or two drinks of an alcoholic beverage (beer, wine, liquor)	3.8	8.3	8.2	7.6	5.9	7.3	6.7	8.0	8.3	6.4	8.7	7.6	8.4
Take one or two drinks nearly every day	20.3	31.3	28.2	27.0	24.8	25.1	24.8	24.3	21.8	21.7	23.4	21.0	20.1
Take four or five drinks nearly every day	65.7	70.9	67.8	66.2	62.8	65.6	63.0	62.1	61.1	59.9	60.7	58.8	57.8
Have five or more drinks once or twice each weekend	35.9	47.1	48.3	46.5	45.2	49.5	43.0	42.8	43.1	42.7	43.6	42.2	43.5
Smoke one or more packs of cigarettes per day	63.7	68.2	69.5	67.6	65.6	68.2	68.7	70.8	70.8	73.1	73.3	74.2	72.1
Take steroids	NA	69.9	69.1	66.1	66.4	67.6	67.2	68.1	62.1	57.9	58.9	57.1	55.0

Note: These data are from a series of nationwide surveys of high school seniors conducted by the University of Michigan's Institute for Social Research for the National Institute on Drug Abuse from 1975 through 2003. The survey design is a multistage random sample of high school seniors in public and private schools. Depending on the survey year, approximately 65% of the schools initially invited to participate agreed to do so. Completed questionnaires were obtained from approximately 83% of all sampled students in participating schools each year. Beginning in 1991, eighth and tenth grade students also were included in the survey. All percentages reported are based on weighted cases; the Ns that are shown in the tables also refer to the number of weighted cases. Readers interested in responses to this question for 1975 through 1979, 1981 through 1989, 1991, and 1992 should consult previous editions of SOURCEBOOK. For survey methodology and definitions of terms, see Appendix 6.

[a]Answer alternatives were: (1) no risk, (2) slight risk, (3) moderate risk, (4) great risk, and (5) can't say, drug unfamiliar.

Source: Lloyd D. Johnston et al., *Monitoring the Future National Survey Results on Drug Use, 1975-2003*, Vol. 1, Secondary School Students (Bethesda, MD: U.S. Department of Health and Human Services, 2004), pp. 314, 315. Table adapted by SOURCEBOOK staff.

Table 2.80

Eighth and tenth graders' perceptions of the harmfulness of drug use, alcohol use, and cigarette smoking

By type of drug and frequency of use, United States, 1991, 1995, and 2000-2003

Question: "How much do you think people risk harming themselves (physically or in other ways), if they . . . ?"

(Percent responding "great risk"[a])

Type of drug and frequency of use	Eighth graders 1991 (N=17,400)	1995 (N=17,501)	2000 (N=16,700)	2001 (N=16,200)	2002 (N=15,100)	2003 (N=16,500)	Tenth graders 1991 (N=14,700)	1995 (N=17,006)	2000 (N=14,300)	2001 (N=14,000)	2002 (N=14,300)	2003 (N=15,800)
Try marijuana once or twice	40.4%	28.9%	29.0%	27.7%	28.2%	30.2%	30.0%	21.5%	18.5%	17.9%	19.9%	21.1%
Smoke marijuana occasionally	57.9	45.9	47.4	46.3	46.0	48.6	48.6	35.4	32.4	31.2	32.0	34.9
Smoke marijuana regularly	83.8	73.0	74.8	72.2	71.7	74.2	82.1	67.9	64.7	62.8	60.8	63.9
Try inhalants once or twice[b]	35.9	36.4	41.2	45.6	42.8	40.3	37.8	41.6	46.6	49.9	48.7	47.7
Take inhalants regularly[b]	65.6	64.8	69.9	71.6	69.9	67.4	69.8	71.8	75.0	76.4	73.4	72.2
Try LSD once or twice[c]	NA	36.7	34.0	31.6	29.6	27.9	NA	44.7	43.0	41.3	40.1	40.8
Take LSD regularly[c]	NA	64.4	57.5	52.9	49.3	48.2	NA	75.5	72.0	68.8	64.9	63.0
Try MDMA (ecstasy) once or twice[d]	NA	NA	NA	35.8	38.9	41.9	NA	NA	NA	39.4	43.5	49.7
Take MDMA (ecstasy) occasionally[d]	NA	NA	NA	55.5	61.8	65.8	NA	NA	NA	64.8	67.3	71.7
Try crack once or twice[b]	62.8	50.8	48.5	48.6	47.4	48.7	70.4	60.9	56.1	57.1	57.4	57.6
Take crack occasionally[b]	82.2	72.1	70.1	70.0	69.7	70.3	87.4	81.2	76.9	77.3	75.7	76.4
Try cocaine powder once or twice[b]	55.5	44.9	43.3	43.9	43.2	43.7	59.1	53.5	48.8	50.6	51.3	51.8
Take cocaine powder occasionally[b]	77.0	66.4	65.5	65.8	64.9	65.8	82.2	75.6	70.9	72.3	71.0	71.4
Try heroin once or twice without using a needle[c]	NA	60.1	62.0	61.1	62.6	62.7	NA	70.7	71.7	72.0	72.2	70.6
Take heroin occasionally without using a needle[c]	NA	76.8	78.6	78.5	78.5	77.8	NA	85.1	85.2	85.4	83.4	83.5
Try one or two drinks of an alcoholic beverage (beer, wine, liquor)	11.0	11.6	11.9	12.2	12.5	12.6	9.0	9.3	9.6	9.8	11.5	11.5
Take one or two drinks nearly every day	31.8	30.5	30.4	30.0	29.6	29.9	36.1	31.7	32.3	31.5	31.0	30.9
Have five or more drinks once or twice each weekend	59.1	54.1	55.9	56.1	56.4	56.5	54.7	52.0	51.0	50.7	51.7	51.6
Smoke one or more packs of cigarettes per day[b]	51.6	49.8	58.8	57.1	57.5	57.7	60.3	57.0	65.9	64.7	64.3	65.7

Note: See Note, table 2.79. Readers interested in responses to this question for 1992 through 1994, and 1996 through 1999 should consult previous editions of SOURCEBOOK. For survey methodology and definitions of terms, see Appendix 6.

Source: Lloyd D. Johnston et al., *Monitoring the Future National Survey Results on Drug Use, 1975-2003*, Vol. 1, Secondary School Students (Bethesda, MD: U.S. Department of Health and Human Services, 2004), p. 313. Table adapted by SOURCEBOOK staff.

[a]Answer alternatives were: (1) no risk, (2) slight risk, (3) moderate risk, (4) great risk, and (5) can't say, drug unfamiliar.
[b]Data for 2000-2003 are based on two-thirds of N indicated due to changes in questionnaire forms.
[c]Data for 1995 are based on one of two forms; N is one-half of N indicated. Data for 2000-2003 are based on one-third of N indicated due to changes in questionnaire forms.
[d]Data based on one-third of N indicated due to changes in questionnaire forms.

Table 2.81

Young adults' perceptions of the harmfulness of drug use, alcohol use, and cigarette smoking

By type of drug, frequency of use, and age group, United States, 1991-2003

Question: "How much do you think people risk harming themselves (physically or in other ways), if they...?"

(Percent responding "great risk"[a])

Age groups

Type of drug and frequency of use	1991 (N=533)	1992 (N=527)	1993 (N=480)	1994 (N=490)	1995 (N=500)	1996 (N=469)	1997 (N=465)	1998 (N=431)	1999 (N=447)	2000 (N=424)	2001 (N=430)	2002 (N=395)	2003 (N=402)
Try marijuana once or twice	19.1%	19.7%	19.4%	18.8%	13.3%	16.9%	14.8%	13.4%	12.5%	14.3%	11.9%	13.3%	17.1%
Smoke marijuana occasionally	30.2	29.5	30.3	31.3	25.5	25.6	22.0	22.0	19.8	25.8	18.0	21.0	24.1
Smoke marijuana regularly	75.0	69.3	69.2	65.0	62.1	61.3	60.6	53.4	55.2	58.0	49.6	56.7	57.8
Try LSD once or twice	48.0	45.6	42.4	42.3	40.3	44.4	40.1	38.7	38.1	37.9	37.5	35.3	39.7
Take LSD regularly	86.6	87.0	81.3	81.0	80.5	82.4	83.6	78.6	82.2	81.6	79.2	81.1	78.6
Try MDMA (ecstasy) once or twice	48.8	46.4	45.0	51.1	48.3	46.7	45.5	42.7	37.6	37.9	40.5	46.8	50.1
Try cocaine once or twice	58.7	56.1	60.5	63.8	57.7	61.9	55.5	55.4	52.8	56.7	48.9	55.5	55.0
Take cocaine occasionally	72.6	74.9	75.4	78.0	73.4	76.6	76.1	71.2	68.0	72.4	70.0	69.9	70.3
Take cocaine regularly	93.5	92.9	91.7	92.2	91.5	92.2	91.6	88.7	88.5	90.7	85.1	88.3	87.4
Try crack once or twice	66.9	65.4	63.5	70.1	61.9	65.2	62.0	59.3	56.1	52.9	54.1	54.1	55.1
Take crack occasionally	82.7	81.9	83.6	84.3	78.8	83.5	79.1	79.1	75.5	74.9	72.3	75.3	75.3
Take crack regularly	95.6	93.4	96.2	96.0	94.2	94.7	93.3	92.8	92.3	91.1	89.6	91.1	93.8
Try heroin once or twice	59.9	59.8	58.9	60.8	58.9	61.0	63.9	60.7	63.5	63.2	64.0	63.1	64.6
Take heroin occasionally	80.2	81.6	78.8	79.0	77.9	82.1	84.7	80.4	82.5	82.0	83.6	82.2	84.9
Take heroin regularly	91.5	92.2	89.2	91.2	89.9	94.0	93.7	92.4	92.8	94.0	91.3	92.6	93.9
Try amphetamines once or twice	32.8	34.5	33.3	36.3	32.9	36.8	30.1	31.7	33.7	35.0	34.2	38.1	40.2
Take amphetamines regularly	77.1	73.5	73.5	71.6	72.2	75.8	72.3	71.9	72.4	73.4	71.1	72.7	75.0
Try crystal methamphetamine (ice)	58.6	57.7	57.5	61.4	58.9	61.1	56.4	55.8	50.6	49.2	52.5	56.5	60.0
Try barbiturates once or twice	33.5	33.5	33.4	35.0	30.5	34.1	31.4	27.7	28.5	30.3	30.0	30.7	32.7
Take barbiturates regularly	75.5	73.6	71.1	69.4	66.4	70.7	69.5	65.1	64.7	64.6	61.8	64.5	63.8
Try one or two drinks of an alcoholic beverage (beer, wine, liquor)	5.4	5.8	6.6	6.5	4.5	3.3	3.2	4.2	5.7	5.4	4.8	6.6	7.5
Take one or two drinks nearly every day	29.1	30.2	28.0	27.5	24.0	23.0	24.2	22.1	23.9	22.1	19.6	22.7	19.8
Take four or five drinks nearly every day	75.5	71.8	72.1	70.3	72.5	68.5	71.4	70.4	69.9	69.9	64.5	71.1	66.4
Have five or more drinks once or twice each weekend	40.8	41.8	42.4	41.9	39.9	40.7	36.6	42.0	37.2	38.9	37.2	37.8	40.4
Smoke one or more packs of cigarettes per day	77.9	72.6	76.0	71.2	71.6	73.8	76.3	77.2	75.7	77.1	76.6	80.6	77.8

Note: See Note, table 2.79. "Young adults" includes high school graduates 1 to 10 years beyond high school. Readers interested in responses to this question for 1980 through 1990 should consult previous editions of SOURCEBOOK. Some data have been revised by the Source and may differ from previous editions of SOURCEBOOK. For survey methodology and definitions of terms, see Appendix 6.

Source: Lloyd D. Johnston et al., *Monitoring the Future National Survey Results on Drug Use, 1975-2003*, Vol. 2, College Students and Adults Ages 19-40 (Bethesda, MD: U.S. Department of Health and Human Services, 2004), pp. 172-175. Table adapted by SOURCEBOOK staff.

[a]Answer alternatives were: (1) no risk, (2) slight risk, (3) moderate risk, (4) great risk, and (5) can't say, drug unfamiliar.

	23 to 26 years old								27 to 30 years old							
	1996 (N=438)	1997 (N=420)	1998 (N=413)	1999 (N=418)	2000 (N=400)	2001 (N=392)	2002 (N=382)	2003 (N=401)	1996 (N=422)	1997 (N=434)	1998 (N=416)	1999 (N=400)	2000 (N=377)	2001 (N=384)	2002 (N=369)	2003 (N=380)
	18.5%	15.1%	16.7%	16.4%	13.1%	13.0%	15.1%	15.3%	16.2%	16.1%	16.4%	16.1%	14.4%	17.3%	16.2%	18.0%
	27.3	26.4	26.8	26.4	24.9	20.5	24.5	22.2	28.1	26.0	25.8	25.3	25.8	25.0	30.2	27.9
	62.7	64.0	62.7	60.1	60.3	55.1	53.7	56.7	67.3	65.0	63.6	66.1	64.0	61.7	63.5	64.7
	46.1	46.6	45.7	49.3	44.9	48.5	45.7	43.8	50.1	52.0	52.0	49.9	46.4	46.7	44.9	47.5
	84.7	85.6	82.1	85.4	84.1	86.0	85.3	84.3	87.0	87.2	90.5	87.8	85.3	86.9	85.3	87.5
	50.4	50.5	47.7	50.0	46.7	45.7	45.6	45.9	50.6	48.8	50.4	50.9	48.9	53.6	52.0	58.8
	57.2	63.1	60.2	62.6	63.1	62.4	61.0	55.4	53.6	54.6	60.5	61.7	59.9	60.9	58.8	56.4
	71.3	76.5	74.2	77.8	76.2	74.2	75.4	68.3	67.8	73.8	73.2	75.4	76.5	78.1	74.3	72.6
	90.6	93.2	92.9	92.7	92.9	91.9	91.5	88.5	91.6	92.7	93.0	92.4	92.3	94.5	91.2	92.9
	68.6	64.7	67.3	64.6	63.2	59.8	60.9	58.5	66.7	68.5	66.5	65.0	62.9	69.3	67.4	66.0
	85.9	80.8	84.2	81.6	84.0	80.1	82.2	77.1	81.3	85.3	81.7	79.8	81.6	84.4	81.5	81.9
	96.1	91.4	95.6	94.4	95.6	93.4	94.7	92.2	94.3	96.0	94.3	95.2	93.5	96.8	94.2	94.4
	63.5	67.3	67.3	68.0	70.7	71.9	69.8	70.6	66.4	67.9	69.7	70.1	67.4	68.2	70.9	72.3
	82.4	86.5	83.9	88.5	86.6	88.4	90.0	88.3	83.8	85.8	86.6	87.1	86.5	86.4	87.9	87.4
	92.7	94.4	93.4	93.7	94.8	95.9	96.3	96.5	92.1	93.8	95.0	93.7	94.2	94.5	95.9	94.9
	34.9	37.8	40.9	41.8	39.9	41.6	38.0	38.3	36.2	34.5	37.6	36.3	39.4	38.5	39.0	40.5
	78.5	79.1	77.5	78.7	79.0	77.7	77.9	80.1	75.6	77.4	81.1	82.6	80.8	79.9	79.8	81.5
	64.1	60.7	58.2	61.3	60.1	59.2	57.7	58.6	59.1	59.8	59.9	61.0	59.7	66.4	62.5	66.6
	35.8	37.3	40.3	39.4	37.0	38.5	34.7	36.5	37.2	35.7	36.7	35.2	36.3	40.9	37.3	38.6
	77.1	75.2	73.9	75.1	73.8	73.1	73.1	72.8	74.1	77.1	79.9	80.7	75.5	78.2	75.4	79.0
	4.8	4.4	4.4	6.6	3.5	5.5	5.1	5.7	4.7	4.0	6.2	5.9	4.7	5.5	3.1	6.9
	22.0	20.2	21.0	26.0	21.7	23.5	23.4	19.1	24.0	24.8	20.8	25.3	22.0	22.7	21.7	21.4
	72.0	75.1	69.3	72.8	71.7	75.8	74.9	71.1	76.1	79.3	75.7	75.1	77.4	72.8	76.2	70.6
	39.1	37.4	41.1	40.2	34.9	39.0	36.8	36.3	41.5	40.0	40.2	41.9	37.9	41.6	40.6	42.5
	76.0	77.6	76.5	80.9	79.7	83.9	85.1	83.6	73.0	80.3	80.9	80.7	78.4	82.7	80.6	82.0

Table 2.82

Respondents' perceptions of the harmfulness of selected drug use behaviors

By age group, United States, 2002 and 2003

Question: "How much do you think people risk harming themselves physically and in other ways when they do each of the following activities?"

(Percent responding "great risk"[a])

	Total 2002	Total 2003	12 to 17 years 2002	12 to 17 years 2003	18 to 25 years 2002	18 to 25 years 2003	26 years and older 2002	26 years and older 2003
Marijuana								
Smoke once a month	38.3%	39.6%	32.4%	34.9%	23.5%	24.8%	41.7%	42.9%
Smoke once or twice a week	51.3	52.8	51.5	54.4	35.5	36.8	54.1	55.4
Cocaine								
Use once a month	71.5	71.0	50.5	51.4	64.1	63.6	75.7	75.0
Use once or twice a week	89.4	89.0	79.8	80.7	87.2	86.6	91.1	90.6
Heroin								
Try once or twice	82.4	82.2	58.5	58.8	78.0	77.5	86.5	86.2
Use once or twice a week	93.9	93.9	82.5	82.6	93.6	93.5	95.5	95.5
LSD								
Try once or twice	73.7	73.4	52.6	53.4	62.4	63.0	78.5	77.9
Use once or twice a week	88.8	88.7	76.2	76.9	84.8	85.3	91.2	90.9
Alcohol								
Four or five drinks nearly every day	69.4	68.9	62.2	61.6	62.1	61.1	71.7	71.2
Five or more drinks once or twice a week	42.3	41.7	38.2	38.5	33.2	31.9	44.5	43.9
Cigarettes								
Smoke one or more packs per day	71.1	71.4	63.1	64.2	65.2	65.7	73.3	73.4

Note: These data are from the 2002 and 2003 National Survey on Drug Use and Health (NSDUH). The NSDUH is an annual survey of the civilian, noninstitutionalized population of the United States age 12 and older, and is sponsored by the U.S. Department of Health and Human Services, Substance Abuse and Mental Health Services Administration. Prior to 2002, the survey was called the National Household Survey on Drug Abuse (NHSDA). Due to methodological changes beginning with the 2002 NSDUH, estimates from the 2002 and 2003 surveys should not be compared with estimates from 2001 and earlier NHSDAs. For the 2002 NSDUH, a response rate of 78.9% yielded 68,126 completed interviews. For the 2003 NSDUH, a response rate of 77.4% yielded 67,784 completed interviews. For information on survey methodology, see Appendix 7.

[a]Answer alternatives to the question were "no risk," "slight risk," "moderate risk," and "great risk."

Source: U.S. Department of Health and Human Services, Substance Abuse and Mental Health Services Administration, *Results from the 2003 National Survey on Drug Use and Health: National Findings* (Rockville, MD: U.S. Department of Health and Human Services, 2004), p. 225. Table adapted by SOURCEBOOK staff.

Table 2.83

High school seniors' perceptions of availability of drugs

By type of drug, United States, 1980, 1990, and 1993-2003

Question: "How difficult do you think it would be for you to get each of the following types of drugs, if you wanted some?"

(Percent responding "fairly easy" or "very easy"[a])

Type of drug	Class of 1980 (N=3,240)	Class of 1990 (N=2,549)	Class of 1993 (N=2,670)	Class of 1994 (N=2,526)	Class of 1995 (N=2,552)	Class of 1996 (N=2,340)	Class of 1997 (N=2,517)	Class of 1998 (N=2,520)	Class of 1999 (N=2,215)	Class of 2000 (N=2,095)	Class of 2001 (N=2,120)	Class of 2002 (N=2,138)	Class of 2003 (N=2,391)
Marijuana	89.0%	84.4%	83.0%	85.5%	88.5%	88.7%	89.6%	90.4%	88.9%	88.5%	88.5%	87.2%	87.1%
Amyl and butyl nitrites	NA	24.4	25.9	26.7	26.0	23.9	23.8	25.1	21.4	23.3	22.5	22.3	19.7
LSD	35.3	40.7	49.2	50.8	53.8	51.3	50.7	48.8	44.7	46.9	44.7	39.6	33.6
PCP	NA	27.7	31.7	31.4	31.0	30.5	30.0	30.7	26.7	28.8	27.2	25.8	21.9
Other psychedelics/hallucinogens[b]	35.0	28.3	33.5	33.8	35.8	33.9	33.9	35.1	29.5	34.5	48.5	47.7	47.2
MDMA (ecstasy)	NA	22.0	28.1	31.2	34.2	36.9	38.8	38.2	40.1	51.4	61.5	59.1	57.5
Cocaine powder	NA	49.0	45.4	43.7	43.8	44.4	43.3	45.7	43.7	44.6	40.7	40.2	37.4
Crack	NA	42.4	43.6	40.5	41.9	40.7	40.6	43.8	41.1	42.6	40.2	38.5	35.3
Cocaine	47.9	54.5	48.5	46.6	47.7	48.1	48.5	51.3	47.6	47.8	46.2	44.6	43.3
Heroin	21.2	31.9	33.7	34.1	35.1	32.2	33.8	35.6	32.1	33.5	32.3	29.0	27.9
Other narcotics (including methadone)	29.4	38.1	37.5	38.0	39.8	40.0	38.9	42.8	40.8	43.9	40.5	44.0	39.3
Amphetamines	61.3	59.7	61.5	62.0	62.8	59.4	59.8	60.8	58.1	57.1	57.1	57.4	55.0
Crystal methamphetamine (ice)	NA	24.1	26.6	25.6	27.0	26.9	27.6	29.8	27.6	27.8	28.3	28.3	26.1
Barbiturates	49.1	45.9	44.5	43.3	42.3	41.4	40.0	40.7	37.9	37.4	35.7	36.6	35.3
Tranquilizers	59.1	44.7	41.1	39.2	37.8	36.0	35.4	36.2	32.7	33.8	33.1	32.9	29.8
Steroids	NA	NA	44.8	42.9	45.5	40.3	41.7	44.5	44.6	44.8	44.4	45.5	40.7

Note: See Note, table 2.79. Readers interested in responses to this question for 1975 through 1979, 1981 through 1989, 1991, and 1992 should consult previous editions of SOURCEBOOK. For survey methodology and definitions of terms, see Appendix 6.

Source: Lloyd D. Johnston et al., *Monitoring the Future National Survey Results on Drug Use, 1975-2003*, Vol. 1, Secondary School Students (Bethesda, MD: U.S. Department of Health and Human Services, 2004), p. 365. Table adapted by SOURCEBOOK staff.

[a]Answer alternatives were: (1) probably impossible, (2) very difficult, (3) fairly difficult, (4) fairly easy, and (5) very easy.
[b]In 2001, the question text was changed from "other psychedelics" to "other hallucinogens" and "shrooms" was added to the list of examples. These changes likely explain the increase in the 2001 result.

Table 2.84

Eighth and tenth graders' perceptions of availability of drugs

By type of drug, United States, 1992, 1995, and 2000-2003

Question: "How difficult do you think it would be for you to get each of the following types of drugs, if you wanted some?"

(Percent responding "fairly easy" or "very easy"[a])

Type of drug	Eighth graders 1992 (N=8,355)	1995 (N=15,496)	2000 (N=15,180)	2001 (N=14,804)	2002 (N=13,972)	2003 (N=15,583)	Tenth graders 1992 (N=7,014)	1995 (N=16,209)	2000 (N=13,690)	2001 (N=13,518)	2002 (N=13,694)	2003 (N=15,225)
Marijuana	42.3%	52.4%	47.0%	48.1%	46.6%	44.8%	65.2%	78.1%	77.7%	77.4%	75.9%	73.9%
LSD	21.5	23.5	17.0	17.6	15.2	14.0	33.6	39.8	32.9	31.2	26.8	23.1
PCP[b]	18.0	19.0	16.0	15.4	14.1	13.7	23.7	24.7	25.0	21.6	20.8	19.4
MDMA (ecstasy)[c]	NA	NA	NA	23.8	22.8	21.6	NA	NA	NA	41.4	41.0	36.3
Crack	25.6	28.7	24.9	24.4	23.7	22.5	33.7	34.6	34.0	30.6	31.3	29.6
Cocaine powder	25.7	27.8	23.9	23.9	22.5	21.6	35.0	35.3	34.5	31.0	31.8	29.6
Heroin	19.7	21.1	16.5	16.9	16.0	15.6	24.3	24.6	22.3	20.1	19.9	18.8
Other narcotics[b]	19.8	20.3	15.6	15.0	14.7	15.0	26.9	27.8	27.2	25.8	25.4	23.5
Amphetamines	32.2	33.4	25.5	26.2	24.4	24.4	43.4	47.7	40.9	40.6	39.6	36.1
Crystal methamphetamine (ice)[b]	16.0	16.0	14.9	13.9	13.3	14.1	18.8	20.7	22.8	19.9	20.5	19.0
Barbiturates	27.4	26.5	19.7	20.7	19.4	19.3	38.0	38.8	32.4	32.8	32.4	28.8
Tranquilizers	22.9	21.3	16.2	17.8	16.9	17.3	31.6	30.6	27.6	28.5	28.3	25.6
Alcohol	76.2	74.9	70.6	70.6	67.9	67.0	88.6	89.7	87.7	87.7	84.8	83.4
Steroids	24.0	23.8	22.3	23.1	22.0	21.7	37.6	34.8	35.4	33.1	33.2	30.6

Note: See Note, table 2.79. Readers interested in responses to this question for 1993, 1994, and 1996 through 1999 should consult previous editions of SOURCEBOOK. For survey methodology and definitions of terms, see Appendix 6.

Source: Lloyd D. Johnston et al., *Monitoring the Future National Survey Results on Drug Use, 1975-2003*, Vol. 1, Secondary School Students (Bethesda, MD: U.S. Department of Health and Human Services, 2004), p. 364. Table adapted by SOURCEBOOK staff.

[a]Answer alternatives were: (1) probably impossible, (2) very difficult, (3) fairly difficult, (4) fairly easy, (5) very easy, and (6) can't say, drug unfamiliar.
[b]Beginning in 1995, data are based on one of two questionnaire forms; N is one-half of N indicated.
[c]Data are based on one of two questionnaire forms; N is one-half of N indicated.

Table 2.85

High school seniors disapproving of drug use, alcohol use, and cigarette smoking

By type of drug and frequency of use, United States, 1980, 1990, and 1993-2003

Question: "Do you disapprove of people (who are 18 or older) doing each of the following?"

(Percent responding "disapprove" or "strongly disapprove"[a])

Type of drug and frequency of use	Class of 1980 (N=3,261)	Class of 1990 (N=2,566)	Class of 1993 (N=2,723)	Class of 1994 (N=2,588)	Class of 1995 (N=2,603)	Class of 1996 (N=2,399)	Class of 1997 (N=2,601)	Class of 1998 (N=2,545)	Class of 1999 (N=2,310)	Class of 2000 (N=2,150)	Class of 2001 (N=2,144)	Class of 2002 (N=2,160)	Class of 2003 (N=2,442)
Try marijuana once or twice	39.0%	67.8%	63.3%	57.6%	56.7%	52.5%	51.0%	51.6%	48.8%	52.5%	49.1%	51.6%	53.4%
Smoke marijuana occasionally	49.7	80.5	75.5	68.9	66.7	62.9	63.2	64.4	62.5	65.8	63.2	63.4	64.2
Smoke marijuana regularly	74.6	91.0	87.6	82.3	81.9	80.0	78.8	81.2	78.6	79.7	79.3	78.3	78.7
Try LSD once or twice	87.3	89.8	85.9	82.5	81.1	79.6	80.5	82.1	83.0	82.4	81.8	84.6	85.5
Take LSD regularly	96.7	96.3	95.8	94.3	92.5	93.2	92.9	93.5	94.3	94.2	94.0	94.0	94.4
Try MDMA (ecstasy) once or twice	NA	NA	NA	NA	NA	NA	82.2	82.5	82.1	81.0	79.5	83.6	84.7
Try cocaine once or twice	76.3	91.5	92.7	91.6	90.3	90.0	88.0	89.5	89.1	88.2	88.1	89.0	89.3
Take cocaine regularly	91.1	96.7	97.5	96.6	96.1	95.6	96.0	95.6	94.9	95.5	94.9	95.0	95.8
Try crack once or twice	NA	92.3	89.9	89.5	91.4	87.4	87.0	86.7	87.6	87.5	87.0	87.8	86.6
Take crack occasionally	NA	94.3	92.8	92.8	94.0	91.2	91.3	90.9	92.3	91.9	91.6	91.5	90.8
Take crack regularly	NA	94.9	93.4	93.1	94.1	93.0	92.3	91.9	93.2	92.8	92.2	92.4	91.2
Try cocaine powder once or twice	NA	87.9	86.6	87.1	88.3	83.1	83.0	83.1	84.3	84.1	83.3	83.8	83.6
Take cocaine powder occasionally	NA	92.1	91.2	91.0	92.7	89.7	89.3	88.7	90.0	90.3	89.8	90.2	88.9
Take cocaine powder regularly	NA	93.7	93.0	92.5	93.8	92.9	91.5	91.1	92.3	92.6	92.5	92.2	90.7
Try heroin once or twice	93.5	95.1	94.4	93.2	92.8	92.1	92.3	93.7	93.5	93.0	93.1	94.1	94.1
Take heroin occasionally	96.7	96.7	97.0	96.2	95.7	95.0	95.4	96.1	95.7	96.0	95.4	95.6	95.9
Take heroin regularly	97.6	97.5	97.5	97.1	96.4	96.3	96.4	96.6	96.4	96.6	96.2	96.2	97.1
Try amphetamines once or twice	75.4	85.3	84.2	81.3	82.2	79.9	81.3	82.5	81.9	82.1	82.3	83.8	85.8
Take amphetamines regularly	93.0	95.5	96.0	94.1	94.3	93.5	94.3	94.0	93.7	94.1	93.4	93.5	94.0
Try barbiturates once or twice	83.9	90.5	89.7	87.5	87.3	84.9	86.4	86.0	86.6	85.9	85.9	86.6	87.8
Take barbiturates regularly	95.4	96.4	97.0	96.1	95.2	94.8	95.3	94.6	94.7	95.2	94.5	94.7	94.4
Try one or two drinks of an alcoholic beverage (beer, wine, liquor)	16.0	29.4	30.1	28.4	27.3	26.5	26.1	24.5	24.6	25.2	26.6	26.3	27.2
Take one or two drinks nearly every day	69.0	77.9	77.8	73.1	73.3	70.8	70.0	69.4	67.2	70.0	69.2	69.1	68.9
Take four or five drinks nearly every day	90.8	91.9	90.6	89.8	88.8	89.4	88.6	86.7	86.9	88.4	86.4	87.5	86.3
Have five or more drinks once or twice each weekend	55.6	68.9	70.1	65.1	66.7	64.7	65.0	63.8	62.7	65.2	62.9	64.7	64.2
Smoke one or more packs of cigarettes per day	70.8	72.8	70.6	69.8	68.2	67.2	67.1	68.8	69.5	70.1	71.6	73.6	74.8
Take steroids	NA	90.8	92.1	91.9	91.0	91.7	91.4	90.8	88.9	88.8	86.4	86.8	86.0

Note: See Note, table 2.79. Readers interested in responses to this question for 1975 through 1979, 1981 through 1989, 1991, and 1992 should consult previous editions of SOURCEBOOK. For survey methodology and definitions of terms, see Appendix 6.

Source: Lloyd D. Johnston et al., *Monitoring the Future National Survey Results on Drug Use, 1975-2003*, Vol. 1, Secondary School Students (Bethesda, MD: U.S. Department of Health and Human Services, 2004), pp. 317, 318. Table adapted by SOURCEBOOK staff.

[a] Answer alternatives were: (1) don't disapprove, (2) disapprove, and (3) strongly disapprove.

Table 2.86

Eighth and tenth graders disapproving of drug use, alcohol use, and cigarette smoking

By type of drug and frequency of use, United States, 1991, 1995, and 2000-2003

Question: "Do you disapprove of people who . . .?"

(Percent responding "disapprove" or "strongly disapprove"[a])

Type of drug and frequency of use	Eighth graders						Tenth graders					
	1991 (N=17,400)	1995 (N=17,600)	2000 (N=16,700)	2001 (N=16,200)	2002 (N=15,100)	2003 (N=16,500)	1991 (N=14,800)	1995 (N=17,000)	2000 (N=14,300)	2001 (N=14,000)	2002 (N=14,300)	2003 (N=15,800)
Try marijuana once or twice	84.6%	70.7%	72.5%	72.4%	73.3%	73.8%	74.6%	59.8%	54.9%	54.8%	57.8%	58.1%
Smoke marijuana occasionally	89.5	79.7	80.6	80.6	80.9	81.5	83.7	70.0	67.2	66.2	68.3	68.4
Smoke marijuana regularly	92.1	85.1	85.3	84.5	85.3	85.7	90.4	81.1	79.1	78.0	78.6	78.8
Try inhalants once or twice[b]	84.9	81.8	85.4	86.6	86.1	85.1	85.2	84.5	87.5	87.8	88.6	87.7
Take inhalants regularly[b]	90.6	88.8	90.2	90.5	90.4	89.8	91.0	90.9	91.8	91.3	91.8	91.0
Try LSD once or twice[c]	NA	71.6	66.7	64.6	62.6	61.0	NA	77.9	77.0	75.4	74.6	74.4
Take LSD regularly[c]	NA	75.8	69.3	67.0	65.5	63.5	NA	84.8	82.1	80.8	79.4	77.6
Try MDMA (ecstasy) once or twice[d]	NA	NA	NA	69.0	74.3	77.7	NA	NA	NA	72.6	77.4	81.0
Take MDMA (ecstasy) occasionally[d]	NA	NA	NA	73.6	78.6	81.3	NA	NA	NA	81.0	84.6	86.3
Try crack once or twice[b]	91.7	85.9	85.4	86.0	86.2	86.4	92.5	88.7	87.1	86.9	88.0	87.6
Take crack occasionally[b]	93.3	89.8	88.8	89.8	89.6	89.8	94.3	91.7	90.9	90.6	91.0	91.0
Try cocaine powder once or twice[b]	91.2	85.3	84.8	85.6	85.8	85.6	90.8	86.8	84.8	85.3	86.4	85.9
Take cocaine powder occasionally[b]	93.1	89.7	88.8	89.6	89.9	89.8	94.0	91.4	89.9	90.2	89.9	90.4
Try heroin once or twice without using a needle[c]	NA	85.8	87.2	87.2	87.8	86.9	NA	89.7	90.1	89.1	89.2	89.3
Take heroin occasionally without using a needle[c]	NA	88.5	88.9	88.9	89.6	89.0	NA	91.6	92.3	90.8	90.7	90.6
Try one or two drinks of an alcoholic beverage (beer, wine, liquor)	51.7	48.0	48.7	49.8	51.1	49.7	37.6	36.1	33.4	34.7	37.7	36.8
Take one or two drinks nearly every day	82.2	75.9	77.8	77.4	78.3	77.1	81.7	75.4	73.8	73.8	74.9	74.2
Have five or more drinks once or twice each weekend	85.2	80.7	81.2	81.6	81.9	81.9	76.7	72.2	68.2	69.2	71.5	71.6
Smoke one or more packs of cigarettes per day[b]	82.8	78.6	81.9	83.5	84.6	84.6	79.4	73.2	76.7	78.2	80.6	81.4

Note: See Note, table 2.79. Readers interested in responses to this question for 1992 through 1994, and 1996 through 1999 should consult previous editions of SOURCEBOOK. The Ns are approximate. For survey methodology and definitions of terms, see Appendix 6.

[a]Answer alternatives were: (1) don't disapprove, (2) disapprove, (3) strongly disapprove, and (6) can't say, drug unfamiliar.
[b]Data for 2000-2003 are based on two-thirds of N indicated due to changes in questionnaire forms.
[c]Data for 1995 are based on one of two questionnaire forms; N is one-half of N indicated. In 2000-2003, N is one-third of N indicated due to changes in questionnaire forms.
[d]Data are based on one-third of N indicated due to changes in questionnaire forms.

Source: Lloyd D. Johnston et al., *Monitoring the Future National Survey Results on Drug Use, 1975-2003*, Vol. 1, Secondary School Students (Bethesda, MD: U.S. Department of Health and Human Services, 2004), p. 316. Table adapted by SOURCEBOOK staff.

Table 2.87

High school seniors favoring prohibition of drug use, alcohol use, and cigarette smoking

By type of drug and place of use, United States, 1975-2003

Question: "Do you think that people (who are 18 or older) should be prohibited by law from doing each of the following?"

(Percent responding "yes"[a])

Class of	Smoke marijuana In private	Smoke marijuana In public places	Take LSD In private	Take LSD In public places	Take heroin In private	Take heroin In public places	Take amphetamines or barbiturates In private	Take amphetamines or barbiturates In public places	Get drunk In private	Get drunk In public places	Smoke cigarettes in certain specified public places
1975[b]	32.8%	63.1%	67.2%	85.8%	76.3%	90.1%	57.2%	79.6%	14.1%	55.7%	NA
1976	27.5	59.1	65.1	81.9	72.4	84.8	53.5	76.1	15.6	50.7	NA
1977	26.8	58.7	63.3	79.3	69.2	81.0	52.8	73.7	18.6	49.0	42.0%
1978	25.4	59.5	62.7	80.7	68.8	82.5	52.2	75.8	17.4	50.3	42.2
1979	28.0	61.8	62.4	81.5	68.5	84.0	53.4	77.3	16.8	50.4	43.1
1980	28.9	66.1	65.8	82.8	70.3	83.8	54.1	76.1	16.7	48.3	42.8
1981	35.4	67.4	62.6	80.7	68.8	82.4	52.0	74.2	19.6	49.1	43.0
1982	36.6	72.8	67.1	82.1	69.3	82.5	53.5	75.5	19.4	50.7	42.0
1983	37.8	73.6	66.7	82.8	69.7	83.7	52.8	76.7	19.9	52.2	40.5
1984	41.6	75.2	67.9	82.4	69.8	83.4	54.4	76.8	19.7	51.1	39.2
1985	44.7	78.2	70.6	84.8	73.3	85.8	56.3	78.3	19.8	53.1	42.8
1986	43.8	78.9	69.0	84.9	71.7	85.0	56.8	79.1	18.5	52.2	45.1
1987	47.6	79.7	70.8	85.2	75.0	86.2	59.1	79.8	18.6	53.2	44.4
1988	51.8	81.3	71.5	86.0	74.2	86.6	60.2	80.2	19.2	53.8	48.4
1989	51.5	80.0	71.6	84.4	74.4	85.2	61.1	79.2	20.2	52.6	44.5
1990	56.0	81.9	72.9	84.9	76.4	86.7	64.5	81.6	23.0	54.6	47.3
1991	51.6	79.8	68.1	83.9	72.8	85.4	59.7	79.7	22.0	54.3	44.9
1992	52.4	78.3	67.2	82.2	71.4	83.3	60.5	78.5	24.4	54.1	47.6
1993	48.0	77.3	63.5	82.1	70.7	84.5	57.4	78.0	22.1	53.6	45.9
1994	42.9	72.5	63.2	80.5	70.1	82.9	55.7	76.4	21.0	54.3	47.3
1995	44.0	72.9	64.3	81.5	72.2	84.8	57.5	77.6	21.6	54.5	45.1
1996	40.4	70.0	62.0	79.2	70.8	82.3	54.6	74.3	21.4	52.8	43.4
1997	38.8	69.4	61.2	80.3	70.6	84.3	54.6	76.5	20.5	51.7	41.3
1998	39.8	72.2	64.7	82.7	73.9	86.4	58.5	77.4	20.2	51.2	41.1
1999	39.3	71.5	62.6	80.4	72.9	84.2	55.1	76.1	20.5	52.8	43.2
2000	38.8	72.1	62.9	80.4	71.1	83.9	56.0	75.4	21.5	51.9	45.1
2001	39.1	68.3	63.1	78.8	70.6	81.7	55.9	74.5	22.6	50.6	44.2
2002	38.4	67.6	64.2	79.9	73.6	83.7	56.0	73.6	21.0	48.6	43.8
2003	40.3	68.6	64.2	79.1	73.1	83.2	55.8	74.4	21.4	50.1	45.5

Note: See Note, table 2.79. Sample sizes vary from year to year. The Ns for the years presented range from 2,146 to 3,783; for the class of 2003, the N is 2,450. For survey methodology and definitions of terms, see Appendix 6.

Source: Lloyd D. Johnston et al., *Monitoring the Future National Survey Results on Drug Use, 1975-2003*, Vol. 1, Secondary School Students (Bethesda, MD: U.S. Department of Health and Human Services, 2004), p. 319. Table adapted by SOURCEBOOK staff.

[a]Answer alternatives were: (1) no, (2) not sure, and (3) yes.
[b]The 1975 question asked about people who are "20 or older."

Table 2.88
High school seniors' attitudes toward the legalization of marijuana use

United States, 1975-2003

Question: "There has been a great deal of public debate about whether marijuana use should be legal. Which of the following policies would you favor?"

(Percent favoring policy)

Class of	Using marijuana should be entirely legal	It should be a minor violation like a parking ticket but not a crime	It should be a crime	Don't know
1975	27.3%	25.3%	30.5%	16.8%
1976	32.6	29.0	25.4	13.0
1977	33.6	31.4	21.7	13.4
1978	32.9	30.2	22.2	14.6
1979	32.1	30.1	24.0	13.8
1980	26.3	30.9	26.4	16.4
1981	23.1	29.3	32.1	15.4
1982	20.0	28.2	34.7	17.1
1983	18.9	26.3	36.7	18.1
1984	18.6	23.6	40.6	17.2
1985	16.6	25.7	40.8	16.9
1986	14.9	25.9	42.5	16.7
1987	15.4	24.6	45.3	14.8
1988	15.1	21.9	49.2	13.9
1989	16.6	18.9	50.0	14.6
1990	15.9	17.4	53.2	13.6
1991	18.0	19.2	48.6	14.3
1992	18.7	18.0	47.6	15.7
1993	22.8	18.7	43.4	15.1
1994	26.8	19.0	39.4	14.8
1995	30.4	18.0	37.3	14.4
1996	31.2	21.0	33.8	13.9
1997	30.8	20.7	34.0	14.5
1998	27.9	24.3	32.6	15.2
1999	27.3	23.7	32.5	16.5
2000	31.2	23.4	30.2	15.2
2001	29.2	24.5	31.1	15.3
2002	30.8	24.2	29.1	15.9
2003	29.5	25.8	29.8	14.9

Note: See Note, table 2.79. Sample sizes vary from year to year. The Ns for the years presented range from 2,143 to 3,710; for the class of 2003, the N is 2,444. For survey methodology and definitions of terms, see Appendix 6.

Source: Lloyd D. Johnston et al., *Monitoring the Future National Survey Results on Drug Use, 1975-2003*, Vol. 1, Secondary School Students (Bethesda, MD: U.S. Department of Health and Human Services, 2004), p. 320. Table adapted by SOURCEBOOK staff.

Table 2.89
High school seniors' attitudes toward legalization of the sale of marijuana if the use of marijuana were legal

United States, 1975-2003

Question: "If it were legal for people to USE marijuana, should it also be legal to SELL marijuana?"

Class of	No	Yes, but only to adults	Yes, to anyone	Don't know
1975	27.8%	37.1%	16.2%	18.9%
1976	23.0	49.8	13.3	13.9
1977	22.5	52.1	12.7	12.7
1978	21.8	53.6	12.0	12.6
1979	22.9	53.2	11.3	12.6
1980	25.0	51.8	9.6	13.6
1981	27.7	48.6	10.5	13.2
1982	29.3	46.2	10.7	13.8
1983	27.4	47.6	10.5	14.6
1984	30.9	45.8	10.6	12.8
1985	32.6	43.2	11.2	13.1
1986	33.0	42.2	10.4	14.4
1987	36.0	41.2	9.2	13.6
1988	36.8	39.9	10.5	12.8
1989	38.8	37.9	9.2	14.1
1990	40.1	38.8	9.6	11.6
1991	36.8	41.4	9.4	12.5
1992	37.8	39.5	9.6	13.1
1993	36.7	40.7	10.1	12.5
1994	33.1	41.7	11.6	13.7
1995	32.3	43.4	11.7	12.6
1996	29.4	46.7	11.1	12.8
1997	29.1	44.8	12.5	13.7
1998	30.2	42.4	11.9	15.5
1999	30.2	42.9	12.1	14.7
2000	27.4	45.5	13.4	13.6
2001	30.0	43.6	12.0	14.3
2002	29.1	43.6	13.6	13.7
2003	30.5	43.2	11.6	14.7

Note: See Notes, tables 2.79 and 2.88. For survey methodology and definitions of terms, see Appendix 6.

Source: Lloyd D. Johnston et al., *Monitoring the Future National Survey Results on Drug Use, 1975-2003*, Vol. 1, Secondary School Students (Bethesda, MD: U.S. Department of Health and Human Services, 2004), p. 320. Table adapted by SOURCEBOOK staff.

Table 2.90

College freshmen reporting that marijuana should be legalized

By sex, United States, 1969-2003

(Percent indicating "agree strongly" or "agree somewhat")

	Marijuana should be legalized		
	Total	Male	Female
1969	26.2%	28.7%	23.4%
1970	40.6	43.1	37.3
1971	40.4	43.4	37.2
1972	47.6	50.3	44.6
1973	48.3	50.9	45.6
1974	45.6	48.2	42.8
1975	46.1	49.4	42.7
1976	47.3	49.4	45.1
1977	51.3	55.0	47.5
1978	47.8	50.4	45.1
1979	44.6	47.4	41.9
1980	37.1	39.7	34.8
1981	32.5	35.4	29.9
1982	27.8	30.7	25.0
1983	24.5	27.3	21.9
1984	22.7	25.5	20.1
1985	21.4	24.4	18.6
1986	20.8	24.2	17.7
1987	19.1	22.8	15.7
1988	19.8	23.4	16.6
1989	16.7	19.9	13.8
1990	18.8	21.7	16.2
1991	21.2	24.1	18.6
1992	24.8	28.2	21.8
1993	29.3	32.6	26.5
1994	32.7	36.4	29.6
1995	33.4	37.1	30.3
1996	32.4	36.1	29.4
1997	33.1	36.7	30.1
1998	32.7	37.7	28.6
1999	32.4	37.2	28.4
2000	34.2	40.4	29.1
2001	36.5	42.9	31.4
2002	39.7	45.8	34.7
2003	38.8	44.3	34.3

Note: These figures are taken from the Cooperative Institutional Research Program Freshman Survey, which is conducted annually by the Higher Education Research Institute (HERI) at the University of California, Los Angeles. The survey covers a wide range of student characteristics including demographic and background information, high school activities, college plans, values, attitudes, and beliefs. Each fall, the HERI surveys approximately 300,000 full-time students entering the freshman classes from a nationally representative sample of colleges and universities in the United States. Both 2-year and 4-year institutions were included in the data for 1969-99. Beginning in 2000, the survey includes only 4-year colleges and universities (baccalaureate institutions). Inclusion of 2-year institutions was discontinued due to declining participation rates and increased need for data adjustment. In order to facilitate comparisons over time, 2-year institutions were removed from the sample and data for years prior to 2000 were recalculated by the Source. The data presented include only 4-year (baccalaureate-granting) institutions for all years and therefore will differ from previous editions of SOURCEBOOK.

From 1966 to 1970, approximately 15% of the Nation's institutions of higher education were selected by sampling procedures to participate in the program. Beginning in 1971, a stratified sample was selected from all institutions that have entering freshman classes and that respond to the U.S. Department of Education's Higher Education General Information Survey. An institution is considered eligible if it was operating at the time of the survey and if it had a full-time freshman class of at least 25 students. The data presented are weighted estimates of all first-time, full-time students entering 4-year institutions in the fall of each year. Published reports on trends over 35 years or reports on individual annual survey results can be obtained by writing to the Higher Education Research Institute, 3005 Moore Hall, UCLA, Los Angeles, CA 90095-1521.

Response categories were "agree strongly," "agree somewhat," "disagree somewhat," and "disagree strongly." The text or format of the questions or responses may differ slightly in different years.

Source: Alexander W. Astin et al., *The American Freshman: Thirty-Five Year Trends*, Higher Education Research Institute (Los Angeles: University of California, 2002), pp. 60, 61, 106, 107, 152, 153; and Linda J. Sax et al., *The American Freshman: National Norms for Fall 2002*, Higher Education Research Institute, pp. 36, 56, 76; *2003*, pp. 34, 54, 74 (Los Angeles: University of California). Table adapted by SOURCEBOOK staff. Reprinted by permission.

Table 2.91

College freshmen reporting that abortion should be legal

By sex, United States, 1977-2003

(Percent indicating "agree strongly" or "agree somewhat")

	Abortion should be legal		
	Total	Male	Female
1977	55.6%	55.6%	55.6%
1978	56.3	56.0	56.6
1979	53.7	53.7	53.8
1980	53.7	53.4	54.0
1981	54.5	53.5	55.3
1982	55.7	54.2	57.2
1983	56.0	55.6	56.4
1984	55.4	54.8	55.9
1985	56.4	55.3	57.3
1986	60.3	59.2	61.4
1987	60.3	59.9	60.6
1988	59.2	58.9	59.4
1989	65.7	64.1	67.1
1990	65.5	64.2	66.7
1991	64.6	63.3	65.7
1992	67.2	65.9	68.3
1993	64.1	62.4	65.5
1994	60.9	59.4	62.1
1995	59.9	58.4	61.1
1996	57.7	56.8	58.5
1997	53.7	53.2	54.1
1998	54.3	53.7	54.7
1999	53.2	53.3	53.2
2000	53.9	54.5	53.5
2001	55.0	55.1	54.8
2002	53.6	54.2	53.2
2003	54.5	55.0	54.1

Note: See Note, table 2.90.

Source: Alexander W. Astin et al., *The American Freshman: Thirty-Five Year Trends*, Higher Education Research Institute (Los Angeles: University of California, 2002), pp. 58, 59, 104, 105, 150, 151; and Linda J. Sax et al., *The American Freshman: National Norms for Fall 2002*, Higher Education Research Institute, pp. 36, 56, 76; *2003*, pp. 34, 54, 74 (Los Angeles: University of California). Table adapted by SOURCEBOOK staff. Reprinted by permission.

Table 2.92

College freshmen reporting there is too much concern in the courts for the rights of criminals

By sex, United States, 1969-83 and 1987-2003

(Percent indicating "agree strongly" or "agree somewhat")

	There is too much concern in the courts for the rights of criminals		
	Total	Male	Female
1969	53.8%	60.0%	46.4%
1970	50.7	56.3	44.0
1971	46.0	52.0	39.4
1972	47.7	54.6	40.0
1973	47.9	54.1	41.4
1974	49.6	55.5	43.3
1975	52.5	59.0	45.7
1976	58.1	63.8	52.2
1977	62.4	67.5	57.2
1978	64.4	69.5	59.4
1979	61.3	66.7	56.1
1980	65.0	69.7	60.6
1981	68.1	73.4	63.2
1982	69.3	73.8	65.0
1983	68.1	72.2	64.3
1987	68.0	71.2	65.1
1988	68.2	71.4	65.4
1989	68.1	71.2	65.3
1990	65.1	68.5	62.2
1991	64.5	67.2	62.0
1992	65.2	67.5	63.1
1993	67.1	69.4	65.2
1994	72.4	74.1	71.1
1995	73.2	74.1	72.6
1996	71.7	73.2	70.4
1997	70.8	71.4	70.3
1998	72.3	73.5	71.3
1999	71.2	72.5	70.0
2000	66.5	67.8	65.5
2001	64.4	65.8	63.2
2002	64.0	65.8	62.5
2003	61.1	63.3	59.3

Note: See Note, table 2.90.

Source: Alexander W. Astin et al., *The American Freshman: Thirty-Five Year Trends*, Higher Education Research Institute (Los Angeles: University of California, 2002), pp. 60, 61, 106, 107, 152, 153; and Linda J. Sax et al., *The American Freshman: National Norms for Fall 2002*, Higher Education Research Institute, pp. 36, 56, 76; *2003*, pp. 34, 54, 74 (Los Angeles: University of California). Table adapted by SOURCEBOOK staff. Reprinted by permission.

Table 2.93

College freshmen reporting that the death penalty should be abolished

By sex, United States, 1969, 1970, 1971, and 1978-2003

(Percent indicating "agree strongly" or "agree somewhat")

	The death penalty should be abolished		
	Total	Male	Female
1969	56.4%	52.1%	61.4%
1970	59.4	56.1	63.4
1971	60.2	55.6	65.3
1978	33.6	27.5	39.5
1979	35.6	28.8	42.1
1980	34.8	28.1	41.1
1981	30.7	25.2	35.8
1982	29.2	24.0	34.3
1983	29.7	24.8	34.4
1984	26.8	22.7	30.7
1985	27.6	23.4	31.6
1986	26.0	21.7	30.0
1987	24.3	20.6	27.8
1988	23.7	20.2	26.9
1989	22.0	18.9	24.9
1990	23.1	19.6	26.2
1991	22.4	19.4	25.0
1992	22.8	19.9	25.4
1993	22.8	19.6	25.5
1994	21.2	18.5	23.4
1995	22.0	19.1	24.4
1996	23.0	19.4	25.9
1997	24.4	20.9	27.4
1998	24.1	20.6	27.0
1999	26.7	23.0	29.7
2000	31.2	27.4	34.3
2001	32.2	28.2	35.5
2002	32.1	28.1	35.4
2003	32.6	28.8	35.8

Note: See Note, table 2.90.

Source: Alexander W. Astin et al., *The American Freshman: Thirty-Five Year Trends*, Higher Education Research Institute (Los Angeles: University of California, 2002), pp. 60, 61, 106, 107, 152, 153; and Linda J. Sax et al., *The American Freshman: National Norms for Fall 2002*, Higher Education Research Institute, pp. 36, 56, 76; *2003*, pp. 34, 54, 74 (Los Angeles: University of California). Table adapted by SOURCEBOOK staff. Reprinted by permission.

Page 180 intentionally left blank.

Table 2.94
College freshmen reporting that homosexual relationships should be legally prohibited

By sex, United States, 1976-2003

(Percent indicating "agree strongly" or "agree somewhat")

	It is important to have laws prohibiting homosexual relationships		
	Total	Male	Female
1976	43.6%	51.6%	35.5%
1977	46.6	54.2	38.8
1978	44.5	52.5	36.8
1979	45.1	53.3	37.4
1980	47.5	56.3	39.3
1981	46.1	55.1	37.9
1982	44.2	53.6	35.2
1983	45.5	54.5	37.0
1984	44.7	54.7	35.4
1985	44.2	54.1	34.8
1986	48.7	58.7	39.6
1987	50.4	60.1	41.6
1988	46.4	57.0	36.9
1989	42.4	54.1	32.0
1990	40.6	52.1	30.5
1991	38.6	49.8	28.7
1992	32.9	43.4	23.6
1993	32.8	44.1	23.2
1994	30.8	41.9	21.6
1995	27.9	39.1	18.5
1996	31.7	42.5	22.5
1997	31.2	41.5	22.7
1998	29.5	38.9	21.7
1999	28.1	37.6	20.3
2000	27.2	36.0	20.1
2001	24.9	33.5	18.0
2002	24.8	32.6	18.5
2003	26.1	34.6	19.2

Note: See Note, table 2.90.

Source: Alexander W. Astin et al., *The American Freshman: Thirty-Five Year Trends*, Higher Education Research Institute (Los Angeles: University of California, 2002), pp. 58, 59, 104, 105, 150, 151; and Linda J. Sax et al., *The American Freshman: National Norms for Fall 2002*, Higher Education Research Institute, pp. 36, 56, 76; *2003*, pp. 34, 54, 74 (Los Angeles: University of California). Table adapted by SOURCEBOOK staff. Reprinted by permission.

Table 2.95
College freshmen reporting that the Federal Government should do more to control the sale of handguns

By sex, United States, 1989-2003

(Percent indicating "agree strongly" or "agree somewhat")

	The Federal Government should do more to control the sale of handguns		
	Total	Male	Female
1989	79.8%	69.7%	88.8%
1990	79.5	68.9	88.8
1991	80.9	71.0	89.8
1992	82.4	73.0	90.7
1993	83.0	73.3	91.3
1994	81.6	71.9	89.7
1995	82.8	73.2	90.8
1996	82.9	74.0	90.3
1997	83.2	73.6	91.2
1998	84.1	75.1	91.6
1999	83.8	74.6	91.3
2000	82.0	72.6	89.6
2001	80.8	71.6	88.1
2002	77.8	69.1	84.8
2003	76.5	67.6	83.7

Note: See Note, table 2.90.

Source: Alexander W. Astin et al., *The American Freshman: Thirty-Five Year Trends*, Higher Education Research Institute (Los Angeles: University of California, 2002), pp. 61, 107, 153; and Linda J. Sax et al., *The American Freshman: National Norms for Fall 2002*, Higher Education Research Institute, pp. 36, 56, 76; *2003*, pp. 34, 54, 74 (Los Angeles: University of California). Table adapted by SOURCEBOOK staff. Reprinted by permission.

Table 2.96
Attitudes toward legalization of doctor-assisted suicide

United States, selected years 1996-2004

Question: "When a person has a disease that cannot be cured and is living in severe pain, do you think doctors should or should not be allowed by law to assist the patient to commit suicide if the patient requests it?"

	Yes, should be allowed	No, should not be allowed	No opinion
1996	52%	42%	6%
January 1997	58	37	5
June 1997	57	35	8
1998	59	39	2
1999	61	35	4
2001	68	27	5
2002	62	34	4
2003[a]	62	36	2
2004[a]	65	31	4

Note: Sample sizes vary from year to year; the data for 2004 are based on telephone interviews with a randomly selected national sample of 481 adults, 18 years of age and older, conducted May 2-4, 2004. Results for certain years, where indicated, are from a half sample. Data for the other years presented are based on full samples, which are comprised of approximately 1,000 respondents. For a discussion of public opinion survey sampling procedures, see Appendix 5.

[a]Asked of a half sample.

Source: The Gallup Organization, Inc., *The Gallup Poll* [Online]. Available: http://www.gallup.com/poll/ [July 16, 2004]. Table adapted by SOURCEBOOK staff. Reprinted by permission.

Table 2.97

Attitudes toward laws regulating the distribution of pornography

By demographic characteristics, United States, selected years 1987-2002

Question: "Which of these statements comes closest to your feelings about pornography laws: There should be laws against the distribution of pornography whatever the age; there should be laws against the distribution of pornography to persons under 18; or there should be no laws forbidding the distribution of pornography?"

	1987 Whatever the age	1987 To persons under 18	1987 No laws	1988 Whatever the age	1988 To persons under 18	1988 No laws	1989 Whatever the age	1989 To persons under 18	1989 No laws	1990 Whatever the age	1990 To persons under 18	1990 No laws	1991 Whatever the age	1991 To persons under 18	1991 No laws
National	40%	55%	4%	43%	50%	5%	40%	54%	5%	41%	52%	6%	40%	55%	4%
Sex															
Male	26	67	5	33	59	6	29	63	7	33	59	6	26	66	6
Female	50	46	3	51	43	4	49	46	3	47	47	5	49	47	3
Race															
White	41	54	4	45	49	5	41	54	4	42	51	5	41	54	4
Black/other	33	61	3	35	58	6	38	52	7	34	57	7	31	60	6
Age															
18 to 20 years	26	74	0	23	71	6	36	56	8	17	65	13	16	79	0
21 to 29 years	25	70	5	28	67	4	27	68	3	29	67	3	30	66	3
30 to 49 years	32	63	4	38	57	4	30	65	4	36	60	4	33	63	4
50 years and older	36	60	4	32	61	7	59	33	6	53	36	8	54	38	5
Education[a]															
College	32	63	4	37	58	4	34	59	5	36	57	7	36	59	4
High school graduate	43	53	3	46	47	5	43	53	4	44	51	5	42	53	4
Less than high school graduate	56	34	7	55	30	6	59	29	7	47	38	5	51	43	4
Income															
$50,000 and over	NA	NA	NA	NA	NA	NA	NA	NA	NA	NA	NA	NA	NA	NA	NA
$30,000 to $49,999	NA	NA	NA	NA	NA	NA	NA	NA	NA	NA	NA	NA	NA	NA	NA
$20,000 to $29,999	NA	NA	NA	NA	NA	NA	NA	NA	NA	NA	NA	NA	NA	NA	NA
Under $20,000	NA	NA	NA	NA	NA	NA	NA	NA	NA	NA	NA	NA	NA	NA	NA
Occupation															
Professional/business	35	59	4	40	54	4	37	58	4	38	55	6	35	60	4
Clerical/support	51	46	3	53	44	2	48	48	3	47	50	4	45	51	4
Manual/service	39	55	4	41	51	6	39	53	6	40	52	5	41	53	4
Farming/agriculture	38	58	5	56	31	12	44	38	12	35	59	6	25	65	5
Region															
Northeast	57	37	4	58	32	5	36	56	5	32	62	5	34	61	3
Midwest	39	55	5	45	48	3	39	56	4	38	54	7	41	54	5
South	43	52	4	48	45	5	44	49	6	49	44	5	39	54	5
West	39	55	4	44	52	4	40	56	4	38	55	6	44	53	3
Religion															
Protestant	43	53	3	48	46	4	46	50	4	46	48	5	43	52	3
Catholic	40	56	3	40	55	3	34	61	2	39	56	4	38	58	4
Jewish	20	65	15	13	65	17	24	71	6	20	53	20	4	82	9
None	16	71	11	21	64	12	22	59	16	22	66	9	18	66	11
Politics															
Republican	44	51	4	46	48	3	42	53	4	43	50	5	43	54	2
Democrat	41	54	4	44	49	6	44	51	5	44	47	7	38	55	4
Independent	34	61	4	39	54	5	34	58	5	34	60	5	38	56	5

Note: See Note, table 2.15. The "don't know" category has been omitted; therefore percents may not sum to 100. Readers interested in responses to this question for previous years should consult previous editions of SOURCEBOOK. For a discussion of public opinion survey sampling procedures, see Appendix 5.

Source: National Opinion Research Center, "General Social Surveys, 1972-2002," Storrs, CT: The Roper Center for Public Opinion Research, University of Connecticut. (Machine-readable data files.) Table constructed by SOURCEBOOK staff.

[a] Beginning in 1996, education categories were revised slightly and therefore are not directly comparable to data presented for prior years.

	1993			1994			1996			1998			2000			2002	
	Laws forbidding distribution		No laws forbidding distribution	Laws forbidding distribution		No laws forbidding distribution	Laws forbidding distribution		No laws forbidding distribution	Laws forbidding distribution		No laws forbidding distribution	Laws forbidding distribution		No laws forbidding distribution	Laws forbidding distribution		No laws forbidding distribution
	What-ever the age	To persons under 18		What-ever the age	To persons under 18		What-ever the age	To persons under 18		What-ever the age	To persons under 18		What-ever the age	To persons under 18		What-ever the age	To persons under 18	
	42%	54%	3%	37%	60%	3%	38%	58%	4%	38%	57%	4%	36%	60%	3%	38%	56%	5%
	32	62	5	26	68	5	25	70	4	27	67	5	24	72	3	31	62	7
	48	48	2	45	52	2	48	48	4	47	49	3	45	51	3	43	52	4
	44	53	3	38	58	3	39	56	4	39	56	4	36	60	3	39	56	5
	31	60	6	31	65	3	31	64	3	32	63	3	34	59	5	32	60	6
	28	59	10	15	79	3	23	70	6	30	66	3	18	77	4	29	59	12
	24	72	3	25	72	2	25	72	2	17	79	4	17	78	4	17	75	8
	33	64	3	28	69	3	30	66	3	33	64	3	29	68	2	32	64	4
	60	34	3	54	41	4	54	39	5	54	39	5	52	43	4	54	40	5
	36	60	3	30	66	3	32	63	4	32	64	3	31	65	3	34	61	4
	46	49	3	42	56	2	41	57	2	44	51	4	41	55	3	40	52	8
	55	39	4	54	34	9	48	43	6	44	49	6	42	52	3	48	48	3
	35	60	5	32	65	2	31	65	3	34	63	3	30	67	3	35	60	5
	37	60	2	34	63	3	34	62	3	39	57	4	32	66	2	39	54	6
	41	53	4	35	60	4	39	56	4	32	65	2	34	61	4	35	58	6
	47	49	2	41	55	3	39	54	4	42	51	6	44	51	3	41	54	4
	38	58	3	32	64	3	34	62	4	35	61	4	31	65	3	34	61	4
	48	48	4	43	55	1	41	56	3	45	50	4	46	50	3	40	55	5
	42	54	3	35	61	4	38	57	3	35	60	3	34	61	3	38	55	6
	42	53	5	38	52	5	45	47	3	52	48	0	49	49	3	61	39	0
	38	56	5	32	63	4	34	60	5	32	62	5	31	66	3	35	59	6
	40	56	3	34	63	2	40	56	3	40	57	3	35	61	4	38	57	4
	47	49	2	43	53	3	42	53	3	41	54	4	43	53	2	44	51	4
	38	57	4	32	64	3	30	65	4	36	60	4	27	66	5	30	62	7
	49	47	2	43	54	2	45	51	3	46	50	3	44	53	2	46	50	4
	35	62	3	32	66	2	30	65	4	33	62	4	31	66	2	34	61	4
	20	80	0	20	76	5	24	63	11	19	72	6	19	79	2	10	75	15
	15	75	9	17	75	7	18	73	6	18	74	6	16	76	7	21	68	11
	52	45	3	43	55	2	43	53	4	43	53	3	42	56	2	47	50	3
	41	55	3	36	61	2	36	59	4	37	58	4	36	59	4	32	62	5
	35	60	4	33	63	4	35	61	3	36	59	4	32	63	4	37	57	7

Public attitudes toward crime and criminal justice-related topics 183

Table 2.98

Attitudes toward the legality of homosexual relations

United States, selected years 1977-2004

Question: "Do you think homosexual relations between consenting adults should or should not be legal?"

	Legal	Not legal	Don't know/ refused
1977	43%	43%	14%
1982	45	39	16
1985	44	47	9
1986	33	54	13
1987	33	55	12
1988	35	57	11
1989	47	36	17
1992	48	44	8
1996	44	47	9
1999	50	43	7
2001	54	42	4
2002	52	43	5
May 2003	60	35	5
July 2003	50	44	6
2004	52	43	5

Note: Sample sizes vary from year to year; the data for 2004 are based on telephone interviews with a randomly selected national sample of 1,000 adults, 18 years of age and older, conducted May 2-4, 2004. For a discussion of public opinion survey sampling procedures, see Appendix 5.

Source: The Gallup Organization, Inc., *The Gallup Poll* [Online]. Available: http://www.gallup.com/poll/ [June 8, 2004]. Reprinted by permission.

Table 2.99

Attitudes toward the legality of homosexual relations

By demographic characteristics, United States, 2004

Question: "Do you think homosexual relations between consenting adults should or should not be legal?"

	Legal	Not legal	Don't know/ refused
National	52%	43%	5%
Sex			
Male	50	45	5
Female	55	41	4
Race			
White	55	41	4
Nonwhite	44	50	6
Black	36	59	5
Age			
18 to 29 years	59	41	0
30 to 49 years	58	34	8
50 to 64 years	52	46	2
50 years and older	45	51	4
65 years and older	35	57	8
Education			
College post graduate	68	28	4
College graduate	71	24	5
Some college	58	37	5
High school graduate or less	37	58	5
Income			
$75,000 and over	65	30	5
$50,000 to $74,999	53	42	5
$30,000 to $49,999	54	43	3
$20,000 to $29,999	47	45	8
Under $20,000	39	58	3
Community			
Urban area	56	38	6
Suburban area	55	40	5
Rural area	42	55	3
Region			
East	58	35	7
Midwest	56	41	3
South	40	56	4
West	63	33	4
Politics			
Republican	43	53	4
Democrat	59	37	4
Independent	56	38	6

Note: See Note, table 2.98. For a discussion of public opinion survey sampling procedures, see Appendix 5.

Source: Table constructed by SOURCEBOOK staff from data provided by The Gallup Organization, Inc. Reprinted by permission.

Table 2.100

Attitudes toward the legality of abortion

United States, selected years 1975-2004

Question: "Do you think abortions should be legal under any circumstances, legal only under certain circumstances, or illegal in all circumstances?"

	Always legal	Legal under certain circumstances	Never legal	No opinion
1975	21%	54%	22%	3%
1977	22	55	19	4
1979	22	54	19	5
1980	25	53	18	4
1981	23	52	21	4
1983	23	58	16	3
1985	21	55	21	3
1988	24	57	17	2
April 1989	27	50	18	5
July 1989	29	51	17	3
1990	31	53	12	4
May 1991	32	50	17	1
September 1991	33	49	14	4
January 1992	31	53	14	2
June 1992	34	48	13	5
1993	32	51	13	4
March 1994	31	51	15	3
September 1994	33	52	13	2
February 1995	33	50	15	2
September 1995	31	54	12	3
July 1996	25	58	15	2
September 1996	24	52	17	7
August 1997	22	61	15	2
November 1997	26	55	17	2
1998	23	59	17	1
1999	27	55	16	2
January 2000	26	56	15	3
March 2000	28	51	19	2
May 2001	26	58	15	1
August 2001	26	56	17	1
February 2002	26	54	18	2
May 2002	25	51	22	2
January 2003	24	57	18	1
October 2003	26	55	17	2
2004	24	56	19	1

Note: Sample sizes vary from year to year; the data for 2004 are based on telephone interviews with a randomly selected national sample of 1,000 adults, 18 years of age and older, conducted May 2-4, 2004. For a discussion of public opinion survey sampling procedures, see Appendix 5.

Source: The Gallup Organization, Inc., *The Gallup Poll* [Online]. Available: http://www.gallup.com/poll/ [June 8, 2004]; and data provided by The Gallup Organization, Inc. Table adapted by SOURCEBOOK staff. Reprinted by permission.

Table 2.101

Attitudes toward the legality of abortion

By demographic characteristics, United States, 2004

Question: "Do you think abortions should be legal under any circumstances, legal only under certain circumstances, or illegal in all circumstances?"

	Always legal	Legal under certain circumstances	Never legal
National	24%	56%	19%
Sex			
Male	19	62	18
Female	28	51	20
Race			
White	24	58	17
Nonwhite	23	50	25
Black	25	42	31
Age			
18 to 29 years	29	50	21
30 to 49 years	24	56	19
50 to 64 years	22	60	17
50 years and older	21	59	19
65 years and older	19	58	22
Education			
College post graduate	36	55	9
College graduate	30	61	9
Some college	28	53	17
High school graduate or less	14	58	27
Income			
$75,000 and over	33	56	10
$50,000 to $74,999	26	54	20
$30,000 to $49,999	24	56	20
$20,000 to $29,999	16	65	19
Under $20,000	13	54	33
Community			
Urban area	30	52	17
Suburban area	24	57	18
Rural area	16	59	24
Region			
East	29	54	16
Midwest	19	62	17
South	16	58	24
West	35	49	16
Politics			
Republican	12	65	23
Democrat	35	47	17
Independent	23	58	17

Note: See Note, table 2.100. The "no opinion" category has been omitted; therefore percents may not sum to 100. For a discussion of public opinion survey sampling procedures, see Appendix 5.

Source: Table constructed by SOURCEBOOK staff from data provided by The Gallup Organization, Inc. Reprinted by permission.

Table 2.102
Attitudes toward whether there should be stricter laws and regulations to protect the environment

United States, selected years 1992-2003

Question: "For each statement, please tell me if you completely agree with it, mostly agree with it, mostly disagree with it or completely disagree with it: There needs to be stricter laws and regulations to protect the environment."

	Completely agree	Mostly agree	Mostly disagree	Completely disagree
1992	55%	35%	7%	2%
1994	46	36	13	4
1997	41	40	13	5
1999	41	42	12	4
2002	42	41	12	4
2003	46	40	10	3

Note: See Note, table 2.46. The "don't know" category has been omitted; therefore percents may not sum to 100. For a discussion of public opinion survey sampling procedures, see Appendix 5.

Source: The Pew Research Center for the People & the Press, *The 2004 Political Landscape: Evenly Divided and Increasingly Polarized* (Washington, DC: The Pew Research Center for the People & the Press, 2003), p. T-42. Table adapted by SOURCEBOOK staff. Reprinted by permission.

Section 3

Nature and distribution of known offenses

Data presented in this section describe the type and extent of criminal activity in the United States. The level of crime is measured through officially recorded data, victimization surveys, and self-reports of criminal involvement. It is well documented that many crimes are not reported to the police. Therefore, surveys of the population and selected subgroups have been used to augment the data provided through official law enforcement records. Two methods have been most commonly used: (1) surveys of household members to determine the rate of criminal victimization, characteristics of victims, and perceived characteristics of offenders; and (2) self-report surveys of the general population, or particular subgroups, to determine the proportion and characteristics of persons who have committed criminal offenses.

The section begins with information from the National Crime Victimization Survey (NCVS), which is an annual national probability survey of households in the United States sponsored by the Bureau of Justice Statistics. Information is provided on the extent and nature of completed and attempted crimes, frequency of occurrence, characteristics of victims and offenders, victim-offender relationships, the circumstances surrounding criminal incidents, and reasons for reporting or not reporting crimes to the police.

The next set of tables is based on data from the Monitoring the Future Project at the University of Michigan's Institute for Social Research. This project conducts annual nationwide surveys of secondary school students' experiences of victimization and involvement in delinquent activity occurring at school and elsewhere. These data include student involvement in traffic violations and crashes while under the influence of alcohol or drugs. Also shown are figures on the prevalence and frequency of drug and alcohol use among eighth and tenth graders, high school seniors, college students, and young adults in the United States. Use of marijuana, hashish, inhalants, hallucinogens (LSD, PCP), cocaine and crack, heroin, stimulants, sedatives, tranquilizers, alcohol, steroids, and cigarettes is examined. This segment also incorporates self-report data collected by PRIDE Surveys on students' (grades 6 through 12) victimization experiences, involvement with delinquent behavior, and alcohol and drug use. The Youth Risk Behavior Surveillance System, a nationwide survey of youth conducted by the Centers for Disease Control and Prevention (CDC), is the source of information for high school students' involvement in a wide scope of risk-related behaviors including fighting and weapons possession at school. These tables are followed by reports of violent crime, bullying, hate-related behavior, and gangs at school, from data jointly collected by the U.S. Departments of Education and Justice. A series of tables present statistics on the prevalence of binge drinking on college campuses, associated violence, and other alcohol-related problems.

Section 3 also covers the prevalence of drug and alcohol use among the Nation's population age 12 and older from the National Survey on Drug Use and Health. Figures for various types of drugs are presented as well as reported problems associated with drug and alcohol use. The next series of tables present data from U.S. Department of Defense surveys measuring illicit drug use among U.S. military personnel. These data include branch of military, type of drug, and recency of use. Also included are data from the Drug Abuse Warning Network (DAWN) focusing on drug abuse-related emergency department episodes. Results of public opinion surveys by The Gallup Organization, asking about alcohol use and related problems, are shown. Information on alcohol-related driving behavior, including involvement in motor vehicle crashes and associated fatalities completes this segment.

The final part of Section 3 incorporates numerous tables displaying statistics on officially recorded crime. The Federal Bureau of Investigation collects information on crimes known to the police through its ongoing Uniform Crime Reporting (UCR) Program. The number and rate of offenses known to police are tabulated by State and for large U.S. cities for the eight Index crimes: murder and nonnegligent manslaughter, forcible rape, robbery, aggravated assault, burglary, larceny-theft, motor vehicle theft, and arson. Tables displaying information on bias-motivated (hate) crimes and offenses occurring in Federal parks are included. The next set of tables provides details about murder victims and offenders based on the Federal Bureau of Investigation's Supplementary Homicide Reports, followed by two tables focusing on violence between intimate partners. Data on homicides and other violent crimes occurring in the workplace and rates of suicide for various subgroups of the population are shown, as is information on the civilians and law enforcement officers killed as a result of the terrorist attacks on Sept. 11, 200. New this year is a table displaying trend data on sniper attacks in the U.S.

Trend tables on robbery, assault, burglary, larceny-theft, and motor vehicle theft present more than 25 years of UCR data. Information on financial institution fraud and Federal bank robberies is provided in this section as are numerous tabulations for the number of law enforcement officers assaulted and killed in the United States. These include detailed data on the circumstances of the incidents.

Section 3 concludes with information on arson, dollar losses due to incendiary or suspicious fires, bombing incidents, information on terrorist incidents and casualties resulting from terrorism, and the results of airline passenger screening.

Table 3.1

Estimated average number, rate, and percent change in rate of personal and property victimization

By type of crime, United States, 2000-01 and 2002-03[a]

Type of crime	Average number of victimizations (in thousands) 2000-01	Average number of victimizations (in thousands) 2002-03	Victimization rate (per 1,000 persons age 12 and older or per 1,000 households) 2000-01	Victimization rate 2002-03	Percent change 2000-01 to 2002-03[b]
All crimes	25,054,520	23,624,410	X	X	X
Personal crimes[c]	6,264,440	5,541,610	27.5	23.5	-14.3%
Crimes of violence	6,033,280	5,371,570	26.5	22.8	-13.8
Completed violence	1,936,170	1,704,040	8.5	7.2	-14.8
Attempted/threatened violence	4,097,110	3,667,520	18.0	15.6	-13.3
Rape/sexual assault	254,600	223,290	1.1	0.9	-15.1
Rape/attempted rape	146,700	142,380	0.6	0.6	-6.0
Rape	88,030	81,310	0.4	0.3	-10.5
Attempted rape	58,670	61,060	0.3	0.3	0.8
Sexual assault	107,900	80,910	0.5	0.3	-27.4
Robbery	681,230	554,310	3.0	2.4	-21.2
Completed/property taken	473,400	381,880	2.1	1.6	-21.9
With injury	167,100	165,090	0.7	0.7	-4.3
Without injury	306,300	216,780	1.3	0.9	-31.5
Attempted to take property	207,830	172,440	0.9	0.7	-19.6
With injury	66,720	48,160	0.3	0.2	-30.1
Without injury	141,110	124,290	0.6	0.5	-14.7
Assault	5,097,450	4,593,970	22.4	19.5	-12.7
Aggravated	1,257,330	1,045,610	5.5	4.4	-19.5
With injury	368,810	338,930	1.6	1.4	-11.0
Threatened with weapon	888,520	706,680	3.9	3.0	-23.0
Simple	3,840,110	3,548,360	16.8	15.1	-10.5
With minor injury	916,980	837,770	4.0	3.6	-11.5
Without injury	2,923,130	2,710,590	12.8	11.5	-10.2
Personal theft[d]	231,170	170,050	1.0	0.7	-28.8
Property crimes	18,790,080	18,082,800	172.4	161.1	-6.6
Household burglary	3,291,700	3,225,670	30.2	28.7	-4.9
Completed	2,798,080	2,703,900	25.7	24.1	-6.2
Forcible entry	1,047,230	1,016,990	9.6	9.1	-5.7
Unlawful entry without force	1,750,840	1,686,910	16.1	15.0	-6.5
Attempted forcible entry	493,620	521,770	4.5	4.6	2.6
Motor vehicle theft	972,890	1,010,610	8.9	9.0	0.9
Completed	682,980	772,070	6.3	6.9	9.8
Attempted	289,910	238,550	2.7	2.1	-20.1
Theft	14,525,500	13,846,520	133.3	123.4	-7.5
Completed[e]	13,986,000	13,379,380	128.4	119.2	-7.1
Less than $50	4,701,510	4,188,440	43.1	37.3	-13.5
$50 to $249	5,055,100	4,603,610	46.4	41.0	-11.6
$250 or more	3,176,160	3,323,300	29.1	29.6	1.6
Attempted	539,490	467,140	5.0	4.2	-15.9

Note: The National Crime Victimization Survey (NCVS) is conducted annually for the U.S. Department of Justice, Bureau of Justice Statistics by the U.S. Census Bureau. These estimates are based on data derived from a continuous survey of a representative sample of housing units in the United States. For the 2003 survey, approximately 149,040 residents in 83,660 housing units were interviewed. Response rates were 92% of eligible housing units and 86% of eligible individuals in interviewed households. For the 2002 survey, approximately 76,050 residents in 42,340 housing units were interviewed. Response rates were 92% of eligible housing units and 87% of eligible individuals in interviewed households. For the 2001 survey, approximately 79,950 residents in 43,680 housing units were interviewed. Response rates were 93% of eligible housing units and 89% of individuals in interviewed households. For the 2000 survey, approximately 159,420 residents in 86,800 housing units were interviewed. Response rates were 93% of eligible housing units and 90% of individuals in interviewed households. In 2000, the total U.S. population age 12 and older was 226,804,610; in 2001, it was 229,215,290; in 2002 it was 231,589,260; and in 2003 it was 239,305,990. The total number of households in the United States in 2000 was 108,352,960; in 2001, it was 109,568,450; in 2002 it was 110,323,840; and in 2003 it was 114,136,930. Readers should note that the NCVS is based on interviews with victims and therefore cannot measure murder.

[a]"Since 1995, the NCVS has undergone sample reductions because of the escalating costs of data collection. At the same time, the rate of violence has continued to decline. The combination of the two--fewer survey respondents and less crime--has resulted in a diminished ability to detect statistically significant year-to-year changes in rates" (Source, p. 3). Presentation of 2-year averages for counts and rates permits over time comparisons that are more reliable. For survey methodology and definitions of terms, see Appendix 8.

[a]Detail may not add to total because of rounding.
[b]Percent change was calculated using unrounded rates.
[c]Does not include murder or manslaughter.
[d]Includes pocket picking, purse snatching, and attempted purse snatching.
[e]Includes thefts with unknown losses.

Source: U.S. Department of Justice, Bureau of Justice Statistics, *Criminal Victimization, 2003*, NCJ 205455 (Washington, DC: U.S. Department of Justice, September 2004), p. 3.

Table 3.2

Estimated number and rate of violent and property victimization

By type of crime, United States, 2002 and 2003[a]

Type of crime	Number of victimizations 2002	Number of victimizations 2003	Victimization rate (per 1,000 persons age 12 and older or per 1,000 households) 2002	2003
All crimes	23,036,030	24,212,800	X	X
Violent crimes[b]	5,341,410	5,401,720	23.1	22.6
Rape/sexual assault	247,730	198,850	1.1	0.8
Robbery	512,490	596,130	2.2	2.5
Assault	4,581,190	4,606,740	19.8	19.3
Aggravated	990,110	1,101,110	4.3	4.6
Simple	3,591,090	3,505,630	15.5	14.6
Property crimes	17,539,220	18,626,380	159.0	163.2
Household burglary	3,055,720	3,395,620	27.7	29.8
Motor vehicle theft	988,760	1,032,470	9.0	9.0
Theft	13,494,750	14,198,290	122.3	124.4

Note: See Note, table 3.1. For survey methodology and definitions of terms, see Appendix 8.

[a]Detail may not add to total because of rounding.
[b]Does not include murder or manslaughter.

Source: U.S. Department of Justice, Bureau of Justice Statistics, *Criminal Victimization, 2003*, NCJ 205455 (Washington, DC: U.S. Department of Justice, September 2004), p. 2.

Table 3.3

Estimated rate of criminal victimization and percent change in rate

By type of crime, United States, 1993, 1994, 1999-2003[a]

Type of crime	1993	1994	1999	2000	2001	2002	2003	Percent change 1993 to 2003[b]
Personal crimes[c]	52.2	54.1	33.7	29.1	25.9	23.7	23.3	-55.4%
Crimes of violence	49.9	51.8	32.8	27.9	25.1	23.1	22.6	-54.7
Completed violence	15.0	15.4	10.1	9.0	8.0	7.6	6.9	-54.0
Attempted/threatened violence	34.9	36.4	22.6	18.9	17.1	15.5	15.7	-55.0
Rape/sexual assault	2.5	2.1	1.7	1.2	1.1	1.1	0.8	-68.0
Rape/attempted rape	1.6	1.4	0.9	0.6	0.6	0.7	0.5	-68.8
Rape	1.0	0.7	0.6	0.4	0.4	0.4	0.3	-70.0
Attempted rape	0.7	0.7	0.3	0.2	0.3	0.3	0.2	-71.4
Sexual assault	0.8	0.6	0.8	0.5	0.4	0.3	0.3	-62.5
Robbery	6.0	6.3	3.6	3.2	2.8	2.2	2.5	-58.3
Completed/property taken	3.8	4.0	2.4	2.3	1.9	1.7	1.6	-57.9
With injury	1.3	1.4	0.8	0.7	0.8	0.7	0.7	-46.2
Without injury	2.5	2.6	1.5	1.6	1.1	0.9	0.9	-64.0
Attempted to take property	2.2	2.3	1.2	0.9	0.9	0.5	0.9	-59.1
With injury	0.4	0.6	0.3	0.3	0.3	0.2	0.2	-50.0
Without injury	1.8	1.7	0.9	0.6	0.6	0.4	0.7	-61.1
Assault	41.4	43.3	27.4	23.5	21.2	19.8	19.3	-53.4
Aggravated	12.0	11.9	6.7	5.7	5.3	4.3	4.6	-61.7
With injury	3.4	3.3	2.0	1.5	1.7	1.4	1.5	-55.9
Threatened with weapon	8.6	8.6	4.7	4.2	3.6	2.9	3.1	-64.0
Simple	29.4	31.5	20.8	17.8	15.9	15.5	14.6	-50.3
With minor injury	6.1	6.8	4.4	4.4	3.7	3.9	3.2	-47.5
Without injury	23.3	24.7	16.3	13.4	12.2	11.6	11.4	-51.1
Personal theft[d]	2.3	2.4	0.9	1.2	0.8	0.7	0.8	-65.2
Property crimes	318.9	310.2	198.0	178.1	166.9	159.0	163.2	-48.8
Household burglary	58.2	56.3	34.1	31.8	28.7	27.7	29.8	-48.8
Completed	47.2	46.1	28.6	26.9	24.5	23.5	24.6	-47.9
Forcible entry	18.1	16.9	11.0	9.6	9.6	9.2	8.9	-50.8
Unlawful entry without force	29.1	29.2	17.6	17.3	14.9	14.3	15.7	-46.0
Attempted forcible entry	10.9	10.2	5.5	4.9	4.1	4.2	5.1	-53.2
Motor vehicle theft	19.0	18.8	10.0	8.6	9.2	9.0	9.0	-52.6
Completed	12.4	12.5	7.5	5.9	6.6	7.1	6.7	-46.0
Attempted	6.6	6.3	2.4	2.7	2.6	1.9	2.3	-65.2
Theft	241.7	235.1	153.9	137.7	129.0	122.3	124.4	-48.5
Completed[e]	230.1	224.3	149.0	132.0	124.8	118.2	120.2	-47.8
Less than $50	98.7	93.5	53.2	43.4	42.9	37.9	36.7	-62.8
$50 to $249	76.1	77.0	54.0	48.9	43.9	40.4	41.6	-45.3
$250 or more	41.6	41.8	31.7	29.3	29.0	29.6	29.6	-28.8
Attempted	11.6	10.8	5.0	5.7	4.2	4.1	4.2	-63.8

Victimization rate (per 1,000 persons age 12 and older or per 1,000 households)

Note: See Note, table 3.1. Victimization rates may differ from those reported previously because the estimates are now based on data collected in each calendar year rather than data about events within a calendar year. For survey methodology and definitions of terms, see Appendix 8.

[a] Detail may not add to total because of rounding.
[b] Differences between annual rates shown do not take into account any changes that may have occurred during interim years. Percent change calculated using unrounded rates.
[c] Does not include murder or manslaughter.
[d] Includes pocket picking, purse snatching, and attempted purse snatching.
[e] Includes thefts with unknown losses.

Source: U.S. Department of Justice, Bureau of Justice Statistics, *Criminal Victimization 2001: Changes 2000-01 with Trends 1993-2001*, Bulletin NCJ 194610 (Washington, DC: U.S. Department of Justice, September 2002), p. 11; and U.S. Department of Justice, Bureau of Justice Statistics, *Criminal Victimization, 2002*, NCJ 199994, p. 5; *2003*, NCJ 205455, p. 5 (Washington, DC: U.S. Department of Justice). Table adapted by SOURCEBOOK staff.

Table 3.4

Estimated rate (per 1,000 persons age 12 and older) of personal victimization

By type of crime and selected characteristics of victim, United States, 2003

Victim characteristics	Population	All crimes of violence[a]	Rape/ sexual assault	Robbery	Assault Total	Assault Aggravated	Assault Simple	Personal theft[b]
Sex								
Male	116,041,090	26.3	0.2[c]	3.2	23.0	5.9	17.1	0.4
Female	123,264,890	19.0	1.5	1.9	15.7	3.3	12.4	1.1
Race[d]								
White	197,577,400	21.5	0.8	1.9	18.8	4.2	14.7	0.6
Black	28,561,780	29.1	0.8[c]	5.9	22.3	6.0	16.3	1.7
Other	11,120,220	16.0	0.2[c]	3.4	12.4	5.4	7.0	0.9[c]
Two or more races	2,046,590	67.7	5.8[c]	8.1[c]	53.7	21.3	32.4	2.7[c]
Ethnicity[d]								
Hispanic	30,275,550	24.2	0.4[c]	3.1	20.8	4.6	16.1	1.1[c]
Non-Hispanic	207,263,340	22.3	0.9	2.4	19.0	4.6	14.4	0.7
Age								
12 to 15 years	17,084,330	51.6	1.2[c]	5.2	45.3	8.9	36.4	1.5[c]
16 to 19 years	16,210,780	53.0	1.3[c]	5.1	46.6	11.9	34.7	1.4[c]
20 to 24 years	19,786,270	43.3	1.7	6.4	35.3	9.8	25.5	1.6
25 to 34 years	39,449,790	26.4	1.6	2.5	22.3	6.0	16.3	1.0
35 to 49 years	65,780,190	18.5	0.6	1.7	16.1	3.8	12.3	0.5
50 to 64 years	46,736,200	10.3	0.4[c]	1.4	8.5	1.6	7.0	0.3[c]
65 years and older	34,258,430	2.0	0.1[c]	0.7[c]	1.2	0.1[c]	1.1	0.5[c]
Household income								
Under $7,500	8,335,120	49.9	1.6[c]	9.0	39.3	10.8	28.5	1.2[c]
$7,500 to $14,999	15,893,630	30.8	1.8[c]	4.0	25.0	7.9	17.0	1.1[c]
$15,000 to $24,999	24,560,390	26.3	0.8[c]	4.0	21.5	4.5	17.0	0.7[c]
$25,000 to $34,999	24,252,930	24.9	0.9[c]	2.2	21.8	5.0	16.9	0.8[c]
$35,000 to $49,999	32,082,950	21.4	0.9[c]	2.1	18.3	4.8	13.5	0.7[c]
$50,000 to $74,999	35,174,290	22.9	0.5[c]	2.0	20.4	5.2	15.2	0.5[c]
$75,000 and over	47,855,860	17.5	0.5[c]	1.7	15.4	2.7	12.6	1.0
Marital status								
Never married	76,429,290	41.6	1.6	5.2	34.8	8.7	26.1	1.4
Married	120,862,960	10.2	0.2[c]	0.8	9.2	1.8	7.4	0.3
Divorced/separated	25,907,600	35.1	1.9	3.5	29.7	7.8	21.9	0.7[c]
Widowed	14,297,780	3.5	0.0[c]	1.1[c]	2.5	0.1[c]	2.3	0.8[c]
Region								
Northeast	44,525,430	21.0	0.2[c]	2.7	18.1	3.9	14.2	1.1
Midwest	55,886,090	23.6	1.5	2.7	19.4	4.6	14.8	1.0
South	86,489,420	21.1	0.9	2.5	17.8	4.4	13.4	0.5
West	52,405,050	25.2	0.6[c]	2.1	22.5	5.6	16.9	0.6
Residence								
Urban	66,466,630	28.2	0.8	3.7	23.8	5.4	18.3	1.3
Suburban	115,814,150	21.3	1.0	2.3	18.1	4.3	13.7	0.7
Rural	57,025,210	18.6	0.6	1.6	16.4	4.2	12.2	0.3[c]

Note: See Note, table 3.1. For survey methodology and definitions of terms, see Appendix 8.

[a]Does not include murder or manslaughter.
[b]Includes pocket picking, purse snatching, and attempted purse snatching.
[c]Estimate is based on 10 or fewer sample cases.
[d]Beginning in 2003, race and ethnicity categories are not directly comparable to previous years. For more information on this change, see Appendix 8.

Source: U.S. Department of Justice, Bureau of Justice Statistics, *Criminal Victimization, 2003*, NCJ 205455 (Washington, DC: U.S. Department of Justice, September 2004), p. 7, Table 6 and p. 8. Table adapted by SOURCEBOOK staff.

Table 3.5

Estimated number and rate (per 1,000 persons age 12 and older) of personal victimization

By type of crime and sex of victim, United States, 2002[a]

Type of crime	Both sexes Number	Both sexes Rate	Male Number	Male Rate	Female Number	Female Rate
All personal crimes	5,496,810	23.7	2,927,520	26.1	2,569,300	21.5
Crimes of violence	5,341,410	23.1	2,857,930	25.5	2,483,480	20.8
Completed violence	1,753,090	7.6	816,240	7.3	936,850	7.8
Attempted/threatened violence	3,588,320	15.5	2,041,690	18.2	1,546,630	13.0
Rape/sexual assault	247,730	1.1	31,640	0.3	216,090	1.8
Rape/attempted rape	167,860	0.7	22,610[b]	0.2[b]	145,240	1.2
Rape	90,390	0.4	4,100[b]	0.0[b]	86,290	0.7
Attempted rape[c]	77,470	0.3	18,520[b]	0.2[b]	58,950	0.5
Sexual assault[d]	79,870	0.3	9,030[b]	0.1[b]	70,840	0.6
Robbery	512,490	2.2	323,530	2.9	188,960	1.6
Completed/property taken	385,880	1.7	237,350	2.1	148,530	1.2
With injury	169,980	0.7	102,860	0.9	67,130	0.6
Without injury	215,890	0.9	134,490	1.2	81,400	0.7
Attempted to take property	126,610	0.5	86,180	0.8	40,430	0.3
With injury	42,600	0.2	31,470	0.3	11,130[b]	0.1[b]
Without injury	84,020	0.4	54,710	0.5	29,300[b]	0.2[b]
Assault	4,581,190	19.8	2,502,760	22.3	2,078,440	17.4
Aggravated	990,110	4.3	588,430	5.2	401,670	3.4
With injury	316,260	1.4	166,930	1.5	149,330	1.3
Threatened with weapon	673,850	2.9	421,510	3.8	252,350	2.1
Simple	3,591,090	15.5	1,914,320	17.1	1,676,760	14.0
With minor injury	906,580	3.9	405,670	3.6	500,910	4.2
Without injury	2,684,510	11.6	1,508,650	13.4	1,175,860	9.9
Purse snatching/pocket picking	155,400	0.7	69,590	0.6	85,810	0.7
Population age 12 and older	231,589,260	X	112,241,930	X	119,347,330	X

Note: See Note, table 3.1. For survey methodology and definitions of terms, see Appendix 8.

Source: U.S. Department of Justice, Bureau of Justice Statistics, *Criminal Victimization in the United States, 2002 Statistical Tables*, NCJ 200561, Table 2 [Online]. Available: http://www.ojp.usdoj.gov/bjs/pub/pdf/cvus02.pdf [Mar. 3, 2004].

[a]Detail may not add to total because of rounding.
[b]Estimate is based on about 10 or fewer sample cases.
[c]Includes verbal threats of rape.
[d]Includes threats.

Table 3.6

Estimated rate (per 1,000 persons in each age group) of personal victimization

By type of crime and age of victim, United States, 2002[a]

Type of crime	12 to 15	16 to 19	20 to 24	25 to 34	35 to 49	50 to 64	65 and older
All personal crimes	45.3	58.8	49.0	26.8	18.8	11.0	4.0
Crimes of violence	44.4	58.2	47.4	26.3	18.1	10.7	3.4
Completed violence	12.8	20.7	16.4	9.0	5.5	3.5	1.2
Attempted/threatened violence	31.7	37.6	31.0	17.3	12.6	7.2	2.2
Rape/sexual assault	2.1	5.5	2.9	0.6[b]	0.5[b]	0.2[b]	0.1[b]
Rape/attempted rape	0.8[b]	4.6	2.0	0.6[b]	0.3[b]	0.0[b]	0.1[b]
Rape	0.5[b]	2.7	1.4[b]	0.2[b]	0.1[b]	0.0[b]	0.0[b]
Attempted rape[c]	0.2[b]	2.0	0.6[b]	0.4[b]	0.2[b]	0.0[b]	0.1[b]
Sexual assault[d]	1.3[b]	0.9[b]	0.9[b]	0.1[b]	0.2[b]	0.2[b]	0.1[b]
Robbery	3.0	4.0	4.7	2.8	1.5	1.6	1.0
Completed/property taken	1.8[b]	3.1	3.6	2.1	1.2	1.2	0.8[b]
With injury	0.9[b]	1.6[b]	1.8	0.7[b]	0.5	0.6[b]	0.2[b]
Without injury	0.9[b]	1.5[b]	1.8	1.4	0.7	0.6[b]	0.6[b]
Attempted to take property	1.2[b]	0.9[b]	1.1[b]	0.7[b]	0.3[b]	0.4[b]	0.2[b]
With injury	0.2[b]	0.4[b]	0.1[b]	0.4[b]	0.2[b]	0.0[b]	0.1[b]
Without injury	1.0[b]	0.5[b]	1.0[b]	0.3[b]	0.1[b]	0.3[b]	0.1[b]
Assault	39.3	48.6	39.8	22.8	16.1	8.9	2.2
Aggravated	5.0	11.9	10.1	5.2	3.5	1.7	0.7[b]
With injury	1.0[b]	3.9	3.8	1.9	0.9	0.6[b]	0.1[b]
Threatened with weapon	4.0	8.0	6.3	3.3	2.5	1.0	0.6[b]
Simple	34.3	36.7	29.7	17.6	12.7	7.2	1.5
With minor injury	8.8	10.2	6.7	4.7	3.2	1.5	0.3[b]
Without injury	25.6	26.5	23.0	12.9	9.4	5.7	1.3
Purse snatching/pocket picking	0.9[b]	0.6[b]	1.6[b]	0.5[b]	0.7	0.3[b]	0.6[b]
Population in each age group	16,676,560	16,171,800	19,317,740	37,329,720	65,263,580	43,746,850	33,083,000

Note: See Note, table 3.1. For survey methodology and definitions of terms, see Appendix 8.

Source: U.S. Department of Justice, Bureau of Justice Statistics, *Criminal Victimization in the United States, 2002 Statistical Tables*, NCJ 200561, Table 3 [Online]. Available: http://www.ojp.usdoj.gov/bjs/pub/pdf/cvus02.pdf [Mar. 3, 2004].

[a]Detail may not add to total because of rounding.
[b]Estimate is based on about 10 or fewer sample cases.
[c]Includes verbal threats of rape.
[d]Includes threats.

Table 3.7

Estimated rate (per 1,000 persons in each age group) of personal victimization

By sex and age of victim, and type of crime, United States, 2002[a]

Sex and age of victim	Total population	Crimes of violence	Completed violence	Attempted/ threatened violence	Rape/ sexual assault[b]	Robbery Total	Robbery With injury	Robbery Without injury	Assault Total	Assault Aggravated	Assault Simple	Purse snatching/ pocket picking
Male												
12 to 15 years	8,603,860	46.1	13.2	33.0	0.0[c]	4.9	1.8[c]	3.1[c]	41.2	5.4	35.8	1.8[c]
16 to 19 years	8,210,100	58.4	16.6	41.7	0.8[c]	4.9	3.0[c]	1.9[c]	52.6	16.3	36.3	1.2[c]
20 to 24 years	9,583,970	56.7	18.2	38.5	0.4[c]	7.2	2.5[c]	4.7	49.1	13.2	35.9	1.9[c]
25 to 34 years	18,406,060	29.4	8.6	20.8	0.1[c]	3.2	0.8[c]	2.4	26.0	6.6	19.4	0.4[c]
35 to 49 years	32,213,630	18.7	4.9	13.9	0.4[c]	2.0	1.1	0.9[c]	16.3	3.1	13.2	0.4[c]
50 to 64 years	21,052,670	11.4	3.0	8.4	0.3[c]	1.6	0.5[c]	1.1[c]	9.5	2.0	7.5	0.4[c]
65 years and older	14,171,630	3.9	1.0[c]	2.9	0.0[c]	1.0[c]	0.6[c]	0.3[c]	2.9	1.2[c]	1.7[c]	0.0[c]
Female												
12 to 15 years	8,072,700	42.6	12.3	30.3	4.3	0.9[c]	0.3[c]	0.6[c]	37.3	4.5	32.8	0.0[c]
16 to 19 years	7,961,700	58.1	24.8	33.2	10.4	3.2[c]	1.0[c]	2.2[c]	44.5	7.4	37.1	0.0[c]
20 to 24 years	9,733,770	38.3	14.6	23.7	5.4	2.2[c]	1.3[c]	0.9[c]	30.7	7.0	23.7	1.3[c]
25 to 34 years	18,923,660	23.2	9.3	13.9	1.1[c]	2.4	1.4[c]	1.0[c]	19.8	3.9	15.9	0.7[c]
35 to 49 years	33,049,950	17.6	6.2	11.4	0.6[c]	1.1	0.3[c]	0.8[c]	16.0	3.9	12.1	1.0
50 to 64 years	22,694,180	10.0	3.9	6.1	0.1[c]	1.5	0.8[c]	0.7[c]	8.4	1.4	7.0	0.3[c]
65 years and older	18,911,370	3.0	1.4[c]	1.6	0.2[c]	1.1[c]	0.1[c]	1.0[c]	1.7	0.2[c]	1.4[c]	1.1[c]

Note: See Note, table 3.1. For survey methodology and definitions of terms, see Appendix 8.

[a] Detail may not add to total because of rounding.
[b] Includes verbal threats of rape and threats of sexual assault.
[c] Estimate is based on about 10 or fewer sample cases.

Source: U.S. Department of Justice, Bureau of Justice Statistics, *Criminal Victimization in the United States, 2002 Statistical Tables*, NCJ 200561, Table 4 [Online]. Available: http://www.ojp.usdoj.gov/bjs/pub/pdf/cvus02.pdf [Mar. 3, 2004].

Table 3.8

Estimated number and rate (per 1,000 persons age 12 and older) of personal victimization

By type of crime and race of victim, United States, 2002[a]

Type of crime	White Number	White Rate	Black Number	Black Rate	Other Number	Other Rate
All personal crimes	4,525,090	23.5	824,530	28.6	147,190	15.1
Crimes of violence	4,392,620	22.8	805,440	27.9	143,350	14.7
Completed violence	1,430,510	7.4	271,200	9.4	51,380	5.3
Attempted/threatened violence	2,962,110	15.4	534,230	18.5	91,980	9.4
Rape/sexual assault	163,790	0.8	72,020	2.5	11,920[b]	1.2[b]
Rape/attempted rape	103,350	0.5	55,460	1.9	9,050[b]	0.9[b]
Rape	65,440	0.3	20,980[b]	0.7[b]	3,980[b]	0.4[b]
Attempted rape[c]	37,910	0.2	34,480	1.2	5,070[b]	0.5[b]
Sexual assault[d]	60,440	0.3	16,560[b]	0.6[b]	2,870[b]	0.3[b]
Robbery	370,800	1.9	118,040	4.1	23,650[b]	2.4[b]
Completed/property taken	275,550	1.4	98,310	3.4	12,020[b]	1.2[b]
With injury	119,810	0.6	43,780	1.5	6,390[b]	0.7[b]
Without injury	155,740	0.8	54,520	1.9	5,630[b]	0.6[b]
Attempted to take property	95,250	0.5	19,740[b]	0.7[b]	11,630[b]	1.2[b]
With injury	34,750	0.2	5,230[b]	0.2[b]	2,620[b]	0.3[b]
Without injury	60,490	0.3	14,510[b]	0.5[b]	9,010[b]	0.9[b]
Assault	3,858,030	20.0	615,370	21.3	107,790	11.0
Aggravated	788,040	4.1	192,900	6.7	9,170[b]	0.9[b]
With injury	267,900	1.4	45,960	1.6	2,390[b]	0.2[b]
Threatened with weapon	520,140	2.7	146,930	5.1	6,780[b]	0.7[b]
Simple	3,069,990	15.9	422,480	14.6	98,620	10.1
With minor injury	780,230	4.0	93,360	3.2	32,990	3.4
Without injury	2,289,760	11.9	329,110	11.4	65,630	6.7
Purse snatching/pocket picking	132,460	0.7	19,100[b]	0.7[b]	3,840[b]	0.4[b]
Population age 12 and older	192,956,980	X	28,871,440	X	9,760,850	X

Note: See Note, table 3.1. For survey methodology and definitions of terms, see Appendix 8.

[a] Detail may not add to total because of rounding.
[b] Estimate is based on about 10 or fewer sample cases.
[c] Includes verbal threats of rape.
[d] Includes threats.

Source: U.S. Department of Justice, Bureau of Justice Statistics, *Criminal Victimization in the United States, 2002 Statistical Tables*, NCJ 200561, Table 5 [Online]. Available: http://www.ojp.usdoj.gov/bjs/pub/pdf/cvus02.pdf [Mar. 3, 2004].

Table 3.9

Estimated number and rate (per 1,000 persons age 12 and older) of personal victimization

By type of crime and ethnicity of victim, United States, 2002[a]

Type of crime	Total[b] Number	Total[b] Rate	Hispanic Number	Hispanic Rate	Non-Hispanic Number	Non-Hispanic Rate
All personal crimes	5,496,810	23.7	647,290	24.0	4,823,750	23.8
Crimes of violence	5,341,410	23.1	637,320	23.6	4,678,330	23.0
Completed violence	1,753,090	7.6	235,600	8.7	1,501,500	7.4
Attempted/threatened violence	3,588,320	15.5	401,720	14.9	3,176,830	15.6
Rape/sexual assault	247,730	1.1	19,670[c]	0.7[c]	228,060	1.1
Rape/attempted rape	167,860	0.7	15,700[c]	0.6[c]	152,150	0.7
Rape	90,390	0.4	6,420[c]	0.2[c]	83,970	0.4
Attempted rape[d]	77,470	0.3	9,280[c]	0.3[c]	68,190	0.3
Sexual assault[e]	79,870	0.3	3,960[c]	0.1[c]	75,910	0.4
Robbery	512,490	2.2	85,490	3.2	424,820	2.1
Completed/property taken	385,880	1.7	63,830	2.4	322,050	1.6
With injury	169,980	0.7	14,690[c]	0.5[c]	155,290	0.8
Without injury	215,890	0.9	49,140	1.8	166,750	0.8
Attempted to take property	126,610	0.5	21,660[c]	0.8[c]	102,780	0.5
With injury	42,600	0.2	2,280[c]	0.1[c]	40,320	0.2
Without injury	84,020	0.4	19,380[c]	0.7[c]	62,460	0.3
Assault	4,581,190	19.8	532,160	19.7	4,025,440	19.8
Aggravated	990,110	4.3	163,510	6.1	826,590	4.1
With injury	316,260	1.4	62,160	2.3	254,090	1.3
Threatened with weapon	673,850	2.9	101,350	3.8	572,500	2.8
Simple	3,591,090	15.5	368,650	13.7	3,198,840	15.8
With minor injury	906,580	3.9	99,220	3.7	791,370	3.9
Without injury	2,684,510	11.6	269,430	10.0	2,407,480	11.9
Purse snatching/pocket picking	155,400	0.7	9,980[c]	0.4[c]	145,420	0.7
Population age 12 and older	231,589,260	X	26,991,490	X	203,062,880	X

Note: See Note, table 3.1. For survey methodology and definitions of terms, see Appendix 8.

[a]Detail may not add to total because of rounding.
[b]Includes data on persons whose ethnicity was not ascertained, which are not shown separately.
[c]Estimate is based on about 10 or fewer sample cases.
[d]Includes verbal threats of rape.
[e]Includes threats.

Source: U.S. Department of Justice, Bureau of Justice Statistics, *Criminal Victimization in the United States, 2002 Statistical Tables*, NCJ 200561, Table 7 [Online]. Available: http://www.ojp.usdoj.gov/bjs/pub/pdf/cvus02.pdf [Mar. 3, 2004].

Table 3.10

Estimated number and rate (per 1,000 persons age 12 and older) of personal victimization

By type of crime, and sex and race of victim, United States, 2002[a]

Type of crime	Male White Number	Male White Rate	Male Black Number	Male Black Rate	Female White Number	Female White Rate	Female Black Number	Female Black Rate
All personal crimes	2,459,570	26.1	386,130	29.3	2,065,520	20.9	438,400	27.9
Crimes of violence	2,394,330	25.4	381,780	29.0	1,998,290	20.3	423,650	27.0
Completed violence	683,120	7.2	107,160	8.1	747,390	7.6	164,040	10.4
Attempted/threatened violence	1,711,210	18.1	274,620	20.9	1,250,900	12.7	259,610	16.5
Rape/sexual assault[b]	19,160[c]	0.2[c]	9,610[c]	0.7[c]	144,630	1.5	62,410	4.0
Robbery	235,360	2.5	75,490	5.7	135,440	1.4	42,560	2.7
Completed/property taken	173,570	1.8	60,170	4.6	101,980	1.0	38,130	2.4
With injury	76,890	0.8	25,970[c]	2.0[c]	42,920	0.4	17,810[c]	1.1[c]
Without injury	96,680	1.0	34,210	2.6	59,060	0.6	20,320[c]	1.3[c]
Attempted to take property	61,790	0.7	15,310[c]	1.2[c]	33,460	0.3	4,420[c]	0.3[c]
With injury	25,720[c]	0.3[c]	3,130[c]	0.2[c]	9,040[c]	0.1[c]	2,100[c]	0.1[c]
Without injury	36,070	0.4	12,180[c]	0.9[c]	24,430[c]	0.2[c]	2,330[c]	0.1[c]
Assault	2,139,810	22.7	296,680	22.5	1,718,230	17.4	318,690	20.3
Aggravated	485,760	5.2	98,030	7.4	302,290	3.1	94,860	6.0
With injury	145,280	1.5	19,260[c]	1.5[c]	122,620	1.2	26,710[c]	1.7[c]
Threatened with weapon	340,480	3.6	78,770	6.0	179,660	1.8	68,160	4.3
Simple	1,654,050	17.5	198,650	15.1	1,415,940	14.4	223,820	14.3
With minor injury	357,970	3.8	27,730[c]	2.1[c]	42,250	4.3	65,630	4.2
Without injury	1,296,080	13.7	170,920	13.0	993,690	10.1	158,190	10.1
Purse snatching/pocket picking	65,240	0.7	4,340[c]	0.3[c]	67,220	0.7	14,750[c]	0.9[c]
Population age 12 and older	94,313,900	X	13,164,830	X	98,643,080	X	15,706,600	X

Note: See Note, table 3.1. Table excludes data on persons of "other" races. For survey methodology and definitions of terms, see Appendix 8.

[a]Detail may not add to total because of rounding.
[b]Includes verbal threats of rape and threats of sexual assault.
[c]Estimate is based on about 10 or fewer sample cases.

Source: U.S. Department of Justice, Bureau of Justice Statistics, *Criminal Victimization in the United States, 2002 Statistical Tables*, NCJ 200561, Table 6 [Online]. Available: http://www.ojp.usdoj.gov/bjs/pub/pdf/cvus02.pdf [Mar. 3, 2004].

Table 3.11

Estimated rate (per 1,000 persons in each age group) of personal victimization

By race and age of victim, and type of crime, United States, 2002[a]

Race and age of victim	Total population	Crimes of violence	Completed violence	Attempted/ threatened violence	Rape/ sexual assault[b]	Robbery Total	Robbery With injury	Robbery Without injury	Assault Total	Assault Aggravated	Assault Simple	Purse snatching/ pocket picking
White												
12 to 15 years	12,991,380	47.5	13.6	33.9	2.0[c]	2.6	1.1[c]	1.5[c]	43.0	5.3	37.6	1.2[c]
16 to 19 years	13,032,600	56.6	19.9	36.7	3.4	4.2	2.3[c]	2.0[c]	49.0	10.9	38.1	0.8[c]
20 to 24 years	15,676,290	49.8	18.0	31.8	3.1	4.8	2.1	2.7	41.9	11.2	30.7	1.9[c]
25 to 34 years	30,125,710	26.4	9.1	17.2	0.7[c]	2.5	1.0[c]	1.5	23.2	4.8	18.4	0.3[c]
35 to 49 years	54,144,220	18.3	5.5	12.8	0.3[c]	1.4	0.6[c]	0.8	16.6	3.3	13.3	0.7
50 to 64 years	37,611,120	10.3	3.1	7.2	0.1[c]	1.1	0.4[c]	0.8[c]	9.1	1.6	7.5	0.3[c]
65 years and older	29,375,650	2.8	0.7[c]	2.1	0.2[c]	0.5[c]	0.2[c]	0.3[c]	2.2	0.6[c]	1.6	0.7[c]
Black												
12 to 15 years	2,937,540	39.6	9.7[c]	29.8	3.0[c]	4.5[c]	1.5[c]	3.0[c]	32.0	4.7[c]	27.4	0.0[c]
16 to 19 years	2,405,340	73.9	28.9	45.0	18.1	4.3[c]	1.3[c]	3.0[c]	51.5	21.1	30.4	0.0[c]
20 to 24 years	2,670,870	34.5	7.3[c]	27.2	1.5[c]	2.8[c]	0.0[c]	2.8[c]	30.3	7.1[c]	23.1	0.0[c]
25 to 34 years	5,223,930	31.9	10.6	21.3	0.7[c]	5.6[c]	2.2[c]	3.5[c]	25.5	9.2	16.3	1.9[c]
35 to 49 years	8,261,960	19.5	6.0	13.6	1.0[c]	2.1[c]	1.3[c]	0.8[c]	16.5	5.9	10.5	0.8[c]
50 to 64 years	4,513,150	14.4	6.5[c]	7.9	0.9[c]	5.1[c]	3.3[c]	1.8[c]	8.4	1.7[c]	6.6[c]	0.0[c]
65 years and older	2,858,650	9.2[c]	6.9[c]	2.3[c]	0.0[c]	5.9[c]	1.4[c]	4.5[c]	3.3[c]	1.6[c]	1.8[c]	0.8[c]

Note: See Note, table 3.1. Table excludes data on persons of "other" races. For survey methodology and definitions of terms, see Appendix 8.

Source: U.S. Department of Justice, Bureau of Justice Statistics, *Criminal Victimization in the United States, 2002 Statistical Tables*, NCJ 200561, Table 9 [Online]. Available: http://www.ojp.usdoj.gov/bjs/pub/pdf/cvus02.pdf [Mar. 3, 2004].

[a]Detail may not add to total because of rounding.
[b]Includes verbal threats of rape and threats of sexual assault.
[c]Estimate is based on about 10 or fewer sample cases.

Table 3.12

Estimated rate (per 1,000 persons age 12 and older) of personal victimization

By type of crime and annual household income of victim, United States, 2002[a]

Type of crime	Less than $7,500	$7,500 to $14,999	$15,000 to $24,999	$25,000 to $34,999	$35,000 to $49,999	$50,000 to $74,999	$75,000 or more
All personal crimes	47.2	32.0	30.8	27.4	26.0	19.3	19.7
Crimes of violence	45.5	31.5	30.0	27.0	25.6	18.7	19.0
Completed violence	18.7	12.0	11.4	9.3	6.7	4.9	5.6
Attempted/threatened violence	26.8	19.5	18.6	17.7	18.8	13.8	13.4
Rape/sexual assault	2.5[b]	3.2	2.1	1.2[b]	0.9[b]	0.2[b]	0.4[b]
Rape/attempted rape	2.3[b]	2.7	1.3	0.8[b]	0.3[b]	0.1[b]	0.2[b]
Rape	0.6[b]	1.4[b]	1.0[b]	0.3[b]	0.1[b]	0.1[b]	0.1[b]
Attempted rape[c]	1.7[b]	1.3[b]	0.2[b]	0.5[b]	0.2[b]	0.0[b]	0.1[b]
Sexual assault[d]	0.3[b]	0.4[b]	0.8[b]	0.4[b]	0.6[b]	0.1[b]	0.2[b]
Robbery	6.3	4.1	2.9	2.9	2.2	2.1	1.0
Completed/property taken	5.0	2.4	2.4	1.9	1.9	1.5	0.8
With injury	2.4[b]	1.3[b]	1.1[b]	0.8[b]	0.5[b]	0.3[b]	0.4[b]
Without injury	2.7[b]	1.1[b]	1.3	1.1[b]	1.4	1.2	0.4[b]
Attempted to take property	1.3[b]	1.7[b]	0.5[b]	1.0[b]	0.3[b]	0.6[b]	0.2[b]
With injury	0.3[b]	0.9[b]	0.1[b]	0.4[b]	0.0[b]	0.2[b]	0.1[b]
Without injury	1.0[b]	0.8[b]	0.4[b]	0.6[b]	0.3[b]	0.4[b]	0.1[b]
Assault	36.7	24.2	25.0	22.9	22.4	16.5	17.6
Aggravated	11.2	5.8	6.1	4.1	5.2	2.5	2.8
With injury	4.2	2.4	1.8	1.5	1.3	0.5[b]	0.9
Threatened with weapon	7.0	3.3	4.3	2.5	3.9	2.0	1.9
Simple	25.5	18.4	18.9	18.9	17.2	14.0	14.8
With minor injury	8.6	5.6	5.7	5.2	3.1	2.8	3.7
Without injury	16.9	12.8	13.3	13.7	14.1	11.2	11.2
Purse snatching/pocket picking	1.7[b]	0.5[b]	0.8[b]	0.3[b]	0.4[b]	0.6[b]	0.7
Population age 12 and older	8,347,650	15,608,210	23,872,200	24,104,810	31,655,160	33,713,640	43,139,380

Note: See Note, table 3.1. Table excludes data on persons whose family income level was not ascertained. For survey methodology and definitions of terms, see Appendix 8.

[a]Detail may not add to total because of rounding.
[b]Estimate is based on about 10 or fewer sample cases.
[c]Includes verbal threats of rape.
[d]Includes threats.

Source: U.S. Department of Justice, Bureau of Justice Statistics, *Criminal Victimization in the United States, 2002 Statistical Tables*, NCJ 200561, Table 14 [Online]. Available: http://www.ojp.usdoj.gov/bjs/pub/pdf/cvus02.pdf [Mar. 3, 2004].

Table 3.13

Estimated rate (per 1,000 persons age 12 and older) of personal victimization

By type of crime, size of population, and locality of residence, United States, 2002[a]

Type of crime	All areas	Total Urban	Total Suburban	50,000 to 249,999 Urban	50,000 to 249,999 Suburban	250,000 to 499,999 Urban	250,000 to 499,999 Suburban	500,000 to 999,999 Urban	500,000 to 999,999 Suburban	1,000,000 or more Urban	1,000,000 or more Suburban	Rural
Personal crimes	23.7	34.4	20.6	37.9	16.2	39.6	20.7	34.4	26.8	28.7	19.4	17.6
Crimes of violence	23.1	33.1	20.0	37.5	15.9	38.3	19.9	33.0	26.1	26.9	18.8	17.5
Completed violence	7.6	11.6	6.3	11.9	5.0	17.0	6.0	12.2	8.9	8.3	5.4	5.4
Attempted/threatened violence	15.5	21.6	13.7	25.6	10.8	21.3	13.9	20.8	17.2	18.5	13.3	12.1
Rape/sexual assault[b]	1.1	2.2	0.7	2.4	0.4[c]	0.6[c]	1.2	2.7	0.6[c]	2.4	0.5[c]	0.6
Robbery	2.2	4.3	1.8	2.6	1.8	7.6	1.6	5.0	2.0	3.8	1.7	0.7
Completed/property taken	1.7	3.3	1.3	2.0	1.3	6.8	1.2	3.6	1.7	2.6	0.8[c]	0.5[c]
With injury	0.7	1.2	0.7	0.8[c]	0.9	3.4	0.7[c]	1.3[c]	0.7[c]	0.5[c]	0.4[c]	0.3[c]
Without injury	0.9	2.1	0.6	1.2[c]	0.4[c]	3.4	0.5[c]	2.3	1.1	2.2	0.4[c]	0.2[c]
Attempted to take property	0.5	1.0	0.5	0.7[c]	0.5[c]	0.9[c]	0.4[c]	1.4[c]	0.3[c]	1.2[c]	0.9[c]	0.1[c]
With injury	0.2	0.2[c]	0.2[c]	0.1[c]	0.3[c]	0.0[c]	0.2[c]	0.5[c]	0.1[c]	0.2[c]	0.3[c]	0.0[c]
Without injury	0.4	0.8	0.2[c]	0.5[c]	0.2[c]	0.9[c]	0.2[c]	0.9[c]	0.2[c]	0.9[c]	0.5[c]	0.1[c]
Assault	19.8	26.7	17.6	32.6	13.7	30.1	17.1	25.3	23.5	20.7	16.6	16.2
Aggravated	4.3	6.5	3.5	6.3	3.4	9.7	2.6	6.3	5.2	5.3	2.5	3.3
With injury	1.4	2.0	1.1	1.5[c]	0.9[c]	4.3	1.2	2.1[c]	1.4	1.3[c]	0.8[c]	1.2
Threatened with weapon	2.9	4.5	2.4	4.7	2.5	5.4	1.5	4.2	3.8	4.0	1.7	2.1
Simple	15.5	20.2	14.1	26.3	10.3	20.3	14.4	19.0	18.3	15.4	14.1	12.9
With minor injury	3.9	5.1	3.6	7.1	2.7	5.3	3.0	4.5	5.4	3.5	3.6	3.1
Without injury	11.6	15.1	10.5	19.2	7.6	15.0	11.4	14.5	12.9	11.9	10.5	9.8
Purse snatching/pocket picking	0.7	1.2	0.6	0.4[c]	0.3[c]	1.3[c]	0.8[c]	1.4[c]	0.7[c]	1.9	0.6[c]	0.2[c]
Population age 12 and older	231,589,260	64,533,840	111,164,070	19,377,970	33,918,960	9,774,350	26,924,760	14,047,610	28,545,860	21,333,930	21,774,480	55,891,360

Note: See Note, table 3.1. "Urban" denotes central cities; "suburban" denotes outside central cities; "rural" denotes nonmetropolitan areas. The population range categories shown for "urban" and "suburban" are based on the size of the core city of a Metropolitan Statistical Area (MSA) and do not reflect the population of the entire MSA. For survey methodology and definitions of terms, see Appendix 8.

[a]Detail may not add to total because of rounding.
[b]Includes verbal threats of rape and threats of sexual assault.
[c]Estimate is based on about 10 or fewer sample cases.

Source: U.S. Department of Justice, Bureau of Justice Statistics, *Criminal Victimization in the United States, 2002 Statistical Tables*, NCJ 200561, Table 52 [Online]. Available: http://www.ojp.usdoj.gov/bjs/pub/pdf/cvus02.pdf [Mar. 3, 2004].

Table 3.14

Estimated number and percent distribution of violent victimization incidents

By type of crime and victim-offender relationship, United States, 2002[a]

Type of crime	All incidents Number	All incidents Percent	Involving strangers Number	Involving strangers Percent	Involving nonstrangers Number	Involving nonstrangers Percent
Crimes of violence	4,923,050	100%	2,403,050	48.8%	2,520,000	51.2%
Completed violence	1,605,900	100	696,930	43.4	908,960	56.6
Attempted/threatened violence	3,317,150	100	1,706,110	51.4	1,611,040	48.6
Rape/sexual assault	247,730	100	83,930	33.9	163,800	66.1
Rape/attempted rape	167,860	100	56,010	33.4	111,850	66.6
Rape	90,390	100	33,400	37.0	56,990	63.0
Attempted rape[b]	77,470	100	22,610[c]	29.2[c]	54,860	70.8
Sexual assault[d]	79,870	100	27,920[c]	35.0[c]	51,950	65.0
Robbery	458,460	100	330,540	72.1	127,930	27.9
Completed/property taken	341,910	100	247,510	72.4	94,400	27.6
With injury	159,120	100	98,450	61.9	60,680	38.1
Without injury	182,790	100	149,060	81.6	33,720	18.4
Attempted to take property	116,550	100	83,020	71.2	33,530	28.8
With injury	39,040	100	24,610[c]	63.0[c]	14,430[c]	37.0[c]
Without injury	77,510	100	58,410	75.4	19,100[c]	24.6[c]
Assault	4,216,850	100	1,988,580	47.2	2,228,270	52.8
Aggravated	848,030	100	486,100	57.3	361,940	42.7
With injury	273,670	100	115,610	42.2	158,060	57.8
Threatened with weapon	574,360	100	370,480	64.5	203,880	35.5
Simple	3,368,820	100	1,502,490	44.6	1,866,340	55.4
With minor injury	845,940	100	283,650	33.5	562,280	66.5
Without injury	2,522,890	100	1,218,830	48.3	1,304,050	51.7

Note: See Note, table 3.1. For survey methodology and definitions of terms, see Appendix 8.

[a]Detail may not add to total because of rounding.
[b]Includes verbal threats of rape.
[c]Estimate is based on about 10 or fewer sample cases.
[d]Includes threats.

Source: U.S. Department of Justice, Bureau of Justice Statistics, *Criminal Victimization in the United States, 2002 Statistical Tables*, NCJ 200561, Table 27 [Online]. Available: http://www.ojp.usdoj.gov/bjs/pub/pdf/cvus02.pdf [Mar. 3, 2004].

Table 3.15
Estimated percent distribution of violent victimization

By type of crime and victim-offender relationship, United States, 2002[a]

				Victim-offender relationship								
	Total		Related					Well	Casual	Don't know		Don't know
Type of crime	number of victimizations	Total crimes	Total	Spouse	Ex-spouse	Parent	Own child	Other relatives	known[b]	acquaint-ances	relation-ship	Strangers	number of offenders
Crimes of violence	5,341,410	100%	8.4%	2.6%	1.1%	1.3%	1.0%	2.3%	27.4%	13.8%	4.3%	44.4%	1.7%
Completed violence	1,753,090	100	12.6	5.0	1.3[c]	2.1	1.4[c]	2.8	31.2	10.7	4.4	39.5	1.7[c]
Attempted/threatened violence	3,588,320	100	6.3	1.5	1.0	0.8[c]	0.8[c]	2.1	25.6	15.4	4.2	46.8	1.7
Rape/sexual assault[d]	247,730	100	2.2[c]	0.7[c]	0.0[c]	0.0[c]	0.0[c]	1.6[c]	38.6	25.2	0.9[c]	30.7	2.2[c]
Robbery	512,490	100	6.7	1.9[c]	0.7[c]	2.2[c]	0.4[c]	1.4[c]	18.3	2.0[c]	8.0	62.5	2.5[c]
Completed/property taken	385,880	100	4.9[c]	1.9[c]	0.5[c]	1.3[c]	0.6[c]	0.6[c]	18.7	2.7[c]	7.5[c]	63.0	3.3[c]
Attempted to take property	126,610	100	12.1[c]	2.0[c]	1.4[c]	4.8[c]	0.0[c]	3.9[c]	17.1[c]	0.0[c]	9.8[c]	61.0	0.0[c]
Assault	4,581,190	100	8.9	2.8	1.2	1.2	1.1	2.5	27.9	14.5	4.0	43.1	1.6
Aggravated	990,110	100	9.2	2.8[c]	0.8[c]	2.2[c]	0.8[c]	2.6[c]	21.1	10.4	6.1	50.6	2.7[c]
Simple	3,591,090	100	8.8	2.8	1.4	1.0	1.2	2.5	29.7	15.7	3.4	41.0	1.3

Note: See Note, table 3.1. For survey methodology and definitions of terms, see Appendix 8.

Source: U.S. Department of Justice, Bureau of Justice Statistics, *Criminal Victimization in the United States, 2002 Statistical Tables*, NCJ 200561, Table 34 [Online]. Available: http://www.ojp.usdoj.gov/bjs/pub/pdf/cvus02.pdf [Mar. 3, 2004].

[a]Detail may not add to total because of rounding.
[b]Includes data on offenders well known to the victim whose relationship to the victim could not be ascertained.
[c]Estimate is based on about 10 or fewer sample cases.
[d]Includes verbal threats of rape and threats of sexual assault.

Table 3.16
Victim-offender relationship in violent victimization

By type of crime and sex of victim, United States, 2003[a]

	Violent crime		Rape/ sexual assault		Robbery		Aggravated assault		Simple assault	
Relationship of victim to offender	Number	Percent	Number	Percent	Number	Percent	Number	Percent	Number	Percent
Male victims, total	3,056,160	100%	19,670	100%	365,590	100%	688,420	100%	1,982,480	100%
Nonstranger	1,287,960	42	14,500[b]	74[b]	118,300	32	266,770	39	888,400	45
Intimate	83,750	3	5,940[b]	30[b]	6,130[b]	2[b]	21,910[b]	3[b]	49,780	3
Other relative	138,310	5	0[b]	0[b]	17,250[b]	5[b]	12,490[b]	2[b]	108,570	6
Friend/acquaintance	1,065,900	35	8,560[b]	44[b]	94,910	26	232,370	34	730,050	37
Stranger	1,658,160	54	5,170[b]	26[b]	226,110	62	399,240	58	1,027,630	52
Relationship unknown	110,050	4	0[b]	0[b]	21,180[b]	6[b]	22,420[b]	3[b]	66,450	3
Female victims, total	2,345,550	100	179,170	100	230,540	100	412,690	100	1,523,150	100
Nonstranger	1,562,010	67	125,370	70	110,670	48	274,430	67	1,051,540	69
Intimate	437,990	19	21,440[b]	12[b]	30,990[b]	13[b]	101,400	25	284,170	19
Other relative	230,850	10	13,930[b]	8[b]	17,430[b]	8[b]	40,320	10	159,180	11
Friend/acquaintance	893,170	38	90,000	50	62,260	27	132,720	32	608,190	40
Stranger	745,930	32	53,800	30	103,630	45	131,850	32	456,640	30
Relationship unknown	37,610	2	0[b]	0[b]	16,240[b]	7[b]	6,400[b]	2[b]	14,970[b]	1[b]

Note: See Note, table 3.1. For survey methodology and definitions of terms, see Appendix 8.

Source: U.S. Department of Justice, Bureau of Justice Statistics, *Criminal Victimization, 2003*, NCJ 205455 (Washington, DC: U.S. Department of Justice, September 2004), p. 9, Table 9.

[a]Detail may not add to total because of rounding.
[b]Estimate is based on 10 or fewer sample cases.

Table 3.17

Estimated percent distribution of violent victimization incidents

By type of crime, victim-offender relationship, and type of weapon used, United States, 2002[a]

Type of crime	All incidents Number	All incidents Percent	No weapon used	Weapon used Total	Total firearm	Hand-gun	Other gun	Gun type unknown	Knife	Sharp object	Blunt object	Other weapon	Weapon type unknown	Don't know if weapon present
Crimes of violence	4,923,050	100%	70.3%	21.3%	7.2%	6.0%	1.1%	0.1%[b]	4.4%	1.0%	3.1%	4.0%	1.5%	8.5%
Completed violence	1,605,900	100	67.5	25.7	8.4	7.4	1.1[b]	0.0[b]	3.6	1.7[b]	5.1	5.9	1.1	6.8
Attempted/threatened violence	3,317,150	100	71.6	19.1	6.6	5.3	1.1	0.2[b]	4.8	0.7[b]	2.1	3.1	1.7	9.3
Rape/sexual assault[c]	247,730	100	84.5	7.2[b]	4.6[b]	4.6[b]	0.0[b]	0.0[b]	2.6[b]	0.0[b]	0.0[b]	0.0[b]	0.0[b]	8.4[b]
Robbery	458,460	100	41.3	47.0	25.6	20.5	5.1[b]	0.0[b]	10.2	1.2[b]	2.3[b]	4.4[b]	3.3[b]	11.7
Completed/property taken	341,910	100	40.3	47.2	26.8	22.8	4.0[b]	0.0[b]	9.9	0.6[b]	2.7[b]	3.6[b]	3.7[b]	12.5
With injury	159,120	100	48.1	39.2	11.0[b]	10.3[b]	0.7[b]	0.0[b]	12.8[b]	1.3[b]	4.1[b]	5.4[b]	4.7[b]	12.7[b]
Without injury	182,790	100	33.6	54.2	40.5	33.7	6.9[b]	0.0[b]	7.3[b]	0.0[b]	1.5[b]	2.0[b]	2.8[b]	12.2[b]
Attempted to take property	116,550	100	44.0	46.4	22.2[b]	14.0[b]	8.2[b]	0.0[b]	11.3[b]	2.8[b]	1.1[b]	6.8[b]	2.2[b]	9.6[b]
With injury	39,040	100	37.3[b]	56.0[b]	17.3[b]	7.0[b]	10.3[b]	0.0[b]	22.6[b]	0.0[b]	3.4[b]	6.2[b]	6.4[b]	6.7[b]
Without injury	77,510	100	47.4	41.6	24.7[b]	17.6[b]	7.1[b]	0.0[b]	5.6[b]	4.2[b]	0.0[b]	7.2[b]	0.0[b]	11.1[b]
Assault	4,216,850	100	72.6	19.3	5.3	4.5	0.7[b]	0.1[b]	3.9	1.1	3.3	4.2	1.4	8.1
Aggravated	848,030	100	4.0	96.0	26.5	22.4	3.5[b]	0.6[b]	19.4	5.4	16.6	20.9	7.1	0.0[b]
With injury	273,670	100	12.4	87.6	13.1	11.8	1.3[b]	0.0[b]	7.2[b]	9.1[b]	26.3	30.2	1.8[b]	0.0[b]
Threatened with weapon	574,360	100	X	100.0	33.0	27.5	4.6[b]	0.9[b]	25.2	3.7[b]	12.0	16.5	9.6	0.0[b]
Simple[d]	3,368,820	100	89.9	X	X	X	X	X	X	X	X	X	X	10.1
With minor injury	845,940	100	93.4	X	X	X	X	X	X	X	X	X	X	6.6
Without injury	2,522,890	100	88.7	X	X	X	X	X	X	X	X	X	X	11.3
Involving strangers														
Crimes of violence	2,403,050	100	59.9	28.2	11.3	9.5	1.7	0.1[b]	5.5	1.0[b]	4.2	4.0	2.1	11.8
Rape/sexual assault[c]	83,930	100	70.6	13.5[b]	13.5[b]	13.5[b]	0.0[b]	0.0[b]	0.0[b]	0.0[b]	0.0[b]	0.0[b]	0.0[b]	15.9[b]
Robbery	330,540	100	27.2	58.4	34.9	28.5	6.4[b]	0.0[b]	11.9	1.6[b]	0.9[b]	4.5[b]	4.6[b]	14.4
Aggravated assault	486,100	100	2.5[b]	97.5	30.0	25.2	4.2[b]	0.6[b]	19.2	4.0[b]	20.3	16.5	7.5	0.0[b]
Simple assault[d]	1,502,490	100	85.1	X	X	X	X	X	X	X	X	X	X	14.9
Involving nonstrangers														
Crimes of violence	2,520,000	100	80.1	14.6	3.2	2.7	0.5[b]	0.1[b]	3.4	1.1[b]	2.0	4.1	0.9[b]	5.2
Rape/sexual assault[c]	163,800	100	91.6	3.9[b]	0.0[b]	0.0[b]	0.0[b]	0.0[b]	3.9[b]	0.0[b]	0.0[b]	0.0[b]	0.0[b]	4.5[b]
Robbery	127,930	100	77.6	17.6[b]	1.7[b]	0.0[b]	1.7[b]	0.0[b]	5.8[b]	0.0[b]	6.1[b]	4.0[b]	0.0[b]	4.8[b]
Aggravated assault	361,940	100	6.0[b]	94.0	21.9	18.7	2.6[b]	0.6[b]	19.7	7.4[b]	11.6	26.8	6.6[b]	0.0[b]
Simple assault[d]	1,866,340	100	93.7	X	X	X	X	X	X	X	X	X	X	6.3

Note: See Note, table 3.1. Responses for weapon use are tallied once, based upon a hierarchy. Prior to 1993, multiple responses for weapons were tallied. For survey methodology and definitions of terms, see Appendix 8.

Source: U.S. Department of Justice, Bureau of Justice Statistics, *Criminal Victimization in the United States, 2002 Statistical Tables*, NCJ 200561, Table 66 [Online]. Available: http://www.ojp.usdoj.gov/bjs/pub/pdf/cvus02.pdf [Mar. 3, 2004].

[a] Detail may not add to total because of rounding.
[b] Estimate is based on about 10 or fewer sample cases.
[c] Includes verbal threats of rape and threats of sexual assault.
[d] Simple assault, by definition, does not involve the use of a weapon.

Table 3.18

Estimated percent of violent victimizations in which victim took self-protective measures

By type of crime and victim-offender relationship, United States, 2002

	Victimizations in which self-protective measure was taken		
Type of crime	Total	Involving strangers	Involving nonstrangers
Crimes of violence	70.1%	67.8%	72.4%
Completed violence	71.1	61.4	79.1
Attempted/threatened violence	69.6	70.5	68.7
Rape/sexual assault[a]	82.1	76.3	85.1
Robbery	60.9	51.4	86.7
Completed/property taken	51.0	39.4	83.6
With injury	72.7	63.8	87.4
Without injury	33.9	25.0	77.0[b]
Attempted to take property	91.1	89.5	95.1
With injury	95.7	100.0[b]	89.1[b]
Without injury	88.8	85.2	100.0[b]
Assault	70.5	70.2	70.7
Aggravated	72.1	70.5	74.4
With injury	71.9	73.0	71.0
Threatened with weapon	72.2	69.7	76.9
Simple	70.0	70.1	70.0
With minor injury	78.2	75.1	79.8
Without injury	67.3	68.9	65.7

Note: See Note, table 3.1. For survey methodology and definitions of terms, see Appendix 8.

[a] Includes verbal threats of rape and threats of sexual assault.
[b] Estimate is based on about 10 or fewer sample cases.

Source: U.S. Department of Justice, Bureau of Justice Statistics, *Criminal Victimization in the United States, 2002 Statistical Tables*, NCJ 200561, Table 68 [Online]. Available: http://www.ojp.usdoj.gov/bjs/pub/pdf/cvus02.pdf [Mar. 3, 2004].

Table 3.19

Estimated percent distribution of self-protective measures employed by victims of violent crime

By sex and race of victim, United States, 2002[a]

	Sex			Race[b]	
Self-protective measure	Both sexes	Male	Female	White	Black
Total	100%	100%	100%	100%	100%
Attacked offender with weapon	0.8	0.9[c]	0.7[c]	0.5[c]	2.6[c]
Attacked offender without weapon	9.4	11.4	7.4	9.0	11.4
Threatened offender with weapon	0.8	1.1[c]	0.5[c]	0.8	1.3[c]
Threatened offender without weapon	1.9	2.2	1.6	1.7	3.4[c]
Resisted or captured offender	24.5	27.4	21.4	23.8	28.0
Scared or warned offender	9.3	8.7	9.9	9.2	8.1
Persuaded or appeased offender	11.0	11.6	10.3	11.3	9.0
Ran away or hid	14.1	12.4	15.8	14.5	12.6
Got help or gave alarm	12.0	10.7	13.5	12.6	9.4
Screamed from pain or fear	2.7	1.0[c]	4.6	2.3	4.3
Took other measures	13.5	12.6	14.4	14.4	9.9

Note: See Note, table 3.1. Some respondents may have reported more than one self-protective measure employed. For survey methodology and definitions of terms, see Appendix 8.

[a] Detail may not add to total because of rounding.
[b] Excludes data on persons of "other" races.
[c] Estimate is based on about 10 or fewer sample cases.

Source: U.S. Department of Justice, Bureau of Justice Statistics, *Criminal Victimization in the United States, 2002 Statistical Tables*, NCJ 200561, Table 71 [Online]. Available: http://www.ojp.usdoj.gov/bjs/pub/pdf/cvus02.pdf [Mar. 3, 2004].

Table 3.20

Estimated percent distribution of violent victimizations in which self-protective measures were employed

By person taking measure, type of crime, and outcome of measure, United States, 2002[a]

					Outcome of self-protective measure			
Person taking measure and type of crime	Number of victimizations	Total	Helped situation	Hurt situation	Both helped and hurt situation	Neither helped nor hurt situation	Don't know	Not available
Measure taken by victim								
Crimes of violence	3,744,110	100%	64.8%	9.7%	4.9%	11.8%	8.2%	0.6%[b]
Rape/sexual assault[c]	203,400	100	51.2	24.2	8.2[b]	10.4[b]	6.0[b]	0.0[b]
Robbery	312,260	100	51.2	13.3	6.7[b]	14.6	13.2	0.9[b]
Assault	3,228,450	100	67.0	8.5	4.5	11.6	7.8	0.6[b]
Aggravated	714,150	100	65.9	8.1	6.8	11.5	7.4	0.4[b]
Simple	2,514,300	100	67.3	8.6	3.9	11.6	8.0	0.6[b]
Measure taken by others								
Crimes of violence	3,496,770	100	32.2	10.4	2.3	45.7	8.0	1.5
Rape/sexual assault[c]	73,160	100	45.8	4.7[b]	0.0[b]	36.5[b]	8.5[b]	4.6[b]
Robbery	272,320	100	35.4	7.8[b]	1.0[b]	48.6	7.2[b]	0.0[b]
Assault	3,151,290	100	31.6	10.7	2.4	45.7	8.1	1.5
Aggravated	695,320	100	35.6	11.1	1.2[b]	41.1	9.0	2.1[b]
Simple	2,455,970	100	30.4	10.6	2.8	47.0	7.8	1.4

Note: See Note, table 3.1. Table excludes victimizations in which no self-protective actions were taken. Of those victimizations in which self-protective measures were employed, the victim and/or someone else may have taken action. Therefore, the above categories are not mutually exclusive. For survey methodology and definitions of terms, see Appendix 8.

Source: U.S. Department of Justice, Bureau of Justice Statistics, *Criminal Victimization in the United States, 2002 Statistical Tables*, NCJ 200561, Table 72 [Online]. Available: http://www.ojp.usdoj.gov/bjs/pub/pdf/cvus02.pdf [Mar. 3, 2004].

[a]Detail may not add to total because of rounding.
[b]Estimate is based on about 10 or fewer sample cases.
[c]Includes verbal threats of rape and threats of sexual assault.

Table 3.21

Estimated rate (per 1,000 households) of property victimization

By type of crime and characteristics of household, United States, 2003

			Type of property crime		
Characteristics of household	Number of households	Total	Burglary	Motor vehicle theft	Theft
Household income					
Under $7,500	5,161,000	204.6	58.0	6.3	140.3
$7,500 to $14,999	9,214,180	167.7	42.2	7.3	118.3
$15,000 to $24,999	12,550,810	179.2	38.4	8.9	131.9
$25,000 to $34,999	11,764,020	180.7	35.3	12.3	133.1
$35,000 to $49,999	14,731,780	177.1	27.6	9.5	140.0
$50,000 to $74,999	15,017,300	168.1	24.9	8.4	134.7
$75,000 and over	19,395,640	176.4	20.8	11.9	143.7
Region					
Northeast	21,259,800	122.1	20.5	7.2	94.4
Midwest	27,137,920	160.2	32.5	6.9	120.9
South	41,583,860	160.5	32.2	7.8	120.4
West	24,155,340	207.4	30.6	15.2	161.6
Residence					
Urban	32,515,050	216.3	38.7	13.0	164.7
Suburban	53,701,950	144.8	24.0	9.3	111.6
Rural	27,919,930	136.6	30.5	4.0	102.1
Home ownership					
Owned	78,421,480	143.5	24.5	7.3	111.7
Rented	35,715,440	206.4	41.2	13.0	152.2

Note: See Note, table 3.1. For survey methodology and definitions of terms, see Appendix 8.

Source: U.S. Department of Justice, Bureau of Justice Statistics, *Criminal Victimization, 2003*, NCJ 205455 (Washington, DC: U.S. Department of Justice, September 2004), p. 9, Table 8.

Table 3.22

Estimated number and rate (per 1,000 households) of property victimization

By type of crime and race of head of household, United States, 2002[a]

Type of crime	All races Number	All races Rate	White Number	White Rate	Black Number	Black Rate	Other Number	Other Rate
Property crimes	17,539,220	159.0	14,527,440	157.6	2,434,780	173.7	576,990	139.8
Household burglary	3,055,720	27.7	2,396,810	26.0	578,880	41.3	80,030	19.4
Completed	2,597,310	23.5	2,080,340	22.6	444,040	31.7	72,930	17.7
Forcible entry	1,017,660	9.2	727,180	7.9	260,680	18.6	29,800[b]	7.2[b]
Unlawful entry without force	1,579,650	14.3	1,353,160	14.7	183,360	13.1	43,130	10.4
Attempted forcible entry	458,410	4.2	316,470	3.4	134,840	9.6	7,100[b]	1.7[b]
Motor vehicle theft	988,760	9.0	695,410	7.5	241,670	17.2	51,670	12.5
Completed	780,630	7.1	549,730	6.0	191,610	13.7	39,300	9.5
Attempted	208,120	1.9	145,690	1.6	50,060	3.6	12,380[b]	3.0[b]
Theft	13,494,750	122.3	11,435,220	124.1	1,614,240	115.2	445,290	107.9
Completed	13,039,920	118.2	11,054,970	119.9	1,556,620	111.1	428,320	103.8
Less than $50	4,186,570	37.9	3,646,500	39.6	409,720	29.2	130,360	31.6
$50 to $249	4,455,080	40.4	3,717,980	40.3	598,290	42.7	138,810	33.6
$250 or more	3,270,530	29.6	2,766,820	30.0	396,330	28.3	107,390	26.0
Amount not available	1,127,740	10.2	923,680	10.0	152,290	10.9	51,760	12.5
Attempted	454,830	4.1	380,240	4.1	57,620	4.1	16,970[b]	4.1[b]
Total number of households	110,323,840	X	92,182,320	X	14,013,850	X	4,127,670	X

Note: See Note, table 3.1. For survey methodology and definitions of terms, see Appendix 8.

[a]Detail may not add to total because of rounding.
[b]Estimate is based on about 10 or fewer sample cases.

Source: U.S. Department of Justice, Bureau of Justice Statistics, *Criminal Victimization in the United States, 2002 Statistical Tables*, NCJ 200561, Table 16 [Online]. Available: http://www.ojp.usdoj.gov/bjs/pub/pdf/cvus02.pdf [Mar. 3, 2004].

Table 3.23

Estimated number and rate (per 1,000 households) of property victimization

By type of crime and ethnicity of head of household, United States, 2002[a]

Type of crime	Total[b] Number	Total[b] Rate	Hispanic Number	Hispanic Rate	Non-Hispanic Number	Non-Hispanic Rate
Property crimes	17,539,220	159.0	2,207,780	210.1	15,192,540	153.3
Household burglary	3,055,720	27.7	318,370	30.3	2,711,060	27.4
Completed	2,597,310	23.5	279,860	26.6	2,295,420	23.2
Forcible entry	1,017,660	9.2	134,410	12.8	873,960	8.8
Unlawful entry without force	1,579,650	14.3	145,460	13.8	1,421,460	14.3
Attempted forcible entry	458,410	4.2	38,510	3.7	415,640	4.2
Motor vehicle theft	988,760	9.0	185,660	17.7	789,290	8.0
Completed	780,630	7.1	156,750	14.9	618,020	6.2
Attempted	208,120	1.9	28,900[c]	2.8[c]	171,270	1.7
Theft	13,494,750	122.3	1,703,750	162.1	11,692,180	118.0
Completed	13,039,920	118.2	1,658,360	157.8	11,295,340	114.0
Less than $50	4,186,570	37.9	372,100	35.4	3,781,860	38.2
$50 to $249	4,455,080	40.4	647,180	61.6	3,784,150	38.2
$250 or more	3,270,530	29.6	480,070	45.7	2,769,960	27.9
Amount not available	1,127,740	10.2	159,010	15.1	959,360	9.7
Attempted	454,830	4.1	45,380	4.3	396,850	4.0
Total number of households	110,323,840	X	10,507,570	X	99,104,480	X

Note: See Note, table 3.1. For survey methodology and definitions of terms, see Appendix 8.

[a]Detail may not add to total because of rounding.
[b]Includes data on persons whose ethnicity was not ascertained, which are not shown separately.
[c]Estimate is based on about 10 or fewer sample cases.

Source: U.S. Department of Justice, Bureau of Justice Statistics, *Criminal Victimization in the United States, 2002 Statistical Tables*, NCJ 200561, Table 17 [Online]. Available: http://www.ojp.usdoj.gov/bjs/pub/pdf/cvus02.pdf [Mar. 3, 2004].

Table 3.24

Estimated rate (per 1,000 households) of property victimization

By type of crime and annual household income, United States, 2002[a]

Type of crime	Less than $7,500	$7,500 to $14,999	$15,000 to $24,999	$25,000 to $34,999	$35,000 to $49,999	$50,000 to $74,999	$75,000 or more
Property crimes	188.9	166.7	172.1	161.7	175.4	158.3	169.8
Household burglary	51.4	31.8	33.8	27.8	27.3	24.6	21.0
Completed	39.1	27.0	25.8	24.2	23.0	21.8	18.6
Forcible entry	16.8	11.9	12.4	9.3	8.6	7.0	4.5
Unlawful entry without force	22.3	15.1	13.5	14.9	14.4	14.8	14.1
Attempted forcible entry	12.3	4.8	7.9	3.7	4.2	2.8	2.4
Motor vehicle theft	3.2[b]	8.1	9.9	12.6	11.3	9.2	5.9
Completed	3.2[b]	6.8	8.2	9.2	8.6	7.0	4.5
Attempted	0.0[b]	1.3[b]	1.7[b]	3.5	2.7	2.1	1.4[b]
Theft	134.3	126.8	128.5	121.2	136.9	124.5	142.9
Completed	130.9	124.1	125.6	116.4	133.1	119.0	136.6
Less than $50	34.5	37.5	42.0	40.2	44.7	40.2	44.4
$50 to $249	55.1	46.6	44.7	40.8	43.8	39.9	44.1
$250 or more	32.8	28.7	30.1	26.3	33.8	26.1	36.5
Amount not available	8.4	11.3	8.8	9.0	10.8	12.9	11.5
Attempted	3.4[b]	2.7[b]	2.8	4.8	3.8	5.5	6.3
Total number of households	5,157,750	9,038,620	12,231,090	11,586,530	14,391,310	14,283,610	17,532,840

Note: See Note, table 3.1. Table excludes data on families whose income level was not ascertained. For survey methodology and definitions of terms, see Appendix 8.

[a]Detail may not add to total because of rounding.
[b]Estimate is based on about 10 or fewer sample cases.

Source: U.S. Department of Justice, Bureau of Justice Statistics, *Criminal Victimization in the United States, 2002 Statistical Tables*, NCJ 200561, Table 20 [Online]. Available: http://www.ojp.usdoj.gov/bjs/pub/pdf/cvus02.pdf [Mar. 3, 2004].

Table 3.25

Estimated rate (per 1,000 households) of property victimization

By type of crime, size of population, and locality of residence, United States, 2002[a]

Type of crime	All areas	Total Urban	Total Suburban	50,000 to 249,999 Urban	50,000 to 249,999 Suburban	250,000 to 499,999 Urban	250,000 to 499,999 Suburban	500,000 to 999,999 Urban	500,000 to 999,999 Suburban	1,000,000 or more Urban	1,000,000 or more Suburban	Rural
Property crimes	159.0	215.3	145.3	223.1	137.0	238.7	136.7	202.3	156.3	206.2	154.4	118.3
Household burglary	27.7	40.5	22.4	45.1	20.7	39.3	22.7	45.6	22.2	33.5	25.2	22.6
Completed	23.5	34.1	19.1	37.8	17.2	33.8	18.4	38.0	19.9	28.3	21.6	19.5
Forcible entry	9.2	16.4	6.1	16.3	4.6	18.0	7.8	19.5	5.9	13.5	6.7	6.7
Unlawful entry without force	14.3	17.8	12.9	21.6	12.6	15.8	10.6	18.5	14.0	14.8	14.9	12.9
Attempted forcible entry	4.2	6.4	3.4	7.3	3.4	5.4[b]	4.3	7.5	2.3[b]	5.2	3.5	3.0
Motor vehicle theft	9.0	17.1	7.5	9.3	5.3	19.6	7.2	19.9	8.2	20.7	10.2	2.2
Completed	7.1	13.1	6.0	9.0	4.3	14.9	5.9	15.6	6.8	14.0	7.9	2.0
Attempted	1.9	4.0	1.4	0.3[b]	1.0[b]	4.7[b]	1.3[b]	4.4	1.4[b]	6.6	2.3[b]	0.3[b]
Theft	122.3	157.7	115.4	168.7	111.1	179.9	106.7	136.8	125.9	152.0	119.0	93.5
Completed	118.2	151.5	111.6	164.3	105.7	170.6	103.8	130.7	121.9	145.6	116.6	91.3
Less than $50	37.9	42.5	37.1	49.3	40.6	44.4	34.2	38.6	36.5	38.5	36.4	34.1
$50 to $249	40.4	55.3	36.5	62.2	35.4	57.9	32.0	47.4	40.4	53.5	38.5	30.1
$250 or more	29.6	40.3	28.0	42.5	22.2	49.1	26.9	33.9	33.0	38.5	31.7	20.1
Amount not available	10.2	13.4	10.0	10.3	7.6	19.2	10.7	10.7	12.0	15.1	10.1	7.0
Attempted	4.1	6.2	3.8	4.4	5.4	9.3	2.9	6.2	4.0	6.3	2.4[b]	2.2
Total number of households	110,323,840	31,937,800	51,446,980	9,207,710	15,382,280	4,982,290	12,670,550	7,195,150	13,385,490	10,552,650	10,008,660	26,939,060

Note: See Notes, tables 3.1 and 3.13. For survey methodology and definitions of terms, see Appendix 8.

Source: U.S. Department of Justice, Bureau of Justice Statistics, *Criminal Victimization in the United States, 2002 Statistical Tables*, NCJ 200561, Table 53 [Online]. Available: http://www.ojp.usdoj.gov/bjs/pub/pdf/cvus02.pdf [Mar. 3, 2004].

[a]Detail may not add to total because of rounding.
[b]Estimate is based on about 10 or fewer sample cases.

Table 3.26

Estimated rate (per 1,000 households) of property victimization

By locality of residence, race of head of household, and type of crime, United States, 2002[a]

Locality and race of head of household	Total households	Property crimes	Household burglary	Motor vehicle theft	Theft
All areas					
White	92,182,320	157.6	26.0	7.5	124.1
Black	14,013,850	173.7	41.3	17.2	115.2
Urban					
White	22,867,860	220.0	37.0	15.0	168.1
Black	7,354,200	211.7	53.6	22.8	135.4
Suburban					
White	45,038,270	145.9	22.3	6.6	116.9
Black	4,390,810	150.4	28.9	15.8	105.7
Rural					
White	24,276,190	120.6	22.5	2.3	95.8
Black	2,268,840	95.7	25.5	2.1[b]	68.1

Note: See Notes, tables 3.1 and 3.13. Table excludes data on persons of "other" races. For survey methodology and definitions of terms, see Appendix 8.

[a]Detail may not add to total because of rounding.
[b]Estimate is based on about 10 or fewer sample cases.

Source: U.S. Department of Justice, Bureau of Justice Statistics, *Criminal Victimization in the United States, 2002 Statistical Tables*, NCJ 200561, Table 55 [Online]. Available: http://www.ojp.usdoj.gov/bjs/pub/pdf/cvus02.pdf [Mar. 3, 2004].

Table 3.27

Estimated percent distribution of households experiencing crime

By type of crime, United States, 1994-2000, 2002, and 2003[a]

Type of crime	1994	1995	1996	1997	1998	1999	2000	2002	2003
Any NCVS crime[b]	25.0%	23.4%	22.4%	20.9%	19.1%	17.7%	16.2%	14.6%	14.7%
Violent crime	7.0	6.3	5.9	5.5	5.0	4.4	3.9	3.2	3.0
Rape	0.2	0.2	0.1	0.2	0.1	0.2	0.1	0.1	0.1
Sexual assault	0.1	0.1	0.1	0.1	0.1	0.1	0.1	0.1	0.1
Robbery	1.0	0.9	0.9	0.7	0.6	0.6	0.5	0.4	0.4
Assault	6.0	5.4	5.1	4.8	4.4	3.8	3.4	2.8	2.6
Aggravated	1.9	1.5	1.4	1.4	1.2	1.0	0.9	0.7	0.7
Simple	4.7	4.3	3.9	3.7	3.5	2.9	2.7	2.2	2.0
Purse snatching/pocket picking	0.4	0.3	0.3	0.3	0.2	0.2	0.2	0.1	0.1
Property crime	21.1	19.9	19.0	17.7	16.0	14.9	13.6	12.5	12.7
Household burglary	4.6	4.1	4.0	3.7	3.3	2.9	2.7	2.4	2.6
Motor vehicle theft	1.7	1.5	1.2	1.2	1.0	0.9	0.8	0.8	0.8
Theft	16.9	16.1	15.4	14.1	12.8	12.1	10.9	9.9	10.0
Intimate partner violence[c]	0.8	0.7	0.6	0.7	0.7	0.5	0.5	0.4	0.3
Violence by strangers or household burglary[d]	7.9	7.2	6.7	6.2	5.4	4.9	4.5	3.9	3.9
Vandalism[b]	9.0	8.0	7.9	7.4	6.5	6.2	5.7	4.9	5.1
Households experiencing crime	25,103,670	23,794,200	23,036,300	21,749,300	20,063,900	18,985,700	17,580,900	16,080,430	16,749,820
Total households	100,544,570	101,481,000	102,675,000	103,967,400	105,301,700	107,138,300	108,331,600	110,323,840	114,136,930

Note: These data are from the U.S. Department of Justice, Bureau of Justice Statistics' National Crime Victimization Survey (NCVS). The data reflect the number and percent of households in the United States victimized during a given year. A household is counted only once for each type of crime, regardless of how often the household or household member was victimized during the year. For example, if a particular household was burglarized twice and a member of that household was robbed once during the year, it is counted once for households victimized by burglary, once for households victimized by robbery, and once for the overall measure of households experiencing crime. The NCVS measures crime for which the victim can be interviewed and therefore does not include murder. For survey methodology and definitions of terms, see Appendix 8.

[a]Subcategories may not add to total because of overlap in households experiencing various types of crime.
[b]Vandalism is not included in totals.
[c]These crimes also are included in overall violent crimes. Intimate partners include current and former spouses, boyfriends, and girlfriends.
[d]These crimes also are included in overall violent or property crimes.

Source: U.S. Department of Justice, Bureau of Justice Statistics, *Crime and the Nation's Households, 2000 with Trends, 1994-2000*, Bulletin NCJ 194107, p. 3; *Crime and the Nation's Households, 2002*, Bulletin NCJ 201797, p. 2, Table 1; and p. 3; *2003*, Bulletin NCJ 206348, p. 2, Table 1; and p. 3, Table 5 (Washington, DC: U.S. Department of Justice).

Table 3.28
Estimated percent distribution of violent victimizations by lone offenders

By type of crime and perceived age of offender, United States, 2002[a]

Type of crime	Number of lone-offender victimizations	Total	Under 12	12 to 20 Total	12 to 14	15 to 17	18 to 20	21 to 29	30 and older	Not known and not available
Crimes of violence	4,158,290	100%	2.2%	29.8%	8.9%	11.3%	9.7%	25.7%	37.8%	4.5%
Completed violence	1,290,480	100	2.8	28.7	8.8	9.1	10.8	27.4	35.5	5.6
Attempted/threatened violence	2,867,810	100	1.9	30.3	8.9	12.2	9.1	24.9	38.9	4.0
Rape/sexual assault[b]	202,670	100	0.0[c]	21.2	3.3[c]	5.1[c]	12.8[c]	49.9	28.8	0.0[c]
Robbery	280,000	100	1.4[c]	21.2	1.8[c]	7.5[c]	11.9	38.6	31.1	7.7[c]
Completed/property taken	191,270	100	0.0[c]	16.8	1.3[c]	6.1[c]	9.4[c]	40.0	33.3	9.9[c]
With injury	74,900	100	0.0[c]	14.5[c]	3.3[c]	0.0[c]	11.2[c]	33.7[c]	45.8	5.9[c]
Without injury	116,360	100	0.0[c]	18.3[c]	0.0[c]	10.1[c]	8.2[c]	44.0	25.3[c]	12.5[c]
Attempted to take property	88,730	100	4.5[c]	30.8[c]	3.0[c]	10.5[c]	17.2[c]	35.6	26.4[c]	2.8[c]
With injury	34,610	100	0.0[c]	25.1[c]	0.0[c]	0.0[c]	25.1[c]	32.1[c]	35.6[c]	7.2[c]
Without injury	54,110	100	7.4[c]	34.4[c]	4.9[c]	17.3[c]	12.2[c]	37.8[c]	20.5[c]	0.0[c]
Assault	3,675,610	100	2.4	30.9	9.7	11.9	9.3	23.4	38.8	4.5
Aggravated	720,880	100	3.0[c]	23.9	5.1	6.3	12.6	19.3	46.7	7.0
Simple	2,954,730	100	2.2	32.6	10.8	13.2	8.5	24.4	36.9	3.9

Note: See Note, table 3.1. For survey methodology and definitions of terms, see Appendix 8.

[a]Detail may not add to total because of rounding.
[b]Includes verbal threats of rape and threats of sexual assault.
[c]Estimate is based on about 10 or fewer sample cases.

Source: U.S. Department of Justice, Bureau of Justice Statistics, *Criminal Victimization in the United States, 2002 Statistical Tables*, NCJ 200561, Table 39 [Online]. Available: http://www.ojp.usdoj.gov/bjs/pub/pdf/cvus02.pdf [Mar. 3, 2004].

Table 3.29
Estimated percent distribution of violent victimizations by lone offenders

By type of crime and perceived race of offender, United States, 2002[a]

Type of crime	Number of lone-offender victimizations	Total	White	Black	Other	Not known and not available
Crimes of violence	4,158,290	100%	63.3%	22.8%	13.0%	0.9%
Completed violence	1,290,480	100	61.4	25.8	12.2	0.7[b]
Attempted/threatened violence	2,867,810	100	64.2	21.5	13.4	1.0[b]
Rape/sexual assault[c]	202,670	100	55.8	35.8	8.4[b]	0.0[b]
Robbery	280,000	100	42.4	45.7	12.0	0.0[b]
Completed/property taken	191,270	100	38.7	52.1	9.1[b]	0.0[b]
With injury	74,900	100	35.8[b]	54.2	10.0[b]	0.0[b]
Without injury	116,360	100	40.7	50.8	8.5[b]	0.0[b]
Attempted to take property	88,730	100	50.2	31.7[b]	18.1[b]	0.0[b]
With injury	34,610	100	59.3[b]	32.6[b]	8.1[b]	0.0[b]
Without injury	54,110	100	44.4[b]	31.1[b]	24.5[b]	0.0[b]
Assault	3,675,610	100	65.3	20.4	13.3	1.0
Aggravated	720,880	100	58.0	24.1	17.5	0.5[b]
Simple	2,954,730	100	67.1	19.4	12.3	1.2

Note: See Note, table 3.1. For survey methodology and definitions of terms, see Appendix 8.

[a]Detail may not add to total because of rounding.
[b]Estimate is based on about 10 or fewer sample cases.
[c]Includes verbal threats of rape and threats of sexual assault.

Source: U.S. Department of Justice, Bureau of Justice Statistics, *Criminal Victimization in the United States, 2002 Statistical Tables*, NCJ 200561, Table 40 [Online]. Available: http://www.ojp.usdoj.gov/bjs/pub/pdf/cvus02.pdf [Mar. 3, 2004].

Table 3.30

Estimated percent distribution of violent victimizations by multiple offenders

By type of crime and perceived age of offenders, United States, 2002[a]

Type of crime	Number of multiple-offender victimizations	Total	All under 12	All 12 to 20	All 21 to 29	All 30 and older	Mixed ages	Not known and not available
Crimes of violence	1,091,760	100%	0.5%[b]	37.9%	16.4%	6.6%	26.0%	12.6%
Completed violence	433,470	100	0.0[b]	26.0	20.2	9.9	27.7	16.2
Attempted/threatened violence	658,280	100	0.8[b]	45.7	13.8	4.5[b]	24.9	10.2
Rape/sexual assault[c]	39,580	100	0.0[b]	38.3[b]	10.9[b]	0.0[b]	43.6[b]	7.3[b]
Robbery	219,770	100	0.0[b]	27.7	23.3	7.1[b]	20.9	21.1
Completed/property taken	181,890	100	0.0[b]	25.2	24.3	8.5[b]	19.5	22.5
With injury	89,620	100	0.0[b]	13.3[b]	22.6[b]	11.0[b]	30.9[b]	22.2[b]
Without injury	92,260	100	0.0[b]	36.7	25.9[b]	6.1[b]	8.4[b]	22.8[b]
Attempted to take property	37,870	100	0.0[b]	39.7[b]	18.6[b]	0.0[b]	27.5[b]	14.2[b]
With injury	7,970[b]	100[b]	0.0[b]	65.8[b]	0.0[b]	0.0[b]	34.2[b]	0.0[b]
Without injury	29,900[b]	100[b]	0.0[b]	32.7[b]	23.6[b]	0.0[b]	25.7[b]	18.0[b]
Assault	832,400	100	0.6[b]	40.5	14.8	6.8	26.6	10.7
Aggravated	242,510	100	1.1[b]	26.2	16.6	5.7[b]	38.1	12.3[b]
Simple	589,890	100	0.4[b]	46.4	14.1	7.3	21.8	10.0

Note: See Note, table 3.1. For survey methodology and definitions of terms, see Appendix 8.

[a]Detail may not add to total because of rounding.
[b]Estimate is based on about 10 or fewer sample cases.
[c]Includes verbal threats of rape and threats of sexual assault.

Source: U.S. Department of Justice, Bureau of Justice Statistics, *Criminal Victimization in the United States, 2002 Statistical Tables*, NCJ 200561, Table 45 [Online]. Available: http://www.ojp.usdoj.gov/bjs/pub/pdf/cvus02.pdf [Mar. 3, 2004].

Table 3.31

Estimated percent distribution of violent victimizations by multiple offenders

By type of crime and perceived race of offenders, United States, 2002[a]

Type of crime	Number of multiple-offender victimizations	Total	All white	All black	All other	Mixed races	Not known and not available
Crimes of violence	1,091,760	100%	41.8%	24.1%	13.6%	14.1%	6.4%
Completed violence	433,470	100	34.0	32.4	13.1	15.0	5.5[b]
Attempted/threatened violence	658,280	100	46.9	18.6	14.0	13.5	7.0
Rape/sexual assault[c]	39,580	100	39.8[b]	29.3[b]	10.9[b]	20.0[b]	0.0[b]
Robbery	219,770	100	22.8	42.8	12.0[b]	14.7	7.6[b]
Completed/property taken	181,890	100	22.2	43.5	8.9[b]	16.3[b]	9.2[b]
With injury	89,620	100	21.1[b]	41.2	10.6[b]	16.2[b]	11.0[b]
Without injury	92,260	100	23.3[b]	45.7	7.2[b]	16.4[b]	7.4[b]
Attempted to take property	37,870	100	26.0[b]	39.8[b]	27.0[b]	7.2[b]	0.0[b]
With injury	7,970[b]	100[b]	33.0[b]	32.8[b]	0.0[b]	34.2[b]	0.0[b]
Without injury	29,900[b]	100[b]	24.1[b]	41.7[b]	34.3[b]	0.0[b]	0.0[b]
Assault	832,400	100	46.9	18.9	14.2	13.6	6.4
Aggravated	242,510	100	37.8	22.5	18.5	14.0	7.1[b]
Simple	589,890	100	50.6	17.3	12.5	13.5	6.1

Note: See Note, table 3.1. For survey methodology and definitions of terms, see Appendix 8.

[a]Detail may not add to total because of rounding.
[b]Estimate is based on about 10 or fewer sample cases.
[c]Includes verbal threats of rape and threats of sexual assault.

Source: U.S. Department of Justice, Bureau of Justice Statistics, *Criminal Victimization in the United States, 2002 Statistical Tables*, NCJ 200561, Table 46 [Online]. Available: http://www.ojp.usdoj.gov/bjs/pub/pdf/cvus02.pdf [Mar. 3, 2004].

Table 3.32

Estimated percent distribution of personal and property incidents

By type of crime and place of occurrence, United States, 2002[a]

Type of crime	Number of incidents	Total	At or in respondent's home	Near home	On the street near home	At, in, or near a friend's, relative's, or neighbor's home	Inside a restaurant, bar, or nightclub	Other commercial building	Parking lot or garage	Inside school building/ on school property	In apartment yard, park, field, or playground	On street other than near own home	On public transportation or inside station	Other
Crimes of violence	4,923,050	100%	16.3%	11.0%	4.4%	8.9%	4.2%	7.1%	7.6%	15.1%	2.5%	14.0%	1.0%	7.7%
Completed violence	1,605,900	100	23.0	9.3	3.5	13.0	3.6	4.2	6.9	11.4	2.4	14.1	1.2[b]	7.4
Attempted/threatened violence	3,317,150	100	13.1	11.9	4.9	7.0	4.5	8.6	8.0	16.9	2.6	13.9	0.9[b]	7.9
Rape/sexual assault[c]	247,730	100	26.1	3.4[b]	1.4[b]	17.0	2.8[b]	14.2	2.1[b]	3.8[b]	1.6[b]	13.5	1.2[b]	13.0
Robbery	458,460	100	21.8	7.8	4.4[b]	5.6[b]	1.0[b]	3.0[b]	14.7	3.8[b]	1.9[b]	28.3	2.8[b]	4.8[b]
Completed/property taken	341,910	100	22.1	7.1[b]	4.2[b]	6.4[b]	1.4[b]	4.0[b]	13.8	2.2[b]	1.5[b]	30.7	2.8[b]	3.8[b]
With injury	159,120	100	23.6	6.1[b]	6.4[b]	6.2[b]	0.7[b]	6.2[b]	4.2[b]	1.6[b]	0.0[b]	42.7	2.3[b]	0.0[b]
Without injury	182,790	100	20.7	7.9[b]	2.3[b]	6.6[b]	2.1[b]	2.1[b]	22.1	2.8[b]	2.9[b]	20.2	3.2[b]	7.2[b]
Attempted to take property	116,550	100	21.0[b]	9.9[b]	4.9[b]	3.1[b]	0.0[b]	0.0[b]	17.5[b]	8.4[b]	2.9[b]	21.4[b]	3.0[b]	7.8[b]
With injury	39,040	100	33.6[b]	0.0[b]	6.7[b]	0.0[b]	0.0[b]	0.0[b]	30.2[b]	8.0[b]	0.0[b]	12.4[b]	9.1[b]	0.0[b]
Without injury	77,510	100	14.7[b]	14.8[b]	4.0[b]	4.7[b]	0.0[b]	0.0[b]	11.1[b]	8.6[b]	4.4[b]	26.0[b]	0.0[b]	11.7[b]
Assault	4,216,850	100	15.2	11.8	4.6	8.8	4.6	7.1	7.2	17.0	2.7	12.5	0.8	7.7
Aggravated	848,030	100	15.8	15.0	3.2[b]	9.3	3.5[b]	7.9	8.8	6.8	2.0[b]	18.6	0.4[b]	8.8
Simple	3,368,820	100	15.0	11.0	5.0	8.7	4.9	7.0	6.7	19.6	2.8	10.9	0.8[b]	7.5
Purse snatching/ pocket picking	154,190	100	3.7[b]	3.7[b]	1.4[b]	10.0[b]	9.6[b]	14.9[b]	9.4[b]	6.0[b]	2.1[b]	33.4	4.4[b]	1.5[b]
Motor vehicle theft	988,760	100	1.3[b]	27.3	18.1	3.6	X	X	36.2	0.7[b]	0.0[b]	10.4	X	2.4[b]
Completed	780,630	100	1.2[b]	28.0	15.3	4.2	X	X	35.4	0.9[b]	0.0[b]	12.3	X	2.7[b]
Attempted	208,120	100	1.5[b]	24.8	28.8	1.3[b]	X	X	39.3	0.0[b]	0.0[b]	3.2[b]	X	1.1[b]
Theft	13,494,750	100	9.7	34.3	6.0	2.9	1.8	5.5	15.6	10.9	1.3	3.9	0.8	7.3

Note: See Note, table 3.1. For survey methodology and definitions of terms, see Appendix 8.

Source: U.S. Department of Justice, Bureau of Justice Statistics, *Criminal Victimization in the United States, 2002 Statistical Tables*, NCJ 200561, Table 61 [Online]. Available: http://www.ojp.usdoj.gov/bjs/pub/pdf/cvus02.pdf [Mar. 3, 2004].

[a] Detail may not add to total because of rounding.
[b] Estimate is based on about 10 or fewer sample cases.
[c] Includes verbal threats of rape and threats of sexual assault.

Table 3.33

Estimated percent distribution of personal and property victimization

By type of crime and whether or not reported to police, United States, 2002[a]

Type of crime	Number of victimizations	Total	Yes[b]	No	Not known and not available
All crimes	23,036,030	100%	42.2%	56.5%	1.3%
Personal crimes	5,496,810	100	48.4	49.8	1.7
Crimes of violence	5,341,410	100	48.5	49.7	1.8
Completed violence	1,753,090	100	60.4	39.0	0.6[c]
Attempted/threatened violence	3,588,320	100	42.7	55.0	2.3
Rape/sexual assault	247,730	100	53.7	46.3	0.0[c]
Rape/attempted rape	167,860	100	56.6	43.4	0.0[c]
Rape	90,390	100	57.3	42.7	0.0[c]
Attempted rape[d]	77,470	100	55.8	44.2	0.0[c]
Sexual assault[e]	79,870	100	47.8	52.2	0.0[c]
Robbery	512,490	100	71.2	28.3	0.5[c]
Completed/property taken	385,880	100	75.8	23.6	0.7[c]
With injury	169,980	100	79.8	20.2	0.0[c]
Without injury	215,890	100	72.6	26.2	1.2[c]
Attempted to take property	126,610	100	57.4	42.6	0.0[c]
With injury	42,600	100	92.6	7.4[c]	0.0[c]
Without injury	84,020	100	39.5	60.5	0.0[c]
Assault	4,581,190	100	45.7	52.3	2.0
Aggravated	990,110	100	56.6	40.5	2.8[c]
With injury	316,260	100	61.3	38.7	0.0[c]
Threatened with weapon	673,850	100	54.5	41.4	4.2[c]
Simple	3,591,090	100	42.7	55.6	1.8
With minor injury	906,580	100	54.8	44.2	1.0[c]
Without injury	2,684,510	100	38.6	59.4	2.1
Purse snatching/pocket picking	155,400	100	46.4	53.6	0.0[c]
Completed purse snatching	55,400	100	74.5	25.5[c]	0.0[c]
Attempted purse snatching	2,140[c]	100[c]	100.0[c]	0.0[c]	0.0[c]
Pocket picking	97,860	100	29.3[c]	70.7	0.0[c]
Property crimes	17,539,220	100	40.2	58.6	1.2
Household burglary	3,055,720	100	57.9	41.4	0.7[c]
Completed	2,597,310	100	58.8	40.4	0.8[c]
Forcible entry	1,017,660	100	77.2	21.7	1.1[c]
Unlawful entry without force	1,579,650	100	46.9	52.5	0.6[c]
Attempted forcible entry	458,410	100	52.9	47.1	0.0[c]
Motor vehicle theft	988,760	100	86.1	13.5	0.5[c]
Completed	780,630	100	95.8	3.9[c]	0.3[c]
Attempted	208,120	100	49.4	49.5	1.1[c]
Theft	13,494,750	100	32.8	65.8	1.4
Completed	13,039,920	100	32.7	65.9	1.4
Less than $50	4,186,570	100	17.1	81.8	1.1
$50 to $249	4,455,080	100	28.3	70.6	1.1
$250 or more	3,270,530	100	56.4	42.8	0.8[c]
Amount not available	1,127,740	100	39.5	55.0	5.5
Attempted	454,830	100	36.5	62.5	1.0[c]

Note: See Note, table 3.1. For survey methodology and definitions of terms, see Appendix 8.

[a]Detail may not add to total because of rounding.
[b]Figures in this column represent the percent of victimizations reported to the police, or "police reporting rates."
[c]Estimate is based on about 10 or fewer sample cases.
[d]Includes verbal threats of rape.
[e]Includes threats.

Source: U.S. Department of Justice, Bureau of Justice Statistics, *Criminal Victimization in the United States, 2002 Statistical Tables*, NCJ 200561, Table 91 [Online]. Available: http://www.ojp.usdoj.gov/bjs/pub/pdf/cvus02.pdf [Mar. 3, 2004].

Table 3.34

Estimated percent distribution of reasons for reporting personal and property victimizations to police

By type of crime, United States, 2002[a]

	Personal crimes				Property crimes			
		Crimes of violence				Household	Motor	
Reasons for reporting to police	Total[b]	Total[c]	Robbery	Assault	Total	burglary	vehicle theft	Theft
Number of reasons for reporting victimizations[d]	2,388,410	2,294,390	402,790	1,778,370	9,064,910	2,468,020	1,050,840	5,546,050
Total	100%	100%	100%	100%	100%	100%	100%	100%
Stop or prevent this incident	17.9	18.5	12.9	20.6	7.6	10.4	4.8	6.8
Needed help due to injury	1.7	1.8	2.1[e]	1.8	0.1[e]	0.2[e]	0.0[e]	0.1[e]
To recover property	5.1	4.1	20.5	0.6[e]	24.7	19.9	35.5	24.7
To collect insurance	0.4[e]	0.3[e]	0.6[e]	0.3[e]	5.3	4.0	10.3	4.9
To prevent further crimes by offender against victim	19.1	19.8	11.7	21.5	9.9	12.2	6.1	9.5
To prevent crime by offender against anyone	10.5	10.5	10.5	9.9	6.8	6.4	5.6	7.2
To punish offender	7.2	7.3	8.8	6.8	4.1	4.8	4.9	3.7
To catch or find offender	6.9	6.5	8.2	5.3	7.3	7.5	7.2	7.2
To improve police surveillance	4.4	4.6	5.2[e]	4.7	6.3	7.2	6.8	5.8
Duty to notify police	5.8	5.7	2.8[e]	6.7	6.0	5.5	5.5	6.3
Because it was a crime	14.6	14.4	14.3	14.2	17.7	18.4	11.7	18.6
Some other reason	4.6	4.5	1.8[e]	5.1	3.0	2.2	1.3[e]	3.6
Not available	1.9	2.0	0.6[e]	2.4	1.4	1.2	0.3[e]	1.7

Note: See Note, table 3.1. For survey methodology and definitions of terms, see Appendix 8.

[a]Detail may not add to total because of rounding.
[b]Includes crimes of violence and purse snatching/pocket picking not listed separately.
[c]Includes rape and sexual assault not listed separately.
[d]Some respondents may have cited more than one reason for reporting victimizations to the police.
[e]Estimate is based on about 10 or fewer sample cases.

Source: U.S. Department of Justice, Bureau of Justice Statistics, *Criminal Victimization in the United States, 2002 Statistical Tables*, NCJ 200561, Table 101 [Online]. Available: http://www.ojp.usdoj.gov/bjs/pub/pdf/cvus02.pdf [Mar. 3, 2004]. Table adapted by SOURCEBOOK staff.

Table 3.35

Estimated percent distribution of reasons for not reporting personal and property victimizations to police

By type of crime, United States, 2002[a]

	Personal crimes				Property crimes			
		Crimes of violence				Household	Motor	
Reasons for not reporting to police	Total[b]	Total[c]	Robbery	Assault	Total	burglary	vehicle theft	Theft
Number of reasons for not reporting victimizations[d]	3,200,150	3,105,890	196,020	2,776,190	12,958,170	1,685,780	152,140	11,120,240
Total	100%	100%	100%	100%	100%	100%	100%	100%
Reported to another official	17.0	17.1	9.0[e]	18.4	9.7	3.9	9.9[e]	10.6
Private or personal matter	21.2	21.7	6.9[e]	23.4	5.2	4.9	6.2[e]	5.2
Object recovered; offender unsuccessful	15.7	15.8	10.7[e]	16.5	25.7	21.0	32.0	26.3
Not important enough	4.9	5.1	5.5[e]	5.1	3.4	3.2	1.4[e]	3.4
Insurance would not cover	0.1[e]	0.1[e]	1.4[e]	0.0[e]	2.4	3.0	1.5[e]	2.4
Not aware crime occurred until later	0.6[e]	0.4[e]	0.0[e]	0.3[e]	5.8	9.8	12.5[e]	5.1
Unable to recover property; no ID number	0.8[e]	0.3[e]	1.5[e]	0.3[e]	7.4	4.9	0.0[e]	7.9
Lack of proof	3.8	3.1	14.8[e]	2.3	11.8	13.4	6.4[e]	11.6
Police would not want to be bothered	5.0	4.8	9.2[e]	4.7	8.3	10.5	2.9[e]	8.0
Police inefficient, ineffective, or biased	3.0	3.0	17.9	2.0	3.3	6.7	5.6[e]	2.7
Fear of reprisal	4.5	4.6	4.6[e]	3.5	0.7	1.0[e]	1.4[e]	0.7
Too inconvenient or time consuming	2.6	2.5	4.0[e]	2.6	3.6	3.8	5.6[e]	3.5
Other reasons	20.9	21.3	14.4[e]	21.1	12.7	14.0	14.5[e]	12.5

Note: See Note, table 3.1. For survey methodology and definitions of terms, see Appendix 8.

[a]Detail may not add to total because of rounding.
[b]Includes crimes of violence and purse snatching/pocket picking not listed separately.
[c]Includes rape and sexual assault not listed separately.
[d]Some respondents may have cited more than one reason for not reporting victimizations to the police.
[e]Estimate is based on about 10 or fewer sample cases.

Source: U.S. Department of Justice, Bureau of Justice Statistics, *Criminal Victimization in the United States, 2002 Statistical Tables*, NCJ 200561, Table 102 [Online]. Available: http://www.ojp.usdoj.gov/bjs/pub/pdf/cvus02.pdf [Mar. 3, 2004]. Table adapted by SOURCEBOOK staff.

Table 3.36

Estimated percent of violent victimizations reported to police

By selected victim and household characteristics, 1992-2000 (aggregate)

Characteristics	Violent crimes					Serious violent crime[a]
	All	Rape/ sexual assault	Robbery	Aggravated assault	Simple assault	
Total	43%	31%	57%	55%	38%	53%
Sex						
Male	40	27	52	52	34	51
Female	47	32	66	61	43	55
Race						
White	42	31	56	54	37	51
Black	49	35	59	61	41	58
American Indian	48	47[b]	45	59	43	55
Asian	40	16[b]	55	51	31	50
Hispanic origin						
Hispanic	44	28	48	55	39	50
Non-Hispanic	43	32	58	55	38	53
Age						
12 to 15 years	25	47	32	37	20	37
16 to 19 years	37	27	49	47	32	44
20 to 24 years	45	28	59	56	39	53
25 to 34 years	51	29	64	62	46	59
35 to 49 years	50	32	64	63	45	60
50 to 64 years	49	33	65	58	43	60
65 years and older	53	30[b]	72	51	46	61
Marital status						
Never married	37	30	50	49	31	47
Married	51	39	67	64	44	63
Widowed	54	51[b]	70	59	46	63
Divorced	52	34	65	60	48	58
Separated	54	25	65	61	53	55
Annual household income						
Less than $7,500	48	38	57	60	41	56
$7,500 to $14,999	48	41	54	57	43	54
$15,000 to $24,999	44	28	58	55	39	52
$25,000 to $34,999	43	28	61	53	37	53
$35,000 to $49,999	42	22	57	53	38	51
$50,000 to $74,999	39	38	53	52	33	51
$75,000 or more	37	21	63	53	30	53
Residence						
Urban	45	30	58	55	38	53
Suburban	42	28	54	54	37	51
Rural	45	42	60	57	40	55

Note: These data are from the U.S. Department of Justice, Bureau of Justice Statistics' National Crime Victimization Survey (NCVS). For survey methodology and definitions of terms, see Appendix 8.

[a] Includes rape, sexual assault, robbery, and aggravated assault.
[b] Estimate is based on about 10 or fewer sample cases.

Source: U.S. Department of Justice, Bureau of Justice Statistics, *Reporting Crime to the Police, 1992-2000*, Special Report NCJ 195710 (Washington, DC: U.S. Department of Justice, March 2003), p. 3, Table 2; p. 4, Table 3. Table adapted by SOURCEBOOK staff.

Table 3.37

High school seniors reporting victimization experiences in last 12 months

By type of victimization, United States, 1991-2003

Question: "During the last 12 months, how often..."

Type of victimization	Class of 1991 (N=2,569)	Class of 1992 (N=2,690)	Class of 1993 (N=2,770)	Class of 1994 (N=2,645)	Class of 1995 (N=2,656)	Class of 1996 (N=2,452)	Class of 1997 (N=2,638)	Class of 1998 (N=2,656)	Class of 1999 (N=2,322)	Class of 2000 (N=2,204)	Class of 2001 (N=2,218)	Class of 2002 (N=2,274)	Class of 2003 (N=2,517)
Has something of yours (worth under $50) been stolen?													
Not at all	55.4%	55.4%	55.3%	56.6%	55.4%	52.5%	54.0%	54.7%	54.9%	54.6%	54.6%	55.6%	56.8%
Once	26.2	27.0	25.6	25.3	25.7	27.0	26.8	25.6	27.1	25.2	26.7	26.3	26.7
Twice	10.9	10.6	11.0	11.0	10.7	11.0	11.0	11.1	10.9	10.8	10.2	10.7	9.9
3 or 4 times	5.2	5.0	5.7	5.1	5.2	6.4	5.3	5.9	4.8	6.1	5.2	4.6	4.4
5 or more times	2.3	2.0	2.4	2.1	3.0	3.1	3.0	2.6	2.4	3.4	3.2	2.8	2.2
Has something of yours (worth over $50) been stolen?													
Not at all	77.2	77.5	75.1	76.8	76.0	73.3	74.2	73.4	74.3	74.3	74.3	75.0	74.7
Once	15.7	15.3	17.2	16.8	16.4	17.0	17.2	17.3	18.2	16.6	17.4	17.6	18.0
Twice	4.8	4.6	4.0	4.1	4.7	5.7	5.5	5.5	4.8	6.1	5.3	4.2	4.5
3 or 4 times	1.7	1.9	2.6	1.6	2.1	2.5	2.3	2.3	2.0	2.1	1.7	2.0	1.7
5 or more times	0.6	0.7	1.0	0.7	0.7	1.5	0.8	1.5	0.7	0.9	1.3	1.1	1.1
Has someone deliberately damaged your property (your car, clothing, etc.)?													
Not at all	65.8	66.4	66.1	67.0	66.4	65.6	67.4	67.5	69.2	69.7	67.4	68.6	68.5
Once	21.6	19.8	19.1	19.6	19.5	20.9	19.9	19.3	19.5	17.7	19.6	18.8	20.1
Twice	7.7	9.4	9.2	8.5	8.6	8.8	8.2	7.6	7.7	7.8	6.9	7.4	6.7
3 or 4 times	3.6	3.4	4.2	3.8	3.7	3.0	3.4	3.8	2.5	3.4	4.4	4.0	3.1
5 or more times	1.3	0.9	1.4	1.2	1.8	1.6	1.1	1.8	1.1	1.3	1.6	1.3	1.6
Has someone injured you with a weapon (like a knife, gun, or club)?													
Not at all	94.5	94.3	93.9	94.9	95.0	95.0	94.9	95.0	95.2	95.5	95.0	96.2	94.7
Once	4.1	4.0	3.6	3.5	3.0	2.9	2.8	3.0	2.5	2.8	3.3	2.0	3.0
Twice	0.7	1.4	1.4	1.1	1.1	0.9	1.1	1.0	1.0	1.2	1.1	1.2	0.7
3 or 4 times	0.4	0.1	0.7	0.3	0.5	0.5	0.8	0.6	0.6	0.3	0.3	0.5	0.6
5 or more times	0.3	0.2	0.4	0.2	0.3	0.6	0.4	0.4	0.6	0.2	0.2	0.2	0.9
Has someone threatened you with a weapon, but not actually injured you?													
Not at all	81.4	80.7	79.6	80.9	82.1	81.0	81.8	82.3	84.2	83.8	83.3	84.2	84.1
Once	11.1	10.9	11.5	11.3	9.3	10.7	11.1	9.8	9.3	9.6	11.0	9.2	9.0
Twice	3.9	4.0	3.8	3.7	4.5	4.6	3.3	4.2	3.4	3.2	2.5	3.1	3.6
3 or 4 times	2.0	2.4	2.8	2.4	2.2	1.9	2.3	1.7	1.8	1.6	1.9	2.0	1.6
5 or more times	1.6	2.1	2.3	1.7	1.8	1.9	1.5	2.0	1.3	1.7	1.3	1.4	1.6
Has someone injured you on purpose without using a weapon?													
Not at all	83.8	84.0	83.6	84.9	84.1	84.4	85.4	85.3	85.6	85.7	84.8	85.2	84.0
Once	9.6	9.3	9.2	9.3	9.0	7.9	7.8	8.6	8.3	8.2	7.5	7.4	8.8
Twice	3.1	3.1	3.4	2.7	3.7	3.2	2.7	2.6	2.6	2.1	3.4	3.6	3.0
3 or 4 times	1.9	2.1	2.0	1.7	1.8	2.6	2.1	2.2	2.1	1.8	2.3	2.2	2.2
5 or more times	1.6	1.5	1.8	1.4	1.4	1.9	2.0	1.3	1.3	2.2	2.0	1.7	2.0
Has an unarmed person threatened you with injury, but not actually injured you?													
Not at all	69.1	69.3	69.0	70.1	70.2	69.9	71.7	71.5	72.1	71.9	70.8	73.0	72.7
Once	13.5	13.7	13.1	13.2	12.8	13.4	13.5	12.4	11.3	12.8	14.0	11.7	13.0
Twice	6.8	6.2	7.6	6.8	6.4	6.2	5.3	6.4	6.3	5.5	5.5	6.2	5.8
3 or 4 times	4.9	5.3	4.2	4.5	4.5	4.0	3.8	4.1	5.1	4.3	4.5	3.8	3.1
5 or more times	5.7	5.4	6.1	5.5	6.1	6.5	5.7	5.5	5.2	5.5	5.2	5.2	5.5

Note: These data are from a series of nationwide surveys of high school seniors conducted from 1975 through 2003 by the Monitoring the Future Project at the University of Michigan's Institute for Social Research. The survey design is a multistage random sample of high school seniors in public and private schools throughout the continental United States. All percentages reported are based on weighted cases; the Ns that are shown in the tables also refer to the number of weighted cases. Readers interested in responses to this question for 1976 through 1990 should consult previous editions of SOURCEBOOK. For survey methodology and definitions of terms, see Appendix 6.

Source: Lloyd D. Johnston, Jerald G. Bachman, and Patrick M. O'Malley, *Monitoring the Future 1991*, pp. 109, 110; *1993*, pp. 110, 111; *1995*, pp. 111, 112; *1997*, pp. 107, 108; *1999*, pp. 108, 109 (Ann Arbor, MI: Institute for Social Research, University of Michigan); Jerald G. Bachman, Lloyd D. Johnston, and Patrick M. O'Malley, *Monitoring the Future 1992*, pp. 109, 110; *1994*, pp. 109, 110; *1996*, pp. 105, 106; *1998*, pp. 107, 108; *2000*, pp. 109, 110 (Ann Arbor, MI: Institute for Social Research, University of Michigan); and data provided by the Monitoring the Future Project, Survey Research Center, Lloyd D. Johnston, Jerald G. Bachman, and Patrick M. O'Malley, Principal Investigators. Table adapted by SOURCEBOOK staff. Reprinted by permission.

Table 3.38

High school seniors reporting victimization experiences in last 12 months

By type of victimization and sex, United States, 1991-2003

Question: "During the last 12 months, how often..."

	Class of 1991		Class of 1992		Class of 1993		Class of 1994		Class of 1995		Class of 1996	
Type of victimization	Male (N=1,280)	Female (N=1,205)	Male (N=1,276)	Female (N=1,308)	Male (N=1,294)	Female (N=1,321)	Male (N=1,208)	Female (N=1,302)	Male (N=1,238)	Female (N=1,313)	Male (N=1,142)	Female (N=1,197)
Has something of yours (worth under $50) been stolen?												
Not at all	50.4%	60.9%	49.9%	60.8%	50.9%	60.3%	53.8%	59.5%	50.7%	60.3%	48.4%	57.1%
Once	28.1	23.9	28.8	25.5	25.9	24.4	24.1	26.5	26.2	24.8	26.0	27.9
Twice	12.1	9.8	12.7	8.3	13.1	9.0	12.9	9.1	12.1	9.3	13.1	9.0
3 or 4 times	6.1	4.0	5.7	4.2	6.6	5.0	6.4	3.6	6.7	4.1	8.1	4.4
5 or more times	3.2	1.4	2.9	1.2	3.5	1.3	2.8	1.2	4.3	1.6	4.4	1.6
Has something of yours (worth over $50) been stolen?												
Not at all	73.2	81.6	73.3	82.7	69.0	81.3	73.6	81.0	70.8	82.3	68.8	78.2
Once	18.5	13.1	17.5	12.2	20.8	13.9	19.0	14.4	19.6	12.9	18.0	15.9
Twice	5.6	3.7	6.0	3.1	5.3	2.6	4.6	3.2	6.2	2.9	7.9	3.6
3 or 4 times	1.9	1.2	2.4	1.4	3.3	1.9	2.2	0.9	2.9	1.4	3.2	1.8
5 or more times	0.7	0.4	0.8	0.6	1.6	0.3	0.6	0.5	0.5	0.6	2.1	0.5
Has someone deliberately damaged your property (your car, clothing, etc.)?												
Not at all	59.7	72.3	61.3	71.8	61.6	71.1	61.8	72.1	61.2	71.1	59.6	71.9
Once	24.5	18.8	21.5	18.4	21.7	16.2	22.0	17.2	22.1	17.5	24.6	17.3
Twice	10.0	5.1	11.9	6.8	9.8	8.6	10.9	6.0	10.1	7.2	9.8	7.9
3 or 4 times	3.9	3.1	4.2	2.3	4.8	3.5	4.4	3.3	4.8	2.6	3.7	2.4
5 or more times	1.9	0.7	1.1	0.7	2.2	0.6	0.9	1.4	1.8	1.6	2.3	0.5
Has someone injured you with a weapon (like a knife, gun, or club)?												
Not at all	92.0	97.2	90.8	98.4	91.3	97.1	93.1	96.9	93.0	97.3	92.0	98.6
Once	5.9	2.3	6.2	1.3	4.6	2.1	5.1	1.8	4.2	1.7	4.8	1.1
Twice	1.0	0.4	2.4	0.3	2.6	0.1	1.4	0.9	1.8	0.4	1.4	0.2
3 or 4 times	0.7	0.1	0.3	0.0	0.9	0.4	0.3	0.2	0.6	0.3	1.1	0.1
5 or more times	0.5	0.1	0.3	0.1	0.6	0.3	(a)	0.2	0.4	0.3	0.8	0.1
Has someone threatened you with a weapon, but not actually injured you?												
Not at all	75.2	87.9	73.8	88.3	72.7	86.5	74.3	87.8	74.4	90.4	74.6	88.5
Once	14.0	8.2	13.3	8.6	14.0	8.6	13.4	8.6	12.7	5.6	12.6	8.1
Twice	5.4	2.4	6.3	1.3	4.8	2.9	6.2	1.5	6.4	2.3	7.3	1.7
3 or 4 times	2.9	1.1	3.7	1.0	4.8	1.1	3.7	1.3	3.4	1.0	2.9	0.9
5 or more times	2.6	0.5	2.9	0.7	3.7	0.9	2.4	0.9	3.1	0.6	2.6	0.8
Has someone injured you on purpose without using a weapon?												
Not at all	83.2	84.6	82.8	86.3	82.7	84.9	84.1	85.6	82.7	85.7	82.3	87.0
Once	10.3	8.7	10.8	7.5	10.6	7.3	10.9	8.1	9.8	7.7	9.7	6.3
Twice	3.3	3.0	2.8	3.2	3.2	3.8	2.5	2.7	4.1	3.4	3.7	2.7
3 or 4 times	1.7	2.1	2.5	1.5	1.8	2.0	1.5	2.0	1.9	1.8	2.7	2.3
5 or more times	1.6	1.7	1.2	1.6	1.7	1.9	1.0	1.8	1.6	1.3	1.6	1.7
Has an unarmed person threatened you with injury, but not actually injured you?												
Not at all	62.3	75.9	63.4	75.6	63.5	74.7	63.4	76.5	61.9	77.9	63.9	76.3
Once	14.5	12.7	14.8	12.9	14.4	11.6	14.7	11.7	14.4	11.2	15.6	11.7
Twice	8.8	4.8	8.2	4.5	8.7	6.6	7.8	5.4	8.4	4.9	6.0	6.3
3 or 4 times	5.7	4.0	5.7	4.5	4.4	3.9	6.3	2.9	6.2	2.9	5.8	2.0
5 or more times	8.7	2.5	7.9	2.6	9.0	3.1	7.7	3.5	9.1	3.1	8.7	3.7

Note: See Note, table 3.37. Readers interested in responses to this question for 1976 through 1990 should consult previous editions of SOURCEBOOK. For survey methodology and definitions of terms, see Appendix 6.

[a] Less than 0.05%.

Source: Lloyd D. Johnston, Jerald G. Bachman, and Patrick M. O'Malley, *Monitoring the Future 1991*, pp. 109, 110; *1993*, pp. 110, 111; *1995*, pp. 111, 112; *1997*, pp. 107, 108; *1999*, pp. 108, 109 (Ann Arbor, MI: Institute for Social Research, University of Michigan); Jerald G. Bachman, Lloyd D. Johnston, and Patrick M. O'Malley, *Monitoring the Future 1992*, pp. 109, 110; *1994*, pp. 109, 110; *1996*, pp. 105, 106; *1998*, pp. 107, 108; *2000*, pp. 109, 110 (Ann Arbor, MI: Institute for Social Research, University of Michigan); and data provided by the Monitoring the Future Project, Survey Research Center, Lloyd D. Johnston, Jerald G. Bachman, and Patrick M. O'Malley, Principal Investigators. Table adapted by SOURCEBOOK staff. Reprinted by permission.

	Class of 1997		Class of 1998		Class of 1999		Class of 2000		Class of 2001		Class of 2002		Class of 2003	
	Male (N=1,204)	Female (N=1,304)	Male (N=1,225)	Female (N=1,299)	Male (N=1,111)	Female (N=1,106)	Male (N=1,000)	Female (N=1,097)	Male (N=1,032)	Female (N=1,089)	Male (N=1,094)	Female (N=1,070)	Male (N=1,164)	Female (N=1,246)
	49.3%	57.9%	49.5%	59.4%	50.1%	60.1%	50.1%	59.0%	51.4%	57.8%	52.3%	59.0%	50.8%	62.2%
	26.6	27.4	27.4	23.9	28.1	25.9	26.0	23.6	27.9	25.5	28.0	24.6	27.8	25.6
	13.7	8.6	12.0	10.5	12.6	9.4	12.2	9.9	11.1	9.4	11.9	9.8	12.1	8.2
	6.1	4.4	7.7	4.4	5.5	3.6	7.5	4.9	6.1	4.2	5.1	4.3	5.9	2.9
	4.3	1.7	3.4	1.8	3.7	1.0	4.2	2.6	3.5	3.0	2.7	2.3	3.3	1.1
	69.0	78.6	68.8	78.2	70.6	78.4	71.1	78.1	69.7	79.3	70.1	80.6	69.2	80.5
	20.3	14.7	20.7	14.2	20.0	16.5	16.8	15.4	20.1	14.7	21.5	13.0	20.4	15.1
	7.1	4.2	5.9	4.8	6.1	3.6	8.1	4.3	7.3	3.0	4.8	3.7	6.6	2.6
	2.4	2.1	2.4	2.2	2.1	1.4	2.8	1.4	1.4	1.9	2.5	1.6	2.5	0.9
	1.1	0.4	2.2	0.7	1.2	0.1	1.2	0.7	1.5	1.2	1.0	1.0	1.3	0.9
	59.3	74.6	61.4	73.3	63.6	74.5	62.5	76.3	62.1	72.2	62.4	74.8	60.7	75.5
	24.3	16.3	21.9	17.1	23.2	15.9	20.9	14.8	22.6	17.2	22.1	15.6	24.3	16.7
	10.4	6.1	9.1	5.7	9.0	6.5	10.3	5.6	8.0	5.8	8.6	6.3	8.6	4.9
	4.6	2.3	4.9	2.8	2.6	2.3	4.5	2.4	5.3	3.7	4.8	2.8	4.6	1.7
	1.3	0.8	2.6	1.1	1.7	0.7	1.8	0.9	1.9	1.2	2.1	0.5	1.9	1.1
	92.4	97.8	92.7	97.3	93.9	97.1	92.9	98.1	92.4	97.6	94.8	97.6	91.6	98.0
	3.8	1.7	4.1	1.9	3.6	1.4	4.0	1.7	5.1	1.8	2.5	1.4	4.6	1.4
	1.8	0.3	1.4	0.6	1.0	1.0	2.3	0.0	1.8	0.6	1.6	0.8	1.0	0.2
	1.4	0.1	1.1	0.0	1.0	0.3	0.7	(a)	0.6	0.0	0.8	0.1	1.0	0.3
	0.5	0.1	0.7	0.2	0.6	0.1	0.1	0.1	0.2	0.1	0.3	0.1	1.8	0.1
	74.0	89.0	75.6	88.7	78.6	90.0	76.8	90.8	77.4	89.4	79.4	89.4	77.8	90.6
	14.7	7.9	12.5	7.1	12.1	6.6	12.4	6.4	14.2	7.7	11.6	6.8	12.0	5.8
	5.1	1.7	6.0	2.6	5.0	1.8	5.3	1.2	3.9	1.2	3.4	2.4	5.4	2.0
	3.8	0.8	2.6	0.9	2.6	0.9	2.1	1.2	2.5	1.3	3.1	1.0	2.2	0.9
	2.4	0.7	3.3	0.7	1.8	0.7	3.3	0.4	2.0	0.4	2.5	0.4	2.6	0.6
	84.7	86.6	82.1	88.7	83.9	87.5	81.8	89.3	83.3	86.3	83.9	86.3	81.6	86.1
	8.2	7.3	11.2	5.9	9.9	6.6	10.2	6.6	8.7	6.5	7.8	6.6	10.3	7.6
	3.1	2.2	2.7	2.3	2.5	2.6	3.2	1.0	3.4	3.4	3.8	3.5	3.6	2.5
	1.9	2.1	2.2	2.2	1.9	2.2	2.3	1.4	1.9	2.7	2.8	1.8	2.0	2.4
	2.1	1.8	1.8	0.9	1.7	1.0	2.5	1.8	2.7	1.2	1.7	1.8	2.5	1.4
	64.3	79.0	63.1	79.8	63.9	79.7	64.1	78.9	63.7	77.7	67.3	78.9	66.5	78.2
	16.6	10.5	15.2	9.5	13.1	9.8	13.8	11.7	16.1	12.1	12.6	10.9	14.1	11.9
	6.6	4.2	7.6	5.4	7.9	4.7	8.2	3.3	6.8	4.2	6.8	5.5	7.2	4.6
	4.7	2.7	5.6	2.5	6.4	4.0	5.3	3.4	6.0	3.1	5.4	2.0	4.0	2.5
	7.8	3.6	8.5	2.8	8.7	1.6	8.7	2.7	7.4	3.0	8.0	2.7	8.3	2.8

Nature and distribution of known offenses 213

Table 3.39

High school seniors reporting victimization experiences in last 12 months

By type of victimization and race, United States, 1991-2003

Question: "During the last 12 months, how often..."

Type of victimization	Class of 1991 White (N=1,818)	Class of 1991 Black (N=289)	Class of 1992 White (N=1,806)	Class of 1992 Black (N=368)	Class of 1993 White (N=1,895)	Class of 1993 Black (N=334)	Class of 1994 White (N=1,815)	Class of 1994 Black (N=282)	Class of 1995 White (N=1,841)	Class of 1995 Black (N=282)	Class of 1996 White (N=1,628)	Class of 1996 Black (N=287)
Has something of yours (worth under $50) been stolen?												
Not at all	57.9%	47.3%	58.2%	52.0%	55.6%	54.2%	59.0%	48.7%	57.7%	49.9%	53.9%	46.4%
Once	25.4	25.3	26.2	25.0	25.6	23.0	23.8	29.5	25.4	26.4	26.0	27.1
Twice	10.2	15.6	9.7	11.5	11.1	10.3	10.5	11.2	8.9	13.1	11.5	11.7
3 or 4 times	4.4	7.8	4.6	7.6	5.6	8.1	5.2	5.7	5.2	7.2	6.0	10.1
5 or more times	2.1	3.9	1.4	3.8	2.2	4.3	1.5	4.9	2.7	3.4	2.6	4.6
Has something of yours (worth over $50) been stolen?												
Not at all	80.4	68.8	80.6	71.3	77.5	67.5	79.8	65.8	79.2	65.9	75.1	66.2
Once	14.3	20.5	14.1	18.3	16.5	19.9	15.5	21.8	14.9	23.0	16.2	19.9
Twice	4.0	5.7	3.4	6.4	3.2	5.3	3.3	7.4	4.1	5.0	5.7	8.0
3 or 4 times	1.0	3.4	1.6	2.4	2.1	5.6	1.1	2.5	1.5	5.3	1.9	3.5
5 or more times	0.3	1.6	0.2	1.7	0.8	1.7	0.3	2.5	0.4	0.8	1.0	2.4
Has someone deliberately damaged your property (your car, clothing, etc.)?												
Not at all	66.3	67.3	67.3	73.4	66.4	70.9	66.9	68.9	67.0	68.9	65.6	71.1
Once	21.3	22.8	20.7	14.8	19.7	17.1	21.3	12.8	19.7	15.8	21.7	13.6
Twice	7.8	4.7	8.5	8.0	8.4	7.3	7.6	9.3	8.4	8.0	8.5	9.1
3 or 4 times	3.5	3.6	3.1	2.5	4.2	3.5	3.3	6.1	3.7	4.3	3.0	3.6
5 or more times	1.1	1.6	0.4	1.3	1.4	1.2	0.9	2.9	1.2	3.0	1.3	2.7
Has someone injured you with a weapon (like a knife, gun, or club)?												
Not at all	95.1	92.1	96.0	93.3	95.0	93.6	96.7	87.6	96.1	93.2	95.8	92.1
Once	3.7	5.7	3.0	4.9	3.1	3.9	2.5	8.4	2.4	4.7	2.9	3.8
Twice	0.4	1.8	0.8	1.6	1.4	0.7	0.6	2.6	0.9	1.8	0.7	2.2
3 or 4 times	0.3	0.0	0.1	0.2	0.4	1.4	0.2	1.3	0.4	0.0	0.3	1.2
5 or more times	0.4	0.4	0.1	0.1	0.2	0.4	0.1	0.1	0.2	0.3	0.3	0.7
Has someone threatened you with a weapon, but not actually injured you?												
Not at all	83.5	71.2	83.1	74.1	81.0	76.0	82.6	71.9	84.6	73.2	82.9	79.3
Once	10.3	15.7	9.9	14.0	11.0	14.6	10.4	14.3	8.5	12.2	9.8	10.8
Twice	3.3	6.9	3.5	4.5	3.4	5.0	3.5	5.0	3.8	5.6	4.8	3.1
3 or 4 times	1.3	3.8	2.0	3.7	2.5	2.8	2.2	4.6	1.8	4.7	1.5	5.0
5 or more times	1.6	2.4	1.5	3.7	2.2	1.6	1.3	4.2	1.3	4.3	1.1	1.9
Has someone injured you on purpose without using a weapon?												
Not at all	83.7	83.1	83.9	87.3	83.5	85.6	85.5	80.7	85.3	81.4	86.0	79.3
Once	9.7	9.3	9.8	6.6	10.0	6.9	9.0	11.4	8.1	9.6	6.7	12.8
Twice	3.2	2.3	3.2	2.5	3.4	2.8	2.7	3.0	3.6	5.0	3.4	2.3
3 or 4 times	1.9	2.6	1.9	1.2	1.3	3.2	1.6	3.4	1.6	3.4	2.4	4.6
5 or more times	1.5	2.7	1.2	2.3	1.8	1.6	1.2	1.6	1.4	0.6	1.6	1.1
Has an unarmed person threatened you with injury, but not actually injured you?												
Not at all	68.6	65.7	68.0	73.8	67.5	72.3	69.2	69.0	70.4	68.4	69.0	67.6
Once	12.7	16.1	13.5	12.6	13.7	11.3	14.2	8.6	13.0	13.6	14.6	13.7
Twice	7.0	6.7	7.2	3.0	8.4	6.6	6.3	9.3	6.9	5.6	6.5	9.0
3 or 4 times	5.2	5.7	5.6	4.2	4.4	5.2	5.0	3.7	3.7	7.6	3.7	3.9
5 or more times	6.4	5.7	5.7	6.4	6.1	4.6	5.3	9.6	6.0	4.8	6.1	5.8

Note: See Note, table 3.37. Data are given for those who identify themselves as white or Caucasian and those who identify themselves as black or African-American; data are not given for the other ethnic categories because these groups comprise a small percentage of the sample in any given year (Source, *2000*, p. 10). Readers interested in responses to this question for 1976 through 1990 should consult previous editions of SOURCEBOOK. For survey methodology and definitions of terms, see Appendix 6.

[a] Less than 0.05%.

Source: Lloyd D. Johnston, Jerald G. Bachman, and Patrick M. O'Malley, **Monitoring the Future 1991**, pp. 109, 110; *1993*, pp. 110, 111; *1995*, pp. 111, 112; *1997*, pp. 107, 108; *1999*, pp. 108, 109 (Ann Arbor, MI: Institute for Social Research, University of Michigan); Jerald G. Bachman, Lloyd D. Johnston, and Patrick M. O'Malley, **Monitoring the Future 1992**, pp. 109, 110; *1994*, pp. 109, 110; *1996*, pp. 105, 106; *1998*, pp. 107, 108; *2000*, pp. 109, 110 (Ann Arbor, MI: Institute for Social Research, University of Michigan); and data provided by the Monitoring the Future Project, Survey Research Center, Lloyd D. Johnston, Jerald G. Bachman, and Patrick M. O'Malley, Principal Investigators. Table adapted by SOURCEBOOK staff. Reprinted by permission.

	Class of 1997		Class of 1998		Class of 1999		Class of 2000		Class of 2001		Class of 2002		Class of 2003	
	White (N=1,726)	Black (N=343)	White (N=1,741)	Black (N=326)	White (N=1,594)	Black (N=282)	White (N=1,425)	Black (N=286)	White (N=1,366)	Black (N=239)	White (N=1,440)	Black (N=231)	White (N=1,631)	Black (N=273)
	54.8%	53.3%	57.2%	48.6%	57.2%	53.3%	57.2%	45.8%	57.0%	45.9%	57.0%	56.0%	57.9%	50.9%
	27.6	22.2	25.1	24.2	25.5	28.9	24.0	24.2	25.3	32.1	25.0	25.6	26.8	25.4
	10.6	12.8	10.0	15.1	10.4	8.0	10.6	13.8	9.5	11.7	11.2	10.7	9.5	13.0
	4.6	8.3	5.4	10.0	4.8	7.1	5.9	7.4	4.9	6.3	4.7	4.1	4.1	5.4
	2.4	3.3	2.2	2.0	2.1	2.8	2.3	8.8	3.2	4.0	2.1	3.6	1.6	5.4
	76.4	67.7	76.2	67.0	77.7	63.7	78.4	61.4	77.7	65.8	76.8	70.8	77.1	69.7
	16.6	17.3	16.4	19.2	16.3	25.4	15.2	19.4	16.0	20.2	16.2	19.6	17.1	18.2
	5.2	6.4	4.6	8.3	4.0	6.0	4.6	11.8	4.2	6.8	4.5	5.1	3.8	6.2
	1.3	6.5	1.8	4.1	1.4	3.5	1.4	4.7	1.3	4.3	1.9	2.4	1.3	2.0
	0.5	2.1	1.1	1.4	0.5	1.4	0.4	2.7	0.8	2.9	0.7	2.1	0.7	3.9
	66.9	73.2	68.3	67.9	69.7	69.6	70.0	71.5	65.7	75.7	68.0	76.4	68.6	69.2
	20.5	15.7	20.1	17.0	19.9	18.6	18.7	14.7	21.7	14.4	20.9	11.8	20.5	16.9
	8.8	5.8	7.1	7.3	6.8	9.3	7.7	7.3	7.4	2.9	7.1	7.0	6.5	8.0
	2.8	3.6	3.4	3.6	2.2	1.7	2.5	4.9	4.5	1.6	3.0	4.2	3.4	3.4
	1.0	1.7	1.1	4.1	1.4	0.8	1.0	1.6	0.6	5.4	1.0	0.6	1.1	2.5
	96.3	91.5	96.1	94.2	96.3	93.9	96.4	94.5	95.9	94.7	96.4	95.8	96.2	94.7
	2.2	4.8	2.4	3.9	2.0	3.2	2.4	3.7	2.7	3.4	1.7	3.2	1.9	3.8
	0.8	2.4	0.8	1.5	0.7	0.5	1.0	0.4	1.0	1.9	1.2	0.1	0.6	0.4
	0.6	0.5	0.5	0.3	0.7	0.4	0.1	1.1	0.3	0.0	0.5	0.7	0.7	(a)
	0.1	0.9	0.2	0.1	0.3	1.9	(a)	0.2	0.1	0.0	0.2	0.2	0.7	1.1
	83.9	74.9	83.6	79.2	85.2	82.8	85.6	81.4	83.7	82.3	85.0	79.0	84.9	82.6
	9.8	15.0	8.9	10.9	9.3	11.1	9.2	9.8	10.3	13.3	9.0	11.7	9.0	9.1
	2.5	6.4	4.1	5.4	3.0	3.0	2.5	4.5	2.5	2.2	3.0	3.7	3.4	5.3
	2.3	2.0	1.6	3.0	1.4	1.7	1.3	2.4	2.4	0.8	1.6	2.1	1.1	1.6
	1.5	1.7	1.8	1.4	1.1	1.5	1.4	1.9	1.0	1.3	1.4	3.5	1.6	1.3
	85.5	85.7	86.0	88.5	85.8	86.9	85.6	86.3	84.8	91.6	85.3	87.4	84.2	89.6
	8.0	6.4	7.8	7.4	8.3	9.1	8.6	9.7	7.5	3.0	7.5	5.6	8.9	6.9
	2.7	2.9	2.8	2.3	2.3	1.2	2.1	1.3	3.3	2.8	3.4	3.9	2.7	1.5
	2.0	2.8	2.3	1.6	2.1	1.3	1.7	1.4	2.0	1.6	2.2	0.7	2.2	0.7
	1.7	2.2	1.2	0.2	1.5	1.5	2.1	1.3	2.3	1.0	1.7	2.4	2.1	1.4
	70.5	75.7	70.3	76.4	72.5	71.5	71.5	72.3	69.2	79.3	71.0	80.8	71.5	75.8
	14.0	10.6	12.3	10.4	10.9	13.0	12.6	12.9	14.3	10.3	12.6	6.7	13.8	11.5
	5.1	6.9	7.3	6.8	5.5	8.2	6.0	5.9	5.5	4.1	7.1	5.4	6.1	4.6
	3.7	3.2	4.4	2.6	5.6	3.4	4.6	3.2	5.3	1.4	4.4	1.2	3.0	2.9
	6.7	3.7	5.7	3.8	5.5	4.0	5.4	5.6	5.7	4.9	4.9	5.8	5.6	5.3

Page 216 intentionally blank.

Table 3.40

High school seniors reporting victimization experiences at school in last 12 months

By type of victimization, United States, 1991-2003

Question: "The next questions are about some things which may have happened to you while you were at school (inside or outside or in a school bus). During the last 12 months, how often..."

Type of victimization	Class of 1991 (N=2,582)	Class of 1992 (N=2,684)	Class of 1993 (N=2,773)	Class of 1994 (N=2,642)	Class of 1995 (N=2,658)	Class of 1996 (N=2,455)	Class of 1997 (N=2,648)	Class of 1998 (N=2,608)	Class of 1999 (N=2,357)	Class of 2000 (N=2,216)	Class of 2001 (N=2,201)	Class of 2002 (N=2,250)	Class of 2003 (N=2,523)
Has something of yours (worth under $50) been stolen?													
Not at all	62.7%	66.4%	62.1%	63.9%	64.6%	66.3%	65.3%	67.8%	66.3%	66.9%	64.6%	69.1%	70.6%
Once	25.6	22.0	24.9	24.8	22.8	23.0	24.1	22.9	22.0	23.1	23.4	21.7	19.8
Twice	7.7	8.0	8.0	6.9	7.6	7.1	7.0	5.5	7.0	5.9	7.0	6.1	6.4
3 or 4 times	2.6	2.4	3.6	3.6	3.3	2.6	2.7	2.6	3.2	2.8	2.9	2.4	2.1
5 or more times	1.4	1.2	1.4	0.9	1.7	1.0	0.8	1.2	1.5	1.3	2.0	0.7	1.2
Has something of yours (worth over $50) been stolen?													
Not at all	81.5	83.7	81.4	82.1	81.0	81.9	82.4	82.0	80.0	82.6	78.9	82.4	83.5
Once	13.6	12.3	12.8	13.4	13.8	14.0	12.9	13.7	14.3	13.5	15.0	13.3	12.2
Twice	3.2	2.8	3.6	3.1	3.3	2.7	3.1	3.1	4.3	2.8	3.6	2.7	2.5
3 or 4 times	1.3	0.9	1.4	1.1	1.1	1.0	1.2	0.6	1.0	0.7	1.8	1.1	1.0
5 or more times	0.4	0.2	0.7	0.3	0.8	0.4	0.4	0.5	0.5	0.3	0.7	0.5	0.8
Has someone deliberately damaged your property (your car, clothing, etc.)?													
Not at all	71.7	73.6	74.2	72.8	72.7	74.1	75.3	74.7	74.4	74.8	76.2	77.1	77.8
Once	18.9	18.5	17.3	18.9	18.6	17.6	16.9	18.1	17.7	17.5	16.9	15.6	15.3
Twice	5.8	4.1	5.6	4.8	5.4	5.6	5.3	4.9	4.9	4.7	4.2	4.8	4.5
3 or 4 times	2.5	2.8	2.0	2.8	2.3	2.0	1.8	1.2	2.1	1.9	1.8	2.0	1.4
5 or more times	1.1	1.1	0.9	0.7	1.0	0.7	0.7	1.1	0.9	1.1	0.9	0.5	0.9
Has someone injured you with a weapon (like a knife, gun, or club)?													
Not at all	93.5	94.9	95.3	95.3	95.1	95.1	94.8	95.4	95.3	96.3	94.9	95.9	96.2
Once	3.9	3.2	2.8	2.7	2.8	2.8	3.0	3.1	2.7	2.1	3.0	2.6	2.2
Twice	1.4	1.0	0.8	1.0	1.2	1.2	1.3	0.7	0.9	0.7	0.5	0.5	0.9
3 or 4 times	0.4	0.3	0.6	0.6	0.6	0.5	0.3	0.4	0.7	0.4	0.8	0.3	0.3
5 or more times	0.8	0.5	0.5	0.4	0.3	0.4	0.6	0.4	0.4	0.5	0.8	0.6	0.5
Has someone threatened you with a weapon, but not actually injured you?													
Not at all	83.7	86.0	84.4	85.0	86.7	86.8	89.2	89.0	87.5	89.0	87.1	90.1	88.8
Once	9.3	8.6	8.6	9.0	8.4	8.1	6.8	6.5	8.1	7.0	7.8	5.9	6.5
Twice	3.6	2.8	3.9	3.2	2.1	2.6	1.7	2.3	2.3	1.7	2.5	2.0	2.0
3 or 4 times	1.6	1.7	1.8	1.2	1.4	1.4	0.7	1.6	1.2	1.1	1.5	0.9	1.2
5 or more times	1.7	0.9	1.3	1.6	1.4	1.0	1.6	0.7	0.8	1.3	1.2	1.1	1.4
Has someone injured you on purpose without using a weapon?													
Not at all	84.7	87.2	88.6	88.3	88.4	88.2	87.8	88.9	89.7	89.0	87.3	89.3	89.7
Once	9.0	7.4	6.8	6.5	6.5	7.4	7.5	7.2	6.0	5.9	7.7	5.6	6.0
Twice	3.1	3.2	2.3	2.9	2.2	2.4	2.2	1.8	2.0	2.5	2.1	2.7	2.3
3 or 4 times	1.8	1.1	1.3	1.3	1.6	0.8	1.0	1.0	1.3	1.6	1.3	1.1	0.8
5 or more times	1.5	1.1	1.0	1.0	1.3	1.2	1.5	1.1	1.0	1.1	1.6	1.3	1.3
Has an unarmed person threatened you with injury, but not actually injured you?													
Not at all	74.2	75.4	76.9	76.3	76.5	78.4	78.8	79.5	77.5	78.2	78.4	80.7	81.2
Once	12.6	13.5	10.5	12.6	10.8	11.6	10.6	10.4	11.5	11.6	11.7	10.7	9.4
Twice	4.9	3.8	5.5	4.3	4.9	3.3	4.5	3.7	4.5	3.8	3.8	3.6	3.6
3 or 4 times	3.7	3.8	2.9	3.0	3.6	2.7	2.7	2.7	2.7	2.9	2.5	1.6	2.3
5 or more times	4.7	3.4	4.1	3.8	4.2	4.0	3.4	3.7	3.8	3.4	3.6	3.5	3.5

Note: See Note, table 3.37. Readers interested in responses to this question for 1976 through 1990 should consult previous editions of SOURCEBOOK. For survey methodology and definitions of terms, see Appendix 6.

Source: Lloyd D. Johnston, Jerald G. Bachman, and Patrick M. O'Malley, *Monitoring the Future 1991*, pp. 151, 152; *1993*, pp. 154, 155; *1995*, pp. 155, 156; *1997*, pp. 150, 151; *1999*, pp. 152, 153 (Ann Arbor, MI: Institute for Social Research, University of Michigan); Jerald G. Bachman, Lloyd D. Johnston, and Patrick M. O'Malley, *Monitoring the Future 1992*, pp. 153, 154; *1994*, pp. 153, 154; *1996*, pp. 147, 148; *1998*, pp. 151, 152; *2000*, pp. 153, 154 (Ann Arbor, MI: Institute for Social Research, University of Michigan); and data provided by the Monitoring the Future Project, Survey Research Center, Lloyd D. Johnston, Jerald G. Bachman, and Patrick M. O'Malley, Principal Investigators. Table adapted by SOURCEBOOK staff. Reprinted by permission.

Table 3.41

High school seniors reporting victimization experiences at school in last 12 months

By type of victimization and sex, United States, 1991-2003

Question: "The next questions are about some things which may have happened to you while you were at school (inside or outside or in a school bus). During the last 12 months, how often..."

Type of victimization	Class of 1991 Male (N=1,292)	Class of 1991 Female (N=1,194)	Class of 1992 Male (N=1,267)	Class of 1992 Female (N=1,334)	Class of 1993 Male (N=1,291)	Class of 1993 Female (N=1,377)	Class of 1994 Male (N=1,221)	Class of 1994 Female (N=1,326)	Class of 1995 Male (N=1,225)	Class of 1995 Female (N=1,327)	Class of 1996 Male (N=1,142)	Class of 1996 Female (N=1,207)
Has something of yours (worth under $50) been stolen?												
Not at all	58.7%	67.1%	62.5%	70.2%	61.3%	63.2%	59.1%	68.3%	61.2%	67.8%	62.0%	70.0%
Once	27.2	24.3	23.7	20.6	25.0	25.1	26.5	23.0	24.3	21.5	24.8	21.5
Twice	9.4	5.8	9.6	6.7	8.4	7.4	9.0	5.2	8.2	6.9	8.8	5.6
3 or 4 times	3.0	1.8	3.1	1.8	3.8	3.5	4.1	3.0	3.9	2.7	3.2	2.2
5 or more times	1.7	1.0	1.2	0.8	1.6	0.9	1.3	0.5	2.3	1.2	1.3	0.7
Has something of yours (worth over $50) been stolen?												
Not at all	77.2	86.6	80.6	87.1	78.9	84.3	76.9	87.0	78.2	83.8	78.4	85.1
Once	16.4	10.7	14.6	10.3	14.6	11.0	17.2	9.8	15.5	12.4	16.2	12.0
Twice	4.1	1.6	3.8	1.8	4.0	3.1	4.0	2.2	3.9	2.6	3.7	1.8
3 or 4 times	1.7	0.8	0.6	0.8	1.6	1.3	1.5	0.8	1.4	0.8	1.4	0.6
5 or more times	0.6	0.2	0.4	0.0	0.9	0.3	0.4	0.2	1.0	0.5	0.3	0.5
Has someone deliberately damaged your property (your car, clothing, etc.)?												
Not at all	65.9	78.4	66.4	80.8	70.2	77.8	66.3	79.4	66.9	77.5	67.6	79.9
Once	22.1	15.4	22.9	14.6	18.9	15.9	23.3	14.3	22.4	15.6	21.3	14.1
Twice	7.6	4.1	5.4	2.5	6.9	4.5	6.4	3.5	6.9	4.0	7.5	4.0
3 or 4 times	3.2	1.4	3.5	1.8	2.5	1.4	3.1	2.2	2.6	2.1	3.0	1.2
5 or more times	1.3	0.7	1.9	0.4	1.4	0.4	0.9	0.5	1.1	0.8	0.5	0.8
Has someone injured you with a weapon (like a knife, gun, or club)?												
Not at all	91.3	96.6	91.9	98.2	93.0	98.0	92.2	98.3	92.5	97.7	93.3	96.9
Once	5.0	2.6	5.3	1.0	4.1	1.5	4.6	0.9	4.3	1.5	3.9	1.7
Twice	2.3	0.6	1.6	0.3	1.1	0.3	1.7	0.4	2.0	0.4	1.4	0.9
3 or 4 times	0.4	0.0	0.4	0.3	0.9	0.2	1.1	0.1	0.8	0.3	0.8	0.1
5 or more times	1.0	0.3	0.8	0.3	0.9	0.1	0.4	0.3	0.3	0.2	0.5	0.4
Has someone threatened you with a weapon, but not actually injured you?												
Not at all	78.7	89.7	79.2	92.8	78.6	90.4	78.0	91.5	80.1	92.6	82.7	90.5
Once	11.6	6.8	12.5	4.9	11.6	5.6	12.9	5.6	12.4	5.1	9.9	6.5
Twice	5.1	1.8	3.9	1.7	4.9	2.5	4.6	1.7	2.8	1.4	3.9	1.5
3 or 4 times	2.0	1.0	2.8	0.4	3.0	0.7	1.7	0.7	2.3	0.6	2.1	0.8
5 or more times	2.6	0.7	1.6	0.2	1.9	0.8	2.8	0.5	2.3	0.3	1.4	0.7
Has someone injured you on purpose without using a weapon?												
Not at all	82.7	87.8	84.4	90.0	86.2	91.0	85.0	92.0	84.8	91.8	86.8	89.2
Once	10.7	6.7	8.2	6.6	8.0	5.5	8.2	4.6	8.5	4.7	7.8	7.1
Twice	3.1	3.0	3.8	2.6	2.7	2.0	3.9	1.8	3.1	1.2	3.0	1.9
3 or 4 times	1.6	1.5	1.9	0.2	2.1	0.6	1.7	0.9	2.1	1.1	0.9	0.8
5 or more times	1.8	1.1	1.8	0.5	1.0	0.9	1.3	0.8	1.5	1.2	1.5	1.0
Has an unarmed person threatened you with injury, but not actually injured you?												
Not at all	68.3	80.6	68.6	81.8	70.1	83.0	68.9	83.3	69.1	83.0	73.6	82.7
Once	14.1	11.2	15.3	12.1	12.5	9.2	15.5	9.8	12.3	9.4	11.9	11.2
Twice	6.8	3.2	4.9	2.8	7.0	4.2	5.6	2.9	6.2	3.9	4.4	2.4
3 or 4 times	4.5	2.4	5.7	1.9	4.6	1.4	4.1	1.8	5.9	1.6	4.3	1.2
5 or more times	6.3	2.6	5.5	1.4	5.7	2.2	5.8	2.2	6.4	2.1	5.8	2.4

Note: See Note, table 3.37. Readers interested in responses to this question for 1976 through 1990 should consult previous editions of SOURCEBOOK. For survey methodology and definitions of terms, see Appendix 6.

Source: Lloyd D. Johnston, Jerald G. Bachman, and Patrick M. O'Malley, *Monitoring the Future 1991*, pp. 151, 152; *1993*, pp. 154, 155; *1995*, pp. 155, 156; *1997*, pp. 150, 151; *1999*, pp. 152, 153 (Ann Arbor, MI: Institute for Social Research, University of Michigan); Jerald G. Bachman, Lloyd D. Johnston, and Patrick M. O'Malley, *Monitoring the Future 1992*, pp. 153, 154; *1994*, pp. 153, 154; *1996*, pp. 147, 148; *1998*, pp. 151, 152; *2000*, pp. 153, 154 (Ann Arbor, MI: Institute for Social Research, University of Michigan); and data provided by the Monitoring the Future Project, Survey Research Center, Lloyd D. Johnston, Jerald G. Bachman, and Patrick M. O'Malley, Principal Investigators. Table adapted by SOURCEBOOK staff. Reprinted by permission.

	Class of 1997		Class of 1998		Class of 1999		Class of 2000		Class of 2001		Class of 2002		Class of 2003	
	Male (N=1,252)	Female (N=1,262)	Male (N=1,195)	Female (N=1,279)	Male (N=1,079)	Female (N=1,159)	Male (N=941)	Female (N=1,130)	Male (N=1,011)	Female (N=1,070)	Male (N=983)	Female (N=1,122)	Male (N=1,085)	Female (N=1,252)
	61.9%	69.1%	63.1%	71.8%	63.9%	69.4%	63.0%	70.5%	62.3%	66.5%	65.6%	71.7%	66.2%	74.7%
	26.3	22.1	24.2	22.1	22.1	21.1	24.5	21.9	24.6	22.7	24.5	19.6	21.9	17.6
	7.7	6.1	7.1	4.3	7.4	6.6	7.2	4.7	7.0	7.2	6.6	5.6	7.4	5.7
	3.1	2.1	3.9	1.2	4.3	2.0	3.8	2.0	3.6	2.4	2.6	2.3	2.7	1.6
	1.1	0.6	1.8	0.6	2.3	0.8	1.6	0.9	2.5	1.2	0.6	0.9	1.8	0.4
	78.8	86.3	76.4	87.2	76.6	83.7	77.5	87.6	74.5	83.1	79.1	85.8	80.8	86.3
	15.3	10.5	17.0	10.9	16.0	12.5	17.3	9.8	17.8	12.8	16.6	10.0	14.3	10.7
	3.6	2.3	5.0	1.5	5.3	3.3	3.7	1.9	4.7	2.3	2.6	2.7	2.8	2.1
	1.8	0.7	0.8	0.3	1.3	0.3	1.2	0.3	2.1	1.3	1.1	1.0	1.2	0.5
	0.5	0.3	0.8	0.2	0.8	0.2	0.2	0.3	0.9	0.4	0.6	0.5	0.8	0.4
	71.3	79.5	71.7	78.0	67.6	81.0	68.9	80.3	71.5	81.1	72.6	81.1	71.8	82.8
	18.6	14.9	19.7	16.3	22.6	13.2	22.3	13.9	19.9	13.6	19.3	12.6	19.1	13.0
	7.0	3.7	6.0	3.8	6.7	3.1	5.9	3.3	4.5	4.1	5.3	4.0	5.9	3.0
	2.4	1.3	0.9	1.4	2.2	1.7	1.9	1.8	2.9	0.6	2.5	1.4	1.7	0.9
	0.8	0.7	1.7	0.5	1.0	1.0	1.0	0.8	1.2	0.6	0.2	0.8	1.5	0.3
	92.1	97.7	92.3	98.4	93.2	97.5	93.9	98.7	92.4	97.5	94.1	98.0	94.8	98.3
	4.7	1.3	4.8	1.3	4.0	1.3	3.8	0.7	4.4	1.8	4.1	1.3	3.1	1.3
	1.9	0.8	1.1	0.3	1.1	0.7	0.9	0.5	0.8	0.2	0.9	0.0	1.3	0.2
	0.5	0.1	0.8	0.0	0.9	0.5	0.6	0.0	1.0	0.2	0.2	0.2	0.2	0.1
	0.8	0.1	0.9	0.0	0.8	0.0	0.8	0.1	1.3	0.2	0.7	0.3	0.6	0.2
	85.1	93.4	83.0	94.3	83.2	92.2	85.0	92.7	81.7	92.0	86.8	93.4	83.0	94.1
	8.9	5.0	8.7	4.2	10.7	5.3	8.6	5.8	10.4	5.5	7.9	4.2	9.8	4.2
	2.1	1.1	4.1	0.8	2.7	1.7	2.6	0.5	4.0	1.2	3.6	0.4	2.7	1.0
	1.1	0.4	2.9	0.5	1.7	0.6	1.7	0.6	2.1	0.6	1.1	0.5	1.9	0.5
	2.8	0.1	1.3	0.2	1.7	0.2	2.1	0.3	1.9	0.6	0.5	1.5	2.7	0.2
	85.2	90.7	85.6	92.4	87.7	91.9	87.8	90.4	84.1	90.3	87.3	91.4	87.9	91.6
	9.5	5.4	9.8	4.5	7.4	4.5	6.7	5.2	9.2	6.4	6.9	4.6	6.7	5.2
	2.7	1.8	1.9	1.4	2.4	1.7	2.4	2.4	2.1	1.8	2.3	2.8	2.7	2.0
	1.0	1.0	1.1	1.1	1.2	1.1	1.8	1.4	1.9	0.8	1.8	0.3	1.0	0.6
	1.7	1.1	1.6	0.7	1.3	0.7	1.4	0.7	2.7	0.7	1.7	1.0	1.7	0.6
	72.7	84.8	71.3	87.2	72.2	83.0	72.9	82.6	71.4	84.6	77.3	83.4	74.4	87.4
	12.5	8.7	13.3	7.3	12.0	10.7	13.3	10.3	15.1	8.9	11.5	10.5	11.0	7.8
	6.2	3.1	4.7	2.9	5.3	3.6	5.4	2.7	4.2	3.6	3.6	3.2	5.0	2.4
	3.4	2.0	4.2	1.3	4.0	1.5	3.0	2.6	3.3	1.4	2.3	0.8	3.7	1.0
	5.3	1.5	6.5	1.3	6.5	1.2	5.4	1.7	6.0	1.5	5.3	2.1	5.9	1.3

Nature and distribution of known offenses 219

Table 3.42

High school seniors reporting victimization experiences at school in last 12 months

By type of victimization and race, United States, 1991-2003

Question: "The next questions are about some things which may have happened to you while you were at school (inside or outside or in a school bus). During the last 12 months how often..."

Type of victimization	Class of 1991 White (N=1,808)	Class of 1991 Black (N=301)	Class of 1992 White (N=1,840)	Class of 1992 Black (N=383)	Class of 1993 White (N=1,883)	Class of 1993 Black (N=340)	Class of 1994 White (N=1,814)	Class of 1994 Black (N=291)	Class of 1995 White (N=1,833)	Class of 1995 Black (N=301)	Class of 1996 White (N=1,638)	Class of 1996 Black (N=294)
Has something of yours (worth under $50) been stolen?												
Not at all	62.6%	62.6%	67.2%	59.4%	61.8%	59.3%	63.6%	59.5%	64.3%	65.3%	67.0%	62.2%
Once	26.1	25.4	22.3	25.4	25.7	24.6	24.6	28.8	23.6	17.2	23.6	21.0
Twice	8.1	6.7	6.9	11.9	8.0	7.8	7.3	5.5	7.7	8.6	6.2	8.6
3 or 4 times	2.3	4.2	2.6	3.0	3.4	6.4	3.8	4.5	2.9	7.8	2.2	6.0
5 or more times	0.9	1.0	1.1	0.3	1.1	1.9	0.7	1.7	1.6	1.1	0.9	2.3
Has something of yours (worth over $50) been stolen?												
Not at all	83.6	74.6	85.3	77.4	83.1	73.1	83.1	75.2	82.4	74.8	84.1	70.9
Once	12.3	19.4	11.6	16.4	11.6	18.0	12.7	19.4	12.9	17.6	13.2	18.9
Twice	2.8	3.8	2.3	5.6	3.6	4.7	3.0	2.2	3.2	5.3	1.8	5.6
3 or 4 times	0.9	1.8	0.5	0.4	1.2	3.0	0.9	3.2	1.0	0.8	0.8	2.3
5 or more times	0.4	0.4	0.3	0.2	0.5	1.2	0.3	0.0	0.5	1.6	0.2	2.4
Has someone deliberately damaged your property (your car, clothing, etc.)?												
Not at all	71.6	75.4	74.3	73.7	74.2	73.7	71.7	78.5	72.0	72.7	74.8	74.0
Once	19.4	15.1	18.3	16.2	18.0	15.8	19.6	17.0	19.5	16.8	17.7	14.4
Twice	5.9	2.5	3.4	6.8	5.3	6.3	4.7	3.8	5.6	5.1	5.5	6.5
3 or 4 times	2.2	3.7	2.9	1.3	1.7	2.3	3.2	0.5	2.1	3.8	1.4	3.4
5 or more times	0.8	3.2	1.0	2.0	0.8	1.9	0.8	0.2	0.8	1.7	0.5	1.7
Has someone injured you with a weapon (like a knife, gun, or club)?												
Not at all	94.7	90.4	95.5	94.8	95.7	93.6	96.0	91.9	95.9	91.3	96.3	90.2
Once	3.2	6.4	2.9	3.5	2.5	4.9	2.5	3.2	2.6	4.5	2.5	3.8
Twice	1.5	1.4	1.0	1.5	0.6	1.0	0.5	3.8	1.0	2.7	0.8	3.4
3 or 4 times	0.2	0.2	0.2	0.0	0.7	0.3	0.6	1.1	0.4	1.5	0.1	1.2
5 or more times	0.5	1.6	0.4	0.2	0.5	0.3	0.4	0.0	0.2	0.0	0.4	1.5
Has someone threatened you with a weapon, but not actually injured you?												
Not at all	84.3	79.8	87.7	80.6	86.2	76.5	85.2	81.9	87.7	81.1	87.7	82.9
Once	8.8	12.2	8.1	9.8	7.1	15.0	9.1	10.6	8.1	9.8	8.3	8.6
Twice	3.6	4.2	2.4	6.1	3.8	3.7	3.4	3.1	1.8	3.3	2.3	3.8
3 or 4 times	1.6	2.9	1.2	2.9	1.7	2.4	1.1	1.7	1.2	3.5	0.9	2.9
5 or more times	1.7	0.9	0.6	0.6	1.3	2.3	1.1	2.7	1.2	2.2	0.8	1.9
Has someone injured you on purpose without using a weapon?												
Not at all	84.6	82.9	87.3	86.2	89.0	88.5	88.5	88.5	88.4	90.8	88.8	84.3
Once	9.2	9.5	7.5	6.4	6.5	5.5	6.2	6.2	6.5	4.4	7.3	8.6
Twice	3.1	3.2	3.2	5.3	2.4	2.7	2.8	3.4	2.0	2.9	2.4	3.5
3 or 4 times	1.7	2.2	1.0	1.0	1.4	1.1	1.3	1.9	1.6	1.2	0.6	1.3
5 or more times	1.5	2.2	0.9	1.2	0.7	2.1	1.2	0.0	1.4	0.6	1.0	2.3
Has an unarmed person threatened you with injury, but not actually injured you?												
Not at all	73.5	72.5	74.5	79.5	76.2	77.7	75.3	77.9	74.9	77.1	78.1	78.1
Once	12.4	13.2	13.7	12.4	10.8	13.8	13.2	11.5	11.1	14.4	11.3	13.8
Twice	5.2	5.3	4.1	2.6	5.8	3.1	3.9	6.4	5.1	3.7	3.5	2.6
3 or 4 times	4.0	4.0	4.3	2.6	3.1	1.4	3.1	2.5	4.0	2.3	3.0	2.3
5 or more times	4.9	4.9	3.4	2.9	4.1	3.9	4.5	1.6	4.9	2.4	4.1	3.2

Note: See Notes, tables 3.37 and 3.39. Readers interested in responses to this question for 1976 through 1990 should consult previous editions of SOURCEBOOK. For survey methodology and definitions of terms, see Appendix 6.

[a]Less than 0.05%.

Source: Lloyd D. Johnston, Jerald G. Bachman, and Patrick M. O'Malley, *Monitoring the Future 1991*, pp. 151, 152; *1993*, pp. 154, 155; *1995*, pp. 155, 156; *1997*, pp. 150, 151; *1999*, pp. 152, 153 (Ann Arbor, MI: Institute for Social Research, University of Michigan); Jerald G. Bachman, Lloyd D. Johnston, and Patrick M. O'Malley, *Monitoring the Future 1992*, pp. 153, 154; *1994*, pp. 153, 154; *1996*, pp. 147, 148; *1998*, pp. 151, 152; *2000*, pp. 153, 154 (Ann Arbor, MI: Institute for Social Research, University of Michigan); and data provided by the Monitoring the Future Project, Survey Research Center, Lloyd D. Johnston, Jerald G. Bachman, and Patrick M. O'Malley, Principal Investigators. Table adapted by SOURCEBOOK staff. Reprinted by permission.

	Class of 1997		Class of 1998		Class of 1999		Class of 2000		Class of 2001		Class of 2002		Class of 2003	
	White (N=1,708)	Black (N=323)	White (N=1,721)	Black (N=326)	White (N=1,594)	Black (N=297)	White (N=1,424)	Black (N=292)	White (N=1,381)	Black (N=252)	White (N=1,421)	Black (N=235)	White (N=1,612)	Black (N=288)
	66.1%	65.0%	68.3%	66.4%	67.0%	67.6%	66.5%	68.3%	64.9%	62.9%	70.3%	60.8%	70.8%	73.1%
	23.9	22.5	22.5	25.3	21.4	21.9	24.0	23.7	23.2	23.5	21.6	23.1	20.1	16.8
	6.6	8.2	5.6	4.7	6.5	7.2	6.4	3.3	7.0	6.1	5.4	8.2	5.8	7.2
	2.5	3.7	2.6	2.0	3.4	2.8	2.7	2.7	3.1	3.9	2.2	6.1	2.1	2.1
	0.8	0.7	0.9	1.6	1.7	0.6	0.5	2.0	1.9	3.7	0.4	1.9	1.1	0.8
	84.2	76.8	83.1	77.4	81.0	78.4	83.7	83.6	80.8	71.5	84.7	72.9	84.7	81.4
	12.3	13.7	13.1	16.5	13.8	15.1	13.0	13.2	13.8	21.7	11.9	15.7	12.2	11.8
	2.2	6.5	2.8	4.4	4.4	3.4	2.5	2.1	3.5	2.5	2.5	7.3	2.2	3.2
	0.9	2.8	0.5	0.6	0.8	1.7	0.8	0.0	1.3	2.7	0.6	3.6	0.6	2.6
	0.4	0.3	0.4	1.1	0.1	1.4	0.1	1.2	0.7	1.6	0.3	0.6	0.3	1.1
	74.5	81.2	74.8	78.5	73.3	78.5	75.3	79.7	76.6	83.2	77.2	75.8	77.0	81.4
	18.0	10.0	18.6	15.7	18.1	16.5	18.0	15.8	16.8	11.4	15.9	15.6	16.0	13.5
	4.9	6.0	4.1	4.9	5.3	3.3	4.7	3.3	4.4	2.1	4.8	3.5	5.1	2.7
	1.8	2.6	1.3	0.6	2.1	1.7	1.0	0.9	1.4	1.3	1.7	3.3	1.4	1.3
	0.8	0.3	1.2	0.3	1.1	0.0	1.0	0.3	0.8	2.0	0.4	1.8	0.5	1.1
	95.7	92.9	96.4	93.4	95.8	96.1	96.7	97.2	95.2	95.1	97.1	90.3	96.6	96.3
	3.0	3.4	2.5	5.0	2.8	2.6	2.0	1.8	2.9	4.6	2.1	5.0	2.2	2.3
	0.7	3.1	0.5	0.8	0.9	1.1	0.6	0.9	0.4	0.0	0.2	1.8	0.5	0.8
	0.2	0.4	0.1	0.5	0.3	(a)	0.4	0.1	0.5	0.3	0.1	1.8	0.3	(a)
	0.5	0.3	0.5	0.3	0.2	0.1	0.3	0.0	1.0	0.0	0.4	1.1	0.4	0.5
	90.4	86.3	89.2	85.6	88.3	89.0	89.7	89.2	86.4	87.3	91.8	78.9	88.7	91.2
	6.9	7.0	6.3	8.3	7.3	7.8	7.0	6.8	8.3	10.2	5.2	10.0	7.0	4.7
	1.3	2.3	2.1	3.5	2.3	2.2	1.1	1.8	2.4	0.6	1.7	3.4	1.8	2.6
	0.2	2.8	1.5	2.1	1.3	0.5	1.1	0.2	1.3	0.7	0.6	3.7	1.2	0.9
	1.2	1.5	0.8	0.5	0.7	0.6	1.0	2.0	1.5	1.1	0.8	3.9	1.3	0.7
	88.0	88.9	89.5	89.2	89.2	95.6	89.2	92.8	86.4	88.6	89.9	84.6	90.1	91.4
	7.7	4.1	6.8	5.7	6.7	2.7	5.5	4.7	8.1	7.9	6.0	6.1	6.1	4.5
	2.1	3.1	1.4	2.6	2.0	1.6	2.6	2.3	1.9	2.8	2.5	4.4	2.1	1.3
	1.0	0.4	1.2	1.5	1.1	0.0	1.5	0.1	1.5	(a)	1.1	1.4	0.5	1.6
	1.2	3.5	1.0	1.0	0.9	0.1	1.2	0.1	2.0	0.6	0.6	3.5	1.2	1.2
	77.6	80.7	79.2	78.5	77.1	80.3	77.1	85.1	76.8	83.2	81.4	74.6	80.3	86.0
	11.2	9.3	9.8	14.5	11.6	11.3	11.6	10.7	12.4	7.7	9.8	14.3	10.3	6.8
	4.7	4.1	3.9	2.4	4.9	3.8	4.6	1.2	4.5	1.7	4.1	4.2	3.4	4.3
	2.7	3.4	3.0	1.5	2.6	1.7	2.7	1.0	2.3	4.9	1.6	0.8	2.4	1.0
	3.8	2.6	4.0	3.1	3.8	2.8	4.0	2.0	3.9	2.6	3.2	6.1	3.5	1.9

Nature and distribution of known offenses 221

Table 3.43

High school seniors reporting involvement in selected delinquent activities in last 12 months

United States, 1991-2003

Question: "During the last 12 months, how often have you..."

Delinquent activity	Class of 1991 (N=2,569)	Class of 1992 (N=2,690)	Class of 1993 (N=2,770)	Class of 1994 (N=2,645)	Class of 1995 (N=2,656)	Class of 1996 (N=2,452)	Class of 1997 (N=2,638)	Class of 1998 (N=2,656)	Class of 1999 (N=2,322)	Class of 2000 (N=2,204)	Class of 2001 (N=2,218)	Class of 2002 (N=2,274)	Class of 2003 (N=2,517)
Argued or had a fight with either of your parents?[a]													
Not at all	10.0%	9.3%	12.1%	10.1%	9.8%	11.0%	11.6%	11.9%	9.2%	11.2%	10.2%	12.3%	10.3%
Once	8.9	8.7	9.4	10.3	9.4	9.6	10.3	9.6	10.2	10.1	9.8	10.3	10.5
Twice	12.7	11.7	12.4	12.1	15.1	13.3	13.1	14.1	12.6	13.4	12.3	12.4	13.8
3 or 4 times	24.7	24.7	20.2	24.9	23.2	24.0	22.6	23.7	24.7	23.5	24.4	24.4	22.9
5 or more times	43.6	45.5	45.9	42.7	42.5	42.2	42.4	40.7	43.3	41.8	43.3	40.6	42.5
Hit an instructor or supervisor?													
Not at all	97.0	96.7	96.2	97.0	96.9	96.3	96.4	96.7	96.9	97.1	96.6	97.0	96.8
Once	1.6	1.9	2.2	1.5	1.6	2.0	1.8	1.6	1.4	1.5	2.0	1.4	1.1
Twice	0.7	0.5	0.6	0.9	0.6	0.7	0.8	0.8	0.3	0.4	0.5	0.9	0.9
3 or 4 times	0.2	0.3	0.4	0.2	0.3	0.4	0.3	0.3	0.3	0.4	0.2	0.4	0.2
5 or more times	0.6	0.6	0.6	0.4	0.6	0.6	0.8	0.6	1.1	0.6	0.8	0.4	1.0
Gotten into a serious fight in school or at work?													
Not at all	82.1	81.1	82.3	83.8	85.2	83.3	82.6	83.4	85.3	87.7	83.8	86.3	85.7
Once	10.3	11.5	10.3	9.1	8.2	9.3	10.1	9.8	8.8	7.1	9.2	8.6	7.2
Twice	4.0	4.0	3.6	3.9	3.4	3.9	3.8	3.7	2.8	2.8	3.7	3.0	4.0
3 or 4 times	2.0	1.8	2.4	2.0	2.2	1.6	1.8	1.6	1.7	1.2	2.2	1.6	1.5
5 or more times	1.6	1.7	1.3	1.1	1.0	1.8	1.7	1.6	1.4	1.2	1.1	0.6	1.6
Taken part in a fight where a group of your friends were against another group?													
Not at all	79.6	78.7	77.8	80.7	81.4	79.8	78.5	79.4	80.8	80.3	79.8	82.9	80.2
Once	11.2	11.5	11.2	10.2	10.1	10.8	11.0	10.3	10.8	11.0	11.9	9.3	10.3
Twice	5.0	4.4	5.8	4.0	3.6	4.3	5.1	5.1	4.6	4.8	4.4	4.2	4.7
3 or 4 times	2.5	3.2	2.9	2.8	2.9	2.3	3.4	3.0	2.6	2.1	2.2	2.1	3.0
5 or more times	1.7	2.2	2.3	2.3	2.0	2.8	2.0	2.2	1.2	1.8	1.6	1.5	1.7
Hurt someone badly enough to need bandages or a doctor?													
Not at all	87.1	87.2	86.6	86.6	87.7	85.7	85.4	85.6	86.6	88.1	86.9	88.3	88.0
Once	8.2	7.3	7.1	7.5	6.5	8.4	8.9	7.9	7.6	7.3	7.6	6.2	5.6
Twice	2.3	2.9	2.7	2.5	2.7	2.9	2.7	3.1	2.8	2.0	2.2	3.2	3.1
3 or 4 times	1.1	1.6	1.7	2.1	2.0	1.7	1.6	1.7	1.7	1.1	1.8	1.3	1.7
5 or more times	1.3	1.1	1.8	1.4	1.2	1.4	1.6	1.7	1.3	1.5	1.5	1.1	1.6
Used a knife or gun or some other thing (like a club) to get something from a person?													
Not at all	96.6	95.7	95.4	95.2	96.5	96.3	95.5	95.7	96.2	97.2	97.2	96.8	96.1
Once	1.6	2.2	1.8	2.4	1.9	1.5	1.5	2.2	1.7	1.1	1.4	1.4	1.5
Twice	0.6	1.0	0.9	0.9	0.7	0.7	1.2	0.8	0.7	0.6	0.5	1.0	0.9
3 or 4 times	0.3	0.5	1.2	0.7	0.4	0.6	1.0	0.5	0.6	0.4	0.3	0.2	0.8
5 or more times	0.9	0.5	0.8	0.8	0.6	1.0	0.8	0.9	0.8	0.8	0.6	0.5	0.7
Taken something not belonging to you worth under $50?													
Not at all	68.1	67.4	67.9	69.3	68.6	67.6	65.8	68.8	69.0	69.5	68.7	71.2	72.3
Once	13.7	14.2	13.8	13.1	14.0	14.2	12.5	13.2	12.8	12.3	13.0	12.4	13.4
Twice	7.7	7.5	7.3	6.6	7.2	6.9	9.3	7.4	7.7	7.4	6.9	6.8	5.8
3 or 4 times	4.1	5.6	4.5	5.7	4.6	4.7	5.9	4.9	4.5	5.0	5.1	3.9	4.0
5 or more times	6.5	5.2	6.5	5.3	5.6	6.6	6.4	5.7	6.0	5.8	6.3	5.7	4.4
Taken something not belonging to you worth over $50?													
Not at all	89.9	89.5	88.7	89.0	90.7	87.7	87.2	88.4	89.4	87.5	88.3	89.9	90.4
Once	4.6	5.5	5.0	5.1	3.7	5.3	6.3	5.3	4.7	5.6	5.3	4.8	4.3
Twice	2.1	1.7	2.1	2.1	2.0	2.6	2.6	2.6	2.0	2.5	2.3	2.0	1.6
3 or 4 times	1.7	1.5	1.5	1.4	1.8	1.8	1.6	1.4	1.6	1.6	1.4	1.6	1.3
5 or more times	1.8	1.7	2.8	2.3	1.9	2.6	2.3	2.3	2.3	2.9	2.7	1.7	2.4

See notes at end of table.

Table 3.43

High school seniors reporting involvement in selected delinquent activities in last 12 months

United States, 1991-2003--Continued

Delinquent activity	Class of 1991 (N=2,569)	Class of 1992 (N=2,690)	Class of 1993 (N=2,770)	Class of 1994 (N=2,645)	Class of 1995 (N=2,656)	Class of 1996 (N=2,452)	Class of 1997 (N=2,638)	Class of 1998 (N=2,656)	Class of 1999 (N=2,322)	Class of 2000 (N=2,204)	Class of 2001 (N=2,218)	Class of 2002 (N=2,274)	Class of 2003 (N=2,517)
Taken something from a store without paying for it?													
Not at all	68.9%	69.6%	69.3%	69.7%	70.1%	67.8%	66.6%	70.3%	72.3%	71.3%	69.4%	72.1%	73.2%
Once	11.9	12.6	13.4	11.5	12.0	12.9	11.4	12.5	11.4	11.4	12.0	11.4	12.1
Twice	7.4	6.7	5.8	6.9	6.0	6.5	7.3	6.5	5.6	6.3	6.4	6.5	5.4
3 or 4 times	5.3	5.2	4.9	5.2	5.5	5.2	7.4	4.1	3.9	3.9	5.4	4.0	4.0
5 or more times	6.5	5.9	6.5	6.7	6.4	7.6	7.2	6.4	6.8	7.0	6.8	6.0	5.2
Taken a car that didn't belong to someone in your family without permission of the owner?													
Not at all	93.8	94.0	93.6	94.1	95.2	94.8	93.9	95.2	93.1	94.8	93.3	95.1	94.7
Once	3.3	3.1	3.0	3.0	2.7	2.4	3.4	2.7	4.2	2.7	3.9	2.4	2.3
Twice	1.2	1.4	1.4	1.3	1.0	1.3	1.2	0.9	1.1	1.2	1.2	0.9	1.1
3 or 4 times	1.0	0.7	1.0	0.8	0.6	0.8	0.6	0.6	0.8	0.6	0.8	0.9	0.7
5 or more times	0.7	0.9	1.0	0.7	0.6	0.8	0.9	0.7	0.8	0.7	0.9	0.7	1.2
Taken part of a car without permission of the owner?													
Not at all	93.7	93.9	92.7	94.3	94.9	94.7	94.6	94.9	95.2	94.9	95.3	95.3	94.5
Once	3.3	3.2	3.2	2.9	2.6	2.7	2.2	2.5	1.9	3.0	2.0	2.0	2.8
Twice	1.3	1.2	1.5	1.0	1.2	1.5	1.4	1.2	1.3	1.1	1.2	1.1	1.1
3 or 4 times	0.6	1.0	1.2	0.8	0.6	0.3	0.9	0.6	0.6	0.4	0.5	0.8	0.7
5 or more times	1.0	0.8	1.3	1.0	0.7	0.8	0.9	0.8	1.1	0.6	1.0	0.7	0.8
Gone into some house or building when you weren't supposed to be there?													
Not at all	75.7	74.0	73.7	75.2	76.5	76.0	75.3	75.4	76.4	77.3	75.7	77.4	77.0
Once	10.8	12.1	12.1	11.2	10.9	10.6	10.5	10.6	11.1	10.3	12.4	10.1	10.5
Twice	6.7	6.9	7.0	6.5	6.1	7.1	7.0	6.5	5.6	6.7	6.1	6.2	6.8
3 or 4 times	3.4	3.9	3.4	4.1	3.1	3.5	3.8	3.6	3.6	2.9	2.7	3.2	3.2
5 or more times	3.6	3.2	3.8	3.0	3.3	2.9	3.5	3.9	3.3	2.8	3.1	3.1	2.5
Set fire to someone's property on purpose?													
Not at all	97.9	97.2	96.6	96.8	97.5	97.0	96.9	97.1	97.5	97.2	96.9	96.9	96.2
Once	1.1	1.6	1.5	1.7	1.5	1.5	1.7	1.1	0.8	1.3	1.6	1.3	1.6
Twice	0.4	0.4	0.7	0.5	0.4	0.6	0.4	0.8	0.4	0.8	0.5	0.9	0.9
3 or 4 times	0.1	0.4	0.6	0.5	0.3	0.2	0.2	0.2	0.1	0.2	0.3	0.4	0.3
5 or more times	0.5	0.4	0.6	0.5	0.4	0.7	0.7	0.8	1.2	0.5	0.7	0.4	1.1
Damaged school property on purpose?													
Not at all	87.2	85.3	85.3	86.2	86.0	85.7	84.8	85.7	86.6	86.5	86.0	88.5	86.8
Once	6.5	7.9	6.4	6.5	6.5	7.2	7.7	7.5	6.4	7.3	6.7	5.4	6.3
Twice	3.0	3.5	4.0	3.5	3.2	3.1	3.1	2.6	3.5	3.5	3.7	2.6	3.9
3 or 4 times	1.3	1.2	2.0	2.0	2.6	2.0	2.2	2.0	1.3	1.5	2.0	1.7	1.4
5 or more times	2.0	2.1	2.2	1.9	1.7	2.0	2.2	2.3	2.1	1.4	1.7	1.8	1.6
Damaged property at work on purpose?													
Not at all	93.4	94.0	93.6	94.4	93.8	93.7	93.3	92.7	92.9	92.8	92.7	93.5	93.2
Once	3.2	2.7	2.9	2.3	3.3	3.3	2.8	3.3	3.7	3.8	3.3	2.7	3.3
Twice	1.3	1.3	1.5	1.5	1.2	0.8	1.7	1.6	1.3	1.4	2.1	1.6	1.5
3 or 4 times	0.8	1.0	0.8	0.9	0.7	0.7	1.0	0.9	0.9	0.8	0.5	0.7	1.1
5 or more times	1.3	1.0	1.1	1.0	1.0	1.4	1.1	1.6	1.1	1.1	1.4	1.5	1.0
Been arrested and taken to a police station?													
Not at all	X	X	90.4	91.1	91.0	90.0	90.6	89.8	90.4	90.9	92.0	90.7	92.0
Once	X	X	5.9	5.5	5.9	5.5	5.6	6.9	5.5	5.3	4.7	6.3	4.5
Twice	X	X	1.8	1.7	1.6	2.6	1.9	1.5	2.1	1.8	1.7	1.7	1.9
3 or 4 times	X	X	1.2	1.0	0.7	0.8	1.1	0.6	0.8	1.2	0.8	0.8	0.7
5 or more times	X	X	0.6	0.8	0.7	1.0	0.9	1.2	1.2	0.8	0.8	0.5	0.9

Note: See Note, table 3.37. Readers interested in responses to this question for 1975 through 1990 should consult previous editions of SOURCEBOOK. For survey methodology and definitions of terms, see Appendix 6.

[a]This question was omitted from schools in California beginning in 1997.

Source: Lloyd D. Johnston, Jerald G. Bachman, and Patrick M. O'Malley, *Monitoring the Future 1991*, pp. 106-109; *1993*, pp. 107-110; *1995*, pp. 108-110; *1997*, pp. 105-107; *1999*, pp. 106-108 (Ann Arbor, MI: Institute for Social Research, University of Michigan); Jerald G. Bachman, Lloyd D. Johnston, and Patrick M. O'Malley, *Monitoring the Future 1992*, pp. 106-109; *1994*, pp. 106-109; *1996*, pp. 103-105; *1998*, pp. 105-107; *2000*, pp. 107-109 (Ann Arbor, MI: Institute for Social Research, University of Michigan); and data provided by the Monitoring the Future Project, Survey Research Center, Lloyd D. Johnston, Jerald G. Bachman, and Patrick M. O'Malley, Principal Investigators. Table adapted by SOURCEBOOK staff. Reprinted by permission.

Table 3.44

High school seniors reporting involvement in selected delinquent activities in last 12 months

By sex, United States, 1991-2003

Question: "During the last 12 months, how often have you..."

Delinquent activity	Class of 1991 Male (N=1,280)	Class of 1991 Female (N=1,205)	Class of 1992 Male (N=1,276)	Class of 1992 Female (N=1,308)	Class of 1993 Male (N=1,294)	Class of 1993 Female (N=1,321)	Class of 1994 Male (N=1,208)	Class of 1994 Female (N=1,302)	Class of 1995 Male (N=1,238)	Class of 1995 Female (N=1,313)	Class of 1996 Male (N=1,142)	Class of 1996 Female (N=1,197)
Argued or had a fight with either of your parents?[a]												
Not at all	12.2%	7.0%	11.5%	6.6%	15.5%	8.0%	13.1%	6.3%	13.1%	5.9%	14.0%	7.7%
Once	9.6	8.3	9.7	7.4	11.8	7.3	12.3	8.0	11.2	7.4	10.2	8.9
Twice	13.1	12.2	12.9	10.7	12.2	12.1	11.6	12.9	15.8	14.0	15.2	11.8
3 or 4 times	24.9	25.3	25.3	24.0	18.5	22.1	23.1	27.3	22.4	24.1	22.8	25.7
5 or more times	40.2	47.2	40.6	51.3	42.0	50.5	40.0	45.6	37.5	48.5	37.9	45.9
Hit an instructor or supervisor?												
Not at all	95.3	98.9	94.8	98.9	94.3	98.3	95.0	99.3	95.8	98.3	94.2	98.9
Once	2.4	0.8	2.6	0.8	3.3	1.1	2.4	0.5	1.7	1.0	3.3	0.7
Twice	0.9	0.1	1.0	0.1	1.0	0.1	1.5	0.2	0.8	0.3	0.9	0.2
3 or 4 times	0.4	0.0	0.6	(b)	0.4	0.3	0.3	0.0	0.6	0.1	0.7	0.1
5 or more times	1.0	0.2	0.9	0.2	1.0	0.1	0.7	(b)	1.0	0.3	0.8	0.1
Gotten into a serious fight in school or at work?												
Not at all	76.6	88.1	76.9	85.8	78.4	87.0	80.3	87.9	82.1	88.6	77.4	90.0
Once	12.4	8.2	12.7	10.2	11.2	8.5	10.3	7.6	9.3	7.0	11.8	6.3
Twice	5.5	2.4	5.4	2.5	5.2	2.3	4.9	2.9	4.1	2.5	6.1	1.9
3 or 4 times	2.8	1.0	2.4	0.9	3.1	1.9	2.8	1.0	2.8	1.6	1.9	1.3
5 or more times	2.7	0.3	2.6	0.6	2.1	0.4	1.8	0.6	1.7	0.3	2.9	0.5
Taken part in a fight where a group of your friends were against another group?												
Not at all	73.8	86.4	73.0	85.3	71.0	85.5	75.4	86.0	76.7	86.1	73.0	86.9
Once	13.4	8.7	12.9	9.3	13.8	8.2	10.8	9.6	11.3	9.1	13.3	8.2
Twice	6.8	2.8	6.0	2.8	7.2	4.3	5.9	2.2	4.5	2.6	5.7	3.0
3 or 4 times	3.5	1.2	4.7	1.9	4.1	1.4	3.8	1.7	4.1	1.8	3.4	1.1
5 or more times	2.5	0.9	3.4	0.8	3.9	0.6	4.1	0.5	3.4	0.6	4.6	0.7
Hurt someone badly enough to need bandages or a doctor?												
Not at all	79.1	96.0	78.5	96.0	78.6	95.0	79.1	94.5	79.6	95.9	77.5	94.6
Once	13.4	2.9	11.9	2.8	11.1	3.0	10.8	4.1	10.1	2.8	12.2	4.1
Twice	3.7	0.5	5.2	0.6	4.1	1.4	4.3	0.8	4.2	0.7	4.9	0.9
3 or 4 times	1.9	0.4	2.5	0.4	2.9	0.5	3.6	0.3	3.9	0.3	3.1	0.3
5 or more times	2.0	0.2	1.9	0.2	3.3	0.1	2.3	0.3	2.2	0.3	2.3	0.1
Used a knife or gun or some other thing (like a club) to get something from a person?												
Not at all	94.7	98.8	93.3	98.6	91.9	99.0	92.5	98.3	94.6	98.6	94.1	98.9
Once	2.5	0.6	3.2	0.9	2.6	0.7	3.7	1.1	2.8	0.6	2.5	0.4
Twice	0.9	0.4	1.9	0.2	1.7	0.1	1.4	0.5	1.1	0.3	0.9	0.5
3 or 4 times	0.5	0.2	0.9	0.2	2.2	0.2	1.0	0.1	0.6	0.3	0.9	0.2
5 or more times	1.4	0.1	0.8	0.2	1.6	0.0	1.4	(b)	1.0	0.2	1.6	0.0
Taken something not belonging to you worth under $50?												
Not at all	58.2	78.3	59.7	75.3	59.9	76.5	60.6	77.0	59.6	76.9	61.3	73.3
Once	16.5	10.8	16.6	11.9	15.8	11.9	14.9	11.4	16.5	11.8	16.1	12.9
Twice	9.5	5.7	9.8	5.5	7.7	6.2	8.4	5.0	9.3	4.9	6.9	7.2
3 or 4 times	5.9	2.2	6.4	4.6	5.7	3.1	8.2	3.6	6.1	3.4	6.1	3.1
5 or more times	9.9	3.0	7.5	2.7	11.0	2.3	7.9	3.0	8.5	3.1	9.6	3.6
Taken something not belonging to you worth over $50?												
Not at all	85.0	95.6	84.8	94.9	82.5	95.6	82.6	95.3	85.6	95.5	82.2	93.5
Once	6.2	2.7	8.2	2.7	7.6	2.3	8.2	2.2	5.3	2.1	6.7	3.7
Twice	3.5	0.4	2.3	0.9	3.4	0.6	3.2	1.2	3.5	0.6	4.2	1.2
3 or 4 times	2.8	0.3	2.2	0.5	2.1	0.7	2.2	0.6	2.6	1.1	2.8	0.7
5 or more times	2.5	0.9	2.5	0.9	4.5	0.9	3.8	0.8	3.1	0.8	4.1	1.0

See notes at end of table.

	Class of 1997		Class of 1998		Class of 1999		Class of 2000		Class of 2001		Class of 2002		Class of 2003	
	Male (N=1,204)	Female (N=1,304)	Male (N=1,225)	Female (N=1,299)	Male (N=1,111)	Female (N=1,106)	Male (N=1,000)	Female (N=1,097)	Male (N=1,032)	Female (N=1,089)	Male (N=1,094)	Female (N=1,070)	Male (N=1,164)	Female (N=1,246)
	13.2%	9.9%	14.2%	9.6%	9.8%	7.8%	13.1%	8.1%	13.7%	6.5%	15.1%	8.5%	12.4%	7.6%
	12.4	7.9	11.1	8.2	11.4	8.8	8.4	11.0	9.3	10.1	11.1	9.2	14.1	6.9
	14.0	12.2	15.5	12.5	13.7	11.7	16.1	11.3	12.0	12.6	13.6	10.9	13.8	13.8
	24.7	20.8	22.7	24.9	23.9	26.4	23.2	24.1	23.3	25.6	23.3	25.8	21.6	24.6
	35.8	49.2	36.6	44.9	41.4	45.3	39.2	45.4	41.6	45.2	36.9	45.6	38.2	47.1
	94.5	98.4	95.3	98.6	95.1	99.1	94.9	99.6	95.2	98.3	95.4	98.7	94.8	99.1
	2.9	0.7	2.2	0.5	2.1	0.6	2.9	0.2	2.5	0.9	2.3	0.5	1.6	0.6
	1.0	0.5	1.4	0.3	0.4	0.2	0.6	0.1	0.4	0.5	1.3	0.3	1.3	0.2
	0.3	0.2	0.3	0.3	0.5	0.0	0.7	0.0	0.5	(b)	0.5	0.3	0.4	(b)
	1.2	0.3	0.8	0.3	1.9	0.1	0.9	0.1	1.4	0.2	0.7	0.1	1.9	0.2
	78.5	87.3	78.6	88.6	81.4	89.4	83.8	92.3	80.8	87.3	83.4	90.2	80.6	91.2
	11.8	7.8	12.0	7.6	10.8	6.9	8.7	5.3	10.6	7.6	10.2	6.2	9.8	4.6
	4.9	2.9	4.4	2.6	3.7	1.8	3.5	1.8	4.4	3.1	3.4	2.3	5.3	2.4
	2.3	1.2	2.5	0.7	2.2	1.3	2.1	0.4	2.5	1.5	2.0	1.1	1.5	1.5
	2.5	0.8	2.5	0.5	2.0	0.5	1.9	0.3	1.6	0.5	1.0	0.2	2.8	0.3
	73.1	84.2	74.2	84.7	76.0	85.8	75.1	85.1	76.3	83.0	81.0	85.7	75.4	85.1
	12.5	9.6	12.3	8.3	12.6	9.5	12.8	9.7	11.6	12.4	9.6	8.9	11.8	9.1
	6.0	3.6	6.0	4.5	6.3	2.4	6.3	3.3	5.5	3.1	4.3	3.7	5.6	3.5
	5.0	1.9	3.8	1.8	3.5	1.7	3.1	1.1	3.8	0.9	2.9	1.1	4.2	1.8
	3.4	0.8	3.7	0.7	1.6	0.6	2.6	0.7	2.7	0.6	2.2	0.8	3.0	0.5
	77.0	93.9	77.2	93.9	79.8	94.3	79.9	95.6	79.9	93.9	82.5	94.9	81.1	94.9
	12.9	4.6	12.6	3.2	11.0	3.8	11.4	3.6	10.9	4.0	8.8	2.7	7.6	3.4
	4.7	0.9	5.1	1.0	4.3	1.2	3.8	0.5	3.5	1.1	4.7	1.6	5.5	0.7
	3.0	0.2	2.8	0.9	2.9	0.3	2.2	0.2	3.3	0.5	2.1	0.6	2.8	0.7
	2.4	0.4	2.3	1.0	2.0	0.3	2.7	0.1	2.5	0.6	2.0	0.2	3.0	0.3
	93.6	97.8	93.2	98.2	94.0	98.7	95.5	99.0	95.1	99.3	94.9	99.1	93.5	99.1
	1.6	1.2	3.2	1.2	2.7	0.8	1.5	0.6	2.4	0.4	2.2	0.4	2.5	0.4
	2.1	0.5	1.4	0.2	0.9	0.2	1.0	0.2	0.7	0.3	1.8	0.2	1.3	0.2
	1.8	0.0	0.8	0.2	1.0	0.1	0.6	0.1	0.5	0.1	0.4	0.0	1.6	0.0
	0.9	0.5	1.3	0.3	1.4	0.2	1.3	0.0	1.2	0.0	0.6	0.2	1.0	0.2
	58.4	72.5	61.5	75.5	60.7	76.8	61.3	76.2	63.1	74.3	67.1	75.2	65.8	78.9
	14.2	11.1	14.8	11.8	14.4	11.6	15.3	10.1	14.3	11.6	12.0	12.8	14.8	11.8
	12.0	7.0	9.3	6.0	9.1	6.5	8.0	6.8	6.8	6.8	8.3	5.1	6.8	4.9
	7.2	4.9	6.9	2.8	6.5	2.5	6.2	4.0	6.4	3.9	4.5	3.3	5.4	2.7
	8.1	4.5	7.5	4.0	9.3	2.7	9.2	2.9	9.4	3.5	8.1	3.6	7.2	1.7
	82.3	92.0	83.3	93.3	84.6	94.5	81.0	93.6	83.6	92.7	85.8	94.6	86.3	94.9
	8.2	4.3	7.7	3.1	6.6	2.7	8.3	3.0	7.1	3.9	6.4	2.7	5.7	2.9
	4.1	1.1	4.0	1.0	2.8	1.2	3.5	1.6	3.6	1.0	3.1	1.0	2.0	0.9
	2.2	1.2	1.7	1.3	2.5	0.8	2.5	0.7	1.8	1.0	2.1	0.8	1.9	0.7
	3.1	1.4	3.3	1.3	3.6	0.7	4.7	0.9	4.0	1.4	2.6	1.0	4.1	0.7

Table 3.44

High school seniors reporting involvement in selected delinquent activities in last 12 months

By sex, United States, 1991-2003--Continued

	Class of 1991		Class of 1992		Class of 1993		Class of 1994		Class of 1995		Class of 1996	
Delinquent activity	Male (N=1,280)	Female (N=1,205)	Male (N=1,276)	Female (N=1,308)	Male (N=1,294)	Female (N=1,321)	Male (N=1,208)	Female (N=1,302)	Male (N=1,238)	Female (N=1,313)	Male (N=1,142)	Female (N=1,197)
Taken something from a store without paying for it?												
Not at all	60.4%	78.0%	62.5%	76.5%	62.4%	76.7%	63.9%	74.8%	64.3%	76.0%	63.1%	72.3%
Once	14.7	8.7	14.2	11.3	15.1	11.5	12.7	10.4	12.8	10.8	14.3	11.4
Twice	7.6	7.2	8.6	5.0	6.1	5.1	8.2	6.0	6.7	5.0	6.8	6.7
3 or 4 times	7.7	2.9	6.6	3.8	7.1	3.0	6.2	4.1	7.0	4.4	5.1	5.3
5 or more times	9.7	3.3	8.1	3.4	9.4	3.6	9.0	4.7	9.2	3.9	10.7	4.3
Taken a car that didn't belong to someone in your family without permission of the owner?												
Not at all	91.7	96.1	91.5	96.6	91.2	96.2	91.6	97.3	93.4	97.0	92.6	97.4
Once	3.8	2.9	4.0	2.0	4.3	1.7	3.7	2.1	3.6	1.7	3.1	1.5
Twice	1.8	0.4	1.9	0.8	1.7	1.3	2.3	0.4	1.5	0.5	1.6	0.8
3 or 4 times	1.5	0.4	1.1	0.3	1.4	0.4	1.2	0.1	0.6	0.5	1.7	0.0
5 or more times	1.2	0.3	1.4	0.2	1.4	0.4	1.2	0.1	0.9	0.3	1.0	0.3
Taken part of a car without permission of the owner?												
Not at all	89.4	98.3	90.4	98.0	87.5	97.9	90.3	98.3	91.9	97.7	90.6	99.1
Once	5.6	1.1	4.6	1.4	5.9	0.7	4.5	1.2	4.1	1.3	4.6	0.8
Twice	2.0	0.4	1.9	0.2	2.1	1.0	2.0	0.1	1.9	0.5	2.9	0.0
3 or 4 times	1.1	0.1	1.7	0.3	2.3	0.1	1.3	0.3	1.0	0.2	0.5	0.0
5 or more times	1.9	0.1	1.4	0.1	2.2	0.3	1.8	(b)	1.1	0.3	1.4	0.0
Gone into some house or building when you weren't supposed to be there?												
Not at all	69.3	82.7	68.7	79.6	65.9	82.5	67.8	82.6	70.4	82.9	71.0	81.6
Once	12.8	8.7	12.4	11.8	13.9	9.4	13.0	8.9	12.4	9.1	12.1	9.1
Twice	7.5	6.0	9.4	4.4	8.2	5.4	9.5	4.0	8.2	4.0	8.7	5.2
3 or 4 times	4.9	1.3	5.0	2.4	5.2	1.7	5.4	2.8	4.4	1.9	4.4	2.6
5 or more times	5.6	1.3	4.5	1.8	6.8	0.9	4.3	1.6	4.6	2.1	3.8	1.5
Set fire to someone's property on purpose?												
Not at all	96.4	99.4	95.3	99.1	94.1	99.1	94.7	99.2	96.3	98.8	95.1	99.1
Once	1.6	0.5	2.6	0.6	2.4	0.4	2.6	0.5	2.4	0.6	2.6	0.6
Twice	0.7	0.0	0.7	0.2	1.1	0.4	1.1	0.0	0.5	0.1	1.0	0.2
3 or 4 times	0.3	0.0	0.6	0.1	1.0	0.1	1.0	0.1	0.4	0.2	0.3	0.0
5 or more times	1.0	0.1	0.8	(b)	1.3	0.0	0.5	0.2	0.4	0.3	0.9	0.1
Damaged school property on purpose?												
Not at all	81.2	93.5	79.7	91.5	77.7	92.8	78.9	92.6	78.6	92.6	79.4	92.5
Once	8.7	4.1	10.0	5.2	8.6	4.3	8.8	4.5	9.1	4.1	9.6	4.8
Twice	4.5	1.4	5.1	2.0	6.2	1.9	5.6	1.5	4.8	1.7	4.5	1.4
3 or 4 times	2.0	0.4	1.4	0.8	3.3	0.7	3.3	0.9	4.3	1.1	3.1	1.0
5 or more times	3.6	0.5	3.7	0.5	4.2	0.3	3.4	0.5	3.2	0.5	3.3	0.3
Damaged property at work on purpose?												
Not at all	89.2	98.2	90.5	97.8	89.5	98.0	90.7	98.0	89.8	97.6	89.6	98.2
Once	4.9	1.1	4.0	1.2	4.4	1.2	3.7	0.9	5.6	1.0	5.1	1.4
Twice	2.1	0.2	1.9	0.6	2.6	0.4	2.6	0.5	1.9	0.6	1.3	0.3
3 or 4 times	1.4	0.2	1.7	0.3	1.4	0.3	1.4	0.4	1.0	0.3	1.5	0.1
5 or more times	2.4	0.3	1.9	0.1	2.1	0.1	1.6	0.3	1.7	0.4	2.4	0.1
Been arrested and taken to a police station?												
Not at all	X	X	X	X	85.5	95.5	86.8	95.5	85.9	96.2	85.7	94.8
Once	X	X	X	X	8.2	3.3	7.1	3.6	8.8	2.9	7.3	3.9
Twice	X	X	X	X	2.8	0.8	2.8	0.6	2.7	0.6	3.9	0.9
3 or 4 times	X	X	X	X	2.4	0.2	1.8	0.2	1.3	0.2	1.5	0.3
5 or more times	X	X	X	X	1.0	0.2	1.5	0.1	1.3	0.2	1.6	0.1

Note: See Note, table 3.37. Readers interested in responses to this question for 1975 through 1990 should consult previous editions of SOURCEBOOK. For survey methodology and definitions of terms, see Appendix 6.

[a]This question was omitted from schools in California beginning in 1997.
[b]Less than 0.05%.

Source: Lloyd D. Johnston, Jerald G. Bachman, and Patrick M. O'Malley, **Monitoring the Future 1991**, pp. 106-109; **1993**, pp. 107-110; **1995**, pp. 108-110; **1997**, pp. 105-107; **1999**, pp. 106-108 (Ann Arbor, MI: Institute for Social Research, University of Michigan); Jerald G. Bachman, Lloyd D. Johnston, and Patrick M. O'Malley, **Monitoring the Future 1992**, pp. 106-109; **1994**, pp. 106-109; **1996**, pp. 103-105; **1998**, pp. 105-107; **2000**, pp. 107-109 (Ann Arbor, MI: Institute for Social Research, University of Michigan); and data provided by the Monitoring the Future Project, Survey Research Center, Lloyd D. Johnston, Jerald G. Bachman, and Patrick M. O'Malley, Principal Investigators. Table adapted by SOURCEBOOK staff. Reprinted by permission.

	Class of 1997		Class of 1998		Class of 1999		Class of 2000		Class of 2001		Class of 2002		Class of 2003	
	Male (N=1,204)	Female (N=1,304)	Male (N=1,225)	Female (N=1,299)	Male (N=1,111)	Female (N=1,106)	Male (N=1,000)	Female (N=1,097)	Male (N=1,032)	Female (N=1,089)	Male (N=1,094)	Female (N=1,070)	Male (N=1,164)	Female (N=1,246)
	62.4%	70.1%	66.5%	73.9%	68.0%	76.8%	66.5%	75.6%	66.0%	73.0%	70.1%	74.2%	69.1%	77.2%
	12.3	10.7	12.7	12.1	11.5	11.8	12.1	10.4	12.6	11.2	11.2	12.2	12.8	11.6
	8.7	6.5	7.3	5.9	6.7	4.3	7.2	5.8	6.4	6.5	7.4	5.7	5.0	5.9
	7.9	7.1	4.8	3.7	4.9	3.1	3.6	4.4	4.8	5.5	3.8	3.8	5.4	2.7
	8.7	5.7	8.7	4.4	9.0	4.1	10.6	3.9	10.2	3.8	7.5	4.2	7.7	2.6
	91.6	96.2	93.5	97.1	91.4	95.2	92.2	97.0	90.3	95.9	93.1	97.3	92.0	97.6
	4.0	3.0	3.5	1.7	4.9	3.3	3.5	2.0	4.7	3.0	2.7	2.0	3.0	1.5
	2.0	0.3	1.4	0.4	1.3	0.9	1.8	0.5	1.9	0.6	1.3	0.5	1.8	0.4
	1.2	0.1	0.9	0.2	1.2	0.2	1.2	0.2	1.3	0.4	1.6	0.0	1.1	0.2
	1.2	0.5	0.7	0.6	1.2	0.5	1.3	0.3	1.8	0.1	1.2	0.2	2.1	0.3
	90.9	98.1	92.1	98.2	93.0	97.4	92.0	97.7	92.7	98.0	93.0	97.9	91.0	97.9
	3.6	0.8	4.1	0.7	2.5	1.1	4.0	1.9	3.3	0.8	2.9	0.9	4.5	1.2
	2.6	0.3	1.6	0.5	2.1	0.5	1.9	0.3	1.6	0.7	1.6	0.6	1.9	0.3
	1.7	0.2	1.1	0.1	0.8	0.3	0.8	0.1	0.7	0.4	1.0	0.5	1.3	0.1
	1.2	0.6	1.1	0.5	1.6	0.6	1.3	0.0	1.8	0.2	1.4	0.1	1.3	0.4
	69.4	81.2	69.4	81.0	69.4	83.3	70.8	83.2	68.7	82.2	73.5	81.2	71.0	82.7
	12.2	8.5	10.7	10.1	12.1	10.1	11.9	8.8	13.9	11.0	11.2	9.0	13.3	7.8
	8.6	5.6	8.5	4.8	8.7	2.8	9.0	4.5	8.7	3.5	7.2	5.2	8.2	5.3
	5.2	2.5	6.3	1.4	4.9	2.2	4.4	1.7	4.1	1.4	4.4	2.2	3.7	2.8
	4.7	2.2	5.1	2.7	4.9	1.5	3.9	1.7	4.5	1.8	3.7	2.3	3.7	1.4
	95.2	98.7	95.8	98.9	96.2	99.2	94.6	99.4	94.5	99.2	95.3	98.8	93.3	99.1
	2.7	0.8	1.5	0.4	1.1	0.5	2.4	0.3	2.7	0.6	1.9	0.6	2.7	0.6
	0.5	(b)	0.9	0.3	0.8	0.1	1.7	0.1	1.0	0.1	1.5	0.4	1.7	(b)
	0.4	0.0	0.5	(b)	0.2	0.0	0.3	0.1	0.6	0.1	0.6	0.2	0.4	0.1
	1.1	0.4	1.3	0.3	1.8	0.3	1.0	0.0	1.2	0.0	0.8	(b)	2.0	0.2
	78.8	90.4	79.5	91.8	79.8	93.7	78.7	93.0	78.1	93.2	84.2	93.4	80.1	93.6
	10.3	5.7	9.6	5.2	9.4	3.8	11.5	3.8	9.4	4.1	7.2	3.8	8.8	3.8
	4.3	1.8	3.7	1.6	5.0	1.9	5.1	2.0	5.7	1.9	3.3	1.7	6.2	1.6
	3.0	1.4	3.4	0.7	2.5	0.2	2.0	0.9	3.6	0.7	2.4	0.3	2.1	0.7
	3.6	0.6	3.8	0.8	3.3	0.4	2.7	0.2	3.1	0.2	2.9	0.8	2.8	0.3
	90.0	96.7	87.4	97.6	88.2	98.1	87.2	97.6	88.9	96.6	88.9	98.4	88.9	97.4
	3.9	1.7	5.8	1.1	5.9	1.3	6.3	1.7	4.3	2.2	4.5	0.9	5.0	1.7
	2.6	0.8	2.9	0.2	2.1	0.4	2.5	0.5	3.6	0.6	2.4	0.5	2.2	0.7
	1.8	0.3	1.4	0.3	1.9	0.1	1.7	0.0	0.7	0.3	1.3	0.1	2.1	(b)
	1.7	0.4	2.6	0.8	2.0	0.1	2.3	0.2	2.6	0.3	2.9	0.2	1.8	0.2
	85.7	95.5	84.7	95.4	87.4	94.4	86.9	94.8	87.7	96.3	86.5	95.7	88.4	95.9
	8.2	3.0	9.6	3.8	6.4	4.1	6.6	3.9	7.4	2.3	9.0	3.2	6.4	2.6
	3.1	0.7	2.5	0.3	3.1	0.9	2.9	0.6	2.3	0.9	2.2	0.9	2.8	0.9
	1.7	0.2	1.1	0.1	1.4	0.3	2.2	0.4	1.4	0.2	1.5	0.1	1.0	0.3
	1.3	0.5	2.1	0.4	1.7	0.3	1.4	0.3	1.1	0.3	0.9	0.1	1.4	0.2

Table 3.45

High school seniors reporting involvement in selected delinquent activities in last 12 months

By race, United States, 1991-2003

Question: "During the last 12 months, how often have you..."

	Class of 1991 White (N=1,818)	Class of 1991 Black (N=289)	Class of 1992 White (N=1,806)	Class of 1992 Black (N=368)	Class of 1993 White (N=1,895)	Class of 1993 Black (N=334)	Class of 1994 White (N=1,815)	Class of 1994 Black (N=282)	Class of 1995 White (N=1,841)	Class of 1995 Black (N=282)	Class of 1996 White (N=1,628)	Class of 1996 Black (N=287)
Delinquent activity												
Argued or had a fight with either of your parents?[a]												
Not at all	6.8%	22.4%	5.5%	23.9%	7.7%	25.9%	6.0%	23.8%	6.6%	22.9%	7.2%	26.6%
Once	7.7	8.4	7.5	11.1	8.5	11.3	9.0	12.9	8.9	9.8	8.9	9.2
Twice	11.9	15.0	11.1	12.3	12.5	12.7	12.4	13.5	15.9	13.1	14.0	13.3
3 or 4 times	26.1	24.4	24.3	24.0	21.1	17.0	26.5	20.3	23.9	21.6	25.0	20.8
5 or more times	47.6	29.9	51.5	28.7	50.2	33.0	46.1	29.5	44.7	32.5	44.9	30.0
Hit an instructor or supervisor?												
Not at all	97.3	95.9	97.2	96.4	96.9	96.1	97.5	95.2	97.7	95.2	97.1	94.0
Once	1.5	1.9	1.8	2.2	1.9	1.7	1.1	2.9	1.0	3.2	1.7	2.9
Twice	0.5	0.8	0.5	0.8	0.6	0.3	0.8	1.0	0.6	0.6	0.4	2.4
3 or 4 times	0.1	0.5	0.2	0.5	0.3	1.0	0.2	0.3	0.1	0.9	0.4	0.4
5 or more times	0.5	0.8	0.4	0.1	0.3	1.0	0.4	0.7	0.6	0.1	0.3	0.4
Gotten into a serious fight in school or at work?												
Not at all	83.1	76.8	82.1	80.6	82.8	83.5	85.3	77.5	86.4	82.0	84.9	81.4
Once	9.7	13.6	10.8	12.7	10.3	9.2	8.3	11.7	7.3	11.4	9.0	11.3
Twice	4.0	5.3	4.3	2.7	3.6	4.2	3.5	6.5	3.2	3.5	3.3	3.7
3 or 4 times	1.7	2.1	1.7	1.9	2.3	1.7	1.8	3.0	2.1	2.4	1.4	1.4
5 or more times	1.6	2.2	1.2	2.1	1.0	1.4	1.1	1.4	1.1	0.7	1.4	2.2
Taken part in a fight where a group of your friends were against another group?												
Not at all	80.8	76.5	79.3	76.3	78.7	75.4	81.7	74.0	82.3	76.7	81.1	79.7
Once	11.3	9.7	11.6	12.8	11.1	9.0	10.1	10.8	10.2	9.4	11.1	9.5
Twice	4.6	6.6	4.1	4.4	6.0	8.5	4.1	3.6	3.1	7.0	3.5	6.0
3 or 4 times	2.2	3.9	2.8	3.7	2.5	2.4	2.5	6.5	2.4	5.2	2.1	2.4
5 or more times	1.2	3.3	2.2	2.8	1.8	4.6	1.5	5.1	1.9	1.7	2.2	2.4
Hurt someone badly enough to need bandages or a doctor?												
Not at all	88.2	84.4	87.9	84.7	87.5	85.5	88.0	77.0	88.9	83.9	87.3	84.4
Once	7.7	10.0	7.3	7.8	7.2	6.2	6.9	12.2	5.7	7.6	7.8	8.1
Twice	2.0	1.7	2.9	2.9	2.9	2.0	2.1	5.6	2.7	2.8	2.6	3.5
3 or 4 times	1.1	0.7	1.3	1.9	1.4	2.0	1.8	2.7	1.7	4.3	1.6	2.1
5 or more times	0.9	3.2	0.6	2.8	1.0	4.3	1.2	2.5	1.0	1.3	0.7	1.8
Used a knife or gun or some other thing (like a club) to get something from a person?												
Not at all	97.4	94.1	97.1	93.2	96.0	94.2	96.4	90.2	97.5	92.8	97.5	93.1
Once	1.4	1.7	1.5	2.9	1.2	3.1	1.8	5.0	1.5	3.4	1.4	2.7
Twice	0.3	2.1	0.9	1.5	1.0	0.6	0.7	1.4	0.3	2.2	0.4	1.4
3 or 4 times	0.1	0.5	0.3	1.3	1.0	1.3	0.5	0.9	0.3	0.8	0.3	2.2
5 or more times	0.8	1.6	0.2	1.0	0.8	0.9	0.6	2.6	0.4	0.7	0.4	0.6
Taken something not belonging to you worth under $50?												
Not at all	67.2	74.9	65.3	79.0	66.1	78.3	69.4	65.7	69.4	69.9	67.8	68.1
Once	13.9	11.2	14.9	7.8	15.4	8.4	13.1	13.9	14.2	8.4	14.4	10.2
Twice	7.9	6.5	9.2	3.9	7.2	3.4	6.7	5.5	6.9	8.5	7.0	8.2
3 or 4 times	3.8	3.0	5.7	5.3	5.0	2.8	5.3	7.8	4.6	5.2	4.5	7.8
5 or more times	7.2	4.5	5.0	4.0	6.3	7.0	5.6	7.1	4.9	7.9	6.3	5.8
Taken something not belonging to you worth over $50?												
Not at all	90.5	93.2	89.9	92.2	89.2	90.6	90.2	84.1	91.6	87.6	90.0	82.1
Once	4.4	3.0	5.2	3.4	5.4	2.1	4.5	7.8	3.5	4.0	4.7	7.3
Twice	2.1	1.4	1.7	1.6	1.8	1.8	1.6	3.4	1.8	3.7	1.8	5.6
3 or 4 times	1.3	1.6	1.4	1.7	1.2	1.4	1.3	1.8	1.5	2.1	1.5	2.6
5 or more times	1.7	0.8	1.8	1.2	2.4	4.1	2.4	3.0	1.7	2.6	2.0	2.4

See notes at end of table.

	Class of 1997		Class of 1998		Class of 1999		Class of 2000		Class of 2001		Class of 2002		Class of 2003	
	White (N=1,726)	Black (N=343)	White (N=1,741)	Black (N=326)	White (N=1,564)	Black (N=282)	White (N=1,425)	Black (N=286)	White (N=1,366)	Black (N=239)	White (N=1,440)	Black (N=231)	White (N=1,631)	Black (N=273)
	7.4%	28.5%	8.9%	23.4%	5.4%	26.8%	6.4%	28.1%	6.9%	22.3%	9.8%	21.9%	6.9%	24.3%
	9.4	12.9	8.9	10.5	9.5	12.9	8.1	17.2	9.2	11.6	9.4	14.4	9.6	14.6
	13.3	13.4	14.0	17.5	12.5	11.8	13.8	12.2	11.5	11.9	11.9	12.8	15.4	8.9
	24.5	15.2	25.7	15.1	26.1	20.8	25.2	17.4	26.1	19.0	26.0	17.0	23.7	19.4
	45.4	29.9	42.6	33.5	46.5	27.8	46.5	25.1	46.3	35.3	42.9	33.9	44.4	32.8
	96.9	94.6	97.5	97.3	97.7	98.0	97.9	95.2	97.1	96.7	97.2	96.7	97.5	98.5
	1.7	1.9	1.2	1.8	0.8	1.6	1.3	3.0	1.8	2.4	1.8	0.8	0.9	0.5
	0.6	2.1	0.9	0.4	0.2	(b)	0.3	0.4	0.1	0.4	0.7	1.4	0.4	0.4
	0.2	(b)	0.1	0.5	0.2	0.1	0.2	(b)	0.2	(b)	0.2	0.4	0.2	0.3
	0.5	1.3	0.4	0.0	1.0	(b)	0.3	(b)	0.8	(b)	0.2	(b)	1.0	(b)
	84.9	79.3	85.5	79.0	86.2	88.5	89.3	85.8	84.7	81.5	87.7	83.8	87.9	81.6
	8.6	12.6	9.0	13.7	8.7	6.1	6.9	6.6	8.8	10.2	7.8	9.7	6.8	9.0
	3.5	4.0	2.9	4.6	2.5	3.3	2.2	5.2	3.4	3.3	2.6	4.4	3.5	5.0
	1.8	2.0	1.7	0.8	1.5	1.6	1.1	0.9	2.4	3.6	1.6	0.7	1.0	3.5
	1.2	2.1	0.9	1.8	1.1	0.5	0.5	1.5	0.7	1.5	0.2	1.5	0.8	0.9
	80.0	76.8	79.9	79.2	82.2	82.7	81.2	82.2	80.8	80.5	83.8	82.7	82.2	78.6
	10.2	11.9	10.6	9.5	10.3	11.5	11.6	6.3	11.2	8.4	9.1	7.4	10.5	11.2
	5.0	4.1	5.2	6.3	4.1	3.8	4.5	5.1	4.4	5.5	4.0	2.3	3.8	3.6
	3.4	3.6	2.8	2.4	2.7	1.8	1.8	1.8	2.2	4.0	2.1	3.9	2.2	5.6
	1.4	3.7	1.5	2.6	0.7	0.2	0.8	4.6	1.5	1.5	1.0	3.8	1.3	1.1
	87.9	83.2	86.8	82.7	88.8	85.5	89.2	86.0	88.5	85.0	88.4	84.9	89.8	85.6
	7.5	7.8	7.4	10.4	6.5	9.1	6.9	7.6	7.0	5.9	6.4	7.0	5.4	7.7
	2.3	4.2	3.1	3.7	2.4	3.0	2.3	1.8	2.1	3.3	3.2	3.9	2.6	2.7
	1.2	2.7	1.7	1.5	1.4	1.5	1.1	1.4	1.3	3.7	1.2	2.1	1.1	2.9
	1.1	2.1	1.0	1.7	0.9	0.9	0.6	3.2	1.1	2.1	0.8	2.1	1.2	1.2
	96.6	91.7	97.1	92.6	97.7	94.7	98.3	95.4	97.8	96.9	97.4	95.8	97.6	97.2
	1.1	2.3	1.3	4.9	0.9	2.6	0.6	2.2	1.1	1.9	1.5	1.8	1.0	1.5
	1.0	3.0	0.6	2.0	0.4	1.2	0.5	0.2	0.4	0.5	0.6	1.7	0.6	0.4
	0.7	1.4	0.5	0.4	0.6	0.7	0.3	1.1	0.3	0.3	0.3	0.1	0.2	0.3
	0.6	1.6	0.5	0.2	0.4	0.7	0.3	1.2	0.4	0.5	0.2	0.7	0.5	0.6
	66.0	69.0	69.3	74.3	69.3	75.6	69.4	74.3	69.6	71.7	70.3	78.3	73.1	78.8
	12.8	9.4	13.3	11.7	13.5	9.3	12.8	7.2	12.1	12.5	12.4	9.7	13.0	10.6
	9.5	8.3	7.3	6.3	7.9	4.2	6.8	10.6	6.5	7.8	7.6	5.9	5.4	5.2
	6.0	4.7	5.1	4.1	4.4	4.6	5.0	4.6	5.4	2.1	3.8	2.2	4.1	2.5
	5.7	8.7	5.0	3.6	4.9	6.2	5.9	3.3	6.4	5.9	5.8	3.9	4.4	2.9
	89.2	83.2	90.8	87.2	91.3	87.3	89.4	87.0	89.9	88.1	90.0	91.7	91.6	93.0
	5.4	6.6	4.3	5.7	3.9	6.5	5.3	4.5	5.0	5.3	4.7	3.8	4.3	2.3
	2.2	3.6	2.0	3.9	1.8	1.0	2.1	3.1	1.7	2.4	2.2	0.6	1.3	1.6
	1.2	3.5	1.5	1.2	1.7	0.6	1.0	3.4	1.4	1.6	1.5	2.0	1.2	0.5
	2.0	3.1	1.6	2.0	1.3	4.6	2.3	2.1	2.0	2.6	1.6	1.8	1.6	2.6

Table 3.45

High school seniors reporting involvement in selected delinquent activities in last 12 months

By race, United States, 1991-2003--Continued

Delinquent activity	Class of 1991 White (N=1,818)	Class of 1991 Black (N=289)	Class of 1992 White (N=1,806)	Class of 1992 Black (N=368)	Class of 1993 White (N=1,895)	Class of 1993 Black (N=334)	Class of 1994 White (N=1,815)	Class of 1994 Black (N=282)	Class of 1995 White (N=1,841)	Class of 1995 Black (N=282)	Class of 1996 White (N=1,628)	Class of 1996 Black (N=287)
Taken something from a store without paying for it?												
Not at all	68.3%	74.5%	70.0%	74.0%	69.4%	73.4%	71.0%	65.1%	72.1%	62.2%	69.1%	64.5%
Once	12.1	9.4	12.3	10.6	13.6	8.9	10.8	12.0	11.7	13.6	12.3	12.8
Twice	7.1	6.8	6.6	5.8	5.6	5.5	7.4	7.4	5.2	6.3	7.2	6.3
3 or 4 times	5.3	4.1	5.5	5.0	5.5	3.9	4.6	5.5	5.5	5.7	5.0	6.9
5 or more times	7.1	5.2	5.6	4.6	5.9	8.3	6.1	10.0	5.5	12.2	6.4	9.6
Taken a car that didn't belong to someone in your family without permission of the owner?												
Not at all	94.4	92.2	95.1	91.9	94.7	93.4	95.4	89.7	96.1	90.7	95.6	94.0
Once	3.2	4.2	2.3	4.6	2.9	1.1	2.6	4.1	2.3	3.2	2.3	2.2
Twice	1.1	1.2	1.4	1.0	1.1	1.7	1.0	2.6	0.6	3.4	0.9	2.9
3 or 4 times	0.9	1.4	0.5	1.4	0.7	1.3	0.3	2.2	0.6	1.1	0.7	0.7
5 or more times	0.5	1.1	0.8	1.1	0.6	2.5	0.7	1.4	0.3	1.5	0.4	0.3
Taken part of a car without permission of the owner?												
Not at all	94.6	91.8	94.7	95.0	93.3	92.7	95.3	88.5	95.8	90.4	95.8	94.5
Once	3.1	4.6	2.7	3.2	3.1	2.6	2.2	6.9	2.1	4.9	2.5	2.1
Twice	1.0	1.8	0.9	0.8	1.3	2.1	1.0	1.2	1.0	2.0	1.0	2.2
3 or 4 times	0.5	0.5	1.2	0.6	1.1	1.2	0.6	1.5	0.4	1.3	0.2	0.8
5 or more times	0.9	1.2	0.5	0.4	1.1	1.4	0.8	2.0	0.6	1.3	0.4	0.3
Gone into some house or building when you weren't supposed to be there?												
Not at all	75.0	78.6	71.7	81.1	72.8	80.5	75.5	72.4	77.5	74.9	75.5	79.8
Once	11.6	8.0	13.1	8.0	12.5	9.0	11.0	9.7	10.8	11.3	11.5	6.7
Twice	6.8	5.2	8.1	3.6	7.1	3.4	6.6	6.2	5.9	5.2	6.9	8.3
3 or 4 times	3.2	3.6	4.1	4.1	3.7	3.2	4.3	5.7	3.3	2.0	3.9	2.4
5 or more times	3.4	4.6	2.9	3.2	4.0	3.9	2.5	6.0	2.5	6.7	2.1	2.8
Set fire to someone's property on purpose?												
Not at all	98.1	98.3	97.3	98.2	96.8	96.6	97.1	95.6	97.8	96.7	97.5	96.0
Once	1.0	0.8	1.8	0.7	1.4	2.1	1.7	2.3	1.3	2.1	1.2	2.6
Twice	0.3	0.6	0.4	0.3	0.7	0.9	0.6	0.0	0.3	0.2	0.6	0.9
3 or 4 times	(b)	0.3	0.3	0.3	0.6	0.2	0.4	1.3	0.3	0.2	0.2	0.0
5 or more times	0.5	0.0	0.2	0.6	0.6	0.3	0.2	0.8	0.3	0.8	0.5	0.5
Damaged school property on purpose?												
Not at all	87.4	88.0	85.8	88.2	84.7	89.2	86.6	81.5	85.7	87.0	86.1	85.8
Once	6.9	4.0	8.1	5.6	6.6	4.5	6.2	8.3	6.7	6.2	7.1	7.9
Twice	2.4	4.3	3.0	3.9	4.1	2.6	3.6	4.3	3.4	2.6	2.9	3.6
3 or 4 times	1.1	2.0	1.0	1.4	2.0	2.2	2.1	3.5	2.7	2.0	2.4	1.7
5 or more times	2.1	1.6	2.0	0.9	2.5	1.5	1.4	2.4	1.5	2.1	1.6	0.9
Damaged property at work on purpose?												
Not at all	93.4	95.7	93.8	96.3	93.7	94.1	94.5	90.5	93.8	93.9	94.5	91.4
Once	3.1	2.1	2.8	1.7	3.1	2.8	2.5	3.2	3.5	2.7	3.1	4.9
Twice	1.2	1.7	1.4	0.5	1.5	1.0	1.6	1.3	1.3	0.2	0.7	1.4
3 or 4 times	0.9	0.0	1.2	0.9	0.7	1.1	0.7	2.9	0.5	1.4	0.8	0.7
5 or more times	1.4	0.5	0.8	0.6	1.0	0.9	0.7	2.1	0.8	1.8	1.0	1.6
Been arrested or taken to a police station?												
Not at all	X	X	X	X	91.0	90.6	91.5	88.5	92.0	87.7	91.7	87.0
Once	X	X	X	X	5.7	6.1	5.4	6.2	5.7	7.8	5.1	5.5
Twice	X	X	X	X	1.5	2.0	1.6	2.8	1.6	1.2	2.1	4.6
3 or 4 times	X	X	X	X	1.3	1.1	0.9	0.6	0.2	2.5	0.6	1.4
5 or more times	X	X	X	X	0.8	0.5	0.7	2.0	0.5	0.9	0.5	1.4

Note: See Notes, tables 3.37 and 3.39. Readers interested in responses to this question for 1976 through 1990 should consult previous editions of SOURCEBOOK. For survey methodology and definitions of terms, see Appendix 6.

[a]This question was omitted from schools in California beginning in 1997.
[b]Less than 0.05%.

Source: Lloyd D. Johnston, Jerald G. Bachman, and Patrick M. O'Malley, *Monitoring the Future 1991*, pp. 106-109; *1993*, pp. 107-110; *1995*, pp. 108-110; *1997*, pp. 105-107; *1999*, pp. 106-108 (Ann Arbor, MI: Institute for Social Research, University of Michigan); Jerald G. Bachman, Lloyd D. Johnston, and Patrick M. O'Malley, *Monitoring the Future 1992*, pp. 106-109; *1994*, pp. 106-109; *1996*, pp. 103-105; *1998*, pp. 105-107; *2000*, pp. 107-109 (Ann Arbor, MI: Institute for Social Research, University of Michigan); and data provided by the Monitoring the Future Project, Survey Research Center, Lloyd D. Johnston, Jerald G. Bachman, and Patrick M. O'Malley, Principal Investigators. Table adapted by SOURCEBOOK staff. Reprinted by permission.

	Class of 1997		Class of 1998		Class of 1999		Class of 2000		Class of 2001		Class of 2002		Class of 2003	
	White (N=1,726)	Black (N=343)	White (N=1,741)	Black (N=326)	White (N=1,564)	Black (N=282)	White (N=1,425)	Black (N=286)	White (N=1,366)	Black (N=239)	White (N=1,440)	Black (N=231)	White (N=1,631)	Black (N=273)
	67.6%	65.7%	72.6%	70.5%	74.5%	71.6%	72.3%	69.2%	70.4%	71.1%	72.8%	73.3%	76.6%	69.7%
	11.7	9.6	12.4	10.7	10.1	13.4	11.3	10.4	11.2	12.8	10.4	14.3	11.2	12.5
	7.3	9.3	6.3	6.6	5.6	3.8	5.6	9.0	6.2	5.3	6.6	5.1	4.3	7.7
	7.0	7.5	3.5	5.9	3.8	2.4	4.2	5.1	4.6	3.9	4.2	2.6	3.7	3.5
	6.4	7.9	5.3	6.3	6.0	8.7	6.6	6.3	7.5	6.8	6.0	4.8	4.2	6.6
	95.6	88.2	96.6	94.5	93.7	92.2	96.3	92.2	93.6	94.8	96.0	94.3	96.0	95.0
	2.5	5.8	2.2	3.1	4.2	3.9	2.6	2.7	3.9	1.1	2.2	2.4	1.9	2.2
	0.9	2.3	0.5	1.5	0.9	2.3	0.5	2.4	1.2	1.5	0.6	0.4	0.7	1.2
	0.5	2.2	0.3	0.9	0.7	1.1	0.4	1.1	0.8	0.5	0.7	2.9	0.3	1.2
	0.6	1.5	0.4	0.0	0.5	0.6	0.3	1.6	0.5	2.0	0.5	(b)	1.1	0.5
	95.2	92.8	95.8	95.0	96.5	94.8	95.4	95.6	96.2	94.0	96.0	96.4	95.7	94.8
	1.9	2.1	2.2	2.4	1.6	1.5	3.0	3.3	1.8	3.1	1.6	1.5	2.2	3.0
	1.4	2.5	1.2	0.8	0.7	2.8	0.7	0.4	1.1	0.9	0.9	0.1	1.0	0.7
	0.9	1.4	0.4	1.5	0.5	0.4	0.4	0.0	0.4	0.2	0.9	0.8	0.4	0.5
	0.6	1.2	0.4	0.2	0.7	0.5	0.5	0.7	0.5	1.8	0.6	1.2	0.7	0.9
	74.1	79.8	75.1	77.7	76.0	81.1	76.7	79.9	74.4	79.6	76.3	75.2	77.1	80.4
	11.9	6.5	11.0	11.9	11.8	6.3	10.3	10.0	13.1	10.1	11.5	10.5	11.3	6.6
	7.2	7.8	6.8	5.3	6.0	6.5	7.2	4.7	6.4	4.8	6.6	4.5	6.2	6.0
	3.8	3.1	4.0	3.3	3.3	2.0	3.4	2.9	3.6	0.6	3.4	3.9	3.4	3.0
	2.9	2.8	3.2	1.7	2.8	4.1	2.5	2.6	2.5	5.0	2.1	5.9	2.1	3.9
	97.6	97.3	98.3	98.4	98.1	96.8	97.5	97.5	97.3	97.7	97.0	95.1	96.6	97.3
	1.1	2.2	0.9	0.9	0.5	0.8	1.2	0.7	1.4	1.5	1.2	2.5	1.5	1.8
	0.1	0.1	0.3	0.2	0.4	0.7	0.5	0.9	0.4	0.0	0.9	1.2	0.8	0.3
	0.3	0.1	0.1	0.5	0.2	0.0	0.2	0.4	0.4	0.0	0.4	1.1	0.3	(b)
	0.8	0.3	0.4	0.0	0.8	1.7	0.5	0.4	0.5	0.8	0.3	0.2	0.8	0.6
	84.7	88.3	86.1	86.0	87.2	86.7	86.2	87.9	85.5	90.2	87.9	88.5	87.4	90.8
	8.3	6.0	7.8	7.2	6.3	4.9	7.7	6.9	7.6	3.2	6.0	5.3	6.6	2.8
	3.3	1.8	2.7	2.5	3.6	4.4	3.1	3.1	3.0	5.1	2.6	2.8	3.7	3.5
	2.1	1.5	2.0	1.8	1.2	0.8	1.7	1.3	2.5	0.0	1.6	1.0	1.1	1.4
	1.5	2.4	1.4	2.4	1.6	3.1	1.2	0.8	1.4	1.6	1.9	2.3	1.3	1.4
	93.2	93.7	92.5	96.4	93.2	95.3	93.1	91.7	92.8	93.9	92.8	94.7	93.3	95.3
	2.8	3.5	3.8	1.0	3.6	1.8	3.1	7.2	3.6	1.9	2.9	3.1	2.9	3.3
	1.8	1.3	1.7	0.4	1.1	1.0	1.6	0.4	2.1	3.1	1.6	1.6	1.7	(b)
	1.1	1.3	0.7	0.9	1.1	0.7	1.1	0.5	0.3	0.3	0.8	0.5	1.0	0.5
	1.2	0.3	1.3	1.3	1.0	1.1	1.2	0.2	1.2	0.8	1.9	0.2	1.1	0.8
	91.6	87.3	90.3	90.9	90.8	92.7	92.1	89.7	92.7	87.6	90.5	90.7	92.9	91.4
	4.9	7.2	7.0	5.1	5.6	4.7	5.0	5.9	5.0	5.8	6.3	6.4	4.2	5.4
	1.9	2.6	1.5	1.4	2.0	1.7	1.3	2.6	1.3	3.9	1.8	1.3	1.8	1.5
	0.7	2.8	0.5	1.3	0.9	0.3	0.8	1.1	0.7	1.9	1.0	0.9	0.6	0.7
	0.9	(b)	0.8	1.2	0.7	0.6	0.8	0.8	0.3	0.8	0.3	0.7	0.5	1.0

Table 3.46

High school seniors reporting receiving traffic ticket or warning for a moving violation in last 12 months

United States, 1991-2003

Question: "Within the last 12 months how many times, if any, have you received a ticket (or been stopped and warned) for moving violations, such as speeding, running a stop light, or improper passing?"

Number of tickets/warnings	Class of 1991 (N=15,483)	Class of 1992 (N=16,251)	Class of 1993 (N=16,763)	Class of 1994 (N=15,929)	Class of 1995 (N=15,876)	Class of 1996 (N=14,824)	Class of 1997 (N=15,963)	Class of 1998 (N=15,780)	Class of 1999 (N=14,056)	Class of 2000 (N=13,286)	Class of 2001 (N=13,304)	Class of 2002 (N=13,544)	Class of 2003 (N=15,200)
None	68.4%	69.1%	71.3%	70.5%	68.9%	68.9%	68.9%	68.2%	66.7%	68.8%	68.2%	69.5%	71.0%
Once	19.2	18.6	17.8	17.7	19.1	18.4	19.1	18.8	19.6	19.1	19.3	18.4	17.4
Twice	6.9	7.1	6.7	6.8	6.7	7.2	6.9	7.4	7.6	6.9	7.1	7.0	6.8
Three times	3.1	2.9	2.3	2.8	3.1	3.2	2.8	3.0	3.3	2.9	3.1	2.9	2.7
Four or more times	2.3	2.3	1.9	2.3	2.2	2.3	2.3	2.5	2.8	2.3	2.3	2.3	2.1

Note: See Note, table 3.37. Readers interested in responses to this question for 1976 through 1990 should consult previous editions of SOURCEBOOK. For survey methodology and definitions of terms, see Appendix 6.

Source: Lloyd D. Johnston, Jerald G. Bachman, and Patrick M. O'Malley, *Monitoring the Future 1991*, p. 22; *1993*, p. 22; *1995*, p. 22; *1997*, p. 22; *1999*, p. 22 (Ann Arbor, MI: Institute for Social Research, University of Michigan); Jerald G. Bachman, Lloyd D. Johnston, and Patrick M. O'Malley, *Monitoring the Future 1992*, p. 22; *1994*, p. 22; *1996*, p. 22; *1998*, p. 22; *2000*, p. 22 (Ann Arbor, MI: Institute for Social Research, University of Michigan); and data provided by the Monitoring the Future Project, Survey Research Center, Lloyd D. Johnston, Jerald G. Bachman, and Patrick M. O'Malley, Principal Investigators. Table adapted by SOURCEBOOK staff. Reprinted by permission.

Table 3.47

High school seniors reporting receiving traffic ticket or warning for a moving violation in last 12 months

By sex, United States, 1991-2003

Question: "Within the last 12 months how many times, if any, have you received a ticket (or been stopped and warned) for moving violations, such as speeding, running a stop light, or improper passing?"

Number of tickets/warnings	Class of 1991 Male (N=7,617)	Class of 1991 Female (N=7,277)	Class of 1992 Male (N=7,582)	Class of 1992 Female (N=8,053)	Class of 1993 Male (N=7,708)	Class of 1993 Female (N=8,310)	Class of 1994 Male (N=7,095)	Class of 1994 Female (N=8,075)	Class of 1995 Male (N=7,293)	Class of 1995 Female (N=7,891)	Class of 1996 Male (N=6,806)	Class of 1996 Female (N=7,261)
None	59.9%	77.0%	61.1%	76.5%	64.4%	77.7%	62.9%	77.2%	61.4%	75.4%	62.1%	75.4%
Once	22.3	16.1	21.6	15.9	20.0	15.6	20.3	15.6	22.0	16.8	20.5	16.4
Twice	9.4	4.4	9.5	4.8	8.9	4.8	9.0	4.8	8.7	4.8	9.3	5.1
Three times	4.5	1.8	4.2	1.7	3.5	1.3	4.1	1.7	4.3	2.0	4.4	2.1
Four or more times	3.9	0.7	3.7	1.0	3.3	0.6	3.7	0.8	3.6	1.0	3.7	1.0

Note: See Note, table 3.37. Readers interested in responses to this question for 1976 through 1990 should consult previous editions of SOURCEBOOK. For survey methodology and definitions of terms, see Appendix 6.

Source: Lloyd D. Johnston, Jerald G. Bachman, and Patrick M. O'Malley, *Monitoring the Future 1991*, p. 22; *1993*, p. 22; *1995*, p. 22; *1997*, p. 22; *1999*, p. 22 (Ann Arbor, MI: Institute for Social Research, University of Michigan); Jerald G. Bachman, Lloyd D. Johnston, and Patrick M. O'Malley, *Monitoring the Future 1992*, p. 22; *1994*, p. 22; *1996*, p. 22; *1998*, p. 22; *2000*, p. 22 (Ann Arbor, MI: Institute for Social Research, University of Michigan); and data provided by the Monitoring the Future Project, Survey Research Center, Lloyd D. Johnston, Jerald G. Bachman, and Patrick M. O'Malley, Principal Investigators. Table adapted by SOURCEBOOK staff. Reprinted by permission.

Table 3.48

High school seniors reporting receiving traffic ticket or warning for a moving violation in last 12 months

By race, United States, 1991-2003

Question: "Within the last 12 months, how many times, if any, have you received a ticket (or been stopped and warned) for moving violations such as speeding, running a stop light, or improper passing?"

Number of tickets/warnings	Class of 1991 White (N=10,754)	Class of 1991 Black (N=1,757)	Class of 1992 White (N=11,029)	Class of 1992 Black (N=2,244)	Class of 1993 White (N=11,274)	Class of 1993 Black (N=2,045)	Class of 1994 White (N=10,786)	Class of 1994 Black (N=1,761)	Class of 1995 White (N=11,012)	Class of 1995 Black (N=1,693)	Class of 1996 White (N=9,890)	Class of 1996 Black (N=1,719)
None	65.4%	81.8%	65.4%	82.9%	67.8%	83.1%	67.0%	83.0%	65.8%	81.1%	65.7%	78.2%
Once	21.0	11.1	21.2	10.3	19.7	10.9	19.6	10.4	21.0	11.7	20.6	13.0
Twice	7.4	4.2	7.5	4.8	7.7	4.2	7.6	4.2	7.3	4.3	7.6	5.7
Three times	3.5	1.8	3.3	1.4	2.7	1.1	3.2	1.3	3.4	1.9	3.6	1.9
Four or more times	2.6	1.1	2.6	0.6	2.1	0.7	2.5	1.1	2.5	1.0	2.5	1.2

Note: See Notes, tables 3.37 and 3.39. Readers interested in responses to this question for 1976 through 1990 should consult previous editions of SOURCEBOOK. For survey methodology and definitions of terms, see Appendix 6.

Source: Lloyd D. Johnston, Jerald G. Bachman, and Patrick M. O'Malley, *Monitoring the Future 1991*, p. 22; *1993*, p. 22; *1995*, p. 22; *1997*, p. 22; *1999*, p. 22 (Ann Arbor, MI: Institute for Social Research, University of Michigan); Jerald G. Bachman, Lloyd D. Johnston, and Patrick M. O'Malley, *Monitoring the Future 1992*, p. 22; *1994*, p. 22; *1996*, p. 22; *1998*, p. 22; *2000*, p. 22 (Ann Arbor, MI: Institute for Social Research, University of Michigan); and data provided by the Monitoring the Future Project, Survey Research Center, Lloyd D. Johnston, Jerald G. Bachman, and Patrick M. O'Malley, Principal Investigators. Table adapted by SOURCEBOOK staff. Reprinted by permission.

	Class of 1997		Class of 1998		Class of 1999		Class of 2000		Class of 2001		Class of 2002		Class of 2003	
	Male (N=7,269)	Female (N=7,793)	Male (N=7,286)	Female (N=7,618)	Male (N=6,485)	Female (N=6,804)	Male (N=5,991)	Female (N=6,492)	Male (N=5,962)	Female (N=6,543)	Male (N=5,992)	Female (N=6,679)	Male (N=6,736)	Female (N=7,554)
	61.5%	75.5%	60.8%	75.1%	58.8%	74.3%	61.5%	75.4%	61.4%	74.6%	63.0%	75.5%	65.9%	75.4%
	21.6	16.9	21.1	16.9	22.2	17.1	22.2	16.4	22.0	17.0	20.6	16.4	18.7	16.4
	8.9	5.1	9.5	5.3	10.2	5.3	8.3	5.5	8.7	5.5	8.7	5.2	8.4	5.3
	4.1	1.7	4.5	1.6	4.4	2.1	4.4	1.6	4.3	1.8	4.2	1.8	3.7	1.8
	3.9	0.8	4.1	1.1	4.4	1.3	3.7	1.1	3.5	1.0	3.5	1.1	3.2	1.1

	Class of 1997		Class of 1998		Class of 1999		Class of 2000		Class of 2001		Class of 2002		Class of 2003	
	White (N=10,210)	Black (N=2,001)	White (N=10,280)	Black (N=1,885)	White (N=9,499)	Black (N=1,692)	White (N=8,447)	Black (N=1,707)	White (N=8,187)	Black (N=1,567)	White (N=8,396)	Black (N=1,443)	White (N=9,722)	Black (N=1,739)
	65.5%	79.2%	63.4%	82.5%	63.3%	78.7%	65.5%	78.1%	63.9%	77.2%	64.9%	83.0%	67.3%	80.4%
	21.1	13.2	21.7	10.6	21.9	11.4	21.4	14.4	22.0	15.3	21.3	9.7	19.8	12.0
	7.8	4.3	8.5	3.9	8.3	5.4	7.6	4.7	8.0	4.6	8.0	4.4	7.5	4.4
	3.1	2.1	3.4	1.8	3.4	2.5	3.1	1.5	3.6	1.4	3.4	1.5	3.1	1.6
	2.6	1.3	3.0	1.2	3.1	1.9	2.5	1.2	2.5	1.5	2.5	1.5	2.3	1.6

Table 3.49

High school seniors reporting receiving traffic ticket or warning for a moving violation in last 12 months while under the influence of alcohol or drugs

By type of drug, United States, 1991-2003

Question: "How many of these tickets or warnings occurred after you were..."

Type of drug	Class of 1991	Class of 1992	Class of 1993	Class of 1994	Class of 1995	Class of 1996	Class of 1997	Class of 1998	Class of 1999	Class of 2000	Class of 2001	Class of 2002	Class of 2003
Drinking alcoholic beverages?													
None	90.0%	91.2%	92.3%	91.1%	91.1%	91.2%	90.8%	91.1%	92.2%	92.6%	92.4%	92.2%	94.0%
One	8.2	6.3	5.8	6.6	6.7	6.3	6.7	6.8	6.2	5.7	5.4	6.4	4.8
Two	1.5	1.7	1.4	1.4	1.4	1.5	1.5	1.6	1.1	1.2	1.6	1.1	0.8
Three	0.2	0.5	0.2	0.6	0.4	0.5	0.3	0.2	0.2	0.2	0.3	0.1	0.1
Four or more	0.2	0.3	0.2	0.4	0.4	0.6	0.7	0.4	0.3	0.3	0.4	0.3	0.3
Smoking marijuana or hashish?													
None	97.1	97.9	96.6	94.9	94.7	93.3	93.1	93.6	93.8	93.7	94.5	94.7	94.5
One	2.1	1.1	2.6	3.6	3.6	4.8	4.1	4.3	4.5	4.4	3.5	3.4	4.2
Two	0.5	0.5	0.5	0.8	0.8	1.1	1.4	1.3	1.0	1.2	1.1	1.1	0.8
Three	0.1	0.2	0.1	0.2	0.4	0.2	0.5	0.3	0.3	0.2	0.4	0.4	0.2
Four or more	0.1	0.4	0.3	0.4	0.6	0.6	0.8	0.4	0.5	0.4	0.4	0.4	0.3
Using other illegal drugs?													
None	99.1	99.0	98.9	98.6	98.4	97.9	97.7	97.8	98.3	98.8	98.0	98.0	98.4
One	0.7	0.3	0.8	0.9	1.2	1.4	1.2	1.4	1.3	0.7	1.4	1.5	0.9
Two	0.1	0.4	0.2	0.2	0.2	0.3	0.5	0.3	0.2	0.3	0.4	0.3	0.3
Three	0.1	0.1	0.0	0.0	0.1	0.1	0.2	0.2	0.0	0.1	0.1	0.1	0.0
Four or more	0.1	0.2	0.1	0.3	0.2	0.2	0.3	0.2	0.1	0.1	0.1	0.2	0.3

Note: See Note, table 3.37. This question was asked of respondents who reported receiving one or more traffic tickets (or warnings). See table 3.46 for the screen question. Readers interested in responses to this question for 1976 through 1990 should consult previous editions of SOURCEBOOK. For survey methodology and definitions of terms, see Appendix 6.

Source: Lloyd D. Johnston, Jerald G. Bachman, and Patrick M. O'Malley, *Monitoring the Future 1991*, pp. 22, 23; *1993*, p. 23; *1995*, p. 23; *1997*, pp. 22, 23; *1999*, pp. 22, 23 (Ann Arbor, MI: Institute for Social Research, University of Michigan); Jerald G. Bachman, Lloyd D. Johnston, and Patrick M. O'Malley, *Monitoring the Future 1992*, pp. 22, 23; *1994*, p. 23; *1996*, pp. 22, 23; *1998*, pp. 22, 23; *2000*, pp. 22, 23 (Ann Arbor, MI: Institute for Social Research, University of Michigan); and data provided by the Monitoring the Future Project, Survey Research Center, Lloyd D. Johnston, Jerald G. Bachman, and Patrick M. O'Malley, Principal Investigators. Table adapted by SOURCEBOOK staff. Reprinted by permission.

Table 3.50

High school seniors reporting receiving traffic ticket or warning for a moving violation in last 12 months while under the influence of alcohol or drugs

By type of drug and sex, United States, 1991-2003

Question: "How many of these tickets or warnings occurred after you were..."

Type of drug	Class of 1991 Male	Class of 1991 Female	Class of 1992 Male	Class of 1992 Female	Class of 1993 Male	Class of 1993 Female	Class of 1994 Male	Class of 1994 Female	Class of 1995 Male	Class of 1995 Female	Class of 1996 Male	Class of 1996 Female
Drinking alcoholic beverages?												
None	88.6%	92.5%	89.1%	94.8%	90.4%	95.3%	88.4%	94.9%	89.1%	94.3%	89.1%	94.4%
One	9.0	6.5	7.6	4.2	7.1	3.9	8.4	4.4	7.9	4.8	7.4	4.6
Two	1.8	1.0	2.3	0.8	1.9	0.7	1.9	0.6	1.9	0.7	2.3	0.5
Three	0.3	0.0	0.5	0.3	0.3	0.1	0.8	0.1	0.7	0.1	0.5	0.4
Four or more	0.3	0.0	0.5	0.0	0.4	0.0	0.5	0.0	0.4	0.1	0.7	0.2
Smoking marijuana or hashish?												
None	96.4	98.5	97.3	98.8	95.6	97.9	94.2	96.5	93.4	96.9	91.3	96.6
One	2.5	1.1	1.2	0.7	3.2	1.6	4.0	3.0	4.1	2.5	6.1	2.6
Two	0.7	0.3	0.7	0.2	0.6	0.3	1.1	0.4	1.1	0.3	1.5	0.5
Three	0.2	(a)	0.3	0.2	0.1	0.1	0.3	0.0	0.6	0.1	0.2	0.2
Four or more	0.2	0.0	0.5	0.1	0.4	0.1	0.4	0.1	0.8	0.2	0.8	0.1
Using other illegal drugs?												
None	98.8	99.5	99.0	99.4	98.8	99.1	98.4	99.2	98.1	99.3	97.4	99.1
One	0.8	0.4	0.3	0.3	0.9	0.6	0.9	0.8	1.3	0.6	1.9	0.5
Two	0.1	0.1	0.5	0.1	0.2	0.1	0.4	0.0	0.3	0.0	0.4	0.2
Three	0.1	0.1	(a)	0.1	0.0	(a)	0.0	0.0	0.1	0.0	0.1	0.1
Four or more	0.1	0.0	0.2	0.1	0.1	(a)	0.3	0.1	0.1	0.1	0.3	0.1

Note: See Note, table 3.37. This question was asked of respondents who reported receiving one or more traffic tickets (or warnings). See table 3.47 for the screen question. Readers interested in responses to this question for 1976 through 1990 should consult previous editions of SOURCEBOOK. For survey methodology and definitions of terms, see Appendix 6.

[a]Less than 0.05%.

Source: Lloyd D. Johnston, Jerald G. Bachman, and Patrick M. O'Malley, *Monitoring the Future 1991*, pp. 22, 23; *1993*, p. 23; *1995*, p. 23; *1997*, pp. 22, 23; *1999*, pp. 22, 23 (Ann Arbor, MI: Institute for Social Research, University of Michigan); Jerald G. Bachman, Lloyd D. Johnston, and Patrick M. O'Malley, *Monitoring the Future 1992*, pp. 22, 23; *1994*, p. 23; *1996*, pp. 22, 23; *1998*, pp. 22, 23; *2000*, pp. 22, 23 (Ann Arbor, MI: Institute for Social Research, University of Michigan); and data provided by the Monitoring the Future Project, Survey Research Center, Lloyd D. Johnston, Jerald G. Bachman, and Patrick M. O'Malley, Principal Investigators. Table adapted by SOURCEBOOK staff. Reprinted by permission.

	Class of 1997		Class of 1998		Class of 1999		Class of 2000		Class of 2001		Class of 2002		Class of 2003	
	Male	Female	Male	Female	Male	Female	Male	Female	Male	Female	Male	Female	Male	Female
	89.0%	93.6%	89.1%	94.3%	90.4%	94.8%	91.2%	95.2%	90.7%	94.9%	89.6%	95.8%	92.0%	96.4%
	7.6	5.1	7.8	4.8	7.6	4.3	6.5	3.8	6.4	3.6	8.2	3.9	6.3	3.2
	2.1	0.7	2.3	0.6	1.5	0.6	1.6	0.7	2.1	1.1	1.7	0.1	1.1	0.4
	0.3	0.2	0.3	0.1	0.1	0.3	0.2	0.2	0.4	0.2	0.1	(a)	0.1	0.1
	0.9	0.4	0.5	0.2	0.5	0.1	0.5	0.0	0.5	0.2	0.3	0.2	0.5	(a)
	91.4	95.5	92.3	95.9	92.9	95.0	91.9	96.4	93.4	96.7	93.1	97.1	92.5	97.2
	5.1	2.9	4.9	3.2	4.8	3.9	5.6	2.6	4.0	2.5	4.3	2.2	5.5	2.3
	1.7	0.8	1.9	0.4	1.2	0.7	1.6	0.7	1.4	0.6	1.5	0.4	1.1	0.4
	0.7	0.2	0.5	0.1	0.4	0.1	0.4	0.1	0.7	0.1	0.5	0.2	0.4	0.1
	1.0	0.6	0.5	0.3	0.7	0.2	0.5	0.2	0.5	0.2	0.5	0.2	0.5	0.0
	97.2	98.6	97.2	99.0	98.0	98.7	98.5	99.2	97.6	98.7	97.4	98.9	98.0	99.3
	1.3	0.9	2.0	0.4	1.4	1.1	0.8	0.4	1.6	1.1	1.8	0.9	1.0	0.7
	0.7	0.1	0.4	0.2	0.3	0.2	0.4	0.3	0.5	0.2	0.4	0.1	0.4	0.0
	0.2	0.2	0.2	0.2	0.1	0.0	0.1	0.1	0.2	0.1	0.2	(a)	0.0	(a)
	0.4	0.2	0.2	0.3	0.2	0.0	0.2	0.0	0.1	0.0	0.2	0.2	0.6	(a)

Table 3.51

High school seniors reporting receiving traffic ticket or warning for a moving violation in last 12 months while under the influence of alcohol or drugs

By type of drug and race, United States, 1991-2003

Question: "How many of these tickets or warnings occurred after you were. . ."

Type of drug	Class of 1991 White	Class of 1991 Black	Class of 1992 White	Class of 1992 Black	Class of 1993 White	Class of 1993 Black	Class of 1994 White	Class of 1994 Black	Class of 1995 White	Class of 1995 Black	Class of 1996 White	Class of 1996 Black
Drinking alcoholic beverages?												
None	89.3%	95.7%	91.3%	95.2%	92.0%	96.9%	90.9%	94.4%	91.0%	92.3%	91.3%	93.5%
One	8.6	3.4	6.3	2.7	6.2	1.7	6.8	3.9	6.8	7.4	6.3	4.1
Two	1.7	0.6	1.7	2.0	1.4	1.5	1.3	0.6	1.6	0.3	1.6	1.0
Three	0.1	0.3	0.5	0.1	0.2	0.0	0.5	0.4	0.4	0.0	0.4	0.9
Four or more	0.2	0.0	0.2	0.0	0.2	0.0	0.4	0.6	0.2	0.0	0.5	0.5
Smoking marijuana or hashish?												
None	97.1	98.3	98.0	98.2	96.3	97.9	95.1	94.4	94.8	96.3	93.1	95.2
One	2.1	0.9	1.2	0.4	2.8	1.7	3.6	3.3	3.6	2.3	5.1	2.4
Two	0.5	0.4	0.4	1.4	0.4	0.4	0.8	1.0	0.7	1.5	1.2	1.5
Three	0.2	0.4	0.2	0.0	0.1	0.0	0.2	0.7	0.4	0.0	0.2	0.4
Four or more	0.1	0.0	0.3	0.0	0.3	0.0	0.4	0.6	0.5	0.0	0.4	0.5
Using other illegal drugs?												
None	98.9	100.0	99.2	98.7	99.0	99.3	98.7	97.8	98.8	99.7	98.3	97.8
One	0.8	0.0	0.2	1.2	0.8	0.4	0.8	1.5	0.9	0.0	1.3	0.1
Two	0.1	0.0	0.4	0.0	0.2	0.3	0.3	0.0	0.1	0.0	0.3	1.1
Three	(a)	0.0	(a)	0.0	0.0	0.0	0.0	0.0	0.1	0.0	0.1	0.4
Four or more	0.1	0.0	0.1	0.1	0.1	0.0	0.2	0.6	0.1	0.3	0.1	0.5

Note: See Notes, tables 3.37 and 3.39. This question was asked of respondents who reported receiving one or more traffic tickets (or warnings). See table 3.48 for the screen question. Readers interested in responses to this question for 1976 through 1990 should consult previous editions of SOURCEBOOK. For survey methodology and definitions of terms, see Appendix 6.

[a]Less than 0.05%.

Source: Lloyd D. Johnston, Jerald G. Bachman, and Patrick M. O'Malley, *Monitoring the Future 1991*, pp. 22, 23; *1993*, p. 23; *1995*, p. 23; *1997*, pp. 22, 23; *1999*, pp. 22, 23 (Ann Arbor, MI: Institute for Social Research, University of Michigan); Jerald G. Bachman, Lloyd D. Johnston, and Patrick M. O'Malley, *Monitoring the Future 1992*, pp. 22, 23; *1994*, p. 23; *1996*, pp. 22, 23; *1998*, pp. 22, 23; *2000*, pp. 22, 23 (Ann Arbor, MI: Institute for Social Research, University of Michigan); and data provided by the Monitoring the Future Project, Survey Research Center, Lloyd D. Johnston, Jerald G. Bachman, and Patrick M. O'Malley, Principal Investigators. Table adapted by SOURCEBOOK staff. Reprinted by permission.

Table 3.52

High school seniors reporting involvement in driving accidents in last 12 months

United States, 1991-2003

Question: "During the last 12 months, how many accidents have you had while you were driving (whether or not you were responsible)?"

Number of accidents	Class of 1991 (N=15,483)	Class of 1992 (N=16,251)	Class of 1993 (N=16,763)	Class of 1994 (N=15,929)	Class of 1995 (N=15,876)	Class of 1996 (N=14,824)	Class of 1997 (N=15,963)	Class of 1998 (N=15,780)	Class of 1999 (N=14,056)	Class of 2000 (N=13,286)	Class of 2001 (N=13,304)	Class of 2002 (N=13,544)	Class of 2003 (N=15,200)
None	75.7%	76.9%	76.1%	75.7%	75.3%	74.1%	74.4%	74.4%	75.1%	75.1%	75.5%	75.5%	75.8%
One	18.3	17.5	18.2	18.6	18.7	19.1	19.3	19.3	18.7	18.7	18.4	18.8	18.4
Two	4.5	4.1	4.4	4.3	4.3	4.9	4.7	4.7	4.4	4.8	4.4	4.0	4.3
Three	1.1	1.0	0.9	1.0	1.2	1.3	1.0	1.0	1.3	1.1	1.2	1.2	1.0
Four or more	0.4	0.4	0.5	0.4	0.6	0.6	0.6	0.5	0.5	0.3	0.4	0.4	0.4

Note: See Note, table 3.37. Respondents were informed that "accident" refers to "a collision involving property damage or personal injury - not bumps or scratches in parking lots" (Source, *1992*, p. 23). Readers interested in responses to this question for 1976 through 1990 should consult previous editions of SOURCEBOOK. For survey methodology and definitions of terms, see Appendix 6.

Source: Lloyd D. Johnston, Jerald G. Bachman, and Patrick M. O'Malley, *Monitoring the Future 1991*, p. 23; *1993*, p. 23; *1995*, p. 23; *1997*, p. 23, *1999*, p. 23 (Ann Arbor, MI: Institute for Social Research, University of Michigan); Jerald G. Bachman, Lloyd D. Johnston, and Patrick M. O'Malley, *Monitoring the Future 1992*, p. 23; *1994*, p. 23; *1996*, p. 23; *1998*, p. 23; *2000*, p. 23 (Ann Arbor, MI: Institute for Social Research, University of Michigan); and data provided by the Monitoring the Future Project, Survey Research Center, Lloyd D. Johnston, Jerald G. Bachman, and Patrick M. O'Malley, Principal Investigators. Table adapted by SOURCEBOOK staff. Reprinted by permission.

	Class of 1997		Class of 1998		Class of 1999		Class of 2000		Class of 2001		Class of 2002		Class of 2003	
	White	Black	White	Black	White	Black	White	Black	White	Black	White	Black	White	Black
	90.1%	95.8%	90.7%	96.6%	91.9%	96.3%	92.3%	95.2%	92.1%	96.5%	91.7%	98.0%	93.5%	95.3%
	7.4	2.6	7.2	1.7	6.7	1.5	6.3	1.3	5.5	1.5	7.0	1.1	5.4	4.2
	1.7	0.8	1.6	1.0	1.1	1.7	1.1	2.0	1.7	1.8	1.1	(a)	0.9	0.1
	0.3	0.5	0.2	0.0	0.1	0.0	0.1	0.9	0.4	(a)	0.1	(a)	0.1	(a)
	0.6	0.3	0.3	0.7	0.2	0.5	0.2	0.6	0.4	0.1	0.1	0.9	0.2	0.3
	92.6	96.0	93.7	94.9	94.3	94.9	93.9	94.6	94.6	96.3	94.8	94.3	94.4	96.4
	4.8	1.9	4.4	3.4	4.2	2.7	4.7	2.3	3.5	1.3	3.7	2.1	4.1	2.7
	1.5	1.3	1.3	1.2	0.9	1.1	1.0	1.8	1.1	1.9	0.9	2.7	0.9	0.3
	0.5	0.3	0.3	0.3	0.3	0.2	0.1	0.4	0.4	0.1	0.4	(a)	0.3	0.3
	0.6	0.6	0.3	0.2	0.4	1.1	0.2	0.9	0.4	0.4	0.2	0.9	0.2	0.3
	97.8	98.2	98.0	99.1	98.3	99.9	99.2	96.5	98.1	99.3	98.0	98.8	98.7	98.8
	1.3	0.8	1.3	0.3	1.4	0.0	0.6	1.9	1.4	0.7	1.6	0.3	0.8	0.9
	0.6	0.8	0.4	(a)	0.2	0.0	0.2	0.2	0.3	0.0	0.3	(a)	0.3	(a)
	0.2	0.0	0.2	0.3	0.0	0.0	0.0	0.7	0.1	0.0	0.1	(a)	0.0	(a)
	0.2	0.3	0.2	0.2	0.1	0.1	0.0	0.7	0.0	0.0	0.0	0.9	0.2	0.3

Table 3.53
High school seniors reporting involvement in driving accidents while under the influence of alcohol or drugs in last 12 months

By type of drug, United States, 1991-2003

Question: "How many of these accidents occurred after you were..."

Type of drug	Class of 1991	Class of 1992	Class of 1993	Class of 1994	Class of 1995	Class of 1996	Class of 1997	Class of 1998	Class of 1999	Class of 2000	Class of 2001	Class of 2002	Class of 2003
Drinking alcoholic beverages?													
None	93.5%	93.4%	94.7%	94.6%	94.6%	94.8%	94.4%	94.5%	94.6%	95.6%	95.0%	95.9%	96.4%
One	5.7	5.4	4.3	4.4	4.5	4.3	4.4	4.3	4.7	3.6	4.0	3.4	2.8
Two	0.7	0.7	0.8	0.6	0.5	0.4	0.6	0.9	0.3	0.5	0.5	0.4	0.5
Three	0.1	0.2	0.2	0.2	0.1	0.2	0.2	0.1	0.1	0.1	0.3	0.2	0.1
Four or more	0.1	0.4	0.1	0.2	0.2	0.2	0.5	0.2	0.3	0.2	0.2	0.1	0.2
Smoking marijuana or hashish?													
None	98.1	98.2	97.8	97.6	97.0	96.5	95.7	96.1	95.9	96.0	96.3	96.5	97.4
One	1.3	1.2	1.7	1.7	2.4	2.7	3.2	3.1	3.5	3.0	2.6	2.8	1.9
Two	0.3	0.2	0.4	0.3	0.3	0.4	0.5	0.5	0.4	0.5	0.7	0.4	0.3
Three	0.1	0.1	0.1	0.2	0.1	0.1	0.2	0.1	0.1	0.2	0.3	0.2	0.1
Four or more	0.1	0.3	0.0	0.2	0.1	0.2	0.4	0.2	0.1	0.3	0.2	0.0	0.2
Using other illegal drugs?													
None	99.2	98.9	98.9	99.1	99.0	98.9	98.6	98.6	98.6	98.8	98.4	98.4	99.2
One	0.6	0.6	0.8	0.6	0.6	0.8	0.8	0.9	1.2	0.8	1.1	1.2	0.2
Two	0.1	0.1	0.2	0.1	0.3	0.1	0.3	0.3	0.1	0.1	0.3	0.2	0.2
Three	0.0	0.1	0.1	0.0	(a)	0.0	0.1	0.0	0.1	0.1	0.1	0.1	0.1
Four or more	0.1	0.4	0.0	0.2	0.1	0.3	0.2	0.2	0.1	0.1	0.1	0.1	0.2

Note: See Notes, tables 3.37 and 3.52. This question was asked of respondents who reported involvement in one or more accidents. See table 3.52 for the screen question. Readers interested in responses to this question for 1976 through 1990 should consult previous editions of SOURCEBOOK. For survey methodology and definitions of terms, see Appendix 6.

[a]Less than 0.05%.

Source: Lloyd D. Johnston, Jerald G. Bachman, and Patrick M. O'Malley, **Monitoring the Future 1991**, p. 23; **1993**, pp. 23, 24; **1995**, pp. 23, 24; **1997**, p. 23; **1999**, p. 23 (Ann Arbor, MI: Institute for Social Research, University of Michigan); Jerald G. Bachman, Lloyd D. Johnston, and Patrick M. O'Malley, **Monitoring the Future 1992**, p. 23; **1994**, pp. 23, 24; **1996**, p. 23; **1998**, p. 23; **2000**, p. 23 (Ann Arbor, MI: Institute for Social Research, University of Michigan); and data provided by the Monitoring the Future Project, Survey Research Center, Lloyd D. Johnston, Jerald G. Bachman, and Patrick M. O'Malley, Principal Investigators. Table adapted by SOURCEBOOK staff. Reprinted by permission.

Table 3.54

Students reporting problem behaviors

By grade level of respondent, 2002-2003[a]

	Never	Seldom	Some- times	Often	A lot
Have you been in trouble with the police?	75.0%	13.3%	6.3%	2.3%	2.9%
Grades 6 to 8	78.1	11.3	5.6	2.3	2.9
Grades 9 to 12	72.1	15.4	7.1	2.4	3.0
12th grade	71.5	16.2	6.9	2.1	3.3
Do you take part in gang activities?	87.9	4.7	3.1	1.4	2.8
Grades 6 to 8	87.3	5.2	3.4	1.6	2.5
Grades 9 to 12	88.5	4.2	2.9	1.3	3.1
12th grade	89.2	3.6	2.5	1.0	3.8
Have you thought about committing suicide?	70.6	14.2	8.7	2.9	3.5
Grades 6 to 8	75.3	11.8	7.2	2.6	3.1
Grades 9 to 12	65.9	16.7	10.2	3.3	3.9
12th grade	65.1	18.0	10.4	2.7	3.9
Have you been caught using alcohol?	82.0	7.2	5.4	2.3	3.0
Grades 6 to 8	88.9	4.8	2.9	1.4	1.9
Grades 9 to 12	75.3	9.5	7.7	3.3	4.1
12th grade	68.8	11.4	9.7	4.4	5.6
Have you been caught using drugs?	88.7	4.6	2.9	1.5	2.4
Grades 6 to 8	92.1	3.3	1.9	1.0	1.8
Grades 9 to 12	85.4	5.9	3.8	1.9	3.0
12th grade	83.1	6.7	4.4	2.4	3.4
Have you threatened to harm a teacher?	91.6	4.4	2.0	0.8	1.2
Grades 6 to 8	92.7	3.9	1.6	0.7	1.1
Grades 9 to 12	90.5	4.9	2.4	0.9	1.4
12th grade	89.7	4.8	2.4	0.9	2.2
Have you threatened to harm one or both of your parents, guardian, etc.?	88.8	6.1	2.8	1.0	1.3
Grades 6 to 8	90.3	5.1	2.4	0.9	1.2
Grades 9 to 12	87.3	7.0	3.2	1.1	1.4
12th grade	87.4	6.6	3.0	1.0	2.1

Note: These data are from a survey of 6th through 12th grade students conducted between August 2002 and June 2003 by PRIDE Surveys. Participating schools are sent the PRIDE questionnaire with explicit instructions for administering the anonymous, self-report survey. Schools that administer the PRIDE questionnaire do so voluntarily or in compliance with a school district or State request. For the 2002-2003 academic year, survey results are based on students from 24 States. The following States participated in the 2002-2003 PRIDE survey: Alabama, Arkansas, Colorado, Georgia, Illinois, Indiana, Kentucky, Louisiana, Massachusetts, Michigan, Mississippi, New Jersey, New Mexico, New York, North Carolina, Ohio, Oklahoma, Pennsylvania, Tennessee, Texas, Virginia, Washington, West Virginia, and Wisconsin. To prevent any one State from having a disproportionate influence on the summary results, random samples of students were drawn from those States where disproportionately large numbers of students were surveyed. Therefore, no State comprises more than 10% of the sample. The results presented are based on a sample consisting of 109,919 students drawn from the total number of students who completed the PRIDE questionnaire.

[a]Percents may not add to 100 because of rounding.

Source: PRIDE Surveys, "2002-2003 PRIDE Surveys National Summary, Grades 6 through 12," Bowling Green, KY: PRIDE Surveys, 2003. (Mimeographed.) P. 166, Table 8.15; p. 167, Table 8.16; p. 171, Table 8.30; p. 172, Tables 8.31 and 8.32; p. 174, Tables 8.38 and 8.39. Table adapted by SOURCEBOOK staff. Reprinted by permission.

Table 3.55

High school students reporting involvement in delinquent and risk-related behaviors, and drug, alcohol, and cigarette use

United States, selected years, 1991-2003

(Percent reporting engaging in or experiencing the behavior)

	1991	1993	1995	1997	1999	2001	2003
Delinquent/risk-related behavior							
Rode with a driver who had been drinking alcohol[a]	39.9%	35.3%	38.8%	36.6%	33.1%	30.7%	30.2%
Drove after drinking alcohol[a]	16.7	13.5	15.4	16.9	13.1	13.3	12.1
Carried a weapon[b]	26.1	22.1	20.0	18.3	17.3	17.4	17.1
Carried a gun[c]	NA	7.9	7.6	5.9	4.9	5.7	6.1
In a physical fight[d]	42.5	41.8	38.7	36.6	35.7	33.2	33.0
Felt unsafe at school or on way to or from school[c]	NA	4.4	4.5	4.0	5.2	6.6	5.4
Carried a weapon on school property[b]	NA	11.8	9.8	8.5	6.9	6.4	6.1
Threatened or injured with a weapon on school property[d]	NA	7.3	8.4	7.4	7.7	8.9	9.2
Engaged in a physical fight on school property[d]	NA	16.2	15.5	14.8	14.2	12.5	12.8
Seriously considered suicide[e]	29.0	24.1	24.1	20.5	19.3	19.0	16.9
Made a suicide plan[a]	18.6	19.0	17.7	15.7	14.5	14.8	16.5
Attempted suicide[d]	7.3	8.6	8.7	7.7	8.3	8.8	8.5
Drug, alcohol, cigarette use							
Marijuana use, lifetime[f]	31.3	32.8	42.4	47.1	47.2	42.4	40.2
Marijuana use, current[a]	14.7	17.7	25.3	26.2	26.7	23.9	22.4
Cocaine use, lifetime[g]	5.9	4.9	7.0	8.2	9.5	9.4	8.7
Cocaine use, current[a]	1.7	1.9	3.1	3.3	4.0	4.2	4.1
Illegal steroid use, lifetime[f]	2.7	2.2	3.7	3.1	3.7	5.0	6.1
Inhalant use, lifetime[h]	NA	NA	20.3	16.0	14.6	14.7	12.1
Alcohol use, current[c]	50.8	48.0	51.6	50.8	50.0	47.1	44.9
Episodic heavy drinking[i]	31.3	30.0	32.6	33.4	31.5	29.9	28.3
Cigarette use, lifetime[j]	70.1	69.5	71.3	70.2	70.4	63.9	58.4
Cigarette use, current[c]	27.5	30.5	34.8	36.4	34.8	28.5	21.9
Cigarette use, frequent[k]	12.7	13.8	16.1	16.7	16.8	13.8	9.7
On school property							
Alcohol use[c]	NA	5.2	6.3	5.6	4.9	4.9	5.2
Marijuana use[a]	NA	5.6	8.8	7.0	7.2	5.4	5.8
Offered, sold, or given an illegal drug[e]	NA	24.0	32.1	31.7	30.2	28.5	28.7

Note: These data are from the national school-based survey conducted biennially as part of the Youth Risk Behavior Surveillance System (YRBSS). The data were collected and analyzed by the U.S. Department of Health and Human Services, Centers for Disease Control and Prevention. For survey methodology and sampling procedures, see Appendix 5.

[a] One or more times during the 30 days preceding the survey.
[b] Carried a weapon (e.g., a gun, knife, or club) on 1 or more of the 30 days preceding the survey.
[c] On 1 or more of the 30 days preceding the survey.
[d] One or more times during the 12 months preceding the survey.
[e] During the 12 months preceding the survey.
[f] Ever used.
[g] Ever tried any form of cocaine (e.g., powder, crack, or freebase).
[h] Ever sniffed glue, breathed the contents of aerosol spray cans, or inhaled any paints or sprays to get high.
[i] Drank five or more drinks of alcohol in a row on 1 or more of the 30 days preceding the survey.
[j] Ever tried cigarette smoking, even one or two puffs.
[k] Smoked cigarettes on 20 or more of the 30 days preceding the survey.

Source: U.S. Department of Health and Human Services, Centers for Disease Control and Prevention, *Trend Fact Sheets: Prevalence Trends, 1991-2003* [Online]. Available: http://www.cdc.gov/healthyyouth/yrbs/factsheets.htm [Aug. 31, 2004]; Jo Anne Grunbaum et al., "Youth Risk Behavior Surveillance--United States, 2001," CDC Surveillance Summaries, *Morbidity and Mortality Weekly Report* 51 No. SS-4 (Washington, DC: USGPO, June 28, 2002), pp. 25-27, 29, 31, 33, 38, 40, 42, 46; and Jo Anne Grunbaum et al., "Youth Risk Behavior Surveillance--United States, 2003," CDC Surveillance Summaries, *Morbidity and Mortality Weekly Report* 53 No. SS-2 (Washington, DC: USGPO, May 21, 2004), pp. 33-69. Table adapted by SOURCEBOOK staff.

Table 3.56

High school students reporting involvement in delinquent and risk-related behaviors

By sex, race, ethnicity, and grade level, United States, 2003

(Percent reporting engaging in or experiencing the behavior)

	Total	Sex Male	Sex Female	Race, ethnicity White, non-Hispanic	Race, ethnicity Black, non-Hispanic	Race, ethnicity Hispanic	Grade level 9th grade	Grade level 10th grade	Grade level 11th grade	Grade level 12th grade
Rode with a driver who had been drinking alcohol[a]	30.2%	29.2%	31.1%	28.5%	30.9%	36.4%	28.2%	29.3%	30.5%	33.3%
Drove after drinking alcohol[a]	12.1	15.0	8.9	12.9	9.1	11.7	6.2	9.2	15.3	19.8
Carried a weapon[b]	17.1	26.9	6.7	16.7	17.3	16.5	18.0	15.9	18.2	15.5
Carried a gun[c]	6.1	10.2	1.6	5.9	6.0	5.4	5.8	5.9	6.3	5.7
In a physical fight[d]	33.0	40.5	25.1	30.5	39.7	36.1	38.6	33.5	30.9	26.5
Injured in a physical fight[d,e]	4.2	5.7	2.6	2.9	5.5	5.2	5.0	4.2	3.6	3.1
Physically hurt by a boyfriend or girlfriend on purpose[f]	8.9	8.9	8.8	7.0	13.9	9.3	8.1	8.8	8.1	10.1
Forced to have sexual intercourse	9.0	6.1	11.9	7.3	12.3	10.4	8.0	9.4	9.2	9.1
Seriously considered suicide[f]	16.9	12.8	21.3	16.5	12.5	18.1	16.9	18.3	16.4	15.5
Made a suicide plan[f]	16.5	14.1	18.9	16.2	10.4	17.6	17.7	16.3	16.2	14.9
Attempted suicide[d]	8.5	5.4	11.5	6.9	8.4	10.6	10.1	9.1	7.3	6.1
Suicide attempt required medical attention[f]	2.9	2.4	3.2	1.7	3.7	5.0	3.5	2.6	2.4	2.1

Note: See Note, table 3.55. For survey methodology and sampling procedures, see Appendix 5.

[a] One or more times during the 30 days preceding the survey.
[b] Carried a weapon (e.g., a gun, knife, or club) on 1 or more of the 30 days preceding the survey.
[c] On 1 or more of the 30 days preceding the survey.
[d] One or more times during the 12 months preceding the survey.
[e] Injured seriously enough to be treated by a doctor or nurse.
[f] During the 12 months preceding the survey.

Source: Jo Anne Grunbaum et al., "Youth Risk Behavior Surveillance--United States, 2003," CDC Surveillance Summaries, *Morbidity and Mortality Weekly Report* 53 No. SS-2 (Washington, DC: USGPO, May 21, 2004), pp. 33, 35, 37, 39, 45, 47. Table adapted by SOURCEBOOK staff.

Table 3.57

High school students reporting victimization experiences and involvement in delinquent activities on school property

By sex, race, ethnicity, and grade level, United States, 2003

(Percent reporting engaging in or experiencing the behavior)

	Total	Sex Male	Sex Female	Race, ethnicity White, non-Hispanic	Race, ethnicity Black, non-Hispanic	Race, ethnicity Hispanic	Grade level 9th grade	Grade level 10th grade	Grade level 11th grade	Grade level 12th grade
Felt unsafe at school or on way to or from school[a]	5.4%	5.5%	5.3%	3.1%	8.4%	9.4%	6.9%	5.2%	4.5%	3.8%
On school property										
Property stolen or deliberately damaged[b,c]	29.8	33.1	26.2	28.2	30.4	32.3	34.8	30.5	27.2	24.2
Threatened or injured with a weapon[c]	9.2	11.6	6.5	7.8	10.9	9.4	12.1	9.2	7.3	6.3
Carried a weapon[d]	6.1	8.9	3.1	5.5	6.9	6.0	5.3	6.0	6.6	6.4
Engaged in a physical fight[c]	12.8	17.1	8.0	10.0	17.1	16.7	18.0	12.8	10.4	7.3
Cigarette use[e]	8.0	8.2	7.6	8.9	5.9	6.0	7.5	7.7	8.2	8.3
Alcohol use[f]	5.2	6.0	4.2	3.9	5.8	7.6	5.1	5.6	5.0	4.5
Marijuana use[g]	5.8	7.6	3.7	4.5	6.6	8.2	6.6	5.2	5.6	5.0
Offered, sold, or given an illegal drug[c]	28.7	31.9	25.0	27.5	23.1	36.5	29.5	29.2	29.9	24.9

Note: See Note, table 3.55. For survey methodology and sampling procedures, see Appendix 5.

[a] On 1 or more of the 30 days preceding the survey.
[b] For example, a car, clothing, or books.
[c] One or more times during the 12 months preceding the survey.
[d] Carried a weapon (e.g., a gun, knife, or club) on 1 or more of the 30 days preceding the survey.
[e] Ever tried smoking, even one or two puffs.
[f] Drank alcohol on 1 or more of the 30 days preceding the survey.
[g] One or more times during the 30 days preceding the survey.

Source: Jo Anne Grunbaum et al., "Youth Risk Behavior Surveillance--United States, 2003," CDC Surveillance Summaries, *Morbidity and Mortality Weekly Report* 53 No. SS-2 (Washington, DC: USGPO, May 21, 2004), pp. 41, 43, 67, 69. Table adapted by SOURCEBOOK staff.

Table 3.58

Students reporting involvement in delinquent activities at school

By grade level of respondent, 2002-2003[a]

Question: "While at school have you. . .?"

	Never	One time	2 to 5 times	6 or more times
Carried a gun	96.3%	1.2%	0.6%	1.8%
Grades 6 to 8	96.9	1.2	0.5	1.5
Grades 9 to 12	95.7	1.3	0.8	2.2
12th grade	94.8	1.4	0.8	3.0
Carried a knife, club or other weapon	85.0	6.7	3.5	4.8
Grades 6 to 8	87.7	6.7	2.6	3.0
Grades 9 to 12	82.4	6.6	4.3	6.6
12th grade	82.1	5.5	4.2	8.1
Threatened a student with a gun, knife or club	94.6	2.2	1.2	1.9
Grades 6 to 8	95.6	2.0	1.0	1.4
Grades 9 to 12	93.7	2.5	1.5	2.4
12th grade	93.6	2.3	1.2	2.9
Threatened to hurt a student by hitting, slapping or kicking	62.6	11.1	12.8	13.6
Grades 6 to 8	62.6	12.0	12.0	13.3
Grades 9 to 12	62.5	10.1	13.6	13.8
12th grade	67.1	8.9	12.1	11.9
Hurt a student by using a gun, knife or club	96.5	1.2	0.8	1.5
Grades 6 to 8	97.2	1.0	0.6	1.2
Grades 9 to 12	95.8	1.5	0.9	1.8
12th grade	95.1	1.5	1.0	2.4
Hurt a student by hitting, slapping or kicking	68.3	11.6	10.8	9.3
Grades 6 to 8	66.6	12.9	10.9	9.6
Grades 9 to 12	69.9	10.4	10.8	9.0
12th grade	75.2	8.3	8.9	7.5

Note: See Note, table 3.54.

[a]Percents may not add to 100 because of rounding.

Source: PRIDE Surveys, "2002-2003 PRIDE Surveys National Summary, Grades 6 through 12," Bowling Green, KY: PRIDE Surveys, 2003. (Mimeographed.) Pp. 212, 213. Table adapted by SOURCEBOOK staff. Reprinted by permission.

Table 3.59

Students reporting victimization experiences at school

By grade level of respondent, 2002-2003[a]

Question: "While at school have you. . .?"

	Never	One time	2 to 5 times	6 or more times
Been threatened with a gun, knife or club by a student	88.3%	6.0%	3.1%	2.6%
Grades 6 to 8	88.4	6.3	2.9	2.4
Grades 9 to 12	88.2	5.7	3.2	2.8
12th grade	89.4	4.8	2.6	3.2
Had a student threaten to hit, slap or kick you	60.3	14.7	13.8	11.2
Grades 6 to 8	58.1	15.6	14.1	12.2
Grades 9 to 12	62.5	13.8	13.5	10.2
12th grade	68.1	12.2	11.0	8.7
Been afraid a student may hurt you	76.3	12.5	6.6	4.6
Grades 6 to 8	74.2	13.4	7.0	5.3
Grades 9 to 12	78.4	11.6	6.1	3.8
12th grade	82.5	9.3	4.6	3.6
Been hurt by a student using a gun, knife or club	96.2	1.6	0.8	1.4
Grades 6 to 8	96.6	1.6	0.7	1.1
Grades 9 to 12	95.8	1.7	0.9	1.7
12th grade	95.5	1.6	0.8	2.1
Been hurt by a student who hit, slapped or kicked you	78.0	10.8	6.3	4.9
Grades 6 to 8	73.9	12.8	7.5	5.9
Grades 9 to 12	82.1	8.9	5.1	4.0
12th grade	85.8	6.6	3.8	3.8

Note: See Note, table 3.54.

[a]Percents may not add to 100 because of rounding.

Source: PRIDE Surveys, "2002-2003 PRIDE Surveys National Summary, Grades 6 through 12," Bowling Green, KY: PRIDE Surveys, 2003. (Mimeographed.) Pp. 214, 215. Table adapted by SOURCEBOOK staff. Reprinted by permission.

Table 3.60

Number and rate (per 1,000 students) of nonfatal violent crimes against students age 12 to 18 occurring at school

By type of crime and student characteristics, United States, 1995, 1999-2001[a]

Student characteristics	1995 Violent[b]	1995 Serious violent[c]	1999 Violent[b]	1999 Serious violent[c]	2000 Violent[b]	2000 Serious violent[c]	2001 Violent[b]	2001 Serious violent[c]
Number of offenses								
Total	1,290,000	222,500	884,100	185,600	699,800	128,400	763,700	160,900
Sex								
Male	779,400	144,800	513,000	111,200	468,000	98,900	424,700	88,800
Female	510,500	77,600	371,200	74,300	231,800	29,600[d]	339,100	72,200
Age								
12 to 14 years	850,400	145,900	543,200	127,000	384,100	57,200	423,600	84,400
15 to 18 years	439,600	76,600	340,900	58,600	315,700	71,200	340,100	76,500
Race, ethnicity								
White, non-Hispanic	917,800	123,000	582,200	95,300	457,800	60,000	511,700	88,600
Black, non-Hispanic	190,500	53,300	178,200	58,900	110,300	19,800[d]	108,800	30,500[d]
Hispanic	151,300	36,900	84,100	25,700	116,400	43,100	138,400	39,300
Other, non-Hispanic	25,100	9,300[d]	31,000	5,600[d]	10,000[d]	2,500[d]	4,900[d]	2,500[d]
Community								
Urban	342,000	95,200	215,100	63,700	167,800	56,700	222,000	52,500
Suburban	709,800	93,400	514,900	110,400	393,500	54,200	406,400	81,100
Rural	238,100	33,800	154,100	11,400[d]	138,600	17,500[d]	135,400	27,300[d]
Rate per 1,000 students								
Total	50	9	33	7	26	5	28	6
Sex								
Male	59	11	37	8	33	7	30	6
Female	41	6	28	6	18	2[d]	26	5
Age								
12 to 14 years	73	13	46	11	32	5	35	7
15 to 18 years	31	5	23	4	21	5	22	5
Race, ethnicity								
White, non-Hispanic	54	7	34	6	26	3	29	5
Black, non-Hispanic	47	13	43	14	26	5[d]	25	7[d]
Hispanic	46	11	21	6	29	11	33	9
Other, non-Hispanic	23	9[d]	26	5[d]	8[d]	2[d]	4[d]	2[d]
Community								
Urban	49	14	29	9	22	7	29	7
Suburban	57	7	36	8	28	4	28	6
Rural	39	5	28	2[d]	26	3[d]	25	5[d]

Note: These data are from the National Crime Victimization Survey (NCVS) conducted for the U.S. Department of Justice, Bureau of Justice Statistics by the U.S. Census Bureau. The data presented are estimates based on a continuous survey of a representative sample of households in the United States and therefore are subject to sampling variation. "At school" is defined as in the school building, on school property, or going to and from school. For more information on the NCVS, see Note, table 3.1 and Appendix 8.

[a]Numbers are rounded to the nearest 100; due to rounding or missing cases, detail may not add to total.
[b]Includes rape, sexual assault, robbery, and aggravated and simple assault.
[c]Includes rape, sexual assault, robbery, and aggravated assault. Serious violent crimes also are included in violent crimes.
[d]Estimate is based on fewer than 10 cases.

Source: Jill F. DeVoe et al., *Indicators of School Crime and Safety: 2003*, NCES 2004-004/NCJ 201257 (Washington, DC: U.S. Departments of Education and Justice, 2003), pp. 56-62. Table adapted by SOURCEBOOK staff.

Table 3.61

Students age 12 to 18 reporting victimization, bullying, hate-related behavior, and gangs at school

By student characteristics, United States, 2001

Student characteristics	Criminal victimization				Bullying	Hate-related behavior		Street gangs present at school
	Total[a]	Theft	Violent[b]	Serious violent[c]		Target of hate-related words	Saw hate-related graffiti	
Total	5.5%	4.2%	1.8%	0.4%	7.9%	12.3%	35.5%	20.1%
Sex								
Male	6.1	4.5	2.1	0.5	8.6	12.8	34.9	21.4
Female	4.9	3.8	1.5	0.4	7.1	11.7	36.1	18.8
Race, ethnicity								
White, non-Hispanic	5.8	4.2	2.0	0.4	8.5	12.1	36.2	15.5
Black, non-Hispanic	6.1	5.0	1.3	0.5	5.9	13.9	33.6	28.6
Hispanic	4.6	3.7	1.5	0.8	7.8	11.0	35.1	32.0
Other, non-Hispanic	3.1	2.9	0.4	(d)	6.6	13.6	32.1	21.4
Grade								
6th	5.9	4.0	2.6	0.1	14.3	12.1	34.9	11.2
7th	5.8	3.4	2.6	0.6	13.0	14.1	34.9	15.7
8th	4.3	3.3	1.3	0.3	9.2	13.0	36.7	17.3
9th	7.9	6.2	2.4	0.8	8.6	12.1	35.7	24.3
10th	6.5	5.7	1.2	0.4	4.6	13.1	36.2	23.6
11th	4.8	3.8	1.6	0.3	4.3	12.7	36.1	24.2
12th	2.9	2.3	0.9	0.3	2.4	7.9	33.0	21.1
Community								
Urban	5.9	4.5	1.7	0.5	6.9	11.9	35.7	28.9
Suburban	5.7	4.3	1.7	0.4	8.1	12.4	36.0	18.3
Rural	4.7	3.4	2.0	0.5	8.7	12.4	33.8	13.3
Type of school								
Public	5.7	4.4	1.9	0.5	8.0	12.7	37.3	21.6
Private	3.4	2.5	1.0	(d)	7.3	8.2	16.8	4.9

Note: These data are from the School Crime Supplement (SCS) to the National Crime Victimization Survey (NCVS). The NCVS is a continuous survey of a representative sample of households in the United States conducted for the U.S. Department of Justice, Bureau of Justice Statistics by the U.S. Census Bureau. The SCS is an additional questionnaire fielded with the 2001 NCVS and was administered to a nationally representative sample of 8,374 students 12 to 18 years of age. Eligible respondents were asked the supplemental SCS questions only after completing the NCVS interview. Persons eligible for the SCS were those NCVS respondents who were enrolled in grades 6 through 12 at a school leading to a high school diploma and had attended school at any time during the 6 months preceding the interview. "At school" includes in the school building, on school property, on a school bus, or going to and from school. These data are not directly comparable to data presented in table 3.60 because those data are derived from the larger NCVS dataset rather than the SCS. The data presented are survey estimates and therefore are subject to sampling variation.

[a]Total victimization is a combination of violent victimization and theft. If the student reported an incident of either, he or she is counted as having experienced "total" victimization. If the student reported having experienced both, he or she is counted once under "total" victimization.
[b]Includes rape, sexual assault, robbery, and aggravated and simple assault.
[c]Includes rape, sexual assault, robbery, and aggravated assault. Serious violent crimes also are included in violent crimes.
[d]No cases of this type occurred in the data.

Source: Jill F. DeVoe et al., *Indicators of School Crime and Safety: 2003*, NCES 2004-004/NCJ 201257 (Washington, DC: U.S. Departments of Education and Justice, 2003), pp. 71, 74, 86-88. Table adapted by SOURCEBOOK staff.

Table 3.62

High school students reporting drug, alcohol, and cigarette use

By sex, race, ethnicity, and grade level, United States, 2003

(Percent reporting engaging in the behavior)

	Total	Sex		Race, ethnicity			Grade level			
		Male	Female	White, non-Hispanic	Black, non-Hispanic	Hispanic	9th grade	10th grade	11th grade	12th grade
Marijuana use, lifetime[a]	40.2%	42.7%	37.6%	39.8%	43.3%	42.7%	30.7%	40.4%	44.5%	48.5%
Marijuana use, current[b]	22.4	25.1	19.3	21.7	23.9	23.8	18.5	22.0	24.1	25.8
Cocaine use, lifetime[c]	8.7	9.5	7.7	8.7	3.2	12.5	6.8	8.5	9.0	10.5
Cocaine use, current[b]	4.1	4.6	3.5	3.8	2.2	5.7	3.6	3.7	4.1	4.7
Illegal steroid use, lifetime[a]	6.1	6.8	5.3	6.2	3.6	7.2	7.1	6.1	5.6	4.9
Injected illegal drugs, lifetime[d]	3.2	3.8	2.5	2.5	2.4	3.9	3.2	3.2	2.8	3.0
Heroin use, lifetime[e]	3.3	4.3	2.0	2.6	2.6	3.9	3.5	2.9	3.0	2.9
Methamphetamine use, lifetime[f]	7.6	8.3	6.8	8.1	3.1	8.3	6.7	7.5	8.0	8.0
Ecstasy use, lifetime[g]	11.1	11.6	10.4	11.0	6.0	13.0	10.9	9.0	11.4	12.8
Sniffed or inhaled intoxicating substances, lifetime[h]	12.1	12.6	11.4	12.8	7.0	12.7	13.6	11.1	11.0	11.8
Sniffed or inhaled intoxicating substances, current[i]	3.9	4.3	3.4	3.6	3.0	4.3	5.4	3.5	3.1	2.7
Alcohol use, lifetime[j]	74.9	73.7	76.1	75.4	71.4	79.5	65.0	75.7	78.6	83.0
Alcohol use, current[k]	44.9	43.8	45.8	47.1	37.4	45.6	36.2	43.5	47.0	55.9
Episodic heavy drinking[l]	28.3	29.0	27.5	31.8	15.3	28.9	19.8	27.4	31.8	37.2
Cigarette use, lifetime[m]	58.4	58.7	58.1	58.1	58.4	61.9	52.0	58.3	60.0	65.4
Cigarette use, current[n]	21.9	21.8	21.9	24.9	15.1	18.4	17.4	21.8	23.6	26.2
Cigarette use, frequent[o]	9.7	9.6	9.7	11.8	5.5	5.5	6.3	9.2	11.2	13.1
Before age 13										
Smoked whole cigarette	18.3	20.0	16.4	18.9	15.3	18.3	19.3	20.1	16.0	16.5
Drank alcohol[p]	27.8	32.0	23.3	25.7	31.2	30.2	36.4	28.5	23.0	20.3
Tried marijuana	9.9	12.6	6.9	8.7	12.1	10.7	11.7	10.8	8.1	7.8

Note: See Note, table 3.55. For survey methodology and sampling procedures, see Appendix 5.

[a] Ever used.
[b] One or more times during the 30 days preceding the survey.
[c] Ever tried any form of cocaine (e.g., powder, crack, or freebase).
[d] Ever injected illegal drugs. Respondents were classified as injecting-drug users only if they (a) reported injecting-drug use not prescribed by a physician and (b) answered "one or more times" to any of these questions: "During your life, how many times have you used any form of cocaine including powder, crack, or freebase?"; "During your life, how many times have you used heroin, (also called smack, junk, or China White)?"; "During your life, how many times have you used methamphetamines (also called speed, crystal, crank, or ice)?"; "During your life, how many times have you taken steroid pills or shots without a doctor's prescription?"
[e] Ever used heroin (also called smack, junk, or China White).
[f] Ever used methamphetamines (also called speed, crystal, crank, or ice).
[g] Ever used ecstasy (also called MDMA).
[h] Ever sniffed glue or breathed the contents of aerosol spray cans or inhaled any paints or sprays to become intoxicated.
[i] Ever sniffed glue or breathed the contents of aerosol spray cans or inhaled any paints or sprays to become intoxicated one or more times during the 30 days preceding the survey.
[j] Ever had one or more drinks of alcohol.
[k] Drank alcohol on 1 or more of the 30 days preceding the survey.
[l] Drank five or more drinks of alcohol on at least one occasion on 1 or more of the 30 days preceding the survey.
[m] Ever tried cigarette smoking, even one or two puffs.
[n] On 1 or more of the 30 days preceding the survey.
[o] Smoked cigarettes on 20 or more of the 30 days preceding the survey.
[p] More than a few sips.

Source: Jo Anne Grunbaum et al., "Youth Risk Behavior Surveillance--United States, 2003," CDC Surveillance Summaries, *Morbidity and Mortality Weekly Report* 53 No. SS-2 (Washington, DC: USGPO, May 21, 2004), pp. 49-65. Table adapted by SOURCEBOOK staff.

Table 3.63

Students reporting use of alcohol and drugs

By grade level of respondent and frequency of use, 2002-2003

	Grades 6 to 8 (N=54,520)		Grades 9 to 12 (N=55,399)		12th grade (N=8,385)	
	Annual use[a]	Monthly use[b]	Annual use[a]	Monthly use[b]	Annual use[a]	Monthly use[b]
Any alcohol	37.0%	13.7%	63.0%	35.0%	70.1%	44.6%
Beer	25.7	9.9	49.3	28.2	56.9	36.8
Wine coolers	28.5	10.1	45.8	20.9	48.7	24.1
Liquor	19.1	8.0	48.3	26.9	58.3	36.3
Any illicit drugs	15.8	9.0	32.7	21.0	37.8	25.2
Marijuana	11.7	7.1	30.0	19.1	35.5	22.9
Cocaine[c]	3.1	1.9	6.3	3.8	8.6	5.3
Inhalants	5.9	2.7	5.7	3.2	5.7	3.7
Hallucinogens[d]	2.6	1.7	5.7	3.3	7.8	4.5
Heroin	2.3	1.6	3.8	2.6	5.0	3.6
Steroids	2.5	1.6	3.7	2.6	4.8	3.6
Ecstasy	3.1	NA	6.7	NA	8.9	NA

Note: See Note, table 3.54.

[a] Used one or more times in the past year.
[b] Used once a month or more in the past year.
[c] Includes crack.
[d] Includes LSD and PCP.

Source: PRIDE Surveys, "2002-2003 PRIDE Surveys National Summary, Grades 6 through 12," Bowling Green, KY: PRIDE Surveys, 2003. (Mimeographed.) Pp. 11, 12, 17. Table adapted by SOURCEBOOK staff. Reprinted by permission.

Table 3.64

Reported alcohol use and most recent use among students

By sex, college plans, region, and population density, United States, 2003

Questions: "On how many occasions have you had alcoholic beverages to drink, more than just a few sips, in your lifetime? On how many occasions have you had alcoholic beverages to drink, more than just a few sips, during the last 12 months? On how many occasions have you had alcoholic beverages to drink, more than just a few sips, during the last 30 days?"

	Ever used			Used in last 12 months			Used in last 30 days		
	Eighth grade	Tenth grade	Twelfth grade	Eighth grade	Tenth grade	Twelfth grade	Eighth grade	Tenth grade	Twelfth grade
Total	45.6%	66.0%	76.6%	37.2%	59.3%	70.1%	19.7%	35.4%	47.5%
Sex									
Male	45.4	64.3	76.8	36.6	57.5	71.0	19.4	35.3	51.7
Female	45.5	67.5	76.5	37.6	61.0	69.3	19.8	35.3	43.8
College plans									
None or under 4 years	63.1	75.9	82.6	54.1	69.8	76.2	35.3	46.6	55.4
Complete 4 years	43.6	64.5	74.9	35.3	57.7	68.5	18.1	33.6	45.2
Region									
Northeast	43.0	70.0	79.9	35.8	64.2	74.6	18.4	38.7	51.6
North Central	47.7	63.9	78.0	40.4	58.2	71.8	21.9	34.4	50.8
South	48.6	67.6	73.8	38.8	59.5	66.1	20.8	34.8	43.0
West	38.8	62.3	76.1	30.7	55.6	70.1	16.0	34.1	47.0
Population density									
Large SMSA	45.5	65.1	74.2	36.6	58.1	67.7	18.2	33.1	43.0
Other SMSA	44.4	65.9	77.6	36.4	59.6	71.4	19.4	35.6	49.6
Non-SMSA	47.9	67.7	77.8	39.5	60.7	70.9	22.3	38.3	49.6

Note: These data are from a series of nationwide surveys of high school seniors conducted by the University of Michigan's Institute for Social Research for the National Institute on Drug Abuse from 1975 through 2003. The survey design is a multistage random sample of high school seniors in public and private schools. Depending on the survey year, approximately 65% of the schools initially invited to participate agreed to do so. Completed questionnaires were obtained from approximately 83% of all sampled students in participating schools each year. Beginning in 1991, eighth and tenth grade students also were included in the survey. All percentages reported are based on weighted cases; the Ns that are shown in the tables also refer to the approximate number (i.e., rounded to the nearest hundred) of weighted cases. The number of respondents for 2003 were approximately 16,500 for eighth graders, 15,800 for tenth graders, and 14,600 for twelfth graders, excluding cases with missing data. For survey methodology and definitions of terms, see Appendix 6.

Source: Lloyd D. Johnston et al., *Monitoring the Future National Survey Results on Drug Use, 1975-2003*, Vol. 1, Secondary School Students (Bethesda, MD: U.S. Department of Health and Human Services, 2004), pp. 106, 110, 114. Table adapted by SOURCEBOOK staff.

Table 3.65

Reported use of any illicit drug and most recent use among students

By sex, college plans, region, and population density, United States, 2003

Questions: "On how many occasions, if any, have you used. . .in your lifetime? On how many occasions, if any, have you used. . .during the last 12 months? On how many occasions, if any, have you used. . .during the last 30 days?"

	Ever used			Used in last 12 months			Used in last 30 days		
	Eighth grade	Tenth grade	Twelfth grade	Eighth grade	Tenth grade	Twelfth grade	Eighth grade	Tenth grade	Twelfth grade
Total	22.8%	41.4%	51.1%	16.1%	32.0%	39.3%	9.7%	19.5%	24.1%
Sex									
Male	23.6	42.4	54.1	16.4	33.2	41.3	10.2	21.0	27.3
Female	21.8	40.2	47.7	15.5	30.8	36.7	8.9	18.0	20.6
College plans									
None or under 4 years	44.5	57.7	60.2	34.7	48.6	46.8	24.7	34.7	30.6
Complete 4 years	20.4	38.6	47.9	14.0	29.2	36.6	8.1	17.0	21.9
Region									
Northeast	18.5	40.4	53.8	13.1	32.6	43.7	8.1	20.2	28.3
North Central	22.5	37.7	52.7	15.7	28.8	40.0	9.1	17.2	23.9
South	25.2	44.2	46.7	18.1	34.0	34.8	11.2	21.3	21.8
West	22.9	42.7	53.7	15.6	32.3	41.4	8.9	19.0	24.2
Population density									
Large SMSA	22.3	40.7	47.6	14.3	30.5	35.7	8.5	17.4	21.9
Other SMSA	22.2	41.2	54.3	16.2	32.4	42.7	9.5	19.8	26.7
Non-SMSA	24.7	43.0	49.6	18.1	33.5	37.6	11.7	22.1	22.4

Note: See Note, table 3.64. For twelfth graders, use of "any illicit drug" includes any use of marijuana, LSD, other hallucinogens, crack, other cocaine, or heroin, or any use of other narcotics, amphetamines, barbiturates, or tranquilizers not under a doctor's orders. For eighth and tenth graders, the use of other narcotics and barbiturates is excluded, because these younger respondents appear to overreport use (perhaps because they include the use of nonprescription drugs in their answers). For survey methodology and definitions of terms, see Appendix 6.

Source: Lloyd D. Johnston et al., *Monitoring the Future National Survey Results on Drug Use, 1975-2003*, Vol. 1, Secondary School Students (Bethesda, MD: U.S. Department of Health and Human Services, 2004), pp. 103, 107, 111. Table adapted by SOURCEBOOK staff.

Table 3.66

Reported use of any illicit drug in last 12 months among students

By sex, race, ethnicity, and college plans, United States, 1991-2003 and 1975-2003

Question: "On how many occasions, if any, have you used. . .during the last 12 months?"

	Percent reporting use of any illicit drug in last 12 months							College plans	
		Sex		Race, ethnicity[a]			None or under	Complete
	Total	Male	Female	White	Black	Hispanic	4 years	4 years
Eighth graders								
1991	11.3%	11.7%	11.0%	NA	NA	NA	22.8%	9.5%
1992	12.9	11.9	13.6	11.8%	7.9%	18.1%	25.6	10.9
1993	15.1	15.2	14.9	13.6	9.3	20.6	30.7	12.8
1994	18.5	19.4	17.6	15.7	13.0	24.6	34.6	16.3
1995	21.4	22.3	20.2	19.2	15.8	26.7	38.4	19.1
1996	23.6	23.6	23.3	22.4	17.5	26.9	40.3	21.0
1997	22.1	22.6	21.3	23.0	18.1	26.5	39.6	19.9
1998	21.0	21.3	20.4	21.5	18.1	26.7	41.3	18.4
1999	20.5	21.3	19.7	19.9	18.6	27.4	39.9	18.0
2000	19.5	19.7	19.0	19.1	18.3	25.1	38.9	17.1
2001	19.5	21.3	17.5	19.0	16.7	24.3	38.5	17.2
2002	17.7	19.2	16.3	18.3	15.1	24.8	36.8	15.7
2003	16.1	16.4	15.5	16.5	14.6	22.8	34.7	14.0
Tenth graders								
1991	21.4	21.6	21.1	NA	NA	NA	32.7	18.9
1992	20.4	20.4	20.1	22.4	10.8	23.6	32.0	17.8
1993	24.7	25.1	24.0	23.7	11.9	26.3	37.7	21.9
1994	30.0	31.8	28.0	27.9	18.5	30.3	43.2	27.0
1995	33.3	33.7	32.5	32.6	23.6	34.3	47.3	30.8
1996	37.5	38.8	36.3	36.5	27.3	40.0	52.4	35.0
1997	38.5	40.1	36.8	39.3	30.2	41.3	55.2	35.7
1998	35.0	35.3	34.7	38.2	28.9	38.1	50.5	32.2
1999	35.9	37.0	34.6	36.4	28.4	38.4	51.8	33.2
2000	36.4	39.4	33.5	36.9	29.7	39.3	53.5	33.9
2001	37.2	39.6	35.0	37.6	30.5	38.8	52.7	34.6
2002	34.8	35.9	33.7	37.6	28.5	36.2	51.5	32.1
2003	32.0	33.2	30.8	35.0	27.3	33.8	48.6	29.2
Twelfth graders								
1975	45.0	49.0	41.4	NA	NA	NA	NA	NA
1976	48.1	52.6	43.0	NA	NA	NA	50.6	44.3
1977	51.1	55.4	46.7	50.4	40.8	49.9	54.3	46.8
1978	53.8	58.6	48.7	53.5	42.8	49.5	55.5	50.5
1979	54.2	58.1	50.1	55.2	41.5	48.4	56.8	50.5
1980	53.1	56.0	49.8	54.9	40.5	48.1	56.5	49.7
1981	52.1	53.6	50.8	54.4	39.0	46.8	55.8	48.6
1982	49.4	51.8	46.3	50.7	36.4	42.7	53.4	45.5
1983	47.4	49.7	44.4	49.3	38.5	42.0	50.8	43.7
1984	45.8	48.0	42.8	47.4	37.8	43.1	50.3	41.4
1985	46.3	48.3	43.8	47.6	35.9	43.9	50.1	43.1
1986	44.3	45.7	42.3	47.2	33.3	42.8	48.6	41.2
1987	41.7	43.2	39.7	45.2	28.9	38.9	46.7	39.0
1988	38.5	40.6	36.1	43.0	25.0	35.4	42.0	36.5
1989	35.4	37.7	32.8	40.3	21.3	30.1	40.9	32.6
1990	32.5	34.3	30.1	37.5	17.0	26.4	37.8	29.6
1991	29.4	32.1	26.2	33.9	14.7	29.4	33.9	27.1
1992	27.1	29.0	24.7	30.5	14.5	30.3	33.5	24.4
1993	31.0	33.5	27.9	31.4	16.6	28.8	34.9	29.2
1994	35.8	38.6	32.7	35.5	23.5	31.2	40.8	33.6
1995	39.0	41.5	35.8	39.0	29.6	35.5	44.1	36.7
1996	40.2	43.4	36.2	40.8	32.4	38.0	46.2	37.8
1997	42.4	44.1	40.0	42.8	33.0	41.2	48.8	40.1
1998	41.4	45.2	37.2	44.0	32.3	41.9	47.3	39.1
1999	42.1	45.0	38.9	43.3	32.8	42.5	47.9	40.3
2000	40.9	43.4	38.0	42.8	32.7	44.8	45.1	38.8
2001	41.4	43.8	38.4	43.1	31.7	41.8	46.2	39.6
2002	41.0	43.5	37.8	43.6	30.4	39.0	46.2	39.3
2003	39.3	41.3	36.7	42.8	28.3	35.8	46.8	36.6

Note: See Note, table 3.64. For twelfth graders, use of "any illicit drug" includes any use of marijuana, LSD, other hallucinogens, crack, other cocaine, or heroin, or any use of other narcotics, amphetamines, barbiturates, or tranquilizers not under a doctor's orders. For eighth and tenth graders, the use of other narcotics and barbiturates is excluded, because these younger respondents appear to overreport use (perhaps because they include the use of nonprescription drugs in their answers) (Source, p. 452). For survey methodology and definitions of terms, see Appendix 6.

[a]To derive percentages for each racial/ethnic subgroup, data for the specified year and the previous year are combined to increase subgroup sample sizes and provide more stable estimates.

Source: Lloyd D. Johnston et al., *Monitoring the Future National Survey Results on Drug Use, 1975-2003*, Vol. 1, Secondary School Students (Bethesda, MD: U.S. Department of Health and Human Services, 2004), pp. 452, 453. Table adapted by SOURCEBOOK staff.

Table 3.67

Reported use of any illicit drug other than marijuana in last 12 months among students

By sex, race, ethnicity, and college plans, United States, 1991-2003 and 1975-2003

Question: "On how many occasions, if any, have you used. . .during the last 12 months?"

Percent reporting use of any illicit drug other than marijuana in last 12 months

	Total	Sex Male	Sex Female	Race, ethnicity[a] White	Race, ethnicity[a] Black	Race, ethnicity[a] Hispanic	College plans None or under 4 years	College plans Complete 4 years
Eighth graders								
1991	8.4%	8.0%	8.8%	NA	NA	NA	16.3%	7.2%
1992	9.3	8.0	10.4	9.0%	4.9%	12.2%	18.5	8.0
1993	10.4	9.2	11.5	10.0	5.0	13.7	21.3	8.9
1994	11.3	10.1	12.3	10.8	5.9	15.2	21.2	9.9
1995	12.6	11.5	13.5	12.6	5.7	15.3	25.3	10.9
1996	13.1	11.0	14.7	13.9	5.3	14.7	23.0	11.6
1997	11.8	10.8	12.6	13.5	4.7	13.6	22.1	10.6
1998	11.0	9.6	12.1	12.5	4.0	13.5	23.8	9.4
1999	10.5	9.7	11.2	11.5	4.1	14.5	23.4	9.0
2000	10.2	9.1	10.9	11.1	3.8	13.9	22.7	8.7
2001	10.8	10.0	11.2	10.6	3.9	12.2	21.5	9.5
2002	8.8	8.1	9.3	10.3	4.4	11.9	19.7	7.6
2003	8.8	7.9	9.4	9.3	4.4	10.8	20.0	7.5
Tenth graders								
1991	12.2	11.2	13.1	NA	NA	NA	19.6	10.7
1992	12.3	11.1	13.2	13.7	4.3	11.8	20.2	10.5
1993	13.9	13.4	14.3	14.4	4.6	13.7	23.1	12.0
1994	15.2	14.1	16.0	15.4	5.4	16.1	24.0	13.3
1995	17.5	15.8	18.9	17.7	5.4	16.9	27.5	15.7
1996	18.4	17.2	19.6	20.0	4.5	18.8	29.5	16.5
1997	18.2	17.2	19.1	20.5	4.8	19.1	29.6	16.3
1998	16.6	15.6	17.5	19.7	4.7	17.5	27.8	14.6
1999	16.7	15.9	17.3	18.7	4.5	17.9	27.3	15.0
2000	16.7	16.7	16.6	18.6	4.2	17.8	27.7	15.0
2001	17.9	18.3	17.4	19.2	4.7	15.8	32.1	15.5
2002	15.7	15.1	16.4	18.9	5.7	15.7	27.1	14.0
2003	13.8	13.0	14.3	17.2	4.7	15.2	23.8	12.1
Twelfth graders								
1975	26.2	25.9	26.2	NA	NA	NA	NA	NA
1976	25.4	25.7	24.4	NA	NA	NA	28.7	20.9
1977	26.0	26.3	25.3	26.6	14.2	23.8	30.1	20.8
1978	27.1	27.9	25.7	27.7	13.4	23.5	30.0	22.7
1979	28.2	29.4	26.3	28.8	13.0	23.3	31.8	23.5
1980	30.4	30.2	30.0	30.6	13.8	24.7	35.5	25.5
1981	34.0	32.8	34.3	34.5	13.2	27.6	38.3	30.1
1982	30.1	31.0	28.3	32.1	14.5	25.5	34.0	26.0
1983	28.4	28.9	27.3	31.2	15.2	25.2	32.3	24.7
1984	28.0	28.2	26.9	30.2	12.9	26.2	32.9	23.3
1985	27.4	27.9	26.2	29.6	12.0	27.2	31.6	24.1
1986	25.9	26.2	24.8	28.2	12.1	26.2	31.3	22.2
1987	24.1	24.3	23.3	26.6	11.1	23.0	28.8	21.3
1988	21.1	22.2	19.3	24.4	10.3	20.5	24.5	19.0
1989	20.0	21.0	18.5	22.5	8.6	17.7	25.5	17.2
1990	17.9	19.2	16.0	21.0	6.5	15.6	23.1	15.2
1991	16.2	17.0	14.8	18.7	5.7	15.8	20.1	14.3
1992	14.9	15.5	13.8	17.1	5.3	15.1	19.5	13.0
1993	17.1	17.8	15.8	17.9	4.8	15.6	19.8	15.9
1994	18.0	18.5	16.9	19.4	6.1	16.5	22.9	16.0
1995	19.4	20.7	17.3	20.3	6.9	17.9	23.9	17.5
1996	19.8	21.7	16.8	21.2	6.0	19.7	24.2	17.9
1997	20.7	21.7	18.8	22.3	6.4	18.9	25.8	18.4
1998	20.2	21.7	18.0	23.1	7.1	17.5	26.5	17.8
1999	20.7	22.5	18.5	22.9	6.8	18.5	24.4	19.4
2000	20.4	21.5	18.6	22.7	6.4	21.2	24.7	18.5
2001	21.6	23.3	19.0	23.0	6.3	18.2	24.5	19.9
2002	20.9	22.0	19.0	24.1	6.0	6.1	27.2	19.0
2003	19.8	21.1	17.9	23.0	6.3	16.0	26.5	17.4

Note: See Notes, tables 3.64 and 3.66. For survey methodology and definitions of terms, see Appendix 6.

[a]To derive percentages for each racial/ethnic subgroup, data for the specified year and the previous year are combined to increase subgroup sample sizes and provide more stable estimates.

Source: Lloyd D. Johnston et al., *Monitoring the Future National Survey Results on Drug Use, 1975-2003*, Vol. 1, Secondary School Students (Bethesda, MD: U.S. Department of Health and Human Services, 2004), pp. 454, 455. Table adapted by SOURCEBOOK staff.

Table 3.68

Reported drug and alcohol use in last 12 months among high school seniors

By type of drug, United States, 1991-2003

Question: "On how many occasions, if any, have you used. . .during the last 12 months?"

(Percent who used in last 12 months)

Type of drug	Class of 1991 (N=15,000)	Class of 1992 (N=15,800)	Class of 1993 (N=16,300)	Class of 1994 (N=15,400)	Class of 1995 (N=15,400)	Class of 1996 (N=14,300)	Class of 1997 (N=15,400)	Class of 1998 (N=15,200)	Class of 1999 (N=13,600)	Class of 2000 (N=12,800)	Class of 2001 (N=12,800)	Class of 2002 (N=12,900)	Class of 2003 (N=14,600)
Marijuana/hashish	23.9%	21.9%	26.0%	30.7%	34.7%	35.8%	38.5%	37.5%	37.8%	36.5%	37.0%	36.2%	34.9%
Inhalants[a]	6.6	6.2	7.0	7.7	8.0	7.6	6.7	6.2	5.6	5.9	4.5	4.5	3.9
Adjusted[a,b]	6.9	6.4	7.4	8.2	8.4	8.5	7.3	7.1	6.0	6.2	4.9	4.9	4.5
Amyl and butyl nitrites[c]	0.9	0.5	0.9	1.1	1.1	1.6	1.2	1.4	0.9	0.6	0.6	1.1	0.9
Hallucinogens[d]	5.8	5.9	7.4	7.6	9.3	10.1	9.8	9.0	9.4	8.1	9.1	6.6	5.9
Adjusted[e]	6.1	6.2	7.8	7.8	9.7	10.7	10.0	9.2	9.8	8.7	9.7	7.2	6.5
LSD	5.2	5.6	6.8	6.9	8.4	8.8	8.4	7.6	8.1	6.6	6.6	3.5	1.9
PCP[c]	1.4	1.4	1.4	1.6	1.8	2.6	2.3	2.1	1.8	2.3	1.8	1.1	1.3
MDMA (ecstasy)[f]	NA	NA	NA	NA	NA	4.6	4.0	3.6	5.6	8.2	9.2	7.4	4.5
Cocaine	3.5	3.1	3.3	3.6	4.0	4.9	5.5	5.7	6.2	5.0	4.8	5.0	4.8
Crack	1.5	1.5	1.5	1.9	2.1	2.1	2.4	2.5	2.7	2.2	2.1	2.3	2.2
Other cocaine[g]	3.2	2.6	2.9	3.0	3.4	4.2	5.0	4.9	5.8	4.5	4.4	4.4	4.2
Heroin[h]	0.4	0.6	0.5	0.6	1.1	1.0	1.2	1.0	1.1	1.5	0.9	1.0	0.8
Other narcotics[i,j]	3.5	3.3	3.6	3.8	4.7	5.4	6.2	6.3	6.7	7.0	6.7	9.4	9.3
Amphetamines[i]	8.2	7.1	8.4	9.4	9.3	9.5	10.2	10.1	10.2	10.5	10.9	11.1	9.9
Methamphetamine[k]	NA	NA	NA	NA	NA	NA	NA	NA	4.7	4.3	3.9	3.6	3.2
Crystal methamphetamine[k]	1.4	1.3	1.7	1.8	2.4	2.8	2.3	3.0	1.9	2.2	2.5	3.0	2.0
Sedatives[i,l]	3.6	2.9	3.4	4.2	4.9	5.3	5.4	6.0	6.3	6.3	5.9	7.0	6.2
Barbiturates[l]	3.4	2.8	3.4	4.1	4.7	4.9	5.1	5.5	5.8	6.2	5.7	6.7	6.0
Methaqualone[i,m]	0.5	0.6	0.2	0.8	0.7	1.1	1.0	1.1	1.1	0.3	0.8	0.9	0.6
Tranquilizers[d,i]	3.6	2.8	3.5	3.7	4.4	4.6	4.7	5.5	5.8	5.7	6.9	7.7	6.7
Alcohol[n]	77.7	76.8	72.7	73.0	73.7	72.5	74.8	74.3	73.8	73.2	73.3	71.5	70.1
Steroids[o]	1.4	1.1	1.2	1.3	1.5	1.4	1.4	1.7	1.8	1.7	2.4	2.5	2.1

Note: See Note, table 3.64. Data for the categories "inhalants" and "hallucinogens" are underestimated because some users of amyl and butyl nitrites, and PCP fail to report in these drug categories. Since 1979, the survey addresses this issue by asking specific questions about amyl and butyl nitrites (inhalants) and PCP (a hallucinogen) on one survey alternate form. The results of this survey are used to adjust for underreporting in these drug categories. "Crack" is a highly potent and addictive form of cocaine. "Other cocaine" refers to noncrack forms of this drug. Readers interested in responses to this question for 1975 through 1990 should consult previous editions of SOURCEBOOK. Some data have been revised by the Source and may differ from previous editions of SOURCEBOOK. For survey methodology and definitions of terms, see Appendix 6.

[a]Data based on five questionnaire forms in 1991-98; N is five-sixths of N indicated. Beginning in 1999, data are based on three questionnaire forms; N is one-half of N indicated.
[b]Adjusted for underreporting of amyl and butyl nitrites.
[c]Data based on a single questionnaire form; N is one-sixth of N indicated.
[d]In 2001, the question text was changed on half of the questionnaire forms. The 2001 data are based on the changed forms only; N is one-half of N indicated. Beginning in 2002, all forms include the revised wording and data are based on all six forms.
[e]Adjusted for underreporting of PCP.
[f]Data based on a single questionnaire form; N is one-sixth of N indicated. Beginning in 2002, data are based on two forms; N is one-third of N indicated.
[g]Data based on four questionnaire forms beginning in 1991; N is two-thirds of N indicated.

[h]Beginning in 1995, the heroin question was changed in half of the questionnaire forms. Separate questions were asked for use with injection and without injection. Data presented here represent the combined data from all forms.
[i]Only drug use that was not under a doctor's orders is included here.
[j]In 2002, the question text was changed on half of the questionnaire forms. The list of examples of narcotics other than heroin was updated by replacing "Talwin," "laudanum," and "paregoric" with "Vicodin," "OxyContin," and "Percocet." The 2002 data are based on the changed forms only; N is one-half of N indicated. Beginning in 2003, all forms include the revised wording and data are based on all six forms.
[k]Data based on two questionnaire forms; N is one-third of N indicated.
[l]Sedatives data are a combination of barbiturate and methaqualone data. Beginning in 1991, six forms of barbiturate data are adjusted by one form of methaqualone data.
[m]Data based on a single questionnaire form; N is one-sixth of N indicated.
[n]Data based on six questionnaire forms in 1991 and 1992. In 1993, the question was changed slightly in three of six forms to indicate that a "drink" meant "more than a few sips." The 1993 data are based on the changed forms only; N is one-half of N indicated. Beginning in 1994, all forms include the revised wording and data are based on all six forms.
[o]Data based on two questionnaire forms; N is one-third of N indicated.

Source: Lloyd D. Johnston et al., *Monitoring the Future National Survey Results on Drug Use, 1975-2003*, Vol. 1, Secondary School Students (Bethesda, MD: U.S. Department of Health and Human Services, 2004), p. 175. Table adapted by SOURCEBOOK staff.

Table 3.69

Reported drug use, alcohol use, and cigarette use in last 30 days among high school seniors

By type of drug, United States, 1991-2003

Question: "On how many occasions, if any, have you used...during the last 30 days?"

(Percent who used in last 30 days)

Type of drug	Class of 1991 (N=15,000)	Class of 1992 (N=15,800)	Class of 1993 (N=16,300)	Class of 1994 (N=15,400)	Class of 1995 (N=15,400)	Class of 1996 (N=14,300)	Class of 1997 (N=15,400)	Class of 1998 (N=15,200)	Class of 1999 (N=13,600)	Class of 2000 (N=12,800)	Class of 2001 (N=12,800)	Class of 2002 (N=12,900)	Class of 2003 (N=14,600)
Marijuana/hashish	13.8%	11.9%	15.5%	19.0%	21.2%	21.9%	23.7%	22.8%	23.1%	21.6%	22.4%	21.5%	21.2%
Inhalants[a]	2.4	2.3	2.5	2.7	3.2	2.5	2.5	2.3	2.0	2.2	1.7	1.5	1.5
Adjusted[a,b]	2.6	2.5	2.8	2.9	3.5	2.9	2.9	3.1	2.4	2.4	2.1	1.8	2.3
Amyl and butyl nitrites[c]	0.4	0.3	0.6	0.4	0.4	0.7	0.7	1.0	0.4	0.3	0.5	0.6	0.7
Hallucinogens[d]	2.2	2.1	2.7	3.1	4.4	3.5	3.9	3.8	3.5	2.6	3.3	2.3	1.8
Adjusted[e]	2.4	2.3	3.3	3.2	4.6	3.8	4.1	4.1	3.9	3.0	3.5	2.7	2.7
LSD	1.9	2.0	2.4	2.6	4.0	2.5	3.1	3.2	2.7	1.6	2.3	0.7	0.6
PCP[c]	0.5	0.6	1.0	0.7	0.6	1.3	0.7	1.0	0.8	0.9	0.5	0.4	0.6
MDMA (ecstasy)[f]	NA	NA	NA	NA	NA	2.0	1.6	1.5	2.5	3.6	2.8	2.4	1.3
Cocaine	1.4	1.3	1.3	1.5	1.8	2.0	2.3	2.4	2.6	2.1	2.1	2.3	2.1
Crack	0.7	0.6	0.7	0.8	1.0	1.0	0.9	1.0	1.1	1.0	1.1	1.2	0.9
Other cocaine[g]	1.2	1.0	1.2	1.3	1.3	1.6	2.0	2.0	2.5	1.7	1.8	1.9	1.8
Heroin[h]	0.2	0.3	0.2	0.3	0.6	0.5	0.5	0.5	0.5	0.7	0.4	0.5	0.4
Other narcotics[i,j]	1.1	1.2	1.3	1.5	1.8	2.0	2.3	2.4	2.6	2.9	3.0	4.0	4.1
Amphetamines[i]	3.2	2.8	3.7	4.0	4.0	4.1	4.8	4.6	4.5	5.0	5.6	5.5	5.0
Methamphetamine[k]	NA	NA	NA	NA	NA	NA	NA	NA	1.7	1.9	1.5	1.7	1.7
Crystal methamphetamine[k]	0.6	0.5	0.6	0.7	1.1	1.1	0.8	1.2	0.8	1.0	1.1	1.2	0.8
Sedatives[i,l]	1.5	1.2	1.3	1.8	2.3	2.3	2.1	2.8	2.8	3.1	3.0	3.4	3.0
Barbiturates[i]	1.4	1.1	1.3	1.7	2.2	2.1	2.1	2.6	2.6	3.0	2.8	3.2	2.9
Methaqualone[i,m]	0.2	0.4	0.1	0.4	0.4	0.6	0.3	0.6	0.4	0.2	0.5	0.3	0.4
Tranquilizers[d,i]	1.4	1.0	1.2	1.4	1.8	2.0	1.8	2.4	2.5	2.6	2.9	3.3	2.8
Alcohol[n]	54.0	51.3	48.6	50.1	51.3	50.8	52.7	52.0	51.0	50.0	49.8	48.6	47.5
Steroids[o]	0.8	0.6	0.7	0.9	0.7	0.7	1.0	1.1	0.9	0.8	1.3	1.4	1.3
Cigarettes	28.3	27.8	29.9	31.2	33.5	34.0	36.5	35.1	34.6	31.4	29.5	26.7	24.4

Note: See Note, table 3.64. Data for the categories "inhalants" and "hallucinogens" are underestimated because some users of amyl and butyl nitrites, and PCP fail to report in these drug categories. Since 1979, the survey addresses this issue by asking specific questions about amyl and butyl nitrites (inhalants) and PCP (a hallucinogen) on one survey alternate form. The results of this survey are used to adjust for underreporting in these drug categories. "Crack" is a highly potent and addictive form of cocaine. "Other cocaine" refers to noncrack forms of this drug. Readers interested in responses to this question for 1975 through 1990 should consult previous editions of SOURCEBOOK. Some data have been revised by the Source and may differ from previous editions of SOURCEBOOK. For survey methodology and definitions of terms, see Appendix 6.

[a]Data based on five questionnaire forms in 1991-98; N is five-sixths of N indicated. Beginning in 1999, data are based on three questionnaire forms; N is one-half of N indicated.
[b]Adjusted for underreporting of amyl and butyl nitrites.
[c]Data based on a single questionnaire form; N is one-sixth of N indicated.
[d]In 2001, the question text was changed on half of the questionnaire forms. The 2001 data are based on the changed forms only; N is one-half of N indicated. Beginning in 2002, all forms include the revised wording and data are based on all six forms.
[e]Adjusted for underreporting of PCP.
[f]Data based on a single questionnaire form; N is one-sixth of N indicated. Beginning in 2002, data are based on two forms; N is one-third of N indicated.
[g]Data based on four questionnaire forms beginning in 1991; N is two-thirds of N indicated.

[h]Beginning in 1995, the heroin question was changed in half of the questionnaire forms. Separate questions were asked for use with injection and without injection. Data presented here represent the combined data from all forms.
[i]Only drug use that was not under a doctor's orders is included here.
[j]In 2002, the question text was changed on half of the questionnaire forms. The list of examples of narcotics other than heroin was updated by replacing "Talwin," "laudanum," and "paregoric" with "Vicodin," "OxyContin," and "Percocet." The 2002 data are based on the changed forms only; N is one-half of N indicated. Beginning in 2003, all forms include the revised wording and data are based on all six forms.
[k]Data based on two questionnaire forms; N is one-third of N indicated.
[l]Sedatives data are a combination of barbiturate and methaqualone data. Beginning in 1991, six forms of barbiturate data are adjusted by one form of methaqualone data.
[m]Data based on a single questionnaire form; N is one-sixth of N indicated.
[n]Data based on six questionnaire forms in 1991 and 1992. In 1993, the question was changed slightly in three of six forms to indicate that a "drink" meant "more than a few sips." The 1993 data are based on the changed forms only; N is one-half of N indicated for 1993. Beginning in 1994, all forms include the revised wording and data are based on all six forms.
[o]Data based on two questionnaire forms; N is one-third of N indicated.

Source: Lloyd D. Johnston et al., *Monitoring the Future National Survey Results on Drug Use, 1975-2003*, Vol. 1, Secondary School Students (Bethesda, MD: U.S. Department of Health and Human Services, 2004), p. 176. Table adapted by SOURCEBOOK staff.

Table 3.70

Reported drug use and most recent use among students

By type of drug and grade level, United States, 1991-2003

Type of drug	1991	1992	1993	1994	1995	1996	1997	1998	1999	2000	2001	2002	2003
Ever used													
Marijuana/hashish													
Eighth grade	10.2%	11.2%	12.6%	16.7%	19.9%	23.1%	22.6%	22.2%	22.0%	20.3%	20.4%	19.2%	17.5%
Tenth grade	23.4	21.4	24.4	30.4	34.1	39.8	42.3	39.6	40.9	40.3	40.1	38.7	36.4
Twelfth grade	36.7	32.6	35.3	38.2	41.7	44.9	49.6	49.1	49.7	48.8	49.0	47.8	46.1
Inhalants[a]													
Eighth grade	17.6	17.4	19.4	19.9	21.6	21.2	21.0	20.5	19.7	17.9	17.1	15.2	15.8
Tenth grade	15.7	16.6	17.5	18.0	19.0	19.3	18.3	18.3	17.0	16.6	15.2	13.5	12.7
Twelfth grade[b]	17.6	16.6	17.4	17.7	17.4	16.6	16.1	15.2	15.4	14.2	13.0	11.7	11.2
Hallucinogens[a,c]													
Eighth grade	3.2	3.8	3.9	4.3	5.2	5.9	5.4	4.9	4.8	4.6	5.2	4.1	4.0
Tenth grade	6.1	6.4	6.8	8.1	9.3	10.5	10.5	9.8	9.7	8.9	8.9	7.8	6.9
Twelfth grade	9.6	9.2	10.9	11.4	12.7	14.0	15.1	14.1	13.7	13.0	14.7	12.0	10.6
LSD													
Eighth grade	2.7	3.2	3.5	3.7	4.4	5.1	4.7	4.1	4.1	3.9	3.4	2.5	2.1
Tenth grade	5.6	5.8	6.2	7.2	8.4	9.4	9.5	8.5	8.5	7.6	6.3	5.0	3.5
Twelfth grade	8.8	8.6	10.3	10.5	11.7	12.6	13.6	12.6	12.2	11.1	10.9	8.4	5.9
MDMA (ecstasy)													
Eighth grade[d]	NA	NA	NA	NA	NA	3.4	3.2	2.7	2.7	4.3	5.2	4.3	3.2
Tenth grade[d]	NA	NA	NA	NA	NA	5.6	5.7	5.1	6.0	7.3	8.0	6.6	5.4
Twelfth grade[e]	NA	NA	NA	NA	NA	6.1	6.9	5.8	8.0	11.0	11.7	10.5	8.3
Cocaine													
Eighth grade	2.3	2.9	2.9	3.6	4.2	4.5	4.4	4.6	4.7	4.5	4.3	3.6	3.6
Tenth grade	4.1	3.3	3.6	4.3	5.0	6.5	7.1	7.2	7.7	6.9	5.7	6.1	5.1
Twelfth grade	7.8	6.1	6.1	5.9	6.0	7.1	8.7	9.3	9.8	8.6	8.2	7.8	7.7
Amphetamines[f]													
Eighth grade	10.5	10.8	11.8	12.3	13.1	13.5	12.3	11.3	10.7	9.9	10.2	8.7	8.4
Tenth grade	13.2	13.1	14.9	15.1	17.4	17.7	17.0	16.0	15.7	15.7	16.0	14.9	13.1
Twelfth grade	15.4	13.9	15.1	15.7	15.3	15.3	16.5	16.4	16.3	15.6	16.2	16.8	14.4
Methamphetamine													
Eighth grade[g]	NA	NA	NA	NA	NA	NA	NA	NA	4.5	4.2	4.4	3.5	3.9
Tenth grade[g]	NA	NA	NA	NA	NA	NA	NA	NA	7.3	6.9	6.4	6.1	5.2
Twelfth grade[h]	NA	NA	NA	NA	NA	NA	NA	NA	8.2	7.9	6.9	6.7	6.2
Used in last 12 months													
Marijuana/hashish													
Eighth grade	6.2	7.2	9.2	13.0	15.8	18.3	17.7	16.9	16.5	15.6	15.4	14.6	12.8
Tenth grade	16.5	15.2	19.2	25.2	28.7	33.6	34.8	31.1	32.1	32.2	32.7	30.3	28.2
Twelfth grade	23.9	21.9	26.0	30.7	34.7	35.8	38.5	37.5	37.8	36.5	37.0	36.2	34.9
Inhalants[a]													
Eighth grade	9.0	9.5	11.0	11.7	12.8	12.2	11.8	11.1	10.3	9.4	9.1	7.7	8.7
Tenth grade	7.1	7.5	8.4	9.1	9.6	9.5	8.7	8.0	7.2	7.3	6.6	5.8	5.4
Twelfth grade[b]	6.6	6.2	7.0	7.7	8.0	7.6	6.7	6.2	5.6	5.9	4.5	4.5	3.9
Hallucinogens[a,c]													
Eighth grade	1.9	2.5	2.6	2.7	3.6	4.1	3.7	3.4	2.9	2.8	3.4	2.6	2.6
Tenth grade	4.0	4.3	4.7	5.8	7.2	7.8	7.6	6.9	6.9	6.1	6.2	4.7	4.1
Twelfth grade	5.8	5.9	7.4	7.6	9.3	10.1	9.8	9.0	9.4	8.1	9.1	6.6	5.9
LSD													
Eighth grade	1.7	2.1	2.3	2.4	3.2	3.5	3.2	2.8	2.4	2.4	2.2	1.5	1.3
Tenth grade	3.7	4.0	4.2	5.2	6.5	6.9	6.7	5.9	6.0	5.1	4.1	2.6	1.7
Twelfth grade	5.2	5.6	6.8	6.9	8.4	8.8	8.4	7.6	8.1	6.6	6.6	3.5	1.9
MDMA (ecstasy)													
Eighth grade[d]	NA	NA	NA	NA	NA	2.3	2.3	1.8	1.7	3.1	3.5	2.9	2.1
Tenth grade[d]	NA	NA	NA	NA	NA	4.6	3.9	3.3	4.4	5.4	6.2	4.9	3.0
Twelfth grade[e]	NA	NA	NA	NA	NA	4.6	4.0	3.6	5.6	8.2	9.2	7.4	4.5
Cocaine													
Eighth grade	1.1	1.5	1.7	2.1	2.6	3.0	2.8	3.1	2.7	2.6	2.5	2.3	2.2
Tenth grade	2.2	1.9	2.1	2.8	3.5	4.2	4.7	4.7	4.9	4.4	3.6	4.0	3.3
Twelfth grade	3.5	3.1	3.3	3.6	4.0	4.9	5.5	5.7	6.2	5.0	4.8	5.0	4.8
Amphetamines[f]													
Eighth grade	6.2	6.5	7.2	7.9	8.7	9.1	8.1	7.2	6.9	6.5	6.7	5.5	5.5
Tenth grade	8.2	8.2	9.6	10.2	11.9	12.4	12.1	10.7	10.4	11.1	11.7	10.7	9.0
Twelfth grade	8.2	7.1	8.4	9.4	9.3	9.5	10.2	10.1	10.2	10.5	10.9	11.1	9.9
Methamphetamine													
Eighth grade[g]	NA	NA	NA	NA	NA	NA	NA	NA	3.2	2.5	2.8	2.2	2.5
Tenth grade[g]	NA	NA	NA	NA	NA	NA	NA	NA	4.6	4.0	3.7	3.9	3.3
Twelfth grade[h]	NA	NA	NA	NA	NA	NA	NA	NA	4.7	4.3	3.9	3.6	3.2

See notes at end of table.

Table 3.70

Reported drug use and most recent use among students

By type of drug and grade level, United States, 1991-2003--Continued

Type of drug	1991	1992	1993	1994	1995	1996	1997	1998	1999	2000	2001	2002	2003
Used in last 30 days													
Marijuana/hashish													
Eighth grade	3.2%	3.7%	5.1%	7.8%	9.1%	11.3%	10.2%	9.7%	9.7%	9.1%	9.2%	8.3%	7.5%
Tenth grade	8.7	8.1	10.9	15.8	17.2	20.4	20.5	18.7	19.4	19.7	19.8	17.8	17.0
Twelfth grade	13.8	11.9	15.5	19.0	21.2	21.9	23.7	22.8	23.1	21.6	22.4	21.5	21.2
Inhalants[a]													
Eighth grade	4.4	4.7	5.4	5.6	6.1	5.8	5.6	4.8	5.0	4.5	4.0	3.8	4.1
Tenth grade	2.7	2.7	3.3	3.6	3.5	3.3	3.0	2.9	2.6	2.6	2.4	2.4	2.2
Twelfth grade[b]	2.4	2.3	2.5	2.7	3.2	2.5	2.5	2.3	2.0	2.2	1.7	1.5	1.5
Hallucinogens[a,c]													
Eighth grade	0.8	1.1	1.2	1.3	1.7	1.9	1.8	1.4	1.3	1.2	1.6	1.2	1.2
Tenth grade	1.6	1.8	1.9	2.4	3.3	2.8	3.3	3.2	2.9	2.3	2.1	1.6	1.5
Twelfth grade	2.2	2.1	2.7	3.1	4.4	3.5	3.9	3.8	3.5	2.6	3.3	2.3	1.8
LSD													
Eighth grade	0.6	0.9	1.0	1.1	1.4	1.5	1.5	1.1	1.1	1.0	1.0	0.7	0.6
Tenth grade	1.5	1.6	1.6	2.0	3.0	2.4	2.8	2.7	2.3	1.6	1.5	0.7	0.6
Twelfth grade	1.9	2.0	2.4	2.6	4.0	2.5	3.1	3.2	2.7	1.6	2.3	0.7	0.6
MDMA (ecstasy)													
Eighth grade[d]	NA	NA	NA	NA	NA	1.0	1.0	0.9	0.8	1.4	1.8	1.4	0.7
Tenth grade[d]	NA	NA	NA	NA	NA	1.8	1.3	1.3	1.8	2.6	2.6	1.8	1.1
Twelfth grade[e]	NA	NA	NA	NA	NA	2.0	1.6	1.5	2.5	3.6	2.8	2.4	1.3
Cocaine													
Eighth grade	0.5	0.7	0.7	1.0	1.2	1.3	1.1	1.4	1.3	1.2	1.2	1.1	0.9
Tenth grade	0.7	0.7	0.9	1.2	1.7	1.7	2.0	2.1	1.8	1.8	1.3	1.6	1.3
Twelfth grade	1.4	1.3	1.3	1.5	1.8	2.0	2.3	2.4	2.6	2.1	2.1	2.3	2.1
Amphetamines[f]													
Eighth grade	2.6	3.3	3.6	3.6	4.2	4.6	3.8	3.3	3.4	3.4	3.2	2.8	2.7
Tenth grade	3.3	3.6	4.3	4.5	5.3	5.5	5.1	5.1	5.0	5.4	5.6	5.2	4.3
Twelfth grade	3.2	2.8	3.7	4.0	4.0	4.1	4.8	4.6	4.5	5.0	5.6	5.5	5.0
Methamphetamine													
Eighth grade[g]	NA	NA	NA	NA	NA	NA	NA	NA	1.1	0.8	1.3	1.1	1.2
Tenth grade[g]	NA	NA	NA	NA	NA	NA	NA	NA	1.8	2.0	1.5	1.8	1.4
Twelfth grade[h]	NA	NA	NA	NA	NA	NA	NA	NA	1.7	1.9	1.5	1.7	1.7

Note: See Notes, tables 3.64 and 3.68. Approximate weighted Ns range from 15,100 to 18,600 for the eighth grade surveys, 13,600 to 17,000 for the tenth grade surveys, and 12,800 to 16,300 for the twelfth grade surveys. For survey methodology and definitions of terms, see Appendix 6.

[a] Inhalants are unadjusted for underreporting of amyl and butyl nitrites; hallucinogens are unadjusted for underreporting of PCP.
[b] For twelfth graders, data based on five questionnaire forms in 1991-98; N is five-sixths of N indicated. Beginning in 1999, data are based on three of six questionnaire forms; N is one-half of N indicated.
[c] In 2001, the question text was changed on half of the questionnaire forms. The 2001 data are based on the changed forms only; N is one-half of N indicated. Beginning in 2002, all forms include the revised wording and data are based on all six forms.
[d] Data based on one of two forms in 1996; N is one-half of N indicated. In 1997-2001, data are based on one-third of N indicated due to changes on the questionnaire forms. Beginning in 2002, data are based on two of four forms; N is one-half of N indicated.
[e] For twelfth graders, data based on one questionnaire form in 1996-2001; N is one-sixth of N indicated. Beginning in 2002, data are based on two questionnaire forms; N is one-third of N indicated.
[f] Only drug use that was not under a doctor's orders is included here.
[g] Data based on one of four questionnaire forms; N is one-third of N indicated.
[h] Data based on two of six questionnaire forms; N is one-third of N indicated.

Source: Lloyd D. Johnston et al., *Monitoring the Future National Survey Results on Drug Use, 1975-2003*, Vol. 1, Secondary School Students (Bethesda, MD: U.S. Department of Health and Human Services, 2004), pp. 178-184. Table adapted by SOURCEBOOK staff.

Table 3.71

Reported drug use, alcohol use, and cigarette use in last 12 months among college students

By type of drug, United States, 1988-2003

Question: "On how many occasions, if any, have you used...during the last 12 months?"

Percent who used in last 12 months

Type of drug	1988	1989	1990	1991	1992	1993	1994	1995	1996	1997	1998	1999	2000	2001	2002	2003
Marijuana	34.6%	33.6%	29.4%	26.5%	27.7%	27.9%	29.3%	31.2%	33.1%	31.6%	35.9%	35.2%	34.0%	35.6%	34.7%	33.7%
Inhalants[a]	4.1	3.7	3.9	3.5	3.1	3.8	3.0	3.9	3.6	4.1	3.0	3.2	2.9	2.8	2.0	1.8
Hallucinogens[b]	5.3	5.1	5.4	6.3	6.8	6.0	6.2	8.2	6.9	7.7	7.2	7.8	6.7	7.5	6.3	7.4
LSD	3.6	3.4	4.3	5.1	5.7	5.1	5.2	6.9	5.2	5.0	4.4	5.4	4.3	4.0	2.1	1.4
MDMA (ecstasy)[c]	NA	2.3	2.3	0.9	2.0	0.8	0.5	2.4	2.8	2.4	3.9	5.5	9.1	9.2	6.8	4.4
Cocaine	10.0	8.2	5.6	3.6	3.0	2.7	2.0	3.6	2.9	3.4	4.6	4.6	4.8	4.7	4.8	5.4
Crack[d]	1.4	1.5	0.6	0.5	0.4	0.6	0.5	1.1	0.6	0.4	1.0	0.9	0.9	0.9	0.4	1.3
Heroin	0.2	0.1	0.1	0.1	0.1	0.1	0.1	0.3	0.4	0.3	0.6	0.2	0.5	0.4	0.1	0.2
Other narcotics[e,f]	3.1	3.2	2.9	2.7	2.7	2.5	2.4	3.8	3.1	4.2	4.2	4.3	4.5	5.7	5.9	8.7
Amphetamines[e]	6.2	4.6	4.5	3.9	3.6	4.2	4.2	5.4	4.2	5.7	5.1	5.8	6.6	7.2	7.0	7.1
Crystal methamphetamine[g]	NA	NA	0.1	0.1	0.2	0.7	0.8	1.1	0.4	0.8	1.0	0.5	0.5	0.6	0.8	0.9
Barbiturates[e]	1.1	1.0	1.4	1.2	1.4	1.5	1.2	2.0	2.3	3.0	2.5	3.2	3.7	3.8	3.7	4.1
Tranquilizers[b,e]	3.1	2.6	3.0	2.4	2.9	2.4	1.8	2.9	2.8	3.8	3.9	3.8	4.2	5.1	6.7	6.9
Alcohol[h]	89.6	89.6	89.0	88.3	86.9	85.1	82.7	83.2	83.0	82.4	84.6	83.6	83.2	83.0	82.9	81.7
Cigarettes	36.6	34.2	35.5	35.6	37.3	38.8	37.6	39.3	41.4	43.6	44.3	44.5	41.3	39.0	38.3	35.2

Note: See Note, table 3.64. These data are from a followup survey of respondents 1 to 4 years past high school who are presently enrolled in college. Included are those registered as full-time students in March of the year in question and who report that they are enrolled in a 2- or 4-year college. Those individuals previously in college and those who have already completed college are excluded. The approximate N for each year is as follows: 1988, 1,310; 1989, 1,300; 1990, 1,400; 1991, 1,410; 1992, 1,490; 1993, 1,490; 1994, 1,410; 1995, 1,450; 1996, 1,450; 1997, 1,480; 1998, 1,440; 1999, 1,440; 2000, 1,350; 2001, 1,340; 2002, 1,260; 2003, 1,270. Readers interested in responses to this question for 1980 through 1987 should consult previous editions of SOURCEBOOK. Some data have been revised by the Source and may differ from previous editions of SOURCEBOOK.

Since 1982, new questions were introduced on the use of controlled and non-controlled stimulants in order to exclude over-the-counter amphetamines, which were believed to have been inflating the statistic for earlier years. Figures presented for "stimulants" are based on the data obtained from these new questions. For survey methodology and definitions of terms, see Appendix 6.

[a]This drug was asked about in four of the five questionnaire forms in 1988 and 1989, in five of the six questionnaire forms in 1990-98, and in three of the six questionnaire forms beginning in 1999.

[b]In 2001, the question text was changed on half of the questionnaire forms. The 2001 data are based on the changed forms only. Beginning in 2002, all forms include the revised wording.

[c]This drug was asked about in two of the five questionnaire forms in 1989, in two of the six questionnaire forms in 1990-2001, and in three of the six questionnaire forms beginning in 2002.

[d]This drug was asked about in two of the five questionnaire forms in 1988 and 1989, in all six questionnaire forms in 1990-2001, and in five of the six questionnaire forms beginning in 2002.

[e]Only drug use that was not under a doctor's orders is included here.

[f]In 2002, the question text was changed on half of the questionnaire forms. The list of examples of narcotics other than heroin was updated by replacing "Talwin," "laudanum," and "paregoric" with "Vicodin," "OxyContin," and "Percocet." The 2002 data are based on the changed forms only; N is one-half of N indicated. Beginning in 2003, all forms include the revised wording and data are based on all six forms.

[g]This drug was asked about in two of the six questionnaire forms.

[h]In 1993 and 1994, the question was changed slightly in half of the questionnaire forms to indicate that a "drink" meant "more than a few sips." Data for 1993 and 1994 are from the revised and unrevised forms combined. Beginning in 1995, all forms include the revised wording.

Source: Lloyd D. Johnston et al., *Monitoring the Future National Survey Results on Drug Use, 1975-2003*, Vol. 2, College Students and Adults Ages 19-45 (Bethesda, MD: U.S. Department of Health and Human Services, 2004), p. 237. Table adapted by SOURCEBOOK staff.

Table 3.72

Reported drug use, alcohol use, and cigarette use in last 30 days among college students

By type of drug, United States, 1988-2003

Question: "On how many occasions, if any, have you used...during the last 30 days?"

Type of drug	1988	1989	1990	1991	1992	1993	1994	1995	1996	1997	1998	1999	2000	2001	2002	2003
Marijuana	16.8%	16.3%	14.0%	14.1%	14.6%	14.2%	15.1%	18.6%	17.5%	17.7%	18.6%	20.7%	20.0%	20.2%	19.7%	19.3%
Inhalants[a]	1.3	0.8	1.0	0.9	1.1	1.3	0.6	1.6	0.8	0.7	0.6	1.5	0.9	0.4	0.7	0.4
Hallucinogens[b]	1.7	2.3	1.4	1.2	2.3	2.5	2.1	3.3	1.9	2.1	2.1	2.0	1.4	1.8	1.2	1.8
LSD	1.1	1.4	1.1	0.8	1.8	1.6	1.8	2.5	0.9	1.1	1.5	1.2	0.9	1.0	0.2	0.2
MDMA (ecstasy)[c]	NA	0.3	0.6	0.2	0.4	0.3	0.2	0.7	0.7	0.8	0.8	2.1	2.5	1.5	0.7	1.0
Cocaine	4.2	2.8	1.2	1.0	1.0	0.7	0.6	0.7	0.8	1.6	1.6	1.2	1.4	1.9	1.6	1.9
Crack[d]	0.5	0.2	0.1	0.3	0.1	0.1	0.1	0.1	0.1	0.2	0.2	0.3	0.3	0.1	0.3	0.4
Heroin	0.1	0.1	0.0	0.1	0.0	(e)	0.0	0.1	(e)	0.2	0.1	0.1	0.2	0.1	0.0	(e)
Other narcotics[f,g]	0.8	0.7	0.5	0.6	1.0	0.7	0.4	1.2	0.7	1.3	1.1	1.0	1.7	1.7	1.6	2.3
Amphetamines[f]	1.8	1.3	1.4	1.0	1.1	1.5	1.5	2.2	0.9	2.1	1.7	2.3	2.9	3.3	3.0	3.1
Crystal methamphetamine[h]	NA	NA	0.0	0.0	0.0	0.3	0.5	0.3	0.1	0.2	0.3	0.0	0.0	0.1	0.0	0.3
Barbiturates[f]	0.5	0.2	0.2	0.3	0.7	0.4	0.4	0.5	0.8	1.2	1.1	1.1	1.1	1.5	1.7	1.7
Tranquilizers[b,f]	1.1	0.8	0.5	0.6	0.6	0.4	0.4	0.5	0.7	1.2	1.3	1.1	2.0	1.5	3.0	2.8
Alcohol[i]	77.0	76.2	74.5	74.7	71.4	70.1	67.8	67.5	67.0	65.8	68.1	69.9	67.4	67.0	68.9	66.2
Cigarettes	22.6	21.1	21.5	23.2	23.5	24.5	23.5	26.8	27.9	28.3	30.0	30.6	28.2	25.7	26.7	22.5

Note: See Notes, tables 3.64 and 3.71. Readers interested in responses to this question for 1980 through 1987 should consult previous editions of SOURCEBOOK. Some data have been revised by the Source and may differ from previous editions of SOURCEBOOK. For survey methodology and definitions of terms, see Appendix 6.

[a]This drug was asked about in four of the five questionnaire forms in 1988 and 1989, in five of the six questionnaire forms in 1990-98, and in three of the six questionnaire forms beginning in 1999.
[b]In 2001, the question text was changed on half of the questionnaire forms. The 2001 data are based on the changed forms only. Beginning in 2002, all forms include the revised wording.
[c]This drug was asked about in two of the five questionnaire forms in 1989, in two of the six questionnaire forms in 1990-2001, and in three of the six questionnaire forms beginning in 2002.
[d]This drug was asked about in two of the five questionnaire forms in 1988 and 1989, in all six forms in 1990-2001, and in five of the six questionnaire forms beginning in 2002.
[e]Less than 0.05%.
[f]Only drug use that was not under a doctor's orders is included here.
[g]In 2002, the question text was changed on half of the questionnaire forms. The list of examples of narcotics other than heroin was updated by replacing "Talwin," "laudanum," and "paregoric" with "Vicodin," "OxyContin," and "Percocet." The 2002 data are based on the changed forms only; N is one-half of N indicated. Beginning in 2003, all forms include the revised wording and data are based on all six forms.
[h]This drug was asked about in two of the six questionnaire forms.
[i]In 1993 and 1994, the question was changed slightly in half of the questionnaire forms to indicate that a "drink" meant "more than a few sips." Data for 1993 and 1994 are from the revised and unrevised forms combined. Beginning in 1995, all forms include the revised wording.

Source: Lloyd D. Johnston et al., *Monitoring the Future National Survey Results on Drug Use, 1975-2003*, Vol. 2, College Students and Adults Ages 19-45 (Bethesda, MD: U.S. Department of Health and Human Services, 2004), p. 238. Table adapted by SOURCEBOOK staff.

Table 3.73

Reported daily use in last 30 days of drugs, alcohol, and cigarettes among college students

By type of drug, United States, 1988-2003

Type of drug	1988	1989	1990	1991	1992	1993	1994	1995	1996	1997	1998	1999	2000	2001	2002	2003
Marijuana	1.8%	2.6%	1.7%	1.8%	1.6%	1.9%	1.8%	3.7%	2.8%	3.7%	4.0%	4.0%	4.6%	4.5%	4.1%	4.7%
Cocaine	0.1	(a)	0.0	(a)	0.0	0.0	0.1	0.0	0.0	0.0	0.0	0.0	0.0	0.0	0.0	(a)
Amphetamines[b]	(a)	(a)	0.0	0.1	0.0	0.1	0.1	0.1	(a)	0.2	0.1	0.1	0.1	0.2	0.1	0.3
Alcohol																
Daily[c]	4.9	4.0	3.8	4.1	3.7	3.9	3.7	3.0	3.2	4.5	3.9	4.5	3.6	4.7	5.0	4.3
5 or more drinks in a row in last 2 weeks	43.2	41.7	41.0	42.8	41.4	40.2	40.2	38.6	38.3	40.7	38.9	40.0	39.3	40.9	40.1	38.5
Cigarettes																
Daily	12.4	12.2	12.1	13.8	14.1	15.2	13.2	15.8	15.9	15.2	18.0	19.3	17.8	15.0	15.9	13.8
Half-pack or more per day	7.3	6.7	8.2	8.0	8.9	8.9	8.0	10.2	8.5	9.1	11.3	11.0	10.1	7.8	7.9	7.6

Note: See Notes, tables 3.64 and 3.71. Readers interested in responses to this question for 1980 through 1987 should consult previous editions of SOURCEBOOK. Some data have been revised by the Source and may differ from previous editions of SOURCEBOOK. For survey methodology and definitions of terms, see Appendix 6.

[a]Less than 0.05%.
[b]Only drug use that was not under a doctor's orders is included here.
[c]In 1993 and 1994, the question was changed slightly in half of the questionnaire forms to indicate that a "drink" meant "more than a few sips." Data for 1993 and 1994 are from the revised and unrevised forms combined. Beginning in 1995, all forms include the revised wording.

Source: Lloyd D. Johnston et al., *Monitoring the Future National Survey Results on Drug Use, 1975-2003*, Vol. 2, College Students and Adults Ages 19-45 (Bethesda, MD: U.S. Department of Health and Human Services, 2004), p. 239. Table adapted by SOURCEBOOK staff.

Table 3.74

Reported drug use, alcohol use, and cigarette use in last 12 months among young adults

By type of drug, United States, 1988-2003

Question: "On how many occasions, if any, have you used...during the last 12 months?"

Type of drug	\multicolumn{16}{c}{Percent who used in last 12 months}
	1988	1989	1990	1991	1992	1993	1994	1995	1996	1997	1998	1999	2000	2001	2002	2003
Marijuana	31.8%	29.0%	26.1%	23.8%	25.2%	25.1%	25.5%	26.5%	27.0%	26.8%	27.4%	27.6%	27.9%	29.2%	29.3%	29.0%
Inhalants[a]	1.8	1.9	1.9	2.0	1.9	2.1	2.1	2.4	2.2	2.3	2.1	2.3	2.1	1.7	1.6	1.4
Hallucinogens[b]	3.9	3.6	4.1	4.5	5.0	4.5	4.8	5.6	5.6	5.8	5.2	5.4	5.4	5.4	4.7	5.2
Adjusted[c]	3.9	NA	4.2	4.6	5.1	4.6	4.9	5.7	5.6	5.9	5.2	5.5	5.5	5.5	4.7	5.2
LSD	2.9	2.7	3.3	3.8	4.3	3.8	4.0	4.6	4.5	4.4	3.5	4.0	3.7	3.4	1.8	1.2
PCP[d]	0.4	NA	0.2	0.3	0.3	0.2	0.3	0.3	0.2	0.5	0.6	0.6	0.3	0.5	0.3	0.3
MDMA (ecstasy)[e]	NA	1.4	1.5	0.8	1.0	0.8	0.7	1.6	1.7	2.1	2.9	3.6	7.2	7.5	6.2	4.5
Cocaine	13.8	10.8	8.6	6.2	5.7	4.7	4.3	4.4	4.1	4.6	4.9	5.4	5.4	5.8	5.8	6.6
Crack[f]	3.1	2.5	1.6	1.2	1.4	1.3	1.1	1.1	1.1	1.0	1.1	1.4	1.2	1.3	1.0	1.0
Other cocaine[g]	11.9	10.3	8.1	5.4	5.1	3.9	3.6	3.9	3.8	4.3	4.5	4.8	4.8	5.3	5.6	6.1
Heroin	0.2	0.2	0.1	0.1	0.2	0.2	0.1	0.4	0.4	0.3	0.4	0.4	0.4	0.5	0.2	0.4
Other narcotics[h,i]	2.7	2.8	2.7	2.5	2.5	2.2	2.5	3.0	2.9	3.3	3.4	3.8	4.1	5.0	7.1	8.5
Amphetamines[h]	7.3	5.8	5.2	4.3	4.1	4.0	4.5	4.6	4.2	4.6	4.5	4.7	5.4	5.8	5.9	5.8
Crystal methamphetamine[j]	NA	NA	0.4	0.3	0.4	0.8	0.9	1.2	0.9	0.9	1.1	0.9	1.2	1.1	1.4	1.3
Barbiturates[h]	1.8	1.7	1.9	1.8	1.6	1.9	1.8	2.1	2.2	2.4	2.5	2.8	3.4	3.7	3.9	3.9
Tranquilizers[b,h]	4.2	3.7	3.7	3.5	3.4	3.1	2.9	3.4	3.2	3.1	3.8	3.7	4.6	5.5	7.0	6.8
Alcohol[k]	88.6	88.1	87.4	86.9	86.2	85.3	83.7	84.7	84.0	84.3	84.0	84.1	84.0	84.3	84.9	83.3
Steroids[l]	NA	0.5	0.3	0.5	0.4	0.3	0.4	0.5	0.3	0.5	0.4	0.6	0.4	0.4	0.4	0.5
Cigarettes	37.7	38.0	37.1	37.7	37.9	37.8	38.3	38.8	40.3	41.8	41.6	41.1	40.9	41.1	39.1	38.6

Note: See Notes, tables 3.64 and 3.71. "Young adults" includes high school graduates 1 to 10 years beyond high school. These data present the prevalence for young adults combined. The approximate N for each year is as follows: 1988, 6,700; 1989, 6,600; 1990, 6,700; 1991, 6,600; 1992, 6,800; 1993, 6,700; 1994, 6,500; 1995, 6,400; 1996, 6,300; 1997, 6,400; 1998, 6,200; 1999, 6,000; 2000, 5,700; 2001, 5,800; 2002, 5,300; 2003, 5,300. Readers interested in responses to this question for 1986 and 1987 should consult previous editions of SOURCEBOOK. Some data have been revised by the Source and may differ from previous editions of SOURCEBOOK. For survey methodology and definitions of terms, see Appendix 6.

[a]This drug was asked about in four of the five questionnaire forms in 1988 and 1989, in five of the six questionnaire forms in 1990-98, and in three of the six questionnaire forms beginning in 1999.
[b]In 2001, the question text was changed on half of the questionnaire forms. The 2001 data are based on the changed forms only. Beginning in 2002, all forms include the revised wording.
[c]Adjusted for underreporting of PCP.
[d]This drug was asked about in one of the five questionnaire forms in 1988, and in one of the six questionnaire forms beginning in 1990.
[e]This drug was asked about in two of the six questionnaire forms in 1990-2001, and in three of the six questionnaire forms beginning in 2002.
[f]This drug was asked about in two of the five questionnaire forms in 1988 and 1989, in all six questionnaire forms in 1990-2001, and in five of the six questionnaire forms beginning in 2002.
[g]This drug was asked about in one of the five questionnaire forms in 1988 and 1989, and in four of the six questionnaire forms beginning in 1990.
[h]Only drug use that was not under a doctor's orders is included here.
[i]In 2002, the question text was changed on half of the questionnaire forms. The list of examples of narcotics other than heroin was updated by replacing "Talwin," "laudanum," and "paregoric" with "Vicodin," "OxyContin," and "Percocet." The 2002 data are based on the changed forms only; N is one-half of N indicated. Beginning in 2003, all forms include the revised wording and data are based on all six forms.
[j]This drug was asked about in two of the six questionnaire forms.
[k]In 1993 and 1994, the question was changed slightly in half of the questionnaire forms to indicate that a "drink" meant "more than a few sips." Data for 1993 and 1994 are from the revised and unrevised forms combined. Beginning in 1995, all forms include the revised wording.
[l]This drug was asked about in one of the five questionnaire forms in 1989, and two of the six questionnaire forms beginning in 1990.

Source: Lloyd D. Johnston et al., *Monitoring the Future National Survey Results on Drug Use, 1975-2003*, Vol. 2, College Students and Adults Ages 19-45 (Bethesda, MD: U.S. Department of Health and Human Services, 2004), p. 134. Table adapted by SOURCEBOOK staff.

Table 3.75

Reported drug use, alcohol use, and cigarette use in last 30 days among young adults

By type of drug, United States, 1988-2003

Question: "On how many occasions, if any, have you used...during the last 30 days?"

Percent who used in last 30 days

Type of drug	1988	1989	1990	1991	1992	1993	1994	1995	1996	1997	1998	1999	2000	2001	2002	2003
Marijuana	17.9%	15.5%	13.9%	13.5%	13.3%	13.4%	14.1%	14.0%	15.1%	15.0%	14.9%	15.6%	16.1%	16.7%	16.9%	17.3%
Inhalants[a]	0.6	0.5	0.6	0.5	0.6	0.7	0.5	0.7	0.5	0.5	0.7	0.8	0.5	0.4	0.5	0.3
Hallucinogens[b]	1.1	1.1	0.9	1.1	1.5	1.2	1.4	1.7	1.2	1.5	1.4	1.3	1.2	1.2	0.9	1.2
Adjusted[c]	1.1	NA	1.0	1.2	1.6	1.2	1.4	1.7	1.3	1.5	1.5	1.3	1.2	1.2	0.9	1.2
LSD	0.8	0.8	0.6	0.8	1.1	0.8	1.1	1.3	0.7	0.9	1.0	0.8	0.8	0.7	0.3	0.2
PCP[d]	0.3	NA	0.2	0.1	0.2	0.2	0.1	0.0	0.1	0.1	0.2	0.2	0.0	0.0	0.1	0.1
MDMA (ecstasy)[e]	NA	0.4	0.2	0.1	0.3	0.3	0.2	0.4	0.3	0.6	0.8	1.3	1.9	1.8	1.3	0.8
Cocaine	5.7	3.8	2.4	2.0	1.8	1.4	1.3	1.5	1.2	1.5	1.7	1.9	1.7	2.2	2.2	2.4
Crack[f]	1.2	0.7	0.4	0.4	0.4	0.4	0.3	0.2	0.3	0.3	0.3	0.4	0.4	0.4	0.3	0.3
Other cocaine[g]	4.8	3.4	2.1	1.8	1.7	1.1	1.0	1.3	1.1	1.5	1.5	1.6	1.5	1.8	2.0	2.1
Heroin	0.1	0.1	0.1	(h)	0.1	0.1	0.1	0.1	0.1	0.1	0.1	0.1	0.1	0.1	0.3	(h)	0.1
Other narcotics[i,j]	0.7	0.7	0.7	0.6	0.7	0.7	0.6	0.9	0.7	0.9	0.9	1.2	1.4	1.7	2.9	2.9
Amphetamines[i]	2.7	2.1	1.9	1.5	1.5	1.5	1.7	1.7	1.5	1.7	1.7	1.9	2.3	2.4	2.5	2.5
Crystal methamphetamine[k]	NA	NA	0.1	(h)	0.1	0.3	0.5	0.3	0.3	0.3	0.3	0.4	0.4	0.4	0.5	0.4
Barbiturates[i]	0.7	0.5	0.6	0.5	0.5	0.6	0.6	0.8	0.8	0.9	0.9	1.1	1.3	1.7	1.5	1.5
Tranquilizers[b,i]	1.4	1.2	1.1	0.9	1.0	1.0	0.8	1.1	0.7	1.1	1.2	1.3	1.8	2.1	2.8	2.4
Alcohol[l]	74.0	72.4	71.2	70.6	69.0	68.3	67.7	68.1	66.7	67.5	66.9	68.2	66.8	67.2	68.3	67.0
Steroids[m]	NA	0.2	0.1	0.2	0.1	0.0	0.1	0.2	0.2	0.2	0.2	0.3	0.1	0.1	0.1	0.2
Cigarettes	28.9	28.6	27.7	28.2	28.3	28.0	28.0	29.2	30.1	29.9	30.9	30.3	30.1	30.2	29.2	28.4

Note: See Notes, tables 3.64, 3.71, and 3.74. Readers interested in responses to this question for 1986 and 1987 should consult previous editions of SOURCEBOOK. Some data have been revised by the Source and may differ from previous editions of SOURCEBOOK. For survey methodology and definitions of terms, see Appendix 6.

[a]This drug was asked about in four of the five questionnaire forms in 1988 and 1989, in five of the six questionnaire forms in 1990-98, and in three of the six questionnaire forms beginning in 1999.
[b]In 2001, the question text was changed on half of the questionnaire forms. The 2001 data are based on the changed forms only. Beginning in 2002, all forms include the revised wording.
[c]Adjusted for underreporting of PCP.
[d]This drug was asked about in one of the five questionnaire forms in 1988, and in one of the six questionnaire forms beginning in 1990.
[e]This drug was asked about in two of the six questionnaire forms in 1990-2001, and in three of the six questionnaire forms beginning in 2002.
[f]This drug was asked about in two of the five questionnaire forms in 1988 and 1989, in all six questionnaire forms in 1990-2001, and in five of the six questionnaire forms beginning in 2002.

[g]This drug was asked about in one of the five questionnaire forms in 1988 and 1989, and in four of the six questionnaire forms beginning in 1990.
[h]Less than 0.05%.
[i]Only drug use that was not under a doctor's orders is included here.
[j]In 2002, the question text was changed on half of the questionnaire forms. The list of examples of narcotics other than heroin was updated by replacing "Talwin," "laudanum," and "paregoric" with "Vicodin," "OxyContin," and "Percocet." The 2002 data are based on the changed forms only; N is one-half of N indicated. Beginning in 2003, all forms include the revised wording and data are based on all six forms.
[k]This drug was asked about in two of the six questionnaire forms.
[l]In 1993 and 1994, the question was changed slightly in half of the questionnaire forms to indicate that a "drink" meant "more than a few sips." Data for 1993 and 1994 are from the revised and unrevised forms combined. Beginning in 1995, all forms include the revised wording.
[m]This drug was asked about in one of the five questionnaire forms in 1989, and in two of the six questionnaire forms beginning in 1990.

Source: Lloyd D. Johnston et al., *Monitoring the Future National Survey Results on Drug Use, 1975-2003*, Vol. 2, College Students and Adults Ages 19-45 (Bethesda, MD: U.S. Department of Health and Human Services, 2004), p. 135. Table adapted by SOURCEBOOK staff.

Table 3.76

Reported daily use within last 30 days of drugs, alcohol, and cigarettes among young adults

By type of drug, United States, 1988-2003

	Percent using daily in last 30 days															
Type of drug	1988	1989	1990	1991	1992	1993	1994	1995	1996	1997	1998	1999	2000	2001	2002	2003
Marijuana	3.3%	3.2%	2.5%	2.3%	2.3%	2.4%	2.8%	3.3%	3.3%	3.8%	3.7%	4.4%	4.2%	5.0%	4.5%	5.3%
Cocaine	0.2	0.1	(a)	0.1	(a)	0.1	(a)	0.1	(a)	(a)	(a)	0.1	(a)	0.1	(a)	(a)
Amphetamines[b]	0.1	0.1	0.1	0.1	0.1	0.1	0.1	0.2	0.1	0.1	0.1	0.2	0.1	0.2	0.2	0.3
Alcohol																
Daily[c]	6.1	5.5	4.7	4.9	4.5	4.5	3.9	3.9	4.0	4.6	4.0	4.8	4.1	4.4	4.7	5.1
5 or more drinks in a row in last 2 weeks	35.2	34.8	34.3	34.7	34.2	34.4	33.7	32.6	33.6	34.4	34.1	35.8	34.7	35.9	35.9	35.8
Cigarettes																
Daily	22.7	22.4	21.3	21.7	20.9	20.8	20.7	21.2	21.8	20.6	21.9	21.5	21.8	21.2	21.2	20.3
Half-pack or more per day	17.7	17.3	16.7	16.0	15.7	15.5	15.3	15.7	15.3	14.6	15.6	15.1	15.1	14.6	14.2	13.9

Note: See Notes, tables 3.64, 3.71, and 3.74. For drugs not included in this table, daily use was below 0.2% in all years. Readers interested in responses to this question for 1986 and 1987 should consult previous editions of SOURCEBOOK. Some data have been revised by the Source and may differ from previous editions of SOURCEBOOK. For survey methodology and definitions of terms, see Appendix 6.

[a]Less than 0.05%.
[b]Only drug use that was not under a doctor's orders is included here.

[c]In 1993 and 1994, the question was changed slightly in half of the questionnaire forms to indicate that a "drink" meant "more than a few sips." Data for 1993 and 1994 are from the revised and unrevised forms combined. Beginning in 1995, all forms include the revised wording.

Source: Lloyd D. Johnston, et al., *Monitoring the Future National Survey Results on Drug Use, 1975-2003*, Vol. 2, College Students and Adults Ages 19-45 (Bethesda, MD: U.S. Department of Health and Human Services, 2004), p. 136. Table adapted by SOURCEBOOK staff.

Table 3.77

Reported drinking behaviors among college students

By sex, United States, 1993, 1997, 1999, and 2001[a]

(Percent reporting the behavior)

Drinking behavior	1993 (N=15,282)	1997 (N=14,428)	1999 (N=13,954)	2001 (N=10,904)
Abstainer[b]	16.4%	19.6%	19.8%	19.3%
Male	15.7	18.9	20.5	20.1
Female	17.0	20.3	19.2	18.7
Drank in past year	83.6	80.3	79.8	80.7
Male	84.2	81.0	79.0	79.9
Female	82.9	79.7	80.5	81.3
Nonbinge drinking[c]	39.7	37.2	35.7	36.3
Male	35.1	32.6	29.4	31.3
Female	44.0	41.4	41.4	40.4
Binge drinking[d]	43.9	43.2	44.5	44.4
Male	49.2	48.5	50.2	48.6
Female	39.0	38.4	39.4	40.9
Occasional binge drinking[e]	24.3	22.2	21.9	21.6
Male	26.8	25.3	24.9	23.4
Female	21.9	19.4	19.2	20.0
Frequent binge drinking[f]	19.7	21.0	22.6	22.8
Male	22.4	23.2	25.3	25.2
Female	17.1	18.9	20.3	20.9

Note: These data are from the 1993, 1997, 1999, and 2001 College Alcohol Studies, conducted by the Harvard School of Public Health. The colleges and universities in the study were selected from the American Council on Education's list of accredited 4-year colleges and universities, using probability sampling proportionate to the size of the institution. This resulted in the inclusion of a cross-section of institutions in terms of type, size, and location. Random samples of full-time undergraduate students were provided from each college participating in the study. In each of the study years, students were mailed questionnaires asking about their drinking behaviors in the previous year, month, and 2-week period before completion of the questionnaire. The data presented are from 119 colleges that participated in all four surveys. The inclusion criteria for data analysis differed from previous survey years, i.e., six schools were reintroduced that had participated in earlier surveys but had been excluded from previous analyses. Therefore, data presented for 1993, 1997, and 1999 have been revised by the Source and may differ from previous editions of SOURCEBOOK.

[a]Subcategories may not add to total because of rounding.
[b]Students who did not consume alcohol in the past year.
[c]Students who consumed alcohol in the past year but did not binge in the previous 2-week period.
[d]Students who consumed five or more drinks in a row for men and four or more in a row for women, on one or more occasions during the 2 weeks prior to the survey.
[e]Students who binged one or two times in the previous 2-week period.
[f]Students who binged three or more times in the previous 2-week period.

Source: Henry Wechsler et al., "Trends in College Binge Drinking During a Period of Increased Prevention Efforts," *Journal of American College Health*, Vol. 50 (March 2002), p. 207, Table 2 [Online]. Available: http://www.hsph.harvard.edu/cas/Documents/trends/Trends.pdf [Dec. 14, 2004]. Table adapted by SOURCEBOOK staff.

Table 3.78

Prevalence of binge drinking among college students

By selected characteristics, United States, 1993, 1997, 1999, and 2001

Characteristics	1993	1997	1999	2001
All students	43.9%	43.2%	44.5%	44.4%
Sex				
Male	49.2	48.5	50.2	48.6
Female	39.0	38.4	39.4	40.9
Race, ethnicity				
White	49.5	48.2	50.1	50.2
Black	16.7	18.5	17.5	21.7
Asian/Pacific Islander	23.1	24.4	23.3	26.2
Native American Indian/other	39.3	37.9	42.6	33.6
Hispanic	39.7	37.7	41.0	34.4
Non-Hispanic	44.3	43.7	44.8	45.2
Age				
20 years or younger	45.5	44.6	44.9	43.6
21 to 23 years	48.1	47.5	50.3	50.2
24 years or older	28.5	28.8	29.1	30.9
Year in school				
Freshman	42.9	42.8	42.0	42.4
Sophomore	45.4	44.6	44.9	42.8
Junior	44.4	44.8	46.3	45.9
Senior	42.8	41.7	45.6	44.9
Living arrangement				
Non-substance-free residence hall	46.7	45.8	44.5	45.3
Substance-free residence hall	34.7	32.5	32.1	35.3
Fraternity/sorority house	83.4	82.6	80.3	75.4
Off campus, alone or with a roommate	54.1	53.5	56.2	54.5
Off campus with a spouse	18.5	20.8	22.9	26.5
Off campus with parents	29.7	28.3	29.8	30.1
Fraternity/sorority member	67.4	67.4	65.2	64.3

Note: See Note, table 3.77. Some data have been revised by the Source and may differ from previous editions of SOURCEBOOK.

Source: Henry Wechsler et al., "Trends in College Binge Drinking During a Period of Increased Prevention Efforts," *Journal of American College Health*, Vol. 50 (March 2002), p. 207, Table 2 and p. 208 [Online]. Available: http://www.hsph.harvard.edu/cas/Documents/trends/Trends.pdf [Dec. 14, 2004]. Table adapted by SOURCEBOOK staff.

Table 3.79

Drinking behaviors among college students reporting alcohol consumption in past year

By sex, United States, 1993, 1997, 1999, and 2001

(Percent reporting the behavior in the past year)

Drinking behavior	Total 1993	Total 1997	Total 1999	Total 2001	Male 1993	Male 1997	Male 1999	Male 2001	Female 1993	Female 1997	Female 1999	Female 2001
Drank on 10 or more occasions in the past 30 days	18.1%	21.1%	23.1%	22.6%	23.9%	27.2%	30.1%	29.2%	12.3%	15.1%	16.4%	16.8%
Was drunk three or more times in the past month	23.4	29.0	30.2	29.4	28.0	33.6	35.8	34.9	18.9	24.4	25.0	24.6
Drinks to get drunk[a]	39.9	53.5	47.7	48.2	44.4	59.1	53.8	55.2	35.6	48.4	42.4	42.4

Note: See Note, table 3.77. This table includes only those students who reported drinking alcohol in the past year. Some data have been revised by the Source and may differ from previous editions of SOURCEBOOK.

[a]Students reporting that getting drunk is an important reason for drinking.

Source: Henry Wechsler et al., "Trends in College Binge Drinking During a Period of Increased Prevention Efforts," *Journal of American College Health*, Vol. 50 (March 2002), p. 209, Table 4 [Online]. Available: http://www.hsph.harvard.edu/cas/Documents/trends/Trends.pdf [Dec. 14, 2004]. Table adapted by SOURCEBOOK staff.

Table 3.80

Alcohol-related problems among college students

United States, 1993, 1997, 1999, and 2001

Problem	1993	1997	1999	2001
Missed a class	26.9%	31.1%	29.9%	29.5%
Got behind in school work	20.5	24.1	24.1	21.6
Did something you regret	32.1	37.0	36.1	35.0
Forgot where you were or what you did	24.7	27.4	27.1	26.8
Argued with friends	19.6	24.0	22.5	22.9
Engaged in unplanned sexual activities	19.2	23.3	21.6	21.3
Did not use protection when you had sex	9.8	11.2	10.3	10.4
Damaged property	9.3	11.7	10.8	10.7
Got into trouble with campus or local police	4.6	6.4	5.8	6.5
Got hurt or injured	9.3	12.0	12.4	12.8
Required medical treatment for an overdose	0.5	0.6	0.6	0.8
Drove after drinking alcohol	26.6	29.5	28.8	29.0
Had five or more different alcohol-related problems	16.6	20.8	19.9	20.3

Note: See Note, table 3.77. This table includes only those students who reported drinking alcohol in the past year and reported having the problem one or more times since the beginning of the school year. Some data have been revised by the Source and may differ from previous editions of SOURCEBOOK.

Source: Henry Wechsler et al., "Trends in College Binge Drinking During a Period of Increased Prevention Efforts," *Journal of American College Health*, Vol. 50 (March 2002), p. 210 [Online]. Available: http://www.hsph.harvard.edu/cas/Documents/trends/Trends.pdf [Dec. 14, 2004]. Table adapted by SOURCEBOOK staff.

Table 3.81

Binge drinking among underage and legal age college students

By living arrangement, United States, 2001

Living arrangement	Total	Underage (N=4,231)	Legal age (N=4,547)
Off campus with parents	29.9%	24.9%	35.7%
Substance-free residence hall	35.5	35.8	33.8
Off campus without parents	53.9	49.6	56.2
Non-substance-free residence hall	49.9	50.7	47.1
Fraternity/sorority house	76.0	69.9	83.4
Controlled living arrangement[a]	32.0	30.3	35.4
Uncontrolled living arrangement[b]	53.1	51.1	55.5

Note: See Note, table 3.77. These data are limited to students participating in the 2001 College Alcohol Study who were 23 years of age and younger. "Underage" students are those under 21 years of age; "legal age" students are those 21 to 23 years of age. "Binge drinking" is the consumption of five or more drinks in a row for men and four or more drinks in a row for women, on one or more occasions during the 2 weeks prior to the survey.

[a]Includes substance-free residence hall and off campus with parents.
[b]Includes non-substance-free residence hall, off campus without parents, and fraternity/sorority house.

Source: Henry Wechsler et al., "Underage College Students' Drinking Behavior, Access to Alcohol, and the Influence of Deterrence Policies," *Journal of American College Health*, Vol. 50 (March 2002), p. 227 [Online]. Available: http://www.hsph.harvard.edu/cas/Documents/underminimum/DrinkingBehavior.pdf [Dec. 14, 2004]. Table adapted by SOURCEBOOK staff.

Table 3.82

Alcohol-related effects experienced by underage college students

By living arrangement, United States, 2001

	Living arrangement				
Effect experienced	Off campus with parents	Substance-free residence	Off campus without parents	Non-substance-free residence hall	Fraternity/ sorority house
Been insulted/humiliated	17.9%	31.0%	32.4%	36.4%	45.0%
Had a serious argument/quarrel	18.7	24.6	29.9	27.8	46.9
Been pushed, hit/assaulted	8.2	13.1	13.1	14.8	20.5
Had property damaged	8.0	15.2	23.0	19.1	28.3
Had to take care of drunken student	34.7	55.9	60.1	64.6	83.7
Had studying/sleeping interrupted	16.3	55.9	50.1	62.4	77.0
Experienced unwanted sexual advance	15.0	25.1	30.6	29.9	34.5
Been victim of sexual assault or date rape[a]	0.8	2.1	1.4	2.5	6.8
Experienced at least one of the above problems	48.3	78.1	77.3	86.5	98.0

Note: See Notes, tables 3.77 and 3.81.

[a]Female respondents only.

Source: Henry Wechsler et al., "Underage College Students' Drinking Behavior, Access to Alcohol, and the Influence of Deterrence Policies," *Journal of American College Health*, Vol. 50 (March 2002), p. 228 [Online]. Available: http://www.hsph.harvard.edu/cas/Documents/underminimum/DrinkingBehavior.pdf [Dec. 14, 2004]. Table adapted by SOURCEBOOK staff.

Table 3.83

College students and underage college students reporting alcohol use

By frequency of use, United States, 1998-2002

	College students' alcohol use			Underage college students' alcohol use	
	In past year	In past 30 days	Binge drinking[a]	In past year	In past 30 days
1998	85.2%	73.1%	45.6%	83.3%	70.4%
1999	85.1	73.2	46.8	83.4	70.7
2000	84.1	72.1	46.5	82.2	69.1
2001	85.3	74.4	49.7	83.6	71.8
2002	85.2	73.4	47.7	82.2	70.3

Note: These data are from the Core Alcohol and Drug Survey, a series of surveys of college students conducted by the Core Institute, Southern Illinois University at Carbondale. These data are from samples of 2- and 4-year colleges and universities in the United States. The 1998 survey included 30,965 students from 64 colleges; the 1999 survey, 65,033 students from 157 colleges; the 2000 survey, 55,026 students from 132 colleges; the 2001 survey, 54,444 students from 131 colleges; and the 2002 survey, 54,367 students from 125 colleges. Only institutions employing random sampling techniques to collect data representative of their campuses are included. Comparisons across years should be undertaken with caution because participating institutions varied from year to year.

[a]"Binge" drinking is defined as five or more drinks on the same occasion at least once during the 2 weeks prior to the survey.

Source: Core Institute, Southern Illinois University at Carbondale, *Core Alcohol and Drug Survey* [Online]. Available: http://www.siu.edu/departments/coreinst/public_html/1998.htm; http://www.siu.edu/departments/coreinst/public_html/1999.htm; http://www.siu.edu/departments/coreinst/public_html/2000.htm; http://www.siu.edu/departments/coreinst/public_html/2001.htm; and http://www.siu.edu/departments/coreinst/public_html/2002.htm [June 16, 2004]. Table adapted by SOURCEBOOK staff.

Table 3.84

College students reporting drug use

By type of drug, United States, 1998-2002

| | Percent of college students reporting drug use ||||||||||
| | 1998 || 1999 || 2000 || 2001 || 2002 ||
	In past year	In past 30 days	In past year	In past 30 days	In past year	In past 30 days	In past year	In past 30 days	In past year	In past 30 days
Marijuana	32.4%	18.8%	32.5%	18.7%	33.6%	20.0%	36.4%	21.9%	35.7%	20.7%
Cocaine	4.4	1.8	3.8	1.6	5.0	2.1	5.1	2.4	5.5	2.5
Amphetamines	6.5	2.9	6.3	3.1	7.6	3.8	8.5	4.5	9.3	5.1
Sedatives	3.4	1.6	3.0	1.4	4.1	1.9	4.4	2.2	4.7	2.3
Hallucinogens	7.3	2.4	6.6	2.2	6.6	2.0	6.3	2.1	5.2	1.4
Opiates	1.6	0.8	1.4	0.7	1.5	0.7	2.1	1.0	1.8	0.8
Inhalants	2.2	0.9	2.3	1.0	1.9	0.8	2.2	1.0	1.7	0.8
Designer drugs	3.8	1.4	5.5	2.5	9.1	3.7	9.1	2.9	7.7	2.1
Steroids	0.6	0.5	0.7	0.5	0.8	0.6	0.9	0.7	0.8	0.6
Other	2.3	1.0	2.2	0.9	2.5	1.1	2.5	1.2	2.5	1.1

Note: See Note, table 3.83.

Source: Core Institute, Southern Illinois University at Carbondale, *Core Alcohol and Drug Survey* [Online]. Available: http://www.siu.edu/departments/coreinst/public_html/1998.htm; http://www.siu.edu/departments/coreinst/public_html/1999.htm; http://www.siu.edu/departments/coreinst/public_html/2000.htm; http://www.siu.edu/departments/coreinst/public_html/2001.htm; and http://www.siu.edu/departments/coreinst/public_html/2002.htm [June 16, 2004]. Table adapted by SOURCEBOOK staff.

Table 3.85

College students reporting experiences of violence or harassment and involvement of alcohol or drugs before the experience

United States, 1995-2002

Question: "Indicate whether any of the following have happened to you within the last year while you were in and around campus. If you answered yes, indicate if you had consumed alcohol or other drugs shortly before these incidents."

(Percent reporting experience; percent reporting consumption of alcohol or drugs shortly before)

| | Happened to respondent |||||||| Respondent reporting consumption of alcohol or drugs shortly before incident[a] ||||||||
	1995	1996	1997	1998	1999	2000	2001	2002	1995	1996	1997	1998	1999	2000	2001	2002
Threats of physical violence	10.7%	9.4%	10.8%	13.3%	10.6%	9.5%	10.3%	9.6%	50.1%	50.6%	57.9%	43.4%	54.4%	34.2%	58.8%	34.2%
Ethnic or racial harassment	6.9	7.1	6.7	8.7	5.3	5.4	5.6	5.7	13.6	11.5	16.1	10.5	11.3	15.5	17.9	13.5
Actual physical violence	5.2	4.8	5.3	8.1	5.1	5.1	5.1	4.7	66.0	62.9	69.1	42.7	43.6	38.0	68.3	67.3
Forced sexual touching or fondling	5.2	4.7	6.2	8.6	5.9	5.2	5.8	5.0	69.9	70.7	75.8	50.8	52.3	40.4	76.0	74.0
Theft involving force or threat of force	1.9	1.8	1.7	4.8	1.7	1.7	1.9	1.9	46.8	42.2	50.2	16.8	20.2	24.3	54.4	47.9

Note: See Note, table 3.83.

[a]Percents are of those respondents reporting experiences of violence or harassment.

Source: Cheryl A. Presley, Jami S. Leichliter, and Philip W. Meilman, *Alcohol and Drugs on American College Campuses: A Report to College Presidents* (Carbondale, IL: Core Institute, Southern Illinois University, 1998), p. 10; and Core Institute, Southern Illinois University at Carbondale, *Core Alcohol and Drug Survey* [Online]. Available: http://www.siu.edu/departments/coreinst/public_html/1998.htm; http://www.siu.edu/departments/coreinst/public_html/1999.htm; http://www.siu.edu/departments/coreinst/public_html/2000.htm; http://www.siu.edu/departments/coreinst/public_html/2001.htm; and http://www.siu.edu/departments/coreinst/public_html/2002.htm [June 16, 2004]. Table adapted by SOURCEBOOK staff.

Table 3.86

Estimated prevalence of drug use during lifetime

By type of drug and age group, United States, 2002 and 2003

(Percent reporting use during lifetime)

Type of drug	Total 2002	Total 2003	12 to 17 years 2002	12 to 17 years 2003	18 to 25 years 2002	18 to 25 years 2003	26 years and older 2002	26 years and older 2003
Any illicit drug[a]	46.0%	46.4%	30.9%	30.5%	59.8%	60.5%	45.7%	46.1%
Marijuana and hashish	40.4	40.6	20.6	19.6	53.8	53.9	40.8	41.2
Cocaine	14.4	14.7	2.7	2.6	15.4	15.0	15.9	16.3
Crack	3.6	3.3	0.7	0.6	3.8	3.8	3.9	3.6
Heroin	1.6	1.6	0.4	0.3	1.6	1.6	1.7	1.7
Hallucinogens	14.6	14.5	5.7	5.0	24.2	23.3	14.1	14.2
LSD	10.4	10.3	2.7	1.6	15.9	14.0	10.5	10.8
PCP	3.2	3.0	0.9	0.8	2.7	3.0	3.5	3.3
Ecstasy	4.3	4.6	3.3	2.4	15.1	14.8	2.6	3.1
Inhalants	9.7	9.7	10.5	10.7	15.7	14.9	8.6	8.6
Nonmedical use of any psychotherapeutic[b]	19.8	20.1	13.7	13.4	27.7	29.0	19.3	19.5
Pain relievers	12.6	13.1	11.2	11.2	22.1	23.7	11.1	11.5
Tranquilizers	8.2	8.5	3.4	3.5	11.2	12.3	8.3	8.5
Stimulants	9.0	8.8	4.3	4.0	10.8	10.8	9.3	9.0
Methamphetamine	5.3	5.2	1.5	1.3	5.7	5.2	5.7	5.7
Sedatives	4.2	4.0	1.0	1.0	2.1	1.8	5.1	4.8
Any illicit drug other than marijuana[c]	29.9	29.9	21.4	21.3	40.1	40.2	29.3	29.3

Note: These data are from the 2002 and 2003 National Survey on Drug Use and Health (NSDUH). The NSDUH is an annual survey of the civilian, noninstitutionalized population of the United States age 12 and older, and is sponsored by the U.S. Department of Health and Human Services, Substance Abuse and Mental Health Services Administration. Prior to 2002, the survey was called the National Household Survey on Drug Abuse (NHSDA). Due to methodological changes beginning with the 2002 NSDUH, estimates from the 2002 and 2003 surveys should not be compared with estimates from 2001 and earlier NHSDAs. For the 2002 NSDUH, a response rate of 78.9% yielded 68,126 completed interviews. For the 2003 NSDUH, a response rate of 77.4% yielded 67,784 completed interviews. For information on survey methodology, see Appendix 7.

[a] Includes use at least once of marijuana or hashish, cocaine (including crack), heroin, hallucinogens (including LSD, PCP, and ecstasy), inhalants, or any prescription-type psychotherapeutic used nonmedically.
[b] Includes nonmedical use of any prescription-type pain reliever, stimulant, sedative, or tranquilizer; does not include over-the-counter drugs.
[c] Includes use at least once of any of these listed drugs, regardless of marijuana/hashish use; marijuana/hashish users who also have used any of the other listed drugs are included.

Source: U.S. Department of Health and Human Services, Substance Abuse and Mental Health Services Administration, *Results from the 2003 National Survey on Drug Use and Health: National Findings* (Rockville, MD: U.S. Department of Health and Human Services, 2004), pp. 189-192. Table adapted by SOURCEBOOK staff.

Table 3.87

Estimated prevalence of drug use during the last 12 months

By type of drug and age group, United States, 2002 and 2003

(Percent reporting use during last 12 months)

	Total		Age group					
			12 to 17 years		18 to 25 years		26 years and older	
Type of drug	2002	2003	2002	2003	2002	2003	2002	2003
Any illicit drug[a]	14.9%	14.7%	22.2%	21.8%	35.5%	34.6%	10.4%	10.3%
Marijuana and hashish	11.0	10.6	15.8	15.0	29.8	28.5	7.0	6.9
Cocaine	2.5	2.5	2.1	1.8	6.7	6.6	1.8	1.9
Crack	0.7	0.6	0.4	0.4	0.9	0.9	0.7	0.6
Heroin	0.2	0.1	0.2	0.1	0.4	0.3	0.1	0.1
Hallucinogens	2.0	1.7	3.8	3.1	8.4	6.7	0.7	0.6
LSD	0.4	0.2	1.3	0.6	1.8	1.1	0.1	0.0
PCP	0.1	0.1	0.4	0.4	0.3	0.4	0.0	0.0
Ecstasy	1.3	0.9	2.2	1.3	5.8	3.7	0.5	0.3
Inhalants	0.9	0.9	4.4	4.5	2.2	2.1	0.2	0.2
Nonmedical use of any psychotherapeutic[b]	6.2	6.3	9.2	9.2	14.2	14.5	4.5	4.5
Pain relievers	4.7	4.9	7.6	7.7	11.4	12.0	3.1	3.3
Tranquilizers	2.1	2.1	2.3	2.3	4.9	5.3	1.5	1.5
Stimulants	1.4	1.2	2.6	2.3	3.7	3.5	0.8	0.6
Methamphetamine	0.7	0.6	0.9	0.7	1.7	1.6	0.4	0.4
Sedatives	0.4	0.3	0.6	0.5	0.5	0.5	0.4	0.3
Any illicit drug other than marijuana[c]	8.7	8.5	13.5	13.4	20.2	19.7	6.0	5.9

Note: See Note, table 3.86. For information on survey methodology, see Appendix 7.

[a]Includes use at least once in last 12 months of marijuana or hashish, cocaine (including crack), heroin, hallucinogens (including LSD, PCP, and ecstasy), inhalants, or any prescription-type psychotherapeutic used nonmedically.
[b]Includes nonmedical use of any prescription-type pain reliever, stimulant, sedative, or tranquilizer; does not include over-the-counter drugs.
[c]Includes use at least once of any of these listed drugs, regardless of marijuana/hashish use; marijuana/hashish users who also have used any of the other listed drugs are included.

Source: U.S. Department of Health and Human Services, Substance Abuse and Mental Health Services Administration, *Results from the 2003 National Survey on Drug Use and Health: National Findings* (Rockville, MD: U.S. Department of Health and Human Services, 2004), pp. 189-192. Table adapted by SOURCEBOOK staff.

Table 3.88

Estimated prevalence of drug use during the last 30 days

By type of drug and age group, United States, 2002 and 2003

(Percent reporting use during last 30 days)

	Total		Age group					
			12 to 17 years		18 to 25 years		26 years and older	
Type of drug	2002	2003	2002	2003	2002	2003	2002	2003
Any illicit drug[a]	8.3%	8.2%	11.6%	11.2%	20.2%	20.3%	5.8%	5.6%
Marijuana and hashish	6.2	6.2	8.2	7.9	17.3	17.0	4.0	4.0
Cocaine	0.9	1.0	0.6	0.6	2.0	2.2	0.7	0.8
Crack	0.2	0.3	0.1	0.1	0.2	0.2	0.3	0.3
Heroin	0.1	0.1	0.0	0.1	0.1	0.1	0.1	0.0
Hallucinogens	0.5	0.4	1.0	1.0	1.9	1.7	0.2	0.1
LSD	0.0	0.1	0.2	0.2	0.1	0.2	0.0	0.0
PCP	0.0	0.0	0.1	0.1	0.0	0.1	0.0	B
Ecstasy	0.3	0.2	0.5	0.4	1.1	0.7	0.1	0.1
Inhalants	0.3	0.2	1.2	1.3	0.5	0.4	0.1	0.1
Nonmedical use of any psychotherapeutic[b]	2.6	2.7	4.0	4.0	5.4	6.0	2.0	1.9
Pain relievers	1.9	2.0	3.2	3.2	4.1	4.7	1.3	1.3
Tranquilizers	0.8	0.8	0.8	0.9	1.6	1.7	0.6	0.6
Stimulants	0.5	0.5	0.8	0.9	1.2	1.3	0.4	0.3
Methamphetamine	0.3	0.3	0.3	0.3	0.5	0.6	0.2	0.2
Sedatives	0.2	0.1	0.2	0.2	0.2	0.2	0.2	0.1
Any illicit drug other than marijuana[c]	3.7	3.7	5.7	5.7	7.9	8.4	2.7	2.6

Note: See Note, table 3.86. For information on survey methodology, see Appendix 7.

[a]Includes use at least once in the last 30 days of marijuana or hashish, cocaine (including crack), heroin, hallucinogens (including LSD, PCP, and ecstasy), inhalants, or any prescription-type psychotherapeutic used nonmedically.
[b]Includes nonmedical use of any prescription-type pain reliever, stimulant, sedative, or tranquilizer; does not include over-the-counter drugs.
[c]Includes use at least once of any of these listed drugs, regardless of marijuana/hashish use; marijuana/hashish users who also have used any of the other listed drugs are included.

Source: U.S. Department of Health and Human Services, Substance Abuse and Mental Health Services Administration, *Results from the 2003 National Survey on Drug Use and Health: National Findings* (Rockville, MD: U.S. Department of Health and Human Services, 2004), pp. 189-192. Table adapted by SOURCEBOOK staff.

Table 3.89

Prevalence of any illicit drug use among military personnel

By branch of service and recency of use, United States, selected years 1980-2002

Branch of service and recency of use	1980	1982	1985	1988	1992	1995	1998	2002
Total								
Past 30 days	27.6%	19.0%	8.9%	4.8%	3.4%	3.0%	2.7%	3.4%
Past 12 months	36.7	26.6	13.4	8.9	6.2	6.5	6.0	6.9
Army								
Past 30 days	30.7	26.2	11.5	6.9	3.9	4.0	4.5	4.8
Past 12 months	39.4	32.4	16.6	11.8	7.7	9.2	9.8	10.4
Navy								
Past 30 days	33.7	16.2	10.3	5.4	4.0	3.6	1.8	3.7
Past 12 months	43.2	28.1	15.9	11.3	6.6	7.3	4.2	7.1
Marine Corps								
Past 30 days	37.7	20.6	9.9	4.0	5.6	3.6	3.3	3.8
Past 12 months	48.0	29.9	14.7	7.8	10.7	7.3	7.2	7.9
Air Force								
Past 30 days	14.5	11.9	4.5	2.1	1.2	1.0	1.2	1.0
Past 12 months	23.4	16.4	7.2	3.8	2.3	2.5	2.4	1.8

Note: These data are from a series of eight surveys sponsored by the U.S. Department of Defense. All military personnel who were on active duty at the time of data collection for each survey year were included in the sampling frames, except for recruits, academy cadets, and persons who were absent without leave, incarcerated, or undergoing a permanent change of station. The final sample for the 2002 survey consisted of 12,756 military personnel (3,269 Army, 3,625 Navy, 3,008 Marine Corps, and 2,854 Air Force) who completed anonymous self-administered questionnaires. Participants were selected to represent males and females in all pay grades of the active force throughout the world. Data primarily were collected from participants in group sessions at military installations or by mail for those not attending the sessions. The overall response rate for 2002 was 55.6%. The data were weighted to represent all active-duty personnel.

"Any illicit drug use" was defined as nonmedical use of marijuana/hashish, phencyclidine (PCP), LSD or other hallucinogens, cocaine, amphetamines or other stimulants, tranquilizers or other depressants, barbiturates or other sedatives, heroin or other opiates, analgesics or other narcotics, inhalants, designer drugs, and gamma hydroxybutyrate (GHB).

Source: Robert M. Bray et al., *2002 Department of Defense Survey of Health Related Behaviors Among Military Personnel* [Online], p. 5-2. Available: http://www.tricare.osd.mil/main/news/2002wwfinalreport.pdf [July 30, 2004]. Table adapted by SOURCEBOOK staff.

Table 3.90

Prevalence of illicit drug use among military personnel

By branch of service, type of drug, and recency of use, United States, 2002

Type of drug and recency of use	Total	Army	Navy	Marine Corps	Air Force
Any illicit drugs[a]					
Past 30 days	3.4%	4.8%	3.7%	3.8%	1.0%
Past 12 months	6.9	10.4	7.1	7.9	1.8
Any illicit drug except marijuana[b]					
Past 30 days	2.4	3.3	2.8	2.7	0.8
Past 12 months	4.4	6.6	4.4	5.2	1.2
Marijuana/hashish					
Past 30 days	1.7	2.5	2.1	1.8	0.3
Past 12 months	4.5	6.8	4.8	5.5	0.8
Cocaine					
Past 30 days	0.7	0.9	1.1	0.5	0.1
Past 12 months	1.5	2.0	1.8	2.0	0.2
PCP					
Past 30 days	0.4	0.5	0.7	0.1	(c)
Past 12 months	0.5	0.7	0.9	0.3	(c)
LSD/hallucinogens					
Past 30 days	0.5	0.7	0.7	0.5	0.2
Past 12 months	1.2	1.5	1.3	1.8	0.2
Amphetamines/stimulants					
Past 30 days	0.8	1.1	1.3	0.3	0.1
Past 12 months	1.2	1.7	1.7	0.9	0.2
Tranquilizers					
Past 30 days	0.7	1.1	0.8	0.6	0.2
Past 12 months	1.1	1.7	1.0	1.2	0.3
Barbiturates/sedatives					
Past 30 days	0.6	0.8	0.8	0.3	0.2
Past 12 months	0.7	1.1	1.0	0.7	0.2
Heroin/other opiates					
Past 30 days	0.4	0.5	0.8	0.2	(c)
Past 12 months	0.5	0.7	0.9	0.4	(c)
Analgesics					
Past 30 days	1.0	1.2	1.5	1.1	0.4
Past 12 months	1.5	2.0	1.9	1.4	0.5
Inhalants					
Past 30 days	0.6	0.8	0.9	0.6	0.2
Past 12 months	1.0	1.3	1.2	0.9	0.3
"Designer" drugs					
Past 30 days	0.7	1.0	1.0	0.7	(c)
Past 12 months	1.6	2.5	1.6	2.0	0.1
Steroids					
Past 30 days	0.7	0.9	1.0	0.7	0.1
Past 12 months	0.9	1.1	1.1	1.2	0.2
Gamma hydroxybutyrate (GHB)					
Past 30 days	0.4	0.5	0.7	0.2	(c)
Past 12 months	0.5	0.6	0.9	0.5	(c)

Note: See Note, table 3.89.

[a] Nonmedical use one or more times of any of the listed classes of drugs, excluding steroids.
[b] Nonmedical use one or more times of any of the listed classes of drugs, excluding marijuana and steroids.
[c] Estimate rounds to zero.

Source: Robert M. Bray et al., *2002 Department of Defense Survey of Health Related Behaviors Among Military Personnel* [Online], p. 5-6. Available: http://www.tricare.osd.mil/main/news/2002wwfinalreport.pdf [July 30, 2004]. Table adapted by SOURCEBOOK staff.

Table 3.91

Prevalence of heavy alcohol use in the past 30 days among military personnel

By branch of service, United States, selected years 1980-2002

	1980	1982	1985	1988	1992	1995	1998	2002
Total	20.8%	24.1%	23.0%	17.2%	15.5%	17.4%	15.4%	18.1%
Army	20.3	24.7	25.5	19.7	17.7	18.4	17.2	18.8
Navy	25.6	27.7	25.0	14.7	14.2	19.1	13.5	18.3
Marine Corps	28.6	30.6	29.4	24.4	26.0	28.6	23.0	27.7
Air Force	14.3	17.7	16.5	14.5	10.6	10.4	11.7	12.3

Note: See Note, table 3.89. "Heavy alcohol use" was defined as consumption of five or more drinks on the same occasion at least once a week in the past 30 days. The method for computing drinking levels (including heavy alcohol use) was revised in 1998. Heavy alcohol use estimates made after 1995 take into account 32- and 40-ounce containers. Estimates for heavy alcohol use prior to 1998 did not take into account 40-ounce containers therefore the 1998 and 2002 estimates are not directly comparable to previous years.

Source: Robert M. Bray et al., *2002 Department of Defense Survey of Health Related Behaviors Among Military Personnel* [Online], p. 4-5. Available: http://www.tricare.osd.mil/main/news/2002wwfinalreport.pdf [July 30, 2004]. Table adapted by SOURCEBOOK staff.

Table 3.92

Drug abuse-related emergency department episodes

By patient and episode characteristics, United States, 1994-2002

Patient and episode characteristics	1994	1995	1996	1997	1998	1999	2000	2001	2002
Total number of drug episodes	518,880	513,429	513,841	526,671	542,250	554,570	601,392	638,345	670,307
Rate per 100,000 population	225	221	218	221	225	228	243	252	261
Sex									
Male	263,823	255,968	257,472	269,845	281,195	291,943	309,520	333,239	355,155
Female	250,182	252,128	250,753	251,963	256,098	257,860	281,712	296,305	308,098
Unknown	4,875	5,333	5,616	4,863	4,956	4,766	10,160	8,800	7,054
Race, ethnicity									
White, non-Hispanic	278,747	277,460	273,611	283,886	295,178	309,909	334,675	351,110	372,727
Black, non-Hispanic	141,351	139,386	135,295	134,894	136,471	132,901	133,727	139,371	142,974
Hispanic	50,368	47,350	55,024	52,695	57,162	56,783	68,272	79,517	79,098
Other race[a]	6,038	5,533	6,017	6,094	5,379	5,584	5,160	5,209	4,499
Unknown	42,377	43,699	43,895	49,102	48,060	49,394	59,559	63,138	71,008
Age									
6 to 17 years	61,294	62,215	64,986	63,157	59,875	53,810	64,460	62,704	64,142
18 to 25 years	112,273	103,699	98,611	104,549	103,367	109,562	123,294	127,110	140,475
26 to 34 years	151,419	143,922	139,530	138,882	138,467	131,183	135,460	145,408	145,806
35 years and older	190,446	202,214	209,857	218,364	239,132	259,206	277,139	301,721	318,799
Unknown	B	1,379	857	1,719	1,410	809	1,038	1,401	1,084
Drug use motive									
Psychic effect	85,656	90,996	97,175	94,329	97,389	105,366	118,686	129,007	132,711
Dependence	165,961	163,988	167,370	178,556	189,091	202,690	217,118	228,994	239,653
Suicide	199,554	200,944	191,090	191,112	189,634	174,786	192,861	194,185	189,198
Other	5,530	4,747	5,060	5,686	5,482	7,503	8,406	10,273	9,178
Unknown motive	62,180	52,754	53,145	56,987	60,653	64,225	64,321	75,886	99,567
Reason for emergency department contact									
Unexpected reaction	66,529	57,371	61,899	68,677	71,168	78,336	92,497	108,309	131,315
Overdose	269,442	271,546	252,636	244,553	244,894	232,123	264,036	263,951	258,931
Chronic effects	56,307	60,165	53,382	49,273	49,884	49,884	52,164	53,256	57,047
Withdrawal	14,051	15,127	15,009	15,176	17,978	25,910	22,497	24,603	29,229
Seeking detoxification	52,329	50,479	59,921	67,886	73,042	72,959	90,623	99,126	103,674
Accident, injury	16,452	16,184	17,991	20,399	19,016	20,537	16,072	18,469	19,706
Other	21,602	23,902	27,278	28,001	37,568	47,666	36,183	38,607	36,310
Unknown reason	22,168	18,656	25,726	32,706	28,475	27,155	27,321	32,025	34,094
Patient disposition									
Treated and released	NA	237,696	242,646	254,084	255,768	259,267	274,725	299,835	319,378
Admitted to hospital	NA	258,239	255,955	253,850	268,964	276,316	306,064	319,077	331,240
Left against medical advice	NA	10,770	8,940	11,243	9,907	10,998	12,330	12,273	13,974
Died	NA	1,359	1,122	932	1,368	1,270	1,541	1,258	1,618
Unknown	NA	5,366	5,177	6,563	6,242	6,719	6,732	5,902	4,097

Note: These data were collected through the Drug Abuse Warning Network (DAWN) sponsored by the Substance Abuse and Mental Health Services Administration. The data are weighted, estimates representing all drug abuse-related emergency department episodes from a stratified random sample of non-Federal, short-stay hospitals with 24-hour emergency departments in the 48 contiguous States, the District of Columbia, and 21 metropolitan areas. These data are estimates derived from a sample and therefore subject to sampling variation. Some data have been revised by the Source and may differ from previous editions of SOURCEBOOK. For information on methodology, estimation procedures, and data limitations, see Appendix 9.

[a]Includes American Indians, Alaska Natives, Asians, Native Hawaiians, other Pacific Islanders, and other racial/ethnic groups.

Source: U.S. Department of Health and Human Services, Substance Abuse and Mental Health Services Administration, *Emergency Department Trends from the Drug Abuse Warning Network, Preliminary Estimates January-June 2001 with Revised Estimates 1994-2000*, Drug Abuse Warning Network Series: D-20, pp. T-103, T-137, T-173; *Emergency Department Trends from the Drug Abuse Warning Network, Final Estimates 1995-2002*, Drug Abuse Warning Network Series: D-24, pp. T-161, T-217, T-275 (Rockville, MD: U.S. Department of Health and Human Services). Table adapted by SOURCEBOOK staff.

Table 3.93

Type of drug mentioned in drug abuse-related emergency department episodes

By patient and episode characteristics, United States, 1999-2002

Patient and episode characteristics	Marijuana/hashish 1999	2000	2001	2002	Heroin 1999	2000	2001	2002	Cocaine/crack 1999	2000	2001	2002	Methamphetamine/speed 1999	2000	2001	2002
Total number of drug mentions	87,068	96,426	110,512	119,472	82,192	94,804	93,064	93,519	168,751	174,881	193,034	199,198	10,447	13,505	14,923	17,696
Sex																
Male	58,043	61,621	71,591	76,526	55,561	62,719	62,075	61,470	109,271	113,355	125,424	128,017	6,054	8,381	8,130	10,512
Female	28,208	33,334	37,781	41,707	26,054	30,146	30,023	31,173	58,253	59,314	65,713	69,852	4,312	4,841	6,680	6,565
Unknown	817	1,471	1,139	1,239	578	B	966	876	1,227	2,212	1,898	1,329	B	B	B	B
Race, ethnicity																
White, non-Hispanic	45,395	49,015	57,836	65,979	31,827	38,426	40,104	39,937	56,724	59,820	71,531	79,715	7,180	18,600	11,019	12,191
Black, non-Hispanic	25,607	26,446	29,455	30,943	28,646	30,934	28,706	28,721	78,017	75,889	80,022	79,889	B	837	369	863
Hispanic	9,064	11,739	12,877	13,512	11,779	14,944	14,075	12,823	20,456	23,728	25,117	23,805	1,489	2,177	1,967	1,580
Other race[a]	716	602	875	621	440	376	381	434	709	850	720	958	B	318	154	142
Unknown	6,285	8,624	9,470	8,418	9,501	10,125	9,798	11,605	12,846	14,594	15,644	14,832	982	1,573	1,414	2,920
Age																
6 to 17 years	12,930	15,792	16,559	18,876	676	1,052	834	813	3,299	4,402	3,514	3,502	844	1,122	1,323	1,234
18 to 25 years	27,266	30,413	33,365	36,896	14,901	18,065	17,451	17,626	25,264	25,753	28,666	30,808	3,289	3,711	4,651	5,769
26 to 34 years	21,410	21,841	25,323	25,279	20,153	23,742	22,868	22,253	54,058	51,007	53,693	52,743	2,988	4,211	4,704	4,682
35 years and older	25,387	28,271	35,123	38,327	46,356	51,698	51,827	52,643	85,869	93,357	106,810	111,937	3,316	4,456	4,170	6,003
Unknown	75	108	142	94	106	247	85	B	261	362	351	208	10	B	B	8
Drug use motive																
Psychic effect	31,725	36,970	38,694	39,901	5,789	5,657	7,029	7,556	32,661	34,231	38,861	34,273	2,516	3,412	3,618	3,823
Dependence	29,760	30,762	33,817	34,302	67,272	79,383	76,791	76,508	99,250	103,351	108,887	108,483	6,705	8,004	7,462	10,044
Suicide	10,055	11,454	14,130	13,753	2,750	2,719	3,432	3,376	15,254	15,999	17,148	19,159	523	711	1,827	1,513
Other	B	615	1,258	1,060	174	457	198	429	473	604	792	708	7	B	B	B
Unknown motive	15,048	16,626	22,612	B	6,207	6,588	5,614	5,651	21,114	20,696	27,345	36,575	696	1,203	1,431	2,061
Reason for emergency department contact																
Unexpected reaction	23,139	31,218	36,626	45,223	8,666	8,751	9,790	10,163	37,004	43,725	49,840	56,075	2,869	3,104	3,378	3,570
Overdose	16,629	18,722	22,469	22,533	15,413	15,667	15,850	15,921	25,499	27,792	28,692	29,582	1,883	2,423	3,976	4,317
Chronic effects	6,889	8,620	9,834	10,583	15,221	16,151	14,896	16,684	23,328	24,926	25,945	27,054	1,281	2,522	2,313	2,596
Withdrawal	B	1,401	1,840	1,419	9,016	10,400	8,899	9,132	5,422	3,221	4,561	4,193	B	B	B	B
Seeking detoxification	11,907	14,109	14,580	13,917	26,471	36,070	35,345	34,317	43,111	49,527	53,853	54,778	1,190	B	1,741	3,377
Accident, injury	6,986	5,632	6,130	6,731	1,635	1,775	1,604	1,520	7,816	6,815	7,586	7,121	102	407	425	320
Other	13,192	10,521	12,242	11,986	3,835	3,943	3,943	2,809	16,773	11,151	12,069	11,741	B	B	B	1,386
Unknown reason	5,995	6,202	6,791	7,081	1,935	2,047	2,736	2,974	9,797	7,726	10,489	8,653	389	511	590	B
Patient disposition																
Treated and released	49,462	52,146	59,841	65,268	44,572	50,121	51,944	51,742	88,153	87,093	96,557	93,349	6,797	8,578	8,912	11,218
Admitted to hospital	35,043	41,715	47,606	51,661	33,388	40,106	37,277	37,569	74,518	82,255	90,647	100,480	3,106	4,121	5,596	6,000
Left against medical advice	1,474	1,518	1,979	1,763	3,332	3,396	2,742	3,305	3,696	3,139	3,785	3,988	447	451	164	436
Died	B	60	B	B	360	339	257	470	451	B	366	B	2	B	B	5
Unknown	959	987	901	693	540	843	844	432	1,934	1,957	1,680	951	B	226	B	38

Note: See Note, table 3.92. For 1999, there were an estimated total of 554,570 episodes involving 1,013,688 drug mentions; for 2000, an estimated total of 601,392 episodes involving 1,098,915 drug mentions; for 2001, an estimated total of 638,345 episodes involving 1,165,148 drug mentions; and for 2002, an estimated total of 670,307 episodes involving 1,209,938 drug mentions. A "drug mention" refers to a substance that was mentioned during a drug-related emergency department episode. In addition to alcohol-in-combination, up to four substances may be reported for each emergency department drug abuse episode; thus, the total number of mentions exceeds the total number of episodes. It should be noted that a particular drug mentioned may or may not be the confirmed "cause" of the episode in multiple-drug abuse cases. Even when only one substance is reported for an episode, allowance still should be made for reportable drugs not mentioned or for other contributory factors. (Source, p. 131.)

Some data have been revised by the Source and may differ from previous editions of SOURCEBOOK. For information on methodology, estimation procedures, and data limitations, see Appendix 9.

[a]Includes American Indians, Alaska Natives, Asians, Native Hawaiians, other Pacific Islanders, and other racial/ethnic groups.

Source: U.S. Department of Health and Human Services, Substance Abuse and Mental Health Services Administration, *Emergency Department Trends from the Drug Abuse Warning Network, Final Estimates 1995-2002*, Drug Abuse Warning Network Series: D-24 (Rockville, MD: U.S. Department of Health and Human Services, 2003), pp. T-189, T-191, T-193, T-197, T-245, T-247, T-249, T-253. Table adapted by SOURCEBOOK staff.

Table 3.94

Type and rate (per 100,000 population) of drug mentioned in drug abuse-related emergency department episodes

By patient characteristics, United States, 1999-2002

Patient characteristics	Marijuana/hashish				Heroin				Cocaine/crack				Methamphetamine/speed			
	1999	2000	2001	2002	1999	2000	2001	2002	1999	2000	2001	2002	1999	2000	2001	2002
Total rate of drug mentions[a]	36	39	44	47	34	38	37	36	69	71	76	78	4	5	6	7
Sex																
Male	49	52	58	61	47	52	50	49	93	95	102	103	5	7	7	8
Female	22	26	29	32	21	24	23	24	46	46	50	53	3	4	5	5
Age																
12 to 17 years	55	67	68	77	3	5	3	3	14	19	14	14	4	5	5	5
18 to 25 years	97	105	99	109	53	62	52	52	89	89	85	91	12	13	14	17
26 to 34 years	64	66	83	82	60	72	75	72	162	155	176	171	9	13	15	15
35 years and older	19	21	25	27	34	37	37	37	64	68	76	79	2	3	3	4

Note: See Notes, tables 3.92 and 3.93. Some data have been revised by the Source and may differ from previous editions of SOURCEBOOK. For information on methodology, estimation procedures, and data limitations, see Appendix 9.

[a]Total rate includes patients whose sex or age was unknown.

Source: U.S. Department of Health and Human Services, Substance Abuse and Mental Health Services Administration, *Emergency Department Trends from the Drug Abuse Warning Network, Final Estimates 1995-2002*, Drug Abuse Warning Network Series: D-24 (Rockville, MD: U.S. Department of Health and Human Services, 2003), pp. T-445, T-447, T-449, T-453. Table adapted by SOURCEBOOK staff.

Table 3.95
Reported alcohol use

By sex, United States, selected years 1939-2004

Question: "Do you have occasion to use alcoholic beverages such as liquor, wine or beer, or are you a total abstainer?"

(Percent of respondents reporting that they use alcoholic beverages)

	National	Male	Female
1939	58%	70%	45%
1945	67	75	60
1946	67	NA	NA
1947	63	72	54
1949	58	66	49
1950	60	NA	NA
1951	59	70	46
1952	60	68	53
1956	60	NA	NA
1957	58	67	50
1958	55	66	45
1960	62	NA	NA
1964	63	NA	NA
1966	65	70	61
1969	64	NA	NA
1974	68	77	61
1976	71	NA	NA
1977	71	77	65
1978	71	75	64
1979	69	74	64
1981	70	75	66
1982	65	69	61
1983	65	71	58
1984	64	73	57
1985	67	72	62
1987	65	72	57
1988	63	72	55
1989	56	64	48
1990	57	64	51
1992	64	72	57
1994	65	70	61
1996	61	66	55
1997	61	63	58
1999	64	70	58
2000	64	67	60
2001	62	68	55
2002	66	72	60
2003	62	68	57
2004	62	66	58

Note: Sample sizes vary from year to year; the data for 2004 are based on telephone interviews with a randomly selected national sample of 1,005 adults, 18 years of age and older, conducted July 8-11, 2004. For a discussion of public opinion survey sampling procedures, see Appendix 5.

Source: George Gallup, Jr., *The Gallup Report*, Report No. 288, p. 14; *The Gallup Poll Monthly*, No. 303, p. 4; No. 317, p. 46 (Princeton, NJ: The Gallup Poll); *The Gallup Poll* (Princeton, NJ: The Gallup Poll, June 16, 1994), p. 2; The Gallup Organization, Inc., *The Gallup Poll* [Online]. Available: http://www.gallup.com/poll/releases/pr001204.asp [Dec. 11, 2000]; http://www.gallup.com/poll/releases/pr020809.asp [Sept. 4, 2002]; http://www.gallup.com/poll/topics/alcohol.asp [July 23, 2003]; and data provided by The Gallup Organization, Inc. Table adapted by SOURCEBOOK staff. Reprinted by permission.

Table 3.96

Reported alcohol use

By demographic characteristics, United States, 2004

Question: "Do you have occasion to use alcoholic beverages such as liquor, wine or beer, or are you a total abstainer?"

	Yes	No, total abstainer
National	62%	38%
Sex		
Male	66	34
Female	58	42
Race		
White	65	35
Nonwhite	53	47
Black	42	58
Age		
18 to 29 years	61	39
30 to 49 years	70	30
50 to 64 years	60	40
50 years and older	55	45
65 years and older	48	52
Education		
College post graduate	76	24
College graduate	77	23
Some college	64	36
High school graduate or less	51	49
Income		
$75,000 and over	78	22
$50,000 to $74,999	70	30
$30,000 to $49,999	60	40
$20,000 to $29,999	45	55
Under $20,000	39	61
Community		
Urban area	61	39
Suburban area	69	31
Rural area	48	52
Region		
East	72	28
Midwest	60	40
South	54	46
West	65	35
Politics		
Republican	59	41
Democrat	67	33
Independent	60	40

Note: See Note, table 3.95. The "don't know/refused" category has been omitted; therefore percents may not sum to 100. For a discussion of public opinion survey sampling procedures, see Appendix 5.

Source: Table constructed by SOURCEBOOK staff from data provided by The Gallup Organization, Inc. Reprinted by permission.

Table 3.97

Respondents reporting whether they drink more than they should

By demographic characteristics, United States, 2004

Question: "Do you sometimes drink more alcoholic beverages than you think you should?"

	Yes	No
National	25%	75%
Sex		
Male	30	70
Female	20	80
Race		
White	25	75
Nonwhite	27	72
Black	19	81
Age		
18 to 29 years	33	67
30 to 49 years	31	69
50 to 64 years	16	83
50 years and older	13	86
65 years and older	9	91
Education		
College post graduate	28	71
College graduate	20	80
Some college	29	71
High school graduate or less	22	77
Income		
$75,000 and over	32	68
$50,000 to $74,999	20	80
$30,000 to $49,999	24	75
$20,000 to $29,999	30	70
Under $20,000	24	76
Community		
Urban area	23	77
Suburban area	26	74
Rural area	28	72
Region		
East	28	72
Midwest	22	78
South	24	75
West	27	73
Politics		
Republican	30	70
Democrat	23	76
Independent	21	79

Note: See Note, table 3.95. This question was asked of the 62% of respondents answering "yes" to the question: "Do you have occasion to use alcoholic beverages such as liquor, wine or beer, or are you a total abstainer?" presented in table 3.96. The "don't know/refused" category has been omitted; therefore percents may not sum to 100. For a discussion of public opinion survey sampling procedures, see Appendix 5.

Source: Table constructed by SOURCEBOOK staff from data provided by The Gallup Organization, Inc. Reprinted by permission.

Table 3.98

Alcohol use and underage alcohol use in the last 30 days

By age group, level of use, and demographic characteristics, United States, 2002 and 2003

(Percent reporting use in last 30 days)

	Total						Under 21 years					
	Any use		"Binge" use[a]		Heavy use[a]		Any use		"Binge" use[a]		Heavy use[a]	
	2002	2003	2002	2003	2002	2003	2002	2003	2002	2003	2002	2003
Total	51.0%	50.1%	22.9%	22.6%	6.7%	6.8%	28.8%	29.0%	19.3%	19.2%	6.2%	6.1%
Sex												
Male	57.4	57.3	31.2	30.9	10.8	10.4	29.6	29.9	21.8	21.7	8.1	7.9
Female	44.9	43.2	15.1	14.8	3.0	3.4	28.0	28.1	16.7	16.5	4.2	4.3
Age group												
12 to 17 years	17.6	17.7	10.7	10.6	2.5	2.6	X	X	X	X	X	X
18 to 25 years	60.5	61.4	40.9	41.6	14.9	15.1	X	X	X	X	X	X
26 years and older	53.9	52.5	21.4	21.0	5.9	5.9	X	X	X	X	X	X
Race, ethnicity												
White, non-Hispanic	55.0	54.4	23.4	23.6	7.5	7.7	32.8	33.2	22.7	22.8	7.9	8.0
Black, non-Hispanic	39.9	37.9	21.0	19.0	4.4	4.5	19.3	18.2	9.8	9.1	2.0	1.6
American Indian or Alaska Native	44.7	42.0	27.9	29.6	8.7	10.0	32.4	26.0	22.6	20.8	3.1	4.0
Native Hawaiian or other Pacific Islander	B	43.3	25.2	29.8	8.3	10.4	B	B	B	B	1.5	5.7
Asian	37.1	39.8	12.4	11.0	2.6	2.3	15.5	18.2	8.6	9.6	1.8	3.1
More than one race	49.9	44.4	19.8	21.8	7.5	6.1	28.1	27.7	19.8	16.5	8.2	2.9
Hispanic	42.8	41.5	24.8	24.2	5.9	5.2	25.0	25.6	16.8	16.9	4.3	4.1

Note: See Note, table 3.86. For information on survey methodology, see Appendix 7.

[a]"Binge" alcohol use is defined as drinking five or more drinks on the same occasion on at least 1 day in the past 30 days. "Occasion" means at the same time or within a couple hours of each other. Heavy alcohol use is defined as drinking five or more drinks on the same occasion on each of 5 or more days in the past 30 days; all heavy alcohol users are also "binge" alcohol users.

Source: U.S. Department of Health and Human Services, Substance Abuse and Mental Health Services Administration, *Results from the 2003 National Survey on Drug Use and Health: National Findings* (Rockville, MD: U.S. Department of Health and Human Services, 2004), pp. 208, 212. Table adapted by SOURCEBOOK staff.

Table 3.99

Respondents reporting whether drinking has ever been a source of family trouble

United States, selected years 1947-2004

Question: "Has drinking ever been a cause of trouble in your family?"

	Yes	No
1947	15%	85%
1950	14	86
1966	12	88
1974	12	88
1976	17	83
1978	22	78
1981	22	78
1984	18	82
1985	21	79
1987	24	76
1989	19	81
1990	23	76
1992	24	76
1994	27	72
1996	23	77
1997	30	70
1999	36	64
2000	36	64
2001	36	64
2002	28	72
2003	31	69
2004	37	63

Note: See Note, table 3.95. The "don't know/refused" category has been omitted; therefore percents may not sum to 100. For a discussion of public opinion survey sampling procedures, see Appendix 5.

Source: George Gallup, Jr., *The Gallup Poll Monthly*, No. 384 (Princeton, NJ: The Gallup Poll, September 1997), p. 24; The Gallup Organization, Inc., *The Gallup Poll* [Online]. Available: http://www.gallup.com/poll/topics/alcohol.asp [July 23, 2003]; and data provided by The Gallup Organization, Inc. Table adapted by SOURCEBOOK staff. Reprinted by permission.

Table 3.100

Respondents reporting whether drinking has ever been a source of family trouble

By demographic characteristics, United States, 2004

Question: "Has drinking ever been a cause of trouble in your family?"

	Yes	No
National	37%	63%
Sex		
Male	36	64
Female	38	62
Race		
White	39	61
Nonwhite	31	69
Black	26	74
Age		
18 to 29 years	29	71
30 to 49 years	39	61
50 to 64 years	41	59
50 years and older	39	61
65 years and older	37	63
Education		
College post graduate	31	69
College graduate	29	71
Some college	36	64
High school graduate or less	44	56
Income		
$75,000 and over	32	68
$50,000 to $74,999	35	65
$30,000 to $49,999	42	58
$20,000 to $29,999	44	56
Under $20,000	43	57
Community		
Urban area	37	63
Suburban area	36	64
Rural area	40	60
Region		
East	32	68
Midwest	35	65
South	34	66
West	49	51
Politics		
Republican	35	65
Democrat	38	62
Independent	40	60

Note: See Note, table 3.95. The "don't know/refused" category has been omitted; therefore percents may not sum to 100. For a discussion of public opinion survey sampling procedures, see Appendix 5.

Source: Table constructed by SOURCEBOOK staff from data provided by The Gallup Organization, Inc. Reprinted by permission.

Table 3.101

Respondents reporting whether drug abuse has ever been a source of family trouble

By demographic characteristics, United States, 2003

Question: "Has drug abuse ever been a cause of trouble in your family?"

	Yes	No
National	24%	76%
Sex		
Male	18	82
Female	28	72
Race		
White	23	77
Nonwhite	24	76
Black	27	73
Age		
18 to 29 years	31	69
30 to 49 years	25	75
50 to 64 years	25	75
50 years and older	18	81
65 years and older	10	90
Education		
College post graduate	24	76
College graduate	23	76
Some college	29	71
High school graduate or less	19	81
Income		
$75,000 and over	21	79
$50,000 to $74,999	18	82
$30,000 to $49,999	29	71
$20,000 to $29,999	26	74
Less than $20,000	25	74
Community		
Urban area	26	74
Suburban area	23	77
Rural area	22	77
Region		
East	22	78
Midwest	21	78
South	24	76
West	26	74
Politics		
Republican	20	80
Democrat	26	73
Independent	24	76

Note: These data are based on telephone interviews with a randomly selected national sample of 1,017 adults, 18 years of age and older, conducted Oct. 6-8, 2003. The "don't know/refused" category has been omitted; therefore percents may not sum to 100. For a discussion of public opinion survey sampling procedures, see Appendix 5.

Source: Table constructed by SOURCEBOOK staff from data provided by The Gallup Organization, Inc. Reprinted by permission.

Table 3.102

Respondents reporting having driven a vehicle under the influence of alcohol or drugs during the last 12 months

By demographic characteristics, United States, 2002 and 2003

	\multicolumn{6}{c}{Respondents reporting that they drove under the influence in the last 12 months}
	\multicolumn{2}{c}{Total}	\multicolumn{2}{c}{Under influence of alcohol in the last 12 months}	\multicolumn{2}{c}{Under influence of illicit drugs in the last 12 months[a]}
	2002	2003	2002	2003	2002	2003
Total	15.2%	14.6%	14.2%	13.6%	4.7%	4.6%
Sex						
Male	20.0	19.5	18.8	18.2	6.3	6.6
Female	10.8	9.9	9.9	9.3	3.1	2.8
Age group						
12 to 17 years	5.4	4.9	4.0	3.8	3.8	3.4
18 to 25 years	29.6	28.2	26.6	25.3	14.7	14.1
26 years and older	14.1	13.5	13.5	12.9	3.0	3.1
Race, ethnicity						
White, non-Hispanic	17.3	16.5	16.2	15.4	5.0	5.0
Black, non-Hispanic	10.5	9.8	9.6	8.8	4.5	4.1
American Indian or Alaska Native	16.4	17.0	15.3	15.4	6.3	6.7
Native Hawaiian or other Pacific Islander	11.2	14.1	11.1	13.6	3.1	9.7
Asian	5.9	7.7	5.7	7.3	1.3	2.0
More than one race	11.9	16.6	10.2	14.1	5.8	7.0
Hispanic	11.2	10.3	10.5	9.7	3.7	3.4

Note: See Note, table 3.86. For information on survey methodology, see Appendix 7.

[a] Includes use at least once in the last 12 months of marijuana or hashish, cocaine (including crack), heroin, hallucinogens (including PCP and LSD), inhalants, or any prescription-type psychotherapeutic used nonmedically.

Source: U.S. Department of Health and Human Services, Substance Abuse and Mental Health Services Administration, *Results from the 2003 National Survey on Drug Use and Health: National Findings* (Rockville, MD: U.S. Department of Health and Human Services, 2004), p. 254. Table adapted by SOURCEBOOK staff.

Table 3.103

Total fatalities and fatalities in alcohol-related motor vehicle crashes

By highest blood alcohol concentration level in the crash, United States, 1982-2002[a]

	Total fatalities in motor vehicle crashes	Total fatalities in alcohol-related crashes		Blood alcohol concentration level					
				0.00		0.01 to 0.07		0.08 or more	
		Number	Percent	Number	Percent	Number	Percent	Number	Percent
1982	43,945	26,173	60%	17,773	40%	2,927	7%	23,246	53%
1983	42,589	24,635	58	17,955	42	2,594	6	22,041	52
1984	44,257	24,762	56	19,496	44	3,046	7	21,715	49
1985	43,825	23,167	53	20,659	47	3,081	7	20,086	46
1986	46,087	25,017	54	21,070	46	3,546	8	21,471	47
1987	46,390	24,094	52	22,297	48	3,398	7	20,696	45
1988	47,087	23,833	51	23,254	49	3,234	7	20,599	44
1989	45,582	22,424	49	23,159	51	2,893	6	19,531	43
1990	44,599	22,587	51	22,012	49	2,980	7	19,607	44
1991	41,508	20,159	49	21,349	51	2,560	6	17,599	42
1992	39,250	18,290	47	20,960	53	2,443	6	15,847	40
1993	40,150	17,908	45	22,242	55	2,361	6	15,547	39
1994	40,716	17,308	43	23,409	57	2,322	6	14,985	37
1995	41,817	17,732	42	24,085	58	2,490	6	15,242	36
1996	42,065	17,749	42	24,316	58	2,486	6	15,263	36
1997	42,013	16,711	40	25,302	60	2,290	5	14,421	34
1998	41,501	16,673	40	24,828	60	2,465	6	14,207	34
1999	41,717	16,572	40	25,145	60	2,321	6	14,250	34
2000	41,945	17,380	41	24,565	59	2,511	6	14,870	35
2001	42,196	17,400	41	24,796	59	2,542	6	14,858	35
2002	42,815	17,419	41	25,396	59	2,401	6	15,019	35

Note: These data are based on information from two of the National Highway Traffic Safety Administration's data systems: the Fatality Analysis Reporting System (FARS) and the National Automotive Sampling System - General Estimates System (GES). FARS contains data from a census of fatal traffic crashes occurring in the 50 States, the District of Columbia, and Puerto Rico. FARS data include crashes involving motor vehicles traveling on a trafficway customarily open to the public and resulting in the death of a vehicle occupant or a nonmotorist within 30 days of the crash. GES data are obtained from a nationally representative probability sample selected from all police-reported crashes. To be eligible for the GES sample, a police accident report must be completed and the crash must involve at least one motor vehicle traveling on a trafficway, and result in property damage, injury, or death.

A fatal crash is defined as alcohol-related or alcohol-involved if either a driver or a nonmotorist (usually a pedestrian) had a measurable or estimated blood alcohol concentration (BAC) of 0.01 or more grams per deciliter. BAC values are estimated by the Source when alcohol test results are unknown.

Beginning in 2001, the Source changed the BAC categories. The "0.01 to 0.09" category was changed to "0.01 to 0.07" and the "0.10 or more" category was changed to "0.08 or more." The data for 1982-2000 were revised to reflect these new categories. Some data have been revised by the Source and may differ from previous editions of SOURCEBOOK.

[a]Detail may not add to total because of rounding.

Source: U.S. Department of Transportation, National Highway Traffic Safety Administration, *Traffic Safety Facts 2002* (Washington, DC: U.S. Department of Transportation, 2004), p. 32. Table adapted by SOURCEBOOK staff.

Table 3.104

Blood alcohol concentration level of motor vehicle drivers involved in fatal crashes

By age, United States, 1990-2002

Blood alcohol concentration	1990	1991	1992	1993	1994	1995	1996	1997	1998	1999	2000	2001	2002
Ages 15 and younger													
0.01 or more	19%	18	18	14	16	14	13	11	15	13	15	16	14
0.08 or more	14%	11	11	9	12	9	9	8	11	10	10	12	9
Total number	409	364	350	383	397	410	413	345	361	333	320	293	336
Ages 16 to 20													
0.01 or more	33%	30	27	24	24	21	23	22	22	22	24	23	23
0.08 or more	25%	23	21	18	18	16	17	17	17	17	18	18	17
Total number	8,821	8,002	7,192	7,256	7,723	7,725	7,824	7,719	7,767	7,985	8,024	7,992	8,082
Ages 21 to 24													
0.01 or more	46%	45	42	40	39	38	38	36	37	38	38	39	39
0.08 or more	39%	38	35	34	33	32	31	30	32	31	32	33	33
Total number	7,195	6,748	6,323	6,406	6,291	6,263	6,205	5,705	5,613	5,639	5,950	6,037	6,285
Ages 25 to 34													
0.01 or more	43%	41	40	37	36	35	34	32	32	32	33	32	33
0.08 or more	37%	36	35	32	31	30	30	27	28	28	28	28	28
Total number	15,764	14,151	13,049	13,038	12,891	13,048	12,889	12,453	11,925	11,763	11,739	11,584	11,416
Ages 35 to 44													
0.01 or more	33%	32	31	30	29	30	29	29	28	28	30	29	29
0.08 or more	30%	28	27	27	26	26	25	26	24	25	26	25	26
Total number	10,177	9,482	9,284	9,738	9,951	10,677	10,955	10,904	11,241	11,059	11,132	11,261	10,896
Ages 45 to 54													
0.01 or more	24%	23	22	21	21	21	21	20	21	20	22	22	22
0.08 or more	20%	20	19	18	18	18	18	17	18	17	18	19	19
Total number	5,867	5,458	5,672	5,970	6,493	6,815	7,127	7,522	7,690	7,708	8,234	8,346	8,517
Ages 55 to 64													
0.01 or more	17%	16	16	17	15	16	15	14	14	14	15	14	15
0.08 or more	14%	13	13	14	12	14	12	11	11	11	12	12	12
Total number	4,068	3,695	3,688	3,824	3,828	4,079	4,237	4,394	4,478	4,608	4,766	4,714	5,063
Ages 65 to 74													
0.01 or more	12%	12	12	10	11	10	11	10	9	10	11	9	9
0.08 or more	9%	9	9	8	9	8	8	8	7	7	8	7	7
Total number	3,161	3,017	3,024	3,031	3,194	3,251	3,319	3,401	3,399	3,251	3,134	3,156	3,076
Ages 75 and older													
0.01 or more	8%	7	6	7	6	6	6	6	6	6	6	6	6
0.08 or more	5%	4	4	4	4	4	5	4	4	4	4	4	4
Total number	2,340	2,454	2,450	2,817	2,867	2,989	3,068	3,314	3,291	3,346	3,147	3,290	3,195

Note: See Note, table 3.103. The "0.01 or more" category includes the "0.08 or more" category. Some data have been revised by the Source and may differ from previous editions of SOURCEBOOK.

Source: U.S. Department of Transportation, National Highway Traffic Safety Administration, *Traffic Safety Facts 2002* (Washington, DC: U.S. Department of Transportation, 2004), p. 36. Table adapted by SOURCEBOOK staff.

Table 3.105
Total fatalities and fatalities in alcohol-related motor vehicle crashes

By highest blood alcohol concentration level in the crash and jurisdiction, 2002[a]

Jurisdiction	Total fatalities in motor vehicle crashes	Total fatalities in alcohol-related crashes Number	Total fatalities in alcohol-related crashes Percent	BAC 0.00 Number	BAC 0.00 Percent	BAC 0.01 to 0.07 Number	BAC 0.01 to 0.07 Percent	BAC 0.08 or more Number	BAC 0.08 or more Percent
Total[b]	42,815	17,419	41%	25,396	59%	2,401	6%	15,019	35%
Alabama	1,033	413	40	620	60	43	4	370	36
Alaska	87	35	41	52	59	2	2	34	39
Arizona	1,117	477	43	640	57	58	5	420	38
Arkansas	640	242	38	398	62	35	5	207	32
California	4,078	1,612	40	2,466	60	300	7	1,312	32
Colorado	742	307	41	435	59	39	5	268	36
Connecticut	322	140	43	182	57	17	5	123	38
Delaware	124	51	41	73	59	8	6	43	34
District of Columbia	47	25	52	22	48	3	5	22	47
Florida	3,132	1,276	41	1,856	59	177	6	1,099	35
Georgia	1,523	529	35	994	65	90	6	439	29
Hawaii	119	50	42	69	58	10	8	41	34
Idaho	264	91	34	173	66	17	7	74	28
Illinois	1,411	648	46	763	54	97	7	552	39
Indiana	792	269	34	523	66	46	6	223	28
Iowa	404	131	32	273	68	24	6	107	27
Kansas	512	229	45	283	55	23	5	205	40
Kentucky	915	301	33	614	67	39	4	263	29
Louisiana	875	413	47	462	53	62	7	351	40
Maine	216	51	24	165	76	4	2	47	22
Maryland	659	265	40	394	60	49	7	216	33
Massachusetts	459	221	48	238	52	30	6	192	42
Michigan	1,277	490	38	787	62	68	5	422	33
Minnesota	657	255	39	402	61	46	7	209	32
Mississippi	885	332	38	553	62	41	5	292	33
Missouri	1,208	525	43	683	57	68	6	457	38
Montana	270	127	47	143	53	21	8	106	39
Nebraska	307	117	38	190	62	21	7	97	31
Nevada	381	171	45	210	55	23	6	148	39
New Hampshire	127	51	40	76	60	5	4	46	36
New Jersey	773	299	39	474	61	45	6	254	33
New Mexico	449	215	48	234	52	27	6	189	42
New York	1,522	478	31	1,044	69	77	5	400	26
North Carolina	1,575	601	38	974	62	67	4	533	34
North Dakota	97	48	50	49	50	8	8	40	41
Ohio	1,418	562	40	856	60	66	5	496	35
Oklahoma	734	249	34	485	66	35	5	215	29
Oregon	436	179	41	257	59	26	6	153	35
Pennsylvania	1,614	656	41	958	59	88	5	568	35
Rhode Island	84	46	55	38	45	8	9	38	45
South Carolina	1,053	551	52	502	48	64	6	487	46
South Dakota	180	92	51	88	49	13	7	80	44
Tennessee	1,175	471	40	704	60	61	5	410	35
Texas	3,725	1,745	47	1,980	53	194	5	1,551	42
Utah	328	73	22	255	78	7	2	67	20
Vermont	78	27	35	51	65	5	6	22	28
Virginia	914	371	41	544	59	48	5	323	35
Washington	659	298	45	361	55	32	5	265	40
West Virginia	439	180	41	259	59	20	5	160	36
Wisconsin	803	364	45	440	55	39	5	325	40
Wyoming	176	70	39	107	61	7	4	62	35
Puerto Rico[b]	510	241	47	270	53	42	8	199	39

Note: See Note, table 3.103.

[a]Detail may not add to total because of rounding.
[b]Data for Puerto Rico are not included in the totals.

Source: U.S. Department of Transportation, National Highway Traffic Safety Administration, *Traffic Safety Facts 2002* (Washington, DC: U.S. Department of Transportation, 2004), pp. 160, 161. Table adapted by SOURCEBOOK staff.

Table 3.106

Estimated number and rate (per 100,000 inhabitants) of offenses known to police

By offense, United States, 1960-2002

	Total Crime Index[a]	Violent crime[b]	Property crime[b]	Murder and non-negligent manslaughter	Forcible rape	Robbery	Aggravated assault	Burglary	Larceny-theft	Motor vehicle theft
Number of offenses										
1960	3,384,200	288,460	3,095,700	9,110	17,190	107,840	154,320	912,100	1,855,400	328,200
1961	3,488,000	289,390	3,198,600	8,740	17,220	106,670	156,760	949,600	1,913,000	336,000
1962	3,752,200	301,510	3,450,700	8,530	17,550	110,860	164,570	994,300	2,089,600	366,800
1963	3,109,500	316,970	3,792,500	8,640	17,650	116,470	174,210	1,086,400	2,297,800	408,300
1964	4,564,600	364,220	4,200,400	9,360	21,420	130,390	203,050	1,213,200	2,514,400	472,800
1965	4,739,400	387,390	4,352,000	9,960	23,410	138,690	215,330	1,282,500	2,572,600	496,900
1966	5,223,500	430,180	4,793,300	11,040	25,820	157,990	235,330	1,410,100	2,822,000	561,200
1967	5,903,400	499,930	5,403,500	12,240	27,620	202,910	257,160	1,632,100	3,111,600	659,800
1968	6,720,200	595,010	6,125,200	13,800	31,670	262,840	286,700	1,858,900	3,482,700	783,600
1969	7,410,900	661,870	6,749,000	14,760	37,170	298,850	311,090	1,981,900	3,888,600	878,500
1970	8,098,000	738,820	7,359,200	16,000	37,990	349,860	334,970	2,205,000	4,225,800	928,400
1971	8,588,200	816,500	7,771,700	17,780	42,260	387,700	368,760	2,399,300	4,424,200	948,200
1972	8,248,800	834,900	7,413,900	18,670	46,850	376,290	393,090	2,375,500	4,151,200	887,200
1973	8,718,100	875,910	7,842,200	19,640	51,400	384,220	420,650	2,565,500	4,347,900	928,800
1974	10,253,400	974,720	9,278,700	20,710	55,400	442,400	456,210	3,039,200	5,262,500	977,100
1975	11,292,400	1,039,710	10,252,700	20,510	56,090	470,500	492,620	3,265,300	5,977,700	1,009,600
1976	11,349,700	1,004,210	10,345,500	18,780	57,080	427,810	500,530	3,108,700	6,270,800	966,000
1977	10,984,500	1,029,580	9,955,000	19,120	63,500	412,610	534,350	3,071,500	5,905,700	977,700
1978	11,209,000	1,085,550	10,123,400	19,560	67,610	426,930	571,460	3,128,300	5,991,000	1,004,100
1979	12,249,500	1,208,030	11,041,500	21,460	76,390	480,700	629,480	3,327,700	6,601,000	1,112,800
1980	13,408,300	1,344,520	12,063,700	23,040	82,990	565,840	672,650	3,795,200	7,136,900	1,131,700
1981	13,423,800	1,361,820	12,061,900	22,520	82,500	592,910	663,900	3,779,700	7,194,400	1,087,800
1982	12,974,400	1,322,390	11,652,000	21,010	78,770	553,130	669,480	3,447,100	7,142,500	1,062,400
1983	12,108,630	1,258,087	10,850,543	19,308	78,918	506,567	653,294	3,129,851	6,712,759	1,007,933
1984	11,881,755	1,273,282	10,608,473	18,692	84,233	485,008	685,349	2,984,434	6,591,874	1,032,165
1985	12,430,357	1,327,767	11,102,590	18,976	87,671	497,874	723,246	3,073,348	6,926,380	1,102,862
1986	13,211,869	1,489,169	11,722,700	20,613	91,459	542,775	834,322	3,241,410	7,257,153	1,224,137
1987	13,508,708	1,483,999	12,024,709	20,096	91,111	517,704	855,088	3,236,184	7,499,851	1,288,674
1988	13,923,086	1,566,221	12,356,865	20,675	92,486	542,968	910,092	3,218,077	7,705,872	1,432,916
1989	14,251,449	1,646,037	12,605,412	21,500	94,504	578,326	951,707	3,168,170	7,872,442	1,564,800
1990	14,475,613	1,820,127	12,655,486	23,438	102,555	639,271	1,054,863	3,073,909	7,945,670	1,635,907
1991	14,872,883	1,911,767	12,961,116	24,703	106,593	687,732	1,092,739	3,157,150	8,142,228	1,661,738
1992	14,438,191	1,932,274	12,505,917	23,760	109,062	672,478	1,126,974	2,979,884	7,915,199	1,610,834
1993	14,144,794	1,926,017	12,218,777	24,526	106,014	659,870	1,135,607	2,834,808	7,820,909	1,563,060
1994	13,989,543	1,857,670	12,131,873	23,326	102,216	618,949	1,113,179	2,712,774	7,879,812	1,539,287
1995	13,862,727	1,798,792	12,063,935	21,606	97,470	580,509	1,099,207	2,593,784	7,997,710	1,472,441
1996	13,493,863	1,688,540	11,805,323	19,645	96,252	535,594	1,037,049	2,506,400	7,904,685	1,394,238
1997	13,194,571	1,636,096	11,558,475	18,208	96,153	498,534	1,023,201	2,460,526	7,743,760	1,354,189
1998	12,485,714	1,533,887	10,951,827	16,974	93,144	447,186	976,583	2,332,735	7,376,311	1,242,781
1999	11,634,378	1,426,044	10,208,334	15,522	89,411	409,371	911,740	2,100,739	6,955,520	1,152,075
2000	11,608,070	1,425,486	10,182,584	15,586	90,178	408,016	911,706	2,050,992	6,971,590	1,160,002
2001	11,876,669	1,439,480	10,437,189	16,037[c]	90,863	423,557	909,023	2,116,531	7,092,267	1,228,391
2002	11,877,218	1,426,325	10,450,893	16,204	95,136	420,637	894,348	2,151,875	7,052,922	1,246,096
Rate (per 100,000 inhabitants)[d]										
1960	1,887.2	160.9	1,726.3	5.1	9.6	60.1	86.1	508.6	1,034.7	183.0
1961	1,906.1	158.1	1,747.9	4.8	9.4	58.3	85.7	518.9	1,045.4	183.6
1962	2,019.8	162.3	1,857.5	4.6	9.4	59.7	88.6	535.2	1,124.8	197.4
1963	2,180.3	168.2	2,012.1	4.6	9.4	61.8	92.4	576.4	1,219.1	216.6
1964	2,388.1	190.6	2,197.5	4.9	11.2	68.2	106.2	634.7	1,315.5	247.4
1965	2,449.0	200.2	2,248.8	5.1	12.1	71.7	111.3	662.7	1,329.3	256.8
1966	2,670.8	220.0	2,450.9	5.6	13.2	80.8	120.3	721.0	1,442.9	286.9
1967	2,989.7	253.2	2,736.5	6.2	14.0	102.8	130.2	826.6	1,575.8	334.1
1968	3,370.2	298.4	3,071.8	6.9	15.9	131.8	143.8	932.3	1,746.6	393.0
1969	3,680.0	328.7	3,351.3	7.3	18.5	148.4	154.5	984.1	1,930.9	436.2
1970	3,984.5	363.5	3,621.0	7.9	18.7	172.1	164.8	1,084.9	2,079.3	456.8
1971	4,164.7	396.0	3,768.8	8.6	20.5	188.0	178.8	1,163.5	2,145.5	459.8
1972	3,961.4	401.0	3,560.4	9.0	22.5	180.7	188.8	1,140.8	1,993.6	426.1
1973	4,154.4	417.4	3,737.0	9.4	24.5	183.1	200.5	1,222.5	2,071.9	442.6
1974	4,850.4	461.1	4,389.3	9.8	26.2	209.3	215.8	1,437.7	2,489.5	462.2
1975	5,298.5	487.8	4,810.7	9.6	26.3	220.8	231.1	1,532.1	2,804.8	473.7
1976	5,287.3	467.8	4,819.5	8.8	26.6	199.3	233.2	1,448.2	2,921.3	450.0
1977	5,077.6	475.9	4,601.7	8.8	29.4	190.7	240.0	1,419.8	2,729.9	451.9
1978	5,140.3	497.8	4,642.5	9.0	31.0	195.8	262.1	1,434.6	2,747.4	460.5
1979	5,565.5	548.9	5,016.6	9.7	34.7	218.4	286.0	1,511.9	2,999.1	505.6
1980	5,950.0	596.6	5,353.3	10.2	36.8	251.1	298.5	1,684.1	3,167.0	502.2
1981	5,850.0	593.5	5,256.5	9.8	36.0	258.4	289.3	1,647.2	3,135.3	474.1
1982	5,600.5	570.8	5,029.7	9.1	34.0	238.8	289.0	1,488.0	3,083.1	458.6
1983	5,179.2	538.1	4,641.1	8.3	33.8	216.7	279.4	1,338.7	2,871.3	431.1
1984	5,038.4	539.9	4,498.5	7.9	35.7	205.7	290.6	1,265.5	2,795.2	437.7
1985	5,224.5	558.1	4,666.4	8.0	36.8	209.3	304.0	1,291.7	2,911.2	463.5
1986	5,501.9	620.1	4,881.8	8.6	38.1	226.0	347.4	1,349.8	3,022.1	509.8
1987	5,575.5	612.5	4,963.0	8.3	37.6	213.7	352.9	1,335.7	3,095.4	531.9
1988	5,694.5	640.6	5,054.0	8.5	37.8	222.1	372.2	1,316.2	3,151.7	586.1
1989	5,774.0	669.9	5,107.1	8.7	38.3	234.3	385.6	1,283.6	3,189.6	634.0
1990	5,802.7	729.6	5,073.1	9.4	41.1	256.3	422.9	1,232.2	3,185.1	655.8

See notes on next page.

278 Sourcebook of criminal justice statistics 2003

Table 3.106
Estimated number and rate (per 100,000 inhabitants) of offenses known to police

By offense, United States, 1960-2002--Continued

	Total Crime Index[a]	Violent crime[b]	Property crime[b]	Murder and non-negligent manslaughter	Forcible rape	Robbery	Aggravated assault	Burglary	Larceny-theft	Motor vehicle theft
Rate (per 100,000 inhabitants)[d]--continued										
1991	5,898.4	758.2	5,140.2	9.8	42.3	272.7	433.4	1,252.1	3,229.1	659.0
1992	5,661.4	757.7	4,903.7	9.3	42.8	263.7	441.9	1,168.4	3,103.6	631.6
1993	5,487.1	747.1	4,740.0	9.5	41.1	256.0	440.5	1,099.7	3,033.9	606.3
1994	5,373.8	713.6	4,660.2	9.0	39.3	237.8	427.6	1,042.1	3,026.9	591.3
1995	5,274.9	684.5	4,590.5	8.2	37.1	220.9	418.3	987.0	3,043.2	560.3
1996	5,087.6	636.6	4,451.0	7.4	36.3	201.9	391.0	945.0	2,980.3	525.7
1997	4,927.3	611.0	4,316.3	6.8	35.9	186.2	382.1	918.8	2,891.8	505.7
1998	4,620.1	567.6	4,052.5	6.3	34.5	165.5	361.4	863.2	2,729.5	459.9
1999	4,266.5	523.0	3,743.6	5.7	32.8	150.1	334.3	770.4	2,550.7	422.5
2000	4,124.8	506.5	3,618.3	5.5	32.0	145.0	324.0	728.8	2,477.3	412.2
2001	4,162.6	504.5	3,658.1	5.6[c]	31.8	148.5	318.6	741.8	2,485.7	430.5
2002	4,118.8	494.6	3,624.1	5.6	33.0	145.9	310.1	746.2	2,445.8	432.1

Note: These data were compiled by the Federal Bureau of Investigation through the Uniform Crime Reporting (UCR) Program. On a monthly basis, law enforcement agencies (police, sheriffs, and State police) report the number of offenses that become known to them in the following crime categories: murder and nonnegligent manslaughter, forcible rape, robbery, aggravated assault, burglary, larceny-theft, motor vehicle theft, and arson. A count of these crimes, which are known as Part I offenses, is taken from records of all complaints of crime received by law enforcement agencies from victims or other sources and/or from officers who discovered the offenses. Whenever complaints of crime are determined through investigation to be unfounded or false, they are eliminated from an agency's count (Source, *2002*, p. 442).

The UCR Program uses seven crime categories to establish a "crime index." Crime index offenses include murder and nonnegligent manslaughter, forcible rape, robbery, aggravated assault, burglary, larceny-theft, and motor vehicle theft; the "Total Crime Index" is a simple sum of the index offenses. Arson was designated as a Part I Index offense in October 1978; data collection began in 1979. However, due to the incompleteness of arson reporting by police, arson data are not displayed nor are they included in the Total Crime Index of the offenses known to the police.

The figures in this table are subject to updating by the UCR Program and therefore may differ from previous editions of SOURCEBOOK. The number of agencies reporting and populations represented may vary from year to year. This table and tables 3.107 and 3.108 present data from all law enforcement agencies in the UCR Program, including those submitting less than 12 months of data. Estimates for nonreporting areas are included and are based on agencies reporting.

Due to ongoing National Incident-Based Reporting System (NIBRS) conversion efforts as well as other reporting problems, complete data were not available for a small number of States for certain years. As a result, the Source estimated State totals for these States for the years in question, but did not include these States in detailed breakdowns of the data. For instance, in 2002, complete data were not available for Illinois and Kentucky. Therefore, estimates for these States were included in tables displaying State totals by offense type. However, these States were omitted from tables displaying detailed breakdowns. For definitions of offenses and a list of States supplying incomplete data for selected years, see Appendix 3.

[a]Because of rounding, the offenses may not add to totals.
[b]Violent crimes are offenses of murder and nonnegligent manslaughter, forcible rape, robbery, and aggravated assault. Property crimes are offenses of burglary, larceny-theft, and motor vehicle theft. Data are not included for the property crime of arson.
[c]The murders and nonnegligent manslaughters that occurred as a result of the events of Sept. 11, 2001 are not included in this table.
[d]All rates were calculated on the number of offenses before rounding.

Source: U.S. Department of Justice, Federal Bureau of Investigation, *Crime in the United States, 1975*, p. 49, Table 2; *1995*, p. 58; *2002*, p. 66 (Washington, DC: USGPO). Table adapted by SOURCEBOOK staff.

Table 3.107
Estimated number and rate (per 100,000 inhabitants) of offenses known to police

By offense and extent of urbanization, 2002

Area	Population[a]	Total Crime Index	Violent crime[b]	Property crime[b]	Murder and non-negligent manslaughter	Forcible rape	Robbery	Aggravated assault	Burglary	Larceny-theft	Motor vehicle theft
United States, total	288,368,698	11,877,218	1,426,325	10,450,893	16,204	95,136	420,637	894,348	2,151,875	7,052,922	1,246,096
Rate per 100,000 inhabitants	X	4,118.8	494.6	3,624.1	5.6	33.0	145.9	310.1	746.2	2,445.8	432.1
Metropolitan Statistical Area	231,376,218										
Area actually reporting[c]	94.3%	9,482,136	1,163,636	8,318,500	13,100	72,708	369,834	707,994	1,658,078	5,570,764	1,089,658
Estimated totals	100.0%	10,201,622	1,262,359	8,939,263	14,235	78,236	401,140	768,748	1,778,174	6,007,505	1,153,584
Rate per 100,000 inhabitants	X	4,409.1	545.6	3,863.5	6.2	33.8	173.4	332.3	768.5	2,596.4	498.6
Other cities	22,475,044										
Area actually reporting[c]	85.5%	881,650	79,845	801,805	617	7,464	11,981	59,783	157,232	603,408	41,165
Estimated totals	100.0%	1,016,773	90,586	926,187	717	8,679	13,746	67,444	181,014	698,507	46,666
Rate per 100,000 inhabitants	X	4,524.0	403.1	4,121.0	3.2	38.6	61.2	300.1	805.4	3,107.9	207.6
Rural	34,517,436										
Area actually reporting[c]	84.7%	582,496	65,962	516,534	1,046	6,937	5,045	52,934	169,192	306,754	40,588
Estimated totals	100.0%	658,823	73,380	585,443	1,252	8,221	5,751	58,156	192,687	346,910	45,846
Rate per 100,000 inhabitants	X	1,908.7	212.6	1,696.1	3.6	23.8	16.7	168.5	558.2	1,005.0	132.8

Note: See Note, table 3.106. These figures are aggregated from individual State statistics presented in table 3.108. These data include estimated offense totals for agencies submitting less than 12 months of offense reports (Source, p. 449). Complete data for 2002 were not available for Illinois and Kentucky; crime counts for these States were estimated by the Source. For definitions of offenses and areas, see Appendix 3.

[a]Populations are U.S. Census Bureau 2002 provisional estimates as of July 1, 2002 and are subject to change.
[b]Violent crimes are offenses of murder and nonnegligent manslaughter, forcible rape, robbery, and aggravated assault. Property crimes are offenses of burglary, larceny-theft, and motor vehicle theft. Data are not included for the property crime of arson.
[c]The percentage representing "area actually reporting" is based on the population covered by law enforcement agencies providing 3 or more months of crime reports to the FBI.

Source: U.S. Department of Justice, Federal Bureau of Investigation, *Crime in the United States, 2002* (Washington, DC: USGPO, 2003), p. 67, Table 2. Table adapted by SOURCEBOOK staff.

Table 3.108

Estimated number and rate (per 100,000 inhabitants) of offenses known to police

By offense, jurisdiction, and extent of urbanization, 2002

Jurisdiction	Population	Total Crime Index	Violent crime[a]	Property crime[b]	Murder and non-negligent manslaughter	Forcible rape	Robbery	Aggravated assault	Burglary	Larceny-theft	Motor vehicle theft
ALABAMA											
Metropolitan Statistical Area	3,136,510										
Area actually reporting	93.2%	146,135	14,368	131,767	231	1,197	4,970	7,970	30,511	90,531	10,725
Estimated totals	100.0%	155,153	15,126	140,027	240	1,256	5,210	8,420	32,145	96,566	11,316
Cities outside metropolitan areas	539,598										
Area actually reporting	82.2%	25,276	2,469	22,807	24	195	484	1,766	4,993	16,610	1,204
Estimated totals	100.0%	30,749	3,003	27,746	29	237	589	2,148	6,074	20,207	1,465
Rural	810,400										
Area actually reporting	73.6%	10,626	1,327	9,299	25	126	120	1,056	3,210	5,272	817
Estimated totals	100.0%	14,429	1,802	12,627	34	171	163	1,434	4,359	7,159	1,109
State total	4,486,508	200,331	19,931	180,400	303	1,664	5,962	12,002	42,578	123,932	13,890
Rate per 100,000 inhabitants	X	4,465.2	444.2	4,020.9	6.8	37.1	132.9	267.5	949.0	2,762.3	309.6
ALASKA											
Metropolitan Statistical Area	267,280										
Area actually reporting	100.0%	13,670	1,721	11,949	18	254	382	1,067	1,521	9,255	1,173
Cities outside metropolitan areas	167,350										
Area actually reporting	95.0%	8,727	1,122	7,605	5	134	73	910	1,015	5,901	689
Estimated totals	100.0%	9,181	1,180	8,001	5	141	77	957	1,068	6,208	725
Rural	209,156										
Area actually reporting	100.0%	4,894	726	4,168	10	116	30	570	1,319	2,276	573
State total	643,786	27,745	3,627	24,118	33	511	489	2,594	3,908	17,739	2,471
Rate per 100,000 inhabitants	X	4,309.7	563.4	3,746.3	5.1	79.4	76.0	402.9	607.0	2,755.4	383.8
ARIZONA											
Metropolitan Statistical Area	4,814,487										
Area actually reporting	98.3%	322,139	27,408	294,731	364	1,499	7,804	17,741	53,694	185,611	55,426
Estimated totals	100.0%	327,109	27,729	299,380	367	1,520	7,876	17,966	54,662	188,571	56,147
Cities outside metropolitan areas	305,238										
Area actually reporting	98.8%	13,860	1,146	12,714	8	54	91	993	2,353	9,487	874
Estimated totals	100.0%	14,030	1,160	12,870	8	55	92	1,005	2,382	9,603	885
Rural	336,728										
Area actually reporting	100.0%	7,328	1,282	6,046	12	33	32	1,205	2,043	3,367	636
State total	5,456,453	348,467	30,171	318,296	387	1,608	8,000	20,176	59,087	201,541	57,668
Rate per 100,000 inhabitants	X	6,386.3	552.9	5,833.4	7.1	29.5	146.6	369.8	1,082.9	3,693.6	1,056.9
ARKANSAS											
Metropolitan Statistical Area	1,339,146										
Area actually reporting	100.0%	74,398	7,326	67,072	95	525	2,044	4,662	13,879	48,670	4,523
Cities outside metropolitan areas	509,713										
Area actually reporting	98.4%	26,046	2,878	23,168	20	132	393	2,333	5,668	16,197	1,303
Estimated totals	100.0%	26,468	2,924	23,544	20	134	399	2,371	5,760	16,460	1,324
Rural	861,220										
Area actually reporting	97.1%	11,467	1,215	10,252	26	92	79	1,018	3,487	5,827	938
Estimated totals	100.0%	11,806	1,251	10,555	27	95	81	1,048	3,590	5,999	966
State total	2,710,079	112,672	11,501	101,171	142	754	2,524	8,081	23,229	71,129	6,813
Rate per 100,000 inhabitants	X	4,157.5	424.4	3,733.1	5.2	27.8	93.1	298.2	857.1	2,624.6	251.4
CALIFORNIA											
Metropolitan Statistical Area	33,953,585										
Area actually reporting	100.0%	1,348,339	204,139	1,144,200	2,352	9,809	64,453	127,525	229,182	696,315	218,703
Cities outside metropolitan areas	501,198										
Area actually reporting	100.0%	21,249	2,323	18,926	20	202	375	1,726	4,468	12,416	2,042
Rural	661,250										
Area actually reporting	100.0%	15,284	1,926	13,358	23	187	140	1,576	4,778	6,961	1,619
State total	35,116,033	1,384,872	208,388	1,176,484	2,395	10,198	64,968	130,827	238,428	715,692	222,364
Rate per 100,000 inhabitants	X	3,943.7	593.4	3,350.3	6.8	29.0	185.0	372.6	679.0	2,038.1	633.2
COLORADO											
Metropolitan Statistical Area	3,779,831										
Area actually reporting	95.6%	166,005	13,589	152,416	158	1,740	3,314	8,377	27,280	103,999	21,137
Estimated totals	100.0%	174,593	14,220	160,373	164	1,821	3,464	8,771	28,431	109,651	22,291
Cities outside metropolitan areas	313,320										
Area actually reporting	86.6%	13,287	992	12,295	5	151	83	753	1,801	10,007	487
Estimated totals	100.0%	15,351	1,146	14,205	6	174	96	870	2,081	11,561	563
Rural	413,391										
Area actually reporting	87.9%	5,061	449	4,612	8	62	15	364	1,005	3,333	274
Estimated totals	100.0%	5,992	516	5,476	9	71	19	417	1,166	3,981	329
State total	4,506,542	195,936	15,882	180,054	179	2,066	3,579	10,058	31,678	125,193	23,183
Rate per 100,000 inhabitants	X	4,347.8	352.4	3,995.4	4.0	45.8	79.4	223.2	702.9	2,778.0	514.4

See notes at end of table.

Table 3.108

Estimated number and rate (per 100,000 inhabitants) of offenses known to police

By offense, jurisdiction, and extent of urbanization, 2002--Continued

Jurisdiction	Population	Total Crime Index	Violent crime[a]	Property crime[b]	Murder and non-negligent manslaughter	Forcible rape	Robbery	Aggravated assault	Burglary	Larceny-theft	Motor vehicle theft
CONNECTICUT											
Metropolitan Statistical Area	2,897,041										
Area actually reporting	100.0%	93,997	9,455	84,542	75	661	3,926	4,793	14,651	58,934	10,957
Cities outside metropolitan areas	60,995										
Area actually reporting	100.0%	2,628	235	2,393	2	13	56	164	539	1,711	143
Rural	502,467										
Area actually reporting	100.0%	7,094	1,077	6,017	3	56	78	940	1,898	3,647	472
State total	3,460,503	103,719	10,767	92,952	80	730	4,060	5,897	17,088	64,292	11,572
Rate per 100,000 inhabitants	X	2,997.2	311.1	2,686.1	2.3	21.1	117.3	170.4	493.8	1,857.9	334.4
DELAWARE											
Metropolitan Statistical Area	645,993										
Area actually reporting	99.9%	26,417	3,961	22,456	19	266	1,035	2,641	4,222	15,409	2,825
Estimated totals	100.0%	26,458	3,966	22,492	19	266	1,036	2,645	4,228	15,437	2,827
Cities outside metropolitan areas	37,573										
Area actually reporting	100.0%	2,303	293	2,010	2	15	69	207	408	1,517	85
Rural	123,819										
Area actually reporting	100.0%	3,042	577	2,465	5	77	49	446	719	1,601	145
State total	807,385	31,803	4,836	26,967	26	358	1,154	3,298	5,355	18,555	3,057
Rate per 100,000 inhabitants	X	3,939.0	599.0	3,340.0	3.2	44.3	142.9	408.5	663.3	2,298.2	378.6
DISTRICT OF COLUMBIA[c]											
Metropolitan Statistical Area	570,898										
Area actually reporting	100.0%	45,799	9,322	36,477	264	262	3,834	4,962	5,170	21,708	9,599
Cities outside metropolitan areas	NONE										
Rural	NONE										
Total	570,898	45,799	9,322	36,477	264	262	3,834	4,962	5,170	21,708	9,599
Rate per 100,000 inhabitants	X	8,022.3	1,632.9	6,389.4	46.2	45.9	671.6	869.2	905.6	3,802.4	1,681.4
FLORIDA											
Metropolitan Statistical Area	15,515,922										
Area actually reporting	99.2%	854,239	121,332	732,907	869	6,225	31,484	82,754	164,155	483,463	85,289
Estimated totals	100.0%	859,847	122,124	737,723	874	6,273	31,647	83,330	165,296	486,611	85,816
Cities outside metropolitan areas	240,207										
Area actually reporting	98.8%	16,556	2,120	14,436	9	105	457	1,549	3,610	9,962	864
Estimated totals	100.0%	16,750	2,144	14,606	9	106	462	1,567	3,653	10,079	874
Rural	957,020										
Area actually reporting	100.0%	29,360	4,453	24,907	28	374	472	3,579	8,293	14,788	1,826
State total	16,713,149	905,957	128,721	777,236	911	6,753	32,581	88,476	177,242	511,478	88,516
Rate per 100,000 inhabitants	X	5,420.6	770.2	4,650.4	5.5	40.4	194.9	529.4	1,060.5	3,060.3	529.6
GEORGIA											
Metropolitan Statistical Area	5,925,447										
Area actually reporting	99.0%	283,284	28,554	254,730	473	1,535	11,664	14,882	53,571	169,095	32,064
Estimated totals	100.0%	286,953	28,856	258,097	476	1,548	11,767	15,065	54,153	171,571	32,373
Cities outside metropolitan areas	915,341										
Area actually reporting	92.3%	50,888	5,642	45,246	47	303	1,155	4,137	8,539	34,476	2,231
Estimated totals	100.0%	55,159	6,115	49,044	51	328	1,252	4,484	9,256	37,370	2,418
Rural	1,719,522										
Area actually reporting	90.4%	39,504	3,885	35,619	71	210	373	3,231	9,509	23,178	2,932
Estimated totals	100.0%	43,718	4,300	39,418	79	232	413	3,576	10,523	25,650	3,245
State total	8,560,310	385,830	39,271	346,559	606	2,108	13,432	23,125	73,932	234,591	38,036
Rate per 100,000 inhabitants	X	4,507.2	458.8	4,048.4	7.1	24.6	156.9	270.1	863.7	2,740.4	444.3
HAWAII											
Metropolitan Statistical Area	900,433										
Area actually reporting	100.0%	57,271	2,601	54,670	18	304	1,072	1,207	8,932	37,250	8,488
Cities outside metropolitan areas	NONE										
Rural	344,465										
Area actually reporting	100.0%	17,967	661	17,306	6	68	138	449	3,790	12,094	1,422
State total	1,244,898	75,238	3,262	71,976	24	372	1,210	1,656	12,722	49,344	9,910
Rate per 100,000 inhabitants	X	6,043.7	262.0	5,781.7	1.9	29.9	97.2	133.0	1,021.9	3,963.7	796.0
IDAHO											
Metropolitan Statistical Area	526,430										
Area actually reporting	100.0%	20,859	1,682	19,177	13	267	153	1,249	3,443	14,390	1,344
Cities outside metropolitan areas	379,717										
Area actually reporting	97.9%	14,642	1,010	13,632	9	126	69	806	2,284	10,572	776
Estimated totals	100.0%	14,949	1,031	13,918	9	129	70	823	2,332	10,794	792
Rural	434,984										
Area actually reporting	98.9%	6,665	699	5,966	14	100	17	568	1,647	3,833	486
Estimated totals	100.0%	6,739	706	6,033	14	101	17	574	1,666	3,876	491
State total	1,341,131	42,547	3,419	39,128	36	497	240	2,646	7,441	29,060	2,627
Rate per 100,000 inhabitants	X	3,172.5	254.9	2,917.5	2.7	37.1	17.9	197.3	554.8	2,166.8	195.9
ILLINOIS[d]											
State total	12,600,620	506,086	78,214	427,872	949	4,298	25,272	47,695	81,123	301,892	44,857
Rate per 100,000 inhabitants	X	4,016.4	620.7	3,395.6	7.5	34.1	200.6	378.5	643.8	2,395.9	356.0

See notes at end of table.

Table 3.108

Estimated number and rate (per 100,000 inhabitants) of offenses known to police

By offense, jurisdiction, and extent of urbanization, 2002--Continued

Jurisdiction	Population	Total Crime Index	Violent crime[a]	Property crime[b]	Murder and non-negligent manslaughter	Forcible rape	Robbery	Aggravated assault	Burglary	Larceny-theft	Motor vehicle theft
INDIANA											
Metropolitan Statistical Area	4,446,634										
Area actually reporting	89.7%	173,239	17,786	155,453	305	1,391	5,971	10,119	31,422	107,426	16,605
Estimated totals	100.0%	183,586	18,576	165,010	312	1,470	6,102	10,692	33,404	114,178	17,428
Cities outside metropolitan areas	590,072										
Area actually reporting	81.7%	23,587	1,183	22,404	19	149	259	756	3,547	17,616	1,241
Estimated totals	100.0%	28,872	1,447	27,425	23	182	317	925	4,342	21,564	1,519
Rural	1,122,362										
Area actually reporting	56.0%	10,372	1,108	9,264	15	107	108	878	2,723	5,790	751
Estimated totals	100.0%	18,508	1,978	16,530	27	191	193	1,567	4,859	10,331	1,340
State total	6,159,068	230,966	22,001	208,965	362	1,843	6,612	13,184	42,605	146,073	20,287
Rate per 100,000 inhabitants	X	3,750.0	357.2	3,392.8	5.9	29.9	107.4	214.1	691.7	2,371.7	329.4
IOWA											
Metropolitan Statistical Area	1,330,865										
Area actually reporting	98.4%	67,221	5,761	61,460	30	555	1,026	4,150	11,123	46,145	4,192
Estimated totals	100.0%	67,944	5,801	62,143	30	559	1,032	4,180	11,213	46,711	4,219
Cities outside metropolitan areas	710,725										
Area actually reporting	91.8%	23,511	1,904	21,607	5	180	119	1,600	4,475	16,101	1,031
Estimated totals	100.0%	25,622	2,075	23,547	5	196	130	1,744	4,877	17,546	1,124
Rural	895,170										
Area actually reporting	98.5%	7,582	504	7,078	9	41	7	447	2,514	4,091	473
Estimated totals	100.0%	7,699	512	7,187	9	42	7	454	2,553	4,154	480
State total	2,936,760	101,265	8,388	92,877	44	797	1,169	6,378	18,643	68,411	5,823
Rate per 100,000 inhabitants	X	3,448.2	285.6	3,162.6	1.5	27.1	39.8	217.2	634.8	2,329.5	198.3
KANSAS											
Metropolitan Statistical Area	1,536,604										
Area actually reporting	95.8%	64,646	5,817	58,829	48	560	1,523	3,686	10,711	43,642	4,476
Estimated totals	100.0%	69,861	6,592	63,269	58	586	1,837	4,111	11,738	46,324	5,207
Cities outside metropolitan areas	682,033										
Area actually reporting	91.7%	28,872	2,384	26,488	11	288	263	1,822	4,887	20,322	1,279
Estimated totals	100.0%	31,474	2,599	28,875	12	314	287	1,986	5,327	22,154	1,394
Rural	497,247										
Area actually reporting	95.4%	9,219	991	8,228	8	129	39	815	2,494	5,151	583
Estimated totals	100.0%	9,662	1,038	8,624	8	135	41	854	2,614	5,399	611
State total	2,715,884	110,997	10,229	100,768	78	1,035	2,165	6,951	19,679	73,877	7,212
Rate per 100,000 inhabitants	X	4,087.0	376.6	3,710.3	2.9	38.1	79.7	255.9	724.6	2,720.2	265.5
KENTUCKY[d]											
State total	4,092,891	118,799	11,418	107,381	184	1,088	3,063	7,083	27,855	70,776	8,750
Rate per 100,000 inhabitants	X	2,902.6	279.0	2,623.6	4.5	26.6	74.8	173.1	680.6	1,729.2	213.8
LOUISIANA											
Metropolitan Statistical Area	3,380,522										
Area actually reporting	98.8%	186,021	22,968	163,053	529	1,262	6,409	14,768	36,188	108,417	18,448
Estimated totals	100.0%	188,429	23,226	165,203	530	1,274	6,459	14,963	36,620	110,010	18,573
Cities outside metropolitan areas	372,005										
Area actually reporting	67.2%	15,170	2,156	13,014	12	77	284	1,783	2,849	9,641	524
Estimated totals	100.0%	22,579	3,210	19,369	18	115	423	2,654	4,240	14,349	780
Rural	730,119										
Area actually reporting	88.7%	15,539	2,886	12,653	40	124	214	2,508	3,982	7,932	739
Estimated totals	100.0%	17,520	3,254	14,266	45	140	241	2,828	4,490	8,943	833
State total	4,482,646	228,528	29,690	198,838	593	1,529	7,123	20,445	45,350	133,302	20,186
Rate per 100,000 inhabitants	X	5,098.1	662.3	4,435.7	13.2	34.1	158.9	456.1	1,011.7	2,973.7	450.3
MAINE											
Metropolitan Statistical Area	488,483										
Area actually reporting	99.9%	15,213	610	14,603	7	167	156	280	2,678	11,351	574
Estimated totals	100.0%	15,225	610	14,615	7	167	156	280	2,680	11,361	574
Cities outside metropolitan areas	428,325										
Area actually reporting	99.4%	13,414	575	12,839	4	141	94	336	2,231	10,107	501
Estimated totals	100.0%	13,502	579	12,923	4	142	95	338	2,246	10,173	504
Rural	377,656										
Area actually reporting	100.0%	5,654	207	5,447	3	68	19	117	2,039	3,057	351
State total	1,294,464	34,381	1,396	32,985	14	377	270	/35	6,965	24,591	1,429
Rate per 100,000 inhabitants	X	2,656.0	107.8	2,548.2	1.1	29.1	20.9	56.8	538.1	1,899.7	110.4
MARYLAND											
Metropolitan Statistical Area	5,060,926										
Area actually reporting	100.0%	244,746	39,609	205,137	493	1,240	13,033	24,843	37,148	134,608	33,381
Cities outside metropolitan areas	108,964										
Area actually reporting	100.0%	8,287	1,303	6,984	9	63	276	955	1,314	5,386	284
Rural	288,247										
Area actually reporting	100.0%	6,087	1,103	4,984	11	67	108	917	1,303	3,326	355
State total	5,458,137	259,120	42,015	217,105	513	1,370	13,417	26,715	39,765	143,320	34,020
Rate per 100,000 inhabitants	X	4,747.4	769.8	3,977.6	9.4	25.1	245.8	489.5	728.5	2,625.8	623.3

See notes at end of table.

282 *Sourcebook of criminal justice statistics 2003*

Table 3.108

Estimated number and rate (per 100,000 inhabitants) of offenses known to police

By offense, jurisdiction, and extent of urbanization, 2002--Continued

Jurisdiction	Population	Total Crime Index	Violent crime[a]	Property crime[b]	Murder and non-negligent manslaughter	Forcible rape	Robbery	Aggravated assault	Burglary	Larceny-theft	Motor vehicle theft
MASSACHUSETTS											
Metropolitan Statistical Area	6,166,938										
Area actually reporting	95.5%	184,978	29,255	155,723	168	1,642	6,944	20,501	30,464	99,669	25,590
Estimated totals	100.0%	190,894	29,971	160,923	170	1,689	7,054	21,058	31,503	103,287	26,133
Cities outside metropolitan areas	251,236										
Area actually reporting	87.4%	6,918	962	5,956	3	77	99	783	1,517	4,044	395
Estimated totals	100.0%	7,970	1,153	6,817	3	88	113	949	1,736	4,629	452
Rural	9,627										
Area actually reporting	100.0%	26	13	13	0	0	2	11	4	6	3
State total	6,427,801	198,890	31,137	167,753	173	1,777	7,169	22,018	33,243	107,922	26,588
Rate per 100,000 inhabitants	X	3,094.2	484.4	2,609.8	2.7	27.6	111.5	342.5	517.2	1,679.0	413.6
MICHIGAN											
Metropolitan Statistical Area	8,261,532										
Area actually reporting	99.4%	340,257	49,949	290,308	643	4,059	11,668	33,579	59,841	183,112	47,355
Estimated totals	100.0%	341,916	50,097	291,819	644	4,074	11,697	33,682	60,103	184,194	47,522
Cities outside metropolitan areas	590,393										
Area actually reporting	89.2%	18,818	1,261	17,557	7	336	66	852	2,545	14,336	676
Estimated totals	100.0%	21,099	1,414	19,685	8	377	74	955	2,853	16,074	758
Rural	1,198,521										
Area actually reporting	98.3%	25,898	2,747	23,151	26	897	75	1,749	7,876	13,857	1,418
Estimated totals	100.0%	26,351	2,795	23,556	26	913	76	1,780	8,014	14,099	1,443
State total	10,050,446	389,366	54,306	335,060	678	5,364	11,847	36,417	70,970	214,367	49,723
Rate per 100,000 inhabitants	X	3,874.1	540.3	3,333.8	6.7	53.4	117.9	362.3	706.1	2,132.9	494.7
MINNESOTA											
Metropolitan Statistical Area	3,533,926										
Area actually reporting	99.4%	138,855	11,309	127,546	95	1,599	3,816	5,799	20,598	95,543	11,405
Estimated totals	100.0%	139,550	11,342	128,208	95	1,606	3,824	5,817	20,688	96,073	11,447
Cities outside metropolitan areas	559,457										
Area actually reporting	99.4%	22,009	1,158	20,851	5	335	74	744	2,861	16,956	1,034
Estimated totals	100.0%	22,137	1,164	20,973	5	337	74	748	2,878	17,055	1,040
Rural	926,337										
Area actually reporting	100.0%	15,767	922	14,845	12	330	39	541	4,468	9,022	1,355
State total	5,019,720	177,454	13,428	164,026	112	2,273	3,937	7,106	28,034	122,150	13,842
Rate per 100,000 inhabitants	X	3,535.1	267.5	3,267.6	2.2	45.3	78.4	141.6	558.5	2,433.4	275.8
MISSISSIPPI											
Metropolitan Statistical Area	1,033,431										
Area actually reporting	82.8%	51,618	3,950	47,668	104	478	1,917	1,451	11,734	30,627	5,307
Estimated totals	100.0%	57,587	4,309	53,278	116	540	2,007	1,646	13,124	34,402	5,752
Cities outside metropolitan areas	657,437										
Area actually reporting	79.3%	32,095	2,402	29,693	52	264	738	1,348	7,177	20,882	1,634
Estimated totals	100.0%	40,481	3,030	37,451	66	333	931	1,700	9,052	26,338	2,061
Rural	1,180,914										
Area actually reporting	41.4%	8,850	1,043	7,807	34	105	173	731	3,071	4,028	708
Estimated totals	100.0%	21,374	2,519	1,885	82	254	418	1,765	7,417	9,728	1,710
State total	2,871,782	119,442	9,858	109,584	264	1,127	3,356	5,111	29,593	70,468	9,523
Rate per 100,000 inhabitants	X	4,159.2	343.3	3,815.9	9.2	39.2	116.9	178.0	1,030.5	2,453.8	331.6
MISSOURI											
Metropolitan Statistical Area	3,847,277										
Area actually reporting	99.7%	211,121	23,892	187,229	267	1,089	6,644	15,892	32,331	129,332	25,566
Estimated totals	100.0%	211,647	23,936	187,711	267	1,091	6,653	15,925	32,403	129,699	25,609
Cities outside metropolitan areas	761,234										
Area actually reporting	99.3%	31,434	3,494	27,940	20	193	300	2,981	4,904	21,876	1,160
Estimated totals	100.0%	31,662	3,519	28,143	20	194	302	3,003	4,940	22,035	1,168
Rural	1,064,068										
Area actually reporting	100.0%	17,768	3,102	14,666	44	180	69	2,809	5,378	8,187	1,101
State total	5,672,579	261,077	30,557	230,520	331	1,465	7,024	21,737	42,721	159,921	27,878
Rate per 100,000 inhabitants	X	4,602.4	538.7	4,063.8	5.8	25.8	123.8	383.2	753.1	2,819.2	491.5
MONTANA											
Metropolitan Statistical Area	307,963										
Area actually reporting	87.3%	13,675	914	12,761	6	57	192	659	1,343	10,616	802
Estimated totals	100.0%	14,565	1,017	13,548	6	62	202	747	1,438	11,245	865
Cities outside metropolitan areas	178,045										
Area actually reporting	72.6%	6,349	573	5,776	3	59	34	477	508	4,971	297
Estimated totals	100.0%	8,744	789	7,955	4	81	47	657	700	6,846	409
Rural	423,445										
Area actually reporting	64.8%	5,601	902	4,699	4	61	22	815	746	3,623	330
Estimated totals	100.0%	8,639	1,391	7,248	6	94	34	1,257	1,151	5,588	509
State total	909,453	31,948	3,197	28,751	16	237	283	2,661	3,289	23,679	1,783
Rate per 100,000 inhabitants	X	3,512.9	351.5	3,161.4	1.8	26.1	31.1	292.6	361.6	2,603.7	196.1

See notes at end of table.

Table 3.108

Estimated number and rate (per 100,000 inhabitants) of offenses known to police

By offense, jurisdiction, and extent of urbanization, 2002--Continued

Jurisdiction	Population	Total Crime Index	Violent crime[a]	Property crime[b]	Murder and non-negligent manslaughter	Forcible rape	Robbery	Aggravated assault	Burglary	Larceny-theft	Motor vehicle theft
NEBRASKA											
Metropolitan Statistical Area	909,259										
Area actually reporting	97.3%	50,855	4,452	46,403	35	307	1,242	2,868	6,214	34,840	5,349
Estimated totals	100.0%	51,466	4,486	46,980	35	310	1,248	2,893	6,303	35,277	5,400
Cities outside metropolitan areas	412,276										
Area actually reporting	90.4%	14,890	592	14,298	8	105	85	394	2,284	11,431	583
Estimated totals	100.0%	16,475	655	15,820	9	116	94	436	2,527	12,648	645
Rural	407,645										
Area actually reporting	93.1%	5,273	267	5,006	4	35	16	212	1,395	3,272	339
Estimated totals	100.0%	5,665	287	5,378	4	38	17	228	1,499	3,515	364
State total	1,729,180	73,606	5,428	68,178	48	464	1,359	3,557	10,329	51,440	6,409
Rate per 100,000 inhabitants	X	4,256.7	313.9	3,942.8	2.8	26.8	78.6	205.7	597.3	2,974.8	370.6
NEVADA											
Metropolitan Statistical Area	1,901,003										
Area actually reporting	100.0%	90,821	13,043	77,778	174	845	5,047	6,977	17,449	43,289	17,040
Cities outside metropolitan areas	46,975										
Area actually reporting	100.0%	1,849	115	1,734	2	15	15	83	380	1,248	106
Rural	225,513										
Area actually reporting	100.0%	5,082	698	4,384	5	68	56	569	1,122	2,922	340
State total	2,173,491	97,752	13,856	83,896	181	928	5,118	7,629	18,951	47,459	17,486
Rate per 100,000 inhabitants	X	4,497.5	637.5	3,860.0	8.3	42.7	235.5	351.0	871.9	2,183.5	804.5
NEW HAMPSHIRE											
Metropolitan Statistical Area	772,025										
Area actually reporting	80.5%	15,278	1,244	14,034	7	224	323	690	2,487	10,359	1,188
Estimated totals	100.0%	17,848	1,435	16,413	7	261	347	820	2,911	12,120	1,382
Cities outside metropolitan areas	441,658										
Area actually reporting	66.8%	6,778	385	6,393	2	116	42	225	1,221	4,815	357
Estimated totals	100.0%	10,153	577	9,576	3	174	63	337	1,829	7,212	535
Rural	61,373										
Area actually reporting	100.0%	305	44	261	2	11	c	28	98	136	27
State total	1,275,056	28,306	2,056	26,250	12	446	413	1,185	4,838	19,468	1,944
Rate per 100,000 inhabitants	X	2,220.0	161.2	2,058.7	0.9	35.0	32.4	92.9	379.4	1,526.8	152.5
NEW JERSEY											
Metropolitan Statistical Area	8,590,300										
Area actually reporting	99.9%	258,903	32,110	226,793	337	1,347	13,882	16,544	43,877	147,217	35,699
Estimated totals	100.0%	259,789	32,168	227,621	337	1,347	13,905	16,579	43,898	147,984	35,739
Cities outside metropolitan areas	NONE										
Rural	NONE										
State total	8,590,300	259,789	32,168	227,621	337	1,347	13,905	16,579	43,898	147,984	35,739
Rate per 100,000 inhabitants	X	3,024.2	374.5	2,649.7	3.9	15.7	161.9	193.0	511.0	1,722.7	416.0
NEW MEXICO											
Metropolitan Statistical Area	1,060,156										
Area actually reporting	87.0%	55,962	7,558	48,404	76	527	1,672	5,283	10,584	32,541	5,279
Estimated totals	100.0%	59,826	8,381	51,445	83	583	1,774	5,941	11,519	34,292	5,634
Cities outside metropolitan areas	442,777										
Area actually reporting	90.3%	24,373	3,616	20,757	35	242	334	3,005	5,156	14,624	977
Estimated totals	100.0%	26,984	4,004	22,980	39	268	370	3,327	5,708	16,190	1,082
Rural	352,126										
Area actually reporting	82.8%	6,118	1,105	5,013	25	146	51	883	1,994	2,422	597
Estimated totals	100.0%	7,386	1,334	6,052	30	176	62	1,066	2,407	2,924	721
State total	1,855,059	94,196	13,719	80,477	152	1,027	2,206	10,334	19,634	53,406	7,437
Rate per 100,000 inhabitants	X	5,077.8	739.5	4,338.2	8.2	55.4	118.9	557.1	1,058.4	2,878.9	400.9
NEW YORK											
Metropolitan Statistical Area	17,639,788										
Area actually reporting	90.5%	470,354	88,373	381,981	862	3,215	35,621	48,675	64,789	272,759	44,433
Estimated totals	100.0%	502,782	91,371	411,411	894	3,478	36,332	50,667	69,911	295,019	46,481
Cities outside metropolitan areas	607,003										
Area actually reporting	86.1%	16,156	1,387	14,769	3	132	197	1,055	2,462	11,889	418
Estimated totals	100.0%	18,760	1,611	17,149	4	153	229	1,225	2,859	13,805	485
Rural	910,741										
Area actually reporting	92.1%	14,346	1,886	12,460	10	234	85	1,557	3,619	8,473	368
Estimated totals	100.0%	15,579	2,048	13,531	11	254	92	1,691	3,930	9,201	400
State total	19,157,532	537,121	95,030	442,091	909	3,885	36,653	53,583	76,700	318,025	47,366
Rate per 100,000 inhabitants	X	2,803.7	496.0	2,307.7	4.7	20.3	191.3	279.7	400.4	1,660.1	247.2

See notes at end of table.

284 *Sourcebook of criminal justice statistics 2003*

Table 3.108

Estimated number and rate (per 100,000 inhabitants) of offenses known to police

By offense, jurisdiction, and extent of urbanization, 2002--Continued

Jurisdiction	Population	Total Crime Index	Violent crime[a]	Property crime[b]	Murder and non-negligent manslaughter	Forcible rape	Robbery	Aggravated assault	Burglary	Larceny-theft	Motor vehicle theft
NORTH CAROLINA											
Metropolitan Statistical Area	5,619,995										
Area actually reporting	99.3%	282,298	28,800	253,498	373	1,543	9,864	17,020	65,851	168,529	19,118
Estimated totals	100.0%	284,500	28,953	255,547	374	1,552	9,909	17,118	66,280	170,055	19,212
Cities outside metropolitan areas	810,696										
Area actually reporting	95.6%	54,791	5,224	49,567	52	291	1,519	3,362	12,354	34,847	2,366
Estimated totals	100.0%	57,283	5,461	51,822	54	304	1,588	3,515	12,916	36,432	2,474
Rural	1,889,455										
Area actually reporting	95.8%	48,895	4,506	44,389	115	326	678	3,387	19,483	21,860	3,046
Estimated totals	100.0%	51,043	4,704	46,339	120	340	708	3,536	20,339	22,820	3,180
State total	8,320,146	392,826	39,118	353,708	548	2,196	12,205	24,169	99,535	229,307	24,866
Rate per 100,000 inhabitants	X	4,721.4	470.2	4,251.2	6.6	26.4	146.7	290.5	1,196.3	2,756.0	298.9
NORTH DAKOTA											
Metropolitan Statistical Area	280,387										
Area actually reporting	99.1%	9,430	299	9,131	2	94	41	162	1,282	7,218	631
Estimated totals	100.0%	9,528	301	9,227	2	95	41	163	1,297	7,294	636
Cities outside metropolitan areas	144,198										
Area actually reporting	88.3%	3,666	128	3,538	2	41	15	70	477	2,859	202
Estimated totals	100.0%	4,149	144	4,005	2	46	17	79	540	3,236	229
Rural	209,525										
Area actually reporting	84.5%	1,336	44	1,292	1	19	0	24	343	820	129
Estimated totals	100.0%	1,581	51	1,530	1	22	0	28	406	971	153
State total	634,110	15,258	496	14,762	5	163	58	270	2,243	11,501	1,018
Rate per 100,000 inhabitants	X	2,406.2	78.2	2,328.0	0.8	25.7	9.1	42.6	353.7	1,813.7	160.5
OHIO											
Metropolitan Statistical Area	9,269,065										
Area actually reporting	87.5%	376,175	35,708	340,467	468	4,018	16,627	14,595	79,941	222,822	37,704
Estimated totals	100.0%	408,945	37,428	371,517	486	4,304	17,253	15,385	85,684	245,901	39,932
Cities outside metropolitan areas	795,592										
Area actually reporting	79.5%	30,482	1,474	29,008	15	268	404	787	5,256	22,644	1,108
Estimated totals	100.0%	38,347	1,854	36,493	19	337	508	990	6,612	28,487	1,394
Rural	1,356,610										
Area actually reporting	62.5%	13,640	529	13,111	13	105	69	342	4,295	7,915	901
Estimated totals	100.0%	21,812	846	20,966	21	168	110	547	6,868	12,657	1,441
State total	11,421,267	469,104	40,128	428,976	526	4,809	17,871	16,922	99,164	287,045	42,767
Rate per 100,000 inhabitants	X	4,107.3	351.3	3,755.9	4.6	42.1	156.5	148.2	868.2	2,513.3	374.5
OKLAHOMA											
Metropolitan Statistical Area	2,123,513										
Area actually reporting	100.0%	122,845	12,688	110,157	104	1,124	2,614	8,846	24,466	75,589	10,102
Cities outside metropolitan areas	699,127										
Area actually reporting	100.0%	32,564	3,524	29,040	24	327	313	2,860	7,285	20,109	1,646
Rural	671,074										
Area actually reporting	100.0%	10,306	1,375	8,931	35	122	39	1,179	3,420	4,487	1,024
State total	3,493,714	165,715	17,587	148,128	163	1,573	2,966	12,885	35,171	100,185	12,772
Rate per 100,000 inhabitants	X	4,743.2	503.4	4,239.8	4.7	45.0	84.9	368.8	1,006.7	2,867.6	365.6
OREGON											
Metropolitan Statistical Area	2,575,588										
Area actually reporting	99.9%	137,598	8,793	128,805	53	989	2,444	5,307	19,095	95,330	14,380
Estimated totals	100.0%	137,645	8,795	128,850	53	989	2,445	5,308	19,101	95,364	14,385
Cities outside metropolitan areas	443,276										
Area actually reporting	97.1%	23,232	1,030	22,202	5	160	240	625	3,658	17,228	1,316
Estimated totals	100.0%	23,933	1,061	22,872	5	165	247	644	3,768	17,748	1,356
Rural	502,651										
Area actually reporting	100.0%	9,865	442	9,423	14	84	50	294	2,827	5,813	783
State total	3,521,515	171,443	10,298	161,145	72	1,238	2,742	6,246	25,696	118,925	16,524
Rate per 100,000 inhabitants	X	4,868.4	292.4	4,576.0	2.0	35.2	77.9	177.4	729.7	3,377.1	469.2
PENNSYLVANIA											
Metropolitan Statistical Area	10,437,252										
Area actually reporting	90.6%	289,525	43,374	246,151	564	3,005	16,123	23,682	44,675	172,421	29,055
Estimated totals	100.0%	312,507	45,563	266,944	584	3,166	16,685	25,128	47,667	188,670	30,607
Cities outside metropolitan areas	805,839										
Area actually reporting	76.1%	16,064	1,795	14,269	10	195	264	1,326	2,271	11,265	733
Estimated totals	100.0%	21,122	2,360	18,762	13	256	347	1,744	2,986	14,812	964
Rural	1,092,000										
Area actually reporting	100.0%	16,817	1,655	15,162	27	309	131	1,188	4,957	8,959	1,246
State total	12,335,091	350,446	49,578	300,868	624	3,731	17,163	28,060	55,610	212,441	32,817
Rate per 100,000 inhabitants	X	2,841.0	401.9	2,439.1	5.1	30.2	139.1	227.5	450.8	1,722.2	266.0
PUERTO RICO											
Metropolitan Statistical Area	3,252,499										
Area actually reporting	100.0%	79,618	11,997	67,621	698	207	8,184	2,908	20,346	35,251	12,024
Cities outside metropolitan areas	606,307										
Area actually reporting	100.0%	11,165	1,474	9,691	76	34	794	570	4,391	4,389	911
Total	3,858,806	90,783	13,471	77,312	774	241	8,978	3,478	24,737	39,640	12,935
Rate per 100,000 inhabitants	X	2,352.6	349.1	2,003.5	20.1	6.2	232.7	90.1	641.1	1,027.3	335.2

See notes at end of table.

Table 3.108

Estimated number and rate (per 100,000 inhabitants) of offenses known to police

By offense, jurisdiction, and extent of urbanization, 2002--Continued

Jurisdiction	Population	Total Crime Index	Violent crime[a]	Property crime[b]	Murder and non-negligent manslaughter	Forcible rape	Robbery	Aggravated assault	Burglary	Larceny-theft	Motor vehicle theft
RHODE ISLAND											
Metropolitan Statistical Area	1,003,857										
Area actually reporting	100.0%	35,952	2,827	33,125	37	356	892	1,542	5,980	22,362	4,783
Cities outside metropolitan areas	65,868										
Area actually reporting	100.0%	2,358	188	2,170	1	23	23	141	431	1,660	79
Rural	NONE										
Area actually reporting	100.0%	83	36	47	3	16	1	16	4	29	14
State total	1,069,725	38,393	3,051	35,342	41	395	916	1,699	6,415	24,051	4,876
Rate per 100,000 inhabitants	X	3,589.1	285.2	3,303.8	3.8	36.9	85.6	158.8	599.7	2,248.3	455.8
SOUTH CAROLINA											
Metropolitan Statistical Area	2,873,545										
Area actually reporting	99.8%	158,519	22,943	135,576	205	1,384	4,509	16,845	30,200	92,031	13,345
Estimated totals	100.0%	158,894	22,985	135,909	205	1,386	4,517	16,877	30,257	92,285	13,367
Cities outside metropolitan areas	311,683										
Area actually reporting	98.4%	23,583	4,386	19,197	31	147	606	3,602	4,114	14,118	965
Estimated totals	100.0%	23,972	4,458	19,514	32	149	616	3,661	4,182	14,351	981
Rural	921,955										
Area actually reporting	100.0%	34,703	6,318	28,385	61	424	641	5,192	9,306	16,560	2,519
State total	4,107,183	217,569	33,761	183,808	298	1,959	5,774	25,730	43,745	123,196	16,867
Rate per 100,000 inhabitants	X	5,297.3	822.0	4,475.3	7.3	47.7	140.6	626.5	1,065.1	2,999.5	410.7
SOUTH DAKOTA											
Metropolitan Statistical Area	263,131										
Area actually reporting	93.8%	8,988	725	8,263	3	215	82	425	1,448	6,428	387
Estimated totals	100.0%	9,439	753	8,686	3	226	84	440	1,519	6,764	403
Cities outside metropolitan areas	214,373										
Area actually reporting	88.6%	5,222	301	4,921	4	71	16	210	849	3,820	252
Estimated totals	100.0%	5,893	340	5,553	5	80	18	237	958	4,311	284
Rural	283,559										
Area actually reporting	65.7%	1,321	169	1,152	2	36	10	121	366	699	87
Estimated totals	100.0%	2,010	257	1,753	3	55	15	184	557	1,064	132
State total	761,063	17,342	1,350	15,992	11	361	117	861	3,034	12,139	819
Rate per 100,000 inhabitants	X	2,278.7	177.4	2,101.3	1.4	47.4	15.4	113.1	398.7	1,595.0	107.6
TENNESSEE											
Metropolitan Statistical Area	3,935,464										
Area actually reporting	100.0%	228,278	33,438	194,840	340	1,820	8,726	22,552	46,561	125,860	22,419
Cities outside metropolitan areas	656,434										
Area actually reporting	99.9%	36,531	4,236	32,295	28	244	532	3,432	6,679	23,639	1,977
Estimated totals	100.0%	36,574	4,241	32,333	28	244	533	3,436	6,687	23,667	1,979
Rural	1,205,391										
Area actually reporting	100.0%	26,109	3,883	22,226	52	226	154	3,451	8,000	12,083	2,143
State total	5,797,289	290,961	41,562	249,399	420	2,290	9,413	29,439	61,248	161,610	26,541
Rate per 100,000 inhabitants	X	5,018.9	716.9	4,302.0	7.2	39.5	162.4	507.8	1,056.5	2,787.7	457.8
TEXAS											
Metropolitan Statistical Area	18,479,316										
Area actually reporting	99.9%	1,035,510	116,035	919,475	1,165	7,536	36,665	70,669	188,088	633,518	97,869
Estimated totals	100.0%	1,036,268	116,090	920,178	1,165	7,541	36,679	70,705	188,238	634,024	97,916
Cities outside metropolitan areas	1,486,837										
Area actually reporting	99.2%	62,401	6,215	56,186	50	623	696	4,846	13,294	40,038	2,854
Estimated totals	100.0%	62,653	6,244	56,409	50	625	697	4,872	13,341	40,202	2,866
Rural	1,813,740										
Area actually reporting	100.0%	31,371	3,684	27,687	87	342	204	3,051	11,023	14,766	1,898
State total	21,779,893	1,130,292	126,018	1,004,274	1,302	8,508	37,580	78,628	212,602	688,992	102,680
Rate per 100,000 inhabitants	X	5,189.6	578.6	4,611.0	6.0	39.1	172.5	361.0	976.1	3,163.4	471.4
UTAH											
Metropolitan Statistical Area	1,772,063										
Area actually reporting	99.8%	88,281	4,596	83,685	34	723	1,096	2,743	12,621	64,067	6,997
Estimated totals	100.0%	88,399	4,601	83,798	34	724	1,097	2,746	12,639	64,153	7,006
Cities outside metropolitan areas	293,306										
Area actually reporting	96.5%	9,775	563	9,212	6	152	28	377	1,521	7,263	428
Estimated totals	100.0%	10,127	583	9,544	6	157	29	391	1,576	7,525	443
Rural	250,887										
Area actually reporting	96.6%	4,447	294	4,153	7	60	14	213	878	3,011	264
Estimated totals	100.0%	4,603	304	4,299	7	62	14	221	909	3,117	273
State total	2,316,256	103,129	5,488	97,641	47	943	1,140	3,358	15,124	74,795	7,722
Rate per 100,000 inhabitants	X	4,452.4	236.9	4,215.5	2.0	40.7	49.2	145.0	653.0	3,229.1	333.4

See notes at end of table.

Table 3.108

Estimated number and rate (per 100,000 inhabitants) of offenses known to police

By offense, jurisdiction, and extent of urbanization, 2002--Continued

Jurisdiction	Population	Total Crime Index	Violent crime[a]	Property crime[b]	Murder and non-negligent manslaughter	Forcible rape	Robbery	Aggravated assault	Burglary	Larceny-theft	Motor vehicle theft
VERMONT											
Metropolitan Statistical Area	163,177										
Area actually reporting	100.0%	5,417	216	5,201	8	16	34	158	1,128	3,858	215
Cities outside metropolitan areas	206,092										
Area actually reporting	99.4%	6,187	272	5,915	1	68	33	170	1,013	4,653	249
Estimated totals	100.0%	6,224	273	5,951	1	68	33	171	1,019	4,681	251
Rural	247,323										
Area actually reporting	100.0%	3,959	169	3,790	4	42	10	113	1,342	2,145	303
State total	616,592	15,600	658	14,942	13	126	77	442	3,489	10,684	769
Rate per 100,000 inhabitants	X	2,530.0	106.7	2,423.3	2.1	20.4	12.5	71.7	565.9	1,732.8	124.7
VIRGINIA											
Metropolitan Statistical Area	5,695,993										
Area actually reporting	99.6%	195,402	18,151	177,251	304	1,435	6,492	9,920	25,657	134,985	16,609
Estimated totals	100.0%	196,372	18,251	178,121	305	1,443	6,520	9,983	25,768	135,664	16,689
Cities outside metropolitan areas	449,150										
Area actually reporting	92.7%	14,081	1,174	12,907	15	125	216	818	1,902	10,393	612
Estimated totals	100.0%	15,185	1,266	13,919	16	135	233	882	2,051	11,208	660
Rural	1,148,399										
Area actually reporting	99.4%	17,378	1,729	15,649	67	259	207	1,196	3,915	10,612	1,122
Estimated totals	100.0%	17,482	1,739	15,743	67	261	208	1,203	3,938	10,676	1,129
State total	7,293,542	229,039	21,256	207,783	388	1,839	6,961	12,068	31,757	157,548	18,478
Rate per 100,000 inhabitants	X	3,140.3	291.4	2,848.9	5.3	25.2	95.4	165.5	435.4	2,160.1	253.3
WASHINGTON											
Metropolitan Statistical Area	5,044,509										
Area actually reporting	97.9%	257,184	18,287	238,897	146	2,166	5,365	10,610	44,484	157,459	36,954
Estimated totals	100.0%	261,666	18,554	243,112	148	2,210	5,433	10,763	45,291	160,226	37,595
Cities outside metropolitan areas	463,899										
Area actually reporting	90.7%	29,773	1,372	28,401	10	285	262	815	4,782	21,958	1,661
Estimated totals	100.0%	32,838	1,513	31,325	11	314	289	899	5,274	24,219	1,832
Rural	560,588										
Area actually reporting	100.0%	15,427	897	14,530	25	210	75	587	4,383	9,081	1,066
State total	6,068,996	309,931	20,964	288,967	184	2,734	5,797	12,249	54,948	193,526	40,493
Rate per 100,000 inhabitants	X	5,106.8	345.4	4,761.4	3.0	45.0	95.5	201.8	905.4	3,188.8	667.2
WEST VIRGINIA											
Metropolitan Statistical Area	762,826										
Area actually reporting	91.8%	22,873	1,968	20,905	19	166	416	1,367	4,570	14,150	2,185
Estimated totals	100.0%	25,084	2,156	22,928	20	180	458	1,498	4,938	15,629	2,361
Cities outside metropolitan areas	278,400										
Area actually reporting	81.1%	6,428	567	5,861	6	39	88	434	1,185	4,369	307
Estimated totals	100.0%	7,921	699	7,222	8	48	108	535	1,460	5,384	378
Rural	760,647										
Area actually reporting	97.3%	11,978	1,329	10,649	28	97	89	1,115	3,189	6,333	1,127
Estimated totals	100.0%	12,315	1,366	10,949	29	100	91	1,146	3,279	6,511	1,159
State total	1,801,873	45,320	4,221	41,099	57	328	657	3,179	9,677	27,524	3,898
Rate per 100,000 inhabitants	X	2,515.2	234.3	2,280.9	3.2	18.2	36.5	176.4	537.1	1,527.5	216.3
WISCONSIN											
Metropolitan Statistical Area	3,692,594										
Area actually reporting	97.4%	134,920	10,363	124,557	135	956	4,572	4,700	19,851	93,057	11,649
Estimated totals	100.0%	136,716	10,437	126,279	136	967	4,588	4,746	20,143	94,399	11,737
Cities outside metropolitan areas	718,125										
Area actually reporting	99.0%	25,127	1,012	24,115	2	147	85	778	3,156	20,105	854
Estimated totals	100.0%	25,371	1,022	24,349	2	148	86	786	3,187	20,300	862
Rural	1,030,477										
Area actually reporting	97.6%	14,547	761	13,786	16	119	38	588	4,487	8,460	839
Estimated totals	100.0%	14,900	779	14,121	16	122	39	602	4,596	8,666	859
State total	5,441,196	176,987	12,238	164,749	154	1,237	4,713	6,134	27,926	123,365	13,458
Rate per 100,000 inhabitants	X	3,252.7	224.9	3,027.8	2.8	22.7	86.6	112.7	513.2	2,267.2	247.3
WYOMING											
Metropolitan Statistical Area	149,614										
Area actually reporting	100.0%	6,626	367	6,259	5	54	51	257	988	4,957	314
Cities outside metropolitan areas	208,723										
Area actually reporting	98.4%	8,560	649	7,911	4	56	35	554	994	6,592	325
Estimated totals	100.0%	8,697	660	8,037	4	57	36	563	1,010	6,697	330
Rural	140,366										
Area actually reporting	100.0%	2,535	337	2,198	6	37	6	288	450	1,649	99
State total	498,703	17,858	1,364	16,494	15	148	93	1,108	2,448	13,303	743
Rate per 100,000 inhabitants	X	3,580.9	273.5	3,307.4	3.0	29.7	18.6	222.2	490.9	2,667.5	149.0

Note: See Note, table 3.106. These data include estimated offense totals for agencies submitting less than 12 months of offense reports (Source, p. 449). For definitions of offenses and areas, see Appendix 3.

[a]Violent crimes are offenses of murder and nonnegligent manslaughter, forcible rape, robbery, and aggravated assault.
[b]Property crimes are offenses of burglary, larceny-theft, and motor vehicle theft. Data are not included for the property crime of arson.
[c]Includes offenses reported by the Zoological Police and the Metro Transit Police.
[d]Complete data were not available for Illinois and Kentucky; crime counts for these States were estimated by the Source.

Source: U.S. Department of Justice, Federal Bureau of Investigation, *Crime in the United States, 2002* (Washington, DC: USGPO, 2003), pp. 78-88. Table adapted by SOURCEBOOK staff.

Table 3.109

Offenses known to police

By offense and size of place, 2001 and 2002

(2002 estimated population)

Population group	Total Crime Index	Violent crime[a]	Property crime[b]	Murder and non-negligent man-slaughter[c]	Forcible rape	Robbery	Aggravated assault	Burglary	Larceny-theft	Motor vehicle theft
TOTAL ALL AGENCIES 12,270 agencies; total population 255,383,586:										
2001	10,781,626	1,327,864	9,453,762	14,888	80,223	400,324	832,429	1,915,952	6,394,800	1,143,010
2002	10,758,229	1,308,757	9,449,472	15,031	83,631	395,474	814,621	1,942,577	6,350,026	1,156,869
Percent change	-0.2	-1.4	(d)	1.0	4.2	-1.2	-2.1	1.4	-0.7	1.2
TOTAL CITIES 8,618 cities; total population 171,734,038:										
2001	8,565,743	1,072,524	7,493,219	11,823	59,203	356,474	645,024	1,407,365	5,138,943	946,911
2002	8,523,610	1,052,260	7,471,350	11,750	61,551	350,974	627,985	1,420,872	5,101,814	948,664
Percent change	-0.5	-1.9	-0.3	-0.6	4.0	-1.5	-2.6	1.0	-0.7	0.2
Group I 69 cities, 250,000 and over; population 51,949,588:										
2001	3,255,232	546,105	2,709,127	6,880	21,373	209,681	308,171	517,254	1,709,386	482,487
2002	3,220,348	532,902	2,687,446	6,823	21,773	205,183	299,123	515,935	1,692,484	479,027
Percent change	-1.1	-2.4	-0.8	-0.8	1.9	-2.1	-2.9	-0.3	-1.0	-0.7
10 cities, 1,000,000 and over; population 24,682,265:										
2001	1,298,118	262,710	1,035,408	3,222	7,239	103,827	148,422	188,589	648,583	198,236
2002	1,288,482	257,755	1,030,727	3,090	7,385	102,672	144,608	188,526	645,634	196,567
Percent change	-0.7	-1.9	-0.5	-4.1	2.0	-1.1	-2.6	(d)	-0.5	-0.8
21 cities, 500,000 to 999,999; population 13,963,253:										
2001	1,014,346	146,304	868,042	1,911	7,038	53,223	84,132	169,262	554,602	144,178
2002	1,005,707	140,595	865,112	1,926	7,303	50,280	81,086	169,540	552,076	143,496
Percent change	-0.9	-3.9	-0.3	0.8	3.8	-5.5	-3.6	0.2	-0.5	-0.5
38 cities, 250,000 to 499,999; population 13,304,070:										
2001	942,768	137,091	805,677	1,747	7,096	52,631	75,617	159,403	506,201	140,073
2002	926,159	134,552	791,607	1,807	7,085	52,231	73,429	157,869	494,774	138,964
Percent change	-1.8	-1.9	-1.7	3.4	-0.2	-0.8	-2.9	-1.0	-2.3	-0.8
Group II 166 cities, 100,000 to 249,999; population 24,834,622:										
2001	1,398,173	158,920	1,239,253	1,850	9,252	55,373	92,445	241,215	837,554	160,484
2002	1,409,516	156,772	1,252,744	1,906	10,066	54,243	90,557	245,410	844,408	162,926
Percent change	0.8	-1.4	1.1	3.0	8.8	-2.0	-2.0	1.7	0.8	1.5
Group III 387 cities, 50,000 to 99,999; population 26,758,653:										
2001	1,188,578	129,564	1,059,014	1,118	9,190	38,967	80,289	204,585	735,536	118,893
2002	1,195,535	128,209	1,067,326	1,198	9,456	38,858	78,697	205,909	739,275	122,142
Percent change	0.6	-1.0	0.8	7.2	2.9	-0.3	-2.0	0.6	0.5	2.7
Group IV 701 cities, 25,000 to 49,999; population 24,448,049:										
2001	1,001,664	92,139	909,525	766	7,435	24,776	59,162	166,915	662,089	80,521
2002	989,433	90,670	898,763	763	7,683	24,372	57,852	168,453	650,184	80,126
Percent change	-1.2	-1.6	-1.2	-0.4	3.3	-1.6	-2.2	0.9	-1.8	-0.5
Group V 1,538 cities, 10,000 to 24,999; population 24,424,834:										
2001	925,269	79,164	846,105	666	6,753	17,481	54,264	150,759	634,399	60,947
2002	919,341	78,131	841,210	600	7,019	18,050	52,462	154,921	624,962	61,327
Percent change	-0.6	-1.3	-0.6	-9.9	3.9	3.3	-3.3	2.8	-1.5	0.6
Group VI 5,757 cities, under 10,000; population 19,318,292:										
2001	796,827	66,632	730,195	543	5,200	10,196	50,693	126,637	559,979	43,579
2002	789,437	65,576	723,861	460	5,554	10,268	49,294	130,244	550,501	43,116
Percent change	-0.9	-1.6	-0.9	-15.3	6.8	0.7	-2.8	2.8	-1.7	-1.1

See notes at end of table.

Table 3.109

Offenses known to police

By offense and size of place, 2001 and 2002--Continued

Population group	Total Crime Index	Violent crime[a]	Property crime[b]	Murder and non-negligent manslaughter[c]	Forcible rape	Robbery	Aggravated assault	Burglary	Larceny-theft	Motor vehicle theft
SUBURBAN COUNTIES 1,259 agencies; population 55,661,496:										
2001	1,672,347	193,253	1,479,094	2,050	14,739	39,076	137,388	354,044	965,598	159,452
2002	1,688,437	195,127	1,493,310	2,289	15,524	39,763	137,551	363,406	959,610	170,294
Percent change	1.0	1.0	1.0	11.7	5.3	1.8	0.1	2.6	-0.6	6.8
RURAL COUNTIES[e] 2,393 agencies; population 27,988,052:										
2001	543,536	62,087	481,449	1,015	6,281	4,774	50,017	154,543	290,259	36,647
2002	546,182	61,370	484,812	992	6,556	4,737	49,085	158,299	288,602	37,911
Percent change	0.5	-1.2	0.7	-2.3	4.4	-0.8	-1.9	2.4	-0.6	3.4
SUBURBAN AREAS[f] 5,893 agencies; population 101,022,671:										
2001	3,279,354	325,394	2,953,960	3,082	25,157	72,353	224,802	605,950	2,060,715	287,295
2002	3,277,268	323,799	2,953,469	3,259	26,079	72,917	221,544	619,687	2,035,813	297,969
Percent change	-0.1	-0.5	(d)	5.7	3.7	0.8	-1.4	2.3	-1.2	3.7

Note: See Note, table 3.106. These data represent all law enforcement agencies submitting complete reports for at least 6 common months in 2001 and 2002 (Source, p. 450). Forcible rape figures furnished by the State-level Uniform Crime Reporting (UCR) Program administered by the Delaware State Bureau of Investigation for 2001 and the Illinois Department of State Police for 2001 and 2002 were not in accordance with national UCR guidelines and were excluded by the Source from the forcible rape, violent crime, and Total Crime Index categories. Complete data were not available for Illinois and Kentucky for 2001 and 2002. Crime counts for these States were estimated by the Source. For definitions of offenses, and suburban and rural areas, see Appendix 3.

[a]Violent crimes are offenses of murder and nonnegligent manslaughter, forcible rape, robbery, and aggravated assault.
[b]Property crimes are offenses of burglary, larceny-theft, and motor vehicle theft. Data are not included for the property crime of arson.
[c]The murders and nonnegligent manslaughters that occurred as a result of the events of Sept. 11, 2001 are not included in this table.
[d]Less than 0.1%.
[e]Includes State police agencies with no county breakdown.
[f]Includes law enforcement agencies in cities with less than 50,000 inhabitants and county law enforcement agencies that are within a Metropolitan Statistical Area; excludes all metropolitan agencies associated with a central city. The agencies associated with suburban areas also will appear in other groups within this table.

Source: U.S. Department of Justice, Federal Bureau of Investigation, *Crime in the United States, 2002* (Washington, DC: USGPO, 2003), pp. 200, 201. Table adapted by SOURCEBOOK staff.

Table 3.110

Offenses known to police in cities over 100,000 population

2001 and 2002

City	Year	Population	Total Crime Index	Murder and non-negligent manslaughter	Forcible rape	Robbery	Aggravated assault	Burglary	Larceny-theft	Motor vehicle theft	Arson
Abilene, TX	2001	118,561	5,186	2	66	88	227	1,084	3,504	215	37
	2002	121,089	5,394	4	63	111	266	1,289	3,432	229	37
Akron, OH[a]	2001	NA	NA	NA	NA	NA	NA	NA	NA	NA	NA
	2002	218,377	13,101	19	156	655	361	3,069	7,383	1,458	112
Albuquerque, NM	2001	451,098	39,541	34	219	1,610	3,396	6,585	23,535	4,162	179
	2002	457,488	35,762	51	293	1,295	3,250	5,452	21,371	4,050	77
Alexandria, VA[a]	2001	NA	NA	NA	NA	NA	NA	NA	NA	NA	NA
	2002	132,180	5,165	3	21	176	212	482	3,532	739	16
Allentown, PA	2001	106,685	5,237	8	46	295	269	1,111	3,052	456	41
	2002	107,101	5,944	9	58	294	254	1,212	3,615	502	81
Amarillo, TX	2001	177,567	13,627	19	98	277	1,008	2,533	8,747	945	56
	2002	181,355	13,473	7	109	330	1,033	2,468	8,566	960	66
Amherst Town, NY	2001	111,169	2,010	0	3	31	50	171	1,645	110	5
	2002	112,024	1,940	0	9	44	48	194	1,558	87	NA
Anaheim, CA	2001	334,110	11,225	8	91	484	733	1,798	6,328	1,783	47
	2002	340,065	12,198	17	80	465	827	1,995	6,945	1,869	50
Anchorage, AK	2001	263,588	13,214	10	210	384	1,144	1,606	8,648	1,212	103
	2002	267,280	13,670	18	254	382	1,067	1,521	9,255	1,173	141
Ann Arbor, MI	2001	114,625	3,880	1	25	125	201	739	2,626	163	18
	2002	115,309	3,727	5	26	87	183	859	2,385	182	35
Arlington, TX	2001	340,525	24,551	15	145	687	1,282	3,552	16,345	2,525	58
	2002	347,789	23,594	14	152	794	1,242	3,638	15,746	2,008	73
Arvada, CO	2001	104,919	3,784	0	23	37	130	466	2,783	345	40
	2002	107,028	4,148	2	17	48	107	519	3,098	357	48
Athens-Clarke County, GA	2001	102,843	6,855	8	26	156	261	1,069	4,956	379	35
	2002	105,007	6,693	7	53	158	223	1,042	4,779	431	35
Atlanta, GA	2001	426,511	52,195	144	367	4,341	5,956	8,731	25,721	6,935	128
	2002	435,494	49,451	152	276	4,168	5,373	8,554	23,706	7,222	151
Aurora, CO	2001	283,876	17,224	17	224	496	937	1,834	10,871	2,845	102
	2002	289,584	18,075	16	256	549	1,031	2,161	10,745	3,317	130
Aurora, IL[b]	2001	143,715	NA	8	NA	256	605	1,064	3,672	356	32
	2002	145,078	NA	25	NA	158	538	1,017	3,979	317	40
Austin, TX	2001	671,462	43,210	26	262	1,171	1,670	7,439	29,276	3,366	144
	2002	685,784	42,979	25	256	1,174	1,748	6,916	29,725	3,135	152
Bakersfield, CA	2001	251,648	10,255	22	34	324	460	2,035	6,226	1,154	247
	2002	256,134	11,846	22	47	355	647	2,436	6,941	1,398	149
Baltimore, MD	2001	660,826	63,488	256	296	5,747	8,500	10,899	29,615	8,175	426
	2002	671,028	55,820	253	178	4,714	8,644	8,759	26,716	6,556	344
Baton Rouge, LA[c]	2001	227,637	20,149	46	62	1,071	1,368	3,716	12,128	1,758	169
	2002	228,515	18,949	59	133	1,107	1,371	4,070	10,763	1,446	193
Beaumont, TX	2001	116,450	8,845	10	158	361	585	1,692	5,512	527	59
	2002	118,934	10,443	7	172	408	563	1,722	7,015	556	66
Bellevue, WA	2001	111,314	4,667	0	21	59	82	535	3,431	539	35
	2002	112,819	4,640	0	26	48	66	606	3,349	545	39
Berkeley, CA	2001	104,652	9,470	1	17	398	326	1,453	6,054	1,221	51
	2002	106,518	10,271	7	28	407	287	1,514	6,687	1,341	48
Birmingham, AL	2001	243,762	21,085	73	206	1,084	1,664	4,079	11,928	2,051	251
	2002	244,972	21,265	65	239	1,186	1,697	4,389	11,640	2,049	211
Boise, ID	2001	189,671	8,730	2	84	78	471	1,347	6,163	585	68
	2002	192,561	8,748	6	92	84	497	1,318	6,209	542	78
Boston, MA	2001	591,944	37,385	65	361	2,523	4,412	4,222	17,608	8,194	NA
	2002	596,444	35,706	60	369	2,533	3,994	3,830	17,824	7,096	NA
Bridgeport, CT	2001	140,328	8,162	16	69	608	1,217	1,266	2,876	2,110	161
	2002	141,780	8,551	12	65	555	1,063	1,401	3,920	1,535	129
Brownsville, TX	2001	142,893	11,910	7	27	180	595	1,066	9,574	461	35
	2002	145,941	12,759	1	32	181	592	1,207	10,266	480	26
Buffalo, NY	2001	293,187	19,894	64	229	1,600	1,816	3,965	9,669	2,551	444
	2002	295,441	19,017	43	185	1,627	1,902	3,857	9,115	2,288	406
Burbank, CA	2001	102,180	3,377	3	7	122	198	503	2,013	531	10
	2002	104,001	3,216	1	10	100	162	501	1,851	591	24
Cambridge, MA	2001	101,837	4,416	1	15	181	273	688	2,740	518	NA
	2002	102,611	4,306	6	11	195	285	720	2,664	425	NA
Cape Coral, FL	2001	104,936	3,670	2	13	34	297	855	2,293	176	31
	2002	106,963	4,086	3	17	42	327	1,081	2,394	222	25
Carrollton, TX	2001	112,063	3,842	2	2	52	135	802	2,491	358	23
	2002	114,453	4,289	1	18	90	148	819	2,802	411	40
Cedar Rapids, IA	2001	120,628	7,473	3	57	99	248	1,318	5,381	367	19
	2002	121,189	7,233	2	57	104	267	1,111	5,387	305	15
Chandler, AZ[a]	2001	NA	NA	NA	NA	NA	NA	NA	NA	NA	NA
	2002	187,795	11,204	3	46	149	321	1,893	7,447	1,345	63
Charlotte-Mecklenberg, NC	2001	636,459	49,757	66	293	2,996	4,420	10,285	27,291	4,406	317
	2002	646,864	48,597	67	289	2,893	4,334	10,516	25,860	4,638	455

See notes at end of table.

Table 3.110

Offenses known to police in cities over 100,000 population

2001 and 2002--Continued

City	Year	Population	Total Crime Index	Murder and non-negligent man-slaughter	Forcible rape	Robbery	Aggravated assault	Burglary	Larceny-theft	Motor vehicle theft	Arson
Chattanooga, TN	2001	156,941	19,320	26	86	765	1,929	3,270	11,042	2,202	78
	2002	158,507	15,867	24	112	625	1,638	2,574	9,462	1,432	72
Chesapeake, VA[a]	2001	NA	NA	NA	NA	NA	NA	NA	NA	NA	NA
	2002	205,235	8,756	6	65	321	971	1,438	5,351	604	18
Chicago, IL[b]	2001	2,910,709	NA	666	NA	18,433	25,533	25,966	97,496	27,694	1,004
	2002	2,938,299	NA	648	NA	18,532	24,842	25,552	96,380	25,245	1,022
Chula Vista, CA	2001	176,781	7,644	8	69	242	610	1,009	3,999	1,707	58
	2002	179,932	7,463	5	50	257	579	1,068	3,733	1,771	86
Cincinnati, OH	2001	331,880	27,817	55	358	2,075	1,402	6,297	14,283	3,347	537
	2002	333,273	29,205	64	388	2,412	1,329	6,461	14,526	4,025	452
Clarksville, TN	2001	105,378	4,794	6	57	90	372	653	3,445	171	9
	2002	105,419	5,962	6	44	82	462	768	4,330	270	20
Clearwater, FL	2001	111,606	6,642	4	56	230	736	1,188	3,979	449	38
	2002	113,761	6,544	7	51	270	795	1,181	3,799	441	37
Cleveland, OH	2001	479,263	33,065	77	624	3,298	2,425	7,937	12,925	5,779	539
	2002	481,274	33,209	80	619	3,263	2,402	8,096	13,250	5,499	489
Colorado Springs, CO	2001	370,661	19,475	14	257	494	1,142	3,070	13,155	1,343	137
	2002	378,114	21,817	25	275	497	1,235	4,063	14,137	1,585	139
Columbia, SC	2001	117,756	10,574	15	62	442	781	1,426	6,863	985	29
	2002	119,036	10,307	10	83	497	949	1,639	6,213	916	NA
Columbus, GA	2001	190,262	12,143	9	18	440	524	1,803	8,473	876	11
	2002	194,265	12,382	20	25	359	427	1,937	8,595	1,019	50
Columbus, OH	2001	712,748	68,547	81	602	3,364	2,349	15,740	38,835	7,576	476
	2002	715,739	66,261	81	673	3,503	2,242	16,066	36,063	7,633	223
Concord, CA	2001	124,043	5,573	0	16	158	324	750	3,563	762	10
	2002	126,254	5,661	3	22	143	260	767	3,490	976	4
Coral Springs, FL	2001	120,595	3,604	2	13	73	157	648	2,393	318	6
	2002	122,923	3,918	2	25	87	178	681	2,613	332	8
Corona, CA	2001	127,288	4,218	3	19	149	153	681	2,500	713	21
	2002	129,557	4,430	8	24	169	148	736	2,551	794	33
Corpus Christi, TX	2001	283,750	22,534	19	224	582	1,640	3,999	14,555	1,515	124
	2002	289,803	21,237	19	243	511	1,290	3,581	14,147	1,446	149
Costa Mesa, CA	2001	110,745	4,021	4	28	155	203	554	2,595	482	15
	2002	112,718	3,826	2	14	98	156	511	2,620	425	16
Dallas, TX	2001	1,215,553	111,006	240	660	8,330	8,546	20,635	53,611	18,984	1,655
	2002	1,241,481	112,040	196	656	8,041	8,125	20,351	56,306	18,365	1,567
Daly City, CA	2001	105,547	2,300	5	25	146	175	213	1,253	483	8
	2002	107,428	2,199	2	27	113	160	221	1,232	444	11
Dayton, OH	2001	166,478	16,952	30	152	1,090	796	4,018	7,497	3,369	202
	2002	167,176	15,932	42	193	1,066	728	3,903	7,311	2,689	176
Denver, CO	2001	569,653	30,272	45	317	1,250	1,462	5,642	14,621	6,935	345
	2002	581,105	32,132	51	324	1,193	1,539	6,117	15,467	7,441	283
Des Moines, IA	2001	198,468	12,610	11	89	298	352	1,301	9,549	1,010	66
	2002	199,390	13,776	9	113	290	364	1,676	10,313	1,011	72
Detroit, MI	2001	956,283	90,193	395	652	7,096	12,804	15,096	29,613	24,537	1,634
	2002	961,987	85,035	402	708	6,288	12,542	14,399	26,839	23,857	2,429
Downey, CA	2001	109,318	3,715	5	20	208	200	490	1,793	999	22
	2002	111,266	3,651	1	17	195	224	556	1,594	1,064	16
Durham, NC	2001	190,217	15,132	28	77	980	769	3,457	8,723	1,098	47
	2002	193,328	14,461	30	75	942	763	3,088	8,483	1,080	38
Elizabeth, NJ	2001	121,571	7,164	5	16	548	279	912	3,403	2,001	11
	2002	123,088	7,149	13	30	571	291	1,050	3,400	1,794	16
El Monte, CA	2001	118,120	3,778	10	24	281	434	589	1,546	894	40
	2002	120,225	3,592	7	39	265	437	647	1,392	805	13
El Paso, TX	2001	576,453	30,814	20	203	775	3,388	2,553	22,039	1,836	126
	2002	588,750	26,998	14	221	575	3,082	2,221	18,887	1,998	110
Erie, PA	2001	103,768	4,269	4	52	227	203	734	2,828	221	48
	2002	104,173	3,560	4	71	196	179	702	2,241	167	41
Escondido, CA	2001	136,041	5,194	2	31	167	376	851	2,826	941	23
	2002	138,466	5,495	4	40	165	399	960	3,111	816	21
Eugene, OR	2001	139,967	9,415	2	55	203	327	1,247	6,893	688	113
	2002	141,928	9,308	2	56	155	256	1,209	6,824	806	100
Evansville, IN	2001	122,267	6,667	8	52	164	483	1,164	4,327	469	67
	2002	123,153	6,154	2	53	134	473	1,112	4,067	313	65
Fayetteville, NC	2001	123,074	9,861	18	62	464	235	2,485	5,780	817	54
	2002	125,087	10,594	20	54	435	634	2,273	6,480	698	43
Flint, MI[d]	2001	125,601	10,962	41	95	508	1,364	2,695	4,291	1,968	138
	2002	126,351	9,714	30	101	449	1,133	2,261	4,398	1,342	87
Fontana, CA	2001	131,325	3,969	10	41	234	625	746	1,297	1,016	39
	2002	133,665	4,312	7	45	274	587	843	1,337	1,219	37
Fort Collins, CO	2001	121,864	4,695	0	86	35	248	662	3,448	216	36
	2002	124,315	5,371	0	99	35	302	738	3,990	207	31
Fort Lauderdale, FL	2001	156,346	12,581	29	48	837	767	2,439	7,049	1,412	48
	2002	159,365	11,681	12	39	669	687	2,482	6,418	1,374	54

See notes at end of table.

Nature and distribution of known offenses 291

Table 3.110

Offenses known to police in cities over 100,000 population

2001 and 2002--Continued

City	Year	Population	Total Crime Index	Murder and non negligent man-slaughter	Forcible rape	Robbery	Aggravated assault	Burglary	Larceny-theft	Motor vehicle theft	Arson
Fort Wayne, IN	2001	206,886	13,291	23	92	609	348	2,013	9,016	1,190	111
	2002	208,386	12,152	24	113	454	255	2,030	8,268	1,008	117
Fort Worth, TX	2001	546,828	40,466	67	332	1,389	2,076	7,971	24,675	3,956	305
	2002	558,493	44,797	53	321	1,648	2,221	9,736	26,881	3,937	268
Fremont, CA	2001	207,193	6,152	0	19	144	236	1,000	4,045	708	41
	2002	210,886	5,704	3	32	134	221	1,018	3,686	610	25
Fresno, CA	2001	435,600	34,681	40	202	1,362	2,492	5,203	18,398	6,984	548
	2002	443,363	33,909	42	158	1,479	2,101	4,476	18,478	7,175	707
Fullerton, CA	2001	128,345	4,555	3	25	157	184	719	2,914	553	25
	2002	130,632	4,774	1	33	124	203	778	3,055	580	32
Garden Grove, CA	2001	168,266	5,176	5	32	302	460	681	2,785	911	38
	2002	171,266	5,430	6	18	218	550	848	2,875	915	35
Garland, TX	2001	220,665	9,568	9	45	274	264	2,141	5,802	1,033	57
	2002	225,371	9,734	11	44	286	287	1,868	6,349	889	43
Gary, IN	2001	103,325	6,132	82	77	461	281	1,742	2,249	1,240	NA
	2002	104,074	5,812	60	58	420	219	1,543	2,271	1,241	NA
Gilbert, AZ	2001	113,475	4,651	0	21	46	62	1,464	2,663	395	36
	2002	116,663	5,284	5	23	44	112	1,378	3,249	473	46
Glendale, AZ	2001	226,348	14,410	17	66	426	705	2,509	7,531	3,156	72
	2002	232,707	15,475	17	65	405	866	2,438	7,889	3,795	91
Glendale, CA[e]	2001	198,596	4,491	5	22	180	235	987	2,313	749	46
	2002	202,136	4,535	9	21	186	279	913	2,392	735	50
Grand Prairie, TX	2001	130,319	6,928	6	51	128	199	1,095	4,278	1,171	54
	2002	133,099	7,924	3	68	193	259	1,291	4,804	1,306	34
Grand Rapids, MI[c]	2001	198,842	12,026	12	53	552	1,431	2,582	6,719	677	66
	2002	200,029	11,292	8	75	508	1,588	2,309	6,124	680	99
Green Bay, WI	2001	103,042	3,712	3	35	36	198	675	2,561	204	11
	2002	103,791	3,762	1	63	73	252	635	2,468	270	22
Greensboro, NC	2001	227,700	15,962	20	89	896	864	3,258	9,871	964	79
	2002	231,424	15,128	28	103	702	806	2,946	9,392	1,151	104
Hampton, VA	2001	148,696	6,815	10	35	283	276	991	4,129	1,091	38
	2002	150,885	6,209	9	38	291	269	961	3,772	869	35
Hartford, CT	2001	122,274	10,789	25	64	889	615	1,569	5,798	1,829	142
	2002	123,540	10,870	25	57	891	574	1,572	5,571	2,180	164
Hayward, CA	2001	142,632	5,525	10	43	275	213	851	2,784	1,349	61
	2002	145,174	5,508	9	42	324	225	791	2,756	1,361	75
Henderson, NV	2001	184,844	5,728	9	99	195	220	1,434	2,863	908	31
	2002	190,761	5,781	4	104	200	146	1,470	2,705	1,152	56
Hialeah, FL	2001	232,286	12,248	9	40	461	1,059	1,596	6,513	2,570	63
	2002	236,772	12,217	9	48	431	1,012	1,609	7,029	2,079	44
Hollywood, FL	2001	142,968	9,250	7	51	393	592	1,235	5,834	1,138	41
	2002	145,729	9,171	11	44	392	576	1,205	5,917	1,026	35
Honolulu, HI	2001	885,605	48,442	20	293	999	1,141	7,340	33,052	5,597	396
	2002	900,433	57,271	18	304	1,072	1,207	8,932	37,250	8,488	429
Houston, TX	2001	1,997,965	141,987	267	945	9,921	12,286	25,108	69,371	24,089	1,758
	2002	2,040,583	149,247	256	892	11,212	12,598	26,905	73,445	23,939	1,696
Huntington Beach, CA	2001	193,117	4,500	0	44	94	205	1,002	2,608	547	48
	2002	196,559	4,385	3	36	84	216	856	2,715	475	33
Huntsville, AL	2001	158,830	11,413	15	109	345	570	1,802	7,802	770	41
	2002	159,618	10,167	5	82	315	559	1,714	6,718	774	45
Independence, MO	2001	113,986	8,889	6	27	144	491	1,157	6,220	844	53
	2002	114,854	8,483	6	33	124	489	1,210	5,833	788	48
Indianapolis, IN[c]	2001	798,251	41,058	112	442	2,787	4,087	9,043	18,224	6,363	279
	2002	804,034	48,503	112	441	2,937	4,028	9,662	24,821	6,502	389
Inglewood, CA[c]	2001	114,672	4,586	38	36	639	610	839	1,550	874	36
	2002	116,716	4,107	28	61	507	329	690	1,522	970	24
Irvine, CA	2001	145,731	3,396	0	9	44	80	904	2,054	305	7
	2002	148,328	3,624	1	20	62	78	867	2,339	257	16
Irving, TX	2001	195,963	9,993	10	58	281	467	1,387	6,561	1,229	44
	2002	200,144	10,812	5	47	250	501	1,634	7,077	1,298	49
Jackson, MS	2001	185,122	18,586	50	218	1,044	654	4,683	8,972	2,965	96
	2002	186,012	17,648	49	182	1,074	497	4,377	8,669	2,800	73
Jacksonville, FL	2001	754,679	51,250	75	287	2,195	4,831	9,903	28,827	5,132	311
	2002	769,253	51,021	90	277	2,016	4,660	9,173	29,391	5,414	297
Jersey City, NJ	2001	242,055	12,527	25	89	1,301	1,438	2,350	4,911	2,413	48
	2002	245,075	12,182	21	86	1,381	1,419	2,285	4,694	2,296	31
Joliet, IL[b]	2001	106,760	NA	5	NA	209	477	887	3,128	387	65
	2002	107,772	NA	7	NA	183	405	851	3,025	290	70
Kansas City, MO	2001	444,267	49,959	103	319	2,367	4,292	7,454	27,126	8,298	493
	2002	447,650	44,942	83	300	2,011	3,660	7,978	24,161	6,749	478
Knoxville, TN	2001	175,441	11,069	15	139	637	1,314	1,717	5,951	1,296	141
	2002	177,191	11,983	21	74	553	1,308	2,135	6,680	1,212	138
Lafayette, LA	2001	110,170	8,167	5	74	195	771	1,332	5,318	472	41
	2002	110,594	8,431	3	85	171	784	1,391	5,503	494	32
Lakewood, CO	2001	148,028	8,454	7	94	164	244	1,035	5,829	1,081	58
	2002	151,005	8,938	1	80	144	207	1,277	6,084	1,145	40

See notes at end of table.

Table 3.110

Offenses known to police in cities over 100,000 population

2001 and 2002--Continued

City	Year	Population	Total Crime Index	Murder and non-negligent manslaughter	Forcible rape	Robbery	Aggravated assault	Burglary	Larceny-theft	Motor vehicle theft	Arson
Lancaster, CA	2001	120,924	4,747	7	56	263	837	1,159	1,909	516	55
	2002	123,079	5,123	12	57	313	980	1,179	1,893	689	63
Lansing, MI	2001	119,756	7,212	8	178	227	940	994	4,382	483	68
	2002	120,471	6,601	11	169	245	867	1,065	3,837	407	52
Laredo, TX	2001	180,583	13,056	8	39	200	874	1,791	9,125	1,019	87
	2002	184,435	12,952	7	58	203	839	1,898	9,064	883	77
Las Vegas, NV[c]	2001	1,117,763	50,570	133	447	3,667	3,302	10,083	22,394	10,544	268
	2002	1,153,546	56,810	137	494	3,776	4,574	11,136	24,204	12,489	270
Lexington, KY[e]	2001	262,045	13,032	24	120	721	718	2,516	8,155	778	58
	2002	263,807	12,521	15	117	626	671	2,439	8,004	649	31
Lincoln, NE	2001	225,841	15,041	6	88	154	1,054	1,970	11,194	575	26
	2002	227,943	15,005	6	98	179	992	2,014	11,190	526	26
Little Rock, AR	2001	184,413	16,866	34	92	617	1,130	3,630	9,841	1,522	168
	2002	185,646	20,680	41	116	884	1,370	4,826	11,930	1,513	148
Livonia, MI	2001	101,075	3,113	1	21	71	112	429	2,202	277	23
	2002	101,678	2,779	7	33	61	112	400	1,938	228	25
Long Beach, CA	2001	470,099	18,467	49	125	1,417	1,822	3,232	7,876	3,946	267
	2002	478,478	19,303	67	144	1,505	1,910	3,405	8,530	3,742	253
Los Angeles, CA	2001	3,763,486	189,278	588	1,409	17,166	33,080	25,695	79,521	31,819	2,348
	2002	3,830,561	190,992	654	1,415	17,197	32,429	25,374	79,813	34,110	2,091
Louisville, KY	2001	257,739	15,673	25	78	989	823	3,390	7,934	2,434	249
	2002	259,472	15,439	35	49	995	958	3,519	7,710	2,173	216
Lowell, MA	2001	105,668	4,510	4	37	122	687	650	2,052	958	NA
	2002	106,472	4,258	7	47	158	637	630	1,957	822	NA
Lubbock, TX	2001	204,093	14,063	10	100	317	2,042	2,847	8,068	679	66
	2002	208,447	14,371	11	133	303	2,067	2,979	8,307	571	65
Macon, GA	2001	99,601	10,590	18	60	275	351	2,291	6,272	1,323	60
	2002	101,696	10,433	16	63	240	319	2,288	6,296	1,211	80
Madison, WI	2001	209,537	8,299	6	63	295	344	1,354	5,530	707	75
	2002	211,061	8,847	3	90	266	396	1,564	5,898	630	127
Manchester, NH	2001	109,032	3,520	0	53	118	86	597	2,356	310	53
	2002	110,406	3,545	0	44	116	82	617	2,441	245	54
McAllen, TX	2001	108,829	8,989	3	11	124	336	1,567	6,235	713	32
	2002	111,150	8,982	4	12	178	339	1,074	6,684	691	58
Memphis, TN[e]	2001	655,898	65,479	158	480	4,338	5,886	15,874	29,207	9,536	262
	2002	662,441	65,846	151	517	4,240	5,538	16,340	29,841	9,219	275
Mesa, AZ[c]	2001	410,026	27,508	17	106	452	1,941	4,313	16,121	4,558	35
	2002	421,547	33,335	22	129	590	2,146	4,957	20,405	5,086	67
Mesquite, TX	2001	127,349	6,542	4	3	147	312	646	4,554	876	102
	2002	130,065	6,480	9	5	135	298	689	4,528	816	52
Miami, FL	2001	371,863	35,291	66	118	2,719	4,307	6,218	16,635	5,228	259
	2002	379,044	33,952	65	96	2,706	4,361	5,962	15,886	4,876	228
Milwaukee, WI	2001	601,229	45,748	127	295	2,913	2,128	6,680	25,712	7,893	453
	2002	605,600	46,315	111	326	3,197	2,148	6,922	26,424	7,187	382
Minneapolis, MN	2001	386,726	26,820	43	399	1,943	1,716	4,092	14,548	4,079	259
	2002	390,415	26,630	47	362	1,794	1,920	4,433	14,641	3,433	261
Mobile, AL[f]	2001	255,551	19,875	42	95	840	552	4,653	12,284	1,409	92
	2002	256,542	17,949	40	107	752	477	3,590	11,534	1,449	NA
Modesto, CA[c]	2001	192,366	11,976	17	104	381	659	1,829	7,580	1,406	120
	2002	195,795	12,981	5	71	344	593	1,819	8,426	1,723	46
Montgomery, AL	2001	202,350	15,791	26	102	652	676	3,252	9,928	1,155	NA
	2002	203,355	17,617	30	118	698	629	3,812	10,640	1,690	NA
Moreno Valley, CA	2001	145,027	6,588	3	33	312	853	1,635	2,869	883	21
	2002	147,612	6,902	7	51	278	907	1,446	3,087	1,126	35
Naperville, IL[b]	2001	129,009	NA	0	NA	25	67	254	2,057	74	24
	2002	130,232	NA	1	NA	13	62	334	1,921	93	15
Nashville, TN	2001	555,059	50,155	64	427	2,521	6,063	7,842	27,837	5,401	228
	2002	560,596	46,018	61	403	2,081	6,138	7,468	25,082	4,785	162
Newark, NJ	2001	275,823	18,748	90	91	1,837	1,819	2,552	6,324	6,035	415
	2002	279,269	17,814	65	88	1,567	1,473	2,253	6,033	6,335	247
New Haven, CT[g]	2001	124,334	9,844	19	56	768	1,072	1,348	5,190	1,391	21
	2002	NA	NA	NA	NA	NA	NA	NA	NA	NA	NA
New Orleans, LA	2001	484,289	36,057	213	209	2,778	2,677	5,262	16,187	8,731	NA
	2002	486,157	31,206	258	162	1,994	2,142	4,759	14,325	7,566	NA
Newport News, VA	2001	182,930	9,784	30	97	448	750	1,508	5,788	1,163	113
	2002	185,622	9,936	20	106	420	805	1,636	5,715	1,234	117
New York, NY[h]	2001	8,023,018	266,587	3,472	1,530	28,202	37,893	31,563	133,938	29,989	NA
	2002	8,084,693	250,630	587	1,689	27,229	34,334	30,102	129,655	27,034	NA
Norfolk, VA	2001	238,020	14,966	31	127	809	633	1,728	10,123	1,515	24
	2002	241,523	15,476	41	115	709	488	1,758	10,738	1,627	23
North Las Vegas, NV	2001	121,719	6,817	20	50	433	850	1,336	2,824	1,304	40
	2002	125,616	7,367	19	57	449	769	1,525	3,029	1,519	68

See notes at end of table.

Nature and distribution of known offenses 293

Table 3.110

Offenses known to police in cities over 100,000 population

2001 and 2002--Continued

City	Year	Population	Total Crime Index	Murder and non-negligent man-slaughter	Forcible rape	Robbery	Aggravated assault	Burglary	Larceny-theft	Motor vehicle theft	Arson
Norwalk, CA	2001	105,218	3,656	7	19	219	556	544	1,436	875	21
	2002	107,093	3,576	10	22	194	520	639	1,340	851	20
Oakland, CA	2001	406,908	27,627	84	295	2,125	2,826	3,696	13,081	5,520	328
	2002	414,161	29,875	108	249	2,452	2,852	4,252	13,703	6,259	354
Oceanside, CA	2001	164,022	5,887	4	86	258	722	1,071	3,074	672	44
	2002	166,945	6,964	5	75	285	751	1,109	3,824	915	40
Oklahoma City, OK	2001	507,517	45,875	45	405	1,090	2,643	8,405	29,771	3,516	222
	2002	512,448	49,929	38	445	1,169	2,562	8,314	33,686	3,715	228
Omaha, NE	2001	390,456	29,507	25	157	868	1,658	3,107	19,382	4,310	255
	2002	394,090	28,781	26	173	998	1,632	3,220	18,490	4,242	268
Ontario, CA	2001	160,943	8,546	10	74	388	717	1,082	4,432	1,843	95
	2002	163,812	8,296	7	55	391	595	1,139	4,390	1,719	108
Orange, CA	2001	131,215	3,692	0	18	125	209	467	2,435	438	37
	2002	133,554	3,872	1	17	108	151	628	2,435	532	25
Orlando, FL	2001	190,769	22,363	15	135	1,086	2,449	3,529	12,842	2,307	60
	2002	194,454	21,133	15	121	1,034	2,449	3,710	11,602	2,202	53
Overland Park, KS[a]	2001	NA	NA	NA	NA	NA	NA	NA	NA	NA	NA
	2002	150,603	5,186	2	26	46	290	559	3,712	551	27
Oxnard, CA	2001	173,524	5,250	6	38	393	375	917	3,062	459	48
	2002	176,617	5,373	10	36	353	449	913	3,034	578	41
Palmdale, CA	2001	118,838	4,312	8	48	178	673	896	1,932	577	43
	2002	120,956	5,374	7	56	245	847	961	2,521	737	82
Pasadena, CA	2001	136,425	5,240	4	34	268	370	899	3,157	508	46
	2002	138,857	4,881	3	25	255	374	959	2,803	462	60
Pasadena, TX	2001	144,889	6,919	3	52	153	555	1,270	4,057	829	78
	2002	147,979	7,184	7	68	154	390	1,379	4,402	784	84
Paterson, NJ	2001	150,465	8,004	16	15	673	598	1,964	3,059	1,679	10
	2002	152,340	6,842	15	29	653	468	1,595	2,645	1,437	19
Pembroke Pines, FL	2001	140,988	5,079	3	14	130	203	620	3,470	639	12
	2002	143,711	4,751	3	20	121	234	675	3,091	607	29
Peoria, AZ	2001	112,096	5,332	3	22	73	242	1,102	3,018	872	15
	2002	115,245	5,877	0	34	64	184	955	3,439	1,201	15
Peoria, IL[b]	2001	113,509	NA	14	NA	345	536	1,840	5,649	932	105
	2002	114,585	NA	9	NA	380	437	1,841	5,590	860	85
Philadelphia, PA	2001	1,518,302	93,878	309	1,014	9,604	10,477	11,629	45,318	15,527	NA
	2002	1,524,226	83,392	288	1,035	8,869	9,865	11,244	38,789	13,302	NA
Phoenix, AZ	2001	1,366,542	104,975	209	400	4,629	5,294	16,673	55,190	22,580	421
	2002	1,404,938	109,916	177	410	4,075	5,561	16,855	57,214	25,624	501
Pittsburgh, PA	2001	341,414	19,708	55	134	1,384	1,391	3,246	10,766	2,732	173
	2002	342,529	19,737	47	148	1,616	1,983	3,298	10,108	2,537	114
Plano, TX	2001	227,069	8,987	4	23	113	448	1,417	6,440	542	45
	2002	231,912	9,020	6	40	145	478	1,326	6,505	520	22
Pomona, CA	2001	152,251	6,131	19	54	418	1,046	951	2,489	1,154	27
	2002	154,964	6,132	18	77	448	805	886	2,681	1,217	28
Portland, OR	2001	537,081	43,183	21	305	1,267	2,963	5,592	28,358	4,677	385
	2002	544,604	43,327	20	354	1,294	2,844	5,702	27,933	5,180	496
Portsmouth, VA	2001	102,117	6,650	12	30	473	584	1,515	3,370	666	15
	2002	103,620	7,015	11	38	425	524	1,316	4,058	643	20
Providence, RI	2001	175,374	14,185	23	111	595	714	2,284	7,387	3,071	344
	2002	177,162	13,864	23	109	550	620	2,186	7,515	2,861	324
Provo, UT	2001	106,891	3,844	0	43	18	98	558	2,929	198	21
	2002	109,079	3,657	0	37	23	105	514	2,789	189	17
Pueblo, CO	2001	104,886	6,466	5	49	146	608	1,131	4,170	357	60
	2002	106,995	6,145	6	27	164	528	1,144	3,893	383	63
Raleigh, NC	2001	280,791	18,585	10	91	804	1,282	3,983	11,087	1,328	101
	2002	285,383	17,833	19	106	697	1,144	3,836	10,692	1,339	90
Rancho Cucamonga, CA	2001	130,117	3,805	1	17	123	156	811	2,089	608	36
	2002	132,436	3,966	2	29	99	149	744	2,372	571	35
Reno, NV[d]	2001	190,218	10,989	6	98	407	704	1,435	7,399	940	42
	2002	196,307	11,626	9	126	450	899	1,288	7,748	1,106	64
Richmond, CA	2001	101,060	7,190	18	47	410	540	1,230	3,448	1,497	95
	2002	102,861	7,838	29	38	471	660	1,051	3,534	2,055	88
Richmond, VA	2001	200,842	18,207	72	117	1,430	1,127	2,943	9,455	3,063	166
	2002	203,799	18,002	77	118	1,289	1,122	2,966	9,926	2,504	191
Riverside, CA	2001	259,908	14,518	20	95	622	1,422	2,225	7,896	2,238	220
	2002	264,540	15,161	20	94	616	1,296	2,525	8,140	2,470	238
Rochester, NY	2001	220,177	16,156	40	84	921	618	2,459	9,719	2,315	NA
	2002	221,871	16,911	42	107	972	665	2,467	9,853	2,805	330
Rockford, IL[b]	2001	150,877	NA	11	NA	446	672	2,502	8,143	1,017	34
	2002	152,307	NA	20	NA	518	631	3,234	8,015	1,197	37
Sacramento, CA	2001	414,582	30,691	40	169	1,440	1,660	5,068	15,977	6,337	440
	2002	421,971	30,780	47	185	1,734	1,581	5,019	15,548	6,666	333
Saint Louis, MO	2001	350,336	52,635	148	120	3,140	4,256	8,128	28,000	8,843	711
	2002	353,004	50,429	111	136	2,818	4,434	7,059	26,036	9,835	585
Saint Paul, MN	2001	290,234	19,046	9	221	680	1,326	3,009	11,457	2,344	236
	2002	293,002	17,803	13	192	973	1,181	3,232	10,041	2,171	208

See notes at end of table.

294 Sourcebook of criminal justice statistics 2003

Table 3.110

Offenses known to police in cities over 100,000 population

2001 and 2002--Continued

City	Year	Population	Total Crime Index	Murder and non-negligent man-slaughter	Forcible rape	Robbery	Aggravated assault	Burglary	Larceny-theft	Motor vehicle theft	Arson
Saint Petersburg, FL	2001	254,664	20,534	21	149	1,147	3,059	3,678	10,418	2,062	133
	2002	259,582	20,914	23	124	1,027	3,249	3,628	10,550	2,313	119
Salem, OR	2001	138,984	11,120	4	81	160	88	1,395	8,515	877	27
	2002	140,931	12,389	6	79	156	103	1,415	9,277	1,353	23
Salinas, CA	2001	153,867	6,979	15	56	399	799	843	4,102	765	53
	2002	156,609	6,834	20	59	367	692	757	4,013	926	58
Salt Lake City, UT	2001	184,723	16,438	18	121	481	546	2,209	11,401	1,662	65
	2002	188,504	19,059	11	109	478	635	2,512	13,337	1,977	87
San Antonio, TX	2001	1,170,622	96,498	100	492	2,146	6,808	14,018	66,694	6,240	576
	2002	1,195,592	94,132	100	464	2,114	7,091	13,368	65,251	5,744	533
San Bernardino, CA	2001	188,847	12,803	30	89	829	1,449	2,299	5,868	2,239	139
	2002	192,212	13,755	42	102	886	1,454	2,340	6,226	2,705	109
San Diego, CA	2001	1,246,136	50,444	50	342	1,729	5,284	7,219	25,050	10,770	201
	2002	1,268,346	50,124	47	330	1,627	5,189	7,639	24,577	10,715	206
San Francisco, CA[a]	2001	NA	NA	NA	NA	NA	NA	NA	NA	NA	NA
	2002	805,269	42,671	68	210	3,208	2,573	5,947	24,468	6,197	227
San Jose, CA	2001	913,513	25,163	22	329	712	4,501	2,939	13,567	3,093	497
	2002	927,821	24,139	26	379	827	2,902	3,026	13,642	3,337	258
Santa Ana, CA	2001	344,258	12,066	24	55	942	823	1,396	6,263	2,563	203
	2002	350,393	12,038	23	66	871	970	1,225	6,485	2,398	159
Santa Clara, CA	2001	104,263	3,350	0	20	45	217	420	2,412	236	45
	2002	106,121	3,228	4	19	62	226	417	2,188	312	29
Santa Clarita, CA	2001	153,896	3,161	3	23	79	210	662	1,831	353	53
	2002	156,639	3,195	6	24	90	185	611	1,844	435	34
Santa Rosa, CA	2001	150,338	5,854	3	72	123	309	773	4,050	524	45
	2002	153,018	6,531	6	93	167	359	974	4,213	719	43
Savannah, GA	2001	134,682	12,458	26	70	840	602	2,080	7,400	1,440	53
	2002	137,516	11,595	32	58	650	449	1,985	6,884	1,537	27
Scottsdale, AZ	2001	209,686	9,905	10	58	196	355	2,660	5,251	1,375	58
	2002	215,578	10,134	1	63	171	248	2,786	5,487	1,378	51
Seattle, WA	2001	572,345	46,091	25	164	1,594	2,367	6,684	26,502	8,755	216
	2002	580,089	46,432	26	152	1,576	2,338	7,290	26,742	8,308	211
Shreveport, LA	2001	199,986	15,616	31	111	534	1,253	3,368	9,200	1,119	130
	2002	200,757	16,389	40	119	667	1,218	3,350	9,346	1,649	146
Simi Valley, CA	2001	113,420	1,746	6	11	37	99	361	1,040	192	13
	2002	115,442	1,756	0	7	26	105	355	1,100	163	20
Sioux Falls, SD	2001	124,263	4,130	2	76	38	208	681	2,943	182	38
	2002	124,997	4,189	1	115	52	228	652	2,946	195	53
South Bend, IN	2001	108,396	9,122	21	78	487	302	1,932	5,603	699	57
	2002	109,182	8,203	20	93	354	353	1,826	4,983	574	69
Spokane, WA	2001	198,744	17,073	7	79	440	883	3,101	10,792	1,771	50
	2002	201,433	15,895	20	83	379	820	2,660	10,248	1,685	62
Springfield, IL[b]	2001	112,019	NA	14	NA	243	744	1,830	5,366	418	59
	2002	113,081	NA	5	NA	342	846	1,736	6,095	349	60
Springfield, MA	2001	152,806	12,798	10	99	503	2,665	2,697	5,087	1,737	156
	2002	153,967	14,299	12	107	585	2,400	3,808	5,117	2,270	125
Springfield, MO	2001	152,515	14,141	10	60	262	657	2,182	10,066	904	93
	2002	153,675	12,066	4	102	222	733	1,882	8,352	771	84
Stamford, CT	2001	117,754	3,086	1	13	141	116	357	2,095	363	6
	2002	118,971	2,398	2	14	147	117	249	1,571	298	3
Sterling Heights, MI	2001	125,127	3,552	0	20	37	203	387	2,631	274	10
	2002	125,873	3,377	1	30	35	180	397	2,489	245	20
Stockton, CA	2001	248,301	19,728	30	144	1,030	2,092	2,871	10,558	3,003	115
	2002	252,727	21,114	36	141	1,171	2,345	2,965	11,003	3,453	74
Sunnyvale, CA	2001	134,209	2,698	0	18	59	103	289	1,995	234	17
	2002	136,601	2,569	2	24	70	96	322	1,837	218	30
Syracuse, NY	2001	147,577	9,413	15	41	568	936	1,802	5,166	885	113
	2002	148,712	9,791	23	43	551	902	1,930	5,060	1,282	118
Tacoma, WA	2001	196,638	18,370	15	143	743	1,211	2,920	10,033	3,305	123
	2002	199,299	20,182	19	171	715	1,277	3,032	11,728	3,240	115
Tallahassee, FL	2001	154,527	12,151	7	127	428	1,247	2,265	7,227	850	26
	2002	157,511	11,880	9	151	384	1,073	2,262	7,188	813	34
Tampa, FL	2001	311,310	34,848	34	212	2,359	4,011	6,096	15,586	6,550	197
	2002	317,322	35,380	37	204	2,334	3,714	6,283	16,088	6,720	134
Tempe, AZ	2001	164,088	16,534	5	72	327	533	2,273	10,497	2,827	37
	2002	168,699	17,819	10	75	344	811	2,360	11,004	3,215	41
Thousand Oaks, CA	2001	119,179	1,888	1	10	33	130	308	1,276	130	20
	2002	121,304	2,030	0	18	35	105	364	1,359	149	24
Toledo, OH[d]	2001	314,183	27,105	18	185	1,312	1,535	6,299	14,006	3,750	373
	2002	315,501	26,717	28	185	1,378	1,592	5,811	14,510	3,213	487
Topeka, KS[d]	2001	122,660	11,530	22	84	358	611	2,046	7,632	777	18
	2002	123,627	11,294	8	73	409	499	1,767	7,863	675	NA
Torrance, CA	2001	140,510	4,366	4	24	210	171	744	2,582	631	26
	2002	143,014	4,541	2	23	211	248	708	2,712	637	23

See notes at end of table.

Table 3.110

Offenses known to police in cities over 100,000 population

2001 and 2002--Continued

City	Year	Population	Total Crime Index	Murder and non-negligent manslaughter	Forcible rape	Robbery	Aggravated assault	Burglary	Larceny-theft	Motor vehicle theft	Arson
Tucson, AZ	2001	503,461	49,757	42	321	1,698	2,762	6,553	31,217	7,164	355
	2002	517,607	50,171	47	338	1,350	2,974	6,717	32,539	6,206	328
Tulsa, OK	2001	394,125	29,354	34	256	776	3,481	5,863	15,308	3,636	250
	2002	397,953	30,119	26	243	901	3,153	6,313	15,918	3,565	246
Vallejo, CA	2001	118,930	7,249	4	53	344	758	1,176	3,963	951	67
	2002	121,049	7,117	7	45	326	704	1,194	3,768	1,073	46
Vancouver, WA[c]	2001	145,846	7,962	4	76	132	475	1,067	5,745	463	61
	2002	147,819	7,773	1	100	155	276	1,196	5,189	856	39
Ventura, CA	2001	102,791	3,357	2	28	91	160	565	2,280	231	13
	2002	104,623	3,648	2	30	90	164	621	2,478	263	9
Virginia Beach, VA	2001	431,819	16,135	12	110	368	350	2,285	12,078	932	181
	2002	438,175	16,067	3	132	443	376	2,290	11,981	842	175
Waco, TX	2001	116,307	10,361	7	100	269	527	1,875	6,787	796	60
	2002	118,788	11,001	14	58	277	596	2,197	7,143	716	32
Warren, MI	2001	138,976	5,633	5	63	191	559	769	2,584	1,462	58
	2002	139,805	5,358	8	68	204	577	870	2,483	1,148	52
Washington, DC	2001	571,822	44,041	232	188	3,940	5,568	5,009	21,434	7,670	95
	2002	570,898	44,349	264	262	3,731	4,854	5,167	20,903	9,168	109
Waterbury, CT	2001	107,886	6,872	7	38	277	224	1,299	4,147	880	16
	2002	109,002	6,524	4	48	283	248	1,246	3,926	769	12
West Covina, CA	2001	107,033	4,793	2	18	152	199	560	2,962	900	46
	2002	108,940	4,238	2	25	136	199	532	2,573	771	30
West Valley, UT[c]	2001	110,682	6,950	2	64	116	281	887	4,998	602	25
	2002	112,948	6,889	3	59	98	275	883	4,843	728	35
Wichita, KS	2001	345,081	23,534	17	183	742	1,501	4,422	14,953	1,716	NA
	2002	347,801	24,104	20	208	796	1,344	4,459	15,523	1,754	NA
Wichita Falls, TX	2001	106,562	8,185	4	21	256	590	1,502	5,314	498	31
	2002	108,834	8,532	11	31	246	710	1,726	5,327	481	35
Winston-Salem, NC[e]	2001	188,937	16,037	15	120	701	930	3,444	9,798	1,029	15
	2002	192,027	14,669	15	116	549	934	3,311	8,757	987	115
Worcester, MA[g]	2001	173,469	8,212	7	117	363	935	1,152	4,421	1,217	72
	2002	NA	NA	NA	NA	NA	NA	NA	NA	NA	NA
Yonkers, NY	2001	196,447	5,419	6	15	473	441	837	2,746	901	65
	2002	197,957	4,676	13	11	419	450	746	2,225	812	47

Note: See Note, table 3.106. Arson is shown only if 12 months of arson data were received. The Total Crime Index is the sum of the Crime Index offenses, not including arson. Cities are included in the table if the population was 100,000 or more in either of the years presented. Complete data were not available for Illinois and Kentucky for 2001 and 2002. For definitions of offenses, see Appendix 3.

[a]Figures not reported for 2001.
[b]Forcible rape figures furnished by the State-level Uniform Crime Reporting (UCR) program administered by the Illinois Department of State Police were not in accordance with national UCR guidelines. Therefore, the figures were excluded from the forcible rape and Total Crime Index categories.
[c]Due to reporting changes, annexations, and/or incomplete data, 2002 figures are not comparable to earlier years.

[d]Due to reporting changes, annexations, and/or incomplete data, 2001 and 2002 figures are not comparable to earlier years.
[e]Due to reporting changes, annexations, and/or incomplete data, 2001 figures are not comparable to earlier years.
[f]The population for the city of Mobile, AL includes 55,864 inhabitants from the jurisdiction of the Mobile County Sheriff's Department.
[g]Figures not reported for 2002.
[h]The murder and nonnegligent manslaughter figure includes 2,823 deaths reported as a result of the events of Sept. 11, 2001.

Source: U.S. Department of Justice, Federal Bureau of Investigation, *Crime in the United States, 2001*, pp. 118-164; *2002*, pp. 120-165 (Washington, DC: USGPO). Table adapted by SOURCEBOOK staff.

Table 3.111

Number of offenses known to police and average loss incurred

By selected offenses and type of target, United States, 2002

(12,524 agencies; 2002 estimated population 236,622,152)

Offense and type of target	Number of offenses 2002	Percent change over 2001[a]	Percent[b]	Average property loss (in dollars)
Murder[c]	12,904	2.2%	100.0%	NA
Forcible rape	77,639	4.2	100.0	NA
Robbery	324,938	-1.1	100.0	$1,281
Street/highway	139,037	-2.9	42.8	1,045
Commercial house	47,344	-1.3	14.6	1,676
Gas or service station	8,690	-7.6	2.7	679
Convenience store	20,990	-4.8	6.5	665
Residence	43,800	4.4	13.5	1,340
Bank	7,485	-6.5	2.3	4,763
Miscellaneous	57,592	2.7	17.7	1,340
Burglary	1,793,362	2.0	100.0	1,549
Residence (dwelling)	1,180,063	3.0	65.8	1,482
Night	348,538	2.4	19.4	1,177
Day	561,688	4.3	31.3	1,567
Unknown	269,837	1.3	15.0	1,698
Nonresidence (store, office, etc.)	613,299	-0.1	34.2	1,678
Night	260,525	(d)	14.5	1,449
Day	190,651	0.1	10.6	1,525
Unknown	162,123	-0.4	9.0	2,227
Larceny-theft (except motor vehicle theft)	5,808,133	(d)	100.0	699
By type				
Pocket-picking	26,707	-5.0	0.5	328
Purse-snatching	32,011	3.0	0.6	332
Shoplifting	811,709	2.2	14.0	187
From motor vehicles (except accessories)	1,536,453	2.9	26.5	692
Motor vehicle accessories	622,384	4.7	10.7	432
Bicycles	227,970	-3.5	3.9	257
From buildings	727,395	-5.4	12.5	1,013
From coin-operated machines	43,103	1.8	0.7	250
All others	1,780,401	-2.2	30.7	984
By value				
Over $200	2,301,455	0.7	39.6	1,682
$50 to $200	1,310,879	-1.5	22.6	114
Under $50	2,195,799	0.1	37.8	18
Motor vehicle theft	1,039,490	2.2	100.0	6,701

Note: See Note, table 3.106. "Commercial house" refers to nonresidential structures, with the exception of gas stations, convenience stores, and banking-type institutions. "Loss" refers to property taken during the commission of the offense only. All offenses, including those that involve no loss of property, were used in compiling "average loss." These data are based on law enforcement agencies submitting complete reports for at least 6 months in 2002 (Source, p. 451). Complete data were not available for Illinois and Kentucky; crime counts for these States were estimated by the Source. For definitions of offenses, see Appendix 3.

[a]Percent change calculations are based only on agencies submitting 6 or more common months of data for both 2001 and 2002. As a result, direct comparisons should not be made with similar data presented in previous editions of SOURCEBOOK.
[b]Because of rounding, percents may not add to total.
[c]The murders and nonnegligent manslaughters that occurred as a result of the events of Sept. 11, 2001 are not included in the figures used to calculate percent change.
[d]Less than 0.1%.

Source: U.S. Department of Justice, Federal Bureau of Investigation, *Crime in the United States, 2002* (Washington, DC: USGPO, 2003), p. 217, Table 23.

Table 3.112

Bias-motivated (hate) crimes known to police

By offense, United States, 2002

	Offenses	Victims[a]	Known offenders[b]
Total	8,832	9,222	7,314[c]
Crimes against persons	6,091	6,139	6,359
Murder and nonnegligent manslaughter	11	11	15
Forcible rape	8	8	16
Robbery	131	179	269
Aggravated assault	1,035	1,035	1,498
Simple assault	1,791	1,791	2,436
Intimidation	3,105	3,105	2,117
Other[d]	10	10	8
Crimes against property	2,692	3,034	1,154
Burglary	131	163	86
Larceny-theft	151	157	95
Motor vehicle theft	9	9	3
Arson	38	47	27
Destruction/damage/vandalism	2,347	2,642	927
Other[d]	16	16	16
Other[d]	49	49	61

Note: These data reflect the number of bias-motivated offenses reported to the Federal Bureau of Investigation's (FBI) Uniform Crime Reporting Program. In accordance with the Hate Crime Statistics Act of 1990, the FBI defines a crime motivated by bias against race, religion, ethnic/national origin, disability, or sexual orientation as a bias-motivated or hate crime. For 2002, a total of 12,073 law enforcement agencies in 49 States and the District of Columbia participated in the Hate Crime Data Collection Program. Hawaii did not participate. These figures include data from law enforcement agencies submitting less than 12 months of data to the FBI (Source, pp. 3, 23). Data from this source have been updated by the FBI and may differ from those reported in *Crime in the United States, 2002*.

[a]May include persons, businesses, institutions, or society as a whole.
[b]"Known offender" does not imply that the identity of the suspect is known, rather that an attribute of the suspect has been identified, distinguishing him/her from an unknown offender.
[c]The actual number of known offenders is 7,314. Some offenders, however, committed more than one offense per incident and are counted more than once. Therefore subcategories will not add to total.
[d]Includes offenses other than those listed that are collected as part of the National Incident-Based Reporting System.

Source: U.S. Department of Justice, Federal Bureau of Investigation, *Hate Crime Statistics 2002*, FBI Uniform Crime Reports (Washington, DC: U.S. Department of Justice, 2003), p. 10. Table adapted by SOURCEBOOK staff.

Table 3.113

Bias motivations in hate crimes known to police

United States, 2002

Bias motivation	Incidents	Offenses	Victims[a]	Known offenders[b]
Total	7,462	8,832	9,222	7,314
Race	3,642	4,393	4,580	4,011
Anti-white	719	888	910	1,064
Anti-black	2,486	2,967	3,076	2,510
Anti-American Indian/Alaskan Native	62	68	72	52
Anti-Asian/Pacific Islander	217	268	280	242
Anti-multi-racial group	158	202	242	143
Ethnicity	1,102	1,345	1,409	1,247
Anti-Hispanic	480	601	639	656
Anti-other ethnicity/national origin	622	744	770	591
Religion	1,426	1,576	1,659	568
Anti-Jewish	931	1,039	1,084	317
Anti-Catholic	53	58	71	21
Anti-Protestant	55	57	58	34
Anti-Islamic	155	170	174	103
Anti-other religious group	198	217	237	73
Anti-multi-religious group	31	32	32	18
Anti-atheism/agnosticism/etc.	3	3	3	2
Sexual orientation	1,244	1,464	1,513	1,438
Anti-male homosexual	825	957	984	1,022
Anti-female homosexual	172	207	221	172
Anti-homosexual	222	259	267	225
Anti-heterosexual	10	26	26	6
Anti-bisexual	15	15	15	13
Disability	45	47	50	47
Anti-physical	20	20	20	21
Anti-mental	25	27	30	26
Multiple biases[c]	3	7	11	3

Note: See Note, table 3.112.

[a] May include persons, businesses, institutions, or society as a whole.
[b] "Known offender" does not imply that the identity of the suspect is known, rather that an attribute of the suspect has been identified, distinguishing him/her from an unknown offender.
[c] A hate crime in which two or more offense types were committed as a result of two or more bias motivations.

Source: U.S. Department of Justice, Federal Bureau of Investigation, *Hate Crime Statistics 2002*, FBI Uniform Crime Reports (Washington, DC: U.S. Department of Justice, 2003), p. 9. Table adapted by SOURCEBOOK staff.

Table 3.114

Race of suspected offender in bias-motivated (hate) crimes known to police

By type of bias motivation, United States, 2002

Bias motivation	Total offenses	White	Black	American Indian/Alaskan Native	Asian/ Pacific Islander	Multi-racial group	Unknown race
Total	8,832	3,712	1,082	46	61	218	651
Race	4,393	2,040	639	29	38	127	344
Anti-white	888	130	497	8	11	34	71
Anti-black	2,967	1,689	84	14	26	72	217
Anti-American Indian/Alaskan Native	68	31	1	2	0	1	9
Anti-Asian/Pacific Islander	268	104	38	4	1	15	22
Anti-multi-racial group	202	86	19	1	0	5	25
Ethnicity	1,345	647	178	8	9	29	73
Anti-Hispanic	601	323	111	0	0	5	25
Anti-other ethnicity/national origin	744	324	67	8	9	24	48
Religion	1,576	327	46	1	8	13	138
Anti-Jewish	1,039	179	15	1	4	5	98
Anti-Catholic	58	10	1	0	2	1	3
Anti-Protestant	57	17	3	0	0	0	7
Anti-Islamic	170	59	19	0	1	7	9
Anti-other religious group	217	50	6	0	1	0	17
Anti-multi-religious group	32	11	1	0	0	0	4
Anti-atheism/agnosticism/etc.	3	1	1	0	0	0	0
Sexual orientation	1,464	679	210	8	6	46	88
Anti-male homosexual	957	458	151	4	5	30	50
Anti-female homosexual	207	94	25	2	0	7	12
Anti-homosexual	259	118	29	2	1	8	25
Anti-heterosexual	26	6	0	0	0	0	1
Anti-bisexual	15	3	5	0	0	1	0
Disability	47	17	9	0	0	3	5
Anti-physical	20	9	6	0	0	0	2
Anti-mental	27	8	3	0	0	3	3
Multiple biases[a]	7	2	0	0	0	0	3

Note: See Note, table 3.112. This table excludes 3,062 hate crime offenses for which no information about the offender was available.

[a] A hate crime in which two or more offense types were committed as a result of two or more bias motivations.

Source: U.S. Department of Justice, Federal Bureau of Investigation, *Hate Crime Statistics 2002*, FBI Uniform Crime Reports (Washington, DC: U.S. Department of Justice, 2003), p. 14. Table adapted by SOURCEBOOK staff.

Table 3.115

Offenses in Federal parks known to park rangers and park police

By offense, 1975-2002

	Total offenses	Total annual visitation (in thousands)	Homicide[a]	Forcible rape[b]	Robbery	Aggravated assault	Burglary[b]	Larceny-theft	Motor vehicle theft	Arson[c]
1975	7,697	238,849	10	84	779	385	1,031	5,156	252	X
1976	7,521	267,827	10	66	281	470	954	5,570	170	X
1977	7,763	261,584	17	60	238	458	1,097	5,662	231	X
1978	8,247	283,090	12	91	261	494	1,188	5,986	215	X
1979	8,561	282,435	15	87	264	505	1,330	6,124	236	X
1980	9,074	300,324	16	89	294	643	1,552	6,230	250	X
1981	8,319	329,663	19	87	303	575	1,391	5,451	296	197
1982	7,892	344,448	30	83	330	607	1,083	5,468	220	71
1983	7,617	335,646	19	81	306	542	1,238	5,125	200	106
1984	6,612	332,507	18	57	266	527	717	4,766	178	83
1985	7,318	346,200	19	70	309	483	892	5,147	235	163
1986	7,945	364,600	24	88	261	637	922	5,732	179	102
1987	6,417	372,800	15	79	197	543	926	4,259	294	104
1988	6,195	368,000	20	79	215	300	801	4,378	313	89
1989	6,532	351,900	9	73	123	441	1,009	4,548	213	116
1990	7,009	337,900	24	92	184	448	1,180	4,643	310	128
1991	7,203	358,295	28	78	209	390	1,118	5,004	251	125
1992	7,212	360,352	23	71	222	386	928	5,204	241	137
1993	6,452	387,707	25	62	197	367	747	4,681	210	163
1994	4,508	380,156	20	37	208	337	389	3,180	201	136
1995	6,009	387,804	16	50	138	318	830	4,309	198	150
1996	5,992	399,765	24	40	146	299	677	4,465	177	164
1997	6,352	419,795	17	44	119	265	499	5,105	219	84
1998	5,640	435,637	12	46	108	368	506	4,385	130	85
1999	5,164	436,296	11	34	142	202	515	3,988	164	108
2000	4,428	429,800	13	50	91	292	576	3,159	145	102
2001	4,328	424,100	10	37	70	212	488	3,277	130	104
2002	3,876	421,200	14	44	47	257	456	2,812	148	98

Note: The National Park Service is responsible for the administration of 384 park areas that are owned by the Federal Government. Three urban park areas are policed by the U.S. Park Police; other park areas are policed by the U.S. Park Rangers. In some park areas law enforcement responsibilities are shared with other police agencies, e.g., State police, sheriff departments, and city/town police. These data exclude offenses handled by other agencies. The offense categories listed above are the Uniform Crime Reporting Program Part I offenses; see Appendix 3 for definitions. Note, however, that prior to 1994 these offenses were not counted in the Federal Bureau of Investigation's figures. In 1975, the "Human Kindness Day" activities held in Washington, DC accounted for approximately 500 robbery incidents. Some data have been revised by the Source and may differ from previous editions of SOURCEBOOK.

[a] Includes negligent and nonnegligent manslaughter.
[b] Includes attempts.
[c] Included in tabulations as a Part I offense beginning in 1981.

Source: Table provided to SOURCEBOOK staff by the U.S. Department of the Interior, National Park Service.

Table 3.116
Offenses in Federal parks known to park rangers and park police, and reported by other law enforcement agencies

By offense, 2002

Offense	Park rangers	Park police	Other law enforcement agencies
Total, all offenses	89,573	11,639	578
Part I offenses, total	3,113	763	82
Homicide			
Murder and nonnegligent manslaughter	7	2	2
Manslaughter by negligence	5	0	2
Forcible rape			
Rape by force	28	4	4
Attempted forcible rape	12	0	0
Robbery			
Firearm	2	8	0
Knife or cutting instrument	1	2	0
Strong arm; hands, fist, feet, etc.	9	16	0
Other dangerous weapon	1	8	0
Aggravated assault			
Firearm	14	9	3
Knife or cutting instrument	15	18	2
Other dangerous weapon	25	15	0
Hands, fist, feet, etc.	88	73	6
Burglary			
Forcible entry	241	21	12
Unlawful entry[a]	97	25	2
Attempted forcible entry	67	5	1
Larceny-theft[b]	2,281	531	26
Motor vehicle theft			
Automobiles	107	16	9
Trucks and buses	10	0	2
Other vehicles	14	1	2
Arson			
Structural	19	2	2
Mobile	15	7	1
Other	55	0	6
Part II offenses, total	86,460	10,876	496
Other assaults	232	143	14
Forgery and counterfeiting	65	57	7
Fraud	70	34	2
Embezzlement	16	2	2
Stolen property; buying, receiving, possessing	209	331	20
Vandalism	2,723	390	15
Weapons; carrying, possessing, etc.	1,310	431	8
Prostitution and commercialized vice	17	19	0
Sex offenses	281	182	6
Drug sale/manufacture	249	35	23
Drug possession	2,626	1,996	38
Offenses against family and children	108	56	1
Gambling	3	1	0
Driving while intoxicated	1,143	620	24
Liquor laws	4,007	1,019	7
Drunkenness	729	57	18
Disorderly conduct	1,952	737	10
Archaeological Resource Protection Act violations	497	1	3
All other offenses	67,241	3,029	291
Suspicion	1,055	1,730	4
Curfew and loitering	492	4	0
Runaways	28	2	1
Thefts	1,407	0	2

Note: See Note, table 3.115. For definitions of offenses, see Appendix 3.

[a] No force used.
[b] Excludes motor vehicle theft.

Source: Table provided to SOURCEBOOK staff by the U.S. Department of the Interior, National Park Service.

Table 3.117
Percent distribution of murders and nonnegligent manslaughters known to police

By type of weapon used, United States, 1964-2002

Year	Number of murders and nonnegligent manslaughters	Total[a]	Firearm	Knife or other cutting instrument	Blunt object (club, hammer, etc.)	Personal weapons (hands, fists, feet, etc.)[b]	Non-personal weapons[c]	Other weapon or weapon not stated[d]
1964	7,990	100%	55%	24%	5%	10%	3%	2%
1965	8,773	100	57	23	6	10	3	1
1966	9,552	100	59	22	5	9	2	1
1967	11,114	100	63	20	5	9	2	1
1968	12,503	100	65	18	6	8	2	1
1969	13,575	100	65	19	4	8	3	1
1970	13,649	100	66	18	4	8	3	1
1971	16,183	100	66	19	4	8	2	1
1972	15,832	100	66	19	4	8	2	1
1973	17,123	100	66	17	5	8	2	2
1974	18,632	100	67	17	5	8	1	1
1975	18,642	100	65	17	5	9	2	2
1976	16,605	100	64	18	5	8	2	3
1977	18,033	100	62	19	5	8	2	3
1978	18,714	100	64	19	5	8	2	3
1979	20,591	100	63	19	5	8	2	3
1980	21,860	100	62	19	5	8	2	4
1981	20,053	100	62	19	5	7	2	3
1982	19,485	100	60	21	5	8	2	3
1983	18,673	100	58	22	6	9	2	3
1984	16,689	100	59	21	6	8	3	4
1985	17,545	100	59	21	6	8	3	4
1986	19,257	100	59	20	6	9	2	4
1987	17,859	100	59	20	6	8	2	4
1988	18,269	100	61	19	6	8	2	4
1989	18,954	100	62	18	6	7	2	4
1990	20,045	100	64	18	5	7	2	4
1991	21,505	100	66	16	5	7	2	4
1992	22,540	100	68	14	5	6	2	5
1993	23,271	100	70	13	4	6	2	5
1994	22,076	100	70	13	4	7	2	5
1995	20,043	100	68	13	4	7	3	5
1996	15,848	100	68	14	5	7	2	5
1997	15,289	100	68	13	5	8	2	5
1998	14,088	100	65	13	5	8	2	6
1999	12,658	100	65	13	6	8	2	5
2000	12,943	100	66	13	5	8	2	6
2001[e]	13,752	100	63	13	5	7	3	9
2002	14,054	100	67	13	5	8	2	6

Note: See Note, table 3.106. In trend tables "constructed" or "adapted" by SOURCEBOOK staff from *Crime in the United States*, the data are from the first year in which the data are reported. It should be noted that the number of agencies reporting and the populations represented vary from year to year.

The Uniform Crime Reporting Program requests that supplementary information be transmitted to the FBI when a murder or nonnegligent manslaughter has been committed. The actual number of offenses presented in the tables displaying characteristics of murders and nonnegligent manslaughters known to the police may differ from figures in other tables that reflect data from only the initial report of the offense. For example, supplementary data were provided by contributing agencies for 14,054 of the estimated total of 16,204 murders and nonnegligent manslaughters in 2002 (Source, *2002*, pp. 19, 20).

For information on States supplying incomplete data for selected years, see Appendix 3.

[a] Because of rounding, percents may not add to total.
[b] Includes beatings, strangulations, and "pushed."
[c] Includes poison, explosives, fire, narcotics, and asphyxiation.
[d] Beginning in 1991, this category includes drownings.
[e] The murders and nonnegligent manslaughters that occurred as a result of the events of Sept. 11, 2001 are not included in this table.

Source: U.S. Department of Justice, Federal Bureau of Investigation, *Crime in the United States*, *1964*, p. 104, Table 16; *1965*, p. 106, Table 16; *1966*, p. 107, Table 20; *1967*, p. 112, Table 20; *1968*, p. 108, Table 20; *1969*, p. 106, Table 21; *1970*, p. 188, Table 21; *1971*, p. 114, Table 21; *1972*, p. 188, Table 24; *1973*, p. 8; *1974*, p. 18; *1975*, p. 18; *1976*, p. 10; *1977*, p. 11; *1978*, p. 12; *1979*, p. 11; *1980*, p. 12; *1981*, p. 11; *1982*, p. 11; *1983*, p. 10; *1984*, p. 10; *1985*, p. 10; *1986*, p. 10; *1987*, p. 10; *1988*, p. 12; *1989*, p. 11; *1990*, p. 12; *1991*, p. 18; *1992*, p. 18, Table 2.10; *1993*, p. 18, Table 2.11; *1994*, p. 18, Table 2.11; *1995*, p. 18, Table 2.11; *1996*, p. 18, Table 2.11; *1997*, p. 20, Table 2.11; *1998*, p. 18, Table 2.11; *1999*, p. 18, Table 2.11; *2000*, p. 19, Table 2.11; *2001*, p. 23, Table 2.11; *2002*, p. 23, Table 2.11 (Washington, DC: USGPO). Table constructed by SOURCEBOOK staff.

Table 3.118

Percent distribution of murders and nonnegligent manslaughters known to police

By type of weapon used and region, 2002

		Type of weapon used			
Region	Total[a]	Firearm	Knife or other cutting instrument	Unknown or other dangerous weapon	Personal weapons (hands, fists, feet, etc.)[b]
Total	100.0%	66.7%	12.6%	14.1%	6.6%
Northeast	100.0	62.6	17.4	12.6	7.5
Midwest	100.0	66.4	10.3	16.5	6.8
South	100.0	66.9	12.1	14.6	6.4
West	100.0	68.9	12.3	12.4	6.4

Note: See Notes, tables 3.106 and 3.117. In this table, strangulations are classified in the "unknown or other dangerous weapon" category rather than in the category "personal weapons," as was done in table 3.117. For a list of States in regions, see Appendix 3.

[a]Because of rounding, percents may not add to total.
[b]Includes "pushed."

Source: U.S. Department of Justice, Federal Bureau of Investigation, *Crime in the United States, 2002* (Washington, DC: USGPO, 2003), p. 23, Table 2.9.

Table 3.119

Murders and nonnegligent manslaughters known to police

By type of weapon used and age of victim, United States, 2002

Age of victim	Total	Firearm	Knife or other cutting instrument	Blunt object (club, hammer, etc.)	Personal weapons (hands, fists, feet, etc.)[a]	Poison	Explosives	Fire	Narcotics	Strangulation	Asphyxiation	Other weapon or weapon not stated[b]
Total	14,054	9,369	1,767	666	933	23	11	104	48	143	103	887
Under 18 years[c]	1,357	661	90	52	299	5	5	21	11	16	41	156
Under 22 years[c]	3,398	2,358	256	94	345	6	5	29	14	23	47	221
18 years and older[c]	12,406	8,568	1,646	595	607	18	6	76	36	125	58	671
Infant (under 1 year)	180	9	4	12	91	0	1	0	3	0	19	41
1 to 4 years	328	45	10	19	166	2	1	7	3	2	12	61
5 to 8 years	86	26	14	2	11	2	2	7	1	2	7	12
9 to 12 years	92	56	11	2	4	1	0	2	0	3	0	13
13 to 16 years	390	299	30	11	17	0	0	5	3	6	2	17
17 to 19 years	1,184	972	101	23	32	1	1	3	4	6	3	38
20 to 24 years	2,756	2,244	250	55	72	0	3	9	7	7	5	104
25 to 29 years	2,059	1,628	227	42	56	0	0	11	2	16	7	70
30 to 34 years	1,587	1,168	197	45	57	0	2	14	5	15	4	80
35 to 39 years	1,337	864	193	74	78	2	0	7	5	25	11	78
40 to 44 years	1,137	663	221	63	84	3	1	9	1	13	8	71
45 to 49 years	856	461	151	80	74	0	0	8	1	15	3	63
50 to 54 years	566	312	101	48	50	2	0	3	2	3	1	44
55 to 59 years	353	172	66	46	23	0	0	1	0	7	2	36
60 to 64 years	245	107	41	37	16	0	0	7	1	7	4	25
65 to 69 years	162	67	27	20	15	1	0	0	3	5	5	19
70 to 74 years	156	53	35	28	14	0	0	0	0	6	2	18
75 years and older	289	83	57	40	46	9	0	4	6	3	4	37
Unknown	291	140	31	19	27	0	0	7	1	2	4	60

Note: See Notes, tables 3.106 and 3.117.

[a]Includes "pushed."
[b]Includes drownings.
[c]Does not include unknown ages.

Source: U.S. Department of Justice, Federal Bureau of Investigation, *Crime in the United States, 2002* (Washington, DC: USGPO, 2003), p. 23, Table 2.11.

Table 3.120

Murders and nonnegligent manslaughters known to police

By victim-offender relationship and circumstances of the offense, United States, 2002

(- represents zero)

Circumstances	Total	Husband	Wife	Mother	Father	Son	Daughter	Brother	Sister	Other family	Acquaintance
Total	14,054	133	601	113	110	239	210	87	20	271	3,217
Felony type, total	2,314	4	17	4	3	8	9	4	1	32	586
Rape	43	-	-	-	-	-	1	-	1	3	11
Robbery	1,092	-	-	-	2	-	-	2	-	13	221
Burglary	96	-	1	-	-	-	-	-	-	4	21
Larceny-theft	15	-	-	-	-	-	-	-	-	-	2
Motor vehicle theft	16	-	-	1	-	-	-	-	-	-	1
Arson	59	-	1	1	-	1	2	-	-	1	9
Prostitution and commercialized vice	8	-	-	-	-	-	-	-	-	-	3
Other sex offenses	8	-	-	-	-	1	1	-	-	-	3
Narcotic drug laws	657	-	1	-	1	-	-	1	-	1	245
Gambling	5	-	-	-	-	-	-	-	-	-	2
Other - not specified	315	4	14	2	-	6	5	1	-	10	68
Suspected felony type	67	-	-	1	-	-	-	-	-	-	6
Other than felony type, total	7,097	109	516	93	88	199	184	69	17	202	2,179
Romantic triangle	130	1	9	-	-	1	-	1	-	9	57
Child killed by babysitter	38	-	-	-	-	1	2	-	-	7	23
Brawl due to influence of alcohol	153	1	6	-	3	-	2	-	-	5	68
Brawl due to influence of narcotics	84	-	2	-	1	-	-	2	-	3	36
Argument over money or property	203	-	4	5	1	-	-	-	-	7	104
Other arguments	3,527	81	334	45	47	52	29	51	11	111	1,154
Gangland killings	73	-	-	-	-	-	-	-	-	-	23
Juvenile gang killings	911	-	-	-	-	-	-	-	-	1	221
Institutional killings	12	-	-	-	-	-	-	-	-	-	9
Sniper attack	11	-	1	-	-	-	-	-	-	-	-
Other - not specified	1,955	26	160	43	36	145	151	15	6	59	484
Unknown	4,576	20	68	15	19	32	17	14	2	37	446

Note: See Notes, tables 3.106 and 3.117. Law enforcement agencies are requested to describe the circumstances of murders and nonnegligent manslaughters. These descriptions are categorized by the Uniform Crime Reporting Program. These data include murder and nonnegligent manslaughter victims for which supplementary homicide data were received. "Felony type" refers to killings that occur in conjunction with the commission of another felony, such as robbery or burglary.

[a]Column headers refer to victims.

Source: U.S. Department of Justice, Federal Bureau of Investigation, *Crime in the United States, 2002* (Washington, DC: USGPO, 2003), p. 24. Table adapted by SOURCEBOOK staff.

Friend	Boyfriend	Girlfriend	Neighbor	Employee	Employer	Stranger	Unknown relationship
352	154	444	110	5	10	1,963	6,015
50	8	18	16	-	1	595	958
2	-	-	1	-	-	7	17
10	4	1	11	-	-	396	432
1	1	1	1	-	1	39	26
-	-	-	-	-	-	8	5
1	-	-	-	-	-	7	6
3	-	3	-	-	-	17	21
-	-	-	-	-	-	2	3
-	-	2	-	-	-	-	1
22	2	2	-	-	-	67	315
-	-	-	-	-	-	1	2
11	1	9	3	-	-	51	130
1	-	-	-	-	-	2	57
257	134	348	77	4	7	999	1,615
10	2	14	1	-	-	15	10
3	-	-	-	-	-	1	1
10	1	4	-	-	-	41	12
3	-	3	1	-	-	8	25
13	-	3	8	-	1	17	40
170	105	243	48	4	3	496	543
-	-	-	-	-	-	20	30
-	-	-	-	-	-	200	489
-	-	-	-	-	-	1	2
-	-	-	-	-	-	7	3
48	26	81	19	-	3	193	460
44	12	78	17	1	2	367	3,385

Table 3.121

Percent distribution of murders and nonnegligent manslaughters known to police

By age of victim, United States, 1964, 1974, 1984, 1989-2002

Age of victim	1964	1974	1984	1989	1990	1991	1992	1993	1994	1995	1996	1997	1998	1999	2000	2001[a]	2002
Number of murders and nonnegligent manslaughters	7,990	18,632	16,689	18,954	20,045	21,505	22,540	23,271	22,076	20,043	15,848	15,289	14,088	12,658	12,943	13,752	14,054
Total[b]	100%	100%	100%	100%	100%	100%	100%	100%	100%	100%	100%	100%	100%	100%	100%	100%	100%
Infant (under 1 year)	2	1	1	1	1	1	1	1	1	1	2	1	2	2	2	2	1
1 to 4 years	3	2	2	2	2	2	2	2	2	2	2	2	2	2	2	2	2
5 to 8 years[c]	1	1	1	1	1	1	1	1	(d)	1	1	1	1	1	1	1	1
9 to 12 years[c]	2	1	1	1	1	1	2	2	1	1	1	1	1	1	(d)	1	1
13 to 16 years[c]	7	9	7	11	12	13	13	13	4	5	4	4	3	4	3	3	3
17 to 19 years[c]	X	X	X	X	X	X	X	X	10	11	11	10	10	10	9	9	8
20 to 24 years	12	16	16	17	17	18	19	19	19	18	17	19	18	18	18	19	20
25 to 29 years	12	15	17	17	17	16	15	15	15	14	14	14	14	14	14	15	15
30 to 34 years	12	12	13	14	14	13	14	13	13	13	12	12	11	11	11	11	11
35 to 39 years	12	9	10	10	10	10	10	10	10	10	11	10	10	10	10	10	10
40 to 44 years	10	8	7	7	7	7	7	7	7	8	8	8	8	8	9	8	8
45 to 49 years	8	7	5	4	4	5	5	5	5	5	6	6	5	6	6	6	6
50 to 54 years	6	6	4	3	3	3	3	3	3	3	3	3	3	4	4	4	4
55 to 59 years	4	4	3	2	2	2	2	2	2	2	2	2	2	2	3	2	2
60 to 64 years	3	4	3	2	2	2	2	2	2	2	2	2	2	2	2	2	2
65 to 69 years	2	2	2	2	1	1	1	1	1	1	1	1	1	1	1	1	1
70 to 74 years	1	1	2	1	1	1	1	1	1	1	1	1	1	1	1	1	1
75 years and older	2	2	2	2	2	2	2	2	2	2	2	2	2	2	2	2	2
Unknown	2	2	2	1	2	2	1	1	2	2	1	2	2	2	2	2	2

Note: See Notes, tables 3.106 and 3.117. For information on States supplying incomplete data for selected years, see Appendix 3.

[a]The murders and nonnegligent manslaughters that occurred as a result of the events of Sept. 11, 2001 are not included in this table.
[b]Because of rounding, percents may not add to total.
[c]In 1994, these age categories were changed by the Source; previously the age groups were "5 to 9 years," "10 to 14 years," and "15 to 19 years."
[d]Less than 0.5%.

Source: U.S. Department of Justice, Federal Bureau of Investigation, *Crime in the United States, 1964*, p. 104, Table 17; *1974*, p. 17, Table 17; *1984*, p. 8; *1987*, p. 9; *1989*, p. 10; *1990*, p. 11; *1991*, p. 16, Table 2.4; *1992*, p. 16, Table 2.4; *1993*, p. 16, Table 2.5; *1994*, p. 16, Table 2.5; *1995*, p. 16, Table 2.5; *1996*, p. 16, Table 2.5; *1997*, p. 18, Table 2.5; *1998*, p. 16, Table 2.5; *1999*, p. 16, Table 2.5; *2000*, p. 17, Table 2.5; *2001*, p. 21, Table 2.5; *2002*, p. 21, Table 2.5 (Washington, DC: USGPO). Table constructed by SOURCEBOOK staff.

Table 3.122
Percent distribution of murders and nonnegligent manslaughters known to police

By sex of victim, United States, 1964-2002

	Number of murders and nonnegligent manslaughters	Total[a]	Sex of victim Male	Sex of victim Female
1964	7,990	100%	74%	26%
1965	8,773	100	74	26
1966	9,552	100	74	26
1967	11,114	100	75	25
1968	12,503	100	78	22
1969	13,575	100	78	22
1970	13,649	100	78	22
1971	16,183	100	79	21
1972	15,832	100	78	22
1973	17,123	100	77	23
1974	18,632	100	77	23
1975	18,642	100	76	24
1976	16,605	100	76	24
1977	18,033	100	75	25
1978	18,714	100	76	24
1979	20,591	100	77	23
1980	21,860	100	77	23
1981	20,053	100	77	23
1982	19,485	100	76	24
1983	18,673	100	76	24
1984	16,689	100	75	25
1985	17,545	100	74	26
1986	19,257	100	75	25
1987	17,859	100	74	26
1988	18,269	100	75	25
1989	18,954	100	76	24
1990	20,045	100	78	22
1991	21,505	100	78	22
1992	22,540	100	78	22
1993	23,271	100	77	23
1994	22,076	100	78	22
1995	20,043	100	77	23
1996	15,848	100	77	23
1997	15,289	100	77	23
1998	14,088	100	75	24
1999	12,658	100	76	24
2000	12,943	100	76	24
2001[b]	13,752	100	76	23
2002	14,054	100	77	23

Note: See Notes, tables 3.106 and 3.117. For information on States supplying incomplete data for selected years, see Appendix 3.

[a]Because of rounding, percents may not add to total.
[b]The murders and nonnegligent manslaughters that occurred as a result of the events of Sept. 11, 2001 are not included in this table.

Source: U.S. Department of Justice, Federal Bureau of Investigation, *Crime in the United States, 1964*, p. 104, Table 17; *1965*, p. 106, Table 17; *1966*, p. 107, Table 21; *1967*, p. 112, Table 21; *1968*, p. 108, Table 21; *1969*, p. 106, Table 22; *1970*, p. 118, Table 22; *1971*, p. 114, Table 22; *1972*, p. 118, Table 25; *1973*, p. 8; *1974*, p. 17; *1975*, p. 17; *1976*, p. 11; *1977*, p. 12; *1978*, p. 9; *1979*, p. 10; *1980*, p. 11; *1981*, p. 10; *1982*, p. 8; *1983*, p. 8; *1984*, p. 8; *1985*, p. 9; *1986*, p. 9; *1987*, p. 9; *1988*, p. 11; *1989*, p. 10; *1990*, p. 11; *1991*, p. 16, Table 2.4; *1992*, p. 16, Table 2.4; *1993*, p. 16, Table 2.5; *1994*, p. 16, Table 2.5; *1995*, p. 16, Table 2.5; *1996*, p. 16, Table 2.5; *1997*, p. 18, Table 2.5; *1998*, p. 16, Table 2.5; *1999*, p. 16, Table 2.5; *2000*, p. 17, Table 2.5; *2001*, p. 21, Table 2.5; *2002*, p. 21, Table 2.5 (Washington, DC: USGPO). Table constructed by SOURCEBOOK staff.

Table 3.123
Percent distribution of murders and nonnegligent manslaughters known to police

By race of victim, United States, 1964-2002

	Number of murders and nonnegligent manslaughters	Total[a]	White	Black	All other (including race unknown)
1964	7,990	100%	45%	54%	1%
1965	8,773	100	45	54	1
1966	9,552	100	45	54	1
1967	11,114	100	45	54	1
1968	12,503	100	45	54	1
1969	13,575	100	44	55	2
1970	13,649	100	44	55	1
1971	16,183	100	44	55	2
1972	15,832	100	45	53	2
1973	17,123	100	47	52	1
1974	18,632	100	48	50	2
1975	18,642	100	51	47	2
1976	16,605	100	51	47	2
1977	18,033	100	52	45	2
1978	18,714	100	54	44	2
1979	20,591	100	54	43	2
1980	21,860	100	53	42	4
1981	20,053	100	54	44	2
1982	19,485	100	55	42	2
1983	18,673	100	55	42	3
1984	16,689	100	56	41	3
1985	17,545	100	56	42	3
1986	19,257	100	53	44	3
1987	17,859	100	52	45	3
1988	18,269	100	49	48	3
1989	18,954	100	48	49	3
1990	20,045	100	48	49	3
1991	21,505	100	47	50	2
1992	22,540	100	47	50	3
1993	23,271	100	46	51	3
1994	22,076	100	46	51	3
1995	20,043	100	48	48	4
1996	15,848	100	48	48	4
1997	15,289	100	48	48	4
1998	14,088	100	49	47	4
1999	12,658	100	49	46	4
2000	12,943	100	48	48	4
2001[b]	13,752	100	49	47	4
2002	14,054	100	48	48	4

Note: See Notes, tables 3.106 and 3.117. For information on States supplying incomplete data for selected years, see Appendix 3.

[a]Because of rounding, percents may not add to total.
[b]The murders and nonnegligent manslaughters that occurred as a result of the events of Sept. 11, 2001 are not included in this table.

Source: U.S. Department of Justice, Federal Bureau of Investigation, *Crime in the United States, 1964*, p. 104, Table 17; *1965*, p. 106, Table 17; *1966*, p. 107, Table 21; *1967*, p. 112, Table 21; *1968*, p. 108, Table 21; *1969*, p. 106, Table 22; *1970*, p. 118, Table 22; *1971*, p. 114, Table 21; *1972*, p. 118, Table 25; *1973*, p. 8; *1974*, p. 17; *1975*, p. 17; *1976*, p. 11; *1977*, p. 12; *1978*, p. 9; *1979*, p. 10; *1980*, p. 11; *1981*, p. 10; *1982*, p. 8; *1983*, p. 8; *1984*, p. 8; *1985*, p. 9; *1986*, p. 9; *1987*, p. 9; *1988*, p. 11; *1989*, p. 10; *1990*, p. 11; *1991*, p. 16, Table 2.4; *1992*, p. 16, Table 2.4; *1993*, p. 16, Table 2.5; *1994*, p. 16, Table 2.5; *1995*, p. 16, Table 2.5; *1996*, p. 16, Table 2.5; *1997*, p. 18, Table 2.5; *1998*, p. 16, Table 2.5; *1999*, p. 16, Table 2.5; *2000*, p. 17, Table 2.5; *2001*, p. 21, Table 2.5; *2002*, p. 21, Table 2.5 (Washington, DC: USGPO). Table constructed by SOURCEBOOK staff.

Table 3.124
Murders and nonnegligent manslaughters known to police

By sex, race, and age of victim, United States, 2002

Age of victim	Total	Sex of victim			Race of victim			
		Male	Female	Unknown	White	Black	Other	Unknown
Total	14,054	10,779	3,251	24	6,757	6,730	377	190
Under 18 years[a]	1,357	867	489	1	689	610	45	13
Under 22 years[a]	3,398	2,624	772	2	1,581	1,683	104	30
18 years and older[a]	12,406	9,703	2,699	4	5,945	6,009	331	121
Infant (under 1 year)	180	96	84	0	102	71	4	3
1 to 4 years	328	180	147	1	176	134	14	4
5 to 8 years	86	35	51	0	50	33	3	0
9 to 12 years	92	50	42	0	53	35	4	0
13 to 16 years	390	281	109	0	180	196	11	3
17 to 19 years	1,184	1,018	166	0	519	615	39	11
20 to 24 years	2,756	2,356	398	2	1,115	1,560	58	23
25 to 29 years	2,059	1,746	313	0	809	1,173	48	29
30 to 34 years	1,587	1,212	375	0	667	851	54	15
35 to 39 years	1,337	976	359	2	676	624	23	14
40 to 44 years	1,137	812	325	0	621	470	40	6
45 to 49 years	856	624	232	0	487	337	25	7
50 to 54 years	566	412	154	0	333	214	16	3
55 to 59 years	353	246	107	0	237	98	14	4
60 to 64 years	245	181	64	0	170	60	10	5
65 to 69 years	162	103	59	0	116	44	2	0
70 to 74 years	156	96	60	0	115	35	4	2
75 years and older	289	146	143	0	208	69	7	5
Unknown	291	209	63	19	123	111	1	56

Note: See Notes, tables 3.106 and 3.117.

[a]Does not include unknown ages.

Source: U.S. Department of Justice, Federal Bureau of Investigation, *Crime in the United States, 2002* (Washington, DC: USGPO, 2003), p. 21, Table 2.5. Table adapted by SOURCEBOOK staff.

Table 3.125
Rate (per 100,000 persons in each group) of murder and nonnegligent manslaughter victimization

By age, sex, and race of victim, United States, 1976-2002

	Total	Age						Sex		Race		
		13 years and younger	14 to 17 years	18 to 24 years	25 to 34 years	35 to 49 years	50 years and older	Male	Female	White	Black	Other
1976	8.8	1.8	4.5	13.8	15.4	12.6	6.8	13.6	4.2	5.1	37.1	4.9
1977	8.8	1.9	4.9	14.3	15.5	12.3	6.6	13.7	4.2	5.4	36.2	4.7
1978	9.0	1.9	5.1	14.6	16.1	12.2	6.3	14.0	4.1	5.6	35.1	4.0
1979	9.7	1.8	5.2	16.5	17.5	12.8	6.7	15.4	4.4	6.1	37.5	4.1
1980	10.2	1.8	5.9	17.5	18.5	13.2	6.8	16.2	4.5	6.3	37.7	5.7
1981	9.8	1.9	5.0	16.0	17.5	13.0	6.7	15.6	4.3	6.2	36.4	6.1
1982	9.1	2.0	4.8	15.0	15.7	11.8	6.2	14.1	4.3	5.9	32.3	6.5
1983	8.3	1.8	4.5	13.8	14.6	10.5	5.5	12.8	3.9	5.3	29.4	6.4
1984	7.9	1.7	4.2	13.2	13.8	10.0	5.1	12.1	3.9	5.2	27.2	5.5
1985	8.0	1.8	4.9	13.2	13.9	9.9	5.0	12.2	4.0	5.2	27.6	5.5
1986	8.6	2.0	5.2	15.3	15.2	10.1	5.0	13.2	4.1	5.4	31.5	6.2
1987	8.3	1.8	5.8	15.5	14.7	9.4	4.9	12.6	4.2	5.1	30.7	5.2
1988	8.5	2.0	6.5	16.4	15.3	9.2	4.7	12.9	4.2	4.9	33.5	4.0
1989	8.7	2.1	7.9	18.2	15.6	9.2	4.6	13.6	4.0	5.0	35.1	4.3
1990	9.4	2.0	9.7	21.1	16.7	9.9	4.4	15.0	4.0	5.4	37.6	4.2
1991	9.8	2.1	11.1	23.9	16.7	10.0	4.5	15.7	4.2	5.5	39.3	6.0
1992	9.3	2.0	11.3	23.4	16.1	9.4	4.2	14.9	4.0	5.3	37.2	5.4
1993	9.5	2.2	12.1	24.4	16.1	9.5	4.2	15.0	4.2	5.3	38.7	5.5
1994	9.0	2.0	11.2	23.6	15.4	8.9	3.8	14.4	3.8	5.0	36.4	4.6
1995	8.2	1.9	11.0	21.5	13.8	8.2	3.8	12.9	3.7	4.8	31.6	4.9
1996	7.4	1.9	9.1	19.5	12.4	7.7	3.4	11.7	3.3	4.3	28.3	4.1
1997	6.8	1.7	7.3	19.1	11.4	6.8	3.2	10.7	3.0	3.9	26.0	4.1
1998	6.3	1.7	6.2	17.5	10.7	6.5	2.8	9.7	3.0	3.8	23.0	2.9
1999	5.7	1.6	5.9	15.4	9.9	5.9	2.6	8.8	2.7	3.5	20.5	3.3
2000	5.5	1.4	4.8	15.0	10.3	5.7	2.5	8.6	2.6	3.3	20.5	2.7
2001	5.6	1.5	4.6	15.4	10.7	5.6	2.6	8.8	2.6	3.4	20.4	2.8
2002	5.6	1.5	4.5	15.3	11.0	5.7	2.5	8.8	2.6	3.3	20.8	2.7

Note: These data are from the Federal Bureau of Investigation's (FBI) Supplementary Homicide Reports (SHR), a component of the Uniform Crime Reporting Program. SHRs are incident-based reports, rather than the monthly aggregates that comprise the FBI Crime Index. Not all agencies that report aggregate offense data to the FBI also submit supplemental homicide data. On average, about 91% of homicides reported to the FBI are included in the SHR database. To account for homicides for which SHR data were not available, the victim-based analyses include SHR data that have been weighted to match national and State estimates prepared by the FBI. Rates are calculated from U.S. Census Bureau, Current Populations Reports. Deaths resulting from the events of Sept. 11, 2001 are not included in any of the analyses that generated these tables. Some data have been revised by the Source and may differ from previous editions of SOURCEBOOK.

Source: U.S. Department of Justice, Bureau of Justice Statistics, "Homicide Trends in the United States" [Online]. Available: http://www.ojp.usdoj.gov/bjs/homicide/homtrnd.htm [Sept. 30, 2004]. Table adapted by SOURCEBOOK staff.

Table 3.126

Rate (per 100,000 persons in each group) of murder and nonnegligent manslaughter victimization

By age, sex, and race of victim, United States, 1976-2002

	14 to 17 years				18 to 24 years				25 years and older			
	Male		Female		Male		Female		Male		Female	
	White	Black	White	Black	White	Black	White	Black	White	Black	White	Black
1976	3.7	24.2	2.1	6.3	11.3	89.8	4.2	25.1	9.8	97.2	3.0	19.3
1977	4.1	22.4	2.4	8.7	12.5	86.9	4.4	24.5	9.9	94.1	3.1	17.2
1978	4.7	21.9	2.5	7.6	13.3	86.4	4.4	23.7	10.4	90.3	3.1	16.5
1979	4.9	23.2	2.3	7.8	16.0	90.9	5.2	24.0	11.0	95.7	3.2	18.2
1980	5.1	26.3	2.6	6.8	16.2	96.7	5.3	23.5	11.4	94.8	3.3	17.1
1981	4.3	23.0	2.4	6.0	14.9	89.7	4.9	20.4	11.3	93.2	3.3	16.0
1982	4.0	22.3	1.9	7.5	13.9	82.6	5.2	17.7	10.4	79.5	3.3	14.4
1983	3.8	21.4	2.0	5.2	12.7	75.0	4.2	19.4	9.4	70.7	3.1	13.0
1984	3.5	18.4	2.1	6.4	11.9	68.0	5.1	18.2	9.1	64.6	3.0	12.4
1985	3.9	23.7	1.9	7.3	12.1	73.3	4.2	16.5	8.9	62.4	3.2	13.2
1986	4.1	26.8	2.3	6.5	13.3	87.9	4.7	19.7	9.0	70.2	3.1	14.1
1987	3.7	36.2	2.2	7.1	12.3	96.4	4.6	19.6	8.5	64.0	3.3	14.4
1988	3.9	43.3	2.2	7.2	12.3	109.5	4.5	20.8	8.1	69.2	3.0	14.8
1989	5.3	54.3	2.1	8.6	13.4	128.3	4.4	20.0	8.2	70.5	2.8	14.7
1990	7.5	59.0	2.5	10.3	16.7	151.0	4.0	20.5	8.7	74.4	2.9	14.3
1991	8.5	71.9	2.5	9.4	18.2	173.7	4.6	23.4	8.8	72.7	2.8	15.0
1992	9.0	67.3	2.4	12.8	17.4	171.8	4.4	20.8	8.4	67.6	2.8	14.4
1993	9.1	76.4	2.7	12.7	17.2	183.5	4.3	24.1	8.1	68.3	3.0	14.5
1994	8.7	71.6	2.0	10.0	17.8	176.2	3.8	20.7	7.7	64.3	2.6	13.7
1995	8.6	63.2	2.7	11.9	17.3	148.9	4.2	17.1	6.9	56.4	2.7	12.2
1996	7.9	52.2	2.0	8.9	15.4	138.2	3.3	15.4	6.5	50.0	2.4	11.3
1997	5.7	42.0	1.7	7.2	14.5	136.5	3.5	15.4	5.9	45.5	2.1	9.9
1998	5.7	32.8	1.9	5.9	14.5	117.4	3.4	14.3	5.3	40.6	2.2	9.3
1999	5.1	31.0	1.7	5.9	12.5	102.4	3.4	12.9	5.0	36.5	2.0	7.9
2000	4.1	25.8	1.4	4.5	12.1	100.6	2.9	13.5	4.7	38.1	2.0	7.6
2001	3.8	26.3	1.4	3.9	12.9	104.0	3.2	10.1	4.8	37.5	2.0	7.6
2002	3.6	22.6	1.5	6.1	12.7	102.3	2.9	11.8	4.7	39.0	1.9	7.4

Note: See Note, table 3.125. Some data have been revised by the Source and may differ from previous editions of SOURCEBOOK.

Source: U.S. Department of Justice, Bureau of Justice Statistics, "Homicide Trends in the United States" [Online]. Available: http://www.ojp.usdoj.gov/bjs/homicide/homtrnd.htm [Sept. 30, 2004]. Table adapted by SOURCEBOOK staff.

Table 3.127

Estimated rate (per 100,000 persons in each group) of offenders committing murder and nonnegligent manslaughter

By age, sex, and race of offender, United States, 1976-2002

	Age						Sex		Race		
	13 years and younger	14 to 17 years	18 to 24 years	25 to 34 years	35 to 49 years	50 years and older	Male	Female	White	Black	Other
1976	0.2	11.4	22.9	19.4	10.7	3.7	16.3	3.0	4.9	46.5	4.6
1977	0.2	10.7	22.8	18.6	10.9	3.7	16.3	2.9	5.1	44.3	4.9
1978	0.3	10.5	24.0	18.9	10.9	3.5	16.9	2.7	5.3	44.5	3.8
1979	0.2	12.3	26.8	20.4	11.3	3.7	18.6	2.9	5.8	47.6	5.0
1980	0.2	12.9	30.0	22.6	12.8	3.6	20.6	3.1	6.5	51.4	6.9
1981	0.2	12.1	26.6	20.2	12.3	3.5	19.0	2.8	6.0	45.8	6.4
1982	0.2	11.1	25.1	19.1	10.9	3.1	17.6	2.6	5.6	41.1	6.4
1983	0.2	10.2	23.0	17.4	9.8	2.7	16.0	2.4	5.3	36.2	6.2
1984	0.2	9.1	22.2	16.9	9.1	2.8	15.4	2.2	5.3	33.0	5.3
1985	0.2	10.5	22.2	16.0	9.1	2.8	15.3	2.1	5.1	33.9	5.8
1986	0.2	12.7	24.4	17.5	9.4	2.7	16.7	2.1	5.3	37.8	6.0
1987	0.2	12.9	25.2	16.3	8.9	2.7	16.2	2.1	5.2	36.5	5.0
1988	0.2	16.8	27.9	16.3	8.6	2.6	17.0	2.0	5.0	41.2	4.5
1989	0.3	18.5	31.6	16.5	8.0	2.3	17.6	2.0	5.1	42.0	4.7
1990	0.2	25.7	36.1	17.5	8.2	2.3	19.6	2.0	5.7	46.5	4.2
1991	0.3	28.1	42.7	18.0	7.5	2.1	20.8	2.1	5.6	51.3	5.4
1992	0.3	28.0	39.5	16.5	7.2	2.1	19.4	1.8	5.2	46.9	5.7
1993	0.3	31.3	42.8	15.6	7.0	2.2	20.0	1.9	5.2	49.2	5.6
1994	0.4	31.1	40.7	14.9	6.8	1.8	19.0	1.8	5.1	45.4	5.1
1995	0.3	25.1	37.7	13.9	6.4	1.8	17.3	1.5	4.9	39.3	5.3
1996	0.2	21.0	36.8	12.8	5.8	1.7	15.6	1.6	4.5	35.8	4.8
1997	0.2	17.5	33.9	12.3	5.2	1.7	14.3	1.4	4.1	32.1	4.5
1998	0.2	13.7	31.7	12.0	5.3	1.5	13.1	1.4	4.2	27.7	3.9
1999	0.2	11.1	28.4	10.9	4.8	1.5	11.8	1.2	3.6	25.3	3.9
2000	0.1	9.5	28.0	11.6	4.8	1.4	11.6	1.2	3.5	25.5	3.3
2001	0.1	9.3	28.4	12.1	4.8	1.3	11.8	1.2	3.6	25.6	3.0
2002	0.1	9.0	26.8	12.8	4.9	1.4	11.7	1.2	3.6	24.9	2.9

Note: See Note, table 3.125. These data are estimates based on characteristics of known offenders from the Federal Bureau of Investigation's Supplementary Homicide Reports and an imputation procedure for cases where information on the offender was unknown because no suspects were identified (unsolved cases). The imputation procedure used to adjust for unsolved homicides is based on characteristics of the victim, circumstances of the incident, and year the incident occurred. Some data have been revised by the Source and may differ from previous editions of SOURCEBOOK.

Source: U.S. Department of Justice, Bureau of Justice Statistics, "Homicide Trends in the United States" [Online]. Available: http://www.ojp.usdoj.gov/bjs/homicide/homtrnd.htm [Sept. 30, 2004]. Table adapted by SOURCEBOOK staff.

Table 3.128

Estimated rate (per 100,000 persons in each group) of offenders committing murder and nonnegligent manslaughter

By age, sex, and race of offender, United States, 1976-2002

	14 to 17 years				18 to 24 years				25 years and older			
	Male		Female		Male		Female		Male		Female	
	White	Black	White	Black	White	Black	White	Black	White	Black	White	Black
1976	10.9	80.3	1.4	11.2	21.0	180.6	2.5	29.4	9.0	100.6	1.5	22.1
1977	11.2	73.8	1.3	7.0	21.8	169.7	2.6	29.8	9.2	96.1	1.4	20.9
1978	11.0	70.1	1.1	7.7	23.6	178.1	2.6	27.3	9.5	96.0	1.4	19.2
1979	13.5	78.4	1.1	9.0	26.8	197.3	2.8	27.0	10.2	101.4	1.5	18.8
1980	13.9	83.5	1.0	8.2	30.2	212.0	2.9	32.5	11.4	108.6	1.6	19.5
1981	11.6	82.6	1.2	8.1	27.2	185.6	2.5	23.8	10.9	96.4	1.5	17.6
1982	11.6	69.0	1.2	5.9	24.5	174.4	2.6	24.1	10.4	84.9	1.5	15.1
1983	11.0	57.3	1.5	7.2	23.9	149.8	2.3	21.9	9.5	76.1	1.3	13.1
1984	10.0	52.6	1.2	6.0	25.3	129.6	2.7	18.5	9.6	71.3	1.2	12.3
1985	10.4	68.9	0.9	7.1	23.2	143.1	2.5	18.0	9.3	68.7	1.2	12.0
1986	13.0	79.8	1.2	5.7	25.1	161.6	2.2	20.2	9.5	76.9	1.2	12.6
1987	11.8	87.3	1.3	6.8	24.4	177.1	2.5	16.5	9.3	69.2	1.2	11.1
1988	14.6	125.1	1.0	7.5	23.3	218.6	2.5	20.6	8.8	72.6	1.1	10.2
1989	16.7	135.0	1.1	6.9	26.9	249.7	2.7	19.0	8.6	67.8	1.1	10.8
1990	22.0	194.0	1.5	6.9	30.9	290.0	2.8	19.1	9.2	70.3	1.1	10.1
1991	22.8	213.6	1.3	10.5	32.9	364.1	2.6	22.0	8.8	68.8	1.0	10.2
1992	23.3	208.5	1.4	11.2	31.8	325.3	2.3	17.2	8.0	65.6	0.9	8.8
1993	22.8	253.0	1.3	9.2	32.7	361.6	2.3	20.1	7.9	60.7	1.1	8.1
1994	24.8	235.1	1.6	9.6	32.7	337.5	2.2	17.7	7.5	55.1	1.0	7.8
1995	22.0	178.6	1.3	7.6	32.0	300.3	2.1	13.0	7.2	51.2	0.9	6.3
1996	18.3	142.8	1.8	8.9	31.6	281.5	2.7	15.7	6.4	47.1	0.9	6.2
1997	16.3	116.7	1.5	4.5	29.5	251.9	2.8	15.9	5.9	45.1	0.8	5.3
1998	14.1	80.2	1.2	5.3	29.7	226.2	2.5	13.3	6.1	39.6	0.9	5.1
1999	10.5	68.3	1.4	6.1	24.8	212.1	2.4	10.7	5.4	36.3	0.8	4.3
2000	8.0	63.2	1.2	5.3	24.6	210.3	2.0	11.5	5.4	38.1	0.8	4.1
2001	8.2	60.8	1.0	5.2	26.0	206.6	2.2	12.6	5.4	38.8	0.7	4.2
2002	9.2	54.5	0.9	3.7	24.9	191.1	2.6	11.0	5.5	40.9	0.7	3.7

Note: See Notes, tables 3.125 and 3.127. Some data have been revised by the Source and may differ from previous editions of SOURCEBOOK.

Source: U.S. Department of Justice, Bureau of Justice Statistics, "Homicide Trends in the United States" [Online]. Available: http://www.ojp.usdoj.gov/bjs/homicide/homtrnd.htm [Sept. 30, 2004]. Table adapted by SOURCEBOOK staff.

Table 3.129

Murders and nonnegligent manslaughters known to police

By race and sex of victim and offender, United States, 2002

Characteristics of victim	Total	Characteristics of offender						
		Race				Sex		
		White	Black	Other	Unknown	Male	Female	Unknown
Total	7,005	3,309	3,386	180	130	6,151	722	132
Race								
White	3,582	3,000	483	58	41	3,169	372	41
Black	3,137	227	2,852	11	47	2,768	320	49
Other	192	51	28	109	4	169	19	4
Unknown	94	31	23	2	38	45	11	38
Sex								
Male	4,931	2,192	2,545	121	73	4,328	528	75
Female	1,980	1,086	818	57	19	1,778	183	19
Unknown	94	31	23	2	38	45	11	38

Note: See Notes, tables 3.106 and 3.117. These data pertain only to the 7,005 murders and nonnegligent manslaughters that involved a single offender and a single victim.

Source: U.S. Department of Justice, Federal Bureau of Investigation, *Crime in the United States, 2002* (Washington, DC: USGPO, 2003), p. 22, Table 2.8.

Table 3.130

Percent distribution of U.S. population, and murder and nonnegligent manslaughter victims and offenders

By age, sex, and race, United States, 1976-2002

	14 to 24 year old white males			14 to 24 year old black males			All others		
	Population	Victims	Offenders	Population	Victims	Offenders	Population	Victims	Offenders
1976	8.9%	8.7%	16.3%	1.3%	9.2%	18.8%	89.8%	82.1%	64.9%
1977	8.9	9.5	16.9	1.3	9.0	18.0	89.8	81.6	65.1
1978	8.8	10.1	17.5	1.3	8.9	18.4	89.9	81.1	64.1
1979	8.8	10.8	18.3	1.3	8.7	18.8	89.9	80.5	62.9
1980	8.6	10.4	18.1	1.3	9.0	18.5	90.1	80.6	63.4
1981	8.5	9.7	17.3	1.4	8.9	18.6	90.2	81.4	64.1
1982	8.3	9.6	16.8	1.3	8.8	18.2	90.4	81.6	64.9
1983	8.1	9.5	17.5	1.3	8.8	16.9	90.6	81.7	65.6
1984	7.9	9.0	18.3	1.3	8.2	15.2	90.9	82.8	66.4
1985	7.7	9.0	16.9	1.3	8.9	17.3	91.1	82.2	65.7
1986	7.5	8.9	17.0	1.3	9.7	18.0	91.3	81.4	65.0
1987	7.3	8.2	16.3	1.2	11.1	20.0	91.5	80.6	63.7
1988	7.1	7.9	15.3	1.2	12.3	24.1	91.7	79.9	60.6
1989	6.9	8.4	16.7	1.2	13.9	25.8	91.9	77.8	57.5
1990	6.7	9.8	17.6	1.2	14.7	28.1	92.1	75.6	54.2
1991	6.5	10.0	17.2	1.2	16.1	31.8	92.3	73.9	51.0
1992	6.4	10.0	17.7	1.1	16.4	31.1	92.5	73.6	51.1
1993	6.4	9.6	17.4	1.1	17.4	34.5	92.5	73.0	48.1
1994	6.3	10.2	18.5	1.1	17.5	33.7	92.6	72.3	47.9
1995	6.2	10.7	19.1	1.1	16.2	31.6	92.6	73.1	49.3
1996	6.1	10.4	19.3	1.1	16.2	30.8	92.7	73.4	49.9
1997	6.1	10.0	19.3	1.1	16.6	29.3	92.8	73.5	51.4
1998	6.1	10.7	20.1	1.1	15.2	26.7	92.8	74.1	53.2
1999	6.1	10.4	18.4	1.1	14.9	27.8	92.8	74.8	53.8
2000	6.1	10.0	17.7	1.1	14.8	27.8	92.7	75.2	54.4
2001	6.1	10.3	18.7	1.2	15.2	27.3	92.7	74.5	54.1
2002	6.2	10.3	18.6	1.2	14.9	25.5	92.7	74.9	55.9

Note: See Notes, tables 3.125 and 3.127. Some data have been revised by the Source and may differ from previous editions of SOURCEBOOK.

Source: U.S. Department of Justice, Bureau of Justice Statistics, "Homicide Trends in the United States" [Online]. Available: http://www.ojp.usdoj.gov/bjs/homicide/homtrnd.htm [Sept. 30, 2004]. Table adapted by SOURCEBOOK staff.

Table 3.131

Murders and nonnegligent manslaughters by intimates of the victims

By sex and race of victim, and victim-offender relationship, United States, 1976-2002

	Sex		Sex and race						Victim-offender relationship		
			Male			Female					Boyfriend/
	Male	Female	White	Black	Other	White	Black	Other	Spouse	Ex-spouse	girlfriend
1976	1,357	1,600	493	846	12	849	714	20	2,174	123	662
1977	1,294	1,437	479	804	5	831	570	17	2,017	110	603
1978	1,202	1,482	490	703	7	868	583	14	1,940	116	629
1979	1,262	1,506	535	712	10	883	594	13	1,940	146	683
1980	1,221	1,549	493	718	5	913	588	34	1,911	115	744
1981	1,278	1,572	554	703	18	952	591	27	1,946	136	768
1982	1,141	1,480	510	619	10	946	504	29	1,722	136	763
1983	1,113	1,462	508	594	10	910	513	37	1,676	128	770
1984	989	1,442	443	530	15	938	467	34	1,501	97	833
1985	957	1,546	427	518	12	1,005	492	48	1,580	111	811
1986	985	1,586	448	529	5	1,000	532	52	1,542	127	901
1987	933	1,494	424	498	8	968	486	35	1,489	96	841
1988	854	1,582	376	459	15	1,007	527	36	1,467	100	869
1989	903	1,415	371	512	11	883	474	42	1,326	78	913
1990	859	1,501	393	441	18	952	490	45	1,371	110	879
1991	779	1,518	359	413	7	931	520	55	1,297	82	918
1992	722	1,455	337	369	10	890	509	48	1,262	81	834
1993	708	1,581	330	362	12	989	542	43	1,232	94	964
1994	692	1,405	318	359	11	900	463	35	1,145	91	861
1995	546	1,317	251	285	9	872	387	50	1,023	60	780
1996	515	1,324	259	248	8	862	422	28	1,008	73	759
1997	451	1,217	239	202	9	761	401	40	867	72	728
1998	515	1,317	275	225	12	881	394	38	975	76	787
1999	426	1,218	223	190	11	814	338	61	839	62	743
2000	442	1,252	230	193	18	855	335	49	902	67	725
2001	399	1,202	206	181	11	804	343	50	836	56	711
2002	388	1,202	215	163	8	775	366	52	804	57	731

Note: See Note, table 3.125. "Intimates" include spouses, ex-spouses, boyfriends, and girlfriends. Some data have been revised by the Source and may differ from previous editions of SOURCEBOOK.

Source: U.S. Department of Justice, Bureau of Justice Statistics, "Homicide Trends in the United States" [Online]. Available: http://www.ojp.usdoj.gov/bjs/homicide/homtrnd.htm [Sept. 30, 2004]. Table adapted by SOURCEBOOK staff.

Table 3.132

Estimated rate (per 1,000 persons age 12 and older) of nonfatal intimate partner violence and percent change in rate

By sex of victim, 1993-2001

Sex of victim	1993	1994	1995	1996	1997	1998	1999	2000	2001	Percent change 1993 to 2001
Total	5.8	5.5	4.9	4.7	4.3	4.8	3.5	2.8	3.0	-48.4%
Male	1.6	1.7	1.1	1.4	1.0	1.5	1.1	0.8	0.9	-41.8
Female	9.8	9.1	8.5	7.8	7.5	7.8	5.8	4.7	5.0	-49.3

Note: These data are from the U.S. Department of Justice, Bureau of Justice Statistics' National Crime Victimization Survey (NCVS). Nonfatal violence includes rape, sexual assault, robbery, aggravated assault, and simple assault. These data do not include fatal violence. "Intimate partners" include current or former spouses, boyfriends, or girlfriends. Percent changes are based on unrounded rates. For survey methodology and definitions of terms, see Appendix 8.

Source: U.S. Department of Justice, Bureau of Justice Statistics, *Intimate Partner Violence, 1993-2001*, Crime Data Brief NCJ 197838 (Washington, DC: U.S. Department of Justice, February 2003), p. 2.

Table 3.133

Murder and nonnegligent manslaughters resulting from the Sept. 11, 2001 terrorist attacks

By sex and race of victim, and location

Race of victim	Total	Male	Female	Unknown
All locations, total	3,047	2,303	739	5
White	2,435	1,908	527	0
Black	286	170	116	0
Other	187	127	60	0
Unknown	139	98	36	5
World Trade Center, total	2,823	2,175	648	0
White	2,279	1,811	468	X
Black	234	148	86	X
Other	184	124	60	X
Unknown	126	92	34	X
Pentagon, total	184	108	71	5
White	120	79	41	0
Black	49	11	28	0
Other	2	2	0	0
Unknown	13	6	2	5
Somerset County, PA, total	40	20	20	0
White	36	18	18	X
Black	3	1	2	X
Other	1	1	0	X

Note: The Uniform Crime Reporting (UCR) Program is limited in its ability to report the offenses committed on Sept. 11, 2001. For the most part, the data associated with the events of Sept. 11, 2001 are not included in tables from *Crime in the United States, 2001*. The number of deaths is so great that combining these figures with traditional crime statistics would distort many types of measurements based on UCR data. Though the deaths resulting from these events may not meet the traditional definition of criminal homicide, the UCR program has classified those deaths for the purposes of presenting these data as murder and nonnegligent manslaughter. (Source: pp. iii, 302, 303).

Source: U.S. Department of Justice, Federal Bureau of Investigation, *Crime in the United States, 2001* (Washington, DC: USGPO, 2002), p. 302.

Table 3.134

Sniper-attack murder incidents, victims, and offenders

By type of firearm, 1982-2001

				Type of firearm				
Year	Incidents	Victims	Offenders[a]	Handgun (pistol, revolver, etc.)	Rifle	Shotgun	Type not stated	Other, unknown gun
Total	327	379	224	208	75	23	19	3
1982	12	15	8	6	2	2	2	0
1983	17	17	8	7	4	4	2	0
1984	18	37	16	7	7	4	0	0
1985	10	10	5	5	5	0	0	0
1986	9	9	4	1	6	0	2	0
1987	28	36	17	12	12	2	2	0
1988	47	55	32	32	9	6	0	0
1989	46	49	28	37	8	1	0	0
1990	40	41	24	29	4	3	4	0
1991	10	12	5	7	3	0	0	0
1992	31	33	14	26	3	0	2	0
1993	6	6	3	4	2	0	0	0
1994	2	2	5	1	0	0	0	1
1995	11	12	6	6	2	1	0	2
1996	8	8	13	4	1	0	3	0
1997	4	4	1	4	0	0	0	0
1998	10	15	15	7	3	0	0	0
1999	5	5	4	5	0	0	0	0
2000	8	8	5	7	1	0	0	0
2001[b]	5	5	11	1	3	0	2	0

Note: These data are from the Federal Bureau of Investigation's Supplementary Homicide Reports (SHR), which are comprised of additional data submitted by participating law enforcement agencies for the offenses of murder and nonnegligent manslaughter only. "Sniper attack" is an available designation on the SHR reporting form. However, the Source cautions that there is no uniform definition of sniper attacks for law enforcement agencies to follow. Reporting agencies are required to select only one circumstance. If a sniper attack occurred in conjunction with another offense type such as a gangland killing or romantic triangle, the agency may have selected one of these designations. The above data include only those incidents in which sniper attack was designated by the reporting agency, the victim was killed, and the weapon reported on the SHR form was a firearm. (Source, p. 315.)

[a] Includes only offenders for whom age, sex and/or race was reported by law enforcement.
[b] In 2001, one incident involved more than one weapon type.

Source: U.S. Department of Justice, Federal Bureau of Investigation, *Crime in the United States, 2002* (Washington, DC: USGPO, 2003), p. 315, Table 5.13; p. 316, Table 5.15. Table adapted by SOURCEBOOK staff.

Table 3.135

Workplace homicides

By victim characteristics, type of event, and selected occupation and industry,
United States, 1992-2002[a]

	1992	1993	1994	1995	1996	1997	1998	1999	2000	2001[b]	2002[c]
Total	1,044	1,074	1,080	1,036	927	860	714	651	677	639	609
Victim characteristics											
Employee status											
Wage and salary workers[d]	793	786	818	823	675	632	526	485	488	470	449
Self-employed[e]	251	288	262	213	252	228	188	166	189	169	160
Sex											
Male	862	884	895	790	751	715	550	525	543	513	473
Female	182	190	185	246	176	145	164	126	134	126	136
Age											
Under 16 years	(f)	6	(f)	(f)	(f)	(f)	(f)	(f)	(f)	(f)	(f)
16 to 17 years	11	11	10	6	8	9	(f)	8	(f)	(f)	(f)
18 to 19 years	19	16	27	26	21	16	12	11	14	14	10
20 to 24 years	105	89	102	70	74	60	44	49	41	45	34
25 to 34 years	271	294	280	264	220	215	178	145	142	136	147
35 to 44 years	275	295	290	258	228	216	199	166	177	174	167
45 to 54 years	186	194	205	215	189	171	139	155	165	151	147
55 to 64 years	116	108	104	127	120	120	82	74	100	81	76
65 years and older	56	61	61	65	65	51	52	38	31	34	24
Race, ethnicity											
White	597	583	592	578	504	500	399	346	344	331	309
Black	192	164	210	206	171	146	128	116	118	113	111
Asian or Pacific Islander	105	128	129	100	105	104	74	85	84	72	54
American Indian, Eskimo, or Aleut	(f)	6	7	5	6	(f)	(f)	(f)	(f)	(f)	(f)
Other or unspecified	14	8	(f)	17	11	5	10	5	20	13	26
Hispanic[g]	132	185	139	130	130	101	99	95	108	106	107
Type of event											
Shooting	852	884	934	762	761	708	574	509	533	505	469
Stabbing	90	95	60	67	80	73	61	62	66	58	58
Hitting, kicking, beating	52	35	47	46	50	48	48	48	37	36	34
Other	30	48	31	153	29	26	24	26	38	38	38
Major occupation											
Managerial and professional specialty occupations	185	162	149	200	184	156	132	117	141	120	104
Technical, sales, and administrative support jobs	353	404	426	381	332	305	239	197	235	203	210
Service occupations	228	212	251	216	188	181	146	156	130	171	156
Police and detectives	62	68	70	81	55	66	53	47	49	62	57
Guards	56	55	76	61	52	43	39	36	33	38	37
Farming, forestry, and fishing	15	11	17	20	18	10	19	19	14	11	13
Precision production, craft, and repair jobs	43	67	39	40	37	36	41	35	38	34	28
Operators, fabricators, and laborers	211	204	178	160	154	162	130	118	113	96	96
Major industry											
Agriculture, forestry, fishing	15	13	18	19	18	9	19	19	12	9	(f)
Construction	20	20	16	15	12	14	20	6	21	26	18
Manufacturing	32	46	33	44	40	43	38	26	25	32	24
Transportation and public utilities	117	126	118	98	76	110	69	70	65	52	49
Taxicabs	86	96	87	68	50	74	48	51	42	33	27
Wholesale trade	25	25	20	25	24	21	21	26	16	6	18
Retail trade	503	525	530	422	437	395	287	264	310	280	263
Grocery stores	166	176	196	152	146	141	95	78	111	92	77
Eating and drinking places	145	145	135	121	135	109	69	95	91	93	86
Gasoline service stations	41	53	41	36	23	34	25	17	14	16	17
Finance, insurance, real estate	37	35	31	53	41	28	22	34	21	20	28
Services	175	155	193	141	169	146	139	136	127	125	110
Detective and armored car services	23	32	49	27	29	21	18	17	16	21	19
Government[h]	104	124	104	212	100	88	94	66	78	88	83
Federal	11	18	12	109	11	7	16	7	6	9	5
State	11	20	12	17	20	19	22	11	11	10	16
Local	80	86	80	84	69	60	56	48	61	68	61

See notes on next page.

Table 3.135

Workplace homicides

By victim characteristics, type of event, and selected occupation and industry,
United States, 1992-2002[a]--Continued

Note: These data were collected through the Census of Fatal Occupational Injuries conducted annually by the Bureau of Labor Statistics in cooperation with numerous Federal, State, and local agencies. Data were compiled from various Federal, State, and local administrative sources including death certificates, workers' compensation reports and claims, medical examiner reports, police reports, news reports, and reports to various regulatory agencies.

The Census of Fatal Occupational Injuries, therefore, includes data for all fatal work injuries, whether they are covered by the Occupational Safety and Health Administration (OSHA), another Federal or State agency, or are outside the scope of regulatory coverage. Federal agencies participating in the census include OSHA, the Employment Standards Administration, the Mine Safety and Health Administration, the Federal Aviation Administration, the Federal Railroad Administration, the Department of Energy, and the U.S. Coast Guard. State and local agencies participating in the census include State and local police departments; State vital statistics registrars; State departments of health, labor, and industries; State farm bureaus; and local coroners and medical examiners. Multiple sources were used because studies have shown that no single source captures all job-related fatalities. Source documents were matched so that each fatality is counted only once. To ensure that a fatality was work related, information was verified from two or more independent source documents or from a source document and a followup questionnaire.

[a] Detail may not add to total because of the omission of miscellaneous categories.
[b] The workplace homicides that occurred as a result of the events of Sept. 11, 2001 are not included in this table.
[c] Data for 2002 are preliminary.
[d] May include volunteers and other workers receiving compensation.
[e] Includes paid and unpaid family workers, and may include owners of incorporated businesses or members of partnerships.
[f] No data reported or data did not meet publication criteria specified by the Source.
[g] Persons identified as Hispanic may be of any race; therefore detail will not add to total.
[h] Includes fatalities to workers employed by government agencies regardless of industry.

Source: Table adapted by SOURCEBOOK staff from data provided by U.S. Department of Labor, Bureau of Labor Statistics.

Table 3.136

Suicide rate (per 100,000 persons in each age group)

By age, United States, 1980, 1985, 1990-2002

Age	1980	1985	1990	1991	1992	1993	1994	1995	1996	1997	1998	1999	2000	2001	2002
Total	11.83	12.38	12.39	12.22	11.95	12.06	11.96	11.90	11.65	11.41	11.31	10.71	12.40	12.46	12.74
10 to 14 years	0.76	1.62	1.50	1.50	1.68	1.70	1.70	1.75	1.57	1.59	1.65	1.24	1.51	1.30	1.23
15 to 19 years	8.53	9.87	11.14	11.02	10.76	10.85	11.00	10.40	9.74	9.45	8.89	8.18	8.15	7.95	7.44
20 to 24 years	16.09	15.39	15.11	14.87	14.91	15.74	16.30	16.03	14.47	13.61	13.57	12.68	12.84	11.93	12.28
25 to 29 years	16.43	15.52	15.04	14.90	14.21	15.20	15.80	15.18	14.82	14.36	14.03	13.17	13.11	12.59	12.82
30 to 34 years	15.17	15.04	15.33	15.47	14.87	14.96	15.02	15.61	14.25	14.29	13.66	13.73	12.52	12.94	12.60
35 to 39 years	15.27	14.36	15.51	15.05	15.06	15.03	15.45	14.94	15.40	15.06	15.20	14.58	13.97	14.27	14.40
40 to 44 years	15.22	14.89	14.72	14.28	15.06	15.21	15.11	15.47	15.68	15.55	15.52	14.28	15.25	15.18	16.17
45 to 49 years	15.41	15.54	14.90	15.65	14.66	14.24	14.43	14.67	15.11	15.17	15.28	14.55	15.01	15.69	16.33
50 to 54 years	16.45	15.92	14.59	15.25	14.65	14.92	14.31	14.44	14.73	14.16	14.31	13.77	14.20	14.56	15.11
55 to 59 years	16.23	17.20	16.16	15.48	14.70	14.61	13.37	12.94	14.21	14.48	13.76	13.03	12.83	13.99	14.60
60 to 64 years	15.45	16.45	15.93	15.39	14.98	14.65	13.39	13.62	13.10	12.37	12.23	11.58	11.60	11.99	12.35
65 to 69 years	16.12	16.92	16.54	15.68	15.59	14.97	13.89	14.48	14.35	13.22	13.12	12.56	11.38	12.70	12.49
70 to 74 years	17.69	20.81	19.50	18.34	17.52	17.89	16.96	17.27	15.80	15.71	15.20	14.64	13.94	13.88	14.54
75 to 79 years	19.54	23.26	23.77	22.23	21.70	20.80	20.55	19.55	18.62	18.45	17.64	17.46	16.56	16.40	16.56
80 to 84 years	18.17	24.98	26.23	25.55	24.70	24.56	22.55	22.49	22.16	20.61	22.86	19.45	19.46	18.90	19.36
85 years and older	19.03	19.38	21.94	23.80	21.60	22.68	22.90	21.49	20.18	20.79	20.99	19.19	19.39	17.36	18.07

Note: These data are based on information from all death certificates filed in the 50 States and the District of Columbia. The mortality data files are maintained by the National Center for Health Statistics at the Centers for Disease Control and Prevention. Rates for decennial years were calculated using U.S. Census Bureau decennial census counts; population estimates produced by the Census Bureau were used for noncensus years.

Suicide rates for ages under 10 years have been omitted because of low incidence. A category including cases where the age is unknown also has been omitted; this category also comprises a small number of cases each year. Some data have been revised by the Source and may differ from previous editions of SOURCEBOOK.

Source: U.S. Department of Health and Human Services, Centers for Disease Control and Prevention, National Center for Injury Prevention and Control [Online]. Available: http://www.cdc.gov/ncipc/data/us8179/suic.htm, http://www.cdc.gov/ncipc/data/us8582/suic.htm, http://www.cdc.gov/ncipc/data/us8986/suic.htm, http://www.cdc.gov/ncipc/data/us9390/suic.htm, http://www.cdc.gov/ncipc/data/us9794/suic.htm [Feb. 9, 2000]; http://webapp.cdc.gov/sasweb/ncipc/mortrate.html [June 4, 2001]; http://webapp.cdc.gov/sasweb/ncipc/mortrate.html [Mar. 19, 2002]; http://webapp.cdc.gov/sasweb/ncipc/mortrate10.html [Apr. 4, 2003]; and http://webapp.cdc.gov/sasweb/ncipc/mortrate10.html [Dec. 7, 2004]. Table adapted by SOURCEBOOK staff.

Table 3.137

Suicide rate (per 100,000 persons in each age group)

By age, sex, and race, United States, 2002

Age	Total	Sex Male	Sex Female	Race White	Race Black	Race Other	White Male	White Female	Black Male	Black Female	Other Male	Other Female
Total	12.74	20.94	4.91	14.10	6.21	7.27	23.02	5.48	11.13	1.85	11.06	3.70
10 to 14 years	1.23	1.81	0.62	1.29	0.97	1.26[a]	1.87	0.68	1.57	0.35[a]	1.81[a]	0.69[a]
15 to 19 years	7.44	12.23	2.36	8.17	4.04	6.54	13.44	2.57	6.89	1.09[a]	9.95	2.96[a]
20 to 24 years	12.28	20.63	3.49	13.10	9.06	9.67	21.86	3.72	16.00	2.28	15.68	3.48
25 to 29 years	12.82	20.84	4.52	13.59	10.34	9.29	21.56	5.13	19.47	1.96	15.36	3.29
30 to 34 years	12.60	20.31	4.76	13.75	8.27	7.88	21.81	5.34	15.19	2.04	12.10	3.78
35 to 39 years	14.40	22.78	6.03	15.92	8.14	7.99	24.81	6.84	14.49	2.49	12.50	3.66
40 to 44 years	16.17	24.76	7.70	18.20	7.14	6.62	27.66	8.68	11.55	3.25	9.28	4.15
45 to 49 years	16.33	24.89	8.02	18.45	5.89	6.92	27.65	9.31	10.99	1.47[a]	10.35	3.86
50 to 54 years	15.11	23.84	6.75	16.80	5.87	7.54	26.43	7.38	9.25	3.00	10.10	5.31
55 to 59 years	14.60	23.54	6.19	16.12	4.64	7.75	25.71	6.94	8.65	1.35[a]	12.45	3.59[a]
60 to 64 years	12.35	20.46	4.99	13.59	5.05	4.70	22.50	5.35	8.14	2.64[a]	5.81[a]	3.71[a]
65 to 69 years	12.49	21.95	4.32	13.70	3.51	8.54	23.80	4.81	7.74	0.37[a]	13.89	4.12[a]
70 to 74 years	14.54	27.87	3.88	15.67	6.56	5.78[a]	30.10	3.91	12.35	2.68[a]	5.26[a]	6.16[a]
75 to 79 years	16.56	34.26	4.06	17.56	6.69	12.77	36.22	4.20	13.84	1.37[a]	19.97[a]	7.58[a]
80 to 84 years	19.36	44.08	4.36	20.87	3.67[a]	10.18[a]	47.29	4.71	10.74[a]	0.00[a]	17.74[a]	4.93[a]
85 years and older	18.07	51.14	3.82	19.20	5.95[a]	12.57[a]	54.46	3.98	19.36[a]	0.82[a]	20.67[a]	7.73[a]

Note: See Note, table 3.136.

[a] Rate based on 20 or fewer deaths.

Source: U.S. Department of Health and Human Services, Centers for Disease Control and Prevention, National Center for Injury Prevention and Control [Online]. Available: http://webapp.cdc.gov/sasweb/ncipc/mortrate10.html [Dec. 8, 2004].

Table 3.138
Suicide rate (per 100,000 persons in each age group) for persons 15 to 24 years of age

By age and sex, United States, 1950, 1960, 1970, 1980, 1990, 1993-2002

Age and sex	1950	1960	1970	1980	1990	1993	1994	1995	1996	1997	1998	1999	2000	2001	2002
15 to 19 years of age	2.7	3.6	5.9	8.5	11.1	10.9	11.0	10.4	9.7	9.4	8.9	8.2	8.2	8.0	7.4
Male	3.5	5.6	8.8	13.8	18.1	17.5	18.1	17.3	15.6	15.2	14.6	13.3	13.2	12.9	12.2
Female	1.8	1.6	2.9	3.0	3.7	3.8	3.5	3.1	3.6	3.4	2.9	2.8	2.8	2.7	2.4
20 to 24 years of age	6.2	7.1	12.2	16.1	15.1	15.7	16.3	16.0	14.5	13.6	13.6	12.7	12.8	11.9	12.3
Male	9.3	11.5	19.2	26.8	25.7	26.6	28.5	27.7	24.8	23.0	23.0	21.6	22.0	20.4	20.6
Female	3.3	2.9	5.6	5.5	4.1	4.4	3.9	4.3	3.7	3.7	3.8	3.5	3.3	3.1	3.5

Note: See Note, table 3.136. Some data have been revised by the Source and may differ from previous editions of SOURCEBOOK.

Source: U.S. Department of Health and Human Services, Centers for Disease Control and Prevention, "Programs for the Prevention of Suicide Among Adolescents and Young Adults," *Morbidity and Mortality Weekly Report* (Washington, DC: USGPO, Apr. 22, 1994), p. 3; and U.S. Department of Health and Human Services, Centers for Disease Control and Prevention, National Center for Injury Prevention and Control [Online]. Available: http://www.cdc.gov/ncipc/data/us9390/suic.htm, http://www.cdc.gov/ncipc/data/us9794/suic.htm [Feb. 9, 2000]; http://webapp.cdc.gov/sasweb/ncipc/mortrate.html [June 4, 2001]; http://webapp.cdc.gov/sasweb/ncipc/mortrate10.html [Mar. 19, 2002]; http://webapp.cdc.gov/sasweb/ncipc/mortrate10.html [Apr. 4, 2003]; and http://webapp.cdc.gov/sasweb/ncipc/mortrate10.html [Dec. 7, 2004]. Table adapted by SOURCEBOOK staff.

Table 3.139
Firearm suicide rate (per 100,000 persons in each age group)

By age, United States, 1980, 1985, 1990-2002

Age	1980	1985	1990	1991	1992	1993	1994	1995	1996	1997	1998	1999	2000	2001	2002
Total	6.78	7.30	7.57	7.35	7.12	7.35	7.21	7.04	6.85	6.56	6.45	7.10	7.01	6.87	6.89
10 to 14 years	0.43	0.82	0.83	0.88	0.95	1.01	1.00	0.97	0.85	0.66	0.80	0.53	0.55	0.43	0.41
15 to 19 years	5.38	5.96	7.50	7.43	7.29	7.33	7.77	6.97	6.15	5.95	5.56	4.94	4.51	4.14	3.65
20 to 24 years	9.92	9.24	9.58	9.54	9.55	10.30	10.66	9.98	8.98	8.29	8.05	7.43	7.41	6.53	6.62
25 to 29 years	9.16	8.85	9.04	8.59	8.13	9.04	9.14	8.58	8.31	7.83	7.63	7.10	6.85	6.66	6.44
30 to 34 years	8.09	7.94	8.46	8.22	7.73	8.27	8.04	8.09	7.21	7.39	6.79	6.74	6.28	6.28	5.68
35 to 39 years	8.54	7.55	8.06	7.82	7.70	7.73	7.88	7.61	7.84	7.54	7.44	7.17	6.83	6.42	6.65
40 to 44 years	8.13	8.23	8.06	7.59	7.74	7.93	7.77	7.80	7.91	7.56	7.52	6.65	7.38	7.02	7.44
45 to 49 years	8.26	8.81	8.74	8.84	8.20	7.97	8.10	7.75	8.14	7.83	7.83	7.55	7.49	7.47	7.77
50 to 54 years	9.05	9.54	8.63	8.98	8.53	9.13	8.27	8.43	8.66	7.92	7.48	7.39	7.92	7.99	7.91
55 to 59 years	9.07	10.19	10.25	9.46	9.40	9.29	8.25	8.13	8.68	9.03	8.40	8.22	7.52	8.42	8.65
60 to 64 years	9.10	10.36	10.30	9.64	9.33	9.82	8.88	9.04	8.56	7.93	8.09	7.63	7.80	7.99	8.10
65 to 69 years	9.97	11.20	11.52	10.80	10.82	10.19	9.62	9.98	10.20	9.36	8.89	8.75	8.39	8.98	8.83
70 to 74 years	10.98	14.40	13.51	13.14	12.84	12.58	12.05	12.41	11.68	11.11	11.36	10.99	10.40	10.25	10.68
75 to 79 years	11.48	15.41	17.09	16.06	15.08	14.97	15.07	14.48	13.50	13.18	13.22	12.91	12.37	12.38	12.35
80 to 84 years	10.41	16.13	17.79	17.60	16.42	17.54	15.93	15.86	15.84	14.58	16.58	13.70	14.16	14.14	14.35
85 years and older	10.09	10.91	13.11	13.97	12.83	14.08	14.03	13.61	13.29	12.76	13.40	12.55	12.99	12.12	12.03

Note: See Note, table 3.136.

Source: U.S. Department of Health and Human Services, Centers for Disease Control and Prevention, National Center for Injury Prevention and Control [Online]. Available: http://www.cdc.gov/ncipc/data/us8179/farmsuic.htm, http://www.cdc.gov/ncipc/data/us8582/farmsuic.htm, http://www.cdc.gov/ncipc/data/us8986/farmsuic.htm, http://www.cdc.gov/ncipc/data/us9390/farmsuic.htm, http://www.cdc.gov/ncipc/data/us9794/farmsuic.htm [Feb. 9, 2000]; http://webapp.cdc.gov/sasweb/ncipc/mortrate.html [June 4, 2001]; http://webapp.cdc.gov/sasweb/ncipc/mortrate10.html [Mar. 19, 2002]; http://webapp.cdc.gov/sasweb/ncipc/mortrate10.html [Apr. 4, 2003]; and http://webapp.cdc.gov/sasweb/ncipc/mortrate10.html [Dec. 7, 2004]. Table adapted by SOURCEBOOK staff.

Table 3.140

Percent distribution of robberies known to police

By type of weapon used, United States, 1974-2002

	Total[a]	Firearm	Knife or other cutting instrument	Other weapon	Strong-armed
1974	100%	45%	13%	8%	34%
1975	100	45	12	8	35
1976	100	43	13	8	36
1977	100	42	13	8	37
1978	100	41	13	9	37
1979	100	40	13	9	38
1980	100	40	13	9	38
1981	100	40	13	9	38
1982	100	40	14	9	37
1983	100	37	14	10	40
1984	100	36	13	9	42
1985	100	35	13	9	42
1986	100	34	14	10	43
1987	100	33	14	10	44
1988	100	33	14	10	43
1989	100	33	13	10	43
1990	100	37	12	10	42
1991	100	40	11	9	40
1992	100	40	11	10	40
1993	100	42	10	10	38
1994	100	42	10	10	39
1995	100	41	9	9	41
1996	100	41	9	12	39
1997	100	40	8	13	38
1998	100	38	9	13	40
1999	100	40	8	10	42
2000	100	41	8	10	40
2001	100	42	9	10	39
2002	100	42	9	9	40

Note: See Note, table 3.106. In trend tables "constructed" or "adapted" by SOURCEBOOK staff from *Crime in the United States*, the data are from the first year in which the data are reported. It should be noted that the number of agencies reporting and the populations represented vary from year to year. Also, the percent distributions are based on offense reports for which the FBI received detailed information from local law enforcement agencies and exclude jurisdictions for which the FBI generated estimated offense totals. For data on the estimated total number of offenses occurring in the United States for each Index crime, see table 3.106. For information on States supplying incomplete data for selected years, see Appendix 3.

[a]Because of rounding, percents may not add to total.

Source: U.S. Department of Justice, Federal Bureau of Investigation, *Crime in the United States, 1974*, p. 26; *1975*, p. 26; *1976*, p. 21; *1977*, p. 19; *1978*, p. 19; *1979*, p. 19; *1980*, p. 19; *1981*, p. 18; *1982*, p. 18; *1983*, p. 18; *1984*, p. 18; *1985*, p. 18; *1986*, p. 18; *1987*, p. 18; *1988*, p. 21; *1989*, p. 20; *1990*, p. 21; *1991*, p. 29, Table 2.21; *1992*, p. 29, Table 2.21; *1993*, p. 29, Table 2.22; *1994*, p. 29, Table 2.22; *1995*, p. 29, Table 2.22; *1996*, p. 29, Table 2.22; *1997*, p. 31, Table 2.22; *1998*, p. 29, Table 2.22; *1999*, p. 29, Table 2.22; *2000*, p. 31, Table 2.22; *2001*, p. 35; *2002*, p. 35 (Washington, DC: USGPO). Table constructed by SOURCEBOOK staff.

Table 3.141

Percent distribution of robberies known to police

By type of weapon used and region, 2002

Region	Total[a]	Firearm	Knife or other cutting instrument	Other weapon	Strong-armed
Total	100.0%	42.1%	8.7%	9.3%	39.9%
Northeast	100.0	34.0	10.8	8.3	46.9
Midwest	100.0	43.8	6.5	9.7	40.0
South	100.0	47.8	7.8	9.7	34.7
West	100.0	36.3	10.3	9.1	44.3

Note: See Note, table 3.106. For a list of States in regions, see Appendix 3.

[a]Because of rounding, percents may not add to total.

Source: U.S. Department of Justice, Federal Bureau of Investigation, *Crime in the United States, 2002* (Washington, DC: USGPO, 2003), p. 35.

Table 3.142

Percent distribution of robberies known to police

By place of occurrence, United States, 1973-2002

	Total[a]	Street/highway	Commercial house	Gas or service station	Convenience store	Residence	Bank	Miscellaneous
1973	100%	49%	17%	4%	6%	11%	1%	14%
1974	100	50	17	3	6	12	1	11
1975	100	51	16	4	6	12	1	10
1976	100	47	15	5	6	12	1	14
1977	100	46	15	6	7	12	1	14
1978	100	47	14	6	7	11	1	13
1979	100	49	14	4	7	11	2	13
1980	100	52	14	4	7	11	2	11
1981	100	52	13	4	6	11	1	12
1982	100	54	12	4	6	11	1	12
1983	100	54	11	3	6	11	1	13
1984	100	54	12	3	6	11	1	13
1985	100	55	12	3	6	10	1	12
1986	100	56	12	3	5	10	1	12
1987	100	54	13	3	6	10	1	12
1988	100	54	12	3	6	10	1	13
1989	100	55	12	3	6	10	1	13
1990	100	56	12	3	6	10	2	12
1991	100	56	12	3	6	10	2	12
1992	100	56	12	2	5	10	2	13
1993	100	55	12	2	5	10	2	13
1994	100	55	12	2	5	11	1	14
1995	100	54	12	2	5	11	2	13
1996	100	51	14	2	6	11	2	14
1997	100	50	14	2	6	12	2	15
1998	100	49	14	2	6	12	2	15
1999	100	48	14	2	6	12	2	16
2000	100	46	14	3	6	12	2	16
2001	100	44	14	3	7	13	2	17
2002	100	43	15	3	6	14	2	18

Note: See Notes, tables 3.106 and 3.140. "Commercial house" refers to nonresidential structures, with the exception of gas stations, convenience stores, and banking-type institutions. For information on States supplying incomplete data for selected years, see Appendix 3.

[a]Because of rounding, percents may not add to total.

Source: U.S. Department of Justice, Federal Bureau of Investigation, *Crime in the United States, 1973*, p. 120, Table 22; *1974*, p. 178, Table 26; *1975*, p. 178, Table 26; *1976*, p. 21; *1977*, p. 19; *1978*, p. 17; *1979*, p. 16; *1980*, p. 17; *1981*, p. 16; *1982*, p. 17; *1983*, p. 18; *1984*, p.18; *1985*, p.18; *1986*, p. 18; *1987*, p. 18; *1988*, p. 19; *1989*, p.18; *1990*, p. 19; *1991*, p. 27, Table 2.19; *1992*, p. 27, Table 2.19; *1993*, p. 27, Table 2.20; *1994*, p. 27, Table 2.20; *1995*, p. 27, Table 2.20; *1996*, p. 27, Table 2.20; *1997*, p. 29, Table 2.20; *1998*, p. 27, Table 2.20; *1999*, p. 28, Table 2.20; *2000*, p. 30, Table 2.20; *2001*, p. 33; *2002*, p. 32, Table 2.20 (Washington, DC: USGPO). Table adapted by SOURCEBOOK staff.

Table 3.143
Percent distribution of aggravated assaults known to police

By type of weapon used, United States, 1964-2002

		Type of weapon used			
	Total[a]	Firearm	Knife or other cutting instrument	Other weapons (clubs, blunt objects, etc.)	Personal weapons (hands, fists, feet, etc.)
1964	100%	15%	40%	23%	22%
1965	100	17	36	22	25
1966	100	19	34	22	25
1967	100	21	33	22	24
1968	100	23	31	24	22
1969	100	24	30	25	22
1970	100	24	28	24	23
1971	100	25	27	24	24
1972	100	25	26	23	25
1973	100	26	25	23	27
1974	100	25	24	23	27
1975	100	25	24	25	27
1976	100	24	24	26	27
1977	100	23	23	27	26
1978	100	22	23	28	27
1979	100	23	22	28	27
1980	100	24	22	28	27
1981	100	24	22	28	26
1982	100	22	23	28	26
1983	100	21	24	29	26
1984	100	21	23	31	25
1985	100	21	23	31	25
1986	100	21	22	32	25
1987	100	21	21	32	25
1988	100	21	20	31	27
1989	100	22	20	32	27
1990	100	23	20	32	26
1991	100	24	18	31	27
1992	100	25	18	31	26
1993	100	25	18	31	26
1994	100	24	18	32	26
1995	100	23	18	33	26
1996	100	22	18	34	26
1997	100	20	18	35	27
1998	100	19	18	36	27
1999	100	18	18	35	29
2000	100	18	18	36	28
2001	100	18	18	36	28
2002	100	19	18	35	28

Note: See Notes, tables 3.106 and 3.140. For information on States supplying incomplete data for selected years, see Appendix 3.

[a]Because of rounding, percents may not add to total.

Source: U.S. Department of Justice, Federal Bureau of Investigation, *Crime in the United States, 1964*, p. 9; *1965*, p. 8; *1966*, p. 9; *1967*, p. 11; *1968*, p. 10; *1969*, p. 10; *1970*, p. 12; *1971*, p. 12; *1972*, p. 10; *1973*, p. 11; *1974*, p. 20; *1975*, p. 20; *1976*, p. 13; *1977*, p. 21; *1978*, p. 21; *1979*, p. 20; *1980*, p. 21; *1981*, p. 20; *1982*, p. 22; *1983*, p. 23; *1984*, p. 23; *1985*, p. 23; *1986*, p. 22; *1987*, p. 23; *1988*, p. 24; *1989*, p. 23; *1990*, p. 24; *1991*, p. 32, Table 2.23; *1992*, p. 32, Table 2.23; *1993*, p. 32, Table 2.24; *1994*, p. 32, Table 2.24; *1995*, p. 32, Table 2.24; *1996*, p. 32, Table 2.24; *1997*, p. 34, Table 2.24; *1998*, p. 32, Table 2.24; *1999*, p. 33, Table 2.24; *2000*, p. 35, Table 2.24; *2001*, p. 38; *2002*, p. 38, Table 2.24 (Washington, DC: USGPO). Table constructed by SOURCEBOOK staff.

Table 3.144
Percent distribution of aggravated assaults known to police

By type of weapon used and region, 2002

		Type of weapon used			
Region	Total[a]	Firearm	Knife or other cutting instrument	Other weapons (clubs, blunt objects, etc.)	Personal weapons (hands, fists, feet, etc.)
Total	100.0%	19.0%	17.8%	35.4%	27.7%
Northeast	100.0	14.1	18.4	34.4	33.1
Midwest	100.0	18.0	17.2	34.7	30.1
South	100.0	21.0	19.5	37.6	21.9
West	100.0	18.0	15.2	32.6	34.3

Note: See Note, table 3.106. For a list of States in regions, see Appendix 3.

[a]Because of rounding, percents may not add to total.

Source: U.S. Department of Justice, Federal Bureau of Investigation, *Crime in the United States, 2002* (Washington, DC: USGPO, 2003), p. 38, Table 2.24.

Table 3.145
Percent distribution of burglaries known to police

By place and time of occurrence, United States, 1976-2002

		Residence (dwelling)			Non-residence (store, office, etc.)		
	Total[a]	Night	Day	Unknown	Night	Day	Unknown
1976	100%	22%	25%	16%	23%	5%	9%
1977	100	23	26	16	21	5	9
1978	100	22	26	16	20	6	10
1979	100	21	26	16	21	6	10
1980	100	21	28	17	18	5	10
1981	100	22	29	17	18	5	9
1982	100	22	27	16	19	6	10
1983	100	23	26	18	18	6	10
1984	100	22	27	18	17	6	10
1985	100	21	27	18	17	6	10
1986	100	22	28	18	17	6	10
1987	100	21	28	18	16	6	10
1988	100	21	29	18	16	7	10
1989	100	20	28	17	16	8	10
1990	100	21	29	16	16	8	9
1991	100	21	28	17	16	8	10
1992	100	21	29	16	16	9	9
1993	100	21	29	16	16	8	10
1994	100	20	30	17	15	9	9
1995	100	20	29	17	14	9	10
1996	100	20	28	19	15	8	11
1997	100	19	28	19	15	8	11
1998	100	19	29	19	14	8	11
1999	100	19	29	18	14	9	11
2000	100	19	30	16	15	11	10
2001	100	19	30	16	15	11	10
2002	100	19	31	15	14	11	9

Note: See Notes, tables 3.106 and 3.140. For information on States supplying incomplete data for selected years, see Appendix 3.

[a]Because of rounding, percents may not add to total.

Source: U.S. Department of Justice, Federal Bureau of Investigation, *Crime in the United States, 1976*, p. 159, Table 18; *1977*, p. 159, Table 18; *1978*, p. 174, Table 18; *1979*, p. 176, Table 18; *1980*, p. 179, Table 18; *1981*, p. 150, Table 17; *1982*, p. 155, Table 17; *1983*, p. 158, Table 17; *1984*, p. 151, Table 18; *1985*, p. 153, Table 18; *1986*, p. 153, Table 18; *1987*, p. 152, Table 18; *1988*, p. 156, Table 18; *1989*, p. 160, Table 18; *1990*, p. 162, Table 18; *1991*, p. 201, Table 23; *1992*, p. 205, Table 23; *1993*, p. 205, Table 23; *1994*, p. 205, Table 23; *1995*, p. 196, Table 23; *1996*, p. 202, Table 23; *1997*, p. 210, Table 23; *1998*, p. 197, Table 23; *1999*, p. 199, Table 23; *2000*, p. 204, Table 23; *2001*, p. 218, Table 23; *2002*, p. 217, Table 23 (Washington, DC: USGPO). Table constructed by SOURCEBOOK staff.

Table 3.146

Percent distribution of larceny-thefts known to police

By type of target, United States, 1973-2002

	Total[a]	Pocket-picking	Purse-snatching	Shop-lifting	From motor vehicles (except accessories)	Motor vehicle accessories	Bicycles	From buildings	From coin-operated machines	All others
1973	100%	1%	2%	11%	17%	16%	17%	17%	1%	18%
1974	100	1	2	11	18	16	17	17	1	17
1975	100	1	2	11	18	19	13	17	1	18
1976	100	1	2	10	20	22	10	15	1	18
1977	100	1	2	11	17	20	11	16	1	20
1978	100	1	2	11	17	19	11	17	1	21
1979	100	1	1	11	17	19	11	16	1	22
1980	100	1	2	11	17	19	10	17	1	23
1981	100	1	2	11	18	19	9	17	1	22
1982	100	1	1	12	19	20	9	16	1	21
1983	100	1	1	13	19	19	8	16	1	22
1984	100	1	1	13	19	18	8	16	1	22
1985	100	1	1	14	20	17	8	16	1	23
1986	100	1	1	15	21	17	7	15	1	22
1987	100	1	1	15	21	17	6	15	1	23
1988	100	1	1	15	22	16	6	15	1	23
1989	100	1	1	16	22	16	6	15	1	24
1990	100	1	1	16	22	15	6	14	1	24
1991	100	1	1	16	22	14	6	14	1	24
1992	100	1	1	16	23	14	6	14	1	25
1993	100	1	1	15	23	14	6	13	1	26
1994	100	1	1	15	24	13	6	13	1	27
1995	100	1	1	15	24	12	6	12	1	28
1996	100	(b)	1	15	25	11	6	13	1	29
1997	100	1	1	15	26	10	6	14	1	28
1998	100	1	1	15	26	10	5	13	1	29
1999	100	1	1	14	26	10	5	14	1	29
2000	100	1	1	14	25	10	4	13	1	32
2001	100	(b)	1	14	26	10	4	13	1	31
2002	100	1	1	14	26	11	4	12	1	31

Note: See Notes, tables 3.106 and 3.140. For information on States supplying incomplete data for selected years, see Appendix 3.

[a]Because of rounding, percents may not add to total.
[b]Less than 0.5%.

Source: U.S. Department of Justice, Federal Bureau of Investigation, *Crime in the United States, 1973*, p. 120, Table 22; *1974*, p. 178, Table 26; *1975*, p. 178, Table 26; *1976*, p. 159, Table 18; *1977*, p. 159, Table 18; *1978*, p. 174, Table 18; *1979*, p. 176, Table 18; *1980*, p. 179, Table 18; *1981*, p. 150, Table 17; *1982*, p. 155, Table 17; *1983*, p. 158, Table 17; *1984*, p. 151, Table 18; *1985*, p. 153, Table 18; *1986*, p. 153, Table 18; *1987*, p. 152, Table 18; *1988*, p. 156, Table 18; *1989*, p. 160, Table 18; *1990*, p. 162, Table 18; *1991*, p. 201, Table 23; *1992*, p. 205, Table 23; *1993*, p. 205, Table 23; *1994*, p. 205, Table 23; *1995*, p. 196, Table 23; *1996*, p. 202, Table 23; *1997*, p. 210, Table 23; *1998*, p. 197, Table 23; *1999*, p. 199, Table 23; *2000*, p. 204, Table 23; *2001*, p. 218, Table 23; *2002*, p. 217, Table 23 (Washington, DC: USGPO). Table constructed by SOURCEBOOK staff.

Table 3.147
Motor vehicle registrations and thefts

United States, 1980-2002

	Number of motor vehicle registrations	Estimated number of motor vehicle thefts	Ratio of vehicles stolen to registered	Thefts per 100,000 registrations
1980	161,614,294	1,131,700	1:143	700
1981	164,287,643	1,087,800	1:151	662
1982	165,298,024	1,062,400	1:156	643
1983	167,718,000	1,007,933	1:166	601
1984	169,446,281	1,032,165	1:164	609
1985	175,709,000	1,102,862	1:159	628
1986	181,890,000	1,224,137	1:149	673
1987	186,137,000	1,288,674	1:144	692
1988	183,930,000	1,432,916	1:128	779
1989	188,981,016	1,564,800	1:121	828
1990	194,502,000	1,635,907	1:119	841
1991	194,897,000	1,661,738	1:117	853
1992	193,775,000	1,610,834	1:120	831
1993	198,041,338	1,563,060	1:127	789
1994	201,763,492	1,539,287	1:131	763
1995	205,297,050	1,472,441	1:139	717
1996	210,236,393	1,394,238	1:151	663
1997	211,580,033	1,354,189	1:156	640
1998	215,496,003	1,242,781	1:173	577
1999	220,461,056	1,152,075	1:191	523
2000	225,821,241	1,160,002	1:195	514
2001	235,331,382	1,228,391	1:192	522
2002	234,624,135	1,246,096	1:188	531

Note: Data on motor vehicle thefts were obtained from the Federal Bureau of Investigation. Figures for number of thefts include motorcycles; beginning in 1993, figures for number of registrations also include motorcycles. Some data have been revised by the Source and may differ from previous editions of SOURCEBOOK.

Source: U.S. Department of Transportation, Federal Highway Administration, *Highway Statistics 1999*, p. II-3; *2000*, p. II-3; *2001*, p. II-3; *2002*, p. II-3 (Washington, DC: U.S. Department of Transportation); and U.S. Department of Justice, Federal Bureau of Investigation, *Crime in the United States, 1999*, p. 64; *2001*, p. 64; *2002*, p. 66 (Washington, DC: USGPO). Table constructed by SOURCEBOOK staff.

Table 3.148
Financial institution fraud and failure matters handled by the U.S. Department of Justice

United States, 1986-2003

	Cases pending Total	Cases pending Major cases[b]	Convictions[a] Total	Convictions[a] Major cases[b]	Indictments	Dollar amounts (in millions) Recovered	Dollar amounts (in millions) Restitution	Dollar amounts (in millions) Fine	Failed financial institutions under investigation at end of fiscal year
1986	7,286	2,948	1,957	533	X	X	X	X	202
1987	7,622	3,393	2,309	740	X	X	X	X	282
1988	7,385	3,446	2,197	851	X	X	X	X	357
1989	7,819	3,605	2,174	791	X	X	X	X	404
1990	7,613	3,672	2,461	1,043	X	X	X	X	530
1991	8,678	4,336	2,559	986	2,784	$59.4	$490.7	$7.8	670
1992	9,772	5,071	2,751	1,136	3,064	67.1	402.7	14.6	740
1993	10,088	5,405	3,233	1,407	3,446	89.6	1,333.5	10.5	651
1994	9,286	4,926	2,926	1,348	2,867	240.6	865.0	10.4	531
1995	8,641	4,413	2,616	1,298	2,880	185.1	1,139.9	16.8	395
1996	8,574	4,070	2,510	1,255	2,630	67.2	359.1	442.7	247
1997	8,512	3,859	2,551	1,342	2,437	41.2	537.1	25.7	200
1998	8,577	3,709	2,613	1,207	2,691	62.4	491.0	5.5	142
1999	8,799	3,855	2,878	1,488	2,869	114.5	834.3	77.8	129
2000	8,638	4,081	2,783	1,394	2,877	48.5	589.0	8.0	99
2001	8,184	4,383	2,702	1,363	2,738	45.8	754.2	15.2	97
2002	7,305	4,287	2,397	1,328	2,471	28.2	1,983.8	7.6	71
2003	5,869	4,027	2,053	1,286	1,918	15.1	3,128.0	35.6	67

Note: Financial institutions include banks, savings and loans, and credit unions. Prior to 1992, data for cases pending and convictions are reported on a fiscal year basis, data for dollar losses are reported on a calendar year basis, and data for failed financial institutions under investigation are as of February of each year. Beginning in 1992, all data are reported for the Federal fiscal year. Some data have been revised by the Source and may differ from previous editions of SOURCEBOOK.

[a] Includes pre-trial diversions.
[b] A major case is defined as a case involving a failed financial institution, or where the amount of reported loss or exposure is $100,000 or more.

Source: U.S. Department of Justice, Criminal Division, *Attacking Financial Institution Fraud, Annual Report, Fiscal Year 1992* (Washington, DC: U.S. Department of Justice, 1993), pp. 131, 133; and U.S. Department of Justice, Federal Bureau of Investigation, *Financial Institution Fraud and Failure Report, Fiscal Years 2000 & 2001* [Online], pp. 6, 9, 15, 22, 26. Available: http://www.fbi.gov/publications/financial/2000-01fif.pdf [Jan. 9, 2003]; *2003* [Online], pp. 5, 8, 12, 17, 20. Available: http://www.fbi.gov/publications/financial/2003fif/fif03.pdf [Jan. 21, 2004]. Table adapted by SOURCEBOOK staff.

Table 3.149

Violations of the Federal Bank Robbery and Incidental Crimes Statute

By type of violation, United States, 1985-2002

	Robbery	Burglary	Larceny	Extortion
1985	5,427	359	209	106
1986	5,672	397	209	78
1987	6,078	312	187	73
1988	6,549	288	158	67
1989	6,691	273	142	65
1990	7,837	279	119	72
1991	9,388	298	124	57
1992	9,063	361	88	48
1993	8,647	310	78	39
1994	7,029	271	84	33
1995	6,758	234	75	36
1996	8,046	290	47	40
1997	7,876	413	83	42
1998	7,584	313	94	34
1999	6,599	315	74	22
2000	7,127	341	78	30
2001	8,496	304	59	31
2002	7,688	254	62	26

Note: These bank crime statistics were compiled by the Federal Bureau of Investigation. Violations of the Federal Bank Robbery and Incidental Crimes Statute include robbery, burglary (entry of bank and/or theft from bank during non-business hours), and larceny (theft not involving direct confrontation between offender and bank personnel or customers) of commercial banks, mutual savings banks, savings and loan institutions, credit unions, and armored carrier companies. Extortion violations also are investigated under the statute and include extortion and kidnaping of bank officials or their families.

Source: U.S. Department of Justice, Federal Bureau of Investigation, "Bank Crime Statistics, Federally Insured Financial Institutions, January 1, 1985-December 31, 1985," p. 13; "January 1, 1986-December 31, 1986," p. 13; "January 1, 1987-December 31, 1987," p. 13; "January 1, 1988-December 31, 1988," p. 13; "January 1, 1989-December 31, 1989," p. 13; "January 1, 1990-December 31, 1990," p. 13; "January 1, 1991-December 31, 1991," p. 12; "January 1, 1992-December 31, 1992," p. 11; "January 1, 1993-December 31, 1993," p. 10; "January 1, 1994-December 31, 1994," p. 10; "January 1, 1995-December 31, 1995," p. 11; "January 1, 1996-December 31, 1996," p. 11; "January 1, 1997-December 31, 1997," p. 12 ; "January 1, 1998-December 31, 1998," p. 11; "January 1, 1999-December 31, 1999," p. 11 ; "January 1, 2000-December 31, 2000," p. 10; "January 1, 2001-December 31, 2001," p. 10; "January 1, 2002-December 31, 2002," p. 9. Washington, DC: U.S. Department of Justice. (Mimeographed.) Table adapted by SOURCEBOOK staff.

Table 3.150
Violations of the Federal Bank Robbery and Incidental Crimes Statute

By type of violation and jurisdiction, 1999-2002

Jurisdiction	1999 Robbery	1999 Burglary	1999 Larceny	1999 Extortion	2000 Robbery	2000 Burglary	2000 Larceny	2000 Extortion	2001 Robbery	2001 Burglary	2001 Larceny	2001 Extortion	2002 Robbery	2002 Burglary	2002 Larceny	2002 Extortion
Total	6,599	315	74	22	7,127	341	78	30	8,496	304	59	31	7,688	254	62	26
Alabama	69	6	2	0	77	2	0	0	91	1	3	0	99	2	1	0
Alaska	23	0	2	0	3	2	1	1	6	1	0	0	8	3	0	0
Arizona	246	0	0	0	184	6	0	0	211	2	0	2	173	1	0	1
Arkansas	18	6	0	0	18	9	2	0	32	3	0	0	33	4	4	0
California	1,249	18	12	0	1,279	13	7	4	1,480	32	3	0	1,380	28	4	1
Colorado	85	3	13	1	149	7	7	0	121	6	1	0	134	11	3	1
Connecticut	26	5	0	0	16	0	0	0	69	2	1	0	73	3	1	0
Delaware	26	1	0	0	24	1	0	0	33	0	0	0	23	0	0	0
District of Columbia	21	0	0	0	12	0	0	0	22	0	0	0	28	0	0	0
Florida	467	21	1	2	510	28	1	5	561	7	4	0	523	5	1	0
Georgia	145	7	0	3	174	13	1	0	195	4	0	0	237	6	0	0
Guam	0	0	0	0	0	0	0	0	0	0	0	0	0	0	0	0
Hawaii	50	0	0	0	37	3	0	0	38	0	0	0	37	1	1	2
Idaho	14	0	0	1	12	2	0	0	14	0	0	0	20	0	0	0
Illinois	153	7	1	2	180	24	4	1	219	20	3	3	249	11	0	4
Indiana	94	2	2	1	137	10	2	0	182	4	0	2	137	5	0	0
Iowa	46	2	0	0	50	0	1	0	59	4	0	1	44	2	1	0
Kansas	56	1	0	1	48	2	0	0	71	9	1	0	43	9	5	0
Kentucky	63	0	0	0	65	5	0	0	80	0	0	1	74	2	0	0
Louisiana	60	1	0	0	86	2	0	1	113	7	2	0	80	9	2	1
Maine	4	0	0	0	3	0	0	0	6	0	0	0	12	0	1	0
Maryland	196	2	3	1	167	5	0	0	291	2	0	0	297	0	0	0
Massachusetts	150	0	0	0	153	5	0	0	270	12	1	1	232	7	0	0
Michigan	292	18	2	0	324	12	11	1	317	17	2	3	243	9	2	1
Minnesota	65	8	3	0	88	7	3	0	99	3	0	0	67	1	0	0
Mississippi	47	8	0	0	63	6	1	0	67	2	2	1	58	8	0	0
Missouri	82	6	2	0	93	1	2	0	123	2	5	3	137	11	5	0
Montana	7	1	0	0	4	0	0	0	3	0	0	0	5	1	1	0
Nebraska	37	8	0	0	44	3	0	0	64	1	0	0	32	4	0	0
Nevada	130	16	0	0	178	11	0	0	204	0	0	0	170	2	2	0
New Hampshire	21	1	0	0	15	0	0	0	11	0	0	0	17	1	0	1
New Jersey	95	8	1	0	136	2	3	0	104	3	0	1	108	0	1	0
New Mexico	51	2	0	0	45	0	0	0	129	1	2	0	87	0	3	0
New York	321	41	2	0	300	65	0	0	427	30	3	0	395	13	0	0
North Carolina	221	24	3	1	288	14	15	1	380	22	3	0	248	11	3	1
North Dakota	0	1	0	0	1	0	0	0	6	0	0	0	0	1	0	0
Ohio	395	21	1	0	400	4	4	1	490	5	1	4	333	7	4	1
Oklahoma	20	8	0	0	23	4	1	1	40	11	0	2	41	9	2	0
Oregon	204	2	3	0	150	0	1	1	153	10	1	0	128	5	1	1
Pennsylvania	288	7	3	3	334	22	2	6	329	6	5	1	344	4	5	2
Puerto Rico	9	0	0	0	11	0	0	0	11	0	0	0	27	0	1	0
Rhode Island	15	0	0	0	13	0	0	0	23	0	0	0	37	0	0	0
South Carolina	93	8	2	1	121	8	0	0	142	9	0	0	101	6	0	1
South Dakota	2	1	1	0	3	1	0	0	7	0	0	0	8	0	0	0
Tennessee	118	6	5	0	135	7	3	0	152	15	3	0	135	19	2	6
Texas	223	13	6	2	331	11	5	2	377	20	6	2	393	10	3	2
Utah	31	6	0	3	46	5	0	3	81	4	0	0	74	3	1	0
Vermont	2	1	0	0	13	1	0	0	8	0	0	0	3	0	0	0
Virgin Islands	0	0	0	0	0	0	0	0	0	0	0	0	1	0	0	0
Virginia	182	5	2	1	148	2	0	2	183	3	0	0	188	1	0	0
Washington	320	6	2	0	314	5	0	0	287	7	4	1	285	9	0	0
West Virginia	6	0	0	0	6	0	1	0	11	1	3	0	10	1	0	0
Wisconsin	61	7	0	0	115	9	0	0	100	16	0	3	71	9	2	0
Wyoming	0	0	0	0	1	2	0	0	4	0	0	0	6	0	0	0

Note: See Note, table 3.149.

Source: U.S. Department of Justice, Federal Bureau of Investigation, "Bank Crime Statistics, Federally Insured Financial Institutions, January 1, 1999-December 31, 1999," pp. 11-13; "January 1, 2000-December 31, 2000," pp. 10-12; "January 1, 2001-December 31, 2001," pp. 10-12; "January 1, 2002-December 31, 2002," pp. 9-11. Washington, DC: U.S. Department of Justice. (Mimeographed.) Table adapted by SOURCEBOOK staff.

Table 3.151

Injuries, deaths, and hostages taken during violations of the Federal Bank Robbery and Incidental Crimes Statute

By type of victim, United States, 1999-2002

Type of victim	1999 Injuries	1999 Deaths	1999 Hostages taken	2000 Injuries	2000 Deaths	2000 Hostages taken	2001 Injuries	2001 Deaths	2001 Hostages taken	2002 Injuries	2002 Deaths	2002 Hostages taken
Total	149	27	100	166	23	108	160	14	51	164	28	136
Customer	23	0	16	35	1	38	31	1	2	18	1	26
Employee	78	2	67	81	1	46	92	2	34	88	6	101
Employee family	0	1	5	0	0	4	2	0	2	0	0	1
Perpetrator	15	22	X	23	19	X	19	9	X	28	18	X
Law officer	11	0	0	13	0	0	6	1	0	15	0	0
Guard	9	2	1	7	1	3	6	1	4	11	2	3
Other	13	0	11	7	1	17	4	0	9	4	1	5

Note: See Note, table 3.149.

Source: U.S. Department of Justice, Federal Bureau of Investigation, "Bank Crime Statistics, Federally Insured Financial Institutions, January 1, 1999-December 31, 1999," pp. 5, 6; "January 1, 2000-December 31, 2000," p. 5; "January 1, 2001-December 31, 2001," p. 5; "January 1, 2002-December 31, 2002," p. 5. Washington, DC: U.S. Department of Justice. (Mimeographed.) Table adapted by SOURCEBOOK staff.

Table 3.152

Assaults on Federal officers

By department and agency, 1991-2002

Department and agency	1991	1992	1993	1994	1995	1996	1997	1998	1999	2000	2001[a]	2002
Total	683	661	770	1,028	744	556	628	653	627	528	590	374
U.S. Department of Homeland Security[b]												
Bureau of Immigration and Customs Enforcement	296	228[c]	210	260	180	194	233	200	214	242	286	54[d]
U.S. Customs Service	66	7	67	128	138	77	61	141	76	55	52	45
U.S. Secret Service	29	37	35	66	46	24	31	26	23	12	17	14
U.S. Department of the Interior												
Bureau of Indian Affairs	0	110	104	133	0	36	41	38	37	2	0	63
National Park Service	96	57	95	207	105	0	74	91	66	99	104	97
U.S. Department of Justice												
Bureau of Alcohol, Tobacco, Firearms and Explosives[e]	31	36	69	42	112	66	50	38	13	7	2	3
Drug Enforcement Administration	47	66	94	87	65	64	44	33	73	55	28	28
Federal Bureau of Investigation	31	50	28	31	40	53	37	22	59	25	33	48
U.S. Marshals Service	30	32	26	17	14	9	24	45	38	7	31	1
U.S. Department of the Treasury												
Internal Revenue Service	1	9	10	17	10	4	7	0	0	0	3	0
Treasury Inspector General for Tax Administration	NA	NA	NA	NA	NA	NA	NA	NA	9	2	9	3
U.S. Capitol Police	17	5	7	9	7	4	2	7	6	7	6	10
U.S. Postal Inspection Service	39	24	25	31	27	25	24	12	13	15	19	8

Note: These data include law enforcement officers killed or assaulted in the line of duty who were employed by the U.S. Departments of the Interior, Justice, Treasury, and the newly established U.S. Department of Homeland Security; the U.S. Capitol Police; and the U.S. Postal Inspection Service. Within these 6 Federal departments are 13 agencies, bureaus, or services, that employ the majority of the personnel responsible for protecting government officials, and enforcing and investigating violations of Federal laws. The Federal Bureau of Investigation's Uniform Crime Reporting Program annually contacts these departments and requests information on officers who were killed or assaulted in the line of duty. All assaults and threats of assault are included in the analysis even if no injury to an officer resulted, as are assaults that resulted in the death of an officer (Source, *2002*, p. 87).

Some data have been revised by the Source and may differ from previous editions of SOURCEBOOK.

[a]Deaths of two Federal officers resulting from the events of Sept. 11, 2001 are not included.
[b]The U.S. Department of Homeland Security (DHS) was established as a result of the Homeland Security Act of 2002. The U.S. Bureau of Immigration and Customs Enforcement, formerly the Immigration and Naturalization Service, was moved from the U.S. Department of Justice (DOJ) to DHS. The U.S. Customs Service and the U.S. Secret Service were moved from the U.S. Department of the Treasury to the DHS.
[c]Data reported by the Immigration and Naturalization Service include the Border Patrol Division only.
[d]Data for 2002 are based only on victim officers who discharged their service weapons.
[e]In accordance with the Homeland Security Act, the Bureau of Alcohol, Tobacco, Firearms and Explosives, formerly the Bureau of Alcohol, Tobacco and Firearms, was moved from the U.S. Department of the Treasury to the DOJ.

Source: U.S. Department of Justice, Federal Bureau of Investigation, *Law Enforcement Officers Killed and Assaulted, 1992*, p. 73; *1994*, p. 79; *1996*, p. 79; *1999*, p. 89; *2001*, p. 100; *2002*, p. 91; FBI Uniform Crime Reports (Washington, DC: U.S. Department of Justice). Table adapted by SOURCEBOOK staff.

Table 3.153

Assaults on Federal officers

By extent of injury and type of weapon used, 1977-2002

	Total victims	Firearm	Personal weapon	Knife	Blunt object	Threat	Vehicle	Bomb	Other
Total, 1977-2002	17,367	2,137	5,593	380	770	5,672	1,165	84	1,566
Killed, total	72	56	2	3	2	X	1	7	1
1977	0	0	0	0	0	X	0	0	0
1978	1	0	1	0	0	X	0	0	0
1979	5	5	0	0	0	X	0	0	0
1980	2	2	0	0	0	X	0	0	0
1981	1	1	0	0	0	X	0	0	0
1982	2	2	0	0	0	X	0	0	0
1983	7	4	0	2	1	X	0	0	0
1984	2	1	0	1	0	X	0	0	0
1985	1	0	0	0	1	X	0	0	0
1986	6	6	0	0	0	X	0	0	0
1987	1	1	0	0	0	X	0	0	0
1988[a]	4	3	0	0	0	X	0	0	1
1989	2	2	0	0	0	X	0	0	0
1990	4	3	0	0	0	X	1	0	0
1991[b]	1	1	0	0	0	X	0	0	0
1992[c]	4	4	0	0	0	X	0	0	0
1993	4	4	0	0	0	X	0	0	0
1994	4	4	0	0	0	X	0	0	0
1995[b]	8	1	0	0	0	X	0	7	0
1996	3	2	1	0	0	X	0	0	0
1997	2	2	0	0	0	X	0	0	0
1998	6	6	0	0	0	X	0	0	0
1999	1	1	0	0	0	X	0	0	0
2000	0	0	0	0	0	X	0	0	0
2001[d]	0	0	0	0	0	X	0	0	0
2002	1	1	0	0	0	X	0	0	0
Injured, total	3,557	278	2,272	104	230	6	310	26	331
1977	140	13	88	8	22	0	8	1	0
1978	121	8	91	5	13	0	4	0	0
1979	126	15	91	3	14	0	1	0	2
1980	118	6	85	11	7	0	8	0	1
1981	133	17	80	7	19	0	8	0	2
1982	123	13	73	8	4	0	7	1	17
1983	78	8	43	7	4	0	4	0	12
1984	60	7	41	3	0	0	3	0	6
1985	62	6	46	1	1	0	5	0	3
1986	58	8	35	6	2	0	3	0	4
1987	36	11	17	1	0	0	7	0	0
1988[a]	55	6	40	2	2	0	3	0	2
1989	130	7	88	5	17	0	11	0	2
1990	151	9	90	5	23	0	19	0	5
1991[b]	189	7	137	2	19	0	14	0	10
1992[c]	176	9	118	4	14	0	26	0	5
1993	215	20	150	0	6	2	14	7	16
1994	314	23	185	7	7	4	30	0	58
1995[b]	271	9	129	0	5	0	29	11	88
1996	116	22	69	2	2	0	14	0	7
1997	157	9	89	6	5	0	16	6	26
1998	175	3	129	0	4	0	26	0	13
1999	171	32	108	3	4	0	13	0	11
2000	124	5	80	1	4	0	12	0	22
2001	126	4	67	2	22	0	17	0	14
2002	132	1	103	5	10	0	8	0	5

See notes at end of table.

Table 3.153

Assaults on Federal officers

By extent of injury and type of weapon used, 1977-2002--Continued

	Total victims	Firearm	Personal weapon	Knife	Blunt object	Threat	Vehicle	Bomb	Other
No injury, total	13,738	1,803	3,319	273	538	5,666	854	51	1,234
1977	740	109	216	21	15	346	32	1	0
1978	649	83	157	14	26	336	28	4	1
1979	491	48	139	3	15	271	13	0	2
1980	604	64	154	8	18	326	23	1	10
1981	594	107	117	11	18	312	16	0	13
1982	587	69	104	16	11	324	26	0	37
1983	495	50	81	12	14	312	9	0	17
1984	610	61	112	11	1	387	17	0	21
1985	745	60	110	4	13	518	14	2	24
1986	565	41	116	14	2	357	10	2	23
1987	534	40	151	18	24	247	36	4	14
1988[a]	643	50	108	6	12	431	25	1	10
1989	429	91	154	13	42	73	31	0	25
1990	509	58	173	11	135	80	48	2	2
1991[b]	393	77	97	17	59	101	35	1	6
1992[c]	481	89	144	10	51	143	37	0	7
1993	551	84	188	7	11	168	30	1	62
1994	711	94	196	22	29	166	58	2	144
1995[b]	465	86	80	4	3	177	48	0	67
1996	437	89	92	9	1	159	29	2	56
1997	469	104	104	4	3	69	51	22	112
1998	472	57	124	9	9	88	66	1	118
1999	455	67	126	10	5	91	42	0	114
2000	404	51	91	6	2	52	38	5	159
2001	464	42	115	2	6	67	53	0	179
2002	241	32	70	11	13	65	39	0	11

Note: See Note, table 3.152. Beginning in 1984, data include assaults on officers of the U.S. Capitol Police. Data for this agency are not available for years prior to 1984. Beginning in 1991, assault statistics from the Bureau of Prisons, Executive Office for United States Attorneys, and the judicial branch were no longer collected. Therefore, data from 1991 and beyond are not directly comparable with preceding years. Some data have been revised by the Source and may differ from previous editions of SOURCEBOOK.

[a] Does not include 1988 data from the Bureau of Prisons where 23 officers were assaulted with weapons and 123 without weapons.

[b] No reports concerning assaults on Bureau of Indian Affairs officers were received for 1991 and 1995. The data for 1991 do not include 96 National Park Service victim officers and 4 Immigration and Naturalization Service victim officers for whom type of weapon was not reported.

[c] Data reported by the Immigration and Naturalization Service include the Border Patrol Division only.

[d] Deaths of two Federal officers resulting from the events of Sept. 11, 2001 are not included.

Source: U.S. Department of Justice, Federal Bureau of Investigation, *Assaults on Federal Officers, 1981*, FBI Uniform Crime Reports (Washington, DC: USGPO, 1982), p. 5, Table 3; and U.S. Department of Justice, Federal Bureau of Investigation, *Law Enforcement Officers Killed and Assaulted, 1985*, p. 54; *1990*, p. 53; *1993*, p. 79; *1999*, p. 91; *2002*, p. 93; FBI Uniform Crime Reports (Washington, DC: U.S. Department of Justice). Table adapted by SOURCEBOOK staff.

Table 3.154
Law enforcement officers killed

United States, 1972-2002

	Officers killed in the line of duty	
	Feloniously	Accidentally
Total	2,553	1,896
1972	117	NA
1973	134	42
1974	132	47
1975	129	56
1976	111	29
1977	93	32
1978	93	52
1979	106	58
1980	104	61
1981	91	66
1982	92	72
1983	80	72
1984	72	75
1985	78	70
1986	66	67
1987	74	74
1988	78	77
1989	66	79
1990	66	67
1991	71	53
1992	64	66
1993	70	59
1994	80	62
1995	74	59
1996	61	52
1997	71	63
1998	61	82
1999	42	65
2000	51	84
2001	70[a]	78
2002	56	77

Note: These data are from the Federal Bureau of Investigation's (FBI) Uniform Crime Reporting (UCR) Program. Federal, State, and local law enforcement agencies participating in the UCR Program submit data on any sworn officer killed feloniously or accidentally in the line of duty within their jurisdictions. FBI field divisions and legal attaché offices also report such incidents occurring in the United States and its territories, as well as those in which a United States law enforcement officer dies while assigned to duties in another country (Source, *2002*, p. 5). Some data have been revised by the Source and may differ from previous editions of SOURCEBOOK.

[a]Does not include the deaths of 72 law enforcement officers resulting from the events of Sept. 11, 2001.

Source: U.S. Department of Justice, Federal Bureau of Investigation, *Law Enforcement Officers Killed, 1981*, FBI Uniform Crime Reports (Washington, DC: USGPO, 1982), p. 12; *Law Enforcement Officers Killed and Assaulted, 1982*, pp. 10, 40; *1992*, pp. 23, 57; *2002*, pp. 9, 59; FBI Uniform Crime Reports (Washington, DC: U.S. Department of Justice). Table constructed by SOURCEBOOK staff.

Table 3.155

Law enforcement officers feloniously killed

By circumstances at scene of incident, United States, 1979-2002

Circumstances at scene of incident	1979	1980	1981	1982	1983	1984	1985	1986	1987	1988	1989	1990	1991	1992	1993	1994	1995	1996	1997	1998	1999	2000	2001	2002
Total	106	104	91	92	80	72	78	66	74	78	66	66	71	64	70	80	74	61	71	61	42	51	70[a]	56
Disturbance calls	17	12	19	18	15	8	13	7	23	7	13	10	17	11	10	8	8	4	14	16	7	8	14	9
Bar fights, persons with firearms, etc.	13	6	14	11	10	7	6	5	10	4	5	5	8	2	5	4	2	1	3	7	6	4	5	4
Family quarrels	4	6	5	7	5	1	7	2	13	3	8	5	9	9	5	4	6	3	11	9	1	4	9	5
Arrest situations	47	49	38	36	31	33	29	26	27	33	24	30	14	27	28	34	21	26	22	16	12	12	24	10
Burglaries in progress/pursuing burglary suspects	7	8	6	3	4	2	4	1	6	3	0	1	3	5	1	4	4	3	5	0	0	3	3	0
Robberies in progress/pursuing robbery suspects	19	22	17	14	11	9	12	9	4	7	8	13	4	11	9	18	7	12	11	3	4	1	4	4
Drug-related matters	6	9	2	5	6	4	6	7	4	12	7	5	3	3	3	4	4	3	1	7	2	3	8	3
Attempting other arrests	15	10	13	14	10	18	7	9	13	11	9	11	4	8	15	8	6	8	5	6	6	5	9	3
Civil disorders (mass disobedience, riot, etc.)	0	0	0	1	0	0	0	0	0	0	0	0	0	0	0	0	0	0	0	0	0	0	0	0
Handling, transporting, custody of prisoners	3	1	1	3	3	3	4	5	6	2	6	2	6	2	1	1	4	0	4	4	2	2	2	0
Investigating suspicious persons/circumstances	9	16	10	11	10	12	9	11	5	23	10	9	10	7	15	15	17	13	10	6	7	6	8	8
Ambush situations	11	7	9	9	9	8	7	4	4	6	4	8	11	7	5	8	14	6	12	10	6	10	10	15
Entrapment/premeditation	8	2	5	7	6	4	5	2	3	2	2	2	5	5	3	1	6	2	5	4	4	2	3	4
Unprovoked attack	3	5	4	2	3	4	2	2	1	4	2	6	6	2	2	7	8	4	7	6	2	8	7	11
Mentally deranged assailants	4	2	2	2	1	0	0	3	1	1	2	1	0	0	1	4	1	1	1	0	0	0	3	4
Traffic pursuits/stops	15	17	12	12	11	8	16	10	8	6	7	6	13	10	10	10	9	11	8	9	8	13	9	10

Note: See Note, table 3.154. These data include Federal, State, and local law enforcement officers feloniously killed in the line of duty. Some data have been revised by the Source and may differ from previous editions of SOURCEBOOK.

Source: U.S. Department of Justice, Federal Bureau of Investigation, *Law Enforcement Officers Killed and Assaulted, 1987*, p. 17; *1997*, p. 29; *2002*, p. 22; FBI Uniform Crime Reports (Washington, DC: U.S. Department of Justice). Table adapted by SOURCEBOOK staff.

[a]Does not include the deaths of 72 law enforcement officers resulting from the events of Sept. 11, 2001.

Table 3.156

Law enforcement officers feloniously killed

By circumstances at scene of incident and type of assignment, United States, 1993-2002 (aggregate)

Circumstances at scene of incident	Total	2-officer vehicle	1-officer vehicle Alone	1-officer vehicle Assisted	Foot patrol Alone	Foot patrol Assisted	Other[a] Alone	Other[a] Assisted	Off-duty
Total	636[b]	84	189	131	8	7	37	96	84
Disturbance calls	98	17	28	34	1	0	3	6	9
Bar fights, persons with firearms, etc.	41	7	7	19	0	0	1	2	5
Family quarrels	57	10	21	15	1	0	2	4	4
Arrest situations	205	24	33	42	1	6	6	55	38
Burglaries in progress/pursuing burglary suspects	23	3	9	5	0	0	1	2	3
Robberies in progress/pursuing robbery suspects	73	9	11	16	0	2	1	5	29
Drug-related matters	38	4	2	1	0	2	4	24	1
Attempting other arrests	71	8	11	20	1	2	0	24	5
Civil disorders (mass disobedience, riot, etc.)	0	X	X	X	X	X	X	X	X
Handling, transporting, custody of prisoners	20	2	9	1	0	0	4	4	0
Investigating suspicious persons/circumstances	105	16	41	12	3	1	4	12	16
Ambush situations	96	11	22	12	3	0	17	11	20
Entrapment/premeditation	34	3	10	4	1	0	4	2	10
Unprovoked attack	62	8	12	8	2	0	13	9	10
Mentally deranged assailants	15	0	2	8	0	0	0	5	0
Traffic pursuits/stops	97	14	54	22	0	0	3	3	1

Note: See Notes, tables 3.154 and 3.155.

[a]Includes detectives, undercover officers, and officers on special assignments and other types of assignments not listed.
[b]Does not include the deaths of 72 law enforcement officers resulting from the events of Sept. 11, 2001.

Source: U.S. Department of Justice, Federal Bureau of Investigation, *Law Enforcement Officers Killed and Assaulted, 2002*, FBI Uniform Crime Reports (Washington, DC: U.S. Department of Justice, 2003), p. 28.

Table 3.157

Law enforcement officers feloniously killed

By circumstances at scene of incident and type of assignment, United States, 2002

Circumstances at scene of incident	Total	2-officer vehicle	1-officer vehicle Alone	1-officer vehicle Assisted	Foot patrol Alone	Foot patrol Assisted	Other[a] Alone	Other[a] Assisted	Off-duty
Total	56	6	17	15	1	0	2	10	5
Disturbance calls	9	2	1	5	0	X	0	1	0
Bar fights, persons with firearms, etc.	4	0	1	3	0	X	0	0	0
Family quarrels	5	2	0	2	0	X	0	1	0
Arrest situations	10	1	1	1	0	X	0	5	2
Burglaries in progress/pursuing burglary suspects	0	X	X	X	X	X	X	X	X
Robberies in progress/pursuing robbery suspects	4	1	0	1	0	X	0	0	2
Drug-related matters	3	0	0	0	0	X	0	3	0
Attempting other arrests	3	0	1	0	0	X	0	2	0
Civil disorders (mass disobedience, riot, etc.)	0	X	X	X	X	X	X	X	X
Handling, transporting, custody of prisoners	0	X	X	X	X	X	X	X	X
Investigating suspicious persons/circumstances	8	0	4	2	0	X	0	2	0
Ambush situations	15	2	3	3	1	X	2	1	3
Entrapment/premeditation	4	0	0	0	0	X	1	1	2
Unprovoked attack	11	2	3	3	1	X	1	0	1
Mentally deranged assailants	4	0	1	3	0	X	0	0	0
Traffic pursuits/stops	10	1	7	1	0	X	0	1	0

Note: See Notes, tables 3.154 and 3.155.

[a]Includes detectives, undercover officers, and officers on special assignments and other types of assignments not listed.

Source: U.S. Department of Justice, Federal Bureau of Investigation, *Law Enforcement Officers Killed and Assaulted, 2002*, FBI Uniform Crime Reports (Washington, DC: U.S. Department of Justice, 2003), p. 26.

Table 3.158

Percent distribution of law enforcement officers feloniously killed

By selected characteristics of officers, United States, 1984-2002[a]

Characteristics of officers killed	1984 (N=72)	1985 (N=78)	1986 (N=66)	1987 (N=73)	1988 (N=78)	1989 (N=66)	1990 (N=65)	1991 (N=71)	1992 (N=62)	1993 (N=70)	1994 (N=76)	1995 (N=74)	1996 (N=55)	1997 (N=65)	1998 (N=61)	1999 (N=42)	2000 (N=51)	2001 (N=70)[b]	2002 (N=56)
Sex																			
Male	94%	96%	98%	100%	97%	97%	98%	96%	100%	94%	96%	99%	96%	100%	90%	93%	98%	96%	86%
Female	6	4	2	0	3	3	2	4	0	6	4	1	4	0	10	7	2	4	14
Race																			
White	85	88	89	90	91	89	80	87	82	86	84	84	80	80	87	88	76	87	91
Black	14	10	11	10	9	11	18	13	16	14	14	12	15	17	11	7	22	11	7
Other[c]	1	1	0	0	0	0	2	0	2	0	1	4	5	3	2	5	0	1	2
Age																			
Under age 25	6	5	8	11	15	4	5	7	6	6	8	8	4	2	11	2	10	9	2
25 to 30 years	28	26	30	26	15	20	14	27	21	37	26	26	35	26	30	24	22	24	20
31 to 40 years	40	35	29	32	40	38	42	37	39	33	38	24	40	35	28	55	35	40	50
Over 40 years	26	35	33	32	30	38	40	30	34	21	28	42	22	37	31	19	33	27	29
Length of service																			
Less than 1 year of service	4	6	3	8	4	3	3	6	6	3	11	12	4	6	3	2	6	1	0
1 to 4 years of service	30	20	33	22	31	23	26	38	22	34	20	20	38	17	33	26	33	26	21
5 to 10 years of service	40	24	30	29	22	29	26	24	24	24	34	27	33	48	26	38	22	30	36
Over 10 years of service	24	49	32	41	40	44	45	31	44	34	36	41	24	28	36	33	39	43	41
In uniform	75	73	67	79	68	67	63	73	64	81	63	66	78	75	79	74	80	69	84
Wearing protective body armor	24	19	24	25	26	32	25	34	27	56	47	46	56	42	57	64	61	59	66

Note: See Notes, tables 3.154 and 3.155. The Ns presented and the distribution of characteristics are based on the known number of victim officers at the time the initial FBI report is published. The Ns presented above may therefore differ from other tables that include totals subsequently revised by the Source.

[a]Percents may not add to 100 because of rounding. Also, for some years, age, race, or length of service was not reported for a small number of cases. Percents are computed on total number of cases and therefore may not total 100.

[b]Does not include the deaths of 72 law enforcement officers resulting from the events of Sept. 11, 2001.

[c]Includes Asian, Pacific Islander, American Indian, and Alaskan Native.

Source: U.S. Department of Justice, Federal Bureau of Investigation, *Law Enforcement Officers Killed and Assaulted, 1984*, p. 20; *1985*, p. 21; *1986*, p. 22; *1987*, p. 20; *1988*, p. 20; *1989*, p. 21; *1990*, p. 20; *1991*, p. 31; *1992*, p. 35; *1993*, p. 35; *1994*, p. 37; *1995*, p. 35; *1996*, p. 35; *1997*, p. 35; *1998*, p. 39; *1999*, p. 37; *2000*, p. 37; *2001*, p. 41; *2002*, p. 14; p. 15, Table 7; and p. 16, Table 9; FBI Uniform Crime Reports (Washington, DC: U.S. Department of Justice). Table constructed by SOURCEBOOK staff.

Table 3.159
Law enforcement officers feloniously killed in Sept. 11, 2001 terrorist attacks

By selected characteristics of officers

Officer characteristics	Number
Total	72
Sex	
Male	70
Female	2
Race	
White	59
Black	12
Not reported	1
Age	
Under age 25	0
25 to 30 years	8
31 to 40 years	31
Over 40 years	33
Length of service	
Less than 1 year of service	0
1 to 4 years of service	7
5 to 10 years of service	20
Over 10 years of service	43
Not reported	2

Note: These data include 71 law enforcement officers killed at the World Trade Center in New York and 1 officer that died in the plane crash in Somerset County, Pennsylvania.

Source: U.S. Department of Justice, Federal Bureau of Investigation, *Law Enforcement Officers Killed and Assaulted, 2001*, FBI Uniform Crime Reports (Washington, DC: U.S. Department of Justice, 2002), p. 65.

Table 3.160
Persons identified in the felonious killing of law enforcement officers

By demographic characteristics and prior record, United States, 1993-2002 (aggregate) and 2002[a]

Characteristics of persons identified	1993 to 2002 Number	1993 to 2002 Percent	2002 Number	2002 Percent
Total	785	100%	61	100%
Sex				
Male	750	96	59	97
Female	22	3	2	3
Not reported	13	2	0	X
Race				
White	417	53	37	61
Black	307	39	24	39
Other[b]	29	4	0	X
Not reported	32	4	0	X
Age				
Under age 18	83	11	2	3
18 to 24 years	290	37	24	39
25 to 30 years	150	19	10	16
31 to 40 years	117	15	12	20
Over 40 years	109	14	13	21
Not reported	36	5	0	X
Prior record[c]				
Prior criminal arrest	528	67	48	79
Convicted on prior criminal charges	373	48	36	59
Prior arrest for crime of violence	245	31	18	30
On parole or probation at time of killing	158	20	15	25
Prior arrest on murder charge	22	3	2	3
Prior arrest on drug law violation	252	32	28	46
Prior arrest for assaulting an officer or resisting arrest	146	19	10	16
Prior arrest for weapons violation	240	31	19	31

Note: See Notes, tables 3.154 and 3.155.

[a] Percents may not add to 100 because of rounding.
[b] Includes Asian, Pacific Islander, American Indian, and Alaskan Native.
[c] Offenders may fall into multiple categories for prior record therefore detail will not add to total.

Source: U.S. Department of Justice, Federal Bureau of Investigation, *Law Enforcement Officers Killed and Assaulted, 2002*, FBI Uniform Crime Reports (Washington, DC: U.S. Department of Justice, 2003), p. 41, Table 38; p. 42, Table 39; and p. 43. Table constructed by SOURCEBOOK staff.

Table 3.161
Persons identified in the felonious killing of law enforcement officers

By type of disposition, United States, 1991-2000 (aggregate)[a]

Type of disposition	Number	Percent
Persons identified	844	100%
Fugitives	9	1
Justifiably killed	101	12
Murdered while at large	1	(b)
Committed suicide	62	7
Died under other circumstances	6	1
Arrested and charged	665	79
Persons arrested and charged	665	100%
Guilty of murder	464	70
Guilty of a lesser offense related to murder	58	9
Guilty of crime other than murder	35	5
Acquitted or otherwise dismissed	45	7
Committed to psychiatric institution	14	2
Case pending or disposition unknown	37	6
Died in custody prior to sentencing	8	1
Other	4	1

Note: See Notes, tables 3.154 and 3.155.

[a] Percents may not add to 100 because of rounding.
[b] Less than 0.5%.

Source: U.S. Department of Justice, Federal Bureau of Investigation, *Law Enforcement Officers Killed and Assaulted, 2002*, FBI Uniform Crime Reports (Washington, DC: U.S. Department of Justice, 2003), p. 44. Table adapted by SOURCEBOOK staff.

Table 3.162
Law enforcement officers accidentally killed

By circumstances at scene of incident, United States, 1980-2002

					Circumstances at scene of incident					
					Struck by vehicles		Accidental shootings			
	Total	Automobile accidents	Motorcycle accidents	Aircraft accidents	Traffic stops, road blocks, etc.	Directing traffic, assisting motorists, etc.	Crossfires, mistaken identities, firearm mishaps	Training sessions	Self-inflicted, cleaning mishaps	Other (falls, drownings, etc.)
Total	1,580	776	119	168	134	176	66	19	12	110
1980	61	35	2	6	6	6	4	0	1	1
1981	66	21	3	11	12	11	3	0	3	2
1982	72	22	6	11	12	11	3	1	1	5
1983	72	28	8	10	10	8	1	3	1	3
1984	75	34	6	11	6	6	5	1	1	5
1985	70	32	3	8	9	10	3	1	1	3
1986	67	24	5	12	2	10	8	2	0	4
1987	74	36	5	5	7	11	4	1	0	5
1988	77	35	6	7	7	9	6	0	1	6
1989	79	43	5	10	8	4	4	0	0	5
1990	67	27	10	7	6	9	4	1	0	3
1991	53	24	6	7	5	3	1	0	0	7
1992	66	34	5	5	6	5	3	0	0	8
1993	59	38	1	9	1	3	2	3	0	2
1994	62	32	8	10	3	4	1	1	0	3
1995	59	33	3	8	1	9	2	0	0	3
1996	52	33	4	1	4	3	1	1	0	5
1997	63	33	4	4	4	11	1	0	0	6
1998	82	49	3	4	4	10	3	0	0	9
1999	65	41	6	4	3	6	2	1	0	2
2000	84	42	6	7	7	7	1	1	1	12
2001	78	38	7	5	7	12	2	2	1	4
2002	77	42	7	6	4	8	2	0	1	7

Note: See Note, table 3.154. These data include Federal, State, and local law enforcement officers who lost their lives due to accidents occurring while performing official duties. Some data have been revised by the Source and may differ from previous editions of SOURCEBOOK.

Source: U.S. Department of Justice, Federal Bureau of Investigation, *Law Enforcement Officers Killed and Assaulted, 1989*, p. 47; *1999*, p. 63; *2002*, p. 65; FBI Uniform Crime Reports (Washington, DC: U.S. Department of Justice). Table adapted by SOURCEBOOK staff.

Table 3.163
Law enforcement officers assaulted

By circumstances at scene of incident and type of weapon, United States, 2002[a]

Circumstances at scene of incident	Total	Firearm	Knife or cutting instrument	Other dangerous weapon	Personal weapon
Total	58,066	1,889	1,056	8,326	46,795
Percent of total	100%	3.3	1.8	14.3	80.6
Disturbance calls (family quarrels, bar fights, persons with firearms, etc.)	18,063	554	486	1,766	15,257
Percent	100%	3.1	2.7	9.8	84.5
Burglaries in progress/ pursuing burglary suspects	820	33	14	193	580
Percent	100%	4.0	1.7	23.5	70.7
Robberies in progress/ pursuing robbery suspects	505	111	11	100	283
Percent	100%	22.0	2.2	19.8	56.0
Attempting other arrests	9,464	207	117	1,109	8,031
Percent	100%	2.2	1.2	11.7	84.9
Civil disorders (mass disobedience, riot, etc.)	656	10	2	90	554
Percent	100%	1.5	0.3	13.7	84.5
Handling, transporting, custody of prisoners	7,759	26	55	616	7,062
Percent	100%	0.3	0.7	7.9	91.0
Investigating suspicious persons/ circumstances	5,702	289	100	911	4,402
Percent	100%	5.1	1.8	16.0	77.2
Ambush situations	199	53	6	42	98
Percent	100%	26.6	3.0	21.1	49.2
Mentally deranged assailants	982	68	87	127	700
Percent	100%	6.9	8.9	12.9	71.3
Traffic pursuits/stops	6,412	271	50	2,222	3,869
Percent	100%	4.2	0.8	34.7	60.3
All other	7,504	267	128	1,150	5,959
Percent	100%	3.6	1.7	15.3	79.4

Note: These data are based on 9,987 agencies reporting assaults to the Federal Bureau of Investigation's Uniform Crime Reporting Program for all 12 months of 2002. These agencies cover approximately 75% of the total U.S. population. In 2002, data for Illinois, Montana, Vermont, and West Virginia were not available for inclusion in the tabulations. (Source, pp. 73, 75.)

[a]Percents may not add to 100 because of rounding.

Source: U.S. Department of Justice, Federal Bureau of Investigation, *Law Enforcement Officers Killed and Assaulted, 2002*, FBI Uniform Crime Reports (Washington, DC: U.S. Department of Justice, 2003), p. 83.

Table 3.164
Law enforcement officers assaulted

By circumstances at scene of incident and type of assignment, United States, 2002[a]

Circumstances at scene of incident	Total	2-officer vehicle	1-officer vehicle Alone	1-officer vehicle Assisted	Detective, special assignment Alone	Detective, special assignment Assisted	Other Alone	Other Assisted
Total	58,066	10,142	13,645	22,998	1,142	2,113	2,453	5,573
Percent of total	100%	100%	100%	100%	100%	100%	100%	100%
Disturbance calls (family quarrels, bar fights, persons with firearms, etc.)	18,063	3,468	4,005	8,851	197	285	349	908
Percent	31.1	34.2	29.4	38.5	17.3	13.5	14.2	16.3
Burglaries in progress/pursuing burglary suspects	820	141	167	406	25	16	21	44
Percent	1.4	1.4	1.2	1.8	2.2	0.8	0.9	0.8
Robberies in progress/pursuing robbery suspects	505	127	103	181	16	27	25	26
Percent	0.9	1.3	0.8	0.8	1.4	1.3	1.0	0.5
Attempting other arrests	9,464	1,687	2,171	3,809	211	578	323	685
Percent	16.3	16.6	15.9	16.6	18.5	27.4	13.2	12.3
Civil disorders (mass disobedience, riot, etc.)	656	90	122	238	21	41	29	115
Percent	1.1	0.9	0.9	1.0	1.8	1.9	1.2	2.1
Handling, transporting, custody of prisoners	7,759	810	1,311	2,197	173	275	719	2,274
Percent	13.4	8.0	9.6	9.6	15.1	13.0	29.3	40.8
Investigating suspicious persons/circumstances	5,702	1,397	1,442	1,833	134	346	205	345
Percent	9.8	13.8	10.6	8.0	11.7	16.4	8.4	6.2
Ambush situations	199	43	63	25	4	12	18	34
Percent	0.3	0.4	0.5	0.1	0.4	0.6	0.7	0.6
Mentally deranged assailants	982	180	180	485	15	29	27	66
Percent	1.7	1.8	1.3	2.1	1.3	1.4	1.1	1.2
Traffic pursuits/stops	6,412	1,216	1,985	2,711	97	140	73	190
Percent	11.0	12.0	14.5	11.8	8.5	6.6	3.0	3.4
All other	7,504	983	2,096	2,262	249	364	664	886
Percent	12.9	9.7	15.4	9.8	21.8	17.2	27.1	15.9

Note: See Note, table 3.163.

[a]Percents may not add to 100 because of rounding.

Source: U.S. Department of Justice, Federal Bureau of Investigation, *Law Enforcement Officers Killed and Assaulted, 2002*, FBI Uniform Crime Reports (Washington, DC: U.S. Department of Justice, 2003), p. 78.

Table 3.165

Assaults on law enforcement officers and percent sustaining personal injury

By type of weapon used, 1980-2002

	Total victims	Firearm	Personal weapon	Knife or cutting instrument	Other dangerous weapon
Total					
1980	57,847	3,295	47,484	1,653	5,415
1981	57,174	3,334	47,304	1,733	4,803
1982	55,775	2,642	46,802	1,452	4,879
1983	62,324	3,067	51,901	1,829	5,527
1984	60,153	2,654	50,689	1,662	5,148
1985	61,724	2,793	51,953	1,715	5,263
1986	64,259	2,852	54,072	1,614	5,721
1987	63,842	2,789	53,807	1,561	5,685
1988	58,916	2,760	49,209	1,368	5,579
1989	62,172	3,154	51,861	1,379	5,778
1990	72,091	3,651	59,370	1,647	7,423
1991	64,803	3,619	52,451	1,536	7,197
1992	81,150	4,445	66,013	2,093	8,599
1993	62,933	3,880	50,412	1,486	7,155
1994	64,967	3,174	53,086	1,510	7,197
1995	57,762	2,354	47,638	1,356	6,414
1996	46,608	1,878	38,790	871	5,069
1997	52,149	2,110	43,268	971	5,800
1998	60,673	2,126	50,034	1,098	7,415
1999	55,971	1,772	45,640	999	7,560
2000	58,398	1,749	47,502	1,015	8,132
2001	57,463	1,841	46,221	1,168	8,233
2002	58,066	1,889	46,795	1,056	8,326
Percent sustaining personal injury					
1980	37.2%	22.5%	38.2%	34.4%	38.0%
1981	35.5	18.3	36.2	34.3	40.6
1982	30.7	16.4	30.7	27.0	39.1
1983	33.4	21.8	33.4	31.4	40.2
1984	33.6	20.1	33.5	30.0	42.2
1985	33.7	20.8	33.9	27.4	41.1
1986	33.7	22.3	33.9	29.9	38.3
1987	33.3	21.7	33.5	30.7	38.4
1988	35.8	27.3	35.6	32.4	42.1
1989	35.2	30.2	35.0	30.5	40.8
1990	36.3	29.4	36.2	29.6	42.6
1991	37.1	30.2	36.9	30.2	43.0
1992	36.5	25.5	36.9	30.3	40.9
1993	36.3	27.7	37.1	31.6	36.2
1994	35.8	26.6	36.4	29.3	36.7
1995	30.1	19.3	30.7	23.9	31.1
1996	32.1	24.8	31.5	30.7	39.4
1997	30.4	23.1	30.6	25.4	32.1
1998	30.7	20.7	31.3	23.7	30.2
1999	28.0	11.9	29.0	17.5	27.1
2000	28.1	11.4	29.2	15.2	26.9
2001	28.3	10.3	29.7	15.3	26.1
2002	28.4	12.2	29.8	17.1	25.7

Note: These data are based on agencies reporting assaults to the Federal Bureau of Investigation's Uniform Crime Reporting Program; the number of agencies reporting and percent of total population represented vary from year to year. Data for 2002 are based on 9,987 agencies covering approximately 75% of the total population. Data for previous years are from agencies covering from 63% to 85% of the total population. Some data have been revised by the Source and may differ from previous editions of SOURCEBOOK.

Source: U.S. Department of Justice, Federal Bureau of Investigation, **Law Enforcement Officers Killed and Assaulted, 1989**, p. 55; **1999**, p. 80; **2002**, p. 79; FBI Uniform Crime Reports (Washington, DC: U.S. Department of Justice). Table adapted by SOURCEBOOK staff.

Table 3.166

Estimated number of structure fires and intentionally set structure fires, and resulting civilian fire deaths and value of property damage

United States, 2002

	Structure fires		
	Estimated number of fires	Estimated number of civilian fire deaths	Estimated value of property damage (in thousands)
Total, all fires in structures	519,000	2,775	$8,742,000
Total, intentionally set structure fires	44,500	350	919,000

Note: These data are weighted estimates from an annual survey of fire departments conducted by the National Fire Protection Association (NFPA). All U.S. fire departments that protect communities of 100,000 population or more are included in the sample. For departments that protect communities of less than 100,000 population, the sample is stratified by community size. A total of 3,460 fire departments responded to the 2002 survey. Readers are advised to consult the Source for more detailed information on methodology and weighting procedures.

"Civilians" include anyone other than a fire fighter. "Property damage" includes all forms of direct loss to contents, structure, machinery, etc., but does not include indirect losses, such as interruption of business or temporary shelter provisions. (Source, p. 33.)

Source: Michael J. Karter, Jr., **Fire Loss in the United States During 2002** (Quincy, MA: National Fire Protection Association, 2003), pp. 3, 8, 15. Table constructed by SOURCEBOOK staff. Reprinted with permission from NFPA, Fire Analysis and Research. Copyright 2003 National Fire Protection Association, Quincy, MA 02169.

Table 3.167

Estimated number of intentionally set structure fires, and resulting civilian fire deaths and value of property damage

United States, 1977-2002

	Intentionally set structure fires		
	Estimated number	Estimated civilian fire deaths	Estimated property damage (in millions)
1977	86,500	480	$636
1978	87,000	520	650
1979	88,500	435	787
1980	92,000	590	1,158
1981	88,000	555	1,142
1982	77,500	720	1,088
1983	72,500	565	946
1984	66,000	385	883
1985	68,500	455	1,069
1986	71,000	505	1,162
1987	65,500	465	1,109
1988	63,000	570	1,022
1989	59,500	460	1,057
1990	58,500	565	875
1991	62,000	365	1,072
1992	58,000	465	1,493
1993	54,000	415	1,839
1994	53,000	410	964
1995	57,500	570	981
1996	52,500	330	897
1997	52,000	340	802
1998	46,500	355	816
1999	43,500	290	828
2000	45,500	375	792
2001[a]	45,500	330	1,013
2002	44,500	350	919

Note: See Note, table 3.166. This table has been revised by the Source due to a change in survey methodology beginning with the 2001 data. Data for 1977-2000 have been adjusted to include only intentionally set structure fires and are comparable to the figures for 2001 and later.

[a]Does not include events of Sept. 11, 2001, which resulted in 2,451 civilian deaths and property loss valued at $33,440,000,000.

Source: Michael J. Karter, Jr., **Fire Loss in the United States During 2002** (Quincy, MA: National Fire Protection Association, 2003), p. 15; and data provided by Michael J. Karter, Jr., National Fire Protection Association. Reprinted with permission from NFPA, Fire Analysis and Research. National Fire Protection Association, Quincy, MA 02169.

Table 3.168

Arson offenses and average value of property damage

By type of target, 2002

(12,414 agencies; 2002 estimated population 225,428,667)

Target	Number of offenses	Percent[a]	Average damage
Total	66,308	100.0%	$11,253
Total structure	27,373	41.3	20,818
Single occupancy residential	11,789	17.8	18,535
Other residential	4,821	7.3	21,846
Storage	1,940	2.9	15,627
Industrial/manufacturing	333	0.5	71,376
Other commercial	2,735	4.1	45,927
Community/public	3,140	4.7	11,181
Other structure	2,615	3.9	11,933
Total mobile	21,920	33.1	6,073
Motor vehicles	20,736	31.3	5,781
Other mobile	1,184	1.8	11,183
Other	17,015	25.7	2,536

Note: Arson was designated as a Part I Index Offense in October 1978; data collection began in 1979. In 2002, 12,454 law enforcement agencies reported 74,921 arson offenses to the Uniform Crime Reporting Program. The data presented above are from 12,414 agencies that furnished detailed reports such as type of structure and estimated value of property damage. Readers should be aware that these data do not represent the Nation's total arson experience (Source, p. 57). For a definition of arson, see Appendix 3.

[a]Because of rounding, percents may not add to total.

Source: U.S. Department of Justice, Federal Bureau of Investigation, *Crime in the United States, 2002* (Washington, DC: USGPO, 2003), p. 58. Table adapted by SOURCEBOOK staff.

Table 3.169

Arson of structures and percent not in use

By type of structure, 2002

(12,414 agencies; 2002 estimated population 225,428,667)

	Arson of structures	
Structure	Number	Percent not in use
Total	27,373	18.2%
Single occupancy residential	11,789	19.7
Other residential	4,821	14.8
Storage	1,940	19.7
Industrial/manufacturing	333	22.8
Other commercial	2,735	15.4
Community/public	3,140	13.6
Other structure	2,615	24.3

Note: See Note, table 3.168. Structures not in use are structures that were uninhabited or abandoned at the time the arson occurred. For a definition of arson, see Appendix 3.

Source: U.S. Department of Justice, Federal Bureau of Investigation, *Crime in the United States, 2002* (Washington, DC: USGPO, 2003), p. 58.

Table 3.170

Bombing incidents known to police

By type of incident and device, value of property damage, and outcome of incident, United States, 1973-99

	Total actual and attempted bombings	Actual Explosive	Actual Incendiary	Attempted Explosive	Attempted Incendiary	Accidental Explosive	Accidental Incendiary	Property damage (dollar value in thousands)[a]	Persons injured	Deaths
Total	45,573	26,366	9,354	6,615	2,931	140	8	$883,959	6,779	840
1973	1,955	742	787	253	173	NA	NA	7,262	187	22
1974	2,044	893	758	236	157	NA	NA	9,887	207	24
1975	2,074	1,088	613	238	135	NA	NA	27,004[b]	326[b]	69[b]
1976	1,570	852	405	188	125	NA	NA	11,265	212	50
1977	1,318	867	248	118	85	NA	NA	8,943	162	22
1978	1,301	768	349	105	79	NA	NA	9,161	135	18
1979	1,220	728	305	104	83	NA	NA	9,273	173	22
1980	1,249	742	336	99	72	NA	NA	12,562	160	34
1981	1,142	637	315	92	98	NA	NA	67,082[b]	133[b]	30
1982	795	485	194	77	39	NA	NA	7,203	99	16
1983	687	442	127	77	41	NA	NA	6,343	100	12
1984	803	518	127	118	40	NA	NA	5,619	112	6
1985	847	575	102	113	57	NA	NA	6,352	144	28
1986	858	580	129	101	48	NA	NA	3,405	185	14
1987	848	600	104	102	42	NA	NA	4,201	107	21
1988	977[c]	593	156	161	40	NA	NA	2,257	145	20
1989	1,208[d]	641	203	243	91	NA	NA	5,000	202	11
1990	1,582	931	267	254	130	NA	NA	9,600	222	27
1991	2,499	1,551	423	395	130	NA	NA	6,440	230	29
1992	2,989	1,911	582	384	112	NA	NA	12,500	349	26
1993	2,980	1,880	538	375	187	NA	NA	518,000[e]	1,323[e]	49
1994	3,163	1,916	545	522	180	NA	NA	7,500	308	31
1995	2,577	1,562	406	417	192	NA	NA	105,100[f]	744[f]	193[f]
1996	2,573	1,457	427	504	185	NA	NA	5,000	336	23
1997	2,217	1,212	378	473	154	NA	NA	9,000	204	18
1998	2,300[g]	1,225	307	488	142	69	6	6,000	160	16
1999	1,797[h]	970	223	378	114	71	2	2,000	114	9

Note: Prior to 1988, detailed information concerning bombing incidents occurring in the United States, Puerto Rico, Guam, and the Virgin Islands was gathered by the Federal Bureau of Investigation's (FBI) Uniform Crime Reporting Program. Since 1988, the FBI Bomb Data Center has collected these data. Reports of bombing incidents are gathered from State and local public safety agencies, the U.S. Postal Inspection Service, Military Explosive Ordnance Disposal units, and the Bureau of Alcohol, Tobacco and Firearms.

Bombing incidents refer to actual and attempted detonations of explosive or incendiary devices in violation of a State, local, or Federal law. Prior to 1990, these tabulations excluded threats to bomb, hoax bomb devices, accidental explosions, recoveries of explosive or incendiary devices, and such misdemeanor offenses as the illegal use of fireworks. Beginning in 1990, only bomb threats and such violations as the illegal use of fireworks were excluded from the tabulations.

[a]Detail may not add to total because of rounding. Beginning in 1985, the Source presented only rounded dollar values.
[b]Includes major bombing incidents resulting in an unusually high number of personal injuries and deaths, or substantial damage to property.
[c]Includes 27 incidents involving combination devices.
[d]Includes 30 incidents involving combination devices.
[e]These figures include $510,000,000 in property damage and 1,042 persons injured resulting from the bombing of the World Trade Center in New York City on Feb. 26, 1993.
[f]These figures include $100,000,000 in property damage, 518 persons injured, and 168 deaths resulting from the bombing of the Alfred P. Murrah Federal building in Oklahoma City on Apr. 19, 1995.
[g]Includes 63 incidents involving combination devices.
[h]Includes 39 incidents involving combination devices.

Source: U.S. Department of Justice, Federal Bureau of Investigation, **Bomb Summary 1982**, FBI Uniform Crime Reports (Washington, DC: USGPO, 1983), Table 1; U.S. Department of Justice, Federal Bureau of Investigation, **1993 Bomb Summary** (Washington, DC: U.S. Department of Justice, 1994), p. 15; U.S. Department of Justice, Federal Bureau of Investigation, "1994 Bombing Incidents," FBI Explosives Unit-Bomb Data Center General Information Bulletin 95-2, Washington, DC: U.S. Department of Justice, 1995. (Mimeographed.) P. 3; U.S. Department of Justice, Federal Bureau of Investigation, **1996 Bomb Summary**, FBI Bomb Data Center General Information Bulletin 96-1, p. 6; **1997 Bomb Summary**, FBI Bomb Data Center General Information Bulletin 97-1, p. 7 (Washington, DC: U.S. Department of Justice); and U.S. Department of Justice, Federal Bureau of Investigation, **1999 Bombing Incidents**, FBI Bomb Data Center General Information Bulletin 99-1 (Washington, DC: U.S. Department of Justice, 2003), p. 7. Table adapted by SOURCEBOOK staff.

Table 3.171

Bombing incidents known to police

By type of target and device, and value of property damage, United States, 1999

Type of target	Explosive	Incendiary	Explosive and incendiary	Property damage
Total	1,041	225	11	$1,852,991
Residential properties				
Private residences	201	105	2	249,025
Mailboxes	400	8	2	39,969
Commercial properties				
Commercial business	53	19	0	172,460
Restaurants	8	4	0	205,150
Office buildings	2	1	0	700
Financial institutions				
Banks	1	1	0	35,000
ATMs	1	0	0	0
Vehicles	60	44	1	200,906
Utilities	13	1	0	7,970
Hospitals	1	2	0	3,500
Other targets				
Local/State government facilities	9	1	0	1,300
Judicial facilities	1	0	0	0
Educational facilities	63	12	0	68,475
Church	4	0	0	20,030
Person	23	6	1	92,230
Other	96	14	4	31,055
Unknown	34	5	1	10,911
Accidental explosion/no target	71	2	0	714,310

Note: See Note, table 3.170.

Source: U.S. Department of Justice, Federal Bureau of Investigation, *1999 Bombing Incidents*, FBI Bomb Data Center General Information Bulletin 99-1 (Washington, DC: U.S. Department of Justice, 2003), p. 16.

Table 3.172

Bombing incidents known to police

By type of incident and device, and region and jurisdiction, 1999

Region and jurisdiction	Explosive Actual	Explosive Attempted	Explosive Accidental	Incendiary Actual	Incendiary Attempted	Incendiary Accidental	Explosive and incendiary Actual	Explosive and incendiary Attempted	Explosive and incendiary Accidental
East	46	24	9	11	8	0	1	1	0
Connecticut	2	0	0	2	0	X	0	0	X
Maine	0	2	0	0	1	X	0	0	X
Massachusetts	8	6	2	4	2	X	0	0	X
New Hampshire	0	0	0	0	0	X	0	0	X
New Jersey	15	4	1	3	0	X	1	1	X
New York	12	4	5	2	0	X	0	0	X
Pennsylvania	7	7	1	0	5	X	0	0	X
Rhode Island	0	0	0	0	0	X	0	0	X
Vermont	2	1	0	0	0	X	0	0	X
North Central	174	97	16	94	35	0	4	9	0
Illinois	46	24	6	64	21	X	2	3	X
Indiana	23	14	1	0	1	X	0	1	X
Iowa	23	11	0	4	0	X	1	2	X
Kansas	14	3	2	2	1	X	0	0	X
Michigan	16	29	2	1	1	X	0	1	X
Minnesota	17	2	2	11	3	X	0	1	X
Missouri	23	3	0	2	3	X	1	0	X
Nebraska	0	5	1	1	1	X	0	0	X
North Dakota	4	0	1	0	0	X	0	0	X
Ohio	8	6	1	9	4	X	0	1	X
South Dakota	0	0	0	0	0	X	0	0	X
Wisconsin	0	0	0	0	0	X	0	0	X
South	262	110	20	56	33	0	4	7	0
Alabama	4	3	0	1	1	X	0	0	X
Arkansas	3	3	3	0	0	X	0	0	X
Delaware	1	0	0	0	1	X	0	0	X
District of Columbia	0	0	0	0	0	X	0	0	X
Florida	144	30	5	12	8	X	2	1	X
Georgia	1	9	0	0	0	X	0	0	X
Kentucky	8	3	1	0	1	X	0	1	X
Louisiana	2	2	1	4	1	X	0	0	X
Maryland	14	7	4	4	6	X	1	0	X
Mississippi	1	0	0	0	0	X	0	0	X
North Carolina	3	3	0	2	1	X	0	0	X
Oklahoma	6	8	1	3	2	X	0	1	X
South Carolina	8	8	1	1	2	X	0	1	X
Tennessee	21	18	1	14	4	X	0	0	X
Texas	29	11	1	6	4	X	1	1	X
Virginia	12	4	1	4	2	X	0	2	X
West Virginia	1	0	1	0	0	X	0	0	X
Puerto Rico	4	1	0	5	0	X	0	0	X
Virgin Islands	0	0	0	0	0	X	0	0	X
West	489	147	26	61	38	2	2	11	0
Alaska	0	0	0	0	0	0	0	0	X
Arizona	43	17	0	6	3	0	0	1	X
California	123	58	14	33	16	1	1	3	X
Colorado	24	6	0	8	8	0	0	0	X
Hawaii	2	0	0	0	0	0	0	0	X
Idaho	4	2	0	0	0	0	0	0	X
Montana	0	0	0	0	0	0	0	0	X
Nevada	10	6	0	3	2	0	0	1	X
New Mexico	2	2	0	2	1	0	0	0	X
Oregon	14	23	0	1	1	0	0	0	X
Utah	48	8	4	0	1	0	0	2	X
Washington	218	24	8	8	6	1	1	4	X
Wyoming	1	1	0	0	0	0	0	0	X
Guam	0	0	0	0	0	0	0	0	X

Note: See Note, table 3.170.

Source: U.S. Department of Justice, Federal Bureau of Investigation, *1999 Bombing Incidents*, FBI Bomb Data Center General Information Bulletin 99-1 (Washington, DC: U.S. Department of Justice, 2003), pp. 10-13. Table adapted by SOURCEBOOK staff.

Table 3.173

Terrorist incidents and preventions

United States, 1980-2001

	Terrorist incidents	Suspected terrorist incidents	Terrorism preventions
Total	294	55	133
1980	29	0	1
1981	42	4	0
1982	51	1	3
1983	31	2	6
1984	13	3	9
1985	7	6	23
1986	25	2	9
1987	9	8	5
1988	9	5	3
1989	4	16	7
1990	7	1	5
1991	5	1	5
1992	4	0	0
1993	12	2	7
1994	1	1	0
1995	1	1	2
1996	3	0	5
1997	4	0	21
1998	5	0	12
1999	10	2	7
2000	8	0	1
2001	14	0	2

Note: A terrorist incident is a violent act, or an act dangerous to human life, in violation of the criminal laws of the United States or of any State, to intimidate or coerce a government, the civilian population, or any segment thereof, in furtherance of political or social objectives. A terrorism prevention is a documented instance in which a violent act by a known or suspected terrorist group or individual with the means and a proven propensity for violence is successfully interdicted through investigative activity. (Source, p. iv.) A suspected terrorist incident is a potential act of terrorism in which responsibility for the act cannot be attributed at the time to a known or suspected terrorist group or individual. Some data have been revised by the Source and may differ from previous editions of SOURCEBOOK.

Source: U.S. Department of Justice, Federal Bureau of Investigation, *Terrorism 2000/2001* [Online]. Available: http://www.fbi.gov/publications/terror/terror2000_2001.pdf [Sept. 14, 2004], p. 10. Table adapted by SOURCEBOOK staff.

Table 3.174

Terrorist incidents

By type of incident and region, United States, 1980-2001 (aggregate)

	Number
Total	482
Type of incident	
Bombing attacks[a]	324
Arson	33
Assassinations	21
Malicious destruction of property; sabotage	19
Shootings	19
Robbery; attempted robbery	15
Hostile takeover	10
Assaults	6
Weapons of mass destruction	6
Hijackings; aircraft attacks[b]	3
Kidnaping	2
Rocket attacks	2
Other	22
Region[c]	
Northeast	144
North Central	56
South	72
West	97
Puerto Rico	103
Other/unknown	12

Note: See Note, table 3.173.

[a]Includes detonated and undetonated devices, tear gas, pipebombs, letterbombs, and firebombs.
[b]Includes the aircraft attacks of Sept. 11, 2001, which are counted by the Source as a single terrorist incident.
[c]These figures sum to 484 because although designated as a single act of terrorism, the aircraft attacks of Sept. 11, 2001 have been designated as one terrorist incident in the Northeast and one terrorist incident in the South. Similarly, although the anthrax mailings that occurred from September through November 2001 have been categorized as a single act of terrorism, the incidents have been designated as one terrorist incident in the Northeast and one terrorist incident in the South.

Source: U.S. Department of Justice, Federal Bureau of Investigation, *Terrorism 2000/2001* [Online]. Available: http://www.fbi.gov/publications/terror/terror2000_2001.pdf [Sept. 14, 2004], pp. 7, 12. Table adapted by SOURCEBOOK staff.

Table 3.175

U.S. citizen casualties resulting from international terrorism

By type of casualty, 1981-2003

	Total	U.S. citizens Killed	U.S. citizens Wounded
Total	2,939	670	2,269
1981	47	7	40
1982	19	8	11
1983	386	271	115
1984	42	11	31
1985	195	38	157
1986	112	12	100
1987	54	7	47
1988	231	192	39
1989	34	16	18
1990	43	9	34
1991	23	7	16
1992	3	2	1
1993	1,011[a]	7	1,004
1994	11	6	5
1995	70	10	60
1996	535[b]	25	510
1997	27	6	21
1998	23	12	11
1999	12	6	6
2000	70	23	47
2001[c]	2,779	2,689	90
2002	64	27	37
2003	64	35	29

Note: Terrorism is defined as premeditated, politically motivated violence perpetrated against noncombatant targets by subnational groups or clandestine agents, usually intended to influence an audience. International terrorism involves citizens or territory of more than one country. (Source, *2003*, p. xii.) Most attacks that have occurred during Operation Iraqi Freedom and Operation Enduring Freedom do not meet this definition of international terrorism because they were directed at military forces on duty. Only those incidents directed against civilians and unarmed military personnel while off duty are considered terrorist attacks. (Source, *2003*, p. 2.) Some data have been revised by the Source and may differ from previous editions of SOURCEBOOK.

[a]The bombing of the World Trade Center in New York City on Feb. 26, 1993 accounts for this increase.
[b]The bombing of the Al Khubar U.S. military housing complex near Dhahran, Saudi Arabia on June 25, 1996 accounts for this increase.
[c]These figures may not include complete counts of persons killed and wounded in the Sept. 11, 2001 terrorist attacks and are subject to revision.

Source: U.S. Department of State, *Patterns of Global Terrorism: 1987*, p.1; *1988*, p. 4; *1995*, p. 71; *2000*, p. 87; *2003*, p. 180 (Washington, DC: U.S. Department of State); and data provided by U.S. Department of State [Online]. Available: http://www.state.gov/s/ct/rls/pgtrpt/2003/33777.htm [June 22, 2004]. Table adapted by SOURCEBOOK staff.

Table 3.176

Terrorist attacks against the United States internationally

By type of event, 1994-2003

Type of event	1994	1995	1996	1997	1998	1999	2000	2001	2002	2003
Total	66	99	73	123	111	169	200	219	77	60
Armed attack	9	8	3	5	5	11	4	1	8	7
Arson	0	6	7	2	1	6	2	0	0	2
Assault	1	0	1	0	0	0	0	0	0	0
Bombing[a]	43	65	55	108	96	111	179	207	66	43
Firebombing	2	0	1	0	5	12	1	1	0	2
Hijacking	NA	NA	NA	NA	NA	NA	NA	1	0	1
Kidnaping/hostage	10	11	6	8	4	21	11	6	3	3
Vandalism	1	9	0	0	0	0	0	3	0	0
Other	NA	NA	NA	NA	NA	8	3	0	0	2

Note: See Note, table 3.175. Includes attacks against U.S. facilities and attacks in which U.S. citizens suffered casualties.

[a]Includes suicide bombing.

Source: U.S. Department of State, *Patterns of Global Terrorism: 1994*, p. 67; *1995*, p. 73; *1996*, p. 74; *1997*, p. 86; *1998*, p. 96; *1999*, p. 106; *2000*, p. 88; *2001*, p. 176; *2002*, p. 166; *2003*, p. 181 (Washington, DC: U.S. Department of State); and data provided by U.S. Department of State [Online]. Available: http://www.state.gov/s/ct/rls/pgtrpt/2003/33777.htm [June 22, 2004]. Table adapted by SOURCEBOOK staff.

Table 3.177
Results of airline passenger screening

United States, 1977-2000

	Persons screened (in millions)	Weapons detected Total	Handguns	Long guns	Other[a]	Other dangerous articles[a]	Explosive/ incendiary devices[b]	Persons arrested For carrying firearms/ explosives	For giving false information
1977	508.8	2,034	1,730	64	240	NA	5	810	44
1978	579.7	2,058	1,827	67	164	NA	3	896	64
1979	592.5	2,161	1,962	55	144	NA	3	1,060	47
1980	585.0	2,022	1,878	36	108	NA	8	1,031	32
1981	598.5	2,255	2,124	44	87	NA	11	1,187	49
1982	630.2	2,676	2,559	57	60	NA	1	1,314	27
1983	709.1	2,784	2,634	67	83	NA	4	1,282	34
1984	775.6	2,957	2,766	100	91	NA	6	1,285	27
1985	992.9	2,987	2,823	90	74	NA	12	1,310	42
1986	1,055.3	3,241	2,981	146	114	NA	11	1,415	89
1987	1,095.6	3,252	3,012	99	141	NA	14	1,581	81
1988	1,054.9	2,773	2,591	74	108	NA	11	1,493	222
1989	1,113.3	2,879	2,397	92	390	NA	26	1,436	83
1990	1,145.1	2,853	2,490	59	304	NA	15	1,336	18
1991	1,015.1	1,919	1,597	47	275	NA	94	893	28
1992	1,110.8	2,608	2,503	105	NA	2,341	167	1,282	13
1993	1,150.0	2,798	2,707	91	NA	3,867	251	1,354	31
1994	1,261.3	2,994	2,860	134	NA	6,051	505	1,433	35
1995	1,263.0	2,390	2,230	160	NA	4,414	631	1,194	68
1996	1,496.9	2,155	1,999	156	NA	NA	NA	999	131
1997	1,659.7	2,067	1,905	162	NA	NA	NA	924	72
1998	1,666.5	1,515	1,401	114	NA	NA	NA	660	86
1999	1,767.0	1,552	1,421	131	NA	NA	NA	633	58
2000	1,812.0	1,937	1,643	294	NA	NA	NA	600	61

Note: Screening consists of "the systematic examination of persons and property using weapons-detecting procedures or facilities (electronic or physical search) for the purpose of detecting weapons and dangerous articles and to prevent their unauthorized introduction into sterile areas or aboard aircraft." (Source, *1993*, p. 42.) Some data have been revised by the Source and may differ from previous editions of SOURCEBOOK.

[a]Prior to 1992, the weapons category "other" included items such as starter pistols, flare pistols, and BB guns. Beginning in 1992, this category was expanded to include stunning devices, chemical agents, martial arts equipment, knives, bludgeons, and certain other designated items, and renamed "other dangerous articles." Reporting of this category was discontinued by the Source in 1996 due to inconsistent reporting.

[b]From 1992 to 1994, the method of counting "explosive/incendiary devices" was revised. Individual items were counted rather than packages (i.e., one box of firecrackers counted as 20 firecrackers; one box of ammunition counted as 50 cartridges). Reporting of this category was discontinued by the Source in 1996 due to inconsistent reporting.

Source: U.S. Department of Transportation, Federal Aviation Administration, *Semiannual Report to Congress on the Effectiveness of the Civil Aviation Security Program, July 1 to December 31, 1978*, Exhibit 10; *July 1 to December 31, 1982*, Exhibit 10; *July 1 to December 31, 1984*, Exhibit 7; *July 1 to December 31, 1989*, p. 11 (Washington, DC: U.S. Department of Transportation); U.S. Department of Transportation, Federal Aviation Administration, *Annual Report to Congress on Civil Aviation Security, January 1, 1993-December 31, 1993*, p. 9; *January 1, 1995-December 31, 1995*, p. 11 (Washington, DC: U.S. Department of Transportation); and data provided by the U.S. Department of Transportation, Federal Aviation Administration and Bureau of Transportation Statistics [Online]. Available: http://www.bts.gov/publications/national_transportation_statistics/2003/html/table_02_16.html [May 24, 2004]. Table adapted by SOURCEBOOK staff.

Section 4

Characteristics and distribution of persons arrested

This section features arrest data from the Uniform Crime Reporting (UCR) Program, the Federal Bureau of Investigation's ongoing nationwide data collection program. Information on criminal offenses known to, and arrests made by, law enforcement agencies across the country are reported to the UCR Program. These data represent the most comprehensive source of arrest information currently available due to a consistently high participation rate by law enforcement agencies. Detailed data on total arrests for each of the Part I and Part II UCR offenses are presented. These tables include arrests in cities, suburban areas, and rural counties, and are displayed by age, sex, and race of arrestees. By-State counts of arrests are shown for the eight Index offenses: murder and nonnegligent manslaughter, forcible rape, robbery, aggravated assault, burglary, larceny-theft, motor vehicle theft, and arson. These figures are provided for the total population and for persons under age 18. In addition, tables displaying trends spanning over 30 years show arrest rates for the eight Index crimes, as well as rates of violent and property crime indices by geographic region.

Offenses cleared by arrest and the proportion of Index crimes cleared by arrest are included in the next part of the section. Tables show trends in clearance by arrest for the last 31 years, and clearances displayed by population size, geographic region, and for persons under 18 years of age (including arson). Additionally, there is information on juveniles taken into police custody and the manner of handling of juvenile detainees. The final UCR tables presented in this section display 31-year trends and by-State counts of alcohol-related arrests.

These tables are followed by information from the National Institute of Justice-sponsored Arrestee Drug Abuse Monitoring (ADAM) Program, which collects data on the prevalence of drug use among adult arrestees processed at booking facilities throughout the United States. These data report the prevalence of arrestee drug use for 43 participating U.S. cities and counties. Additional tables from the ADAM Program provide information on arrestees reporting receiving drug treatment and the percent reporting recent binge alcohol use. Next, the number of Federal arrests by offense type and arresting agency are displayed in tables from the Bureau of Justice Statistics-sponsored Federal Justice Statistics Program. Information on characteristics of persons arrested by Federal agencies also is presented.

Included in the last segment of this section are data from the Federal-wide Drug Seizure System, which provide counts of drugs seized by Federal agencies. A series of tables, some of which provide more than 25 years of data, present the activities of the Drug Enforcement Administration (DEA), including information on drugs removed from the domestic market, seizures of domestically cultivated marijuana, seizures of illegal drug laboratories, arrests made by the DEA and characteristics of persons arrested, and the type and value of assets seized. Drug and property seizures made by the former U.S. Customs Service also are presented. Finally, information on the law enforcement activities of the U.S. Citizenship and Immigration Services, formerly the Immigration and Naturalization Service, is shown, including data on the number of deportable aliens located and removed from the United States.

Table 4.1

Estimated number of arrests[a]

By offense charged, United States, 2002

Offense charged	
Total[b]	13,741,438
Murder and nonnegligent manslaughter	14,158
Forcible rape	28,288
Robbery	105,774
Aggravated assault	472,290
Burglary	288,291
Larceny-theft	1,160,085
Motor vehicle theft	148,943
Arson	16,635
Violent crime[c]	620,510
Property crime[d]	1,613,954
Total Crime Index[e]	2,234,464
Other assaults	1,288,682
Forgery and counterfeiting	115,735
Fraud	337,404
Embezzlement	18,552
Stolen property; buying, receiving, possessing	126,422
Vandalism	276,697
Weapons; carrying, possessing, etc.	164,446
Prostitution and commercialized vice	79,733
Sex offenses (except forcible rape and prostitution)	95,066
Drug abuse violations	1,538,813
Gambling	10,506
Offenses against family and children	140,286
Driving under the influence	1,461,746
Liquor laws	653,819
Drunkenness	572,735
Disorderly conduct	669,938
Vagrancy	27,295
All other offenses (except traffic)	3,662,159
Suspicion (not included in total)	8,899
Curfew and loitering law violations	141,252
Runaways	125,688

Note: These data were compiled by the Federal Bureau of Investigation through the Uniform Crime Reporting (UCR) Program. On a monthly basis, law enforcement agencies report the number of offenses that become known to them in the following crime categories: murder and nonnegligent manslaughter, manslaughter by negligence, forcible rape, robbery, aggravated assault, burglary, larceny-theft, motor vehicle theft, and arson. All of these crime categories, except manslaughter by negligence, are used to establish a crime index. The "Total Crime Index" is a simple sum of the index offenses. Arson was designated a Part I Index offense in October 1978. Data collection began in 1979. Unlike the tables from *Crime in the United States* presented in Section 3, arrest statistics for the crime of arson are complete and appear in the "Total Crime Index" and "Property crime" total.

Arrest statistics are compiled as part of this monthly data collection effort. Participating law enforcement agencies are instructed to count one arrest each time a person is taken into custody, notified, or cited for criminal infractions other than traffic violations. Annual arrest figures do not measure the number of individuals taken into custody because one person may be arrested several times during the year for the same type of offense or for different offenses. A juvenile is counted as a person arrested when he/she commits an act that would be a criminal offense if committed by an adult. Two offense categories, "curfew and loitering" and "runaway," are tabulated only for juveniles. Violations of local juvenile acts other than runaway and curfew and loitering law violations are included in the "all other offenses" classification (U.S. Department of Justice, Federal Bureau of Investigation, *Uniform Crime Reporting Handbook* (Washington, DC: USGPO, 1984), p. 60).

Data in this table are estimates based on arrest statistics for all law enforcement agencies in the Uniform Crime Reporting Program, including those submitting reports for less than 12 months in 2002 (Source, p. 451). Because of reporting problems at the State level, only limited arrest data were provided by Illinois, Kentucky, Nevada, and South Carolina and no arrest data were available from the District of Columbia. Complete arrest data for New York City also were not available. Arrest totals for these States, New York City, and the District of Columbia were estimated by the Source for inclusion in the above table. Subsequent tables, displaying detailed breakdowns of persons arrested, contain limited or no data for these States, New York City, and the District of Columbia (Source, p. 444).

For definitions of offenses, see Appendix 3.

[a]Data are based on all reporting agencies and estimates for unreported areas.
[b]Because of rounding, figures may not add to total. Total does not include suspicion.
[c]Violent crimes are offenses of murder and nonnegligent manslaughter, forcible rape, robbery, and aggravated assault.
[d]Property crimes are offenses of burglary, larceny-theft, motor vehicle theft, and arson.
[e]Includes arson.

Source: U.S. Department of Justice, Federal Bureau of Investigation, *Crime in the United States, 2002* (Washington, DC: USGPO, 2003), p. 234, Table 29.

Table 4.2

Arrest rates (per 100,000 inhabitants)

By offense, 1971-2002

(Rate per 100,000 inhabitants)

	Total Crime Index[a]	Violent crime[b]	Property crime[c]	Murder and non-negligent manslaughter	Forcible rape	Robbery	Aggravated assault	Burglary	Larceny-theft	Motor vehicle theft	Arson
1971	897.1	175.8	721.4	9.4	10.7	65.4	90.3	202.9	434.2	84.2	X
1972	881.5	186.5	695.0	9.4	12.1	68.1	97.0	196.0	423.1	76.0	X
1973	883.4	187.3	696.1	9.3	12.4	65.7	99.9	204.1	415.6	76.4	X
1974	1,098.0	219.7	878.3	10.3	13.3	80.9	115.2	254.1	544.2	80.0	X
1975	1,059.6	206.7	852.9	9.2	12.3	72.4	112.8	250.7	535.1	67.1	X
1976	1,016.8	193.1	823.7	8.0	12.4	62.8	109.8	231.8	528.8	63.1	X
1977	1,039.4	202.7	836.7	9.0	13.5	64.2	116.0	238.1	527.8	70.9	X
1978	1,047.6	215.5	832.2	9.1	13.6	68.3	124.4	234.6	523.6	74.0	X
1979	1,057.2	212.5	844.7	8.9	14.3	63.9	125.4	228.8	536.8	70.2	9.0
1980	1,055.8	214.4	841.4	9.0	14.1	67.0	124.3	230.4	539.8	62.3	8.9
1981	1,070.0	216.8	853.2	9.5	14.0	68.8	124.5	228.4	558.8	57.0	9.0
1982	1,148.9	236.9	912.0	9.9	15.1	73.7	138.2	232.9	612.1	58.0	9.0
1983	1,071.9	221.1	850.8	9.0	15.0	66.8	130.3	207.1	582.5	52.6	8.6
1984	1,019.8	212.5	807.3	7.6	15.8	60.4	128.8	185.9	561.4	51.9	8.2
1985	1,046.5	212.4	834.0	7.8	15.7	59.3	129.6	188.1	580.7	56.9	8.3
1986	1,091.8	234.5	857.3	8.1	15.7	62.6	148.1	189.2	595.6	64.7	7.8
1987	1,120.1	233.8	886.4	8.3	15.5	60.9	149.1	185.3	621.0	72.5	7.5
1988	1,123.5	243.8	879.7	8.6	15.1	58.9	161.2	175.6	615.4	81.0	7.7
1989	1,173.1	268.6	904.4	9.0	15.3	66.9	177.4	178.4	627.3	91.4	7.3
1990	1,203.2	290.7	912.5	9.5	16.0	70.4	194.8	176.3	641.4	87.0	7.7
1991	1,198.8	293.0	905.8	9.8	16.0	73.3	194.0	173.1	639.8	85.1	7.9
1992	1,162.4	300.5	861.9	9.1	15.6	71.9	203.8	168.6	605.5	80.3	7.6
1993	1,131.6	302.9	828.8	9.5	15.2	71.7	206.5	158.0	584.4	78.8	7.5
1994	1,148.4	310.7	837.7	8.9	14.3	70.8	216.6	154.1	595.5	80.1	8.1
1995	1,140.3	315.2	825.0	8.5	13.5	70.2	223.0	148.8	592.7	75.9	7.6
1996	1,081.8	288.6	793.2	7.6	12.8	64.1	204.1	139.1	577.3	69.5	7.2
1997	1,042.9	273.6	769.3	7.0	12.1	51.3	203.2	134.2	564.2	63.3	7.5
1998	954.0	258.8	695.2	6.6	11.8	46.9	193.5	125.5	505.6	57.5	6.5
1999	880.0	244.5	635.5	5.7	10.9	42.8	185.1	112.1	462.2	54.9	6.3
2000	821.8	228.2	593.6	4.8	9.8	39.7	173.9	104.0	429.5	54.2	5.9
2001	807.3	225.6	581.8	4.9	9.6	39.8	171.2	103.3	418.6	53.3	6.6
2002	788.4	217.9	570.5	4.9	9.8	37.7	165.5	100.5	412.0	52.3	5.8

Note: See Note, table 4.1. The number of agencies reporting and the populations represented vary from year to year. Due to National Incident-Based Reporting System conversion efforts beginning in 1991, complete arrest data were not available for a small number of States for certain years. See Appendix 3 for a list of States omitted. Arson was designated an Index property crime in October 1978. Data collection began in 1979. For definitions of offenses, see Appendix 3.

[a]Includes arson beginning in 1979.
[b]Violent crimes are offenses of murder and nonnegligent manslaughter, forcible rape, robbery, and aggravated assault.
[c]Property crimes are offenses of burglary, larceny-theft, motor vehicle theft, and arson.

Source: U.S. Department of Justice, Federal Bureau of Investigation, *Crime in the United States, 1971*, p. 116; *1972*, p. 120; *1973*, p. 122; *1974*, p. 180; *1975*, p. 180; *1976*, p. 173; *1977*, p. 172; *1978*, p. 186; *1979*, p. 188; *1980*, p. 192; *1981*, p. 163; *1982*, p. 168; *1983*, p. 171; *1984*, p. 164; *1985*, p. 165; *1986*, p. 165; *1987*, p. 165; *1988*, p. 169; *1989*, p. 173; *1990*, p. 175; *1991*, p. 214; *1992*, p. 218; *1993*, p. 218; *1994*, p. 218; *1995*, p. 209; *1996*, p. 215; *1997*, p. 223; *1998*, p. 211; *1999*, p. 213; *2000*, p. 217; *2001*, p. 235; *2002*, p. 235 (Washington, DC: USGPO). Table adapted by SOURCEBOOK staff.

Table 4.3

Number and rate (per 100,000 inhabitants) of arrests

By offense charged and size of place, 2002

Offense charged	Total (10,372 agencies; population 205,122,185)	Total city arrests (7,507 cities; population 142,375,961)	Cities Group I (54 cities, 250,000 and over; population 38,631,295)	Group II (134 cities, 100,000 to 249,999; population 20,337,915)	Group III (322 cities, 50,000 to 99,999; population 22,278,495)	Group IV (625 cities, 25,000 to 49,999; population 21,842,796)	Group V (1,368 cities, 10,000 to 24,999; population 21,747,999)	Group VI (5,004 cities under 10,000; population 17,537,461)	Counties Suburban counties[a] (916 agencies; population 40,822,218)	Rural counties (1,949 agencies; population 21,924,006)	Suburban areas[b] (5,060 agencies; population 85,923,394)
Total[c]	9,811,831	7,361,064	2,124,721	994,018	1,094,374	975,460	1,056,146	1,116,345	1,568,199	882,568	3,627,108
Rate per 100,000 inhabitants	4,783.4	5,170.2	5,500.0	4,887.5	4,912.2	4,465.8	4,856.3	6,365.5	3,841.5	4,025.6	4,221.3
Murder and nonnegligent manslaughter	10,107	7,467	4,022	1,093	862	529	471	490	1,754	886	2,660
Rate	4.9	5.2	10.4	5.4	3.9	2.4	2.2	2.8	4.3	4.0	3.1
Forcible rape	20,162	14,515	4,980	2,059	2,062	1,797	1,857	1,760	3,476	2,171	6,893
Rate	9.8	10.2	12.9	10.1	9.3	8.2	8.5	10.0	8.5	9.9	8.0
Robbery	77,342	66,834	29,940	11,185	9,638	6,858	5,682	3,531	8,494	2,014	20,577
Rate	37.7	46.9	77.5	55.0	43.3	31.4	26.1	20.1	20.8	9.2	23.9
Aggravated assault	339,437	260,392	99,328	41,276	37,833	30,000	26,458	25,497	55,158	23,887	110,807
Rate	165.5	182.9	257.1	203.0	169.8	137.3	121.7	145.4	135.1	109.0	129.0
Burglary	206,136	151,343	42,217	25,095	25,204	19,458	19,884	19,485	33,920	20,873	72,415
Rate	100.5	106.3	109.3	123.4	113.1	89.1	91.4	111.1	83.1	95.2	84.3
Larceny-theft	845,009	716,186	188,616	106,453	122,677	108,759	109,372	80,309	95,596	33,227	293,756
Rate	412.0	503.0	488.2	523.4	550.7	497.9	502.9	457.9	234.2	151.6	341.9
Motor vehicle theft	107,187	85,662	42,141	12,934	9,569	6,953	7,058	7,007	15,052	6,473	29,520
Rate	52.3	60.2	109.1	63.6	43.0	31.8	32.5	40.0	36.9	29.5	34.4
Arson	11,833	8,372	2,064	1,242	1,273	1,152	1,371	1,270	2,392	1,069	4,894
Rate	5.8	5.9	5.3	6.1	5.7	5.3	6.3	7.2	5.9	4.9	5.7
Violent crime[d]	447,048	349,208	138,270	55,613	50,395	39,184	34,468	31,278	68,882	28,958	140,937
Rate	217.9	245.3	357.9	273.4	226.2	179.4	158.5	178.3	168.7	132.1	164.0
Property crime[e]	1,170,165	961,563	275,038	145,724	158,723	136,322	137,685	108,071	146,960	61,642	400,585
Rate	570.5	675.4	712.0	716.5	712.4	624.1	633.1	616.2	360.0	281.2	466.2
Total Crime Index[f]	1,617,213	1,310,771	413,308	201,337	209,118	175,506	172,153	139,349	215,842	90,600	541,522
Rate	788.4	920.6	1,069.9	990.0	938.7	803.5	791.6	794.6	528.7	413.2	630.2
Other assaults	921,676	691,820	201,815	103,551	100,389	91,462	96,509	98,094	151,178	78,678	329,934
Rate	449.3	485.9	522.4	509.2	450.6	418.7	443.8	559.3	370.3	358.9	384.0
Forgery and counterfeiting	83,111	63,725	15,285	9,175	10,653	9,329	10,627	8,656	12,866	6,520	30,751
Rate	40.5	44.8	39.6	45.1	47.8	42.7	48.9	49.4	31.5	29.7	35.8
Fraud	233,087	121,969	18,506	13,595	18,624	18,389	25,464	27,391	71,794	39,324	112,608
Rate	113.6	85.7	47.9	66.8	83.6	84.2	117.1	156.2	175.9	179.4	131.1
Embezzlement	13,416	10,337	2,005	1,848	2,209	1,578	1,606	1,091	2,151	928	4,727
Rate	6.5	7.3	5.2	9.1	9.9	7.2	7.4	6.2	5.3	4.2	5.5
Stolen property; buying, receiving, possessing	91,280	71,788	22,776	10,286	12,384	10,287	9,034	7,021	13,977	5,515	33,825
Rate	44.5	50.4	59.0	50.6	55.6	47.1	41.5	40.0	34.2	25.2	39.4
Vandalism	198,550	155,656	40,568	21,305	23,714	21,473	24,252	24,344	27,787	15,107	72,884
Rate	96.8	109.3	105.0	104.8	106.4	98.3	111.5	138.8	68.1	68.9	84.8
Weapons; carrying, possessing, etc.	118,312	93,030	34,824	14,098	13,284	10,551	9,767	10,506	17,307	7,975	38,959
Rate	57.7	65.3	90.1	69.3	59.6	48.3	44.9	59.9	42.4	36.4	45.3
Prostitution and commercialized vice	58,758	56,686	40,661	8,620	4,189	2,062	862	292	1,929	143	4,773
Rate	28.6	39.8	105.3	42.4	18.8	9.4	4.0	1.7	4.7	0.7	5.6
Sex offenses (except forcible rape and prostitution)	67,833	49,745	19,639	6,735	7,164	5,653	5,471	5,083	11,865	6,223	22,771
Rate	33.1	34.9	50.8	33.1	32.2	25.9	25.2	29.0	29.1	28.4	26.5
Drug abuse violations	1,103,017	838,900	305,079	130,137	118,287	97,171	92,402	95,824	172,912	91,205	372,988
Rate	537.7	589.2	789.7	639.9	530.9	444.9	424.9	546.4	423.6	416.0	434.1
Gambling	7,525	6,216	4,222	439	618	264	296	377	658	651	1,281
Rate	3.7	4.4	10.9	2.2	2.8	1.2	1.4	2.1	1.6	3.0	1.5
Offenses against family and children	97,716	53,532	10,108	6,588	9,340	9,117	9,656	8,723	29,443	14,741	47,539
Rate	47.6	37.6	26.2	32.4	41.9	41.7	44.4	49.7	72.1	67.2	55.3
Driving under the influence	1,020,377	632,092	133,013	70,136	84,470	93,099	115,918	135,456	215,764	172,521	442,751
Rate	497.4	444.0	344.3	344.9	379.2	426.2	533.0	772.4	528.5	786.9	515.3
Liquor laws	463,849	368,132	60,397	36,373	53,809	46,070	69,035	102,448	49,729	45,988	176,569
Rate	226.1	258.6	156.3	178.8	241.5	210.9	317.4	584.2	121.8	209.8	205.5
Drunkenness	413,808	347,469	83,907	49,505	51,344	49,840	53,590	59,283	41,471	24,868	140,222
Rate	201.7	244.1	217.2	243.4	230.5	228.2	246.4	338.0	101.6	113.4	163.2
Disorderly conduct	482,827	415,817	101,985	43,442	62,883	53,946	71,839	81,722	40,754	26,256	174,655
Rate	235.4	292.1	264.0	213.6	282.3	247.0	330.3	466.0	99.8	119.8	203.3
Vagrancy	19,678	17,378	9,294	1,995	1,621	946	1,388	2,134	1,713	587	4,941
Rate	9.6	12.2	24.1	9.8	7.3	4.3	6.4	12.2	4.2	2.7	5.8

See notes at end of table.

Table 4.3

Number and rate (per 100,000 inhabitants) of arrests

By offense charged and size of place, 2002--Continued

		Cities							Counties		
Offense charged	Total (10,372 agencies; population 205,122,185)	Total city arrests (7,507 cities; population 142,375,961)	Group I (54 cities, 250,000 and over; population 38,631,295)	Group II (134 cities, 100,000 to 249,999; population 20,337,915)	Group III (322 cities, 50,000 to 99,999; population 22,278,495)	Group IV (625 cities, 25,000 to 49,999; population 21,842,796)	Group V (1,368 cities, 10,000 to 24,999; population 21,747,999)	Group VI (5,004 cities under 10,000; population 17,537,461)	Suburban counties[a] (916 agencies; population 40,822,218)	Rural counties (1,949 agencies; population 21,924,006)	Suburban areas[b] (5,060 agencies; population 85,923,394)
All other offenses (except traffic)	2,606,294	1,892,117	541,924	245,919	284,227	261,584	265,427	293,036	466,910	247,267	1,018,349
Rate	1,270.6	1,329.0	1,402.8	1,209.2	1,275.8	1,197.6	1,220.5	1,670.9	1,143.8	1,127.8	1,185.2
Suspicion (not included in totals)	7,670	6,781	4,887	274	315	224	593	488	730	159	1,617
Rate	3.7	4.8	12.7	1.3	1.4	1.0	2.7	2.8	1.8	0.7	1.9
Curfew and loitering law violations	103,155	97,467	49,158	6,936	13,397	7,998	10,888	9,090	4,654	1,034	22,511
Rate	50.3	68.5	127.2	34.1	60.1	36.6	50.1	51.8	11.4	4.7	26.2
Runaways	90,349	66,417	16,247	11,998	12,650	9,135	9,962	6,425	17,495	6,437	32,548
Rate	44.0	46.6	42.1	59.0	56.8	41.8	45.8	36.6	42.9	29.4	37.9

Note: See Note, table 4.1. This table presents data from all law enforcement agencies submitting complete reports for 12 months in 2002 (Source, p. 451). Population figures are estimates calculated from U.S. Census Bureau data. For definitions of offenses, suburban areas, and rural counties, see Appendix 3.

[a] Includes only suburban county law enforcement agencies.
[b] Includes law enforcement agencies in cities with less than 50,000 inhabitants and county law enforcement agencies that are within a Metropolitan Statistical Area; excludes all metropolitan agencies associated with a central city. The agencies associated with suburban areas also will appear in other groups within this table.

[c] Does not include suspicion.
[d] Violent crimes are offenses of murder and nonnegligent manslaughter, forcible rape, robbery, and aggravated assault.
[e] Property crimes are offenses of burglary, larceny-theft, motor vehicle theft, and arson.
[f] Includes arson.

Source: U.S. Department of Justice, Federal Bureau of Investigation, *Crime in the United States, 2002* (Washington, DC: USGPO, 2003), pp. 236, 237.

Table 4.4

Percent distribution of total U.S. population and persons arrested for all offenses

By age group, United States, 2002

Age group	U.S. resident population	Persons arrested
14 years and younger	21.0%	5.2%
15 to 19 years	7.1	21.3
20 to 24 years	7.0	19.9
25 to 29 years	6.6	12.3
30 to 34 years	7.3	10.9
35 to 39 years	7.6	10.4
40 to 44 years	8.0	8.9
45 to 49 years	7.4	5.5
50 to 54 years	6.5	2.9
55 to 59 years	5.2	1.4
60 to 64 years	4.0	0.6
65 years and older	12.3	0.6

Note: See Note, table 4.1. This table presents data from all law enforcement agencies submitting complete reports for 12 months in 2002 (Source, U.S. Department of Justice, p. 452). Because of rounding, percents may not add to 100.

Source: U.S. Department of Justice, Federal Bureau of Investigation, *Crime in the United States, 2002* (Washington, DC: USGPO, 2003), pp. 244, 245; and U.S. Department of Commerce, U.S. Census Bureau [Online]. Available: http://www.census.gov/popest/archives/2000s/vintage_2002/NA-EST2002-ASRO-01.html [Sept. 10, 2004]. Table constructed by SOURCEBOOK staff.

Table 4.5

Arrests

By offense charged, age group, and State, 2002

State	Total all offenses[a]	Total Crime Index[b]	Violent crime[c]	Property crime[d]	Murder and non-negligent man-slaughter	Forcible rape	Robbery	Aggravated assault	Burglary	Larceny-theft	Motor vehicle theft	Arson
Alabama: 279 agencies; population 3,782,265:												
Under 18	11,861	3,912	592	3,320	26	36	231	299	486	2,650	163	21
Total all ages	195,820	25,619	6,730	18,889	300	370	1,709	4,351	2,849	14,691	1,242	107
Alaska: 27 agencies; population 585,475:												
Under 18	5,102	2,212	216	1,996	3	14	38	161	260	1,501	225	10
Total all ages	31,730	5,626	1,272	4,354	27	78	144	1,023	492	3,401	442	19
Arizona: 84 agencies; population 5,164,982:												
Under 18	50,583	13,508	1,592	11,916	19	17	266	1,290	1,638	8,918	1,189	171
Total all ages	298,631	48,900	9,040	39,860	271	191	1,497	7,081	4,903	29,643	5,055	259
Arkansas: 93 agencies; population 1,404,187:												
Under 18	9,410	2,517	272	2,245	1	8	56	207	284	1,890	63	8
Total all ages	107,467	11,877	2,903	8,974	48	93	443	2,319	1,234	7,333	349	58
California: 681 agencies; population 34,678,046:												
Under 18	227,266	66,812	15,351	51,461	216	344	4,455	10,336	14,498	29,248	6,610	1,105
Total all ages	1,412,566	298,772	128,951	169,821	1,865	2,541	16,838	107,707	48,759	92,024	27,177	1,861
Colorado: 144 agencies; population 3,653,314:												
Under 18	44,035	10,300	973	9,327	8	55	183	727	994	6,765	1,373	195
Total all ages	222,108	33,788	5,842	27,946	120	436	800	4,486	2,841	21,889	2,895	321
Connecticut: 88 agencies; population 2,420,548:												
Under 18	14,345	3,795	556	3,239	2	38	162	354	490	2,402	269	78
Total all ages	99,005	17,013	3,753	13,260	52	221	1,015	2,465	1,893	10,285	943	139
Delaware: 36 agencies; population 687,929:												
Under 18	5,206	1,288	245	1,043	2	21	57	165	258	702	55	28
Total all ages	25,217	4,986	1,228	3,758	12	117	231	868	826	2,729	156	47
District of Columbia[e]: 2 agencies;												
Under 18	277	62	23	39	0	0	13	10	2	8	29	0
Total all ages	4,303	140	63	77	0	0	26	37	2	34	41	0
Florida: 595 agencies; population 16,589,355:												
Under 18	123,260	47,936	9,222	38,714	44	310	2,120	6,748	9,542	24,824	4,103	245
Total all ages	912,998	182,530	53,630	128,900	730	2,218	9,470	41,212	27,271	88,464	12,593	572
Georgia: 271 agencies; population 4,188,014:												
Under 18	26,900	7,792	1,295	6,497	69	43	356	827	1,150	4,752	529	66
Total all ages	232,233	39,589	11,249	28,340	493	377	2,168	8,211	4,647	21,408	2,023	262
Hawaii: 2 agencies; population 960,506:												
Under 18	9,850	1,997	292	1,705	0	13	167	112	158	1,344	193	10
Total all ages	45,929	6,970	1,148	5,822	26	122	432	568	569	4,028	1,201	24
Idaho: 111 agencies; population 1,303,441:												
Under 18	16,699	4,004	260	3,744	3	17	24	216	421	3,060	181	82
Total all ages	72,595	9,121	1,362	7,759	33	107	135	1,087	1,027	6,229	395	108
Illinois[f]: 1 agency; population 2,938,299:												
Under 18	38,810	10,983	3,062	7,921	49	119	1,180	1,714	1,225	3,170	3,459	67
Total all ages	199,430	41,490	9,885	31,605	520	630	2,995	5,740	3,395	18,487	9,542	181
Indiana: 149 agencies; population 4,227,126:												
Under 18	33,841	8,426	1,681	6,745	15	39	209	1,418	847	5,309	511	78
Total all ages	196,964	32,336	10,730	21,606	250	222	1,403	8,855	3,174	16,504	1,771	157

See notes at end of table.

Table 4.5
Arrests

By offense charged, age group, and State, 2002--Continued

State	Total all offenses[a]	Total Crime Index[b]	Violent crime[c]	Property crime[d]	Murder and non-negligent man-slaughter	Forcible rape	Robbery	Aggravated assault	Burglary	Larceny-theft	Motor vehicle theft	Arson
Iowa: 192 agencies; population 2,665,086:												
Under 18	20,944	6,587	731	5,856	8	25	81	617	748	4,707	298	103
Total all ages	112,438	18,840	4,198	14,642	47	112	413	3,626	2,021	11,830	639	152
Kansas: 183 agencies; population 1,318,620:												
Under 18	9,500	2,154	262	1,892	2	28	25	207	317	1,415	114	46
Total all ages	54,136	6,050	1,251	4,799	19	98	97	1,037	751	3,734	242	72
Kentucky[f]: 18 agencies; population 953,247:												
Under 18	5,717	1,925	289	1,636	1	4	73	211	332	1,091	191	22
Total all ages	61,176	10,226	3,202	7,024	51	99	524	2,528	1,255	4,916	800	53
Louisiana: 153 agencies; population 3,185,679:												
Under 18	35,560	9,132	1,550	7,582	21	95	252	1,192	1,597	5,601	287	97
Total all ages	216,444	39,138	10,157	28,981	288	512	1,282	8,075	5,339	22,164	1,256	222
Maine: 180 agencies; population 1,291,128:												
Under 18	9,277	2,968	140	2,828	0	24	39	77	577	2,022	192	37
Total all ages	54,880	8,171	787	7,384	5	126	170	486	1,477	5,436	403	68
Maryland: 139 agencies; population 3,197,675:												
Under 18	25,518	7,229	1,119	6,110	3	45	362	709	1,233	4,097	595	185
Total all ages	161,317	24,028	5,497	18,531	85	263	1,220	3,929	3,366	13,284	1,570	311
Massachusetts: 239 agencies; population 4,660,489:												
Under 18	17,395	5,576	2,098	3,478	5	42	385	1,666	736	2,354	347	41
Total all ages	114,657	26,930	11,348	15,582	79	384	1,545	9,340	2,791	11,760	923	108
Michigan: 557 agencies; population 9,625,166:												
Under 18	46,096	13,115	1,986	11,129	21	161	360	1,444	1,732	8,442	824	131
Total all ages	371,037	51,794	18,103	33,691	607	1,008	2,560	13,928	6,043	25,140	2,075	433
Minnesota: 302 agencies; population 4,155,118:												
Under 18	42,874	10,997	906	10,091	17	141	116	632	990	8,391	604	106
Total all ages	164,144	26,316	3,697	22,619	73	614	457	2,553	2,516	18,614	1,329	160
Mississippi: 92 agencies; population 1,542,712:												
Under 18	14,003	3,458	223	3,235	10	25	100	88	632	2,405	168	30
Total all ages	116,670	15,033	2,414	12,619	135	238	653	1,388	2,290	9,451	641	237
Missouri: 302 agencies; population 4,763,516:												
Under 18	38,813	10,907	1,637	9,270	32	98	358	1,149	1,470	6,512	1,075	213
Total all ages	304,921	54,487	15,112	39,375	393	582	2,180	11,957	5,937	29,220	3,686	532
Montana: 67 agencies; population 598,495:												
Under 18	5,953	1,656	111	1,545	1	3	12	95	114	1,296	117	18
Total all ages	21,579	4,440	782	3,658	10	33	64	675	271	3,127	234	26
Nebraska: 224 agencies; population 1,570,139:												
Under 18	15,772	4,404	198	4,206	4	11	85	98	332	3,561	231	82
Total all ages	93,355	11,970	1,333	10,637	42	149	332	810	953	9,075	490	119
Nevada[f]: 3 agencies; population 1,540,614:												
Under 18	12,489	4,072	390	3,682	9	19	210	152	451	2,765	432	34
Total all ages	115,128	18,783	2,761	16,022	85	172	1,142	1,362	3,943	10,186	1,833	60
New Hampshire: 113 agencies; population 819,288:												
Under 18	7,165	1,146	115	1,031	0	12	17	86	187	757	61	26
Total all ages	34,348	2,896	518	2,378	5	64	93	356	421	1,792	124	41

See notes at end of table.

Table 4.5

Arrests

By offense charged, age group, and State, 2002--Continued

State	Total all offenses[a]	Total Crime Index[b]	Violent crime[c]	Property crime[d]	Murder and non-negligent man-slaughter	Forcible rape	Robbery	Aggravated assault	Burglary	Larceny-theft	Motor vehicle theft	Arson
New Jersey: 525 agencies; population 8,312,552:												
Under 18	62,093	13,027	3,309	9,718	22	123	1,261	1,903	1,914	6,978	558	268
Total all ages	368,619	51,333	15,268	36,065	253	640	4,203	10,172	6,344	27,716	1,566	439
New Mexico: 53 agencies; population 1,187,172:												
Under 18	9,201	2,181	461	1,720	7	24	52	378	235	1,340	133	12
Total all ages	76,539	8,677	3,014	5,663	81	130	361	2,442	926	4,304	392	41
New York[g]: 361 agencies; population 6,333,908:												
Under 18	43,790	12,590	2,196	10,394	24	75	730	1,367	2,183	7,075	914	222
Total all ages	264,833	47,530	11,190	36,340	208	587	2,535	7,860	6,138	27,418	2,380	404
North Carolina: 356 agencies; population 6,907,574:												
Under 18	45,879	14,336	2,370	11,966	50	69	658	1,593	2,863	8,414	514	175
Total all ages	447,259	76,017	21,729	54,288	622	685	3,768	16,654	13,929	37,819	2,115	425
North Dakota: 65 agencies; population 569,346:												
Under 18	7,025	1,420	39	1,381	0	15	8	16	151	1,074	143	13
Total all ages	25,221	2,810	161	2,649	6	32	20	103	276	2,113	237	23
Ohio: 317 agencies; population 6,468,915:												
Under 18	46,858	9,741	1,397	8,344	16	152	370	859	1,560	5,866	718	200
Total all ages	247,868	38,944	9,534	29,410	200	687	1,892	6,755	5,210	22,081	1,733	386
Oklahoma: 297 agencies; population 3,424,485:												
Under 18	22,805	6,770	958	5,812	13	55	157	733	978	4,205	528	101
Total all ages	161,363	22,663	6,098	16,565	173	426	745	4,754	3,013	11,577	1,739	236
Oregon: 125 agencies; population 2,943,092:												
Under 18	24,840	6,500	440	6,060	5	27	146	262	818	4,614	466	162
Total all ages	111,337	25,543	2,795	22,748	77	220	881	1,617	2,554	17,514	2,454	226
Pennsylvania: 728 agencies; population 10,433,778:												
Under 18	100,243	19,298	4,641	14,657	38	283	1,504	2,816	2,770	9,615	1,922	350
Total all ages	421,600	74,338	23,269	51,069	492	1,362	6,196	15,219	9,663	35,048	5,571	787
Rhode Island: 47 agencies; population 1,046,290:												
Under 18	7,681	1,902	284	1,618	7	22	70	185	317	1,054	161	86
Total all ages	42,140	6,034	1,259	4,775	27	123	254	855	842	3,458	366	109
South Carolina[f]: 109 agencies; population 2,223,424:												
Under 18	15,696	4,804	1,000	3,804	19	59	155	767	716	2,817	217	54
Total all ages	120,025	20,597	6,613	13,984	171	317	873	5,252	2,552	10,651	647	134
South Dakota: 82 agencies; population 527,406:												
Under 18	5,954	1,144	52	1,092	0	4	2	46	167	848	53	24
Total all ages	28,112	2,917	494	2,423	6	82	30	376	405	1,854	132	32
Tennessee: 337 agencies; population 4,936,496:												
Under 18	26,686	5,963	1,065	4,898	11	48	192	814	704	3,735	409	50
Total all ages	234,995	36,020	11,267	24,753	284	332	1,224	9,427	3,566	18,797	2,113	277
Texas: 948 agencies; population 21,447,682:												
Under 18	180,017	42,091	5,175	36,916	67	420	1,449	3,239	6,419	27,717	2,432	348
Total all ages	1,036,323	154,229	31,844	122,385	801	2,310	6,865	21,868	18,498	93,853	9,187	847
Utah: 107 agencies; population 2,201,721:												
Under 18	28,450	7,658	506	7,152	8	42	64	392	488	6,224	338	102
Total all ages	121,200	20,091	1,768	18,323	48	163	291	1,266	1,488	15,821	857	157

See notes at end of table.

Table 4.5

Arrests

By offense charged, age group, and State, 2002--Continued

State	Total all offenses[a]	Total Crime Index[b]	Violent crime[c]	Property crime[d]	Murder and non-negligent manslaughter	Forcible rape	Robbery	Aggravated assault	Burglary	Larceny-theft	Motor vehicle theft	Arson
Vermont: 48 agencies; population 532,178:												
Under 18	1,851	489	29	460	0	8	0	21	108	298	50	4
Total all ages	13,757	1,826	334	1,492	9	62	2	261	305	1,054	114	19
Virginia: 279 agencies; population 6,286,697:												
Under 18	32,989	6,927	897	6,030	17	57	247	576	903	4,449	481	197
Total all ages	251,047	30,532	6,276	24,256	222	405	1,341	4,308	3,525	18,915	1,449	367
Washington: 208 agencies; population 5,108,516:												
Under 18	38,772	13,456	1,370	12,086	9	167	388	806	1,943	9,038	900	205
Total all ages	237,512	42,765	7,133	35,632	102	837	1,541	4,653	5,088	27,988	2,195	361
West Virginia: 249 agencies; population 918,517:												
Under 18	1,739	566	51	515	1	2	7	41	99	353	53	10
Total all ages	25,781	3,508	848	2,660	25	37	56	730	481	1,939	198	42
Wisconsin: 337 agencies; population 4,944,040:												
Under 18	114,131	20,771	2,040	18,731	112	209	566	1,153	2,243	15,188	1,133	167
Total all ages	409,682	52,229	10,219	42,010	351	708	1,655	7,505	4,994	34,546	2,146	324
Wyoming: 62 agencies; population 487,292:												
Under 18	6,231	1,039	63	976	0	3	5	55	105	824	36	11
Total all ages	34,060	3,281	619	2,662	8	58	41	512	354	2,129	119	60

Note: See Note, table 4.1. This table presents data from all law enforcement agencies submitting complete reports for 12 months in 2002 (Source, p. 453). Complete data were not available for the District of Columbia, Illinois, Kentucky, Nevada, South Carolina, and New York City. Data displayed for these jurisdictions are for a limited number of agencies. Population figures are estimates calculated from U.S. Census Bureau data. Direct comparisons of arrest totals listed in this table should not be made with prior years (Source, p. 298). For definitions of offenses, see Appendix 3.

[a]Does not include traffic arrests. For a list of included offenses, see table 4.1.
[b]Includes arson.
[c]Violent crimes are offenses of murder and nonnegligent manslaughter, forcible rape, robbery, and aggravated assault.
[d]Property crimes are offenses of burglary, larceny-theft, motor vehicle theft, and arson.
[e]Includes arrests reported by the Zoological Police and the Metro Transit Police only; these agencies have no population associated with them.
[f]Limited number of agencies reporting for 2002.
[g]Complete 12-month arrest figures for New York City were not available for 2002.

Source: U.S. Department of Justice, Federal Bureau of Investigation, *Crime in the United States, 2002* (Washington, DC: USGPO, 2003), pp. 292-299.

Page 352 intentionally left blank.

Table 4.6
Arrests

By offense charged and age group, United States, 1993 and 2002

(7,596 agencies; 1993 estimated population 157,011,564; 2002 estimated population 175,384,794)

Offense charged	Total all ages 1993	Total all ages 2002	Percent change	Under 18 years of age 1993	Under 18 years of age 2002	Percent change	18 years of age and older 1993	18 years of age and older 2002	Percent change
Total[a]	8,581,290	8,413,983	-1.9%	1,564,326	1,393,752	-10.9%	7,016,964	7,020,231	(b)
Murder and nonnegligent manslaughter	15,125	8,933	-40.9	2,485	886	-64.3	12,640	8,047	-36.3%
Forcible rape	23,509	17,394	-26.0	3,928	2,887	-26.5	19,581	14,507	-25.9
Robbery	96,877	69,405	-28.4	26,505	16,338	-38.4	70,372	53,067	-24.6
Aggravated assault	320,814	299,286	-6.7	49,427	38,082	-23.0	271,387	261,204	-3.8
Burglary	253,751	178,477	-29.7	89,511	54,393	-39.2	164,240	124,084	-24.4
Larceny-theft	959,452	729,825	-23.9	307,926	216,434	-29.7	651,526	513,391	-21.2
Motor vehicle theft	128,552	94,608	-26.4	57,740	28,664	-50.4	70,812	65,944	-6.9
Arson	12,646	10,055	-20.5	6,451	4,957	-23.2	6,195	5,098	-17.7
Violent crime[c]	456,325	395,018	-13.4	82,345	58,193	-29.3	373,980	336,825	-9.9
Property crime[d]	1,354,401	1,012,965	-25.2	461,628	304,448	-34.0	892,773	708,517	-20.6
Total Crime Index[e]	1,810,726	1,407,983	-22.2	543,973	362,641	-33.3	1,266,753	1,045,342	-17.5
Other assaults	733,037	782,294	6.7	126,489	143,933	13.8	606,548	638,361	5.2
Forgery and counterfeiting	66,364	71,842	8.3	5,341	3,070	-42.5	61,023	68,772	12.7
Fraud	218,695	195,925	-10.4	6,449	5,258	-18.5	212,246	190,667	-10.2
Embezzlement	7,910	11,815	49.4	510	883	73.1	7,400	10,932	47.7
Stolen property; buying, receiving, possessing	101,613	76,137	-25.1	28,808	15,766	-45.3	72,805	60,371	-17.1
Vandalism	209,095	169,842	-18.8	97,968	65,360	-33.3	111,127	104,482	-6.0
Weapons; carrying, possessing, etc.	175,998	104,418	-40.7	42,530	22,615	-46.8	133,468	81,803	-38.7
Prostitution and commercialized vice	61,811	51,275	-17.0	755	958	26.9	61,056	50,317	-17.6
Sex offenses (except forcible rape and prostitution)	69,072	59,193	-14.3	13,387	12,198	-8.9	55,685	46,995	-15.6
Drug abuse violations	710,922	974,082	37.0	73,413	116,781	59.1	637,509	857,301	34.5
Gambling	10,348	6,500	-37.2	1,715	1,053	-38.6	8,633	5,447	-36.9
Offenses against family and children	67,930	79,059	16.4	3,520	5,208	48.0	64,410	73,851	14.7
Driving under the influence	984,141	879,210	-10.7	8,878	12,921	45.5	975,263	866,289	-11.2
Liquor laws	316,919	385,611	21.7	75,836	88,574	16.8	241,083	297,037	23.2
Drunkenness	509,543	362,979	-28.8	11,705	11,452	-2.2	497,838	351,527	-29.4
Disorderly conduct	483,676	398,728	-17.6	103,747	112,844	8.8	379,929	285,884	-24.8
Vagrancy	13,581	15,702	15.6	2,254	1,346	-40.3	11,327	14,356	26.7
All other offenses (except traffic)	1,834,511	2,209,668	20.4	221,650	239,171	7.9	1,612,861	1,970,497	22.2
Suspicion (not included in totals)	6,231	2,252	-63.9	1,239	708	-42.9	4,992	1,544	-69.1
Curfew and loitering law violations	68,042	91,984	35.2	68,042	91,984	35.2	X	X	X
Runaways	127,356	79,736	-37.4	127,356	79,736	-37.4	X	X	X

Note: See Note, table 4.1. This table presents data from all law enforcement agencies submitting complete reports for 12 months in 1993 and 2002 (Source, p. 451). Population figures are estimates calculated from U.S. Census Bureau data. For definitions of offenses, see Appendix 3.

[a]Does not include suspicion.
[b]Less than 0.1%.
[c]Violent crimes are offenses of murder and nonnegligent manslaughter, forcible rape, robbery, and aggravated assault.
[d]Property crimes are offenses of burglary, larceny-theft, motor vehicle theft, and arson.
[e]Includes arson.

Source: U.S. Department of Justice, Federal Bureau of Investigation, *Crime in the United States, 2002* (Washington, DC: USGPO, 2003), p. 238.

Table 4.7

Arrests

By offense charged and age, United States, 2002

(10,372 agencies; 2002 estimated population 205,122,185)

Offense charged	Total all ages	Under 15 years	Under 18 years	18 years and older	Under 10 years	10 to 12 years	13 to 14 years	15 years	16 years	17 years	18 years	19 years
Total	9,819,501	510,226	1,624,192	8,195,309	19,904	120,097	370,225	306,678	381,909	425,379	478,836	502,251
Percent[a]	100.0%	5.2	16.5	83.5	0.2	1.2	3.8	3.1	3.9	4.3	4.9	5.1
Murder and nonnegligent manslaughter	10,107	101	973	9,134	0	17	84	140	274	458	568	676
Forcible rape	20,162	1,243	3,361	16,801	42	336	865	562	672	884	1,028	1,029
Robbery	77,342	4,323	17,893	59,449	85	789	3,449	3,408	4,532	5,630	6,228	5,617
Aggravated assault	339,437	15,846	44,281	295,156	699	4,350	10,797	7,948	9,722	10,765	12,052	12,786
Burglary	206,136	22,389	61,843	144,293	1,153	5,804	15,432	11,515	13,349	14,590	15,620	13,143
Larceny-theft	845,009	95,090	248,861	596,148	3,538	25,799	65,753	46,317	53,323	54,131	51,524	43,421
Motor vehicle theft	107,187	8,227	32,544	74,643	65	1,006	7,156	7,698	8,531	8,088	7,766	6,763
Arson	11,833	3,728	5,851	5,982	552	1,350	1,826	855	671	597	494	435
Violent crime[b]	447,048	21,513	66,508	380,540	826	5,492	15,195	12,058	15,200	17,737	19,876	20,108
Percent[a]	100.0%	4.8	14.9	85.1	0.2	1.2	3.4	2.7	3.4	4.0	4.4	4.5
Property crime[c]	1,170,165	129,434	349,099	821,066	5,308	33,959	90,167	66,385	75,874	77,406	75,404	63,762
Percent[a]	100.0%	11.1	29.8	70.2	0.5	2.9	7.7	5.7	6.5	6.6	6.4	5.4
Total Crime Index[d]	1,617,213	150,947	415,607	1,201,606	6,134	39,451	105,362	78,443	91,074	95,143	95,280	83,870
Percent[a]	100.0%	9.3	25.7	74.3	0.4	2.4	6.5	4.9	5.6	5.9	5.9	5.2
Other assaults	921,676	71,697	168,996	752,680	2,813	20,123	48,761	31,230	33,653	32,416	29,604	30,983
Forgery and counterfeiting	83,111	457	3,652	79,459	34	70	353	479	984	1,732	3,391	4,186
Fraud	233,087	1,178	6,434	226,653	102	225	851	885	1,611	2,760	5,610	8,342
Embezzlement	13,416	90	1,005	12,411	2	20	68	72	259	584	876	926
Stolen property; buying, receiving, possessing	91,280	5,044	18,819	72,461	138	982	3,924	3,550	4,600	5,625	6,133	5,937
Vandalism	198,550	32,888	75,955	122,595	2,565	10,049	20,274	13,179	14,988	14,900	13,082	10,862
Weapons; carrying, possessing, etc.	118,312	8,647	25,288	93,024	438	2,166	6,043	4,615	5,379	6,647	7,509	7,177
Prostitution and commercialized vice	58,758	165	1,095	57,663	2	24	139	170	281	479	1,567	1,802
Sex offenses (except forcible rape and prostitution)	67,833	7,226	13,877	53,956	427	2,144	4,655	2,352	2,128	2,171	2,565	2,534
Drug abuse violations	1,103,017	21,836	133,754	969,263	284	2,609	18,943	23,031	36,904	51,983	70,713	72,105
Gambling	7,525	171	1,114	6,411	0	32	139	200	308	435	456	486
Offenses against family and children	97,716	2,442	6,572	91,144	343	612	1,487	1,279	1,406	1,445	1,959	2,232
Driving under the influence	1,020,377	370	15,214	1,005,163	113	23	234	631	3,810	10,403	24,662	33,317
Liquor laws	463,849	10,132	106,014	357,835	152	752	9,228	15,826	30,702	49,354	76,275	81,666
Drunkenness	413,808	1,679	13,529	400,279	87	143	1,449	2,101	3,245	6,504	12,401	13,721
Disorderly conduct	482,827	56,314	139,048	343,779	1,487	14,502	40,325	27,667	27,941	27,126	23,628	21,274
Vagrancy	19,678	402	1,519	18,159	10	62	330	297	369	451	685	581
All other offenses (except traffic)	2,606,294	76,025	282,025	2,324,269	3,118	15,459	57,448	54,407	70,007	81,586	102,123	119,925
Suspicion	7,670	294	1,171	6,499	6	52	236	220	298	359	317	325
Curfew and loitering law violations	103,155	29,070	103,155	X	523	5,127	23,420	23,323	29,066	21,696	X	X
Runaways	90,349	33,152	90,349	X	1,126	5,470	26,556	22,721	22,896	11,580	X	X

Note: See Note, table 4.1. This table presents data from all law enforcement agencies submitting complete reports for 12 months in 2002 (Source, p. 452). Population figures are estimates calculated from U.S. Census Bureau data. For definitions of offenses, see Appendix 3.

[a]Because of rounding, percents may not add to total.
[b]Violent crimes are offenses of murder and nonnegligent manslaughter, forcible rape, robbery, and aggravated assault.
[c]Property crimes are offenses of burglary, larceny-theft, motor vehicle theft, and arson.
[d]Includes arson.

Source: U.S. Department of Justice, Federal Bureau of Investigation, *Crime in the United States, 2002* (Washington, DC: USGPO, 2003), pp. 244, 245.

20 years	21 years	22 years	23 years	24 years	25 to 29 years	30 to 34 years	35 to 39 years	40 to 44 years	45 to 49 years	50 to 54 years	55 to 59 years	60 to 64 years	65 years and older
472,286	425,790	393,201	346,552	312,996	1,212,258	1,073,614	1,023,543	876,049	543,956	281,008	132,915	61,634	58,420
4.8	4.3	4.0	3.5	3.2	12.3	10.9	10.4	8.9	5.5	2.9	1.4	0.6	0.6
698	658	575	542	471	1,590	999	783	591	455	230	144	69	85
906	901	722	733	622	2,465	2,429	2,158	1,622	994	520	304	166	202
4,671	4,187	3,445	2,933	2,486	8,624	7,322	6,179	4,417	2,051	789	291	113	96
13,018	13,725	13,437	12,393	11,708	48,211	43,290	40,344	33,587	20,285	10,299	5,054	2,434	2,533
10,280	8,856	7,520	6,274	5,588	20,067	17,854	16,388	12,323	6,379	2,479	903	317	302
34,862	29,605	26,005	22,331	19,294	77,250	75,980	74,348	62,966	39,451	20,386	9,403	4,527	4,795
5,550	4,795	4,235	3,565	3,176	11,525	9,745	8,067	5,213	2,582	1,048	395	134	84
328	274	245	201	194	781	735	754	649	450	232	107	61	42
19,293	19,471	18,179	16,601	15,287	60,890	54,040	49,464	40,217	23,785	11,838	5,793	2,782	2,916
4.3	4.4	4.1	3.7	3.4	13.6	12.1	11.1	9.0	5.3	2.6	1.3	0.6	0.7
51,020	43,530	38,005	32,371	28,252	109,623	104,314	99,557	81,151	48,862	24,145	10,808	5,039	5,223
4.4	3.7	3.2	2.8	2.4	9.4	8.9	8.5	6.9	4.2	2.1	0.9	0.4	0.4
70,313	63,001	56,184	48,972	43,539	170,513	158,354	149,021	121,368	72,647	35,983	16,601	7,821	8,139
4.3	3.9	3.5	3.0	2.7	10.5	9.8	9.2	7.5	4.5	2.2	1.0	0.5	0.5
31,671	34,362	33,987	31,248	29,302	121,664	113,791	107,750	88,571	51,417	25,272	11,800	5,494	5,764
4,508	4,066	3,967	3,721	3,350	14,226	12,699	10,649	7,633	4,079	1,884	647	259	194
9,519	9,377	9,837	9,016	8,579	39,305	38,137	33,058	25,363	15,175	7,813	3,986	1,776	1,760
774	718	604	524	460	1,890	1,661	1,488	1,172	620	382	194	84	38
5,175	4,527	3,967	3,330	2,990	11,006	9,500	8,068	6,194	3,266	1,437	526	226	179
8,599	8,437	7,129	5,918	4,944	17,588	14,125	12,420	9,567	5,224	2,476	1,138	500	586
6,517	6,263	5,634	4,888	4,182	14,878	10,399	8,515	6,861	4,620	2,697	1,466	681	737
1,795	1,888	1,937	1,878	1,856	8,358	10,545	10,600	8,110	4,166	1,691	733	348	389
2,337	2,281	1,964	1,857	1,634	6,701	7,014	7,335	6,288	4,380	2,734	1,814	1,147	1,371
65,632	58,791	53,195	45,625	40,327	147,495	120,515	110,963	93,072	54,064	23,606	8,348	3,024	1,788
440	377	354	339	279	888	571	500	471	368	330	214	165	173
2,464	2,977	3,131	3,050	3,181	15,448	16,326	16,144	12,502	6,566	2,912	1,223	536	493
37,656	50,189	48,676	44,500	40,684	156,792	134,311	128,625	120,640	83,515	49,980	26,735	13,114	11,767
67,454	13,320	9,180	6,662	5,554	18,374	15,404	17,138	17,855	13,396	7,935	4,089	1,907	1,626
13,853	18,425	16,684	14,456	12,982	50,553	47,954	55,553	57,678	41,299	23,422	11,523	5,561	4,214
20,047	22,963	19,922	16,285	14,034	48,603	39,438	39,193	35,128	21,893	11,175	5,236	2,548	2,412
540	551	525	475	418	1,820	2,090	2,597	3,108	2,257	1,338	695	284	195
122,713	122,989	116,063	103,558	94,428	365,226	319,836	303,002	253,687	154,460	77,702	35,864	16,127	16,566
279	288	261	250	273	930	944	924	781	544	239	83	32	29
X	X	X	X	X	X	X	X	X	X	X	X	X	X
X	X	X	X	X	X	X	X	X	X	X	X	X	X

Characteristics and distribution of persons arrested 355

Table 4.8
Arrests

By offense charged and sex, United States, 2002

(10,372 agencies; 2002 estimated population 205,122,185)

Offense charged	Total number	Male Number	Male Percent	Female Number	Female Percent	Percent distribution of offenses charged[a] Total	Male	Female
Total	9,819,501	7,559,435	77.0%	2,260,066	23.0%	100.0%	100.0%	100.0%
Murder and nonnegligent manslaughter	10,107	9,015	89.2	1,092	10.8	0.1	0.1	(b)
Forcible rape	20,162	19,884	98.6	278	1.4	0.2	0.3	(b)
Robbery	77,342	69,369	89.7	7,973	10.3	0.8	0.9	0.4
Aggravated assault	339,437	270,905	79.8	68,532	20.2	3.5	3.6	3.0
Burglary	206,136	178,806	86.7	27,330	13.3	2.1	2.4	1.2
Larceny-theft	845,009	532,274	63.0	312,735	37.0	8.6	7.0	13.8
Motor vehicle theft	107,187	89,463	83.5	17,724	16.5	1.1	1.2	0.8
Arson	11,833	10,031	84.8	1,802	15.2	0.1	0.1	0.1
Violent crime[c]	447,048	369,173	82.6	77,875	17.4	4.6	4.9	3.4
Property crime[d]	1,170,165	810,574	69.3	359,591	30.7	11.9	10.7	15.9
Total Crime Index[e]	1,617,213	1,179,747	72.9	437,466	27.1	16.5	15.6	19.4
Other assaults	921,676	701,562	76.1	220,114	23.9	9.4	9.3	9.7
Forgery and counterfeiting	83,111	49,788	59.9	33,323	40.1	0.8	0.7	1.5
Fraud	233,087	127,896	54.9	105,191	45.1	2.4	1.7	4.7
Embezzlement	13,416	6,740	50.2	6,676	49.8	0.1	0.1	0.3
Stolen property; buying, receiving, possessing	91,280	74,958	82.1	16,322	17.9	0.9	1.0	0.7
Vandalism	198,550	165,574	83.4	32,976	16.6	2.0	2.2	1.5
Weapons; carrying, possessing, etc.	118,312	108,759	91.9	9,553	8.1	1.2	1.4	0.4
Prostitution and commercialized vice	58,758	20,127	34.3	38,631	65.7	0.6	0.3	1.7
Sex offenses (except forcible rape and prostitution)	67,833	62,234	91.7	5,599	8.3	0.7	0.8	0.2
Drug abuse violations	1,103,017	903,656	81.9	199,361	18.1	11.2	12.0	8.8
Gambling	7,525	6,749	89.7	776	10.3	0.1	0.1	(b)
Offenses against family and children	97,716	73,756	75.5	23,960	24.5	1.0	1.0	1.1
Driving under the influence	1,020,377	842,770	82.6	177,607	17.4	10.4	11.1	7.9
Liquor laws	463,849	348,869	75.2	114,980	24.8	4.7	4.6	5.1
Drunkenness	413,808	355,973	86.0	57,835	14.0	4.2	4.7	2.6
Disorderly conduct	482,827	364,695	75.5	118,132	24.5	4.9	4.8	5.2
Vagrancy	19,678	16,158	82.1	3,520	17.9	0.2	0.2	0.2
All other offenses (except traffic)	2,606,294	2,036,108	78.1	570,186	21.9	26.5	26.9	25.2
Suspicion	7,670	6,103	79.6	1,567	20.4	0.1	0.1	0.1
Curfew and loitering law violations	103,155	70,874	68.7	32,281	31.3	1.1	0.9	1.4
Runaways	90,349	36,339	40.2	54,010	59.8	0.9	0.5	2.4

Note: See Notes, tables 4.1 and 4.7. Estimates by the U.S. Census Bureau indicate that on July 1, 2002, males comprised 49.1% and females 50.9% of the total U.S. resident population (U.S. Department of Commerce, U.S. Census Bureau, "Annual Resident Population Estimates of the United States by Sex, Race and Hispanic or Latino Origin: April 1; 2000 to July 1, 2002" [Online]. Available: http://www.census.gov/popest/archives/2000s/vintage_2002/NA-EST2002-ASRO-02.html [Sept. 10, 2004].) For definitions of offenses, see Appendix 3.

[a]Because of rounding, percents may not add to total.
[b]Less than 0.1%.
[c]Violent crimes are offenses of murder and nonnegligent manslaughter, forcible rape, robbery, and aggravated assault.
[d]Property crimes are offenses of burglary, larceny-theft, motor vehicle theft, and arson.
[e]Includes arson.

Source: U.S. Department of Justice, Federal Bureau of Investigation, *Crime in the United States, 2002* (Washington, DC: USGPO, 2003), p. 251. Table adapted by SOURCEBOOK staff.

Table 4.9

Arrests

By offense charged, sex, and age group, United States, 2001 and 2002

(8,787 agencies; 2001 estimated population 177,579,561; 2002 estimated population 179,500,199)

Offense charged	Male Total 2001	Male Total 2002	Male Percent change	Male Under 18 2001	Male Under 18 2002	Male Under 18 Percent change	Female Total 2001	Female Total 2002	Female Percent change	Female Under 18 2001	Female Under 18 2002	Female Under 18 Percent change
Total[a]	6,541,353	6,540,340	(b)	1,012,899	977,219	-3.5%	1,924,010	1,965,008	2.1%	409,049	401,830	-1.8%
Murder and nonnegligent manslaughter	7,557	7,563	0.1%	710	724	2.0	1,123	952	-15.2	89	87	-2.2
Forcible rape	17,019	17,343	1.9	2,840	2,793	-1.7	206	196	-4.9	43	49	14.0
Robbery	60,195	59,516	-1.1	13,692	13,498	-1.4	6,898	7,007	1.6	1,302	1,358	4.3
Aggravated assault	242,573	240,305	-0.9	30,781	29,513	-4.1	61,138	60,648	-0.8	9,366	9,026	-3.6
Burglary	157,719	158,932	0.8	50,063	48,168	-3.8	25,290	25,230	-0.2	6,955	6,336	-8.9
Larceny-theft	463,925	463,111	-0.2	136,458	131,809	-3.4	270,551	274,001	1.3	87,641	85,613	-2.3
Motor vehicle theft	71,080	73,837	3.9	22,593	21,334	-5.6	14,045	14,612	4.0	4,877	4,576	-6.2
Arson	10,118	8,982	-11.2	5,235	4,741	-9.4	1,925	1,615	-16.1	727	612	-15.8
Violent crime[c]	327,344	324,727	-0.8	48,023	46,528	-3.1	69,365	68,803	-0.8	10,800	10,520	-2.6
Property crime[d]	702,842	704,862	0.3	214,349	206,052	-3.9	311,811	315,458	1.2	100,200	97,137	-3.1
Total Crime Index[e]	1,030,186	1,029,589	-0.1	262,372	252,580	-3.7	381,176	384,261	0.8	111,000	107,657	-3.0
Other assaults	622,322	617,297	-0.8	100,278	100,612	0.3	191,470	195,594	2.2	46,173	47,821	3.6
Forgery and counterfeiting	43,716	43,760	0.1	2,446	2,026	-17.2	29,417	29,212	-0.7	1,392	1,148	-17.5
Fraud	108,347	107,450	-0.8	3,623	3,373	-6.9	90,175	91,268	1.2	1,855	1,711	-7.8
Embezzlement	6,729	6,310	-6.2	706	535	-24.2	6,612	6,291	-4.9	535	391	-26.9
Stolen property; buying, receiving, possessing	69,350	69,215	-0.2	15,148	14,422	-4.8	15,131	15,018	-0.7	2,940	2,687	-8.6
Vandalism	142,512	142,967	0.3	57,962	56,483	-2.6	27,696	28,827	4.1	8,756	8,950	2.2
Weapons; carrying, possessing, etc.	93,886	93,550	-0.4	20,224	19,075	-5.7	8,301	8,126	-2.1	2,325	2,308	-0.7
Prostitution and commercialized vice	16,376	16,575	1.2	260	299	15.0	30,401	30,554	0.5	533	527	-1.1
Sex offenses (except forcible rape and prostitution)	52,118	52,596	0.9	10,509	10,566	0.5	3,971	3,932	-1.0	845	860	1.8
Drug abuse violations	770,247	767,873	-0.3	99,623	92,127	-7.5	169,882	173,969	2.4	19,568	18,532	-5.3
Gambling	3,981	3,841	-3.5	375	441	17.6	585	640	9.4	24	23	-4.2
Offenses against family and children	64,309	65,150	1.3	3,780	3,401	-10.0	19,858	20,982	5.7	2,154	2,162	0.4
Driving under the influence	714,540	724,469	1.4	10,340	10,607	2.6	145,010	154,298	6.4	2,288	2,535	10.8
Liquor laws	301,748	296,394	-1.8	60,992	58,568	-4.0	94,599	95,350	0.8	29,305	29,108	-0.7
Drunkenness	343,540	323,737	-5.8	10,464	9,678	-7.5	54,909	53,117	-3.3	2,817	2,698	-4.2
Disorderly conduct	290,123	284,538	-1.9	75,390	76,639	1.7	94,114	95,013	1.0	32,639	34,355	5.3
Vagrancy	14,448	15,529	7.5	1,284	1,049	-18.3	3,199	3,379	5.6	337	329	-2.4
All other offenses (except traffic)	1,757,527	1,790,117	1.9	181,775	175,355	-3.5	478,468	501,061	4.7	64,527	63,912	-1.0
Suspicion (not included in totals)	1,560	1,981	27.0	421	656	55.8	472	609	29.0	204	277	35.8
Curfew and loitering law violations	59,527	56,826	-4.5	59,527	56,826	-4.5	26,550	25,177	-5.2	26,550	25,177	-5.2
Runaways	35,821	32,557	-9.1	35,821	32,557	-9.1	52,486	48,939	-6.8	52,486	48,939	-6.8

Note: See Note, table 4.1. This table presents data from all law enforcement agencies submitting complete reports for 12 months in 2001 and 2002 (Source, p. 452). Population figures are estimates calculated from U.S. Census Bureau data. For definitions of offenses, see Appendix 3.

[a]Does not include suspicion.
[b]Less than 0.1%.
[c]Violent crimes are offenses of murder and nonnegligent manslaughter, forcible rape, robbery, and aggravated assault.
[d]Property crimes are offenses of burglary, larceny-theft, motor vehicle theft, and arson.
[e]Includes arson.

Source: U.S. Department of Justice, Federal Bureau of Investigation, *Crime in the United States, 2002* (Washington, DC: USGPO, 2003), p. 243.

Table 4.10

Arrests

By offense charged, age group, and race, United States, 2002

(10,370 agencies; 2002 estimated population 205,108,615)

	Total arrests					Percent[a]				
Offense charged	Total	White	Black	American Indian or Alaskan Native	Asian or Pacific Islander	Total	White	Black	American Indian or Alaskan Native	Asian or Pacific Islander
Total	9,797,385	6,923,390	2,633,632	130,636	109,727	100.0%	70.7%	26.9%	1.3%	1.1%
Murder and nonnegligent manslaughter	10,099	4,814	5,047	115	123	100.0	47.7	50.0	1.1	1.2
Forcible rape	20,127	12,766	6,852	240	269	100.0	63.4	34.0	1.2	1.3
Robbery	77,280	34,109	41,837	471	863	100.0	44.1	54.1	0.6	1.1
Aggravated assault	338,850	214,992	115,789	4,069	4,000	100.0	63.4	34.2	1.2	1.2
Burglary	205,873	144,958	56,647	1,992	2,276	100.0	70.4	27.5	1.0	1.1
Larceny-theft	843,066	572,515	246,946	10,345	13,260	100.0	67.9	29.3	1.2	1.6
Motor vehicle theft	107,031	64,625	39,114	1,156	2,136	100.0	60.4	36.5	1.1	2.0
Arson	11,808	9,067	2,537	100	104	100.0	76.8	21.5	0.8	0.9
Violent crime[b]	446,356	266,681	169,525	4,895	5,255	100.0	59.7	38.0	1.1	1.2
Property crime[c]	1,167,778	791,165	345,244	13,593	17,776	100.0	67.7	29.6	1.2	1.5
Total Crime Index[d]	1,614,134	1,057,846	514,769	18,488	23,031	100.0	65.5	31.9	1.1	1.4
Other assaults	919,691	610,946	286,787	12,201	9,757	100.0	66.4	31.2	1.3	1.1
Forgery and counterfeiting	82,882	57,125	24,148	458	1,151	100.0	68.9	29.1	0.6	1.4
Fraud	232,336	157,763	71,538	1,431	1,604	100.0	67.9	30.8	0.6	0.7
Embezzlement	13,379	9,153	3,959	64	203	100.0	68.4	29.6	0.5	1.5
Stolen property; buying, receiving, possessing	91,150	53,535	35,986	611	1,018	100.0	58.7	39.5	0.7	1.1
Vandalism	198,139	150,437	42,757	2,804	2,141	100.0	75.9	21.6	1.4	1.1
Weapons; carrying, possessing, etc.	118,148	73,140	42,810	879	1,319	100.0	61.9	36.2	0.7	1.1
Prostitution and commercialized vice	58,659	33,650	23,455	364	1,190	100.0	57.4	40.0	0.6	2.0
Sex offenses (except forcible rape and prostitution)	67,761	50,378	15,745	680	958	100.0	74.3	23.2	1.0	1.4
Drug abuse violations	1,101,547	728,797	357,725	6,848	8,177	100.0	66.2	32.5	0.6	0.7
Gambling	7,525	2,033	5,136	38	318	100.0	27.0	68.3	0.5	4.2
Offenses against family and children	97,393	66,440	28,180	1,266	1,507	100.0	68.2	28.9	1.3	1.5
Driving under the influence	1,017,504	893,395	99,548	15,460	9,101	100.0	87.8	9.8	1.5	0.9
Liquor laws	462,215	405,275	41,204	11,397	4,339	100.0	87.7	8.9	2.5	0.9
Drunkenness	412,735	345,448	55,598	9,563	2,126	100.0	83.7	13.5	2.3	0.5
Disorderly conduct	481,932	321,117	149,393	7,883	3,589	100.0	66.6	31.0	1.6	0.7
Vagrancy	19,669	12,223	6,888	419	139	100.0	62.1	35.0	2.1	0.7
All other offenses (except traffic)	2,599,658	1,751,450	778,558	37,377	32,273	100.0	67.4	29.9	1.4	1.2
Suspicion	7,647	4,130	3,128	108	281	100.0	54.0	40.9	1.4	3.7
Curfew and loitering law violations	103,054	70,738	29,717	1,083	1,516	100.0	68.6	28.8	1.1	1.5
Runaways	90,227	68,371	16,603	1,214	4,039	100.0	75.8	18.4	1.3	4.5

See notes at end of table.

Table 4.10
Arrests

By offense charged, age group, and race, United States, 2002--Continued

	Arrests of persons under 18 years of age					Percent[a]				
Offense charged	Total	White	Black	American Indian or Alaskan Native	Asian or Pacific Islander	Total	White	Black	American Indian or Alaskan Native	Asian or Pacific Islander
Total	1,620,594	1,158,776	415,854	20,383	25,581	100.0%	71.5%	25.7%	1.3%	1.6%
Murder and nonnegligent manslaughter	972	446	487	23	16	100.0	45.9	50.1	2.4	1.6
Forcible rape	3,355	2,079	1,207	37	32	100.0	62.0	36.0	1.1	1.0
Robbery	17,878	6,895	10,537	91	355	100.0	38.6	58.9	0.5	2.0
Aggravated assault	44,185	26,877	16,217	535	556	100.0	60.8	36.7	1.2	1.3
Burglary	61,754	44,680	15,558	689	827	100.0	72.4	25.2	1.1	1.3
Larceny-theft	248,202	173,910	65,667	3,443	5,182	100.0	70.1	26.5	1.4	2.1
Motor vehicle theft	32,487	18,949	12,428	445	665	100.0	58.3	38.3	1.4	2.0
Arson	5,837	4,711	1,026	48	52	100.0	80.7	17.6	0.8	0.9
Violent crime[b]	66,390	36,297	28,448	686	959	100.0	54.7	42.8	1.0	1.4
Property crime[c]	348,280	242,250	94,679	4,625	6,726	100.0	69.6	27.2	1.3	1.9
Total Crime Index[d]	414,670	278,547	123,127	5,311	7,685	100.0	67.2	29.7	1.3	1.9
Other assaults	168,641	106,119	58,518	1,942	2,062	100.0	62.9	34.7	1.2	1.2
Forgery and counterfeiting	3,644	2,845	711	33	55	100.0	78.1	19.5	0.9	1.5
Fraud	6,418	4,242	2,051	47	78	100.0	66.1	32.0	0.7	1.2
Embezzlement	1,004	696	287	1	20	100.0	69.3	28.6	0.1	2.0
Stolen property; buying, receiving, possessing	18,769	10,612	7,761	134	262	100.0	56.5	41.4	0.7	1.4
Vandalism	75,781	61,373	12,594	919	895	100.0	81.0	16.6	1.2	1.2
Weapons; carrying, possessing, etc.	25,239	16,945	7,751	207	336	100.0	67.1	30.7	0.8	1.3
Prostitution and commercialized vice	1,094	479	597	6	12	100.0	43.8	54.6	0.5	1.1
Sex offenses (except forcible rape and prostitution)	13,857	9,986	3,603	107	161	100.0	72.1	26.0	0.8	1.2
Drug abuse violations	133,494	97,766	33,208	1,152	1,368	100.0	73.2	24.9	0.9	1.0
Gambling	1,114	127	955	0	32	100.0	11.4	85.7	X	2.9
Offenses against family and children	6,554	4,837	1,541	56	120	100.0	73.8	23.5	0.9	1.8
Driving under the influence	15,155	14,138	628	267	122	100.0	93.3	4.1	1.8	0.8
Liquor laws	105,652	97,372	4,629	2,656	995	100.0	92.2	4.4	2.5	0.9
Drunkenness	13,508	12,155	995	258	100	100.0	90.0	7.4	1.9	0.7
Disorderly conduct	138,847	88,761	47,261	1,708	1,117	100.0	63.9	34.0	1.2	0.8
Vagrancy	1,518	1,147	346	14	11	100.0	75.6	22.8	0.9	0.7
All other offenses (except traffic)	281,184	210,704	62,641	3,261	4,578	100.0	74.9	22.3	1.2	1.6
Suspicion	1,170	816	330	7	17	100.0	69.7	28.2	0.6	1.5
Curfew and loitering law violations	103,054	70,738	29,717	1,083	1,516	100.0	68.6	28.8	1.1	1.5
Runaways	90,227	68,371	16,603	1,214	4,039	100.0	75.8	18.4	1.3	4.5

See notes at end of table.

Table 4.10

Arrests

By offense charged, age group, and race, United States, 2002--Continued

	Arrests of persons 18 years of age and older					Percent[a]				
Offense charged	Total	White	Black	American Indian or Alaskan Native	Asian or Pacific Islander	Total	White	Black	American Indian or Alaskan Native	Asian or Pacific Islander
Total	8,176,791	5,764,614	2,217,778	110,253	84,146	100.0%	70.5%	27.1%	1.3%	1.0%
Murder and nonnegligent manslaughter	9,127	4,368	4,450	92	107	100.0	47.9	50.0	1.0	1.2
Forcible rape	16,772	10,687	5,645	203	237	100.0	63.7	33.7	1.2	1.4
Robbery	59,402	27,214	31,300	380	508	100.0	45.8	52.7	0.6	0.9
Aggravated assault	294,665	188,115	99,572	3,534	3,444	100.0	63.8	33.8	1.2	1.2
Burglary	144,119	100,278	41,089	1,303	1,449	100.0	69.6	28.5	0.9	1.0
Larceny-theft	594,864	398,605	181,279	6,902	8,078	100.0	67.0	30.5	1.2	1.4
Motor vehicle theft	74,544	45,676	26,686	711	1,471	100.0	61.3	35.8	1.0	2.0
Arson	5,971	4,356	1,511	52	52	100.0	73.0	25.3	0.9	0.9
Violent crime[b]	379,966	230,384	141,077	4,209	4,196	100.0	60.6	37.1	1.1	1.1
Property crime[c]	819,498	548,915	250,565	8,968	11,050	100.0	67.0	30.6	1.1	1.3
Total Crime Index[d]	1,199,464	779,299	391,642	13,177	15,346	100.0	65.0	32.7	1.1	1.3
Other assaults	751,050	504,827	228,269	10,259	7,695	100.0	67.2	30.4	1.4	1.0
Forgery and counterfeiting	79,238	54,280	23,437	425	1,096	100.0	68.5	29.6	0.5	1.4
Fraud	225,918	153,521	69,487	1,384	1,526	100.0	68.0	30.8	0.6	0.7
Embezzlement	12,375	8,457	3,672	63	183	100.0	68.3	29.7	0.5	1.5
Stolen property; buying, receiving, possessing	72,381	42,923	28,225	477	756	100.0	59.3	39.0	0.7	1.0
Vandalism	122,358	89,064	30,163	1,885	1,246	100.0	72.8	24.7	1.5	1.0
Weapons; carrying, possessing, etc.	92,909	56,195	35,059	672	983	100.0	60.5	37.7	0.7	1.1
Prostitution and commercialized vice	57,565	33,171	22,858	358	1,178	100.0	57.6	39.7	0.6	2.0
Sex offenses (except forcible rape and prostitution)	53,904	40,392	12,142	573	797	100.0	74.9	22.5	1.1	1.5
Drug abuse violations	968,053	631,031	324,517	5,696	6,809	100.0	65.2	33.5	0.6	0.7
Gambling	6,411	1,906	4,181	38	286	100.0	29.7	65.2	0.6	4.5
Offenses against family and children	90,839	61,603	26,639	1,210	1,387	100.0	67.8	29.3	1.3	1.5
Driving under the influence	1,002,349	879,257	98,920	15,193	8,979	100.0	87.7	9.9	1.5	0.9
Liquor laws	356,563	307,903	36,575	8,741	3,344	100.0	86.4	10.3	2.5	0.9
Drunkenness	399,227	333,293	54,603	9,305	2,026	100.0	83.5	13.7	2.3	0.5
Disorderly conduct	343,085	232,356	102,132	6,175	2,422	100.0	67.7	29.8	1.8	0.7
Vagrancy	18,151	11,076	6,542	405	128	100.0	61.0	36.0	2.2	0.7
All other offenses (except traffic)	2,318,474	1,540,746	715,917	34,116	27,695	100.0	66.5	30.9	1.5	1.2
Suspicion	6,477	3,314	2,798	101	264	100.0	51.2	43.2	1.6	4.1
Curfew and loitering law violations	X	X	X	X	X	X	X	X	X	X
Runaways	X	X	X	X	X	X	X	X	X	X

Note: See Notes, tables 4.1 and 4.7. Estimates by the U.S. Census Bureau indicate that on July 1, 2002, whites comprised 80.7%, blacks 12.7%, and other racial categories 6.6% of the total U.S. resident population (U.S. Department of Commerce, U.S. Census Bureau, "Annual Resident Population Estimates of the United States by Sex, Race and Hispanic or Latino Origin: April 1, 2000 to July 1, 2002" [Online]. Available: http://www.census.gov/popest/archives/2000s/vintage_2002/NA-EST2002-ASRO-02.html [Sept. 10, 2004.]) For definitions of offenses, see Appendix 3.

[a]Because of rounding, percents may not add to total.
[b]Violent crimes are offenses of murder and nonnegligent manslaughter, forcible rape, robbery, and aggravated assault.
[c]Property crimes are offenses of burglary, larceny-theft, motor vehicle theft, and arson.
[d]Includes arson.

Source: U.S. Department of Justice, Federal Bureau of Investigation, *Crime in the United States, 2002* (Washington, DC: USGPO, 2003), pp. 252-254.

Table 4.11
Arrests in cities

By offense charged and sex, 2002

(7,507 agencies; 2002 estimated population 142,375,961)

Offense charged	Persons arrested					Percent distribution of offenses charged[a]		
	Total number	Male Number	Male Percent	Female Number	Female Percent	Total	Male	Female
Total	7,367,845	5,650,215	76.7%	1,717,630	23.3%	100.0%	100.0%	100.0%
Murder and nonnegligent manslaughter	7,467	6,730	90.1	737	9.9	0.1	0.1	(b)
Forcible rape	14,515	14,319	98.6	196	1.4	0.2	0.3	(b)
Robbery	66,834	59,901	89.6	6,933	10.4	0.9	1.1	0.4
Aggravated assault	260,392	206,175	79.2	54,217	20.8	3.5	3.6	3.2
Burglary	151,343	130,543	86.3	20,800	13.7	2.1	2.3	1.2
Larceny-theft	716,186	446,007	62.3	270,179	37.7	9.7	7.9	15.7
Motor vehicle theft	85,662	71,392	83.3	14,270	16.7	1.2	1.3	0.8
Arson	8,372	7,083	84.6	1,289	15.4	0.1	0.1	0.1
Violent crime[c]	349,208	287,125	82.2	62,083	17.8	4.7	5.1	3.6
Property crime[d]	961,563	655,025	68.1	306,538	31.9	13.1	11.6	17.8
Total Crime Index[e]	1,310,771	942,150	71.9	368,621	28.1	17.8	16.7	21.5
Other assaults	691,820	525,945	76.0	165,875	24.0	9.4	9.3	9.7
Forgery and counterfeiting	63,725	38,064	59.7	25,661	40.3	0.9	0.7	1.5
Fraud	121,969	69,148	56.7	52,821	43.3	1.7	1.2	3.1
Embezzlement	10,337	5,152	49.8	5,185	50.2	0.1	0.1	0.3
Stolen property; buying, receiving, possessing	71,788	58,787	81.9	13,001	18.1	1.0	1.0	0.8
Vandalism	155,656	129,281	83.1	26,375	16.9	2.1	2.3	1.5
Weapons; carrying, possessing, etc.	93,030	85,550	92.0	7,480	8.0	1.3	1.5	0.4
Prostitution and commercialized vice	56,686	19,054	33.6	37,632	66.4	0.8	0.3	2.2
Sex offenses (except forcible rape and prostitution)	49,745	45,112	90.7	4,633	9.3	0.7	0.8	0.3
Drug abuse violations	838,900	689,595	82.2	149,305	17.8	11.4	12.2	8.7
Gambling	6,216	5,705	91.8	511	8.2	0.1	0.1	(b)
Offenses against family and children	53,532	37,165	69.4	16,367	30.6	0.7	0.7	1.0
Driving under the influence	632,092	518,288	82.0	113,804	18.0	8.6	9.2	6.6
Liquor laws	368,132	277,453	75.4	90,679	24.6	5.0	4.9	5.3
Drunkenness	347,469	299,821	86.3	47,648	13.7	4.7	5.3	2.8
Disorderly conduct	415,817	314,636	75.7	101,181	24.3	5.6	5.6	5.9
Vagrancy	17,378	14,416	83.0	2,962	17.0	0.2	0.3	0.2
All other offenses (except traffic)	1,892,117	1,475,991	78.0	416,126	22.0	25.7	26.1	24.2
Suspicion	6,781	5,420	79.9	1,361	20.1	0.1	0.1	0.1
Curfew and loitering law violations	97,467	67,169	68.9	30,298	31.1	1.3	1.2	1.8
Runaways	66,417	26,313	39.6	40,104	60.4	0.9	0.5	2.3

Note: See Note, table 4.1. This table presents data from all city law enforcement agencies submitting complete reports for 12 months in 2002 (Source, p. 452). Population figures are estimates calculated from U.S. Census Bureau data. For definitions of offenses and city areas, see Appendix 3.

[a]Because of rounding, percents may not add to total.
[b]Less than 0.1%.
[c]Violent crimes are offenses of murder and nonnegligent manslaughter, forcible rape, robbery, and aggravated assault.
[d]Property crimes are offenses of burglary, larceny-theft, motor vehicle theft, and arson.
[e]Includes arson.

Source: U.S. Department of Justice, Federal Bureau of Investigation, *Crime in the United States, 2002* (Washington, DC: USGPO, 2003), p. 260. Table adapted by SOURCEBOOK staff.

Table 4.12

Arrests in cities

By offense charged, age group, and race, 2002

(7,505 agencies; 2002 estimated population 142,362,391)

	Total arrests					Percent[a]				
Offense charged	Total	White	Black	American Indian or Alaskan Native	Asian or Pacific Islander	Total	White	Black	American Indian or Alaskan Native	Asian or Pacific Islander
Total	7,351,904	5,006,302	2,155,660	94,160	95,782	100.0%	68.1%	29.3%	1.3%	1.3%
Murder and nonnegligent manslaughter	7,463	3,073	4,225	56	109	100.0	41.2	56.6	0.8	1.5
Forcible rape	14,491	8,394	5,719	143	235	100.0	57.9	39.5	1.0	1.6
Robbery	66,784	28,509	37,104	362	809	100.0	42.7	55.6	0.5	1.2
Aggravated assault	259,904	156,085	97,791	2,585	3,443	100.0	60.1	37.6	1.0	1.3
Burglary	151,127	101,169	46,761	1,199	1,998	100.0	66.9	30.9	0.8	1.3
Larceny-theft	714,476	479,268	213,858	9,165	12,185	100.0	67.1	29.9	1.3	1.7
Motor vehicle theft	85,542	47,798	34,947	820	1,977	100.0	55.9	40.9	1.0	2.3
Arson	8,350	6,131	2,065	64	90	100.0	73.4	24.7	0.8	1.1
Violent crime[b]	348,642	196,061	144,839	3,146	4,596	100.0	56.2	41.5	0.9	1.3
Property crime[c]	959,495	634,366	297,631	11,248	16,250	100.0	66.1	31.0	1.2	1.7
Total Crime Index[d]	1,308,137	830,427	442,470	14,394	20,846	100.0	63.5	33.8	1.1	1.6
Other assaults	690,184	436,318	236,676	8,860	8,330	100.0	63.2	34.3	1.3	1.2
Forgery and counterfeiting	63,514	42,648	19,475	359	1,032	100.0	67.1	30.7	0.6	1.6
Fraud	121,544	79,736	39,815	730	1,263	100.0	65.6	32.8	0.6	1.0
Embezzlement	10,313	6,826	3,262	51	174	100.0	66.2	31.6	0.5	1.7
Stolen property; buying, receiving, possessing	71,676	39,420	30,923	424	909	100.0	55.0	43.1	0.6	1.3
Vandalism	155,325	114,440	36,907	2,099	1,879	100.0	73.7	23.8	1.4	1.2
Weapons; carrying, possessing, etc.	92,913	54,496	36,674	583	1,160	100.0	58.7	39.5	0.6	1.2
Prostitution and commercialized vice	56,590	32,164	22,974	345	1,107	100.0	56.8	40.6	0.6	2.0
Sex offenses (except forcible rape and prostitution)	49,696	35,208	13,161	488	839	100.0	70.8	26.5	1.0	1.7
Drug abuse violations	837,806	521,279	305,106	4,431	6,990	100.0	62.2	36.4	0.5	0.8
Gambling	6,216	1,260	4,648	36	272	100.0	20.3	74.8	0.6	4.4
Offenses against family and children	53,340	35,434	15,613	879	1,414	100.0	66.4	29.3	1.6	2.7
Driving under the influence	630,312	549,723	64,823	9,119	6,647	100.0	87.2	10.3	1.4	1.1
Liquor laws	367,105	317,097	36,736	9,407	3,865	100.0	86.4	10.0	2.6	1.1
Drunkenness	346,480	286,560	49,843	8,127	1,950	100.0	82.7	14.4	2.3	0.6
Disorderly conduct	415,023	270,582	134,755	6,411	3,275	100.0	65.2	32.5	1.5	0.8
Vagrancy	17,373	10,688	6,160	394	131	100.0	61.5	35.5	2.3	0.8
All other offenses (except traffic)	1,887,888	1,223,700	610,826	24,990	28,372	100.0	64.8	32.4	1.3	1.5
Suspicion	6,773	3,687	2,698	107	281	100.0	54.4	39.8	1.6	4.1
Curfew and loitering law violations	97,377	66,156	28,883	1,010	1,328	100.0	67.9	29.7	1.0	1.4
Runaways	66,319	48,453	13,232	916	3,718	100.0	73.1	20.0	1.4	5.6

See notes at end of table.

Table 4.12

Arrests in cities

By offense charged, age group, and race, 2002--Continued

	Arrests of persons under 18 years of age					Percent[a]				
Offense charged	Total	White	Black	American Indian or Alaskan Native	Asian or Pacific Islander	Total	White	Black	American Indian or Alaskan Native	Asian or Pacific Islander
Total	1,325,223	925,182	360,857	16,185	22,999	100.0%	69.8%	27.2%	1.2%	1.7%
Murder and nonnegligent manslaughter	788	341	422	9	16	100.0	43.3	53.6	1.1	2.0
Forcible rape	2,502	1,411	1,039	23	29	100.0	56.4	41.5	0.9	1.2
Robbery	15,983	6,011	9,559	78	335	100.0	37.6	59.8	0.5	2.1
Aggravated assault	35,526	20,815	13,848	380	483	100.0	58.6	39.0	1.1	1.4
Burglary	46,511	32,072	13,242	480	717	100.0	69.0	28.5	1.0	1.5
Larceny-theft	216,960	150,757	58,284	3,137	4,782	100.0	69.5	26.9	1.4	2.2
Motor vehicle theft	26,732	14,436	11,362	332	602	100.0	54.0	42.5	1.2	2.3
Arson	4,484	3,527	869	39	49	100.0	78.7	19.4	0.9	1.1
Violent crime[b]	54,799	28,578	24,868	490	863	100.0	52.2	45.4	0.9	1.6
Property crime[c]	294,687	200,792	83,757	3,988	6,150	100.0	68.1	28.4	1.4	2.1
Total Crime Index[d]	349,486	229,370	108,625	4,478	7,013	100.0	65.6	31.1	1.3	2.0
Other assaults	132,643	80,911	48,488	1,459	1,785	100.0	61.0	36.6	1.1	1.3
Forgery and counterfeiting	2,855	2,197	580	28	50	100.0	77.0	20.3	1.0	1.8
Fraud	4,657	3,140	1,423	28	66	100.0	67.4	30.6	0.6	1.4
Embezzlement	845	574	252	1	18	100.0	67.9	29.8	0.1	2.1
Stolen property; buying, receiving, possessing	15,788	8,442	7,003	108	235	100.0	53.5	44.4	0.7	1.5
Vandalism	60,619	48,200	10,915	711	793	100.0	79.5	18.0	1.2	1.3
Weapons; carrying, possessing, etc.	21,015	13,849	6,714	150	302	100.0	65.9	31.9	0.7	1.4
Prostitution and commercialized vice	1,026	436	575	5	10	100.0	42.5	56.0	0.5	1.0
Sex offenses (except forcible rape and prostitution)	10,197	6,957	3,042	56	142	100.0	68.2	29.8	0.5	1.4
Drug abuse violations	108,335	76,464	29,864	837	1,170	100.0	70.6	27.6	0.8	1.1
Gambling	1,077	112	933	0	32	100.0	10.4	86.6	X	3.0
Offenses against family and children	4,787	3,423	1,200	51	113	100.0	71.5	25.1	1.1	2.4
Driving under the influence	10,034	9,279	481	178	96	100.0	92.5	4.8	1.8	1.0
Liquor laws	79,698	72,719	4,027	2,083	869	100.0	91.2	5.1	2.6	1.1
Drunkenness	11,556	10,333	889	242	92	100.0	89.4	7.7	2.1	0.8
Disorderly conduct	120,547	76,616	41,487	1,408	1,036	100.0	63.6	34.4	1.2	0.9
Vagrancy	1,119	816	280	14	9	100.0	72.9	25.0	1.3	0.8
All other offenses (except traffic)	224,166	165,992	51,654	2,415	4,105	100.0	74.0	23.0	1.1	1.8
Suspicion	1,077	743	310	7	17	100.0	69.0	28.8	0.6	1.6
Curfew and loitering law violations	97,377	66,156	28,883	1,010	1,328	100.0	67.9	29.7	1.0	1.4
Runaways	66,319	48,453	13,232	916	3,718	100.0	73.1	20.0	1.4	5.6

See notes at end of table.

Table 4.12
Arrests in cities

By offense charged, age group, and race, 2002--Continued

	Arrests of persons 18 years of age and older					Percent[a]				
Offense charged	Total	White	Black	American Indian or Alaskan Native	Asian or Pacific Islander	Total	White	Black	American Indian or Alaskan Native	Asian or Pacific Islander
Total	6,026,681	4,081,120	1,794,803	77,975	72,783	100.0%	67.7%	29.8%	1.3%	1.2%
Murder and nonnegligent manslaughter	6,675	2,732	3,803	47	93	100.0	40.9	57.0	0.7	1.4
Forcible rape	11,989	6,983	4,680	120	206	100.0	58.2	39.0	1.0	1.7
Robbery	50,801	22,498	27,545	284	474	100.0	44.3	54.2	0.6	0.9
Aggravated assault	224,378	135,270	83,943	2,205	2,960	100.0	60.3	37.4	1.0	1.3
Burglary	104,616	69,097	33,519	719	1,281	100.0	66.0	32.0	0.7	1.2
Larceny-theft	497,516	328,511	155,574	6,028	7,403	100.0	66.0	31.3	1.2	1.5
Motor vehicle theft	58,810	33,362	23,585	488	1,375	100.0	56.7	40.1	0.8	2.3
Arson	3,866	2,604	1,196	25	41	100.0	67.4	30.9	0.6	1.1
Violent crime[b]	293,843	167,483	119,971	2,656	3,733	100.0	57.0	40.8	0.9	1.3
Property crime[c]	664,808	433,574	213,874	7,260	10,100	100.0	65.2	32.2	1.1	1.5
Total Crime Index[d]	958,651	601,057	333,845	9,916	13,833	100.0	62.7	34.8	1.0	1.4
Other assaults	557,541	355,407	188,188	7,401	6,545	100.0	63.7	33.8	1.3	1.2
Forgery and counterfeiting	60,659	40,451	18,895	331	982	100.0	66.7	31.1	0.5	1.6
Fraud	116,887	76,596	38,392	702	1,197	100.0	65.5	32.8	0.6	1.0
Embezzlement	9,468	6,252	3,010	50	156	100.0	66.0	31.8	0.5	1.6
Stolen property; buying, receiving, possessing	55,888	30,978	23,920	316	674	100.0	55.4	42.8	0.6	1.2
Vandalism	94,706	66,240	25,992	1,388	1,086	100.0	69.9	27.4	1.5	1.1
Weapons; carrying, possessing, etc.	71,898	40,647	29,960	433	858	100.0	56.5	41.7	0.6	1.2
Prostitution and commercialized vice	55,564	31,728	22,399	340	1,097	100.0	57.1	40.3	0.6	2.0
Sex offenses (except forcible rape and prostitution)	39,499	28,251	10,119	432	697	100.0	71.5	25.6	1.1	1.8
Drug abuse violations	729,471	444,815	275,242	3,594	5,820	100.0	61.0	37.7	0.5	0.8
Gambling	5,139	1,148	3,715	36	240	100.0	22.3	72.3	0.7	4.7
Offenses against family and children	48,553	32,011	14,413	828	1,301	100.0	65.9	29.7	1.7	2.7
Driving under the influence	620,278	540,444	64,342	8,941	6,551	100.0	87.1	10.4	1.4	1.1
Liquor laws	287,407	244,378	32,709	7,324	2,996	100.0	85.0	11.4	2.5	1.0
Drunkenness	334,924	276,227	48,954	7,885	1,858	100.0	82.5	14.6	2.4	0.6
Disorderly conduct	294,476	193,966	93,268	5,003	2,239	100.0	65.9	31.7	1.7	0.8
Vagrancy	16,254	9,872	5,880	380	122	100.0	60.7	36.2	2.3	0.8
All other offenses (except traffic)	1,663,722	1,057,708	559,172	22,575	24,267	100.0	63.6	33.6	1.4	1.5
Suspicion	5,696	2,944	2,388	100	264	100.0	51.7	41.9	1.8	4.6
Curfew and loitering law violations	X	X	X	X	X	X	X	X	X	X
Runaways	X	X	X	X	X	X	X	X	X	X

Note: See Notes, tables 4.1 and 4.11. For definitions of offenses and city areas, see Appendix 3.

[a] Because of rounding, percents may not add to total.
[b] Violent crimes are offenses of murder and nonnegligent manslaughter, forcible rape, robbery, and aggravated assault.
[c] Property crimes are offenses of burglary, larceny-theft, motor vehicle theft, and arson.
[d] Includes arson.

Source: U.S. Department of Justice, Federal Bureau of Investigation, *Crime in the United States, 2002* (Washington, DC: USGPO, 2003), pp. 261-263.

Table 4.13
Arrests in suburban areas[a]

By offense charged and sex, 2002

(5,060 agencies; 2002 estimated population 85,923,394)

Offense charged	Persons arrested						Percent distribution of offenses charged[b]		
	Total number	Male		Female		Total	Male	Female
		Number	Percent	Number	Percent			
Total	3,628,725	2,789,848	76.9%	838,877	23.1%	100.0%	100.0%	100.0%
Murder and nonnegligent manslaughter	2,660	2,290	86.1	370	13.9	0.1	0.1	(c)
Forcible rape	6,893	6,813	98.8	80	1.2	0.2	0.2	(c)
Robbery	20,577	18,397	89.4	2,180	10.6	0.6	0.7	0.3
Aggravated assault	110,807	89,568	80.8	21,239	19.2	3.1	3.2	2.5
Burglary	72,415	63,444	87.6	8,971	12.4	2.0	2.3	1.1
Larceny-theft	293,756	185,275	63.1	108,481	36.9	8.1	6.6	12.9
Motor vehicle theft	29,520	24,701	83.7	4,819	16.3	0.8	0.9	0.6
Arson	4,894	4,239	86.6	655	13.4	0.1	0.2	0.1
Violent crime[d]	140,937	117,068	83.1	23,869	16.9	3.9	4.2	2.8
Property crime[e]	400,585	277,659	69.3	122,926	30.7	11.0	10.0	14.7
Total Crime Index[f]	541,522	394,727	72.9	146,795	27.1	14.9	14.1	17.5
Other assaults	329,934	249,781	75.7	80,153	24.3	9.1	9.0	9.6
Forgery and counterfeiting	30,751	18,676	60.7	12,075	39.3	0.8	0.7	1.4
Fraud	112,608	60,734	53.9	51,874	46.1	3.1	2.2	6.2
Embezzlement	4,727	2,375	50.2	2,352	49.8	0.1	0.1	0.3
Stolen property; buying, receiving, possessing	33,825	27,756	82.1	6,069	17.9	0.9	1.0	0.7
Vandalism	72,884	61,605	84.5	11,279	15.5	2.0	2.2	1.3
Weapons; carrying, possessing, etc.	38,959	35,629	91.5	3,330	8.5	1.1	1.3	1.4
Prostitution and commercialized vice	4,773	2,150	45.0	2,623	55.0	0.1	0.1	0.3
Sex offenses (except forcible rape and prostitution)	22,771	21,573	94.7	1,198	5.3	0.6	0.8	0.1
Drug abuse violations	372,988	303,862	81.5	69,126	18.5	10.3	10.9	8.2
Gambling	1,281	1,035	80.8	246	19.2	(c)	(c)	(c)
Offenses against family and children	47,539	37,449	78.8	10,090	21.2	1.3	1.3	1.2
Driving under the influence	442,751	363,493	82.1	79,258	17.9	12.2	13.0	9.4
Liquor laws	176,569	131,374	74.4	45,195	25.6	4.9	4.7	5.4
Drunkenness	140,222	118,735	84.7	21,487	15.3	3.9	4.3	2.6
Disorderly conduct	174,655	131,265	75.2	43,390	24.8	4.8	4.7	5.2
Vagrancy	4,941	4,097	82.9	844	17.1	0.1	0.1	0.1
All other offenses (except traffic)	1,018,349	793,434	77.9	224,915	22.1	28.1	28.4	26.8
Suspicion	1,617	1,258	77.8	359	22.2	(c)	(c)	(c)
Curfew and loitering law violations	22,511	15,275	67.9	7,236	32.1	0.6	0.5	0.9
Runaways	32,548	13,565	41.7	18,983	58.3	0.9	0.5	2.3

Note: See Note, table 4.1. This table presents data from all suburban law enforcement agencies submitting complete reports for 12 months in 2002 (Source, p. 453). Population figures are estimates calculated from U.S. Census Bureau data. For definitions of offenses and suburban areas, see Appendix 3.

[a] Includes law enforcement agencies in cities with less than 50,000 inhabitants and county law enforcement agencies that are within a Metropolitan Statistical Area; excludes all metropolitan agencies associated with a central city.
[b] Because of rounding, percents may not add to total.
[c] Less than 0.1%.
[d] Violent crimes are offenses of murder and nonnegligent manslaughter, forcible rape, robbery, and aggravated assault.
[e] Property crimes are offenses of burglary, larceny-theft, motor vehicle theft, and arson.
[f] Includes arson.

Source: U.S. Department of Justice, Federal Bureau of Investigation, *Crime in the United States, 2002* (Washington, DC: USGPO, 2003), p. 287. Table adapted by SOURCEBOOK staff.

Table 4.14

Arrests in suburban areas[a]

By offense charged, age group, and race, 2002

(5,058 agencies; 2002 estimated population 85,883,296)

Offense charged	Total arrests					Percent[b]				
	Total	White	Black	American Indian or Alaskan Native	Asian or Pacific Islander	Total	White	Black	American Indian or Alaskan Native	Asian or Pacific Islander
Total	3,615,828	2,782,303	782,253	24,226	27,046	100.0%	76.9%	21.6%	0.7%	0.7%
Murder and nonnegligent manslaughter	2,655	1,634	979	18	24	100.0	61.5	36.9	0.7	0.9
Forcible rape	6,876	5,045	1,720	60	51	100.0	73.4	25.0	0.9	0.7
Robbery	20,546	10,929	9,394	100	123	100.0	53.2	45.7	0.5	0.6
Aggravated assault	110,549	81,098	27,590	783	1,078	100.0	73.4	25.0	0.7	1.0
Burglary	72,302	55,893	15,529	351	529	100.0	77.3	21.5	0.5	0.7
Larceny-theft	292,150	207,164	79,719	1,822	3,445	100.0	70.9	27.3	0.6	1.2
Motor vehicle theft	29,414	21,522	7,347	211	334	100.0	73.2	25.0	0.7	1.1
Arson	4,882	4,147	669	30	36	100.0	84.9	13.7	0.6	0.7
Violent crime[c]	140,626	98,706	39,683	961	1,276	100.0	70.2	28.2	0.7	0.9
Property crime[d]	398,748	288,726	103,264	2,414	4,344	100.0	72.4	25.9	0.6	1.1
Total Crime Index[e]	539,374	387,432	142,947	3,375	5,620	100.0	71.8	26.5	0.6	1.0
Other assaults	328,973	244,642	79,658	2,165	2,508	100.0	74.4	24.2	0.7	0.8
Forgery and counterfeiting	30,587	22,036	8,181	85	285	100.0	72.0	26.7	0.3	0.9
Fraud	112,207	76,367	34,920	311	609	100.0	68.1	31.1	0.3	0.5
Embezzlement	4,708	3,323	1,319	9	57	100.0	70.6	28.0	0.2	1.2
Stolen property; buying, receiving, possessing	33,774	22,664	10,586	176	348	100.0	67.1	31.3	0.5	1.0
Vandalism	72,582	60,410	11,125	480	567	100.0	83.2	15.3	0.7	0.8
Weapons; carrying, possessing, etc.	38,857	27,774	10,535	177	371	100.0	71.5	27.1	0.5	1.0
Prostitution and commercialized vice	4,765	3,390	1,183	24	168	100.0	71.1	24.8	0.5	3.5
Sex offenses (except forcible rape and prostitution)	22,724	18,589	3,818	102	215	100.0	81.8	16.8	0.4	0.9
Drug abuse violations	372,099	287,395	80,984	1,535	2,185	100.0	77.2	21.8	0.4	0.6
Gambling	1,281	777	451	1	52	100.0	60.7	35.2	0.1	4.1
Offenses against family and children	47,287	33,653	13,215	210	209	100.0	71.2	27.9	0.4	0.4
Driving under the influence	441,014	397,403	37,794	2,743	3,074	100.0	90.1	8.6	0.6	0.7
Liquor laws	175,359	159,228	12,443	1,865	1,823	100.0	90.8	7.1	1.1	1.0
Drunkenness	139,943	125,140	12,608	1,483	712	100.0	89.4	9.0	1.1	0.5
Disorderly conduct	174,151	131,394	40,429	1,158	1,170	100.0	75.4	23.2	0.7	0.7
Vagrancy	4,938	3,193	1,691	18	36	100.0	64.7	34.2	0.4	0.7
All other offenses (except traffic)	1,014,702	731,850	268,447	7,881	6,524	100.0	72.1	26.5	0.8	0.6
Suspicion	1,595	1,040	545	3	7	100.0	65.2	34.2	0.2	0.4
Curfew and loitering law violations	22,386	17,940	4,094	137	215	100.0	80.1	18.3	0.6	1.0
Runaways	32,522	26,663	5,280	288	291	100.0	82.0	16.2	0.9	0.9

See notes at end of table.

Table 4.14

Arrests in suburban areas[a]

By offense charged, age group, and race, 2002--Continued

	Arrests of persons under 18 years of age					Percent[b]				
Offense charged	Total	White	Black	American Indian or Alaskan Native	Asian or Pacific Islander	Total	White	Black	American Indian or Alaskan Native	Asian or Pacific Islander
Total	600,579	469,669	121,133	3,949	5,828	100.0%	78.2%	20.2%	0.7%	1.0%
Murder and nonnegligent manslaughter	194	112	82	0	0	100.0	57.7	42.3	X	X
Forcible rape	1,205	858	332	10	5	100.0	71.2	27.6	0.8	0.4
Robbery	4,502	2,110	2,331	19	42	100.0	46.9	51.8	0.4	0.9
Aggravated assault	15,575	10,838	4,451	134	152	100.0	69.6	28.6	0.9	1.0
Burglary	22,526	17,799	4,408	128	191	100.0	79.0	19.6	0.6	0.8
Larceny-theft	85,377	61,835	21,588	601	1,353	100.0	72.4	25.3	0.7	1.6
Motor vehicle theft	8,402	5,993	2,186	78	145	100.0	71.3	26.0	0.9	1.7
Arson	2,619	2,278	311	13	17	100.0	87.0	11.9	0.5	0.6
Violent crime[c]	21,476	13,918	7,196	163	199	100.0	64.8	33.5	0.8	0.9
Property crime[d]	118,924	87,905	28,493	820	1,706	100.0	73.9	24.0	0.7	1.4
Total Crime Index[e]	140,400	101,823	35,689	983	1,905	100.0	72.5	25.4	0.7	1.4
Other assaults	64,189	45,527	17,791	395	476	100.0	70.9	27.7	0.6	0.7
Forgery and counterfeiting	1,423	1,145	249	11	18	100.0	80.5	17.5	0.8	1.3
Fraud	2,679	1,725	918	6	30	100.0	64.4	34.3	0.2	1.1
Embezzlement	389	291	91	0	7	100.0	74.8	23.4	X	1.8
Stolen property; buying, receiving, possessing	7,117	4,632	2,329	45	111	100.0	65.1	32.7	0.6	1.6
Vandalism	30,265	26,197	3,654	164	250	100.0	86.6	12.1	0.5	0.8
Weapons; carrying, possessing, etc.	8,804	6,645	2,035	34	90	100.0	75.5	23.1	0.4	1.0
Prostitution and commercialized vice	122	76	43	1	2	100.0	62.3	35.2	0.8	1.6
Sex offenses (except forcible rape and prostitution)	5,062	4,029	990	14	29	100.0	79.6	19.6	0.3	0.6
Drug abuse violations	50,260	42,743	6,902	241	374	100.0	85.0	13.7	0.5	0.7
Gambling	137	65	72	0	0	100.0	47.4	52.6	X	X
Offenses against family and children	2,718	2,159	541	6	12	100.0	79.4	19.9	0.2	0.4
Driving under the influence	6,279	5,988	220	37	34	100.0	95.4	3.5	0.6	0.5
Liquor laws	45,669	42,965	1,790	482	432	100.0	94.1	3.9	1.1	0.9
Drunkenness	5,775	5,389	297	56	33	100.0	93.3	5.1	1.0	0.6
Disorderly conduct	57,776	41,168	15,946	270	392	100.0	71.3	27.6	0.5	0.7
Vagrancy	656	512	137	3	4	100.0	78.0	20.9	0.5	0.6
All other offenses (except traffic)	115,622	91,726	21,999	775	1,122	100.0	79.3	19.0	0.7	1.0
Suspicion	329	261	66	1	1	100.0	79.3	20.1	0.3	0.3
Curfew and loitering law violations	22,386	17,940	4,094	137	215	100.0	80.1	18.3	0.6	1.0
Runaways	32,522	26,663	5,280	288	291	100.0	82.0	16.2	0.9	0.9

See notes at end of table.

Table 4.14

Arrests in suburban areas[a]

By offense charged, age group, and race, 2002--Continued

Offense charged	Arrests of persons 18 years of age and older					Percent[b]				
	Total	White	Black	American Indian or Alaskan Native	Asian or Pacific Islander	Total	White	Black	American Indian or Alaskan Native	Asian or Pacific Islander
Total	3,015,249	2,312,634	661,120	20,277	21,218	100.0%	76.7%	21.9%	0.7%	0.7%
Murder and nonnegligent manslaughter	2,461	1,522	897	18	24	100.0	61.8	36.4	0.7	1.0
Forcible rape	5,671	4,187	1,388	50	46	100.0	73.8	24.5	0.9	0.8
Robbery	16,044	8,819	7,063	81	81	100.0	55.0	44.0	0.5	0.5
Aggravated assault	94,974	70,260	23,139	649	926	100.0	74.0	24.4	0.7	1.0
Burglary	49,776	38,094	11,121	223	338	100.0	76.5	22.3	0.4	0.7
Larceny-theft	206,773	145,329	58,131	1,221	2,092	100.0	70.3	28.1	0.6	1.0
Motor vehicle theft	21,012	15,529	5,161	133	189	100.0	73.9	24.6	0.6	0.9
Arson	2,263	1,869	358	17	19	100.0	82.6	15.8	0.8	0.8
Violent crime[c]	119,150	84,788	32,487	798	1,077	100.0	71.2	27.3	0.7	0.9
Property crime[d]	279,824	200,821	74,771	1,594	2,638	100.0	71.8	26.7	0.6	0.9
Total Crime Index[e]	398,974	285,609	107,258	2,392	3,715	100.0	71.6	26.9	0.6	0.9
Other assaults	264,784	199,115	61,867	1,770	2,032	100.0	75.2	23.4	0.7	0.8
Forgery and counterfeiting	29,164	20,891	7,932	74	267	100.0	71.6	27.2	0.3	0.9
Fraud	109,528	74,642	34,002	305	579	100.0	68.1	31.0	0.3	0.5
Embezzlement	4,319	3,032	1,228	9	50	100.0	70.2	28.4	0.2	1.2
Stolen property; buying, receiving, possessing	26,657	18,032	8,257	131	237	100.0	67.6	31.0	0.5	0.9
Vandalism	42,317	34,213	7,471	316	317	100.0	80.8	17.7	0.7	0.7
Weapons; carrying, possessing, etc.	30,053	21,129	8,500	143	281	100.0	70.3	28.3	0.5	0.9
Prostitution and commercialized vice	4,643	3,314	1,140	23	166	100.0	71.4	24.6	0.5	3.6
Sex offenses (except forcible rape and prostitution)	17,662	14,560	2,828	88	186	100.0	82.4	16.0	0.5	1.1
Drug abuse violations	321,839	244,652	74,082	1,294	1,811	100.0	76.0	23.0	0.4	0.6
Gambling	1,144	712	379	1	52	100.0	62.2	33.1	0.1	4.5
Offenses against family and children	44,569	31,494	12,674	204	197	100.0	70.7	28.4	0.5	0.4
Driving under the influence	434,735	391,415	37,574	2,706	3,040	100.0	90.0	8.6	0.6	0.7
Liquor laws	129,690	116,263	10,653	1,383	1,391	100.0	89.6	8.2	1.1	1.1
Drunkenness	134,168	119,751	12,311	1,427	679	100.0	89.3	9.2	1.1	0.5
Disorderly conduct	116,375	90,226	24,483	888	778	100.0	77.5	21.0	0.8	0.7
Vagrancy	4,282	2,681	1,554	15	32	100.0	62.6	36.3	0.4	0.7
All other offenses (except traffic)	899,080	640,124	246,448	7,106	5,402	100.0	71.2	27.4	0.8	0.6
Suspicion	1,266	779	479	2	6	100.0	61.5	37.8	0.2	0.5
Curfew and loitering law violations	X	X	X	X	X	X	X	X	X	X
Runaways	X	X	X	X	X	X	X	X	X	X

Note: See Notes, tables 4.1 and 4.13. For definitions of offenses and suburban areas, see Appendix 3.

[a]Includes law enforcement agencies in cities with less than 50,000 inhabitants and county law enforcement agencies that are within a Metropolitan Statistical Area; excludes all metropolitan agencies associated with a central city.
[b]Because of rounding, percents may not add to total.
[c]Violent crimes are offenses of murder and nonnegligent manslaughter, forcible rape, robbery, and aggravated assault.
[d]Property crimes are offenses of burglary, larceny-theft, motor vehicle theft, and arson.
[e]Includes arson.

Source: U.S. Department of Justice, Federal Bureau of Investigation, *Crime in the United States, 2002* (Washington, DC: USGPO, 2003), pp. 288-290.

Table 4.15

Arrests in rural counties

By offense charged and sex, 2002

(1,949 agencies; 2002 estimated population 21,924,006)

Offense charged	Persons arrested					Percent distribution of offenses charged[a]		
	Total number	Male		Female		Total	Male	Female
		Number	Percent	Number	Percent			
Total	882,727	694,371	78.7%	188,356	21.3%	100.0%	100.0%	100.0%
Murder and nonnegligent manslaughter	886	776	87.6	110	12.4	0.1	0.1	0.1
Forcible rape	2,171	2,143	98.7	28	1.3	0.2	0.3	(b)
Robbery	2,014	1,824	90.6	190	9.4	0.2	0.3	0.1
Aggravated assault	23,887	19,800	82.9	4,087	17.1	2.7	2.9	2.2
Burglary	20,873	18,548	88.9	2,325	11.1	2.4	2.7	1.2
Larceny-theft	33,227	24,091	72.5	9,136	27.5	3.8	3.5	4.9
Motor vehicle theft	6,473	5,435	84.0	1,038	16.0	0.7	0.8	0.6
Arson	1,069	911	85.2	158	14.8	0.1	0.1	0.1
Violent crime[c]	28,958	24,543	84.8	4,415	15.2	3.3	3.5	2.3
Property crime[d]	61,642	48,985	79.5	12,657	20.5	7.0	7.1	6.7
Total Crime Index[e]	90,600	73,528	81.2	17,072	18.8	10.3	10.6	9.1
Other assaults	78,678	60,730	77.2	17,948	22.8	8.9	8.7	9.5
Forgery and counterfeiting	6,520	3,778	57.9	2,742	42.1	0.7	0.5	1.5
Fraud	39,324	20,180	51.3	19,144	48.7	4.5	2.9	10.2
Embezzlement	928	462	49.8	466	50.2	0.1	0.1	0.2
Stolen property; buying, receiving, possessing	5,515	4,612	83.6	903	16.4	0.6	0.7	0.5
Vandalism	15,107	12,749	84.4	2,358	15.6	1.7	1.8	1.3
Weapons; carrying, possessing, etc.	7,975	7,363	92.3	612	7.7	0.9	1.1	0.3
Prostitution and commercialized vice	143	93	65.0	50	35.0	(b)	(b)	(b)
Sex offenses (except forcible rape and prostitution)	6,223	5,889	94.6	334	5.4	0.7	0.8	0.2
Drug abuse violations	91,205	74,004	81.1	17,201	18.9	10.3	10.7	9.1
Gambling	651	543	83.4	108	16.6	0.1	0.1	0.1
Offenses against family and children	14,741	12,101	82.1	2,640	17.9	1.7	1.7	1.4
Driving under the influence	172,521	144,579	83.8	27,942	16.2	19.5	20.8	14.8
Liquor laws	45,988	33,999	73.9	11,989	26.1	5.2	4.9	6.4
Drunkenness	24,868	21,104	84.9	3,764	15.1	2.8	3.0	2.0
Disorderly conduct	26,256	19,738	75.2	6,518	24.8	3.0	2.8	3.5
Vagrancy	587	416	70.9	171	29.1	0.1	0.1	0.1
All other offenses (except traffic)	247,267	195,146	78.9	52,121	21.1	28.0	28.1	27.7
Suspicion	159	135	84.9	24	15.1	(b)	(b)	(b)
Curfew and loitering law violations	1,034	651	63.0	383	37.0	0.1	0.1	0.2
Runaways	6,437	2,571	39.9	3,866	60.1	0.7	0.4	2.1

Note: See Note, table 4.1. This table presents data from all rural county law enforcement agencies submitting complete reports for 12 months in 2002 (Source, p. 453). Population figures are estimates calculated from U.S. Census Bureau data. For definitions of offenses and rural counties, see Appendix 3.

[a]Because of rounding, percents may not add to total.
[b]Less than 0.1%.
[c]Violent crimes are offenses of murder and nonnegligent manslaughter, forcible rape, robbery, and aggravated assault.
[d]Property crimes are offenses of burglary, larceny-theft, motor vehicle theft, and arson.
[e]Includes arson.

Source: U.S. Department of Justice, Federal Bureau of Investigation, *Crime in the United States, 2002* (Washington, DC: USGPO, 2003), p. 278. Table adapted by SOURCEBOOK staff.

Table 4.16

Arrests in rural counties

By offense charged, age group, and race, 2002

(1,949 agencies; 2002 estimated population 21,924,006)

Offense charged	Total arrests					Percent[a]				
	Total	White	Black	American Indian or Alaskan Native	Asian or Pacific Islander	Total	White	Black	American Indian or Alaskan Native	Asian or Pacific Islander
Total	880,037	727,920	120,859	25,918	5,340	100.0%	82.7%	13.7%	2.9%	0.6%
Murder and nonnegligent manslaughter	885	603	233	44	5	100.0	68.1	26.3	5.0	0.6
Forcible rape	2,167	1,733	359	60	15	100.0	80.0	16.6	2.8	0.7
Robbery	2,013	1,032	912	61	8	100.0	51.3	45.3	3.0	0.4
Aggravated assault	23,826	17,894	4,733	1,050	149	100.0	75.1	19.9	4.4	0.6
Burglary	20,848	17,154	2,973	616	105	100.0	82.3	14.3	3.0	0.5
Larceny-theft	33,168	27,313	4,878	690	287	100.0	82.3	14.7	2.1	0.9
Motor vehicle theft	6,463	5,498	671	238	56	100.0	85.1	10.4	3.7	0.9
Arson	1,067	919	126	20	2	100.0	86.1	11.8	1.9	0.2
Violent crime[b]	28,891	21,262	6,237	1,215	177	100.0	73.6	21.6	4.2	0.6
Property crime[c]	61,546	50,884	8,648	1,564	450	100.0	82.7	14.1	2.5	0.7
Total Crime Index[d]	90,437	72,146	14,885	2,779	627	100.0	79.8	16.5	3.1	0.7
Other assaults	78,505	62,552	12,989	2,446	518	100.0	79.7	16.5	3.1	0.7
Forgery and counterfeiting	6,515	5,200	1,216	68	31	100.0	79.8	18.7	1.0	0.5
Fraud	39,211	31,505	7,102	507	97	100.0	80.3	18.1	1.3	0.2
Embezzlement	922	786	122	7	7	100.0	85.2	13.2	0.8	0.8
Stolen property; buying, receiving, possessing	5,509	4,334	1,051	111	13	100.0	78.7	19.1	2.0	0.2
Vandalism	15,058	12,927	1,537	506	88	100.0	85.8	10.2	3.4	0.6
Weapons; carrying, possessing, etc.	7,951	6,394	1,325	198	34	100.0	80.4	16.7	2.5	0.4
Prostitution and commercialized vice	143	103	30	5	5	100.0	72.0	21.0	3.5	3.5
Sex offenses (except forcible rape and prostitution)	6,208	5,467	546	152	43	100.0	88.1	8.8	2.4	0.7
Drug abuse violations	91,027	75,764	13,238	1,608	417	100.0	83.2	14.5	1.8	0.5
Gambling	651	363	283	2	3	100.0	55.8	43.5	0.3	0.5
Offenses against family and children	14,712	10,960	3,446	290	16	100.0	74.5	23.4	2.0	0.1
Driving under the influence	172,083	150,707	14,882	5,142	1,352	100.0	87.6	8.6	3.0	0.8
Liquor laws	45,728	43,033	1,155	1,377	163	100.0	94.1	2.5	3.0	0.4
Drunkenness	24,824	21,824	1,880	1,069	51	100.0	87.9	7.6	4.3	0.2
Disorderly conduct	26,224	20,964	4,029	1,153	78	100.0	79.9	15.4	4.4	0.3
Vagrancy	583	461	99	20	3	100.0	79.1	17.0	3.4	0.5
All other offenses (except traffic)	246,127	195,837	40,599	8,234	1,457	100.0	79.6	16.5	3.3	0.6
Suspicion	158	101	57	0	0	100.0	63.9	36.1	X	X
Curfew and loitering law violations	1,033	824	28	44	137	100.0	79.8	2.7	4.3	13.3
Runaways	6,428	5,668	360	200	200	100.0	88.2	5.6	3.1	3.1

See notes at end of table.

Table 4.16

Arrests in rural counties

By offense charged, age group, and race, 2002--Continued

	Arrests of persons under 18 years of age					Percent[a]				
Offense charged	Total	White	Black	American Indian or Alaskan Native	Asian or Pacific Islander	Total	White	Black	American Indian or Alaskan Native	Asian or Pacific Islander
Total	89,838	77,428	8,642	2,766	1,002	100.0%	86.2%	9.6%	3.1%	1.1%
Murder and nonnegligent manslaughter	64	32	18	14	0	100.0	50.0	28.1	21.9	X
Forcible rape	301	248	41	9	3	100.0	82.4	13.6	3.0	1.0
Robbery	222	122	90	8	2	100.0	55.0	40.5	3.6	0.9
Aggravated assault	2,176	1,637	425	89	25	100.0	75.2	19.5	4.1	1.1
Burglary	5,413	4,752	458	160	43	100.0	87.8	8.5	3.0	0.8
Larceny-theft	7,284	6,312	663	182	127	100.0	86.7	9.1	2.5	1.7
Motor vehicle theft	2,037	1,800	133	80	24	100.0	88.4	6.5	3.9	1.2
Arson	320	288	26	6	0	100.0	90.0	8.1	1.9	X
Violent crime[b]	2,763	2,039	574	120	30	100.0	73.8	20.8	4.3	1.1
Property crime[c]	15,054	13,152	1,280	428	194	100.0	87.4	8.5	2.8	1.3
Total Crime Index[d]	17,817	15,191	1,854	548	224	100.0	85.3	10.4	3.1	1.3
Other assaults	9,243	7,147	1,701	288	107	100.0	77.3	18.4	3.1	1.2
Forgery and counterfeiting	264	238	24	2	0	100.0	90.2	9.1	0.8	X
Fraud	482	409	55	14	4	100.0	84.9	11.4	2.9	0.8
Embezzlement	36	32	3	0	1	100.0	88.9	8.3	X	2.8
Stolen property; buying, receiving, possessing	666	572	81	11	2	100.0	85.9	12.2	1.7	0.3
Vandalism	4,900	4,419	304	143	34	100.0	90.2	6.2	2.9	0.7
Weapons; carrying, possessing, etc.	924	725	154	40	5	100.0	78.5	16.7	4.3	0.5
Prostitution and commercialized vice	12	8	4	0	0	100.0	66.7	33.3	X	X
Sex offenses (except forcible rape and prostitution)	1,286	1,121	111	42	12	100.0	87.2	8.6	3.3	0.9
Drug abuse violations	7,324	6,498	533	204	89	100.0	88.7	7.3	2.8	1.2
Gambling	11	7	4	0	0	100.0	63.6	36.4	X	X
Offenses against family and children	550	511	35	3	1	100.0	92.9	6.4	0.5	0.2
Driving under the influence	2,687	2,514	73	83	17	100.0	93.6	2.7	3.1	0.6
Liquor laws	12,076	11,467	145	437	27	100.0	95.0	1.2	3.6	0.2
Drunkenness	653	621	20	10	2	100.0	95.1	3.1	1.5	0.3
Disorderly conduct	5,802	4,403	1,165	211	23	100.0	75.9	20.1	3.6	0.4
Vagrancy	261	240	20	0	1	100.0	92.0	7.7	X	0.4
All other offenses (except traffic)	17,355	14,792	1,961	486	116	100.0	85.2	11.3	2.8	0.7
Suspicion	28	21	7	0	0	100.0	75.0	25.0	X	X
Curfew and loitering law violations	1,033	824	28	44	137	100.0	79.8	2.7	4.3	13.3
Runaways	6,428	5,668	360	200	200	100.0	88.2	5.6	3.1	3.1

See notes at end of table.

Table 4.16

Arrests in rural counties

By offense charged, age group, and race, 2002--Continued

	Arrests of persons 18 years of age and older					Percent[a]				
Offense charged	Total	White	Black	American Indian or Alaskan Native	Asian or Pacific Islander	Total	White	Black	American Indian or Alaskan Native	Asian or Pacific Islander
Total	790,199	650,492	112,217	23,152	4,338	100.0%	82.3%	14.2%	2.9%	0.5%
Murder and nonnegligent manslaughter	821	571	215	30	5	100.0	69.5	26.2	3.7	0.6
Forcible rape	1,866	1,485	318	51	12	100.0	79.6	17.0	2.7	0.6
Robbery	1,791	910	822	53	6	100.0	50.8	45.9	3.0	0.3
Aggravated assault	21,650	16,257	4,308	961	124	100.0	75.1	19.9	4.4	0.6
Burglary	15,435	12,402	2,515	456	62	100.0	80.3	16.3	3.0	0.4
Larceny-theft	25,884	21,001	4,215	508	160	100.0	81.1	16.3	2.0	0.6
Motor vehicle theft	4,426	3,698	538	158	32	100.0	83.6	12.2	3.6	0.7
Arson	747	631	100	14	2	100.0	84.5	13.4	1.9	0.3
Violent crime[b]	26,128	19,223	5,663	1,095	147	100.0	73.6	21.7	4.2	0.6
Property crime[c]	46,492	37,732	7,368	1,136	256	100.0	81.2	15.8	2.4	0.6
Total Crime Index[d]	72,620	56,955	13,031	2,231	403	100.0	78.4	17.9	3.1	0.6
Other assaults	69,262	55,405	11,288	2,158	411	100.0	80.0	16.3	3.1	0.6
Forgery and counterfeiting	6,251	4,962	1,192	66	31	100.0	79.4	19.1	1.1	0.5
Fraud	38,729	31,096	7,047	493	93	100.0	80.3	18.2	1.3	0.2
Embezzlement	886	754	119	7	6	100.0	85.1	13.4	0.8	0.7
Stolen property; buying, receiving, possessing	4,843	3,762	970	100	11	100.0	77.7	20.0	2.1	0.2
Vandalism	10,158	8,508	1,233	363	54	100.0	83.8	12.1	3.6	0.5
Weapons; carrying, possessing, etc.	7,027	5,669	1,171	158	29	100.0	80.7	16.7	2.2	0.4
Prostitution and commercialized vice	131	95	26	5	5	100.0	72.5	19.8	3.8	3.8
Sex offenses (except forcible rape and prostitution)	4,922	4,346	435	110	31	100.0	88.3	8.8	2.2	0.6
Drug abuse violations	83,703	69,266	12,705	1,404	328	100.0	82.8	15.2	1.7	0.4
Gambling	640	356	279	2	3	100.0	55.6	43.6	0.3	0.5
Offenses against family and children	14,162	10,449	3,411	287	15	100.0	73.8	24.1	2.0	0.1
Driving under the influence	169,396	148,193	14,809	5,059	1,335	100.0	87.5	8.7	3.0	0.8
Liquor laws	33,652	31,566	1,010	940	136	100.0	93.8	3.0	2.8	0.4
Drunkenness	24,171	21,203	1,860	1,059	49	100.0	87.7	7.7	4.4	0.2
Disorderly conduct	20,422	16,561	2,864	942	55	100.0	81.1	14.0	4.6	0.3
Vagrancy	322	221	79	20	2	100.0	68.6	24.5	6.2	0.6
All other offenses (except traffic)	228,772	181,045	38,638	7,748	1,341	100.0	79.1	16.9	3.4	0.6
Suspicion	130	80	50	0	0	100.0	61.5	38.5	X	X
Curfew and loitering law violations	X	X	X	X	X	X	X	X	X	X
Runaways	X	X	X	X	X	X	X	X	X	X

Note: See Notes, tables 4.1 and 4.15. For definitions of offenses and rural counties, see Appendix 3.

[a]Because of rounding, percents may not add to total.
[b]Violent crimes are offenses of murder and nonnegligent manslaughter, forcible rape, robbery, and aggravated assault.
[c]Property crimes are offenses of burglary, larceny-theft, motor vehicle theft, and arson.
[d]Includes arson.

Source: U.S. Department of Justice, Federal Bureau of Investigation, *Crime in the United States, 2002* (Washington, DC: USGPO, 2003), pp. 279-281.

Table 4.17

Arrest rates (per 100,000 inhabitants) for violent crimes

By offense charged and region, 1971-2002

(Rate per 100,000 inhabitants)

	Murder and nonnegligent manslaughter				Forcible rape				Robbery				Aggravated assault			
	Northeast	Midwest	South	West	Northeast	Midwest	South	West	Northeast	Midwest	South	West	Northeast	Midwest	South	West
1971	7.1	8.8	12.7	8.6	8.5	9.6	12.2	13.1	83.4	55.3	54.4	73.0	81.2	59.0	119.5	111.3
1972	6.8	7.8	13.3	10.1	10.0	10.1	13.7	16.4	82.2	54.0	58.6	84.7	83.7	63.1	125.0	134.4
1973	7.9	7.0	12.8	9.1	12.1	9.4	13.5	15.5	84.8	41.3	59.3	85.9	96.5	58.8	120.2	134.7
1974	6.5	10.2	14.3	11.1	12.3	11.1	15.2	15.8	87.2	69.0	75.5	96.9	108.6	74.7	134.1	164.7
1975	6.9	6.9	13.1	9.2	11.9	9.2	14.0	14.4	91.2	53.2	69.3	81.8	109.1	64.1	139.2	145.2
1976	6.3	6.4	11.7	4.5	12.0	9.8	13.7	13.8	84.6	44.6	56.9	67.7	106.3	62.5	135.6	136.9
1977	5.9	7.8	11.7	9.5	13.2	11.6	14.5	14.8	83.7	52.3	53.2	76.8	117.3	59.5	137.1	154.7
1978	7.4	7.3	11.5	9.2	15.1	10.9	14.2	14.8	110.7	46.7	52.5	75.3	149.2	57.9	144.7	152.1
1979	5.6	9.1	11.9	10.3	12.8	11.9	15.2	17.8	79.4	46.6	56.6	82.8	114.3	67.7	151.9	174.4
1980	6.3	7.5	11.1	10.4	12.9	12.1	14.8	17.1	91.9	48.1	54.4	85.1	118.1	64.5	147.0	170.5
1981	6.3	7.5	11.3	12.6	13.1	12.4	14.6	16.1	98.6	48.7	55.7	84.2	115.2	69.7	148.5	163.5
1982	7.1	10.0	11.1	10.8	13.5	15.2	15.6	16.0	102.0	63.1	55.3	83.9	129.6	82.5	158.7	161.3
1983	6.6	8.0	10.4	10.2	14.3	14.6	15.4	15.7	101.7	49.5	54.7	70.4	127.7	77.8	155.1	148.5
1984	6.1	5.8	9.5	8.0	16.1	15.1	16.3	15.2	103.4	37.9	48.9	56.8	139.4	84.9	141.4	143.5
1985	6.1	5.7	9.3	9.0	15.3	15.6	16.3	15.4	96.2	34.8	47.8	63.1	136.1	85.5	143.7	145.8
1986	6.3	6.5	9.4	9.2	15.4	14.9	16.3	15.7	105.0	34.5	51.7	69.2	154.1	93.2	151.3	191.3
1987	6.5	9.1	8.5	8.6	15.0	16.4	15.2	15.2	103.1	42.2	47.5	63.6	161.1	94.6	140.8	207.2
1988	6.6	9.7	9.1	8.7	13.9	15.3	15.5	15.3	99.7	40.3	44.1	64.1	171.5	115.1	138.9	226.7
1989	6.9	10.2	9.5	9.0	14.4	16.2	15.2	15.2	116.4	45.9	47.7	68.9	182.2	131.0	152.3	252.6
1990	6.8	8.9	11.1	9.8	13.8	15.7	17.3	16.2	117.8	41.2	57.8	77.9	182.7	131.1	186.9	272.6
1991	7.7	10.2	11.3	9.4	14.5	17.2	16.7	15.3	120.7	45.5	57.2	77.2	188.3	128.6	183.4	265.0
1992	6.8	9.5	10.4	8.8	14.6	17.0	16.4	14.3	114.1	45.3	60.4	75.6	186.9	129.5	210.0	267.7
1993	7.0	9.7	11.3	8.5	13.8	16.7	16.3	13.3	115.9	44.8	62.1	71.8	190.8	131.4	213.0	270.3
1994	6.6	10.0	10.2	8.2	12.7	17.3	15.5	12.0	110.5	48.2	59.9	69.9	186.2	147.5	222.5	282.2
1995	6.9	9.4	9.4	7.7	13.0	15.7	14.6	10.7	126.6	45.0	57.6	67.7	212.7	151.1	217.0	288.2
1996	5.6	9.3	8.6	6.9	11.8	15.6	13.5	10.8	100.7	49.2	49.3	63.7	177.1	166.1	187.7	270.6
1997	3.2	8.9	8.6	5.9	9.8	14.0	13.2	10.7	46.9	44.6	51.4	58.7	152.8	156.6	189.0	285.1
1998	3.7	9.6	7.5	5.7	10.5	13.6	12.7	10.4	51.2	39.6	43.5	52.3	157.9	155.5	176.2	259.9
1999	3.3	8.7	6.1	4.8	10.0	13.9	11.0	9.7	48.2	39.9	37.6	46.2	153.4	149.4	163.0	245.6
2000	3.1	4.6	6.3	4.4	9.9	10.9	10.0	9.0	45.3	33.2	37.3	42.6	146.5	129.8	155.2	235.4
2001	3.2	5.3	6.0	4.5	9.6	11.0	9.7	8.9	45.4	34.5	38.0	41.5	140.4	136.4	148.4	234.2
2002	3.2	5.7	5.7	4.6	10.0	11.2	10.1	8.4	44.7	32.1	35.5	40.0	131.1	144.5	145.5	222.6

Note: See Notes, tables 4.1 and 4.2. For a list of States in regions and definitions of offenses, see Appendix 3.

Source: U.S. Department of Justice, Federal Bureau of Investigation, *Crime in the United States*, *1971*, p. 35; *1972*, p. 35; *1973*, p. 34; *1974*, p. 45; *1975*, p. 41; *1976*, p. 172; *1977*, p. 171; *1978*, p. 185; *1979*, p. 187; *1980*, p. 190; *1981*, p. 161; *1982*, p. 166; *1983*, p. 169; *1984*, p. 162; *1985*, p. 165; *1986*, p. 165; *1987*, p. 165; *1988*, p. 169; *1989*, p. 173; *1990*, p. 175; *1991*, p. 214; *1992*, p. 218; *1993*, p. 218; *1994*, p. 218; *1995*, p. 209; *1996*, p. 215; *1997*, p. 223; *1998*, p. 211; *1999*, p. 213; *2000*, p. 217; *2001*, p. 235; *2002*, p. 235 (Washington, DC: USGPO). Table adapted by SOURCEBOOK staff.

Table 4.18

Arrest rates (per 100,000 inhabitants) for property crimes

By offense charged and region, 1971-2002

(Rate per 100,000 inhabitants)

	Burglary				Larceny-theft				Motor vehicle theft				Arson			
	Northeast	Midwest	South	West	Northeast	Midwest	South	West	Northeast	Midwest	South	West	Northeast	Midwest	South	West
1971	173.7	170.7	204.8	295.2	302.1	455.8	445.2	572.1	72.1	69.5	67.5	151.2	X	X	X	X
1972	164.0	157.9	200.3	306.7	281.8	447.2	431.0	593.5	66.6	61.2	62.3	137.4	X	X	X	X
1973	189.6	154.3	193.9	314.2	280.8	424.6	425.7	572.6	77.1	58.9	60.6	126.0	X	X	X	X
1974	207.9	213.5	269.5	361.5	398.0	586.0	542.5	680.9	67.3	62.3	66.7	139.9	X	X	X	X
1975	222.0	186.5	271.0	344.3	393.7	528.8	571.7	658.1	63.1	49.9	56.8	112.2	X	X	X	X
1976	232.9	170.2	241.5	307.2	423.8	491.9	550.4	692.3	65.9	46.4	51.1	115.0	X	X	X	X
1977	243.6	178.8	233.8	320.8	452.0	507.9	521.3	658.1	66.4	57.7	53.6	125.4	X	X	X	X
1978	259.6	166.7	231.5	304.5	475.7	485.9	515.9	646.2	77.9	55.4	57.5	124.0	X	X	X	X
1979	221.0	163.2	237.9	315.8	447.4	499.5	537.9	697.5	60.6	52.2	58.1	129.2	9.9	8.1	7.9	11.2
1980	226.1	167.2	239.0	303.5	463.5	535.1	516.3	674.8	60.1	46.0	50.2	107.4	9.8	8.3	8.1	9.8
1981	213.4	172.5	235.0	305.9	474.2	558.2	541.7	685.9	55.2	42.8	47.8	93.9	9.2	8.6	8.5	10.5
1982	199.5	188.8	234.5	304.9	492.4	661.6	590.4	735.4	57.8	49.4	47.6	83.7	9.0	11.5	7.5	9.9
1983	177.9	166.2	209.7	275.9	475.8	593.9	566.4	703.1	49.5	41.7	46.0	78.1	8.5	9.1	7.8	9.3
1984	159.6	139.3	194.3	247.9	466.2	545.8	549.9	692.6	50.0	38.3	49.5	71.2	8.0	8.0	7.1	10.2
1985	156.7	133.0	197.6	258.7	477.9	549.5	572.2	723.5	47.7	38.4	53.0	90.9	8.8	7.9	7.2	9.9
1986	151.1	129.6	206.7	253.9	478.5	563.4	590.7	738.4	54.8	43.4	60.0	101.7	8.0	7.7	7.1	8.8
1987	151.7	136.5	204.9	235.8	514.9	622.7	602.1	739.2	67.3	50.3	66.3	109.2	7.8	7.7	6.4	8.6
1988	145.2	131.3	182.7	234.9	511.6	625.8	579.3	730.6	77.1	60.6	64.7	124.4	7.6	8.2	6.9	8.2
1989	153.6	135.5	181.9	239.8	527.1	650.2	599.4	729.0	90.7	73.1	73.1	134.2	7.2	7.6	6.7	7.9
1990	145.1	121.4	192.9	229.0	533.3	626.9	647.0	729.0	79.7	56.3	81.0	128.5	7.2	8.0	7.4	8.4
1991	142.0	127.8	182.7	223.9	536.0	660.4	650.0	693.8	78.6	56.0	78.2	122.4	7.1	7.7	8.0	8.3
1992	137.0	122.4	174.8	222.2	499.8	610.1	607.5	686.6	69.6	52.7	72.7	122.5	7.1	8.6	6.8	8.7
1993	126.2	110.4	168.7	206.4	466.4	577.7	598.2	666.1	65.7	57.0	71.7	118.1	6.8	8.0	7.1	8.5
1994	120.0	113.9	165.5	194.0	468.7	593.9	635.0	643.4	61.3	64.4	74.8	114.6	6.9	9.5	7.1	9.5
1995	125.5	108.5	156.2	180.7	509.7	586.1	610.1	627.6	58.5	67.2	67.9	105.9	6.7	9.3	6.4	9.1
1996	108.6	111.4	147.2	172.9	438.1	638.4	612.6	600.2	50.2	83.1	57.2	88.9	5.8	8.5	6.7	8.1
1997	109.8	101.7	142.7	161.9	456.8	606.8	589.9	568.7	37.5	71.4	55.1	83.5	6.8	7.8	7.8	7.5
1998	101.6	95.3	134.5	148.8	427.8	527.6	528.5	515.7	42.3	68.1	49.1	70.9	6.7	7.2	6.1	6.6
1999	86.9	90.6	118.3	133.8	383.5	466.6	509.6	461.7	39.2	80.3	41.2	62.1	6.5	7.2	5.9	6.0
2000	81.0	81.1	109.6	126.0	360.9	460.4	458.6	424.1	36.2	73.4	43.0	64.9	5.8	5.6	5.6	6.3
2001	82.2	78.0	108.9	124.9	357.8	460.8	448.0	399.0	35.3	64.0	41.5	70.2	5.9	5.6	6.0	8.3
2002	83.3	81.5	103.5	121.2	345.8	441.4	444.9	394.4	34.6	54.9	39.2	74.9	5.9	5.9	5.6	5.8

Note: See Notes, tables 4.1 and 4.2. Arson was designated an Index property crime in October 1978. Data collection began in 1979. For a list of States in regions and definitions of offenses, see Appendix 3.

Source: U.S. Department of Justice, Federal Bureau of Investigation, *Crime in the United States, 1971*, p. 35; *1972*, p. 35; *1973*, p. 34; *1974*, p. 45; *1975*, p. 41; *1976*, p. 172; *1977*, p. 171; *1978*, p. 185; *1979*, p. 187; *1980*, p. 190; *1981*, p. 161; *1982*, p. 166; *1983*, p. 169; *1984*, p. 162; *1985*, p. 165; *1986*, p. 165; *1987*, p. 165; *1988*, p. 169; *1989*, p. 173; *1990*, p. 175; *1991*, p. 214; *1992*, p. 218; *1993*, p. 218; *1994*, p. 218; *1995*, p. 209; *1996*, p. 215; *1997*, p. 223; *1998*, p. 211; *1999*, p. 213; *2000*, p. 217; *2001*, p. 235; *2002*, p. 235 (Washington, DC: USGPO). Table adapted by SOURCEBOOK staff.

Table 4.19

Offenses known to police and percent cleared by arrest[a]

By offense and population group, 2002

(2002 estimated population)

Population group	Total Crime Index	Violent crime[b]	Property crime[c]	Murder and non-negligent manslaughter	Forcible rape	Robbery	Aggravated assault	Burglary	Larceny-theft	Motor vehicle theft
Total all agencies										
12,862 agencies; population 240,070,262:										
Offenses known	10,121,721	1,184,453	8,937,268	13,561	80,515	343,023	747,354	1,842,930	6,014,290	1,080,048
Percent cleared by arrest	20.0%	46.8	16.5	64.0	44.5	25.7	56.5	13.0	18.0	13.8
Total cities										
9,130 cities; population 159,128,836:										
Offenses known	7,966,962	934,424	7,032,538	10,371	59,085	299,891	565,077	1,341,162	4,812,396	878,980
Percent cleared by arrest	19.7%	44.5	16.4	62.0	43.4	25.0	54.6	12.3	18.1	12.8
Group I										
65 cities, 250,000 and over; population 40,220,526:										
Offenses known	2,746,733	425,109	2,321,624	5,643	19,771	158,573	241,122	455,961	1,442,526	423,137
Percent cleared by arrest	16.8%	38.6	12.8	57.8	44.0	21.4	49.1	10.5	14.3	10.3
8 cities, 1,000,000 and over; population 13,659,273:										
Offenses known	846,653	149,894	696,759	1,855	5,696	56,911	85,432	132,872	419,599	144,288
Percent cleared by arrest	17.4%	38.6	12.9	61.9	42.9	22.2	48.7	10.7	14.8	9.2
21 cities, 500,000 to 999,999; population 13,866,854:										
Offenses known	977,046	145,515	851,531	2,020	7,443	52,147	83,905	170,288	539,734	141,509
Percent cleared by arrest	15.6%	37.2	11.9	54.5	43.7	19.8	47.0	9.4	13.1	10.3
36 cities, 250,000 to 499,999; population 12,694,399:										
Offenses known	903,034	129,700	773,334	1,768	6,632	49,515	71,785	152,801	483,193	137,340
Percent cleared by arrest	17.5%	40.3	13.7	57.1	45.2	22.3	51.9	11.4	15.1	11.3
Group II										
158 cities, 100,000 to 249,999; population 23,822,400:										
Offenses known	1,320,491	145,837	1,174,654	1,698	9,645	50,401	84,093	226,441	793,631	154,582
Percent cleared by arrest	18.6%	44.4	15.3	61.7	43.1	26.4	55.0	11.4	17.1	11.9
Group III										
381 cities, 50,000 to 99,999; population 26,328,413:										
Offenses known	1,187,713	126,887	1,060,826	1,189	9,443	38,358	77,897	203,511	738,564	118,751
Percent cleared by arrest	20.4%	46.9	17.3	67.3	41.9	27.6	56.7	12.3	19.4	12.3
Group IV										
682 cities, 25,000 to 49,999; population 23,803,053:										
Offenses known	965,387	87,974	877,413	746	7,388	23,742	56,098	163,955	637,193	76,265
Percent cleared by arrest	21.7%	49.8	18.8	72.3	40.4	30.9	58.7	12.8	20.8	15.4
Group V										
1,555 cities, 10,000 to 24,999; population 24,675,220:										
Offenses known	929,803	79,815	849,988	612	7,156	18,290	53,757	156,697	631,531	61,760
Percent cleared by arrest	23.9%	53.4	21.1	70.6	44.9	32.9	61.3	15.3	22.6	20.8
Group VI										
6,289 cities under 10,000; population 20,279,224:										
Offenses known	816,835	68,802	748,033	483	5,682	10,527	52,110	134,597	568,951	44,485
Percent cleared by arrest	22.9%	58.9	19.6	73.7	46.2	34.9	65.1	16.3	19.8	26.3
Suburban counties										
1,279 agencies; population 54,106,364:										
Offenses known	1,636,611	191,377	1,445,234	2,227	15,051	38,727	135,372	349,563	930,563	165,108
Percent cleared by arrest	20.8%	54.0	16.4	66.6	47.0	29.5	61.6	14.0	17.4	15.7

See notes at end of table.

Table 4.19

Offenses known to police and percent cleared by arrest[a]

By offense and population group, 2002--Continued

Population group	Total Crime Index	Violent crime[b]	Property crime[c]	Murder and non-negligent manslaughter	Forcible rape	Robbery	Aggravated assault	Burglary	Larceny-theft	Motor vehicle theft
Rural counties 2,453 agencies; population 26,835,062:										
Offenses known	518,148	58,652	459,496	963	6,379	4,405	46,905	152,205	271,331	35,960
Percent cleared by arrest	23.2%	61.4	18.3	78.9	49.8	41.4	64.5	16.6	17.9	27.9
Suburban areas[d] 6,120 agencies; population 99,561,928:										
Offenses known	3,226,405	320,382	2,906,023	3,210	25,562	71,803	219,807	604,584	2,010,471	290,968
Percent cleared by arrest	21.3%	53.4	17.8	67.5	45.7	29.9	61.7	14.1	19.1	16.2

Note: See Note, table 4.1. "An offense is 'cleared by arrest' or solved for crime reporting purposes when at least one person is: (1) arrested; (2) charged with the commission of the offense; and (3) turned over to the court for prosecution." The prosecution can follow arrest, court summons, or police notice. An offense is also counted as cleared by arrest if any of the following "exceptional" conditions pertain: (1) suicide of the offender; (2) double murder; (3) deathbed confession; (4) offender killed by police or citizen; (5) confession by offender already in custody or serving a sentence; (6) an offender prosecuted in another jurisdiction for a different offense and that jurisdiction does not release offender to first jurisdiction; (7) extradition denied; (8) victim refuses to cooperate in prosecution; (9) warrant is outstanding for felon but before arrest the offender dies of natural causes or as a result of an accident, or is killed in the commission of another offense; or, (10) handling of a juvenile offender either orally or by written notice to parents in instances involving minor offenses where no referral to juvenile court is made as a matter of publicly accepted police policy. (U.S. Department of Justice, Federal Bureau of Investigation, *Uniform Crime Reporting Handbook* (Washington, DC: USGPO, 1984), pp. 41, 42.) It should be noted that the arrest of one person can clear several crimes or several persons may be arrested to clear one crime.

Arson was designated an Index property crime in October 1978. Due to the incompleteness of arson reporting by police for offenses known, arson data are not included in this table. This table presents data from all law enforcement agencies submitting complete reports for at least 6 months in 2002 (Source, p. 451). Population figures are estimates calculated from U.S. Census Bureau data. For definitions of offenses, city and suburban areas, and rural counties, see Appendix 3.

[a]Includes offenses cleared by exceptional means.
[b]Violent crimes are offenses of murder and nonnegligent manslaughter, forcible rape, robbery, and aggravated assault.
[c]Property crimes are offenses of burglary, larceny-theft, and motor vehicle theft. Data are not included for the property crime of arson.
[d]Includes law enforcement agencies in cities with less than 50,000 inhabitants and county law enforcement agencies that are within a Metropolitan Statistical Area; excludes all metropolitan agencies associated with a central city. The agencies associated with suburban areas also will appear in other groups within this table.

Source: U.S. Department of Justice, Federal Bureau of Investigation, *Crime in the United States, 2002* (Washington, DC: USGPO, 2003), pp. 223, 224. Table adapted by SOURCEBOOK staff.

Table 4.20

Offenses known to police and percent cleared by arrest[a]

By type of offense, United States, 1971-2002

	Total Crime Index		Violent crime[b]		Property crime[c]	
	Offenses known to police	Percent cleared by arrest	Offenses known to police	Percent cleared by arrest	Offenses known to police	Percent cleared by arrest
1971	5,377,735	20.9%	473,126	46.5%	3,126,936	15.7%
1972	5,345,468	22.0	506,938	48.8	3,189,111	16.1
1973	6,412,766	21.2	685,982	45.2	5,726,784	18.3
1974	7,226,079	21.3	750,341	45.2	6,475,738	18.5
1975	8,198,613	21.0	797,688	44.7	7,400,925	18.5
1976	8,647,303	20.5	791,409	45.5	7,855,894	18.0
1977	8,007,135	21.0	773,328	45.8	7,233,807	18.3
1978	8,431,644	20.8	830,565	45.5	7,601,079	18.1
1979	9,143,082	19.8	914,576	43.7	8,228,506	17.1
1980	12,483,038	19.2	1,242,511	43.6	11,240,527	16.5
1981	12,715,894	19.5	1,275,135	42.9	11,440,759	16.9
1982	11,932,744	20.1	1,195,533	45.4	10,737,211	17.3
1983	11,403,141	20.6	1,166,888	46.5	10,236,253	17.7
1984	11,121,418	21.0	1,172,616	47.4	9,948,802	17.9
1985	11,762,540	20.9	1,240,134	47.6	10,522,406	17.8
1986	12,734,405	20.7	1,445,965	46.3	11,288,440	17.5
1987	12,502,268	20.9	1,354,012	47.4	11,148,256	17.7
1988	12,059,648	20.7	1,355,693	45.7	10,703,955	17.5
1989	12,124,462	21.1	1,364,705	45.8	10,759,757	18.0
1990	13,468,228	21.6	1,700,303	45.6	11,767,925	18.1
1991	13,334,099	21.2	1,682,487	44.7	11,651,612	17.8
1992	13,644,294	21.4	1,854,630	44.6	11,789,664	17.7
1993	12,863,631	21.1	1,772,279	44.2	11,091,352	17.4
1994	12,586,227	21.4	1,720,302	45.3	10,865,925	17.7
1995	11,859,129	21.2	1,531,703	45.4	10,327,426	17.6
1996	10,419,304	21.8	1,293,408	47.4	9,125,896	18.1
1997	10,928,483	21.6	1,343,642	48.3	9,584,841	17.9
1998	9,583,738	21.3	1,178,388	49.1	8,405,350	17.4
1999	9,659,727	21.4	1,164,380	50.0	8,495,347	17.5
2000	9,366,936	20.5	1,131,923	47.5	8,235,013	16.7
2001	8,884,332	19.6	1,024,134	46.2	7,860,198	16.2
2002	10,121,721	20.0	1,184,453	46.8	8,937,268	16.5

Note: See Notes, tables 4.1, 4.2, and 4.19. This table presents data from all law enforcement agencies submitting complete reports for 12 months or fewer in 1971-80 and at least 6 months in 1981-2002. For definitions of offenses, see Appendix 3.

[a]Includes offenses cleared by exceptional means.
[b]Violent crimes are offenses of murder and nonnegligent manslaughter, forcible rape, robbery, and aggravated assault.
[c]Property crimes are offenses of burglary, larceny-theft, and motor vehicle theft. Data are not included for the property crime of arson.

Source: U.S. Department of Justice, Federal Bureau of Investigation, *Crime in the United States, 1971*, p. 104; *1972*, p. 107; *1973*, p. 109; *1974*, p. 166; *1975*, p. 166; *1976*, p. 162; *1977*, p. 162; *1978*, p. 177; *1979*, p. 179; *1980*, p. 182; *1981*, p. 153; *1982*, p. 158; *1983*, p. 161; *1984*, p. 154; *1985*, p. 156; *1986*, p. 156; *1987*, p. 155; *1988*, p. 159; *1989*, p. 163; *1990*, p. 165; *1991*, p. 204; *1992*, p. 208; *1993*, p. 208; *1994*, p. 208; *1995*, p. 199; *1996*, p. 205; *1997*, p. 213; *1998*, p. 201; *1999*, p. 203; *2000*, p. 207; *2001*, p. 222; *2002*, p. 223 (Washington, DC: USGPO). Table constructed by SOURCEBOOK staff.

Table 4.21

Percent of offenses known to police that were cleared by arrest[a]

By extent of urbanization and type of offense, 1972-2002

	Cities			Suburban[b]			Rural		
	Total Crime Index	Violent crime[c]	Property crime[d]	Total Crime Index	Violent crime[c]	Property crime[d]	Total Crime Index	Violent crime[c]	Property crime[d]
1972	20.6%	48.8%	16.1%	17.2%	50.3%	14.0%	25.2%	70.2%	20.1%
1973	21.2	45.2	18.3	19.2	51.2	17.0	23.5	69.5	19.3
1974	21.3	45.2	18.5	19.5	50.0	17.3	24.0	69.7	19.7
1975	21.0	44.7	18.5	19.7	50.0	17.6	23.6	70.1	19.4
1976	20.5	45.5	18.0	19.1	51.3	16.9	22.7	69.5	18.7
1977	21.0	45.8	18.3	19.3	50.9	16.9	23.1	69.2	18.8
1978	20.8	45.5	18.1	19.4	49.9	17.0	22.7	67.9	18.4
1979	19.8	43.7	17.1	19.0	49.3	16.6	22.8	67.0	18.8
1980	19.2	41.7	16.6	18.6	48.4	16.2	20.5	64.9	16.7
1981	19.5	40.9	17.0	19.4	48.7	17.0	20.7	63.8	17.0
1982	20.0	43.5	17.3	20.4	50.9	17.8	22.1	66.4	18.1
1983	20.5	44.5	17.7	21.1	52.3	18.4	22.1	66.9	18.0
1984	21.0	45.5	18.0	21.7	53.8	18.8	22.3	65.7	18.1
1985	20.9	45.7	17.9	21.1	53.2	18.2	22.9	67.0	18.4
1986	20.7	44.6	17.5	21.1	51.7	18.3	22.0	63.9	17.7
1987	21.0	46.0	17.9	21.2	51.3	18.4	21.6	61.8	17.6
1988	20.7	44.2	17.7	21.2	51.7	18.4	21.9	63.5	17.8
1989	21.3	44.4	18.2	21.4	51.3	18.7	22.2	61.7	18.2
1990	21.7	43.9	18.3	21.8	51.7	18.7	22.3	61.3	18.1
1991	21.3	42.9	18.1	21.7	51.2	18.6	22.9	63.0	18.6
1992	21.5	43.1	18.0	21.9	51.1	18.6	23.0	60.7	18.4
1993	21.2	42.5	17.6	21.7	51.0	18.3	22.9	60.7	18.3
1994	21.5	43.5	17.8	22.0	52.5	18.5	23.6	60.9	18.7
1995	21.1	43.5	17.7	22.1	52.7	18.6	23.2	60.9	18.6
1996	21.8	45.9	18.3	22.3	53.7	19.1	24.3	62.3	19.8
1997	21.4	46.2	17.9	22.5	54.5	18.9	23.9	62.2	19.2
1998	21.3	47.7	17.5	21.9	54.5	18.4	23.4	60.2	18.7
1999	21.4	48.3	17.6	22.0	54.4	18.4	23.4	61.4	18.4
2000	20.2	45.4	16.8	21.6	53.8	17.9	23.7	61.3	18.7
2001	19.4	44.0	16.2	20.5	53.5	17.2	23.0	62.0	18.1
2002	19.7	44.5	16.4	21.3	53.4	17.8	23.2	61.4	18.3

Note: See Notes, tables 4.1, 4.2, and 4.19. For definitions of offenses, city and suburban areas, and rural counties, see Appendix 3.

[a]Includes offenses cleared by exceptional means.
[b]Includes city law enforcement agencies with less than 50,000 inhabitants and county law enforcement agencies that are within a Metropolitan Statistical Area; excludes all metropolitan agencies associated with a central city. The agencies associated with suburban areas also will appear in other groups within this table.
[c]Violent crimes are offenses of murder and nonnegligent manslaughter, forcible rape, robbery, and aggravated assault.
[d]Property crimes are offenses of burglary, larceny-theft, and motor vehicle theft. Data are not included for the property crime of arson.

Source: U.S. Department of Justice, Federal Bureau of Investigation, *Crime in the United States, 1972*, pp. 107, 108; *1973*, pp. 109, 110; *1974*, pp. 166, 167; *1975*, pp. 166, 167; *1976*, pp. 162, 163; *1977*, pp. 162, 163; *1978*, pp. 177, 178; *1979*, pp. 179, 180; *1980*, pp. 182, 183; *1981*, pp. 153, 154; *1982*, pp. 158, 159; *1983*, pp. 161, 162; *1984*, pp. 154, 155; *1985*, pp. 156, 157; *1986*, pp. 156, 157; *1987*, pp. 155, 156; *1988*, pp. 159, 160; *1989*, pp. 163, 164; *1990*, pp. 165, 166; *1991*, pp. 204, 205; *1992*, pp. 208, 209; *1993*, pp. 208, 209; *1994*, pp. 208, 209; *1995*, pp. 199, 200; *1996*, pp. 205, 206; *1997*, pp. 213, 214; *1998*, pp. 201, 202; *1999*, pp. 203, 204; *2000*, pp. 207, 208; *2001*, pp. 222, 223; *2002*, pp. 223, 224 (Washington, DC: USGPO). Table constructed by SOURCEBOOK staff.

Table 4.22

Number of offenses known to police that were cleared by arrest and percent of clearances from arrest of persons under 18 years of age[a]

By offense and population group, 2002

(2002 estimated population)

Population group	Total Crime Index	Violent crime[b]	Property crime[c]	Murder and non-negligent manslaughter	Forcible rape	Robbery	Aggravated assault	Burglary	Larceny-theft	Motor vehicle theft
Total all agencies 11,912 agencies; population 212,703,198:										
Total clearances	1,715,344	460,834	1,254,510	7,473	30,521	73,815	349,025	199,395	929,658	125,457
Percent under 18 years of age	18.0%	11.9	20.3	5.0	12.0	14.1	11.6	17.3	21.2	18.2
Total cities 8,647 cities; population 144,084,799:										
Total clearances	1,366,819	356,903	1,009,916	5,599	22,632	64,405	264,267	142,839	769,020	98,057
Percent under 18 years of age	18.6%	12.1	20.9	5.4	11.6	14.2	11.7	17.3	21.9	18.5
Group I 56 cities, 250,000 and over; population 35,189,022:										
Total clearances	391,212	138,430	252,782	2,774	7,594	29,021	99,041	39,903	175,057	37,822
Percent under 18 years of age	15.2%	10.2	17.8	5.1	9.1	13.8	9.4	14.4	18.3	19.3
8 cities, 1,000,000 and over; population 13,659,273:										
Total clearances	147,518	57,801	89,717	1,148	2,443	12,617	41,593	14,217	62,174	13,326
Percent under 18 years of age	13.8%	9.2	16.8	5.1	8.5	13.8	7.9	13.2	17.6	16.8
15 cities, 500,000 to 999,999; population 9,791,298:										
Total clearances	101,556	34,923	66,633	680	2,355	6,396	25,492	10,067	46,297	10,269
Percent under 18 years of age	14.9%	10.5	17.2	3.7	8.9	14.9	9.8	14.7	16.8	21.1
33 cities, 250,000 to 499,999; population 11,738,451:										
Total clearances	142,138	45,706	96,432	946	2,796	10,008	31,956	15,619	66,586	14,227
Percent under 18 years of age	16.7%	11.4	19.3	6.0	9.9	13.1	11.2	15.3	20.0	20.2
Group II 140 cities, 100,000 to 249,999; population 21,144,564:										
Total clearances	208,095	54,414	153,681	935	3,543	11,455	38,481	22,045	116,431	15,205
Percent under 18 years of age	18.2%	11.6	20.5	5.7	9.4	13.8	11.3	16.2	21.8	17.1
Group III 342 cities, 50,000 to 99,999; population 23,701,295:										
Total clearances	211,407	51,078	160,329	713	3,454	9,113	37,798	21,363	126,249	12,717
Percent under 18 years of age	21.1%	13.5	23.5	5.8	13.1	16.3	13.0	17.6	25.0	19.2
Group IV 628 cities, 25,000 to 49,999; population 21,868,627:										
Total clearances	184,190	38,302	145,888	458	2,640	6,269	28,935	18,054	117,778	10,056
Percent under 18 years of age	21.1%	13.9	22.9	5.9	13.3	15.2	13.7	19.4	23.8	19.2
Group V 1,429 cities, 10,000 to 24,999; population 22,716,911:										
Total clearances	197,861	37,283	160,578	385	2,898	5,239	28,761	21,259	128,035	11,284
Percent under 18 years of age	20.0%	13.7	21.5	5.2	16.0	13.6	13.5	18.0	22.5	17.1
Group VI 6,052 cities under 10,000; population 19,464,380:										
Total clearances	174,054	37,396	136,658	334	2,503	3,308	31,251	20,215	105,470	10,973
Percent under 18 years of age	19.6%	14.2	21.1	5.7	13.2	13.5	14.5	21.5	21.3	17.6

See notes at end of table.

Table 4.22

Number of offenses known to police that were cleared by arrest and percent of clearances from arrest of persons under 18 years of age[a]

By offense and population group, 2002--Continued

Population group	Total Crime Index	Violent crime[b]	Property crime[c]	Murder and non-negligent manslaughter	Forcible rape	Robbery	Aggravated assault	Burglary	Larceny-theft	Motor vehicle theft
Suburban counties 1,053 agencies; population 44,134,049:										
Total clearances	244,872	72,856	172,016	1,185	5,088	7,968	58,615	34,919	118,309	18,788
Percent under 18 years of age	16.4%	12.3	18.1	4.0	12.8	14.4	12.1	17.6	18.6	16.1
Rural counties 2,212 agencies; population 24,484,350:										
Total clearances	103,653	31,075	72,578	689	2,801	1,442	26,143	21,637	42,329	8,612
Percent under 18 years of age	14.5%	9.6	16.5	4.2	13.8	7.4	9.5	16.6	15.9	19.7
Suburban areas[d] 5,581 agencies; population 85,992,422:										
Total clearances	548,995	130,615	418,380	1,768	9,178	16,460	103,209	65,999	314,949	37,432
Percent under 18 years of age	18.5%	13.6	20.0	4.8	13.9	14.6	13.5	18.6	20.7	16.5

Note: See Notes, tables 4.1 and 4.19. For definitions of offenses, city and suburban areas, and rural counties, see Appendix 3.

[a]Includes offenses cleared by exceptional means.
[b]Violent crimes are offenses of murder and nonnegligent manslaughter, forcible rape, robbery, and aggravated assault.
[c]Property crimes are offenses of burglary, larceny-theft, and motor vehicle theft. Data are not included for the property crime of arson.
[d]Includes law enforcement agencies in cities with less than 50,000 inhabitants and county law enforcement agencies that are within a Metropolitan Statistical Area; excludes all metropolitan agencies associated with a central city. The agencies associated with suburban areas also will appear in other groups within this table.

Source: U.S. Department of Justice, Federal Bureau of Investigation, *Crime in the United States, 2002* (Washington, DC: USGPO, 2003), pp. 229, 230. Table adapted by SOURCEBOOK staff.

Table 4.23

Percent of offenses known to police that were cleared by arrest of persons under 18 years of age[a]

By type of offense, United States, 1972-2002

	Total Crime Index	Violent crime[b]	Property crime[c]
1972	27.3%	13.2%	33.8%
1973	30.6	12.2	35.9
1974	31.3	12.5	36.3
1975	30.0	12.8	34.4
1976	28.6	12.2	32.7
1977	28.4	11.8	32.8
1978	28.1	11.7	32.6
1979	26.6	11.6	30.9
1980	24.4	11.2	28.2
1981	21.4	9.8	24.7
1982	20.6	9.5	23.8
1983	20.1	9.5	23.2
1984	20.1	9.8	23.3
1985	20.1	9.6	23.4
1986	19.1	9.0	22.6
1987	18.1	8.5	21.3
1988	18.1	8.9	20.9
1989	17.8	9.5	20.3
1990	19.2	11.2	22.0
1991	19.3	11.4	22.1
1992	20.0	12.8	22.6
1993	20.5	13.4	23.3
1994	21.7	14.2	24.6
1995	22.1	14.1	25.0
1996	20.6	12.8	23.4
1997	20.2	12.4	23.0
1998	18.9	12.1	21.4
1999	19.3	12.4	21.8
2000	19.3	12.2	22.1
2001	18.6	12.1	21.1
2002	18.0	11.9	20.3

Note: See Notes, tables 4.1, 4.2, and 4.19. For definitions of offenses, see Appendix 3.

[a]Includes offenses cleared by exceptional means.
[b]Violent crimes are offenses of murder and nonnegligent manslaughter, forcible rape, robbery, and aggravated assault.
[c]Property crimes are offenses of burglary, larceny-theft, and motor vehicle theft. Data are not included for the property crime of arson.

Source: U.S. Department of Justice, Federal Bureau of Investigation, *Crime in the United States, 1972*, pp. 110, 111; *1973*, pp. 112, 113; *1974*, pp. 170, 171; *1975*, pp. 170, 171; *1976*, pp. 168, 169; *1977*, pp. 167, 168; *1978*, pp. 182, 183; *1979*, pp. 184, 185; *1980*, pp. 187, 188; *1981*, pp. 158, 159; *1982*, pp. 163, 164; *1983*, pp. 166, 167; *1984*, pp. 159, 160; *1985*, pp. 161, 162; *1986*, pp. 161, 162; *1987*, pp. 161, 162; *1988*, pp. 165, 166; *1989*, p. 169; *1990*, pp. 171, 172; *1991*, pp. 210, 211; *1992*, pp. 214, 215; *1993*, pp. 214, 215; *1994*, pp. 214, 215; *1995*, pp. 205, 206; *1996*, pp. 211, 212; *1997*, pp. 219, 220; *1998*, pp. 207, 208; *1999*, pp. 209, 210; *2000*, pp. 213, 214; *2001*, pp. 228, 229; *2002*, pp. 229, 230 (Washington, DC: USGPO). Table constructed by SOURCEBOOK staff.

Table 4.24

Arsons cleared by arrest and clearances by arrest of persons under 18 years of age[a]

By type of target, United States, 2002

(12,414 agencies; 2002 estimated population 225,428,667)

Target	Number of offenses	Percent of offenses cleared by arrest	Percent of clearances by arrest of persons under 18 years of age
Total	66,308	16.9%	42.1%
Total structure	27,373	22.4	40.3
Single occupancy residential	11,789	22.3	31.2
Other residential	4,821	22.2	30.7
Storage	1,940	20.2	54.0
Industrial/manufacturing	333	18.6	29.0
Other commercial	2,735	17.7	27.6
Community/public	3,140	33.0	71.8
Other structure	2,615	17.7	47.1
Total mobile	21,920	7.2	23.6
Motor vehicles	20,736	6.9	21.9
Other mobile	1,184	13.6	39.1
Other	17,015	20.4	53.5

Note: See Notes, tables 4.1 and 4.19. These data are from the 12,414 agencies that furnished detailed arson reports to the Uniform Crime Reporting Program for 2002. Users should be aware that these data do not represent the Nation's total arson experience and differ from those reported in other arrest tables displaying arson because only arson clearances reported by property classification are included. For the definition of arson, see Appendix 3.

[a]Includes offenses cleared by exceptional means.

Source: U.S. Department of Justice, Federal Bureau of Investigation, *Crime in the United States, 2002* (Washington, DC: USGPO, 2003), p. 58. Table adapted by SOURCEBOOK staff.

Table 4.25

Juveniles taken into police custody

By method of disposition and population group, 2002[a]

(2002 estimated population)

Population group	Total[b]	Handled within department and released	Referred to juvenile court jurisdiction	Referred to welfare agency	Referred to other police agency	Referred to criminal or adult court
Total all agencies						
6,073 agencies; total population 130,229,927						
Number	732,282	132,825	532,940	4,779	10,183	51,555
Percent	100.0%	18.1	72.8	0.7	1.4	7.0
Total cities						
4,577 cities; total population 92,489,061:						
Number	611,897	115,191	444,336	3,956	7,901	40,513
Percent	100.0%	18.8	72.6	0.6	1.3	6.6
Group I						
32 cities, 250,000 and over; population 23,601,703:						
Number	122,767	24,627	93,612	525	1,638	2,365
Percent	100.0%	20.1	76.3	0.4	1.3	1.9
Group II						
88 cities, 100,000 to 249,999; population 13,193,782:						
Number	81,448	13,344	61,791	636	1,143	4,534
Percent	100.0%	16.4	75.9	0.8	1.4	5.6
Group III						
235 cities, 50,000 to 99,999; population 16,120,073						
Number	111,816	26,075	78,439	533	1,822	4,947
Percent	100.0%	23.3	70.2	0.5	1.6	4.4
Group IV						
405 cities, 25,000 to 49,999; population 14,310,637:						
Number	94,913	17,183	68,483	1,187	1,769	6,291
Percent	100.0%	18.1	72.2	1.3	1.9	6.6
Group V						
896 cities, 10,000 to 24,999; population 14,336,965:						
Number	105,574	18,232	74,556	553	670	11,563
Percent	100.0%	17.3	70.6	0.5	0.6	11.0
Group VI						
2,921 cities under 10,000; population 10,925,901:						
Number	95,379	15,730	67,455	522	859	10,813
Percent	100.0%	16.5	70.7	0.5	0.9	11.3
Suburban counties						
568 agencies; population 25,198,464:						
Number	86,648	13,068	64,180	478	1,745	7,177
Percent	100.0%	15.1	74.1	0.6	2.0	8.3
Rural counties						
928 agencies; population 12,542,402:						
Number	33,737	4,566	24,424	345	537	3,865
Percent	100.0%	13.5	72.4	1.0	1.6	11.5
Suburban areas[c]						
3,286 agencies; population 62,227,924:						
Number	321,746	60,621	227,447	1,826	3,557	28,295
Percent	100.0%	18.8	70.7	0.6	1.1	8.8

Note: See Notes, tables 4.1 and 4.7. For definitions of city and suburban areas, and rural counties, see Appendix 3.

Source: U.S. Department of Justice, Federal Bureau of Investigation, *Crime in the United States, 2002* (Washington, DC: USGPO, 2003), p. 291.

[a]Because of rounding, percents may not add to total.
[b]Includes all offenses except traffic and neglect cases.
[c]Includes law enforcement agencies in cities with less than 50,000 inhabitants and county law enforcement agencies that are within a Metropolitan Statistical Area; excludes all metropolitan agencies associated with a central city. The agencies associated with suburban areas also will appear in other groups within this table.

Table 4.26
Percent distribution of juveniles taken into police custody

By method of disposition, United States, 1972-2002[a]

	Referred to juvenile court jurisdiction	Handled within department and released	Referred to criminal or adult court	Referred to other police agency	Referred to welfare agency
1972	50.8%	45.0%	1.3%	1.6%	1.3%
1973	49.5	45.2	1.5	2.3	1.4
1974	47.0	44.4	3.7	2.4	2.5
1975	52.7	41.6	2.3	1.9	1.4
1976	53.4	39.0	4.4	1.7	1.6
1977	53.2	38.1	3.9	1.8	3.0
1978	55.9	36.6	3.8	1.8	1.9
1979	57.3	34.6	4.8	1.7	1.6
1980	58.1	33.8	4.8	1.7	1.6
1981	58.0	33.8	5.1	1.6	1.5
1982	58.9	32.5	5.4	1.5	1.6
1983	57.5	32.8	4.8	1.7	3.1
1984	60.0	31.5	5.2	1.3	2.0
1985	61.8	30.7	4.4	1.2	1.9
1986	61.7	29.9	5.5	1.1	1.8
1987	62.0	30.3	5.2	1.0	1.4
1988	63.1	29.1	4.7	1.1	1.9
1989	63.9	28.7	4.5	1.2	1.7
1990	64.5	28.3	4.5	1.1	1.6
1991	64.2	28.1	5.0	1.0	1.7
1992	62.5	30.1	4.7	1.1	1.7
1993	67.3	25.6	4.8	0.9	1.5
1994	63.2	29.5	4.7	1.0	1.7
1995	65.7	28.4	3.3	0.9	1.7
1996	68.6	23.3	6.2	0.9	0.9
1997	66.9	24.6	6.6	0.8	1.1
1998	69.2	22.2	6.8	0.9	1.0
1999	69.2	22.5	6.4	1.0	0.8
2000	70.8	20.3	7.0	1.1	0.8
2001	72.4	19.0	6.5	1.4	0.7
2002	72.8	18.1	7.0	1.4	0.7

Note: See Notes, tables 4.1 and 4.2. These data include all offenses except traffic and neglect cases.

[a]Because of rounding, percents may not add to 100.

Source: U.S. Department of Justice, Federal Bureau of Investigation, *Crime in the United States, 1972*, p. 116; *1973*, p. 119; *1974*, p. 177; *1975*, p. 177; *1976*, p. 220; *1977*, p. 219; *1978*, p. 228; *1979*, p. 230; *1980*, p. 258; *1981*, p. 233; *1982*, p. 242; *1983*, p. 245; *1984*, p. 238; *1985*, p. 240; *1986*, p. 240; *1987*, p. 225; *1988*, p. 229; *1989*, p. 233; *1990*, p. 235; *1991*, p. 278; *1992*, p. 282; *1993*, p. 282; *1994*, p. 282; *1995*, p. 265; *1996*, p. 271; *1997*, p. 279; *1998*, p. 267; *1999*, p. 269; *2000*, p. 273; *2001*, p. 291; *2002*, p. 291 (Washington, DC: USGPO). Table constructed by SOURCEBOOK staff.

Table 4.27
Arrests for alcohol-related offenses and driving under the influence

United States, 1970-2002

(In thousands)

	Alcohol-related offenses	Driving under the influence
1970	2,849	424
1971	2,914	490
1972	2,835	604
1973	2,539	654
1974	2,297	617
1975	3,044	909
1976	2,790	838
1977	3,303	1,104
1978	3,406	1,205
1979	3,455	1,232
1980	3,535	1,304
1981	3,745	1,422
1982	3,640	1,405
1983	3,729	1,613
1984	3,153	1,347
1985	3,418	1,503
1986	3,325	1,459
1987	3,248	1,410
1988	2,995	1,294
1989	3,180	1,333
1990	3,270	1,391
1991	3,000	1,289
1992	3,061	1,320
1993	2,886	1,229
1994	2,698	1,080
1995	2,578	1,033
1996	2,677	1,014
1997	2,510	986
1998	2,451	969
1999	2,238	931
2000	2,218	916
2001	2,224	947
2002	2,401	1,020

Note: See Notes, tables 4.1 and 4.2. This table presents data from all law enforcement agencies submitting complete reports for 12 months. Alcohol-related offenses include driving under the influence, liquor law violations, drunkenness, disorderly conduct, and vagrancy. For definitions of offenses, see Appendix 3.

Source: U.S. Department of Justice, Federal Bureau of Investigation, *Crime in the United States, 1970*, p. 126; *1971*, p. 122; *1972*, p. 126; *1973*, p. 128; *1974*, p. 186; *1975*, p. 188; *1976*, p. 181; *1977*, p. 180; *1978*, p. 194; *1979*, p. 196; *1980*, p. 200; *1981*, p. 171; *1982*, pp. 176, 177; *1983*, pp. 179, 180; *1984*, pp. 172, 173; *1985*, pp. 174, 175; *1986*, pp. 174, 175; *1987*, pp. 174, 175; *1988*, pp. 178, 179; *1989*, pp. 182, 183; *1990*, pp. 184, 185; *1991*, pp. 223, 224; *1992*, pp. 227, 228; *1993*, pp. 227, 228; *1994*, pp. 227, 228; *1995*, pp. 218, 219; *1996*, pp. 224, 225; *1997*, pp. 232, 233; *1998*, pp. 220, 221; *1999*, pp. 222, 223; *2000*, pp. 226, 227; *2001*, pp. 244, 245; *2002*, pp. 244, 245 (Washington, DC: USGPO). Table constructed by SOURCEBOOK staff.

Table 4.28

Arrests for alcohol-related offenses

By offense and State, 2002

		Alcohol-related arrests						
State	All arrests	Total	Percent of all arrests	Driving under the influence	Liquor law violations	Drunken-ness	Disorderly conduct	Vagrancy
Total	10,452,151	2,522,356	24.1%	1,067,185	487,123	431,939	515,007	21,102
Alabama	195,820	34,219	17.5	13,869	6,503	9,715	3,808	324
Alaska	31,786	6,722	21.2	4,723	1,144	53	801	1
Arizona	298,631	83,736	28.0	41,417	24,896	0	16,669	754
Arkansas	109,681	24,497	22.3	9,822	1,653	9,034	3,351	637
California	1,417,641	325,461	23.0	178,688	25,359	99,587	17,311	4,516
Colorado	227,807	57,928	25.4	23,673	18,527	367	14,537	824
Connecticut	134,562	27,558	20.5	7,575	1,655	7	18,274	47
Delaware	34,223	5,333	15.6	198	2,113	328	2,193	501
District of Columbia	4,351	1,751	40.2	28	1,390	49	180	104
Georgia	232,234	53,561	23.1	23,836	7,646	4,377	16,458	1,244
Hawaii	63,019	5,188	8.2	3,731	932	14	511	0
Idaho	73,755	17,653	23.9	9,970	5,209	224	2,236	14
Illinois	199,430	26,175	13.1	5,910	1,050	0	19,215	0
Indiana	197,092	62,685	31.8	26,461	11,686	16,173	8,001	364
Iowa	113,188	38,755	34.2	13,293	12,213	8,412	4,783	54
Kansas	73,588	23,230	31.6	13,150	6,969	258	2,853	0
Kentucky	71,018	17,960	25.3	7,029	1,540	6,499	2,890	2
Louisiana	219,447	37,271	17.0	12,504	3,358	4,082	16,718	609
Maine	54,880	12,108	22.1	6,797	3,597	31	1,683	0
Maryland	311,064	35,651	11.5	22,965	6,531	4	5,958	193
Massachusetts	128,540	28,604	22.2	10,519	3,958	6,746	7,369	12
Michigan	371,655	91,277	24.6	50,153	29,229	613	10,944	338
Minnesota	164,144	62,445	38.0	26,922	25,703	0	9,737	83
Mississippi	122,310	31,756	26.0	12,663	3,253	6,972	8,756	112
Missouri	304,921	62,187	20.4	34,276	11,293	2,142	13,822	654
Montana	21,579	6,682	31.0	2,659	1,998	0	2,019	6
Nebraska	93,710	30,265	32.3	12,896	13,196	0	4,168	5
Nevada	151,826	22,672	14.9	8,958	7,865	296	3,177	2,376
New Hampshire	37,945	13,639	35.9	4,447	3,323	4,819	967	83
New Jersey	368,619	58,654	15.9	23,933	9,526	8	22,902	2,285
New Mexico	76,810	18,014	23.4	10,808	3,166	1,930	2,093	17
New York	358,173	55,628	15.5	32,725	6,013	0	15,795	1,095
North Carolina	441,000	89,607	20.3	57,727	14,969	0	16,663	248
North Dakota	25,468	10,213	40.1	3,341	5,139	276	1,455	2
Ohio	271,857	61,845	22.8	22,495	16,386	6,900	15,856	208
Oklahoma	161,363	51,430	31.9	21,649	3,031	23,792	2,955	3
Oregon	111,337	29,768	26.7	13,214	11,276	0	5,278	0
Pennsylvania	430,567	142,838	33.2	39,854	28,215	20,303	54,000	466
Rhode Island	42,140	6,067	14.4	1,933	1,066	190	2,872	6
South Carolina	212,950	47,635	22.4	13,157	10,086	9,435	14,618	339
South Dakota	36,746	15,562	42.4	5,112	8,110	566	1,745	29
Tennessee	266,072	65,255	24.5	27,488	6,878	20,675	10,161	53
Texas	1,041,883	294,591	28.3	90,283	32,396	132,520	37,397	1,995
Utah	124,115	32,398	26.1	8,002	12,889	5,160	6,158	189
Vermont	14,394	4,798	33.3	3,183	737	3	871	4
Virginia	289,890	66,937	23.1	24,095	10,931	25,139	6,675	97
Washington	237,143	52,875	22.3	34,636	13,645	26	4,524	44
West Virginia	38,035	10,737	28.2	5,567	1,717	2,556	891	6
Wisconsin	409,682	148,894	36.3	34,483	42,587	393	71,285	146
Wyoming	34,060	11,641	34.2	4,368	4,571	1,265	1,424	13

Note: These data are compiled from the Federal Bureau of Investigation's (FBI) Uniform Crime Reporting Program. The data presented in this table differ from those presented in the U.S. Department of Justice, Federal Bureau of Investigation, *Crime in the United States, 2002* (Washington, DC: USGPO, 2003) because this table includes data processed by the FBI after the cutoff date for that publication. According to the Source, in many States where drunkenness and/or vagrancy are not treated as criminal actions, these categories are not permissible causes of arrest. In one respect, these data may be considered conservative estimates of alcohol-related arrests. The FBI classifies arrests by a single offense, using a hierarchical rule. Consequently, crimes committed while intoxicated are categorized under the primary offense. On the other hand, "driving under the influence" includes impairment due to any type of drug; it is not limited to impairment due to alcohol. Data for 2002 were not available for Florida.

Source: Table adapted by SOURCEBOOK staff from table provided by the U.S. Department of Health and Human Services, National Institute on Alcohol Abuse and Alcoholism.

Table 4.29

Percent distribution of arrests for drug abuse violations

By type of drug, United States, 1982-2002[a]

	Total			Heroin/cocaine			Marijuana			Synthetic drugs			Other		
	Total	Sale/manu-facture	Posses-sion	Total	Sale/manu-facture	Posses-sion	Total	Sale/manu-facture	Posses-sion	Total	Sale/manu-facture	Posses-sion	Total	Sale/manu-facture	Posses-sion
1982	100%	20%	80%	13%	4%	9%	72%	10%	62%	4%	1%	2%	12%	5%	7%
1983	100	22	78	23	6	17	61	10	50	3	1	2	13	4	8
1984	100	22	78	26	7	19	59	10	48	3	1	2	12	4	9
1985	100	24	76	30	8	22	55	10	45	3	1	2	12	4	8
1986	100	25	75	41	13	28	44	8	36	3	1	2	13	4	9
1987	100	26	74	46	14	32	40	7	33	3	1	2	12	4	8
1988	100	27	73	52	17	35	34	6	28	3	1	2	11	4	7
1989	100	32	68	54	19	35	29	6	23	2	1	1	15	6	8
1990	100	32	68	54	21	33	30	6	24	2	1	2	14	4	10
1991	100	33	67	55	22	33	28	6	22	2	1	1	14	4	10
1992	100	32	68	53	21	32	32	7	26	2	1	1	13	4	9
1993	100	30	70	50	19	31	34	6	28	2	1	1	14	4	10
1994	100	27	73	47	17	30	36	6	30	2	(b)	1	16	4	12
1995	100	25	75	42	15	28	40	6	34	2	1	2	16	4	12
1996	100	25	75	40	14	26	43	6	36	2	1	1	16	4	12
1997	100	20	80	36	10	25	44	6	38	3	1	2	18	4	14
1998	100	21	79	37	11	26	44	5	38	3	1	2	17	4	13
1999	100	20	80	34	10	24	46	6	40	3	1	2	17	3	14
2000	100	19	81	34	9	24	46	6	41	3	1	2	17	3	14
2001	100	19	81	33	10	23	46	5	40	4	1	3	18	3	14
2002	100	20	80	30	9	21	45	5	40	4	1	3	20	4	16

Note: See Notes, tables 4.1 and 4.2. For definition of drug abuse violations, see Appendix 3.

[a] Because of rounding, percents may not add to total.
[b] Less than 0.5%.

Source: U.S. Department of Justice, Federal Bureau of Investigation, *Crime in the United States, 1982*, p. 165; *1983*, p. 168; *1984*, p. 161; *1985*, p. 163; *1986*, p. 163; *1987*, p. 163; *1988*, p. 167; *1989*, p. 171; *1990*, p. 173; *1991*, p. 212; *1992*, p. 216; *1993*, p. 216; *1994*, p. 216; *1995*, p. 207; *1996*, p. 213; *1997*, p. 221; *1998*, p. 209; *1999*, p. 211; *2000*, p. 216; *2001*, p. 232; *2002*, p. 234 (Washington, DC: USGPO). Table constructed by SOURCEBOOK staff.

Table 4.30

Drug use by adult male arrestees in 43 U.S. cities and counties

By type of drug, 2000-2003

(Percent testing positive)

Primary city	Any drug[a] 2000	2001	2002	2003	Cocaine[b] 2000	2001	2002	2003	Marijuana 2000	2001	2002	2003
Albany, NY	65%	63%	70%	72%	25%	30%	26%	34%	45%	46%	54%	54%
Albuquerque, NM	65	64	62	67	35	37	38	35	47	38	34	42
Anchorage, AK	52	52	61	66	22	19	20	25	38	38	49	52
Atlanta, GA	70	NA	71	72	48	NA	49	50	38	NA	35	42
Birmingham, AL	65	63	64	66	33	29	34	34	45	49	42	45
Boston, MA	NA	NA	NA	80	NA	NA	NA	32	NA	NA	NA	51
Charlotte, NC	68	66	62	66	44	32	34	35	44	48	44	47
Chicago, IL	76	84	85	86	37	41	48	51	46	50	49	53
Cleveland, OH	72	68	72	74	38	35	35	39	49	47	51	49
Dallas, TX	54	52	58	62	28	30	31	33	36	33	35	39
Denver, CO	64	62	62	66	35	34	33	38	41	40	40	42
Des Moines, IA	55	57	56	69	11	9	10	12	41	43	42	49
Detroit, MI	70	64	NA	NA	24	22	NA	NA	50	48	NA	NA
Fort Lauderdale, FL	62	NA	NA	NA	31	NA	NA	NA	43	NA	NA	NA
Honolulu, HI	63	59	63	63	16	11	9	12	30	30	32	31
Houston, TX	57	NA	NA	62	32	NA	NA	23	36	NA	NA	48
Indianapolis, IN	64	66	66	65	31	32	35	35	49	50	47	45
Kansas City, MO	NA	69	NA	NA	NA	34	NA	NA	NA	49	NA	NA
Laredo, TX	59	49	46	NA	45	35	36	NA	28	26	26	NA
Las Vegas, NV	58	60	64	65	22	21	24	22	33	35	35	34
Los Angeles, CA	NA	NA	62	69	NA	NA	32	24	NA	NA	36	41
Miami, FL	63	NA	NA	63	44	NA	NA	47	38	NA	NA	41
Minneapolis, MN	67	69	74	65	26	28	31	28	54	54	54	48
New Orleans, LA	69	68	72	78	35	37	42	48	47	45	47	51
New York, NY	80	76	81	70	49	45	49	36	41	40	44	43
Oklahoma City, OK	71	68	72	71	22	22	26	25	57	51	54	55
Omaha, NE	63	69	61	71	18	20	21	20	48	56	41	51
Philadelphia, PA	72	71	76	67	31	37	39	30	49	43	48	46
Phoenix, AZ	66	69	71	74	32	27	27	23	34	40	42	41
Portland, OR	64	68	66	72	22	27	22	30	36	36	38	38
Rio Arriba, NM	NA	NA	62	77	NA	NA	30	39	NA	NA	38	50
Sacramento, CA	74	73	79	79	18	18	21	22	50	48	51	49
Salt Lake City, UT	54	54	60	56	18	16	19	15	34	34	36	32
San Antonio, TX	53	57	63	60	20	30	32	30	41	41	42	42
San Diego, CA	64	62	64	67	15	14	13	10	39	36	38	41
San Jose, CA	53	62	58	63	12	13	13	13	36	38	34	35
Seattle, WA	64	64	70	67	31	32	38	37	38	35	36	37
Spokane, WA	58	62	65	70	15	18	16	15	40	42	47	44
Tampa, FL	NA	NA	NA	60	NA	NA	NA	30	NA	NA	NA	45
Tucson, AZ	69	63	71	73	41	36	42	42	45	44	47	44
Tulsa, OK	NA	61	70	70	NA	20	22	20	NA	48	52	52
Washington, DC	NA	NA	64	66	NA	NA	28	26	NA	NA	41	37
Woodbury, IA	NA	NA	43	42	NA	NA	12	3	NA	NA	28	34
Median	64	64	64	67	31	29	30	30	41	43	42	44

Note: These data are from the Arrestee Drug Abuse Monitoring (ADAM) program sponsored by the U.S. Department of Justice, National Institute of Justice. ADAM data are collected in booking facilities in participating counties throughout the United States. Each quarter, trained local ADAM staff obtain voluntary and anonymous urine specimens and confidential interviews from a new sample of arrestees. ADAM data are collected on a county-wide basis, however, the primary city in each county is used as the identifier. Readers should note that for a small number of counties, estimates are based on data from only one or two data collection quarters. Readers are encouraged to consult the original Source for information on year-to-year variation in number of data collection quarters completed and arrestees interviewed. For methodology and survey sampling information, see Appendix 10.

[a] Includes cocaine, marijuana, methamphetamine, opiates, and phencyclidine (PCP).

[b] Includes either crack or powder cocaine.

Source: U.S. Department of Justice, National Institute of Justice, *2000 Arrestee Drug Abuse Monitoring: Annual Report*, NCJ 193013, pp. 21, 108; *Drug Use and Related Matters Among Adult Arrestees, 2001*, Table 3; *Preliminary Data on Drug Use and Related Matters Among Adult Arrestees and Juvenile Detainees, 2002*, Tables 3-6; and *Drug and Alcohol Use and Related Matters Among Arrestees 2003*, Tables 3-6 (Washington, DC: U.S. Department of Justice). Table adapted by SOURCEBOOK staff.

Table 4.31

Adult male arrestees in 39 U.S. cities and counties reporting receiving drug or alcohol treatment ever and in past year

By type of treatment, 2003

Primary city	Percent reporting receiving drug or alcohol treatment			
	Outpatient		Inpatient or residential	
	Ever	Past year	Ever	Past year
Albany, NY	40.0%	11.2%	33.3%	9.5%
Albuquerque, NM	24.3	6.0	31.3	5.7
Anchorage, AK	39.4	6.7	43.6	8.8
Atlanta, GA	15.1	1.5	25.7	4.8
Birmingham, AL	13.4	2.9	20.7	2.9
Boston, MA	28.2	12.9	40.2	19.3
Charlotte, NC	16.6	3.1	22.9	5.2
Chicago, IL	20.9	5.7	22.8	5.3
Cleveland, OH	22.0	4.5	29.3	7.0
Dallas, TX	12.8	2.6	20.1	5.5
Denver, CO	23.4	5.0	36.1	7.5
Des Moines, IA	31.0	8.3	32.3	5.6
Honolulu, HI	21.8	3.2	25.4	5.8
Houston, TX	19.3	9.4	24.7	7.6
Indianapolis, IN	27.3	6.3	23.8	2.1
Las Vegas, NV	16.8	3.9	22.9	4.6
Los Angeles, CA	11.5	3.4	15.8	4.7
Miami, FL	17.4	4.2	16.7	3.8
Minneapolis, MN	29.5	5.2	38.3	9.6
New Orleans, LA	7.9	1.8	13.5	4.6
New York, NY	23.3	7.7	30.0	8.3
Oklahoma City, OK	10.9	2.2	29.2	5.7
Omaha, NE	20.2	1.9	26.0	4.8
Philadelphia, PA	22.9	5.9	29.7	7.7
Phoenix, AZ	19.4	4.0	22.1	4.4
Portland, OR	38.2	14.6	42.7	8.4
Rio Arriba, NM	22.1	9.4	43.3	14.6
Sacramento, CA	16.9	5.3	24.5	4.9
Salt Lake City, UT	26.9	5.7	29.5	6.8
San Antonio, TX	12.1	1.6	14.4	2.1
San Diego, CA	18.5	4.3	29.5	7.6
San Jose, CA	21.4	7.7	22.8	6.5
Seattle, WA	30.1	6.7	34.2	5.2
Spokane, WA	34.9	6.1	35.1	3.9
Tampa, FL	18.2	3.8	25.2	4.7
Tucson, AZ	19.3	4.5	26.8	6.0
Tulsa, OK	15.1	2.9	29.8	4.9
Washington, DC	15.3	3.0	23.0	6.2
Woodbury, IA	34.2	1.6	29.8	5.5
Median	20.9	4.5	26.8	5.6

Note: See Note, table 4.30. For methodology and survey sampling information, see Appendix 10.

Source: U.S. Department of Justice, National Institute of Justice, *Drug and Alcohol Use and Related Matters Among Arrestees 2003*, Table 14 (Washington, DC: U.S. Department of Justice, 2004). Table adapted by SOURCEBOOK staff.

Table 4.32

Adult male arrestees in 43 U.S. cities and counties reporting binge drinking in past 30 days

2000-2003

Primary city	Binge drinking in past 30 days[a]			
	2000	2001	2002	2003
Albany, NY	53.2%	55.0%	50.0%	54.4%
Albuquerque, NM	70.2	66.6	68.9	61.1
Anchorage, AK	69.5	66.0	70.4	68.3
Atlanta, GA	42.5	NA	43.7	41.2
Birmingham, AL	48.5	49.4	49.4	44.0
Boston, MA	NA	NA	NA	54.8
Charlotte, NC	47.6	45.7	43.5	38.9
Chicago, IL	44.2	35.1	37.5	37.0
Cleveland, OH	54.1	45.8	53.5	48.6
Dallas, TX	46.1	51.2	45.1	41.1
Denver, CO	62.9	57.3	53.2	54.1
Des Moines, IA	56.1	53.1	52.1	46.6
Detroit, MI	38.4	44.1	NA	NA
Ft. Lauderdale, FL	52.6	NA	NA	NA
Honolulu, HI	46.4	49.3	45.7	47.6
Houston, TX	41.0	NA	NA	47.9
Indianapolis, IN	50.6	49.6	53.0	50.2
Kansas City, MO	NA	42.1	NA	NA
Laredo, TX	64.6	54.8	57.3	NA
Las Vegas, NV	53.6	53.0	52.1	48.3
Los Angeles, CA	NA	NA	43.4	42.4
Miami, FL	40.2	NA	NA	45.1
Minneapolis, MN	54.3	47.7	50.8	51.5
New Orleans, LA	36.0	43.0	41.9	47.0
New York, NY	39.8	31.2	32.4	35.0
Oklahoma City, OK	61.3	55.5	57.9	51.1
Omaha, NE	51.0	45.9	49.2	45.2
Philadelphia, PA	35.4	35.8	38.2	37.4
Phoenix, AZ	54.2	56.2	48.7	45.6
Portland, OR	40.5	43.3	42.7	42.0
Rio Arriba, NM	NA	NA	66.3	65.7
Sacramento, CA	51.7	47.7	52.8	47.7
Salt Lake City, UT	48.6	50.4	49.0	48.1
San Antonio, TX	43.5	54.3	57.0	57.5
San Diego, CA	54.5	54.3	49.7	54.6
San Jose, CA	61.0	50.6	52.0	47.7
Seattle, WA	52.1	53.5	50.1	47.5
Spokane, WA	55.9	59.0	55.6	52.6
Tampa, FL	NA	NA	NA	53.1
Tucson, AZ	59.2	54.7	57.1	54.3
Tulsa, OK	NA	62.3	54.2	56.0
Washington, DC	NA	NA	31.1	25.6
Woodbury, IA	NA	NA	57.7	48.7
Median	51.7	50.6	50.5	47.9

Note: See Note, table 4.30. For methodology and survey sampling information, see Appendix 10.

[a] Consumption of five or more drinks on at least one occasion in the past 30 days.

Source: U.S. Department of Justice, National Institute of Justice, *2000 Arrestee Drug Abuse Monitoring: Annual Report*, NCJ 193013, pp. 52, 124; *Drug Use and Related Matters Among Adult Arrestees, 2001*, Table 10; *Preliminary Data on Drug Use and Related Matters Among Adult Arrestees and Juvenile Detainees, 2002*, Table 10; *Drug and Alcohol Use and Related Matters Among Arrestees 2003*, Table 10 (Washington, DC: U.S. Department of Justice). Table adapted by SOURCEBOOK staff.

Table 4.33

Persons arrested for Federal offenses

By offense, United States, fiscal year 2001[a]

Most serious offense	Number arrested	Percent
All offenses[b]	118,896	100%
Violent offenses	4,843	4.1
Murder, nonnegligent manslaughter	304	0.3
Negligent manslaughter	35	(c)
Assault	1,129	1.0
Robbery	2,800	2.4
Sexual abuse[d]	265	0.2
Kidnaping	161	0.1
Threatening communication	117	0.1
Other violent offenses	32	(c)
Property offenses	16,824	14.3
Fraudulent	13,397	11.4
Embezzlement	1,035	0.9
Fraud[e]	10,288	8.7
Forgery	329	0.3
Counterfeiting	1,745	1.5
Other	3,427	2.9
Burglary	160	0.1
Larceny[f]	2,101	1.8
Motor vehicle theft	360	0.3
Arson and explosives	123	0.1
Transportation of stolen property	543	0.5
Other property offenses[g]	140	0.1
Drug offenses	33,589	28.5
Public-order offenses	9,156	7.8
Regulatory	687	0.6
Antitrust	4	(c)
Food and drug	144	0.1
Civil rights	117	0.1
Other regulatory offenses	422	0.4
Other	8,469	7.2
Tax law violations including tax fraud	938	0.8
Bribery	229	0.2
Perjury, contempt, intimidation	288	0.2
National defense	15	(c)
Escape	888	0.8
Racketeering and extortion	618	0.5
Gambling offenses	119	0.1
Mail or transport of obscene material	460	0.4
Child Support Recovery	371	0.3
Nonviolent sex offenses	512	0.4
Obstruction of justice	420	0.4
Traffic offenses	2,211	1.9
Conspiracy, aiding and abetting, and jurisdictional offenses	499	0.4
All other offenses[h]	901	0.8
Weapons offenses	6,007	5.1
Immigration offenses	24,794	21.0
Supervision violations	18,978	16.1
Material witness[i]	3,679	3.1

Note: These data are from the U.S. Department of Justice, Bureau of Justice Statistics' Federal Justice Statistics Program database. Sources of information include the Executive Office for U.S. Attorneys, the Administrative Office of the United States Courts, the U.S. Sentencing Commission, the U.S. Marshals Service, the Drug Enforcement Administration, and the Federal Bureau of Prisons. Persons arrested by Federal agencies are transferred to the custody of the U.S. Marshals Service for processing, transportation, and detention. Arrest data were derived from the U.S. Marshals Prisoner Tracking System database and reflect persons booked by the U.S. Marshals Service. Only records of arrests made from Oct. 1, 2000 through Sept. 30, 2001 were selected. For methodology and definitions of terms, see Appendix 11.

[a]Percents may not add to 100 because of rounding.
[b]Includes 1,026 suspects for whom an offense category could not be determined. Percent distribution based on the suspects for whom offense category could be determined.
[c]Less than 0.05%.
[d]Includes only violent sex offenses.
[e]Excludes tax fraud.
[f]Excludes transportation of stolen property.
[g]Excludes fraudulent property offenses; includes destruction of property and trespass.
[h]Includes offenses with unclassifiable offense type.
[i]To secure and safeguard a material witness.

Source: U.S. Department of Justice, Bureau of Justice Statistics, *Compendium of Federal Justice Statistics, 2001*, NCJ 201627 (Washington, DC: U.S. Department of Justice, 2003), p. 15.

Table 4.34

Persons arrested for Federal offenses

By Federal agency, United States, fiscal year 2001

					Most serious offense at arrest						
Arresting agency	Number arrested	Violent offenses	Property offenses Fraudulent	Other	Drug offenses	Public-order offenses Regulatory	Other	Weapons offenses	Immigration offenses	Supervision violations	Material witness[a]
All agencies	118,896	4,843	13,397	3,427	33,589	687	8,469	6,007	24,794	18,978	3,679
Department of Agriculture	107	0	41	7	15	21	18	3	0	1	0
Department of Defense	524	22	45	58	35	2	339	6	1	9	0
Department of the Interior	891	96	13	46	96	55	357	30	2	154	0
Bureau of Indian Affairs	170	69	1	12	35	0	12	5	1	35	0
U.S. Park Police	721	27	12	34	61	55	345	25	1	119	0
Department of Justice	84,027	3,679	5,804	1,552	20,933	240	4,729	2,253	24,547	15,937	3,627
Drug Enforcement Administration	11,778	34	64	8	11,400	27	80	68	13	34	14
Federal Bureau of Investigation	11,573	2,356	2,955	563	3,638	78	1,431	260	24	138	44
Immigration and Naturalization Service	28,308	33	382	23	324	0	400	79	23,412	260	3,371
U.S. Marshals Service	32,336	1,253	2,403	956	5,568	135	2,810	1,846	1,097	15,498	198
Other Department of Justice	32	3	0	2	3	0	8	0	1	7	0
Department of State	308	0	273	2	3	0	4	0	24	2	0
Department of the Treasury	14,070	115	2,427	165	7,714	17	590	2,839	77	62	15
Bureau of Alcohol, Tobacco and Firearms	3,666	55	75	59	594	5	48	2,791	5	11	5
U.S. Customs Service	7,772	13	203	40	7,057	10	287	36	62	39	8
Internal Revenue Service	470	4	189	4	51	0	211	1	5	0	2
U.S. Secret Service	2,162	43	1,960	62	12	2	44	11	5	12	0
Federal judiciary	612	10	257	156	35	0	42	7	16	78	3
U.S. Postal Service	1,226	25	622	404	59	3	96	4	0	5	0
Other	17,131	896	3,915	1,037	4,699	349	2,294	865	127	2,730	34
Self-report, subpoena	8,427	150	3,251	674	1,074	201	1,221	295	38	1,467	3
State and local	4,879	571	126	211	1,915	15	515	420	39	1,001	19
Task force	1,367	6	23	3	1,245	2	21	30	7	22	1
Other	2,458	169	515	149	465	131	537	120	43	240	11

Note: See Note, table 4.33. This table displays data by the arresting Federal agency. The arresting agency may be different from the Federal agency that initiated the investigation involving the arrestee. For methodology and definitions of terms, see Appendix 11.

[a]To secure and safeguard a material witness.

Source: U.S. Department of Justice, Bureau of Justice Statistics, *Compendium of Federal Justice Statistics, 2001*, NCJ 201627 (Washington, DC: U.S. Department of Justice, 2003), p. 16.

Table 4.35

Characteristics of persons arrested by Federal agencies

By offense, United States, fiscal year 2001

						Percent of persons arrested for:					
Arrestee characteristics	Number arrested	All offenses	Violent offenses	Property offenses Fraudulent	Other	Drug offenses	Public-order offenses Regulatory	Other	Weapons offenses	Immigration offenses	Supervision violations	Material witness[a]
All arrestees[b]	118,896	100%	4.1%	11.4%	2.9%	28.5%	0.6%	7.2%	5.1%	21.0%	16.1%	3.1%
Sex												
Male	101,637	85.5	91.4	70.4	73.3	84.7	89.4	85.2	96.2	91.7	87.2	81.9
Female	17,249	14.5	8.6	29.6	26.7	15.3	10.6	14.8	3.8	8.3	12.8	18.1
Race												
White	81,858	69.6	41.7	62.6	59.0	66.3	82.6	72.5	45.8	95.5	57.5	92.0
Black	31,934	27.1	45.6	33.7	33.6	31.6	8.7	22.7	52.4	3.2	38.3	4.4
Native American	1,869	1.6	11.5	0.6	3.7	0.7	5.4	1.9	1.1	0.1	3.1	0.1
Asian/Pacific Islander	2,013	1.7	1.2	3.1	3.7	1.3	3.3	2.9	0.7	1.3	1.1	3.5
Age												
Under 19 years	2,462	2.1	5.8	0.7	3.0	2.1	2.0	1.4	1.9	2.5	0.6	7.6
19 to 20 years	7,045	5.9	10.4	3.5	7.4	6.7	4.4	5.2	7.5	6.7	2.8	11.3
21 to 30 years	48,440	40.8	39.0	29.6	32.9	44.1	21.7	30.0	46.5	48.7	36.2	51.4
31 to 40 years	34,474	29.0	26.3	30.1	28.5	28.3	27.8	26.6	24.6	29.9	33.0	21.9
Over 40 years	26,404	22.2	18.5	36.1	28.2	18.8	44.1	36.9	19.4	12.2	27.4	7.8
Citizenship												
U.S. citizen	68,200	62.2	93.1	85.2	92.7	70.1	92.6	89.7	94.3	4.8	85.2	3.4
Not U.S. citizen	41,499	37.8	6.9	14.8	7.3	29.9	7.4	10.3	5.7	95.2	14.8	96.6

Note: See Note, table 4.33. For methodology and definitions of terms, see Appendix 11.

[a]To secure and safeguard a material witness.
[b]Includes persons for whom offense or characteristics are unknown; therefore detail for total number arrested may not add to total.

Source: U.S. Department of Justice, Bureau of Justice Statistics, *Compendium of Federal Justice Statistics, 2001*, NCJ 201627 (Washington, DC: U.S. Department of Justice, 2003), p. 17.

Table 4.36

Federal drug seizures

By type of drug, fiscal years 1989-2003

Fiscal year	Total	Heroin	Cocaine	Marijuana	Hashish
			Pounds seized[a]		
1989	1,343,702	2,415	218,697	1,070,965	51,625
1990	738,004	1,704	235,885	483,353	17,062
1991	926,700	3,067	246,325	499,097	178,211
1992	1,093,366	2,552	303,289	783,477	4,048
1993	1,045,997	3,516	244,315	772,086	26,080
1994	1,355,678	2,898	309,710	1,041,445	1,625
1995	1,576,865	2,569	234,105	1,308,171	32,020
1996	1,718,552	3,373	253,297	1,429,786	32,096
1997	1,796,863	3,121	252,329	1,488,362	53,051
1998	2,047,558	3,499	266,029	1,777,434	596
1999	2,571,355	2,733	284,631	2,282,313	1,678
2000	2,894,200	6,640	248,827	2,614,746	23,987
2001	2,917,796	4,378	239,576	2,673,410	433
2002	2,648,068	6,874	225,758	2,415,243	193
2003	2,952,797	5,643	245,499	2,700,282	1,373

Note: The Federal-wide Drug Seizure System (FDSS) contains information about drug seizures made within the jurisdiction of the United States by the Drug Enforcement Administration, Federal Bureau of Investigation, U.S. Customs Service, and U.S. Border Patrol as well as maritime seizures made by the U.S. Coast Guard. Drug seizures made by other Federal agencies are included in the FDSS database when custody of the drug evidence was transferred to one of these five agencies.

Some data have been revised by the Source and may differ from previous editions of SOURCEBOOK.

[a]Figures are rounded to the nearest pound.

Source: Table adapted by SOURCEBOOK staff from tables provided by the U.S. Department of Justice, Drug Enforcement Administration, Federal-wide Drug Seizure System.

Table 4.37

Drug removals from the domestic market by the Drug Enforcement Administration

By type of drug, fiscal years 1978-2003

Fiscal year	Opium (lbs.)	Heroin (lbs.)	Cocaine (lbs.)	Marijuana (lbs.)	Hashish (lbs.)	Hallucinogens (d.u.)	Depressants (d.u.)	Stimulants (d.u.)	Methadone (d.u.)
1978	27	442	1,009	1,117,422	3,004	4,349,917	311,044	2,901,948	39
1979	4	160	1,139	887,302	43,261	6,439,136	5,671,379	7,711,628	14,998
1980	NA	201	2,590	994,468	5,993	7,522,905	8,337,806	6,434,742	NA
1981	NA	332	4,352	1,935,202	30,162	36,064,329	21,701,603	47,475,580	NA
1982	NA	608	12,493	2,814,787	3,086	1,978,617	5,739,423	4,482,404	NA
1983	263	662	19,625	1,795,875	31,339	58,542,610	2,535,040	11,345,783	NA
1984	18	850	25,344	2,909,393	2,059	596,999	688,491	16,500,791	3,218
1985	45	985	39,969	1,641,626	21,858	4,593,867	664,589	20,709,871	57,903
1986	6	801	59,699	1,819,764	577	16,748,616	1,627,315	27,846,419	70
1987	65	804	81,823	1,429,339	2,368	6,057,338	643,178	26,929,899	920
1988	73	1,841	127,967	1,241,630	83,542	17,530,667	182,215	95,972,547	375,009
1989	13	1,372	181,519	745,255	1,270	13,100,524	564,440	94,333,273	22,164
1990	30	1,405	162,386	310,610	16,878	3,212,636	335,974	143,824,926	23,022
1991	3	2,529	130,776	237,183	1,333	1,824,587	378,352	29,157,571	6,200
1992	54	1,534	173,727	445,942	4,328	3,691,242	917,019	44,428,806	3,580
1993	39	1,592	134,003	314,091	267	2,841,245	179,058	80,462,242	1,618
1994	21	1,048	145,751	337,121	539	1,590,624	25,769,912	130,755,446	3,467
1995	31	1,198	115,261	480,339	30,721	2,326,293	442,740	163,142,631	30,870
1996	52	1,110	76,462	390,173	495	2,353,793	471,651	66,712,308	542
1997	51	735	78,071	472,181	33,940	1,095,225	710,575	124,398,731	5,720
1998	55	719	67,276	543,491	289	913,174	387,930	89,256,386	1,471
1999	147	865	69,256	727,208	1,031	1,208,217	429,118	73,170,334	1,723
2000	83	1,151	109,790	742,524	205	30,041,696	464,981	116,219,298	7,047
2001	31	1,316	125,217	603,063	17	38,957,335	364,801	129,915,379	1,401
2002	40	1,536	123,333	514,773	691	12,034,354	199,377	115,036,979	1,956
2003	314	1,715	142,654	586,669	1,255	2,630,215	207,539	172,194,833	2,693

Note: The notation "d.u." refers to dosage unit. Some data have been revised by the Source and may differ from previous editions of SOURCEBOOK.

Source: Table adapted by SOURCEBOOK staff from tables provided by the U.S. Department of Justice, Drug Enforcement Administration.

Table 4.38

Number of marijuana plants eradicated and seized, arrests made, weapons seized, and value of assets seized

Under the Drug Enforcement Administration's Domestic Cannabis Eradication/Suppression Program, by State, 2003

State	Total cultivated plants eradicated	Outdoor operations: Plots eradicated	Outdoor operations: Cultivated plants eradicated[a]	Indoor operations: Grows seized	Indoor operations: Cultivated plants eradicated	Bulk processed marijuana (in pounds)	Ditchweed[b] eradicated	Number of arrests	Number of weapons seized	Value of assets seized
Total	3,651,106	34,362	3,427,923	2,678	223,183	56,283	243,430,664	8,480	4,176	$25,062,874
Alabama	51,137	1,160	50,917	4	220	0	NA	90	NA	0
Alaska	7,350	4	74	111	7,276	44	NA	157	81	243,278
Arizona	19,574	5	19,339	114	235	5	8	127	31	112,549
Arkansas	72,565	254	71,630	14	935	7	NA	56	45	113,329
California	1,181,957	1,880	1,109,066	451	72,891	9,026	NA	812	869	2,378,403
Colorado	13,981	31	6,618	84	7,363	1	220,217	241	133	1,672,189
Connecticut	3,027	31	1,393	10	1,634	6	NA	16	10	43,100
Delaware	200	5	200	NA	NA	132	NA	4	26	3,806
Florida	37,744	393	21,442	227	16,302	2,100	NA	403	187	503,852
Georgia	46,985	675	46,762	6	223	220	NA	80	98	378,467
Hawaii	392,422	9,662	388,903	9	3,519	553	NA	969	25	36,669
Idaho	13,664	29	8,560	20	5,104	196	NA	71	22	239,210
Illinois	41,806	752	39,440	54	2,366	338	701,503	127	54	210,806
Indiana	31,192	1,715	23,816	166	7,376	636	219,124,925	1,021	96	925,894
Iowa	1,257	18	368	10	889	22	181,421	17	38	17,800
Kansas	14,471	42	13,338	29	1,133	389	619,049	45	23	78,486
Kentucky	527,775	8,264	519,986	56	7,789	6,552	NA	647	590	3,579,876
Louisiana	5,090	127	4,319	36	771	2	NA	80	3	6,750
Maine	16,258	208	14,052	30	2,206	114	NA	165	55	191,463
Maryland	3,445	170	3,409	7	36	14	NA	85	45	101,641
Massachusetts	1,937	61	1,802	3	135	0	NA	10	NA	0
Michigan	24,524	241	21,942	53	2,582	0	NA	140	131	555,512
Minnesota	2,967	8	357	29	2,610	305	3,095,172	37	68	363,760
Mississippi	2,984	53	2,812	11	172	3	NA	55	NA	46,800
Missouri	14,285	346	12,825	70	1,460	805	4,489,850	398	104	614,295
Montana	404	3	210	10	194	271	NA	25	46	1,300
Nebraska	2,632	3	2,056	16	576	83	362,313	26	19	17,429
Nevada	1,877	4	23	19	1,854	38	NA	18	91	64,364
New Hampshire	547	20	332	11	215	123	NA	27	4	1,000
New Jersey	1,260	43	726	19	534	96	NA	39	NA	40,250
New Mexico	1,507	7	1,068	5	439	9	NA	10	1	29,500
New York	99,423	384	95,385	97	4,038	4	387	281	49	1,491,747
North Carolina	34,283	848	32,793	23	1,490	185	NA	125	38	64,877
North Dakota	1,811	4	1,116	19	695	12	3,200,000	31	4	0
Ohio	44,597	1,429	41,183	43	3,414	107	NA	41	87	41,875
Oklahoma	4,297	184	3,008	12	1,289	52	9,995,153	73	96	230,050
Oregon	32,346	316	16,402	199	15,944	914	NA	231	333	2,957,171
Pennsylvania	5,622	318	3,833	49	1,789	46	NA	97	1	21,599
Rhode Island	76	2	16	2	60	28	NA	2	3	198,919
South Carolina	15,038	138	13,396	7	1,642	23	NA	66	59	37,983
South Dakota	340	NA	340	NA	NA	0	33,010	8	NA	74,905
Tennessee	679,105	2,506	678,635	9	470	26,411	NA	476	7	234,760
Texas	33,404	256	21,682	107	11,722	1,897	448,000	86	48	460,138
Utah	173	NA	NA	2	173	1	NA	2	NA	0
Vermont	3,427	191	2,351	25	1,076	606	NA	77	2	11,171
Virginia	11,419	290	8,981	33	2,438	3,396	0	203	35	45,040
Washington	65,675	228	42,118	196	23,557	308	NA	355	379	6,132,981
West Virginia	74,690	793	73,345	46	1,345	131	34,000	114	35	26,933
Wisconsin	8,523	261	5,554	121	2,969	70	925,656	209	105	460,947
Wyoming	33	NA	NA	4	33	2	NA	5	NA	0

Note: These data were collected by the Drug Enforcement Administration (DEA) in conjunction with the Domestic Cannabis Eradication/Suppression Program. This program is a joint Federal and State effort in which the DEA contributes funding, training, equipment, investigative, and aircraft resources to the participating States in the effort to eradicate domestically cultivated marijuana.

[a] May include tended ditchweed; see footnote b.
[b] Ditchweed is a type of marijuana that grows wild.

Source: Table adapted by SOURCEBOOK staff from table provided by the U.S. Department of Justice, Drug Enforcement Administration.

Table 4.39

Seizures of illegal drug laboratories by the Drug Enforcement Administration

By type of drug manufactured, United States, fiscal years 1975-2003

Fiscal year	Total illegal drug laboratories seized	PCP	Metham-phetamine	Amphe-tamine	Methaqualone; meth-cathinone[a]	Hashish oil	LSD	Cocaine	Other hallucin-ogens[b]	Other controlled substances[c]
Total	16,270	550	14,134	656	134	30	26	158	206	376
1975	32	15	11	2	1	0	0	3	0	NA
1976	97	30	36	11	5	4	4	7	0	NA
1977	148	66	46	10	10	6	1	2	7	NA
1978	180	79	69	12	7	5	0	4	4	NA
1979	235	53	137	10	9	4	2	5	15	NA
1980	234	49	126	20	17	1	4	2	15	NA
1981	182	35	87	14	13	2	4	5	10	12
1982	224	47	132	18	7	0	0	6	7	7
1983	226	39	119	25	10	4	0	11	11	7
1984	197	13	121	19	3	3	0	16	3	19
1985	419	23	257	67	5	0	1	29	2	35
1986	509	8	372	66	4	0	2	23	6	28
1987	682	13	561	68	1	1	1	17	2	18
1988	810	20	667	82	4	0	0	9	7	21
1989	852	13	683	101	5	0	0	1	0	49
1990	549	10	449	54	3	0	0	4	10	19
1991	408	5	345	26	1	0	3	3	13	12
1992	335	4	291	15	1	0	0	5	6	13
1993	286	3	237	8	0	0	0	0	12	26
1994	274	12	224	11	0	0	0	1	4	22
1995	330	5	299	4	0	0	0	0	1	21
1996	806	2	776	4	14	0	0	0	6	4
1997	1,311	1	1,289	1	5	0	0	0	10	5
1998	1,175	1	1,157	1	2	0	0	1	4	9
1999	2,158	1	2,122	5	3	0	3	2	15	7
2000	1,905	0	1,873	1	1	0	0	1	17	12
2001	1,208	1	1,176	2	2	0	1	1	7	18
2002	647	3	618	4	1	0	0	0	15	6
2003	420	3	409	0	0	0	0	0	5	3

Note: Laboratory seizures reported here represent only those made by Drug Enforcement Administration personnel and do not include the collaborative efforts of State and local law enforcement officials. Some data have been revised by the Source and may differ from previous editions of SOURCE-BOOK.

[a] Category changed to methcathinone in 1996; prior to 1996, methcathinone was included in "other controlled substances."
[b] Includes MDMA (ecstasy), GHB (gamma-hydroxybutyric acid), etc.
[c] Includes substances such as phenal 2 propanone, a precursor used in making methamphetamine and amphetamine; and methadone, an opiate-type heroin substitute.

Source: Comptroller General of the United States, *Report to the Congress: Stronger Crackdown Needed on Clandestine Laboratories Manufacturing Dangerous Drugs* (Washington, DC: U.S. General Accounting Office, 1981), p. 37; and data provided to SOURCEBOOK staff by the U.S. Department of Justice, Drug Enforcement Administration.

Table 4.40

Arrests by the Drug Enforcement Administration

By type of drug, fiscal years 1992-2003[a]

Fiscal year	Total Number	Total Percent	Heroin[b] Number	Heroin[b] Percent	Cocaine[c] Number	Cocaine[c] Percent	Cannabis[d] Number	Cannabis[d] Percent	Other dangerous drugs[e] Number	Other dangerous drugs[e] Percent
1992	24,874	100%	2,285	9.2%	12,710	51.1%	6,166	24.8%	3,713	14.9%
1993	22,059	100	2,021	9.2	10,984	49.8	5,578	25.3	3,476	15.8
1994	22,081	100	2,015	9.1	11,251	51.0	5,355	24.3	3,460	15.7
1995	24,993	100	2,546	10.2	12,026	48.1	6,231	24.9	4,190	16.8
1996	27,698	100	2,682	9.7	12,674	45.8	6,735	24.3	5,607	20.2
1997	33,626	100	3,090	9.2	14,901	44.3	7,650	22.8	7,985	23.7
1998	37,841	100	3,299	8.7	16,447	43.5	8,066	21.3	10,029	26.5
1999	40,695	100	3,590	8.8	17,038	41.9	8,606	21.1	11,461	28.2
2000	40,324	100	3,610	9.0	16,336	40.5	8,541	21.2	11,837	29.4
2001	35,359	100	3,372	9.5	13,538	38.3	6,976	19.7	11,473	32.4
2002	30,060	100	2,487	8.3	12,010	40.0	5,576	18.5	9,987	33.2
2003	27,198	100	2,329	8.6	10,516	38.7	5,679	20.9	8,674	31.9

Note: Some data have been revised by the Source and may differ from previous editions of SOURCEBOOK.

[a] Percents may not add to 100 because of rounding.
[b] Includes morphine, opium, and other opiate-related substances.
[c] Includes crack.
[d] Includes marijuana, hashish, and hashish oil.
[e] Includes stimulants (e.g., methamphetamine), depressants (e.g., barbiturates), and hallucinogens (e.g., LSD and PCP).

Source: Table adapted by SOURCEBOOK staff from table provided by the U.S. Department of Justice, Drug Enforcement Administration, Defendant Statistical System.

Table 4.41

Characteristics of persons arrested by the Drug Enforcement Administration

By type of drug, United States, fiscal year 2001

	Total arrested		Type of drug					
Arrestee characteristics	Number	Percent	Cocaine powder	Crack cocaine	Marijuana	Methamphet- amine	Opiates	Other or non-drug
All arrestees[a]	32,925	100%	7,534	5,278	6,351	7,220	3,137	3,405
Sex								
Male	27,381	83.4	6,563	4,555	5,360	5,669	2,566	2,668
Female	5,452	16.6	948	714	973	1,528	561	728
Race								
White	22,490	69.5	4,734	1,217	4,807	6,792	2,150	2,790
Black	9,319	28.8	2,582	3,981	1,348	109	892	407
Native American	108	0.3	21	16	30	30	5	6
Asian/Pacific Islander	452	1.4	32	22	45	172	18	163
Ethnicity								
Hispanic	12,183	38.1	3,848	802	2,906	2,269	1,777	581
Non-Hispanic	19,772	61.9	3,526	4,271	3,267	4,762	1,297	2,649
Age								
Under 19 years	196	0.6	37	45	29	24	21	40
19 to 20 years	1,736	5.3	291	321	413	305	156	250
21 to 30 years	14,348	43.8	3,258	2,717	2,784	2,686	1,202	1,701
31 to 40 years	9,726	29.7	2,406	1,378	1,725	2,471	951	795
Over 40 years	6,735	20.6	1,495	801	1,356	1,690	792	601
Citizenship								
U.S. citizen	23,961	77.2	4,893	4,569	4,441	5,361	1,993	2,704
Not U.S. citizen	7,094	22.8	2,191	424	1,616	1,467	958	438

Note: See Note, table 4.33. These data are from the Drug Enforcement Administration's (DEA) Defendant Statistical System. Some persons arrested by the DEA may be transferred to State or local jurisdiction and not to the U.S. Marshals Service. Therefore, counts of DEA arrests presented above will be higher than those reported in table 4.34. For methodology and definitions of terms, see Appendix 11.

[a] Includes persons for whom offense or characteristics are unknown; therefore detail for total number arrested may not add to total.

Source: U.S. Department of Justice, Bureau of Justice Statistics, *Compendium of Federal Justice Statistics, 2001*, NCJ 201627 (Washington, DC: U.S. Department of Justice, 2003), p. 18, Table 1.4.

Table 4.42

Asset seizures by the Drug Enforcement Administration

By type and value of asset seized, fiscal years 1992-2003

Fiscal year	Total	Currency	Other financial instrument	Real property	Vehicle	Vessel	Aircraft	Other conveyance	Other
Number of seizures									
1992	19,868	8,344	741	1,712	5,948	228	53	278	2,564
1993	16,895	7,014	588	1,565	4,737	159	45	323	2,464
1994	13,859	6,641	461	924	3,794	147	37	196	1,650
1995	13,973	7,792	411	753	3,335	99	34	167	1,382
1996	13,554	7,426	831	567	3,099	117	17	133	1,364
1997	15,860	8,123	507	748	3,695	111	24	172	2,480
1998	15,615	8,560	519	372	3,817	120	14	0	2,213
1999	16,341	8,968	474	392	4,032	106	10	0	2,359
2000	16,409	8,816	475	407	4,119	109	15	0	2,468
2001	14,663	7,862	417	366	3,927	102	10	0	1,979
2002	15,730	8,381	520	449	4,439	82	6	0	1,853
2003	15,950	8,581	546	458	4,450	103	5	0	1,807
Value									
1992	$874,889,400	$267,820,145	$154,834,673	$320,631,938	$57,065,862	$12,399,302	$15,828,500	$2,146,124	$44,162,856
1993	688,720,873	250,469,017	50,703,447	255,157,081	48,787,715	9,198,707	33,915,750	4,333,503	36,155,653
1994	650,842,200	316,292,043	47,071,268	172,966,741	39,081,767	18,379,846	10,109,200	1,814,528	45,126,807
1995	650,344,625	274,397,676	180,417,157	98,675,343	40,246,228	11,519,006	9,598,400	1,451,266	34,039,549
1996	499,291,097	275,218,245	59,668,742	88,448,201	40,278,491	8,249,654	5,564,100	1,663,878	20,199,786
1997	551,680,150	284,680,029	73,602,092	108,833,498	47,379,874	5,884,754	8,945,000	1,734,731	20,620,172
1998	540,407,702	364,715,792	34,296,978	55,824,274	49,512,722	4,278,850	3,587,000	X	28,192,086
1999	664,692,772	316,994,186	211,558,504	55,386,156	54,479,853	7,127,446	1,868,000	X	17,278,627
2000	458,911,273	274,484,704	44,098,354	58,667,131	57,685,041	6,336,591	4,011,200	X	13,628,252
2001	428,319,869	272,555,035	14,362,643	58,172,991	59,331,725	8,726,328	2,493,200	X	12,677,947
2002	440,715,331	267,224,074	29,155,556	54,998,344	67,503,719	3,773,266	940,600	X	17,119,772
2003	458,316,226	271,729,492	23,930,878	70,712,793	65,361,297	3,919,734	2,240,900	X	20,421,132

Note: Some data have been revised by the Source and may differ from previous editions of SOURCEBOOK.

Source: Table adapted by SOURCEBOOK staff from tables provided by the U.S. Department of Justice, Drug Enforcement Administration, Computerized Asset Program.

Table 4.43

Drug seizures by the U.S. Customs Service

By type and amount of drugs seized, fiscal years 1975-2001

Fiscal year	Heroin Number of seizures	Heroin Quantity (in pounds)	Cocaine Number of seizures	Cocaine Quantity (in pounds)	Hashish Number of seizures	Hashish Quantity (in pounds)	Marijuana Number of seizures	Marijuana Quantity (in pounds)	Opium[a] Number of seizures	Opium[a] Quantity (in pounds)	Morphine Number of seizures	Morphine Quantity (in pounds)	Other drugs[b] Number of seizures	Other drugs[b] Quantity (in dosage units)
1975	436	114.8	1,011	728.9	4,003	3,400.9	13,792	466,510.3	46	18.6	7	1.2	2,606	11,625,507
1976	437	367.7	1,167	1,029.6	5,162	13,436.7	13,555	759,359.9	72	37.6	15	3.9	2,581	21,418,652
Transition quarter	104	45.3	330	236.1	1,343	469.6	4,620	115,334.4	18	4.4	1	--	836	2,114,245
1977	245	277.7	1,025	952.1	6,323	15,923.0	14,902	1,652,772.7	50	20.2	15	1.4	2,105	7,813,721
1978	179	188.6	846	1,418.7	4,919	22,658.5	12,826	4,616,883.7	51	20.3	6	1.8	2,911	7,683,298
1979	173	122.5	1,259	1,438.1	4,379	50,848.9	12,323	3,583,555.5	41	26.1	21	8.8	3,130	15,912,218
1980	149	268.7	1,307	4,742.9	3,979	14,675.4	12,620	2,361,141.5	33	49.9	15	50.7	3,495	43,000,416
1981	170	234.7	1,372	3,741.1	2,689	17,991.8	14,036	5,109,792.5	52	9.5	75	6.2	3,877	38,947,804
1982	168	289.9	1,364	11,149.5	2,610	58,276.6	11,947	3,958,870.9	265	197.0	165	17.8	3,017	2,339,360
1983	285	593.6	1,731	19,601.5	1,829	2,209.8	12,101	2,732,974.5	103	78.9	199	60.0	2,862	5,592,669
1984	396	664.3	1,625	27,525.8	1,530	42,389.5	12,304	3,274,927.2	429	258.0	156	12.6	2,627	6,819,717
1985	426	784.6	2,164	50,506.4	1,948	22,970.0	12,002	2,389,704.1	1,118	505.0	10	3.3	2,179	22,540,573
1986	406	692.4	2,557	52,520.9	2,158	17,555.4	10,377	2,211,068.1	807	321.2	8	0.6	2,680	1,424,682
1987	527	639.0	2,158	87,898.3	1,930	1,073.2	14,569	1,701,149.6	538	1,014.6	8	4.2	3,345	3,881,793
1988	322	1,350.5	2,333	137,408.4	1,675	94,475.1	11,226	969,966.7	952	1,482.7	12	20.1	2,726	282,317
1989	454	1,056.7	2,059	129,493.2	1,656	51,476.0	10,183	645,858.2	3,384	901.3	26	10.3	2,549	2,622,721
1990	569	1,504.5	2,169	164,727.0	1,961	17,052.7	7,522	222,313.8	6,942	2,047.2	12	8.4	2,733	2,813,241
1991	754	2,757.1	2,138	169,586.1	2,000	177,037.7	8,688	287,519.6	3,594	1,131.6	6	0.3	2,059	2,913,236
1992	940	2,226.4	2,150	243,364.8	1,820	4,046.3	12,081	462,328.9	2,995	1,061.8	3	0.4	2,267	8,261,600
1993	1,010	2,966.2	2,182	175,317.6	1,529	26,089.1	10,961	507,248.7	2,426	2,128.8	11	19.8	2,747	17,864,966
1994	987	2,530.1	2,392	204,514.0	1,558	1,393.4	9,632	559,583.6	1,362	1,946.7	202	12,691.1	3,251	24,104,228
1995	923	2,235.3	2,226	158,313.7	1,284	16,616.8	10,214	642,012.5	462	484.5	367	27,544.0	4,896	5,665,673
1996	1,053	2,895.0	2,451	180,947.0	1,452	36,671.0	12,510	775,065.0	NA	NA	NA	NA	5,800	NA
1997	1,208	2,444.8	2,537	157,924.3	1,528	37,338.4	12,741	726,198.6	NA	NA	NA	NA	6,695	15,790,950
1998	1,049	2,956.9	2,364	157,042.7	1,604	885.3	15,545	955,987.5	NA	NA	NA	NA	8,100	221,657,448
1999	914	1,934.0	2,519	160,677.6	1,278	29,716.4	15,718	1,219,651.9	NA	NA	1,460	94,308.6	21,464	NA
2000	859	2,555.2	2,489	150,036.0	1,799	24,079.7	14,861	1,291,487.4	650	1,288.2	NA	NA	22,315	NA
2001	916	3,622.4	2,698	190,856.4	1,448	776.7	14,587	1,503,940.8	558	2,636.3	NA	NA	18,910	NA

Note: The data presented for 1975 and 1976 coincide with the former Federal fiscal year, the period July 1 to June 30. The transition quarter refers to the period July 1, 1976 to Sept. 30, 1976. The Federal fiscal year is now October 1 to September 30. Beginning in fiscal year 1995, the data include all incidents in which the U.S. Customs Service participated with other Federal, State, or local enforcement agencies. Some data have been revised by the Source and may differ from previous editions of SOURCEBOOK.

[a]Category changed to "opiates" in fiscal year 2000; previously, opiates were included with "other drugs."
[b]Includes amphetamines, barbiturates, LSD, and other drugs. Khat and methamphetamine were added in fiscal year 2000.

Source: U.S. Department of the Treasury, U.S. Customs Service, *Prologue '76* (Washington, DC: U.S. Department of the Treasury, 1976), p. 36; U.S. Department of the Treasury, U.S. Customs Service, *Customs U.S.A., 1980*, p. 33; *1985*, p. 41; *1988*, p. 40; *1989*, p. 40 (Washington, DC: U.S. Department of the Treasury); U.S. Department of the Treasury, U.S. Customs Service, *U.S. Customs Update 1992* (Washington, DC: U.S. Department of the Treasury, 1993), p. 22; U.S. Department of the Treasury, U.S. Customs Service, *U.S. Customs Service: Annual Report FY 1993* (Washington, DC: U.S. Department of the Treasury, 1994), p. 41; and data provided by the U.S. Department of the Treasury, U.S. Customs Service. Table adapted by SOURCEBOOK staff.

Table 4.44

Property seizures by the U.S. Customs Service

By type and value of property seized, fiscal years 1979-2001

(Domestic value in thousands)

	Type of property seized													
	Vehicles		Aircraft		Vessels		Monetary instruments		General merchandise[a]		Arms/ ammunition		Real estate		Intellectual property rights[b]	
Fiscal year	Number of seizures	Domestic value	Number of seizures	Domestic value	Number of seizures	Domestic value	Number of seizures	Domestic value	Number of seizures	Domestic value	Number of seizures	Domestic value	Number of seizures	Domestic value	Number of seizures	Domestic value
---	---	---	---	---	---	---	---	---	---	---	---	---	---	---	---	---
1979	2,829	$9,060	135	$19,979	272	$74,529	1,328	$22,472	24,318	$41,639	NA	NA	NA	NA	NA	NA
1980	3,039	12,269	195	11,584	1,319	91,269	1,257	31,382	19,789	39,606	NA	NA	NA	NA	NA	NA
1981	4,011	14,882	272	32,487	556	46,535	1,554	39,846	23,250	63,491	NA	NA	NA	NA	NA	NA
1982	5,951	35,936	206	34,742	500	44,462	1,802	32,757	27,132	92,015	NA	NA	NA	NA	NA	NA
1983	9,481	63,912	203	19,104	405	33,209	2,066	50,174	36,972	142,824	NA	NA	NA	NA	NA	NA
1984	9,347	62,954	157	50,327	558	49,256	2,088	67,734	33,334	348,796	NA	NA	NA	NA	NA	NA
1985	9,323	80,666	145	150,448	524	41,227	1,114	95,838	32,679	277,339	NA	NA	NA	NA	NA	NA
1986	8,911	74,597	123	17,414	292	14,424	1,370	121,536	30,489	237,850	NA	NA	NA	NA	NA	NA
1987	11,400	84,807	176	112,479	535	23,783	2,138	102,383	40,257	417,750	NA	NA	NA	NA	NA	NA
1988	12,073	97,570	129	204,643	374	122,585	3,064	165,296	23,966	477,938	NA	NA	NA	NA	NA	NA
1989	12,444	100,729	182	204,000	333	58,139	4,102	225,028	22,416	509,601	NA	NA	NA	NA	NA	NA
1990	8,412	84,277	151	102,623	285	17,984	8,960	440,487	34,602	449,019	NA	NA	NA	NA	NA	NA
1991	7,945	62,652	103	43,801	257	30,261	8,555	271,315	26,908	377,105	1,902	$5,763	154	$52,736	NA	NA
1992	8,910	61,021	91	41,933	193	15,293	3,510	219,439	15,064	178,588	1,999	10,333	215	167,244	1,253	$32,492
1993	8,917	71,872	47	6,900	180	9,408	3,550	183,128	14,072	214,356	2,663	3,396	245	77,981	2,005	44,175
1994	8,523	80,902	35	5,290	190	42,474	3,266	217,507	11,881	174,033	2,420	5,002	73	36,540	2,219	38,288
1995	9,269	91,378	36	29,253	192	45,668	3,071	207,737	10,985	513,765	1,719	24,231	172	45,326	2,092	51,683
1996	11,543	104,933	29	7,901	217	9,070	2,964	258,591	13,731	204,181	1,373	9,191	135	25,631	2,236	52,384
1997	10,953	94,287	23	15,158	197	11,839	3,739	240,243	17,573	1,176,551	1,509	7,229	326	38,303	2,117	64,001
1998	13,705	94,537	34	29,212	187	13,821	4,336	426,640	19,327	1,696,333	1,456	6,500	98	26,052	3,567	82,692
1999	13,848	101,456	22	20,755	179	11,893	4,515	444,035	12,667	202,792	1,398	8,796	49	25,471	3,926	120,275
2000	11,997	100,450	19	14,413	174	19,080	3,892	204,090	12,211	160,138	1,140	11,753	75	17,336	3,357	60,252
2001	11,637	74,531	7	550	112	7,822	3,458	161,956	16,291	190,358	702	3,377	42	18,169	3,477	134,971

Note: Some data have been revised by the Source and may differ from previous editions of SOURCEBOOK.

[a] Includes any other type of merchandise brought into the country in violation of the U.S. Customs laws.
[b] Includes any unauthorized use or theft of copyrighted or pirated goods, and counterfeit items and goods not licensed for sale in the United States.

Source: U.S. Department of the Treasury, U.S. Customs Service, *Customs U.S.A., 1980*, p. 32; *1982*, p. 40; *1989*, p. 40 (Washington, DC: U.S. Department of the Treasury); U.S. Department of the Treasury, U.S. Customs Service, *U.S. Customs Update 1992* (Washington, DC: U.S. Department of the Treasury, 1993), p. 22; U.S. Department of the Treasury, U.S. Customs Service, *U.S. Customs Service: Annual Report FY 1993* (Washington, DC: U.S. Department of the Treasury, 1994), p. 41; and data provided by the U.S. Department of the Treasury, U.S. Customs Service. Table adapted by SOURCEBOOK staff.

Table 4.45

Value of asset forfeiture recoveries by U.S. attorneys

United States, 1989-2002

	Value of assets forfeited
1989	$285,000,039
1990	451,870,952
1991	596,879,728
1992	325,786,450
1993	385,000,701
1994	418,224,247
1995	464,666,914
1996	377,527,900
1997	570,656,170
1998	280,808,572
1999	535,767,852
2000	312,676,413
2001[a]	199,043,103
2002	322,246,408

Note: The U.S. attorney is the highest ranking law enforcement official in each of the 94 Federal judicial districts. Each U.S. attorney, under the direction of the U.S. Attorney General, is responsible for establishing law enforcement priorities, and for carrying out the prosecution and litigation activities within their respective districts. Each U.S. attorney also is the chief litigator representing the United States in civil judicial proceedings in the district. U.S. attorneys direct and supervise the work of the assistant U.S. attorneys and staff of the district's offices.

U.S. attorneys' offices utilize both criminal and civil asset forfeiture laws to strip away, through court proceedings, property that was either used for or derived from criminal activity such as narcotics violations, money laundering, racketeering, and fraud as well as property used to facilitate the commission of certain crimes (Source, *Fiscal Year 2002*, p. 36). These data represent the combined value of forfeited cash and property.

[a]Beginning in fiscal year 2001, data reflect changes resulting from the Civil Asset Forfeiture Reform Act (CAFRA) of 2000, which requires numerous procedural modifications governing criminal and civil asset forfeiture. See the Source, *Fiscal Year 2002*, for details.

Source: U.S. Department of Justice, Executive Office for United States Attorneys, *United States Attorneys' Annual Statistical Report: Fiscal Year 1993*, p. 29; *Fiscal Year 2000*, p. 73; *Fiscal Year 2001*, p. 70; *Fiscal Year 2002*, p. 38 (Washington, DC: U.S. Department of Justice). Table adapted by SOURCEBOOK staff.

Table 4.46

Deportable aliens located by the Bureau of Customs and Border Protection and the Bureau of Immigration and Customs Enforcement, and aliens removed from the United States

By type of removal, fiscal years 1961-2003

Fiscal year	Aliens located	Formal[a]	Voluntary departure[b]
1961	88,823	8,181	52,383
1962	92,758	8,025	54,164
1963	88,712	7,763	69,392
1964	86,597	9,167	73,042
1965	110,371	10,572	95,263
1966	138,520	9,680	123,683
1967	161,608	9,728	142,343
1968	212,057	9,590	179,952
1969	283,557	11,030	240,958
1970	345,353	17,469	303,348
1971	420,126	18,294	370,074
1972	505,949	16,883	450,927
1973	655,968	17,346	568,005
1974	788,145	19,413	718,740
1975	766,600	24,432	655,814
1976	875,915	29,226	765,094
Transition quarter[c]	221,824	9,245	190,280
1977	1,042,215	31,263	867,015
1978	1,057,977	29,277	975,515
1979	1,076,418	26,825	966,137
1980	910,361	18,013	719,211
1981	975,780	17,379	823,875
1982	970,246	15,216	812,572
1983	1,251,357	19,211	931,600
1984	1,246,981	18,696	909,833
1985	1,348,749	23,105	1,041,296
1986	1,767,400	24,592	1,586,320
1987	1,190,488	24,336	1,091,203
1988	1,008,145	25,829	911,790
1989	954,243	34,427	830,890
1990	1,169,939	30,039	1,022,533
1991	1,197,875	33,189	1,061,105
1992	1,258,481	43,671	1,105,829
1993	1,327,261	42,542	1,243,410
1994	1,094,719	45,674	1,029,107
1995	1,394,554	50,924	1,313,764
1996	1,649,986	69,680	1,573,428
1997	1,536,520	114,432	1,440,684
1998	1,679,439	173,146	1,570,127
1999	1,714,035	180,902	1,574,682
2000	1,814,729	185,987	1,675,711
2001	1,387,486	177,739	1,254,035
2002	1,062,279	150,084	934,119
2003	1,046,422	186,151	887,115

Note: On Mar. 1, 2003, the Immigration and Naturalization Service transitioned to the U.S. Department of Homeland Security and two bureaus were formed to handle enforcement activities: the Bureau of Customs and Border Protection and the Bureau of Immigration and Customs Enforcement (Source, p. 144). Some data have been revised by the Source and may differ from previous editions of SOURCEBOOK.

[a]Includes deportations pursuant to an order by an immigration judge and exclusions, which involve denial of entry into the United States based on a finding of inadmissibility by an immigration judge or by authority of immigration officials through an expedited removal process.
[b]Includes departure of aliens from the United States without an order of removal and may or may not be preceded by a hearing before an immigration judge. The alien concedes removability but is not barred from seeking future admissibility.
[c]The 3-month period, July 1-Sept. 30, 1976.

Source: U.S. Department of Homeland Security, Office of Immigration Statistics, *2003 Yearbook of Immigration Statistics*, pp. 153, 158 [Online]. Available: http://uscis.gov/graphics/shared/aboutus/statistics/2003yearbook.pdf [Oct. 7, 2004].

Table 4.47

Aliens formally removed from the United States for violation of immigration laws

By reason for removal, fiscal years 1991-2003

Fiscal year	Total	Attempted entry without proper documents or through fraud or misrepresentation	Criminal	Failed to maintain status	Previously removed or ineligible for reentry	Present without authorization[a]	Security	Smuggling or aiding illegal entry	Other	Unknown
1991	33,189	3,058	14,475	1,135	735	13,347	7	28	191	213
1992	43,671	3,630	20,098	1,076	1,008	17,403	31	177	57	191
1993	42,542	2,968	22,470	783	913	15,018	54	208	95	33
1994	45,674	3,482	24,581	716	1,052	15,500	57	218	51	17
1995	50,924	5,822	25,684	611	1,432	17,069	34	196	63	13
1996	69,680	15,412	27,655	708	2,005	23,522	36	275	49	18
1997	114,432	35,737	34,113	1,031	3,302	39,297	30	385	522	15
1998	173,146	79,290	35,946	986	7,103	48,477	15	497	816	16
1999	180,902	91,858	41,995	789	9,287	34,898	10	404	1,651	10
2000	185,987	89,893	41,076	729	11,653	40,254	13	490	1,874	5
2001	177,739	76,212	40,112	714	10,668	47,889	12	507	1,619	6
2002	150,084	41,295	37,723	1,226	12,809	55,322	11	572	1,101	25
2003	186,151	52,014	39,600	1,240	17,630	73,609	12	597	1,442	7

Note: See Note, table 4.46. These data reflect the legal basis for formal removal (including deportation and exclusion) of persons identified as aliens. Some aliens who are criminals may be removed for a reason (charge) other than those listed above. Removal categories have been revised by the Source pursuant to a revision in the law effective Apr. 1, 1997. Some data have been revised by the Source and may differ from previous editions of SOURCEBOOK.

[a]Includes those aliens charged with "entering without inspection" prior to the Apr. 1, 1997 revision in the law.

Source: U.S. Department of Homeland Security, Office of Immigration Statistics, *2003 Yearbook of Immigration Statistics*, p. 160 [Online]. Available: http://uscis.gov/graphics/shared/aboutus/statistics/2003yearbook.pdf [Oct. 7, 2004].

Page 398 intentionally blank.

Section 5

Judicial processing of defendants

This section presents a wide range of statistics on judicial activity for Federal, State, and military courts detailing the judicial processing of adult and juvenile defendants in the United States. The section begins with information on requests for immunity by Federal prosecutors. Court orders for interception of wire, oral, or electronic communications and subsequent arrests and convictions are then presented. Activities of U.S. attorneys follow, including the number of grand jury proceedings, criminal cases handled, and offenses involved.

Activities of the Federal courts are the focus of the next portion of Section 5. Detailed data from the Administrative Office of the United States Courts show criminal cases filed, terminated, and pending in U.S. District Courts, and include trend tables that present these case processing activities over time. Tables also display specific offenses (e.g., weapons and immigration violations, fraud, embezzlement), as well as offense level (e.g., felony, class A misdemeanor).

Information on pretrial detention for Federal defendants follows. Several tables feature information on the number of defendants detained, the length of detention, and detention-related costs incurred by each Federal judicial circuit and district.

The Bureau of Justice Statistics' (BJS) Federal Justice Statistics Program also provides detailed data on the U.S. District Courts, including figures on Federal defendants released or detained prior to trial. Data are displayed by offense type, defendant characteristics, and outcome of pretrial release. Information on the processing of cases in district courts includes the disposition of cases, number of defendants convicted, method of conviction, and type of sentences imposed. Demographic characteristics of defendants sentenced, data on specific offenses, type of disposition, and length of prison sentences also are included in the sentencing data.

Application of U.S. Sentencing Commission guidelines in Federal district courts is the focus of the next segment. These tables enumerate offenders sentenced, offense types, demographic characteristics of defendants (including level of education and status of citizenship), type and length of sentences imposed, fines and restitution ordered, and sentences that depart from the guidelines. Also, a table showing fines and restitution ordered for organizations sentenced in U.S. District Courts is included. A detailed breakdown of defendants charged with and sentenced for violation of Federal drug laws, as well as convictions resulting from arrests by the Drug Enforcement Administration is among the information presented. Counts of antitrust cases filed, length of civil and criminal trials, and amount of time from filing to final disposition of cases in U.S. District Courts concludes this series of tables.

The National Judicial Reporting Program sponsored by BJS is the source of extensive information on judicial activity in State courts shown in the next group of tables. This dataset provides counts of felony convictions and sentences in State courts by offense type, demographic characteristics of defendants, method of conviction, and the type and length of sentences imposed. Information also is presented on defendants sentenced to additional penalties and the length of time from arrest to sentencing for felony cases.

Next are tables from BJS' State Court Processing Statistics Program, which pertain to the processing of felony defendants in the 75 largest counties in the United States. These data inform those interested in judicial processing in large urban areas. A series of tables focusing on juvenile courts and the processing of juvenile defendants follows. Included is information on the characteristics of juvenile offenders and the outcomes of cases.

Section 5 also includes a trend table with more than 25 years of data for types of prisoner petitions filed in U.S. District Courts by State and Federal prisoners. The number of appeals filed in U.S. Courts of Appeal is presented. Tables on the activities of the U.S. Supreme Court show data on cases filed and types of dispositions. Next is a trend table with 50 years of data on requests for executive clemency. Criminal matters handled by the U.S. Postal Inspection Service, processing of immigration law violators, and cases involving abuse of public office during the last quarter century are the topics of tables that appear at the end of this segment.

Data on activity in U.S. military courts conclude this section. Specifically, these tables detail military courts-martial cases for all branches of the U.S. armed forces. Tables provide trend data on general, special, and summary courts-martial, and type of discharge, for each branch of the U.S. military and the Coast Guard.

Table 5.1

Requests for immunity by Federal prosecutors to the U.S. Attorney General and witnesses involved in these requests

By origin of request, fiscal years 1973-2003

	Requests			Witnesses		
	Total	Criminal Division		Total	Criminal Division	
Fiscal year	number	Number	Percent	number	Number	Percent
1973	1,160	769	66%	2,715	1,598	59%
1974	1,410	1,121	80	3,655	2,055	56
1975	1,632	1,259	77	3,733	2,183	58
1976	1,789	1,361	76	3,923	2,366	60
1977	1,798	1,250	70	4,413	1,969	45
1978	1,445	959	66	2,997	1,403	47
1979	1,596	1,163	73	3,204	1,816	57
1980	1,653	1,207	73	3,530	1,892	54
1981	1,686	1,252	74	3,271	2,032	62
1982	1,836	1,394	76	3,810	2,233	59
1983	1,986	1,425	72	4,226	2,243	53
1984	2,378	1,838	77	4,784	2,858	60
1985	2,451	1,898	77	5,146	3,329	65
1986	2,550	1,948	76	5,013	3,267	65
1987	2,359	1,869	79	4,603	3,249	71
1988	2,359	1,821	77	4,702	3,205	68
1989	2,301	1,807	79	4,495	3,249	72
1990	2,049	1,694	83	3,735	2,905	78
1991	1,953	1,561	80	3,377	2,449	73
1992	1,819	1,417	78	3,242	2,309	71
1993	1,959	1,466	75	3,521	2,393	68
1994	1,717	1,262	74	3,279	2,225	68
1995	1,520	1,182	78	2,776	1,987	72
1996	1,493	1,135	76	2,806	2,066	74
1997	1,502	1,108	74	2,737	1,953	71
1998	1,340	1,017	76	2,300	1,616	70
1999	1,196	908	76	2,059	1,444	70
2000	1,206	955	79	2,164	1,584	73
2001	1,132	929	82	1,986	1,558	78
2002	901	717	80	1,546	1,084	70
2003	913	743	81	1,613	1,175	73

Note: These data reflect requests received from Federal prosecutors under 18 U.S.C. 6001-6005, the statute that governs the granting of use immunity. 18 U.S.C. 6003 requires all Federal prosecuting attorneys to receive authorization from the U.S. Attorney General (or representative) before seeking a court order for witness immunity. It should be noted that in some cases in which the authorization is obtained, the prosecutor may decide not to seek the immunity order from the courts. Therefore, the number of witnesses actually granted immunity is probably lower than the data in the table indicate. It should also be noted that data for 1973 and 1974 include a total of 11 requests and 27 witnesses, and 7 requests and 11 witnesses, respectively, falling under an older statute, 18 U.S.C. 2514, which was repealed. "Criminal Division" includes the Criminal Division of the U.S. Department of Justice and the U.S. attorneys. Other requests, not pertaining to the Criminal Division, come from the remaining divisions of the U.S. Department of Justice (e.g., Antitrust, Tax, Civil Division, Civil Rights, and Environment and Natural Resources), as well as from the other Federal agencies (e.g., Federal Trade Commission, Securities and Exchange Commission, and Department of the Army) and from Congress, all of which may request immunity for witnesses. Some data have been revised by the Source and may differ from previous editions of SOURCEBOOK.

Source: Table constructed by SOURCEBOOK staff from data provided by the U.S. Department of Justice, Criminal Division.

Table 5.2

Court-authorized orders for interception of wire, oral, or electronic communications

United States, 1969-2003

	Intercept applications authorized	
	Federal	State
1969	33	268
1970	182	414
1971	285	531
1972	206	649
1973	130	734
1974	121	607
1975	108	593
1976	137	549
1977	77	549
1978	81	489
1979	87	466
1980	81	483
1981	106	483
1982	130	448
1983	208	440
1984	289	512
1985	243	541
1986	250	504
1987	236	437
1988	293	445
1989	310	453
1990	324	548
1991	356	500
1992	340	579
1993	450	526
1994	554	600
1995	532	526
1996	581	568
1997	569	617
1998	566	763
1999	601	749
2000	479	711
2001	486	1,005
2002	497	861
2003	578	864

Note: The Director of the Administrative Office of the United States Courts is required, in accordance with provisions of 18 U.S.C. 2519(1), to transmit to Congress a report regarding applications for orders authorizing or approving the interception of wire, oral, or electronic communications. This report is required to contain information about the number of such orders and any extensions granted. Every State and Federal judge is required to file a written report on each application made. This report is required to contain information on the grants and denials, name of applicant, offense under investigation, type and location of device, and duration of authorized intercept. Prosecuting officials who have applied for intercept orders are required to file reports containing information on the cost of the intercepts; the number of days the device was in operation; the total number of intercepts; the number of incriminating intercepts recorded; whether encryption was encountered in the course of the intercept; and the results of the intercepts in terms of the number of arrests, trials, convictions, and motions to suppress evidence obtained through the use of intercepts. Forty-seven jurisdictions (the Federal Government, the District of Columbia, the Virgin Islands, and 44 States) had statutes authorizing the interception of wire, oral, or electronic communications during 2003; 24 of these jurisdictions had court-authorized orders for interception during 2003 (Source, *2003*, pp. 6, 7).

Source: Administrative Office of the United States Courts, *Report on Applications for Orders Authorizing or Approving the Interception of Wire or Oral Communications for the Period January 1, 1977 to December 31, 1977* (Washington, DC: Administrative Office of the United States Courts, 1978), p. xvi; Administrative Office of the United States Courts, *Report on Applications for Orders Authorizing or Approving the Interception of Wire, Oral, or Electronic Communications for the Period January 1, 1988 to December 31, 1988* (Washington, DC: USGPO, 1989), p. 19; and Administrative Office of the United States Courts, *1999 Wiretap Report*, p. 32; *2003*, p. 32 (Washington, DC: Administrative Office of the United States Courts). Table adapted by SOURCEBOOK staff.

Table 5.3

Court-authorized orders for interception of wire, oral, or electronic communications

By most serious offense under investigation, United States, 2003

Offense	Intercept applications authorized		
	Total	Federal	State
All offenses	1,442	578	864
Narcotics	1,104	502	602
Racketeering	96	43	53
Gambling	49	2	47
Homicide and assault	80	1	79
Kidnaping	7	0	7
Loansharking, usury, and extortion	6	5	1
Larceny, theft, and robbery	50	0	50
Bribery	9	1	8
Other	41	24	17

Note: See Note, table 5.2.

Source: Administrative Office of the United States Courts, *2003 Wiretap Report* (Washington, DC: Administrative Office of the United States Courts, 2004), pp. 19-21. Table adapted by SOURCEBOOK staff.

Table 5.4

Court-authorized orders for interception of wire, oral, or electronic communications

By jurisdiction, 1997-2003

Jurisdiction	1997	1998	1999	2000	2001	2002	2003
Total	1,186	1,329	1,350	1,190	1,491	1,358	1,442
Federal	569	566	601	479	486	497	578
Alaska	0	0	0	0	0	0	0
Arizona	6	6	8	18	10	7	14
California	28	52	76	88	130	143	188
Colorado	4	1	2	5	2	0	2
Connecticut	8	23	15	4	9	0	4
Delaware	0	1	1	0	0	0	1
District of Columbia	0	0	0	0	0	0	0
Florida	57	44	23	43	51	37	45
Georgia	18	9	11	3	7	4	4
Hawaii	0	1	0	0	0	0	0
Idaho	0	0	1	1	0	0	1
Illinois	17	27	50	41	128	25	23
Indiana	0	0	0	0	0	0	0
Iowa	0	0	0	1	0	0	0
Kansas	0	4	4	1	0	0	0
Louisiana	2	3	0	1	0	1	0
Maine[a]	X	X	X	X	0	0	0
Maryland	27	32	6	31	49	54	25
Massachusetts	2	0	15	5	11	8	16
Minnesota	0	1	6	0	1	0	0
Mississippi	4	4	3	0	6	1	3
Missouri	0	0	0	0	0	0	0
Nebraska	4	2	4	0	2	0	0
Nevada	10	13	9	10	0	4	12
New Hampshire	4	1	9	0	1	0	5
New Jersey	70	84	71	45	99	81	117
New Mexico	1	0	0	4	0	3	0
New York	304	373	343	349	425	404	328
North Carolina	0	0	0	0	0	1	0
North Dakota	0	0	0	0	0	0	0
Ohio	2	2	3	6	2	1	2
Oklahoma	0	1	6	4	2	2	0
Oregon	1	1	1	1	2	0	0
Pennsylvania	42	68	69	43	54	79	52
Rhode Island	2	0	0	0	0	0	0
South Carolina[b]	X	X	X	X	X	0	2
South Dakota	0	0	0	0	0	0	0
Tennessee	0	0	1	1	0	0	10
Texas	0	5	4	0	1	2	4
Utah	0	5	2	3	4	4	4
Virgin Islands	0	0	0	0	0	0	0
Virginia	1	0	6	0	4	0	0
Washington	0	0	0	2	1	0	0
West Virginia	0	0	0	0	0	0	0
Wisconsin	3	0	0	1	4	0	2
Wyoming	0	0	0	0	0	0	0

Note: See Note, table 5.2.

[a] Maine did not have legislation authorizing interception of communications prior to 2001.
[b] South Carolina did not have legislation authorizing interception of communications prior to 2002.

Source: Administrative Office of the United States Courts, *1997 Wiretap Report*, pp. 13, 14; *1998*, pp. 13, 14; *1999*, pp. 13, 14; *2000*, pp. 14, 15; *2001*, pp. 14, 15; *2002*, pp. 14, 15; *2003*, pp. 14, 15 (Washington, DC: Administrative Office of the United States Courts). Table constructed by SOURCEBOOK staff.

Table 5.5

Arrests and convictions resulting from court-authorized orders for interception of wire, oral, or electronic communications

United States, 1987-2003

Year arrests and convictions reported	1987 (N=634)	1988 (N=678)	1989 (N=720)	1990 (N=812)	1991 (N=802)	1992 (N=846)	1993 (N=938)	1994 (N=1,100)	1995 (N=1,024)	1996 (N=1,035)	1997 (N=1,094)	1998 (N=1,245)	1999 (N=1,277)	2000 (N=1,139)	2001 (N=1,405)	2002 (N=1,273)	2003 (N=1,367)
1987																	
Arrests	2,226	X	X	X	X	X	X	X	X	X	X	X	X	X	X	X	X
Convictions	506	X	X	X	X	X	X	X	X	X	X	X	X	X	X	X	X
1988																	
Arrests	716	2,486	X	X	X	X	X	X	X	X	X	X	X	X	X	X	X
Convictions	936	543	X	X	X	X	X	X	X	X	X	X	X	X	X	X	X
1989																	
Arrests	186	969	2,804	X	X	X	X	X	X	X	X	X	X	X	X	X	X
Convictions	341	1,192	706	X	X	X	X	X	X	X	X	X	X	X	X	X	X
1990																	
Arrests	54	251	986	2,057	X	X	X	X	X	X	X	X	X	X	X	X	X
Convictions	141	400	823	420	X	X	X	X	X	X	X	X	X	X	X	X	X
1991																	
Arrests	5	106	289	897	2,364	X	X	X	X	X	X	X	X	X	X	X	X
Convictions	23	203	490	550	605	X	X	X	X	X	X	X	X	X	X	X	X
1992																	
Arrests	38	18	120	213	801	2,685	X	X	X	X	X	X	X	X	X	X	X
Convictions	9	66	186	357	827	607	X	X	X	X	X	X	X	X	X	X	X
1993																	
Arrests	19	29	23	83	270	983	2,428	X	X	X	X	X	X	X	X	X	X
Convictions	16	57	111	142	210	895	413	X	X	X	X	X	X	X	X	X	X
1994																	
Arrests	15	0	8	67	155	326	981	2,852	X	X	X	X	X	X	X	X	X
Convictions	11	8	52	111	169	450	912	772	X	X	X	X	X	X	X	X	X
1995																	
Arrests	15	6	8	26	111	67	390	1,165	2,577	X	X	X	X	X	X	X	X
Convictions	12	6	7	81	148	164	538	965	494	X	X	X	X	X	X	X	X
1996																	
Arrests	1	2	7	2	30	40	130	209	1,246	2,464	X	X	X	X	X	X	X
Convictions	1	11	1	2	40	50	233	403	1,112	502	X	X	X	X	X	X	X
1997																	
Arrests	0	0	0	0	35	22	109	79	448	1,069	3,086	X	X	X	X	X	X
Convictions	0	0	2	62	64	1	179	191	740	1,110	542	X	X	X	X	X	X
1998																	
Arrests	0	0	9	9	4	35	70	86	425	402	1,406	3,450	X	X	X	X	X
Convictions	0	0	10	9	8	45	81	163	502	423	1,220	911	X	X	X	X	X
1999																	
Arrests	0	0	1	0	0	20	1	60	40	194	493	1,266	4,372	X	X	X	X
Convictions	0	0	1	0	16	22	2	39	33	205	464	1,214	654	X	X	X	X
2000																	
Arrests	0	0	0	1	0	0	0	1	19	25	176	441	1,600	3,411	X	X	X
Convictions	0	0	0	0	0	0	0	2	29	62	169	596	1,323	736	X	X	X
2001																	
Arrests	0	0	0	0	1	0	1	1	14	37	110	337	428	1,741	3,683	X	X
Convictions	0	0	0	0	1	0	0	5	26	59	87	271	515	1,148	732	X	X
2002																	
Arrests	0	0	0	0	0	20	0	30	28	11	33	114	216	681	1,325	3,060	X
Convictions	0	0	0	0	0	7	0	32	23	9	62	139	235	793	1,316	493	X
2003																	
Arrests	0	0	0	0	0	0	0	1	3	1	19	30	38	142	316	1,067	3,674
Convictions	0	0	0	0	0	0	0	1	4	2	25	23	77	280	572	1,082	843

Note: See Note, table 5.2. Arrests, trials, and convictions resulting from the interceptions of wire, oral, and electronic communication do not always occur within the same year as the implementation of the court order. This table presents arrest and conviction data for the year court-authorized interception began and subsequent years. Some data have been revised by the Source and may differ from previous editions of SOURCEBOOK.

Source: Administrative Office of the United States Courts, *Report on Applications for Orders Authorizing or Approving the Interception of Wire, Oral, or Electronic Communications for the Period January 1, 1992 to December 31, 1992* (Washington, DC: USGPO, 1993), p. 29; and Administrative Office of the United States Courts, *2003 Wiretap Report* (Washington, DC: Administrative Office of the United States Courts, 2004), pp. 32, 38. Table adapted by SOURCEBOOK staff.

Table 5.6

Grand jury proceedings and criminal cases filed and terminated by U.S. attorneys

United States, fiscal years 1980-2002

	Grand jury proceedings	Criminal cases[a] Filed	Criminal cases[a] Terminated
1980	16,592	26,086	NA
1981	16,794	25,830	NA
1982	17,064	26,106	NA
1983	17,765	27,462	NA
1984	17,487	27,292	NA
1985	17,094	27,059	NA
1986	20,111	31,012	NA
1987	19,263	31,593	30,547
1988	20,184	33,294	29,582
1989	23,203	34,865	29,322
1990	23,925	36,042	32,204
1991	25,943	38,374	33,834
1992	25,470	35,263	33,161
1993	23,757	36,995	35,809
1994	20,714	33,307	32,231
1995	22,856	36,878	32,829
1996	23,449	38,250	34,882
1997	25,209	39,291	34,634
1998	30,734	47,277	40,746
1999	32,474	50,779	46,423
2000	34,055	52,887	46,308
2001	36,167	53,339	49,834
2002	39,306	56,658	51,436

Note: The U.S. attorney is the highest ranking law enforcement official in each of the 94 Federal judicial districts. Each U.S. attorney, under the direction of the U.S. Attorney General, is responsible for establishing law enforcement priorities, and for carrying out the prosecution and litigation activities within their respective districts. Each U.S. attorney also is the chief litigator representing the United States in civil judicial proceedings in the district. U.S. attorneys direct and supervise the work of the assistant U.S. attorneys and staff of the district's offices.

[a] Includes cases filed and terminated by U.S. attorneys in U.S. District Courts only; excludes filings and terminations in magistrate courts and appellate courts.

Source: U.S. Department of Justice, Executive Office for United States Attorneys, *United States Attorneys' Annual Statistical Report: Fiscal Year 1980*, p. 1; *Fiscal Year 1981*, p. 1; *Fiscal Year 1982*, p. 1; *Fiscal Year 1983*, p. 1; *Fiscal Year 1984*, p. 1; *Fiscal Year 1987*, p. 1; *Fiscal Year 1991*, pp. 8, 10; *Fiscal Year 1997*, p. 95; *Fiscal Year 1998*, p. 102 (Washington, DC: USGPO); U.S. Department of Justice, Executive Office for United States Attorneys, *United States Attorneys' Annual Statistical Report: Fiscal Year 1985*, p. 1; *Fiscal Year 1988*, p. 1; *Fiscal Year 1989*, pp. 1, 18; *Fiscal Year 1990*, p. 1; *Fiscal Year 1992*, p. 49; *Fiscal Year 1993*, p. 45; *Fiscal Year 1994*, p. 45; *Fiscal Year 1995*, p. 45; *Fiscal Year 1996*, p. 67; *Fiscal Year 1999*, pp. 12, 103; *Fiscal Year 2000*, pp. 11, 103; *Fiscal Year 2001*, pp. 11, 102; *Fiscal Year 2002*, pp. 8, 64 (Washington, DC: U.S. Department of Justice). Table adapted by SOURCEBOOK staff.

Table 5.7

Criminal cases filed and disposed of and number of defendants handled by U.S. attorneys

By offense type, United States, fiscal year 2002

Offense type	Cases Filed[a]	Cases Terminated[b]	Defendants Filed[c]	Defendants Terminated[d]	Guilty	Not guilty[e]	Dismissed[f]	Rule 20[g]	Other
Total	56,658	51,436	77,305	70,492	64,182	568	5,092	506	144
Assimilated crimes[h]	484	295	505	308	200	2	102	4	0
Civil rights prosecutions	81	85	115	135	119	9	5	0	2
Government regulatory offenses	1,541	1,663	2,243	2,476	2,168	19	247	34	8
Copyright violations	38	42	54	82	64	0	18	0	0
Counterfeiting	767	814	1,189	1,291	1,175	5	88	17	6
Customs violations:									
Duty	39	60	45	78	57	1	18	2	0
Currency	97	100	128	114	100	0	12	1	1
Energy pricing and related fraud	0	0	0	3	3	0	0	0	0
Environmental offenses	214	243	326	369	319	9	34	6	1
Health and safety violations	17	20	29	36	30	1	5	0	0
Money laundering:									
Narcotics	72	61	106	111	82	0	29	0	0
Other	105	111	152	147	117	2	25	3	0
Trafficking in contraband cigarettes	5	4	8	6	4	0	2	0	0
Other regulatory offenses	187	208	206	239	217	1	16	5	0
Immigration	13,676	12,357	14,705	13,183	12,580	25	563	9	6
Internal security offenses	27	13	28	14	12	0	0	2	0
Interstate theft	182	189	313	357	322	5	25	5	0
Labor management offenses	101	94	123	105	96	1	6	2	0
Corruption:									
Bribery	10	10	10	10	10	0	0	0	0
Pension benefit	33	28	39	30	29	1	0	0	0
Labor racketeering	8	12	20	19	17	0	2	0	0
Other labor offenses	50	44	54	46	40	0	4	2	0
Drug offenses	17,284	16,318	30,014	28,272	25,944	198	1,971	102	57
Organized Crime Drug Enforcement									
Task Force (OCDETF)	3,044	3,319	8,414	9,233	8,296	59	822	37	19
Non-OCDETF	14,240	12,999	21,600	19,039	17,648	139	1,149	65	38
Dealing	13,993	12,759	21,278	18,753	17,397	138	1,115	65	38
Possession	247	240	322	286	251	1	34	0	0
Official corruption	460	399	668	527	476	7	38	5	1
Federal procurement	32	34	41	46	40	1	3	2	0
Federal program	78	71	117	81	73	0	8	0	0
Federal law enforcement	34	36	44	41	40	1	0	0	0
Other Federal	109	110	131	126	113	2	10	1	0
Local	127	93	226	140	121	3	13	2	1
State	38	30	55	51	49	0	2	0	0
Other official	42	25	54	42	40	0	2	0	0
Organized crime	140	176	336	414	372	3	36	3	0
Terrorism/anti-terrorism	1,046	394	1,112	428	367	1	60	0	0
Theft	1,525	1,521	1,945	1,937	1,748	15	152	19	3
Check/postal	1,103	1,085	1,418	1,376	1,256	6	100	11	3
Motor vehicle theft	53	67	112	142	121	1	15	5	0
Theft of government property	369	369	415	419	371	8	37	3	0
Violent crime	10,070	8,516	11,991	10,142	8,889	184	913	141	15
Violent offenses in Indian country	603	540	660	592	509	19	64	0	0
Non-OCDETF drugs	280	231	477	354	308	3	42	1	0
OCDETF drugs	99	86	191	164	146	3	14	0	1
Organized crime	46	39	130	119	109	6	4	0	0
Other	9,042	7,620	10,533	8,913	7,817	153	789	140	14
Other (non-violent) offenses in Indian country	147	122	182	144	126	3	15	0	0

See notes at end of table.

Table 5.7

Criminal cases filed and disposed of and number of defendants handled by U.S. attorneys

By offense type, United States, fiscal year 2002--Continued

Offense type	Cases Filed[a]	Cases Terminated[b]	Defendants Filed[c]	Defendants Terminated[d]	Guilty	Not guilty[e]	Dispositions Dismissed[f]	Rule 20[g]	Other
White collar crime	6,252	6,073	8,820	8,395	7,575	64	594	121	41
Advance fee schemes[i]	70	66	97	105	90	1	9	5	0
Fraud against business institutions	603	556	924	871	805	12	39	13	2
Antitrust violations	8	20	16	37	36	0	1	0	0
Bank fraud and embezzlement	2,053	2,083	2,760	2,769	2,550	9	168	40	2
Bankruptcy fraud	146	143	166	164	140	2	16	6	0
Commodities fraud	24	21	32	31	28	0	2	0	1
Computer fraud	142	112	223	164	141	3	11	3	6
Consumer fraud	127	141	183	195	170	1	20	3	1
Federal procurement fraud	83	79	114	111	100	1	8	1	1
Federal program fraud	834	772	1,080	1,001	887	6	99	8	1
Health care fraud	361	379	608	554	478	7	57	7	5
Insurance fraud	106	113	179	156	126	5	20	5	0
Other investment fraud	75	69	110	95	87	0	5	3	0
Securities fraud	260	199	443	374	338	4	21	10	1
Tax fraud	524	558	656	701	653	10	33	5	0
Other fraud	836	762	1,229	1,067	946	3	85	12	21
All other	3,642	3,221	4,205	3,655	3,188	32	365	59	11

Note: See Note, table 5.6.

[a]Includes 494 cases initiated by transfer under Rule 20 (see footnote g).
[b]Includes 395 cases terminated by transfer under Rule 20 (see footnote g).
[c]Includes 509 defendants initiated by transfer under Rule 20 (see footnote g).
[d]Includes 506 defendants terminated by transfer under Rule 20 (see footnote g).
[e]Includes 10 verdicts of not guilty by reason of insanity involving 11 defendants.
[f]Includes transfers, dismissals other than by court, pretrial diversions, and proceedings suspended indefinitely by court.
[g]Rule 20 of the Federal Criminal Rules permits the transfer of a case from one district to another for plea and sentencing. That is, if an offender is arrested in one district on an indictment or information originating in another district, the offender may plead guilty and be sentenced in the arresting district.
[h]Laws of States adopted for areas within a Federal jurisdiction (18 U.S.C. 13), e.g., driving while intoxicated on a military base.
[i]Fraud against businesses or individuals involving the payment of a fee in advance for goods, services, or other things of value.

Source: U.S. Department of Justice, Executive Office for United States Attorneys, *United States Attorneys' Annual Statistical Report: Fiscal Year 2002* (Washington, DC: U.S. Department of Justice, 2004), pp. 71, 72. Table adapted by SOURCEBOOK staff.

Table 5.8

Criminal cases commenced, terminated, and pending, and judgeships authorized in U.S. District Courts

1982-2003

	Judgeships authorized	Cases commenced[a] Number	Cases per judgeship	Drug cases	Terminated	Pending[b]
1982	515	32,682	63	4,218	31,889	16,659
1983	515	35,872	70	5,094	33,985	18,546
1984	515	36,845	72	5,606	35,494	19,938
1985	575	39,500	69	6,690	37,139	22,299
1986	575	41,490	72	7,893	39,328	24,453
1987	575	43,292	75	8,878	42,287	25,263
1988	575	43,607	76	10,603	41,878	28,776
1989	575	45,792	80	12,342	42,933	32,666
1990	575	46,568	81	11,547	43,296	35,308
1991	649	47,123	73	11,954	43,073	39,562
1992	649	48,366	75	12,833	44,147	34,078
1993	649	46,786	72	12,238	44,800	28,701
1994	649	45,484	70	11,369	45,129	26,328
1995	649	45,788	71	11,520	41,527	28,738
1996	647	47,889	74	12,092	45,499	32,156
1997	647	50,363	78	13,656	46,887	37,237
1998	646	57,691	89	16,281	51,428	40,277
1999	646	59,923	93	17,483	56,511	42,966
2000	655	62,745	96	17,505	58,102	47,677
2001	665	62,708	94	18,425	58,718	49,696
2002	665	67,000	101	19,215	60,991	55,518
2003	680	70,642	104	18,996	65,628	60,532
Percent change 2002 to 2003	2.2%	5.4%	3.0%	-1.1%	7.6%	9.0%

Note: Data for 1982-87 are reported for the 12-month period ending June 30. Beginning in 1988, data are reported for the Federal fiscal year, which is the 12-month period ending September 30. Some data have been revised by the Source and may differ from previous editions of SOURCEBOOK.

[a]Data for criminal cases commenced include transfers with the exception of drug cases, which exclude transfers.
[b]Beginning in 1993, pending totals exclude cases in which all defendants were fugitives for more than 1 year.

Source: Administrative Office of the United States Courts, *Annual Report of the Director, 1991*, p. 90; *1992*, p. 66; *1997*, p. 20 (Washington, DC: USGPO); and Administrative Office of the United States Courts, *Judicial Business of the United States Courts: 2002 Annual Report of the Director*, p. 23; *2003 Annual Report of the Director*, p. 16 (Washington, DC: USGPO). Table adapted by SOURCEBOOK staff.

Table 5.9
Criminal cases filed, terminated, and pending in U.S. District Courts

1955-2003

	Pending at beginning of reporting period	Total filed Original proceeding[a]	Total filed Received by transfer	Total terminated	Pending at end of reporting period		Pending at beginning of reporting period	Total filed Original proceeding[a]	Total filed Received by transfer	Total terminated	Pending at end of reporting period
1955	10,100	35,310	1,813	38,580	8,643	1980	15,124	27,910	1,022	29,297	14,759
1956	8,643	28,739	1,914	32,053	7,243	1981	14,759	30,353	975	30,221	15,866
1957	7,243	28,120	1,958	29,826	7,495	1982	15,866	31,623	1,059	31,889	16,659
1958	7,495	28,897	1,840	30,781	7,451	1983	16,659	34,681	1,191	33,985	18,546
1959	7,451	28,729	1,924	30,377	7,727	1984	18,587	35,911	934	35,494	19,938
						1985	19,938	38,546	954	37,139	22,299
1960	7,727	28,137	1,691	29,864	7,691	1986	22,299	40,427	1,063	39,333	24,456
1961	7,691	28,460	1,808	29,881	8,078	1987	24,453	42,156	1,136	42,287	25,458
1962	8,078	29,274	1,743	30,013	9,082	1988	25,263	43,503	1,082	42,115	27,733
1963	9,082	29,858	1,888	31,546	9,282	1989	27,722	44,891	1,104	42,810	30,907
1964	9,282	29,944	1,789	31,437	9,578						
1965	9,578	31,569	1,765	32,078	10,834	1990	30,910	47,962	942	44,295	35,519
1966	10,834	29,729	1,765	30,644	11,684	1991	35,021	45,055	680	42,788	37,968
1967	11,684	30,534	1,673	30,350	13,541	1992	39,562	47,472	894	44,147	43,781
1968	13,541	30,714	1,857	31,349	14,763	1993	34,078	45,903	883	44,800	36,064
1969	14,763	33,585	1,828	32,406	17,770	1994	28,701	44,667	806	45,129	29,045
						1995	26,328	45,053	735	41,527	30,589
1970	17,770	38,102	1,857	36,819	20,910	1996	28,738	47,146	743	45,499	31,128
1971	20,910	41,290	1,867	39,582	24,485	1997	32,156	49,655	708	46,887	35,632
1972	24,485	47,043	2,011	48,101	25,438	1998	37,237	57,023	668	51,428	43,500
1973	25,438	40,367	2,067	43,456	24,416	1999	40,277	59,251	672	56,511	43,689
1974	24,416	37,667	2,087	41,526	22,644						
1975	22,644	41,108	2,174	43,515	22,411	2000	42,966	62,152	593	58,102	47,609
1976	22,411	39,147	1,911	43,675	19,794	2001	47,677	62,134	574	58,718	51,667
1977	19,794	40,000	1,589	44,233	17,150	2002	49,696	66,452	548	60,991	55,705
1978	17,150	34,624	1,359	37,286	15,847	2003	55,518	70,092	550	65,628	60,532
1979	15,847	31,536	1,152	33,411	15,124						

Note: Two reporting changes were made during fiscal year 1976. Beginning Oct. 1, 1975, all minor offenses (offenses involving penalties that do not exceed 1 year imprisonment or a fine of more than $1,000), with the exception of most petty offenses (offenses involving penalties that do not exceed 6 months incarceration and/or a fine of not more than $500), are included. Minor offenses are generally disposed of by magistrate judges and, in past years, most of these minor offenses would not have been counted in the workload of the district courts. Second, when the Federal Government's motion to dismiss an original indictment or information is granted, the superseding indictment or information does not become a new case as in the years prior to 1976, but remains the same case. (An indictment is the charging document of the grand jury, and an information is the charging document of the U.S. attorney.) Data for 1955-91 are reported for the 12-month period ending June 30. Beginning in 1992, data are reported for the Federal fiscal year, which is the 12-month period ending September 30. These data were taken from the first year they were reported and do not reflect revisions made in subsequent years. Therefore, these data may differ from figures presented in table 5.8.

"Received by transfer" includes defendants transferred by Rule 20, *Federal Rules of Criminal Procedure*, which provides that defendants who (1) are arrested or held in a district other than that in which an indictment or information is pending against them or in which the warrant for their arrest was issued and (2) state in writing that they wish to plead guilty or nolo contendere, may consent to disposition of the case in the district in which they are arrested or are held, subject to the approval of the U.S. attorney for both districts.

[a]Includes reopens.

Source: Administrative Office of the United States Courts, *Annual Report of the Director, 1981*, p. 94; *1983*, pp. 302, 303; *1985*, pp. 336, 337; *1986*, pp. 232, 233; *1995*, pp. 195, 196; *1998*, pp. 198, 199; *1999*, pp. 192, 193 (Washington, DC: Administrative Office of the United States Courts); Administrative Office of the United States Courts, *Annual Report of the Director, 1982*, pp. 272, 273; *1984*, pp. 310, 311; *1987*, pp. 238, 239; *1988*, pp. 241, 242; *1989*, pp. 239, 240; *1990*, pp. 176, 177; *1991*, pp. 230, 231; *1992*, pp. 232, 233; *1993*, pp. AI111, AI112; *1994*, Table D-1; *1996*, pp. 191, 192; *1997*, pp. 184, 185 (Washington, DC: USGPO); and Administrative Office of the United States Courts, *Judicial Business of the United States Courts: 2001 Annual Report of the Director*, pp. 181-186; *2002 Annual Report of the Director*, pp. 181, 182; *2003 Annual Report of the Director*, pp. 181, 182 (Washington, DC: USGPO). Table constructed by SOURCEBOOK staff.

Table 5.10

Criminal cases filed in U.S. District Courts

By offense, fiscal years 1990, 1994-2003

Offense	1990	1994	1995	1996	1997	1998	1999	2000	2001	2002	2003
Total	47,962	44,678	45,053	47,146	49,655	57,023	59,251	62,152	62,134	66,452	70,092
Miscellaneous general offenses	13,265	12,414	11,114	10,462	10,386	10,856	11,747	12,544	13,190	14,987	16,432
Drunk driving and traffic	8,538	7,080	5,214	5,045	4,974	4,982	5,005	4,679	4,958	5,149	5,084
Weapons and firearms	2,713	3,112	3,621	3,162	3,184	3,641	4,367	5,387	5,845	7,382	9,075
Escape[a]	875	739	697	723	587	564	639	635	582	562	519
Kidnaping	65	68	81	116	99	150	101	111	104	98	124
Bribery	254	283	190	152	168	174	158	145	131	118	101
Extortion, racketeering, and threats	357	509	713	557	572	617	534	557	466	594	479
Gambling and lottery	109	80	26	16	24	22	16	17	6	10	11
Perjury	122	93	85	99	87	126	91	113	137	114	84
Other	232	450	487	592	691	580	836	900	961	960	955
Fraud	7,552	7,098	7,414	7,633	7,874	8,342	7,654	7,788	7,585	8,204	8,092
Drug laws	12,592	11,369	11,520	12,092	13,656	16,281	17,483	17,505	18,425	19,215	18,996
Larceny and theft	3,391	3,337	3,432	3,674	3,299	3,590	3,514	3,414	3,242	3,138	3,103
Forgery and counterfeiting	1,514	1,093	1,001	987	1,156	1,346	1,292	1,203	1,212	1,193	1,078
Embezzlement	2,027	1,575	1,368	1,284	1,172	1,397	1,315	1,200	1,072	1,075	962
Immigration laws	2,390	2,595	3,960	5,526	6,677	9,339	10,641	12,150	11,277	12,576	15,400
Federal statutes	2,325	2,084	2,403	2,317	2,156	2,363	2,241	2,844	2,573	2,384	2,281
Agricultural/conservation acts	276	247	401	313	267	333	277	316	282	232	226
Migratory bird laws	31	39	27	48	22	42	18	52	56	74	126
Civil rights[b]	64	70	73	73	59	77	81	80	76	62	48
Motor Carrier Act	40	11	12	7	8	6	16	5	3	2	3
Antitrust violations	70	43	38	31	34	25	39	43	28	24	11
Food and Drug Act	87	46	55	48	48	47	59	52	70	59	46
Contempt	178	74	69	81	77	80	78	109	158	107	73
National defense laws	106	95	85	62	73	55	68	533	462	147	74
Customs laws	148	88	97	110	97	125	96	97	79	78	72
Postal laws[c]	215	182	202	152	165	152	119	112	135	129	122
Other	1,110	1,189	1,344	1,392	1,306	1,421	1,390	1,445	1,224	1,470	1,480
Robbery	1,379	1,520	1,240	1,365	1,453	1,448	1,295	1,258	1,355	1,292	1,123
Bank	1,323	1,468	1,168	1,291	1,384	1,392	1,250	1,219	1,325	1,239	1,085
Postal	21	35	43	36	29	32	29	25	16	27	20
Other	35	17	29	38	40	24	16	14	14	26	18
Assault[d]	562	563	561	540	527	629	529	665	622	633	811
Motor vehicle theft	243	335	267	232	189	182	189	199	180	152	131
Burglary	104	139	63	65	70	89	72	59	52	44	46
Homicide[d]	176	195	295	344	348	384	383	370	329	370	311
Sex offenses	433	359	412	623	690	777	893	944	1,017	1,187	1,325
Liquor, Internal Revenue	9	2	3	2	2	0	3	9	3	2	1

Note: See Note, table 5.9. These data exclude transfers. Some data have been revised by the Source and may differ from previous editions of SOURCEBOOK.

[a]Includes escape from custody, aiding or abetting an escape, failure to appear in court, and bail jumping.
[b]The data for years prior to 2001 include cases removed from State courts under provisions of the Civil Rights Act, 28 U.S.C. 1443.
[c]Includes obstructing mail, mailing nonmailable material, and other postal regulations.
[d]In 2003, a change in coding caused some cases that previously would have been classified as homicide cases to be reported as aggravated assault cases; therefore, the data for 2003 and thereafter are not comparable to previous years.

Source: Administrative Office of the United States Courts, *Annual Report of the Director, 1990*, pp. 184, 185; *1997*, pp. 196-198 (Washington, DC: USGPO); and Administrative Office of the United States Courts, *Judicial Business of the United States Courts: 2002 Annual Report of the Director*, pp. 193-195; *2003 Annual Report of the Director*, pp. 193-195 (Washington, DC: USGPO). Table adapted by SOURCEBOOK staff.

Table 5.11

Criminal cases filed, terminated, and pending in U.S. District Courts

By type of offense, circuit, and district, fiscal year 2003

| | Pending Oct. 1, 2002 |||| Filed |||||||
| | ||| | | Original proceedings |||||
Circuit and district	Total	Felony	Class A misdemeanor	Other[a]	Total commenced	Total	Felony	Class A misdemeanor	Other[a]	Reopens[b]	Transfers
Total	55,518	47,172	7,842	504	70,642	69,788	58,670	10,764	354	304	550
District of Columbia	1,120	1,053	65	2	549	547	523	24	0	0	2
First Circuit	1,556	1,503	28	25	1,253	1,235	1,194	27	14	7	11
Maine	149	143	6	0	195	193	185	6	2	0	2
Massachusetts	683	664	12	7	417	409	400	9	0	2	6
New Hampshire	144	142	1	1	215	214	211	2	1	0	1
Rhode Island	210	203	7	0	113	113	112	1	0	0	0
Puerto Rico	370	351	2	17	313	306	286	9	11	5	2
Second Circuit	7,065	6,319	687	59	4,028	3,942	3,746	182	14	42	44
Connecticut	354	342	10	2	305	295	283	11	1	3	7
New York:											
Northern	715	525	190	0	388	377	335	41	1	10	1
Eastern	2,064	1,989	74	1	1,331	1,314	1,281	31	2	4	13
Southern	3,318	2,881	381	56	1,373	1,329	1,273	46	10	25	19
Western	450	422	28	0	478	475	428	47	0	0	3
Vermont	164	160	4	0	153	152	146	6	0	0	1
Third Circuit	3,019	2,751	245	23	2,853	2,798	2,498	291	9	13	42
Delaware	191	164	26	1	141	140	99	41	0	0	1
New Jersey	972	786	180	6	1,038	1,013	792	222	0	6	19
Pennsylvania:											
Eastern	898	886	9	3	696	683	671	7	5	3	10
Middle	386	370	16	0	350	346	332	12	2	0	4
Western	277	270	7	0	382	370	363	7	0	4	8
Virgin Islands	295	275	7	13	246	246	242	2	2	0	0
Fourth Circuit	7,322	4,358	2,800	164	8,689	8,621	4,751	3,757	113	30	38
Maryland	1,864	867	956	41	1,593	1,585	512	1,070	3	1	7
North Carolina:											
Eastern	956	405	522	29	1,179	1,175	509	574	92	2	2
Middle	201	197	3	1	385	382	376	6	0	2	1
Western	478	464	4	10	325	315	296	18	1	5	5
South Carolina	808	777	23	8	863	843	812	27	4	9	11
Virginia:											
Eastern	2,304	970	1,274	60	3,438	3,423	1,373	2,041	9	8	7
Western	422	393	15	14	438	435	423	11	1	0	3
West Virginia:											
Northern	122	121	0	1	195	193	185	5	3	1	1
Southern	167	164	3	0	273	270	265	5	0	2	1
Fifth Circuit	7,221	6,847	286	88	12,607	12,517	11,896	538	83	36	54
Louisiana:											
Eastern	212	208	3	1	393	388	322	64	2	2	3
Middle	184	178	4	2	287	284	247	37	0	0	3
Western	220	168	52	0	412	411	326	83	2	0	1
Mississippi:											
Northern	127	121	5	1	126	121	119	2	0	2	3
Southern	243	228	12	3	388	379	356	16	7	1	8
Texas:											
Northern	902	811	49	42	1,015	997	915	66	16	9	9
Eastern	358	355	2	1	625	615	608	7	0	8	2
Southern	2,917	2,793	93	31	4,849	4,838	4,821	12	5	3	8
Western	2,058	1,985	66	7	4,512	4,484	4,182	251	51	11	17
Sixth Circuit	3,556	3,130	400	26	4,476	4,412	3,806	595	11	14	50
Kentucky:											
Eastern	273	269	4	0	407	396	381	15	0	0	11
Western	471	208	259	4	659	651	228	422	1	0	8
Michigan:											
Eastern	678	657	20	1	698	682	666	14	2	0	16
Western	227	224	2	1	340	337	326	11	0	1	2
Ohio:											
Northern	366	359	5	2	516	516	507	8	1	0	0
Southern	407	378	29	0	432	426	379	46	1	1	5
Tennessee:											
Eastern	347	336	11	0	599	595	556	37	2	2	2
Middle	215	213	2	0	267	255	249	4	2	9	3
Western	572	486	68	18	558	554	514	38	2	1	3

See notes at end of table.

	Terminated						Pending Sept. 30, 2003			
		Original proceedings								
Total terminated	Total	Felony	Class A misdemeanor	Other[a]	Reopens[b]	Transfers	Total	Felony	Class A misdemeanor	Other[a]
65,628	64,727	53,476	9,824	1,427	266	635	60,532	51,158	8,832	542
438	437	417	19	1	0	1	1,231	1,157	72	2
1,259	1,238	1,169	35	34	10	11	1,550	1,515	29	6
182	180	167	12	1	0	2	162	159	2	1
360	357	344	9	4	1	2	740	721	16	3
185	180	174	5	1	1	4	174	173	0	1
102	101	100	1	0	1	0	221	214	7	0
430	420	384	8	28	7	3	253	248	4	1
3,690	3,636	3,432	174	30	33	21	7,403	6,633	710	60
314	305	293	12	0	8	1	345	333	9	3
320	317	279	38	0	1	2	783	588	194	1
1,312	1,302	1,257	28	17	8	2	2,083	1,998	84	1
1,199	1,172	1,112	47	13	16	11	3,492	3,055	382	55
425	422	378	44	0	0	3	503	467	36	0
120	118	113	5	0	0	2	197	192	5	0
2,649	2,614	2,334	260	20	6	29	3,223	2,920	281	22
145	144	125	18	1	0	1	187	136	50	1
936	920	706	205	9	4	12	1,074	871	199	4
702	697	681	9	7	0	5	892	883	7	2
270	269	254	14	1	0	1	466	451	14	1
320	311	301	9	1	2	7	339	333	6	0
276	273	267	5	1	0	3	265	246	5	14
7,442	7,342	4,233	2,731	378	24	76	8,569	4,778	3,584	207
1,151	1,148	434	708	6	0	3	2,306	949	1,314	43
937	931	453	342	136	4	2	1,198	459	669	70
370	353	347	6	0	1	16	216	212	3	1
371	360	339	20	1	2	9	432	418	4	10
790	755	693	40	22	10	25	881	846	25	10
2,995	2,973	1,171	1,593	209	7	15	2,747	1,142	1,548	57
376	373	360	13	0	0	3	484	453	16	15
191	189	184	1	4	0	2	126	121	4	1
261	260	252	8	0	0	1	179	178	1	0
11,884	11,799	11,090	536	173	28	57	7,944	7,506	344	94
372	367	303	62	2	1	4	233	222	10	1
146	143	107	36	0	0	3	325	315	8	2
330	319	251	66	2	1	10	302	236	66	0
137	136	129	6	1	1	0	116	113	2	1
386	379	351	22	6	1	6	245	230	10	5
881	863	795	54	14	7	11	1,036	913	76	47
524	516	499	13	4	4	4	459	454	5	0
4,668	4,658	4,571	36	51	2	8	3,098	2,984	83	31
4,440	4,418	4,084	241	93	11	11	2,130	2,039	84	7
4,202	4,137	3,514	602	21	18	47	3,830	3,394	407	29
411	410	394	16	0	0	1	269	265	4	0
674	665	225	432	8	0	9	456	213	238	5
600	592	569	21	2	4	4	776	755	20	1
353	349	326	20	3	1	3	214	210	4	0
551	545	525	16	4	0	6	331	328	2	1
437	431	394	37	0	0	6	402	362	39	1
517	511	474	34	3	1	5	429	416	13	0
189	170	166	4	0	11	8	293	288	3	2
470	464	441	22	1	1	5	660	557	84	19

Table 5.11
Criminal cases filed, terminated, and pending in U.S. District Courts

By type of offense, circuit, and district, fiscal year 2003--Continued

	Pending Oct. 1, 2002				Filed						
						Original proceedings					
Circuit and district	Total	Felony	Class A misdemeanor	Other[a]	Total commenced	Total	Felony	Class A misdemeanor	Other[a]	Reopens[b]	Transfers
Seventh Circuit	2,011	1,911	98	2	2,563	2,533	2,357	168	8	15	15
Illinois:											
Northern	867	847	20	0	884	868	834	34	0	13	3
Central	319	259	60	0	437	434	337	96	1	0	3
Southern	133	130	3	0	302	300	298	1	1	0	2
Indiana:											
Northern	307	302	4	1	322	321	299	20	2	0	1
Southern	132	126	6	0	218	215	207	4	4	0	3
Wisconsin:											
Eastern	184	178	5	1	242	237	227	10	0	2	3
Western	69	69	0	0	158	158	155	3	0	0	0
Eighth Circuit	2,723	2,636	78	9	4,418	4,369	4,151	195	23	11	38
Arkansas:											
Eastern	190	185	5	0	257	256	245	7	4	0	1
Western	93	93	0	0	184	180	175	5	0	0	4
Iowa:											
Northern	310	309	1	0	435	427	423	3	1	5	3
Southern	219	218	1	0	312	310	307	2	1	0	2
Minnesota	259	255	3	1	391	388	373	14	1	0	3
Missouri:											
Eastern	408	366	42	0	829	820	705	115	0	2	7
Western	435	421	13	1	680	676	658	16	2	0	4
Nebraska	515	507	6	2	723	711	691	17	3	1	11
North Dakota	105	96	6	3	227	225	214	5	6	0	2
South Dakota	189	186	1	2	380	376	360	11	5	3	1
Ninth Circuit	11,774	9,944	1,771	59	16,040	15,833	13,731	2,037	65	73	134
Alaska	102	77	24	1	229	226	158	67	1	2	1
Arizona	2,194	2,127	65	2	4,320	4,300	3,799	497	4	7	13
California:											
Northern	1,157	885	272	0	808	795	649	144	2	4	9
Eastern	1,031	849	168	14	958	940	850	90	0	6	12
Central	1,984	1,899	61	24	1,403	1,346	1,309	23	14	23	34
Southern	1,440	1,403	37	0	3,582	3,545	3,525	17	3	17	20
Hawaii	861	281	580	0	616	611	312	299	0	0	5
Idaho	152	147	4	1	257	254	244	9	1	0	3
Montana	327	279	47	1	466	466	374	83	9	0	0
Nevada	601	590	8	3	730	723	674	41	8	3	4
Oregon	584	574	9	1	784	772	760	11	1	2	10
Washington:											
Eastern	378	377	0	1	519	508	495	9	4	7	4
Western	839	336	492	11	1,230	1,214	459	739	16	1	15
Guam	108	105	3	0	112	107	98	7	2	1	4
Northern Marianas	16	15	1	0	26	26	25	1	0	0	0
Tenth Circuit	3,468	2,724	732	12	6,194	6,128	4,957	1,163	8	27	39
Colorado	546	359	186	1	680	680	612	68	0	0	0
Kansas	427	343	84	0	617	610	518	92	0	2	5
New Mexico	1,309	1,026	280	3	2,455	2,429	2,360	68	1	5	21
Oklahoma:											
Northern	150	146	3	1	178	174	168	6	0	2	2
Eastern	45	44	1	0	101	101	97	4	0	0	0
Western	226	136	89	1	860	857	219	636	2	0	3
Utah	633	557	75	1	1,075	1,051	788	261	2	17	7
Wyoming	132	113	14	5	228	226	195	28	3	1	1
Eleventh Circuit	4,683	3,996	652	35	6,972	6,853	5,060	1,787	6	36	83
Alabama:											
Northern	395	361	33	1	566	560	459	101	0	1	5
Middle	193	127	59	7	258	247	189	57	1	3	8
Southern	238	236	2	0	228	226	223	3	0	0	2
Florida:											
Northern	337	218	118	1	600	585	289	296	0	5	10
Middle	1,054	1,020	25	9	1,249	1,215	1,201	13	1	11	23
Southern	1,163	1,150	9	4	1,641	1,618	1,595	22	1	11	12
Georgia:											
Northern	621	528	83	10	801	784	642	141	1	2	15
Middle	254	185	69	0	1,152	1,143	243	900	0	2	7
Southern	428	171	254	3	477	475	219	254	2	1	1

Note: These data include all felony and class A misdemeanor cases but include only those petty offense cases that have been assigned to district court judges. Pending totals exclude each case in which the defendant has been a fugitive since before Oct. 1, 2002.

Source: Administrative Office of the United States Courts, *Judicial Business of the United States Courts: 2003 Annual Report of the Director* (Washington, DC: USGPO, 2004), pp. 181-186.

[a] Primarily petty offenses assigned to a district judge.
[b] Includes appeals from magistrates, reopens, and remands.

	Terminated						Pending Sept. 30, 2003			
		Original proceedings								
Total terminated	Total	Felony	Class A misdemeanor	Other[a]	Reopens[b]	Transfers	Total	Felony	Class A misdemeanor	Other[a]
2,407	2,369	2,193	168	8	14	24	2,167	2,052	112	3
855	836	799	36	1	12	7	896	874	22	0
415	412	321	91	0	0	3	341	273	67	1
245	239	235	2	2	2	4	190	188	2	0
334	333	310	21	2	0	1	295	290	4	1
197	192	185	5	2	0	5	153	148	5	0
217	215	203	11	1	0	2	209	198	10	1
144	142	140	2	0	0	2	83	81	2	0
3,795	3,739	3,472	230	37	12	44	3,346	3,258	79	9
207	202	187	11	4	0	5	240	236	4	0
190	188	181	7	0	0	2	87	85	2	0
358	349	344	4	1	2	7	387	384	1	2
297	294	289	2	3	0	3	234	233	1	0
367	362	347	13	2	2	3	283	277	6	0
754	743	624	119	0	2	9	483	440	43	0
526	519	498	21	0	1	6	589	578	8	3
557	551	527	19	5	2	4	681	673	7	1
209	208	176	20	12	1	0	123	119	4	0
330	323	299	14	10	2	5	239	233	3	3
15,599	15,431	12,716	2,332	383	68	100	12,215	10,598	1,544	73
197	185	116	68	1	1	11	134	102	30	2
4,252	4,238	3,696	524	18	9	5	2,262	2,180	79	3
701	693	552	136	5	2	6	1,264	971	293	0
860	844	633	160	51	3	13	1,129	935	181	13
1,462	1,426	1,307	93	26	19	17	1,925	1,849	48	28
3,528	3,511	3,485	23	3	16	1	1,494	1,453	40	1
891	885	207	677	1	0	6	586	384	202	0
225	223	203	15	5	1	1	184	179	4	1
367	364	266	88	10	2	1	426	379	46	1
711	690	642	33	15	6	15	620	600	20	0
735	722	638	19	65	4	9	633	621	12	0
482	476	464	7	5	4	2	415	407	5	3
1,073	1,064	406	481	177	1	8	996	395	581	20
94	89	82	6	1	0	5	126	122	3	1
21	21	19	2	0	0	0	21	21	0	0
5,679	5,496	4,144	1,047	305	19	164	3,983	3,065	907	11
609	585	474	106	5	2	22	617	423	194	0
495	485	437	47	1	5	5	549	421	128	0
2,379	2,261	1,906	69	286	4	114	1,385	1,100	283	2
178	176	169	7	0	0	2	150	144	5	1
76	74	68	5	1	0	2	70	70	0	0
829	827	197	624	6	0	2	257	156	101	0
928	905	739	164	2	8	15	780	600	178	2
185	183	154	25	4	0	2	175	151	18	6
6,584	6,489	4,762	1,690	37	34	61	5,071	4,282	763	26
556	546	450	96	0	1	9	405	364	40	1
221	214	153	47	14	4	3	230	165	63	2
214	213	210	3	0	0	1	252	248	4	0
532	523	230	292	1	3	6	405	283	121	1
1,123	1,102	1,072	25	5	8	13	1,180	1,155	17	8
1,715	1,687	1,645	36	6	12	16	1,089	1,077	11	1
724	717	593	123	1	4	3	698	582	106	10
1,113	1,108	224	882	2	2	3	293	204	89	0
386	379	185	186	8	0	7	519	204	312	3

Table 5.12

Defendants detained by U.S. District Courts[a]

By circuit and district, fiscal year 2003

Circuit and district	Number of cases closed	Total detention cost (in dollars)	Before initial hearing: Number of defendants	Before initial hearing: Number of days	Before initial hearing: Cost (in dollars)	After initial hearing: Number of defendants	After initial hearing: Number of days	After initial hearing: Cost (in dollars)	Post adjudication: Number of defendants	Post adjudication: Number of days	Post adjudication: Cost (in dollars)
Total	88,735	$544,221,384	37,519	79,258	$4,388,034	52,906	5,027,172	$282,648,580	37,227	4,577,950	$257,184,770
First Circuit	2,401	29,063,269	545	1,482	91,057	1,567	309,331	18,854,712	1,153	168,609	10,117,500
Maine	210	1,289,062	64	186	11,293	106	7,919	480,446	104	13,142	797,323
Massachusetts	663	8,983,920	73	150	9,000	433	105,787	6,347,220	295	43,795	2,627,700
New Hampshire	215	1,187,250	3	3	150	109	12,395	619,750	94	11,347	567,350
Rhode Island	137	1,034,350	28	95	4,750	95	7,691	384,550	82	12,901	645,050
Puerto Rico	1,176	16,568,687	377	1,048	65,864	824	175,539	11,022,746	578	87,424	5,480,077
Second Circuit	6,295	69,887,711	1,955	3,736	241,821	3,679	528,875	34,692,547	2,696	553,677	34,953,343
Connecticut	436	4,477,732	30	89	6,052	241	42,982	2,922,776	137	22,778	1,548,904
New York:											
Northern	516	5,742,170	144	351	24,570	360	42,176	2,952,320	204	39,504	2,765,280
Eastern	2,237	24,133,151	924	1,959	125,376	1,507	158,982	10,174,848	1,058	216,928	13,832,927
Southern	2,262	24,529,635	625	914	52,098	1,112	204,167	11,636,913	981	226,881	12,840,624
Western	632	9,487,968	127	253	24,035	339	67,188	6,243,030	217	34,521	3,220,903
Vermont	212	1,517,055	105	170	9,690	120	13,380	762,660	99	13,065	744,705
Third Circuit	3,599	31,371,571	672	2,134	111,994	1,895	293,532	15,239,920	1,410	306,593	16,019,657
Delaware	192	1,244,650	24	54	2,700	101	12,462	623,100	93	12,377	618,850
New Jersey	1,270	8,707,185	297	768	34,560	546	94,838	4,267,710	435	97,887	4,404,915
Pennsylvania:											
Eastern	1,091	13,462,581	79	301	17,122	647	108,166	6,148,166	514	128,758	7,297,293
Middle	427	3,813,521	43	186	10,848	198	27,026	1,577,234	200	38,133	2,225,439
Western	324	1,324,800	26	84	3,360	141	19,578	783,120	117	13,458	538,320
Virgin Islands	295	2,818,834	203	741	43,404	262	31,462	1,840,590	51	15,980	934,840
Fourth Circuit	8,148	41,955,352	1,234	3,106	158,247	4,098	366,957	19,375,388	3,364	432,266	22,421,717
Maryland	714	6,515,082	153	380	23,117	424	66,149	4,018,619	269	40,713	2,473,346
North Carolina:											
Eastern	1,007	3,680,910	62	308	13,860	351	28,946	1,302,570	397	52,544	2,364,480
Middle	352	2,271,979	9	17	998	266	12,030	703,829	245	26,788	1,567,152
Western	685	8,224,045	115	286	17,732	442	63,156	3,910,643	310	69,285	4,295,670
South Carolina	1,423	5,042,730	229	470	16,450	662	65,542	2,293,970	541	78,066	2,732,310
Virginia:											
Eastern	2,512	8,813,796	290	552	34,705	1,203	61,847	3,884,013	854	77,947	4,895,078
Western	677	4,611,499	255	694	32,618	434	44,804	2,105,788	415	52,619	2,473,093
West Virginia:											
Northern	321	1,007,361	46	169	7,267	115	9,742	418,906	146	13,516	581,188
Southern	457	1,787,950	75	230	11,500	201	14,741	737,050	187	20,788	1,039,400
Fifth Circuit	17,044	73,243,450	10,858	21,383	1,054,262	11,060	749,668	36,335,792	7,019	733,090	35,853,396
Louisiana:											
Eastern	484	2,695,320	174	221	9,945	355	28,593	1,286,685	263	31,082	1,398,690
Middle	151	941,399	40	75	4,339	74	8,467	489,397	60	7,745	447,663
Western	384	1,237,488	109	432	12,528	194	30,861	894,969	91	11,379	329,991
Mississippi:											
Northern	185	644,355	32	57	2,565	75	8,320	374,400	62	5,942	267,390
Southern	498	819,740	169	469	9,380	263	21,401	428,020	200	19,117	382,340
Texas:											
Northern	1,801	8,347,578	758	1,562	91,646	1,141	69,432	4,062,065	686	71,687	4,193,867
Eastern	725	3,668,721	165	499	20,459	472	36,377	1,491,457	418	52,605	2,156,805
Southern	7,047	25,188,649	5,171	8,870	443,500	4,074	237,743	11,885,099	2,103	257,201	12,860,050
Western	5,769	29,700,200	4,240	9,198	459,900	4,412	308,474	15,423,700	3,136	276,332	13,816,600
Sixth Circuit	6,214	27,024,600	838	1,842	89,987	3,061	298,168	13,975,735	2,259	273,536	12,958,878
Kentucky:											
Eastern	567	2,087,460	115	216	9,720	297	21,704	976,680	231	24,468	1,101,060
Western	373	1,851,538	82	173	10,207	162	17,508	1,032,972	113	13,701	808,359
Michigan:											
Eastern	1,189	5,093,423	134	261	15,890	463	44,872	2,716,750	269	38,860	2,360,783
Western	526	2,845,645	63	155	8,525	322	17,736	975,480	295	33,848	1,861,640
Ohio:											
Northern	1,006	4,875,050	60	254	12,700	491	59,541	2,977,050	357	37,706	1,885,300
Southern	854	2,120,400	126	280	10,080	330	27,528	991,008	228	31,092	1,119,312
Tennessee:											
Eastern	738	4,556,374	236	457	21,345	460	47,136	2,191,935	419	50,387	2,343,094
Middle	363	1,699,280	8	14	560	210	24,957	998,280	135	17,511	700,440
Western	598	1,895,430	14	32	960	326	37,186	1,115,580	212	25,963	778,890

See notes at end of table.

Table 5.12

Defendants detained by U.S. District Courts[a]

By circuit and district, fiscal year 2003--Continued

Circuit and district	Number of cases closed	Total detention cost (in dollars)	Before initial hearing Number of defendants	Before initial hearing Number of days	Before initial hearing Cost (in dollars)	After initial hearing Number of defendants	After initial hearing Number of days	After initial hearing Cost (in dollars)	Post adjudication Number of defendants	Post adjudication Number of days	Post adjudication Cost (in dollars)
Seventh Circuit	3,698	$30,211,434	1,071	2,608	$148,668	2,207	300,285	$17,086,858	1,666	223,138	$12,975,908
Illinois:											
Northern	1,501	13,455,188	449	644	39,829	842	131,772	8,129,028	592	85,692	5,286,331
Central	403	3,772,020	150	317	19,020	260	26,220	1,573,200	240	36,330	2,179,800
Southern	389	2,600,370	104	285	12,825	277	29,715	1,337,175	253	27,786	1,250,370
Indiana:											
Northern	447	4,659,879	217	829	48,911	288	35,938	2,120,342	237	42,214	2,490,626
Southern	362	1,880,283	47	113	4,708	200	39,396	1,634,985	61	5,797	240,590
Wisconsin:											
Eastern	396	2,915,019	27	79	5,135	234	27,924	1,802,999	164	17,029	1,106,885
Western	200	928,675	77	341	18,240	106	9,320	489,129	119	8,290	421,306
Eighth Circuit	5,222	38,071,286	1,115	2,829	178,212	3,147	281,406	18,001,865	2,458	287,361	19,891,209
Arkansas:											
Eastern	296	696,240	24	57	1,710	109	15,852	475,560	74	7,299	218,970
Western	239	859,800	125	323	9,690	173	14,320	429,600	149	14,017	420,510
Iowa:											
Northern	452	4,618,380	85	285	18,525	276	28,571	1,857,115	311	42,196	2,742,740
Southern	430	4,392,654	24	51	3,417	311	29,325	1,964,775	283	36,186	2,424,462
Minnesota	602	5,652,240	204	487	38,960	334	30,303	2,424,240	265	39,863	3,189,040
Missouri:											
Eastern	875	4,260,155	22	52	3,163	525	39,479	2,398,422	312	30,593	1,858,570
Western	1,034	10,214,199	159	448	44,800	521	40,171	4,017,100	409	61,756	6,152,299
Nebraska	630	5,155,118	191	510	31,197	477	51,550	3,156,413	362	32,133	1,967,508
North Dakota	270	901,950	122	346	17,300	151	10,961	548,050	91	6,732	336,600
South Dakota	394	1,320,550	159	270	9,450	270	20,874	730,590	202	16,586	580,510
Ninth Circuit	22,223	128,665,961	13,618	28,774	1,692,907	13,460	1,173,941	69,985,049	8,938	944,845	56,988,005
Alaska	225	2,267,503	124	762	81,216	129	8,267	880,933	101	12,250	1,305,354
Arizona	7,245	44,686,564	5,976	9,709	563,122	5,680	397,230	23,039,340	3,952	363,519	21,084,102
California:											
Northern	977	9,202,838	23	92	7,084	622	86,299	6,638,353	265	33,213	2,557,401
Eastern	1,024	884,650	671	1,217	60,850	876	126,786	6,339,300	495	49,690	2,484,500
Central	2,425	12,094,023	1,037	2,580	141,900	1,265	121,792	6,698,560	548	95,733	5,253,563
Southern	5,314	17,930,667	4,251	10,769	613,833	2,034	139,021	7,841,895	1,709	166,227	9,474,939
Hawaii	443	7,203,425	211	359	35,587	291	30,603	3,005,295	190	42,458	4,162,543
Idaho	381	1,696,716	194	456	19,152	248	21,444	900,648	185	18,498	776,916
Montana	425	1,933,161	169	462	20,157	245	20,376	886,768	229	23,581	1,026,236
Nevada	900	6,839,530	398	1,077	66,774	515	66,580	4,127,960	409	42,658	2,644,796
Oregon	852	7,330,860	148	353	21,180	625	88,666	5,319,960	303	33,162	1,989,720
Washington:											
Eastern	429	3,052,920	225	366	21,960	349	28,025	1,681,500	218	22,491	1,349,460
Western	1,424	3,931,332	132	439	27,092	496	32,529	2,006,714	269	30,759	1,897,526
Guam	128	1,396,516	57	131	12,804	70	5,591	546,298	51	9,137	837,414
Northern Marianas	31	215,256	2	2	196	15	732	71,525	14	1,469	143,535
Tenth Circuit	6,005	38,065,004	2,980	5,882	366,424	4,417	343,627	20,551,017	2,721	285,682	17,147,563
Colorado	683	3,459,248	140	314	16,328	515	36,301	1,887,652	277	29,909	1,555,268
Kansas	693	4,834,790	178	499	31,563	433	42,112	2,660,409	334	33,878	2,142,818
New Mexico	2,836	21,428,092	2,317	3,764	255,952	2,454	164,976	11,218,368	1,373	146,379	9,953,772
Oklahoma:											
Northern	251	1,057,040	52	123	4,920	160	12,958	518,320	102	13,345	533,800
Eastern	108	356,264	24	57	2,336	60	3,500	143,293	55	5,145	210,635
Western	565	1,502,820	54	185	8,325	180	13,205	594,225	146	20,006	900,270
Utah	589	3,941,650	85	177	8,850	429	53,942	2,697,100	281	24,714	1,235,700
Wyoming	280	1,485,100	130	763	38,150	186	16,633	831,650	153	12,306	615,300
Eleventh Circuit	7,886	36,661,746	2,633	5,482	254,455	4,315	381,382	18,549,697	3,543	369,153	17,857,594
Alabama:											
Northern	526	1,884,050	51	147	7,350	248	13,581	679,050	199	23,953	1,197,650
Middle	145	582,600	51	89	4,450	65	5,799	289,950	49	5,764	288,200
Southern	377	1,101,632	66	244	7,808	214	12,298	393,536	189	21,884	700,288
Florida:											
Northern	440	1,372,217	109	209	7,786	237	13,886	519,343	224	22,596	845,088
Middle	1,853	13,062,673	322	668	39,592	1,223	114,712	6,815,027	968	104,495	6,208,054
Southern	2,651	13,557,282	1,389	2,699	139,948	1,512	135,599	7,018,629	1,240	123,623	6,398,705
Georgia:											
Northern	889	3,312,606	314	624	20,592	513	59,997	1,979,901	360	39,761	1,312,113
Middle	663	912,866	233	463	15,742	136	12,431	422,654	152	13,955	474,470
Southern	342	875,820	98	339	11,187	167	13,079	431,607	162	13,122	433,026

[a]Excludes the District of Columbia and includes transfers.

Source: Administrative Office of the United States Courts, *Judicial Business of the United States Courts: 2003 Annual Report of the Director* (Washington, DC: USGPO, 2004), pp. 298-300.

Table 5.13

Federal defendants released or detained prior to trial in U.S. District Courts

By offense, United States, fiscal year 2001

Most serious offense charged	Number of defendants Total	Released	Detained	All releases	Financial[a]	Unsecured bond	Personal recognizance	Conditional release	All detentions	Temporary detention[b]	Part of pretrial period	All of pretrial period	Denied bail	Other detentions
All offenses[c]	68,214	31,320	49,199	45.9%	18.2%	47.2%	28.2%	6.3%	72.1%	2.2%	22.0%	11.6%	53.4%	10.8%
Violent offenses	3,225	1,170	2,579	36.3	6.6	36.0	47.9	9.6	80.0	0.7	16.6	3.6	62.8	16.4
Murder, nonnegligent manslaughter	159	48	142	30.2	2.1	22.9	75.0	0.0	89.3	0.7	16.9	2.1	66.2	14.1
Negligent manslaughter	14	11	8	78.6	0.0	0.0	100.0	0.0	57.1	B	B	B	B	B
Assault	820	518	456	63.2	3.5	27.4	51.4	17.8	55.6	0.0	30.3	3.1	51.5	15.1
Robbery	1,845	408	1,677	22.1	11.3	53.2	31.1	4.4	90.9	0.8	11.3	4.3	66.8	16.8
Sexual abuse[d]	253	149	174	58.9	4.7	25.5	69.1	0.7	68.8	0.0	32.8	0.6	53.4	13.2
Kidnaping	100	26	91	26.0	11.5	38.5	46.2	3.8	91.0	3.3	13.2	2.2	60.4	20.9
Threats against the President	34	10	31	29.4	B	B	B	B	91.2	0.0	9.7	0.0	64.5	25.8
Property offenses	13,170	10,322	4,960	78.4	10.2	54.8	33.0	2.0	37.7	0.9	38.6	5.8	41.6	13.0
Fraudulent offenses	10,361	8,120	3,901	78.4	11.1	58.4	29.4	1.2	37.7	1.0	38.6	6.1	41.4	12.9
Embezzlement	1,394	1,292	220	92.7	3.4	55.3	39.3	2.0	15.8	1.4	51.8	7.3	29.5	10.0
Fraud[e]	7,541	5,775	2,998	76.6	13.0	57.6	28.4	1.1	39.8	1.0	36.8	6.1	42.9	13.1
Forgery	208	162	85	77.9	8.6	65.4	25.9	0.0	40.9	0.0	45.9	4.7	37.6	11.8
Counterfeiting	1,218	891	598	73.2	10.2	66.8	22.2	0.8	49.1	0.7	41.6	6.0	38.8	12.9
Other offenses	2,809	2,202	1,059	78.4	7.0	41.7	46.3	5.0	37.7	0.8	38.6	4.6	42.3	13.7
Burglary	127	62	92	48.8	6.5	33.9	59.7	0.0	72.4	0.0	30.4	3.3	44.6	21.7
Larceny[f]	2,103	1,773	652	84.3	6.0	39.7	48.6	5.8	31.0	0.5	45.2	4.9	37.9	11.5
Motor vehicle theft	227	118	149	52.0	15.3	55.1	28.0	1.7	65.6	1.3	22.8	4.7	55.0	16.1
Arson and explosives	122	73	76	59.8	8.2	63.0	28.8	0.0	62.3	3.9	27.6	1.3	53.9	13.2
Transportation of stolen property	145	107	64	73.8	16.8	57.0	26.2	0.0	44.1	0.0	29.7	9.4	45.3	15.6
Other property offenses[g]	85	69	26	81.2	4.3	31.9	58.0	5.8	30.6	0.0	46.2	0.0	30.8	23.1
Drug offenses	26,802	10,968	22,430	40.9	29.3	46.3	20.5	4.0	83.7	2.3	25.2	9.7	53.2	9.5
Trafficking	24,458	9,740	20,864	39.8	30.4	48.2	18.1	3.3	85.3	2.0	25.2	10.1	53.5	9.2
Other	2,344	1,228	1,566	52.4	20.6	31.1	39.3	9.0	66.8	6.9	25.4	4.3	49.4	14.0
Public-order offenses	7,275	5,227	2,960	71.8	11.0	39.3	35.5	14.3	40.7	1.0	28.3	4.7	47.8	18.1
Regulatory offenses	2,286	1,591	1,027	69.6	14.1	46.0	34.7	5.2	44.9	1.6	29.0	7.4	39.8	22.2
Agriculture	106	104	8	98.1	1.9	33.7	52.9	11.5	7.5	B	B	B	B	B
Antitrust	9	9	0	B	B	B	B	B	B	X	X	X	X	X
Food and drug	50	43	16	86.0	16.3	46.5	30.2	7.0	32.0	0.0	50.0	6.3	37.5	6.3
Transportation	68	52	26	76.5	5.8	44.2	46.2	3.8	38.2	0.0	30.8	0.0	69.2	0.0
Civil rights	77	64	21	83.1	10.9	70.3	18.8	0.0	27.3	0.0	23.8	0.0	52.4	23.8
Communications	68	62	14	91.2	8.1	54.8	37.1	0.0	20.6	0.0	42.9	7.1	35.7	14.3
Customs laws	92	71	57	77.2	31.0	49.3	19.7	0.0	62.0	0.0	52.6	12.3	35.1	0.0
Postal laws	149	137	32	91.9	2.2	56.2	36.5	5.1	21.5	0.0	62.5	3.1	21.9	12.5
Other regulatory offenses	1,667	1,049	853	62.9	16.6	43.9	34.1	5.4	51.2	1.9	25.2	7.7	40.0	25.2
Other offenses	4,989	3,636	1,933	72.9	9.6	36.4	35.8	18.2	38.7	0.7	28.0	3.3	52.1	15.9
Tax law violations including tax fraud	533	516	82	96.8	4.8	60.9	33.5	0.8	15.4	0.0	78.0	2.4	14.6	4.9
Bribery	153	129	59	84.3	22.5	45.0	32.6	0.0	38.6	0.0	54.2	3.4	40.7	1.7
Perjury, contempt, intimidation	199	137	105	68.8	13.1	56.2	29.2	1.5	52.8	1.0	36.2	3.8	43.8	15.2
National defense	85	65	29	76.5	15.4	32.3	9.2	43.1	34.1	0.0	24.1	3.4	58.6	13.8
Escape	621	92	573	14.8	19.6	40.2	30.4	9.8	92.3	0.9	6.8	1.7	70.7	19.9
Racketeering and extortion	743	424	480	57.1	34.4	47.4	16.7	1.4	64.6	0.8	24.8	2.7	58.5	13.1
Gambling offenses	45	44	5	97.8	11.4	45.5	43.2	0.0	11.1	B	B	B	B	B
Liquor offenses	7	7	2	B	B	B	B	B	B	B	B	B	B	B
Nonviolent sex offenses	628	467	276	74.4	11.1	45.6	32.1	11.1	43.9	0.4	40.2	4.3	39.5	15.6
Mail or transport of obscene material	57	46	25	80.7	15.2	71.7	10.9	2.2	43.9	0.0	48.0	4.0	36.0	12.0
Traffic offenses	1,223	1,145	110	93.6	1.0	16.9	41.0	41.0	9.0	1.8	47.3	9.1	25.5	16.4
Migratory birds	28	28	3	100.0	0.0	21.4	60.7	17.9	10.7	B	B	B	B	B
All other offenses[h]	667	536	184	80.4	5.0	27.2	51.7	16.0	27.6	0.5	32.6	4.9	39.7	22.3
Weapons offenses	4,214	1,900	3,204	45.1	14.9	53.8	29.5	1.8	76.0	1.3	23.5	2.6	56.8	15.8
Immigration offenses	13,405	1,658	12,998	12.4	30.5	32.6	10.0	26.8	97.0	3.4	9.3	22.4	56.9	8.0

See notes on next page.

Table 5.13

Federal defendants released or detained prior to trial in U.S. District Courts

By offense, United States, fiscal year 2001--Continued

Note: These data are from the U.S. Department of Justice, Bureau of Justice Statistics' Federal Justice Statistics Program database. Sources of information include the Executive Office for U.S. Attorneys, the Administrative Office of the United States Courts, the U.S. Sentencing Commission, the U.S. Marshals Service, the Drug Enforcement Administration, and the Federal Bureau of Prisons. The Administrative Office of the United States Courts also maintains data collected by the Federal Pretrial Services Agency (PSA), the U.S. Courts of Appeals, and the Federal probation and supervision service.

Tables presenting pretrial release and detention information were created from the PSA data files. The data describe 68,214 defendants who terminated pretrial services during fiscal year 2001 and whose cases were filed by complaint, indictment, or information. "Released" defendants includes some defendants who also were detained prior to trial; "detained" defendants includes some defendants who also were released prior to trial. Total includes defendants for whom release status data were unavailable. For methodology and definitions of terms, see Appendix 11.

[a] Includes deposit bond, surety bond, and collateral bond.
[b] Held under 18 U.S.C. 3142 pending deportation, action on prior pretrial release, or probation or parole review.
[c] Includes 138 defendants for whom offense category could not be determined, 98 of whom were released, 63 of whom were detained.
[d] Includes only violent sex offenses.
[e] Excludes tax fraud.
[f] Excludes transportation of stolen property.
[g] Excludes fraudulent property offenses; includes destruction of property and trespass.
[h] Includes offenses with unclassifiable offense type.

Source: U.S. Department of Justice, Bureau of Justice Statistics, *Compendium of Federal Justice Statistics, 2001*, NCJ 201627 (Washington, DC: U.S. Department of Justice, 2003), pp. 42, 44. Table adapted by SOURCEBOOK staff.

Table 5.14

Federal pretrial detention hearings and defendants ordered detained in U.S. District Courts

By characteristics, United States, fiscal year 2001

Defendant characteristics	Number of defendants	Defendants with pretrial detention hearings			
		Number of defendants		Percent of defendants with hearings held	Of defendants with hearings held, percent ordered detained
		Hearings held	Ordered detained		
All defendants[a]	68,214	35,657	26,263	52.3%	73.7%
Sex					
Male	57,385	31,951	24,054	55.7	75.3
Female	10,756	3,687	2,196	34.3	59.6
Race					
White	46,999	24,225	18,246	51.5	75.3
Black	17,576	9,555	6,837	54.4	71.6
Native American	1,272	712	417	56.0	58.6
Asian/Pacific Islander	1,580	849	536	53.7	63.1
Ethnicity					
Hispanic	28,233	17,835	14,422	63.2	80.9
Non-Hispanic	39,542	17,654	11,730	44.6	66.4
Age					
16 to 18 years	1,304	718	511	55.1	71.2
19 to 20 years	4,080	2,106	1,577	51.6	74.9
21 to 30 years	27,549	15,846	11,843	57.5	74.7
31 to 40 years	19,582	10,540	7,920	53.8	75.1
Over 40 years	15,546	6,397	4,383	41.1	68.5
Education					
Less than high school graduate	20,095	11,964	8,607	59.5	71.9
High school graduate	16,663	7,944	5,164	47.7	65.0
Some college	9,902	3,765	2,210	38.0	58.7
College graduate	4,180	1,122	641	26.8	57.1
Marital status					
Never married	21,522	11,652	8,179	54.1	70.2
Divorced/separated	9,442	4,299	2,754	45.5	64.1
Married	16,448	7,117	4,700	43.3	66.0
Common law	4,647	2,670	1,809	57.5	67.8
Other	16,155	9,919	8,821	61.4	88.9
Employment status at arrest					
Unemployed	22,509	12,972	9,175	57.6	70.7
Employed	29,559	12,521	7,989	42.4	63.8
Criminal record					
No convictions[b]	20,132	8,155	5,550	40.5	68.1
Prior conviction					
Misdemeanor only	11,223	5,068	3,303	45.2	65.2
Felony					
Nonviolent	15,150	9,160	7,077	60.5	77.3
Violent	11,062	7,422	5,924	67.1	79.8
Number of prior convictions					
1	11,090	5,544	3,951	50.0	71.3
2 to 4	15,366	8,943	6,715	58.2	75.1
5 or more	10,979	7,163	5,638	65.2	78.7

Note: See Note, table 5.13. For methodology and definitions of terms, see Appendix 11.

[a] Includes defendants for whom these characteristics were unknown.
[b] Includes only those defendants whose PSA records explicitly showed no prior convictions.

Source: U.S. Department of Justice, Bureau of Justice Statistics, *Compendium of Federal Justice Statistics, 2001*, NCJ 201627 (Washington, DC: U.S. Department of Justice, 2003), p. 47. Table adapted by SOURCEBOOK staff.

Table 5.15

Federal defendants released or detained prior to trial in U.S. District Courts

By characteristics, United States, fiscal year 2001

Defendant characteristics	Number of defendants	Defendants released		Defendants detained	
		Number	Percent	Number	Percent
All defendants[a]	68,214	31,320	45.9%	49,199	72.1%
Sex					
Male	57,385	23,568	41.1	43,721	76.2
Female	10,756	7,712	71.7	5,439	50.6
Race					
White	46,999	20,333	43.3	34,770	74.0
Black	17,576	8,843	50.3	12,166	69.2
Native American	1,272	820	64.5	844	66.4
Asian/Pacific Islander	1,580	907	57.4	968	61.3
Ethnicity					
Hispanic	28,233	6,558	23.2	25,953	91.9
Non-Hispanic	39,542	24,523	62.0	23,006	58.2
Age					
16 to 18 years	1,304	605	46.4	1,009	77.4
19 to 20 years	4,080	1,878	46.0	2,993	73.4
21 to 30 years	27,549	10,972	39.8	21,555	78.2
31 to 40 years	19,582	8,444	43.1	14,618	74.7
Over 40 years	15,546	9,329	60.0	8,945	57.5
Education					
Less than high school graduate	20,095	7,821	38.9	16,463	81.9
High school graduate	16,663	10,064	60.4	10,474	62.9
Some college	9,902	7,098	71.7	5,078	51.3
College graduate	4,180	3,331	79.7	1,553	37.2
Marital status					
Never married	21,522	10,893	50.6	15,376	71.4
Divorced/separated	9,442	5,590	59.2	5,989	63.4
Married	16,448	9,940	60.4	9,702	59.0
Common law	4,647	2,065	44.4	3,643	78.4
Other	16,155	2,832	17.5	14,489	89.7
Employment status at arrest					
Unemployed	22,509	9,976	44.3	17,321	77.0
Employed	29,559	18,699	63.3	17,207	58.2
Criminal record					
No convictions[b]	20,132	12,160	60.4	11,570	57.5
Prior conviction					
Misdemeanor only	11,223	6,670	59.4	7,203	64.2
Felony					
Nonviolent	15,150	4,882	32.2	12,725	84.0
Violent	11,062	2,823	25.5	9,890	89.4
Number of prior convictions					
1	11,090	5,415	48.8	7,861	70.9
2 to 4	15,366	5,902	38.4	12,329	80.2
5 or more	10,979	3,058	27.9	9,628	87.7

Note: See Note, table 5.13. "Released" defendants includes some defendants who also were detained prior to trial; "detained" defendants includes some defendants who also were released prior to trial. Total includes defendants for whom release status data were unavailable. For methodology and definitions of terms, see Appendix 11.

[a] Includes defendants for whom these characteristics were unknown.
[b] Includes only those defendants whose PSA records explicitly showed no prior convictions.

Source: U.S. Department of Justice, Bureau of Justice Statistics, *Compendium of Federal Justice Statistics, 2001*, NCJ 201627 (Washington, DC: U.S. Department of Justice, 2003), pp. 43, 45. Table adapted by SOURCEBOOK staff.

Table 5.16

Behavior of Federal defendants released prior to trial in U.S. District Courts

By offense, type of release, and characteristics, United States, fiscal year 2001

Most serious offense charged, type of release, and defendant characteristics	Number of released defendants	No violation	At least one	Failed to appear	New offense charged Felony	New offense charged Misdemeanor	Technical violations of bail conditions	Release revoked
All defendants[a]	31,320	81.2%	18.8%	2.6%	1.9%	1.9%	17.3%	6.8%
Offense charged								
Violent offenses	1,170	77.0	23.0	2.8	2.1	2.7	22.2	12.6
Property offenses	10,322	87.3	12.7	1.4	1.6	1.4	11.3	4.8
Fraudulent offenses	8,120	88.2	11.8	1.4	1.5	1.3	10.5	4.3
Other offenses	2,202	84.2	15.8	1.5	1.8	1.8	14.4	6.3
Drug offenses	10,968	72.0	28.0	3.9	2.5	2.6	26.1	9.8
Public-order offenses	5,227	91.5	8.5	1.6	0.5	0.9	7.7	2.3
Regulatory offenses	1,591	91.8	8.2	1.0	0.7	1.1	7.5	2.1
Other offenses	3,636	91.4	8.6	1.9	0.4	0.9	7.8	2.4
Weapons offenses	1,900	69.9	30.1	2.5	4.4	3.6	28.2	12.8
Immigration offenses	1,658	86.9	13.1	4.1	1.3	0.8	11.3	3.7
Type of release								
Financial release	5,710	75.5	24.5	4.6	2.7	2.7	21.8	7.1
Unsecured bond	14,795	81.3	18.7	2.3	2.1	1.9	17.2	6.9
Personal recognizance	8,838	81.3	18.7	1.5	1.4	1.8	17.7	8.0
Conditional release	1,977	96.8	3.2	3.1	0.0	0.0	3.2	0.1
Sex								
Male	23,568	80.2	19.8	2.6	2.1	2.1	18.3	7.4
Female	7,712	84.3	15.7	2.3	1.3	1.3	14.5	5.1
Race								
White	20,333	82.8	17.2	2.6	1.6	1.6	15.8	6.1
Black	8,843	76.7	23.3	2.7	2.8	2.5	21.4	8.3
Native American	820	76.2	23.8	1.0	1.8	3.4	22.9	15.6
Asian/Pacific Islander	907	90.0	10.0	0.9	0.4	0.8	9.8	3.7
Ethnicity								
Hispanic	6,558	79.9	20.1	4.8	1.6	1.7	18.1	5.2
Non-Hispanic	24,523	81.5	18.5	2.0	2.0	1.9	17.2	7.3
Age								
16 to 18 years	605	73.2	26.8	3.6	4.1	4.0	24.8	12.1
19 to 20 years	1,878	74.5	25.5	3.1	3.6	2.7	23.9	10.4
21 to 30 years	10,972	77.0	23.0	3.1	2.4	2.6	21.2	8.1
31 to 40 years	8,444	80.7	19.3	2.7	1.7	1.8	17.7	7.2
Over 40 years	9,329	88.4	11.6	1.7	1.0	0.9	10.7	4.0
Education								
Less than high school graduate	7,821	72.4	27.6	4.3	3.0	2.9	25.2	10.4
High school graduate	10,064	79.5	20.5	2.3	2.0	2.1	19.1	7.4
Some college	7,098	84.4	15.6	1.6	1.5	1.5	14.3	5.8
College graduate	3,331	92.0	8.0	0.8	1.0	0.9	7.3	2.5

Note: See Note, table 5.13. Data describe defendants whose pretrial services were terminated in fiscal year 2001. A defendant with more than one type of violation appears in more than one column. A defendant with more than one of the same type of violation appears only once in that column. Therefore, the sum of individual violations exceeds the total. Not all violations resulted in revocation. For methodology and definitions of terms, see Appendix 11.

[a] Includes defendants for whom offense category or characteristics could not be determined.

Source: U.S. Department of Justice, Bureau of Justice Statistics, *Compendium of Federal Justice Statistics, 2001*, NCJ 201627 (Washington, DC: U.S. Department of Justice, 2003), pp. 48, 49. Table adapted by SOURCEBOOK staff.

Table 5.17

Disposition of cases terminated in U.S. District Courts

By offense, United States, fiscal year 2001

Most serious offense charged	Total defendants	Percent of all defendants convicted	Convicted Total	Guilty plea	Nolo contendere	Trial Jury	Trial Non-jury	Not convicted Total	Dismissed	Trial Jury[a]	Trial Non-jury
All offenses[b]	77,145	88.8%	68,533	64,894	274	2,313	1,052	8,612	7,621	507	484
Felonies	66,112	91.5	60,467	58,039	23	2,272	133	5,645	5,059	496	90
Violent offenses	2,977	90.3	2,687	2,512	2	164	9	290	240	46	4
Murder, nonnegligent manslaughter	404	86.1	348	304	0	40	4	56	47	7	2
Negligent manslaughter	1	B	0	0	0	0	0	1	1	0	0
Assault	316	81.3	257	229	2	25	1	59	46	12	1
Robbery	1,689	94.1	1,590	1,530	0	57	3	99	84	14	1
Sexual abuse[c]	382	88.2	337	311	0	25	1	45	34	11	0
Kidnaping	163	87.1	142	125	0	17	0	21	20	1	0
Threats against the President	22	59.1	13	13	0	0	0	9	8	1	0
Property offenses	13,950	90.6	12,640	12,124	5	491	20	1,310	1,182	108	20
Fraudulent offenses	11,563	90.8	10,498	10,097	5	380	16	1,065	973	75	17
Embezzlement	933	91.6	855	827	0	27	1	78	72	6	0
Fraud[d]	9,028	90.6	8,180	7,837	5	323	15	848	769	64	15
Forgery	107	92.5	99	93	0	6	0	8	6	1	1
Counterfeiting	1,495	91.2	1,364	1,340	0	24	0	131	126	4	1
Other offenses	2,387	89.7	2,142	2,027	0	111	4	245	209	33	3
Burglary	64	84.4	54	52	0	2	0	10	9	1	0
Larceny[e]	1,591	90.8	1,445	1,378	0	63	4	146	126	17	3
Motor vehicle theft	112	90.2	101	96	0	5	0	11	10	1	0
Arson and explosives	239	83.7	200	181	0	19	0	39	29	10	0
Transportation of stolen property	310	89.0	276	254	0	22	0	34	30	4	0
Other property offenses[f]	71	93.0	66	66	0	0	0	5	5	0	0
Drug offenses	28,227	91.6	25,854	24,889	9	922	34	2,373	2,142	198	33
Trafficking	26,501	91.5	24,253	23,353	7	863	30	2,248	2,030	186	32
Possession and other	1,726	92.8	1,601	1,536	2	59	4	125	112	12	1
Public-order offenses	4,402	87.1	3,836	3,586	3	236	11	566	483	67	16
Regulatory offenses	1,166	84.8	989	951	1	35	2	177	145	27	5
Agriculture	109	80.7	88	79	0	8	1	21	18	2	1
Antitrust	34	94.1	32	32	0	0	0	2	2	0	0
Food and drug	48	89.6	43	40	0	3	0	5	5	0	0
Transportation	128	79.7	102	99	0	2	1	26	14	12	0
Civil rights	87	69.0	60	55	0	5	0	27	15	10	2
Communications	62	95.2	59	56	0	3	0	3	3	0	0
Customs laws	70	85.7	60	56	0	4	0	10	9	0	1
Postal laws	44	77.3	34	33	1	0	0	10	10	0	0
Other regulatory offenses	584	87.5	511	501	0	10	0	73	69	3	1
Other offenses	3,236	88.0	2,847	2,635	2	201	9	389	338	40	11
Tax law violations including tax fraud	484	95.5	462	433	1	25	3	22	16	5	1
Bribery	237	89.5	212	201	0	11	0	25	19	4	2
Perjury, contempt, intimidation	334	83.2	278	243	0	35	0	56	44	9	3
National defense	46	93.5	43	35	0	8	0	3	3	0	0
Escape	497	84.5	420	400	1	18	1	77	75	1	1
Racketeering and extortion	827	83.9	694	627	0	66	1	133	113	18	2
Gambling offenses	25	100.0	25	25	0	0	0	0	0	0	0
Liquor offenses	7	B	7	5	0	2	0	0	0	0	0
Nonviolent sex offenses	498	94.2	469	442	0	24	3	29	27	2	0
Mail or transport of obscene material	11	100.0	11	10	0	1	0	0	0	0	0
Traffic offenses	29	89.7	26	22	0	3	1	3	3	0	0
Migratory birds	4	B	4	3	0	1	0	0	0	0	0
Other felonies[g]	237	82.7	196	189	0	7	0	41	38	1	2
Weapons offenses	5,814	90.0	5,231	4,829	3	363	36	583	508	62	13
Immigration offenses	10,742	95.1	10,219	10,099	1	96	23	523	504	15	4
Misdemeanors[h]	10,952	73.0	7,995	6,789	251	38	917	2,957	2,552	11	394

Note: See Note, table 5.13. These data are from the Administrative Office of the United States Courts' master data files. Only records with cases that terminated during fiscal year 2001 were selected. For methodology and definitions of terms, see Appendix 11.

[a] Includes mistrials.
[b] Includes 81 defendants for whom offense category could not be determined, 71 of whom were convicted, 10 of whom were not convicted.
[c] Includes only violent sex offenses.
[d] Excludes tax fraud.
[e] Excludes transportation of stolen property.
[f] Excludes fraudulent property offenses; includes destruction of property and trespass.
[g] Includes felonies with unclassifiable offense type.
[h] Includes misdemeanors, petty offenses, and unknown offense level.

Source: U.S. Department of Justice, Bureau of Justice Statistics, *Compendium of Federal Justice Statistics, 2001*, NCJ 201627 (Washington, DC: U.S. Department of Justice, 2003), p. 58.

Table 5.18
Federal defendants convicted in U.S. District Courts

By offense and characteristics, United States, fiscal year 2001[a]

Defendant characteristics	Total number of convicted defendants	Percent of defendants convicted of:								
		All offenses[b]	Felonies							Mis-demeanors
			Violent offenses	Property offenses: Fraudulent	Property offenses: Other	Drug offenses	Public-order offenses: Regulatory	Public-order offenses: Other	Weapons offenses	Immigration offenses	
All offenders[c]	68,533	68,533	2,604	10,359	1,990	25,088	1,410	2,937	4,925	10,050	9,100
Sex											
Male	51,535	85.3%	92.9%	74.1%	74.2%	86.1%	76.1%	86.5%	96.6%	94.8%	74.9%
Female	8,898	14.7	7.1	25.9	25.8	13.9	23.9	13.5	3.4	5.2	25.1
Race											
White	40,877	76.6	54.7	71.2	69.5	77.3	83.0	82.5	55.3	95.7	70.0
Black	9,997	18.7	21.6	22.5	20.8	20.5	9.0	10.9	41.6	2.6	21.4
Native American	1,022	1.9	21.0	0.8	5.2	0.8	1.7	1.7	1.7	0.4	2.8
Asian/Pacific Islander	1,322	2.5	2.6	5.0	4.2	1.2	5.6	4.6	1.3	1.1	5.4
Other	138	0.3	0.2	0.5	0.2	0.2	0.6	0.2	0.2	0.2	0.4
Ethnicity											
Hispanic	23,904	39.6	8.6	17.5	11.9	43.9	34.4	16.8	13.5	91.0	23.9
Non-Hispanic	36,482	60.4	91.4	82.5	88.1	56.1	65.6	83.2	86.5	9.0	76.1
Age											
16 to 18 years	421	0.7	1.9	0.1	0.4	0.9	0.1	0.2	0.6	0.5	2.1
19 to 20 years	2,764	4.8	8.7	2.3	4.8	5.4	4.9	1.6	6.4	3.6	7.5
21 to 30 years	22,982	39.6	38.2	29.3	33.9	44.3	26.9	23.5	47.5	43.5	36.6
31 to 40 years	17,404	30.0	29.6	30.4	30.5	29.2	28.8	28.2	26.8	35.9	25.7
Over 40 years	14,408	24.9	21.7	37.9	30.4	20.2	39.3	46.5	18.7	16.5	28.1
Citizenship											
U.S. citizen	39,568	66.5	94.9	81.6	91.2	69.0	70.5	87.1	92.7	9.5	75.9
Not U.S. citizen	19,963	33.5	5.1	18.4	8.8	31.0	29.5	12.9	7.3	90.5	24.1
Education											
Less than high school graduate	24,918	45.0	37.7	20.7	27.3	50.7	33.0	23.8	47.9	80.0	25.5
High school graduate	17,235	31.2	40.1	32.1	38.1	32.0	31.8	33.1	38.6	14.2	38.6
Some college	9,584	17.3	18.8	30.5	25.3	14.7	22.1	23.9	11.7	4.5	24.0
College graduate	3,587	6.5	3.5	16.7	9.3	2.7	13.2	19.3	1.7	1.3	11.9
Criminal record											
No convictions	24,310	40.2	31.0	54.2	44.9	44.5	66.4	53.7	14.3	19.0	47.0
Prior adult convictions[d]	36,162	59.8	69.0	45.8	55.1	55.5	33.6	46.3	85.7	81.0	53.0

Note: See Note, table 5.13. These data were created by matching the Administrative Office of the United States Courts master data files with the U.S. Sentencing Commission monitoring system files (which are limited to defendants sentenced under the Federal sentencing guidelines) and the Federal Pretrial Services Agency's data files. Offenders were classified by the most serious offense charged. For methodology and definitions of terms, see Appendix 11.

[a] Percents may not add to 100 because of rounding.
[b] Includes defendants for whom offense category could not be determined.
[c] Includes offenders for whom these characteristics could not be determined.
[d] For some defendants, prior adult convictions are limited to those used in calculating sentences under the Federal sentencing guidelines (see Source, p. 62).

Source: U.S. Department of Justice, Bureau of Justice Statistics, *Compendium of Federal Justice Statistics, 2001*, NCJ 201627 (Washington, DC: U.S. Department of Justice, 2003), p. 61.

Table 5.19

Sentences imposed in cases terminated in U.S. District Courts

By offense, United States, fiscal year 2001

Most serious conviction offense	Total number of convicted offenders[b]	Incarcer- ation[c]	Probation[d]	Fine only	Incarceration[a] Mean	Incarceration[a] Median	Probation[a] Mean	Probation[a] Median
All offenses[e]	68,533	74.5%	17.5%	4.1%	56.5	35.0	33.8	36.0
Felonies	59,363	83.4	13.1	0.4	58.0	37.0	40.7	36.0
Violent offenses	2,604	92.1	6.9	0.1	90.8	63.0	41.2	36.0
Murder, nonnegligent manslaughter	280	88.6	8.6	0.4	84.9	46.0	43.3	39.0
Assault	225	76.0	17.8	0.4	37.6	30.0	31.6	36.0
Robbery	1,659	96.4	3.8	0.0	98.3	70.0	43.5	36.0
Sexual abuse[f]	306	89.9	10.1	0.0	87.8	66.5	47.1	53.0
Kidnaping	121	79.3	15.7	0.0	88.2	60.0	41.3	36.0
Threats against the President	13	69.2	23.1	0.0	B	B	B	B
Property offenses	12,349	62.7	31.5	1.0	24.1	15.0	41.2	36.0
Fraudulent offenses	10,359	63.1	30.6	1.1	22.2	15.0	40.7	36.0
Embezzlement	780	59.4	30.4	1.9	16.5	8.0	39.9	36.0
Fraud[g]	8,328	63.9	29.7	1.1	22.9	15.0	41.0	36.0
Forgery	105	55.2	40.0	1.0	19.6	12.0	41.5	36.0
Counterfeiting	1,146	60.9	36.4	0.1	20.5	15.0	39.4	36.0
Other offenses	1,990	60.7	36.2	0.4	34.7	18.0	43.3	36.0
Burglary	59	88.1	6.8	0.0	23.2	19.5	B	B
Larceny[h]	1,393	54.2	41.8	0.5	28.3	18.0	44.4	36.0
Motor vehicle theft	101	77.2	23.8	0.0	26.9	19.5	29.3	33.0
Arson and explosives	159	85.5	13.2	0.0	86.2	48.0	38.0	36.0
Transportation of stolen property	234	69.7	29.1	0.0	33.7	23.0	42.8	36.0
Other property offenses[i]	44	52.3	47.7	0.0	20.1	12.0	38.3	36.0
Drug offenses	25,088	92.0	5.6	0.2	73.8	51.0	42.6	36.0
Trafficking	23,248	92.1	5.4	0.2	73.5	51.0	43.3	36.0
Possession and other	1,840	89.8	8.0	0.4	79.0	60.0	36.6	36.0
Public-order offenses	4,347	61.8	34.9	1.0	39.3	24.0	38.3	36.0
Regulatory offenses	1,410	42.3	51.1	1.8	23.5	15.0	33.9	36.0
Agriculture	67	41.8	55.2	1.5	22.5	13.5	36.0	36.0
Antitrust	28	25.0	67.9	7.1	B	B	40.4	36.0
Food and drug	52	34.6	61.5	1.9	17.7	13.5	37.5	36.0
Transportation	93	26.9	64.5	4.3	14.9	7.0	34.3	36.0
Civil rights	59	83.1	16.9	1.7	60.4	31.0	B	B
Communications	60	18.3	81.7	0.0	7.4	5.0	30.0	24.0
Customs laws	94	54.3	26.6	2.1	16.2	13.0	42.6	24.0
Postal laws	37	13.5	86.5	0.0	B	B	27.2	24.0
Other regulatory offenses	920	43.8	49.6	1.5	21.8	18.0	33.7	36.0
Other offenses	2,937	71.1	27.2	0.6	43.8	27.0	42.3	36.0
Tax law violations including tax fraud	492	56.1	44.3	0.6	21.8	15.0	38.6	36.0
Bribery	219	38.4	58.0	0.9	26.7	14.0	49.8	60.0
Perjury, contempt, intimidation	220	65.9	32.3	0.5	34.1	24.0	34.8	36.0
National defense	31	48.4	32.3	16.1	47.8	35.5	B	B
Escape	451	89.1	8.4	0.2	19.9	12.0	31.2	36.0
Racketeering and extortion	822	78.1	20.1	0.2	74.3	51.0	41.4	36.0
Gambling offenses	8	B	B	B	B	B	B	B
Liquor offenses	5	B	B	B	B	B	B	B
Nonviolent sex offenses	491	85.5	14.3	0.4	45.4	33.0	49.0	48.0
Mail or transport of obscene material	21	76.2	23.8	0.0	47.4	30.0	B	B
Traffic offenses	27	74.1	18.5	3.7	30.0	21.0	B	B
Migratory birds	3	B	B	B	X	X	B	B
Other felonies[j]	147	42.9	53.7	0.0	27.5	15.0	48.7	60.0
Weapons offenses	4,925	92.2	8.3	0.1	86.9	54.0	40.8	36.0
Immigration offenses	10,050	90.2	3.8	0.2	29.2	24.0	39.0	36.0
Misdemeanors[k]	9,100	16.6	45.4	28.4	10.0	6.0	20.6	12.0

Note: See Notes, tables 5.13 and 5.17. Total includes offenders whose offense category or sentence could not be determined. For methodology and definitions of terms, see Appendix 11.

[a]Excludes life, death, and indeterminate sentences. These excluded cases represent 1% of all incarcerations.
[b]Includes offenders receiving incarceration, probation, split or mixed sentences, and fines. Not represented in the percentage columns, but also included in the totals, are offenders receiving deportation, suspended sentences, sealed sentences, imprisonment of 4 days or less, and no sentences.
[c]All sentences to incarceration, including split, mixed, life, and indeterminate sentences.
[d]Includes offenders with split and mixed sentences.
[e]Includes offenders whose sentence could not be determined and 70 defendants for whom offense category could not be determined.
[f]Includes only violent sex offenses.
[g]Excludes tax fraud.
[h]Excludes transportation of stolen property.
[i]Excludes fraudulent property offenses; includes destruction of property and trespass.
[j]Includes felonies with unclassifiable offense type.
[k]Includes misdemeanors, petty offenses, and unknown offense level.

Source: U.S. Department of Justice, Bureau of Justice Statistics, *Compendium of Federal Justice Statistics, 2001*, NCJ 201627 (Washington, DC: U.S. Department of Justice, 2003), pp. 69, 70. Table adapted by SOURCEBOOK staff.

Table 5.20

Federal offenders sentenced to incarceration in U.S. District Courts

By offense and characteristics, United States, fiscal year 2001

Offender characteristics	Total number of convicted offenders	Percent of convicted offenders sentenced to incarceration								
		All offenses	Felonies								Mis-demeanors
			Violent offenses	Property offenses		Drug offenses	Public-order offenses		Weapons offenses	Immigration offenses	
				Fraudulent	Other		Regulatory	Other			
All offenders[a]	68,533	74.5%	92.1%	63.1%	60.7%	92.0%	42.3%	71.1%	92.2%	90.2%	16.6%
Sex											
Male	51,535	83.0	94.2	67.3	67.6	93.7	48.4	74.3	93.1	91.7	26.6
Female	8,898	59.4	77.4	52.5	39.5	81.9	30.4	53.4	71.4	69.8	15.1
Race											
White	40,877	80.2	92.4	64.4	62.6	91.1	43.3	71.2	88.5	91.5	27.3
Black	9,997	79.2	95.1	59.6	51.9	94.6	41.3	75.9	95.5	77.6	18.9
Native American	1,022	71.7	89.3	40.3	51.2	75.9	55.0	73.2	94.0	54.3	29.4
Asian/Pacific Islander	1,322	57.2	84.6	55.9	58.6	91.8	26.2	60.4	96.0	61.0	5.6
Other	138	64.5	B	57.5	B	89.2	B	B	B	63.6	7.1
Ethnicity											
Hispanic	23,904	87.5	89.9	67.8	68.2	93.6	47.2	66.5	93.1	91.8	46.9
Non-Hispanic	36,482	74.4	93.3	62.5	59.2	90.9	42.1	72.5	92.3	78.0	16.6
Age											
16 to 18 years	421	71.0	81.4	B	B	86.5	B	B	96.3	73.9	16.9
19 to 20 years	2,764	78.2	94.9	50.9	48.3	89.8	53.3	82.9	96.0	83.1	17.4
21 to 30 years	22,982	83.5	94.1	61.6	55.8	92.6	49.4	80.6	94.7	91.0	29.6
31 to 40 years	17,404	82.2	93.0	65.1	64.9	92.8	45.6	73.1	90.9	92.1	31.2
Over 40 years	14,408	73.8	92.3	62.1	62.8	91.1	38.9	65.0	87.1	89.1	20.7
Citizenship											
U.S. citizen	39,568	76.2	93.7	62.1	59.6	90.8	41.4	72.3	92.3	74.2	19.1
Not U.S. citizen	19,963	87.4	79.7	68.2	68.1	95.0	50.4	64.4	94.2	92.4	42.4
Education											
Less than high school graduate	24,918	87.9	92.7	63.8	64.7	94.0	54.8	78.5	94.1	92.3	36.0
High school graduate	17,235	78.4	94.1	61.8	58.3	92.0	39.0	70.8	92.0	86.8	19.0
Some college	9,584	71.2	92.7	63.3	56.3	88.0	40.4	69.0	87.1	74.8	15.4
College graduate	3,587	61.0	87.2	59.8	64.9	82.2	33.5	65.8	87.7	69.8	16.8
Criminal record											
No convictions	24,310	68.5	85.5	54.0	47.6	88.8	37.5	60.5	78.5	73.6	12.0
Prior adult conviction[b]	36,162	87.0	96.4	74.6	70.7	94.7	56.4	84.2	94.7	94.5	34.1

Note: See Notes, tables 5.13 and 5.18. By definition, corporations are excluded from data displaying offender characteristics but included in the data for "all offenders." Offenders are classified by the most serious offense of conviction. Life sentences and indeterminate sentences are included. These percentages reflect the percent of convicted persons having a particular characteristic who were incarcerated. For example, 83% of all convicted males were incarcerated and 94.2% of males convicted of a violent offense were incarcerated. For methodology and definitions of terms, see Appendix 11.

[a]Includes corporations and offenders for whom offense or characteristics were unknown.

[b]For some offenders, prior adult convictions are limited to those used in calculating sentences under the Federal sentencing guidelines (see Source, p. 75).

Source: U.S. Department of Justice, Bureau of Justice Statistics, *Compendium of Federal Justice Statistics, 2001*, NCJ 201627 (Washington, DC: U.S. Department of Justice, 2003), p. 72.

Table 5.21

Mean and median length of sentences imposed on Federal offenders sentenced to incarceration in U.S. District Courts

By offense and characteristics, United States, fiscal year 2001

(In months)

Offender characteristics	Violent offenses Mean	Violent offenses Median	Property: Fraudulent Mean	Property: Fraudulent Median	Property: Other Mean	Property: Other Median	Drug offenses Mean	Drug offenses Median	Public-order: Regulatory Mean	Public-order: Regulatory Median	Public-order: Other Mean	Public-order: Other Median	Weapons Mean	Weapons Median	Immigration Mean	Immigration Median
All offenders[a]	90.8	63.0	22.2	15.0	34.7	18.0	73.8	51.0	23.5	15.0	43.8	27.0	86.9	54.0	29.2	24.0
Sex																
Male	90.7	63.0	23.4	15.0	34.8	21.0	77.3	57.0	22.1	15.0	44.5	27.0	86.7	53.0	29.6	26.0
Female	42.5	37.0	16.4	12.0	23.3	14.0	44.7	33.0	18.3	15.0	28.4	18.0	55.4	30.0	19.8	13.0
Race																
White	84.2	63.0	22.3	15.0	34.5	19.0	59.3	40.0	19.9	15.0	41.0	27.0	73.8	46.0	29.0	24.0
Black	108.8	77.0	21.4	15.0	29.9	18.0	102.2	77.0	22.2	21.0	43.4	24.0	86.6	57.0	38.5	41.0
Native American	62.8	37.0	21.9	12.0	23.8	19.5	56.3	30.0	38.7	18.0	35.2	22.5	71.5	60.0	20.7	18.0
Asian/Pacific Islander	70.7	54.0	20.8	13.0	21.3	12.0	75.0	57.0	23.5	18.0	54.8	35.0	228.3	67.5	18.7	12.0
Other	B	B	25.7	16.0	B	B	64.2	38.5	B	B	B	B	B	B	35.4	28.5
Ethnicity																
Hispanic	86.9	63.0	17.1	12.0	30.1	21.0	57.8	37.0	16.1	13.0	46.3	21.0	67.5	44.0	29.4	24.0
Non-Hispanic	88.0	63.0	23.0	15.0	33.3	18.0	85.8	60.0	24.7	18.0	42.2	27.0	88.7	55.0	26.9	21.0
Age																
16 to 18 years	75.5	63.5	B	B	B	B	27.2	18.0	B	B	B	B	86.3	72.0	15.1	12.0
19 to 20 years	76.3	52.0	13.3	12.0	38.0	18.0	44.6	30.0	20.2	19.5	59.2	45.5	69.2	42.0	16.3	12.0
21 to 30 years	82.1	57.0	18.9	13.0	30.3	18.0	73.1	51.0	21.2	18.0	50.8	30.0	83.2	52.0	27.6	24.0
31 to 40 years	97.1	70.0	21.3	15.0	34.5	18.0	79.2	57.0	24.1	15.0	45.5	27.0	95.5	57.0	34.5	30.0
Over 40 years	93.0	66.0	26.4	18.0	33.0	21.0	74.7	55.0	19.4	15.0	36.0	24.0	84.4	46.0	32.8	30.0
Citizenship																
U.S. citizen	87.5	63.0	23.0	15.0	33.2	18.0	81.2	60.0	24.5	18.0	42.4	27.0	86.1	54.0	21.4	18.0
Not U.S. citizen	92.6	57.0	18.7	12.0	30.1	19.0	56.6	37.0	16.2	13.0	47.0	27.0	81.7	36.0	30.1	27.0
Education																
Less than high school graduate	91.4	60.0	21.6	15.0	29.5	18.0	70.0	48.0	20.4	15.0	55.1	30.0	79.5	51.0	31.5	27.0
High school graduate	88.2	64.5	21.6	15.0	33.3	18.0	79.1	60.0	24.4	18.0	42.3	27.0	93.6	57.0	32.7	30.0
Some college	83.2	60.0	21.8	15.0	33.2	18.0	73.2	48.0	22.4	15.0	39.2	27.0	89.6	54.0	26.7	20.5
College graduate	70.8	46.0	27.3	18.0	37.4	27.0	63.5	46.0	18.6	12.0	31.6	24.0	65.4	30.0	23.5	18.0
Criminal record																
No convictions	60.7	41.0	19.8	12.0	33.2	18.0	51.1	37.0	19.2	13.0	39.2	26.0	76.4	34.0	12.8	10.0
Prior adult conviction[b]	98.8	70.0	23.8	16.0	32.7	20.0	90.1	63.0	24.5	18.0	45.8	27.0	87.1	55.0	32.2	30.0

Note: See Notes, tables 5.13 and 5.18. Data exclude offenders sentenced to life sentences and indeterminate sentences; and include prison portion of split or mixed sentences. By definition, corporations are excluded from data displaying offender characteristics but included in the data for "all offenders." For methodology and definitions of terms, see Appendix 11.

[a] Includes corporations and offenders for whom offense category or characteristics were unknown.
[b] For some offenders, prior adult convictions are limited to those used in calculating sentences under the Federal sentencing guidelines (see Source, p. 77).

Source: U.S. Department of Justice, Bureau of Justice Statistics, *Compendium of Federal Justice Statistics, 2001*, NCJ 201627 (Washington, DC: U.S. Department of Justice, 2003), pp. 73, 74. Table adapted by SOURCEBOOK staff.

Table 5.22

Defendants disposed of in U.S. District Courts

By type of disposition, 1945-2003

	Total defendants	Not convicted				Convicted and sentenced			
		Total	Dismissed[a]	Acquitted by Court	Acquitted by Jury	Total	Plea of guilty or nolo contendere	Convicted by Court	Convicted by Jury
1945	43,755	7,641	6,462	331	848	36,114	30,817	3,082	2,215
1946	38,872	6,693	5,599	259	835	32,179	27,385	3,250	1,544
1947	38,180	5,592	4,512	279	801	32,588	29,138	2,336	1,114
1948	35,431	4,911	3,990	225	696	30,520	27,833	1,672	1,015
1949	37,318	4,245	3,332	297	616	33,073	30,447	1,628	998
1950	38,835	4,210	3,268	276	666	34,625	31,739	1,731	1,155
1951	42,286	4,096	3,204	309	583	38,190	35,271	1,795	1,124
1952	39,947	3,904	2,947	296	661	36,043	32,734	2,002	1,307
1953	39,234	4,349	3,220	409	720	34,885	31,336	2,207	1,342
1954	44,447	4,903	3,617	501	785	39,544	35,560	2,308	1,678
1955	40,235	5,184	3,832	450	902	35,501	31,148	2,077	1,826
1956	33,216	4,320	3,125	425	770	28,896	25,029	2,227	1,640
1957	31,284	3,544	2,426	348	770	27,740	23,867	2,343	1,530
1958	32,055	3,717	2,606	378	733	28,338	24,256	2,475	1,607
1959	32,125	3,736	2,667	321	748	28,389	24,793	2,089	1,507
1960	31,984	3,828	2,629	340	859	28,156	24,245	2,179	1,732
1961	32,671	4,046	2,887	291	868	28,625	24,830	2,124	1,671
1962	33,110	4,599	3,374	390	835	28,511	24,639	1,997	1,875
1963	34,845	5,042	3,735	544	763	29,803	25,924	2,005	1,874
1964	33,381	4,211	2,936	559	716	29,170	26,273	942	1,955
1965	33,718	4,961	3,789	463	709	28,757	25,923	961	1,873
1966	31,975	4,661	3,570	397	694	27,314	24,127	1,066	2,121
1967	31,535	5,191	4,196	409	586	26,344	23,121	1,040	2,173
1968	31,843	6,169	4,981	484	704	25,674	22,055	1,184	2,435
1969	32,796	5,993	4,867	483	643	26,803	23,138	1,152	2,513
1970	36,356	8,178	6,608	703	867	28,178	24,111	1,290	2,777
1971	44,615	12,512	10,655	687	1,170	32,103	27,544	1,416	3,143
1972	49,516	12,296	10,219	690	1,387	37,220	31,714	1,847	3,659
1973	46,724	11,741	9,757	661	1,323	34,983	29,009	1,873	4,101
1974	48,014	11,784	10,019	508	1,257	36,230	30,660	1,785	3,785
1975	49,212	11,779	10,274	397	1,108	37,433	31,816	1,580	4,037
1976	51,612	11,500	9,752	508	1,240	40,112	34,041	1,587	4,484
1977	53,188	11,732	9,952	598	1,382	41,456	35,323	1,629	4,504
1978	45,922	9,417	7,792	311	1,314	36,505	31,112	1,431	3,962
1979	41,175	8,262	6,791	303	1,168	32,913	27,295	2,006	3,612
1980	36,560	7,962	6,633	283	1,046	28,598	23,111	1,851	3,636
1981	38,127	8,259	6,981	266	1,012	29,868	24,322	1,867	3,679
1982	40,466	8,214	7,051	255	938	32,252	27,392	1,205	3,655
1983	43,329	7,738	6,566	281	891	35,591	30,523	1,286	3,782
1984	44,501	8,397	7,022	327	1,048	36,104	31,461	969	3,674
1985	47,360	8,830	7,484	415	931	38,530	33,823	994	3,713
1986	50,040	9,300	7,894	461	945	40,740	35,448	1,139	4,153
1987	54,168	10,226	8,802	446	978	43,942	38,440	1,371	4,131
1988	52,791	9,889	8,379	453	1,057	42,902	37,514	1,267	4,121
1989	54,643	10,119	8,420	638	1,061	44,524	38,681	1,225	4,618
1990	56,519	9,794	8,193	630	971	46,725	40,452	1,063	5,210
1991	56,747	9,979	8,372	603	1,004	46,768	41,213	699	4,856
1992	59,644	9,384	7,769	560	1,055	50,260	44,632	576	5,052
1993	61,309	9,586	8,284	396	906	51,723	46,541	500	4,682
1994	59,625	9,908	8,669	545	693	49,717	45,429	491	3,797
1995	54,980	8,207	7,112	482	613	46,773	43,103	467	3,203
1996	60,255	7,985	7,083	340	562	52,270	48,196	461	3,613
1997	63,148	7,500	6,607	400	493	55,648	51,918	499	3,231
1998	67,934	8,049	6,968	594	487	59,885	56,256	601	3,028
1999	73,481	8,666	7,649	553	464	64,815	61,626	487	2,702
2000	75,071	8,035	6,992	603	440	67,036	63,863	632	2,541
2001	75,650	7,919	7,017	479	423	67,731	64,402	1,035	2,294
2002	78,835	7,953	7,217	336	400	70,882	68,188	423	2,271
2003	83,530	8,680	7,957	293	430	74,850	72,110	327	2,413

Note: See Note, table 5.9. The District of Columbia is excluded from these data through 1973. The territorial courts of the Virgin Islands, Canal Zone, and Guam are excluded through 1976. Data for 1945-91 are reported for the 12-month period ending June 30. Beginning in 1992, data are reported for the Federal fiscal year, which is the 12-month period ending September 30. Beginning in 1991, defendants charged in two or more cases that were terminated during the year are reported only once.

[a] Prior to 2001, these data included defendants who were committed pursuant to 28 U.S.C. 2902 of the Narcotic Addict Rehabilitation Act.

Source: Administrative Office of the United States Courts, *Federal Offenders in the United States District Courts July 1973-June 1974* (Washington, DC: Administrative Office of the United States Courts, 1977), p. H-1; Administrative Office of the United States Courts, *Annual Report of the Director, 1979*, p. 108; *1981*, p. 101, Table 46; *1983*, p. 171; *1985*, p. 180; *1986*, pp. 271-278; *1995*, pp. 225-227; *1998*, pp. 228-230; *1999*, pp. 222-224 (Washington, DC: Administrative Office of the United States Courts); Administrative Office of the United States Courts, *Annual Report of the Director, 1982*, p. 141; *1987*, pp. 294-304; *1988*, pp. 297-304; *1989*, pp. 295-302; *1990*, pp. 204-207; *1991*, pp. 256, 257, 262, 263; *1992*, pp. 269-272, 276-279; *1993*, Tables D-5, D-7; *1994*, Tables D-5, D-7; *1996*, pp. 221-223; *1997*, pp. 214-216 (Washington, DC: USGPO); and Administrative Office of the United States Courts, *Judicial Business of the United States Courts: 2000 Annual Report of the Director*, pp. 221, 223; *2001 Annual Report of the Director*, pp. 211-213; *2002 Annual Report of the Director*, pp. 211-213; *2003 Annual Report of the Director*, pp. 211-213 (Washington, DC: USGPO). Table adapted by SOURCEBOOK staff.

Table 5.23

Defendants sentenced in U.S. District Courts

By type and length of sentence, 1945-2003

			Type of sentence									Average sentence to imprisonment (in months)[f]	Average sentence to probation (in months)[g]
			Imprisonment										
			Regular sentences[a]										
	Total[b]	Total regular	1 through 12 months	13 through 35 months	36 through 60 months	Over 60 months	Split sentence[c]	Indeterminate[d]	Probation	Fine	Other[e]		
1945	17,095	X	10,522	3,634	2,017	922	X	X	14,359	4,660	X	16.5	NA
1946	15,393	X	9,316	3,610	1,809	658	X	X	12,691	4,095	X	18.6	NA
1947	15,146	X	9,033	3,679	1,746	688	X	X	13,318	4,124	X	17.3	NA
1948	13,505	X	8,033	3,329	1,517	626	X	X	14,014	3,001	X	17.6	NA
1949	14,730	X	9,389	3,378	1,392	571	X	X	15,161	3,182	X	15.8	NA
1950	14,998	X	8,910	3,799	1,588	701	X	X	16,603	3,024	X	17.5	NA
1951	15,568	X	9,215	3,758	1,805	790	X	X	19,855	2,767	X	18.1	NA
1952	15,963	X	9,094	3,817	2,072	980	X	X	17,687	2,393	X	19.1	NA
1953	16,355	X	8,969	4,213	2,164	1,009	X	X	15,811	2,719	X	19.4	NA
1954	19,221	X	10,977	4,546	2,487	1,211	X	X	17,517	2,806	X	18.9	NA
1955	17,542	X	8,942	4,584	2,724	1,292	X	X	14,584	2,945	X	21.9	NA
1956	13,576	X	5,681	4,217	2,478	1,200	X	X	12,365	2,955	X	24.9	NA
1957	13,798	X	5,473	4,018	2,635	1,672	X	X	11,434	2,508	X	28.0	NA
1958	14,101	X	5,382	4,029	2,861	1,829	X	X	11,617	2,620	X	28.2	NA
1959	14,350	X	5,024	3,680	3,237	1,849	(c)	X	11,379	2,660	X	29.2	NA
1960	14,170	X	5,024	3,877	3,288	1,981	(c)	X	11,081	2,905	X	29.6	NA
1961	14,462	X	4,057	4,753	3,481	2,171	(c)	X	10,714	2,772	677	31.0	NA
1962	14,042	X	4,088	4,441	3,418	2,095	(c)	X	11,071	2,618	780	32.0	NA
1963	13,639	X	2,949	4,218	3,228	2,076	1,168	X	12,047	2,847	1,270	32.3	NA
1964	13,273	X	2,992	4,085	3,094	1,987	1,115	X	11,634	2,689	1,574	31.9	NA
1965	13,668	X	3,748	3,139	3,262	2,252	1,267	X	10,779	2,477	1,833	33.5	NA
1966	13,282	X	3,549	2,926	3,332	2,092	1,383	X	10,256	2,356	1,420	32.9	NA
1967	13,085	X	3,236	2,837	3,411	2,381	1,220	X	9,435	2,293	1,531	36.5	NA
1968	12,610	X	2,473	2,413	3,568	2,915	1,241	X	9,820	1,816	1,428	42.2	NA
1969	12,847	X	2,771	2,252	3,500	3,012	1,312	X	9,991	1,682	2,283	42.0	NA
1970	12,415	X	2,753	2,253	3,290	2,775	1,344	X	11,387	1,935	2,441	41.1	NA
1971	14,378	X	2,820	2,599	3,326	3,482	2,151	X	13,243	1,789	2,693	42.1	NA
1972	16,832	X	4,450	2,645	3,695	3,569	2,473	X	15,395	2,232	2,761	38.1	NA
1973	17,540	X	3,384	2,912	4,141	4,220	2,883	X	15,026	1,866	551	15.4	NA
1974	17,180	X	3,333	2,880	4,107	3,960	2,900	X	16,623	2,078	349	42.2	NA
1975	17,301	X	3,337	2,825	4,437	4,387	2,315	X	17,913	1,876	343	45.5	NA
1976	18,477	X	3,530	3,096	4,731	4,862	2,258	X	18,208	3,199	228	47.2	NA
1977	19,552	13,772	4,016	2,938	2,953	3,865	3,217	1,604	16,135	5,409	360	34.7	32.8
1978	17,426	12,234	3,284	2,804	2,792	3,354	3,263	1,132	14,525	4,279	285	48.6	32.4
1979	14,580	9,818	2,320	2,344	2,389	2,765	3,234	887	13,459	4,368	506	49.0	32.3
1980	13,191	8,484	2,016	1,936	1,945	2,587	3,012	1,123	11,053	3,916	438	51.9	33.1
1981	13,700	8,906	2,192	1,904	1,906	2,906	3,069	1,232	12,173	3,507	488	55.3	31.7
1982	15,857	10,673	2,202	2,313	2,422	3,736	3,538	1,163	12,723	3,395	277	58.6	32.2
1983	17,886	11,979	2,503	2,671	2,543	4,262	3,973	1,496	14,097	3,220	388	57.2	33.5
1984	17,710	11,828	2,282	2,666	2,628	4,252	4,063	1,482	13,880	3,977	537	58.0	35.0
1985	18,679	12,910	2,285	2,886	2,995	4,744	4,084	1,494	14,404	4,830	617	60.2	35.2
1986	20,261	15,004	2,393	3,251	3,529	5,831	4,397	1,200	15,230	4,232	657	64.6	35.5
1987	23,344	17,556	2,661	3,850	3,942	7,103	4,524	1,257	16,023	4,368	207	65.4	35.2
1988	22,473	17,605	3,070	3,721	3,291	7,523	4,014	848	16,057	4,087	285	66.1	34.0
1989	24,867	21,485	5,057	5,301	3,463	7,664	2,676	706	14,997	4,193	467	58.6	32.9
1990	27,796	25,768	6,701	6,466	3,305	9,296	1,716	312	14,196	4,176	557	59.2	32.7
1991	29,189	28,809	7,896	6,667	5,123	9,123	NA	NA	13,754	3,772	53	69.6	42.7
1992	32,866	31,895	8,281	8,073	5,650	9,891	NA	NA	13,299	3,985	109	65.6	32.3
1993	35,001	33,664	8,493	8,241	6,790	10,140	NA	NA	12,775	3,870	77	63.9	32.1
1994	33,554	32,075	7,856	8,116	6,535	9,568	NA	NA	12,409	3,650	52	64.1	32.3
1995	32,439	31,112	7,806	8,226	5,807	9,273	NA	NA	11,288	2,875	171	66.4	32.5
1996	37,579	35,556	8,597	9,606	6,811	10,542	NA	NA	11,526	2,929	229	61.4	32.3
1997	41,105	38,419	9,086	11,054	7,547	10,732	NA	NA	11,656	2,672	215	58.8	32.7
1998	45,166	42,085	9,750	12,004	8,359	11,972	NA	NA	11,708	2,732	279	58.8	32.7
1999	50,076	46,653	10,667	13,092	9,842	13,052	NA	NA	11,986	2,495	258	57.7	33.1
2000	53,047	49,536	11,306	13,860	10,686	13,684	NA	NA	11,517	2,241	231	56.6	33.0
2001	53,910	50,318	10,953	14,279	11,165	13,921	NA	NA	11,160	2,351	310	56.5	33.0
2002	56,686	52,776	10,965	15,802	11,229	14,780	NA	NA	11,474	2,427	295	56.9	33.5
2003	61,102	56,737	11,628	16,587	12,415	16,107	NA	NA	10,997	2,435	316	58.6	32.2

See notes on next page.

Table 5.23

Defendants sentenced in U.S. District Courts

By type and length of sentence, 1945-2003--Continued

Note: See Notes, tables 5.9 and 5.22. Data for 1945-91 are reported for the 12-month period ending June 30. Beginning in 1992, data are reported for the Federal fiscal year, which is the 12-month period ending September 30.

Prior to 1977, the periods reported for lengths of sentences to imprisonment were 1 year and 1 day and under, over 1 year and 1 day to 3 years, 3 to 5 years, and 5 years and over. Beginning in 1977, the periods reported for lengths of sentences to imprisonment are 1 through 12 months, 13 through 35 months, 36 through 59 months, and 60 months and over. Beginning in 1991, two of the periods reported for lengths of sentences to imprisonment changed. The period 36 through 59 months changed to 36 through 60 months, and the period 60 months and over changed to over 60 months.

[a] Includes sentences of more than 6 months that are to be followed by a term of probation (mixed sentences). Beginning in 1991, includes sentences of at least 1 month that may be followed by a term of probation.

[b] Prior to 1989, total includes Youth Corrections Act and youthful offender sentences not separately enumerated. From 1979-85, total includes Federal Juvenile Delinquency Act sentences not separately enumerated. Beginning in 1991, total includes life sentences, death sentences, and cases with either no sentence, a suspended sentence, a sealed sentence, deportation, or imprisonment of 4 days or less.

[c] A "split sentence" is a sentence on a one-count indictment of 6 months or less in a jail-type institution followed by a term of probation, 18 U.S.C. 3651 approved Aug. 23, 1958 (72 Stat. 834). Included are mixed sentences involving confinement for 6 months or less on one count to be followed by a term of probation on one or more counts. For 1959-62, split sentences were included in prison terms of 1 year and 1 day and under (see Note).

[d] 18 U.S.C. 4205B(1) and (2).

[e] From 1945-60, "other" was included with sentences of probation. From 1986-90, "other" included deportation, suspended sentences, imprisonment for 4 days or less, time already served, remitted and suspended fines, and life sentences. Beginning in 1991, "other" includes supervised releases, probation of 4 days or less, suspended sentences, sealed sentences, and no sentence.

[f] From 1977-90, split sentences, Youth Corrections Act and youthful offender sentences, and life sentences were not included in computing average sentence. Beginning in 1991, deportation, suspended sentences, sealed sentences, imprisonment of 4 days or less, no sentence, life sentences, and death sentences were not included in computing average sentence.

[g] From 1986-90, split sentences, indeterminate sentences, and Youth Corrections Act and youthful offender sentences were not included in computing average sentences. Beginning in 1991, supervised releases, probation of 4 days or less, suspended sentences, sealed sentences, and no sentence were not included in computing the average sentence.

Source: Administrative Office of the United States Courts, *Federal Offenders in the United States District Courts July 1973-June 1974* (Washington, DC: Administrative Office of the United States Courts, 1977), p. H-1; Administrative Office of the United States Courts, *Annual Report of the Director, 1979*, p. 108; *1981*, p. 101, Table 46; *1983*, p. 171; *1985*, p. 180; *1986*, pp. 271-278; *1995*, pp. 228-231; *1998*, pp. 231-234; *1999*, pp. 225-228 (Washington, DC: Administrative Office of the United States Courts); Administrative Office of the United States Courts, *Annual Report of the Director, 1982*, p. 141; *1987*, pp. 294-304; *1988*, pp. 297-304; *1989*, pp. 295-302; *1990*, pp. 204-207; *1991*, pp. 256, 257, 262, 263; *1992*, pp. 269-272, 276-279; *1993*, Tables D-5, D-7; *1994*, Tables D-5, D-7; *1996*, pp. 224-227; *1997*, pp. 217-220 (Washington, DC: USGPO); and Administrative Office of the United States Courts, *Judicial Business of the United States Courts: 2000 Annual Report of the Director*, pp. 224-227; *2001 Annual Report of the Director*, pp. 214-217; *2002 Annual Report of the Director*, pp. 214-217; *2003 Annual Report of the Director*, pp. 214-217 (Washington, DC: USGPO). Table adapted by SOURCEBOOK staff.

Table 5.24

Defendants disposed of in U.S. District Courts

By offense and type of disposition, fiscal year 2003

		Not convicted				Convicted and sentenced				
	Total			Acquitted by			Plea	Plea of nolo	Convicted by	
Offense	defendants	Total	Dismissed	Court	Jury	Total	of guilty	contendere	Court	Jury
Total	83,530	8,680	7,957	293	430	74,850	71,683	427	327	2,413
GENERAL OFFENSES										
Homicide	247	30	24	1	5	217	192	0	1	24
Murder-first degree	186	27	23	0	4	159	136	0	1	22
Murder-second degree	21	1	0	0	1	20	19	0	0	1
Manslaughter	40	2	1	1	0	38	37	0	0	1
Robbery	1,499	71	59	4	8	1,428	1,366	1	5	56
Bank	1,445	69	57	4	8	1,376	1,317	1	5	53
Postal	28	1	1	0	0	27	25	0	0	2
Other	26	1	1	0	0	25	24	0	0	1
Assault	786	183	168	4	11	603	556	4	13	30
Burglary	53	9	9	0	0	44	41	0	0	3
Bank	0	X	X	X	X	X	X	X	X	X
Postal	15	0	X	X	X	15	13	0	0	2
Interstate shipments	0	X	X	X	X	X	X	X	X	X
Other	38	9	9	0	0	29	28	0	0	1
Larceny and theft	3,211	773	754	9	10	2,438	2,293	60	10	75
Bank	234	10	9	0	1	224	219	1	0	4
Postal	510	28	26	1	1	482	475	1	0	6
Interstate shipments	314	47	44	1	2	267	233	0	0	34
Other U.S. property	1,600	482	472	7	3	1,118	1,037	57	8	16
Transport stolen property	202	27	24	0	3	175	161	0	1	13
Other	351	179	179	0	0	172	168	1	1	2
Embezzlement	1,038	89	81	4	4	949	926	1	1	21
Bank	431	35	33	0	2	396	393	1	0	2
Postal	259	21	19	0	2	238	232	0	0	6
Other	348	33	29	4	0	315	301	0	1	13
Fraud	11,066	860	764	20	76	10,206	9,788	10	16	392
Income tax	470	27	25	0	2	443	413	0	1	29
Lending institution	1,422	98	83	6	9	1,324	1,268	0	2	54
Postal	1,521	163	146	2	15	1,358	1,263	4	4	87
Veterans and allotments	10	1	1	0	0	9	8	1	0	0
Securities and Exchange	145	13	9	1	3	132	112	0	0	20
Social Security	718	123	122	0	1	595	582	1	0	12
False personation	31	3	2	0	1	28	26	0	1	1
Nationality laws	266	21	21	0	0	245	242	0	0	3
Passport fraud	498	30	29	0	1	468	462	0	2	4
False claims and statements	1,901	142	128	4	10	1,759	1,715	1	1	42
Other	4,084	239	198	7	34	3,845	3,697	3	5	140
Motor vehicle theft	176	21	20	0	1	155	136	0	1	18
Forgery and counterfeiting	1,275	138	130	2	6	1,137	1,099	0	1	37
Transport forged securities	0	X	X	X	X	X	X	X	X	X
Postal forgery	0	X	X	X	X	X	X	X	X	X
Other forgery	98	14	13	1	0	84	83	0	0	1
Counterfeiting	1,177	124	117	1	6	1,053	1,016	0	1	36
Sex offenses	1,158	104	90	2	12	1,054	992	0	4	58
Sexual abuse	463	55	43	2	10	408	369	0	2	37
Other	695	49	47	0	2	646	623	0	2	21
Drug laws	29,457	2,471	2,329	18	124	26,986	25,918	43	53	972
Miscellaneous general offenses	15,283	3,000	2,670	210	120	12,283	11,270	297	155	561
Bribery	132	17	13	1	3	115	110	0	0	5
Drunk driving and traffic	4,744	1,653	1,481	172	0	3,091	2,709	273	108	1
Escape[a]	598	82	81	1	0	516	504	1	0	11
Extortion, racketeering, threats	1,122	117	104	10	3	1,005	916	0	1	88
Gambling and lottery	15	2	2	0	0	13	11	0	0	2
Kidnaping	106	26	19	1	6	80	57	0	0	23
Perjury	88	13	12	0	1	75	61	0	0	14
Weapons and firearms	7,612	826	703	19	104	6,786	6,344	3	29	410
Other	866	264	255	6	3	602	558	20	17	7
SPECIAL OFFENSES										
Immigration laws	15,296	496	482	2	12	14,800	14,699	2	25	74
Liquor, Internal Revenue	2	0	X	X	X	2	2	0	0	0
Federal statutes	2,983	435	377	17	41	2,548	2,405	9	42	92
Agricultural/conservation acts	270	81	76	3	2	189	180	1	5	3
Antitrust violations	16	0	X	X	X	16	14	0	0	2
Food and Drug Act	79	8	8	0	0	71	70	0	0	1
Migratory bird laws	167	6	6	0	0	161	158	0	2	1
Motor Carrier Act	1	0	X	X	X	1	1	0	0	0
National defense laws	1	0	X	X	X	1	1	0	0	0
Civil rights	91	32	11	1	20	59	47	0	0	12
Contempt	50	5	5	0	0	45	41	3	1	0
Customs laws	123	19	19	0	0	104	98	0	1	5
Postal laws[b]	167	12	11	1	0	155	154	1	0	0
Other	2,018	272	241	12	19	1,746	1,641	4	33	68

See notes at end of table.

Table 5.24

Defendants disposed of in U.S. District Courts

By offense and type of disposition, fiscal year 2003--Continued

Note: Data include defendants in all felony and class A misdemeanor cases, but include only those petty offense defendants whose cases were assigned to district court judges. Defendants charged in two or more cases that were terminated during the year are reported only once. Data exclude 733 transfers and 1,323 terminations for defendants charged in more than one case during the year.

[a] Includes escape from custody, aiding and abetting an escape, failure to appear in court, and bail jumping.

[b] Includes obstructing mail, mailing nonmailable material, and other postal regulations.

Source: Administrative Office of the United States Courts, *Judicial Business of the United States Courts: 2003 Annual Report of the Director* (Washington, DC: USGPO, 2004), pp. 211-213.

Table 5.25

Defendants sentenced in U.S. District Courts

By offense, and type and length of sentence, fiscal year 2003

											Type of sentence
		Imprisonment									
			Regular sentences[a]								
Offense	Total defendants sentenced	Total imprisonment	6 months or less	7 through 12 months	13 through 35 months	36 through 60 months	Over 60 months	Average sentence in months[b]	Life	Death	Other[c]
Total	74,850	61,102	6,477	5,151	16,587	12,415	16,107	58.6	241	1	4,123
GENERAL OFFENSES											
Homicide	217	202	10	12	28	31	96	108.6	18	0	7
Murder-first degree	159	150	5	4	12	19	85	134.7	18	0	7
Murder-second degree	20	19	0	1	3	6	9	82.7	0	0	0
Manslaughter	38	33	5	7	13	6	2	24.6	0	0	0
Robbery	1,428	1,388	11	16	118	389	834	106.0	5	0	15
Bank	1,376	1,343	11	14	112	375	814	107.1	5	0	12
Postal	27	22	0	1	2	4	12	83.6	0	0	3
Other	25	23	0	1	4	10	8	58.8	0	0	0
Assault	603	404	81	40	128	73	48	32.7	0	0	34
Burglary	44	40	3	3	19	10	3	29.7	0	0	2
Bank	0	X	X	X	X	X	X	X	X	X	X
Postal	15	15	0	0	8	4	2	33.9	0	0	1
Interstate shipments	0	X	X	X	X	X	X	X	X	X	X
Other	29	25	3	3	11	6	1	27.3	0	0	1
Larceny and theft	2,438	1,065	225	191	341	106	113	29.8	0	0	89
Bank	224	79	18	14	19	15	10	30.8	0	0	3
Postal	482	325	79	74	115	13	4	15.6	0	0	40
Interstate shipments	267	232	17	25	73	47	66	57.8	0	0	4
Other U.S. property	1,118	227	76	46	56	10	7	15.4	0	0	32
Transport stolen property	175	129	15	18	60	15	18	32.2	0	0	3
Other	172	73	20	14	18	6	8	30.4	0	0	7
Embezzlement	949	502	163	65	127	24	16	16.9	0	0	107
Bank	396	289	104	23	64	7	5	13.2	0	0	86
Postal	238	35	17	8	5	1	0	9.9	0	0	4
Other	315	178	42	34	58	16	11	23.1	0	0	17
Fraud	10,206	6,866	1,519	975	2,277	815	341	25.2	0	0	939
Income tax	443	257	65	63	92	24	10	20.0	0	0	3
Lending institution	1,324	1,155	223	134	419	123	76	25.1	0	0	180
Postal	1,358	907	127	129	372	178	77	34.8	0	0	24
Veterans and allotments	9	1	0	1	0	0	0	12.0	0	0	0
Securities and Exchange	132	99	8	4	33	27	20	59.7	0	0	7
Social Security	595	309	99	38	59	14	9	16.8	0	0	90
False personation	28	18	8	3	2	1	0	12.0	0	0	4
Nationality laws	245	229	53	29	91	24	0	15.9	0	0	32
Passport fraud	468	395	97	22	19	9	2	10.0	0	0	246
False claims and statements	1,759	1,205	445	187	308	65	10	14.2	0	0	190
Other	3,845	2,291	394	365	882	350	137	28.4	0	0	163
Motor vehicle theft	155	135	3	10	34	23	51	129.8	9	1	4
Forgery and counterfeiting	1,137	767	114	154	327	87	34	22.3	0	0	51
Transport forged securities	0	X	X	X	X	X	X	X	X	X	X
Postal forgery	0	X	X	X	X	X	X	X	X	X	X
Other forgery	84	39	12	1	15	2	2	19.4	0	0	7
Counterfeiting	1,053	728	102	153	312	85	32	22.4	0	0	44
Sex offenses	1,054	964	22	31	374	234	292	72.7	2	0	9
Sexual abuse	408	367	9	9	90	61	189	113.7	2	0	7
Other	646	597	13	22	284	173	103	48.1	0	0	2
Drug laws	26,986	25,060	1,143	1,489	4,781	5,967	10,557	80.2	157	0	966
Miscellaneous general offenses	12,283	8,312	502	529	2,137	1,988	2,764	71.9	40	0	352
Bribery	115	64	14	13	23	4	2	18.4	0	0	8
Drunk driving and traffic	3,091	325	101	23	20	6	3	10.0	0	0	172
Escape[f]	516	480	97	116	191	52	8	19.6	0	0	16
Extortion, racketeering, threats	1,005	852	51	49	212	219	263	74.5	16	0	42
Gambling and lottery	13	11	3	0	7	0	0	16.6	0	0	1
Kidnaping	80	74	2	5	12	5	42	163.3	5	0	3
Perjury	75	51	10	9	16	11	3	26.8	0	0	2
Weapons and firearms	6,786	6,295	178	286	1,614	1,676	2,437	78.2	19	0	85
Other	602	160	46	28	42	15	6	19.0	0	0	23

See notes at end of table.

	Probation						
Total	6 months or less	7 through 12 months	13 through 35 months	36 months and over	Average sentence in months[d]	Other[e]	Fine only
11,313	532	2,351	2,022	6,092	32.2	316	2,435
15	0	3	3	9	36.6	0	0
9	0	3	2	4	29.3	0	0
1	0	0	0	1	60.0	0	0
5	0	0	1	4	45.0	0	0
40	0	2	4	32	41.3	2	0
33	0	1	4	26	40.2	2	0
5	0	1	0	4	40.8	0	0
2	0	0	0	2	60.0	0	0
172	17	49	37	66	25.8	3	27
4	0	0	0	4	44.8	0	0
X	X	X	X	X	X	X	X
0	X	X	X	X	X	X	X
X	X	X	X	X	X	X	X
4	0	0	0	4	44.8	0	0
1,233	109	261	197	659	32.5	7	140
145	4	12	19	108	40.1	2	0
157	2	14	26	113	36.4	2	0
35	2	7	3	22	34.9	1	0
759	92	197	116	352	30.3	2	132
46	3	3	8	32	42.8	0	0
91	6	28	25	32	25.5	0	8
441	8	57	96	267	34.4	13	6
107	3	16	18	60	31.2	10	0
198	3	28	52	114	32.9	1	5
136	2	13	26	93	38.9	2	1
3,289	62	319	621	2,215	37.9	72	51
186	8	19	38	120	35.0	1	0
168	3	10	20	119	40.4	16	1
446	3	30	52	357	42.5	4	5
8	1	2	1	4	30.4	0	0
32	0	3	3	26	62.5	0	1
283	5	28	53	188	38.2	9	3
10	0	2	5	2	24.0	1	0
16	0	1	3	8	26.3	4	0
73	1	12	19	28	25.7	13	0
531	13	73	130	295	32.4	20	23
1,536	28	139	297	1,068	38.8	4	18
20	0	0	7	13	39.2	0	0
370	6	17	83	258	38.6	6	0
X	X	X	X	X	X	X	X
X	X	X	X	X	X	X	X
45	0	1	7	37	44.1	0	0
325	6	16	76	221	37.8	6	0
88	4	8	3	71	46.3	2	2
40	3	4	3	30	43.8	0	1
48	1	4	0	41	48.3	2	1
1,844	48	384	332	1,017	32.2	63	82
2,101	194	882	309	678	24.3	38	1,870
50	1	6	16	27	35.9	0	1
1,075	130	740	103	88	14.4	14	1,691
35	3	8	9	12	22.0	3	1
150	3	13	32	102	39.0	0	3
2	0	0	0	2	36.0	0	0
6	0	0	3	3	53.0	0	0
24	0	3	8	13	39.5	0	0
485	10	44	103	311	35.9	17	6
274	47	68	35	120	31.0	4	168

Table 5.25

Defendants sentenced in U.S. District Courts

By offense, and type and length of sentence, fiscal year 2003--Continued

		Type of sentence								
		Imprisonment									
		Regular sentences[a]									
Offense	Total defendants sentenced	Total imprison-ment	6 months or less	7 through 12 months	13 through 35 months	36 through 60 months	Over 60 months	Average sentence in months[b]	Life	Death	Other[c]
SPECIAL OFFENSES											
Immigration laws	14,800	14,231	2,477	1,503	5,551	2,526	834	26.1	1	0	1,339
Liquor, Internal Revenue	2	0	X	X	X	X	X	X	X	X	X
Federal statutes	2,548	1,166	204	133	345	142	124	40.1	9	0	209
Agricultural/conservation acts	189	38	18	2	11	2	2	25.8	0	0	3
Antitrust violations	16	4	2	2	0	0	0	7.0	0	0	0
Food and Drug Act	71	18	4	3	2	1	4	171.9	0	0	4
Migratory bird laws	161	1	1	0	0	0	0	3.0	0	0	0
Motor Carrier Act	1	0	X	X	X	X	X	X	X	X	X
National defense laws	1	0	X	X	X	X	X	X	X	X	X
Civil rights	59	50	3	6	18	9	13	60.1	1	0	0
Contempt	45	26	7	7	3	3	4	39.5	0	0	2
Customs laws	104	76	13	11	22	8	0	19.0	0	0	22
Postal laws[g]	155	20	10	2	0	2	0	9.7	0	0	6
Other	1,746	933	146	100	289	117	101	39.4	8	0	172

Note: See Note, table 5.24.

[a]Includes sentences of at least 1 month that may be followed by a term of probation (mixed sentences).
[b]Excludes life sentences, death sentences, deportation, suspended sentences, sealed sentences, imprisonment of 4 days or less, and no sentence.
[c]Includes deportation, suspended sentences, sealed sentences, imprisonment of 4 days or less, and no sentence.
[d]Excludes supervised release, probation of 4 days or less, suspended sentences, sealed sentences, and no sentence.
[e]Includes supervised release, probation of 4 days or less, suspended sentences, sealed sentences, and no sentence.
[f]Includes escape from custody, aiding or abetting an escape, failure to appear in court, and bail jumping.
[g]Includes obstructing mail, mailing nonmailable material, and other postal regulations.

Source: Administrative Office of the United States Courts, *Judicial Business of the United States Courts: 2003 Annual Report of the Director* (Washington, DC: USGPO, 2004), pp. 214-217.

		Probation					
	6 months or less	7 through 12 months	13 through 35 months	36 months and over	Average sentence in months[d]	Other[e]	Fine only
Total							
566	21	55	82	314	28.8	94	3
2	1	1	0	0	9.0	0	0
1,128	62	313	248	489	28.3	16	254
104	7	26	36	35	26.8	0	47
8	0	3	2	1	15.0	2	4
46	1	14	16	15	24.6	0	7
53	9	27	11	6	15.9	0	107
1	0	0	1	0	24.0	0	0
1	0	1	0	0	12.0	0	0
9	1	0	2	6	36.7	0	0
17	4	5	6	2	19.1	0	2
25	0	6	3	16	33.4	0	3
131	10	42	32	47	24.8	0	4
733	30	189	139	361	30.4	14	80

Table 5.26

Offenders sentenced in U.S. District Courts under the U.S. Sentencing Commission guidelines

By primary offense, sex, race, and ethnicity, fiscal year 2002

		Sex					Race, ethnicity							
	Total	Male		Female		Total	White		Black		Hispanic[a]		Other[b]	
Primary offense	cases	Number	Percent	Number	Percent	cases	Number	Percent	Number	Percent	Number	Percent	Number	Percent
Total	63,779	54,854	86.0%	8,925	14.0%	62,437	19,212	30.8%	15,352	24.6%	25,607	41.0%	2,266	3.6%
Murder	83	76	91.6	7	8.4	84	29	34.5	15	17.9	10	11.9	30	35.7
Manslaughter	59	49	83.1	10	16.9	59	4	6.8	2	3.4	2	3.4	51	86.4
Kidnaping, hostage-taking	66	62	93.9	4	6.1	65	23	35.4	10	15.4	19	29.2	13	20.0
Sexual abuse	212	207	97.6	5	2.4	210	68	32.4	14	6.7	12	5.7	116	55.2
Assault	489	440	90.0	49	10.0	466	150	32.2	70	15.0	74	15.9	172	36.9
Robbery	1,631	1,501	92.0	130	8.0	1,617	713	44.1	759	46.9	123	7.6	22	1.4
Arson	65	62	95.4	3	4.6	64	43	67.2	9	14.1	3	4.7	9	14.1
Drug offenses														
Trafficking	25,335	22,013	86.9	3,322	13.1	25,084	6,592	26.3	6,821	27.2	11,107	44.3	564	2.2
Communication facility	458	365	79.7	93	20.3	455	120	26.4	162	35.6	162	35.6	11	2.4
Simple possession	583	492	84.4	91	15.6	498	243	48.8	134	26.9	107	21.5	14	2.8
Firearms	5,173	4,991	96.5	182	3.5	5,107	1,913	37.5	2,459	48.1	613	12.0	122	2.4
Burglary, breaking and entering	43	42	97.7	1	2.3	43	18	41.9	3	7.0	3	7.0	19	44.2
Auto theft	162	159	98.1	3	1.9	161	101	62.7	38	23.6	19	11.8	3	1.9
Larceny	2,236	1,421	63.6	815	36.4	2,130	1,059	49.7	650	30.5	267	12.5	154	7.2
Fraud	7,086	5,218	73.6	1,868	26.4	6,877	3,333	48.5	2,134	31.0	1,105	16.1	305	4.4
Embezzlement	732	309	42.2	423	57.8	707	403	57.0	186	26.3	68	9.6	50	7.1
Forgery, counterfeiting	1,466	1,123	76.6	343	23.4	1,446	590	40.8	597	41.3	220	15.2	39	2.7
Bribery	168	139	82.7	29	17.3	162	83	51.2	20	12.3	50	30.9	9	5.6
Tax	622	520	83.6	102	16.4	607	435	71.7	77	12.7	51	8.4	44	7.2
Money laundering	939	761	81.0	178	19.0	921	414	45.0	150	16.3	312	33.9	45	4.9
Racketeering, extortion	825	758	91.9	67	8.1	802	337	42.0	224	27.9	184	22.9	57	7.1
Gambling, lottery	104	90	86.5	14	13.5	103	77	74.8	5	4.9	2	1.9	19	18.4
Civil rights	93	89	95.7	4	4.3	90	56	62.2	17	18.9	16	17.8	1	1.1
Immigration	11,673	11,066	94.8	607	5.2	11,549	596	5.2	349	3.0	10,389	90.0	215	1.9
Pornography, prostitution	664	653	98.3	11	1.7	656	561	85.5	23	3.5	40	6.1	32	4.9
Prison offenses	317	279	88.0	38	12.0	303	93	30.7	105	34.7	92	30.4	13	4.3
Administration of justice offenses	1,102	782	71.0	320	29.0	1,062	428	40.3	190	17.9	386	36.3	58	5.5
Environmental, wildlife	139	129	92.8	10	7.2	129	100	77.5	2	1.6	14	10.9	13	10.1
National defense	10	10	100.0	0	X	9	2	22.2	2	22.2	5	55.6	0	X
Antitrust	17	16	94.1	1	5.9	17	14	82.4	2	11.8	0	X	1	5.9
Food and drug	91	82	90.1	9	9.9	84	53	63.1	5	6.0	20	23.8	6	7.1
Other	1,136	950	83.6	186	16.4	870	561	64.5	118	13.6	132	15.2	59	6.8

Note: The sentencing reform provisions of the Comprehensive Crime Control Act, Public Law No. 98-473 (1984), created the U.S. Sentencing Commission. The Commission's primary function is to develop and monitor sentencing policies and practices for the Federal courts. On Apr. 13, 1987, the Commission submitted initial Sentencing Guidelines and Policy Statements to Congress. The guidelines became effective on Nov. 1, 1987, and apply to all offenses committed on or after that date. These data are derived from the U.S. Sentencing Commission's fiscal year 2002 Offender Dataset, which includes information on 64,366 cases sentenced under the Sentencing Reform Act (guideline cases) during fiscal year 2002 (Oct. 1, 2001 through Sept. 30, 2002) for which data were received by the Commission as of Apr. 28, 2004. Given the nature of the data file and reporting requirements, the following types of cases are not included in the data presented here: cases initiated but for which no convictions were obtained, defendants convicted for whom no sentences were yet issued, defendants sentenced but for whom no data were submitted to the Commission, and cases not sentenced under the Sentencing Reform Act (non-guideline cases).

A case or defendant is defined as a single sentencing event for a single defendant (even if multiple indictments or multiple convictions are consolidated for sentencing).

Multiple defendants in a single sentencing event are treated as separate cases. If an individual defendant is sentenced more than once during the fiscal year, each sentencing event is identified as a separate case. (Source, p. A-4.)

Of the 64,366 guideline cases, some were excluded due to missing information. For sex, 587 cases were excluded due to one or both of the following conditions: missing primary offense category, 393; and missing gender information, 327. For race and ethnicity, 1,929 cases were excluded due to one or both of the following conditions: missing primary offense category, 393; and missing race or ethnicity information, 1,860.

Under drug offenses, "communication facility" refers to the use of a device, such as a telephone, in a drug trafficking offense.

[a]Includes both black and white Hispanics.
[b]Includes Native Americans, Alaskan Natives, Asians, and Pacific Islanders.

Source: U.S. Sentencing Commission, *2002 Sourcebook of Federal Sentencing Statistics* (Washington, DC: U.S. Sentencing Commission, 2004), pp. 14, 15. Table adapted by SOURCEBOOK staff.

Table 5.27

Offenders sentenced in U.S. District Courts under the U.S. Sentencing Commission guidelines

By primary offense and age, fiscal year 2002

Primary offense	Total cases	Under 21 years Number	Under 21 years Percent	21 to 25 years Number	21 to 25 years Percent	26 to 30 years Number	26 to 30 years Percent	31 to 35 years Number	31 to 35 years Percent	36 to 40 years Number	36 to 40 years Percent	41 to 50 years Number	41 to 50 years Percent	Over 50 years Number	Over 50 years Percent	Mean age (in years)
Total	62,518	3,190	5.1%	11,541	18.5%	12,490	20.0%	10,716	17.1%	8,532	13.6%	10,534	16.8%	5,515	8.8%	34.3
Murder	83	9	10.8	19	22.9	7	8.4	14	16.9	13	15.7	14	16.9	7	8.4	33.6
Manslaughter	59	5	8.5	15	25.4	12	20.3	9	15.3	6	10.2	11	18.6	1	1.7	31.0
Kidnaping, hostage-taking	66	2	3.0	23	34.8	6	9.1	16	24.2	14	21.2	4	6.1	1	1.5	30.6
Sexual abuse	212	17	8.0	37	17.5	35	16.5	26	12.3	39	18.4	36	17.0	22	10.4	34.8
Assault	488	44	9.0	97	19.9	108	22.1	81	16.6	58	11.9	64	13.1	36	7.4	32.7
Robbery	1,628	137	8.4	354	21.7	300	18.4	245	15.0	237	14.6	261	16.0	94	5.8	32.6
Arson	65	6	9.2	10	15.4	10	15.4	10	15.4	5	7.7	16	24.6	8	12.3	35.6
Drug offenses																
Trafficking	25,252	1,564	6.2	5,227	20.7	5,606	22.2	4,407	17.5	3,288	13.0	3,707	14.7	1,453	5.8	32.7
Communication facility	457	19	4.2	64	14.0	117	25.6	88	19.3	59	12.9	77	16.8	33	7.2	34.1
Simple possession	563	81	14.4	149	26.5	103	18.3	69	12.3	56	9.9	77	13.7	28	5.0	30.7
Firearms	5,165	293	5.7	1,299	25.2	1,114	21.6	789	15.3	572	11.1	746	14.4	352	6.8	32.5
Burglary, breaking and entering	43	11	25.6	9	20.9	5	11.6	8	18.6	4	9.3	5	11.6	1	2.3	29.1
Auto theft	162	8	4.9	27	16.7	35	21.6	25	15.4	25	15.4	27	16.7	15	9.3	34.7
Larceny	2,236	173	7.7	363	16.2	307	13.7	332	14.8	302	13.5	441	19.7	318	14.2	36.2
Fraud	6,826	107	1.6	705	10.3	940	13.8	1,109	16.2	994	14.6	1,678	24.6	1,293	18.9	39.5
Embezzlement	730	23	3.2	129	17.7	99	13.6	99	13.6	105	14.4	166	22.7	109	14.9	37.1
Forgery, counterfeiting	1,456	113	7.8	356	24.5	302	20.7	246	16.9	171	11.7	188	12.9	80	5.5	31.7
Bribery	168	2	1.2	8	4.8	11	6.5	24	14.3	26	15.5	46	27.4	51	30.4	43.3
Tax	617	1	0.2	14	2.3	19	3.1	45	7.3	68	11.0	189	30.6	281	45.5	48.9
Money laundering	937	7	0.7	61	6.5	115	12.3	152	16.2	146	15.6	236	25.2	220	23.5	41.4
Racketeering, extortion	823	21	2.6	145	17.6	150	18.2	147	17.9	101	12.3	133	16.2	126	15.3	36.6
Gambling, lottery	102	0	X	1	1.0	6	5.9	8	7.8	9	8.8	31	30.4	47	46.1	49.8
Civil rights	93	2	2.2	12	12.9	18	19.4	18	19.4	19	20.4	15	16.1	9	9.7	35.7
Immigration	10,844	402	3.7	1,906	17.6	2,577	23.8	2,244	20.7	1,738	16.0	1,607	14.8	370	3.4	32.8
Pornography, prostitution	664	11	1.7	70	10.5	81	12.2	96	14.5	107	16.1	163	24.5	136	20.5	40.0
Prison offenses	315	10	3.2	45	14.3	65	20.6	61	19.4	50	15.9	51	16.2	33	10.5	35.1
Administration of justice offenses	1,087	42	3.9	185	17.0	173	15.9	170	15.6	142	13.1	213	19.6	162	14.9	36.6
Environmental, wildlife	136	1	0.7	8	5.9	6	4.4	16	11.8	10	7.4	41	30.1	54	39.7	47.6
National defense	10	0	X	1	10.0	2	20.0	1	10.0	0	X	3	30.0	3	30.0	42.9
Antitrust	17	0	X	0	X	1	5.9	0	X	3	17.6	4	23.5	9	52.9	52.3
Food and drug	90	1	1.1	1	1.1	13	14.4	7	7.8	17	18.9	26	28.9	25	27.8	43.5
Other	1,124	78	6.9	201	17.9	147	13.1	154	13.7	148	13.2	258	23.0	138	12.3	36.1

Note: See Note, table 5.26. Of the 64,366 guideline cases, 1,848 cases were excluded due to one or both of the following conditions: missing primary offense category, 393; and missing date of birth, 1,758.

Source: U.S. Sentencing Commission, *2002 Sourcebook of Federal Sentencing Statistics* (Washington, DC: U.S. Sentencing Commission, 2004), p. 16.

Table 5.28

Offenders sentenced in U.S. District Courts under the U.S. Sentencing Commission guidelines

By primary offense and education level, fiscal year 2002

Primary offense	Total cases	Less than high school graduate Number	Less than high school graduate Percent	High school graduate Number	High school graduate Percent	Some college Number	Some college Percent	College graduate Number	College graduate Percent
Total	58,519	26,856	45.9%	18,049	30.8%	9,906	16.9%	3,708	6.3%
Murder	82	37	45.1	35	42.7	5	6.1	5	6.1
Manslaughter	59	30	50.8	22	37.3	7	11.9	0	X
Kidnaping, hostage-taking	63	35	55.6	21	33.3	6	9.5	1	1.6
Sexual abuse	205	63	30.7	77	37.6	38	18.5	27	13.2
Assault	453	173	38.2	165	36.4	98	21.6	17	3.8
Robbery	1,612	547	33.9	717	44.5	296	18.4	52	3.2
Arson	63	20	31.7	28	44.4	12	19.0	3	4.8
Drug offenses									
Trafficking	24,510	12,412	50.6	7,959	32.5	3,468	14.1	671	2.7
Communication facility	447	213	47.7	157	35.1	65	14.5	12	2.7
Simple possession	450	138	30.7	190	42.2	86	19.1	36	8.0
Firearms	5,071	2,367	46.7	2,027	40.0	598	11.8	79	1.6
Burglary, breaking and entering	43	23	53.5	15	34.9	5	11.6	0	X
Auto theft	159	68	42.8	57	35.8	30	18.9	4	2.5
Larceny	2,052	496	24.2	820	40.0	573	27.9	163	7.9
Fraud	6,480	1,180	18.2	1,877	29.0	2,096	32.3	1,327	20.5
Embezzlement	702	56	8.0	295	42.0	263	37.5	88	12.5
Forgery, counterfeiting	1,439	474	32.9	525	36.5	372	25.9	68	4.7
Bribery	159	22	13.8	29	18.2	53	33.3	55	34.6
Tax	599	73	12.2	138	23.0	164	27.4	224	37.4
Money laundering	900	217	24.1	258	28.7	244	27.1	181	20.1
Racketeering, extortion	795	289	36.4	284	35.7	160	20.1	62	7.8
Gambling, lottery	102	34	33.3	41	40.2	17	16.7	10	9.8
Civil rights	90	19	21.1	33	36.7	23	25.6	15	16.7
Immigration	8,966	7,027	78.4	1,266	14.1	493	5.5	180	2.0
Pornography, prostitution	654	82	12.5	211	32.3	222	33.9	139	21.3
Prison offenses	287	106	36.9	126	43.9	49	17.1	6	2.1
Administration of justice offenses	1,010	383	37.9	312	30.9	205	20.3	110	10.9
Environmental, wildlife	126	35	27.8	40	31.7	28	22.2	23	18.3
National defense	9	2	22.2	2	22.2	2	22.2	3	33.3
Antitrust	17	1	5.9	3	17.6	6	35.3	7	41.2
Food and drug	83	18	21.7	15	18.1	22	26.5	28	33.7
Other	832	216	26.0	304	36.5	200	24.0	112	13.5

Note: See Note, table 5.26. Of the 64,366 guideline cases, 5,847 were excluded due to one or both of the following conditions: missing primary offense category, 393; and missing education information, 5,847.

Source: U.S. Sentencing Commission, *2002 Sourcebook of Federal Sentencing Statistics* (Washington, DC: U.S. Sentencing Commission, 2004), p. 18.

Table 5.29

Sentences imposed in U.S. District Courts under the U.S. Sentencing Commission guidelines

By primary offense and type of sentence, fiscal year 2002

		Imprisonment						Probation					
		Total receiving imprisonment		Prison only		Prison/ community split sentence[a]		Total receiving probation		Probation and confinement		Probation only	
Primary offense	Total cases	Number	Percent	Number	Percent	Number	Percent	Number	Percent	Number	Percent	Number	Percent
Total	63,292	54,370	85.9%	52,117	82.3%	2,253	3.6%	8,922	14.1%	3,151	5.0%	5,771	9.1%
Murder	84	83	98.8	82	97.6	1	1.2	1	1.2	0	X	1	1.2
Manslaughter	58	56	96.6	50	86.2	6	10.3	2	3.4	1	1.7	1	1.7
Kidnaping, hostage-taking	65	64	98.5	63	96.9	1	1.5	1	1.5	1	1.5	0	X
Sexual abuse	206	185	89.8	179	86.9	6	2.9	21	10.2	10	4.9	11	5.3
Assault	483	388	80.3	370	76.6	18	3.7	95	19.7	34	7.0	61	12.6
Robbery	1,620	1,596	98.5	1,580	97.5	16	1.0	24	1.5	16	1.0	8	0.5
Arson	64	60	93.8	58	90.6	2	3.1	4	6.3	1	1.6	3	4.7
Drug offenses													
Trafficking	25,209	24,128	95.7	23,568	93.5	560	2.2	1,081	4.3	455	1.8	626	2.5
Communication facility	456	387	84.9	379	83.1	8	1.8	69	15.1	33	7.2	36	7.9
Simple possession	572	193	33.7	187	32.7	6	1.0	379	66.3	26	4.5	353	61.7
Firearms	5,132	4,741	92.4	4,575	89.1	166	3.2	391	7.6	152	3.0	239	4.7
Burglary, breaking and entering	43	37	86.0	31	72.1	6	14.0	6	14.0	2	4.7	4	9.3
Auto theft	161	126	78.3	119	73.9	7	4.3	35	21.7	16	9.9	19	11.8
Larceny	2,206	946	42.9	805	36.5	141	6.4	1,260	57.1	399	18.1	861	39.0
Fraud	7,012	4,779	68.2	4,073	58.1	706	10.1	2,233	31.8	912	13.0	1,321	18.8
Embezzlement	721	394	54.6	274	38.0	120	16.6	327	45.4	98	13.6	229	31.8
Forgery, counterfeiting	1,446	884	61.1	790	54.6	94	6.5	562	38.9	247	17.1	315	21.8
Bribery	165	82	49.7	65	39.4	17	10.3	83	50.3	25	15.2	58	35.2
Tax	618	333	53.9	261	42.2	72	11.7	285	46.1	125	20.2	160	25.9
Money laundering	931	735	78.9	699	75.1	36	3.9	196	21.1	77	8.3	119	12.8
Racketeering, extortion	818	757	92.5	740	90.5	17	2.1	61	7.5	23	2.8	38	4.6
Gambling, lottery	104	31	29.8	22	21.2	9	8.7	73	70.2	32	30.8	41	39.4
Civil rights	89	57	64.0	53	59.6	4	4.5	32	36.0	11	12.4	21	23.6
Immigration	11,616	11,179	96.2	11,093	95.5	86	0.7	437	3.8	120	1.0	317	2.7
Pornography, prostitution	662	608	91.8	598	90.3	10	1.5	54	8.2	28	4.2	26	3.9
Prison offenses	316	290	91.8	278	88.0	12	3.8	26	8.2	11	3.5	15	4.7
Administration of justice offenses	1,088	695	63.9	636	58.5	59	5.4	393	36.1	125	11.5	268	24.6
Environmental, wildlife	133	46	34.6	39	29.3	7	5.3	87	65.4	25	18.8	62	46.6
National defense	10	8	80.0	8	80.0	0	X	2	20.0	0	X	2	20.0
Antitrust	17	9	52.9	8	47.1	1	5.9	8	47.1	6	35.3	2	11.8
Food and drug	89	21	23.6	14	15.7	7	7.9	68	76.4	13	14.6	55	61.8
Other	1,098	472	43.0	420	38.3	52	4.7	626	57.0	127	11.6	499	45.4

Note: See Note, table 5.26. Of the 64,366 guideline cases, 1,074 cases were excluded due to one or more of the following conditions: missing primary offense category, 393; missing sentencing information, 707; and cases in which a defendant received no imprisonment or probation, 301.

[a] A term of imprisonment followed by supervised release with a condition of community confinement, home detention, or intermittent confinement.

Source: U.S. Sentencing Commission, *2002 Sourcebook of Federal Sentencing Statistics* (Washington, DC: U.S. Sentencing Commission, 2004), p. 28.

Table 5.30

Length of sentences to imprisonment imposed in U.S. District Courts for U.S. Sentencing Commission guideline cases

By type of offense, fiscal years 1997-2002

(In months)

	Violent offenses[a]		Drug offenses[b]		White collar offenses[c]	
	Average length	Median length	Average length	Median length	Average length	Median length
1997	104.7	70	80.7	56	20.2	13
1998	105.7	70	78.0	56	19.2	12
1999	97.9	63	75.0	48	20.4	12
2000	102.0	63	74.3	51	20.5	12
2001	89.5	63	71.6	48	20.8	15
2002	NA	NA	73.6	51	21.5	15

Note: See Note, table 5.26. These data include prison sentences only and exclude any imposition of home detention, community confinement, or intermittent confinement (Source, *2002*, p. A-4). Some data have been revised by the Source and may differ from previous editions of SOURCEBOOK.

[a]Includes murder, manslaughter, kidnaping, sexual abuse, assault, bank robbery, and arson.
[b]Includes drug trafficking, drug communication facilities, and simple possession.
[c]Includes fraud, embezzlement, forgery, counterfeiting, bribery, tax offenses, and money laundering.

Source: U.S. Sentencing Commission, *2001 Sourcebook of Federal Sentencing Statistics*, p. 32; *2002*, p. 32 (Washington, DC: U.S. Sentencing Commission). Table adapted by SOURCEBOOK staff.

Table 5.31

Length of sentences to imprisonment imposed in U.S. District Courts for U.S. Sentencing Commission guideline cases

By primary offense, fiscal year 2002

Primary offense	Total cases	Sentences to imprisonment Average length (in months)	Median length (in months)
Total	52,694	55.4	33.0
Murder	82	237.2	180.5
Manslaughter	56	39.6	27.0
Kidnaping, hostage-taking	62	181.5	120.0
Sexual abuse	185	62.0	36.0
Assault	378	39.3	27.0
Robbery	1,589	92.2	71.0
Arson	60	93.0	60.0
Drug offenses			
Trafficking	23,976	74.4	57.0
Communication facility	381	50.9	48.0
Simple possession	164	19.2	6.0
Firearms	4,673	70.8	44.0
Burglary, breaking and entering	37	21.1	16.0
Auto theft	124	60.6	24.0
Larceny	936	15.2	12.0
Fraud	4,498	20.0	15.0
Embezzlement	389	7.8	4.0
Forgery, counterfeiting	876	17.4	14.0
Bribery	78	26.4	13.5
Tax	327	17.3	12.0
Money laundering	729	47.6	33.0
Racketeering, extortion	744	87.8	60.0
Gambling, lottery	30	11.9	10.0
Civil rights	56	42.1	24.0
Immigration	10,254	26.0	24.0
Pornography, prostitution	605	53.3	33.0
Prison offenses	283	18.8	14.0
Administration of justice offenses	666	23.5	15.5
Environmental, wildlife	43	10.6	10.0
National defense	8	149.0	56.5
Antitrust	9	14.3	12.0
Food and drug	21	20.1	12.0
Other	375	20.9	12.0

Note: See Notes, tables 5.26 and 5.30. Of the 64,366 guideline cases, 9,373 cases with 0 months of prison ordered were excluded. In addition, 2,299 cases were excluded due to one or more of the following conditions: missing primary offense category, 384; missing criminal history category, 1,444; and missing or indeterminable sentencing information, 1,051.

Source: U.S. Sentencing Commission, *2002 Sourcebook of Federal Sentencing Statistics* (Washington, DC: U.S. Sentencing Commission, 2004), p. 30.

Table 5.32

Fines and restitution ordered in U.S. District Courts for U.S. Sentencing Commission guideline cases

By primary offense, fiscal year 2002

Primary offense	Total cases	No fine or restitution ordered Number	Percent	Restitution ordered/no fine Number	Percent	Fine ordered/ no restitution Number	Percent	Both fine and restitution ordered Number	Percent	Amount of payment ordered (dollar amount) Total cases	Mean	Median	Total
Total	62,660	46,219	73.8%	8,210	13.1%	7,435	11.9%	796	1.3%	16,433	$345,929	$5,000	$5,684,656,762
Murder	79	43	54.4	26	32.9	8	10.1	2	2.5	36	3,003,150	6,733	108,113,398
Manslaughter	55	26	47.3	24	43.6	2	3.6	3	5.5	29	5,406	3,201	156,787
Kidnaping, hostage-taking	65	43	66.2	18	27.7	1	1.5	3	4.6	22	27,119	3,466	596,617
Sexual abuse	208	141	67.8	28	13.5	37	17.8	2	1.0	67	6,527	1,200	437,322
Assault	482	344	71.4	85	17.6	47	9.8	6	1.2	138	10,929	1,635	1,508,258
Robbery	1,537	459	29.9	970	63.1	61	4.0	47	3.1	1,078	18,311	5,000	19,739,144
Arson	63	19	30.2	38	60.3	2	3.2	4	6.3	44	319,451	78,852	14,055,857
Drug offenses													
Trafficking	25,212	22,109	87.7	204	0.8	2,858	11.3	41	0.2	3,103	12,303	1,500	38,175,971
Communication facility	456	387	84.9	2	0.4	66	14.5	1	0.2	69	19,997	1,000	1,379,821
Simple possession	585	259	44.3	2	0.3	319	54.5	5	0.9	326	1,031	1,000	336,216
Firearms	5,088	3,999	78.6	248	4.9	824	16.2	17	0.3	1,089	13,302	1,500	14,485,776
Burglary, breaking and entering	38	10	26.3	26	68.4	0	X	2	5.3	28	5,400	1,981	151,208
Auto theft	148	51	34.5	73	49.3	19	12.8	5	3.4	97	54,907	16,000	5,325,975
Larceny	2,144	614	28.6	1,069	49.9	329	15.3	132	6.2	1,528	55,185	7,272	84,323,286
Fraud	6,648	2,212	33.3	3,509	52.8	642	9.7	285	4.3	4,433	698,994	36,452	3,098,638,515
Embezzlement	718	145	20.2	486	67.7	57	7.9	30	4.2	573	70,609	14,860	40,459,061
Forgery, counterfeiting	1,389	626	45.1	565	40.7	147	10.6	51	3.7	762	48,481	2,359	36,942,256
Bribery	165	68	41.2	26	15.8	62	37.6	9	5.5	97	166,030	5,000	16,104,954
Tax	613	234	38.2	111	18.1	235	38.3	33	5.4	379	114,244	10,000	43,298,426
Money laundering	898	538	59.9	187	20.8	160	17.8	13	1.4	360	5,086,647	57,195	1,831,192,869
Racketeering, extortion	791	468	59.2	160	20.2	147	18.6	16	2.0	321	490,806	7,500	157,548,770
Gambling, lottery	104	44	42.3	13	12.5	45	43.3	2	1.9	60	15,544	5,000	932,644
Civil rights	87	48	55.2	21	24.1	12	13.8	6	6.9	39	9,364	2,500	365,199
Immigration	11,632	11,270	96.9	25	0.2	336	2.9	1	(a)	362	14,088	1,000	5,099,969
Pornography, prostitution	661	469	71.0	20	3.0	170	25.7	2	0.3	192	6,682	4,000	1,282,884
Prison offenses	318	279	87.7	3	0.9	35	11.0	1	0.3	39	59,896	500	2,335,961
Administration of justice offenses	1,092	784	71.8	70	6.4	219	20.1	19	1.7	308	280,671	2,000	86,446,737
Environmental, wildlife	138	46	33.3	8	5.8	70	50.7	14	10.1	92	11,258	3,000	1,035,740
National defense	10	8	80.0	1	10.0	1	10.0	0	X	2	X	X	X
Antitrust	17	2	11.8	5	29.4	4	23.5	6	35.3	15	3,997,698	168,000	59,965,464
Food and drug	91	29	31.9	14	15.4	43	47.3	5	5.5	62	18,954	5,000	1,175,117
Other	1,128	445	39.5	173	15.3	477	42.3	33	2.9	683	19,049	700	13,010,679

Note: See Note, table 5.26. Of the 64,366 guideline cases, 1,706 cases were excluded due to one or both of the following conditions: missing primary offense category, 393; and missing information on type of economic sanction for cases in which orders were made, 1,475. A total of 16,433 cases were used to calculate amount of payments ordered. This differs from the 16,441 cases in which fines and/or restitution were ordered due to the exclusion of 8 cases in which the amount of fine and/or restitution was not specified. Fine information includes either fines and/or costs of supervision.

Source: U.S. Sentencing Commission, *2002 Sourcebook of Federal Sentencing Statistics* (Washington, DC: U.S. Sentencing Commission, 2004), p. 33.

[a] Less than 0.05%.

Table 5.33

Fines and restitution ordered for organizations sentenced in U.S. District Courts for U.S. Sentencing Commission guideline cases

By primary offense, fiscal year 2002

Primary offense	Total cases involving organizations[a] Number	Total cases involving organizations[a] Percent	Cases with restitution imposed Number	Cases with restitution imposed Mean	Cases with restitution imposed Median	Cases with fine imposed Number	Cases with fine imposed Mean	Cases with fine imposed Median
Total	252	100.0%	112	$6,292,650	$200,000	165	$2,815,154	$96,000
Administration of justice: contempt, obstruction, perjury	3	1.2	0	X	X	3	53,333	30,000
Antitrust	23	9.1	9	2,894,240	540,000	15	6,235,067	1,100,000
Archeological damage	1	0.4	1	NA	NA	1	NA	NA
Bribery, gratuity, extortion	5	2.0	3	36,921	40,000	2	NA	NA
Contraband	2	0.8	0	X	X	2	NA	NA
Copyright, trademark	2	0.8	2	NA	NA	1	NA	NA
Drugs	3	1.2	0	X	X	2	NA	NA
Environmental								
Water	33	13.1	8	114,845	67,020	29	625,724	75,000
Air	2	0.8	0	X	X	2	NA	NA
Hazardous, toxic pollutants	10	4.0	2	NA	NA	9	99,611	50,000
Wildlife	2	0.8	1	NA	NA	2	NA	NA
Import and export	10	4.0	3	239,333	33,000	10	130,473	101,113
Food, drugs, agricultural, and consumer products	19	7.5	4	119,167	122,232	19	15,400,537	100,000
Fraud	102	40.5	67	10,064,322	306,742	55	950,463	96,000
Gambling	1	0.4	0	X	X	0	X	X
Immigration, naturalization, passports	2	0.8	0	X	X	2	NA	NA
Larceny, theft, embezzlement	2	0.8	2	NA	NA	1	NA	NA
Money laundering	19	7.5	9	98,031	22,918	4	58,750	60,000
Pornography, prostitution	3	1.2	0	X	X	3	351,667	490,000
Racketeering	5	2.0	1	NA	NA	1	NA	NA
Tax	3	1.2	0	X	X	2	NA	NA

Note: See Note, table 5.26. "Organizations" include corporations, partnerships, associations, joint-stock companies, unions, trusts, pension funds, unincorporated organizations, governments and political subdivisions thereof, and non-profit organizations. (Source, p. A-5). Mean and median dollar values include only cases with reported non-zero fine or restitution amounts. In fiscal year 2002, no fine or restitution was ordered in 21 of the 252 cases involving organizations.

[a] Data for cases receiving either fines or restitution will sum to more than the total because some cases received both fines and restitution.

Source: U.S. Sentencing Commission, *2002 Sourcebook of Federal Sentencing Statistics* (Washington, DC: U.S. Sentencing Commission, 2004), p. 96. Table adapted by SOURCEBOOK staff.

Table 5.34

Mode of conviction in U.S. District Courts for U.S. Sentencing Commission guideline cases

By primary offense, fiscal year 2002

Primary offense	Total cases	Plea of guilty Number	Plea of guilty Percent	Trial Number	Trial Percent
Total	63,935	62,084	97.1%	1,851	2.9%
Murder	84	67	79.8	17	20.2
Manslaughter	59	56	94.9	3	5.1
Kidnaping, hostage-taking	64	57	89.1	7	10.9
Sexual abuse	212	202	95.3	10	4.7
Assault	492	450	91.5	42	8.5
Robbery	1,631	1,579	96.8	52	3.2
Arson	64	53	82.8	11	17.2
Drug offenses					
Trafficking	25,361	24,595	97.0	766	3.0
Communication facility	459	458	99.8	1	0.2
Simple possession	592	583	98.5	9	1.5
Firearms	5,173	4,923	95.2	250	4.8
Burglary, breaking and entering	43	41	95.3	2	4.7
Auto theft	162	153	94.4	9	5.6
Larceny	2,250	2,220	98.7	30	1.3
Fraud	7,107	6,880	96.8	227	3.2
Embezzlement	734	729	99.3	5	0.7
Forgery, counterfeiting	1,466	1,449	98.8	17	1.2
Bribery	168	159	94.6	9	5.4
Tax	622	600	96.5	22	3.5
Money laundering	939	870	92.7	69	7.3
Racketeering, extortion	828	769	92.9	59	7.1
Gambling, lottery	104	104	100.0	0	X
Civil rights	93	82	88.2	11	11.8
Immigration	11,730	11,612	99.0	118	1.0
Pornography, prostitution	664	643	96.8	21	3.2
Prison offenses	318	313	98.4	5	1.6
Administration of justice offenses	1,107	1,076	97.2	31	2.8
Environmental, wildlife	140	131	93.6	9	6.4
National defense	10	8	80.0	2	20.0
Antitrust	17	15	88.2	2	11.8
Food and drug	91	91	100.0	0	X
Other	1,151	1,116	97.0	35	3.0

Note: See Note, table 5.26. Of the 64,366 guideline cases, 431 cases were excluded due to one or both of the following conditions: missing primary offense category, 393; and missing information on mode of conviction, 370.

Source: U.S. Sentencing Commission, *2002 Sourcebook of Federal Sentencing Statistics* (Washington, DC: U.S. Sentencing Commission, 2004), p. 24.

Table 5.35

U.S. citizens and non-U.S. citizens sentenced in U.S. District Courts under the U.S. Sentencing Commission guidelines

By primary offense, fiscal year 2002

Primary offense	Total cases	U.S. citizen Number	U.S. citizen Percent	Non-U.S. citizen Number	Non-U.S. citizen Percent
Total	61,634	40,923	66.4%	20,711	33.6%
Murder	82	70	85.4	12	14.6
Manslaughter	59	59	100.0	0	X
Kidnaping, hostage-taking	64	40	62.5	24	37.5
Sexual abuse	209	204	97.6	5	2.4
Assault	458	409	89.3	49	10.7
Robbery	1,620	1,591	98.2	29	1.8
Arson	64	63	98.4	1	1.6
Drug offenses					
Trafficking	24,798	17,292	69.7	7,506	30.3
Communication facility	453	366	80.8	87	19.2
Simple possession	475	442	93.1	33	6.9
Firearms	5,113	4,800	93.9	313	6.1
Burglary, breaking and entering	43	42	97.7	1	2.3
Auto theft	160	142	88.8	18	11.3
Larceny	2,078	1,929	92.8	149	7.2
Fraud	6,703	5,611	83.7	1,092	16.3
Embezzlement	706	689	97.6	17	2.4
Forgery, counterfeiting	1,443	1,281	88.8	162	11.2
Bribery	160	125	78.1	35	21.9
Tax	605	554	91.6	51	8.4
Money laundering	917	668	72.8	249	27.2
Racketeering, extortion	799	683	85.5	116	14.5
Gambling, lottery	102	96	94.1	6	5.9
Civil rights	90	83	92.2	7	7.8
Immigration	11,355	1,028	9.1	10,327	90.9
Pornography, prostitution	657	629	95.7	28	4.3
Prison offenses	291	264	90.7	27	9.3
Administration of justice offenses	1,027	768	74.8	259	25.2
Environmental, wildlife	126	110	87.3	16	12.7
National defense	9	5	55.6	4	44.4
Antitrust	17	16	94.1	1	5.9
Food and drug	85	79	92.9	6	7.1
Other	866	785	90.6	81	9.4

Note: See Note, table 5.26. Of the 64,366 guideline cases, 2,732 cases were excluded due to one or both of the following conditions: missing primary offense category, 393; or missing citizenship information, 2,731.

Source: U.S. Sentencing Commission, *2002 Sourcebook of Federal Sentencing Statistics* (Washington, DC: U.S. Sentencing Commission, 2004), p. 19.

Table 5.36

Sentences within and departing from U.S. Sentencing Commission guidelines in U.S. District Courts

By primary offense, fiscal year 2002

		Within guideline range		Downward departures				Upward departure	
				Substantial assistance departure[a]		Other downward departure			
Primary offense	Total cases	Number	Percent	Number	Percent	Number	Percent	Number	Percent
Total	58,423	37,968	65.0%	10,170	17.4%	9,828	16.8%	457	0.8%
Murder	76	50	65.8	4	5.3	9	11.8	13	17.1
Manslaughter	57	37	64.9	1	1.8	6	10.5	13	22.8
Kidnaping, hostage-taking	57	33	57.9	4	7.0	12	21.1	8	14.0
Sexual abuse	195	142	72.8	2	1.0	37	19.0	14	7.2
Assault	445	347	78.0	12	2.7	70	15.7	16	3.6
Robbery	1,522	1,051	69.1	227	14.9	220	14.5	24	1.6
Arson	59	38	64.4	14	23.7	4	6.8	3	5.1
Drug offenses									
Trafficking	23,949	13,398	55.9	6,565	27.4	3,932	16.4	54	0.2
Communication facility	421	303	72.0	56	13.3	61	14.5	1	0.2
Simple possession	481	458	95.2	17	3.5	4	0.8	2	0.4
Firearms	4,765	3,511	73.7	581	12.2	602	12.6	71	1.5
Burglary, breaking and entering	42	30	71.4	5	11.9	4	9.5	3	7.1
Auto theft	151	93	61.6	41	27.2	14	9.3	3	2.0
Larceny	2,038	1,745	85.6	151	7.4	126	6.2	16	0.8
Fraud	6,378	4,539	71.2	1,135	17.8	633	9.9	71	1.1
Embezzlement	672	588	87.5	24	3.6	58	8.6	2	0.3
Forgery, counterfeiting	1,363	1,094	80.3	159	11.7	97	7.1	13	1.0
Bribery	148	87	58.8	41	27.7	20	13.5	0	X
Tax	557	352	63.2	107	19.2	95	17.1	3	0.5
Money laundering	852	496	58.2	245	28.8	101	11.9	10	1.2
Racketeering, extortion	744	474	63.7	178	23.9	75	10.1	17	2.3
Gambling, lottery	95	57	60.0	27	28.4	11	11.6	0	X
Civil rights	87	60	69.0	16	18.4	11	12.6	0	X
Immigration	10,399	6,861	66.0	248	2.4	3,236	31.1	54	0.5
Pornography, prostitution	613	442	72.1	34	5.5	117	19.1	20	3.3
Prison offenses	297	229	77.1	19	6.4	46	15.5	3	1.0
Administration of justice offenses	1,010	719	71.2	144	14.3	134	13.3	13	1.3
Environmental, wildlife	121	76	62.8	25	20.7	20	16.5	0	X
National defense	9	6	66.7	1	11.1	2	22.2	0	X
Antitrust	16	5	31.3	9	56.3	2	12.5	0	X
Food and drug	77	55	71.4	10	13.0	11	14.3	1	1.3
Other	727	592	81.4	68	9.4	58	8.0	9	1.2

Note: See Note, table 5.26. A case is determined to involve no departure if the sentence imposed is within the guideline range. If a sentence imposed by the court falls outside the guideline range, the court provides reasons for the departure. (Source, p. A-2.) Of the 64,366 guideline cases, 5,943 cases were excluded due to one or both of the following conditions: missing offense type, 393; or missing/inapplicable departure information, 5,682.

[a]Cases departed downward based on a motion by the Government for a reduced sentence due to the defendant's substantial assistance to authorities.

Source: U.S. Sentencing Commission, *2002 Sourcebook of Federal Sentencing Statistics* (Washington, DC: U.S. Sentencing Commission, 2004), p. 56.

Table 5.37

Defendants charged with violation of drug laws in U.S. District Courts

By type of disposition, 1945-2003

	Total defendants	Not convicted				Convicted and sentenced			
				Acquitted by			Plea of guilty or nolo contendere	Convicted by	
		Total	Dismissed[a]	Court	Jury	Total		Court	Jury
1945	1,413	228	197	5	26	1,185	1,062	35	88
1946	1,687	349	305	13	31	1,338	1,218	37	83
1947	1,880	210	153	17	40	1,670	1,517	57	96
1948	1,790	308	237	14	57	1,482	1,324	48	110
1949	1,806	208	148	14	46	1,598	1,404	59	135
1950	2,400	264	184	28	52	2,136	1,907	61	168
1951	2,332	304	234	25	45	2,028	1,745	105	178
1952	2,121	252	184	29	39	1,869	1,523	109	237
1953	2,336	333	237	30	66	2,003	1,589	121	293
1954	2,220	310	239	28	43	1,910	1,491	107	312
1955	2,166	363	279	32	52	1,803	1,386	95	322
1956	1,835	314	221	36	57	1,521	1,168	93	260
1957	1,910	256	184	28	44	1,654	1,264	91	299
1958	1,942	301	217	25	59	1,641	1,138	129	374
1959	1,742	364	267	40	57	1,378	1,005	112	261
1960	1,846	340	263	38	39	1,506	1,155	93	258
1961	1,828	313	248	20	45	1,515	1,171	74	270
1962	1,643	240	175	29	36	1,403	1,022	113	268
1963	1,689	283	222	34	27	1,406	1,040	112	254
1964	1,679	271	205	32	34	1,408	1,039	112	257
1965	2,078	323	257	41	25	1,755	1,384	132	239
1966	2,223	349	280	36	33	1,874	1,469	119	286
1967	2,250	428	363	34	31	1,822	1,424	119	279
1968	2,692	563	466	49	48	2,129	1,664	138	327
1969	3,545	836	716	50	70	2,709	2,239	123	347
1970	3,420	959	886	48	45	2,461	2,030	97	334
1971	5,366	2,204	2,080	43	81	3,162	2,682	94	386
1972	6,848	1,600	1,396	52	152	5,248	4,391	228	629
1973	9,983	2,169	1,905	83	181	7,814	6,297	393	1,124
1974	10,989	2,744	2,430	80	234	8,245	6,666	437	1,142
1975	10,901	2,750	2,454	62	234	8,151	6,531	393	1,227
1976	10,762	2,721	2,404	73	244	8,041	6,324	446	1,271
1977	9,741	2,106	1,754	53	299	7,635	5,970	387	1,278
1978	7,860	2,043	1,729	37	277	5,817	4,440	290	1,087
1979	6,609	1,542	1,297	34	211	5,067	3,662	240	1,165
1980	6,343	1,594	1,337	32	225	4,749	3,450	236	1,063
1981	7,008	1,662	1,385	29	248	5,346	3,757	308	1,281
1982	7,981	1,645	1,360	51	234	6,336	4,798	342	1,196
1983	9,164	1,674	1,393	36	245	7,490	5,774	363	1,353
1984	9,191	1,732	1,421	28	283	7,459	5,793	218	1,448
1985	11,208	1,977	1,609	56	312	9,231	7,511	223	1,497
1986	12,934	2,170	1,811	63	296	10,764	8,888	159	1,717
1987	15,130	2,431	2,047	49	335	12,699	10,655	203	1,841
1988	15,750	2,588	2,168	45	375	13,162	11,044	170	1,948
1989	16,834	2,695	2,299	49	347	14,139	11,686	161	2,292
1990	19,271	3,083	2,610	53	420	16,188	13,067	148	2,973
1991	19,227	2,881	2,444	39	398	16,346	13,554	93	2,699
1992	19,168	2,779	2,323	35	421	16,389	13,577	60	2,752
1993	21,543	2,967	2,534	60	373	18,576	16,018	78	2,480
1994	21,441	2,978	2,592	65	321	18,463	16,276	48	2,139
1995	18,502	2,641	2,358	52	231	15,861	14,345	56	1,460
1996	20,957	2,624	2,376	38	210	18,333	16,620	48	1,665
1997	22,276	2,443	2,224	36	183	19,833	18,315	65	1,453
1998	24,141	2,612	2,371	47	194	21,529	20,042	62	1,425
1999	27,023	2,776	2,567	37	172	24,247	22,936	66	1,245
2000	27,220	2,434	2,210	41	183	24,786	23,630	50	1,106
2001	28,238	2,423	2,212	39	172	25,815	24,852	43	920
2002	29,477	2,351	2,167	41	143	27,126	26,132	53	941
2003	29,457	2,471	2,329	18	124	26,986	25,961	53	972

Note: See Notes, tables 5.9 and 5.22. Data for 1945-91 are reported for the 12-month period ending June 30. Beginning in 1992, data are reported for the Federal fiscal year, which is the 12-month period ending September 30.

[a]From 1968-81 and 1990-2000, defendants who were committed pursuant to 28 U.S.C. 2902 of the Narcotic Addict Rehabilitation Act are included in the dismissed column.

Source: Administrative Office of the United States Courts, *Federal Offenders in the United States District Courts, 1984* (Washington, DC: USGPO, 1986), pp. 42, 43; Administrative Office of the United States Courts, *Federal Offenders in the United States District Courts, 1985* (Washington, DC: Administrative Office of the United States Courts, 1987), pp. 40, 41; Administrative Office of the United States Courts, *Annual Report of the Director, 1997* (Washington, DC: USGPO, 1998), pp. 214-216; Administrative Office of the United States Courts, *Annual Report of the Director, 1998*, pp. 228-230; *1999*, pp. 222-224 (Washington, DC: Administrative Office of the United States Courts); Administrative Office of the United States Courts, *Judicial Business of the United States Courts: 2000 Annual Report of the Director*, pp. 221-223; *2001 Annual Report of the Director*, pp. 211-213; *2002 Annual Report of the Director*, pp. 211-213; *2003 Annual Report of the Director*, pp. 211-213 (Washington, DC: USGPO); and tables provided to SOURCEBOOK staff by the Administrative Office of the United States Courts. Table adapted by SOURCEBOOK staff.

Table 5.38

Defendants sentenced for violation of drug laws in U.S. District Courts

By type and length of sentence, 1945-2003

		Type of sentence									Average sentence to imprisonment (in months)[d]	Average sentence to probation (in months)[e]
		Imprisonment										
		Regular sentences[a]										
	Total	Total regular	1 through 12 months	13 through 35 months	36 through 60 months	Over 60 months	Life sentences	Other[b]	Probation	Fine and other[c]		
1945	861	X	308	360	140	53	NA	X	287	37	22.2	NA
1946	949	X	430	377	108	34	NA	X	369	20	18.7	NA
1947	1,128	X	471	452	161	44	NA	X	504	38	19.7	NA
1948	1,048	X	488	408	122	30	NA	X	411	23	18.6	NA
1949	1,187	X	541	451	152	43	NA	X	398	13	18.9	NA
1950	1,654	X	595	736	218	105	NA	X	471	11	21.9	NA
1951	1,659	X	473	671	328	187	NA	X	345	24	27.1	NA
1952	1,551	X	221	652	402	276	NA	X	312	6	35.2	NA
1953	1,586	X	108	789	358	331	NA	X	403	14	38.4	NA
1954	1,483	X	72	681	360	370	NA	X	411	16	41.3	NA
1955	1,457	X	47	648	360	402	NA	X	329	17	43.5	NA
1956	1,258	X	30	511	341	376	NA	X	250	13	45.8	NA
1957	1,432	X	16	326	248	842	NA	X	220	2	66.0	NA
1958	1,351	X	25	167	141	1,018	NA	X	282	8	69.4	NA
1959	1,151	X	43	126	95	887	NA	X	224	3	74.2	NA
1960	1,232	X	33	145	148	906	NA	X	271	3	72.8	NA
1961	1,258	X	42	126	105	985	NA	X	252	5	74.0	NA
1962	1,173	X	38	129	106	900	NA	X	217	13	70.5	NA
1963	1,085	X	39	144	113	789	NA	X	304	17	70.1	NA
1964	1,076	X	28	142	157	749	NA	X	309	23	63.7	NA
1965	1,257	X	53	186	197	821	NA	X	480	18	60.3	NA
1966	1,272	X	85	154	276	757	NA	X	589	13	61.3	NA
1967	1,180	X	83	139	245	713	NA	X	620	22	62.0	NA
1968	1,368	X	93	141	293	841	NA	X	728	33	64.4	NA
1969	1,581	X	110	179	500	892	NA	X	1,110	18	63.7	NA
1970	1,283	X	101	166	276	740	NA	X	1,156	22	64.8	NA
1971	1,834	X	249	300	428	857	NA	X	1,258	70	58.5	NA
1972	3,050	X	882	396	789	983	NA	X	2,068	130	46.4	NA
1973	5,097	X	1,445	744	1,343	1,565	NA	X	2,591	126	45.5	NA
1974	5,125	X	1,547	792	1,390	1,396	NA	X	3,039	81	43.7	NA
1975	4,887	X	1,366	706	1,441	1,374	NA	X	3,209	55	45.3	NA
1976	5,039	X	1,221	790	1,544	1,484	NA	X	2,927	75	47.6	NA
1977	5,223	X	1,505	886	1,366	1,466	NA	X	2,324	88	47.3	NA
1978	4,119	3,605	885	623	956	1,141	NA	514	1,630	68	51.3	38.6
1979	3,641	2,820	369	614	868	969	NA	821	1,379	47	50.8	37.8
1980	3,479	2,547	281	565	792	909	NA	932	1,232	38	54.5	38.7
1981	3,856	2,865	403	578	748	1,136	NA	991	1,371	119	55.5	36.6
1982	4,586	3,516	383	729	966	1,438	NA	1,070	1,617	133	61.4	34.1
1983	5,449	4,150	447	890	1,011	1,802	NA	1,299	1,893	148	63.8	33.7
1984	5,756	4,306	354	845	1,173	1,934	NA	1,450	1,584	119	65.7	43.2
1985	6,786	5,207	411	1,103	1,459	2,234	NA	1,579	2,039	238	64.8	36.2
1986	8,152	6,601	506	1,271	1,808	3,016	NA	1,551	2,353	259	70.0	38.7
1987	9,907	8,188	613	1,491	2,049	4,035	NA	1,719	2,680	112	73.0	39.9
1988	9,983	8,560	708	1,466	1,577	4,809	NA	1,423	3,042	137	78.0	33.4
1989	11,626	10,838	1,270	2,343	1,844	5,381	NA	788	2,358	155	73.8	32.8
1990	13,838	13,462	1,490	3,047	1,801	7,124	NA	376	2,135	215	79.3	32.3
1991	14,382[f]	14,286	1,687	2,828	3,063	6,708	34	61	1,896	68	95.7	53.4
1992	16,040	15,775	1,810	3,423	3,397	7,145	80	185	2,011	194	87.8	38.7
1993	16,995[f]	16,639	2,097	3,383	4,128	7,031	186	169	1,943	310	83.2	35.8
1994	15,623	15,130	1,836	3,074	3,798	6,422	238	255	1,908	73	84.3	34.4
1995	14,157	13,734	1,606	2,716	3,311	6,101	150	273	1,597	107	88.7	33.6
1996	18,333	16,684	1,643	3,334	4,025	7,113	197	372	1,534	112	82.5	35.0
1997	18,231[f]	17,456	1,687	4,166	4,445	7,158	228	546	1,523	79	79.3	34.9
1998	19,809	19,062	2,100	4,443	4,517	8,002	180	567	1,629	91	78.0	34.9
1999	22,443[f]	21,513	2,670	5,074	5,240	8,529	205	724	1,719	85	74.6	34.2
2000	23,120	22,207	2,523	5,095	5,452	9,137	148	765	1,591	75	75.7	35.1
2001	24,011	23,127	2,780	5,350	5,670	9,327	122	762	1,671	133	73.8	34.5
2002	25,031	23,838	2,825	5,250	5,727	10,036	168	1,025	1,947	148	75.9	33.4
2003	25,060	23,937	2,632	4,781	5,967	10,557	157	966	1,781	145	80.2	32.2

See notes at end of table.

Table 5.38

Defendants sentenced for violation of drug laws in U.S. District Courts

By type and length of sentence, 1945-2003--Continued

Note: See Notes, tables 5.9 and 5.22. Data for 1945-91 are reported for the 12-month period ending June 30. Beginning in 1992, data are reported for the Federal fiscal year, which is the 12-month period ending September 30. Some data have been revised by the Source and may differ from previous editions of SOURCEBOOK.

[a] Includes sentences of more than 6 months that are to be followed by a term of probation (mixed sentences). Beginning in 1991, includes sentences of at least 1 month that may be followed by a term of probation.
[b] From 1978-88, "other" includes split sentences, indeterminate sentences, and Youth Corrections Act and youthful offender sentences. In 1989 and 1990, the category includes split sentences and indeterminate sentences. Beginning in 1991, "other" includes deportation, suspended and sealed sentences, imprisonment of 4 days or less, and no sentence.
[c] Includes supervised release, probation of 4 days or less, suspended sentences, sealed sentences, and no sentence.
[d] From 1978-90, split sentences, Youth Corrections Act and youthful offender sentences, and life sentences are not included in computing average sentence. Beginning in 1991, life sentences, death sentences, deportation, suspended and sealed sentences, imprisonment of 4 days or less, and no sentence also are not included in computing average sentence.
[e] From 1986-90, split sentences, indeterminate sentences, and Youth Corrections Act and youthful offender sentences are not included in computing average sentence. Beginning in 1991, supervised release, probation of 4 days or less, suspended sentences, sealed sentences, and no sentence also are not included in computing the average sentence.
[f] Includes one death sentence.

Source: Administrative Office of the United States Courts, *Federal Offenders in the United States District Courts, 1984* (Washington, DC: USGPO, 1986), pp. 42, 43; Administrative Office of the United States Courts, *Federal Offenders in the United States District Courts, 1985* (Washington, DC: Administrative Office of the United States Courts, 1987), pp. 40, 41; Administrative Office of the United States Courts, *Annual Report of the Director, 1997* (Washington, DC: USGPO, 1998), pp. 217-220; Administrative Office of the United States Courts, *Annual Report of the Director, 1998*, pp. 231-234; *1999*, pp. 225-227 (Washington, DC: Administrative Office of the United States Courts); Administrative Office of the United States Courts, *Judicial Business of the United States Courts: 2000 Annual Report of the Director*, pp. 224-227; *2001 Annual Report of the Director*, pp. 214-217; *2002 Annual Report of the Director*, pp. 214-217; *2003 Annual Report of the Director*, pp. 214-217 (Washington, DC: USGPO); and tables provided to SOURCEBOOK staff by the Administrative Office of the United States Courts. Table adapted by SOURCEBOOK staff.

Table 5.39

Drug offenders sentenced in U.S. District Courts under the U.S. Sentencing Commission guidelines

By offender characteristics, mode of conviction, and drug offense, fiscal year 2002[a]

	Total cases		Powder cocaine		Crack cocaine		Heroin		Marijuana		Methamphetamine[b]		Other	
	Number	Percent	Number	Percent	Number	Percent	Number	Percent	Number	Percent	Number	Percent	Number	Percent
Sex														
Male	22,246	86.7%	5,033	85.7%	4,737	91.5%	1,505	82.8%	6,384	86.3%	3,360	85.3%	1,227	84.5%
Female	3,406	13.3	841	14.3	440	8.5	312	17.2	1,010	13.7	578	14.7	225	15.5
Race, ethnicity														
White	6,886	26.9	1,037	17.7	363	7.0	253	14.0	1,904	25.8	2,369	60.2	960	66.3
Black	7,221	28.2	1,815	30.9	4,203	81.4	409	22.6	597	8.1	42	1.1	155	10.7
Hispanic[c]	10,939	42.7	2,938	50.1	542	10.5	1,114	61.7	4,776	64.7	1,327	33.7	242	16.7
Other[d]	563	2.2	77	1.3	58	1.1	30	1.7	110	1.5	196	5.0	92	6.3
Citizenship														
United States	18,104	70.7	3,802	64.8	4,794	92.7	878	48.4	4,465	60.6	3,015	76.6	1,150	79.4
Non-United States	7,499	29.3	2,066	35.2	376	7.3	936	51.6	2,903	39.4	920	23.4	298	20.6
Mode of conviction														
Guilty plea	22,317	97.2	4,967	96.7	4,403	96.2	1,517	97.9	6,730	98.4	3,456	96.6	1,244	98.4
Trial	633	2.8	172	3.3	175	3.8	33	2.1	112	1.6	121	3.4	20	1.6
Drug offenses														
Drug trafficking	24,842	96.8	5,778	98.3	4,936	95.3	1,769	97.3	7,156	96.7	3,835	97.3	1,368	94.2
Protected locations[e]	318	1.2	30	0.5	177	3.4	21	1.2	31	0.4	39	1.0	20	1.4
Continuing criminal enterprise	37	0.1	12	0.2	5	0.1	1	0.1	12	0.2	5	0.1	2	0.1
Communication facility	26	0.1	9	0.2	8	0.2	2	0.1	2	(f)	4	0.1	1	0.1
Rent/manage drug establishment	67	0.3	7	0.1	18	0.3	7	0.4	9	0.1	23	0.6	3	0.2
Possession	376	1.5	39	0.7	34	0.7	18	1.0	191	2.6	36	0.9	58	4.0

Note: See Note, table 5.26. Of the 64,366 guideline cases, 25,920 were sentenced under drug offense guidelines. Some cases are excluded from the table due to missing information.

[a] Percents may not add to 100 because of rounding.
[b] Includes methamphetamine mixture, methamphetamine actual, ICE, and methamphetamine precursors.
[c] Includes both black and white Hispanics.
[d] Includes Native Americans, Alaskan Natives, Asians, and Pacific Islanders.
[e] Offenses occurring at designated protected locations such as near schools or playgrounds.
[f] Less than 0.05%.

Source: U.S. Sentencing Commission, *2002 Sourcebook of Federal Sentencing Statistics* (Washington, DC: U.S. Sentencing Commission, 2004), pp. 68-71, 73. Table adapted by SOURCEBOOK staff.

Table 5.40

Convictions resulting from arrests by the Drug Enforcement Administration

By type of drug, fiscal years 1992-2003[a]

Fiscal year	Total Number	Total Percent	Heroin[b] Number	Heroin[b] Percent	Cocaine[c] Number	Cocaine[c] Percent	Cannabis[d] Number	Cannabis[d] Percent	Other dangerous drugs[e] Number	Other dangerous drugs[e] Percent
1992	17,308	100%	1,412	8.2%	9,417	54.4%	3,852	22.3%	2,627	15.2%
1993	18,257	100	2,059	11.3	9,580	52.5	4,014	22.0	2,604	14.3
1994	14,760	100	1,358	9.2	7,617	51.6	3,645	24.7	2,140	14.5
1995	14,102	100	1,363	9.7	7,178	50.9	3,340	23.7	2,221	15.7
1996	15,625	100	1,612	10.3	7,442	47.6	3,844	24.6	2,727	17.5
1997	15,765	100	1,596	10.1	7,206	45.7	3,939	25.0	3,024	19.2
1998	18,696	100	1,705	9.1	8,365	44.7	4,449	23.8	4,177	22.3
1999	21,044	100	2,144	10.2	9,398	44.7	4,236	20.1	5,266	25.0
2000	20,917	100	2,209	10.6	9,362	44.8	3,702	17.7	5,644	27.0
2001	21,180	100	1,849	8.7	8,932	42.2	4,281	20.2	6,118	28.9
2002	19,800	100	1,547	7.8	8,052	40.7	3,945	19.9	6,256	31.6
2003	17,296	100	1,371	7.9	7,344	42.5	3,017	17.4	5,564	32.2

Note: Data are reported for the year in which the conviction occurred and may include convictions resulting from arrests made in prior years. Data for all years are revised by the Source as additional information becomes available.

[a]Percents may not add to 100 because of rounding.
[b]Includes morphine, opium, and other opiate-related substances.
[c]Includes crack.
[d]Includes marijuana, hashish, and hashish oil.
[e]Includes stimulants (e.g., methamphetamine), depressants (e.g., barbiturates), and hallucinogens (e.g., LSD and PCP).

Source: Table adapted by SOURCEBOOK staff from table provided by the U.S. Department of Justice, Drug Enforcement Administration, Defendant Statistical System.

Table 5.41

Antitrust cases filed in U.S. District Courts

By type of case, 1975-2003[a]

	Total	U.S. Government cases Number	U.S. Government cases Percent	Private cases Number	Private cases Percent
1975	1,467	92	6.3%	1,375	93.7%
1976	1,574	70	4.4	1,504	95.6
1977	1,689	78	4.6	1,611	95.4
1978	1,507	72	4.8	1,435	95.2
1979	1,312	78	5.9	1,234	94.1
1980	1,535	78	5.1	1,457	94.9
1981	1,434	142	9.9	1,292	90.1
1982	1,148	111	9.7	1,037	90.3
1983	1,287	95	7.4	1,192	92.6
1984	1,201	101	8.4	1,100	91.6
1985	1,142	90	7.9	1,052	92.1
1986	922	84	9.1	838	90.9
1987	858	100	11.6	758	88.4
1988	752	98	13.0	654	87.0
1989	738	99	13.4	639	86.6
1990	542	90	16.6	452	83.4
1991	743	93	12.5	650	87.5
1992	566	85	15.0	481	84.9
1993	724	86	11.9	638	88.1
1994	729	71	9.7	658	90.3
1995	819	75	9.2	744	90.8
1996	720	73	10.1	647	89.9
1997	632	62	9.8	570	90.2
1998	605	57	9.4	548	90.6
1999	684	76	11.1	608	88.9
2000	901	90	10.0	811	90.0
2001	751	44	5.9	707	94.1
2002	850	44	5.2	806	94.8
2003	773	44	5.7	729	94.3

Note: U.S. Government cases include both civil and criminal filings, and include cases where the Government was a plaintiff or a defendant. Data for 1975-91 are reported for the 12-month period ending June 30. Beginning in 1992, data are reported for the Federal fiscal year, which is the 12-month period ending September 30. Data for 1988-91 have been revised by the Source and may differ from previous editions of SOURCEBOOK.

[a]Percents may not add to 100 because of rounding.

Source: Administrative Office of the United States Courts, *Annual Report of the Director, 1985*, p. 156; *1986*, pp. 176, 238; *1995*, pp. 139, 209; *1998*, pp. 143, 212; *1999*, pp. 137, 206 (Washington, DC: Administrative Office of the United States Courts); Administrative Office of the United States Courts, *Annual Report of the Director, 1984*, p. 151; *1987*, pp. 178, 257; *1988*, pp. 181, 260; *1989*, pp. 177, 258; *1990*, pp. 137, 187; *1991*, pp. 190, 243; *1992*, pp. 179, 250; *1993*, pp. A1-55, A53; *1994*, Tables C-2 and D-2; *1996*, pp. 136, 205; *1997*, pp. 129, 198 (Washington, DC: USGPO); and Administrative Office of the United States Courts, *Judicial Business of the United States Courts: 2000 Annual Report of the Director*, pp. 136, 205; *2001 Annual Report of the Director*, pp. 131, 195; *2002 Annual Report of the Director*, pp. 130, 195; *2003 Annual Report of the Director*, pp. 127, 195 (Washington, DC: USGPO). Table adapted by SOURCEBOOK staff.

Table 5.42

Length of civil and criminal trials completed in U.S. District Courts

By circuit and district, fiscal year 2003

Circuit and district	Total number of trials	Civil trials							Criminal trials						
		Total	1 day	2 days	3 days	4 to 9 days	10 to 19 days	20 days and over	Total	1 day	2 days	3 days	4 to 9 days	10 to 19 days	20 days and over
Total	12,948	5,830	2,408	941	686	1,515	241	39	7,118	3,586	1,196	860	1,221	188	67
District of Columbia	221	62	20	14	3	19	4	2	159	65	14	21	50	5	4
First Circuit	451	267	66	40	37	99	23	2	184	70	25	20	50	13	6
Maine	57	24	9	5	3	4	3	0	33	21	5	4	3	0	0
Massachusetts	198	109	17	17	14	49	11	1	89	28	15	9	27	8	2
New Hampshire	32	14	3	1	3	7	0	0	18	9	3	1	5	0	0
Rhode Island	49	39	12	6	4	16	1	0	10	3	0	2	3	2	0
Puerto Rico	115	81	25	11	13	23	8	1	34	9	2	4	12	3	4
Second Circuit	1,147	641	237	99	63	200	32	10	506	178	51	69	163	27	18
Connecticut	136	93	34	12	10	30	5	2	43	12	3	6	14	4	4
New York:															
Northern	79	45	7	11	6	21	0	0	34	14	2	6	7	4	1
Eastern	354	219	103	27	16	56	13	4	135	43	19	29	33	6	5
Southern	471	247	77	44	25	84	13	4	224	69	21	22	96	11	5
Western	68	22	8	3	5	5	1	0	46	23	4	4	10	2	3
Vermont	39	15	8	2	1	4	0	0	24	17	2	2	3	0	0
Third Circuit	927	548	195	96	67	159	28	3	379	187	48	43	77	16	8
Delaware	91	59	21	7	5	23	3	0	32	23	5	3	1	0	0
New Jersey	168	109	35	20	15	28	9	2	59	19	8	4	15	7	6
Pennsylvania:															
Eastern	249	147	36	33	17	53	8	0	102	18	16	21	40	6	1
Middle	230	127	67	15	16	28	1	0	103	83	9	4	4	2	1
Western	161	97	35	17	13	25	6	1	64	37	9	7	11	0	0
Virgin Islands	28	9	1	4	1	2	1	0	19	7	1	4	6	1	0
Fourth Circuit	1,193	385	203	64	39	69	8	2	808	468	148	84	93	11	4
Maryland	210	75	40	8	10	13	3	1	135	67	18	12	34	3	1
North Carolina:															
Eastern	50	10	2	4	1	3	0	0	40	15	12	2	10	1	0
Middle	88	25	12	3	0	9	1	0	63	30	19	10	4	0	0
Western	76	16	10	0	1	5	0	0	60	21	15	12	12	0	0
South Carolina	203	94	50	9	9	24	2	0	109	61	14	22	8	3	1
Virginia:															
Eastern	351	94	44	25	10	12	2	1	257	195	32	13	13	2	2
Western	102	33	22	6	3	2	0	0	69	40	14	5	9	1	0
West Virginia:															
Northern	31	15	9	5	1	0	0	0	16	3	8	4	0	1	0
Southern	82	23	14	4	4	1	0	0	59	36	16	4	3	0	0
Fifth Circuit	1,905	806	420	141	89	148	8	0	1,099	699	206	102	80	9	3
Louisiana:															
Eastern	151	120	47	35	19	19	0	0	31	19	6	1	3	2	0
Middle	97	38	29	3	4	2	0	0	59	55	2	1	1	0	0
Western	89	49	26	12	7	4	0	0	40	14	14	8	4	0	0
Mississippi:															
Northern	68	39	15	12	4	8	0	0	29	15	7	5	2	0	0
Southern	82	51	23	5	9	14	0	0	31	13	11	1	6	0	0
Texas:															
Northern	318	132	66	21	15	26	4	0	186	153	11	5	16	0	1
Eastern	204	111	60	19	7	23	2	0	93	57	13	16	6	0	1
Southern	604	181	112	21	15	33	0	0	423	278	75	36	27	7	0
Western	292	85	42	13	9	19	2	0	207	95	67	29	15	0	1
Sixth Circuit	1,074	483	192	81	63	125	20	2	591	281	112	80	93	20	5
Kentucky:															
Eastern	76	34	7	4	12	10	1	0	42	22	8	3	6	3	0
Western	98	32	15	7	6	3	1	0	66	45	7	5	7	2	0
Michigan:															
Eastern	161	60	11	13	7	26	3	0	101	28	25	17	26	4	1
Western	100	47	27	6	2	10	2	0	53	25	12	6	10	0	0
Ohio:															
Northern	122	73	30	7	11	21	3	1	49	15	8	6	15	4	1
Southern	138	70	34	6	6	20	4	0	68	38	5	9	11	3	2
Tennessee:															
Eastern	103	46	24	10	4	6	1	1	57	35	8	11	1	1	1
Middle	157	79	32	16	13	14	4	0	78	51	9	10	7	1	0
Western	119	42	12	12	2	15	1	0	77	22	30	13	10	2	0

See notes at end of table.

Table 5.42

Length of civil and criminal trials completed in U.S. District Courts

By circuit and district, fiscal year 2003--Continued

Circuit and district	Total number of trials	Civil trials							Criminal trials						
		Total	1 day	2 days	3 days	4 to 9 days	10 to 19 days	20 days and over	Total	1 day	2 days	3 days	4 to 9 days	10 to 19 days	20 days and over
Seventh Circuit	765	393	180	71	45	79	17	1	372	176	62	53	68	12	1
Illinois:															
Northern	254	146	41	26	19	47	12	1	108	29	11	21	37	9	1
Central	83	50	24	11	8	7	0	0	33	18	5	6	4	0	0
Southern	77	38	15	10	3	8	2	0	39	23	3	4	9	0	0
Indiana:															
Northern	114	38	20	8	4	6	0	0	76	52	7	10	5	2	0
Southern	150	84	66	8	4	5	1	0	66	35	20	4	6	1	0
Wisconsin:															
Eastern	47	13	3	2	3	4	1	0	34	9	13	8	4	0	0
Western	40	24	11	6	4	2	1	0	16	10	3	0	3	0	0
Eighth Circuit	947	476	205	86	71	99	12	3	471	188	95	85	94	9	0
Arkansas:															
Eastern	135	90	35	19	16	19	1	0	45	24	5	6	9	1	0
Western	52	43	13	14	9	6	1	0	9	3	3	0	3	0	0
Iowa:															
Northern	81	22	10	3	4	4	1	0	59	28	16	8	7	0	0
Southern	100	15	9	2	0	4	0	0	85	58	7	11	9	0	0
Minnesota	86	50	13	5	6	18	6	2	36	3	2	12	14	5	0
Missouri:															
Eastern	138	90	46	16	12	15	0	1	48	14	12	9	13	0	0
Western	110	74	34	17	6	14	3	0	36	9	12	8	6	1	0
Nebraska	128	55	30	6	9	10	0	0	73	28	8	17	19	1	0
North Dakota	37	11	4	0	4	3	0	0	26	6	8	6	5	1	0
South Dakota	80	26	11	4	5	6	0	0	54	15	22	8	9	0	0
Ninth Circuit	1,832	641	176	98	73	224	59	11	1,191	586	210	127	223	36	9
Alaska	34	13	2	1	2	8	0	0	21	8	2	4	7	0	0
Arizona	189	64	14	11	12	20	6	1	125	52	26	18	24	4	1
California:															
Northern	150	83	17	14	3	32	16	1	67	21	8	4	29	4	1
Eastern	110	39	6	6	3	15	7	2	71	30	17	6	12	4	2
Central	385	204	55	24	26	79	15	5	181	56	25	23	65	11	1
Southern	297	41	13	7	4	12	5	0	256	150	48	28	25	4	1
Hawaii	51	8	1	2	0	4	1	0	43	21	6	3	8	3	2
Idaho	48	14	1	2	2	8	1	0	34	10	6	8	7	3	0
Montana	125	15	6	5	1	3	0	0	110	64	31	9	6	0	0
Nevada	118	55	19	11	6	15	3	1	63	24	17	13	8	1	0
Oregon	150	45	20	8	7	8	2	0	105	81	12	3	9	0	0
Washington:															
Eastern	94	18	11	2	2	2	1	0	76	55	8	2	9	2	0
Western	69	37	10	4	4	16	2	1	32	12	4	5	11	0	0
Guam	7	4	1	1	1	1	0	0	3	1	0	1	1	0	0
Northern Marianas	5	1	0	0	0	1	0	0	4	1	0	0	2	0	1
Tenth Circuit	925	403	141	60	48	142	10	2	522	324	79	57	51	9	2
Colorado	161	88	18	15	9	44	1	1	73	45	7	8	11	1	1
Kansas	198	67	35	6	4	20	1	1	131	102	8	7	11	2	1
New Mexico	143	51	21	5	13	12	0	0	92	62	15	12	3	0	0
Oklahoma:															
Northern	80	48	17	11	6	13	1	0	32	20	4	4	3	1	0
Eastern	41	16	13	1	1	1	0	0	25	18	3	1	2	1	0
Western	101	68	21	10	10	26	1	0	33	13	6	8	5	1	0
Utah	133	37	11	10	4	10	2	0	96	39	34	14	8	1	0
Wyoming	68	28	5	2	1	16	4	0	40	25	2	3	8	2	0
Eleventh Circuit	1,561	725	373	91	88	152	20	1	836	364	146	119	179	21	7
Alabama:															
Northern	147	60	30	10	9	9	2	0	87	59	15	7	5	1	0
Middle	89	49	33	7	3	6	0	0	40	19	7	6	8	0	0
Southern	64	11	3	3	2	3	0	0	53	35	12	4	2	0	0
Florida:															
Northern	149	34	20	7	5	2	0	0	115	84	18	6	7	0	0
Middle	373	220	139	15	16	43	7	0	153	45	34	26	41	4	3
Southern	378	171	61	32	19	53	5	1	207	28	29	50	82	14	4
Georgia:															
Northern	231	112	54	10	16	29	3	0	119	59	17	13	28	2	0
Middle	70	44	22	3	12	4	3	0	26	12	6	5	3	0	0
Southern	60	24	11	4	6	3	0	0	36	23	8	2	3	0	0

Note: This table includes trials conducted by district and appellate judges only. Trials conducted by magistrate judges and sentencing hearings are excluded. Includes trials of miscellaneous cases, hearings on temporary restraining orders and preliminary injunctions, hearings on contested motions, and other contested proceedings in which evidence is introduced.

Source: Administrative Office of the United States Courts, *Judicial Business of the United States Courts: 2003 Annual Report of the Director* (Washington, DC: USGPO, 2004), pp. 165-167.

Table 5.43

Median amount of time from filing to disposition of criminal defendants in U.S. District Courts

By method of disposition, and circuit and district, fiscal year 2003

Circuit and district	Total Number of defendants	Total Median amount of time[a] (in months)	Dismissed Number of defendants	Dismissed Median amount of time[a] (in months)	Plea of guilty Number of defendants	Plea of guilty Median amount of time[a] (in months)	Court (bench) trial Number of defendants	Court (bench) trial Median amount of time[a] (in months)	Jury trial Number of defendants	Jury trial Median amount of time[a] (in months)
Total	83,530	6.2	7,957	6.8	72,110	6.0	620	2.6	2,843	12.3
District of Columbia	515	10.0	46	8.0	428	10.1	1	B	40	13.6
First Circuit	2,078	11.0	162	12.1	1,795	10.7	31	1.5	90	15.9
Maine	196	6.4	15	9.8	169	6.2	2	B	10	10.5
Massachusetts	556	14.2	25	21.8	493	13.0	8	B	30	15.9
New Hampshire	208	8.4	17	7.1	186	8.5	0	X	5	B
Rhode Island	127	6.3	7	B	113	6.3	0	X	7	B
Puerto Rico	991	12.2	98	13.9	834	12.1	21	1.2	38	17.6
Second Circuit	5,403	10.7	216	12.2	4,901	10.3	16	14.9	270	17.9
Connecticut	439	9.4	41	12.2	375	9.1	2	B	21	18.1
New York:										
Northern	417	8.8	9	B	390	8.4	1	B	17	13.9
Eastern	1,907	10.7	38	19.7	1,798	10.3	4	B	67	16.8
Southern	1,903	11.5	76	11.6	1,677	11.0	7	B	143	18.5
Western	525	9.1	23	25.2	485	8.1	2	B	15	27.7
Vermont	212	11.0	29	4.8	176	11.5	0	X	7	B
Third Circuit	3,408	8.9	358	8.0	2,870	8.6	10	8.8	170	14.7
Delaware	168	8.0	17	6.0	141	7.8	0	X	10	11.6
New Jersey	1,038	7.9	120	3.0	870	7.9	2	B	46	21.2
Pennsylvania:										
Eastern	1,079	10.5	68	37.1	929	10.0	3	B	79	14.7
Middle	371	10.7	29	7.7	326	10.5	0	X	16	17.6
Western	444	7.8	51	5.2	385	8.2	0	X	8	B
Virgin Islands	308	1.6	73	20.2	219	0.4	5	B	11	14.6
Fourth Circuit	9,276	5.8	1,757	3.5	7,043	5.9	129	2.6	347	10.2
Maryland	1,316	5.1	457	2.4	784	6.9	23	3.3	52	14.4
North Carolina:										
Eastern	1,055	6.8	230	25.1	790	6.4	8	B	27	10.7
Middle	392	5.2	27	5.8	335	5.0	1	B	29	6.5
Western	734	14.7	98	27.8	589	13.9	0	X	47	20.4
South Carolina	1,227	8.4	149	8.7	1,044	8.3	3	B	31	10.2
Virginia:										
Eastern	3,295	3.5	716	1.9	2,410	3.8	90	2.0	79	7.2
Western	622	8.3	41	9.3	530	8.2	2	B	49	9.7
West Virginia:										
Northern	288	6.2	19	9.9	257	6.2	1	B	11	9.6
Southern	347	6.0	20	3.2	304	6.0	1	B	22	8.2
Fifth Circuit	15,065	5.1	1,001	5.6	13,714	5.0	47	8.7	303	9.0
Louisiana:										
Eastern	568	6.5	28	5.6	530	6.4	1	B	9	B
Middle	167	5.9	14	1.4	148	6.2	2	B	3	B
Western	449	7.3	60	5.9	370	7.3	0	X	19	11.1
Mississippi:										
Northern	183	6.9	9	B	157	6.4	0	X	17	10.7
Southern	532	6.3	55	12.2	459	6.2	1	B	17	9.1
Texas:										
Northern	1,277	5.8	111	6.3	1,129	5.8	4	B	33	7.7
Eastern	716	7.5	66	5.6	614	7.4	2	B	34	10.6
Southern	5,516	4.5	341	4.4	5,060	4.5	24	8.7	91	8.4
Western	5,657	4.9	317	5.9	5,247	4.8	13	6.9	80	7.8
Sixth Circuit	5,799	7.4	665	7.7	4,870	7.2	25	5.9	239	11.3
Kentucky:										
Eastern	552	6.4	48	6.3	469	6.4	3	B	32	11.0
Western	742	6.1	206	7.2	515	5.9	8	B	13	9.0
Michigan:										
Eastern	860	9.8	110	11.9	689	9.4	3	B	58	13.1
Western	483	6.6	32	9.0	416	6.4	1	B	34	9.8
Ohio:										
Northern	963	6.6	43	9.9	901	6.5	3	B	16	11.3
Southern	568	7.1	26	15.0	521	7.1	3	B	18	12.1
Tennessee:										
Eastern	733	6.3	83	5.2	620	6.4	2	B	28	12.5
Middle	288	10.3	24	7.4	244	10.0	0	X	20	13.7
Western	610	8.8	93	7.6	495	8.7	2	B	20	11.0

See notes at end of table.

Table 5.43
Median amount of time from filing to disposition of criminal defendants in U.S. District Courts

By method of disposition, and circuit and district, fiscal year 2003--Continued

Circuit and district	Total Number of defendants	Total Median amount of time[a] (in months)	Dismissed Number of defendants	Dismissed Median amount of time[a] (in months)	Plea of guilty Number of defendants	Plea of guilty Median amount of time[a] (in months)	Court (bench) trial Number of defendants	Court (bench) trial Median amount of time[a] (in months)	Jury trial Number of defendants	Jury trial Median amount of time[a] (in months)
Seventh Circuit	3,430	8.0	230	9.4	3,020	7.7	11	11.0	169	15.1
Illinois:										
Northern	1,346	9.6	78	22.6	1,205	9.1	1	B	62	19.0
Central	473	7.8	51	3.5	407	7.9	1	B	14	15.4
Southern	384	6.8	22	4.1	355	6.8	0	X	7	B
Indiana:										
Northern	440	8.2	40	13.0	367	7.7	2	B	31	15.4
Southern	296	7.8	20	13.0	251	7.4	2	B	23	12.0
Wisconsin:										
Eastern	307	7.5	10	6.1	272	7.4	2	B	23	10.3
Western	184	5.7	9	B	163	5.6	3	B	9	B
Eighth Circuit	4,925	7.3	282	5.9	4,358	7.2	16	12.0	269	10.8
Arkansas:										
Eastern	290	9.4	26	7.9	245	9.2	0	X	19	19.7
Western	202	5.6	2	B	193	5.5	0	X	7	B
Iowa:										
Northern	442	8.9	18	6.5	381	8.7	1	B	42	13.2
Southern	432	7.8	14	4.6	385	7.7	1	B	32	10.7
Minnesota	516	7.8	23	7.0	449	7.6	4	B	40	10.7
Missouri:										
Eastern	896	5.9	63	4.5	805	5.9	4	B	24	8.1
Western	735	8.8	31	5.5	677	8.6	3	B	24	15.4
Nebraska	767	7.7	53	7.3	680	7.6	1	B	33	10.8
North Dakota	260	5.5	16	5.1	223	5.1	1	B	20	9.1
South Dakota	385	5.9	36	5.6	320	5.9	1	B	28	8.3
Ninth Circuit	18,564	5.4	1,985	11.8	16,138	5.1	59	4.6	382	14.3
Alaska	236	5.0	52	2.6	165	5.2	3	B	16	7.7
Arizona	5,196	4.3	212	8.5	4,950	4.3	5	B	29	14.0
California:										
Northern	876	10.6	111	23.1	717	9.6	9	B	39	22.9
Eastern	1,138	8.2	95	15.3	1,023	7.9	2	B	18	21.0
Central	1,990	9.1	134	10.9	1,770	8.6	5	B	81	20.8
Southern	3,816	3.2	143	3.3	3,631	3.2	3	B	39	9.1
Hawaii	994	19.5	524	69.8	453	8.2	3	B	14	15.7
Idaho	329	7.1	42	5.8	268	7.1	0	X	19	9.8
Montana	473	6.9	107	2.7	326	7.3	6	B	34	10.9
Nevada	815	7.6	106	13.4	676	7.4	2	B	31	10.0
Oregon	842	8.5	88	8.9	725	8.2	3	B	26	19.7
Washington:										
Eastern	467	7.3	73	5.4	376	7.5	3	B	15	8.4
Western	1,265	4.7	280	4.6	961	4.7	14	4.6	10	8.8
Guam	98	10.5	13	3.6	81	11.5	0	X	4	B
Northern Marianas	29	6.7	5	B	16	5.2	1	B	7	B
Tenth Circuit	6,302	5.0	644	5.2	5,506	4.9	16	8.9	136	13.5
Colorado	743	7.0	103	5.2	613	7.0	2	B	25	20.1
Kansas	626	7.5	46	4.9	555	7.5	7	B	18	13.8
New Mexico	2,534	3.4	137	15.5	2,374	3.3	0	X	23	16.9
Oklahoma:										
Northern	222	8.6	47	39.0	164	7.9	0	X	11	13.1
Eastern	101	4.6	13	1.5	85	4.9	0	X	3	B
Western	820	1.4	148	0.9	646	1.6	2	B	24	9.9
Utah	1,029	6.1	137	12.3	871	5.7	5	B	16	24.2
Wyoming	227	5.8	13	5.3	198	5.6	0	X	16	7.4
Eleventh Circuit	8,765	5.9	611	6.8	7,467	5.8	259	0.1	428	10.0
Alabama:										
Northern	651	5.8	105	2.9	500	5.9	12	0.8	34	7.2
Middle	254	6.8	31	5.1	191	6.6	2	B	30	10.2
Southern	342	6.6	15	9.1	301	6.4	3	B	23	7.7
Florida:										
Northern	646	4.8	34	2.0	576	4.7	9	B	27	8.1
Middle	1,650	7.0	54	9.4	1,488	6.8	5	B	103	9.9
Southern	2,546	6.2	101	8.1	2,271	5.9	21	15.2	153	13.5
Georgia:										
Northern	978	7.1	119	18.0	822	6.5	6	B	31	10.9
Middle	1,225	0.1	90	4.4	916	0.1	201	0.1	18	10.8
Southern	473	5.0	62	5.3	402	4.9	0	X	9	B

Note: See Note, table 5.24. The median is the number that marks the point below which and above which 50% of all cases fall.

Source: Administrative Office of the United States Courts, *Judicial Business of the United States Courts: 2003 Annual Report of the Director* (Washington, DC: USGPO, 2004), pp. 218-220.

[a] Computed on 10 or more defendants only.

Table 5.44

Felony convictions in State courts

By offense, United States, 2000[a]

Most serious conviction offense	Felony convictions Number	Percent
All offenses	924,700	100%
Violent offenses	173,200	18.7
Murder, nonnegligent manslaughter[b]	8,600	0.9
Murder	6,400	0.7
Nonnegligent manslaughter	2,100	0.2
Sexual assault, rape	31,500	3.4
Rape	10,600	1.1
Other sexual assault	20,900	2.3
Robbery	36,800	4.0
Armed	10,400	1.1
Unarmed	11,000	1.2
Unspecified	15,300	1.7
Aggravated assault	79,400	8.6
Other violent[c]	17,000	1.8
Property offenses	262,000	28.3
Burglary	79,300	8.6
Residential	10,900	1.2
Nonresidential	16,300	1.8
Unspecified	52,100	5.6
Larceny	100,000	10.8
Motor vehicle theft	11,900	1.3
Other theft[d]	88,100	9.5
Fraud, forgery, embezzlement	82,700	8.9
Fraud, embezzlement	40,500	4.4
Forgery	42,200	4.6
Drug offenses	319,700	34.6
Possession	116,300	12.6
Trafficking	203,400	22.0
Marijuana	25,300	2.7
Other	54,400	5.9
Unspecified	123,700	13.4
Weapons offenses	28,200	3.1
Other offenses[e]	141,600	15.3

Note: These data are from the National Judicial Reporting Program (NJRP), a biennial survey of State felony courts. Data were collected for the U.S. Department of Justice, Bureau of Justice Statistics by the U.S. Census Bureau. The 2000 NJRP survey was based on a sample of 344 counties selected to be nationally representative. The sample included the District of Columbia and at least one county from every State except, by chance, Delaware, Montana, and Wyoming. Only offenses that State penal codes define as felonies are included. Excluded are Federal courts and State or local courts that did not adjudicate adult felony cases. Data specifying the conviction offense were available for the estimated total of 924,700 convicted felons. These data are estimates derived from a sample and therefore are subject to sampling variation.

For survey sampling procedures and definitions of terms, see Appendix 12.

[a] Detail may not add to total because of rounding.
[b] In a small number of cases where it was unclear whether the offense was murder or manslaughter, the case was classified under nonnegligent manslaughter.
[c] Includes offenses such as negligent manslaughter and kidnaping.
[d] When vehicle theft could not be distinguished from other theft, the case was coded as other theft. This results in a conservative estimate of vehicle thefts.
[e] Composed of nonviolent offenses such as receiving stolen property and vandalism.

Source: U.S. Department of Justice, Bureau of Justice Statistics, *Felony Sentences in State Courts, 2000*, Bulletin NCJ 198821 (Washington, DC: U.S. Department of Justice, June 2003), p. 2, Table 1.

Table 5.45
Characteristics of felony offenders convicted in State courts

By offense, United States, 2000[a]

		Sex		Race			Age						Mean	Median
Most serious conviction offense	Total	Male	Female	White	Black	Other	Under 20 years	20 to 29 years	30 to 39 years	40 to 49 years	50 to 59 years	60 years and older	(in years)	(in years)
All offenses	100%	83%	17%	54%	44%	2%	8%	39%	30%	18%	4%	1%	32	30
Violent offenses	100	90	10	53	44	3	10	42	27	15	4	2	31	29
Murder, nonnegligent manslaughter	100	91	9	43	54	3	9	49	23	13	4	2	30	27
Sexual assault, rape	100	98	2	68	28	4	7	35	29	18	7	4	34	32
Rape	100	98	2	64	35	1	8	34	30	17	7	4	34	32
Other sexual assault	100	98	2	70	25	5	7	35	29	18	7	4	34	32
Robbery	100	93	7	35	64	1	21	50	20	8	1	(b)	26	23
Aggravated assault	100	86	14	55	42	3	8	41	29	16	5	1	32	30
Other violent[c]	100	89	11	67	31	2	7	37	31	19	5	1	33	32
Property offenses	100	75	25	59	39	2	9	40	30	17	3	1	31	30
Burglary	100	92	8	62	36	2	17	43	25	13	2	(b)	28	26
Larceny, motor vehicle theft	100	75	25	58	40	2	8	38	31	18	4	1	32	31
Motor vehicle theft	100	90	10	63	32	5	13	48	27	10	2	(b)	28	26
Fraud, forgery, embezzlement	100	59	41	58	40	2	3	39	35	18	4	1	33	32
Drug offenses	100	83	17	46	53	1	6	40	30	19	4	1	32	31
Possession	100	81	19	49	50	1	4	34	33	23	5	1	33	33
Trafficking	100	84	16	44	55	1	6	43	28	18	4	1	31	30
Weapons offenses	100	95	5	44	54	2	10	47	23	14	4	2	31	28
Other offenses[d]	100	88	12	66	32	2	6	34	33	20	6	1	33	33

Note: See Note, table 5.44. Data on sex were available for 712,835 of the estimated total of 924,700 convicted felons; figures on race for 618,843; and figures on age for 765,902. For survey sampling procedures and definitions of terms, see Appendix 12.

Source: U.S. Department of Justice, Bureau of Justice Statistics, *Felony Sentences in State Courts, 2000*, Bulletin NCJ 198821 (Washington, DC: U.S. Department of Justice, June 2003), p. 6. Table adapted by SOURCEBOOK staff.

[a]Detail may not add to total because of rounding.
[b]Less than 0.5%.
[c]Includes offenses such as negligent manslaughter and kidnaping.
[d]Composed of nonviolent offenses such as receiving stolen property and vandalism.

Table 5.46
Felony convictions in State courts

By offense and method of conviction, United States, 2000[a]

	Trial						Guilty plea	
	Total		Jury		Bench			
Most serious conviction offense	Number	Percent	Number	Percent	Number	Percent	Number	Percent
All offenses	45,700	5%	29,300	3%	16,400	2%	879,200	95%
Violent offenses	19,700	11	15,300	9	4,400	2	153,500	89
Murder, nonnegligent manslaughter	3,600	42	3,200	38	400	4	5,000	58
Sexual assault, rape	3,700	12	3,100	10	600	2	27,800	88
Rape	2,100	19	1,700	16	400	3	8,600	81
Other sexual assault	1,700	8	1,400	7	300	1	19,300	92
Robbery	4,100	11	3,100	8	1,100	3	32,700	89
Aggravated assault	6,800	9	4,700	6	2,100	3	72,600	91
Other violent[b]	1,500	9	1,200	7	300	2	15,500	91
Property offenses	7,000	3	3,700	2	3,300	1	255,000	97
Burglary	2,800	3	1,800	2	1,000	1	76,500	97
Larceny, motor vehicle theft	2,600	3	1,300	2	1,300	1	97,400	97
Motor vehicle theft	300	2	200	1	100	1	11,700	98
Fraud, forgery, embezzlement	1,700	2	700	1	1,100	1	81,100	98
Drug offenses	12,000	4	6,300	2	5,800	2	307,400	96
Possession	3,300	3	1,400	1	1,900	2	112,700	97
Trafficking	8,700	4	4,800	2	3,900	2	194,700	96
Weapons offenses	2,100	7	1,000	3	1,100	4	26,100	93
Other offenses[c]	4,800	3	3,000	2	1,800	1	137,200	97

Note: See Note, table 5.44. Data on type of conviction were available for 558,871 of the estimated total of 924,700 convicted felons. However, figures include estimates for cases missing a designation on method of conviction. For survey sampling procedures and definitions of terms, see Appendix 12.

[c]Composed of nonviolent offenses such as receiving stolen property and vandalism.

Source: U.S. Department of Justice, Bureau of Justice Statistics, *Felony Sentences in State Courts, 2000*, Bulletin NCJ 198821 (Washington, DC: U.S. Department of Justice, June 2003), p. 8, Table 9; p. 9, Table 10. Table adapted by SOURCEBOOK staff.

[a]Detail may not add to total because of rounding.
[b]Includes offenses such as negligent manslaughter and kidnaping.

Table 5.47

Felony sentences imposed by State courts

By offense, United States, 2000[a]

Most serious conviction offense	Total	Percent of felons sentenced to:			
		Incarceration			Probation
		Total	Prison	Jail	
All offenses	100%	68%	40%	28%	32%
Violent offenses	100	78	54	24	22
Murder, nonnegligent manslaughter	100	95	93	2	5
Sexual assault, rape	100	84	64	20	16
Rape	100	90	70	20	10
Other sexual assault	100	80	60	20	20
Robbery	100	89	74	15	11
Aggravated assault	100	71	40	31	29
Other violent[b]	100	71	42	29	29
Property offenses	100	64	37	27	36
Burglary	100	76	52	24	24
Larceny, motor vehicle theft	100	63	33	30	37
Motor vehicle theft	100	73	41	32	27
Fraud, forgery, embezzlement	100	54	29	25	46
Drug offenses	100	67	38	29	33
Possession	100	64	33	31	36
Trafficking	100	69	41	28	31
Weapons offenses	100	70	41	29	30
Other offenses[c]	100	66	32	34	34

Note: See Note, table 5.44. Data on sentence type were available for 919,387 of the estimated total of 924,700 convicted felons. For persons receiving a combination of sentences, the sentence designation came from the most serious penalty imposed--prison being the most serious, followed by jail, then probation. "Prison" includes sentences to death. Felons receiving a sentence other than incarceration or probation are included in "probation." For survey sampling procedures and definitions of terms, see Appendix 12.

[a] Detail may not add to total because of rounding.
[b] Includes offenses such as negligent manslaughter and kidnaping.
[c] Composed of nonviolent offenses such as receiving stolen property and vandalism.

Source: U.S. Department of Justice, Bureau of Justice Statistics, *Felony Sentences in State Courts, 2000*, Bulletin NCJ 198821 (Washington, DC: U.S. Department of Justice, June 2003), p. 2, Table 2.

Table 5.48

Mean and median maximum length of felony sentences imposed by State courts

By offense, United States, 2000

(In months)

Most serious conviction offense	Maximum sentence length for felons sentenced to:			
	Incarceration			Probation
	Total	Prison	Jail	
Mean sentence				
All offenses	36	55	6	38
Violent offenses	66	91	7	44
Murder, nonnegligent manslaughter	242	248	18	64
Sexual assault, rape	87	108	8	64
Rape	110	136	8	79
Other sexual assault	73	92	8	61
Robbery	82	94	11	52
Aggravated assault	37	59	6	40
Other violent[a]	33	50	7	36
Property offenses	27	42	6	38
Burglary	39	52	7	41
Larceny, motor vehicle theft	21	34	6	37
Motor vehicle theft	18	27	5	37
Fraud, forgery, embezzlement	21	34	6	37
Drug offenses	30	47	6	36
Possession	20	34	5	33
Trafficking	35	52	7	39
Weapons offenses	25	38	7	36
Other offenses[b]	22	38	6	40
Median sentence				
All offenses	16	36	5	36
Violent offenses	36	60	6	36
Murder, nonnegligent manslaughter	264	291	12	60
Sexual assault, rape	48	70	6	60
Rape	72	96	6	60
Other sexual assault	36	60	6	60
Robbery	60	61	10	48
Aggravated assault	16	36	5	36
Other violent[a]	16	34	5	36
Property offenses	12	27	5	36
Burglary	24	36	6	36
Larceny, motor vehicle theft	12	24	5	36
Motor vehicle theft	12	24	4	36
Fraud, forgery, embezzlement	12	24	4	36
Drug offenses	12	36	5	36
Possession	10	24	3	24
Trafficking	18	36	6	36
Weapons offenses	16	24	6	36
Other offenses[b]	12	24	4	36

Note: See Notes, tables 5.44 and 5.47. Means exclude sentences to death or to life in prison. The median sentence is the sentence length that marks the point below which and above which 50% of all sentence lengths fall. Sentence length data were available for 852,616 convicted felons sentenced to incarceration and probation. For survey sampling procedures and definitions of terms, see Appendix 12.

[a] Includes offenses such as negligent manslaughter and kidnaping.
[b] Composed of nonviolent offenses such as receiving stolen property and vandalism.

Source: U.S. Department of Justice, Bureau of Justice Statistics, *Felony Sentences in State Courts, 2000*, Bulletin NCJ 198821 (Washington, DC: U.S. Department of Justice, June 2003), p. 4.

Table 5.49

Felons sentenced to additional penalties by State courts

By offense and type of penalty, United States, 2000

Most serious conviction offense	Fine	Restitution	Treatment[a]	Community service	Other
All offenses	25%	14%	7%	5%	7%
Violent offenses	20	13	7	4	7
Murder, nonnegligent manslaughter	9	11	3	1	3
Sexual assault, rape	19	11	9	3	8
Rape	14	10	8	2	8
Other sexual assault	22	11	9	4	8
Robbery	13	13	3	3	4
Aggravated assault	22	13	8	6	10
Other violent[b]	36	15	6	5	4
Property offenses	24	26	7	6	7
Burglary	21	24	6	5	6
Larceny, motor vehicle theft	24	25	6	7	9
Motor vehicle theft	19	27	5	5	19
Fraud, forgery, embezzlement	27	31	8	6	7
Drug offenses	27	6	7	6	7
Possession	20	4	12	7	12
Trafficking	31	6	5	5	4
Weapons offenses	19	6	4	5	8
Other offenses[c]	27	10	7	6	9

Note: See Note, table 5.44. Additional penalties are penalties imposed in addition to the primary penalty of jail, prison, or probation. Examples of penalties in the category "other" are community control, house arrest, work release, drug testing, and loss of driver's license. Where the data indicated affirmatively that a particular additional penalty was imposed, the case was coded accordingly. Where the data did not indicate affirmatively or negatively, the case was treated as not having an additional penalty. These procedures provide a conservative estimate of the prevalence of additional penalties. Persons receiving more than one type of additional penalty appear under more than one penalty heading. For survey sampling procedures and definitions of terms, see Appendix 12.

[a]Includes any type of counseling, rehabilitation, treatment, or mental hospital confinement.
[b]Includes offenses such as negligent manslaughter and kidnaping.
[c]Composed of nonviolent offenses such as receiving stolen property and vandalism.

Source: U.S. Department of Justice, Bureau of Justice Statistics, *Felony Sentences in State Courts, 2000*, Bulletin NCJ 198821 (Washington, DC: U.S. Department of Justice, June 2003), p. 10.

Table 5.50

Time between arrest and sentencing for felons convicted in State courts

By offense, United States, 2000

Most serious conviction offense	Median time (in days)	Cumulative percent sentenced within:				
		1 week	1 month	3 months	6 months	1 year
All offenses	153	2%	9%	30%	58%	86%
Violent offenses	186	1	5	22	48	81
Murder, nonnegligent manslaughter	369	(b)	1	3	13	50
Sexual assault, rape	220	1	2	13	39	79
Rape	219	1	3	14	41	78
Other sexual assault	220	1	2	12	37	79
Robbery	197	1	4	19	46	82
Aggravated assault	163	2	8	27	55	84
Other violent[a]	155	2	6	27	57	85
Property offenses	142	2	9	31	62	88
Burglary	145	1	9	30	61	87
Larceny, motor vehicle theft	134	2	11	35	64	88
Motor vehicle theft	90	3	16	50	78	93
Fraud, forgery, embezzlement	153	2	7	27	59	88
Drug offenses	145	2	11	34	59	86
Possession	118	4	18	42	65	89
Trafficking	158	1	8	30	56	85
Weapons offenses	151	1	9	31	58	86
Other offenses[b]	153	2	8	28	58	88

Note: See Note, table 5.44. The median marks the point below which and above which 50% of all cases fall. Data on time to dispose of felonies were available for 434,047 of the estimated total of 924,700 convicted felons. For survey sampling procedures and definitions of terms, see Appendix 12.

[a]Includes offenses such as negligent manslaughter and kidnaping.
[b]Composed of nonviolent offenses such as receiving stolen property and vandalism.

Source: U.S. Department of Justice, Bureau of Justice Statistics, **Felony Sentences in State Courts, 2000**, Bulletin NCJ 198821 (Washington, DC: U.S. Department of Justice, June 2003), p. 9, Table 11.

Table 5.51

Arrest offense of felony defendants in the 75 largest counties

United States, 2000[a]

Most serious arrest charge	Felony defendants	
	Number	Percent
All offenses	54,428	100%
Violent offenses	13,546	24.9
Murder	485	0.9
Rape	886	1.6
Robbery	2,930	5.4
Assault	6,607	12.1
Other violent	2,638	4.8
Property offenses	16,083	29.5
Burglary	3,983	7.3
Larceny/theft	4,473	8.2
Motor vehicle theft	1,623	3.0
Forgery	1,819	3.3
Fraud	2,121	3.9
Other property	2,064	3.8
Drug offenses	20,038	36.8
Trafficking	9,360	17.2
Other drug	10,678	19.6
Public-order offenses	4,761	8.7
Weapons	1,418	2.6
Driving-related	1,617	3.0
Other public-order	1,726	3.2

Note: These data were collected by the Pretrial Services Resource Center for the U.S. Department of Justice, Bureau of Justice Statistics as part of the State Court Processing Statistics program. The data are based on 40 of the 75 most populous counties in the United States and a sample of 14,877 felony cases collected from the 40 sampled counties. These cases represent the estimated 54,590 felony cases filed in the 75 counties in May 2000, and the felony defendants involved in these cases. The sample was designed and selected by the U.S. Census Bureau. These data are estimates derived from a sample and therefore are subject to sampling variation.

Data for the specific arrest charge were available for all cases. For methodology, definitions of terms, and crimes within offense categories, see Appendix 13.

[a]Detail may not add to total because of rounding.

Source: U.S. Department of Justice, Bureau of Justice Statistics, **Felony Defendants in Large Urban Counties, 2000**, NCJ 202021 (Washington, DC: U.S. Department of Justice, 2003), p. 2, Table 1.

Table 5.52

Characteristics of felony defendants in the 75 largest counties

By arrest charge, United States, 2000[a]

	Sex			Race, ethnicity					Age							
Most serious arrest charge	Number of defendants	Male	Female	Number of defendants	White, non-Hispanic	Black, non-Hispanic	Other, non-Hispanic	Hispanic, any race	Number of defendants	Under 18 years	18 to 20 years	21 to 24 years	25 to 29 years	30 to 34 years	35 to 39 years	40 years and older
All offenses	54,337	81%	19%	53,522	30%	45%	2%	23%	54,249	3%	15%	16%	16%	15%	14%	21%
Violent offenses	13,518	85	15	13,362	26	46	2	26	13,487	5	16	18	16	13	13	19
Murder	485	96	4	478	21	50	2	27	485	10	17	18	20	13	10	13
Rape	886	99	1	886	32	40	3	25	886	1	18	16	15	15	14	21
Robbery	2,930	91	9	2,906	14	61	2	23	2,927	13	25	18	14	11	9	10
Assault	6,590	81	19	6,530	27	45	2	26	6,578	3	13	18	16	14	14	21
Other violent	2,627	82	18	2,563	35	33	3	29	2,612	1	12	16	17	13	16	26
Property offenses	16,052	75	25	15,557	34	45	3	18	16,038	3	17	15	17	15	14	19
Burglary	3,979	88	12	3,951	34	40	3	23	3,973	4	22	16	15	13	13	17
Larceny/theft	4,463	74	26	4,425	35	47	3	15	4,466	2	17	14	14	14	15	24
Motor vehicle theft	1,623	88	12	1,604	27	36	5	31	1,619	3	21	20	19	14	13	11
Forgery	1,819	63	37	1,796	42	43	2	14	1,812	2	14	16	19	18	15	17
Fraud	2,108	45	55	1,753	36	48	3	13	2,113	1	5	11	21	21	16	25
Other property	2,060	83	17	2,029	33	52	2	13	2,055	4	21	15	17	13	12	18
Drug offenses	20,022	81	19	19,899	27	47	2	24	19,977	2	14	15	16	15	15	22
Trafficking	9,350	83	17	9,299	21	52	2	25	9,316	3	17	17	17	15	13	18
Other drug	10,672	79	21	10,600	33	42	2	23	10,661	1	10	13	15	16	17	26
Public-order offenses	4,745	90	10	4,704	33	40	3	24	4,747	2	10	16	17	13	17	25
Weapons	1,410	93	7	1,404	17	56	2	25	1,411	5	20	22	19	11	11	12
Driving-related	1,613	92	8	1,594	48	28	3	21	1,613	(b)	4	10	17	14	23	32
Other public-order	1,722	85	15	1,706	32	39	2	27	1,724	1	8	15	16	14	15	30

Note: See Note, table 5.51. Data on sex of defendants were available for 99.8% of all cases; data on race, 98%; and data on age, 99.6%. U.S. Census Bureau data for 2000 indicate that the distribution of the population of the 75 largest counties was 58% white, non-Hispanic; 14% black, non-Hispanic; 9% other race, non-Hispanic; and 19% Hispanics of any race. For methodology, definitions of terms, and crimes within offense categories, see Appendix 13.

[a]Detail may not add to total because of rounding.
[b]Less than 0.5%.

Source: U.S. Department of Justice, Bureau of Justice Statistics, *Felony Defendants in Large Urban Counties, 2000*, NCJ 202021 (Washington, DC: U.S. Department of Justice, 2003), p. 4, Table 3 and p. 5, Tables 4 and 5. Table adapted by SOURCEBOOK staff.

Table 5.53

Prior felony convictions of felony defendants in the 75 largest counties

By arrest charge, United States, 2000[a]

		Percent of felony defendants								
			Without prior felony conviction			With prior felony conviction				
				Nonfelony	No prior		Number of prior felony convictions			
Most serious current arrest charge	Number of defendants	Total	Total	only	convictions	Total	1	2 to 4	5 to 9	10 or more
All offenses	52,178	100%	60%	18%	42%	40%	15%	18%	5%	1%
Violent offenses	13,049	100	67	19	48	33	13	15	4	1
Murder	473	100	66	13	53	34	16	15	3	0
Rape	861	100	74	21	53	26	13	8	4	1
Robbery	2,841	100	60	13	47	40	14	19	6	2
Assault	6,375	100	67	21	46	33	14	15	4	1
Other violent	2,499	100	73	20	53	27	12	14	2	0
Property offenses	15,240	100	61	16	45	39	15	16	6	1
Burglary	3,816	100	53	18	35	47	17	19	9	2
Larceny/theft	4,342	100	62	17	45	38	14	17	5	1
Motor vehicle theft	1,551	100	52	15	37	48	18	20	8	1
Forgery	1,737	100	66	17	49	34	13	14	5	1
Fraud	1,884	100	79	14	65	21	10	8	2	1
Other property	1,910	100	63	18	45	37	14	15	5	2
Drug offenses	19,315	100	56	18	38	44	16	21	6	1
Trafficking	9,061	100	56	17	39	44	16	21	5	1
Other drug	10,254	100	56	20	36	44	17	20	6	1
Public-order offenses	4,574	100	54	21	33	46	17	23	5	1
Weapons	1,358	100	57	13	44	43	15	23	5	0
Driving-related	1,568	100	56	33	23	44	16	22	5	1
Other public-order	1,649	100	50	16	34	50	19	24	6	1

Note: See Note, table 5.51. Data on number of prior felony convictions were available for 96% of all cases. For methodology, definitions of terms, and crimes within offense categories, see Appendix 13.

Source: U.S. Department of Justice, Bureau of Justice Statistics, *Felony Defendants in Large Urban Counties, 2000*, NCJ 202021 (Washington, DC: U.S. Department of Justice, 2003), p. 13.

[a]Detail may not add to total because of rounding.

Table 5.54

Felony defendants released before or detained until case disposition in the 75 largest counties

By arrest charge, United States, 2000[a]

Most serious arrest charge	Number of defendants	Percent of felony defendants Total	Released before case disposition	Detained until case disposition
All offenses	52,448	100%	62%	38%
Violent offenses	13,054	100	56	44
Murder	474	100	13	87
Rape	852	100	56	44
Robbery	2,863	100	44	56
Assault	6,333	100	61	39
Other violent	2,533	100	65	35
Property offenses	15,368	100	64	36
Burglary	3,885	100	49	51
Larceny/theft	4,300	100	68	32
Motor vehicle theft	1,598	100	46	54
Forgery	1,714	100	72	28
Fraud	1,956	100	85	15
Other property	1,915	100	71	29
Drug offenses	19,467	100	64	36
Trafficking	9,104	100	62	38
Other drug	10,363	100	66	34
Public-order offenses	4,559	100	66	34
Weapons	1,356	100	70	30
Driving-related	1,577	100	75	25
Other public-order	1,626	100	54	46

Note: See Note, table 5.51. Data on detention/release outcome were available for 96% of all cases. For methodology, definitions of terms, and crimes within offense categories, see Appendix 13.

[a]Detail may not add to total because of rounding.

Source: U.S. Department of Justice, Bureau of Justice Statistics, *Felony Defendants in Large Urban Counties, 2000*, NCJ 202021 (Washington, DC: U.S. Department of Justice, 2003), p. 16, Table 13.

Table 5.55

Type of pretrial release or detention of felony defendants in the 75 largest counties

By arrest charge, United States, 2000[a]

Most serious arrest charge	Financial release — Total financial	Surety bond	Deposit bond	Full cash bond	Property bond	Nonfinancial release — Total nonfinancial	Recognizance	Conditional	Unsecured	Emergency release	Held on bail	Denied bail
All offenses	32%	24%	6%	2%	(b)	30%	16%	8%	6%	(b)	31%	7%
Violent offenses	36	25	8	2	(b)	19	12	6	2	0%	35	9
Murder	8	5	2	0	0%	4	3	1	0	0	41	46
Rape	39	26	7	3	(b)	17	6	5	7	0	36	8
Robbery	27	14	8	2	1	16	12	4	1	0	45	12
Assault	40	29	9	2	(b)	20	11	6	2	0	32	7
Other violent	39	32	4	4	0	26	15	8	1	0	30	5
Property offenses	29	24	5	1	(b)	34	18	8	8	1	30	5
Burglary	27	21	6	1	(b)	22	12	5	4	(b)	44	7
Larceny/theft	32	28	4	1	1	36	19	11	6	(b)	27	5
Motor vehicle theft	22	20	2	1	0	24	12	9	3	1	45	8
Forgery	35	30	4	2	(b)	36	17	11	7	(b)	22	7
Fraud	25	22	4	1	(b)	58	28	6	24	1	12	3
Other property	31	21	7	2	(b)	39	25	7	7	2	25	3
Drug offenses	31	22	7	1	(b)	33	16	11	7	(b)	30	5
Trafficking	36	24	10	1	1	26	14	8	4	(b)	33	5
Other drug	26	21	4	1	(b)	40	18	13	9	(b)	29	5
Public-order offenses	38	26	8	2	(b)	28	18	7	4	1	26	8
Weapons	44	19	18	2	0	25	17	5	6	1	27	3
Driving-related	45	39	5	1	0	31	18	8	4	1	20	4
Other public-order	25	19	3	2	(b)	27	19	7	2	(b)	31	16

Note: See Note, table 5.51. Data on type of pretrial release or detention were available for 87% of all cases. For methodology, definitions of terms, and crimes within offense categories, see Appendix 13.

Source: U.S. Department of Justice, Bureau of Justice Statistics, *Felony Defendants in Large Urban Counties, 2000*, NCJ 202021 (Washington, DC: U.S. Department of Justice, 2003), p. 17, Table 14.

[a]Detail may not add to total because of rounding.
[b]Less than 0.5%.

Table 5.56

Released felony defendants charged with misconduct and rearrested in the 75 largest counties

By arrest charge, United States, 2000[a]

Most serious arrest charge	Felony defendants released prior to case disposition — Number	Percent charged with misconduct[b]	Failed to appear in court — Total	Returned to court	Remained a fugitive	Percent rearrested — Total	Felony	Misdemeanor
All offenses	32,606	32%	22%	16%	6%	16%	10%	6%
Violent offenses	7,313	24	13	9	4	14	7	7
Murder	61	12	6	0	6	6	6	0
Rape	481	12	8	7	2	4	1	3
Robbery	1,256	33	17	10	7	21	14	7
Assault	3,856	23	13	10	4	13	6	7
Other violent	1,659	23	12	8	4	14	6	8
Property offenses	9,820	30	21	15	6	15	10	5
Burglary	1,914	32	21	16	5	16	11	6
Larceny/theft	2,935	31	23	16	7	15	10	4
Motor vehicle theft	731	31	21	16	5	15	12	3
Forgery	1,230	33	22	17	4	17	9	7
Fraud	1,659	18	15	11	5	6	3	3
Other property	1,351	37	25	16	9	22	16	6
Drug offenses	12,463	38	27	20	7	19	12	7
Trafficking	5,612	38	26	19	7	21	15	6
Other drug	6,851	38	28	21	7	17	10	7
Public-order offenses	3,010	30	20	15	4	16	9	7
Weapons	946	29	20	15	5	14	8	6
Driving-related	1,185	31	19	14	5	16	9	7
Other public-order	879	31	20	16	4	18	9	9

Note: See Note, table 5.51. Data were collected for up to 1 year; misconduct and rearrests occurring after the end of the 1-year study period are not included in the table. Data on the court appearance record for the current case were available for 99% of cases involving a defendant released prior to case disposition. All defendants who failed to appear in court and were not returned to the court during the 1-year study period are counted as fugitives. Some of these defendants may have been returned to the court at a later date. Rearrest data were available for 97% of released defendants. Information on rearrests occurring in jurisdictions other than the one granting the pretrial release was not always available. For methodology, definitions of terms, and crimes within offense categories, see Appendix 13.

[a] Detail may not add to total because of rounding.
[b] Misconduct includes failure to appear in court, rearrest for a new offense, or a technical violation of release conditions that resulted in the revocation of pretrial release.

Source: U.S. Department of Justice, Bureau of Justice Statistics, *Felony Defendants in Large Urban Counties, 2000*, NCJ 202021 (Washington, DC: U.S. Department of Justice, 2003), p. 21, Tables 19 and 20, and p. 22, Table 21. Table adapted by SOURCEBOOK staff.

Table 5.57
Adjudication outcome for felony defendants in the 75 largest counties

By arrest charge, United States, 2000[a]

Most serious arrest charge	Number of defendants	Percent of felony defendants										
		Convicted						Not convicted			Other outcome[b]
		Total convicted	Felony			Misdemeanor			Total	Dismissed	Acquitted	
			Total	Plea	Trial	Total	Plea	Trial				
All offenses	47,290	64%	52%	49%	3%	12%	12%	(c)	27%	26%	1%	9%
Violent offenses	11,288	56	42	38	4	14	13	(c)	39	37	2	6
Murder	256	66	64	31	33	2	2	0%	30	28	2	5
Rape	675	60	50	47	2	11	10	(c)	35	33	2	5
Robbery	2,486	58	50	44	6	8	8	(c)	38	35	3	4
Assault	5,635	52	35	32	3	16	16	1	42	40	2	6
Other violent	2,237	62	46	43	3	16	16	(c)	32	31	1	6
Property offenses	14,299	66	50	48	2	15	15	(c)	25	24	(c)	10
Burglary	3,721	72	59	56	2	13	13	(c)	23	23	(c)	5
Larceny/theft	3,839	66	49	46	3	17	16	1	24	23	(c)	10
Motor vehicle theft	1,540	65	56	55	1	9	9	(c)	29	27	1	6
Forgery	1,604	68	53	52	2	15	15	(c)	24	24	(c)	8
Fraud	1,797	52	33	33	(c)	20	19	(c)	18	18	0	30
Other property	1,798	62	45	43	2	17	17	(c)	34	33	1	4
Drug offenses	17,473	65	58	56	2	7	7	(c)	23	23	(c)	11
Trafficking	7,902	74	67	63	4	7	7	(c)	21	20	(c)	6
Other drug	9,571	58	50	49	1	8	8	(c)	26	25	(c)	16
Public-order offenses	4,229	72	56	53	2	17	17	(c)	22	21	1	5
Weapons	1,276	69	56	53	3	13	13	0	27	24	3	4
Driving-related	1,434	86	70	68	2	16	16	(c)	10	10	(c)	4
Other public-order	1,519	63	42	40	2	21	20	(c)	30	29	1	7

Note: See Note, table 5.51. Twelve percent of all cases were still pending adjudication at the end of the 1-year study period and are excluded from the table. Data on adjudication outcome were available for 99% of those cases that had been adjudicated. For methodology, definitions of terms, and crimes within offense categories, see Appendix 13.

[a]Detail may not add to total because of rounding.
[b]Includes diversion and deferred adjudication.
[c]Less than 0.5%.

Source: U.S. Department of Justice, Bureau of Justice Statistics, *Felony Defendants in Large Urban Counties, 2000*, NCJ 202021 (Washington, DC: U.S. Department of Justice, 2003), p. 24, Table 23.

Table 5.58
Conviction offense of felony defendants in the 75 largest counties

United States, 2000

| Most serious conviction offense | Felony defendants ||
	Number	Percent
All offenses	30,138	100%
All felonies	24,398	81.0
Violent offenses	4,298	14.3
Murder	150	0.5
Rape	234	0.8
Robbery	956	3.2
Assault	1,863	6.2
Other violent	1,095	3.6
Property offenses	7,361	24.4
Burglary	1,787	5.9
Larceny/theft	2,171	7.2
Motor vehicle theft	774	2.6
Forgery	911	3.0
Fraud	603	2.0
Other property	1,117	3.7
Drug offenses	10,118	33.6
Trafficking	4,481	14.8
Other drug	5,637	18.7
Public-order offenses	2,529	8.4
Weapons	789	2.6
Driving-related	1,054	3.5
Other public-order	686	2.3
Other felonies	91	0.3
Misdemeanors[a]	5,740	19.0

Note: See Note, table 5.51. Data on conviction offense were available for 100% of cases involving defendants who had been convicted. For methodology, definitions of terms, and crimes within offense categories, see Appendix 13.

[a]Comprised of defendants with a felony arrest charge who were convicted of a misdemeanor.

Source: U.S. Department of Justice, Bureau of Justice Statistics, *Felony Defendants in Large Urban Counties, 2000*, NCJ 202021 (Washington, DC: U.S. Department of Justice, 2003), p. 27, Table 28.

Table 5.59

Type of sentence received by convicted defendants in the 75 largest counties

By conviction offense, United States, 2000[a]

Most serious conviction offense	Number of defendants	Total	Incarceration Total	Prison	Jail	Nonincarceration Total	Probation	Fine
All offenses	28,810	100%	69%	33%	36%	31%	30%	1%
All felonies	23,385	100	73	40	33	27	27	(b)
Violent offenses	4,042	100	79	49	30	21	21	(b)
Murder	117	100	96	96	0	4	4	0
Rape	222	100	75	56	19	25	25	0
Robbery	874	100	86	73	12	14	14	1
Assault	1,781	100	78	42	36	22	22	(b)
Other violent	1,048	100	72	33	39	28	28	0
Property offenses	7,129	100	71	39	33	29	28	(b)
Burglary	1,737	100	78	49	29	22	22	0
Larceny/theft	2,107	100	69	33	36	31	31	(b)
Motor vehicle theft	760	100	84	51	33	16	16	0
Forgery	886	100	59	31	28	41	40	(b)
Fraud	577	100	65	27	38	35	35	0
Other property	1,062	100	70	37	33	30	29	1
Drug offenses	9,661	100	71	36	34	29	29	(b)
Trafficking	4,177	100	72	42	30	28	28	(b)
Other drug	5,483	100	70	32	38	30	29	1
Public-order offenses	2,433	100	74	44	30	26	26	(b)
Weapons	754	100	72	44	28	28	28	0
Driving-related	1,020	100	76	40	36	24	24	0
Other public-order	659	100	73	48	25	27	27	1
Misdemeanors[c]	5,425	100	53	1	53	47	41	6

Note: See Note, table 5.51. Data on type of sentence were available for 93% of cases involving defendants who had been convicted. Sixty-seven percent of jail sentences and 12% of prison sentences included a probation term. Sentences to incarceration or probation may have included a fine, restitution, community service, treatment, or other court-ordered conditions. Sentences to incarceration that were suspended are included in the probation category. Total for all felonies includes cases that could not be classified into one of the four major offense categories. For methodology, definitions of terms, and crimes within offense categories, see Appendix 13.

[a]Detail may not add to total because of rounding.
[b]Less than 0.5%.
[c]Comprised of defendants with a felony arrest charge who were convicted of a misdemeanor.

Source: U.S. Department of Justice, Bureau of Justice Statistics, *Felony Defendants in Large Urban Counties, 2000*, NCJ 202021 (Washington, DC: U.S. Department of Justice, 2003), p. 30.

Table 5.60

Length of prison sentence received by felony defendants in the 75 largest counties

By conviction offense, United States, 2000[a]

Most serious felony conviction offense	Number of defendants	Mean[b]	Median	Total	1 to 24	25 to 48	49 to 72	73 to 120	Over 120[b]	Life
All offenses	9,340	55	32	100%	46%	25%	13%	8%	6%	1%
Violent offenses	1,976	99	60	100	22	26	17	16	16	3
Murder	113	282	180	100	0	3	6	24	35	32
Rape	125	146	84	100	9	29	9	23	28	4
Robbery	642	97	60	100	15	21	24	18	21	1
Assault	748	77	48	100	25	31	16	17	9	2
Other violent	348	74	36	100	39	27	14	7	12	2
Property offenses	2,761	41	24	100	56	24	10	6	3	(c)
Burglary	851	56	36	100	42	28	13	10	6	1
Larceny/theft	696	32	24	100	64	22	8	4	2	0
Motor vehicle theft	386	26	24	100	71	19	7	2	0	0
Forgery	278	40	24	100	56	19	14	6	4	0
Fraud	155	37	24	100	60	24	12	0	4	0
Other property	394	38	24	100	56	25	8	9	2	0
Drug offenses	3,512	45	29	100	50	27	14	6	4	(c)
Trafficking	1,771	61	36	100	32	32	20	10	6	(c)
Other drug	1,741	30	24	100	67	21	7	2	1	(c)
Public-order offenses	1,059	39	24	100	54	25	13	6	2	(c)
Weapons	332	42	36	100	44	30	17	10	0	0
Driving-related	413	38	24	100	55	24	11	7	3	0
Other public-order	313	37	24	100	62	22	13	0	3	1

Note: See Note, table 5.51. Data on length of prison sentence were available for 100% of all cases in which a convicted defendant received a prison sentence. Twelve percent of prison sentences included a probation term and 16% included a fine. Table excludes portions of sentences that were suspended. Total for all offenses includes cases that could not be classified into one of the four major offense categories. For methodology, definitions of terms, and crimes within offense categories, see Appendix 13.

[a]Detail may not add to total because of rounding.
[b]Excludes life sentences.
[c]Less than 0.5%.

Source: U.S. Department of Justice, Bureau of Justice Statistics, *Felony Defendants in Large Urban Counties, 2000*, NCJ 202021 (Washington, DC: U.S. Department of Justice, 2003), p. 32, Table 31.

Table 5.61

Characteristics of juvenile offenders in cases disposed by juvenile courts

By type of offense, United States, 2000[a]

		Type of offense			
	All offenses (N=1,657,533)	Person (N=378,604)	Property (N=678,683)	Drug (N=198,526)	Public-order (N=401,720)
Total	100%	100%	100%	100%	100%
Sex					
Male	75.4	72.5	75.4	83.2	74.1
Female	24.6	27.5	24.6	16.8	25.9
Race					
White	68.6	61.9	69.7	75.4	69.6
Black	28.1	35.1	26.3	22.2	27.3
Other[b]	3.3	3.0	4.0	2.4	3.1
Age at referral to court					
11 years and younger	5.0	7.3	6.3	0.5	2.8
12 years	5.3	7.3	6.0	1.7	4.1
13 years	10.0	12.5	10.9	5.2	8.8
14 years	16.1	17.5	16.8	12.1	15.7
15 years	21.1	20.2	20.8	21.4	22.3
16 years	23.0	19.9	22.0	30.0	24.2
17 years and older	19.4	15.3	17.2	29.0	22.0

Note: These data were collected by the National Center for Juvenile Justice (NCJJ) for the U.S. Department of Justice, Office of Juvenile Justice and Delinquency Prevention. The data are gathered from courts with juvenile jurisdiction in participating States. Information reported is based on national estimates of delinquency cases disposed by juvenile courts in the United States during 2000 (N=1,657,533). The final sample included data reported by 1,991 jurisdictions in 35 States covering 71% of the Nation's youth population. These data were derived from a nonprobability sample of courts; therefore statistical confidence in the estimates cannot be determined. A case disposed refers to a definite action having been taken as the result of a referral to juvenile court, i.e., a plan of treatment was selected or initiated. These data files were developed by NCJJ and originally analyzed for the Juvenile Court Statistics series. For methodology, definitions of terms, and offenses within categories, see Appendix 14.

[a] Percents may not add to 100 because of rounding.
[b] Includes persons having origin in any of the original peoples of North America, the Far East, Southeast Asia, the Indian Subcontinent, or the Pacific Islands. Nearly all Hispanics were included in the "white" racial category.

Source: A. Stahl, T. Finnegan, and W. Kang, "Easy Access to Juvenile Court Statistics: 1985-2000" [Online]. Washington, DC: U.S. Department of Justice, Office of Juvenile Justice and Delinquency Prevention, 2002. Available: http://ojjdp.ncjrs.org/ojstatbb/ezajcs/ [Apr. 15, 2003]. Table constructed by SOURCEBOOK staff.

Table 5.62

Type of offense in cases disposed by juvenile courts

By characteristics of juvenile offenders, United States, 2000[a]

Type of offense	All offenses	Sex		Race			Age at referral to court						
		Male	Female	White	Black	Other[b]	11 years and younger	12 years	13 years	14 years	15 years	16 years	17 years and older
Total	100%	100%	100%	100%	100%	100%	100%	100%	100%	100%	100%	100%	100%
Person	22.8	22.0	25.5	20.6	28.5	20.3	33.4	31.4	28.4	24.7	21.9	19.7	18.0
Property	40.9	41.0	40.8	41.6	38.4	48.7	51.7	46.3	44.3	42.7	40.3	39.1	36.4
Drug	12.0	13.2	8.2	13.2	9.5	8.6	1.3	3.7	6.1	9.0	12.2	15.6	18.0
Public-order	24.2	23.8	25.5	24.6	23.6	22.4	13.6	18.5	21.2	23.6	25.7	25.5	27.6

Note: See Note, table 5.61. For methodology, definitions of terms, and offenses within categories, see Appendix 14.

[a] Percents may not add to 100 because of rounding.
[b] Includes persons having origin in any of the original peoples of North America, the Far East, Southeast Asia, the Indian Subcontinent, or the Pacific Islands. Nearly all Hispanics were included in the "white" racial category.

Source: A. Stahl, T. Finnegan, and W. Kang, "Easy Access to Juvenile Court Statistics: 1985-2000" [Online]. Washington, DC: U.S. Department of Justice, Office of Juvenile Justice and Delinquency Prevention, 2002. Available: http://ojjdp.ncjrs.org/ojstatbb/ezajcs/ [Apr. 16, 2003]. Table constructed by SOURCEBOOK staff.

Table 5.63

Juvenile court case outcomes

By characteristics of juvenile offenders and type of offense, United States, 2000

	Delinquency cases		Petitioned cases		Cases adjudicated delinquent				Nonadjudicated cases[a]			
	Detained prior to juvenile court disposition	Petitioned	Adjudicated delinquent	Transferred/ waived to adult court	Placed out of home	Placed on probation	Dismissed	Other[b]	Placed out of home	Placed on probation	Dismissed	Other[b]
Total	19.5%	57.8%	66.2%	0.6%	24.0%	63.1%	2.5%	10.3%	0.7%	27.5%	47.1%	24.7%
Sex												
Male	20.5	60.8	66.9	0.7	25.4	61.9	2.6	10.2	0.9	26.8	48.5	23.9
Female	16.2	48.6	63.8	B	18.7	67.7	2.5	11.1	0.4	29.3	43.3	27.0
Race												
White	17.5	55.1	67.2	0.5	22.8	63.6	2.2	11.4	0.9	29.2	44.1	25.8
Black	23.8	64.5	64.2	0.8	26.9	61.9	3.4	7.8	0.4	24.0	53.2	22.4
Other[c]	23.6	55.3	67.0	B	22.5	64.3	B	12.0	B	19.6	59.5	20.5
Age at referral to court												
11 years and younger	6.9	36.8	56.0	B	10.8	74.2	B	12.1	B	31.0	46.7	22.2
12 years	13.7	48.0	63.9	B	17.3	71.7	B	8.5	B	30.7	45.2	24.0
13 years	16.7	53.3	67.8	B	20.8	68.7	2.1	8.3	B	30.0	45.4	24.3
14 years	19.1	57.8	68.9	B	24.0	65.8	2.1	8.1	0.7	29.0	45.5	24.8
15 years	21.3	60.3	68.7	B	25.0	64.0	2.6	8.5	0.9	27.2	47.1	24.7
16 years	21.6	59.8	66.8	0.7	25.3	61.7	2.6	10.4	0.9	26.9	46.8	25.3
17 years and older	21.5	63.1	62.4	1.7	26.1	55.3	3.1	15.5	1.1	23.3	50.3	25.3
Type of offense												
Person	23.4	60.5	62.6	0.9	25.1	63.5	3.2	8.1	0.6	26.7	52.9	19.7
Property	15.7	54.8	66.9	0.6	22.4	64.9	2.3	10.4	0.6	28.9	42.9	27.6
Drug	19.0	60.6	67.9	B	20.2	62.3	3.3	14.2	B	28.7	43.9	26.6
Public-order	22.3	58.9	67.9	B	27.5	60.2	2.0	10.3	1.0	24.9	50.4	23.7

Note: See Note, table 5.61. For methodology, definitions of terms, and offenses within categories, see Appendix 14.

Source: A. Stahl, T. Finnegan, and W. Kang, "Easy Access to Juvenile Court Statistics: 1985-2000" [Online]. Washington, DC: U.S. Department of Justice, Office of Juvenile Justice and Delinquency Prevention, 2002. Available: http://ojjdp.ncjrs.org/ojstatbb/ezajcs/ [Apr. 16, 2003]. Table constructed by SOURCEBOOK staff.

[a]Includes petitioned cases that were not adjudicated delinquent and nonpetitioned cases.
[b]Includes dispositions such as fines, restitution, community service, and referrals outside the court for services with minimal or no further court involvement anticipated.
[c]Includes persons having origin in any of the original peoples of North America, the Far East, Southeast Asia, the Indian Subcontinent, or the Pacific Islands. Nearly all Hispanics were included in the "white" racial category.

Table 5.64

Juvenile court case outcomes

By type of offense and race of juvenile offender, United States, 2000

Type of offense and race of offender	Delinquency cases		Petitioned cases		Cases adjudicated delinquent				Nonadjudicated cases[a]			
	Detained prior to juvenile court disposition	Petitioned	Adjudicated delinquent	Transferred/ waived to adult court	Placed out of home	Placed on probation	Dismissed	Other[b]	Placed out of home	Placed on probation	Dismissed	Other[b]
Person												
White	22.5%	57.6%	63.8%	B	24.6%	64.3%	2.8%	8.3%	0.9%	28.4%	50.0%	20.0%
Black	24.2	65.7	60.6	1.1%	26.1	62.2	3.9	7.8	B	23.7	56.1	18.9
Property												
White	14.1	52.9	67.5	0.6	21.5	65.3	1.9	11.4	0.7	30.1	40.1	28.6
Black	19.7	60.3	65.4	B	24.7	64.2	3.4	7.6	B	26.2	47.9	24.9
Drug												
White	15.0	55.7	69.3	B	16.2	64.4	2.9	16.5	B	30.7	39.7	28.7
Black	32.2	77.6	64.2	B	30.9	56.3	B	8.4	B	19.8	57.9	18.0
Public-order												
White	20.3	56.5	68.4	B	26.9	59.9	1.8	11.3	1.2	26.7	47.8	24.1
Black	26.8	64.8	66.9	B	29.3	60.5	2.6	7.6	B	21.2	54.9	23.0

Note: See Note, table 5.61. For methodology, definitions of terms, and offenses within categories, see Appendix 14.

Source: A. Stahl, T. Finnegan, and W. Kang, "Easy Access to Juvenile Court Statistics: 1985-2000" [Online]. Washington, DC: U.S. Department of Justice, Office of Juvenile Justice and Delinquency Prevention, 2002. Available: http://ojjdp.ncjrs.org/ojstatbb/ezajcs/ [Apr. 29, 2003]. Table constructed by SOURCEBOOK staff.

[a]Includes petitioned cases that were not adjudicated delinquent and nonpetitioned cases.
[b]Includes dispositions such as fines, restitution, community service, and referrals outside the court for services with minimal or no further court involvement anticipated.

Table 5.65

Petitions filed in U.S. District Courts by Federal and State prisoners

By type of petition, 1977-2003

		Petitions by Federal prisoners						Petitions by State prisoners				
	Total	Total	Motions to vacate sentence	Habeas corpus	Mandamus, etc.	Civil rights	Prison conditions	Total	Habeas corpus	Mandamus, etc.	Civil rights	Prison conditions
1977	19,537	4,691	1,921	1,745	542	483	NA	14,846	6,866	228	7,752	NA
1978	21,924	4,955	1,924	1,851	544	636	NA	16,969	7,033	206	9,730	NA
1979	23,001	4,499	1,907	1,664	340	588	NA	18,502	7,123	184	11,195	NA
1980	23,287	3,713	1,322	1,465	323	603	NA	19,574	7,031	146	12,397	NA
1981	27,711	4,104	1,248	1,680	342	834	NA	23,607	7,790	178	15,639	NA
1982	29,303	4,328	1,186	1,927	381	834	NA	24,975	8,059	175	16,741	NA
1983	30,775	4,354	1,311	1,914	339	790	NA	26,421	8,532	202	17,687	NA
1984	31,107	4,526	1,427	1,905	372	822	NA	26,581	8,349	198	18,034	NA
1985	33,468	6,262	1,527	3,405	373	957	NA	27,206	8,534	181	18,491	NA
1986	33,765	4,432	1,556	1,679	427	770	NA	29,333	9,045	216	20,072	NA
1987	37,316	4,519	1,669	1,812	313	725	NA	32,797[a]	9,542	276	22,972	NA
1988	38,839	5,130	2,071	1,867	330	862	NA	33,709	9,880	270	23,559	NA
1989	41,481	5,577	2,526	1,818	315	918	NA	35,904	10,554	311	25,039	NA
1990	42,630	6,611	2,970	1,967	525	1,149	NA	36,019	10,823	353	24,843	NA
1991	42,462	6,817	3,328	2,112	378	999	NA	35,645	10,331	268	25,046	NA
1992	48,423	6,997	3,983	1,507	597	910	NA	41,426	11,299	481	29,646	NA
1993	53,451	8,456	5,379	1,467	695	915	NA	44,995	11,587	390	33,018	NA
1994	57,940	7,700	4,628	1,441	491	1,140	NA	50,240	11,918	397	37,925	NA
1995	63,550	8,951	5,988	1,343	510	1,110	NA	54,599	13,632	398	40,569	NA
1996	68,235	13,095	9,729	1,703	444	1,219	NA	55,140	14,726	418	39,996	NA
1997	62,966	14,952	11,675	1,902	401	974	NA	48,014	19,956	397	27,661	NA
1998	54,715	9,937	6,287	2,321	346	641	342	44,778	18,838	461	13,115	12,364
1999	56,603	10,859	5,752	3,590	555	642	320	45,744	20,493	513	13,441	11,291
2000	58,257	11,880	6,341	3,870	628	736	305	46,377	21,349	564	13,415	11,049
2001	58,805	14,619	8,644	4,440	516	732	287	44,186	20,446	641	12,703	10,396
2002	55,295	12,190	6,107	4,483	554	771	275	43,105	19,616	571	13,268	9,650
2003	54,378	11,981	5,832	4,341	551	982	275	42,397	18,872	609	13,708	9,108
Percent change 2002 to 2003	-1.7%	-1.7%	-4.5%	-3.2%	-0.5%	27.4%	0%	-1.6%	-3.8%	6.7%	3.3%	-5.6%

Note: Petitions by Federal prisoners are suits brought against the Federal Government. Petitions by State prisoners are those petitions in which the State or its representative(s) is (are) named as the defendant(s). "Habeas corpus" is a writ utilized to bring a party before a court. In this case, the government must ensure that an individual's imprisonment conforms with the law. "Mandamus" is a writ issued by a superior court to an inferior court or to a public official, directing that a specified action be taken. Prisoners file mandamus petitions in order to compel a government official to perform a duty owed to the prisoner. "Civil rights" petitions are a means to seek relief from constitutional deprivations. Data for 1977-91 are reported for the 12-month period ending June 30. Beginning in 1992, data are reported for the Federal fiscal year, which is the 12-month period ending September 30. Some data have been revised by the Source and may differ from previous editions of SOURCEBOOK.

[a] Includes 7 motions to vacate sentence.

Source: Administrative Office of the United States Courts, *Annual Report of the Director, 1985*, p. 149; *1986*, p. 176; *1995*, p. 139; *1998*, p. 143; *1999*, p. 137 (Washington, DC: Administrative Office of the United States Courts); Administrative Office of the United States Courts, *Annual Report of the Director, 1987*, p. 179; *1988*, p. 182; *1989*, p. 178; *1990*, p. 138; *1991*, p. 191; *1992*, p. 179; *1993*, p. A1-55; *1994*, Table C-2; *1996*, p. 136; *1997*, p. 129 (Washington, DC: USGPO); and Administrative Office of the United States Courts, *Judicial Business of the United States Courts: 2000 Annual Report of the Director*, p. 136; *2001 Annual Report of the Director*, p. 131; *2002 Annual Report of the Director*, p. 130; *2003 Annual Report of the Director*, p. 127 (Washington, DC: USGPO). Table adapted by SOURCEBOOK staff.

Table 5.66

Appeals commenced, terminated, and pending, and judgeships authorized in U.S. Courts of Appeals

1982-2003

	Appeals commenced		Terminated	Pending	Judgeships authorized
	Number	Cases per three-judge panel			
1982	27,946	635	27,984	21,510	132
1983	29,630	673	28,660	22,480	132
1984	31,490	716	31,185	22,785	132
1985	33,360	642	31,387	24,758	156
1986	34,292	659	33,774	25,276	156
1987	35,176	676	34,444	26,008	156
1988	38,239	737	36,213	28,273	156
1989	39,900	767	37,509	30,614	156
1990	40,858	786	38,790	32,299	156
1991	43,027	773	41,640	33,428	167
1992	47,013	845	44,373	35,799	167
1993	50,224	902	47,790	38,156	167
1994	48,322	868	49,184	37,269	167
1995	50,072	899	49,805	37,310	167
1996	51,991	934	50,413	38,774	167
1997	52,319	940	51,194	39,846	167
1998	53,805	967	52,002	41,666	167
1999	54,693	983	54,088	42,225	167
2000	54,697	983	56,512	40,261	167
2001	57,464	1,032	57,422	39,996	167
2002	57,555	1,034	56,586	40,149	167
2003	60,847	1,093	56,396	44,600	167
Percent change 2002 to 2003	5.7%	5.7%	-0.3%	11.1%	0%

Note: These data include criminal and civil appeals from U.S. District Courts, bankruptcy appeals, appeals from administrative agencies, and original proceedings. Three-judge panels represent full panels and hear appeal arguments. Data on the number of judges and cases filed in the Federal Circuit are excluded. Data for 1982-87 are reported for the 12-month period ending June 30. Beginning in 1988, data are reported for the Federal fiscal year, which is the 12-month period ending September 30. Some data have been revised by the Source and may differ from previous editions of SOURCEBOOK.

Source: Administrative Office of the United States Courts, *Annual Report of the Director, 1992*, p. 57, Table 1; *1997*, p. 14, Table 1 (Washington, DC: USGPO); and Administrative Office of the United States Courts, *Judicial Business of the United States Courts: 2002 Annual Report of the Director*, p. 16, Table 1; *2003 Annual Report of the Director*, p. 14, Table 1 (Washington, DC: USGPO). Table adapted by SOURCEBOOK staff.

Table 5.67

Appeals from U.S. District Courts filed in U.S. Courts of Appeals

By nature of suit or offense, 1980, 1985, 1990-2003

Nature of suit or offense	1980	1985	1990	1991	1992	1993	1994	1995	1996	1997	1998	1999	2000	2001	2002	2003
Total cases	19,259	28,560	36,609	37,410	41,543	44,236	42,983	44,365	47,026	45,935	48,057	46,931	46,487	47,327	47,068	46,358
Total civil cases	14,854	23,571	27,116	27,461	30,328	32,374	32,309	34,203	36,137	35,414	37,522	36,680	35,780	36,046	35,499	34,390
U.S. cases	4,654	6,744	6,626	6,663	7,137	7,858	7,533	7,919	8,750	8,986	9,816	9,221	8,695	9,705	9,424	8,589
U.S. plaintiff	869	914	935	991	1,012	985	923	809	728	557	638	634	608	495	466	377
Contract actions	99	99	146	116	165	196	126	95	89	55	50	62	108	62	45	27
Real property actions	101	111	88	98	81	134	102	62	63	37	43	50	29	26	19	23
Civil rights	62	68	121	100	89	53	83	78	80	71	98	64	62	49	57	48
Labor laws	68	68	62	68	59	44	49	37	26	23	25	23	22	25	27	11
All other[a]	539	568	518	609	618	558	563	537	470	371	422	435	387	333	318	268
U.S. defendant	3,785	5,830	5,691	5,672	6,125	6,873	6,610	7,110	8,022	8,429	9,178	8,587	8,087	9,210	8,958	8,212
Contract actions	179	141	133	159	206	232	180	139	131	90	107	106	73	58	68	65
Real property actions	63	77	82	107	91	114	99	97	110	64	74	56	72	57	61	44
Tort actions	324	404	381	384	396	369	376	356	463	350	293	276	273	472	243	256
Civil rights	454	720	693	744	796	899	873	898	948	898	963	990	895	848	876	874
Prisoner petitions:																
Motions to vacate sentence	450	551	1,112	1,154	1,467	1,818	1,774	2,215	3,078	3,870	4,066	3,356	2,671	3,470	3,368	2,907
Habeas corpus[b]	302	531	488	506	432	421	430	462	451	492	677	1,034	1,398	1,612	1,621	1,328
Prisoner civil rights	159	288	408	389	406	416	506	555	624	434	302	303	336	358	384	384
Prison conditions	NA	NA	NA	NA	NA	NA	NA	NA	NA	85[c]	152	154	169	189	186	189
Other prisoner petitions	96	140	253	289	239	247	229	225	293	302	327	364	381	509	506	542
Social Security laws	627	1,188	926	686	683	846	861	925	815	699	862	904	845	710	777	714
Tax suits	197	448	313	332	360	320	306	270	219	248	276	243	189	139	131	167
Environmental matters	NA	102	93	96	99	101	105	110	133	138	113	121	116	127	144	126
Freedom of Information Act	NA	130	93	98	136	142	98	81	94	106	109	78	78	76	65	58
All other[d]	934	1,110	716	728	814	948	773	777	663	653	857	602	591	585	528	558
Private cases	10,200	16,827	20,490	20,798	23,191	24,516	24,776	26,284	27,387	26,428	27,706	27,459	27,085	26,341	26,075	25,801
Federal question	7,728	12,910	16,370	16,668	18,795	19,930	20,824	22,496	23,533	22,630	24,250	24,076	23,885	23,122	23,003	22,640
Contract actions	252	586	561	628	737	631	768	578	642	553	606	633	513	564	445	453
Tort actions	497	749	737	742	750	783	744	813	686	687	666	901	589	641	638	600
Civil rights	2,145	3,648	3,915	3,844	4,339	5,030	5,638	6,001	6,242	6,923	7,405	7,052	6,995	6,393	6,515	5,843
Antitrust	343	310	214	190	162	197	197	164	160	166	169	146	106	121	102	117
Prisoner petitions:																
Habeas corpus[b]	1,020	2,172	3,170	3,391	3,725	3,612	3,642	3,927	4,423	4,475	6,054	6,782	7,234	7,145	7,115	7,304
Prisoner civil rights	1,578	2,772	4,413	4,655	5,396	6,044	6,385	7,528	8,053	5,358	3,814	2,925	2,681	2,585	2,729	2,761
Prison conditions	NA	NA	NA	NA	NA	NA	NA	NA	NA	1,103[c]	1,937	2,178	2,295	2,366	2,269	2,180
Other prisoner petitions	70	78	53	70	71	104	78	69	70	68	92	93	87	109	94	96
Labor laws	417	1,009	1,085	1,079	1,195	1,181	1,179	1,276	1,190	1,160	1,303	1,185	1,108	1,043	969	1,039
Copyright, patent, and trademark	270	275	349	306	377	394	401	443	447	450	491	465	504	497	485	492
Securities, commodities, exchange	NA	290	417	352	428	323	242	224	242	200	177	196	223	212	197	216
Constitutionality of State statutes	NA	104	96	100	117	87	106	123	96	133	129	121	133	99	110	98
All other	1,136	917	1,360	1,311	1,498	1,544	1,444	1,350	1,282	1,354	1,407	1,399	1,417	1,347	1,335	1,441
Diversity of citizenship	2,427	3,878	4,099	4,088	4,333	4,551	3,898	3,753	3,833	3,776	3,443	3,366	3,190	3,210	3,055	3,153
Contract actions	1,362	2,192	2,413	2,419	2,450	2,398	2,292	2,183	2,235	2,259	2,019	1,958	1,969	1,974	1,997	2,060
Tort actions	996	1,538	1,488	1,415	1,663	1,957	1,410	1,414	1,445	1,379	1,296	1,274	1,099	1,111	937	944
All other[e]	69	148	198	254	220	196	196	156	153	138	128	134	122	125	121	149
General local jurisdiction	45	39	21	42	63	35	54	35	21	22	13	17	10	9	17	8
Contract actions	10	NA	8	10	16	8	13	8	2	7	0	6	0	1	1	3
Tort actions	14	NA	3	18	14	14	21	11	3	4	6	7	6	5	3	0
Prisoner petitions	7	NA	1	0	2	0	0	0	4	1	1	2	0	0	0	0
All other[e]	14	NA	9	14	31	13	20	16	12	10	6	2	4	3	13	5
Total criminal cases	4,405	4,989	9,493	9,949	11,215	11,862	10,674	10,162	10,889	10,521	10,535	10,251	10,707	11,281	11,569	11,968
Homicide	52	49	81	66	79	83	126	114	142	140	119	118	97	90	121	79
Assault	NA	67	97	86	80	116	103	103	80	89	79	71	60	49	61	79
Robbery and burglary	310	300	400	463	547	596	528	353	289	305	319	268	312	318	295	269
Larceny and theft	244	242	267	225	238	262	302	250	278	275	269	221	237	241	211	235
Embezzlement and fraud	826	912	1,221	1,387	1,522	1,561	1,426	1,294	1,581	1,526	1,403	1,276	1,339	1,292	1,331	1,418
Motor vehicle theft	64	55	35	38	49	64	135	92	112	76	94	93	70	58	54	54
Drug offenses	1,369	2,063	5,658	5,570	5,936	5,900	5,104	4,499	5,099	4,750	4,845	4,513	4,450	4,529	4,688	4,562
Extortion, racketeering, and threats	251	263	119	136	167	157	150	122	204	218	163	205	201	149	158	167
Firearms, weapons	175	229	526	715	1,092	1,237	1,139	1,034	1,183	1,135	982	1,070	1,035	1,266	1,386	1,681
Forgery and counterfeiting	214	157	172	128	152	132	127	132	140	143	158	153	130	117	164	147
Immigration	NA	64	140	144	209	226	263	277	353	417	693	934	1,357	1,654	1,679	1,821
All other[f]	900	588	777	991	1,144	1,528	1,271	1,892	1,428	1,447	1,411	1,329	1,419	1,518	1,421	1,456

See notes on next page.

Table 5.67

Appeals from U.S. District Courts filed in U.S. Courts of Appeals

By nature of suit or offense, 1980, 1985, 1990-2003--Continued

Note: See Note, table 5.65. These data exclude bankruptcy appeals, appeals from administrative agencies, and original proceedings, and therefore will differ from figures presented in table 5.66. "Private cases" brought in U.S. District Courts include suits wherein litigation is between States and/or private citizens. "Prisoner petitions" included in this category are those filed by State prisoners naming a State or its representative(s) as the defendant(s). "Diversity of citizenship" refers to lawsuits between residents of different States. Since 1987, totals include reopened, remanded, and reinstated appeals as well as original appeals. Data for 1980 and 1985-91 are reported for the 12-month period ending June 30. Beginning in 1992, data are reported for the Federal fiscal year, which is the 12-month period ending September 30.

[a]Includes tort actions; forfeiture and penalty; securities, commodities, and exchange; and tax suits.
[b]Includes death sentence cases.
[c]Collection of data for this category began on Jan. 1, 1997; therefore reported data are for 9 months.
[d]Includes labor suits.
[e]Includes real property actions.
[f]Includes sex offenses, bribery, gambling, lottery, kidnaping, escape, perjury, drunk driving/traffic, other miscellaneous general offenses, and Federal statutes such as agricultural acts and antitrust violations.

Source: Administrative Office of the United States Courts, *Annual Report of the Director, 1980*, pp. 366-369; *1985*, p. 118; *1995*, pp. 122-126; *1998*, pp. 126-130; *1999*, pp. 120-124 (Washington, DC: Administrative Office of the United States Courts); Administrative Office of the United States Courts, *Annual Report of the Director, 1990*, pp. 130-132; *1991*, pp. 183, 184; *1992*, pp. 166-170; *1993*, pp. A1-38--A1-42; *1994*, Table B-7; *1996*, pp. 119-123; *1997*, pp. 112-116 (Washington, DC: USGPO); and Administrative Office of the United States Courts, *Judicial Business of the United States Courts: 2000 Annual Report of the Director*, pp. 114-118; *2001 Annual Report of the Director*, pp. 110-114; *2002 Annual Report of the Director*, pp. 109-113; *2003 Annual Report of the Director*, pp. 106-110 (Washington, DC: USGPO). Table adapted by SOURCEBOOK staff.

Table 5.68

Activities of the U.S. Supreme Court

At conclusion of the October term, 1976-2002

October term	Argued during term	Disposed of by full opinions	Disposed of by per curiam opinions	Set for reargument	Granted review this term	Reviewed and decided without oral argument	Total available for argument at outset of following term
1976	176	154	22	0	169	207	88
1977	172	153	8	9	162	129	75
1978	168	153	8	8	163	110	79
1979	156	143	12	1	154	128	78
1980	154	144	8	2	183	130	102
1981	184	169	10	4	210	134	126
1982	183	174	6	3	179	135	113
1983	184	174	6	4	149	86	80
1984	175	159	11	5	185	82	87
1985	172	161	10	1	187	103	101
1986	175	164	10	1	167	113	91
1987	167	151	9	7	180	95	105
1988	170	156	12	2	147	110	81
1989	146	143	3	0	122	80	57
1990	125	121	4	0	141	115	70
1991	127	120	3	4	120	77	66
1992	116	111	4	0	97	113	46
1993	99	93	6	0	99	70	40
1994	94	91	3	0	93	69	39
1995	90	87	3	0	105	120	52
1996	90	87	3	0	87	82	48
1997[a]	96	93	1	0	90	51	41
1998[a]	90	84	4	2	81	59	30
1999	83	79	2	1	92	54	37
2000	86	83	4	0	99	127	49
2001	88	85	3	0	88	72	47
2002	84	79	5	0	91	66	40

Note: "Per curiam" refers to disposition of a case by the Court that is not accompanied by a full opinion. Some data have been revised by the Source and may differ from previous editions of SOURCEBOOK.

[a]Includes two dismissed cases.

Source: Administrative Office of the United States Courts, *Annual Report of the Director, 1981*, p. A-1; *1986*, p. 135 (Washington, DC: Administrative Office of the United States Courts); Administrative Office of the United States Courts, *Annual Report of the Director, 1991*, p. 161; *1996*, p. 82 (Washington, DC: USGPO); and Administrative Office of the United States Courts, *Judicial Business of the United States Courts: 2002 Annual Report of the Director*, p. 72; *2003 Annual Report of the Director*, p. 69 (Washington, DC: USGPO). Table adapted by SOURCEBOOK staff.

Table 5.69

Cases filed, disposed of, and pending in the U.S. Supreme Court

By method of filing, at conclusion of the October term, 1976-2002

October term	Total	Original	Paid	In forma pauperis	October term	Total	Original	Paid	In forma pauperis
1976					**1990**				
Cases on docket	4,730	8	2,324	2,398	Cases on docket	6,316	14	2,351	3,951
Disposed of	3,918	2	1,852	2,064	Disposed of	5,481	3	2,042	3,436
Remaining on docket	812	6	472	334	Remaining on docket	835	11	309	515
1977					**1991**				
Cases on docket	4,704	14	2,341	2,349	Cases on docket	6,770	12	2,451	4,307
Disposed of	3,867	3	1,911	1,953	Disposed of	5,894	1	2,125	3,768
Remaining on docket	837	11	430	396	Remaining on docket	876	11	326	539
1978					**1992**				
Cases on docket	4,731	17	2,383	2,331	Cases on docket	7,245	12	2,441	4,792
Disposed of	4,017	0	2,021	1,996	Disposed of	6,402	1	2,140	4,261
Remaining on docket	714	17	362	335	Remaining on docket	843	11	301	531
1979					**1993**				
Cases on docket	4,781	23	2,509	2,249	Cases on docket	7,786	12	2,442	5,332
Disposed of	3,889	1	2,050	1,838	Disposed of	6,721	1	2,099	4,621
Remaining on docket	892	22	459	411	Remaining on docket	1,065	11	343	711
1980					**1994**				
Cases on docket	5,144	24	2,749	2,371	Cases on docket	8,100	11	2,515	5,574
Disposed of	4,196	7	2,222	1,950	Disposed of	7,170	2	2,185	4,983
Remaining on docket	948	17	527	421	Remaining on docket	930	9	330	591
1981					**1995**				
Cases on docket	5,311	22	2,935	2,354	Cases on docket	7,565	11	2,456	5,098
Disposed of	4,433	6	2,390	2,037	Disposed of	6,649	5	2,130	4,514
Remaining on docket	878	16	545	317	Remaining on docket	916	6	326	584
1982					**1996**				
Cases on docket	5,079	17	2,170	2,352	Cases on docket	7,602	7	2,430	5,165
Disposed of	4,201	3	2,190	2,008	Disposed of	6,739	2	2,124	4,613
Remaining on docket	878	14	520	344	Remaining on docket	863	5	306	552
1983					**1997**				
Cases on docket	5,100	18	2,688	2,394	Cases on docket	7,692	7	2,432	5,253
Disposed of	4,140	7	2,148	1,985	Disposed of	6,759	1	2,142	4,616
Remaining on docket	960	11	540	409	Remaining on docket	933	6	290	637
1984					**1998**				
Cases on docket	5,006	15	2,575	2,416	Cases on docket	8,083	7	2,387	5,689
Disposed of	4,261	8	2,175	2,078	Disposed of	7,045	2	2,092	4,951
Remaining on docket	745	7	400	338	Remaining on docket	1,038	5	295	738
1985					**1999**				
Cases on docket	5,158	10	2,571	2,577	Cases on docket	8,445	8	2,413	6,024
Disposed of	4,275	2	2,095	2,178	Disposed of	7,369	0	2,096	5,273
Remaining on docket	883	8	476	399	Remaining on docket	1,076	8	317	751
1986					**2000**				
Cases on docket	5,134	12	2,547	2,575	Cases on docket	8,965	9	2,305	6,651
Disposed of	4,360	1	2,105	2,254	Disposed of	7,762	2	2,024	5,736
Remaining on docket	774	11	442	321	Remaining on docket	1,203	7	281	915
1987					**2001**				
Cases on docket	5,268	16	2,577	2,675	Cases on docket	9,176	8	2,210	6,958
Disposed of	4,387	5	2,131	2,251	Disposed of	8,072	1	1,932	6,139
Remaining on docket	881	11	446	424	Remaining on docket	1,104	7	278	819
1988					**2002**				
Cases on docket	5,657	14	2,587	3,056	Cases on docket	9,406	7	2,190	7,209
Disposed of	4,911	2	2,271	2,638	Disposed of	8,388	1	1,899	6,488
Remaining on docket	746	12	316	418	Remaining on docket	1,018	6	291	721
1989									
Cases on docket	5,746	14	2,416	3,316					
Disposed of	4,989	2	2,096	2,891					
Remaining on docket	757	12	320	425					

Note: "Original" refers to those cases that were on the Supreme Court docket previously and were disposed of, but that subsequently were reinstated. For all cases other than "original" ones, a docket filing fee must be "paid." If the petitioner is indigent, the docket filing fee is waived and the case is filed "in forma pauperis."

Source: Administrative Office of the United States Courts, **Annual Report of the Director, 1981**, p. A-1; **1986**, p. 135 (Washington, DC: Administrative Office of the United States Courts); **Annual Report of the Director, 1991**, p. 161; **1996**, p. 82 (Washington, DC: USGPO); and Administrative Office of the United States Courts, **Judicial Business of the United States Courts: 2002 Annual Report of the Director**, p. 72; **2003 Annual Report of the Director**, p. 69 (Washington, DC: USGPO). Table adapted by SOURCEBOOK staff.

Table 5.70

Petitions for review on writ of certiorari to the U.S. Supreme Court filed, terminated, and pending

By circuit and nature of proceeding, fiscal year 2003

Circuit and nature of proceeding	Pending Oct. 1, 2002	Filed	Terminated Granted	Terminated Denied	Dismissed	Pending Sept. 30, 2003	Circuit and nature of proceeding	Pending Oct. 1, 2002	Filed	Terminated Granted	Terminated Denied	Dismissed	Pending Sept. 30, 2003
Total	3,262	6,671	115	6,526	28	3,264	Sixth Circuit	194	543	9	496	5	227
Criminal	927	2,454	20	2,487	3	871	Criminal	42	147	0	135	0	54
U.S. civil	603	1,175	23	1,182	5	568	U.S. civil	25	87	0	80	1	31
Private civil	1,645	2,949	61	2,777	20	1,736	Private civil	124	300	8	272	4	140
Administrative appeals	87	93	11	80	0	89	Administrative appeals	3	9	1	9	0	2
District of Columbia	42	87	1	78	4	46	Seventh Circuit	122	433	4	407	1	143
Criminal	7	11	0	9	0	9	Criminal	40	124	0	120	0	44
U.S. civil	23	47	1	48	1	20	U.S. civil	34	142	2	120	1	53
Private civil	6	16	0	12	3	7	Private civil	48	163	2	164	0	45
Administrative appeals	6	13	0	9	0	10	Administrative appeals	0	4	0	3	0	1
First Circuit	91	69	8	88	0	64	Eighth Circuit	147	365	5	383	0	124
Criminal	24	24	3	26	0	19	Criminal	26	107	1	98	0	34
U.S. civil	19	13	3	20	0	9	U.S. civil	37	71	1	86	0	21
Private civil	47	31	2	41	0	35	Private civil	77	180	0	195	0	62
Administrative appeals	1	1	0	1	0	1	Administrative appeals	7	7	3	4	0	7
Second Circuit	478	295	5	327	1	440	Ninth Circuit	954	1,273	30	1,158	0	1,039
Criminal	130	84	1	97	1	115	Criminal	245	472	1	481	0	235
U.S. civil	70	42	1	45	0	66	U.S. civil	160	132	4	130	0	158
Private civil	273	167	3	184	0	253	Private civil	495	645	19	524	0	597
Administrative appeals	5	2	0	1	0	6	Administrative appeals	54	24	6	23	0	49
Third Circuit	165	426	4	429	2	156	Tenth Circuit	147	318	5	317	0	143
Criminal	40	125	0	129	0	36	Criminal	40	101	1	101	0	39
U.S. civil	30	86	2	86	1	27	U.S. civil	41	65	4	81	0	21
Private civil	92	210	2	209	1	90	Private civil	66	149	0	132	0	83
Administrative appeals	3	5	0	5	0	3	Administrative appeals	0	3	0	3	0	0
Fourth Circuit	213	782	21	763	5	206	Eleventh Circuit	320	777	12	823	7	255
Criminal	53	321	9	321	1	43	Criminal	105	262	1	286	0	80
U.S. civil	56	202	2	192	0	64	U.S. civil	82	195	2	217	1	57
Private civil	100	247	9	235	4	99	Private civil	131	310	9	315	6	111
Administrative appeals	4	12	1	15	0	0	Administrative appeals	2	10	0	5	0	7
Fifth Circuit	389	1,303	11	1,257	3	421							
Criminal	175	676	3	684	1	163							
U.S. civil	26	93	1	77	0	41							
Private civil	186	531	7	494	2	214							
Administrative appeals	2	3	0	2	0	3							

Note: "Writ of certiorari" is an order by the appellate court that is used when the court has discretion on whether to hear an appeal. If the appellate court grants the writ, it has the effect of ordering the lower court to certify the record and send it up to the higher court, which will then hear the appeal. "U.S. civil" filings involve suits against the Federal Government brought in U.S. District Courts. "Private civil" filings involve suits wherein litigation is between States and/or private citizens. "Administrative appeals" include applications for enforcement or petitions for review of orders of an administrative board or agency. Data for the U.S. Court of Appeals for the Federal circuit are not included in the above table. For a list of U.S. District Courts in each circuit, see table 5.11.

Source: Administrative Office of the United States Courts, *Judicial Business of the United States Courts: 2003 Annual Report of the Director* (Washington, DC: USGPO, 2004), pp. 79-81.

Table 5.71

U.S. Supreme Court cases argued and decided on merits

At conclusion of the October term, 1982-2002

October term	Argued Total	Government participating	Government as petitioner or appellant[b]	Government as respondent or appellee[b]	Government as amicus[c]	Government not participating	Decided on merits[a] Total	Government participating	Decided in favor of Government's position[b]	Decided against Government's position[b]	Not classifiable as for or against[b]	Government not participating
Number												
1982	183	131	44	44	43	52	283	172	115	50	7	111
1983	184	118	46	33	39	66	262	150	124	23	3	112
1984	175	114	37	34	43	61	236	146	113	30	3	90
1985	171	106	39	24	43	65	275	139	99	35	5	136
1986	175	104	27	32	45	71	282	140	98	36	6	142
1987	167	106	36	34	36	61	251	135	82	38	15	116
1988	170	91	25	25	41	79	265	122	86	25	11	143
1989	146	89	26	23	40	57	224	108	67	39	2	116
1990	125	77	10	32	35	48	232	107	74	31	2	125
1991	123	84	26	17	41	39	183	103	76	22	5	80
1992	116	88	24	23	41	28	206	126	84	36	6	80
1993	99	70	11	20	39	29	157	97	56	37	4	60
1994	94	64	21	16	27	30	146	84	48	33	3	62
1995	90	68	13	28	27	22	189	129	50	70[d]	9	60
1996	90	68	18	19	31	22	160	103	72	21	10	57
1997	96	70	13	26	31	26	146	83	55	26	2	63
1998	90	76	13	26	37	14	143	94	63	25	6	49
1999	81	58	12	21	25	23	131	77	43	33	1	54
2000	87	67	14	20	33	20	201	151	42	105[e]	4	50
2001	88	75	21	21	33	13	158	92	71	21	0	66
2002	84	71	10	15	46	13	147	89[f]	71	16	2	58
Percent												
1982	100%	72%	34%	34%	33%	28%	100%	61%	67%	29%	4%	39%
1983	100	64	39	28	33	36	100	57	83	15	2	43
1984	100	65	32	30	38	35	100	62	77	21	2	38
1985	100	62	37	23	41	38	100	51	71	25	4	49
1986	100	59	26	31	43	41	100	50	70	26	4	50
1987	100	63	34	32	34	37	100	54	61	28	11	46
1988	100	54	27	27	45	46	100	46	70	20	9	54
1989	100	61	29	26	45	39	100	48	62	36	2	52
1990	100	62	13	42	45	38	100	46	69	29	2	54
1991	100	68	31	20	49	32	100	56	74	21	5	44
1992	100	76	27	26	47	24	100	61	67	29	5	39
1993	100	71	16	29	56	29	100	62	58	38	4	38
1994	100	68	33	25	42	32	100	58	57	39	4	42
1995	100	76	19	41	40	24	100	68	39	54	7	32
1996	100	75	26	28	45	24	100	64	70	20	10	36
1997	100	73	19	37	44	27	100	57	66	31	2	43
1998	100	84	17	34	49	16	100	66	67	27	6	34
1999	100	72	15	26	31	28	100	59	33	25	1	41
2000	100	77	16	23	38	23	100	75	28	69	1	25
2001	100	85	28	28	44	15	100	58	77	23	0	42
2002	100	85	14	21	65	15	100	61	80	18	2	39

Note: These data represent actions taken during the annual terms of the U.S. Supreme Court. "Amicus" refers to a party who is not involved directly in the suit, but who demonstrates an interest in the case by filing a supportive brief. "Decided on merits" refers to a reassessment and resolution of the substantive issues presented in the case, and does not involve active participation of the litigants through the filing of written and oral arguments. Some data have been revised by the Source and may differ from previous editions of SOURCEBOOK.

[a] Includes cases summarily affirmed, reversed, or vacated on the In Forma Pauperis Docket.
[b] Percent is based on the total cases in which the Government participated.
[c] Includes cases in which the Government filed briefs as amicus curiae but did not participate in the argument.
[d] Includes 43 cases that were vacated and remanded for further consideration.
[e] Includes 66 cases that were vacated and remanded for further consideration.
[f] Includes 17 cases that were vacated and remanded and 1 case that was remanded for further consideration.

Source: Table adapted from tables provided to SOURCEBOOK staff by the U.S. Department of Justice, Office of the Solicitor General.

Table 5.72

Executive clemency applications for Federal offenses received, disposed of, and pending in the Office of the U.S. Pardon Attorney

Fiscal years 1953-2003

Fiscal year	Pending from previous fiscal year	Received	Granted Pardons	Granted Commutations	Denied
1953	543[a]	599	97	8	356
1954	681	461	55	7	348
1955	732	662	59	4	684
1956	647	585	192	9	568
1957	463	585	232	4	443
1958	369	406	98	6	302
1959	369	434	117	2	286
1960	398	437	149	5	244
1961	437[a]	481	226	18	266
1962	408	595	166	16	315
1963	506	592	133	45	233
1964	687[a]	921	315	73	437
1965	783	1,008	195	80	569
1966	947	865	364	81	726
1967	641	863	222	23	520
1968	739	749	13	3	415
1969	1,057[a]	724	0	0	505
1970	1,276	459	82	14	698
1971	941	454	157	16	648
1972	574	516	235	20	410
1973	425	485	202	5	341
1974	362	426	187	8	337
1975	256	610	147	9	325
1976	385	742	106	11	442
1977	568[a]	738	129	8	301
1978	868	641	162	3	836
1979	508	710	143	10	448
1980	617	523	155	11	498
1981	474[a]	547	76	7	259
1982	679	462	83	3	547
1983	508	447	91	2	306
1984	556	447	37	5	326
1985	635	407	32	3	279
1986	728	362	55	0	290
1987	745	410	23	0	311
1988	824	384	38	0	497
1989	673[a]	373	41	1	392
1990	616	354	0	0	289
1991	681	318	29	0	681
1992	289	379	0	0	192
1993	476[a]	868	36	2	251
1994	1,048	808	0	0	785
1995	1,071	612	53	3	588
1996	1,039	512	0	0	371
1997	1,174	685	0	0	555
1998	1,304	608	21	0	378
1999	1,512	1,009	34	14	601
2000[b]	1,872	1,388	70	6	1,027
2001[c]	2,153[a]	1,828	218	40	483
2002	3,310	1,248	0	0	2,278
2003	2,281	1,023	7	0	1,050

Note: Article II, Section 2 of the U.S. Constitution authorizes the President to grant executive clemency for Federal criminal offenses. The U.S. Pardon Attorney, in consultation with the Attorney General's office, receives and reviews all petitions for executive clemency, initiates the necessary investigations, and prepares the recommendations of the Attorney General to the President. Clemency may be a reprieve, remission of fine or restitution, commutation, or pardon. A "pardon," which is generally considered only after sentence completion, restores basic civil rights and may aid in the reinstatement of professional or trade licenses that may have been lost as a result of the conviction. A "commutation" is a reduction of sentence. Commutations include remission of fines. Petitions denied also include those that are closed administratively. Cases in which multiple forms of relief were granted are counted in only one category. The figures presented in this table do not include clemency actions on draft resisters, or military deserters and absentees during the Vietnam war era. Some data have been revised by the Source and may differ from previous editions of SOURCEBOOK.

[a] In inaugural years, these figures are for the outgoing Administration.
[b] In addition to the six commutations, President Clinton granted one reprieve of an execution date during fiscal year 2000.
[c] In addition to the 40 commutations, President Clinton granted 1 reprieve of an execution date during fiscal year 2001.

Source: U.S. Department of Justice, Office of the Pardon Attorney [Online]. Available: http://www.usdoj.gov/pardon/actions_administration.htm [July 6, 2004]; and data provided by the U.S. Department of Justice, Office of the Pardon Attorney. Table adapted by SOURCEBOOK staff.

Table 5.73

Arrests and convictions handled by the U.S. Postal Inspection Service

Fiscal years 1981-2003

Fiscal year	Total Arrests	Total Convictions	Mail fraud Arrests	Mail fraud Convictions
1981	5,358	5,410	1,100	1,046
1982	5,658	4,783	1,026	966
1983	6,254	5,019	1,194	938
1984	6,426	5,095	1,272	1,042
1985	7,115	5,570	1,142	887
1986	8,620	6,608	1,435	1,131
1987	9,006	7,732	1,304	1,206
1988	10,470	8,114	1,488	1,015
1989	11,502	9,479	1,543	1,225
1990	12,060	9,614	1,699	1,486
1991	13,513	10,320	1,772	1,297
1992	14,578	11,359	1,904	1,582
1993	14,263	12,428	1,965	1,900
1994	11,514	10,588	1,730	1,571
1995	10,920	10,038	1,538	1,473
1996	10,540	9,097	1,547	1,342
1997	10,668	10,013	1,545	1,533
1998	10,095	9,642	1,396	1,533
1999	10,395	9,337	1,523	1,370
2000	11,356	9,393	1,633	1,377
2001	11,873	9,914	1,691	1,477
2002	10,828	9,588	1,634	1,453
2003	11,161	9,783	1,453	1,387

Note: The U.S. Postal Inspection Service is the law enforcement agency of the U.S. Postal Service. Responsibilities include enforcing over 200 statutes related to crime against the mail, the Postal Service, Postal Service employees, and customers. The Office of Inspector General (OIG), established in 1996, is an independent agency within the Postal Service. The OIG's main responsibilities are to prevent and detect fraud, waste, program abuse and mismanagement; promote efficiency of operations; and conduct investigations of revenue and cost containment issues. The Postal Inspection Service continues to be primarily concerned with the security and integrity of the mail, postal employees, and their environments; and conducts investigations relating to these responsibilities. Data for 1997 to 2000 include the activities of both the Postal Inspection Service and the OIG.

Arrests and convictions include joint investigations with other Federal law enforcement agencies. Convictions reported in a given year may be the result of arrests made during a previous year.

Source: U.S. Postal Service, U.S. Postal Inspection Service, *Semiannual Report, April 1 - September 30, 1991*, p. 55; *April 1 - September 30, 1992*, p. 65; *April 1 - September 30, 1993*, p. 60; *April 1 - September 30, 1994*, p. 63; *April 1 - September 30, 1995*, p. 47; *April 1 - September 30, 1996*, p. 56 (Washington, DC: U.S. Postal Inspection Service); U.S. Postal Service, Office of Inspector General, *Semiannual Report, April 1 - September 30, 1997*, p. 63; *April 1, 1998 - September 30, 1998*, pp. 100, 101; *October 1, 1998 - March 31, 1999*, p. 104; *April 1, 1999 - September 30, 1999*, p. 118; *October 1, 1999 - March 31, 2000*, p. 138; *April 1 - September 30, 2000*, p. 115 (Washington, DC: U.S. Postal Service); U.S. Postal Inspection Service, *2001 Annual Report of Investigations of the United States Postal Inspection Service*, p. 58; *2002*, p. 62; *2003*, p. 75 (Washington, DC: U.S. Postal Inspection Service); and data provided by the U.S. Postal Service, U.S. Postal Inspection Service. Table constructed by SOURCEBOOK staff.

Table 5.74

Arrests and convictions handled by the U.S. Postal Inspection Service

By type of offense, fiscal year 2003

Type of offense	Arrests	Convictions
Total	11,161	9,783
Internal crime		
Narcotics	31	29
Miscellaneous	87	57
External crime		
Burglary	128	115
Robbery	61	70
Assault	356	274
Miscellaneous	448	351
Prohibited mailings		
Pornography/obscenity	320	289
Controlled substances	1,378	1,180
Bombs, threats, hoaxes, and explosive devices	99	82
Miscellaneous	128	125
Revenue and Asset Protection Program		
Financial and expenditure investigations	285	271
Workers' Compensation fraud	50	43
Revenue investigations	68	54
Mail fraud	1,453	1,387
Mail theft	6,269	5,456

Note: See Note, table 5.73. Internal crimes are those involving employees of the U.S. Postal Service and external crimes are those committed by individuals or groups outside the organization. Narcotics cases include both employees and non-employees selling narcotics on postal property. Miscellaneous internal crimes include theft of postal property and sabotage of equipment. Assault includes threats and assaults against on-duty postal employees. Miscellaneous external crimes include counterfeit and contraband postage, money order offenses, vandalism, and arson. Pornography/obscenity includes mailing of child pornography, obscenity, or sexually-oriented advertisements. Controlled substances include narcotics, steroids, drug-related proceeds, and drug paraphernalia. Miscellaneous prohibited mailings include hazardous material, firearms and weapons, intoxicants, extortion, and false documents.

The Revenue and Asset Protection Program (RAPP) was established in 1995 and combines portions of the audit and criminal investigation activities. The objective of RAPP is to give priority to the protection of postal revenue and assets. Activities include reviewing internal controls, examining unfavorable trends and significant variations in activity, and pursuing information received through financial audits, customer complaints, and anonymous tips.

Source: U.S. Postal Inspection Service, *2003 Annual Report of Investigations of the United States Postal Inspection Service* (Washington, DC: U.S. Postal Inspection Service, 2004), p. 75. Table adapted by SOURCEBOOK staff.

Table 5.75

Prosecutions for violations of U.S. immigration and naturalization laws

By type of case and disposition, and aggregate fines and imprisonment imposed,
fiscal years 1990, 1993-2003

Type of case and disposition	1990	1993	1994	1995	1996	1997	1998	1999	2000	2001	2002	2003
Total, all cases	20,079	18,731	14,854	17,035	16,115	19,180	23,826	22,491	22,926	24,316	23,852	24,917
Dismissals[a]	7,310	6,806	4,558	4,836	3,886	2,972	2,281	1,962	2,079	3,169	2,694	2,382
Acquittals	50	240	86	124	108	24	65	58	96	92	114	57
Convictions	12,719	11,685	10,210	12,075	12,121	16,184	21,480	20,471	20,751	21,055	21,044	22,478
Aggregate fines imposed	$2,935,664	$2,613,297	$101,503,303	$955,054	$1,131,709	$760,209	$776,622	$1,275,604	$4,795,872	$12,498,608	$2,171,518	$1,066,176
Aggregate imprisonment (in years)	5,749	6,621	7,513	7,161	6,947	11,353	12,030	14,843	19,003	17,863	16,804	19,643
Immigration cases, total	19,351	15,566	13,068	15,337	14,223	17,807	22,857	21,588	22,071	23,374	23,221	24,152
Dismissals[a]	6,788	5,232	3,814	4,133	3,102	2,566	2,029	1,783	1,983	2,989	2,628	2,286
Acquittals	48	145	74	94	107	22	60	52	81	88	108	46
Convictions	12,515	10,189	9,180	11,110	11,014	15,219	20,768	19,753	20,007	20,297	20,485	21,820
Aggregate fines imposed	$2,872,279	$2,242,129	$316,163	$609,480	$959,214	$310,893	$437,547	$692,477	$3,677,297	$468,718	$707,224	$941,950
Aggregate imprisonment (in years)	5,642	3,873	3,716	5,234	5,436	8,059	10,455	12,922	16,109	14,786	15,613	17,773
Naturalization cases, total	728	695	506	328	176	212	171	206	211	196	171	155
Dismissals[a]	522	326	336	210	43	(b)	42	33	(b)	28	22	(b)
Acquittals	2	82	10	5	0	(b)	0	0	(b)	0	3	(b)
Convictions	204	287	160	113	133	164	129	173	181	168	146	137
Aggregate fines imposed	$63,385	$9,660	$7,080	$13,695	$3,195	$11,579	$7,870	$10,575	$74,545	$26,025	$7,550	$1,650
Aggregate imprisonment (in years)	107	94	36	52	64	77	116	180	101	121	104	118
Other cases, total	NA	2,470	1,280	1,370	1,716	1,161	798	697	644	746	460	610
Dismissals[a]	NA	1,248	408	493	741	(b)	210	146	67	152	44	79
Acquittals	NA	13	2	25	1	(b)	5	6	14	4	3	10
Convictions	NA	1,209	870	852	974	801	583	545	563	590	413	521
Aggregate fines imposed	NA	$361,508	$101,180,060	$331,879	$169,300	$437,737	$331,205	$572,552	$1,044,030	$12,003,865	$1,456,744	$122,576
Aggregate imprisonment (in years)	NA	2,654	3,761	1,875	1,447	3,217	1,459	1,741	2,793	2,956	1,087	1,752

Note: Violations of nationality laws include false representations as citizens of the United States, false statements and procurement of citizenship or naturalization unlawfully, and reproduction of citizenship and naturalization papers. Some data have been revised by the Source and may differ from previous editions of SOURCEBOOK.

[a]Dismissed or otherwise closed.
[b]Beginning with the 1997 data, in order to protect the identity of individuals the Source has suppressed the value in any cell with a count of one or two and associated cells that would reveal such a count through calculation.

Source: U.S. Department of Justice, Immigration and Naturalization Service, *2000 Statistical Yearbook of the Immigration and Naturalization Service*, p. 265 [Online]. Available: http://uscis.gov/graphics/shared/aboutus/statistics/Yearbook2000.pdf [Oct. 7, 2004]; *2001 Statistical Yearbook of the Immigration and Naturalization Service*, p. 269 [Online]. Available: http://uscis.gov/graphics/shared/aboutus/statistics/Yearbook2001.pdf [Oct. 7, 2004]; U.S. Department of Homeland Security, Office of Immigration Statistics, *2003 Yearbook of Immigration Statistics*, p. 180 [Online]. Available: http://uscis.gov/graphics/shared/aboutus/statistics/2003yearbook.pdf [Oct. 7, 2004]; and data provided by the U.S. Department of Justice, Immigration and Naturalization Service. Table adapted by SOURCEBOOK staff.

Table 5.76

Convictions for violations of U.S. immigration and naturalization laws

By offense, fiscal years 1990-2003

Offense	1990	1991	1992	1993	1994	1995	1996	1997	1998	1999	2000	2001	2002	2003
Total	12,529	11,509	9,865	11,685	10,210	12,075	12,121	16,184	21,480	20,471	20,751	21,055	21,042	22,478
Violations of immigration laws	12,325	11,392	9,766	10,189	9,180	11,110	11,014	15,219	20,768	19,753	20,007	20,297	20,483	21,820
Illegal entry of aliens	8,162	7,214	6,341	7,179	6,607	7,430	6,361	9,723	15,050	13,515	12,733	13,378	13,371	14,199
Reentries of deported aliens	444	547	477	767	803	1,475	2,331	2,859	3,149	3,623	4,759	4,315	4,699	4,938
Bringing in, transporting, harboring illegal aliens	1,431	1,498	977	1,008	731	758	1,295	1,182	1,103	1,403	1,700	1,680	1,691	1,612
Fraud and false statements to obtain or confer immigration benefits	NA	NA	NA	132	58	45	28	63	41	36	31	98	119	270
Fraud, forgery, misuse of visas, alien registration, and other documents	289	318	306	83	32	301	254	203	322	366	362	327	196	253
Fraud, forgery, misuse of identification documents	NA	NA	NA	936	918	1,032	681	1,127	1,032	765	363	432	367	390
Fraud and false statements or entries	83	68	109	NA	NA	NA	NA	NA	NA	NA	NA	NA	NA	NA
Alien registration or alien address violations	135	93	39	6	12	NA	NA	NA	NA	NA	NA	NA	NA	NA
Producing, transferring, possessing, stealing, using, or selling false identification documents	597	602	497	NA	NA	NA	NA	NA	NA	NA	NA	NA	NA	NA
Conspiracy to defraud the United States	615	252	121	38	8	NA	12	10	18	8	(a)	(a)	5	6
Employing unauthorized aliens, peonage, false attestations for employment	NA	NA	NA	40	11	52	48	48	48	24	49	(a)	25	72
Other immigration violations	569	334	401	0	0	17	4	4	5	13	(a)	47	10	80
Violations of naturalization laws	204	117	99	287	160	113	133	164	129	173	181	168	146	137
False representation as citizen of the United States	137	69	59	221	130	76	101	105	81	99	93	129	98	101
False statements and procurement of citizenship or naturalization unlawfully	60	36	37	3	2	NA	NA	NA	NA	NA	NA	NA	NA	NA
Reproduction and sale of citizenship and naturalization papers	7	12	3	NA	NA	NA	NA	NA	NA	NA	NA	NA	NA	NA
Fraud, forgery, misuse of citizen naturalization papers	NA	NA	NA	2	3	9	14	22	16	(a)	3	4	7	6
Fraud, forgery, misuse of U.S. passports	NA	NA	NA	61	25	28	18	37	32	42	85	35	41	30
Other naturalization violations	NA	NA	NA	0	0	0	0	0	0	(a)	0	0	0	0
Other violations	NA	NA	NA	1,209	870	852	974	801	583	545	563	590	413	521
Racketeering	NA	NA	NA	692	467	443	662	342	313	263	199	185	122	173
Money laundering and financial fraud	NA	NA	NA	20	11	15	3	(a)	25	3	29	10	17	(a)
Weapons trafficking, unlawful possession	NA	NA	NA	46	44	32	16	29	27	39	64	84	105	67
Drug trafficking	NA	466	498	358	292	272	222	378	146	186	175	226	126	158
Obstructing justice	NA	NA	NA	68	42	46	29	26	33	15	39	57	37	35
Alien prostitution	NA	NA	NA	0	1	5	13	(a)	7	3	4	6	(a)	(a)
Other violations	NA	NA	NA	25	13	39	29	21	32	36	53	22	(a)	63

Note: Some data have been revised by the Source and may differ from previous editions of SOURCEBOOK.

[a]Beginning with the 1997 data, in order to protect the identity of individuals the Source has suppressed the value in any cell with a count of one or two and associated cells that would reveal such a count through calculation.

Source: U.S. Department of Justice, Immigration and Naturalization Service, *2000 Statistical Yearbook of the Immigration and Naturalization Service*, p. 266 [Online]. Available: http://uscis.gov/graphics/shared/aboutus/statistics/Yearbook2000.pdf [Oct. 7, 2004]; *2001 Statistical Yearbook of the Immigration and Naturalization Service*, p. 270 [Online]. Available: http://uscis.gov/graphics/shared/aboutus/statistics/Yearbook2001.pdf [Oct. 7, 2004]; U.S. Department of Homeland Security, Office of Immigration Statistics, *2002 Yearbook of Immigration Statistics*, p. 210 [Online]. Available: http://uscis.gov/graphics/shared/aboutus/statistics/Yearbook2002.pdf [Oct. 7, 2004]; *2003 Yearbook of Immigration Statistics*, p. 181 [Online]. Available: http://uscis.gov/graphics/shared/aboutus/statistics/2003yearbook.pdf [Oct. 7, 2004]; and data provided by the U.S. Department of Justice, Immigration and Naturalization Service. Table adapted by SOURCEBOOK staff.

Table 5.77

Immigration offenders investigated, charged in U.S. District Courts, and admitted to Federal prison

United States, 1985-2000

	Immigration offenders		
	Investigated	Charged	Admitted to Federal prison
1985	7,239	6,744	NA
1986	8,858	8,237	7,440
1987	7,424	6,677	6,571
1988	7,255	6,818	5,170
1989	7,854	7,493	5,870
1990	8,784	8,313	7,488
1991	7,854	6,632	6,228
1992	6,470	5,904	5,108
1993	5,934	5,390	5,036
1994	5,526	5,006	5,514
1995	7,256	6,294	5,873
1996	7,122	6,605	6,252
1997	9,366	8,472	7,300
1998	14,144	12,879	9,762
1999	15,539	14,729	11,857
2000	16,495	15,613	13,151

Note: These data are from the U.S. Department of Justice, Bureau of Justice Statistics' (BJS) Federal Justice Statistics Program, a database comprised of information from various Federal agencies. Immigration offenses are defined according to the BJS filing offense classification procedure followed by the Administrative Office of the United States Courts. The category is composed largely of the following offense types: smuggling, transporting, and harboring aliens; unlawful entry and reentry of aliens; and misuse of visa and other documents. (Source, p. 8.) The data presented are for offenders for whom an immigration offense was the most serious offense.

Source: U.S. Department of Justice, Bureau of Justice Statistics, *Immigration Offenders in the Federal Criminal Justice System, 2000*, Special Report NCJ 191745 (Washington, DC: U.S. Department of Justice, August 2002), p. 10, Appendix for figure 4.

Table 5.78

Nationality of suspects in matters referred to U.S. attorneys for immigration offenses

United States, 2000

		Immigration offenses				
			Unlawful entry or reentry			
Geographic region and nationality	Number	Total	Improper entry	Reentry by removed alien	Smuggling	Misuse of visas/other
Total[a]	16,495	74.9%	24.4%	50.5%	20.2%	4.9%
U.S. citizen	1,110	29.8	13.3	16.5	64.3	6.0
Mexico	9,425	86.6	23.7	62.9	10.8	2.6
Other countries[b]	1,817	82.9	45.5	37.4	9.7	7.5
Asia and Oceania						
China	433	93.1	92.4	0.7	5.1	1.9
Other	165	60.6	35.8	24.9	28.5	10.9
Central America						
Honduras	223	91.9	31.8	60.1	3.6	4.5
El Salvador	113	92.0	40.7	51.3	6.2	1.8
Guatemala	67	77.6	22.4	55.2	1.5	20.9
Other	25	92.0	32.0	60.0	4.0	4.0
Caribbean						
Dominican Republic	190	89.0	13.2	75.8	4.7	6.3
Other	198	85.4	40.4	45.0	9.1	5.6
Europe	134	73.1	29.9	43.3	16.4	10.5
South America						
Colombia	55	70.9	7.3	63.6	10.9	18.2
Other	56	73.2	21.4	51.8	10.7	16.1
Not indicated on arrest record	2,835	78.1	25.5	52.6	13.4	8.5

Note: See Note, table 5.77.

[a] Includes 1,308 suspects for whom an investigation record could not be matched with an arrest record to ascertain nationality.

[b] Includes 158 suspects from other countries not listed.

Source: U.S. Department of Justice, Bureau of Justice Statistics, *Immigration Offenders in the Federal Criminal Justice System, 2000*, Special Report NCJ 191745 (Washington, DC: U.S. Department of Justice, August 2002), p. 2, Table 2.

Table 5.79

Persons indicted, awaiting trial on December 31, and convicted of offenses involving abuse of public office

By level of government, 1973-2002

	Total			Elected or appointed official									Others involved		
				Federal			State			Local					
	In-dicted	Awaiting trial on Dec. 31	Con-victed	In-dicted	Awaiting trial on Dec. 31	Con-victed	In-dicted	Awaiting trial on Dec. 31	Con-victed	In-dicted	Awaiting trial on Dec. 31	Con-victed	In-dicted	Awaiting trial on Dec. 31	Con-victed
Total	28,419	7,997	24,605	12,165	2,262	10,788	2,292	824	1,924	6,825	2,361	5,634	7,137	2,550	6,259
1973	191	18	144	60	2	48	19	0	17	85	2	64	27	14	15
1974	305	5	213	59	1	51	36	0	23	130	4	87	80	0	52
1975	294	27	211	53	5	43	36	5	18	139	15	94	66	2	56
1976	391	199	260	111	1	101	59	30	35	194	98	100	27	70	24
1977	535	210	440	129	32	94	50	33	38	157	62	164	199	83	144
1978	530	205	418	133	42	91	55	20	56	171	72	127	171	71	144
1979	579	178	419	114	21	102	56	29	31	211	63	151	198	65	135
1980	727	213	602	123	16	131	72	28	51	247	82	168	285	87	252
1981	808	231	730	198	23	159	87	36	66	244	102	211	279	70	294
1982	813	186	671	158	38	147	49	18	43	257	58	232	349	72	249
1983	1,076	222	972	460[a]	58	424	81	26	65	270	61	226	265	77	257
1984	931	269	934	408	77	429	58	21	52	203	74	196	262	97	257
1985	1,157	256	997	563	90	470	79	20	66	248	49	221	267	97	240
1986	1,208	246	1,026	596	83	523	88	24	71	232	55	207	292	81	225
1987	1,276	368	1,081	651	118	545	102	26	76	246	89	204	277	135	256
1988	1,274	288	1,067	629	86	529	66	14	69	276	79	229	303	109	240
1989	1,348	375	1,149	695	126	610	71	18	54	269	122	201	313	109	284
1990	1,176	300	1,084	615	103	583	96	28	79	257	98	225	208	71	197
1991	1,452	346	1,194	803	149	665	115	42	77	242	88	180	292	67	272
1992	1,189	380	1,081	624	139	532	81	24	92	232	91	211	252	126	246
1993	1,371	403	1,362	627	133	595	113	39	133	309	132	272	322	99	362
1994	1,165	332	969	571	124	488	99	17	97	248	96	202	247	95	182
1995	1,051	323	878	527	120	438	61	23	61	236	89	191	227	91	188
1996	984	244	902	456	64	459	109	40	83	219	60	190	200	80	170
1997	1,057	327	853	459	83	392	51	20	49	255	118	169	292	106	243
1998	1,174	340	1,014	442	85	414	91	37	58	277	90	264	364	128	278
1999	1,134	329	1,065	480	101	460	115	44	80	237	95	219	302	89	306
2000	1,000	327	938	441	92	422	92	37	91	211	89	183	256	109	242
2001	1,087	437	920	502	131	414	95	75	61	224	110	184	266	121	261
2002	1,136	413	1,011	478	119	429	110	50	132	299	118	262	249	126	188

Note: Questionnaires are sent annually to the U.S. attorneys' offices in each of the Federal judicial districts eliciting data concerning indictments and convictions during the year as well as prosecutions awaiting trial on December 31 of each year. Response rates for the 94 Federal judicial districts are consistently high, yielding an average response rate of 97%. These data cover persons elected or appointed to office and career (staff) government employees; "others involved" include individuals who hold no official position, but who participated in an offense aimed at corrupting another's public office. "Abuse of public office" includes offenses such as fraud, extortion, bribery, conflict of interest, election ballot fraud, and campaign finance offenses. Some data have been revised by the Source and may differ from previous editions of SOURCEBOOK.

[a] The 1983 figures were reviewed to attempt to identify the reason for the substantial increase in prosecutions of Federal officials. The explanation appeared to be two-fold: there had been a greater focus on Federal corruption nationwide, and there appeared to have been more consistent reporting of lower-level employees who abused their office, cases that may have been overlooked in the past. For reference, the U.S. attorneys' offices were told: "For purposes of this questionnaire, a public corruption case includes any case involving abuse of office by a public employee. We are not excluding low-level employees or minor crimes, but rather focusing on the job-relatedness of the offense and whether the offense involves abuse of the public trust placed in the employee."

Source: U.S. Department of Justice, Criminal Division, "Report to Congress on the Activities and Operations of the Public Integrity Section for 1991," pp. 28, 29; "1992," pp. 36, 37; "1999," pp. 38, 39; "2002," pp. 37, 38. Washington, DC: U.S. Department of Justice. (Mimeographed.) Table adapted by SOURCEBOOK staff.

Table 5.80

U.S. Army personnel tried in general, special, and summary courts-martial, and discharges approved

By conviction status, United States, fiscal years 1997-2003

Fiscal year	Type of courts-martial									Discharges approved		
	General			Special[a]			Summary					
	Tried	Convicted	Acquitted	Tried	Convicted	Acquitted	Tried	Convicted	Acquitted	Dishonorable	Dismissal	Bad conduct[b]
1997	741	701	40	325	279	46	396	381	15	152	26	546
1998	685	639	46	287	261	26	489	464	25	138	14	554
1999	737	692	45	432	409	23	487	459	28	142	15	614
2000	731	653	78	393	318	75[c]	666	638	28	123	26	610
2001	770	739	31	357	333	24[c]	672	645	27	67	11	454
2002	788	757	31	602	582	20	858	793	65	106	19	426
2003	689	657	32	665	651	14	858	812	46	115	16	629

Note: Courts-martial have exclusive jurisdiction over military offenses and acts or omissions that violate local criminal law, foreign or domestic, for any persons subject to the Uniform Code of Military Justice (UCMJ). The data presented are for violations of the UCMJ, including acts violating civilian criminal codes that were tried by courts-martial. "General courts-martial" consist of a military judge and not less than five members (jurors), or by request of the accused, the case may be heard by a military judge alone. General courts-martial have jurisdiction to try any person subject to the UCMJ and adjudge any punishment authorized in the Rules for Courts-Martial (RCM) including the death penalty. "Special courts-martial" consist of not less than three members and also may include a military judge. Special courts-martial have jurisdiction to try persons for noncapital offenses and adjudge any punishment except death, dishonorable discharge, dismissal, confinement for more than 1 year, hard labor without confinement for more than 3 months, forfeiture of pay exceeding two-thirds pay per month, or forfeiture exceeding 1 year. "Summary courts-martial" consist of one commissioned officer and the maximum penalty that can be adjudged is confinement for 30 days, forfeiture of two-thirds of 1 month's pay, and reduction to the lowest pay grade.

A "dishonorable discharge" may be adjudged only by general courts-martial and applies to enlisted persons and noncommissioned warrant officers convicted of offenses usually recognized in civilian jurisdictions as felonies, or offenses of a military nature requiring severe punishment. A "dismissal" may be adjudged only by general courts-martial and applies to commissioned officers, warrant officers, cadets, and midshipmen. A "bad-conduct discharge" (BCD) applies only to enlisted persons and may be adjudged by general or special courts-martial. It is less severe than a dishonorable discharge and is designed as punishment for bad conduct, rather than for serious offenses of a military or civilian nature. A BCD also can be applied to persons convicted repeatedly of minor offenses and whose punitive separation appears necessary by the courts-martial. (Source: Joint Service Committee on Military Justice, *Manual for Courts-Martial United States*, 2002 Edition [Online]. Available: http://www.usapa.army.mil/pdffiles/mcm2002.pdf.)

[a]Includes BCD and non-BCD special courts-martial.
[b]Includes bad conduct discharges adjudged by both general and special courts-martial.
[c]Acquittals also include cases withdrawn or dismissed after arraignment.

Source: U.S. Court of Appeals for the Armed Forces, *Annual Reports* [Online]. Available: http://www.armfor.uscourts.gov/Annual.htm [May 26, 2004]. Table constructed by SOURCEBOOK staff.

Table 5.81

U.S. Navy and Marine Corps personnel tried in general, special, and summary courts-martial, and discharges approved

By conviction status, United States, fiscal years 1997-2003

Fiscal year	Type of courts-martial									Discharges approved	
	General			Special[a]			Summary				
	Tried	Convicted	Acquitted	Tried	Convicted	Acquitted	Tried	Convicted	Acquitted	Dishonorable	Bad conduct[b]
1997	548	511	37	2,698	2,586	112	1,631	1,589	42	205	1,976
1998	470	459	11	2,322	2,309	13	1,783	1,762	21	173	1,857
1999	349	317	31	2,102	2,009	93	1,565	1,529	36	114	1,698
2000	428	398	30	2,381	2,298	83	1,883	1,802	81	98	1,659
2001	481	454	27	2,264	2,222	42	2,103	2,074	29	114	1,823
2002	499	481	18	2,188	2,144	44	2,098	2,078	20	164	1,819
2003	315	291	24	1,854	1,815	39	1,990	1,955	35	99	1,596

Note: See Note, table 5.80.

[a]Includes only BCD; the Navy and Marine Corps did not convene non-BCD special courts-martial.
[b]Includes bad conduct discharges adjudged by both general and special courts-martial.

Source: U.S. Court of Appeals for the Armed Forces, *Annual Reports* [Online]. Available: http://www.armfor.uscourts.gov/Annual.htm [May 26, 2004]. Table constructed by SOURCEBOOK staff.

Table 5.82
U.S. Air Force personnel tried in general, special, and summary courts-martial, and discharges approved

By conviction status, United States, fiscal years 1997-2003

Fiscal year	General Tried	General Convicted	General Acquitted	Special[a] Tried	Special[a] Convicted	Special[a] Acquitted	Summary Tried	Summary Convicted	Summary Acquitted	Discharges approved Dishonorable	Discharges approved Bad conduct[b]
1997	527	489	38	405	380	25	70	69	1	87	461
1998	442	411	31	304	288	16	76	73	3	44	322
1999	421	396	25	333	313	20	91	90	1	52	338
2000	438	404	34	320	306	14	139	135	4	36	395
2001	490	463	27	340	318	22	126	125	1	43	443
2002	564	534	30	384	351	19	119	118	1	61	540
2003	351	329	22	471	441	30	101	100	1	85[c]	466

Note: See Note, table 5.80.

[a] Includes both BCD and non-BCD special courts-martial for fiscal year 1997; beginning in fiscal year 1998, the Air Force no longer convenes non-BCD special courts-martial.
[b] Includes bad conduct discharges adjudged by both general and special courts-martial.
[c] Includes 28 officer dismissals.

Source: U.S. Court of Appeals for the Armed Forces, *Annual Reports* [Online]. Available: http://www.armfor.uscourts.gov/Annual.htm [May 26, 2004]. Table constructed by SOURCEBOOK staff.

Table 5.83
U.S. Coast Guard personnel tried in general, special, and summary courts-martial, and discharges approved

By conviction status, United States, fiscal years 1997-2003

Fiscal year	General Tried	General Convicted	General Acquitted	Special[a] Tried	Special[a] Convicted	Special[a] Acquitted	Summary Tried	Summary Convicted	Summary Acquitted	Discharges approved Dishonorable	Discharges approved Bad conduct[b]
1997	6	6	0	9	9	0	10	10	0	2	7
1998	18	17	1	21	20	--	8	8	0	3	12
1999	6	6	0	17	17	0	3	3	0	6	22
2000	10	9	1	23	23	0	11	10	1	2	14
2001	15	15	0	17	17	0	18	18	0	3	16
2002	4	4	0	23	23	0	11	11	0	2	19
2003	8	8	0	18	18	0	20	20	0	1	17

Note: See Note, table 5.80.

[a] Includes only BCD special courts-martial; the Coast Guard did not convene non-BCD special courts-martial.
[b] Includes bad conduct discharges adjudged by both general and special courts-martial.

Source: U.S. Court of Appeals for the Armed Forces, *Annual Reports* [Online]. Available: http://www.armfor.uscourts.gov/Annual.htm [May 26, 2004]. Table constructed by SOURCEBOOK staff.

Page 476 intentionally blank.

Section 6

Persons under correctional supervision

Inmates in local jails, prisoners in State and Federal correctional facilities, and persons on probation and parole are the focus of this section. In addition, data are provided on prisoners under sentence of death and those executed. Much of the material in this section is from the following Bureau of Justice Statistics (BJS)-sponsored data collection programs: the Census of Jails (conducted every 5 years), the Annual Survey of Jails (conducted in non-census years), the Survey of Inmates in Local Jails, the National Prisoner Statistics Program, the Annual Probation and Parole Surveys, the Federal Justice Statistics Program, and the Census of State and Federal Adult Correctional Facilities.

Opening the section are trend tables presenting a view of U.S. correctional populations over time, including numbers of jail inmates, prisoners, probationers, and parolees. These tables are followed by detailed enumerations of adults under Federal and State probation supervision. The number of entries and exits for State and Federal probation supervision are displayed by region and State, and the percent change in the population during the year is calculated. A set of tables provides information specific to persons under Federal community supervision, such as the number under supervision, the number of probation officers, and offenders terminating supervision by type of offense.

Data from the most recent Census of Juveniles in Residential Placement are presented. The census, sponsored by the U.S. Department of Justice, Office of Juvenile Justice and Delinquency Prevention, provides counts of juvenile detainees by race, ethnicity, sex, age, type of offense, and jurisdiction. A new table comparing the 2001 detainee counts in each State with by-State counts from the previous two censuses, 1997 and 1999, is included.

Next in this section are trend tables, covering varying years between 1983 and 2003, on the size of the population in jails and prisons. These tables are followed by more detailed data on jail inmates including the number, sex, and race of jail inmates; confinement status; conviction status; legal status; jails and jail inmates in Indian country; the prevalence of HIV in jail populations; and deaths occurring in jails. Featured this year are data from the latest (2002) Survey of Inmates in Local Jails. These tables display the characteristics of jail inmates, most serious offense, percent reporting drug and alcohol use, and family background while growing up.

The next portion of Section 6 contains several trend tables on prison populations, starting with tables that display the number and rate of sentenced male and female prisoners in State and Federal institutions back to 1925. A 24-year trend table displaying the rates of sentenced prisoners, by region and State is included, as is a table that compares the Federal and State prison populations for 2002 and 2003. This is followed by data from BJS' 2000 Census of State and Federal Adult Correctional Facilities. These tables display the number of prisoners in Federal, State, and private adult correctional facilities by type of facility and selected prisoner characteristics. Also from the 2000 census is a table showing the number of prisoners under age 18 in adult correctional facilities by type of facility, security level, and region. New this year is a trend table covering selected years between 1990 and 2003, that provides counts of prisoners under age 18 in State prisons.

What follows is a series of tables presenting data on a variety of topics from recent BJS reports. Statistics on firearm possession and usage by State and Federal prisoners, the number of female prisoners under jurisdiction of State and Federal correctional authorities, the number of noncitizens in State and Federal prisons, educational attainment of jail inmates and prisoners, and participation in education programs are part of this sequence. There also are recent data on length of sentences for prisoners in State prisons and a long-term study of recidivism in 15 States, which presents recidivism data by demographic characteristics and offense category.

The Federal Bureau of Prisons provides extensive data on Federal prisoners, including prisoner characteristics, commitment offense, type of facility, security level, and the proportion of Federal prisoners incarcerated for drug offenses. Other data show time served to first release by offense type and selected Federal prisoner demographics. Also presented are BJS data on the number of immigration offenders in Federal prison, the number of detainees under U.S. Immigration and Customs Enforcement jurisdiction, the number of registered sex offenders in each State, and a trend table showing counts of prisoners under jurisdiction of military authorities.

Next are tables dealing with post-release supervision. These include the number and rate of persons on parole, movement of the parole population, persons successfully discharged from parole supervision, and persons returned to Federal prison for either a supervision violation or conviction for a new offense.

Information focusing on medical issues in correctional facilities follows. These data include mental health screenings and types of mental health treatment in State prisons. A series of tables also features information on the prevalence of HIV and AIDS among the State and Federal prisoner populations, a new table showing the decline of AIDS-related prisoner deaths, and total prisoner deaths by cause of death.

The final portion of Section 6 presents numerous tables on State and Federal prisoners sentenced to death, movement of prisoners on death row, and persons executed or otherwise removed from death row. Selected characteristics of prisoners with death sentences (e.g., race, ethnicity, sex, age, education) are included in many of these tables. Tables on methods of execution employed by States authorizing the death penalty and executions carried out in the U.S. dating back to 1930 conclude the section.

Table 6.1

Adults on probation, in jail or prison, and on parole

United States, 1980-2003

	Total estimated correctional population[a]	Probation	Jail	Prison	Parole
1980	1,840,400	1,118,097	182,288[b]	319,598	220,438
1981	2,006,600	1,225,934	195,085[b]	360,029	225,539
1982	2,192,600	1,357,264	207,853	402,914	224,604
1983	2,475,100	1,582,947	221,815	423,898	246,440
1984	2,689,200	1,740,948	233,018	448,264	266,992
1985	3,011,500	1,968,712	254,986	487,593	300,203
1986	3,239,400	2,114,621	272,735	526,436	325,638
1987	3,459,600	2,247,158	294,092	562,814	355,505
1988	3,714,100	2,356,483	341,893	607,766	407,977
1989	4,055,600	2,522,125	393,303	683,367	456,803
1990	4,350,300	2,670,234	405,320	743,382	531,407
1991	4,535,600	2,728,472	424,129[c]	792,535	590,442
1992	4,762,600	2,811,611	441,781[c]	850,566	658,601
1993	4,944,000	2,903,061	455,500[c]	909,381	676,100
1994	5,141,300	2,981,022	479,800	990,147	690,371
1995	5,342,900	3,077,861	507,044	1,078,542	679,421
1996	5,490,700	3,164,996	518,492	1,127,528	679,733
1997[d]	5,734,900	3,296,513	567,079	1,176,564	694,787
1998[d]	6,134,200	3,670,441	592,462	1,224,469	696,385
1999[d]	6,340,800	3,779,922	605,943	1,287,172	714,457
2000	6,445,100	3,826,209	621,149	1,316,333	723,898
2001	6,581,700	3,931,731	631,240	1,330,007	732,333
2002	6,759,100	4,024,067	665,475	1,367,856	750,934
2003	6,889,800	4,073,987	691,301	1,387,269[e]	774,588
Percent change 2002 to 2003	1.9%	1.2%	3.9%	2.3%	3.1%

Note: Counts for probation, prison, and parole populations are for December 31 of each year; jail population counts are for June 30 of each year. Counts of adults held in jail facilities for 1993 and 1994 were estimated and rounded to the nearest 100. Data for jail and prison are for inmates under custody and include those held in private facilities. Totals for 1998-2003 exclude probationers held in jail or prison. These data have been revised by the Source based on the most recently reported counts and may differ from previous editions of SOURCEBOOK. For information on methodology and explanatory notes, see Appendix 15.

[a]Because a small number of individuals may have multiple correctional statuses, the totals are rounded to the nearest 100.
[b]Estimated.
[c]Includes an unknown number of persons supervised outside jail facilities.
[d]Coverage of probation agencies was expanded. For counts based on the same reporting agencies, use 3,266,837 in 1997 (to compare with 1996); 3,417,613 in 1998 (to compare with 1997); and 3,772,773 in 1999 (to compare with 1998).
[e]As of June 30, 2003.

Source: U.S. Department of Justice, Bureau of Justice Statistics, *Correctional Populations in the United States, 1994*, NCJ-160091, Table 1.1; *1995*, NCJ-163916, Table 1.1 (Washington, DC: U.S. Department of Justice); U.S. Department of Justice, Bureau of Justice Statistics, *Probation and Parole in 1999*, Press Release NCJ 183508 (Washington, DC: U.S. Department of Justice, July 2000), p. 3, Table 1; U.S. Department of Justice, Bureau of Justice Statistics, *Probation and Parole in the United States, 2002*, Bulletin NCJ 201135, p. 1; *2003*, Bulletin NCJ 205336, p. 1 (Washington, DC: U.S. Department of Justice); and data provided by the U.S. Department of Justice, Bureau of Justice Statistics. Table adapted by SOURCEBOOK staff.

Table 6.2

Adults under correctional supervision

By type of supervision, region, and jurisdiction, 2003

Region and jurisdiction	Total under correctional supervision, Dec. 31, 2003	Number on probation or parole[a]	Number in prison or jail, June 30, 2003	Number under supervision per 100,000 adult residents[b]	Percent of correctional population incarcerated
United States, total	6,889,800	4,811,200	2,078,600	3,173	30.2%
Federal	282,800	117,100	165,800	130	58.6
State	6,607,000	4,694,100	1,912,800	3,042	29.0
Northeast	1,067,000	792,700	274,200	2,588	25.7
Connecticut	74,100	54,800	19,300	2,815	26.0
Maine	13,400	9,900	3,500	1,341	26.4
Massachusetts	153,300	130,800	22,500	3,117	14.6
New Hampshire	9,400	5,300	4,100	974	43.6
New Jersey	183,600	137,500	46,100	2,817	25.1
New York	278,400	180,100	98,200	1,925	35.3
Pennsylvania	315,000	239,500	75,600	3,339	24.0
Rhode Island	27,700	24,200	3,500	3,357	12.8
Vermont	12,000	10,600	1,400	2,559	11.9
Midwest	1,418,300	1,055,300	363,000	2,918	25.6
Illinois	244,400	179,500	65,000	2,609	26.6
Indiana	155,300	118,600	36,700	3,373	23.6
Iowa	36,200	24,000	12,200	1,638	33.7
Kansas	34,400	18,700	15,700	1,715	45.7
Michigan	263,100	195,800	67,400	3,527	25.6
Minnesota	127,900	114,300	13,600	3,411	10.6
Missouri	110,600	70,800	39,800	2,595	36.0
Nebraska	25,800	19,100	6,800	2,009	26.2
North Dakota	5,700	3,700	1,900	1,189	34.0
Ohio	301,400	236,300	65,000	3,530	21.6
South Dakota	11,600	7,200	4,400	2,069	38.2
Wisconsin	101,800	67,300	34,500	2,491	33.9
South	2,730,900	1,879,100	851,800	3,485	31.2
Alabama	74,200	45,100	29,100	2,202	39.2
Arkansas	59,600	41,800	17,800	2,924	29.9
Delaware	26,200	19,400	6,800	4,235	25.9
District of Columbia[c]	15,400	12,300	3,100	3,440	20.3
Florida	423,900	289,100	134,900	3,197	31.8
Georgia	533,500	446,500	87,000	(d)	(d)
Kentucky	63,100	35,700	27,400	2,028	43.4
Louisiana	106,600	58,100	48,400	3,255	45.5
Maryland	128,400	91,600	36,800	3,117	28.6
Mississippi	47,500	20,900	26,600	2,264	56.0
North Carolina	165,500	115,800	49,600	2,589	30.0
Oklahoma	62,100	32,400	29,700	2,372	47.9
South Carolina	79,400	43,300	36,200	2,547	45.5
Tennessee	90,900	49,400	41,400	2,054	45.6
Texas	738,000	524,200	213,800	4,609	29.0
Virginia	102,500	46,500	56,000	1,827	54.6
West Virginia	14,000	6,900	7,100	991	50.5
West	1,390,800	967,000	423,800	2,840	30.5
Alaska	10,900	6,300	4,500	2,382	41.7
Arizona	112,700	71,200	41,600	2,717	36.9
California	725,600	485,000	240,500	2,791	33.2
Colorado	84,700	56,800	27,900	2,486	33.0
Hawaii	25,200	19,900	5,300	2,600	21.0
Idaho	43,600	34,500	9,100	(d)	(d)
Montana	12,500	7,700	4,800	1,817	38.1
Nevada	32,400	16,300	16,100	1,909	49.7
New Mexico	30,100	17,000	13,100	2,211	43.6
Oregon	83,100	64,500	18,600	3,082	22.4
Utah	22,400	11,900	10,500	1,397	46.9
Washington	199,500	170,600	28,900	4,350	14.5
Wyoming	8,100	5,200	2,900	2,186	35.5

Note: Counts were rounded to the nearest 100. Jail counts by State were estimated using the average daily population from Deaths in Custody, 2002 and the Annual Survey of Jails, 2003 (Source, p. 7). For information on methodology and explanatory notes, see Appendix 15.

[a] Excludes 25,497 probationers held in jail and 11,872 probationers held in prison.
[b] Based on the estimated number of adult State residents on Dec. 31, 2003 using the 2000 Census of Population and Housing and adjusting for population change since April 2000.
[c] Excludes prisoners held by the Federal Bureau of Prisons.
[d] Not calculated by the Source.

Source: U.S. Department of Justice, Bureau of Justice Statistics, *Probation and Parole in the United States, 2003*, Bulletin NCJ 205336 (Washington, DC: U.S. Department of Justice, July 2004), p. 7.

Table 6.3

Adults on probation under State and Federal jurisdiction

By region and jurisdiction, 2003

Region and jurisdiction	Probation population Jan. 1, 2003	2003[a] Entries	2003[a] Exits	Probation population Dec. 31, 2003	Percent change in probation population during 2003	Number on probation on Dec. 31, 2003 per 100,000 adult residents
United States, total	4,024,067	2,229,668	2,179,847	4,073,987	1.2%	1,876
Federal	31,330	13,989	14,449	30,599	-2.3	14
State	3,992,737	2,215,679	2,165,398	4,043,388	1.3	1,862
Northeast	629,503	233,044	247,722	614,825	-2.3	1,491
Connecticut	50,984	24,384	23,176	52,192	2.4	1,983
Maine	9,446	6,625	6,216	9,855	4.3	984
Massachusetts[b,c,d]	131,319	56,933	61,117	127,135	(e)	2,585
New Hampshire[f]	3,702	1,480	1,052	4,130	11.6	426
New Jersey	134,290	40,601	50,610	124,281	-7.5	1,907
New York[c]	132,966	39,590	48,261	124,295	-6.5	859
Pennsylvania[d]	130,786	52,072	45,652	137,206	4.9	1,454
Rhode Island	25,914	6,451	6,436	25,929	0.1	3,143
Vermont	10,096	4,908	5,202	9,802	-2.9	2,085
Midwest	937,378	606,152	607,511	936,387	-0.1	1,926
Illinois	141,544	63,000	60,090	144,454	2.1	1,542
Indiana	114,209	94,741	97,324	111,626	-2.3	2,424
Iowa	19,970	14,600	13,685	20,885	4.6	945
Kansas[d]	15,217	23,315	23,981	14,551	-4.4	725
Michigan[d,f]	174,577	130,857	129,029	176,392	1.0	2,364
Minnesota	122,692	59,517	71,484	110,725	-9.8	2,953
Missouri	54,584	26,512	25,486	55,610	1.9	1,305
Nebraska	16,468	15,845	13,901	18,412	11.8	1,432
North Dakota	3,229	2,332	2,059	3,502	8.5	737
Ohio[d,f]	215,186	146,723	142,616	219,658	2.1	2,573
South Dakota	5,088	3,261	3,129	5,236	2.9	933
Wisconsin	54,614	25,449	24,727	55,336	1.3	1,354
South	1,623,038	960,243	910,074	1,673,206	3.1	2,135
Alabama	39,713	15,152	15,213	39,652	-0.2	1,177
Arkansas	27,377	9,168	8,419	28,126	2.7	1,380
Delaware	20,201	13,962	15,242	18,921	-6.3	3,058
District of Columbia[d,f]	9,389	6,597	8,755	7,231	(e)	1,612
Florida[d,f]	291,315	257,539	261,212	287,641	-1.3	2,169
Georgia[f,g]	367,349	230,686	173,650	424,385	(e)	(e)
Kentucky[d]	24,480	16,165	11,949	28,696	17.2	921
Louisiana	36,257	13,875	13,455	36,677	1.2	1,120
Maryland	81,982	39,037	43,144	77,875	-5.0	1,890
Mississippi[d,h]	16,633	8,773	6,290	19,116	14.9	911
North Carolina	112,900	60,782	60,521	113,161	0.2	1,770
Oklahoma[f]	29,881	15,299	16,854	28,326	-5.2	1,082
South Carolina	41,574	14,760	16,287	40,047	-3.7	1,285
Tennessee[d]	42,712	24,256	24,132	42,836	0.3	968
Texas	434,486	200,450	202,947	431,989	-0.6	2,698
Virginia	40,359	30,669	29,365	41,663	3.2	743
West Virginia[d]	6,430	3,072	2,638	6,864	6.7	487
West	802,818	416,241	400,092	818,970	2.0	1,672
Alaska	5,229	973	796	5,406	3.4	1,185
Arizona[f]	66,485	39,115	39,795	65,805	-1.0	1,586
California[f]	358,121	180,636	164,059	374,701	4.6	1,441
Colorado[d,f]	57,328	28,954	30,985	55,297	-3.5	1,623
Hawaii	16,772	7,006	6,126	17,652	5.2	1,822
Idaho[f,i]	31,361	25,360	24,501	32,220	2.7	(e)
Montana	6,703	3,898	3,687	6,914	3.1	1,006
Nevada	12,290	5,869	6,000	12,159	-1.1	716
New Mexico	16,287	7,662	7,813	16,136	-0.9	1,186
Oregon	45,397	16,275	16,847	44,825	-1.3	1,662
Utah	10,646	5,429	5,696	10,379	-2.5	646
Washington[d,f]	171,603	93,132	91,921	172,814	0.7	3,767
Wyoming	4,596	1,932	1,866	4,662	1.4	1,255

Note: These data are from the 2003 Probation and Parole Surveys conducted by the U.S. Department of Justice, Bureau of Justice Statistics. Persons on probation are defined as those who have been placed under the supervision of a State, local, or Federal probation agency resulting from a court order. For information on methodology and definitions of terms, see Appendix 15.

[a] Because of incomplete data, the probation population for some jurisdictions on Dec. 31, 2003 does not equal the population on Jan. 1, 2003, plus entries, minus exits.
[b] Data are for June 30, 2002 and 2003. Some data for June 30, 2002 were estimated.
[c] Due to change in reporting criteria, data are not comparable to previous reports.
[d] Data for entries and exits were estimated for nonreporting agencies.
[e] Not calculated by the Source.
[f] All data were estimated.
[g] Counts include private agency cases and may overstate the number under supervision.
[h] Data are for year ending Dec. 1, 2003.
[i] Data include estimates for misdemeanors based on annual admissions.

Source: U.S. Department of Justice, Bureau of Justice Statistics, *Probation and Parole in the United States, 2003*, Bulletin NCJ 205336 (Washington, DC: U.S. Department of Justice, July 2004), p. 3, Table 2.

Table 6.4

Federal offenders under community supervision

By offense, United States, fiscal year 2001[a]

Most serious conviction offense	Total offenders under supervision Number	Percent	Probation Number	Percent	Supervised release[b] Number	Percent	Parole Number	Percent
All offenses	103,348	100%	30,782	100%	68,496	100%	4,070	100%
Felonies	93,113	90.3	21,104	68.9	67,945	99.3	4,064	100
Violent offenses	6,163	6.0	587	1.9	4,273	6.2	1,303	32.0
Murder, nonnegligent manslaughter	410	0.4	31	0.1	211	0.3	168	4.1
Negligent manslaughter	8	(c)	0	X	6	(c)	2	(c)
Assault	627	0.6	162	0.5	401	0.6	64	1.6
Robbery	4,471	4.3	288	0.9	3,244	4.7	939	23.1
Sexual abuse[d]	403	0.4	92	0.3	277	0.4	34	0.8
Kidnaping	200	0.2	9	(c)	96	0.1	95	2.3
Threats against the President	44	(c)	5	(c)	38	0.1	1	(c)
Property offenses	28,851	28.0	11,458	37.4	17,020	24.9	373	9.2
Fraudulent	23,947	23.2	9,195	30.0	14,555	21.3	197	4.8
Embezzlement	3,174	3.1	953	3.1	2,208	3.2	13	0.3
Fraud[e]	17,993	17.4	6,918	22.6	10,915	15.9	160	3.9
Forgery	466	0.5	253	0.8	198	0.3	15	0.4
Counterfeiting	2,314	2.2	1,071	3.5	1,234	1.8	9	0.2
Other	4,904	4.8	2,263	7.4	2,465	3.6	176	4.3
Burglary	254	0.2	59	0.2	132	0.2	63	1.5
Larceny[f]	3,406	3.3	1,840	6.0	1,501	2.2	65	1.6
Motor vehicle theft	429	0.4	120	0.4	294	0.4	15	0.4
Arson and explosives	341	0.3	66	0.2	257	0.4	18	0.4
Transportation of stolen property	397	0.4	142	0.5	242	0.4	13	0.3
Other property offenses[g]	77	0.1	36	0.1	39	0.1	2	(c)
Drug offenses	42,333	41.0	3,644	11.9	36,771	53.7	1,918	47.2
Trafficking	38,001	36.8	3,301	10.8	32,968	48.2	1,732	42.6
Other drug offenses	4,332	4.2	343	1.1	3,803	5.6	186	4.6
Public-order offenses	8,773	8.5	3,720	12.1	4,747	6.9	306	7.5
Regulatory	2,604	2.5	1,481	4.8	1,089	1.6	34	0.8
Agriculture	85	0.1	54	0.2	30	(c)	1	(c)
Antitrust	24	(c)	19	0.1	5	(c)	0	X
Food and drug	73	0.1	51	0.2	22	(c)	0	X
Transportation	81	0.1	49	0.2	29	(c)	3	0.1
Civil rights	156	0.2	35	0.1	117	0.2	4	0.1
Communications	125	0.1	84	0.3	41	0.1	0	X
Customs laws	156	0.2	75	0.2	81	0.1	0	X
Postal laws	136	0.1	92	0.3	42	0.1	2	(c)
Other regulatory offenses	1,768	1.7	1,022	3.3	722	1.1	24	0.6
Other	6,169	6.0	2,239	7.3	3,658	5.3	272	6.7
Tax law violations including tax fraud	1,421	1.4	777	2.5	635	0.9	9	0.2
Bribery	415	0.4	235	0.8	176	0.3	4	0.1
Perjury, contempt, intimidation	338	0.3	129	0.4	199	0.3	10	0.2
National defense	49	(c)	17	0.1	17	(c)	15	0.4
Escape	291	0.3	48	0.2	223	0.3	20	0.5
Racketeering and extortion	2,113	2.0	436	1.4	1,518	2.2	159	3.9
Gambling offenses	195	0.2	114	0.4	81	0.1	0	X
Nonviolent sex offenses	855	0.8	214	0.7	597	0.9	44	1.1
Mail or transport of obscene material	61	0.1	27	0.1	34	(c)	0	X
Migratory birds	5	(c)	5	(c)	0	X	0	X
Other felonies	426	0.4	237	0.8	178	0.3	11	0.3
Weapons offenses	4,977	4.8	803	2.6	4,017	5.9	157	3.9
Immigration offenses	1,807	1.8	735	2.4	1,069	1.6	3	0.1
Misdemeanors[h]	10,235	9.9	9,678	31.6	551	0.8	6	0.1

Note: These data are from the U.S. Department of Justice, Bureau of Justice Statistics' Federal Justice Statistics Program database. Sources of information include the Executive Office for U.S. Attorneys, the Administrative Office of the United States Courts (AO), the U.S. Sentencing Commission, the U.S. Marshals Service, the Drug Enforcement Administration, the Federal Bureau of Prisons, the Federal Pretrial Services Agency, and the Federal probation and supervision service.

Data on probation, parole, and supervision are from the Federal Probation Supervision Information System maintained by the AO. Only records with offenders under active supervision as of the end of fiscal year 2001 were selected. Corporate defendants were excluded. Total includes 209 felony offenders whose offense category could not be determined. For methodology and definitions of terms, see Appendix 11.

[a]Percents may not add to 100 because of rounding.
[b]Under the Federal Sentencing Reform Act, supervised release replaces parole for Federal offenders sentenced on or after Nov. 1, 1987.
[c]Less than 0.05%.
[d]Includes only violent sex offenses.
[e]Excludes tax fraud.
[f]Excludes transportation of stolen property.
[g]Excludes fraudulent property offenses; includes destruction of property and trespass.
[h]Includes misdemeanors, petty offenses, and unknown offense level.

Source: U.S. Department of Justice, Bureau of Justice Statistics, *Compendium of Federal Justice Statistics, 2001*, NCJ 201627 (Washington, DC: U.S. Department of Justice, 2003), p. 93.

Table 6.5

Persons received for supervision by the Federal Probation System

By type of supervision, 1975-2003[a]

	Total cases		Type of supervision								
	Number	Percent	Court probation	U.S. magistrate judge probation	Supervised release	Pretrial diversion	Parole[b]	Mandatory release	Military parole	Special parole	Bureau of Prisons custody	Received by transfer
1975	36,061	100%	51.8%	13.5%	NA	3.2%	21.9%	6.7%	0.6%	2.4%	NA	NA
1976	35,102	100	52.3	15.3	NA	4.9	17.9	5.5	0.7	3.4	NA	NA
1977	35,098	100	50.0	16.2	NA	5.9	14.9	7.2	0.8	5.0	NA	NA
1978	34,808	100	45.0	16.7	NA	6.1	16.7	9.5	0.5	5.5	NA	NA
1979	33,839	100	41.7	15.4	NA	6.7	20.2	9.5	0.3	6.3	NA	NA
1980	31,410	100	38.8	14.6	NA	6.4	24.4	8.5	0.7	6.6	NA	NA
1981	29,575	100	40.2	18.3	NA	6.8	21.8	6.6	1.1	5.1	NA	NA
1982	31,531	100	42.1	20.5	NA	6.4	18.7	6.2	0.9	5.1	NA	NA
1983	33,784	100	43.2	21.5	NA	6.4	17.5	6.0	0.8	4.6	NA	NA
1984	34,582	100	42.3	21.9	NA	6.3	18.1	6.3	0.7	4.4	NA	NA
1985	35,199	100	42.7	21.8	NA	6.4	16.6	7.1	0.8	4.6	NA	NA
1986	37,583	100	42.0	22.8	NA	5.5	15.7	7.7	1.0	5.2	NA	NA
1987	38,486	100	43.5	21.0	NA	3.8	16.2	8.8	1.1	5.5	NA	NA
1988	37,974	100	41.6	21.5	0.1%	0.0	18.2	10.9	1.3	6.3	NA	NA
1989	38,184	100	37.3	21.8	3.1	NA	19.4	10.8	1.2	6.2	NA	NA
1990	47,546	100	27.1	17.7	10.1	NA	14.6	8.2	1.2	4.8	NA	16.3%
1991	47,720	100	26.5	15.7	18.7	NA	12.3	7.2	1.0	3.9	NA	14.5
1992	49,102	100	24.6	15.6	26.0	NA	8.6	5.3	1.0	3.2	NA	15.7
1993	48,722	100	23.0	15.0	31.1	NA	7.3	4.5	1.0	2.9	NA	15.3
1994	46,273	100	21.3	15.1	37.6	NA	5.5	3.5	0.8	2.2	NA	13.9
1995	45,163	100	19.4	15.3	41.9	NA	4.1	2.6	0.6	1.9	NA	14.2
1996	48,367	100	18.2	15.5	45.5	NA	3.6	1.9	0.5	1.4	NA	13.4
1997	46,190	100	18.5	15.7	47.9	NA	2.8	1.4	0.5	0.9	NA	13.1
1998	45,586	100	17.4	15.6	49.8	NA	2.6	1.0	0.4	0.7	NA	12.4
1999	48,035	100	17.9	14.4	52.9	NA	2.3	1.0	0.4	0.5	NA	10.6
2000	48,653	100	17.2	13.4	55.9	NA	2.3	0.7	0.3	0.4	NA	9.7
2001	50,308	100	16.4	12.4	57.5	NA	1.9	0.5	0.3	NA	1.7%	9.2
2002	54,062	100	16.1	11.5	58.6	NA	2.1	0.4	0.3	NA	2.0	8.9
2003	55,734	100	15.4	10.9	59.5	NA	1.8	0.3	0.3	NA	3.2	8.6

Note: Persons under supervision of the Federal Probation System include persons placed on probation--either by U.S. District Courts, U.S. magistrate judges, or at the request of U.S. attorneys (pretrial diversion/deferred prosecution)--and Federal offenders released from confinement on parole, supervised release, or mandatory release.

Data for 1975-90 represent persons who began supervision in the 12-month period prior to June 30 of the year noted. Beginning in 1991, data are reported for the Federal fiscal year, which is the 12-month period ending September 30. Some data have been revised by the Source and may differ from previous editions of SOURCEBOOK. The Canal Zone, Guam, and the Virgin Islands began reporting data in 1977.

"Supervised release" refers to a specified term of post-release supervision enacted in November 1987 under the Federal Sentencing Guidelines.

"Pretrial diversion" was called "deferred prosecution" in years prior to 1977.

"Special parole" refers to a specified period of parole attached to a term of imprisonment at sentencing. This provision is applicable to violations of certain drug laws (see Drug Abuse Prevention and Control Act of 1970, Public Law 91-513, Oct. 27, 1970, 84 Stat. 1260).

"Bureau of Prisons custody" was added in fiscal year 2001 and includes persons completing incarceration under the jurisdiction of the Federal Bureau of Prisons but who may be in halfway houses or other facilities and supervised by probation officers (Source, *2001*, p. 31).

[a]Percents may not add to 100 because of rounding.
[b]Beginning in fiscal year 2001, this category includes "special parole."

Source: Administrative Office of the United States Courts, *Annual Report of the Director, 1975*, p. 164; *1985*, p. 212; *1986*, p. 43; *1995*, p. 245; *1998*, p. 257; *1999*, p. 251 (Washington, DC: Administrative Office of the United States Courts); Administrative Office of the United States Courts, *Annual Report of the Director, 1988*, p. 39; *1990*, p. 28; *1991*, p. 110; *1993*, p. 28; *1994*, p. 245; *1996*, p. 241; *1997*, p. 237 (Washington, DC: USGPO); and Administrative Office of the United States Courts, *Judicial Business of the United States Courts: 2000 Annual Report of the Director*, p. 250; *2001 Annual Report of the Director*, p. 240; *2002 Annual Report of the Director*, p. 243; *2003 Annual Report of the Director*, p. 242 (Washington, DC: USGPO). Table constructed by SOURCEBOOK staff.

Table 6.6

Movement of persons under supervision of the Federal Probation System

Fiscal year 2003

	Number	Percent[a]
Persons under supervision on Oct. 1, 2002	108,701	X
Total received	55,734	100%
Court probation	8,605	15.4
U.S. magistrate judge probation	6,064	10.9
Supervised release	33,164	59.5
Parole/special parole	985	1.8
Mandatory release	171	0.3
Military parole	147	0.3
Bureau of Prisons custody	1,784	3.2
Received by transfer	4,814	8.6
Total removed	53,814	100%
Court probation	9,125	17.0
U.S. magistrate judge probation	6,337	11.8
Supervised release	30,571	56.8
Parole/special parole	1,234	2.3
Mandatory release	259	0.5
Military parole	170	0.3
Bureau of Prisons custody	1,425	2.6
Removed by transfer	4,693	8.7
Persons under supervision on Sept. 30, 2003	110,621	X

Note: See Note, table 6.5.

[a]Percents may not add to 100 because of rounding.

Source: Administrative Office of the United States Courts, *Judicial Business of the United States Courts: 2003 Annual Report of the Director* (Washington, DC: USGPO, 2004), pp. 242, 243. Table constructed by SOURCEBOOK staff.

Table 6.7

Persons under supervision of the Federal Probation System and authorized probation officers

United States, 1975-2003

	Number of persons under supervision	Number of probation officers
1975	64,261	1,377
1976	64,246	1,452
1977	64,427	1,578
1978	66,681	1,604
1979	66,087	1,604
1980	64,450	1,604
1981	59,016	1,534
1982	58,373	1,637
1983	60,180	1,574
1984	63,092	1,690
1985	65,999	1,758
1986	69,656	1,847
1987	73,432	1,879
1988	76,366	2,046
1989	77,284	2,146
1990	80,592	2,361
1991	83,012	2,802
1992	85,920	3,316
1993	86,823	3,516[a]
1994	89,103	NA
1995	85,822	NA
1996	88,966	3,473
1997	91,434	3,603
1998	93,737	3,842
1999	97,190	3,913
2000	100,395	3,981
2001	104,715	4,345
2002	108,792	4,476
2003	110,621	4,560

Note: See Note, table 6.5. The "number of persons under supervision" data for 1975-87 are reported for the 12-month period ending June 30. Beginning in 1988, these data are reported for the Federal fiscal year, which is the 12-month period ending September 30. The "number of probation officers" data for 1975-90 are reported as of June 30. Beginning in 1991, these data are reported as of September 30. Some data have been revised by the Source and may differ from previous editions of SOURCEBOOK.

[a]Approximate.

Source: Administrative Office of the United States Courts, *Annual Report of the Director, 1980*, p. 15; *1983*, pp. 20, 38; *1985*, pp. 22, 52; *1995*, p. 246; *1998*, p. 258; *1999*, p. 252 (Washington, DC: Administrative Office of the United States Courts); Administrative Office of the United States Courts, *Annual Report of the Director, 1982*, p. 19, Table 19; *1987*, pp. 38, 49; *1989*, pp. 34, 45; *1990*, pp. 27, 41; *1991*, pp. 109, 127; *1992*, pp. 85, 98; *1994*, Table 8; *1996*, p. 242; *1997*, p. 238 (Washington, DC: USGPO); Administrative Office of the United States Courts, *Judicial Business of the United States Courts: 2000 Annual Report of the Director*, p. 251; *2001 Annual Report of the Director*, p. 241; *2002 Annual Report of the Director*, p. 244; *2003 Annual Report of the Director*, p. 243 (Washington, DC: USGPO); and data provided by the Administrative Office of the United States Courts. Table constructed by SOURCEBOOK staff.

Table 6.8

Federal probation terminations

By outcome and offense, United States, fiscal year 2001

			Percent terminating supervision with:				
			Technical violations[a]				
Most serious conviction offense	Number of probation terminations	No violation	Drug use	Fugitive status	Other	New crime[b]	Administrative case closure
All offenses	14,961	80.4%	3.1%	2.4%	6.1%	6.4%	1.6%
Felonies	7,573	82.8	2.8	2.3	4.7	5.6	1.7
Violent offenses	239	71.1	2.1	3.8	9.2	11.7	2.1
Murder, nonnegligent manslaughter	12	41.7	0.0	8.3	33.3	16.7	0.0
Assault	67	62.7	3.0	4.5	10.4	13.4	6.0
Robbery	115	80.0	2.6	2.6	6.1	7.8	0.9
Sexual abuse[c]	38	65.8	0.0	5.3	10.5	18.4	0.0
Kidnaping	4	B	B	B	B	B	B
Threats against the President	3	B	B	B	B	B	B
Property offenses	4,173	83.3	2.8	2.0	5.0	5.2	1.6
Fraudulent offenses	3,380	85.3	2.3	1.7	4.5	4.5	1.6
Embezzlement	366	87.7	2.5	0.8	4.9	3.0	1.1
Fraud[d]	2,496	86.8	1.7	1.6	4.0	4.2	1.8
Forgery	90	75.6	5.6	5.6	6.7	4.4	2.2
Counterfeiting	428	76.2	5.1	2.8	7.0	7.9	0.9
Other offenses	793	75.0	4.7	3.2	7.2	8.2	1.8
Burglary	30	53.3	0.0	20.0	6.7	16.7	3.3
Larceny[e]	621	75.4	5.6	2.4	6.6	8.4	1.6
Motor vehicle theft	40	65.0	5.0	5.0	15.0	7.5	2.5
Arson and explosives	31	74.2	0.0	3.2	12.9	9.7	0.0
Transportation of stolen property	54	90.7	0.0	0.0	5.6	1.9	1.9
Other property offenses[f]	17	76.5	0.0	5.9	5.9	5.9	5.9
Drug offenses	1,167	79.6	4.5	2.7	4.4	6.8	2.1
Trafficking	1,023	79.4	4.8	2.7	4.4	6.6	2.1
Possession and other	144	81.3	2.8	2.1	4.2	7.6	2.1
Public-order offenses	1,425	90.4	1.4	1.5	2.5	2.7	1.5
Regulatory offenses	552	90.2	1.6	1.8	2.4	3.1	0.9
Agriculture	35	94.3	2.9	0.0	0.0	0.0	2.9
Antitrust	5	B	B	B	B	B	B
Food and drug	22	95.5	0.0	0.0	0.0	4.5	0.0
Transportation	24	95.8	0.0	0.0	4.2	0.0	0.0
Civil rights	9	B	B	B	B	B	B
Communications	31	93.5	3.2	0.0	0.0	0.0	3.2
Customs laws	33	93.9	0.0	3.0	0.0	0.0	3.0
Postal laws	37	83.8	0.0	8.1	8.1	0.0	0.0
Other regulatory offenses	356	89.3	2.0	1.7	2.2	4.2	0.6
Other offenses	873	90.5	1.3	1.4	2.5	2.5	1.8
Tax law violations including tax fraud	390	93.6	0.3	0.8	2.3	1.3	1.8
Bribery	90	95.6	0.0	1.1	1.1	1.1	1.1
Perjury, contempt, intimidation	68	92.6	0.0	0.0	1.5	2.9	2.9
National defense	12	83.3	0.0	8.3	0.0	8.3	0.0
Escape	24	62.5	12.5	0.0	12.5	12.5	0.0
Racketeering and extortion	137	87.6	2.9	0.7	3.6	2.9	2.2
Gambling offenses	52	94.2	0.0	1.9	0.0	1.9	1.9
Nonviolent sex offenses	34	76.5	0.0	5.9	2.9	11.8	2.9
Mail or transport of obscene material	6	B	B	B	B	B	B
Migratory birds	3	B	B	B	B	B	B
Other felonies	57	82.5	5.3	5.3	3.5	1.8	1.8
Weapons offenses	255	73.3	3.9	4.7	6.3	10.2	1.6
Immigration offenses	261	73.6	1.9	6.1	5.0	11.9	1.5
Misdemeanors[g]	7,388	77.9	3.5	2.5	7.5	7.1	1.4

Note: See Note, table 6.4. Only records with one or more terminations of active supervision during fiscal year 2001 were selected. Each termination was counted separately. Technical violations and terminations for new crimes are shown only if supervision terminated with incarceration or removal from active supervision for reason of a violation. The data exclude corporate offenders. Total includes 53 felony offenders whose offense category could not be determined. For methodology and definitions of terms, see Appendix 11.

[a] Supervision terminated with incarceration or removal to inactive status for violation of supervision conditions other than charges for new offenses.
[b] Supervision terminated with incarceration or removal to inactive status after arrest for a "major" or "minor" offense.
[c] Includes only violent sex offenses.
[d] Excludes tax fraud.
[e] Excludes transportation of stolen property.
[f] Excludes fraudulent property offenses; includes destruction of property and trespass.
[g] Includes misdemeanors, petty offenses, and unknown offense level.

Source: U.S. Department of Justice, Bureau of Justice Statistics, *Compendium of Federal Justice Statistics, 2001*, NCJ 201627 (Washington, DC: U.S. Department of Justice, 2003), p. 95.

Table 6.9

Number and rate (per 100,000 juveniles age 10 through upper age of jurisdiction) of juveniles in public and private residential custody facilities

By State, 1997, 1999, and 2001[a]

	Juvenile offenders in public and private residential custody facilities					
	Oct. 29, 1997		Oct. 27, 1999		Oct. 24, 2001	
State	Number	Rate	Number	Rate	Number	Rate
United States, total[b]	105,790	359	108,931	361	104,413	336
Alabama	1,685	329	1,589	313	1,617	317
Alaska	352	430	382	445	349	386
Arizona	1,868	349	1,901	328	1,884	300
Arkansas	603	192	705	225	652	209
California	19,899	529	19,072	490	18,145	436
Colorado	1,748	377	1,979	406	1,772	346
Connecticut	1,326	502	1,466	521	630	210
Delaware	311	377	347	402	305	350
District of Columbia	265	560	259	545	171	368
Florida	5,975	385	6,813	416	6,776	388
Georgia	3,622	464	3,729	455	2,942	338
Hawaii	134	102	118	91	103	78
Idaho	242	143	360	213	530	309
Illinois	3,425	279	3,885	312	3,560	279
Indiana	2,485	354	2,650	373	3,235	450
Iowa	1,064	305	1,017	294	1,105	330
Kansas	1,242	380	1,254	381	1,116	344
Kentucky	1,079	235	1,188	264	990	227
Louisiana	2,776	555	2,745	560	2,456	507
Maine	318	219	242	165	227	158
Maryland	1,498	264	1,579	264	1,198	191
Massachusetts	1,065	191	1,188	202	1,324	223
Michigan	3,710	369	4,324	422	3,504	334
Minnesota	1,522	259	1,760	293	1,946	326
Mississippi	756	210	784	220	693	199
Missouri	1,401	245	1,161	202	1,392	243
Montana	302	265	246	218	266	243
Nebraska	741	351	720	341	718	348
Nevada	857	460	789	378	901	380
New Hampshire	186	153	216	168	203	155
New Jersey	2,251	263	2,386	268	2,079	220
New Mexico	778	329	855	363	837	356
New York	4,661	309	4,813	311	4,593	287
North Carolina	1,204	197	1,429	222	1,318	192
North Dakota	272	331	235	292	180	243
Ohio	4,318	329	4,531	344	4,554	344
Oklahoma	808	193	1,123	270	870	215
Oregon	1,462	382	1,549	400	1,508	382
Pennsylvania	3,962	294	3,819	278	4,066	297
Rhode Island	426	394	310	271	311	276
South Carolina	1,583	405	1,650	416	1,398	350
South Dakota	528	535	603	620	496	523
Tennessee	2,118	346	1,534	247	1,655	261
Texas	6,898	317	7,954	356	8,524	364
Utah	768	239	985	310	1,015	328
Vermont	49	68	67	92	62	87
Virginia	2,879	391	3,085	404	2,811	352
Washington	2,216	333	2,094	306	2,054	293
West Virginia	398	198	388	201	475	254
Wisconsin	2,013	356	1,924	338	1,941	343
Wyoming	340	507	310	481	327	531

Note: These data are from the Census of Juveniles in Residential Placement, conducted biennially by the U.S. Department of Justice, Office of Juvenile Justice and Delinquency Prevention. Public and private facilities, secure and nonsecure, that hold alleged or adjudicated juvenile delinquents or status offenders are asked to provide information on each juvenile in residence on a specified reference date. Facilities are asked to include all juveniles under 21 years of age assigned a bed in the residential facility on the reference date as a result of being charged or court adjudicated for an offense. The reference date for the 1997 census was October 29 and the facility response rate was 96%; for the 1999 census it was October 27 and 100%; and for the 2001 census it was October 24 and 89%.

[a]Detail may not add to total because of rounding.
[b]Totals include 3,401 juveniles in 1997, 2,645 juveniles in 1999, and 2,435 juveniles in 2001 in private facilities for whom the State where the offense was committed was not reported; and 174 juveniles in 1999 and 194 juveniles in 2001 in tribal facilities.

Source: Melissa Sickmund, T.J. Sladky, and Wei Kang, "Census of Juveniles in Residential Placement Databook" [Online]. Washington, DC: U.S. Department of Justice, Office of Juvenile Justice and Delinquency Prevention. Available: http://www.ojjdp.ncjrs.org/ojstatbb/cjrp/ [May 17, 2004]. Table adapted by SOURCEBOOK staff.

Table 6.10

Juveniles in public and private residential custody facilities

By race, ethnicity, and offense, United States, on Oct. 24, 2001[a]

Most serious offense	Total	White, non-Hispanic	Black, non-Hispanic	Hispanic	American Indian	Asian	Other
Total	104,413	41,342	40,751	18,012	2,177	1,510	621
Delinquency offenses	99,297	38,775	39,117	17,436	1,980	1,449	537
Violent offenses	34,915	12,897	14,469	6,051	729	555	216
Index offenses[b]	23,696	7,932	10,290	4,452	522	393	105
Other violent	11,219	4,965	4,179	1,599	207	162	108
Property offenses	29,373	12,468	10,809	4,887	609	447	156
Index offenses[c]	24,467	10,362	9,045	4,053	513	381	114
Other property	4,906	2,106	1,764	834	96	63	42
Drug offenses	9,086	2,889	4,353	1,608	114	75	48
Public-order offenses	10,451	4,101	3,960	1,986	204	144	57
Technical violation	15,472	6,420	5,526	2,907	324	231	63
Status offenses[d]	5,116	2,568	1,632	576	198	60	84

Note: See Note, table 6.9.

[a] Detail may not add to total because of rounding.
[b] Includes criminal homicide, violent sexual assault, robbery, and aggravated assault.
[c] Includes burglary, theft, auto theft, and arson.
[d] Status offenses include running away, underage drinking, truancy, curfew violations, and other offenses that are illegal for juveniles but not adults. Care should be exercised when interpreting status offense data because States differ in what they classify as an adjudicable status offense.

Source: Melissa Sickmund, T.J. Sladky, and Wei Kang, "Census of Juveniles in Residential Placement Databook" [Online]. Washington, DC: U.S. Department of Justice, Office of Juvenile Justice and Delinquency Prevention. Available: http://www.ojjdp.ncjrs.org/ojstatbb/cjrp/ [May 17, 2004].

Table 6.11

Juveniles in public and private residential custody facilities

By age and sex, United States, on Oct. 24, 2001[a]

Age	Total Number	Total Percent	Male Number	Male Percent	Female Number	Female Percent
Total	104,413	100%	89,271	85%	15,142	15%
Less than 13 years	1,852	2	1,563	84	288	16
13 years	4,448	4	3,492	79	957	22
14 years	10,499	10	8,205	78	2,295	22
15 years	19,565	19	15,825	81	3,741	19
16 years	26,992	26	23,061	85	3,930	15
17 years	24,988	24	22,131	89	2,856	11
18 years and older	16,069	15	14,994	93	1,074	7

Note: See Note, table 6.9.

[a] Detail may not add to total because of rounding.

Source: Melissa Sickmund, T.J. Sladky, and Wei Kang, "Census of Juveniles in Residential Placement Databook" [Online]. Washington, DC: U.S. Department of Justice, Office of Juvenile Justice and Delinquency Prevention. Available: http://www.ojjdp.ncjrs.org/ojstatbb/cjrp/ [May 17, 2004]. Table adapted by SOURCEBOOK staff.

Table 6.12

Juveniles in public and private residential custody facilities

By sex, race, ethnicity, and State, on Oct. 24, 2001[a]

State	Total	Sex Male	Sex Female	White, non-Hispanic	Black, non-Hispanic	Hispanic	American Indian	Asian	Other	Public	Private
United States, total[b]	104,413	89,271	15,142	41,342	40,751	18,012	2,177	1,510	621	73,328	30,891
Alabama	1,617	1,314	303	711	882	15	0	0	6	840	777
Alaska	349	294	54	135	30	12	147	18	6	252	96
Arizona	1,884	1,545	339	759	177	828	102	21	0	1,602	282
Arkansas	652	519	132	297	321	24	0	3	6	354	297
California	18,145	16,152	1,992	3,846	5,757	7,557	330	600	54	16,548	1,596
Colorado	1,772	1,515	255	882	237	612	33	6	3	942	828
Connecticut	630	525	105	267	198	156	3	6	3	291	339
Delaware	305	267	39	90	189	24	0	0	0	222	84
District of Columbia	171	162	9	6	159	6	0	0	0	90	81
Florida	6,776	5,820	957	2,931	3,327	477	3	21	15	2,880	3,894
Georgia	2,942	2,451	489	909	1,935	81	0	12	3	2,259	681
Hawaii	103	81	24	9	9	12	0	63	12	84	18
Idaho	530	435	96	429	3	81	12	3	3	453	78
Illinois	3,560	3,171	390	1,224	1,929	303	9	84	9	3,003	558
Indiana	3,235	2,514	720	1,989	1,068	144	3	12	21	2,313	924
Iowa	1,105	903	201	837	162	57	24	15	9	372	735
Kansas	1,116	957	159	597	315	114	24	12	57	810	306
Kentucky	990	825	165	690	279	9	3	3	6	771	219
Louisiana	2,456	2,049	408	660	1,767	15	3	6	3	1,968	489
Maine	227	186	42	213	9	3	3	0	0	180	48
Maryland	1,198	1,068	129	459	702	30	0	3	3	597	603
Massachusetts	1,324	1,149	174	576	357	336	3	33	18	540	783
Michigan	3,504	2,871	633	1,788	1,482	150	21	15	48	1,572	1,932
Minnesota	1,946	1,638	306	1,050	447	93	222	111	24	1,005	942
Mississippi	693	555	138	171	516	3	0	0	3	678	15
Missouri	1,392	1,206	186	711	636	27	3	6	6	1,356	36
Montana	266	228	36	183	6	12	60	6	0	162	102
Nebraska	718	525	192	372	198	96	39	6	9	510	210
Nevada	901	732	168	468	231	171	15	12	6	819	84
New Hampshire	203	174	27	144	15	39	3	6	0	132	72
New Jersey	2,079	1,875	204	315	1,371	378	3	9	6	2,022	57
New Mexico	837	708	129	162	63	519	90	3	0	753	84
New York	4,593	3,675	918	1,482	2,607	321	90	42	54	2,517	2,076
North Carolina	1,318	1,140	180	462	759	51	15	18	15	948	369
North Dakota	180	153	27	102	6	3	63	0	3	93	87
Ohio	4,554	4,005	549	2,391	1,947	108	3	12	96	4,050	504
Oklahoma	870	777	93	435	252	54	126	3	0	531	339
Oregon	1,508	1,314	195	1,143	126	150	66	21	6	1,293	213
Pennsylvania	4,066	3,570	495	1,641	1,863	480	3	33	45	1,239	2,826
Rhode Island	311	282	30	123	90	84	9	3	3	183	129
South Carolina	1,398	1,212	186	468	924	3	0	0	0	1,035	363
South Dakota	496	351	147	267	12	6	207	3	3	333	165
Tennessee	1,655	1,338	318	819	786	27	0	12	12	1,149	504
Texas	8,524	7,512	1,011	2,424	2,742	3,294	15	51	0	6,900	1,623
Utah	1,015	846	171	747	42	183	24	15	3	486	528
Vermont	62	57	3	48	6	9	0	0	0	30	33
Virginia	2,811	2,379	432	1,053	1,614	99	3	30	9	2,595	216
Washington	2,054	1,761	291	1,260	345	261	102	84	0	1,905	150
West Virginia	475	399	78	393	72	0	0	0	6	219	255
Wisconsin	1,941	1,620	321	981	771	63	54	60	12	1,272	669
Wyoming	327	186	141	246	12	45	21	3	0	174	153

Note: See Note, table 6.9. These data reflect the State where the offense was committed rather than the State in which the holding facility is located.

Source: Melissa Sickmund, T. J. Sladky, and Wei Kang, "Census of Juveniles in Residential Placement Databook" [Online]. Washington, DC: U.S. Department of Justice, Office of Juvenile Justice and Delinquency Prevention. Available: http://www.ojjdp.ncjrs.org/ojstatbb/cjrp/ [May 17, 2004]. Table adapted by SOURCEBOOK staff.

[a]Detail may not add to total because of rounding.
[b]Total includes 2,435 juvenile offenders in private facilities for whom the State where the offense was committed was not reported and 194 juvenile offenders in tribal facilities.

Table 6.13

Number and rate (per 100,000 residents) of persons in State and Federal prisons and local jails

United States, 1985, 1990-2003

	Total in custody	Prisoners in custody Federal	Prisoners in custody State	Inmates in local jails	Incarceration rate[a]
1985	744,208	35,781	451,812	256,615	313
1990	1,148,702	58,838	684,544	405,320	458
1991	1,219,014	63,930	728,605	426,479	481
1992	1,295,150	72,071	778,495	444,584	505
1993	1,369,185	80,815	828,566	459,804	528
1994	1,476,621	85,500	904,647	486,474	564
1995	1,585,586	89,538	989,004	507,044	601
1996	1,646,020	95,088	1,032,440	518,492	618
1997	1,743,643	101,755	1,074,809	567,079	648
1998	1,816,931	110,793	1,113,676	592,462	669
1999[b]	1,893,115	125,682	1,161,490	605,943	691
2000	1,937,482[c]	133,921	1,176,269	621,149	684
2001	1,961,247[c]	143,337	1,180,155	631,240	685
2002	2,033,022[c]	151,618	1,209,331	665,475	701
2003	2,085,620[c]	161,673	1,226,175	691,301	714
Percent change 2002 to 2003	2.6%	6.6%	1.4%	3.9%	X
Annual average percent increase 1995 to 2003	3.5%	7.7%	2.7%	4.0%	X

Note: Jail counts are for June 30; counts for 1994-2003 exclude persons who were supervised outside of a jail facility. State and Federal prisoner counts are for December 31. Some data have been revised by the Source and may differ from previous editions of SOURCEBOOK. For information on methodology and explanatory notes, see Appendix 4 and Appendix 15.

[a] Number of prison and jail inmates per 100,000 U.S. residents at yearend.
[b] In 1999, 15 States expanded their reporting criteria to include prisoners held in privately operated correctional facilities. For comparisons with previous years, the State count 1,137,544 and the total 1,869,169 should be used for 1999.
[c] Includes Federal prisoners in non-secure privately operated facilities (6,143 in 2000, 6,515 in 2001, 6,598 in 2002, and 6,471 in 2003).

Source: U.S. Department of Justice, Bureau of Justice Statistics, **Prison and Jail Inmates at Midyear 1998**, Bulletin NCJ 173414 (Washington, DC: U.S. Department of Justice, March 1999), p. 2, Table 1; U.S. Department of Justice, Bureau of Justice Statistics, **Prisoners in 2002**, Bulletin NCJ 200248, p. 2; and **2003**, Bulletin NCJ 205335, p. 2, Table 1 (Washington, DC: U.S. Department of Justice). Table adapted by SOURCEBOOK staff.

Table 6.14

Number of jail inmates, average daily population, and rated capacity

By legal status and sex, United States, 1983-2003

	All inmates	1-day counts[a] Total Adults	Male	Female	Juvenile[b]	Average daily population[c]	Rated capacity of jails[d]	Percent of rated capacity occupied[e]
1983	223,551	221,815	206,163	15,652	1,736	227,541	261,556	85%
1984	234,500	233,018	216,275	16,743	1,482	230,641	261,432	90
1985	256,615	254,986	235,909	19,077	1,629	265,010	272,830	94
1986	274,444	272,736	251,235	21,501	1,708	265,517	285,726	96
1987	295,873	294,092	270,172	23,920	1,781	290,300	301,198	98
1988	343,569	341,893	311,594	30,299	1,676	336,017	339,633	101
1989	395,553	393,303	356,050	37,253	2,250	386,845	367,769	108
1990	405,320	403,019	365,821	37,198	2,301	408,075	389,171	104
1991	426,479	424,129	384,628	39,501	2,350	422,609	421,237	101
1992	444,584	441,780	401,106	40,674	2,804	441,889	449,197	99
1993[f]	459,804	455,500	411,500	44,100	4,300	466,155	475,224	97
1994[f]	486,474	479,800	431,300	48,500	6,700	479,757	504,324	96
1995[f]	507,044	499,300	448,000	51,300	7,800	509,828	545,763	93
1996[f]	518,492	510,400	454,700	55,700	8,100	515,432	562,971	92
1997	567,079	557,974	498,678	59,296	9,105	556,586	586,564	97
1998	592,462	584,372	520,581	63,791	8,090	593,808	612,780	97
1999	605,943	596,485	528,998	67,487	9,458	607,978	652,321	93
2000	621,149	613,534	543,120	70,414	7,615	618,319	677,787	92
2001	631,240	623,628	551,007	72,621	7,613	625,966	699,309	90
2002	665,475	658,228	581,411	76,817	7,248	652,082	713,899	93
2003	691,301	684,431	602,781	81,650	6,869	680,760	735,518	94

Note: Data for 1983, 1988, 1993, and 1999 are from the National Jail Census. Data for 1984-87, 1989-92, 1994-98, and 2000-2003 are from the Annual Survey of Jails taken during noncensus years. Both the censuses and the surveys are conducted for the U.S. Department of Justice, Bureau of Justice Statistics by the U.S. Census Bureau. The data from the annual surveys are estimates and therefore are subject to sampling variation. A jail is defined as a locally administered confinement facility that holds inmates beyond arraignment, usually for more than 48 hours, and is administered and staffed by municipal or county employees. Excluded from the censuses and surveys were temporary holding facilities, such as physically separate drunk tanks and police lockups, and other holding facilities that did not hold persons after they were formally charged in court. Also excluded for all years were Connecticut, Delaware, Hawaii, Rhode Island, and Vermont because these States have integrated jail-prison systems. Alaska also was excluded as an integrated system; however, beginning in 1988, locally operated jails in Alaska are included. For methodology and survey sampling procedures, see Appendix 4.

[a] Data for years prior to 1994 include an unknown number of persons who were under jail supervision but not confined. Beginning in 1994, data are based on the number of inmates held in jail facilities.
[b] Juveniles are persons defined by State statute as being under a certain age, usually 18, and subject initially to juvenile court authority even if tried as adults in criminal court. In 1994, the definition was changed to include all persons under age 18.
[c] The average daily population is the sum of the number of inmates in a jail each day for a year, divided by the number of days in the year.
[d] Rated capacity is the number of beds or inmates assigned by a rating official to facilities within each jurisdiction.
[e] The number of inmates divided by rated capacity times 100. Prior to 1994, this ratio may include some inmates not in physical custody, but under the jurisdiction of a local jail, such as inmates on electronic monitoring, under house arrest, or in day reporting or other community supervision programs. Beginning in 1994, the ratio includes only those held in jail.
[f] Detailed data for 1-day counts are estimated and rounded to the nearest 100.

Source: U.S. Department of Justice, Bureau of Justice Statistics, *Jail Inmates, 1985*, NCJ-105586 (Washington, DC: USGPO, 1987), p. 5, Table 1 and p. 7, Table 5; U.S. Department of Justice, Bureau of Justice Statistics, *Jail Inmates 1987*, Bulletin NCJ-114319, p. 2, Table 1 and p. 3, Table 5; *1990*, Bulletin NCJ-129756, p. 1, Table 1 and p. 2, Table 5; *1991*, Bulletin NCJ-134726, p. 2, Table 1 and p. 3, Table 5; *1992*, Bulletin NCJ-143284, p. 2, Table 1 and p. 3, Table 6; *Jails and Jail Inmates 1993-94*, Bulletin NCJ-151651, p. 3 and p. 6, Table 7; *Prison and Jail Inmates at Midyear 1997*, Bulletin NCJ-167247, p. 6, Table 6 and p. 7, Table 8; *1998*, Bulletin NCJ 173414, p. 6, Table 6 and p. 7, Table 8; *1999*, Bulletin NCJ 181643, p. 6, Table 6 and p. 7, Table 9; *2002*, Bulletin NCJ 198877, p. 8, Table 9 and p. 9; *2003*, Bulletin NCJ 203947, p. 8, Table 9 and p. 9 (Washington, DC: U.S. Department of Justice). Table adapted by SOURCEBOOK staff.

Table 6.15

Persons under jail supervision

By confinement status and type of program, United States, 1995-2003

Confinement status and type of program	\multicolumn{9}{c}{Persons under jail supervision}								
	1995	1996	1997	1998	1999	2000	2001	2002	2003
Total	541,913	591,469	637,319	664,847	687,973	687,033	702,044	737,912	762,672
Held in jail	507,044	518,492	567,079	592,462	605,943	621,149	631,240	665,475	691,301
Supervised outside a jail facility[a]	34,869	72,977	70,239	72,385	82,030	65,884	70,804	72,437	71,371
Electronic monitoring	6,788	7,480	8,699	10,827	10,230	10,782	10,017	9,706	12,678
Home detention[b]	1,376	907	1,164	370	518	332	539	1,037	594
Day reporting	1,283	3,298	2,768	3,089	5,080	3,969	3,522	5,010	7,965
Community service	10,253	17,410	15,918	17,518	20,139	13,592	17,561	13,918	17,102
Weekender programs	1,909	16,336	17,656	17,249	16,089	14,523	14,381	17,955	12,111
Other pretrial supervision	3,229	2,135	7,368	6,048	10,092	6,279	6,632	8,702	11,452
Other work programs[c]	9,144	14,469	6,631	7,089	7,780	8,011	5,204	5,190	4,498
Treatment programs[d]	NA	10,425	6,693	5,702	8,500	5,714	5,219	1,256	1,891
Other	887	517	3,342	4,493	3,602	2,682	7,729	9,663	3,080

Note: See Note, table 6.14. For methodology and survey sampling procedures, see Appendix 4.

[a]Excludes persons supervised by a probation or parole agency.
[b]Includes only those without electronic monitoring.
[c]Includes persons in work release programs, work gangs/crews, and other work alternative programs.
[d]Includes persons under drug, alcohol, mental health, and other medical treatment.

Source: U.S. Department of Justice, Bureau of Justice Statistics, *Prison and Jail Inmates at Midyear 2000*, Bulletin NCJ 185989, p. 6; *2003*, Bulletin NCJ 203947, p. 7 (Washington, DC: U.S. Department of Justice).

Table 6.16

Jail inmates

By confinement status, region, and jurisdiction, June 30, 1999

	Persons under jail supervision[a]		Confinement status		
			Confined	Jail population under community supervision	
Region and jurisdiction	Number	Rate per 100,000 U.S. residents[b]		Nonconfined[c]	Serving weekend sentences[d]
United States, total	699,182	256	617,152	65,941	16,089
Federal	11,209	4	11,209	0	0
State	687,973	252	605,943	65,941	16,089
Northeast	95,045	202	90,716	2,519	1,810
Maine	1,291	104	1,113	46	132
Massachusetts	11,125	180	10,774	324	27
New Hampshire	1,705	142	1,592	45	68
New Jersey	18,349	225	16,830	965	554
New York	34,265	188	33,411	208	646
Pennsylvania	28,310	236	26,996	931	383
Midwest	109,976	174	97,652	10,541	1,783
Illinois	19,366	160	16,880	2,121	365
Indiana	14,270	240	12,787	1,180	303
Iowa	3,162	110	2,998	33	131
Kansas	4,524	170	4,378	46	100
Michigan	18,679	190	15,629	2,789	261
Minnesota	6,445	135	5,002	1,337	106
Missouri	7,490	137	6,940	347	203
Nebraska	2,368	142	2,189	147	32
North Dakota	668	105	588	52	28
Ohio	18,703	167	16,638	1,849	216
South Dakota	1,100	149	1,064	17	19
Wisconsin	13,201	252	12,559	623	19
South	321,328	335	284,742	29,307	7,279
Alabama	11,803	269	11,418	103	282
Arkansas	5,398	211	4,832	394	172
District of Columbia	1,660	322	1,653	0	7
Florida	57,685	381	51,080	5,769	836
Georgia	34,861	447	32,835	1,528	498
Kentucky	15,680	396	10,373	5,024	283
Louisiana	26,976	615	25,631	1,260	85
Maryland	21,363	413	10,945	10,131	287
Mississippi	9,018	325	8,886	35	97
North Carolina	14,315	187	13,279	288	748
Oklahoma	7,100	211	6,743	195	162
South Carolina	9,427	243	8,780	203	444
Tennessee	20,557	374	19,629	52	876
Texas	61,182	304	57,930	1,809	1,443
Virginia	21,482	314	18,235	2,290	957
West Virginia	2,821	156	2,493	226	102
West	161,624	269	132,833	23,574	5,217
Alaska	68	11	68	0	0
Arizona	10,737	224	10,320	47	370
California	94,136	284	77,142	12,841	4,153
Colorado	16,094	397	9,004	6,870	220
Idaho	3,102	248	2,809	195	98
Montana	1,550	176	1,521	13	16
Nevada	5,681	313	4,898	718	65
New Mexico	5,439	311	5,217	164	58
Oregon	7,528	227	6,283	1,176	69
Utah	4,514	211	4,024	393	97
Washington	11,691	203	10,542	1,126	23
Wyoming	1,084	225	1,005	31	48

Note: These data are from the 1999 Census of Jails conducted for the U.S. Department of Justice, Bureau of Justice Statistics by the U.S. Census Bureau. The 1999 census included all locally administered jails that held inmates beyond arraignment (usually more than 72 hours) and were staffed by municipal or county employees. Excluded from the census were physically separate temporary holding facilities, such as drunk tanks and police lockups, that do not hold persons after they are formally charged in court. Also excluded were Connecticut, Delaware, Hawaii, Rhode Island, and Vermont because these jurisdictions have State-operated integrated jail/prison systems. Alaska also was excluded for this reason, however, 15 independently operated jails in Alaska were included. For additional information on the Census of Jails, see Appendix 4.

[a] Includes persons confined in jail facilities and those under community supervision.
[b] Based on U.S. Census Bureau estimates of the U.S. resident population for July 1, 1999.
[c] Includes all persons in community-based programs run by jail authorities (e.g., electronic monitoring, house arrest, community service, day reporting, pretrial supervision, and other alternative work programs).
[d] During the weekend prior to June 30, 1999. Includes all persons who serve their sentences of confinement only on weekends (e.g., Friday to Sunday).

Source: U.S. Department of Justice, Bureau of Justice Statistics, *Census of Jails, 1999*, NCJ 186633 (Washington, DC: U.S. Department of Justice, 2001), pp. 14, 19. Table adapted by SOURCEBOOK staff.

Table 6.17

Jail inmates

By sex, race, Hispanic origin, and conviction status, United States, 1990-2003[a]

	Percent of jail inmates													
	1990	1991	1992	1993	1994	1995	1996[b]	1997	1998	1999	2000	2001	2002	2003
Total	100%	100%	100%	100%	100%	100%	100%	100%	100%	100%	100%	100%	100%	100%
Sex														
Male	90.8	90.7	90.8	90.4	90.0	89.8	89.2	89.4	89.2	88.8	88.6	88.4	88.4	88.1
Female	9.2	9.3	9.2	9.6	10.0	10.2	10.8	10.6	10.8	11.2	11.4	11.6	11.6	11.9
Race, Hispanic origin														
White, non-Hispanic	41.8	41.1	40.1	39.3	39.1	40.1	41.6	40.6	41.3	41.3	41.9	43.0	43.8	43.6
Black, non-Hispanic	42.5	43.4	44.1	44.2	43.9	43.5	41.1	42.0	41.2	41.5	41.3	40.6	39.8	39.2
Hispanic	14.3	14.2	14.5	15.1	15.4	14.7	15.6	15.7	15.5	15.5	15.1	14.7	14.7	15.4
Other[c]	1.3	1.2	1.3	1.3	1.6	1.7	1.7	1.8	2.0	1.7	1.6	1.6	1.6	1.8
Conviction status[d]														
Convicted	48.5	NA	NA	NA	NA	44.0	NA	NA	43.2	45.9	44.0	41.5	40.0	39.4
Male	44.1	NA	NA	NA	NA	39.7	NA	NA	38.4	40.8	39.0	36.6	35.4	34.7
Female	4.5	NA	NA	NA	NA	4.3	NA	NA	4.8	5.1	5.0	4.9	4.6	4.7
Unconvicted	51.5	NA	NA	NA	NA	56.0	NA	NA	56.8	54.1	56.0	58.5	59.9	60.6
Male	46.7	NA	NA	NA	NA	50.0	NA	NA	50.6	48.0	50.0	51.9	53.0	53.5
Female	4.8	NA	NA	NA	NA	6.0	NA	NA	6.1	6.1	6.0	6.6	6.9	7.1

Note: See Note, table 6.14. For methodology and survey sampling procedures, see Appendix 4.

[a]Percents may not add to total because of rounding.
[b]Based on all persons under jail supervision; not limited to inmates confined in jail facilities.
[c]Includes Asians, American Indians, Alaska Natives, Native Hawaiians, and other Pacific Islanders.
[d]Data for conviction status include adults only with the exception of 1999, which includes adults and juveniles.

Source: U.S. Department of Justice, Bureau of Justice Statistics, *Prison and Jail Inmates at Midyear 1998*, Bulletin NCJ 173414, p. 6, Table 7 and p. 7; *2000*, Bulletin NCJ 185989, p. 7, Table 9; *2002*, Bulletin NCJ 198877, p. 8, Table 10; *2003*, Bulletin NCJ 203947, p. 8, Table 10 (Washington, DC: U.S. Department of Justice). Table adapted by SOURCEBOOK staff.

Table 6.18
Characteristics of jail inmates

By conviction status, United States, 1983, 1989, 1996, and 2002

	Percent of jail inmates							
	1983	1989	1996	2002 Total	2002 Convicted	2002 Unconvicted	2002 Both[a]
Number of jail inmates	223,552	395,554	507,026	631,241	394,039	182,754	100,495
Sex							
Male	92.9%	90.5%	89.8%	88.4%	87.7%	89.2%	89.6%
Female	7.1	9.5	10.2	11.6	12.3	10.8	10.4
Race, Hispanic origin[b]							
White, non-Hispanic	46.4	38.6	37.4	36.0	39.4	31.0	33.3
Black, non-Hispanic	37.5	41.7	40.9	40.1	37.3	43.0	44.1
Hispanic	14.3	17.4	18.5	18.5	18.5	19.6	16.6
American Indian, Alaska Native	NA	NA	2.4	1.3	1.2	1.4	1.6
Asian, Pacific Islander	NA	NA	0.9	1.1	0.9	1.7	0.9
Other[c]	1.8	2.3	NA	3.0	2.6	3.3	3.6
Age							
17 years and younger	1.3	1.5	2.3	1.8	1.2	2.9	1.6
18 to 24 years	40.4	32.6	28.5	28.1	28.3	28.9	26.4
25 to 34 years	38.6	42.9	37.4	31.9	31.0	31.8	35.4
35 to 44 years	12.4	16.7	23.9	26.0	27.1	24.2	25.2
45 to 54 years	4.9	4.6	6.3	10.0	10.2	9.4	10.4
55 years and older	2.4	1.7	1.5	2.2	2.2	2.8	1.0
Marital status							
Married	21.0	19.0	15.7	16.2	15.8	16.5	17.3
Widowed	1.4	1.0	1.4	1.2	1.1	1.5	1.1
Divorced	15.7	15.1	15.6	15.7	16.3	14.7	15.5
Separated	7.9	8.2	8.7	6.7	7.5	5.6	6.3
Never married	54.1	56.7	58.6	60.1	59.3	61.7	59.8
Education[d]							
8th grade or less	17.7	15.6	13.1	12.3	11.8	14.3	10.6
Some high school	41.3	38.2	33.4	31.6	30.6	32.7	33.4
GED	NA	NA	14.1	17.1	18.2	14.1	18.6
High school diploma	29.2	33.1	25.9	25.9	26.1	26.2	24.6
Some college	11.8	13.1	10.3	10.1	10.5	9.7	9.6
College graduate or more	NA	NA	3.2	2.9	2.8	2.9	3.1
Military service							
Veteran	21.2	15.5	11.7	NA	NA	NA	NA
Nonveteran	78.8	84.5	88.3	NA	NA	NA	NA
U.S. citizenship							
Citizen	NA	NA	91.8	92.2	92.6	89.5	95.8
Noncitizen	NA	NA	8.2	7.8	7.4	10.5	4.2

Note: These data are from the Survey of Inmates in Local Jails conducted for the U.S. Department of Justice, Bureau of Justice Statistics by the U.S. Census Bureau in 1983, 1989, 1996, and 2002. For the 2002 survey, a nationally representative sample of 6,982 inmates in 417 local jails were interviewed between January and April 2002. A jail is defined as a locally operated correctional facility that confines a person before or after adjudication. Inmates sentenced to jail usually have a sentence of 1 year or less, but jails also incarcerate persons in a wide variety of other categories. Jails may also house inmates awaiting transfer to other correctional or mental health facilities, those awaiting trials or sentencing, and those being held in protective custody, for contempt, or as court witnesses. These data are estimates derived from a sample and therefore subject to sampling variation. For information on methodology and survey sampling procedures, see Appendix 4.

[a] Includes inmates with a prior conviction, but no new conviction for the current charge.
[b] Excludes 0.3% of inmates in 1996 and 2002 who did not specify a race.
[c] Prior to 1996, category includes Asians, Pacific Islanders, American Indians, Alaska Natives, and other racial groups. After 1996, category includes inmates specifying more than one race.
[d] Beginning with the 1996 survey, inmates with less than a high school diploma were asked specifically if they had a GED. Those reporting that they had a GED or high school equivalency certificate were classified as high school graduates. Prior to the 1996 survey, GED was a volunteered response.

Source: U.S. Department of Justice, Bureau of Justice Statistics, *Profile of Jail Inmates, 1996*, Special Report NCJ-164620, p. 3; *2002*, Special Report NCJ 201932, p. 2, Table 1 (Washington, DC: U.S. Department of Justice). Table adapted by SOURCEBOOK staff.

Table 6.19

Most serious current offense of jail inmates

By conviction status, United States, 1983, 1989, 1996, and 2002

				Percent of jail inmates			
					2002		
Most serious offense	1983	1989	1996	Total	Convicted	Unconvicted	Both[a]
Number of jail inmates	219,573	380,160	496,752	623,492	342,372	178,035	100,348
Violent offenses	30.7%	22.5%	26.3%	25.4%	21.6%	34.4%	22.3%
Murder, nonnegligent manslaughter	4.1	2.8	2.8	2.0	0.9	5.3	NA
Negligent manslaughter	0.6	0.5	0.4	0.5	0.7	0.4	0.3
Kidnaping	1.3	0.8	0.5	0.7	0.4	1.4	0.6
Rape	1.5	0.8	0.5	0.6	0.6	0.8	0.4
Other sexual assault	2.0	2.6	2.7	2.8	2.7	3.6	1.5
Robbery	11.2	6.7	6.5	5.6	3.9	8.7	5.5
Assault	8.6	7.2	11.6	11.7	10.9	12.5	12.7
Other violent[b]	1.3	1.1	1.3	1.4	1.4	1.6	1.1
Property offenses	38.6	30.0	26.9	24.4	24.9	21.5	27.4
Burglary	14.3	10.7	7.6	6.7	6.4	6.8	8.0
Larceny/theft	11.7	7.9	8.0	7.0	7.6	5.3	7.6
Motor vehicle theft	2.3	2.8	2.6	2.0	2.0	1.6	2.6
Arson	0.8	0.7	0.4	0.3	0.3	0.5	0.1
Fraud	5.0	4.0	4.6	4.9	5.3	4.2	4.7
Stolen property	2.5	2.4	2.1	1.7	1.6	1.4	2.5
Other property[c]	1.9	1.6	1.6	1.8	1.8	1.7	1.9
Drug offenses	9.3	23.0	22.0	24.7	24.0	23.4	30.2
Possession	4.7	9.7	11.5	10.8	10.0	10.4	14.6
Trafficking	4.0	12.0	9.2	12.1	12.6	10.6	13.5
Other drug	0.6	1.3	1.3	1.8	1.5	2.3	2.1
Public-order offenses	20.6	22.8	24.4	24.9	29.1	20.2	19.2
Weapons	2.3	1.9	2.3	2.0	2.1	1.9	2.2
Obstruction of justice	2.0	2.8	4.9	3.9	3.5	5.4	2.7
Traffic violations	2.2	2.7	3.2	3.7	4.7	2.3	2.5
Driving while intoxicated[d]	7.0	8.8	7.4	6.4	8.9	2.3	5.1
Drunkenness, morals[e]	3.4	1.7	2.0	1.7	1.8	1.5	1.8
Violation of parole, probation[f]	2.3	3.0	2.6	2.9	3.5	1.5	3.3
Immigration violations	NA	NA	0.2	1.8	1.8	2.5	0.3
Other public-order[g]	1.6	1.8	1.8	2.5	2.8	2.8	1.2
Other offenses[h]	0.8	1.6	0.5	0.5	0.4	0.6	0.9

Note: See Note, table 6.18. Data exclude inmates for whom offense was unknown. Some data for 1996 have been revised by the Source and may differ from previous editions of SOURCEBOOK. For information on methodology and survey sampling procedures, see Appendix 4.

[a]Includes inmates with a prior conviction, but no new conviction for the current charge.
[b]Includes blackmail, extortion, hit-and-run driving with bodily injury, child abuse, and criminal endangerment.
[c]Includes destruction of property, vandalism, hit-and-run driving without bodily injury, trespassing, and possession of burglary tools.
[d]Includes driving while intoxicated and driving under the influence of drugs or alcohol.
[e]Includes drunkenness, vagrancy, disorderly conduct, unlawful assembly, morals, and commercialized vice.
[f]Includes parole or probation violations, escape, absence without leave (AWOL), and flight to avoid prosecution.
[g]Includes rioting, abandonment, nonsupport, invasion of privacy, liquor law violations, and tax evasion.
[h]Includes juvenile offenses and other unspecified offenses.

Source: U.S. Department of Justice, Bureau of Justice Statistics, *Profile of Jail Inmates, 1996*, Special Report NCJ-164620, p. 4; *2002*, Special Report NCJ 201932, p. 3 (Washington, DC: U.S. Department of Justice). Table adapted by SOURCEBOOK staff.

Table 6.20

Most serious current offense of jail inmates

By sex, race, and Hispanic origin, United States, 2002

	Percent of jail inmates				
	Sex		Race, Hispanic origin		
Most serious offense	Male	Female	White, non-Hispanic	Black, non-Hispanic	Hispanic
Number of jail inmates	551,186	72,306	223,292	249,304	114,562
Violent offenses	26.5%	17.1%	21.8%	26.9%	27.1%
Murder, nonnegligent manslaughter	2.1	1.4	1.2	2.4	2.5
Negligent manslaughter	0.6	0.4	0.4	0.6	0.6
Rape	0.7	NA	0.6	0.5	0.6
Other sexual assault	3.1	0.9	4.0	1.7	2.5
Robbery	5.8	3.6	2.8	7.7	6.0
Assault	12.2	8.0	10.6	11.8	13.0
Other violent[a]	1.3	2.5	1.6	1.3	1.0
Property offenses	23.3	32.4	28.1	24.0	17.5
Burglary	7.2	2.9	8.3	6.3	4.8
Larceny/theft	6.5	10.3	8.1	7.3	4.2
Motor vehicle theft	2.0	1.4	2.2	1.8	2.1
Fraud	3.7	14.0	6.2	4.6	2.9
Stolen property	1.7	1.6	1.6	2.1	1.1
Other property[b]	1.9	1.5	1.3	1.9	2.1
Drug offenses	24.1	29.2	18.5	30.6	27.5
Possession	10.3	14.5	8.6	12.7	12.4
Trafficking	12.3	10.9	7.7	16.3	13.9
Other/unspecified drug	1.5	3.8	2.2	1.6	1.1
Public-order offenses	25.5	20.8	31.0	18.0	27.5
Weapons	2.2	0.6	1.8	2.4	1.9
Obstruction of justice	3.8	4.4	4.4	3.7	3.1
Driving while intoxicated[c]	6.6	4.9	10.9	1.8	7.7
Drunkenness, morals[d]	1.5	3.3	1.9	1.5	1.8
Violation of parole, probation[e]	2.9	3.1	3.6	2.6	2.3
Immigration violations	1.9	0.5	NA	0.6	6.6
Other public-order[f]	2.7	1.5	3.5	2.3	1.5
Other offenses[g]	0.5	0.6	0.7	0.4	NA

Note: See Note, table 6.18. The table excludes inmates for whom offense was unknown but includes offenses for which estimates are not shown separately. For information on methodology and survey sampling procedures, see Appendix 4.

[a] Includes blackmail, extortion, kidnaping, hit-and-run driving with bodily injury, child abuse, and criminal endangerment.
[b] Includes destruction of property, vandalism, arson, hit-and-run driving without bodily injury, trespassing, and possession of burglary tools.
[c] Includes driving while intoxicated and driving under the influence of drugs or alcohol.
[d] Includes drunkenness, vagrancy, disorderly conduct, unlawful assembly, morals, and commercialized vice.
[e] Includes parole or probation violations, escape, absence without leave (AWOL), and flight to avoid prosecution.
[f] Includes rioting, abandonment, nonsupport, invasion of privacy, liquor law violations, and tax evasion.
[g] Includes juvenile offenses and other unspecified offenses.

Source: U.S. Department of Justice, Bureau of Justice Statistics, *Profile of Jail Inmates, 2002*, Special Report NCJ 201932 (Washington, DC: U.S. Department of Justice, July 2004), p. 4, Table 4. Table adapted by SOURCEBOOK staff.

Table 6.21

Percent of jail inmates reporting drug use

By type of drug and frequency of use, United States, 1996 and 2002

	All inmates				Convicted inmates[a]			
	Ever used drugs		Ever used drugs regularly[b]		Used drugs in the month before the offense		Used drugs at the time of the offense	
Type of drug	1996	2002	1996	2002	1996	2002	1996	2002
Any drug	82.4%	82.2%	64.2%	68.7%	54.0%	52.6%	34.9%	28.8%
Marijuana or hashish	78.2	75.7	54.9	57.6	36.0	37.5	18.0	13.6
Cocaine or crack	50.4	48.1	31.0	30.5	22.8	20.7	14.3	10.6
Heroin or opiates	23.9	20.7	11.8	11.9	7.9	7.8	5.1	4.1
Depressants[c]	29.9	21.6	10.4	10.6	5.3	6.1	2.2	2.4
Stimulants[d]	33.6	27.8	16.5	16.8	9.6	11.4	5.6	5.2
Hallucinogens[e]	32.2	32.4	10.5	13.2	4.2	5.9	1.4	1.6
Inhalants	16.8	12.7	4.8	4.1	0.9	1.0	0.3	0.2

Note: See Note, table 6.18. For information on methodology and survey sampling procedures, see Appendix 4.

[a]Includes all inmates with a current conviction or with a prior conviction, but no new conviction for the current charge.
[b]Used drugs at least once a week for at least a month.
[c]Includes barbiturates, tranquilizers, and Quaaludes.
[d]Includes amphetamines and methamphetamine.
[e]Includes LSD, ecstasy, and PCP.

Source: U.S. Department of Justice, Bureau of Justice Statistics, *Profile of Jail Inmates, 2002*, Special Report NCJ 201932 (Washington, DC: U.S. Department of Justice, July 2004), p. 8, Table 12. Table adapted by SOURCEBOOK staff.

Table 6.22

Percent of jail inmates reporting alcohol use

By sex, race, Hispanic origin, and most serious offense, United States, 1996 and 2002

	Percent of jail inmates who drank alcohol			
	Regularly[a]		At the time of the offense[b]	
	1996	2002	1996	2002
Total	66.3%	66.0%	40.8%	34.5%
Sex				
Male	67.7	67.4	41.9	35.7
Female	54.5	55.4	31.1	25.5
Race, Hispanic origin[c]				
White, non-Hispanic	76.5	75.3	48.2	39.5
Black, non-Hispanic	61.0	62.2	33.6	30.5
Hispanic	56.9	56.1	38.2	31.3
Most serious offense				
Violent	67.7	65.7	40.7	37.6
Property	64.3	65.9	33.1	28.5
Drug	59.8	62.9	28.9	22.4
Public-order, excluding driving while intoxicated	68.6	65.0	32.7	32.3

Note: See Note, table 6.18. For information on methodology and survey sampling procedures, see Appendix 4.

[a]Includes inmates who reported ever drinking at least once a week for a month, as well as drinking daily or at least once a week during the year before the current offense.
[b]Includes all inmates with a current conviction or prior conviction.
[c]Jail inmates who identified more than one race are not shown.

Source: U.S. Department of Justice, Bureau of Justice Statistics, *Profile of Jail Inmates, 2002*, Special Report NCJ 201932 (Washington, DC: U.S. Department of Justice, July 2004), p. 7, Table 11.

Table 6.23

Family background of jail inmates while growing up

United States, 1996 and 2002

	Percent of jail inmates	
	1996	2002
Person(s) lived with most of the time		
Both parents	39.7%	43.6%
Mother only	43.3	39.2
Father only	4.9	4.4
Grandparents	7.0	10.3
Other	5.2	2.5
Ever lived in a foster home, agency, or institution	13.6	11.5
Family member ever incarcerated		
Total[a]	46.1	46.3
Father	17.1	18.6
Mother	4.4	7.1
Brother	30.3	31.4
Sister	6.2	8.9
Spouse	3.3	1.8
Child	1.3	3.5
Parent or guardian ever abused alcohol or drugs while inmate was growing up		
Alcohol only	23.1	19.9
Drugs only	1.3	2.1
Both	6.9	8.6

Note: See Note, table 6.18. For information on methodology and survey sampling procedures, see Appendix 4.

[a]Detail may not add to total because more than one response was possible.

Source: U.S. Department of Justice, Bureau of Justice Statistics, *Profile of Jail Inmates, 2002*, Special Report NCJ 201932 (Washington, DC: U.S. Department of Justice, July 2004), p. 10, Table 15.

Table 6.24
Jail inmates

By sex, race, Hispanic origin, region, and jurisdiction, June 30, 1999[a]

		Sex		Race and Hispanic origin			
Region and jurisdiction	Total	Male	Female	White, non-Hispanic	Black, non-Hispanic	Hispanic	Other[b]
National estimate[c]	617,200	548,300	68,900	257,500	255,100	93,600	11,000
United States, total	617,152	548,276	68,876	222,314	220,167	80,795	9,494
Federal	11,209	10,455	754	7,080	3,559	(d)	570
State	605,943	537,821	68,122	215,234	216,608	80,795	8,924
Northeast	90,716	82,023	8,693	29,029	40,140	15,978	841
Maine	1,113	1,013	100	1,009	43	37	24
Massachusetts	10,774	10,291	483	4,761	2,973	2,879	158
New Hampshire	1,592	1,488	104	1,030	156	207	47
New Jersey	16,830	15,053	1,777	3,920	9,554	3,182	78
New York	33,411	30,118	3,293	6,912	15,144	7,114	202
Pennsylvania	26,996	24,060	2,936	11,397	12,270	2,559	332
Midwest	97,652	86,858	10,794	42,457	26,167	3,298	1,814
Illinois	16,880	15,167	1,713	3,118	2,487	415	119
Indiana	12,787	11,692	1,095	6,962	3,113	327	18
Iowa	2,998	2,668	330	1,525	431	192	55
Kansas	4,378	3,950	428	2,216	910	269	34
Michigan	15,629	13,910	1,719	7,125	5,763	539	105
Minnesota	5,002	4,505	497	2,576	1,201	322	416
Missouri	6,940	6,028	912	2,881	1,459	119	33
Nebraska	2,189	1,966	223	1,110	520	354	102
North Dakota	588	537	51	354	16	28	179
Ohio	16,638	14,478	2,160	7,882	6,726	306	24
South Dakota	1,064	879	185	435	22	48	288
Wisconsin	12,559	11,078	1,481	6,273	3,519	379	441
South	284,742	252,569	32,173	95,291	127,765	21,215	1,197
Alabama	11,418	10,227	1,191	3,825	5,959	179	39
Arkansas	4,832	4,210	622	2,582	1,894	248	22
District of Columbia	1,653	1,586	67	57	1,525	71	0
Florida	51,080	44,803	6,277	19,659	21,073	3,843	27
Georgia	32,835	29,458	3,377	8,059	16,749	604	62
Kentucky	10,373	9,331	1,042	6,073	2,832	165	3
Louisiana	25,631	22,937	2,694	4,859	15,367	408	221
Maryland	10,945	9,729	1,216	3,491	7,044	292	48
Mississippi	8,886	8,201	685	1,572	4,057	85	20
North Carolina	13,279	12,063	1,216	3,028	5,740	473	52
Oklahoma	6,743	5,805	938	3,514	2,143	245	442
South Carolina	8,780	7,974	806	2,103	5,117	108	11
Tennessee	19,629	16,978	2,651	8,126	9,945	276	16
Texas	57,930	51,057	6,873	20,364	17,578	13,680	133
Virginia	18,235	16,001	2,234	6,186	10,257	510	97
West Virginia	2,493	2,209	284	1,793	485	28	4
West	132,833	116,371	16,462	48,457	22,536	40,304	5,072
Alaska	68	65	3	11	0	3	32
Arizona	10,320	9,018	1,302	4,204	1,060	2,928	399
California	77,142	67,441	9,701	22,392	16,561	29,664	2,661
Colorado	9,004	8,028	976	3,162	885	2,060	149
Idaho	2,809	2,469	340	1,441	22	376	94
Montana	1,521	1,385	136	852	29	39	173
Nevada	4,898	4,250	648	2,599	1,235	818	183
New Mexico	5,217	4,654	563	942	356	2,058	361
Oregon	6,283	5,449	834	3,782	663	490	134
Utah	4,024	3,516	508	1,655	94	463	97
Washington	10,542	9,206	1,336	6,762	1,602	1,290	715
Wyoming	1,005	890	115	655	29	114	74

Note: See Note, table 6.16. These data represent inmates confined in jail facilities and exclude those under community supervision. For additional information on the Census of Jails, see Appendix 4.

[a]Detail may not add to total because some reporting units could not report data on sex or race/Hispanic origin of inmates.
[b]Includes American Indians, Alaska Natives, Asians, Native Hawaiians, and other Pacific Islanders
[c]National estimates were calculated by summing the item values from reporting jail jurisdictions and then multiplying by a nonresponse adjustment factor. All estimates for inmates were rounded to the nearest 100.
[d]The Federal system did not report data on Hispanic origin of inmates.

Source: U.S. Department of Justice, Bureau of Justice Statistics, **Census of Jails, 1999**, NCJ 186633 (Washington, DC: U.S. Department of Justice, 2001), p. 22.

Table 6.25

Jails and jail inmates in Indian country

By selected characteristics, United States, midyear 1998-2002

	1998	1999	2000	2001	2002
Number of jails	69	69	69	68	70
Rated capacity, total	1,945	2,065	2,076	2,101	2,177
Percent occupied on survey date	76%	78%	86%	91%	92%
Percent occupied on peak day in June	119%	111%	118%	126%	126%
Number of inmates	1,567	1,693	1,853	2,030	2,080
In custody	1,479	1,621	1,775	1,912	2,006
Adults	1,176	1,354	1,498	1,600	1,699
Male	988	1,131	1,214	1,366	1,399
Female	188	223	284	234	300
Juveniles	303	267	277	312	307
Male	227	197	207	212	219
Female	76	70	70	100	88
Under community supervision	88	72	78	118	74
Conviction status[a]					
Convicted	NA	NA	1,072	1,062	1,120
Unconvicted	NA	NA	689	836	857
Offense[a]					
Felony	NA	NA	97	113	107
Misdemeanor	NA	NA	1,560	1,738	1,725
Other	NA	NA	71	61	174
Violent offense	NA	NA	NA	NA	699
Domestic violence	NA	NA	NA	NA	291
DWI/DUI[b]	NA	NA	274	181	226
Drug law violation	NA	NA	133	130	126

Note: These data are from the Survey of Jails in Indian Country (SJIC) sponsored by the U.S. Department of Justice, Bureau of Justice Statistics (BJS). The SJIC was initiated in 1998 as a component of the Annual Survey of Jails, a sample survey of the Nation's local jails also sponsored by BJS. Data were collected by mail questionnaires and through followup phone calls and facsimiles. The SJIC included all confinement facilities, detention centers, jails, and other correctional facilities located in Indian country and operated by tribal authorities or by the Bureau of Indian Affairs. Special jail facilities such as medical, treatment, or release centers; halfway houses; and work farms also are included. "Indian country" is a statutory term that includes all lands within an Indian reservation, dependent Indian communities, and Indian trust allotments. Tribal authority to imprison Indian offenders is limited by statute to 1 year per offense.

[a]Some facilities did not report complete data for conviction status or offense, therefore, these categories may not add to total in custody.
[b]Includes driving while intoxicated and driving while under the influence of drugs or alcohol.

Source: U.S. Department of Justice, Bureau of Justice Statistics, *Jails in Indian Country, 1998 and 1999*, NCJ 173410, p. 2, Tables 2 and 3; p. 4, Table 8; pp. 7, 22; *2001*, Bulletin NCJ 193400, pp. 1, 2, 4; *2002*, Bulletin NCJ 198997, pp. 1, 2, 4 (Washington, DC: U.S. Department of Justice). Table adapted by SOURCEBOOK staff.

Table 6.26
Jail inmates known to be positive for the human immunodeficiency virus (HIV)

By region and State, June 30, 1993 and 1999

Region and State	1993 Total known to be HIV positive	1993 HIV/AIDS cases as a percent of total jail population[a]	1999 Total known to be HIV positive	1999 HIV/AIDS cases as a percent of total jail population[a]
Total	6,711	1.8%	8,615	1.7%
Northeast	2,759	5.3	3,105	3.8
Maine	10	1.4	25	2.3
Massachusetts	420	5.4	426	4.0
New Hampshire	3	0.3	11	0.7
New Jersey	758	9.3	366	2.9
New York	1,296	6.4	1,359	4.3
Pennsylvania	272	1.9	918	3.8
Midwest	556	0.9	612	0.8
Illinois	304	2.2	250	1.6
Indiana	36	0.4	32	0.4
Iowa	14	0.9	17	0.6
Kansas	10	0.4	27	0.8
Michigan	44	0.4	55	0.4
Minnesota	12	0.4	13	0.4
Missouri	23	0.7	61	1.0
Nebraska	7	0.4	8	0.4
North Dakota	1	0.3	NA	NA
Ohio	57	0.5	86	0.7
South Dakota	1	0.2	6	0.8
Wisconsin	47	0.7	57	0.7
South	2,732	1.5	3,822	1.6
Alabama	75	1.3	86	0.9
Arkansas	33	1.2	32	0.9
District of Columbia[b]	169	10.0	126	7.6
Florida	1,027	3.1	936	2.4
Georgia	199	1.0	549	1.8
Kentucky	17	0.3	40	0.5
Louisiana	126	1.2	311	1.4
Maryland	123	1.4	383	3.5
Mississippi	43	1.0	108	1.6
North Carolina	54	0.8	156	1.8
Oklahoma	11	0.4	42	0.6
South Carolina	78	1.6	83	1.1
Tennessee	76	0.6	301	1.7
Texas	521	1.1	333	0.8
Virginia	176	1.4	324	1.8
West Virginia	4	0.3	12	0.5
West	664	0.8	1,076	1.0
Alaska	0	X	2	3.2
Arizona	24	0.6	16	0.6
California	422	0.7	693	1.0
Colorado	23	0.6	38	0.6
Idaho	7	0.6	34	1.3
Montana	8	1.3	11	0.8
Nevada	28	1.1	20	0.4
New Mexico	44	1.6	37	0.7
Oregon	28	0.8	30	0.6
Utah	32	1.7	6	0.2
Washington	47	0.7	168	2.0
Wyoming	1	0.2	21	2.2

Note: These data were collected by the U.S. Department of Justice, Bureau of Justice Statistics through the 1993 and 1999 Census of Jails. The 1999 Census of Jails included 3,365 locally administered confinement facilities that held inmates beyond arraignment and were staffed by municipal or county employees. The census also included 47 jails that were privately operated under contract to local governments. Excluded from the census were temporary holding facilities, such as drunk tanks and police lockups, that do not hold persons after being formally charged in court (usually within 72 hours of arrest). Also excluded were State-operated facilities in Connecticut, Delaware, Hawaii, Rhode Island, and Vermont, which have integrated jail-prison systems.

[a]Based on the number of inmates held in local jails on June 30, excluding those that did not report the number of HIV/AIDS cases.
[b]The District of Columbia jail, part of an integrated system, was included in the 1999 Census. Other district facilities were excluded.

Source: U.S. Department of Justice, Bureau of Justice Statistics, *HIV in Prisons and Jails, 1999*, Bulletin NCJ 187456 (Washington, DC: U.S. Department of Justice, July 2001), p. 8.

Table 6.27
Deaths and AIDS-related deaths among local jail inmates

By region and State, July 1, 1998 to June 30, 1999

Region and State	Deaths from all causes Total	Rate per 100,000 jail inmates[a]	AIDS-related deaths Total	Rate per 100,000 jail inmates[a]	As a percent of all deaths
Total	919	155	78	13	8.5%
Northeast	152	169	26	29	17.1
Maine	3	342	0	X	X
Massachusetts	16	163	3	28	18.8
New Hampshire	4	264	2	132	50.0
New Jersey	18	109	5	33	27.8
New York	66	192	11	32	16.7
Pennsylvania	45	169	5	19	11.1
Midwest	137	144	3	3	2.2
Illinois	15	92	1	6	6.7
Indiana	20	166	0	X	X
Iowa	3	102	0	X	X
Kansas	6	134	0	X	X
Michigan	11	70	0	X	X
Minnesota	9	168	0	X	X
Missouri	14	203	0	X	X
Nebraska	4	262	0	X	X
North Dakota	2	342	0	X	X
Ohio	27	164	2	12	7.4
South Dakota	7	583	0	X	X
Wisconsin	19	163	0	X	X
South	428	156	47	17	11.0
Alabama	20	182	0	X	X
Arkansas	7	184	0	X	X
District of Columbia	18	1,084	5	301	27.8
Florida	61	120	15	30	24.6
Georgia	47	139	11	33	23.4
Kentucky	11	105	0	X	X
Louisiana	19	111	3	17	15.8
Maryland	32	289	2	18	6.3
Mississippi	13	148	0	X	X
North Carolina	20	153	1	8	5.0
Oklahoma	10	149	0	X	X
South Carolina	17	193	1	11	5.9
Tennessee	39	191	3	15	7.7
Texas	76	134	3	5	3.9
Virginia	31	175	3	17	9.7
West Virginia	7	282	0	X	X
West	202	151	2	1	1.0
Alaska	0	X	X	X	X
Arizona	14	132	0	X	X
California	100	129	2	3	2.0
Colorado	17	191	0	X	X
Idaho	3	118	0	X	X
Montana	7	489	0	X	X
Nevada	8	154	0	X	X
New Mexico	8	150	0	X	X
Oregon	15	237	0	X	X
Utah	3	74	0	X	X
Washington	23	219	0	X	X
Wyoming	4	409	0	X	X

Note: See Note, table 6.26.

[a]Based on the number of inmates held in local jails on June 30, 1999.

Source: U.S. Department of Justice, Bureau of Justice Statistics, *HIV in Prisons and Jails, 1999*, Bulletin NCJ 187456 (Washington, DC: U.S. Department of Justice, July 2001), p. 10.

Table 6.28

Number and rate (per 100,000 resident population in each group) of sentenced prisoners under jurisdiction of State and Federal correctional authorities on December 31

By sex, United States, 1925-2003

(Rate per 100,000 resident population in each group)

	Total	Rate	Male Number	Male Rate	Female Number	Female Rate		Total	Rate	Male Number	Male Rate	Female Number	Female Rate
1925	91,669	79	88,231	149	3,438	6	1970	196,429	96	190,794	191	5,635	5
1926	97,991	83	94,287	157	3,704	6	1971	198,061	95	191,732	189	6,329	6
1927	109,983	91	104,983	173	4,363	7	1972	196,092	93	189,823	185	6,269	6
1928	116,390	96	111,836	182	4,554	8	1973	204,211	96	197,523	191	6,004	6
1929	120,496	98	115,876	187	4,620	8	1974	218,466	102	211,077	202	7,389	7
							1975	240,593	111	231,918	220	8,675	8
1930	129,453	104	124,785	200	4,668	8	1976	262,833	120	252,794	238	10,039	9
1931	137,082	110	132,638	211	4,444	7	1977[a]	278,141	126	267,097	249	11,044	10
1932	137,997	110	133,573	211	4,424	7	1977[b]	285,456	129	274,244	255	11,212	10
1933	136,810	109	132,520	209	4,290	7	1978	294,396	132	282,813	261	11,583	10
1934	138,316	109	133,769	209	4,547	7	1979	301,470	133	289,465	264	12,005	10
1935	144,180	113	139,278	217	4,902	8							
1936	145,038	113	139,990	217	5,048	8	1980	315,974	139	303,643	275	12,331	11
1937	152,741	118	147,375	227	5,366	8	1981	353,673	154	339,375	304	14,298	12
1938	160,285	123	154,826	236	5,459	8	1982	395,516	171	379,075	337	16,441	14
1939	179,818	137	173,143	263	6,675	10	1983	419,346	179	401,870	354	17,476	15
							1984	443,398	188	424,193	370	19,205	16
1940	173,706	131	167,345	252	6,361	10	1985	480,568	202	459,223	397	21,345	17
1941	165,439	124	159,228	239	6,211	9	1986	522,084	217	497,540	426	24,544	20
1942	150,384	112	144,167	217	6,217	9	1987	560,812	231	533,990	453	26,822	22
1943	137,220	103	131,054	202	6,166	9	1988	603,732	247	573,587	482	30,145	24
1944	132,456	100	126,350	200	6,106	9	1989	680,907	276	643,643	535	37,264	29
1945	133,649	98	127,609	193	6,040	9							
1946	140,079	99	134,075	191	6,004	8	1990	739,980	297	699,416	575	40,564	32
1947	151,304	105	144,961	202	6,343	9	1991	789,610	313	745,808	606	43,802	34
1948	155,977	106	149,739	205	6,238	8	1992	846,277	332	799,776	642	46,501	36
1949	163,749	109	157,663	211	6,086	8	1993	932,074	359	878,037	698	54,037	41
							1994	1,016,691	389	956,566	753	60,125	45
1950	166,123	109	160,309	211	5,814	8	1995	1,085,022	411	1,021,059	789	63,963	47
1951	165,680	107	159,610	208	6,070	8	1996	1,137,722	427	1,068,123	819	69,599	51
1952	168,233	107	161,994	208	6,239	8	1997	1,194,581	444	1,120,787	853	73,794	54
1953	173,579	108	166,909	211	6,670	8	1998	1,245,402	461	1,167,802	885	77,600	57
1954	182,901	112	175,907	218	6,994	8	1999	1,304,074	463[c]	1,221,611	913	82,463	59
1955	185,780	112	178,655	217	7,125	8							
1956	189,565	112	182,190	218	7,375	9	2000	1,331,278	469[c]	1,246,234	915	85,044	59
1957	195,414	113	188,113	221	7,301	8	2001	1,345,217	470	1,260,033	896	85,184	58
1958	205,643	117	198,208	229	7,435	8	2002	1,380,516	476	1,291,450	906	89,066	60
1959	208,105	117	200,469	228	7,636	8	2003[d]	1,409,280	482	1,316,495	915	92,785	62
1960	212,953	117	205,265	230	7,688	8							
1961	220,149	119	212,268	234	7,881	8							
1962	218,830	117	210,823	229	8,007	8							
1963	217,283	114	209,538	225	7,745	8							
1964	214,336	111	206,632	219	7,704	8							
1965	210,895	108	203,327	213	7,568	8							
1966	199,654	102	192,703	201	6,951	7							
1967	194,896	98	188,661	195	6,235	6							
1968	187,914	94	182,102	187	5,812	6							
1969	196,007	97	189,413	192	6,594	6							

Note: Prison population data are compiled by a yearend census of prisoners in State and Federal institutions. Data for 1925 through 1939 include sentenced prisoners in State and Federal prisons and reformatories whether committed for felonies or misdemeanors. Data for 1940 through 1970 include all adult felons serving sentences in State and Federal institutions. Since 1971, the census has included all adults or youthful offenders sentenced to a State or Federal correctional institution with maximum sentences of over 1 year.

Beginning on Dec. 31, 1978, a distinction was made between prisoners "in custody" and prisoners "under jurisdiction." As defined in a 1978 report (U.S. Department of Justice, Bureau of Justice Statistics, *Prisoners in State and Federal Institutions on December 31, 1978*, NPS Bulletin SD-NPS-PSF-6 (Washington, DC: USGPO, 1980)), "in custody" refers to the direct physical control and responsibility for the body of a confined person. "Under jurisdiction" is defined as follows: A State or Federal prison system has jurisdiction over a person if it retains the legal power to incarcerate the person in one of its own prisons. Jurisdiction is not determined by the prisoner's physical location; jurisdiction is determined by the legal authority to hold the prisoner. Examples of prisoners under the jurisdiction of a given system, but not in its custody, are those housed in local jails, in other States, or in hospitals (including mental health facilities) outside the correctional system; prisoners on work release, furlough, or bail; and State prisoners held in Federal prisons or vice versa. Both custody and jurisdiction figures are shown for 1977 to facilitate year-to-year comparison. The rates for the period before 1980 are based on the civilian population. The civilian population represents the resident population less the armed forces stationed in the United States. Since 1980, the rates are based on the total resident population provided by the U.S. Census Bureau. Some data have been revised by the Source and may differ from previous editions of SOURCEBOOK. For information on methodology and definitions of terms, see Appendix 15.

[a]Custody counts.
[b]Jurisdiction counts.
[c]Rates have been revised and are now based on population estimates from the 2000 decennial census.
[d]Preliminary; subject to revision.

Source: U.S. Department of Justice, Bureau of Justice Statistics, *Prisoners 1925-81*, Bulletin NCJ-85861, p. 2; *Prisoners in 1998*, Bulletin NCJ 175687, p. 3, Table 3 and p. 5, Table 6; *2000*, Bulletin NCJ 188207, p. 5, Table 6; *2001*, Bulletin NCJ 195189, p. 5 and p. 6, Table 7; *2002*, Bulletin NCJ 200248, p. 4 and p. 5, Table 5; *2003*, Bulletin NCJ 205335, p. 4 (Washington, DC: U.S. Department of Justice); and U.S. Department of Justice, Bureau of Justice Statistics, *Correctional Populations in the United States, 1994*, NCJ-160091, Tables 1.8 and 1.9; *1997*, NCJ 177613, Tables 1.8 and 1.9 (Washington, DC: U.S. Department of Justice). Table adapted by SOURCEBOOK staff.

Table 6.29

Rate (per 100,000 resident population) of sentenced prisoners under jurisdiction of State and Federal correctional authorities on December 31

By region and jurisdiction, 1980, 1984-2003

Region and jurisdiction	1980	1984	1985	1986	1987	1988	1989	1990	1991	1992	1993	1994	1995	1996	1997	1998	1999	2000	2001	2002	2003
United States, total	139	188	200	216	228	244	271	292	310	330	350	389	411	427	445	461	476	478	470	476	482
Federal	9	12	14	15	16	17	19	20	22	26	28	30	32	33	35	38	42	45	48	49	52
State	130	176	187	201	211	227	253	272	287	305	322	358	379	393	410	423	434	432	422	427	430
Northeast	87	136	145	157	169	186	215	232	248	261	272	286	301	308	317	328	330	320	304	304	300
Connecticut[a]	68	119	127	135	144	146	194	238	263	268	320	321	318	314	397	372	397	398	387	405	389
Maine	61	72	83	106	106	100	116	118	123	121	116	113	107	108	124	125	133	129	127	141	149
Massachusetts[b]	56	84	88	92	102	109	122	132	143	161	154	174	170	178	278	275	266	252	243	234	233
New Hampshire	35	57	68	76	81	93	103	117	132	160	157	177	174	176	184	182	187	185	188	192	188
New Jersey	76	138	149	157	177	219	251	271	301	290	301	311	340	343	351	382	384	362	331	322	314
New York	123	187	195	216	229	248	285	304	320	340	354	367	378	383	386	397	400	383	355	346	339
Pennsylvania	68	109	119	128	136	149	169	183	192	207	216	235	268	286	291	303	305	307	310	325	330
Rhode Island[a]	65	92	99	103	100	118	146	157	173	170	172	186	186	205	213	220	193	197	181	191	184
Vermont[a]	67	74	82	81	91	98	109	117	124	151	154	168	179	136	140	188	198	218	213	214	226
Midwest	109	144	161	173	184	200	225	239	255	273	282	299	310	327	346	360	367	371	370	373	375
Illinois	94	149	161	168	171	181	211	234	247	271	294	310	317	327	342	357	368	371	355	336	342
Indiana	114	165	175	181	192	202	217	223	226	242	250	258	275	286	301	321	324	335	341	348	370
Iowa	86	97	98	98	101	107	126	139	144	160	174	192	207	222	243	258	252	276	272	284	290
Kansas	106	173	192	217	233	232	222	227	231	238	226	248	274	301	304	310	321	312	318	327	334
Michigan	163	161	196	227	259	298	340	366	388	413	414	427	429	440	457	466	472	480	488	501	489
Minnesota	49	52	56	58	60	64	71	72	78	85	92	100	105	110	113	117	125	128	132	141	155
Missouri	112	175	194	203	218	236	269	287	305	311	308	338	358	409	442	457	477	494	509	529	529
Nebraska	89	95	108	116	123	129	141	140	145	151	153	164	183	194	200	215	217	228	225	228	228
North Dakota	28	54	55	53	57	62	62	67	68	67	70	78	85	101	112	128	137	158	161	161	181
Ohio	125	174	194	209	219	243	279	289	324	347	365	387	400	413	429	432	417	406	398	398	391
South Dakota	88	127	146	160	160	143	175	187	191	208	216	236	252	284	303	329	339	353	370	378	393
Wisconsin	85	105	113	119	126	130	138	149	157	176	166	187	201	238	283	334	375	376	383	391	392
South	188	231	236	248	255	266	292	316	333	355	380	454	483	490	506	520	543	539	526	536	542
Alabama	149	256	267	283	307	300	328	370	394	407	431	450	471	492	500	519	549	549	584	612	635
Arkansas	128	188	195	198	227	230	261	277	317	340	327	345	361	357	392	415	443	458	447	479	476
Delaware[a]	183	263	281	311	326	331	333	323	344	390	394	400	413	428	443	429	493	513	504	453	501
District of Columbia[a,c]	426	649	738	753	905	1,078	1,132	1,148	1,221	1,287	1,549	1,782	1,650	1,611	1,682	1,913	1,314	971	(c)	(c)	(c)
Florida	208	242	247	272	265	278	307	336	344	355	384	406	447	439	437	447	456	462	437	450	463
Georgia	219	254	251	265	282	281	300	327	342	365	387	456	470	462	472	502	532	550	542	552	539
Kentucky	99	128	133	142	147	191	222	241	262	274	274	288	311	331	372	379	385	373	371	380	392
Louisiana	211	310	308	316	346	370	396	427	462	484	522	556	578	615	672	736	776	801	800	794	801
Maryland	183	285	279	280	282	291	323	348	366	381	383	395	404	412	413	418	427	429	422	425	420
Mississippi	132	229	237	249	256	277	293	307	330	327	361	395	452	482	531	574	626	688	715	743	768
North Carolina	244	246	254	257	250	249	250	265	269	290	305	323	384	376	370	358	345	347	335	345	348
Oklahoma	151	236	250	288	296	323	361	381	416	459	506	508	552	591	617	622	662	685	658	667	636
South Carolina	238	284	294	324	344	369	416	451	473	486	488	494	515	532	536	550	543	532	529	555	551
Tennessee	153	154	149	157	156	157	213	207	227	234	250	276	287	292	309	325	408	399	411	430	433
Texas	210	226	226	228	231	240	257	290	297	344	385	637	677	686	717	724	762	730	711	692	702
Virginia	161	185	204	215	217	230	263	279	311	327	346	406	410	404	407	399	447	422	431	460	472
West Virginia	64	82	89	77	77	78	84	85	83	92	98	106	136	149	174	192	196	211	231	250	260
West	105	166	176	197	214	234	256	277	287	299	319	334	358	384	405	417	421	423	408	415	419
Alaska[a]	143	252	288	306	339	355	361	348	345	327	446	317	338	383	420	413	374	341	300	396	401
Arizona	160	247	256	268	307	328	350	375	396	409	430	459	473	479	484	507	495	515	492	513	525
California	98	162	181	212	231	257	283	311	318	339	368	384	416	446	475	483	481	474	453	452	455
Colorado	96	104	103	115	145	174	207	209	249	256	262	289	292	322	342	357	383	403	391	415	430
Hawaii[a]	65	124	134	142	141	136	142	150	153	164	198	202	217	249	288	307	320	302	298	308	325
Idaho	87	127	133	144	144	157	180	190	205	209	234	245	283	319	323	330	385	430	451	461	427
Montana	94	121	136	135	147	158	165	176	183	180	182	204	228	259	255	310	335	348	368	361	393
Nevada	230	380	397	447	432	452	438	444	439	448	434	468	493	515	518	542	509	518	474	483	462
New Mexico	106	133	144	154	174	180	178	196	191	197	206	211	231	261	256	271	270	279	295	309	314
Oregon	120	170	165	176	200	215	235	223	228	174	166	191	206	226	232	260	293	316	327	342	354
Utah	64	84	98	108	110	115	137	142	149	146	152	157	174	195	205	205	245	254	230	233	240
Washington	106	156	156	147	134	124	142	162	182	192	196	201	212	225	233	247	251	251	249	261	260
Wyoming	113	143	148	168	190	199	216	237	237	226	238	254	289	310	326	327	355	349	340	348	372

Note: See Note, table 6.28. Sentenced prisoners are defined as those serving sentences of more than 1 year under the jurisdiction of State and Federal correctional authorities. Population estimates are provided by the U.S. Census Bureau. Some data have been revised by the Source and may differ from previous editions of SOURCEBOOK. For information on methodology and definitions of terms, see Appendix 15.

[a]Prisons and jails form an integrated system. Data include total jail and prison population.
[b]Beginning in 1998, the incarceration rate includes an estimated 6,200 prisoners sentenced to more than 1 year but held in local jails or houses of correction.
[c]As of Dec. 31, 2001, the transfer of responsibility for sentenced felons from the District of Columbia to the Federal Bureau of Prisons was completed. The District of Columbia no longer operates a prison system.

Source: U.S. Department of Justice, Bureau of Justice Statistics, *Prisoners in State and Federal Institutions*, SD-NPS-PSF-8, NCJ-80520 (Washington, DC: USGPO, 1982), p. 16; U.S. Department of Justice, Bureau of Justice Statistics, *Prisoners in 1984*, Bulletin NCJ-97118, p. 2; *1997*, Bulletin NCJ 170014, p. 3, Table 3; *1998*, Bulletin NCJ 175687, p. 3, Table 3; *1999*, Bulletin NCJ 183476, p. 3, Table 5; *2000*, Bulletin NCJ 188207, p. 3, Table 3; *2001*, Bulletin NCJ 195189, p. 4; *2002*, Bulletin NCJ 200248, p. 4; *2003*, Bulletin NCJ 205335, p. 4, Table 4 (Washington, DC: U.S. Department of Justice); and U.S. Department of Justice, Bureau of Justice Statistics, *Correctional Populations in the United States, 1985*, NCJ-103957, Table 5.4; *1986*, NCJ-111611, Table 5.4; *1987*, NCJ-118762, Table 5.4; *1988*, NCJ-124280, Table 5.4; *1989*, NCJ-130445, Table 5.4; *1990*, NCJ-135946, Table 5.4; *1991*, NCJ-142729, Table 5.4; *1992*, NCJ-146413, Table 5.4; *1993*, NCJ-156241, Table 5.4; *1994*, NCJ-160091, Table 5.4; *1995*, NCJ-163916, Table 5.4; *1996*, NCJ 170013, p. 79 (Washington, DC: U.S. Department of Justice). Table adapted by SOURCEBOOK staff.

Table 6.30

Prisoners under jurisdiction of State and Federal correctional authorities

By region and jurisdiction, Dec. 31, 2002 and 2003

Region and jurisdiction	Total 2002	Total 2003	Percent change Dec. 31, 2002 to Dec. 31, 2003
United States, total	1,440,144	1,470,045	2.1%
Federal	163,528	173,059	5.8
State	1,276,616	1,296,986	1.6
Northeast	175,907	173,330	-1.5
Connecticut[a]	20,720	19,846	-4.2
Maine	1,900	2,013	5.9
Massachusetts	10,329	10,232	-0.9
New Hampshire	2,451	2,434	-0.7
New Jersey	27,891	27,246	-2.3
New York	67,065	65,198	-2.8
Pennsylvania	40,168	40,890	1.8
Rhode Island[a]	3,520	3,527	0.2
Vermont[a]	1,863	1,944	4.3
Midwest	245,303	247,388	0.8
Illinois	42,693	43,418	1.7
Indiana	21,611	23,069	6.7
Iowa[b]	8,398	8,546	1.8
Kansas	8,935	9,132	2.2
Michigan	50,591	49,358	-2.4
Minnesota	7,129	7,865	10.3
Missouri	30,099	30,303	0.7
Nebraska	4,058	4,040	-0.4
North Dakota	1,112	1,239	11.4
Ohio	45,646	44,778	-1.9
South Dakota	2,918	3,026	3.7
Wisconsin	22,113	22,614	2.3
South	575,048	587,814	2.2
Alabama	27,947	29,253	4.7
Arkansas	13,091	13,084	-0.1
Delaware[a]	6,778	6,794	0.2
Florida[b,c]	75,210	79,594	5.8
Georgia[b]	47,445	47,208	-0.5
Kentucky	15,820	16,622	5.1
Louisiana	36,032	36,047	0.0
Maryland	24,162	23,791	-1.5
Mississippi	22,705	23,182	2.1
North Carolina	32,832	33,560	2.2
Oklahoma	22,802	22,821	0.1
South Carolina	23,715	23,719	0.0
Tennessee	24,989	25,403	1.7
Texas	162,003	166,911	3.0
Virginia	34,973	35,067	0.3
West Virginia	4,544	4,758	4.7
West	280,358	288,454	2.9
Alaska[a]	4,398	4,527	2.9
Arizona[b]	29,359	31,170	6.2
California	161,361	164,487	1.9
Colorado	18,833	19,671	4.4
Hawaii[a]	5,423	5,828	7.5
Idaho	5,746	5,887	2.5
Montana	3,323	3,620	8.9
Nevada	10,478	10,543	0.6
New Mexico	5,991	6,223	3.9
Oregon	12,085	12,715	5.2
Utah	5,562	5,763	3.6
Washington	16,062	16,148	0.5
Wyoming	1,737	1,872	7.8

Note: See Note, table 6.28. The data in this table represent all prisoners under jurisdiction of State and Federal correctional authorities including unsentenced prisoners and those sentenced to less than 1 year.

As of Dec. 31, 2001, the transfer of responsibility for sentenced felons from the District of Columbia to the Federal Bureau of Prisons was completed. The District of Columbia no longer operates a prison system. For information on methodology and definitions of terms, see Appendix 15.

[a]Prisons and jails form an integrated system. Data include total jail and prison population.
[b]Population figures are based on custody counts.
[c]Jurisdiction counts reported by Florida totaled 82,012 on Dec. 31, 2003.

Source: U.S. Department of Justice, Bureau of Justice Statistics, *Prisoners in 2003*, Bulletin NCJ 205335 (Washington, DC: U.S. Department of Justice, November 2004), p. 3. Table adapted by SOURCEBOOK staff.

Table 6.31

Prisoners in Federal, State, and private adult correctional facilities

By type of facility and sex of prisoner, United States, June 30, 1995 and 2000

	All facilities			Type of facility					
			Percent	Confinement		Percent	Community-based		Percent
	1995	2000	change	1995	2000	change	1995	2000	change
Total	1,023,572	1,305,253	27.5%	992,333	1,244,574	25.4%	31,239	60,679	94.2%
Male	961,210	1,219,225	26.8	932,641	1,166,141	25.0	28,569	53,084	85.8
Female	62,362	86,028	37.9	59,692	78,433	31.4	2,670	7,595	184.5
Federal	80,960	110,974	37.1	80,221	110,974	38.3	739	0	X
Male	75,489	102,737	36.1	74,750	102,737	37.4	739	0	X
Female	5,471	8,237	50.6	5,471	8,237	50.6	0	0	X
State	925,949	1,101,202	18.9	899,376	1,055,746	17.4	26,573	45,456	71.1
Male	871,191	1,031,131	18.4	846,841	990,625	17.0	24,350	40,506	66.3
Female	54,758	70,071	28.0	52,535	65,121	24.0	2,223	4,950	122.7
Private	16,663	93,077	458.6	12,736	77,584	511.3	3,927	15,223	287.6
Male	14,530	85,357	487.5	11,050	72,779	558.6	3,480	12,578	261.4
Female	2,133	7,720	261.9	1,686	5,075	201.0	447	2,645	491.7

Note: These data are from the 2000 Census of State and Federal Adult Correctional Facilities sponsored by the U.S. Department of Justice, Bureau of Justice Statistics. Facilities were included in the census if they were staffed with Federal, State, local, or private employees; housed primarily State or Federal prisoners; were physically, functionally, and administratively separate from other facilities; and were operational on June 30, 2000. Also included were 264 private facilities under contract to State governments or the Federal Bureau of Prisons to house prisoners. Facilities included were prisons and prison farms; reception, diagnostic, and classification centers; road camps; forestry and conservation camps; youthful offender facilities (except those in California); vocational training facilities; drug and alcohol treatment facilities; and State-operated local detention facilities in Alaska, Connecticut, Delaware, Hawaii, Rhode Island, and Vermont. Excluded from the census were jails and other local regional detention facilities; private facilities not exclusively for State or Federal prisoners; facilities for the military, the Immigration and Naturalization Service, the Bureau of Indian Affairs, and the U.S. Marshals Service; and correctional hospital wards not operated by correctional authorities. The "private" facilities included in the census are those with 50% or more of their inmates held for State or Federal authorities. Private facilities with more than 50% of their inmates held for local authorities were classified as jails and excluded from the census.

Correctional facilities were classified as "community-based" if 50% or more of the residents were regularly permitted to leave, unaccompanied, to work or study. These included halfway houses, restitution centers, and prerelease, work release, and study centers. Facilities in which less than 50% of the prisoners regularly left the facility unaccompanied were classified as "confinement" institutions.

Source: U.S. Department of Justice, Bureau of Justice Statistics, *Census of State and Federal Correctional Facilities, 2000*, NCJ 198272 (Washington, DC: U.S. Department of Justice, 2003), p. 1. Table adapted by SOURCEBOOK staff.

Table 6.32

State and Federal prisoners housed in private facilities and local jails

By jurisdiction, on Dec. 31, 2002 and 2003

	Private facilities			Local jails		
	Number		Percent of all prisoners, 2003[a]	Number		Percent of all prisoners, 2003[a]
Jurisdiction	2002	2003		2002	2003	
United States, total	93,912	95,522	6.5%	72,550	73,343	5.0%
Federal[b]	20,274	21,865	12.6	3,377	3,278	1.9
State	73,638	73,657	5.7	69,173	70,065	5.4
Northeast	3,146	3,201	1.8	2,234	1,911	1.1
Connecticut	0	0	X	(c)	(c)	(c)
Maine	8	30	1.5	0	0	X
Massachusetts	0	0	X	375	361	3.5
New Hampshire	0	0	X	11	7	0.3
New Jersey[d]	2,601	2,636	9.7	1,528	1,542	5.7
New York	0	0	X	320	1	X
Pennsylvania	537	535	1.3	0	0	X
Rhode Island[d]	0	0	X	(c)	(c)	(c)
Vermont[d]	0	0	X	(c)	(c)	(c)
Midwest	6,748	4,957	2.0	1,801	2,386	1.0
Illinois	0	0	X	0	0	X
Indiana	843	652	2.8	1,262	1,724	7.5
Iowa	0	0	X	0	0	X
Kansas	0	0	X	0	0	X
Michigan	460	480	1.0	30	42	0.1
Minnesota	0	0	X	221	283	3.6
Missouri	0	0	X	0	0	X
Nebraska	0	0	X	0	0	X
North Dakota	23	0	X	9	44	3.6
Ohio	1,927	1,901	4.2	0	0	X
South Dakota	32	25	0.8	12	29	1.0
Wisconsin	3,463	1,899	8.4	267	264	1.2
South	46,091	48,222	8.2	60,036	60,810	10.3
Alabama	0	1,698	5.8	2,449	1,340	4.6
Arkansas	0	0	X	1,172	1,016	7.8
Delaware	0	0	X	(c)	(c)	(c)
Florida	4,173	4,330	5.4	47	48	0.1
Georgia	4,573	4,589	9.7	4,975	4,949	10.5
Kentucky	1,635	1,640	9.9	3,657	3,969	23.9
Louisiana	2,929	2,918	8.1	16,022	16,549	45.9
Maryland	127	122	0.5	168	234	1.0
Mississippi	3,435	3,463	14.9	4,550	4,724	20.4
North Carolina	186	215	0.6	0	0	X
Oklahoma	6,470	6,022	26.4	1,497	1,869	8.2
South Carolina	21	44	0.2	415	424	1.8
Tennessee	4,200	5,049	19.9	6,717	6,283	24.7
Texas	16,773	16,570	9.9	12,375	13,331	8.0
Virginia	1,569	1,562	4.5	5,024	5,106	14.6
West Virginia	0	0	X	968	968	20.3
West	17,653	17,277	6.0	5,102	4,958	1.7
Alaska	1,360	1,386	30.6	(c)	(c)	(c)
Arizona	1,965	2,323	7.5	232	174	0.6
California	4,649	3,507	2.1	2,591	2,415	1.5
Colorado	2,452	3,013	15.3	160	221	1.1
Hawaii	1,347	1,478	25.4	(c)	(c)	(c)
Idaho	1,266	1,267	21.5	295	239	4.1
Montana	963	1,059	29.3	419	567	15.7
Nevada	434	0	X	177	190	1.8
New Mexico	2,690	2,751	44.2	0	0	X
Oregon	0	0	X	0	0	X
Utah	0	0	X	1,170	1,065	18.5
Washington[d]	0	0	X	0	0	X
Wyoming	527	493	26.3	58	87	4.6

Note: See Notes, tables 6.28 and 6.30. For information on methodology and definitions of terms, see Appendix 15.

[a]Based on the total number of prisoners under State and Federal jurisdiction.
[b]Includes Federal prisoners in non-secure privately operated facilities (6,598 in 2002 and 6,471 in 2003).
[c]Not applicable; prisons and jails form an integrated system.
[d]Prisoners held in other State facilities include interstate compact cases.

Source: U.S. Department of Justice, Bureau of Justice Statistics, **Prisoners in 2003**, Bulletin NCJ 205335 (Washington, DC: U.S. Department of Justice, November 2004), p. 6. Table adapted by SOURCEBOOK staff.

Table 6.33

Rate (per 100,000 U.S. resident population in each group) of sentenced prisoners under jurisdiction of State and Federal correctional authorities

By sex, race, Hispanic origin, and age group, United States, 2003

Rate of sentenced prisoners per 100,000 residents of each group[a]

	Male				Female			
Age group	Total[b]	White, non-Hispanic	Black, non-Hispanic	Hispanic	Total[b]	White, non-Hispanic	Black, non-Hispanic	Hispanic
Total	915	465	3,405	1,231	62	38	185	84
18 to 19 years	597	266	2,068	692	28	15	80	39
20 to 24 years	1,996	932	7,017	2,267	112	71	286	138
25 to 29 years	2,380	1,090	9,262	2,592	147	99	406	152
30 to 34 years	2,074	1,042	7,847	2,440	164	109	456	181
35 to 39 years	1,895	1,017	6,952	2,226	170	106	491	209
40 to 44 years	1,584	873	5,854	1,995	133	82	386	192
45 to 54 years	899	501	3,500	1,329	60	36	190	97
55 years and older	208	141	747	397	8	5	22	16

Note: See Note, table 6.28. For information on methodology and definitions of terms, see Appendix 15.

[a] Based on estimates of the U.S. resident population on July 1, 2003, using intercensal estimates for July 1, 2002 (by sex, race, and Hispanic origin) and adjusted to the July 1, 2003 estimates by sex.
[b] Includes American Indians, Alaska Natives, Asians, Native Hawaiians, and other Pacific Islanders.

Source: U.S. Department of Justice, Bureau of Justice Statistics, *Prisoners in 2003*, Bulletin NCJ 205335 (Washington, DC: U.S. Department of Justice, November 2004), p. 9, Table 12.

Table 6.34

Prisoners in Federal, State, and private adult correctional facilities

By race and Hispanic origin of prisoner, and region, United States, June 30, 2000

	Total	White, non-Hispanic	Black, non-Hispanic	Hispanic	American Indian	Asian/ Pacific Islander[a]	Not reported
Total	1,305,253	453,300	587,300	203,700	13,240	9,670	37,930
Federal[b]	110,974	29,800	44,800	33,200	1,640	1,480	0
State	1,101,202	395,637	506,408	151,810	9,968	6,527	30,852
Private	93,077	27,905	36,066	18,728	1,634	1,662	7,082
Region[c]							
Northeast	171,999	44,367	86,207	37,872	435	885	2,233
Midwest	233,993	103,374	115,423	10,165	2,721	849	1,461
South	518,912	177,688	279,531	49,417	2,006	759	9,511
West	269,375	98,113	61,313	73,084	6,440	5,696	24,729

Note: See Note, table 6.31.

[a] Includes Native Hawaiians.
[b] Federal total was estimated based on Federal Justice Statistics data for Sept. 30, 2000, and rounded to the nearest 100 for whites, blacks, and Hispanics, and to the nearest 10 for American Indians/Alaska Natives, Asian/Pacific Islanders, and not reported categories.
[c] Regional breakdowns exclude prisoners in Federal prisons.

Source: U.S. Department of Justice, Bureau of Justice Statistics, *Census of State and Federal Correctional Facilities, 2000*, NCJ 198272 (Washington, DC: U.S. Department of Justice, 2003), p. 3, Table 4.

Table 6.35
State and Federal prisoners reporting prior possession of firearms

By type of firearm, United States, 1997

	Percent of prisoners					
	Armed during current offense		Ever armed while committing offense		Ever used or possessed firearm	
Type of firearm	State	Federal	State	Federal	State	Federal
Firearm[a]	18.4%	14.8%	25.1%	20.0%	46.9%	48.9%
Handgun	15.3	12.8	21.3	17.2	36.0	38.6
Rifle	1.3	1.3	2.0	1.9	12.4	14.6
Shotgun	2.4	2.0	3.5	3.0	13.7	15.6
Other	0.5	0.6	1.1	0.9	2.7	2.3
No firearm	81.6	85.2	74.9	80.0	53.1	51.1

Note: Data for State prisoners are from the 1997 Survey of Inmates in State Correctional Facilities (SISCF), conducted by the U.S. Census Bureau for the U.S. Department of Justice, Bureau of Justice Statistics (BJS). Data for Federal prisoners are from the 1997 Survey of Inmates in Federal Correctional Facilities (SIFCF), conducted by the U.S. Census Bureau for BJS and the Federal Bureau of Prisons. From June through October 1997, prisoners were interviewed about their current offenses and sentences, criminal histories, family and personal backgrounds, gun possession and use, prior drug and alcohol use and treatment, educational programs, and other services provided while in prison. Similar surveys of State prisoners were conducted in 1974, 1979, 1986, and 1991; Federal prisoners were surveyed for the first time in 1991. The samples for the 1997 surveys were taken from a universe of 1,409 State prisons and 127 Federal prisons enumerated in the 1995 Census of State and Federal Adult Correctional Facilities or opened between completion of the census and June 30, 1996. The sample design for both surveys was a stratified two-stage selection process; first selecting prisons, and second, selecting prisoners in those prisons. A total of 14,285 interviews were completed for the State survey, and 4,041 for the Federal survey, for overall response rates of 92.5% and 90.2% respectively.

[a]Detail does not add to total with firearms because prisoners may have possessed more than one firearm.

Source: U.S. Department of Justice, Bureau of Justice Statistics, *Firearm Use by Offenders*, Special Report NCJ 189369 (Washington, DC: U.S. Department of Justice, November 2001), p. 2, Table 1.

Table 6.36
State and Federal prisoners reporting possession of firearms during current offense

By type of offense, United States, 1991 and 1997

	Prisoners			
	1991		1997	
Current offense	Number	Percent who possessed a firearm during current offense	Number	Percent who possessed a firearm during current offense
State				
All prisoners	700,050	16.3%	1,037,241	18.4%
Violent offense	323,653	29.1	483,713	30.2
Property offense	171,749	3.2	227,726	3.1
Drug offense	148,743	4.1	213,974	8.1
Public-order offense	47,001	16.1	99,396	19.1
Federal				
All prisoners	53,348	11.8	87,466	14.8
Violent offense	9,113	38.0	12,604	35.4
Property offense	7,011	2.1	5,811	2.9
Drug offense	30,788	3.9	54,561	8.7
Public-order offense	4,964	28.5	12,708	27.3

Note: See Note, table 6.35. For a list of offenses included in each category, see table 6.37.

Source: U.S. Department of Justice, Bureau of Justice Statistics, *Firearm Use by Offenders*, Special Report NCJ 189369 (Washington, DC: U.S. Department of Justice, November 2001), p. 3, Table 3.

Table 6.37
State and Federal prisoners reporting possession of firearms during current offense

By offense, United States, 1997

	Prisoners			
	State		Federal	
Current offense	Number	Percent who possessed a firearm during current offense	Number	Percent who possessed a firearm during current offense
Violent offense	483,713	30.2%	12,604	35.4%
Homicide	135,493	42.9	1,273	39.3
Sexual assault	87,687	2.9	679	0
Robbery	145,318	34.5	8,554	40.3
Assault	95,756	31.2	1,108	26.0
Other violent	19,459	27.1	989	22.4
Property offense	227,726	3.1	5,811	2.9
Burglary	111,198	4.0	279	10.1
Other property	116,528	2.3	5,531	2.5
Drug offense	213,974	8.1	54,561	8.7
Possession	91,511	7.8	9,959	7.0
Trafficking	116,578	8.6	39,769	9.1
Other drug	5,885	3.1	4,834	8.7
Public-order offense	99,396	19.1	12,708	27.3
Weapons	25,257	64.9	5,905	51.9
Other public-order	74,139	3.5	6,803	5.9

Note: See Note, table 6.35.

Source: U.S. Department of Justice, Bureau of Justice Statistics, *Firearm Use by Offenders*, Special Report NCJ 189369 (Washington, DC: U.S. Department of Justice, November 2001), p. 3, Table 4.

Table 6.38
Source of firearms possessed by State prisoners during current offense

United States, 1991 and 1997

	Percent of State prisoners who possessed a firearm during current offense	
Source of firearms	1991	1997
Total	100%	100%
Purchased or traded from retail outlet	20.8	13.9
Retail store	14.7	8.3
Pawnshop	4.2	3.8
Flea market	1.3	1.0
Gun show	0.6	0.7
Family or friend	33.8	39.6
Purchased or traded	13.5	12.8
Rented or borrowed	10.1	18.5
Other	10.2	8.3
Street/illegal source	40.8	39.2
Theft or burglary	10.5	9.9
Drug dealer/off street	22.5	20.8
Fence/black market	7.8	8.4
Other	4.6	7.4

Note: See Note, table 6.35.

Source: U.S. Department of Justice, Bureau of Justice Statistics, *Firearm Use by Offenders*, Special Report NCJ 189369 (Washington, DC: U.S. Department of Justice, November 2001), p. 6, Table 8.

Table 6.39
Prisoners under age 18 in State prisons

By sex, United States, midyear 1990, 1995, and 1999-2003

	Prisoners under age 18		
	Total	Male	Female
1990	3,600	NA	NA
1995	5,309	NA	NA
1999	4,194	4,027	167
2000	3,896	3,721	175
2001	3,147	3,010	137
2002	3,038	2,927	111
2003	3,006	2,880	126

Note: See Note, table 6.28. Federal prisons held 39 prisoners under age 18 in 1990, but none in 1995 and 1999 to 2003. For information on methodology and definitions of terms, see Appendix 15.

Source: U.S. Department of Justice, Bureau of Justice Statistics, *Prison and Jail Inmates at Midyear 2003*, Bulletin NCJ 203947 (Washington, DC: U.S. Department of Justice, May 2004), p. 5, Table 5. Table adapted by SOURCEBOOK staff.

Table 6.40
Prisoners under age 18 in State and private adult correctional facilities

By type of facility, security level, and region, United States, June 30, 2000

		All facilities			Type of facility					
					Confinement facilities			Community-based facilities		
	Total	Maximum[a]	Medium	Minimum/low	Maximum[a]	Medium	Minimum/low	Maximum	Medium	Minimum/low
Total	4,095	2,008	1,582	505	2,008	1,490	444	X	92	61
State	3,927	2,007	1,441	479	2,007	1,427	437	X	14	42
Private	168	1	141	26	1	63	7	X	78	19
Region										
Northeast	760	461	233	66	461	231	66	X	2	0
Midwest	699	244	225	230	244	234	197	X	1	33
South	2,150	1,132	819	199	1,132	730	175	X	89	24
West	486	171	305	10	171	305	6	X	0	4

Note: See Note, table 6.31. As of June 30, 2000, there were no persons under age 18 in Federal facilities. Age information was not available for 1,471 State prisoners.

[a]Includes facilities with the security designations super maximum, close, or high.

Source: U.S. Department of Justice, Bureau of Justice Statistics, *Census of State and Federal Correctional Facilities, 2000*, NCJ 198272 (Washington, DC: U.S. Department of Justice, 2003), p. 17.

Table 6.41

Female prisoners under jurisdiction of State and Federal correctional authorities

By region and jurisdiction, on Dec. 31, 1990, 1995, 2000-2003

	Female prisoners Number 1990	1995	2000	2001	2002	2003	Percent change 2002 to 2003	Average annual percent change 1995 to 2003	Incarceration rate, 2003[a]
United States, total	44,065	68,468	93,234	92,979	97,631	101,179	3.6%	5.0%	62
Federal	5,011	7,398	10,245	10,973	11,234	11,635	3.6	5.8	6
State	39,054	61,070	82,989	82,066	86,397	89,544	3.6	4.9	56
Northeast	6,293	8,401	9,082	9,108	9,381	9,108	-2.9	1.0	28
Connecticut	683	975	1,406	1,447	1,694	1,548	-8.6	5.9	46
Maine	44	36	66	59	90	124	37.8	16.7	18
Massachusetts[b]	582	656	663	713	704	708	0.6	1.0	12
New Hampshire	44	109	120	129	144	117	-18.8	0.9	18
New Jersey	1,041	1,307	1,650	1,628	1,586	1,517	-4.4	1.9	34
New York	2,691	3,615	3,280	3,133	2,996	2,914	-2.7	-2.7	29
Pennsylvania	1,006	1,502	1,579	1,711	1,821	1,823	0.1	2.5	29
Rhode Island	166	157	238	193	214	222	3.7	4.4	10
Vermont	36	44	80	95	132	135	2.3	15.0	27
Midwest	7,521	10,864	14,598	14,872	15,306	15,682	2.5	4.7	47
Illinois	1,183	2,196	2,849	2,747	2,520	2,700	7.1	2.6	42
Indiana[b]	681	892	1,452	1,542	1,583	1,758	11.1	8.9	56
Iowa	212	425	592	635	703	716	1.8	6.7	48
Kansas	284	449	504	497	537	629	17.1	4.3	46
Michigan[b]	1,688	1,842	2,131	2,149	2,267	2,198	-3.0	2.2	43
Minnesota	159	217	368	383	455	435	-4.4	9.1	17
Missouri	777	1,174	1,993	2,124	2,274	2,239	-1.5	8.4	76
Nebraska	145	211	266	342	352	323	-8.2	5.5	35
North Dakota	20	29	68	101	103	113	9.7	18.5	34
Ohio	1,947	2,793	2,808	2,829	2,929	2,897	-1.1	0.5	49
South Dakota	77	134	200	220	227	269	18.5	9.1	69
Wisconsin	348	502	1,367	1,303	1,356	1,405	3.6	13.7	47
South	15,366	27,366	39,652	39,135	41,801	43,389	3.8	5.9	74
Alabama	955	1,295	1,826	1,783	1,697	2,003	18.0	5.6	82
Arkansas	435	523	772	851	854	887	3.9	6.8	63
Delaware	226	358	597	591	542	508	-6.3	4.5	53
District of Columbia[c]	606	494	356	NA	NA	NA	NA	NA	NA
Florida	2,664	3,660	4,105	4,282	4,595	5,068	10.3	4.2	58
Georgia	1,243	2,036	2,758	2,834	3,129	3,145	0.5	5.6	71
Kentucky	479	734	1,061	1,138	1,269	1,411	11.2	8.5	63
Louisiana	775	1,424	2,219	2,362	2,298	2,405	0.3	6.8	104
Maryland	877	1,079	1,219	1,207	1,264	1,248	-1.3	1.8	42
Mississippi	448	791	1,669	1,823	2,082	2,163	3.9	13.4	134
North Carolina[b]	945	1,752	1,903	2,042	2,173	2,256	3.8	3.2	37
Oklahoma	1,071	1,815	2,394	2,290	2,338	2,320	-0.8	3.1	127
South Carolina	1,053	1,045	1,420	1,509	1,671	1,576	-5.7	5.3	68
Tennessee[b]	390	637	1,369	1,468	1,735	1,826	5.2	14.1	61
Texas	2,196	7,935	13,622	12,369	13,051	13,487	3.3	6.9	98
Virginia	927	1,659	2,059	2,240	2,641	2,681	1.5	6.2	71
West Virginia	76	129	303	346	362	405	11.9	15.4	42
West	9,874	14,439	19,657	18,891	19,909	21,365	7.3	5.0	61
Alaska	128	243	284	359	349	392	12.3	6.2	55
Arizona	835	1,432	1,964	2,168	2,428	2,656	9.4	8.0	85
California[b]	6,502	9,082	11,161	9,921	9,987	10,656	6.7	2.0	57
Colorado	433	713	1,333	1,375	1,566	1,736	10.9	11.8	77
Hawaii	171	312	561	616	669	685	2.4	10.3	68
Idaho	120	212	493	541	592	592	0.0	13.7	86
Montana	76	112	306	363	345	419	21.4	17.9	91
Nevada	406	530	846	841	851	880	3.4	6.5	79
New Mexico	193	278	511	517	518	576	11.2	9.5	56
Oregon	362	465	596	661	812	883	8.7	8.3	49
Utah	125	161	381	315	371	427	15.1	13.0	35
Washington	435	793	1,065	1,079	1,254	1,288	2.7	6.3	41
Wyoming[b]	88	106	156	135	167	175	4.8	6.5	70

Note: See Note, table 6.28. Some data have been revised by the Source and may differ from previous editions of SOURCEBOOK. For information on methodology, definitions of terms, and jurisdictional explanatory notes, see Appendix 15.

[a] The number of female prisoners with sentences of more than 1 year per 100,000 female U.S. residents.
[b] Average annual percent change from 1995 to 2003 may be slightly overestimated due to a change in reporting from custody to jurisdiction counts.
[c] As of Dec. 31, 2001, the transfer of responsibility for sentenced felons from the District of Columbia to the Federal Bureau of Prisons was completed. The District of Columbia no longer operates a prison system.

Source: U.S. Department of Justice, Bureau of Justice Statistics, *Prisoners in 2000*, Bulletin NCJ 188207, p. 6; *2001*, Bulletin NCJ 195189, p. 7; *2002*, Bulletin NCJ 200248, p. 5, Table 6; *2003*, Bulletin NCJ 205335, p. 5 (Washington, DC: U.S. Department of Justice). Table adapted by SOURCEBOOK staff.

Table 6.42

Noncitizens in State and Federal prisons

United States, at midyear 1998-2003

	Noncitizen prisoners		
	Total	Federal	State
1998	77,099	27,682	49,417
1999	88,811	33,765	55,046
2000	89,676	36,090	53,586
2001	87,917	33,886	54,031
2002	88,677	33,873	54,804
2003	90,700	34,456	56,244

Note: See Note, table 6.28. New York reports foreign-born prisoners rather than noncitizens. For information on methodology and definitions of terms, see Appendix 15.

Source: U.S. Department of Justice, Bureau of Justice Statistics, *Prison and Jail Inmates at Midyear 2003*, Bulletin NCJ 203947 (Washington, DC: U.S. Department of Justice, May 2004), p. 5, Table 6. Table adapted by SOURCEBOOK staff.

Table 6.43

Mean maximum sentence, mean time served, and percent of sentence served for violent offenders[a]

By State, 1993, 1996, and 1999

	Mean maximum sentence (in months)[b]			Mean time served (in months)			Percent of sentence served[c]		
	1993	1996	1999	1993	1996	1999	1993	1996	1999
All States	108	99	103	46	50	53	46%	52%	56%
Truth-in-sentencing States[d]	89	88	93	41	46	50	50	54	58
Arizona	69	71	60	43	48	49	62	68	81
California	58	63	60	33	36	37	57	57	61
Connecticut	71	74	80	38	49	64	54	65	80
Delaware	NA	NA	NA	42	42	46	NA	NA	NA
Florida	74	84	91	31	45	53	42	54	58
Georgia	150	134	117	63	67	76	42	50	65
Illinois	91	99	107	40	45	48	44	45	45
Iowa	192	135	146	39	48	58	20	36	40
Kansas	NA	NA	NA	29	33	41	NA	NA	NA
Louisiana	104	98	96	67	68	45	64	69	48
Maine	NA	NA	NA	43	44	39	NA	NA	NA
Michigan	43	50	52	46	53	59	(e)	(e)	(e)
Minnesota	50	56	60	34	37	39	68	67	65
Mississippi	106	118	128	45	58	57	43	49	44
Missouri	96	98	99	74	78	85	77	80	86
New Jersey	121	108	120	47	46	53	39	43	44
New Mexico	70	67	77	38	37	57	54	56	74
New York	94	96	98	50	53	66	53	56	68
North Carolina	136	121	120	33	44	52	24	36	44
North Dakota	47	60	38	31	47	29	66	78	76
Ohio	237	226	165	61	71	64	26	32	39
Oregon	111	65	62	43	37	42	39	58	67
Pennsylvania	117	119	140	54	61	80	46	51	57
South Carolina	100	90	104	44	44	46	44	48	44
Tennessee	130	121	131	48	58	65	37	48	50
Utah	121	90	100	43	36	35	36	40	36
Virginia	107	97	113	41	50	62	38	51	55
Washington	41	47	49	31	34	38	76	72	78
Wisconsin	84	82	80	41	43	51	49	52	64
Other States	129	113	104	53	54	55	42	48	54
Alabama	NA	NA	NA	NA	NA	NA	NA	NA	NA
Alaska	115	124	88	65	71	63	57	57	72
Arkansas	131	109	157	35	37	56	27	34	36
Colorado	98	89	96	39	40	50	40	45	52
Hawaii	138	124	125	64	57	59	47	46	47
Idaho	104	90	98	59	80	36	57	89	37
Indiana	108	111	102	54	56	46	50	51	45
Kentucky	242	156	196	77	71	(e)	32	45	(e)
Maryland	118	106	99	63	59	57	53	56	58
Massachusetts	123	110	98	51	61	61	42	55	63
Montana	89	119	NA	61	54	60	69	46	NA
Nebraska	118	123	140	55	49	61	47	40	44
Nevada	NA	86	107	NA	34	41	NA	40	39
New Hampshire	98	89	100	36	39	48	37	44	48
Oklahoma	104	110	111	34	42	47	33	38	42
Rhode Island	80	80	68	44	50	46	55	63	67
South Dakota	101	78	72	36	37	29	35	48	40
Texas	157	123	97	48	57	59	31	46	61
Vermont	100	113	121	29	56	54	29	50	45
West Virginia	171	108	139	76	50	62	44	46	45
Wyoming	140	123	137	69	69	55	49	56	40

Note: These data are from the Violent Offender Incarceration and Truth-in-Sentencing Incentive Grant Program. The data include only offenders with a sentence of more than 1 year that have been released for the first time on the current sentence. Excludes persons released from prison by transfer, appeal, or detainer, as well as escapees and deceased prisoners. "Truth-in-sentencing States" include the 29 States and the District of Columbia that had adopted the Federal truth-in-sentencing standard by yearend 2000. This standard requires that Part I violent offenders (defined as the Federal Bureau of Investigation's Uniform Crime Reporting Program offenses of murder and nonnegligent manslaughter, rape, robbery, and aggravated assault) serve not less than 85% of their prison sentence before becoming eligible for release. The result of truth-in-sentencing practices has been to reduce discretionary release of offenders by parole boards in favor of mandatory release according to statutory provisions.

[a]Violent offenders include those serving sentences for murder and nonnegligent manslaughter, rape, robbery, and aggravated assault.
[b]Excludes sentences of life or death.
[c]Based on States that reported both mean maximum sentence and mean time served.
[d]These States met Federal truth-in-sentencing standards. The District of Columbia is excluded.
[e]Not calculated by the Source.

Source: U.S. Department of Justice, Bureau of Justice Statistics, *Trends in State Parole, 1990-2000*, Special Report NCJ 184735 (Washington, DC: U.S. Department of Justice, October 2001), p. 6.

Table 6.44

Mean sentence length and mean time served for first releases from State prison

By offense, United States, 1990 and 1999

	Mean sentence length (in months)[a]		Mean time served (in months)				Total time served (in months)[c]		Percent of sentence served[d]	
			Jail[b]		Prison					
	1990	1999	1990	1999	1990	1999	1990	1999	1990	1999
All offenses	69	65	6	5	22	29	28	34	38.0%	48.7%
Violent offenses	99	87	7	6	39	45	46	51	43.8	55.0
Murder[e]	209	192	9	10	83	96	92	106	43.1	53.1
Manslaughter	88	102	5	6	31	49	37	56	41.0	52.5
Rape	128	124	7	6	55	73	62	79	45.5	58.3
Other sexual assault	77	76	5	6	30	42	36	47	43.8	57.0
Robbery	104	97	7	6	41	48	48	55	42.8	51.6
Assault	64	62	6	6	23	33	30	39	43.9	58.7
Property offenses	65	58	6	5	18	25	24	29	34.4	45.6
Burglary	79	73	6	5	22	31	29	36	33.9	44.3
Larceny/theft	52	45	6	4	14	19	20	24	35.5	46.9
Motor vehicle theft	56	44	7	5	13	20	20	25	33.1	52.5
Fraud	56	49	6	4	14	19	20	23	33.2	41.7
Drug offenses	57	59	6	5	14	22	20	27	32.9	42.8
Possession	61	56	6	5	12	20	18	25	29.0	42.4
Trafficking	60	64	6	5	16	24	22	29	34.8	42.0
Public-order offenses	40	42	5	4	14	19	18	23	42.6	51.1

Note: See Note, table 6.43.

[a]Maximum sentence length for the most serious offense. Excludes sentences of life, life without parole, life plus additional years, and death.
[b]Time served in jail and credited toward the current sentence.
[c]Based on time served in jail and in prison. Detail may not add to total because of rounding.
[d]Based on total sentence length (not shown) for all consecutive sentences.
[e]Includes nonnegligent manslaughter.

Source: U.S. Department of Justice, Bureau of Justice Statistics, *Trends in State Parole, 1990-2000*, Special Report NCJ 184735 (Washington, DC: U.S. Department of Justice, October 2001), p. 5, Table 5.

Table 6.45

Educational attainment for those in State and Federal prisons, in local jails, on probation, and in the general population

United States, selected years[a]

	Prisoners				Local jail inmates		Probationers, 1995	General population, 1997[b]
	State		Federal					
Educational attainment	1991	1997	1991	1997	1989	1996		
8th grade or less	14.3%	14.2%	11.0%	12.0%	15.6%	13.1%	8.4%	7.2%
Some high school	26.9	25.5	12.3	14.5	38.2	33.4	22.2	11.2
GED[c]	24.6	28.5	22.6	22.7	9.2	14.1	11.0	NA
High school diploma	21.8	20.5	25.9	27.0	24.0	25.9	34.8	33.2
Postsecondary/some college	10.1	9.0	18.8	15.8	10.3	10.3	18.8	26.4
College graduate or more	2.3	2.4	9.3	8.1	2.8	3.2	4.8	22.0
Total population	706,173	1,055,495	53,677	88,705	393,111	503,599	2,029,866	192,352,084

Note: These data are from several U.S. Department of Justice, Bureau of Justice Statistics surveys. The data for prisoners are from the Survey of Inmates in State and Federal Correctional Facilities conducted in 1991 and 1997. The data for local jail inmates are from the Survey of Inmates in Local Jails conducted in 1989 and 1996. The data for probationers are from the Survey of Adults on Probation conducted in 1995.

Data for the general population are from the Bureau of Labor Statistics' Current Population Survey, March 1997 supplement.

[a]Percents may not add to 100 because of rounding.
[b]Includes the noninstitutionalized population age 18 and older; probationers have been excluded.
[c]General Educational Development certificate.

Source: U.S. Department of Justice, Bureau of Justice Statistics, *Education and Correctional Populations*, Special Report NCJ 195670 (Washington, DC: U.S. Department of Justice, January 2003), p. 2.

Table 6.46

Participation in education programs for those in State and Federal prisons, in local jails, and on probation

By type of program, United States, selected years[a]

	Prisoners				Local jail inmates, 1996	Probationers, 1995
	State		Federal			
Education program	1991	1997	1991	1997		
Total	56.6%	51.9%	67.0%	56.4%	14.1%	22.9%
Basic	5.3	3.1	10.4	1.9	0.8	0.4
GED[b]/high school	27.3	23.4	27.3	23.0	8.6	7.8
College courses	13.9	9.9	18.9	12.9	1.0	6.1
English as a second language	NA	1.2	NA	5.7	NA	NA
Vocational	31.2	32.2	29.4	31.0	4.8	7.0
Other	2.6	2.6	8.4	5.6	2.1	3.4
Total population	709,042	1,046,136	53,753	87,624	501,159	2,055,942

Note: See Note, table 6.45.

[a]Detail may not add to total due to rounding or inmates' participation in more than one educational program.
[b]General Educational Development certificate.

Source: U.S. Department of Justice, Bureau of Justice Statistics, *Education and Correctional Populations*, Special Report NCJ 195670 (Washington, DC: U.S. Department of Justice, January 2003), p. 4, Table 4.

Table 6.47

Characteristics of prisoners released in 1994 from prisons in 15 States

	Percent of released prisoners
Sex	
Male	91.3%
Female	8.7
Race	
White	50.4
Black	48.5
Other	1.1
Ethnicity	
Hispanic	24.5
Non-Hispanic	75.5
Age at release	
17 years and younger	0.4
18 to 24 years	21.0
25 to 29 years	22.8
30 to 34 years	22.7
35 to 39 years	16.2
40 to 44 years	9.4
45 years and older	7.5
Offense for which prisoner was serving sentence	
Violent	22.5
Property	33.5
Drugs	32.6
Public-order	9.7
Other	1.7
Sentence length (in months)[a]	
Mean	58.9
Median	48.0
Time served before release (in months)[a,b]	
Mean	20.6
Median	13.3
Percent of sentence served before release[b]	38.0
Prior arrest[c]	93.1
Prior conviction[c]	81.4
Prior prison sentence[c]	43.6

Note: These data are from a recidivism study conducted by the U.S. Department of Justice, Bureau of Justice Statistics. The data represent 272,111 prisoners released in 1994 from prisons in 15 States: Arizona, California, Delaware, Florida, Illinois, Maryland, Michigan, Minnesota, New Jersey, New York, North Carolina, Ohio, Oregon, Texas, and Virginia. The 272,111 are an estimated two-thirds of all prisoners released during 1994 in the United States with sentences greater than 1 year. The data presented are based on weighted estimates from a sample of 33,796 prisoners meeting four selection criteria: 1) a RAP sheet was found for the prisoner in the State criminal history repository, 2) the released prisoner was alive during the 3-year followup period, 3) the prisoner's total maximum sentence length was greater than 1 year (missing sentences were treated as greater than 1 year), and 4) the prisoner's 1994 release was not recorded by the State department of corrections as a release to custody/detainer/warrant, absent without leave, escape, transfer, administrative release, or release on appeal. The sample cases were tracked for 3 years from the date of release from prison. Any rearrest, reconviction, or reimprisonment occurring after the 3-year followup period was not included.

[a]Calculation of sentence length and time served is based on "first releases" only and excludes Michigan (which reported minimum sentence) and Ohio (which did not report data to identify "first releases").
[b]Excludes credited jail time.
[c]Does not include the arrest, conviction, or prison sentence for which prisoners were released in 1994.

Source: U.S. Department of Justice, Bureau of Justice Statistics, **Recidivism of Prisoners Released in 1994**, Special Report NCJ 193427 (Washington, DC: U.S. Department of Justice, June 2002), p. 2. Table adapted by SOURCEBOOK staff.

Table 6.48

Recidivism rates of prisoners released in 1994 from prisons in 15 States

By amount of time after release recidivism occurred and outcome

	Cumulative percent of released prisoners who were:		
Time after release	Rearrested	Reconvicted[a]	Returned to prison with new prison sentence[b]
6 months	29.9%	10.6%	5.0%
1 year	44.1	21.5	10.4
2 years	59.2	36.4	18.8
3 years	67.5	46.9	25.4

Note: See Note, table 6.47.

[a]Because of missing data, prisoners released in Ohio were excluded from the calculation of percent reconvicted.
[b]Includes new sentences to State or Federal prisons but not to local jails. Because of missing data, prisoners released in Ohio and Virginia were excluded from the calculation of percent returned to prison with new sentence.

Source: U.S. Department of Justice, Bureau of Justice Statistics, **Recidivism of Prisoners Released in 1994**, Special Report NCJ 193427 (Washington, DC: U.S. Department of Justice, June 2002), p. 3.

Table 6.49

Recidivism rates of prisoners released in 1994 from prisons in 15 States

By selected prisoner characteristics

Prisoner characteristics	Percent of all released prisoners	Rearrested	Reconvicted[a]	Returned to prison with new prison sentence[b]	Returned to prison with or without a new prison sentence[c]
Total	100%	67.5%	46.9%	25.4%	51.8%
Sex					
Male	91.3	68.4	47.6	26.2	53.0
Female	8.7	57.6	39.9	17.3	39.4
Race					
White	50.4	62.7	43.3	22.6	49.9
Black	48.5	72.9	51.1	28.5	54.2
Other	1.1	55.2	34.2	13.3	49.5
Ethnicity					
Hispanic	24.5	64.6	43.9	24.7	51.9
Non-Hispanic	75.5	71.4	50.7	26.8	57.3
Age at release					
17 years and younger	0.3	82.1	55.7	38.6	56.6
18 to 24 years	21.0	75.4	52.0	30.2	52.0
25 to 29 years	22.8	70.5	50.1	26.9	52.5
30 to 34 years	22.7	68.8	48.8	25.9	54.8
35 to 39 years	16.2	66.2	46.3	24.0	52.0
40 to 44 years	9.4	58.4	38.0	18.3	50.0
45 years and older	7.6	45.3	29.7	16.9	40.9

Note: See Note, table 6.47. Of 272,111 released prisoners, data on sex were reported for 100%, race for 97.6%, Hispanic origin for 81.9%, and age at release for 99.9%.

[a] Because of missing data, prisoners released in Ohio were excluded from the calculation of percent reconvicted.

[b] Includes new sentences to State or Federal prisons but not to local jails. Because of missing data, prisoners released in Ohio and Virginia were excluded from the calculation of percent returned to prison with new sentence.

[c] Includes both prisoners with new sentences to State or Federal prisons plus prisoners returned for technical violations. Because of missing data, prisoners released in Arizona, Delaware, Maryland, New Jersey, Ohio, and Virginia were excluded from the calculation of percent returned to prison with or without a new prison sentence. New York State custody records did not always distinguish prison returns from jail returns. Consequently, some persons received in New York jails were probably mistakenly classified as prison returns. Also, California, with a relatively high return-to-prison rate, affects the overall rate of 51.8%. When California is excluded, the return-to-prison rate falls to 40.1%.

Source: U.S. Department of Justice, Bureau of Justice Statistics, *Recidivism of Prisoners Released in 1994*, Special Report NCJ 193427 (Washington, DC: U.S. Department of Justice, June 2002), p. 7.

Table 6.50

Recidivism rates of prisoners released in 1994 from prisons in 15 States

By most serious offense for which released

Most serious offense for which released	Percent of all released prisoners	Rearrested	Reconvicted[a]	Returned to prison with new prison sentence[b]	Returned to prison with or without a new prison sentence[c]
Total	100%	67.5%	46.9%	25.4%	51.8%
Violent offenses	22.5	61.7	39.9	20.4	48.8
Homicide	1.7	40.7	20.5	10.8	31.4
Kidnaping	0.4	59.4	37.8	25.1	29.5
Rape	1.2	46.0	27.4	12.6	43.5
Other sexual assault	2.4	41.4	22.3	10.5	36.0
Robbery	9.9	70.2	46.5	25.0	54.7
Assault	6.5	65.1	44.2	21.0	51.2
Other violent	0.4	51.7	29.8	12.7	40.9
Property offenses	33.5	73.8	53.4	30.5	56.4
Burglary	15.2	74.0	54.2	30.8	56.1
Larceny/theft	9.7	74.6	55.7	32.6	60.0
Motor vehicle theft	3.5	78.8	54.3	31.3	59.1
Arson	0.5	57.7	41.0	20.1	38.7
Fraud	2.9	66.3	42.1	22.8	45.4
Stolen property	1.4	77.4	57.2	31.8	62.1
Other property	0.3	71.1	47.6	28.5	40.0
Drug offenses	32.6	66.7	47.0	25.2	49.2
Possession	7.5	67.5	46.6	23.9	42.6
Trafficking	20.2	64.2	44.0	24.8	46.1
Other/unspecified	4.9	75.5	60.5	28.8	71.8
Public-order offenses	9.7	62.2	42.0	21.6	48.0
Weapons	3.1	70.2	46.6	24.3	55.5
Driving under the influence	3.3	51.5	31.7	16.6	43.7
Other public-order	3.3	65.1	48.0	24.4	43.6
Other offenses	1.7	64.7	42.1	20.7	66.9

Note: See Note, table 6.47.

[a] Because of missing data, prisoners released in Ohio were excluded from the calculation of percent reconvicted.

[b] Includes new sentences to State or Federal prisons but not to local jails. Because of missing data, prisoners released in Ohio and Virginia were excluded from the calculation of percent returned to prison with new sentence.

[c] Includes both prisoners with new sentences to State or Federal prisons plus prisoners returned for technical violations. Because of missing data, prisoners released in Arizona, Delaware, Maryland, New Jersey, Ohio, and Virginia were excluded from the calculation of percent returned to prison with or without a new prison sentence. New York State custody records did not always distinguish prison returns from jail returns. Consequently, some persons received in New York jails were probably mistakenly classified as prison returns. Also, California, with a relatively high return-to-prison rate, affects the overall rate of 51.8%. When California is excluded, the return-to-prison rate falls to 40.1%.

Source: U.S. Department of Justice, Bureau of Justice Statistics, *Recidivism of Prisoners Released in 1994*, Special Report NCJ 193427 (Washington, DC: U.S. Department of Justice, June 2002), p. 8.

Table 6.51

Rearrest rates of prisoners released in 1994 from prisons in 15 States

By most serious offense for which released and charge at rearrest

		Percent of prisoners rearrested within 3 years of release whose most serious offense at time of release was:											
		Violent offenses					**Property offenses**						
Rearrest charge	All offenses[a]	Total[b]	Homicide[c]	Rape[d]	Robbery	Assault[d]	Total[e]	Burglary	Larceny/ theft	Motor vehicle theft	Fraud	Drug offense[f]	Public-order offense[g]
Number of released prisoners	272,111	61,107	4,443	3,138	26,862	17,708	91,061	41,257	26,259	9,478	7,853	88,516	26,329
All charges[a]	67.5%	61.7%	40.7%	46.0%	70.2%	65.1%	73.8%	74.0%	74.6%	78.8%	66.3%	66.7%	62.2%
Violent offenses[b]	21.6	27.5	16.7	18.6	29.6	31.4	21.9	21.9	22.3	26.5	14.8	18.4	18.5
Homicide[c]	0.8	1.1	1.2	0.7	1.1	1.6	0.8	0.7	0.6	2.4	0.5	0.7	0.6
Rape[d]	0.6	1.1	0.0	2.5	1.2	1.0	0.7	0.8	0.5	1.6	0.3	0.3	0.4
Robbery	6.2	8.5	3.4	3.9	13.4	6.1	6.3	5.9	7.3	8.4	3.3	4.9	4.6
Assault[d]	13.7	16.4	11.9	8.7	15.1	22.0	13.7	13.8	14.4	16.1	9.0	12.4	12.1
Property offenses[e]	31.9	25.5	10.8	14.8	32.9	25.6	46.3	45.4	47.8	45.7	44.8	24.0	22.9
Burglary	9.9	6.9	2.0	4.4	8.7	7.7	17.6	23.4	13.9	11.1	9.1	5.5	5.0
Larceny/theft	16.3	12.0	4.1	6.2	16.5	10.6	26.1	23.0	33.9	18.9	23.4	11.5	8.9
Motor vehicle theft	4.5	3.9	1.0	2.3	5.3	4.4	6.0	5.5	4.7	11.5	4.5	3.5	4.1
Fraud	4.7	3.2	2.1	1.8	4.0	3.2	7.1	5.1	6.8	6.6	19.0	3.3	5.1
Drug offenses[f]	30.3	22.6	13.0	11.2	29.4	21.5	27.2	27.6	27.1	33.9	18.5	41.2	22.1
Public-order offenses[g]	28.3	27.4	17.7	20.5	29.3	31.1	29.2	30.3	25.5	33.5	26.3	27.7	31.2

Note: See Note, table 6.47. The numerator for each percent is the number of persons rearrested for a new charge and the denominator is the number released for each type of offense. Detail may not add to totals because persons may be rearrested for more than one type of charge.

[a] Includes any offense type listed in footnotes b through g plus "other" and "unknown" offenses.
[b] Includes homicide, kidnaping, rape, other sexual assault, robbery, assault, and other forms of violence.
[c] Includes murder, voluntary manslaughter, vehicular manslaughter, negligent manslaughter, nonnegligent manslaughter, unspecified manslaughter, and unspecified homicide.
[d] Does not include sexual assault.
[e] Includes burglary, larceny/theft, motor vehicle theft, fraud, forgery, embezzlement, arson, stolen property, and other forms of property offenses.
[f] Includes drug trafficking, drug possession, and other forms of drug offenses.
[g] Includes traffic offenses, weapon offenses, probation and parole violations, court-related offenses, disorderly conduct, and other such offenses.

Source: U.S. Department of Justice, Bureau of Justice Statistics, *Recidivism of Prisoners Released in 1994*, Special Report NCJ 193427 (Washington, DC: U.S. Department of Justice, June 2002), p. 9.

Table 6.52

Recidivism rates of State prisoners released in 1983 and 1994

By offense type

Most serious offense for which released	Percent of prisoners released in:		Percent rearrested within 3 years, among prisoners released in:		Percent reconvicted within 3 years, among prisoners released in:	
	1983	1994	1983	1994	1983	1994
All released prisoners	100%	100%	62.5%	67.5%	46.8%	46.9%
Violent	34.6	22.5	59.6	61.7	41.9	39.9
Property	48.3	33.5	68.1	73.8	53.0	53.4
Drug	9.5	32.6	50.4	66.7	35.3	47.0
Public-order	6.4	9.7	54.6	62.2	41.5	42.0
Other	1.1	1.7	76.8	64.7	62.9	42.1

Note: See Note, table 6.47. These data represent 272,111 prisoners released in 1994 from prisons in 15 States, and 108,580 prisoners released in 1983 from prisons in 11 States. All 11 States from 1983 are among the 15 States represented in 1994.

Source: U.S. Department of Justice, Bureau of Justice Statistics, *Recidivism of Prisoners Released in 1994*, Special Report NCJ 193427 (Washington, DC: U.S. Department of Justice, June 2002), p. 11.

Table 6.53

Characteristics of Federal prisoners

United States, yearend 1995, 1999-2003[a]

	1995		1999		2000		2001		2002		2003	
	Number	Percent	Number	Percent	Number	Percent	Number	Percent	Number	Percent	Number	Percent
Total	100,250	100%	135,246	100%	145,416	100%	156,993	100%	163,528	100%	173,059	100%
Sex												
Male	92,852	92.6	125,333	93.0	135,171	93.0	146,020	93.0	152,294	93.1	161,424	93.3
Female	7,398	7.4	9,913	7.0	10,245	7.1	10,973	7.0	11,234	6.9	11,635	6.7
Race												
White	60,261	60.1	77,719	57.5	83,732	57.6	87,873	56.0	91,851	56.2	97,598	56.4
Black	37,055	37.0	53,048	39.2	57,028	39.2	64,277	40.9	66,504	40.7	69,923	40.4
Other[b]	2,934	2.9	4,479	3.3	4,656	3.2	4,843	3.1	5,173	3.2	5,538	3.2
Ethnicity												
Hispanic	27,559	27.5	42,527	31.4	47,023	32.3	49,722	31.7	52,174	31.9	55,417	32.0
Non-Hispanic	72,691	72.5	92,719	68.6	98,393	67.7	107,271	68.3	111,354	68.1	117,642	68.0
Age												
Less than 18 years	79	0.1	106	0.1	101	0.1	102	0.1	87	0.1	70	(c)
18 to 25 years	13,655	13.6	17,843	13.2	18,688	12.8	19,870	12.7	19,755	12.1	20,085	11.6
26 to 30 years	18,156	18.1	26,818	19.8	28,827	19.8	30,241	19.3	30,738	18.8	31,892	18.4
31 to 35 years	18,907	18.9	25,654	19.0	27,922	19.2	30,571	19.5	32,563	19.9	35,236	20.4
36 to 40 years	16,767	16.7	22,022	16.3	23,882	16.4	25,667	16.4	26,966	16.5	28,526	16.5
41 to 45 years	12,844	12.8	16,698	12.3	18,051	12.4	19,801	12.6	20,812	12.7	22,374	12.9
46 to 50 years	9,129	9.1	11,505	8.5	12,209	8.4	13,462	8.6	14,371	8.8	15,326	8.9
51 to 55 years	5,410	5.4	7,314	5.4	7,868	5.4	8,702	5.5	9,042	5.5	9,442	5.5
56 to 60 years	2,879	2.9	3,980	3.0	4,330	3.0	4,654	3.0	5,039	3.1	5,484	3.2
61 to 65 years	1,441	1.4	1,682	1.2	1,845	1.3	2,056	1.3	2,160	1.3	2,407	1.4
66 years and older	981	1.0	1,624	1.2	1,693	1.2	1,867	1.2	1,995	1.2	2,217	1.3
Region												
Northeast	19,640	19.6	21,082	15.5	24,702	17.0	28,577	18.2	29,078	17.8	28,765	16.6
North Central	14,684	14.6	17,604	13.0	17,421	12.0	21,942	14.0	21,742	13.3	22,630	13.1
Mid-Atlantic	15,267	15.2	23,083	17.0	24,487	16.8	22,176	14.1	23,097	14.1	25,477	14.7
Southeast	17,076	17.0	23,719	17.5	24,801	17.1	26,367	21.5	27,121	16.6	29,207	16.9
South Central	18,967	18.9	31,132	23.0	33,384	23.0	33,791	16.8	35,690	21.8	38,845	22.4
West	14,616	14.6	18,626	14.0	20,621	14.2	24,140	15.4	26,800	16.4	28,135	16.3
Security level												
High	10,322	10.3	13,248	10.0	13,610	9.4	14,873	9.5	18,559	11.4	NA	NA
Medium	25,738	25.7	33,329	24.6	35,160	24.2	39,467	25.1	41,028	25.1	NA	NA
Low	21,710	21.7	34,848	25.7	35,959	24.7	40,188	25.6	41,450	25.4	NA	NA
Minimum	18,570	18.5	20,265	14.9	20,659	14.2	20,215	12.9	20,631	12.6	NA	NA
Administrative[d]	13,198	13.2	16,302	12.1	19,152	13.2	23,968	15.3	25,081	15.3	NA	NA
Contract	10,712	10.7	17,254	12.7	20,876	14.4	18,282	11.6	16,779	10.2	NA	NA
Citizenship												
U.S. citizen	72,765	72.6	94,508	69.8	100,883	69.4	110,539	70.4	115,562	70.7	123,145	71.2
Non-U.S. citizen	25,444	25.4	39,094	29.0	43,474	29.9	45,110	28.7	46,539	28.5	48,739	28.2
Unavailable	2,041	2.0	1,644	1.2	1,059	0.7	1,344	0.9	1,427	0.9	1,175	0.7

Note: These data represent all prisoners under Federal Bureau of Prisons (BOP) jurisdiction, which includes those in BOP-operated facilities and those in contract facilities. Contract facility figures include prisoners housed in secure facilities where the BOP had a direct contract with a private operator and those in secure facilities where there was a sub-contract with a private provider at a local government facility. In addition, prisoners housed in facilities operated by a locality to house short-term detention and juvenile cases are counted here, as well as prisoners in facilities operated by a State that is either under contract or under an intergovernmental agreement with the BOP. Also included are prisoners in community corrections centers and those on home confinement. Subcategories may not add to the total because of missing data for some prisoners.

[a]Percents may not add to total because of rounding.
[b]Includes Asians and Native Americans.
[c]Less than 0.05%.
[d]Includes special populations such as individuals requiring medical treatment or those in pretrial status regardless of security level.

Source: Table adapted by SOURCEBOOK staff from tables provided by the U.S. Department of Justice, Federal Bureau of Prisons.

Table 6.54

Characteristics of Federal prisoners

By type of facility, United States, yearend 2003[a]

	Total		Prisoners confined in:			
			Bureau of Prisons facilities		Contract facilities	
	Number	Percent	Number	Percent	Number	Percent
Total	173,059	100%	146,279	100%	26,780	100%
Sex						
Male	161,424	93.3	135,928	92.9	25,496	95.2
Female	11,635	6.7	10,351	7.1	1,284	4.8
Race						
White	97,598	56.4	77,745	53.2	19,853	74.1
Black	69,923	40.4	64,014	43.8	5,909	22.1
Other[b]	5,538	3.2	4,520	3.1	1,018	3.8
Ethnicity						
Hispanic	55,417	32.0	40,236	27.5	15,181	56.7
Non-Hispanic	117,642	68.0	106,043	72.5	11,599	43.3
Age						
Less than 18 years	70	(c)	0	X	70	0.3
18 to 25 years	20,085	11.6	16,505	11.3	3,580	13.4
26 to 30 years	31,892	18.4	26,997	18.5	4,895	18.3
31 to 35 years	35,236	20.4	29,845	20.4	5,391	20.1
36 to 40 years	28,526	16.5	23,885	16.3	4,641	17.3
41 to 45 years	22,374	12.9	18,854	12.9	3,520	13.1
46 to 50 years	15,326	8.9	13,080	8.9	2,246	8.4
51 to 55 years	9,442	5.5	8,139	5.6	1,303	4.9
56 to 60 years	5,484	3.2	4,844	3.3	640	2.4
61 to 65 years	2,407	1.4	2,142	1.5	265	1.0
66 years and older	2,217	1.3	1,988	1.4	229	0.9
Region						
Northeast	28,765	16.6	27,629	18.9	1,136	4.2
North Central	22,630	13.1	20,803	14.2	1,827	6.8
Mid-Atlantic	25,477	14.7	22,751	15.6	2,726	10.2
Southeast	29,207	16.9	26,234	17.9	2,973	11.1
South Central	38,845	22.4	30,157	20.6	8,688	32.4
West	28,135	16.3	18,705	12.8	9,430	35.2
Citizenship						
U.S. citizen	123,145	71.2	112,069	76.6	11,076	41.4
Non-U.S. citizen	48,739	28.2	33,063	22.6	15,676	58.5
Unavailable	1,175	0.7	1,147	0.8	28	0.1

Note: See Note, table 6.53.

[a]Percents may not add to total because of rounding.
[b]Includes Asians and Native Americans.
[c]Less than 0.05%.

Source: Table adapted by SOURCEBOOK staff from table provided by the U.S. Department of Justice, Federal Bureau of Prisons.

Table 6.55

Security level of facilities housing Federal prisoners

By sex and race of prisoner, United States, yearend 2002[a]

	Total		Male						Female					
			White		Black		Other[b]		White		Black		Other[b]	
	Number	Percent	Number	Percent	Number	Percent	Number	Percent	Number	Percent	Number	Percent	Number	Percent
Total	163,528	100.0%	85,038	100.0%	62,531	100.0%	4,725	100.0%	6,813	100.0%	3,973	100.0%	448	100.0%
Security level														
High[c]	18,559	11.4	7,323	8.6	10,572	16.9	664	14.0	X	X	X	X	X	X
Medium[d]	41,028	25.1	20,073	23.6	19,657	31.4	1,247	26.4	X	X	X	X	X	X
Low	41,450	25.4	21,928	25.8	15,298	24.5	994	21.0	1,865	27.4	1,251	31.5	114	25.4
Minimum	20,631	12.6	9,153	10.8	7,079	11.3	326	6.9	2,431	35.7	1,545	38.9	97	21.6
Administrative[e]	25,081	15.3	15,205	17.9	6,572	10.5	950	20.1	1,578	23.2	691	17.4	136	30.4
Contract	16,779	10.2	11,356	13.4	3,353	5.4	544	11.5	939	13.8	486	12.2	101	22.5

Note: See Note, table 6.53.

[a]Percents may not add to total because of rounding.
[b]Includes Asians and Native Americans.
[c]There are no high security facilities for female prisoners. High security level females are housed in a special unit.
[d]There are no female prisoners classified as medium security and no medium security level facilities for females.
[e]Includes special populations such as individuals requiring medical treatment or those in pretrial status regardless of security level.

Source: Table adapted by SOURCEBOOK staff from table provided by the U.S. Department of Justice, Federal Bureau of Prisons.

Table 6.56

Type of commitment offense among Federal prisoners

By sex and race of prisoner, United States, yearend 2003[a]

	Total		Male						Female					
			White		Black		Other[b]		White		Black		Other[b]	
Offense	Number	Percent	Number	Percent	Number	Percent	Number	Percent	Number	Percent	Number	Percent	Number	Percent
Total	156,702	100%	80,811	100%	60,986	100%	4,235	100%	6,539	100%	3,716	100%	415	100%
Drug	85,800	54.8	41,139	50.9	36,662	60.1	1,164	27.5	4,282	65.5	2,353	63.3	200	48.2
Robbery	10,168	6.5	4,298	5.3	5,349	8.8	154	3.6	167	2.6	194	5.2	6	1.4
Property	7,058	4.5	3,646	4.5	2,369	3.9	403	9.5	408	6.2	198	5.3	34	8.2
Extortion, fraud, bribery	6,915	4.4	3,768	4.7	1,679	2.8	198	4.7	702	10.7	515	13.9	53	12.8
Violent[c]	5,210	3.3	1,190	1.5	2,848	4.7	935	22.1	49	0.8	111	3.0	77	18.6
Weapons, explosives, arson	18,022	11.5	7,689	9.5	9,545	15.6	425	10.0	178	2.7	174	4.7	11	2.6
White collar[d]	1,040	0.7	499	0.6	272	0.4	33	0.8	162	2.5	66	1.8	8	1.9
Immigration	16,582	10.6	15,423	19.1	673	1.1	73	1.7	388	5.9	14	0.4	11	2.6
Court, corrections[e]	712	0.4	367	0.4	187	0.3	16	0.4	92	1.4	44	1.2	6	1.4
Sex offenses	1,617	1.0	397	0.5	475	0.8	730	17.2	9	0.1	4	0.1	2	0.5
National security	86	0.1	59	0.1	11	(f)	4	0.1	7	0.1	5	0.1	0	X
Continuing criminal enterprise	621	0.4	320	0.4	278	0.5	8	0.2	12	0.2	3	0.1	0	X
Other	2,871	1.8	2,016	2.5	638	1.1	92	2.2	83	1.3	35	0.9	7	1.7

Note: See Note, table 6.53. These data include prisoners under Federal Bureau of Prisons jurisdiction for whom offense information was available.

[a]Percents may not add to total because of rounding.
[b]Includes Asians and Native Americans.
[c]Includes crimes such as homicide, aggravated assault, and kidnaping.
[d]Includes banking, insurance, counterfeiting, and embezzlement.
[e]Includes crimes such as harboring a fugitive, possessing or bringing contraband into a prison, and perjury.
[f]Less than 0.05%.

Source: Table adapted by SOURCEBOOK staff from table provided by the U.S. Department of Justice, Federal Bureau of Prisons.

Table 6.57

Federal prison population, and number and percent sentenced for drug offenses

United States, 1970-2004

	Total sentenced and unsentenced population	Sentenced population		
			Drug offenses	
		Total	Number	Percent of total
1970	21,266	20,686	3,384	16.3%
1971	20,891	20,529	3,495	17.0
1972	22,090	20,729	3,523	16.9
1973	23,336	22,038	5,652	25.6
1974	23,690	21,769	6,203	28.4
1975	23,566	20,692	5,540	26.7
1976	27,033	24,135	6,425	26.6
1977	29,877	25,673	6,743	26.2
1978	27,674	23,501	5,981	25.4
1979	24,810	21,539	5,468	25.3
1980	24,252	19,023	4,749	24.9
1981	26,195	19,765	5,076	25.6
1982	28,133	20,938	5,518	26.3
1983	30,214	26,027	7,201	27.6
1984	32,317	27,622	8,152	29.5
1985	36,042	27,623	9,491	34.3
1986	37,542	30,104	11,344	37.7
1987	41,609	33,246	13,897	41.8
1988	41,342	33,758	15,087	44.7
1989	47,568	37,758	18,852	49.9
1990	54,613	46,575	24,297	52.2
1991	61,026	52,176	29,667	56.9
1992	67,768	59,516	35,398	59.5
1993	76,531	68,183	41,393	60.7
1994	82,269	73,958	45,367	61.3
1995	85,865	76,947	46,669	60.7
1996	89,672	80,872	49,096	60.7
1997	95,513	87,294	52,059	59.6
1998	104,507	95,323	55,984	58.7
1999	115,024	104,500	60,399	57.8
2000	123,141	112,329	63,898	56.9
2001	131,419	120,829	67,037	55.5
2002	139,183	128,090	70,009	54.7
2003	148,731	137,536	75,801	55.1
2004[a]	154,706	143,864	77,867	54.1

Note: These data represent prisoners housed in Federal Bureau of Prisons facilities; prisoners housed in contract facilities are not included. Data for 1970-76 are for June 30; beginning in 1977, data are for September 30. Some data have been revised by the Source and may differ from previous editions of SOURCEBOOK.

[a]As of November 2004.

Source: U.S. Department of Justice, Federal Bureau of Prisons [Online]. Available: http://www.bop.gov/fact0598.html [Sept. 9, 2003]; and data provided by the U.S. Department of Justice, Federal Bureau of Prisons.

Table 6.58

Time served to first release by Federal prisoners

By offense, United States, fiscal year 2001

(In months)

Most serious conviction offense	All prisoners — Number of prisoners released	All prisoners — Mean time served	All prisoners — Median time served	Sentences of 1 year or less — Number of prisoners released	Sentences of 1 year or less — Mean time served	Sentences of 1 year or less — Median time served	Sentences over 1 year — Number of prisoners released	Sentences over 1 year — Mean time served	Sentences over 1 year — Median time served	Sentences over 1 year — Percent of sentence served
All offenses	39,428	29.3	20.8	11,083	4.9	4.9	28,345	38.9	27.0	87.8%
Violent offenses	2,006	54.8	43.5	147	5.6	5.9	1,859	58.7	45.9	87.0
Murder, nonnegligent manslaughter	82	80.8	48.9	7	B	B	75	87.8	52.3	84.1
Assault	282	27.9	23.5	72	5.0	5.2	210	35.7	28.3	88.9
Robbery	1,417	59.3	49.7	47	6.4	5.9	1,370	61.1	50.4	87.0
Sexual abuse[a]	163	42.1	26.1	17	4.9	6.0	146	46.4	28.7	87.3
Kidnaping	51	84.3	66.2	2	B	B	49	87.5	67.9	83.4
Threats against the President	11	21.5	22.1	2	B	B	9	B	B	B
Property offenses	6,666	16.1	12.0	2,587	5.1	5.0	4,079	23.0	18.2	88.5
Fraudulent offenses	5,487	15.8	12.0	2,072	5.2	5.0	3,415	22.2	17.4	88.4
Embezzlement	426	9.0	5.0	263	3.9	4.0	163	17.3	13.1	87.6
Fraud[b]	4,435	16.5	12.0	1,588	5.4	5.0	2,847	22.7	18.2	88.5
Forgery	150	12.7	10.2	75	4.3	4.0	75	21.1	15.7	89.2
Counterfeiting	476	15.9	12.2	146	6.2	6.0	330	20.2	15.7	88.4
Other offenses	1,179	17.5	12.0	515	4.5	4.0	664	27.6	20.9	88.9
Burglary	63	21.5	15.7	14	6.0	5.0	49	26.0	18.3	87.7
Larceny[c]	555	11.9	10.0	300	5.3	5.0	255	19.7	15.6	89.7
Motor vehicle theft	88	16.8	13.0	24	7.0	7.8	64	20.5	15.7	88.2
Arson and explosives	42	46.3	34.1	5	B	B	37	51.8	44.8	88.2
Transportation of stolen property	109	22.1	16.6	18	5.4	5.0	91	25.4	20.8	90.3
Other property offenses[d]	322	21.2	12.5	154	2.1	1.3	168	38.7	31.8	87.5
Drug offenses	14,393	41.8	31.4	1,446	6.5	6.0	12,947	45.8	33.3	87.4
Trafficking	14,185	42.3	32.1	1,298	6.7	6.0	12,887	45.8	33.5	87.4
Possession and other	208	11.9	6.0	148	4.3	4.0	60	30.7	18.3	91.0
Public-order offenses	2,978	24.2	15.7	918	4.4	4.2	2,060	33.0	23.6	87.5
Regulatory offenses	646	19.8	13.1	205	5.9	5.0	441	26.2	20.9	88.0
Other offenses	2,332	25.4	15.7	713	3.9	4.0	1,619	34.9	26.1	87.4
Tax law violations including tax fraud	347	15.9	12.0	127	5.2	5.0	220	22.1	15.7	87.7
Bribery	64	12.8	10.4	29	5.6	5.9	35	18.7	13.1	87.0
Perjury, contempt, intimidation	67	18.0	12.2	28	5.4	5.0	39	26.9	20.1	88.5
National defense	20	33.9	23.4	6	B	B	14	45.2	29.2	84.9
Escape	180	17.4	13.1	65	6.0	6.0	115	23.8	18.0	88.7
Racketeering and extortion	966	40.7	32.3	72	6.3	5.9	894	43.5	35.7	86.9
Gambling offenses	2	B	B	2	B	B	0	X	X	X
Nonviolent sex offenses	60	29.1	23.6	8	B	B	52	33.1	26.1	88.5
Mail or transport of obscene material	193	22.8	20.9	14	5.3	6.0	179	24.1	23.5	87.4
Traffic offenses	308	2.4	1.0	294	1.8	0.9	14	16.4	13.9	90.6
Migratory birds	12	16.2	10.2	6	B	B	6	B	B	B
Other	113	13.2	9.0	62	4.5	5.0	51	23.8	18.3	91.5
Weapons offenses	2,171	43.7	34.8	169	6.2	5.3	2,002	46.9	40.0	88.1
Immigration offenses	10,653	15.2	10.0	5,533	4.5	4.0	5,120	26.8	24.8	88.6
Other offenses[e]	561	13.5	10.4	283	3.9	3.0	278	23.4	20.8	88.9

Note: See Note, table 6.4. These data are from the Federal Bureau of Prisons data files. Prisoners and the length of their sentences are classified according to the offense associated with the longest single sentence actually imposed. Prisoners serving consecutive sentences may have total imposed sentences exceeding the longest single sentence length. Accordingly, the time actually served may exceed the longest single imposed sentence. "Time served" is the number of months from the prisoner's arrival into jurisdiction of the Bureau of Prisons until first release from prison, plus any jail time served and credited. The total reported for "all offenses" includes prisoners whose offense category could not be determined. These data exclude prisoners who left Federal prison by extraordinary means, such as death, sentence commutation, and treaty transfer: 4,375 prisoners in fiscal year 2001. For methodology and definitions of terms, see Appendix 11.

[a]Includes only violent sex offenses.
[b]Excludes tax fraud.
[c]Excludes transportation of stolen property.
[d]Excludes fraudulent property offenses; includes destruction of property and trespass.
[e]Offenses not classifiable or not a violation of the U.S. Code.

Source: U.S. Department of Justice, Bureau of Justice Statistics, *Compendium of Federal Justice Statistics, 2001*, NCJ 201627 (Washington, DC: U.S. Department of Justice, 2003), p. 104.

Table 6.59

Mean time served to first release by Federal prisoners

By offense and characteristics, United States, fiscal year 2001

(In months)

Prisoner characteristics	Number of prisoners released	All offenses	Violent offenses	Property offenses Fraudulent	Property offenses Other	Drug offenses	Public-order offenses Regulatory	Public-order offenses Other	Weapons offenses	Immigration offenses
All releases	39,428	29.3	54.8	15.8	17.5	41.8	19.8	25.4	43.7	15.2
Sex										
Male	34,908	30.3	56.8	16.9	18.9	43.5	20.5	26.1	44.0	15.6
Female	4,474	20.9	31.3	11.4	10.6	30.6	15.7	18.8	32.6	8.1
Race										
White	29,479	25.4	57.8	15.8	18.2	36.3	19.0	24.2	40.7	14.9
Black	8,603	42.0	55.3	15.5	16.0	55.4	22.5	27.8	47.5	27.5
Native American	524	35.5	44.6	16.0	17.4	31.1	11.1	18.1	27.9	13.8
Asian/Pacific Islander	776	30.7	39.1	16.2	19.5	51.9	21.7	30.6	37.2	20.0
Ethnicity										
Hispanic	19,036	23.4	59.6	13.1	13.8	36.0	17.4	29.0	37.1	14.7
Non-Hispanic	20,346	34.8	54.2	16.3	18.2	47.2	20.5	24.6	44.8	21.8
Age										
Less than 19 years	329	22.2	41.5	11.3	17.4	24.8	12.9	63.1	58.1	5.5
19 to 20 years	1,894	25.6	51.2	12.2	15.7	32.8	20.5	22.2	42.4	8.2
21 to 30 years	16,172	28.5	53.5	13.7	18.9	40.3	21.4	27.1	43.6	13.8
31 to 40 years	12,030	31.0	61.0	15.9	20.3	44.4	20.5	25.8	45.2	18.1
Over 40 years	8,957	29.2	51.1	17.5	14.3	44.1	18.0	23.7	41.5	16.8
Citizenship										
U.S. citizen	20,627	34.4	55.1	16.4	17.0	43.8	21.4	24.3	44.6	11.9
Not U.S. citizen	18,614	23.7	46.6	13.7	24.2	39.2	14.9	32.4	35.3	15.4

Note: See Notes, tables 6.4 and 6.58. Totals include prisoners whose offense category could not be determined and exclude prisoners released by extraordinary means such as commutation and death. For methodology and definitions of terms, see Appendix 11.

Source: U.S. Department of Justice, Bureau of Justice Statistics, *Compendium of Federal Justice Statistics, 2001*, NCJ 201627 (Washington, DC: U.S. Department of Justice, 2003), p. 106, Table 7.16.

Table 6.60

Immigration offenders in Federal prison and average time to be served

United States, 1985-2000

	Immigration offenders in Federal prison	
	Number	Average time to be served (in months)[a]
1985	1,593	NA
1986	1,799	3.6
1987	1,667	3.6
1988	1,631	4.1
1989	1,729	3.7
1990	1,673	3.6
1991	1,667	4.6
1992	1,654	5.4
1993	2,198	7.3
1994	2,486	9.5
1995	3,420	11.0
1996	4,476	13.9
1997	5,454	15.1
1998	7,430	16.5
1999	10,156	20.0
2000	13,676	20.6

Note: These data are from the U.S. Department of Justice, Bureau of Justice Statistics' (BJS) Federal Justice Statistics Program, a database comprised of information from various Federal agencies. Immigration offenses are defined according to the BJS filing offense classification procedure followed by the Administrative Office of the United States Courts. The category is composed largely of the following offense types: smuggling, transporting, and harboring aliens; unlawful entry and reentry of aliens; and misuse of visa and other documents. (Source, p. 8.) The data presented are for offenders for whom an immigration offense was the most serious offense.

[a]Estimates of time to be served are subject to change. Once committed to the Federal Bureau of Prisons, the term an offender is required to serve may be adjusted for reasons such as assistance to Federal prosecutors and appellate review.

Source: U.S. Department of Justice, Bureau of Justice Statistics, *Immigration Offenders in the Federal Criminal Justice System, 2000*, Special Report NCJ 191745 (Washington, DC: U.S. Department of Justice, August 2002), p. 10, Appendix for figure 5 and Appendix for figure 6. Table adapted by SOURCEBOOK staff.

Table 6.61

Detainees under Bureau of Immigration and Customs Enforcement (ICE) jurisdiction[a]

By type of facility, Dec. 31, 1995, 2000-2003

Type of facility	Number of detainees					Percent change
	1995	2000	2001	2002	2003	2002 to 2003
Total[b]	8,177	19,528	19,137	21,065	23,514	11.6%
ICE-operated facilities	3,776	4,785	4,550	5,087	5,109	0.4
Private facilities under exclusive contract to ICE	652	1,829	1,947	1,936	1,935	-0.1
Federal Bureau of Prisons	1,282	1,444	1,276	1,100	1,338	21.6
Other Federal facilities	181	178	162	130	88	-32.3
Intergovernmental agreements	2,286	11,281	11,201	12,812	15,044	17.4
State prisons	8	369	419	453	477	5.3
Local jails	1,984	8,886	8,681	9,764	11,376	16.5
Other facilities	294	2,026	2,101	2,595	3,191	23.0

Note: See Note, table 6.28.

[a]On Mar. 1, 2003, functions of several border and security agencies including the U.S. Customs Service and the Immigration and Naturalization Service were transferred to the U.S. Department of Homeland Security, Bureau of Immigration and Customs Enforcement.
[b]Detail does not add to total because facility type was unknown for one detainee in 2000 and 2001.

Source: U.S. Department of Justice, Bureau of Justice Statistics, *Prisoners in 2001*, Bulletin NCJ 195189, p. 10, Table 12; *2003*, Bulletin NCJ 205335, p. 9 (Washington, DC: U.S. Department of Justice). Table adapted by SOURCEBOOK staff.

Table 6.62

Drug and alcoholism treatment facilities and clients in treatment

By type of care received and jurisdiction, on Mar. 29, 2002

Jurisdiction[a]	Treatment facilities	All clients Total	Out-patient	Residential	Hospital inpatient	Under 18 Total	Out-patient	Residential	Hospital inpatient	Percent
Total	13,720	1,136,287	1,020,214	102,394	13,679	91,851	80,383	10,342	1,126	8.1%
Alabama	118	10,934	10,047	790	97	557	486	69	2	5.1
Alaska	87	3,004	2,527	464	13	229	202	27	0	7.6
Arizona	212	26,115	24,132	1,763	220	1,650	1,416	231	3	6.3
Arkansas	59	3,789	3,079	667	43	218	184	34	0	5.8
California	1,772	158,653	139,530	18,067	1,056	12,033	11,084	902	47	7.6
Colorado	389	32,764	31,279	1,283	202	2,762	2,483	271	8	8.4
Connecticut	247	20,874	18,532	1,961	381	875	703	140	32	4.2
Delaware	42	4,106	3,896	187	23	210	208	1	1	5.1
District of Columbia	60	5,900	5,232	547	121	196	119	50	27	3.3
Federated States of Micronesia	3	179	167	1	11	13	12	0	1	7.3
Florida	612	47,849	41,906	5,212	731	4,017	3,350	609	58	8.4
Georgia	263	18,973	16,872	1,778	323	986	838	122	26	5.2
Guam	1	253	253	0	0	30	30	0	0	11.9
Hawaii	91	3,642	3,164	422	56	774	690	54	30	21.3
Idaho	67	4,149	3,952	166	31	1,050	1,001	44	5	25.3
Illinois	608	45,375	41,065	3,943	367	3,974	3,398	547	29	8.8
Indiana	288	27,291	26,445	676	170	2,524	2,502	18	4	9.2
Iowa	119	8,262	7,592	617	53	1,151	968	182	1	13.9
Kansas	182	9,311	8,459	805	47	1,055	943	98	14	11.3
Kentucky	308	18,440	17,002	1,096	342	1,081	922	61	98	5.9
Louisiana	167	12,653	10,761	1,607	285	738	528	202	8	5.8
Maine	177	6,621	6,190	295	136	822	783	39	0	12.4
Maryland	345	36,114	33,936	2,043	135	2,835	2,629	182	24	7.9
Massachusetts	352	35,919	31,679	3,622	618	1,485	1,413	65	7	4.1
Michigan	562	44,166	41,014	2,927	225	3,239	3,132	97	10	7.3
Minnesota	263	9,936	6,690	2,914	332	947	608	309	30	9.5
Mississippi	121	5,310	4,163	948	199	268	169	74	25	5.0
Missouri	253	18,507	16,846	1,590	71	1,291	969	296	26	7.0
Montana	52	2,531	2,330	170	31	490	418	65	7	19.4
Nebraska	104	5,397	4,636	670	91	857	792	65	0	15.9
Nevada	77	7,266	6,805	441	20	387	350	37	0	5.3
New Hampshire	64	3,160	2,861	254	45	185	151	32	2	5.9
New Jersey	315	31,696	28,625	2,491	580	2,827	2,460	333	34	8.9
New Mexico	120	10,634	9,880	661	93	870	809	46	15	8.2
New York	1,260	139,434	124,520	12,174	2,740	7,698	7,012	640	46	5.5
North Carolina	283	27,758	26,088	1,353	317	2,484	2,426	53	5	8.9
North Dakota	47	1,878	1,543	285	50	269	208	50	11	14.3
Ohio	515	38,919	35,561	2,865	493	4,304	3,819	485	0	11.1
Oklahoma	149	8,815	7,250	1,488	77	1,067	877	166	24	12.1
Oregon	232	24,290	23,096	1,144	50	2,455	2,236	219	0	10.1
Palau	1	70	66	0	4	1	0	0	1	1.4
Pennsylvania	488	38,734	33,385	4,840	509	3,540	2,861	676	3	9.1
Puerto Rico	111	8,228	5,582	2,580	66	962	709	249	4	11.7
Rhode Island	56	6,173	5,851	308	14	264	223	41	0	4.3
South Carolina	93	12,216	11,650	311	255	1,276	1,261	2	13	10.4
South Dakota	61	2,520	1,861	607	52	483	330	133	20	19.2
Tennessee	190	9,838	8,383	1,223	232	904	716	162	26	9.2
Texas	555	37,274	30,734	5,969	571	2,854	1,826	882	146	7.7
Utah	134	9,079	7,585	1,377	117	1,628	864	709	55	17.9
Vermont	40	2,426	2,187	206	33	466	422	40	4	19.2
Virgin Islands	4	156	113	43	0	14	11	3	0	9.0
Virginia	228	23,734	22,322	1,206	206	2,315	2,150	165	0	9.8
Washington	310	37,353	35,415	1,674	264	3,502	3,163	218	121	9.4
West Virginia	85	4,954	4,430	452	72	562	519	33	10	11.3
Wisconsin	324	20,648	19,247	1,073	328	1,935	1,784	100	51	9.4
Wyoming	54	2,017	1,798	138	81	242	216	14	12	12.0

Note: These data are from the National Survey of Substance Abuse Treatment Services (N-SSATS), which is conducted annually by the Substance Abuse and Mental Health Services Administration. The survey includes both public and private treatment facilities in the 50 States, the District of Columbia, and U.S. territories and protectorates. The reference date for the 2002 N-SSATS was Mar. 29, 2002. A total of 15,459 facilities were eligible for the 2002 survey; data were received for 14,756 facilities for a response rate of 95.5%. After exclusion of responding facilities deemed out of the scope of the survey focus, there were 13,720 eligible respondents for the 2002 N-SSATS. "Clients in treatment" include hospital inpatient and residential clients receiving treatment (and not discharged) on the survey reference date, and outpatient clients enrolled on the reference date who received a substance abuse treatment service during the month prior to the survey.

[a] Data for facilities operated by Federal agencies are included in the States in which the facilities are located.

Source: U.S. Department of Health and Human Services, Substance Abuse and Mental Health Services Administration, *National Survey of Substance Abuse Treatment Services (N-SSATS): 2002* (Rockville, MD: U.S. Department of Health and Human Services, 2003), pp. 65, 124, 125. Table adapted by SOURCEBOOK staff.

Table 6.63

Offenders in State sex offender registries

By State, 1998 and 2001

State	Offenders in registry 1998	Offenders in registry 2001	Percent change 1998 to 2001
Total	263,166	386,112	47%
Alabama	440	3,338	659
Alaska[a]	3,535	4,107	16
Arizona	9,200	11,500	25
Arkansas	958	2,935	206
California[a]	78,000	88,853	14
Colorado	4,326	8,804	104
Connecticut	(b)	2,030	X
Delaware	800	1,688	111
District of Columbia	50	303	506
Florida	9,000	20,000	122
Georgia	1,200	4,564	280
Hawaii	1,000	1,500	50
Idaho	1,710	1,778	4
Illinois[a]	14,300	16,551	16
Indiana	9,500	11,656	23
Iowa	2,240	3,921	75
Kansas	1,200	1,794	50
Kentucky	800	2,000	150
Louisiana	3,455	5,708	65
Maine	275	473	72
Maryland	400	1,400	250
Massachusetts	7,004	(c)	X
Michigan	19,000	26,850	41
Minnesota	7,300	10,610	45
Mississippi	1,063	1,512	42
Missouri	2,800	7,500	168
Montana[d]	1,739	2,088	20
Nebraska	640	1,120	75
Nevada	1,500	2,519	68
New Hampshire	1,500	2,168	45
New Jersey	5,151	7,495	46
New Mexico	450	1,171	160
New York	7,200	11,575	61
North Carolina	2,200	5,922	169
North Dakota	683	766	12
Ohio	1,294	5,423	319
Oklahoma	2,303	4,020	75
Oregon	7,400	9,410	27
Pennsylvania	2,400	4,533	89
Rhode Island	273	1,424	422
South Carolina	2,500	4,924	97
South Dakota	800	1,182	48
Tennessee	2,800	4,561	63
Texas	18,000	29,494	64
Utah	4,733	5,192	10
Vermont	877	1,509	72
Virginia	6,615	9,306	41
Washington	1,400	15,304	993
West Virginia	600	950	58
Wisconsin	10,000	11,999	20
Wyoming	552	682	24

Note: In March 1998, the U.S. Department of Justice, Bureau of Justice Statistics (BJS) established the National Sex Offender Registry Assistance Program (NSOR-AP). As part of BJS' National Criminal History Improvement Program, NSOR-AP assists States in meeting the requirements of the Wetterling Act as amended by Megan's Law and the Pam Lychner Act. The program also provides assistance to allow States to participate in the Federal Bureau of Investigation's permanent National Sex Offender Registry. Readers should be aware that several factors in each State's authorizing legislation significantly influence the size of a State's registry. Among these factors are the number of different offenses requiring registration, the date that triggers the registration mandate, and the duration of the registration requirement.

[a] Number includes more than just registered offenders (for example, never registered but required to do so, offenders in jail, registered but not in compliance).
[b] At the time the survey was conducted in 1998, Connecticut did not have a centralized sex offender registry.
[c] The 2001 count is not included due to a superior court injunction against the Sex Offender Registry Board, prohibiting registration without first providing the offender a hearing. At the time of the survey, Massachusetts estimated that about 17,000 sex offenders would be qualified to register.
[d] Also includes offenders who must register for certain violent offenses.

Source: U.S. Department of Justice, Bureau of Justice Statistics, *Summary of State Sex Offender Registries, 2001*, Fact Sheet NCJ 192265 (Washington, DC: U.S. Department of Justice, March 2002), p. 6.

Table 6.64

Prisoners under jurisdiction of U.S. military authorities

By branch of service, Dec. 31, 1996-2003[a]

Branch of service	1996	1997	1998	1999	2000	2001	2002	2003	Percent change 2002 to 2003
To which prisoners belonged									
Total	2,747	2,772	2,426	2,279	2,420	2,436	2,377	2,165	-8.9%
Air Force	487	575	484	409	413	480	450	391	-13.1
Army	1,106	1,063	862	761	789	804	860	840	-2.3
Marine Corps	685	628	682	565	730	628	565	539	-4.6
Navy	455	490	389	523	474	516	489	377	-22.9
Coast Guard	14	16	9	21	14	8	13	18	38.5
Holding prisoners									
Total	2,747	2,772	2,426	2,279	2,420	2,436	2,377	2,165	-8.9
Air Force[b]	NA	103	128	92	102	126	128	105	-18.0
Army	1,486	1,494	1,115	1,026	994	981	966	967	0.1
Marine Corps	650	571	617	480	563	428	478	441	-7.7
Navy	611	604	526	681	761	901	805	652	-19.0

Note: For information on methodology, see Appendix 15.

[a] Detail may not add to total because of rounding.
[b] Data for 1996 exclude prisoners confined in Air Force facilities.

Source: U.S. Department of Justice, Bureau of Justice Statistics, *Prisoners in 1997*, Bulletin NCJ 170014, p. 2; *1999*, Bulletin NCJ 183476, p. 2, Table 3; *2001*, Bulletin NCJ 195189, p. 11, Table 13; *2003*, Bulletin NCJ 205335, p. 8 (Washington, DC: U.S. Department of Justice). Table adapted by SOURCEBOOK staff.

Table 6.65

Rate (per 100,000 adult residents) of adults on parole

United States, 1981-2003

	Rate per 100,000 adult residents
1981	136
1982	144
1983	147
1984	155
1985	158
1986	184
1987	201
1988	224
1989	248
1990	287
1991	316
1992	336
1993	352
1994	359
1995	361
1996	359
1997[a]	349
1998	352
1999	352
2000	347
2001	350
2002	350
2003	357

Note: See Note, table 6.3. Parole is a period of conditional supervised release following a prison term. Prisoners may be released to parole either by a parole board decision or by mandatory conditional release. Rates were calculated using U.S. Census Bureau population figures for the number of adult residents. For information on methodology and definitions of terms, see Appendix 15.

[a] Due to reporting changes in New Jersey and other jurisdictions, the 1997 rate is not directly comparable to prior years.

Source: U.S. Department of Justice, Bureau of Justice Statistics, *Probation and Parole 1982*, Bulletin NCJ-89874, p. 4; *1983*, Bulletin NCJ-94776, p. 2; *1984*, Bulletin NCJ-100181, p. 4 (Washington, DC: U.S. Department of Justice); U.S. Department of Justice, Bureau of Justice Statistics, *Correctional Populations in the United States, 1985*, NCJ-103957, p. 91; *1986*, NCJ-111611, p. 81; *1987*, NCJ-118762, p. 125; *1988*, NCJ-124280, p. 97; *1989*, NCJ-130445, p. 103; *1990*, NCJ-134946, p. 117; *1992*, NCJ-146413, p. 105; *1993*, NCJ-156241, Table 6.2; *1994*, NCJ-160091, Table 6.2; *1995*, NCJ-163916, Table 6.2 (Washington, DC: U.S. Department of Justice); U.S. Department of Justice, Bureau of Justice Statistics, *Probation and Parole Populations 1997*, Press Release NCJ-172216 (Washington, DC: U.S. Department of Justice, August 1998), p. 4; U.S. Department of Justice, Bureau of Justice Statistics, *Probation and Parole in 1999*, Press Release NCJ 183508 (Washington, DC: U.S. Department of Justice, July 2000), p. 5; U.S. Department of Justice, Bureau of Justice Statistics, *Probation and Parole in the United States, 2000*, Press Release NCJ 188208, p. 5; *2001*, Bulletin NCJ 195669, p. 5; *2002*, Bulletin NCJ 201135, p. 5, Table 5; *2003*, Bulletin NCJ 205336, p. 5, Table 5 (Washington, DC: U.S. Department of Justice); and data provided by the U.S. Department of Justice, Bureau of Justice Statistics. Table constructed by SOURCEBOOK staff.

Table 6.66

Adults on parole under State and Federal jurisdiction

By region and jurisdiction, 2003

Region and jurisdiction	Parole population Jan. 1, 2003	2003[a] Entries	2003[a] Exits	Parole population Dec. 31, 2003	Percent change in parole population during 2003	Number on parole on Dec. 31, 2003 per 100,000 adult residents
United States, total	750,934	492,727	470,538	774,588	3.1%	357
Federal	83,063	33,590	31,088	86,459	4.1	40
State	667,871	459,137	439,450	688,129	3.0	317
Northeast	174,591	77,381	71,903	180,069	3.1	437
Connecticut	2,186	3,260	2,847	2,599	18.9	99
Maine	32	0	0	32	0.0	3
Massachusetts	3,951	6,305	6,552	3,704	-6.3	370
New Hampshire[b]	963	719	482	1,200	24.6	124
New Jersey	12,576	10,322	9,650	13,248	5.3	203
New York	55,990	25,049	25,186	55,853	-0.2	386
Pennsylvania[c]	97,712	30,870	26,338	102,244	4.6	1,084
Rhode Island	384	456	448	392	2.1	48
Vermont	797	400	400	797	0.0	170
Midwest	114,173	95,242	87,882	121,533	6.4	250
Illinois	35,458	32,476	32,926	35,008	-1.3	374
Indiana	5,877	7,304	6,162	7,019	19.4	152
Iowa[d]	2,787	2,787	2,475	3,099	11.2	140
Kansas[d]	3,990	4,146	3,991	4,145	3.9	207
Michigan	17,648	12,579	9,994	20,233	14.6	271
Minnesota	3,577	4,121	4,102	3,596	0.5	96
Missouri	13,533	10,407	8,720	15,220	12.5	357
Nebraska	574	839	763	650	13.2	51
North Dakota	148	585	507	226	52.7	48
Ohio	17,853	11,670	11,096	18,427	3.2	216
South Dakota	1,640	1,451	1,147	1,944	18.5	346
Wisconsin	11,088	6,877	5,999	11,966	7.9	293
South	219,849	104,142	96,351	227,668	3.6	291
Alabama	5,309	4,098	2,457	6,950	30.9	206
Arkansas	12,128	7,379	5,813	13,694	12.9	672
Delaware	551	217	239	529	-4.0	85
District of Columbia[b,c]	5,297	3,136	3,369	5,064	(e)	1,129
Florida	5,223	4,409	4,680	4,952	-5.2	37
Georgia	20,822	11,738	10,391	22,135	6.3	344
Kentucky[d]	5,968	4,719	3,115	7,572	26.9	243
Louisiana	23,049	13,468	11,452	25,065	8.7	766
Maryland	13,271	8,059	7,588	13,742	3.5	334
Mississippi[f]	1,816	1,103	963	1,816	0.0	87
North Carolina	2,805	3,214	3,342	2,677	-4.6	42
Oklahoma[b]	3,573	1,995	1,521	4,047	(e)	155
South Carolina	3,491	1,025	1,306	3,210	-8.0	103
Tennessee	7,949	3,130	3,314	7,967	0.2	180
Texas[b]	103,068	32,847	33,644	102,271	-0.8	639
Virginia	4,530	2,779	2,475	4,834	6.7	86
West Virginia	999	826	682	1,143	14.4	81
West	159,258	182,371	183,313	158,859	-0.3	324
Alaska[d]	900	614	587	927	(e)	203
Arizona[c]	4,587	8,895	8,115	5,367	17.0	129
California[d]	113,185	148,915	152,305	110,338	-2.5	424
Colorado	6,215	5,298	4,954	6,559	5.5	193
Hawaii	2,525	906	1,191	2,240	-11.3	231
Idaho	1,961	1,486	1,118	2,329	18.8	236
Montana[d]	845	601	631	815	-3.6	119
Nevada	3,971	2,956	2,801	4,126	3.9	243
New Mexico	1,962	1,977	1,532	2,407	22.7	177
Oregon	19,090	8,059	7,380	19,769	3.6	733
Utah	3,352	2,300	2,353	3,299	-1.6	205
Washington[b]	95	45	35	105	10.5	2
Wyoming	570	319	311	578	1.4	156

Note: See Notes, tables 6.3 and 6.65. For information on methodology and definitions of terms, see Appendix 15.

[a] Because of incomplete data, the population for some jurisdictions on Dec. 31, 2003 does not equal the population on Jan. 1, 2003, plus entries, minus exits.
[b] All data were estimated.
[c] Data for entries and exits were estimated for nonreporting agencies.
[d] Data do not include parolees in one or more of the following categories: absconder, out of State, or inactive.
[e] Not calculated by the Source.
[f] Data are for year ending Dec. 1, 2003.

Source: U.S. Department of Justice, Bureau of Justice Statistics, *Probation and Parole in the United States, 2003*, Bulletin NCJ 205336 (Washington, DC: U.S. Department of Justice, July 2004), p. 5, Table 5.

Table 6.67

Percent of State parole discharges successfully completing supervision

By method of release from prison, United States, 1990-99

	All discharges[a]	Type of release[b] First release	Type of release[b] Re-release	Method of release[b] Discretionary parole	Method of release[b] Mandatory parole
1990	44.6%	56.4%	14.6%	51.6%	23.8%
1991	46.8	60.7	17.1	52.6	24.9
1992	48.6	57.4	22.5	50.7	29.8
1993	46.9	65.4	23.0	54.8	33.5
1994	44.3	56.7	19.1	52.2	30.4
1995	44.3	63.4	18.0	54.3	28.0
1996	45.2	67.4	19.4	55.9	30.2
1997	43.4	63.4	18.7	55.8	30.8
1998	43.8	62.9	20.5	55.3	32.2
1999	41.9	63.5	21.1	54.1	33.1

[a]Data are from the U.S. Department of Justice, Bureau of Justice Statistics' Annual Parole Survey.
[b]Data are from the U.S. Department of Justice, Bureau of Justice Statistics' National Corrections Reporting Program.

Source: U.S. Department of Justice, Bureau of Justice Statistics, *Trends in State Parole, 1990-2000*, Special Report NCJ 184735 (Washington, DC: U.S. Department of Justice, October 2001), p. 11, Table 16.

Table 6.68

Offenders returning to Federal prison within 3 years of release

United States, 1986-97

Year of release	Number of first releases	First returns to prison within 3 years of release Number	First returns to prison within 3 years of release Percent of releases
Total	215,263	33,855	15.7%
1986	21,493	2,440	11.4
1987	22,889	2,942	12.9
1988	22,237	2,995	13.5
1989	22,221	3,225	14.5
1990	25,389	3,948	15.6
1991	24,685	4,291	17.4
1992	24,280	4,429	18.2
1993	25,224	4,593	18.2
1994	26,845	4,992	18.6

Note: These data are from the U.S. Department of Justice, Bureau of Justice Statistics' Federal Justice Statistics Program, which is a database constructed from source files provided by the Executive Office for United States Attorneys, the Administrative Office of the United States Courts, the United States Sentencing Commission, and the Federal Bureau of Prisons. This study counts the number of Federal prisoners who returned to Federal prison after first release from a U.S. district court commitment. "First returns to prison" include all first releases who were returned for any reason, including those who entered Federal prison as the result of a supervision violation or conviction for a new offense. Federal prisoners who, after first release from a Federal prison, subsequently entered a State prison or local jail were not included in this analysis. Federal offenders released during 1994 represent the final cohort included in the above data. By ending with the 1994 cohort, offenders could be tracked for at least 3 years following release.

Source: U.S. Department of Justice, Bureau of Justice Statistics, *Offenders Returning to Federal Prison, 1986-97*, Special Report NCJ 182991 (Washington, DC: U.S. Department of Justice, September 2000), p. 2.

Table 6.69

Offenders returning to Federal prison within 3 years of release

By demographic characteristics, conviction offense, and type of release, United States, 1986-97 (aggregate)

Characteristics and conviction offense	Number of first releases	Percent returned
Total[a]	215,263	15.7%
Sex		
Male	192,452	16.2
Female	22,382	11.6
Race		
White	168,733	13.4
Black	41,290	24.4
Other	5,240	21.6
Hispanic origin		
Non-Hispanic	81,093	13.7
Hispanic	133,741	17.0
Age		
Under 21 years	9,538	13.9
21 to 40 years	148,504	17.7
Over 40 years	56,783	11.0
Citizenship		
U.S. citizen	80,992	11.1
Not U.S. citizen	133,842	18.5
Conviction offense		
Violent	13,036	32.4
Robbery	8,880	36.3
Other violent	4,156	23.9
Property	48,428	16.6
Fraud	23,970	13.2
Other property	24,448	20.0
Drugs	72,728	13.4
Public-order	79,202	14.7
Weapons	9,203	24.2
Immigration	49,709	14.7
Other public-order	20,290	10.7
Supervision requirement		
Parole or supervised release	130,494	18.4
No supervision required	84,769	11.7

Note: See Note, table 6.68.

[a]Includes observations for which sex, race, Hispanic origin, age, citizenship, or conviction offense may have been missing.

Source: U.S. Department of Justice, Bureau of Justice Statistics, *Offenders Returning to Federal Prison, 1986-97*, Special Report NCJ 182991 (Washington, DC: U.S. Department of Justice, September 2000), pp. 3, 4; p. 5, Table 4. Table adapted by SOURCEBOOK staff.

Table 6.70

Federal supervised release terminations

By outcome and offense, United States, fiscal year 2001

Most serious conviction offense	Number of supervised release terminations	No violation	Drug use	Fugitive status	Other	New crime[b]	Administrative case closure
All offenses	24,966	64.2%	7.6%	4.9%	8.2%	12.8%	2.3%
Felonies	24,323	64.2	7.5	4.9	8.2	12.8	2.3
Violent offenses	1,828	43.6	11.5	8.7	13.8	19.5	2.9
Murder, nonnegligent manslaughter	79	39.2	6.3	12.7	22.8	15.2	3.8
Negligent manslaughter	4	B	B	B	B	B	B
Assault	228	47.8	6.6	10.5	14.0	20.2	0.9
Robbery	1,308	42.4	14.1	8.1	11.9	20.3	3.2
Sexual abuse[c]	163	48.5	2.5	10.4	22.1	14.1	2.5
Kidnaping	19	52.6	10.5	5.3	5.3	21.1	5.3
Threats against the President	27	37.0	3.7	3.7	29.6	22.2	3.7
Property offenses	6,653	70.6	5.8	4.5	8.0	9.3	1.9
Fraudulent offenses	5,480	73.5	5.0	4.0	7.2	8.4	1.8
Embezzlement	741	85.3	2.8	1.6	3.9	4.9	1.5
Fraud[d]	4,022	74.3	4.6	3.8	7.4	8.0	1.9
Forgery	137	64.2	10.2	8.8	7.3	8.8	0.7
Counterfeiting	580	55.0	9.3	7.4	10.0	15.9	2.4
Other offenses	1,173	56.8	9.5	6.6	11.7	13.2	2.1
Burglary	78	35.9	15.4	9.0	20.5	19.2	0.0
Larceny[e]	732	53.7	10.8	7.7	13.3	13.4	1.2
Motor vehicle theft	126	64.3	7.1	4.8	3.2	16.7	4.0
Arson and explosives	102	67.6	2.0	3.9	7.8	13.7	4.9
Transportation of stolen property	104	74.0	7.7	1.9	6.7	6.7	2.9
Other property offenses[f]	31	58.1	6.5	9.7	16.1	0.0	9.7
Drug offenses	11,073	65.4	8.1	4.3	7.1	12.4	2.6
Trafficking	9,894	64.8	8.1	4.4	7.2	12.7	2.7
Possession and other	1,179	70.2	7.7	3.5	6.6	10.2	1.8
Public-order offenses	2,109	77.5	3.8	3.7	6.3	6.9	1.9
Regulatory offenses	572	74.5	4.4	4.4	6.5	8.9	1.4
Agriculture	10	B	B	B	B	B	B
Antitrust	3	B	B	B	B	B	B
Food and drug	6	B	B	B	B	B	B
Transportation	20	85.0	0.0	10.0	0.0	5.0	0.0
Civil rights	49	79.6	2.0	0.0	4.1	12.2	2.0
Communications	21	85.7	9.5	0.0	0.0	4.8	0.0
Customs laws	34	67.6	17.6	8.8	2.9	2.9	0.0
Postal laws	24	54.2	4.2	8.3	20.8	8.3	4.2
Other regulatory offenses	405	74.8	3.2	4.4	7.2	8.9	1.5
Other offenses	1,537	78.7	3.6	3.4	6.2	6.1	2.1
Tax law violations including tax fraud	322	91.6	1.6	1.9	1.2	1.9	1.9
Bribery	65	92.3	3.1	0.0	3.1	1.5	0.0
Perjury, contempt, intimidation	109	76.1	7.3	0.9	7.3	7.3	0.9
National defense	7	B	B	B	B	B	B
Escape	149	41.6	10.1	19.5	12.8	14.8	1.3
Racketeering and extortion	516	82.0	3.5	1.0	6.2	5.0	2.3
Gambling offenses	50	84.0	4.0	0.0	2.0	6.0	4.0
Nonviolent sex offenses	171	73.1	0.0	4.1	9.9	8.8	4.1
Mail or transport of obscene material	25	88.0	0.0	0.0	4.0	4.0	4.0
Migratory birds	3	B	B	B	B	B	B
Other felonies	120	75.0	4.2	3.3	7.5	9.2	0.8
Weapons offenses	1,838	53.4	11.5	5.3	10.6	16.5	2.6
Immigration offenses	790	31.3	5.4	9.2	13.3	39.5	1.3
Misdemeanors[g]	643	63.3	10.4	4.8	8.4	11.7	1.4

Note: See Notes, tables 6.4 and 6.8. Total includes 32 felony offenders whose offense category could not be determined. For methodology and definitions of terms, see Appendix 11.

[a] Supervision terminated with incarceration or removal to inactive status for violation of supervision conditions other than charges for new offenses.
[b] Supervision terminated with incarceration or removal to inactive status after arrest for a "major" or "minor" offense.
[c] Includes only violent sex offenses.
[d] Excludes tax fraud.
[e] Excludes transportation of stolen property.
[f] Excludes fraudulent property offenses; includes destruction of property and trespass.
[g] Includes misdemeanors, petty offenses, and unknown offense level.

Source: U.S. Department of Justice, Bureau of Justice Statistics, *Compendium of Federal Justice Statistics, 2001*, NCJ 201627 (Washington, DC: U.S. Department of Justice, 2003), p. 97.

Table 6.71

Federal parole terminations

By outcome and offense, United States, fiscal year 2001

Most serious conviction offense	Number of parole terminations	No violation	Drug use	Fugitive status	Other	New crime[b]	Administrative case closure
All offenses	1,653	55.8%	10.1%	6.2%	8.8%	13.4%	5.7%
Felonies	1,649	55.8	10.1	6.2	8.7	13.4	5.8
Violent offenses	504	37.5	16.1	9.7	10.9	19.8	6.0
Murder, nonnegligent manslaughter	41	34.1	12.2	9.8	17.1	17.1	9.8
Assault	12	41.7	16.7	8.3	25.0	0.0	8.3
Robbery	403	37.0	17.1	9.7	9.9	20.3	6.0
Sexual abuse[c]	16	43.8	6.3	12.5	12.5	25.0	0.0
Kidnaping	32	43.8	12.5	9.4	9.4	21.9	3.1
Property offenses	185	71.4	4.3	4.3	5.4	9.2	5.4
Fraudulent offenses	101	76.2	3.0	3.0	2.0	8.9	6.9
Embezzlement	4	B	B	B	B	B	B
Fraud[d]	80	78.8	2.5	2.5	1.3	8.8	6.3
Forgery	9	B	B	B	B	B	B
Counterfeiting	8	B	B	B	B	B	B
Other offenses	84	65.5	6.0	6.0	9.5	9.5	3.6
Burglary	28	57.1	10.7	3.6	10.7	7.1	10.7
Larceny[e]	30	76.7	3.3	10.0	3.3	6.7	0.0
Motor vehicle theft	12	50.0	0.0	0.0	16.7	33.3	0.0
Arson and explosives	11	72.7	9.1	0.0	18.2	0.0	0.0
Transportation of stolen property	3	B	B	B	B	B	B
Drug offenses	786	64.4	8.3	5.0	7.1	9.4	5.9
Trafficking	715	63.6	8.7	4.9	6.9	9.8	6.2
Possession and other	71	71.8	4.2	5.6	9.9	5.6	2.8
Public-order offenses	110	60.0	5.5	1.8	12.7	13.6	6.4
Regulatory offenses	10	B	B	B	B	B	B
Other offenses	100	60.0	6.0	2.0	12.0	13.0	7.0
Tax law violations including tax fraud	14	92.9	0.0	0.0	7.1	0.0	0.0
Perjury, contempt, intimidation	6	B	B	B	B	B	B
National defense	1	B	B	B	B	B	B
Escape	13	46.2	15.4	0.0	15.4	23.1	0.0
Racketeering and extortion	47	59.6	6.4	2.1	12.8	12.8	6.4
Gambling offenses	1	B	B	B	B	B	B
Nonviolent sex offenses	10	B	B	B	B	B	B
Other felonies	8	B	B	B	B	B	B
Weapons offenses	62	41.9	11.3	6.5	14.5	22.6	3.2
Immigration offenses	2	B	B	B	B	B	B
Misdemeanors[f]	4	B	B	B	B	B	B

Note: See Notes, tables 6.4 and 6.8. For methodology and definitions of terms, see Appendix 11.

[a] Supervision terminated with incarceration or removal to inactive status for violation of supervision conditions other than charges for new offenses.
[b] Supervision terminated with incarceration or removal to inactive status after arrest for a "major" or "minor" offense.
[c] Includes only violent sex offenses.
[d] Excludes tax fraud.
[e] Excludes transportation of stolen property.
[f] Includes misdemeanors, petty offenses, and unknown offense level.

Source: U.S. Department of Justice, Bureau of Justice Statistics, *Compendium of Federal Justice Statistics, 2001*, NCJ 201627 (Washington, DC: U.S. Department of Justice, 2003), p. 99.

Table 6.72

State correctional facilities providing mental health screening and treatment

By region and State, June 30, 2000

Region and State	Total	Screen prisoners at intake	Conduct psychiatric assessments	Provide 24-hour mental health care	Provide therapy/ counseling	Distribute psychotropic medications	Help released prisoners obtain services	No services provided	No data reported
Total	1,558	1,055	990	776	1,073	1,115	1,006	125	39
Northeast	233	154	163	152	173	178	167	5	3
Connecticut	20	17	17	13	18	16	16	0	0
Maine	8	6	5	3	7	7	6	0	0
Massachusetts	25	20	17	15	21	20	20	0	2
New Hampshire	8	4	5	4	7	7	7	0	0
New Jersey	43	27	24	14	23	30	25	3	0
New York	69	31	52	66	53	43	40	0	0
Pennsylvania	44	36	29	32	29	40	39	2	0
Rhode Island	7	7	7	0	7	7	7	0	0
Vermont	9	6	7	5	8	8	7	0	1
Midwest	301	190	167	140	207	210	196	25	1
Illinois	48	30	30	32	31	31	34	4	0
Indiana	25	17	14	14	15	13	13	4	0
Iowa	30	11	12	12	10	21	23	2	1
Kansas	11	9	8	9	9	10	11	0	0
Michigan	70	39	43	35	40	31	32	10	0
Minnesota	9	1	1	1	8	9	8	0	0
Missouri	28	27	0	0	27	27	27	1	0
Nebraska	9	2	2	0	9	9	0	0	0
North Dakota	3	2	2	1	2	2	2	1	0
Ohio	34	34	34	26	33	32	29	0	0
South Dakota	4	2	3	1	3	4	3	0	0
Wisconsin	30	16	18	9	20	21	14	3	0
South	730	527	497	338	514	535	471	59	17
Alabama	35	16	21	13	21	26	11	3	1
Arkansas	15	12	12	12	12	12	12	3	0
Delaware	9	8	8	2	8	8	5	0	1
District of Columbia	6	2	2	3	2	3	4	2	0
Florida	106	98	90	1	88	88	85	8	0
Georgia	83	54	45	38	41	47	48	6	2
Kentucky	25	15	12	8	13	12	14	1	0
Louisiana	17	12	11	11	10	11	11	0	5
Maryland	26	12	14	13	18	18	22	2	0
Mississippi	28	12	11	5	8	9	2	9	1
North Carolina	80	49	55	31	68	73	61	0	2
Oklahoma	52	37	30	25	33	37	20	4	3
South Carolina	34	19	18	17	21	22	20	5	0
Tennessee	15	14	14	15	15	15	14	0	0
Texas	127	117	114	111	114	118	109	2	2
Virginia	61	44	34	31	34	30	29	14	0
West Virginia	11	6	6	2	8	6	4	0	0
West	294	184	163	146	179	192	172	36	18
Alaska	24	16	10	6	12	19	18	1	1
Arizona	16	15	13	13	14	14	12	0	1
California	86	50	35	28	41	36	38	13	12
Colorado	47	16	30	32	34	38	35	0	3
Hawaii	10	10	9	9	10	9	1	0	0
Idaho	13	7	5	6	5	10	7	1	0
Montana	8	6	5	4	6	6	4	0	1
Nevada	20	11	10	7	10	9	9	7	0
New Mexico	10	10	10	8	10	9	8	0	0
Oregon	13	13	10	7	9	12	11	0	0
Utah	8	6	5	4	5	6	7	0	0
Washington	30	17	15	17	17	17	15	13	0
Wyoming	9	7	6	5	6	7	7	1	0

Note: These data are from the 2000 Census of State and Federal Adult Correctional Facilities, the sixth in a series of facility censuses, sponsored by the U.S. Department of Justice, Bureau of Justice Statistics. The universe of facilities was developed using the 1995 census and updated to identify new facilities and facilities that had closed since June 30, 1995. Facilities identified for the 2000 census include 84 Federal facilities, 1,295 State facilities, 22 facilities under State and local authority, 3 facilities operated by the District of Columbia, and 264 private facilities, in operation on June 30, 2000. Adult correctional facilities include: prisons and penitentiaries; boot camps; prison farms; reception, diagnostic, and classification centers; road camps; forestry and conservation camps; youthful offender facilities (except those in California); vocational training facilities; prison hospitals; drug and alcohol treatment facilities; and State-operated local detention facilities (in Alaska, Connecticut, Delaware, Hawaii, Rhode Island, and Vermont). Data were collected from all facilities resulting in a response rate of 100%.

The data presented are from 1,295 State-operated facilities, 22 facilities under joint State and local authority, 3 facilities operated by the District of Columbia, and 238 private facilities with more than 50% of their prisoners held for State authorities. All 84 Federal facilities and 26 privately operated facilities holding at least 50% of their prisoners for Federal authorities were excluded because data for prisoners receiving mental health treatment in these facilities were not available.

Source: U.S. Department of Justice, Bureau of Justice Statistics, **Mental Health Treatment in State Prisons, 2000**, Special Report NCJ 188215 (Washington, DC: U.S. Department of Justice, July 2001), p. 5.

Table 6.73

Prisoners receiving mental health treatment in State correctional facilities

By region and State, June 30, 2000

Region and State	24-hour care Number	24-hour care Percent	Therapy/counseling Number	Therapy/counseling Percent	Psychotropic medications Number	Psychotropic medications Percent	In all facilities	In facilities reporting data[a]	Percent covered
Total	17,354	1.6%	137,385	12.8%	105,336	9.7%	1,178,807	1,088,023	92.3%
Northeast	1,715	1.0	20,099	12.6	14,840	9.2	171,723	160,938	93.7
Connecticut	341	2.3	2,596	17.8	1,659	11.4	16,984	14,577	85.8
Maine	26	2.8	538	33.0	367	23.5	1,629	1,562	95.9
Massachusetts	309	3.0	2,271	21.8	1,331	12.7	10,500	10,500	100.0
New Hampshire	92	4.9	387	20.7	228	12.2	2,277	1,872	82.2
New Jersey	467	1.8	2,308	9.2	2,541	9.4	27,118	27,118	100.0
New York	262	0.4	6,888	10.2	4,539	6.7	71,662	67,595	94.3
Pennsylvania	178	0.5	4,761	13.0	3,891	10.6	36,895	36,710	99.5
Rhode Island	10	0.3	NA	NA	NA	NA	3,347	0	X
Vermont	30	3.0	350	34.9	284	28.3	1,311	1,004	76.6
Midwest	3,843	1.7	32,461	14.3	21,527	9.3	233,993	230,640	98.6
Illinois	672	1.5	4,374	9.9	2,954	6.7	44,150	44,000	99.7
Indiana	354	1.9	4,281	23.5	2,392	13.1	18,195	18,195	100.0
Iowa	134	1.5	1,293	14.3	1,122	12.4	9,086	9,031	99.4
Kansas	218	2.4	2,075	23.1	1,518	16.9	8,992	8,992	100.0
Michigan	760	1.7	4,678	10.5	2,161	4.8	47,639	45,183	94.8
Minnesota	32	0.4	1,222	16.4	1,312	17.6	7,451	7,451	100.0
Missouri	12	(b)	3,331	11.9	1,054	3.8	27,963	27,963	100.0
Nebraska	84	2.4	982	28.0	691	19.7	3,508	3,508	100.0
North Dakota	NA	NA	NA	NA	247	39.3	992	628	63.3
Ohio	1,042	2.2	7,165	15.0	4,921	10.3	47,915	47,915	100.0
South Dakota	43	1.7	577	22.3	420	16.2	2,591	2,591	100.0
Wisconsin	492	3.2	2,483	20.4	2,735	18.0	15,511	15,183	97.9
South	7,106	1.6	54,119	11.9	41,280	9.1	510,287	452,197	88.6
Alabama	556	2.5	1,768	8.4	1,078	4.9	22,395	22,169	99.0
Arkansas	82	0.8	1,117	10.7	424	4.1	10,465	10,465	100.0
Delaware	2	(b)	801	14.5	739	12.5	6,023	5,910	98.1
District of Columbia	38	1.6	503	21.1	213	8.9	2,574	2,385	92.7
Florida	191	0.3	10,689	14.9	7,764	10.8	71,616	71,616	100.0
Georgia	2,070	4.8	5,302	12.1	4,659	10.6	44,235	43,958	99.4
Kentucky	126	1.0	2,626	21.9	2,296	18.5	12,378	12,378	100.0
Louisiana	201	1.2	5,062	27.0	1,626	8.7	19,167	18,757	97.9
Maryland	253	1.3	2,829	14.9	2,344	12.4	22,821	18,933	83.0
Mississippi	580	3.9	1,607	10.9	1,935	13.1	14,823	14,748	99.5
North Carolina	715	2.5	3,747	13.2	2,783	10.2	30,708	27,406	89.2
Oklahoma	187	0.8	3,349	14.6	2,716	11.8	23,858	23,013	96.5
South Carolina	39	0.2	1,122	5.3	28	1.1	21,277	2,627	12.3
Tennessee	399	2.2	430	6.5	1,811	9.9	18,368	18,368	100.0
Texas	1,638	1.5	9,599	7.7	7,838	6.2	155,099	126,084	81.3
Virginia	0	X	3,215	10.6	2,540	8.4	31,412	30,368	96.7
West Virginia	29	1.0	353	12.6	486	16.1	3,068	3,012	98.2
West	4,690	1.9	30,706	13.5	27,689	11.3	262,804	244,248	92.9
Alaska	93	2.9	286	10.8	238	9.0	3,248	2,657	81.8
Arizona	378	1.4	3,874	14.7	2,194	8.3	27,005	26,360	97.6
California	3,144	2.1	18,863	12.5	15,831	10.5	160,727	150,884	93.9
Colorado	274	1.8	2,213	14.9	2,180	14.2	15,655	15,339	98.0
Hawaii	120	3.2	100	2.7	746	19.8	3,761	3,761	100.0
Idaho	1	(b)	547	14.3	728	19.1	3,961	3,813	96.3
Montana	13	0.6	268	12.0	478	21.4	2,368	2,233	94.3
Nevada	54	0.8	599	10.6	529	7.7	9,296	6,914	74.4
New Mexico	138	2.7	803	15.6	427	8.5	5,158	5,028	97.5
Oregon	65	0.8	2,032	21.8	1,796	19.6	9,933	9,181	92.4
Utah	22	1.8	306	29.0	239	19.8	4,824	1,210	25.1
Washington	381	2.6	NA	NA	1,925	13.1	14,682	14,682	100.0
Wyoming	7	0.3	815	37.3	378	17.3	2,186	2,186	100.0

Note: See Note, table 6.72. Percents are based on the number of prisoners held in facilities reporting data. Totals vary by item: 1,073,455 for 24-hour care, 1,069,605 for therapy/counseling, and 1,088,023 for use of medications.

Source: U.S. Department of Justice, Bureau of Justice Statistics, **Mental Health Treatment in State Prisons, 2000**, Special Report NCJ 188215 (Washington, DC: U.S. Department of Justice, July 2001), p. 6.

[a] Based on facilities reporting use of psychotropic medications.
[b] Less than 0.05%.

Table 6.74

State and Federal prisoners known to be positive for the human immunodeficiency virus (HIV) and confirmed AIDS cases

By region and jurisdiction, 1995-2001

Region and jurisdiction	1995	1996	1997	1998	1999	2000	2001	1995	2001	Confirmed AIDS cases for 2001
United States, total	24,256	23,881	23,886	25,680	25,807	25,333	24,147	2.3%	1.9%	5,754[b]
Federal	822	947	1,030	1,066	1,156	1,302	1,520	0.9	1.2	526
State	23,434	22,934	22,856	24,614	24,651	24,031	22,627	2.4	2.0	5,228
Northeast	12,262	11,090	10,384	10,613	10,030	8,721	8,136	7.8	4.9	1,978
Connecticut	755	690	798	634	632	593	604	5.1	3.5	259
Maine	4	4	NA	11	9	11	15	0.3	0.9	6
Massachusetts	409	393	392	395	346	313	307	3.9	3.0	119
New Hampshire	31	18	17	17	17	23	17	1.5	0.7	3
New Jersey	847	705	867	924	869	771	804	3.7	3.4	183
New York	9,500	8,500	7,500	7,500	7,000	6,000	5,500	13.9	8.1	1,160
Pennsylvania	590	652	697	977	939	900	735	1.8	2.0	199
Rhode Island	126	125	107	140	203	90	148	4.4	4.4	46
Vermont	0	3	6	15	15	20	6	X	0.4	3
Midwest	1,667	1,874	1,849	2,115	2,171	2,252	2,135	0.9	1.0	401
Illinois	583	634	655	694	635	619	593	1.5	1.3	159
Iowa	20	24	34	18	30	27	27	0.3	0.3	8
Kansas	24	16	4	38	41	49	41	0.3	0.5	7
Michigan	379	528	419	546	578	585	584	0.9	1.2	NA
Minnesota	46	24	31	26	32	42	33	1.0	0.5	1
Missouri	173	190	227	235	290	267	262	0.9	0.9	58
Nebraska	19	17	22	23	20	18	24	0.6	0.6	2
North Dakota	2	3	7	3	2	2	4	0.3	0.4	0
Ohio	346	343	365	392	391	478	398	0.8	0.9	121
South Dakota	3	4	1	4	5	4	5	0.2	0.2	2
Wisconsin	72	91	84	136	147	161	164	0.6	0.9	43
South	7,870	8,162	8,639	9,705	10,243	10,767	10,392	1.9	2.2	2,446
Alabama	222	234	212	273	283	419	302	1.1	1.2	26
Arkansas	83	77	86	94	99	101	108	1.0	0.9	23
Delaware	122	NA	248	180	170	127	143	2.5	2.1	NA
District of Columbia[c]	NA	NA	175	268	359	126	X	NA	X	X
Florida	2,193	2,152	2,325	2,461	2,633	2,640	2,602	3.4	3.6	677
Georgia	858	814	861	870	846	938	1,150	2.5	2.5	NA
Kentucky	41	55	55	81	122	124	105	0.4	1.1	9
Louisiana	314	347	397	436	381	500	514	1.8	2.6	NA
Maryland	724	832	766	686	820	998	830	3.4	3.5	213
Mississippi	138	135	189	172	192	230	234	1.4	2.0	60
North Carolina	526	589	519	554	554	588	573	1.9	1.8	185
Oklahoma	115	108	107	NA	122	145	130	0.8	0.9	15
South Carolina	380	422	432	607	617	560	559	2.0	2.6	233
Tennessee	120	131	131	168	185	215	231	0.9	1.7	66
Texas	1,890	1,876	2,126	2,393	2,520	2,492	2,388	1.5	1.8	859
Virginia	134	383	NA	453	330	550	507	0.6	1.7	69
West Virginia	10	7	10	9	10	14	16	0.4	0.5	11
West	1,635	1,808	1,984	2,181	2,207	2,291	1,964	0.8	0.8	403
Alaska	5	10	10	16	16	NA	16	0.2	0.5	1
Arizona	140	205	105	118	144	110	122	0.7	0.4	15
California	1,042	1,136	1,328	1,567	1,570	1,638	1,305	0.8	0.8	229
Colorado	93	94	110	124	131	146	173	1.0	1.2	39
Hawaii	12	23	16	20	30	19	13	0.4	0.3	0
Idaho	11	17	10	13	15	14	14	0.4	0.4	4
Montana	4	6	8	10	10	11	11	0.2	0.6	0
Nevada	147	133	139	121	125	151	127	1.9	1.4	24
New Mexico	24	11	23	31	26	28	27	0.6	0.5	NA
Oregon	29	39	54	35	23	41	30	0.4	0.3	5
Utah	31	31	60	32	34	37	34	0.8	0.8	7
Washington	92	99	119	91	75	90	88	0.8	0.6	79
Wyoming	5	4	2	3	8	6	4	0.4	0.4	0

Columns 2-8: Total known to be HIV positive. Columns 9-10: HIV/AIDS cases as a percent of total custody population[a].

Note: These data were collected by the U.S. Department of Justice, Bureau of Justice Statistics through the National Prisoner Statistics (NPS) program. The NPS program provides yearend data for the prisoner populations of the 50 States, the District of Columbia, and the Federal Bureau of Prisons. These data represent the custody population, which includes only those prisoners housed in a jurisdiction's facilities. Indiana did not report the number of HIV/AIDS cases for 1995-2001. Some data have been revised by the Source and may differ from previous editions of SOURCEBOOK.

[a]Percentages are based on custody counts, except for New Mexico. In 2000 and 2001, New Mexico's percentages are based on its yearend jurisdiction count.

[b]5,754 confirmed AIDS cases are based on reported data. The estimated total number of confirmed AIDS cases is 6,286; this includes estimates for the following States not reporting these data for 2001: Delaware, Georgia, Louisiana, Michigan, and New Mexico. Estimates were based on the most recent data available.

[c]At yearend 2001, responsibility for housing District of Columbia sentenced prisoners was transferred to the Federal Bureau of Prisons.

Source: U.S. Department of Justice, Bureau of Justice Statistics, *HIV in Prisons 1997*, Bulletin NCJ 178284, p. 2; *2001*, Bulletin NCJ 202293, pp. 2, 4 (Washington, DC: U.S. Department of Justice); and U.S. Department of Justice, Bureau of Justice Statistics, *HIV in Prisons and Jails, 1999*, Bulletin NCJ 187456 (Washington, DC: U.S. Department of Justice, July 2001), pp. 2, 3. Table adapted by SOURCEBOOK staff.

Table 6.75

State and Federal prisoners known to be positive for the human immunodeficiency virus (HIV)

By sex, region, and jurisdiction, 2001

	Male HIV cases		Female HIV cases	
Region and jurisdiction	Number	Percent of total custody population	Number	Percent of total custody population
Total reported	21,268	1.9%	2,265	2.9%
Total estimated[a]	21,815	X	2,332	X
Federal	1,400	1.2	120	1.3
State	19,868	2.0	2,145	3.2
Northeast	7,361	4.7	775	9.1
Connecticut	500	3.1	104	8.4
Maine	15	0.9	0	X
Massachusetts	267	2.8	40	5.7
New Hampshire	15	0.7	2	1.3
New Jersey	713	3.2	91	7.1
New York	5,030	7.8	470	14.9
Pennsylvania	691	1.9	44	2.7
Rhode Island	124	3.9	24	12.1
Vermont	6	0.5	0	X
Midwest	1,947	1.0	147	1.2
Illinois	550	1.3	43	1.6
Iowa	23	0.3	4	0.6
Michigan	541	1.2	43	2.0
Minnesota	29	0.5	4	1.2
Missouri	249	0.9	13	0.6
Nebraska	22	0.6	2	0.6
North Dakota	4	0.4	0	X
Ohio	371	0.9	27	1.0
South Dakota	5	0.2	0	X
Wisconsin	153	1.0	11	0.9
South	8,701	2.1	1,118	3.8
Alabama	264	1.1	38	2.3
Arkansas	99	0.9	9	1.2
Delaware	116	1.8	27	4.7
Florida	2,203	3.2	399	9.3
Georgia	1,004	2.3	146	5.2
Kentucky	100	1.1	5	0.8
Louisiana	466	2.5	48	4.6
Maryland	733	3.3	97	8.1
Mississippi	207	2.0	27	2.0
Oklahoma	125	0.9	5	0.4
South Carolina	531	2.6	28	1.9
Tennessee	208	1.6	23	2.6
Texas	2,169	1.8	219	2.4
Virginia	461	1.7	46	2.2
West Virginia	15	0.5	1	0.5
West	1,859	0.8	105	0.6
Alaska	14	0.5	2	0.7
Arizona	104	0.4	18	0.8
California	1,288	0.9	17	0.2
Colorado	154	1.1	19	1.4
Hawaii	13	0.4	0	X
Idaho	12	0.3	2	0.7
Montana	10	0.6	1	0.7
Nevada	93	1.0	34	12.0
New Mexico	26	0.5	1	0.2
Oregon	28	0.3	2	0.3
Utah	30	0.8	4	1.7
Washington	83	0.6	5	0.5
Wyoming	4	0.4	0	X

Note: See Note, table 6.74. At yearend 2001, responsibility for housing District of Columbia sentenced prisoners was transferred to the Federal Bureau of Prisons.

[a]Includes estimates of the number of prisoners with HIV/AIDS by sex for Kansas and North Carolina. Estimates were based on the most recent data available by sex.

Source: U.S. Department of Justice, Bureau of Justice Statistics, *HIV in Prisons, 2001*, Bulletin NCJ 202293 (Washington, DC: U.S. Department of Justice, January 2004), p. 3.

Table 6.76

Number and rate (per 100,000 prisoners) of deaths among State and Federal prisoners

By cause of death, United States, 2001

	Deaths			
	State		Federal	
Cause of death	Number[a]	Rate	Number	Rate
Total	3,008	240	303	198
Natural causes other than AIDS	2,258	180	247	162
AIDS	256	20	22	14
Suicide	173	14	18	12
Accident	46	4	6	4
Execution	58	5	2	1
By another person	49	4	8	5
Other/unspecified	91	7	0	X

Note: See Note, table 6.74.

[a]Detail does not add to total because Louisiana reported 77 deaths but did not provide a breakdown.

Source: U.S. Department of Justice, Bureau of Justice Statistics, *HIV in Prisons, 2001*, Bulletin NCJ 202293 (Washington, DC: U.S. Department of Justice, January 2004), p. 5, Table 4; p. 6, Table 5. Table adapted by SOURCEBOOK staff.

Table 6.77

Number and rate (per 100,000 prisoners) of AIDS-related deaths among State and Federal prisoners

United States, 1991-2001

	AIDS-related deaths			
	State		Federal	
	Number	Rate	Number	Rate
1991	520	71	NA	NA
1992	648	83	NA	NA
1993	761	89	NA	NA
1994	955	104	NA	NA
1995	1,010	100	NA	NA
1996	907	90	NA	NA
1997	538	48	NA	NA
1998	350	30	NA	NA
1999	242	20	NA	NA
2000	185	15	21	14
2001	256	20	22	14

Note: See Note, table 6.74.

Source: U.S. Department of Justice, Bureau of Justice Statistics, *HIV in Prisons, 2001*, Bulletin NCJ 202293 (Washington, DC: U.S. Department of Justice, January 2004), p. 6. Table adapted by SOURCEBOOK staff.

Table 6.78

Number and rate (per 100,000 prisoners) of deaths and AIDS-related deaths among State prisoners

By region and State, 1995 and 2001

	Deaths from all causes				AIDS-related deaths			
	1995		2001		1995		2001	
Region and State	Number	Rate	Number	Rate	Number	Rate	Number	Rate
Total	3,133	311	3,008	240	1,010	100	256	20
Northeast	740	468	452	261	402	254	68	39
Connecticut	42	280	30	159	24	160	5	26
Maine	0	X	8	473	0	X	0	X
Massachusetts	34	296	31	289	14	122	0	X
New Hampshire	2	97	2	86	2	97	0	X
New Jersey	137	535	71	253	66	258	19	68
New York	396	578	179	259	258	376	28	40
Pennsylvania	122	409	124	334	38	127	15	40
Rhode Island	7	223	3	95	0	X	1	32
Vermont	0	X	4	224	0	X	0	X
Midwest	481	252	533	222	63	42	21	9
Illinois	103	273	86	188	31	82	11	24
Indiana	44	280	50	243	1	6	2	10
Iowa	9	158	9	111	0	X	0	X
Kansas	13	188	21	246	0	X	0	X
Michigan	104	251	114	236	NA	NA	5	10
Minnesota	9	189	13	200	1	21	0	X
Missouri	53	280	58	206	4	21	2	7
Nebraska	13	464	8	203	0	X	0	X
North Dakota	1	164	3	278	0	X	0	X
Ohio	114	262	119	260	23	53	0	X
South Dakota	5	275	4	150	0	X	0	X
Wisconsin	13	122	48	229	3	28	1	5
South	1,455	325	1,472	261	432	105	134	29
Alabama	88	438	85	312	20	100	8	29
Arkansas	26	286	48	389	1	11	2	16
Delaware	9	194	18	253	0	X	7	98
District of Columbia	7	67	9	167	NA	NA	1	19
Florida	254	410	183	254	150	242	39	54
Georgia	127	372	100	220	50	147	15	33
Kentucky	29	243	40	260	2	17	0	X
Louisiana	68	270	77	217	NA	NA	NA	NA
Maryland	54	252	70	292	25	117	11	46
Mississippi	42	337	42	203	5	40	2	10
North Carolina	69	257	73	234	28	104	NA	NA
Oklahoma	66	375	77	333	4	23	1	4
South Carolina	63	323	74	332	34	175	5	22
Tennessee	64	429	59	255	12	80	2	9
Texas	399	314	426	259	74	58	32	19
Virginia	83	304	73	240	27	99	9	30
West Virginia	7	287	18	436	0	X	0	X
West	457	217	551	200	113	54	33	12
Alaska	5	154	10	238	0	X	0	X
Arizona	58	277	65	240	0	X	2	7
California	262	199	289	176	91	69	22	13
Colorado	25	232	47	275	6	56	7	41
Hawaii	11	307	7	129	1	28	0	X
Idaho	1	31	18	316	0	X	0	X
Montana	11	581	8	246	0	X	0	X
Nevada	25	334	28	272	6	80	1	10
New Mexico	8	194	12	227	0	X	0	X
Oregon	21	280	23	208	5	67	1	9
Utah	6	183	5	92	0	X	0	X
Washington	23	202	34	223	4	35	0	X
Wyoming	1	76	5	298	0	X	0	X

Note: See Note, table 6.74.

Source: U.S. Department of Justice, Bureau of Justice Statistics, *HIV in Prisons, 2000*, Bulletin NCJ 196023, p. 8; *2001*, Bulletin NCJ 202293, p. 6 (Washington, DC: U.S. Department of Justice).

Table 6.79

Number of murders and nonnegligent manslaughters, persons under death sentence, executions, and other death sentence dispositions

United States, 1972-2003

Year	Murders and nonnegligent manslaughters	Persons under death sentence	Executions under civil authority	Dispositions other than execution[a]
1972	18,670	334	0	391
1973	19,640	134	0	242
1974	20,710	244	0	57
1975	20,510	488	0	78
1976	18,780	420	0	317
1977	19,120	423	1	155
1978	19,560	482	0	150
1979	21,460	593	2	59
1980	23,040	691	0	100
1981	22,520	856	1	79
1982	21,010	1,050	2	68
1983	19,308	1,209	5	111
1984	18,692	1,405	21	63
1985	18,976	1,591	18	84
1986	20,613	1,781	18	73
1987	20,096	1,984	25	90
1988	20,675	2,124	11	128
1989	21,500	2,250	16	102
1990	23,438	2,356	23	108
1991	24,703	2,482	14	116
1992	23,760	2,575	31	124
1993	24,526	2,716	38	108
1994	23,326	2,890	31	112
1995	21,606	3,054	56	105
1996	19,645	3,219	45	99
1997	18,208	3,335	74	89
1998	16,974	3,465	68	93
1999	15,522	3,540	98	112
2000	15,586	3,601	85	76
2001	16,037	3,577	66	109
2002	16,229	3,562	71	108
2003	16,503	3,374	65	267

Note: Data for murders and nonnegligent manslaughters are from the U.S. Department of Justice, Federal Bureau of Investigation's Uniform Crime Reports. Data for persons under sentence of death and death sentence dispositions are from the U.S. Department of Justice, Bureau of Justice Statistics. These data exclude persons held under Armed Forces jurisdiction with a military death sentence for murder. Some data have been revised by the Source and will differ from previous editions of SOURCEBOOK.

In 1972, the Supreme Court ruled that capital punishment, as administered at that time in the United States, was unconstitutional (*Furman v. Georgia*, 408 U.S. 238 (1972)), thus halting further executions. In 1976, the Supreme Court upheld newly enacted death penalty laws in three related decisions (see *Gregg v. Georgia*, 428 U.S. 153 (1976); *Proffitt v. Florida*, 428 U.S. 242 (1976); and *Jurek v. Texas*, 428 U.S. 262 (1976)), thus paving the way for lifting the moratorium on executions in the United States. Executions resumed in January 1977.

[a]Dispositions of death sentences other than by execution include dismissal of indictment, reversal of judgment, commutation, resentencing, order of a new trial, and death.

Source: U.S. Department of Justice, Federal Bureau of Investigation, *Crime in the United States, 1991*, p. 58; *2003*, p. 70 (Washington, DC: USGPO); U.S. Department of Justice, Bureau of Justice Statistics, *Capital Punishment 1982*, National Prisoner Statistics report NCJ-91533, p. 18; *Capital Punishment 1984*, Bulletin NCJ-98399, p. 5; *1996*, Bulletin NCJ-167031, p. 6; *1997*, Bulletin NCJ-172881, p. 6; *1998*, Bulletin NCJ 179012, p. 6; *1999*, Bulletin NCJ 184795, p. 6; *2000*, Bulletin NCJ 190598, p. 6; *2001*, Bulletin NCJ 197020, p. 6; *2002*, Bulletin NCJ 201848, p. 5; *2003*, Bulletin NCJ 206627, p. 5 (Washington, DC: U.S. Department of Justice); U.S. Department of Justice, Bureau of Justice Statistics, *Correctional Populations in the United States, 1985*, NCJ-103957, Table 7.2; *1986*, NCJ-111611, Table 7.2; *1987*, NCJ-118762, Table 7.2; *1988*, NCJ-124280, Table 7.2; *1989*, NCJ-130445, Table 7.2; *1990*, NCJ-135946, Table 7.2; *1991*, NCJ-142729, Table 7.2; *1992*, NCJ-146413, Table 7.2; *1993*, NCJ-156241, Table 7.2; *1994*, NCJ-160091, Table 7.2; *1995*, NCJ-163916, Table 7.2 (Washington, DC: U.S. Department of Justice); and data provided by the U.S. Department of Justice, Bureau of Justice Statistics. Table adapted by SOURCEBOOK staff.

Table 6.80

Prisoners under sentence of death

By race, ethnicity, and jurisdiction, on Apr. 1, 2004

Jurisdiction	Total	White	Black	Hispanic	Native American	Asian
United States[a]	3,487[b]	1,591	1,462	354	39	40
Federal	31	9	21	0	1	0
U.S. military	7	1	5	0	0	1
Alabama	197	103	91	2	0	1
Arizona	130	93	14	19	3	1
Arkansas	39	16	22	1	0	0
California	635	248	228	126	14	19
Colorado	3	0	2	1	0	0
Connecticut	8	4	3	1	0	0
Delaware	19	9	7	3	0	0
Florida	381	219	127	33	1	1
Georgia	114	56	54	3	0	1
Idaho	20	20	0	0	0	0
Illinois	10	5	4	1	0	0
Indiana	39	27	12	0	0	0
Kansas	7	5	2	0	0	0
Kentucky	36	28	7	1	0	0
Louisiana	92	27	62	2	0	1
Maryland	11	4	7	0	0	0
Mississippi	70	32	37	0	0	1
Missouri	58	34	24	0	0	0
Montana	4	4	0	0	0	0
Nebraska	7	5	1	1	0	0
Nevada	87	42	35	9	0	1
New Hampshire	0	X	X	X	X	X
New Jersey	16	9	7	0	0	0
New Mexico	2	2	0	0	0	0
New York	4	2	2	0	0	0
North Carolina	203	74	115	4	8	2
Ohio	210	100	104	2	2	2
Oklahoma	102	54	38	3	7	0
Oregon[b]	31	25	2	2	1	0
Pennsylvania	235	69	146	18	0	2
South Carolina	75	40	35	0	0	0
South Dakota	4	4	0	0	0	0
Tennessee	104	58	41	1	2	2
Texas	454	143	186	120	0	5
Utah	10	6	2	1	1	0
Virginia	26	12	14	0	0	0
Washington	11	6	5	0	0	0
Wyoming	2	2	0	0	0	0

Note: The NAACP Legal Defense and Educational Fund, Inc. collects data on persons on death row. As of Apr. 1, 2004, 38 States, the Federal Government, and the United States military had capital punishment laws; 37 States, the Federal Government, and the United States military had at least 1 prisoner under sentence of death.

[a]Detail will not add to total because prisoners sentenced to death in more than one State are listed in the respective State totals, but each prisoner is counted only once for the national total.

[b]Total includes one prisoner in Oregon whose race/ethnicity was unknown.

Source: NAACP Legal Defense and Educational Fund, Inc., "Death Row U.S.A.: Spring 2004," New York: NAACP Legal Defense and Educational Fund, Inc. 2004. (Mimeographed.) Pp. 1, 30, 31. Table adapted by SOURCEBOOK staff.

Table 6.81
Prisoners under sentence of death

By demographic characteristics, prior felony conviction history, and legal status, United States, on Dec. 31, 1996-2003[a]

	Percent of prisoners							
	1996	1997	1998	1999	2000	2001	2002	2003
<u>Sex</u>								
Male	98.5%	98.7%	98.6%	98.6%	98.5%	98.6%	98.6%	98.6%
Female	1.5	1.3	1.4	1.4	1.5	1.4	1.4	1.4
<u>Race</u>								
White	56.5	56.3	55.2	55.2	55.4	55.0	54.3	55.7
Black	41.9	42.2	43.0	42.9	42.7	42.9	43.7	42.0
Other	1.6	1.6	1.7	1.8	1.9	2.1	2.0	2.3
<u>Hispanic origin</u>								
Hispanic	8.8	9.2	10.0	10.2	10.6	11.2	11.5	12.5
Non-Hispanic	91.2	90.8	90.0	89.8	89.4	88.8	88.5	87.5
<u>Age</u>[b]								
17 years and younger	(c)	0	0	0	0	0	0	0
18 to 19 years	0.5	0.4	0.4	0.5	0.3	0.1	0.1	(c)
20 to 24 years	8.7	8.2	7.7	7.1	6.6	5.4	4.3	3.9
25 to 29 years	14.9	14.9	15.0	14.6	13.6	13.2	12.7	11.9
30 to 34 years	18.5	17.3	16.9	16.8	17.1	17.5	17.0	16.7
35 to 39 years	21.8	21.8	20.6	20.0	19.1	17.9	17.4	17.2
40 to 44 years	14.9	15.6	16.7	17.0	18.2	18.8	19.6	18.2
45 to 49 years	10.6	10.6	10.2	10.5	10.9	11.8	12.7	14.1
50 to 54 years	5.7	6.5	7.5	7.9	8.0	8.5	8.5	8.8
55 to 59 years	2.5	2.6	2.9	3.2	3.5	4.1	4.9	5.8
60 years and older	1.8	1.9	2.1	2.3	2.7	2.6	2.8	3.3
<u>Education</u>								
Grade 8 or less	14.4	14.2	14.3	13.9	14.4	14.5	14.7	15.2
Grades 9 to 11	37.5	37.6	37.6	37.7	37.3	37.2	37.1	37.1
High school graduate/GED	37.8	38.0	38.0	38.2	38.2	38.4	38.5	38.3
Any college	10.2	10.1	10.1	10.1	10.1	9.9	9.7	9.3
<u>Marital status</u>								
Married	24.9	24.5	24.0	22.9	22.6	22.1	22.1	22.5
Divorced or separated	21.3	21.3	20.8	21.2	21.0	21.0	20.8	20.7
Widowed	2.7	2.6	2.7	2.8	2.8	2.6	2.8	2.8
Never married	51.1	51.5	52.5	53.0	53.6	54.3	54.3	54.0
<u>Prior felony conviction history</u>								
Prior felony conviction	65.7	65.3	65.0	64.1	64.0	64.4	64.3	64.5
No prior felony conviction	34.3	34.7	35.0	35.9	36.0	35.6	35.7	35.5
<u>Prior homicide conviction history</u>								
Prior homicide conviction	8.6	8.6	8.6	8.4	8.1	8.0	8.0	8.2
No prior homicide conviction	91.4	91.4	91.4	91.6	91.9	92.0	92.0	91.8
<u>Legal status at time of capital offense</u>								
Charges pending	7.3	7.6	7.2	7.4	7.1	7.3	7.5	7.9
Probation	10.0	10.1	9.9	10.0	10.1	10.3	10.5	10.8
Parole	20.0	19.5	18.1	17.9	17.6	17.5	17.3	16.5
Prison escapee	1.4	1.3	1.3	1.3	1.2	1.1	1.2	1.4
Incarcerated	2.4	2.6	2.9	2.8	2.7	3.0	3.2	3.1
Other status	1.1	1.0	0.9	0.7	0.6	0.5	0.5	0.6
None	57.7	58.0	59.7	60.0	60.6	60.2	59.8	59.7

Note: Thirty-eight States and the Federal Government had death penalty statutes in effect at yearend 1996-2003. Percents are based on those cases for which data were reported. The U.S. military also has a death penalty provision, but the Bureau of Justice Statistics does not collect data for persons under military death sentence.

[a]Percents may not add to 100 because of rounding.
[b]The youngest person under sentence of death in 1996 was a black male in Nevada born in May 1979 and sentenced to death in June 1996; in 1997, a black male in Alabama born in November 1979 and sentenced to death in October 1997; in 1998, a black male in Alabama born in July 1980 and sentenced to death in December 1998; in 1999, a black male in Texas born in December 1981 and sentenced to death in November 1999; in 2000, a white male in Arizona born in April 1982 and sentenced to death in October 2000; in 2001, a black male in North Carolina born in December 1982 and sentenced to death in November 2001; in 2002 and 2003, a white male in Texas, born in April 1984 and sentenced to death in August 2002. The oldest person under sentence of death during the years 1996 to 2003 was a white male in Arizona born in September 1915 and sentenced to death in June 1983.
[c]Less than 0.1%.

Source: U.S. Department of Justice, Bureau of Justice Statistics, *Capital Punishment 1996*, Bulletin NCJ-167031, p. 8, Table 7; p. 9; p. 10, Table 9; *1997*, Bulletin NCJ-172881, p. 8, Table 7; p. 9; p. 10, Table 9; *1998*, Bulletin NCJ 179012, p. 8, Table 7; p. 9; p. 10, Table 9; *1999*, Bulletin NCJ 184795, p. 8, Table 7; p. 9; p. 10, Table 9; *2000*, Bulletin NCJ 190598, p. 8, Table 7; p. 9; p. 10, Table 9; *2001*, Bulletin NCJ 197020, p. 8, Table 7; p. 9; p. 10, Table 9; *2002*, Bulletin NCJ 201848, p. 6; p. 7, Table 7; p. 8; *2003*, Bulletin NCJ 206627, p. 6, Table 5; p. 7, Table 7; p. 8 (Washington, DC: U.S. Department of Justice). Table adapted by SOURCEBOOK staff.

Table 6.82

Prisoners under sentence of death

By race, region, and jurisdiction, on Dec. 31, 2002 and 2003

| | Prisoners under sentence of death on Dec. 31, 2002 ||| Changes during 2003 |||||||||| Prisoners under sentence of death on Dec. 31, 2003 |||
| | | | | Received under sentence of death ||| Removed from death row (excluding executions)[a] ||| Executed ||| | | |
Region and jurisdiction	Total[b]	White	Black	Total[b]	White	Black	Total[b]	White	Black	Total[b]	White	Black	Total[b]	White	Black
United States, total	3,562	1,939	1,551	144	92	44	267	109	157	65	44	20	3,374	1,878	1,418
Federal[c]	23	6	17	2	0	1	1	0	1	1	0	1	23	6	16
State	3,539	1,933	1,534	142	92	43	266	109	156	64	44	19	3,351	1,872	1,402
Northeast	266	97	158	7	4	3	17	7	10	0	0	0	256	94	151
Connecticut	7	4	3	0	0	0	0	0	0	0	0	0	7	4	3
New Hampshire	0	0	0	0	0	0	0	0	0	0	0	0	0	0	0
New Jersey	14	8	6	0	0	0	0	0	0	0	0	0	14	8	6
New York	5	4	1	1	0	1	1	1	0	0	0	0	5	3	2
Pennsylvania	240	81	148	6	4	2	16	6	10	0	0	0	230	79	140
Midwest	486	230	253	14	11	3	178	65	113	7	6	1	315	170	142
Illinois	159	57	102	2	2	0	159	57	102	0	0	0	2	2	0
Indiana	37	26	11	1	1	0	1	0	1	2	2	0	35	25	10
Kansas	5	3	2	1	1	0	0	0	0	0	0	0	6	4	2
Missouri	66	34	32	3	1	2	15	6	9	2	2	0	52	27	25
Nebraska	7	6	1	0	0	0	0	0	0	0	0	0	7	6	1
Ohio	207	99	105	7	6	1	2	1	1	3	2	1	209	102	104
South Dakota	5	5	0	0	0	0	1	1	0	0	0	0	4	4	0
South	1,892	1,020	848	85	58	24	54	25	29	57	38	18	1,866	1,015	825
Alabama	191	100	90	6	5	1	2	1	1	3	3	0	192	101	90
Arkansas	42	17	25	0	0	0	1	0	1	1	0	1	40	17	23
Delaware	14	10	4	2	2	0	0	0	0	0	0	0	16	12	4
Florida	366	234	132	11	11	0	10	5	5	3	2	1	364	238	126
Georgia	115	58	56	1	1	0	2	0	2	3	3	0	111	56	54
Kentucky	36	28	8	0	0	0	1	0	1	0	0	0	35	28	7
Louisiana	90	27	62	1	0	1	4	0	4	0	0	0	87	27	59
Maryland	15	5	10	0	0	0	4	1	3	0	0	0	11	4	7
Mississippi	65	29	35	3	2	1	2	0	2	0	0	0	66	31	34
North Carolina	206	80	118	6	2	4	10	4	6	7	3	3	195	75	113
Oklahoma	112	64	42	9	4	3	5	4	1	14	8	6	102	56	38
South Carolina	72	38	34	5	3	2	6	3	3	0	0	0	71	38	33
Tennessee	96	57	38	6	4	1	6	6	0	0	0	0	96	55	39
Texas	449	260	184	29	20	9	1	1	0	24	17	7	453	262	186
Virginia	23	13	10	6	4	2	0	0	0	2	2	0	27	15	12
West	895	586	275	36	19	13	17	12	4	0	0	0	914	593	284
Arizona	117	100	12	9	5	2	3	2	1	0	0	0	123	103	13
California	613	369	220	19	6	11	3	2	1	0	0	0	629	373	230
Colorado	5	2	2	1	1	0	3	2	0	0	0	0	3	1	2
Idaho	20	20	0	1	1	0	2	2	0	0	0	0	19	19	0
Montana	6	5	0	0	0	0	1	1	0	0	0	0	5	4	0
Nevada	82	48	33	4	4	0	2	0	2	0	0	0	84	52	31
New Mexico	2	2	0	0	0	0	0	0	0	0	0	0	2	2	0
Oregon	27	25	1	2	2	0	1	1	0	0	0	0	28	26	1
Utah	11	8	2	0	0	0	1	1	0	0	0	0	10	7	2
Washington	10	5	5	0	0	0	0	0	0	0	0	0	10	5	5
Wyoming	2	2	0	0	0	0	1	1	0	0	0	0	1	1	0

Note: See Note, table 6.81. Some data for yearend 2002 have been revised by the Source and will differ from previous editions of SOURCEBOOK. Data for "white" and "black" prisoners include Hispanics.

[a] Includes six deaths from natural causes (two each in California and Tennessee and one each in Ohio and Utah); and four deaths from suicide (one each in Georgia, Montana, South Dakota, and Tennessee).

[b] Totals include persons of races other than white and black.

[c] Excludes persons held under Armed Forces jurisdiction with a military death sentence for murder.

Source: U.S. Department of Justice, Bureau of Justice Statistics, *Capital Punishment, 2003*, Bulletin NCJ 206627 (Washington, DC: U.S. Department of Justice, November 2004), p. 5.

Table 6.83

Hispanic and female prisoners under sentence of death

By State, 2002 and 2003

| | Prisoners under sentence of death on Dec. 31, 2002 || Changes during 2003 |||| Prisoners under sentence of death on Dec. 31, 2003 ||
| | | | Received under sentence of death || Removed from death row (including executions)[a] ||| |
	Hispanics	Females	Hispanics	Females	Hispanics	Females	Hispanics	Females
United States, total	363	51	24	2	18	6	369	47
Federal system	2	0	0	0	0	0	2	0
Alabama	1	3	0	0	0	0	1	3
Arizona	17	1	3	0	0	0	20	1
Arkansas	1	0	0	0	0	0	1	0
California	126	14	4	0	0	0	130	14
Colorado	1	0	1	0	1	0	1	0
Connecticut	1	0	0	0	0	0	1	0
Delaware	2	0	0	0	0	0	2	0
Florida	29	1	1	0	0	0	30	1
Georgia	2	1	0	0	0	0	2	1
Idaho	0	1	0	0	0	0	0	1
Illinois	11	4	0	0	11	4	0	0
Indiana	1	1	0	0	0	0	1	1
Kentucky	1	1	0	0	0	0	1	1
Louisiana	1	1	0	0	0	0	1	1
Mississippi	0	1	0	0	0	0	0	1
Nebraska	1	0	0	0	0	0	1	0
Nevada	10	1	0	0	0	0	10	1
New Mexico	1	0	0	0	0	0	1	0
New York	1	0	0	0	0	0	1	0
North Carolina	4	6	0	0	0	2	4	4
Ohio	5	0	0	1	0	0	5	1
Oklahoma	5	0	1	0	1	0	5	0
Oregon	2	0	0	0	0	0	2	0
Pennsylvania	20	5	4	0	1	0	23	5
Tennessee	1	2	0	0	0	0	1	2
Texas	114	8	10	0	3	0	121	8
Utah	3	0	0	0	1	0	2	0
Virginia	0	0	0	1	0	0	0	1

Note: See Note, table 6.81. The following jurisdictions with death penalty statutes reported no Hispanics or females under sentence of death on Dec. 31, 2002 or 2003: Kansas, Maryland, Missouri, Montana, New Hampshire, New Jersey, South Carolina, South Dakota, Washington, and Wyoming. Some data for yearend 2002 have been revised by the Source and will differ from previous editions of SOURCEBOOK.

[a]Includes three Hispanic males in Texas who were executed in 2003.

Source: U.S. Department of Justice, Bureau of Justice Statistics, *Capital Punishment, 2003*, Bulletin NCJ 206627 (Washington, DC: U.S. Department of Justice, November 2004), p. 7, Table 6.

Table 6.84
Prisoners executed

By jurisdiction, 1930-Dec. 31, 2003 (aggregate)

Jurisdiction	Number executed Since 1930	Since 1977[a]
United States, total	4,744	885
Texas	610	313
Georgia	400	34
New York	329	0
California	302	10
North Carolina	293	30
Florida	227	57
South Carolina	190	28
Virginia	181	89
Ohio	180	8
Alabama	163	28
Louisiana	160	27
Mississippi	160	6
Pennsylvania	155	3
Arkansas	143	25
Oklahoma	129	69
Missouri	123	61
Kentucky	105	2
Illinois	102	12
Tennessee	94	1
New Jersey	74	0
Maryland	71	3
Arizona	60	22
Indiana	52	11
Washington	51	4
Colorado	48	1
District of Columbia[b]	40	0
West Virginia[b]	40	0
Nevada	38	9
Federal system	36	3
Massachusetts[b]	27	0
Delaware	25	13
Oregon	21	2
Connecticut	21	0
Utah	19	6
Iowa[b]	18	0
Kansas	15	0
New Mexico	9	1
Montana	8	2
Wyoming	8	1
Nebraska	7	3
Idaho	4	1
Vermont[b]	4	0
New Hampshire	1	0
South Dakota	1	0
Wisconsin[b]	0	0
Rhode Island[b]	0	0
North Dakota[b]	0	0
Minnesota[b]	0	0
Michigan[b]	0	0
Maine[b]	0	0
Hawaii[b]	0	0
Alaska[b]	0	0

Note: See Note, table 6.81.

[a] Executions in the United States resumed in 1977; see Note, table 6.79.
[b] State did not authorize the death penalty as of Dec. 31, 2003.

Source: U.S. Department of Justice, Bureau of Justice Statistics, *Capital Punishment, 2003*, Bulletin NCJ 206627 (Washington, DC: U.S. Department of Justice, November 2004), p. 9, Table 9. Table adapted by SOURCEBOOK staff.

Table 6.85

Prisoners executed under civil authority

By region and jurisdiction, 1930-2003

(- represents zero)

Region and jurisdiction	Total	1930 to 1934	1935 to 1939	1940 to 1944	1945 to 1949	1950 to 1954	1955 to 1959	1960 to 1964	1965 to 1969	1970 to 1979	1980 to 1984	1985	1986	1987	1988	1989	1990	1991	1992
United States	4,744	776	891	645	639	413	304	181	10	3	29	18	18	25	11	16	23	14	31
Federal	36	1	9	7	6	6	3	1	-	-	-	-	-	-	-	-	-	-	-
State	4,708	775	882	638	633	407	301	180	10	3	29	18	18	25	11	16	23	14	31
Northeast	611	155	145	110	74	56	51	17	-	-	-	-	-	-	-	-	-	-	-
Connecticut	21	2	3	5	5	-	5	1	-	-	-	-	-	-	-	-	-	-	-
Maine	X	X	X	X	X	X	X	X	X	X	X	X	X	X	X	X	X	X	X
Massachusetts	27	7	11	6	3	-	-	-	-	-	-	X	X	X	X	X	X	X	X
New Hampshire	1	-	1	-	-	-	-	-	-	-	-	-	-	-	-	-	-	-	-
New Jersey	74	24	16	6	8	8	9	3	-	X	-	-	-	-	-	-	-	-	-
New York	329	80	73	78	36	27	25	10	-	-	-	X	X	X	X	X	X	X	X
Pennsylvania	155	41	41	15	21	19	12	3	-	-	-	-	-	-	-	-	-	-	-
Rhode Island	-	-	-	-	-	-	-	-	-	-	X	X	X	X	X	X	X	X	X
Vermont	4	1	-	-	1	2	-	-	-	-	-	-	-	-	-	-	-	X	X
Midwest	498	105	113	42	64	42	16	16	5	-	1	1	-	-	-	1	5	1	1
Illinois	102	34	27	13	5	8	1	2	-	-	-	-	-	-	-	-	1	-	-
Indiana	52	11	20	2	5	2	-	1	-	-	1	1	-	-	-	-	-	-	-
Iowa	18	1	7	3	4	1	-	2	X	X	X	X	X	X	X	X	X	X	X
Kansas	15	X	-	3	2	5	-	1	4	X	X	X	X	X	X	X	X	X	X
Michigan	-	-	-	-	-	-	-	-	X	X	X	X	X	X	X	X	X	X	X
Minnesota	X	X	X	X	X	X	X	X	X	X	X	X	X	X	X	X	X	X	X
Missouri	123	16	20	6	9	5	2	3	1	-	-	-	-	-	-	-	1	4	1	1
Nebraska	7	-	-	-	2	1	1	-	-	-	-	-	-	-	-	-	-	-	-
North Dakota	-	-	-	-	-	-	-	-	-	-	X	X	X	X	X	X	X	X	X
Ohio	180	43	39	15	36	20	12	7	-	-	-	-	-	-	-	-	-	-	-
South Dakota	1	X	-	-	1	-	-	-	-	-	-	-	-	-	-	-	-	-	-
Wisconsin	X	X	X	X	X	X	X	X	X	X	X	X	X	X	X	X	X	X	X
South	3,031	419	524	413	419	244	183	102	2	1	28	16	18	24	10	13	17	13	26
Alabama	163	19	41	29	21	14	6	4	1	-	1	-	1	1	-	4	1	-	2
Arkansas	143	20	33	20	18	11	7	9	-	-	-	-	-	-	-	-	2	-	2
Delaware	25	2	6	2	2	-	-	-	-	-	-	-	-	-	-	-	-	-	1
District of Columbia	40	15	5	3	13	3	1	-	-	X	X	X	X	X	X	X	X	X	X
Florida	227	15	29	38	27	22	27	12	-	1	9	3	3	1	2	2	4	2	2
Georgia	400	64	73	58	72	51	34	14	-	-	3	3	1	5	1	1	-	1	-
Kentucky	105	18	34	19	15	8	8	1	-	-	-	-	-	-	-	-	-	-	-
Louisiana	160	39	19	24	23	14	13	1	-	-	6	1	-	8	3	-	1	1	-
Maryland	71	6	10	26	19	2	4	1	-	-	-	-	-	-	-	-	-	-	-
Mississippi	160	26	22	34	26	15	21	10	-	-	1	-	-	2	-	1	-	-	-
North Carolina	293	51	80	50	62	14	5	1	-	-	2	-	1	-	-	-	-	1	1
Oklahoma	129	25	9	6	7	4	3	5	1	-	-	-	-	-	-	-	1	-	2
South Carolina	190	37	30	32	29	16	10	8	-	-	-	1	1	-	-	-	1	1	-
Tennessee	94	16	31	19	18	1	7	1	-	-	-	-	-	-	-	-	-	-	-
Texas	610	48	72	38	36	49	25	29	-	-	4	6	10	6	3	4	4	5	12
Virginia	181	8	20	13	22	15	8	6	-	-	2	2	1	1	1	1	3	2	4
West Virginia	40	10	10	2	9	5	4	-	X	X	X	X	X	X	X	X	X	X	X
West	568	96	100	73	76	65	51	45	3	2	-	1	-	1	1	2	1	-	4
Alaska[a]	X	X	X	X	X	X	X	X	X	X	X	X	X	X	X	X	X	X	X
Arizona	60	7	10	6	3	2	6	4	-	-	-	-	-	-	-	-	-	-	1
California	302	51	57	35	45	39	35	29	1	-	-	-	-	-	-	-	-	-	-
Colorado	48	16	9	6	7	1	2	5	1	-	-	-	-	-	-	-	-	-	1
Hawaii[a]	X	X	X	X	X	X	X	X	X	X	X	X	X	X	X	X	X	X	X
Idaho	4	-	-	-	-	2	1	-	-	-	-	-	-	-	-	-	-	-	-
Montana	8	1	4	1	-	-	-	-	-	-	-	-	-	-	-	-	-	-	-
Nevada	38	5	3	5	5	9	-	2	-	1	-	1	-	-	-	-	2	1	-
New Mexico	9	2	-	-	2	2	1	1	-	-	-	-	-	-	-	-	-	-	-
Oregon	21	1	1	6	6	4	-	1	X	-	-	-	-	-	-	-	-	-	-
Utah	19	-	2	3	1	2	4	1	-	1	-	-	-	-	1	1	-	-	1
Washington	51	10	13	9	7	4	2	2	-	-	-	-	-	-	-	-	-	-	-
Wyoming	8	3	1	2	-	-	-	-	1	-	-	-	-	-	-	-	-	-	1

Note: In three States, Maine, Minnesota, and Wisconsin, there were no death penalty statutes in effect for the entire period covered by the table. Alaska and Hawaii have not had the death penalty since 1960, when they were first included as States. For other States, the death penalty may have been abolished or declared unconstitutional, and/or subsequently reinstated. In these cases, an X appears to indicate years when the death penalty was not in effect. For information on methodology, definitions of terms, and explanatory notes, see Appendix 15.

[a]As States, Alaska and Hawaii are included in the series beginning Jan. 1, 1960.

Source: U.S. Department of Justice, Bureau of Justice Statistics, *Correctional Populations in the United States, 1997*, NCJ 177613 (Washington, DC: U.S. Department of Justice, 2000), Table 7.25; and U.S. Department of Justice, Bureau of Justice Statistics [Online]. Available: http://www.ojp.usdoj.gov/bjs/data/exest.wk1 [Aug. 6, 2004]. Table adapted by SOURCEBOOK staff.

1993	1994	1995	1996	1997	1998	1999	2000	2001	2002	2003
38	31	56	45	74	68	98	85	66	71	65
-	-	-	-	-	-	-	-	2	-	1
38	31	56	45	74	68	98	85	64	71	64
-	-	2	-	-	-	1	-	-	-	-
-	-	-	-	-	-	-	-	-	-	-
X	X	X	X	X	X	X	X	X	X	X
X	X	X	X	X	X	X	X	X	X	X
-	-	-	-	-	-	-	-	-	-	-
-	-	-	-	-	-	-	-	-	-	-
X	X	-	-	-	-	-	-	-	-	-
-	-	2	-	-	-	1	-	-	-	-
X	X	X	X	X	X	X	X	X	X	X
X	X	X	X	X	X	X	X	X	X	X
4	3	11	9	10	5	12	5	10	9	7
-	1	5	1	2	1	1	-	-	-	-
-	1	-	1	1	1	1	-	2	-	2
X	X	X	X	X	X	X	X	X	X	X
X	X	-	-	-	-	-	-	-	-	-
X	X	X	X	X	X	X	X	X	X	X
X	X	X	X	X	X	X	X	X	X	X
4	X	6	6	6	3	9	5	7	6	2
-	1	-	1	1	-	-	-	-	-	-
X	X	X	X	X	X	X	X	X	X	X
-	-	-	-	-	-	1	-	1	3	3
-	-	-	-	-	-	-	-	-	-	-
X	X	X	X	X	X	X	X	X	X	X
30	26	41	29	60	55	74	76	50	61	57
-	-	2	1	3	1	2	4	-	2	3
-	5	2	1	4	1	4	2	1	-	1
2	1	1	3	-	-	2	1	2	-	-
X	X	X	X	X	X	X	X	X	X	X
3	1	3	2	1	4	1	6	1	3	3
2	1	2	2	-	1	-	-	4	4	3
-	-	-	-	1	-	1	-	-	-	-
1	-	1	1	1	-	1	1	-	1	-
-	1	-	-	1	1	-	-	-	-	-
-	-	-	-	-	-	-	-	-	2	-
-	1	2	-	-	3	4	1	5	2	7
-	-	3	2	1	4	6	11	18	7	14
-	-	1	6	2	7	4	1	-	3	-
-	-	-	-	-	-	-	1	-	-	-
17	14	19	3	37	20	35	40	17	33	24
5	2	5	8	9	13	14	8	2	4	2
X	X	X	X	X	X	X	X	X	X	X
4	2	2	7	4	8	11	4	4	1	-
X	X	X	X	X	X	X	X	X	X	X
2	-	1	2	2	4	7	3	-	-	-
1	-	-	2	-	1	2	1	1	1	-
-	-	-	-	1	-	-	-	-	-	-
X	X	X	X	X	X	X	X	X	X	X
-	1	-	-	-	-	-	-	-	-	-
-	-	1	-	-	1	-	-	-	-	-
-	-	-	1	-	1	1	-	1	-	-
-	-	-	-	-	-	-	-	1	-	-
-	-	-	1	1	-	-	-	-	-	-
-	-	-	1	-	-	1	-	-	-	-
1	1	-	-	-	1	-	-	1	-	-
-	-	-	-	-	-	-	-	-	-	-

Persons under correctional supervision 541

Table 6.86
Prisoners executed under civil authority

By race and offense, United States, 1930-98

(- represents zero)

	Total				White				Black				Other			
	Total	Murder	Rape	Other offenses[a]	Total	Murder	Rape	Other offenses	Total	Murder	Rape	Other offenses	Total	Murder	Rape	Other offenses
1930-98	4,359	3,734	455	70	2,064	1,977	48	39	2,246	1,810	405	31	49	47	2	-
1998	68	68	-	-	48	48	-	-	18	18	-	-	2	2	-	-
1997	74	74	-	-	45	45	-	-	27	27	-	-	2	2	-	-
1996	45	45	-	-	31	31	-	-	14	14	-	-	-	-	-	-
1995	56	56	-	-	33	33	-	-	22	22	-	-	1	1	-	-
1994	31	31	-	-	20	20	-	-	11	11	-	-	-	-	-	-
1993	38	38	-	-	23	23	-	-	14	14	-	-	1	1	-	-
1992	31	31	-	-	19	19	-	-	11	11	-	-	1	1	-	-
1991	14	14	-	-	7	7	-	-	7	7	-	-	-	-	-	-
1990	23	23	-	-	16	16	-	-	7	7	-	-	-	-	-	-
1989	16	16	-	-	8	8	-	-	8	8	-	-	-	-	-	-
1988	11	11	-	-	6	6	-	-	5	5	-	-	-	-	-	-
1987	25	25	-	-	13	13	-	-	12	12	-	-	-	-	-	-
1986	18	18	-	-	11	11	-	-	7	7	-	-	-	-	-	-
1985	18	18	-	-	11	11	-	-	7	7	-	-	-	-	-	-
1984	21	21	-	-	13	13	-	-	8	8	-	-	-	-	-	-
1983	5	5	-	-	4	4	-	-	1	1	-	-	-	-	-	-
1982	2	2	-	-	1	1	-	-	1	1	-	-	-	-	-	-
1981	1	1	-	-	1	1	-	-	-	-	-	-	-	-	-	-
1980	-	-	-	-	-	-	-	-	-	-	-	-	-	-	-	-
1979	2	2	-	-	2	2	-	-	-	-	-	-	-	-	-	-
1978	-	-	-	-	-	-	-	-	-	-	-	-	-	-	-	-
1977[b]	1	1	-	-	1	1	-	-	-	-	-	-	-	-	-	-
1967	2	2	-	-	1	1	-	-	1	1	-	-	-	-	-	-
1966	1	1	-	-	1	1	-	-	-	-	-	-	-	-	-	-
1965	7	7	-	-	6	6	-	-	1	1	-	-	-	-	-	-
1964	15	9	6	-	8	5	3	-	7	4	3	-	-	-	-	-
1963	21	18	2	1	13	12	-	1	8	6	2	-	-	-	-	-
1962	47	41	4	2	28	26	2	-	19	15	2	2	-	-	-	-
1961	42	33	8	1	20	18	1	1	22	15	7	-	-	-	-	-
1960	56	44	8	4	21	18	-	3	35	26	8	1	-	-	-	-
1959	49	41	8	-	16	15	1	-	33	26	7	-	-	-	-	-
1958	49	41	7	1	20	20	-	-	28	20	7	1	1	1	-	-
1957	65	54	10	1	34	32	2	-	31	22	8	1	-	-	-	-
1956	65	52	12	1	21	20	-	1	43	31	12	-	1	1	-	-
1955	76	65	7	4	44	41	1	2	32	24	6	2	-	-	-	-
1954	81	71	9	1	38	37	1	-	42	33	8	1	1	1	-	-
1953	62	51	7	4	30	25	1	4	31	25	6	-	1	1	-	-
1952	83	71	12	-	36	35	1	-	47	36	11	-	-	-	-	-
1951	105	87	17	1	57	55	2	-	47	31	15	1	1	1	-	-
1950	82	68	13	1	40	36	4	-	42	32	9	1	-	-	-	-
1949	119	107	10	2	50	49	-	1	67	56	10	1	2	2	-	-
1948	119	95	22	2	35	32	1	2	82	61	21	-	2	2	-	-
1947	153	129	23	1	42	40	2	-	111	89	21	1	-	-	-	-
1946	131	107	22	2	46	45	-	1	84	61	22	1	1	1	-	-
1945	117	90	26	1	41	37	4	-	75	52	22	1	1	1	-	-
1944	120	96	24	-	47	45	2	-	70	48	22	-	3	3	-	-
1943	131	118	13	-	54	54	-	-	74	63	11	-	3	1	2	-
1942	147	115	25	7	67	57	4	6	80	58	21	1	-	-	-	-
1941	123	102	20	1	59	55	4	-	63	46	16	1	1	1	-	-
1940	124	105	15	4	49	44	2	3	75	61	13	1	-	-	-	-
1939	160	145	12	3	80	79	-	1	77	63	12	2	3	3	-	-
1938	190	154	25	11	96	89	1	6	92	63	24	5	2	2	-	-
1937	147	133	13	1	69	67	2	-	74	62	11	1	4	4	-	-
1936	195	181	10	4	92	86	2	4	101	93	8	-	2	2	-	-
1935	199	184	13	2	119	115	2	2	77	66	11	-	3	3	-	-
1934	168	154	14	-	65	64	1	-	102	89	13	-	1	1	-	-
1933	160	151	7	2	77	75	1	1	81	74	6	1	2	2	-	-
1932	140	128	10	2	62	62	-	-	75	63	10	2	3	3	-	-
1931	153	137	15	1	77	76	1	-	72	57	14	1	4	4	-	-
1930	155	147	6	2	90	90	-	-	65	57	6	2	-	-	-	-

Note: See Note, table 6.85. For information on methodology, definitions of terms, and explanatory notes, see Appendix 15.

Source: U.S. Department of Justice, Bureau of Justice Statistics, *Correctional Populations in the United States, 1998 Statistical Tables*, NCJ 192929, Table 7.20 [Online]. Available: http://www.ojp.usdoj.gov/bjs/abstract/cpusst.htm [Aug. 10, 2004]. Table adapted by SOURCEBOOK staff.

[a]Includes 25 executed for armed robbery, 20 for kidnaping, 11 for burglary, 6 for sabotage, 6 for aggravated assault, and 2 for espionage.
[b]There were no executions from 1968 through 1976; see Note, table 6.79.

Table 6.87

Methods of execution in States authorizing the death penalty

By State, 2003

Lethal injection	Electrocution	Lethal gas	Hanging	Firing squad
Alabama[a]	Alabama[a]	Arizona[a,b]	Delaware[a,c]	Idaho[a]
Arizona[a,b]	Arkansas[a,d]	California[a]	New Hampshire[a,e]	Oklahoma[a,f]
Arkansas[a,d]	Florida[a]	Missouri[a]	Washington[a]	Utah[a]
California[a]	Kentucky[a,g]	Wyoming[a,h]		
Colorado	Nebraska			
Connecticut	Oklahoma[a,f]			
Delaware[a,c]	South Carolina[a]			
Florida[a]	Tennessee[a,i]			
Georgia	Virginia[a]			
Idaho[a]				
Illinois				
Indiana				
Kansas				
Kentucky[a,g]				
Louisiana				
Maryland				
Mississippi				
Missouri[a]				
Montana				
Nevada				
New Hampshire[a,e]				
New Jersey				
New Mexico				
New York				
North Carolina				
Ohio				
Oklahoma[a,f]				
Oregon				
Pennsylvania				
South Carolina[a]				
South Dakota				
Tennessee[a,i]				
Texas				
Utah[a]				
Virginia[a]				
Washington[a]				
Wyoming[a,h]				

Note: See Note, table 6.81. The method of execution of Federal prisoners is lethal injection, pursuant to 28 CFR, Part 26. For offenses under the Violent Crime Control and Law Enforcement Act of 1994, the method is that of the State in which the conviction took place, pursuant to 18 USC 3596.

[a] Authorizes more than one method of execution.
[b] Arizona authorizes lethal injection for persons whose capital sentence was received after Nov. 15, 1992; for those who were sentenced before that date, the condemned prisoner may select lethal injection or lethal gas.
[c] Delaware authorizes lethal injection for those whose capital offense occurred after June 13, 1986; for those whose offense occurred before that date, the condemned prisoner may select lethal injection or hanging.
[d] Arkansas authorizes lethal injection for those whose capital offense occurred on or after July 4, 1983; for those whose offense occurred before that date, the condemned prisoner may select lethal injection or electrocution.
[e] New Hampshire authorizes hanging only if lethal injection cannot be given.
[f] Oklahoma authorizes electrocution if lethal injection is ever held unconstitutional and firing squad if both lethal injection and electrocution are held unconstitutional.
[g] Kentucky authorizes lethal injection for persons whose capital sentence was received on or after Mar. 31, 1998; for those sentenced before that date, the condemned prisoner may select lethal injection or electrocution.
[h] Wyoming authorizes lethal gas if lethal injection is ever held unconstitutional.
[i] Tennessee authorizes lethal injection for those whose capital offense occurred after Dec. 31, 1998; for those whose offense occurred before that date, the condemned prisoner may select lethal injection or electrocution.

Source: U.S. Department of Justice, Bureau of Justice Statistics, *Capital Punishment, 2003*, Bulletin NCJ 206627 (Washington, DC: U.S. Department of Justice, November 2004), p. 4, Table 2.

Annotated list of sources and references

Only published documents cited by the *Sourcebook* are listed here. Information provided to *Sourcebook* staff in the form of single tables or mimeographed reports are not listed. Some sources are available electronically. The World Wide Web addresses of source publishers are included in the addresses of publishers list that begins on page 561.

Administrative Office of the United States Courts

Judicial Business of the United States Courts: 2003 Annual Report of the Director

(Annual. Washington: USGPO, 2004. 400 pages, 130 tables, 9 figures, 1 appendix.)

Presents data for fiscal 2003 and trend data for 1994-2003. SOURCEBOOK tables 1.84, 1.94, 1.95, 1.97, 5.8-5.12, 5.22-5.25, 5.37, 5.38, 5.41-5.43, 5.65-5.70, 6.5-6.7.

This report is divided into three sections. The first section presents summary information on the business of the Federal judiciary, including caseload trends for the appellate, district, and bankruptcy courts; the probation and pretrial services system; and other components of the Federal judiciary. The second and third sections present supplemental tables and detailed statistical tables presenting data on civil and criminal cases filed, terminated, and pending in U.S. district and appellate courts. Dispositions of criminal cases, length of civil and criminal trials, number of prisoner petitions, and juror utilization are tabulated. Information also is provided for U.S. magistrate judges, U.S. Bankruptcy Courts, the U.S. Supreme Court, the U.S. Court of International Trade, the U.S. Court of Federal Claims, and the Federal Probation System.

2003 Federal Court Management Statistics

(Annual. Washington: Administrative Office of the United States Courts, 2004. 167 pages, 135 tables.)

Presents data for fiscal 1998-2003. SOURCEBOOK table 1.83.

This report presents workload and performance statistics on both civil and criminal matters for each of the U.S. Courts of Appeals and each of the 94 U.S. District Courts. Data for the former include appeals filed, terminated, and pending; number of judgeships; types of appeals; number of opinions; median time from filing to disposition; and other matters pertaining to the appellate courts. Data for the U.S. District Courts include cases filed, terminated, and pending; actions per judgeship; median time from filing to disposition; a juror usage index; and other matters related to activities in U.S. District Courts. As part of the profile, each court is ranked on various dimensions. Two tables presenting a national profile for all U.S. Courts of Appeals and all U.S. District Courts on workload and performance measures also are included.

2003 Wiretap Report

(Annual. Washington: Administrative Office of the United States Courts, 2004. 232 pages, 13 tables, 3 figures, 1 appendix.)

Presents data for 2003 and trend data for 1993-2003. SOURCEBOOK tables 5.2-5.5.

This report details the applications for orders authorizing or approving the interception of wire, oral, or electronic communications, as required by Title 18, United States Code, Section 2519(1). Included are descriptions of the reporting requirements of the statute, regulations for filing reports, and summaries of the reports submitted by judges and prosecuting officials. The tables in the body of the report present data on grants, denials, and authorized length of intercept orders; offenses for which court intercept orders were granted; types of surveillance used; average costs of electronic surveillance; arrests and convictions resulting from electronic surveillance; and a summary of authorized intercepts from 1993 through 2003. The appendix tables contain detailed data from reports filed by Federal and State judges and prosecuting officials on court-authorized electronic surveillance activities during 2003 and on arrests, trials, and convictions as a result of intercepts installed during previous years.

American Judicature Society

Judicial Selection in the United States: A Compendium of Provisions

(Periodic. 2nd edition. Chicago: American Judicature Society, 1993. 194 pages, 15 tables.)

Presents data for 1993. SOURCEBOOK tables 1.91-1.93.

This is the last published resource describing the methods by which judges are selected in the 50 States and the District of Columbia. The book begins with a historical review of judicial selection in the United States and a narrative summary of current practice. A survey of State statutes provides data for 1992 or from the most recent statutory updates available. Data are presented on the selection and retention process for State supreme court justices; intermediate appellate court judges; and general, limited, and special jurisdiction trial court judges. Current provisions for selecting judges through commission plans, partisan elections, and nonpartisan elections also are presented. The book concludes with a State-by-State presentation of relevant statutory citations and a summary of their texts.

Bray, Robert M. et al.

2002 Department of Defense Survey of Health Related Behaviors Among Military Personnel

(Periodic. [Online]. Available: http://www.tricare.osd.mil/main/news/ 2002wwfinalreport.pdf [July 30, 2004]. 347 pages, 84 tables, 4 figures, 8 appendices.)

Presents data for 2002 and trend data for 1980-2002. SOURCEBOOK tables 3.89-3.91.

This report presents results of a survey focusing on health-related behaviors of active-duty military personnel. The survey is the eighth in a series of such surveys sponsored by the U.S. Department of Defense. The findings include detailed estimates of the prevalence of alcohol, illicit drug, and tobacco use as well as the negative effects of alcohol use. Estimates for health behaviors pertaining to fitness and cardiovascular disease reduction, injuries and injury prevention, and sexually transmitted disease reduction are reported. Also included are assessments of the mental health of military personnel, including stress, anxiety, and depression; military job satisfaction; gambling; oral health; and gender-specific health issues. A detailed description of the survey methodology is included and the appendices cover sample design and weighting, estimation procedures, and other technical issues related to measurement and analysis.

DeVoe, Jill F. et al.

Indicators of School Crime and Safety: 2003

(Annual. NCES 2004-004/NCJ 201257. Washington: U.S. Departments of Education and Justice, 2003. 164 pages, 52 tables, 35 figures, 2 appendices.)

Presents data for 1992-2002. SOURCEBOOK tables 2.6, 3.60, 3.61.

This report presents data from multiple data sources. Included are data from the School Survey on Crime and Safety and the National Schools and Staffing Survey, conducted by the National Center for Education Statistics (NCES). The National School-Based Youth Risk Behavior Survey from the Centers for Disease Control and Prevention (CDC), the National Crime Victimization Survey from the Bureau of Justice Statistics (BJS), and the School Crime Supplement jointly produced by the NCES and BJS, also contribute data used in this report. This edition also presents data from the School Associated Violent Death Study developed by CDC in conjunction with BJS and the U.S. Department of Education; the Supplementary Homicide Reports, part of the Uniform Crime Reporting Program administered by the Federal Bureau of Investigation; and the Web-based Injury Statistics Query and Reporting System, from CDC's National Center for Health Statistics.

The report is comprised of five sections. The first section presents data on homicides and suicides of students at school and away from school. The second section deals with nonfatal victimization of students, including the prevalence of being victimized at school, being threatened or injured with a weapon, physical fights on school property, and students being bullied at school. The third section displays data on crimes reported to police by public schools and serious disciplinary actions taken by public schools. The fourth section provides information on nonfatal victimization of teachers at school, including reported threats and physical attacks. Information on the school environment is presented in the last section. This includes data on prevalence of students carrying weapons on school property, students' perceptions of safety at school and avoiding places in school, students' reports of gangs or hate-related behavior at school, principals' reports of discipline problems at school, and the prevalence of alcohol and marijuana availability and use at school. The appendices include technical notes on the data sources and a glossary of terms used in the report.

Executive Office of the President, Office of Management and Budget

The Budget of the United States Government, Fiscal Year 2005

(Annual. [CD-ROM]. Washington: USGPO, 2004.)

Presents data for fiscal 2003-2009 and trend data for fiscal 1946-2004. SOURCEBOOK table 1.12.

This CD-ROM includes six files that comprise the primary sections of the budget. The first, entitled Budget of the United States Government, Fiscal Year 2005 contains the budget message of the President, information on the President's budget and management priorities, and budget overviews organized by agency. The second presents a Budget Appendix, which includes detailed budget estimates by agency. The third, entitled Historical Tables provides data on budget receipts, outlays, surpluses or deficits, Federal debt, and Federal employment from 1940. Next, is a Program Assessment Rating Tool Summary File showing key performance measures for each agency. The fifth file, Analytical Perspectives, highlights specific subject areas and provides other significant presentations of budget data that place the budget in perspective including economic and accounting analyses; information on Federal receipts and collections; analyses of Federal spending; detailed information on Federal borrowing and debt; baseline or current services estimates; and other technical presentations. Finally, Analytical Perspectives CD-ROM Tables that do not appear in the printed budget document are shown here. Also included are numerous additional files and spreadsheets for other topics and selected data tables. Included among the spreadsheets are figures on economic assumptions and Federal aid to State and local governments. Among the various additional files are discussions of the budget system and concepts, and Federal borrowing and debt.

Executive Office of the President, Office of National Drug Control Policy

National Drug Control Strategy: FY 2005 Budget Summary

(Annual. Washington: Executive Office of the President, 2004. 115 pages, 45 tables, 1 figure.)

Presents data for fiscal 2005 and trend data for fiscal 1996-2005. SOURCEBOOK tables 1.14, 1.15.

This report presents detailed information on the budget and objectives of the National Drug Control Strategy developed by the Office of National Drug Control Policy. The Executive Summary highlights major drug control initiatives and Federal funding priorities for fiscal year 2005. The next section includes overview tables showing breakdowns of Federal drug control funding by function and agency. Section three presents detailed agency-by-agency summaries of specific drug control programs, agency budgets organized by strategic goals, program accomplishments, and tables presenting fiscal 2003 final, fiscal 2004 enacted, and fiscal 2005 requested budget authorities.

The Gallup Organization, Inc.

The Gallup Poll

(Princeton, NJ: The Gallup Organization, Inc. Periodicity, contents, and dates of data presented: See below. Available: http://www.gallup.com/.)

SOURCEBOOK tables 2.1, 2.10-2.14, 2.16-2.21, 2.26, 2.28, 2.29, 2.33, 2.34, 2.37, 2.39, 2.40, 2.44, 2.45, 2.48, 2.49, 2.51-2.60, 2.63-2.65, 2.67, 2.69, 2.96, 2.98-2.101, 3.95-3.97, 3.99-3.101.)

The results of public opinion research conducted by The Gallup Organization, Inc. are released daily by The Gallup Poll News Service. Topics examined include business and the economy, politics and elections, social issues and policy, and lifestyles. Also available through Gallup's weekly release, Gallup Poll On Demand, are additional analyses on finance, government and public affairs, healthcare, religion and values, and education and youth. A brief note on sample size, sampling tolerance, and survey dates is included in each release.

Goldman, Sheldon; Elliot Slotnick; Gerard Gryski; Gary Zuk; and Sara Schiavoni

"W. Bush Remaking the Judiciary: Like Father Like Son?"

(*Judicature* 86 (May-June 2003), pp. 282-309. 28 pages, 7 tables.)

Presents data for 1977-2002. SOURCEBOOK tables 1.81, 1.82.

This article reports the results of research on judgeship appointments to Federal district and appeals courts. Background characteristics of judges appointed by President George W. Bush during his presidency are compared with those appointed by Presidents Carter, Reagan, Bush, and Clinton. Recent appointees are highlighted and data comparing traditional and nontraditional appointees during the current Bush administration are provided.

Grunbaum, Jo Anne et al.

"Youth Risk Behavior Surveillance--United States, 2003"

(CDC Surveillance Summaries. *Morbidity and Mortality Weekly Report* 53 No. SS-2. Washington: USGPO, May 21, 2004. 96 pages, 66 tables, 8 figures.)

Presents data for 2003. SOURCEBOOK tables 3.55-3.57, 3.62.

This report presents the results of the 2003 national school-based survey conducted as part of the Youth Risk Behavior Surveillance

System by the U.S. Department of Health and Human Services, Centers for Disease Control and Prevention. Data on the prevalence and incidence of numerous health risk behaviors among high school students are presented. These include students reporting use of safety belts; use of bicycle helmets; riding with a driver who had been drinking; driving after drinking; carrying a weapon; engaging in physical fights; dating violence; school-related violence; thoughts and attempts of suicide; tobacco, alcohol, and drug use; and risk-related sexual behaviors. Other topics covered are students' dietary behaviors and physical activities.

Harris Interactive, Inc.
The Harris Poll

(New York: Harris Interactive Inc. Periodicity, contents, and dates of data presented: See below.)

SOURCEBOOK tables 2.2, 2.9, 2.22, 2.27.

The Harris Poll is a weekly news release of public opinion research conducted by Harris Interactive, Inc. The releases deal with a variety of topics including confidence in selected institutions, Presidential job performance, foreign affairs, business and finance, as well as numerous current political and social issues. A brief note on sample size and survey dates is included in each release.

Johnston, Lloyd D.; Patrick M. O'Malley; Jerald G. Bachman; and John E. Schulenberg
Monitoring the Future National Survey Results on Drug Use, 1975-2003

(Annual. Bethesda, MD: U.S. Department of Health and Human Services, 2004.)

Presents data for 2003 and trend data for 1975-2003. SOURCEBOOK tables 2.79-2.81, 2.83-2.89, 3.64-3.76.

This two-volume report presents the results of the 29th national survey of drug use and related attitudes among American high school seniors, the 13th such survey of 8th and 10th grade students, and a followup survey of young adults, including college students. Volume I contains the results from the secondary school samples of 8th, 10th, and 12th graders. The results from college students and young adults are reported in Volume II. Two major topics treated in the report are trends in drug use among American high school students since 1975 and prevalence of drug use among American high school seniors. Also reported are data on school grade at first use, intensity of "high" produced by drug use, attitudes and beliefs among seniors about various types of drug use, and their perceptions of certain relevant aspects of the social environment, such as parental disapproval of drug use or availability of drugs. Beginning in 1986, data on prevalence and trends in drug use among young adults who have completed high school also are presented.

Karter, Michael J., Jr.
Fire Loss in the United States During 2002

(Annual. Quincy, MA: National Fire Protection Association, 2003. 35 pages, 15 tables, 5 figures.)

Presents data for 2002 and trend data for 1977-2002. SOURCEBOOK tables 3.166, 3.167.

This report presents the results of the annual National Fire Experience Survey conducted from 1977 to 2002 by the National Fire Protection Association. Data are displayed on fire incidence, deaths, injuries, and property loss, by fire type (structural, vehicular, and arson), property use, community size, and geographic region. Also presented are data on the number of fire department responses to fires and other incidents, and a section on the survey methodology.

Moulder, Evelina R.
"Police and Fire Personnel, Salaries, and Expenditures for 2003"

(Annual. In *The Municipal Year Book 2004*, pp. 123-176. Washington: International City/County Management Association, 2004. 54 pages, 17 tables, 1 figure.)

Presents data for 2003 and a trend figure for 1993-2003. SOURCEBOOK tables 1.64, 1.65, 1.69.

This article presents data gathered through a mail survey sent to all municipalities with populations of 10,000 or more in the United States. This annual survey, conducted by the International City/County Management Association, collects data on personnel, salaries, and expenditures for police and fire departments in 2003 as well as minimum staffing requirements for fire departments and fire apparatus. A table presenting detailed data for each of the 1,645 cities responding to the survey is included.

"Salaries of County Officials, 2003"

(Annual. In *The Municipal Year Book 2004*, pp. 102-122. Washington: International City/County Management Association, 2004. 21 pages, 4 tables, 1 figure.)

Presents data for 2003. SOURCEBOOK table 1.71.

This article presents data collected from the 2003 survey of salaries of local government officials conducted by the International City/County Management Association. Salaries are presented by job title, county size, region, county type, and form of government. The survey gathers information on 25 positions; among the positions included are the county manager, chief administrative officer, clerk, chief financial officer, treasurer, risk manager, health officer, engineer, chief law enforcement official, fire chief, superintendent of parks, chief librarian, and the directors of human resources, planning, purchasing, parks and recreation, economic development, public works, human services, public safety, and information services.

"Salaries of Municipal Officials, 2003"

(Annual. In *The Municipal Year Book 2004*, pp. 79-101. Washington: International City/County Management Association, 2004. 23 pages, 6 tables, 1 figure.)

Presents data for 2003. SOURCEBOOK table 1.70.

This article presents data collected from the 2003 survey of salaries of local government officials conducted by the International City/County Management Association. Salaries of municipal officials are presented by job title, city size, region, city type, and form of government. Average salaries of 23 positions are presented: the city manager, chief administrative officer, primary assistant chief administrative officer, clerk, chief financial officer, health officer, treasurer, engineer, chief law enforcement official, fire chief, superintendent of parks, risk manager, chief librarian, and the directors of public safety, public works, economic development, planning, human resources, human services, parks and recreation, information services, recreation, and purchasing.

National Center on Addiction and Substance Abuse at Columbia University
National Survey of American Attitudes on Substance Abuse VIII: Teens and Parents

(Annual. [Online]. Available: http://www.casacolumbia.org/pdshopprov/files/2003_Teen_Survey_8_19_03.pdf [Mar. 1, 2004].)

Presents data for 2003. SOURCEBOOK tables 2.7, 2.8, 2.77.

This report presents the results of surveys of teenagers and parents of teens. The teen survey covers a wide variety of topics including type of school attended, parental status at home (single parent, both parents, stepparent, etc.), family and leisure activities, problems facing teens, tobacco and alcohol use of parents and close friends, teens' own tobacco and alcohol use, drug-free environments at school, harmfulness of drug use and availability of drugs, and several items focusing on the impact of stress, boredom, and the availability of spending money on the risk of teen substance abuse. The survey of parents of teens covers similar topics from a parental perspective, including parental perceptions of problems faced by teens, the quality of their teens' education, school safety, and a number of questions about drug-free schools and drug testing in school. Also included are several questions on parental perceptions of the harmfulness of drugs, parental influence over teen drug use, and parents' confidence in ability to detect their teens' drug use and to respond effectively.

National Survey of American Attitudes on Substance Abuse IX: Teen Dating Practices and Sexual Activity

(Annual. [Online]. Available: http://www.casacolumbia.org/pdshopprov/files/august_2004_casa_teen_survey.pdf [Aug. 31, 2004].)

Presents data for 2004. SOURCEBOOK tables 2.3, 2.78.

This report presents the results of surveys of teenagers and parents of teens. The teen survey covers a wide variety of topics including type of school attended, parental status at home (single parent, both parents, stepparent, etc.), family and religious activities, nature and extent of Internet activity, problems facing teens, tobacco and alcohol use of parents and close friends, teens' own tobacco and alcohol use, drug-free environments at school, availability of drugs generally and at teen parties, and several items focusing on school-related issues and extent of dating activity. The survey of parents of teens covers similar topics from a parental perspective, including parental perceptions of problems faced by teens and school safety, and a number of questions about drug-free schools. Also included are several questions on parental perceptions of teens' dating practices, sexual activity, and drug use, including access to prescription drugs and parents' confidence in ability to detect their teens' drug use.

National Center for State Courts
Survey of Judicial Salaries

(Biannual. Vol. 28, No. 2. Williamsburg, VA: National Center for State Courts, 2004. 16 pages, 6 tables, 1 figure.)

Presents data for 2003. SOURCEBOOK table 1.90.

This report presents judicial salaries for State appellate and general jurisdiction trial courts as well as courts of special and limited jurisdiction, such as probate and family court. A profile for each State shows salary information for chief justices and associate justices of courts of last resort, judges of intermediate appellate and general trial courts, and State court administrators. Salaries for judges or magistrates of courts of limited and special jurisdiction are included, as is the date of the State's last salary adjustment for judicial personnel. Two tables highlight the States that reported salary increases in 2003 for general jurisdiction judges and for intermediate appellate judges. Salary information that accounts for differences in cost of living is provided for general jurisdiction trial court judges, allowing for a direct comparison of salaries across all 50 States. This edition also includes a special section on recalling senior and retired judges to service.

National Opinion Research Center
General Social Surveys, 1972-2002

(Periodic. Storrs, CT: The Roper Center for Public Opinion Research, University of Connecticut, distributors. Contents: See below.)

Presents data for 1972-78, 1980, 1982-91, 1993, 1994, 1996, 1998, 2000, and 2002. SOURCEBOOK tables 2.15, 2.23-2.25, 2.38, 2.41-2.43, 2.47, 2.50, 2.61, 2.62, 2.66, 2.68, 2.97.

This cumulative data file merges all 24 General Social Surveys into a single machine-readable data file with each survey year as a subfile. Interviews were conducted by the National Opinion Research Center during February, March, and April of 1972-78, 1980, 1982-91, 1993, 1994, 1996, 1998, 2000, and 2002. The data are derived from a national probability sample of English-speaking adults, 18 years of age and older, living in non-institutional arrangements in the United States. Survey questions relate to a variety of social issues, including politics, abortion, religion, homosexuality, crime, law enforcement, guns, and capital punishment. A comprehensive codebook entitled *General Social Surveys, 1972-2002: Cumulative Codebook* is published by The Roper Center for Public Opinion Research. Survey methodology and the data program are explained in detail in the codebook.

The Pew Research Center for the People & the Press
The 2004 Political Landscape: Evenly Divided and Increasingly Polarized

(Special. Washington: The Pew Research Center for the People & the Press, 2003. 152 pages, 14 tables, 9 figures.)

Presents data for 2003. SOURCEBOOK tables 2.30-2.32, 2.46, 2.102.

This report presents results from a nationwide survey of adults, 18 years of age and older, conducted in 2003. The survey examined issues related to parties and politics, including party affiliation and early voting intentions. Trend data showing party identification dating back to the 1930s and a discussion of key swing voting groups are included. Numerous topics focusing on political values and attitudes are examined. Included are respondents' attitudes on several foreign policy items (e.g., global engagement, military strength), international threats, and patriotism. Attitudes about success and poverty, including personal empowerment and efficacy; government responsibility (e.g., providing a safety net for the needy); and social and political attitudes about race are discussed. Data on cynicism toward politics and government, trust, and participation in the political process are presented. Public attitudes toward business, government regulation, and labor are shown next. The final sections cover respondents' attitudes about religion, civil liberties, immigration, technology, and the environment. A discussion of survey methodology, the questionnaires, and results from the October News Interest Index also are included.

Rose, Lowell C. and Alec M. Gallup

"The 35th Annual Phi Delta Kappa/Gallup Poll of the Public's Attitudes Toward the Public Schools"

(Annual. *Phi Delta Kappan* (September 2003), pp. 41-56. 16 pages, 43 tables, 13 figures.)

Presents data for 2003 and data for selected years 1983-2003. SOURCEBOOK table 2.4.

This article presents the results of an annual public opinion survey on attitudes toward public schools. Data are provided on a variety of topics including improving the public schools, biggest problems facing local schools, grading the schools, public versus nonpublic schools, school choice, school vouchers, teachers' salaries, academic achievement gaps, standardized testing, and school size. A major focus of the 2003 poll is the Federal No Child Left Behind Act passed in 2002, which increases the Federal Government's role in State and local education. Summary charts addressing policy implications are included in this edition. A brief explanation of the composition of the sample and the research procedure also is provided.

Sax, Linda J.; Alexander W. Astin; Jennifer A. Lindholm; William S. Korn; Victor B. Saenz; and Kathryn M. Mahoney

The American Freshman: National Norms for Fall 2003

(Annual. Higher Education Research Institute. Los Angeles: University of California, 2003. 184 pages, 5 tables, 10 figures, 6 appendices.)

Presents data for 2003 and trend data for 1966-2003. SOURCEBOOK tables 2.90-2.95.

This report presents the results of a national survey of students attending colleges and universities as first-time, full-time freshmen in fall 2003. The survey examines social issues and activism, professional interests and goals, economic concerns and their effect on college choice, lifetime goals such as social and financial success, activities during high school, and attitudes toward a variety of political and social issues. These data are based on the responses of 276,449 students at 413 of the Nation's 4-year colleges and universities. A discussion of survey methodology, the data collection instruments, and a list of participating colleges and universities are included.

U.S. Department of Health and Human Services, Substance Abuse and Mental Health Services Administration

Emergency Department Trends from the Drug Abuse Warning Network, Final Estimates 1995-2002

(Annual. Drug Abuse Warning Network Series: D-24. Rockville, MD: U.S. Department of Health and Human Services, 2003. 620 pages, 309 tables, 18 figures, 6 appendices.)

Presents data for 2002 and trend data for 1995-2002. SOURCEBOOK tables 3.92-3.94.

This report presents annual and semi-annual estimates of drug abuse-related emergency department episodes for 1995-2002. The data were compiled by the Substance Abuse and Mental Health Services Administration through the Drug Abuse Warning Network (DAWN). National estimates of the number of hospital emergency department episodes directly related to use of illegal drugs or the nonmedical use of legal drugs are presented. Estimates are provided for demographic and episodic characteristics as well as type of drug involved. Detailed breakdowns are presented for numerous drugs including cocaine/crack, heroin, marijuana/hashish, amphetamines, methamphetamine, ecstasy, LSD, PCP, and inhalants. These data also are presented for 21 large U.S. metropolitan areas. The appendices include a detailed discussion of the DAWN methodology, revisions to the measurement of race and ethnicity, and error sources in the DAWN data. Also included is a glossary of terms, the Multum license agreement, and a copy of the DAWN emergency department report form.

National Survey of Substance Abuse Treatment Services (N-SSATS): 2002

(Annual. Rockville, MD: U.S. Department of Health and Human Services, 2003. 147 pages, 69 tables, 7 figures, 3 appendices.)

Presents data for 2002 and trend data for 1996-2002. SOURCEBOOK table 6.62.

This report presents data from national censuses of substance abuse treatment facilities in the 50 States, the District of Columbia, and the U.S. Territories. These data were collected through the National Survey of Substance Abuse Treatment Services (N-SSATS) administered by the Substance Abuse and Mental Health Services Administration. Detailed data are presented on trends in facility characteristics including number of facilities, facilities dispensing methadone, facility ownership, programs for special populations, and managed care. Information also is presented on facility characteristics including type of care offered, type of services provided, programs for special groups (e.g., adolescents and HIV patients), type of payment accepted, and funding sources. Data for clients include number of clients broken down by type of care received and substance problem treated. The final chapter displays detailed facility and client data for the 50 States and the other jurisdictions included in the survey. The appendices include a copy of the questionnaire sent to facilities, item response rates for the 2002 survey, and background information for the N-SSATS.

Results from the 2003 National Survey on Drug Use and Health: National Findings

(Annual. Rockville, MD: U.S. Department of Health and Human Services, 2004. 254 pages, 57 figures, 84 tables, 7 appendices.)

Presents data for 2002 and 2003 and trend data for 1965-2002. SOURCEBOOK tables 2.82, 3.86-3.88, 3.98, 3.102.

This report presents findings from the 2002 and 2003 National Surveys on Drug Use and Health (NSDUH), including national estimates of rates of drug use, numbers of users, and numerous other measures of substance use and related problems in the U.S. population. The data are presented in nine chapters that focus on the following topics: use of illicit drugs, alcohol, and tobacco broken down by several key characteristics such as demographics, employment status, and frequency of use; trends in initiation of substance use; youth prevention-related issues including perceptions of risk and attitudes about school; substance dependence, abuse, and treatment; and the prevalence and treatment of mental health problems. The technical appendices include a description of the survey, statistical methods and measurement information, key NSDUH definitions, a listing of other data sources, references, sample size and population tables, and detailed prevalence tables.

U.S. Department of Homeland Security, Office of Immigration Statistics

2003 Yearbook of Immigration Statistics

(Annual. Washington: USGPO, 2004 [Online]. Available: http://uscis.gov/graphics/shared/aboutus/statistics/2003yearbook.pdf [Oct. 7, 2004]. 195 pages, 60 tables, 12 figures, 4 appendices.)

Presents data for fiscal 2003 and trend data for 1820-2003. SOURCEBOOK tables 4.46, 4.47, 5.75, 5.76.

This report presents data on immigrants applying for legal status in the United States and law enforcement activities involving locating and removing deportable aliens. The report is divided into eight chapters and a glossary. The first two chapters provide an introduction to the report and highlights from the 2003 data. Chapters three through seven are each devoted to one of the five legal status categories available to immigrants. Chapter three provides detailed data on aliens granted lawful permanent residence (i.e., green-card recipients) and includes a brief discussion of preferential statuses and numeric limitations imposed. Chapters four and five are devoted to refugees and asylees seeking legal status because of persecution abroad. The next chapter includes information on persons coming to the U.S. as temporary admissions. These include nonimmigrants such as tourists, students, and businesspersons; and parolees, which are persons who initially appear inadmissible but are granted temporary admission for a special circumstance such as medical need. Chapter seven shows detailed data on persons becoming U.S. citizens through the naturalization process. Chapter eight focuses on the enforcement activities of the Department of Homeland Security to prevent illegal entry into the U.S. and to apprehend and remove deportable aliens. Included is a discussion of border patrol activities, investigations of immigration law violations, and the removal process. The appendices include the fiscal 2003 immigration limits, a description of the data sources, and geographic definitions.

U.S. Department of Justice, Bureau of Justice Assistance

Edward Byrne Memorial State and Local Law Enforcement Assistance Program Brief: Fiscal Year 2002

(Annual. Washington: U.S. Department of Justice, 2002. 7 pages, 1 table.)

Presents data for fiscal 2002. SOURCEBOOK table 1.16.

This report describes the Edward Byrne Memorial State and Local Law Enforcement Assistance Program. The program provides funds to States and units of local government to improve the functioning of criminal justice systems and enhance drug control efforts. The legislatively authorized program purposes are discussed, including the types of activities and projects to which jurisdictions may allocate the formula grant funds. Brief discussions of procedures for allocating the fiscal 2002 funds as well as the legislatively mandated evaluation activities also are included. Finally, a table presenting the dollar amount of formula grant funds allocated to each State and the percentage to be passed through to local jurisdictions is provided.

U.S. Department of Justice, Bureau of Justice Statistics

Background Checks for Firearm Transfers, 2003

(Annual. Bulletin NCJ 204428. Washington: U.S. Department of Justice, September 2004. 15 pages, 11 tables, 2 appendices.)

Presents data for 2003 and trend data for 1994-2003. SOURCEBOOK tables 1.110, 1.111.

This report provides information on background checks for firearm transfers conducted by State and local agencies or the Federal Bureau of Investigation through the National Instant Criminal Background Check System (NICS). The data include national estimates of the total number of applications received and rejected, the reasons for rejection, and estimates of applications and rejections for each type of approval system. Also provided is information about appeals of rejected applications and arrest of persons denied (for falsified applications or outstanding warrant). Provisions of the Federal Gun Control Act and the Brady Act are discussed, and an overview of the national firearm check system is included. Also provided is a table that presents major changes in State laws related to firearms sales from 1999 to 2003. Detailed information for the Bureau of Justice Statistics-sponsored Firearm Inquiry Statistics Program, which collects the data for background checks conducted by State and local agencies, is included. The appendices detail the methodology, type of agency responsible for background checks by type of firearm, and a by-State listing of the State and local agencies conducting background checks.

Capital Punishment, 2003

(Annual. Bulletin NCJ 206627. Washington: U.S. Department of Justice, November 2004. 12 pages, 11 tables, 4 figures.)

Presents data for 2003 and trend data for 1930-2003. SOURCEBOOK tables 6.79, 6.81-6.84, 6.87.

This bulletin presents data on prisoners sentenced to death, current methods of execution, and recent changes in capital punishment legislation. Prisoner information includes sex, race, ethnicity, age, education, marital status, and criminal history. The number of executions occurring in each jurisdiction since 1930 is presented. Data on prisoners removed from death row by means other than execution also are included.

Census of Jails, 1999

(Periodic. NCJ 186633. Washington: U.S. Department of Justice, September 2001. 48 pages, 50 tables, 1 figure.)

Presents data for 1999 and trend data for selected years 1983-99. SOURCEBOOK tables 1.98-1.101, 1.105, 6.16, 6.24.

This report presents results from the 1999 Census of Jails sponsored by the U.S. Department of Justice, Bureau of Justice Statistics. Detailed data are presented for jail facility characteristics, staff and correctional officers, jail programs and procedures, and persons under jurisdiction of jail authorities on June 30, 1999. The facility data include number of jails, number of jail jurisdictions, rated capacity, occupied capacity, jails under court order or consent decree, and size of jails. Information focusing on staff and correctional officers includes occupational category and demographic characteristics (sex, race, Hispanic origin). Data for jail programs and procedures include mental health delivery systems; screening policies for tuberculosis; testing policies for HIV; suicide prevention procedures; and jails offering work, educational, and counseling programs. Data presented for jail inmates include number of persons under jail supervision, inmates confined in facilities, and number under community supervision. Also shown are inmate demographic characteristics, conviction status, new admissions, HIV cases, suspected tuberculosis cases, and inmate deaths.

Census of State and Federal Correctional Facilities, 2000

(Periodic. NCJ 198272. Washington: U.S. Department of Justice, 2003. 19 pages, 30 tables.)

Presents data for 2000 and selected data for 1995. SOURCEBOOK tables 1.102-1.104, 6.31, 6.34, 6.40.

This report presents results from the 2000 Census of State and Federal Adult Correctional Facilities sponsored by the U.S. Department of Justice, Bureau of Justice Statistics. The census is conducted approximately every 5 years and includes all adult correctional institutions operated by State and Federal authorities along with private facilities operating under contract to government authorities. The census collects information on facilities, prisoners, and staff. Earlier censuses were conducted in 1974, 1979, 1984, 1990, and 1995. Facility information includes the number and type of correctional facilities nationwide, facility operators, average daily populations, rated capacities, and facility size and age. Also included are the number of facilities offering work, education, and counseling programs, and the number of boot camp programs. Data on prisoners include the number of prisoners under custody; sex, race, and Hispanic origin breakdowns; security levels; deaths in correctional facilities; and counts of special populations including prisoners under age 18 and non-citizens in custody. Staff data include number of employees by occupational category and facility type, as well as sex, race, and Hispanic origin breakdowns. Other topics covered include assaults and other prisoner violations, prisoner-to-employee ratios, and facilities under court order. Comparisons are made, when possible, with findings from the 1995 census.

Census of State and Local Law Enforcement Agencies, 2000

(Periodic. Bulletin NCJ 194066. Washington: U.S. Department of Justice, October 2002. 15 pages, 16 tables, 8 figures.)

Presents data for 2000 and trend data for 1992, 1996, and 2000. SOURCEBOOK tables 1.27-1.32.

This report presents data from the 2000 Census of State and Local Law Enforcement Agencies sponsored by the U.S. Department of Justice, Bureau of Justice Statistics and the Office of Community Oriented Policing Services. The 2000 census included all full-time law enforcement agencies that employed at least one full-time sworn officer with general arrest powers, or the equivalent in part-time officers. Data are presented on the number of agencies and the number of full- and part-time employees, both sworn and nonsworn for local police agencies, sheriffs' offices, State police agencies, and special jurisdiction agencies (e.g., college and university police, State capitol police, etc.). The employee and agency counts are presented by State, and the Nation's largest local agencies, sheriffs' offices, and special jurisdiction agencies are separately listed according to the number of full-time officers employed. Data also are presented on selected areas of duty, i.e., patrol, investigation, jail operation, and court operation.

Compendium of Federal Justice Statistics, 2001

(Annual. NCJ 201627. Washington: U.S. Department of Justice, 2003. 123 pages, 53 tables, 31 figures.)

Presents data for fiscal 2001. SOURCEBOOK tables 4.33-4.35, 4.41, 5.13-5.21, 6.4, 6.8, 6.58, 6.59, 6.70, 6.71.

This report presents detailed information on the processing of cases in the Federal criminal justice system during fiscal 2001. The data are from the Federal Justice Statistics Program database, which is constructed from files provided by the Executive Office for U.S. Attorneys, the Administrative Office of the United States Courts, the Federal Pretrial Services Agency, the U.S. Marshals Service, the Drug Enforcement Administration, the U.S. Sentencing Commission, the Federal probation and supervision service, and the Federal Bureau of Prisons. Information is provided on arrests for Federal offenses by offense category, arresting agency, and arrestee demographics; prosecutorial decisionmaking by U.S. attorneys; type and outcome of pretrial release or detention; disposition of cases; type and length of sentences imposed; and appeals processed. In addition, detailed data are provided for persons under Federal correctional supervision. These tables include number of persons under community supervision; outcomes of probation, parole, and supervised release; number and characteristics of Federal prisoners; and time served by released Federal prisoners. A description of the methodology and a glossary of terms are included.

Correctional Populations in the United States, 1998 Statistical Tables

(Periodic. NCJ 192929. Washington: U.S. Department of Justice [Online]. Available: http://www.ojp.usdoj.gov/bjs/abstract/cpusst.htm [Aug. 10, 2004]. 88 tables.)

Presents data for 1998 and trend data for 1930-98. SOURCEBOOK table 6.86.

This set of tables presents data on persons under supervision of all major components of the correctional system including persons under probation and parole supervision; persons confined in jails, State and Federal prisons, and military correctional facilities; and persons under sentence of death. The data include jurisdiction-level counts of prisoners, probationers, and parolees, by sex, race, Hispanic origin, admission type, release type, and sentence length. Data are also provided on persons under jail jurisdiction in the Nation, as well as the 25 largest jail jurisdictions. Jail information includes the number of inmates by sex, race, Hispanic origin, juvenile status, and conviction status, and the total jail capacity and percent occupied at midyear. The tables also include data on characteristics of prisoners under sentence of death, reported separately for those who entered prison and those who were removed from under a death sentence during the year. Finally, the tables include detailed data on correctional facilities operated by the U.S. military and characteristics of persons confined under military authority at yearend. Copies of the questionnaires used to collect the data and detailed jurisdictional notes are included.

Crime and the Nation's Households, 2003

(Periodic. Bulletin NCJ 206348. Washington: U.S. Department of Justice, October 2004. 4 pages, 5 tables, 2 figures.)

Presents data for 2003 and trend data for 1994-2003. SOURCEBOOK table 3.27.

This bulletin presents data from the National Crime Victimization Survey (NCVS) on the impact of crime on households in the United States. Data are presented on the number and percent of households experiencing violent crime, including rape, sexual assault, robbery, and assault; purse snatching/pocket picking; property crime, including burglary, motor vehicle theft, and theft; intimate partner violence; and vandalism. The data are displayed by race of household head, size of household, place of residence, and region. A brief methodology section describes the households-experiencing-crime indicators.

Criminal Victimization, 2003

(Annual. NCJ 205455. Washington: U.S. Department of Justice, September 2004. 12 pages, 10 tables, 14 figures.)

Presents data for 2003 and trend data for 1993-2003. SOURCEBOOK tables 3.1-3.4, 3.16, 3.21.

This report presents information on criminal victimization in the United States from the National Crime Victimization Survey (NCVS). The NCVS collects data on nonfatal crimes against persons age 12 and older, reported and nonreported to the police. Data presented include levels and rates of victimization for the personal crimes of rape, sexual assault, robbery, assault, and personal theft, and the property crimes of household burglary, motor vehicle theft, and theft. Violent crime rates are presented for several victim characteristics including age, sex, race, and income. Property crime rates are presented for characteristics of household. This report also includes a comparison of 2-year average annual rates for personal and property crimes, which facilitates comparisons of statistically significant year-to-year changes.

Criminal Victimization in the United States, 2002 Statistical Tables

(Annual. NCJ 200561. Washington: U.S. Department of Justice [Online]. Available: http://www.ojp.usdoj.gov/bjs/pub/pdf/cvus02.pdf [Mar. 3, 2004]. 113 tables.)

Presents data for 2002. SOURCEBOOK tables 3.5-3.15, 3.17-3.20, 3.22-3.26, 3.28-3.35.

This set of tables presents data on criminal victimization in the United States during 2002 and is part of an ongoing series prepared from the National Crime Victimization Survey (NCVS) program. The 2002 NCVS collected data from a nationally representative sample of approximately 76,050 persons in 42,000 households. The NCVS gathers information on personal victimization including rape, sexual assault, robbery, assault, and purse snatching and pocket picking. Also gathered are data on property crimes including burglary, motor vehicle theft, and theft. The statistical tables are divided into six sections: demography of victims, victims and offenders, geography, the crime event, victims and the criminal justice system, and series victimizations. Also included is a detailed discussion of the survey methodology and a glossary of terms used in the tables.

Education and Correctional Populations

(Special. Special Report NCJ 195670. Washington: U.S. Department of Justice, January 2003. 12 pages, 16 tables.)

Presents data for 1997 and other selected years. SOURCEBOOK tables 1.109, 6.45, 6.46.

This special report presents data from several U.S. Department of Justice, Bureau of Justice Statistics surveys of prisoners, jail inmates, and probationers; the Bureau of Labor Statistics' Current Population Survey; and the National Center for Educational Statistics' National Adult Literacy Survey. The report compares educational attainment of State and Federal prisoners, local jail inmates, and persons on probation to that of the general population. Educational attainment is presented for various demographic groups (e.g., sex, race, ethnicity, age, citizenship, and military service), as well as for other social and economic factors. Data comparing dropping out of school for those in local jails and the general population also are discussed. Additionally, data describing the availability of educational programs for those housed in State and Federal prisons and in local jails, and their participation in educational and vocational programs since incarceration are presented.

Federal Law Enforcement Officers, 2002

(Periodic. Bulletin NCJ 199995. Washington: U.S. Department of Justice, August 2003. 17 pages, 10 tables, 4 figures.)

Presents data for 2002. SOURCEBOOK tables 1.72-1.75.

This bulletin presents data provided by Federal agencies in response to a survey conducted by the U.S. Department of Justice, Bureau of Justice Statistics. The report presents information on full-time Federal law enforcement personnel with Federal arrest authority who were authorized to carry firearms in the performance of their duties. Data are presented on the number of Federal officers employed by each agency; sex, race, and ethnicity breakdowns of Federal officers; the major States of employment for agencies employing 750 or more officers; and the number of Federal officers per 100,000 residents in each State. Assaults on Federal officers in selected large agencies are reported, as are data on Federal officers stationed in the U.S. Territories. Also included are a table listing the primary States of employment for officers of eight large Federal agencies and the website addresses for numerous Federal law enforcement agencies.

The survey was conducted prior to the enactment of legislation creating the Department of Homeland Security. However, the report includes a discussion of changes to Federal law enforcement resulting from the Homeland Security Act of 2002.

Felony Defendants in Large Urban Counties, 2000

(Biennial. NCJ 202021. Washington: U.S. Department of Justice, 2003. 46 pages, 43 tables, 22 figures, 1 appendix.)

Presents data for 2000. SOURCEBOOK tables 5.51-5.60.

This report presents data on the processing of felony defendants in the State courts of the 75 most populous counties in the United States. The data are from the State Court Processing Statistics (SCPS) program (formerly the National Pretrial Reporting Program) sponsored by the U.S. Department of Justice, Bureau of Justice Statistics. Information from the 2000 SCPS is presented on demographic characteristics, arrest charge, criminal history, pretrial release and detention, adjudication outcome, and sentencing of felony defendants in the 75 largest counties. A methodology section describes the SCPS program sampling and provides definitions of offenses and related terms used in the report.

Felony Sentences in State Courts, 2000

(Biennial. Bulletin NCJ 198821. Washington: U.S. Department of Justice, June 2003. 12 pages, 12 tables, 3 figures.)

Presents data for 2000 and trend data for selected years 1992-2000. SOURCEBOOK tables 5.44-5.50.

This bulletin presents data on felony sentences imposed by State courts. The data are from the National Judicial Reporting Program administered by the U.S. Department of Justice, Bureau of Justice Statistics. The results are based on case processing in a nationally representative sample of 344 counties. Information presented includes number of felony convictions and types of sentences imposed by State courts. Data on sentence length, estimated time to be served, and demographic characteristics of persons convicted of felonies are included. Processing information including method of conviction (jury, bench, plea) and average time between arrest and sentencing is presented, as is information on the imposition of additional penalties (e.g., restitution, treatment, etc.) by State courts.

Firearm Use by Offenders

(Special. Special Report NCJ 189369. Washington: U.S. Department of Justice, November 2001. 15 pages, 17 tables.)

Presents data for 1991 and 1997. SOURCEBOOK tables 6.35-6.38.

This report presents data from surveys of inmates in State and Federal correctional facilities conducted by the U.S. Census Bureau for the U.S. Department of Justice, Bureau of Justice Statistics and the Federal Bureau of Prisons. The report provides highlights from the surveys regarding firearm use by offenders, detailed tables, survey sampling and statistical methodology, and firearm definitions. Data presented include the possession, use, source, and types of firearms used by offenders during their current offense, and selected characteristics of these offenders such as age, sex, ethnicity, family background, criminal history, prior sentences, and type of current offense.

HIV in Prisons, 2001

(Annual. Bulletin NCJ 202293. Washington: U.S. Department of Justice, January 2004. 8 pages, 6 tables, 2 figures.)

Presents data for 2001 and trend data for 1991-2001. SOURCEBOOK tables 6.74-6.78.

This report presents information on HIV infection and AIDS cases in State and Federal prisons. The data include the number of prisoners known to be HIV positive and confirmed AIDS cases for the 50 States, the District of Columbia, and the Federal Bureau of Prisons. Number and rate of total prisoner deaths and AIDS-related deaths also are presented for each State, the Federal prison system, and the District of Columbia for selected years. The incidence of AIDS cases and related deaths among prisoners is compared to the general U.S. population. A methodology section discusses the sources of data for the information provided.

Immigration Offenders in the Federal Criminal Justice System, 2000

(Special. Special Report NCJ 191745. Washington: U.S. Department of Justice, August 2002. 11 pages, 19 tables, 10 figures.)

Presents data for 2000 and trend data for 1985-2000. SOURCEBOOK tables 5.77, 5.78, 6.60.

This report presents information on offenders charged with immigration offenses. The data are from the U.S. Department of Justice, Bureau of Justice Statistics' Federal Justice

Statistics Program. Included are trend data on the number of offenders investigated, charged, and sent to Federal prison for immigration offenses. The nationality of suspects investigated, type of immigration offense, demographic characteristics, and criminal history of offenders is presented. Also included are data on sentence types and average time to be served for those convicted of immigration offenses. Finally, selected information for noncitizens in the Federal criminal justice system is shown, including number of noncitizens charged, type of offense (primarily drugs or immigration offenses), and the number of noncitizens in Federal prisons.

Intimate Partner Violence, 1993-2001

(Periodic. Crime Data Brief NCJ 197838. Washington: U.S. Department of Justice, February 2003. 2 pages, 3 tables, 1 figure.)

Presents data for 1993-2001. SOURCEBOOK table 3.132.

This data brief presents information on nonlethal victimizations perpetrated by intimate partners. The data are from the Bureau of Justice Statistics' National Crime Victimization Survey. Offenses included are rape, sexual assault, robbery, aggravated assault, and simple assault. Information is presented for female and male victims. Also included is a table presenting the number of murder victims killed by intimate partners; these data are from the Federal Bureau of Investigations' Supplementary Homicide Reports.

Jails in Indian Country, 2002

(Annual. Bulletin NCJ 198997. Washington: U.S. Department of Justice, November 2003. 12 pages, 7 tables, 1 figure.)

Presents data for 2002 and trend data for 1998, 2000-2002. SOURCEBOOK table 6.25.

This report presents data from the fifth Survey of Jails in Indian Country, a data collection effort initiated in 1998 by the U.S. Department of Justice, Bureau of Justice Statistics. Summary tables present aggregate data for all Indian country jails surveyed in 2001 and 2002, and selected data from the 1998 and 2000 surveys. These data include number of adult and juvenile inmates, type of supervision, inmate movements, and staff characteristics. Facility characteristics include rated capacities, percent occupied, jails operating above 150% of capacity, the 10 largest jails, and facilities under court order or consent decree. An additional set of tables lists the jail facilities surveyed and provides detailed data for each.

Justice Expenditure and Employment Statistics

(Annual. Washington: U.S. Department of Justice. Contents: See below. Available: http://www.ojp.usdoj.gov/bjs/eande.htm.)

Presents data for 2001 and trend data for 1982-2001. SOURCEBOOK tables 1.1-1.11, 1.17-1.26.

These tables display detailed criminal justice expenditure and employment data for 2001 and national trend data for 1982 to 2001. The data were compiled from existing data sources and from annual surveys of government finances and employment conducted by the U.S. Census Bureau. Detailed data are presented for Federal, State, and local governments on three categories of criminal justice activities: police protection; judicial, including courts, legal services, prosecution, and public defense; and corrections. The data include national and by-State expenditures by governments for criminal justice-related activities and number of personnel employed for these functions. Selected data are shown for counties with populations of 500,000 or more and cities with populations of 300,000 or more. Also available is supporting text material providing a description of the methodology; definitions of concepts, categories, and terms; differences affecting comparability over time; and information about the relative standard errors associated with the survey estimates.

Law Enforcement Management and Administrative Statistics, 2000: Data for Individual State and Local Agencies with 100 or More Officers

(Special. NCJ 203350. Washington: U.S. Department of Justice, 2004. 272 pages, 40 tables, 4 figures, 1 appendix.)

Presents data for 2000. SOURCEBOOK tables 1.59-1.62.

This monograph presents data from the 2000 Law Enforcement Management and Administrative Statistics (LEMAS) program of the U.S. Department of Justice, Bureau of Justice Statistics. The 2000 LEMAS survey was mailed to all State and local law enforcement agencies that reported employing 100 or more sworn officers in a 1996 Bureau of Justice Statistics census of State and local law enforcement agencies. In addition, a sample of agencies with fewer than 100 officers received a slightly abbreviated version of the questionnaire. This report presents data for 804 agencies with 100 or more full-time officers and 35 or more full-time officers whose regularly assigned duties included responding to calls for service. This includes 49 State police agencies, 32 county police departments, 501 municipal police departments, and 222 sheriffs' offices. Detailed data are presented on personnel including full- and part-time, and sworn and civilian employees; expenditures and pay; community policing; operations; equipment; computers and information systems; and agency policies and programs. A copy of the survey questionnaire is included.

Local Police Departments 2000

(Periodic. NCJ 196002. Washington: U.S. Department of Justice, 2003. 28 pages, 59 tables, 24 figures.)

Presents data for 2000 and trend data for 1990, 1997, 1999, and 2000. SOURCEBOOK tables 1.33, 1.35, 1.37, 1.39, 1.41, 1.43, 1.45, 1.47, 1.49, 1.51, 1.53.

This report presents data from the 2000 Law Enforcement Management and Administrative Statistics (LEMAS) survey sponsored by the U.S. Department of Justice, Bureau of Justice Statistics and the Office of Community Oriented Policing Services. The data represent the nearly 13,000 local police departments operated by municipal, county, or tribal governments. Information presented includes number and type of personnel, budgets and salary levels, operations, community policing initiatives, equipment, use of computer and information systems, and written policies and procedures.

Mental Health Treatment in State Prisons, 2000

(Special. Special Report NCJ 188215. Washington: U.S. Department of Justice, July 2001. 8 pages, 8 tables, 1 appendix.)

Presents data for 2000. SOURCEBOOK tables 6.72, 6.73.

This special report presents data on mental health services and treatment in State prisons. The data are from the 2000 Census of State and Federal Adult Correctional Facilities, sponsored by the U.S. Department of Justice, Bureau of Justice Statistics. Information is provided on mental health screening for prisoners, the number of prisoners receiving mental health treatment, and type of treatment provided (e.g., 24-hour mental health care, therapy/counseling, psychotropic medications). Data are provided by type of facility (e.g., confinement or community-based, public or private, male or female only prisoner populations, population size, and security level), and are broken down by State and region.

Offenders Returning to Federal Prison, 1986-97

(Special. Special Report NCJ 182991. Washington: U.S. Department of Justice, September 2000. 10 pages, 7 tables, 5 figures.)

Presents data for 1986-97. SOURCEBOOK tables 6.68, 6.69.

This report presents data on Federal offenders returning to prison within 3 years of release. The data include the number of Federal prison releases and the number and percent of offenders returned to prison from 1986 to 1997. The data are displayed by offense type, demographic characteristics, reason for return to prison, and time served prior to release. Returns of offenders sentenced before and after implementation of Federal sentencing guidelines are compared. A methodology section describes the data sources and the study.

Police Departments in Large Cities, 1990-2000

(Special. Special Report NCJ 175703. Washington: U.S. Department of Justice, May 2002. 16 pages, 28 tables, 5 figures.)

Presents data for 1990 and 2000. SOURCEBOOK tables 1.55-1.58.

This report presents data from the 1990 and 2000 Law Enforcement Management and Administrative Statistics (LEMAS) surveys sponsored by the U.S. Department of Justice, Bureau of Justice Statistics and the Federal Bureau of Investigation's (FBI) Uniform Crime Reporting Program (UCR). Data are included for police departments in 62 cities with populations of 250,000 or more residents in both of the survey years. Information is provided on police department staffing levels including minority and female employment in police departments, officer education and training requirements, operating budgets, officer salaries and special pay, types of special units operated, drug enforcement activities, sidearm and armor policies, types of vehicles operated, and computerization of information systems. FBI Crime Index data are compared with police employment levels from the LEMAS surveys for each of the 62 cities included in the report.

Prison and Jail Inmates at Midyear 2003

(Annual. Bulletin NCJ 203947. Washington: U.S. Department of Justice, May 2004. 14 pages, 14 tables, 2 figures.)

Presents data for 2003 and trend data for 1990-2003. SOURCEBOOK tables 6.14, 6.15, 6.17, 6.39, 6.42.

This bulletin presents data from the 2003 National Prisoner Statistics program and the 2003 Annual Survey of Jails as well as trend data from both programs. Information presented includes the number of prisoners held in State and Federal prisons and in local jails, prisoners under jurisdiction of State and Federal correctional authorities, changes in the number of prisoners under jurisdiction of State and Federal correctional authorities, prisoners admitted to and released from State and Federal jurisdiction, prisoners held in private facilities, the number of State prisoners under age 18, and the number of noncitizens held in State and Federal prisons. Data for local jails include jail population trends, capacity figures, characteristics of jail inmates, confinement status, type of supervision program, and figures for the 50 largest jail jurisdictions. A brief discussion of the two data sources is included.

Prisoners in 2003

(Annual. Bulletin NCJ 205335. Washington: U.S. Department of Justice, November 2004. 12 pages, 12 tables.)

Presents data for 2003 and trend data for 1995-2003. SOURCEBOOK tables 6.13, 6.28-6.30, 6.32, 6.33, 6.41, 6.61, 6.64.

This report presents data on prisoners under the jurisdiction of State and Federal adult correctional authorities. The total number of prisoners, prisoners sentenced to more than 1 year, and rates of incarceration are presented for each State, the Federal prison system, and four geographic regions. Changes in the number of sentenced prisoners from 1995 to 2003 also are shown for the States, regions, and the Federal prison system. Data are provided for prisoners under military jurisdiction, State and Federal prisoners held in private facilities and local jails, prisoners in custody in the U.S. Territories, and State and Federal prison capacities. Also shown are incarceration rates by sex, race, Hispanic origin, and age of prisoners. The number of Immigration and Customs Enforcement (ICE) detainees also is provided along with facility type for 1995, 2002, and 2003. The methodology section discusses the data collection programs and variations among jurisdictions in reported data.

Probation and Parole in the United States, 2003

(Annual. Bulletin NCJ 205336. Washington: U.S. Department of Justice, July 2004. 8 pages, 9 tables.)

Presents data for 2003 and trend data for 1995-2003. SOURCEBOOK tables 6.1-6.3, 6.65, 6.66.

This bulletin presents data from the Annual Probation and Parole Surveys conducted by the U.S. Department of Justice, Bureau of Justice Statistics. Included are counts of persons under probation and parole supervision in each State, the District of Columbia, and the Federal system. Data from the most recent survey, the 2003 survey, show probation and parole counts for Jan. 1 and Dec. 31, 2003, entries to and exits from supervision during 2003, and rates of persons under each type of community supervision per 100,000 adult residents. Also shown are data on characteristics of adults on probation and parole, including demographic characteristics, offense type, and supervision status. The top 10 States are ranked according to those with the largest community corrections populations, the largest percent increase, and the highest and lowest rates of persons under community supervision. Figures also are provided for the total number of persons under correctional supervision in the United States, i.e., probation, jail, prison, and parole populations combined.

Profile of Jail Inmates, 2002

(Special. Special Report NCJ 201932. Washington: U.S. Department of Justice, July 2004. 12 pages, 19 tables.)

Presents data for 2002 and selected data for 1996. SOURCEBOOK tables 6.18-6.23.

This special report presents data from the 2002 Survey of Inmates in Local Jails sponsored by the U.S. Department of Justice, Bureau of Justice Statistics. Interviews were conducted from a nationally representative sample of over 6,900 inmates in 417 jails. Inmates provided extensive information on current offenses and sentences, conviction status, time served, criminal history, drug and alcohol use and treatment, family background, and individual characteristics including demographic and employment history data. Inmates also reported on experiences of physical or sexual abuse prior to admission to jail and whether they had been under a restraining order prior to admission.

Prosecutors in State Courts, 2001

(Periodic. Bulletin NCJ 193441. Washington: U.S. Department of Justice, May 2002. 12 pages, 14 tables, 2 figures.)

Presents data for 2001. SOURCEBOOK tables 1.85-1.88.

This bulletin presents data from the 2001 National Survey of Prosecutors (NSP) sponsored by the U.S. Department of Justice, Bureau of Justice Statistics. The 2001 NSP was a census of all chief prosecutors that tried felony cases in State courts of general jurisdiction. The report presents data on staffing and budget in prosecutors' offices; annual salary and length of service for chief prosecutors; types of felony, non-felony, and computer-related crimes prosecuted; criminal cases closed and percent convicted; proceedings against juveniles in criminal court; work-related threats and assaults received by members of prosecutors' offices; security measures used for protection; use of DNA evidence; and community-related activities engaged in by prosecutors' offices. A comparison of staffing and budget in prosecutors' offices for 1992, 1994, 1996, and 2001 also is provided. A methodology section discusses respondent selection, data collection, survey response, and data imputation. An appendix table provides a by-State listing of the number, title, areas of jurisdiction, and manner of selection of chief prosecutors.

Recidivism of Prisoners Released in 1994

(Special. Special Report NCJ 193427. Washington: U.S. Department of Justice, June 2002. 16 pages, 13 tables, 1 figure.)

Presents data for prisoners released in 1994. SOURCEBOOK tables 6.47-6.52.

This special report presents data from a U.S. Department of Justice, Bureau of Justice Statistics study on recidivism of prisoners who were released from prison in 1994 in 15 States. The study tracked prisoners who had been sentenced to more than 1 year of incarceration, and examined their recidivism for a period of 3 years after their release in 1994, using four measures: rearrest, reconviction, resentence to prison, and return to prison with or without a new sentence. Highlights of the study are presented, along with a profile of released prisoners, the number and type of both in-State and out-of-State rearrest charges, and States in which out-of-State rearrests occurred. Also shown are recidivism rates at different time periods after release and by various characteristics, including prisoner sex, race, ethnicity, and age; most serious offense for which prisoners were released; charge at rearrest; number of prior arrests; and the amount of time served before first release. The report includes a comparison of recidivism rates of prisoners released in 1994 with those from an earlier study involving prisoners released in 1983. A methodology section discusses the data sources, sampling methodology, and definitions of offenses examined in the study.

Reporting Crime to the Police, 1992-2000

(Special. Special Report NCJ 195710. Washington: U.S. Department of Justice, March 2003. 8 pages, 9 tables, 3 figures.)

Presents data for 1992-2000. SOURCEBOOK table 3.36.

This special report presents estimates of the number and percent of crimes reported to the police. The data are from the National Crime Victimization Survey sponsored by the U.S. Department of Justice, Bureau of Justice Statistics. Estimates of violent and property crimes reported to the police for 2000 are presented, and reporting of violent crime is examined in more detail for the years 1992-2000. Tables showing percentages of violent crimes reported to police are broken down by numerous victim characteristics including sex, race, age, Hispanic origin, income, and others. Also included are percentages of violent victimizations reported to police based on whether injury resulted, the presence of a weapon, victim-offender relationship, and several offender characteristics. Finally, reasons for reporting and not reporting violence to the police, and factors associated with reporting to police are discussed.

Sheriffs' Offices 2000

(Periodic. NCJ 196534. Washington: U.S. Department of Justice, 2003. 28 pages, 59 tables, 24 figures.)

Presents data for 2000 and trend data for 1990, 1997, 1999, and 2000. SOURCEBOOK tables 1.34, 1.36, 1.38, 1.40, 1.42, 1.44, 1.46, 1.48, 1.50, 1.52, 1.54.

This report presents data from the 2000 Law Enforcement Management and Administrative Statistics (LEMAS) survey sponsored by the U.S. Department of Justice, Bureau of Justice Statistics and the Office of Community Oriented Policing Services. The data represent more than 3,000 sheriffs' offices operated by county or independent city governments. Information presented includes number and type of personnel, budgets and salary levels, operations, community policing initiatives, equipment, use of computers and information systems, and written policies and procedures.

State Court Prosecutors in Small Districts, 2001

(Special. Special Report NCJ 196020. Washington: U.S. Department of Justice, January 2003. 10 pages, 13 tables, 3 figures.)

Presents data for 2001. SOURCEBOOK table 1.89.

This report presents data from the 2001 National Survey of Prosecutors (NSP) sponsored by the U.S. Department of Justice, Bureau of Justice Statistics. The 2001 NSP was a census of all chief prosecutors that tried felony cases in State courts of general jurisdiction. This special report focuses on full-time prosecutors' offices that served districts with populations under 250,000. Data are presented on staff size and budget for prosecutors' offices; annual salary for chief prosecutors; types of cases handled, including felony, non-felony, and computer-related crime; criminal cases closed and percent convicted; proceedings against juveniles in criminal court; work-related threats and assaults received by members of prosecutors' offices; security measures used for protection; use of DNA evidence; and community-related activities engaged in by prosecutors' offices. Also provided are selected data for offices with part-time chief prosecutors. A methodology section discusses respondent selection, data collection, survey response, and data imputation.

Summary of State Sex Offender Registries, 2001

(Special. Fact Sheet NCJ 192265. Washington: U.S. Department of Justice, March 2002. 12 pages, 4 tables.)

Presents data for 1998 and 2001. SOURCEBOOK table 6.63.

This report provides information on sex offender registries (SOR) in the 50 States and the District of Columbia. Included is information on the organizational location of each State's registry, e.g., the State police, the department of public safety, the attorney general, or the department of corrections. The number of offenders registered for 1998 and 2001 in each State is included. The extent of each State's SOR automation and DNA sample collection is discussed. Finally, detailed information is presented on community notification by law enforcement agencies and the extent to which this is carried out through posting of offender-specific information on the Internet.

Trends in State Parole, 1990-2000

(Special. Special Report NCJ 184735. Washington: U.S. Department of Justice, October 2001. 15 pages, 22 tables, 4 figures.)

Presents trend data for 1990-2000. SOURCEBOOK tables 6.43, 6.44, 6.67.

This report presents information on trends in State parole populations since 1990. Changes in sentencing policies that have resulted in States moving away from discretionary release by parole boards to mandatory release are discussed. The effects of the Federal truth-in-sentencing standard requiring violent offenders to serve not less than 85% of their sentence before release are examined for the States that have adopted this standard. The report compares discretionary and mandatory releases to parole with the type of discharge from parole supervision. Data are presented on the success and failure rates of offenders on parole by criminal history, sentence length, time served in prison, and offense distribution. The report also profiles specific characteristics and needs of offenders reentering the community, including drug and alcohol use history, homelessness, and mental health status.

Tribal Law Enforcement, 2000

(Special. Fact Sheet NCJ 197936. Washington: U.S. Department of Justice, January 2003. 4 pages, 6 tables, 1 figure.)

Presents data for 2000. SOURCEBOOK table 1.63.

This fact sheet presents data from the 2000 Census of State and Local Law Enforcement Agencies sponsored by the U.S. Department of Justice, Bureau of Justice Statistics. The report presents information on tribally operated law enforcement agencies, full-time sworn personnel, and violent and nonviolent crime reported by law enforcement agencies in Indian country. Also included are data on full-time community policing and school resource officers in tribally operated law enforcement agencies.

U.S. Department of Justice, Criminal Division

"Report to Congress on the Activities and Operations of the Public Integrity Section for 2002"

(Annual. Washington: U.S. Department of Justice, 2004. Mimeographed. 43 pages, 3 tables.)

Presents data for 1983-2002. SOURCEBOOK table 5.79.

This report was compiled by the Public Integrity Section of the U.S. Department of Justice. The report is divided into three sections. Part one discusses the operational responsibilities of the Public Integrity Section including litigation matters, special priorities, and legal and technical assistance provided to other agencies. The second section describes each case prosecuted by the Section during 2002. Part three presents nationwide data on the number of Federal, State, and local public officials and others involved who were indicted, convicted, and awaiting trial for each year from 1983 to 2002. Additionally, the number of convictions of individuals involved in abuse of public office is reported by judicial district.

U.S. Department of Justice, Executive Office for United States Attorneys

United States Attorneys' Annual Statistical Report: Fiscal Year 2002

(Annual. Washington: U.S. Department of Justice, 2004. 146 pages, 29 tables, 32 figures.)

Presents data for fiscal 2002 and trend data for fiscal 1993-2002. SOURCEBOOK tables 1.79, 4.45, 5.6, 5.7.

This annual publication is comprised of graphs, tables, and commentary summarizing the civil and criminal caseloads in U.S. attorneys' offices. Section I provides an overview of U.S. attorneys' offices, including staffing and organization. Section II presents data on criminal prosecutions by U.S. attorneys and includes a discussion of priority criminal prosecution areas such as terrorism, firearms, narcotics, corporate fraud, and civil rights. The third section presents information on U.S. attorneys' asset forfeiture litigation. Section IV presents data on civil litigation by U.S. attorneys, including caseloads and types of civil litigation such as bankruptcy and defensive civil litigation. Section V presents data on criminal and civil appeals, including post-sentencing motions. The final section describes the reconciliation of Federal case processing data, which is a Federal effort to simplify data classification and increase consistency in data processing across different Federal agencies. Detailed statistical tables present data for each of the U.S. District Courts.

U.S. Department of Justice, Federal Bureau of Investigation

"Bank Crime Statistics, Federally Insured Financial Institutions, January 1, 2002- December 31, 2002"

(Annual. Washington: U.S. Department of Justice, 2003. Mimeographed. 16 pages, 27 tables.)

Presents data for 2002. SOURCEBOOK tables 3.149-3.151.

This report presents data on crime involving Federally insured financial institutions. Information is provided on violations of Federal bank robbery statutes including extortion and violations involving armored carriers. The data are broken down by characteristics of the banking institutions, offenders, property loss and recovery, community characteristics, deaths, injuries sustained, hostages taken, and State and region of occurrence.

1999 Bombing Incidents

(Annual. FBI Bomb Data Center General Information Bulletin 99-1. Washington: U.S. Department of Justice, 2003. 27 pages, 18 tables, 10 figures.)

Presents data for 1999 and trend data for 1989-99. SOURCEBOOK tables 3.170-3.172.

This report provides information on bombing incidents reported to the Federal Bureau of Investigation's Bomb Data Center. Data on actual, attempted, and accidental bombing incidents are presented by type of device and resulting property damage, injuries, and deaths. Bombing incidents by State and region are listed and data are presented on types of explosives and devices, type of target, and time of occurrence. Information is provided on improvised devices, hoaxes, and on the apparent motivations of those involved in hoaxes and bombing incidents.

Crime in the United States, 2002

(Annual. FBI Uniform Crime Reports. Washington: USGPO, 2003. 470 pages, 139 tables (estimated), 26 figures, 7 appendices.)

Presents data for 2002 and trend data for 1982-2002. SOURCEBOOK tables 1.66-1.68, 3.106-3.111, 3.117-3.124, 3.129, 3.134, 3.140-3.146, 3.168, 3.169, 4.1-4.27, 4.29.

This report begins with a summary of the Uniform Crime Reporting (UCR) Program including a discussion of the redesign of the UCR and recent data collection developments. The next section presents data on Crime Index offenses reported to the police. Each of the eight index offenses (murder and nonnegligent manslaughter, forcible rape, robbery, aggravated assault, burglary, larceny-theft, motor vehicle theft, and arson) is discussed in terms of number of offenses known to the police, 5-year trends, and characteristics of offenses. Also included is a brief section on hate crime. Detailed tabulations present each of the index offenses by State, metropolitan statistical areas, cities and towns over 10,000 population, and suburban and rural counties. Index offenses occurring on college and university campuses also are included.

Section three presents tables on Crime Index offenses cleared by arrest. Data on offenses known to the police and percent cleared by arrest, and percent cleared by arrest of persons under 18 years of age are displayed. The fourth section focuses on arrests and includes the number and rate of persons arrested for Part I and Part II offenses. Arrest data are displayed by sex, age, and race for total number of arrests, arrests in cities, arrests in suburban areas and counties, and arrests in rural counties. Total arrests and arrests of persons under age 18 for both Part I and Part II offenses are shown for each State. Aggregate data for police disposition of juveniles taken into custody also are included.

Section five presents two special reports. The first, focusing on bank robbery in the United States from 1990-2001, examines data from three FBI databases--the UCR, the National Incident-Based Reporting System (NIBRS), and the Bank Crime Statistics in order to assess the convergence of these three sources. A second special report includes information concerning reported sniper attacks from 1982-2001 and is based on data from the FBI's Supplementary Homicide Reports. Section six is devoted to information on law enforcement personnel. The number of law enforcement employees and officers broken down by sex is shown for each State. Also included are tables showing the number of law enforcement employees and officers for U.S. cities, colleges and universities, and suburban and rural counties. The appendices include a discussion of the methodology, definitions of UCR offenses and reporting areas, a discussion of the Nation's two crime measures, a directory of State UCR programs, a national UCR program directory, and a publications list.

Financial Institution Fraud and Failure Report, Fiscal Year 2003

(Annual. Washington: U.S. Department of Justice, 2003. 51 pages, 21 tables, 11 figures.)

Presents data for fiscal 2003 and trend data for fiscal 1999-2003. SOURCEBOOK table 3.148.

This report presents information on financial institution fraud and failure matters handled by the Federal Bureau of Investigation's (FBI) Financial Institution Fraud Unit. Detailed data are presented on the number of failed financial institutions, the number of failure and fraud investigations pending, cases resulting in indictments and convictions, and types of subjects convicted (e.g., bank employee, bank officer, company or corporation). Also included are data on dollar amounts recovered and received from restitutions and fines. Information on seizures and forfeitures is presented. These data are broken down by type of financial institution (i.e., savings and loans, banks, credit unions) and FBI field office.

Hate Crime Statistics 2002

(Annual. FBI Uniform Crime Reports. Washington: U.S. Department of Justice, 2003. 142 pages, 14 tables, 1 appendix.)

Presents data for 2002. SOURCEBOOK tables 3.112-3.114.

These data were collected by the Federal Bureau of Investigation through the Uniform Crime Reporting Program. The report presents information on bias-motivated (hate) crimes known to police. Data are presented on the number of incidents, offenses, victims, and offenders involved in hate crimes. The data include the type of bias motivation, offense type, and location of incidents. Detailed tables present the number of bias-related offenses in each State, county, and participating police agency as well as information about agencies reporting no incidents of hate crime. Bias-related offenses occurring at universities and colleges also are included. Information concerning the number of quarters each agency contributed to the national hate crime program is reported.

Law Enforcement Officers Killed and Assaulted, 2002

(Annual. FBI Uniform Crime Reports. Washington: U.S. Department of Justice, 2003. 102 pages, 70 tables, 5 figures.)

Presents data for 2002 and trend data for 1991-2002. SOURCEBOOK tables 3.152-3.158, 3.160-3.165.

This report contains detailed information including tables, graphs, and descriptive summaries on law enforcement officers feloniously killed and assaulted in the line of duty. Data on officers killed are presented by State and agency; geographic region; population group; circumstances at the scene of the incident; type of assignment; type of weapon and size of ammunition used in the offense; location of the fatal wound; use of body armor; distance between the officer and offender; and the month, day, and time of the attack. Profiles of the victim officers are presented as well as profiles and dispositions of known assailants.

Information also is provided on law enforcement officers accidentally killed. These data are broken down by geographic region, State, several incident and officer characteristics, and circumstances at the scene of the incident.

Data on officers assaulted are presented by geographic region, population group, type of weapon, circumstances at the scene of the incident, type of assignment, percent receiving personal injury, time of day, and percent of cases cleared.

The report presents data on assaults on Federal officers from six sectors of the U.S. Government: the Department of the Interior, the Department of Justice, the Department of the Treasury, the newly established Department of Homeland Security, the U.S. Capitol Police, and the U.S. Postal Inspection Service. This section begins with departmental summaries of incidents involving assaults on Federal officers that occurred during 2002. Data are presented on the number of victim officers and known assailants, officers killed or injured, type of weapon, type of activity in which the officer was engaged at the time of the incident, disposition of known assailants, and geographic region.

Terrorism 2000/2001

(Annual. Washington: U.S. Department of Justice, 2004 [Online]. Available: http://www.fbi.gov/publications/terror/terror2000_2001.pdf [Sept. 14, 2004]. 39 pages, 8 figures, 3 appendices.)

Presents data for 2000 and 2001 and trend data for 1980-2001. SOURCEBOOK tables 3.173, 3.174.

This report presents an overview of terrorist incidents and preventions taking place in the United States and its territories, and FBI investigations into terrorism acts involving U.S. interests around the world. Descriptions of incidents occurring in the United States during 2000 and 2001 are included. The report contains a review of the September 11th terrorist attacks, a discussion of trends in animal rights and environmental extremism, and a review of the USA PATRIOT Act. The appendix provides a chronological summary of terrorist incidents in the U.S. from 1990 to 2001, and figures presenting the number of casualties of terrorism and terrorist activities by region from 1980 through 2001.

U.S. Department of Justice, Federal Bureau of Prisons

State of the Bureau 2003

(Annual. Washington: U.S. Department of Justice, 2004. 60 pages, 3 tables.)

Presents data for 2003. SOURCEBOOK table 1.106.

This report presents information on the correctional institutions operated by the Federal Bureau of Prisons (BOP). Bureau accomplishments for fiscal year 2003 and strategic planning objectives for fiscal year 2004 are reviewed. Brief descriptions of the central and regional offices are provided. Information for each BOP institution, such as location, telephone and fax numbers, security level, average population, and number of staff is included. Also listed is contact information for the Bureau's 28 regional Community Corrections Management Offices. The report concludes with summary statistical data on prisoners committed to BOP custody and BOP personnel.

U.S. Department of Justice, National Institute of Justice

Drug and Alcohol Use and Related Matters Among Arrestees 2003

(Annual. Washington: U.S. Department of Justice, 2004. 33 pages, 28 tables.)

Presents data for 2003. SOURCEBOOK tables 4.30-4.32.

This report presents data on drug use among adult arrestees in 39 U.S. cities and counties. The data are from the Arrestee Drug Abuse Monitoring (ADAM) program, sponsored by the U.S. Department of Justice, National Institute of Justice. Data are based on voluntary urinalysis testing and interviews from samples of arrestees. Information is presented on the use of marijuana, cocaine, methamphetamine, opiates, and PCP. Self-reported patterns of drug-related behaviors such as frequency of use, drug acquisition, failed attempts to purchase drugs, and heavy drinking are included. Also included are estimates of drug, alcohol, and mental health treatment participation.

U.S. Department of Justice, U.S. Marshals Service

FY 2000 Annual Report of the United States Marshals Service

(Annual. Washington: U.S. Department of Justice, 2001. 148 pages, 108 tables, 12 figures.)

Presents data for fiscal 1999 and 2000 and trend data for fiscal 1985-2000. SOURCEBOOK tables 1.77, 1.78.

This report presents data on the missions, workload, operations, resources, and productivity of the U.S. Marshals Service (USMS). Data are shown for the agency as a whole and separately for each district. USMS duties include fugitive investigations, prisoner processing and detention, prisoner production and transportation, protection of the judiciary, witness security, execution of court orders, government seizures, and special operations and analysis. Sections with national data trends, data definitions and sources, staffing allocations, and organizational references also are included.

U.S. Department of State

Patterns of Global Terrorism: 2003

(Annual. Washington: U.S. Department of State, 2004. 197 pages, 9 figures, 7 appendices.)

Presents data for 2003 and trend data for 1982-2003. SOURCEBOOK tables 3.175, 3.176.

This report includes graphs, narrative descriptions, and comments on incidents of international terrorism and politically inspired violence. Information is presented on types of incidents, victims, and terrorist groups. Overviews of counter-terrorist activities and cooperation with the United States' anti-terrorism efforts are provided for numerous countries in eight regions of the world. A discussion of countries engaging in State-sponsored terrorism also is included. The appendices present a chronology of significant terrorist incidents in 2003, detailed background information on organizations that engage in terrorism, U.S. programs and policies, the U.S. military's counterterrorism campaign in 2003, a discussion of countering terrorism on the economic front, and a statistical review of international terrorist incidents.

U.S. Department of Transportation, Federal Aviation Administration

Annual Report to Congress on Civil Aviation Security, January 1, 1995-December 31, 1995

(Annual. Washington: U.S. Department of Transportation, 1996. 20 pages, 2 tables, 1 figure.)

Presents data for 1995 and trend data for 1991-95. SOURCEBOOK table 3.177.

This report contains data on threats against civil aviation, both foreign and domestic, including hijackings, airport bombings, bomb threats, and security incidents. Also presented are data on passenger screening activities and summaries of other ongoing preventive measures. This report covers the 1995 calendar year and provides detailed descriptions of criminal acts against civil aviation committed during that period.

U.S. Department of Transportation, Federal Highway Administration

Highway Statistics 2002

(Annual. Washington: U.S. Department of Transportation, 2003. 174 pages, 103 tables, 3 figures.)

Presents data for 2002. SOURCEBOOK table 3.147.

This report presents information on highway transportation in three general areas: highway use, including the ownership and operation of motor vehicles; highway finance, including the receipts and expenditures for highways by public agencies; and highway function--the extent, characteristics, and performance of public highways, roads, and streets in the Nation. Detailed statistical data are provided on motor fuel use and taxation; motor vehicle ownership; driver licensing; highway-use revenues; State highway finance; highway mileage, performance, and characteristics; Federal aid for highways; highway finance data for local governments; and motor vehicle-related fatalities and injuries. Selected international highway data also are included.

U.S. Department of Transportation, National Highway Traffic Safety Administration

Digest of State Alcohol-Highway Safety Related Legislation, Current as of January 1, 2002

(Annual. Washington: U.S. Department of Transportation, 2002. 577 pages, 2 tables, 2 appendices.)

Presents data for 2002. SOURCEBOOK tables 1.112, 1.113.

This 20th edition of the digest provides a detailed description of the various statutory provisions related to alcohol use and highway safety. The data were collected through an examination of statutory codes of the 50 States, the District of Columbia, American Samoa, Guam, Puerto Rico, and the Virgin Islands. Statutory provisions are examined in the following areas: blood alcohol concentration (BAC) levels as evidence in court, preliminary breath test and implied consent laws, chemical tests authorized under implied consent laws, provisions related to adjudication of driving while intoxicated charges, sanctions for refusal to submit to a BAC test, sanctions following a conviction for driving while intoxicated-related offenses, laws requiring a blood alcohol concentration test on persons killed in traffic crashes, minimum legal drinking age, liability of owners of drinking establishments for serving alcohol to intoxicated patrons and to minors, open container laws, and anti-consumption laws. The appendices present the Uniform Vehicle Code and the Millennium DUI Prevention Act.

Traffic Safety Facts 2002

(Annual. Washington: U.S. Department of Transportation, 2004. 202 pages, 126 tables, 30 figures, 3 appendices.)

Presents data for 2002 and trend data for 1966-2002. SOURCEBOOK tables 3.103-3.105.

This report is based on information from two of the National Highway Traffic Safety Administration's data systems: the Fatality Analysis Reporting System and the National Automotive Sampling System - General Estimates System. Trend information on number and types of motor vehicle crashes, fatalities, characteristics of persons killed, characteristics of incidents, and alcohol involvement is provided. Detailed information on the time, location, circumstances, and alcohol involvement for motor vehicle crashes occurring in 2002 is included. Statistics on drivers, passengers, and pedestrians involved in crashes also are presented. Finally, fatal crash and fatality statistics are tabulated for the 50 States, the District of Columbia, and Puerto Rico.

U.S. Postal Inspection Service

2003 Annual Report of Investigations of the United States Postal Inspection Service

(Annual. Washington: U.S. Postal Inspection Service, 2004. 76 pages, 6 tables, 3 figures.)

Presents data for fiscal 2003 and trend figures for 1999-2003. SOURCEBOOK tables 5.73, 5.74.

This report presents information on the investigative and security-related activities of the U.S. Postal Inspection Service. Data are provided on investigations of crimes under the jurisdiction of the agency including: mail fraud and dangerous mailings, e.g., mail bombs and biohazardous materials; child exploitation; interdiction of drugs and related trafficking; and asset forfeiture and money laundering. Other offense investigations covered are mail theft, identity theft, violent crimes against postal employees, and threats to Postal Service revenue and finances. The report summarizes laws pertaining to the Inspection Service's most important areas of jurisdiction. A special insert describing Postal Inspector's continuing efforts to investigate and deter Workers' Compensation fraud is included. The next section deals with safety and security including safeguarding employees, facilities, and the U.S. mail. Additional topics include management of intelligence information, emergency preparedness and homeland security, consumer education, fraud prevention, legislative action, strategic planning, safety of international mail products, and forensic and technical services. The Inspection Service's fiscal 2003 goals, objectives, and results are reviewed and goals, objectives, and targets for fiscal 2004 are listed.

U.S. Sentencing Commission

2002 Sourcebook of Federal Sentencing Statistics

(Annual. Washington: U.S. Sentencing Commission, 2004. 220 pages, 536 tables (estimated), 13 figures, 2 appendices.)

Presents data for fiscal 2002. SOURCEBOOK tables 5.26-5.36, 5.39.

This publication presents detailed information on the application of Federal sentencing guidelines for fiscal year 2002. The information is presented in nine sections. Section one contains data on the reporting characteristics of the 94 district courts represented in the report. The second section presents data on demographic characteristics and offenses of defendants sentenced according to the Federal sentencing guidelines. Section three contains data on the type and length of sentences imposed in Federal courts. In sections four and five, detailed information is presented on the applications of and departures from the guideline ranges. Section six focuses on drug guideline offenses, including breakdowns by drug type, offender characteristics, and offense-related variables. Sections seven and eight contain data on the sentencing of immigration cases and organizations, respectively. The final section provides detailed information on appeals of cases processed under the sentencing guidelines. The appendices include a description of variables and supplemental tables providing detailed sentencing statistics by judicial district.

Wechsler, Henry; Jae Eun Lee; Meichun Kuo; Mark Seibring; Toben F. Nelson; and Hang Lee

"Trends in College Binge Drinking During a Period of Increased Prevention Efforts"

(*Journal of American College Health*, Vol. 50 (March 2002), pp. 203-217. 15 pages, 10 tables [Online]. Available: http://www.hsph.harvard.edu/cas/Documents/trends/Trends.pdf [Dec. 14, 2004].)

Presents data for 1993, 1997, 1999, and 2001. SOURCEBOOK tables 3.77-3.80.

This article reports the results of four national surveys of college students on drinking practices and related behaviors. The data are from the Harvard School of Public Health's College Alcohol Studies conducted in 1993, 1997, 1999, and 2001. Tables are presented on patterns of alcohol use and drinking styles of college students, and the prevalence of binge drinking by student and college characteristics. The prevalence of alcohol-related problems experienced by college students, the effects of binge drinking on non-binge drinkers in campus housing settings, and the prevalence of heavy drinking at on- and off-campus venues also are presented. The article concludes with tables providing information on college students' exposure to alcohol-related education and consequences imposed by colleges.

Wechsler, Henry; Jae Eun Lee; Toben F. Nelson; and Meichun Kuo

"Underage College Students' Drinking Behavior, Access to Alcohol, and the Influence of Deterrence Policies"

(*Journal of American College Health*, Vol. 50 (March 2002), pp. 223-236. 14 pages, 9 tables [Online]. Available: http://www.hsph.harvard.edu/cas/Documents/underminimum/DrinkingBehavior.pdf [Dec. 14, 2004].)

Presents data for 1993, 1997, 1999, and 2001. SOURCEBOOK tables 3.81, 3.82.

This article presents results from the Harvard School of Public Health's College Alcohol Studies, a series of four national surveys of college students examining drinking practices and related behaviors. Estimates are provided for the number of underage college students consuming alcohol and their patterns of use and drinking styles. Tables are presented on secondhand effects of alcohol use for college students residing in campus housing, the types of venues in which college students report drinking alcohol, and underage students' reports of sources and accessibility to alcohol. Information also is provided on the prevalence of educational awareness campaigns launched by colleges, exposure to college-imposed sanctions for drinking alcohol, underage students' perceptions of the likelihood and consequences of being caught drinking alcohol, and the effects of laws and policies targeting underage drinking on the number of underage binge drinkers in the study.

Page 560 intentionally blank.

Addresses of publishers

Administrative Office of the U.S. Courts
Thurgood Marshall Federal Judiciary
 Building
One Columbus Circle, N.E.
Washington, DC 20544
URL: http://www.uscourts.gov/

American Judicature Society
The Opperman Center at Drake University
2700 University Avenue
Des Moines, IA 50311
URL: http://www.ajs.org/

Core Institute
Center for Alcohol and Other Drug Studies
Student Health Programs
Southern Illinois University at Carbondale
1225 Douglas Drive, Suite 201
Carbondale, IL 62901
URL: http://www.siu.edu/~coreinst/

Executive Office of the President
Office of Management and Budget
725 17th Street, N.W.
Washington, DC 20503
URL: http://www.whitehouse.gov/omb/

Executive Office of the President
Office of National Drug Control Policy
Drug Policy Information Clearinghouse
P.O. Box 6000
Rockville, MD 20849-6000
800-666-3332
URL: http://www.whitehousedrugpolicy.gov/

The Gallup Organization, Inc.
Corporate Headquarters
901 F Street, N.W.
Washington, DC 20004
URL: http://www.gallup.com/

Harris Interactive
135 Corporate Woods
Rochester, NY 14623-1457
URL: http://www.harrisinteractive.com/

Higher Education Research Institute
University of California at Los Angeles
3005 Moore Hall/Box 951521
Los Angeles, CA 90095-1521
URL: http://www.gseis.ucla.edu/heri/heri.html

International City/County Management
 Association
The Municipal Year Book
777 North Capitol Street, N.E.
Suite 500
Washington, DC 20002-4201
URL: http://www.icma.org/

Journal of American College Health
Heldref Publications
1319 18th Street, N.W.
Washington, DC 20036-1802
URL: http://www.heldref.org/jach.php

Judicature
American Judicature Society
The Opperman Center at Drake University
2700 University Avenue
Des Moines, IA 50311
URL: http://www.ajs.org/ajs/publications/
 ajs_judicature.asp

Monitoring the Future Project
Institute for Social Research
Survey Research Center
University of Michigan
Ann Arbor, MI 48106-1248
URL: http://monitoringthefuture.org/

Morbidity and Mortality Weekly Report
Epidemiology Program Office MS E-96
Centers for Disease Control and Prevention
1600 Clifton Road
Atlanta, GA 30333
URL: http://www.cdc.gov/mmwr/

NAACP Legal Defense and Educational
 Fund, Inc.
99 Hudson Street
Suite 1600
New York, NY 10013-2815
URL: http://www.naacpldf.org/

National Center for State Courts
300 Newport Avenue
Williamsburg, VA 23185-4147
URL: http://www.ncsconline.org/

National Center on Addiction and Substance
 Abuse at Columbia University
633 Third Avenue, 19th Floor
New York, NY 10017-6706
URL: http://www.casacolumbia.org/

National Criminal Justice Reference Service
P.O. Box 6000
Rockville, MD 20849-6000
800-851-3420
URL: http://www.ncjrs.org/

National Fire Protection Association
1 Batterymarch Park
Quincy, MA 02169-7471
URL: http://www.nfpa.org/

National Opinion Research Center
1155 East 60th Street
Chicago, IL 60637
URL: http://www.norc.uchicago.edu/

The Pew Research Center for the People
 and the Press
1615 L. Street, N.W.
Suite 700
Washington, DC 20036
URL: http://www.people-press.org

Phi Delta Kappa International
408 North Union Street
P.O. Box 789
Bloomington, IN 47402-0789
URL: http://www.pdkintl.org/

PRIDE Surveys
160 Vanderbilt Court
Bowling Green, KY 42103
URL: http://www.pridesurveys.com/

The Roper Center for Public Opinion
 Research
341 Mansfield Road, Unit 1164
University of Connecticut
Storrs, CT 06269-1164
URL: http://www.ropercenter.uconn.edu/

U.S. Court of Appeals for the Armed Forces
450 E Street, N.W.
Washington, DC 20442
URL: http://www.armfor.uscourts.gov/

U.S. Department of Commerce
U.S. Census Bureau
4700 Silver Hill Road
Washington, DC 20233-0001
URL: http://www.census.gov/

U.S. Department of Defense
TRICARE/Military Health System
Skylines, Suite 810
5111 Leesburg Pike
Falls Church, VA 22041-3206
URL: http//www.tricare.osd.mil

U.S. Department of Education
National Center for Education Statistics
1990 K Street, N.W.
Washington, DC 20006
URL: http://nces.ed.gov/

U.S. Department of Health and Human
 Services
Centers for Disease Control and Prevention
1600 Clifton Road
Atlanta, GA 30333
URL: http://www.cdc.gov/

U.S. Department of Health and Human
 Services
Centers for Disease Control and Prevention
National Center for Injury Prevention and
 Control
Mailstop K65
4770 Buford Highway, N.E.
Atlanta, GA 30341-3724
URL: http://www.cdc.gov/ncipc/

U.S. Department of Health and Human Services
National Institute on Alcohol Abuse and Alcoholism
National Institutes of Health
5635 Fishers Lane, MSC 9304
Bethesda, MD 20892-9304
URL: http://www.niaaa.nih.gov/

U.S. Department of Health and Human Services
National Institute on Drug Abuse
National Institutes of Health
6001 Executive Boulevard, Room 5213
Bethesda, MD 20892-9561
URL: http://www.nida.nih.gov/

U.S. Department of Health and Human Services
Substance Abuse and Mental Health Services Administration
Office of Applied Studies
5600 Fishers Lane
Rockville, MD 20857
URL: http://www.oas.samhsa.gov/

U.S. Department of Homeland Security
U.S. Citizenship and Immigration Services
425 I Street, N.W.
Washington, DC 20536
URL: http://www.uscis.gov/

U.S. Department of Homeland Security
U.S. Customs and Border Protection
1300 Pennsylvania Avenue, N.W.
Washington, DC 20229
URL: http://www.cbp.gov/

U.S. Department of the Interior
National Park Service
1849 C Street, N.W.
Washington, DC 20240
URL: http://www.nps.gov/

U.S. Department of Justice
Bureau of Justice Assistance
810 Seventh Street, N.W.
4th Floor
Washington, DC 20531
URL: http://www.ojp.usdoj.gov/BJA/

U.S. Department of Justice
Bureau of Justice Statistics
810 Seventh Street, N.W.
Washington, DC 20531
URL: http://www.ojp.usdoj.gov/bjs/

U.S. Department of Justice
Criminal Division
Public Integrity Section
950 Pennsylvania Avenue
Washington, DC 20530-0001
URL: http://www.usdoj.gov/criminal/

U.S. Department of Justice
Criminal Division
Witness Immunity Unit
950 Pennsylvania Avenue
Washington, DC 20530-0001
URL: http://www.usdoj.gov/criminal/

U.S. Department of Justice
Drug Enforcement Administration
Mailstop: AXS
2401 Jefferson Davis Highway
Alexandria, VA 22301
URL: http://www.usdoj.gov/dea/

U.S. Department of Justice
Executive Office for United States Attorneys
950 Pennsylvania Avenue, N.W.
Room 2616
Washington, DC 20530-0001
URL: http://www.usdoj.gov/usao/eousa/

U.S. Department of Justice
Federal Bureau of Investigation
J. Edgar Hoover Building
935 Pennsylvania Avenue, N.W.
Washington, DC 20535-0001
URL: http://www.fbi.gov/

U.S. Department of Justice
Federal Bureau of Prisons
320 First Street, N.W.
Washington, DC 20534
URL: http://www.bop.gov/

U.S. Department of Justice
National Institute of Justice
810 Seventh Street, N.W.
Washington, DC 20531
URL: http://www.ojp.usdoj.gov/nij/

U.S. Department of Justice
Office of Justice Programs
810 Seventh Street, N.W.
Washington, DC 20531
URL: http://www.ojp.usdoj.gov/

U.S. Department of Justice
Office of Juvenile Justice and Delinquency Prevention
810 Seventh Street, N.W.
Washington, DC 20531
URL: http://ojjdp.ncjrs.org/

U.S. Department of Justice
Office of the Pardon Attorney
500 First Street, N.W.
Suite 400
Washington, DC 20530
URL: http://www.usdoj.gov/pardon/

U.S. Department of Justice
Office of the Solicitor General
950 Pennsylvania Avenue, N.W.
Washington, DC 20530-0001
URL: http://www.usdoj.gov/osg/

U.S. Department of Justice
U.S. Marshals Service
Washington, DC 20530-1000
URL: http://www.usdoj.gov/marshals/

U.S. Department of Labor
Bureau of Labor Statistics
Postal Square Building
2 Massachusetts Avenue, N.E.
Washington, DC 20212-0001
URL: http://www.bls.gov/

U.S. Department of State
Office of the Coordinator for Counterterrorism
Office of Public Affairs
2201 C Street, N.W.
Room 2509
Washington, DC 20520
URL: http://www.state.gov/s/ct/

U.S. Department of Transportation
Bureau of Transportation Statistics
400 7th Street, S.W.
Room 3103
Washington, DC 20591
URL: http://www.bts.gov/

U.S. Department of Transportation
Federal Aviation Administration
800 Independence Avenue, S.W.
Washington, DC 20591
URL: http://www.faa.gov/

U.S. Department of Transportation
Federal Highway Administration
Office of Highway Policy Information
400 Seventh Street, S.W.
Routing Code: HPPI
Room 3306
Washington, DC 20590
URL: http://www.fhwa.dot.gov/policy/ohpi/

U.S. Department of Transportation
National Highway Traffic Safety Administration
National Center for Statistics and Analysis
400 Seventh Street, S.W.
Washington, DC 20590
URL: http://www-nrd.nhtsa.dot.gov/departments/nrd-30/ncsa

U.S. Government Printing Office
732 North Capitol Street, N.W.
Washington, DC 20401
888-293-6498
URL: http://www.gpoaccess.gov/

U.S. Postal Inspection Service
475 L'Enfant Plaza, S.W.
Washington, DC 20260-0004
URL: http://www.usps.com/postalinspectors/welcome2.htm

U.S. Sentencing Commission
One Columbus Circle, N.E.
Washington, DC 20002-8002
URL: http://www.ussc.gov/

Appendices

1 Justice Expenditure and Employment Data Survey methodology and definitions of terms 564

2 *The Municipal Year Book 2004* Definitions of terms and survey response rates 569

3 *Crime in the United States* Definitions of terms 571

4 Census of Jails, Annual Survey of Jails, and Survey of Inmates in Local Jails Methodology and survey sampling procedures 574

5 Public opinion survey sampling procedures 576

6 Monitoring the Future Survey methodology and definitions of terms 581

7 National Survey on Drug Use and Health Survey methodology 587

8 National Crime Victimization Survey Survey methodology and definitions of terms 589

9 Drug Abuse Warning Network Methodology, estimation procedures, and data limitations 593

10 Arrestee Drug Abuse Monitoring Methodology and survey sampling information 595

11 Federal Justice Statistics Program Methodology and definitions of terms 597

12 National Judicial Reporting Program Survey sampling procedures and definitions of terms 601

13 State Court Processing Statistics Methodology, definitions of terms, and crimes within offense categories 603

14 Juvenile Court Statistics Methodology, definitions of terms, and offenses within categories 605

15 *Correctional Populations in the United States* Survey methodology, definitions of terms, and jurisdictional explanatory notes 608

Appendix 1

Justice Expenditure and Employment Data
Survey methodology and definitions of terms

Note: The following information has been excerpted from U.S. Department of Justice, Bureau of Justice Statistics, *2001 Justice Expenditure and Employment Extracts*, NCJ 202792 [Online]; and *Trends in Justice Expenditure and Employment* [Online]. Available: http://www.ojp.usdoj.gov/bjs/eande.htm.

Historical overview

The Bureau of Justice Statistics (BJS) began the collection of justice expenditure and employment data with fiscal 1971, using a special sample drawn by the U.S. Census Bureau especially for this purpose. The annual Survey of Criminal Justice Expenditure and Employment (CJEE Survey) provided comparable trend data from 1971 to 1979. That survey was the source of detailed, comprehensive statistics on the justice activities of the Federal, State, and local governments. Each annual survey resulted in a preliminary report or BJS Bulletin, a publication of detailed tabulations of national and State-local estimates, as well as individual government data, a volume displaying trends since 1971, and additional data accessible on magnetic tape.

In 1980, BJS discontinued the CJEE Survey for budgetary reasons following the collection of 1979 data. The cancellation of the CJEE Survey left a gap in national criminal justice statistics, which the CJEE Extracts series is designed to fill, albeit on a limited basis. Instead of presenting data based on a separate survey, the CJEE Extracts contains justice expenditure and employment data from the Census Bureau's annual sample surveys of government finances and public employment.

Those Census Bureau surveys traditionally have provided limited data on the justice sectors of police protection (from 1902) and corrections (from 1954), with slightly more data being collected for State governments and the largest local governments. Beginning with 1982 these surveys began collecting "judicial and legal services" data as a separate category, allowing estimation of total justice expenditure and employment from the Census Bureau surveys, using the criminal justice data from the Census Bureau's annual government finance and employment surveys.

Special surveys in 1985, 1988, and 1990 collected CJEE Survey data that are comparable to data for 1971 to 1979. The current Extracts methodology produces considerably less detailed information than is available from those special CJEE Surveys. Another significant difference, which is not as noticeable, relates to the comparability of the CJEE Extracts variables to the variables in those CJEE Surveys. In many instances, variables of the same name are not comparable between the two programs. While great care was taken to adjust the source data to maximize comparability with the CJEE Survey data, some differences remain.

In making trend comparisons, users should limit their analysis to one of the two sources: long-term trends for 1971-79, 1985, 1988, and 1990 from the CJEE Survey series; or more recent trends from 1980 using the CJEE Extracts data.

Sample design

The CJEE Extracts data are assembled from data collected through the Census Bureau's annual surveys of government finances and public employment. The samples of local governments for those surveys are drawn from the most recent available Quinquennial Census of Governments. The samples consist of all large local general purpose governments above a certain population threshold (certainty units) plus a sample below the certainty level. The samples also include certain independent school districts and special districts, for which justice data are not collected. For detailed information about the sample for any given year, contact askbjs@ojp.usdoj.gov.

Survey period

The Federal Government expenditure data are for the fiscal year, which ends on September 30 of the year indicated; for example, 2001 data are for the period Oct. 1, 2000 to Sept. 30, 2001.

The State expenditure data presented cover fiscal years ending June 30 for all States except four whose fiscal years ended as follows: New York, March 31; Texas, August 31; and Alabama and Michigan, September 30 of the year indicated. For local governments, the fiscal years reported are those that closed between July 1 and June 30. Most municipalities and counties end their fiscal years on December 31 or June 30. Thus, some local jurisdictions that ended their fiscal year on December 31 are included in the spreadsheets for the following year. The fiscal years reported for the District of Columbia ended on September 30 of the year indicated.

Some agencies operate on a different fiscal year basis from the parent government. In such instances, figures included are for the agency's fiscal year that ended within the parent government's regular fiscal year.

The employment data are for the month of October for years prior to 1997. Beginning in 1997, employment data are for the month of March.

Data collection

The CJEE Extracts data are from a special compilation of data and sources available from the Census Bureau's regular surveys of government finances and public employment. The recurrent surveys of government finances and public employment provide data on expenditure and employment, by function of the Federal, State, and local governments (counties, cities, townships, independent school districts, and special districts). The data collection procedures of these surveys for the expenditure and employment data are described below.

Annual Government Finances Survey

Federal Government financial data were obtained from actual data presented in the *Budget of the United States Government* for each fiscal year displayed. The methodology for collecting the Federal financial data was changed in 1998. Previously the Census Bureau performed an extensive compilation of the Federal budget data for the purpose of bringing it in line with Census Bureau definitions. Beginning in 1998, the data were taken directly from the *Budget of the United States Government* using definitions of justice functions contained in the budget. The Census Bureau had included justice expenditures of nonjustice agencies. However, most of this expenditure is coded under other-than-justice functions in the Federal budget.

State finance statistics as well as those for large counties and cities were compiled by Census Bureau representatives from official reports and records, with the advice of State and local officers and employees. The data were compiled from State government audits, budgets, and other financial reports, either in printed or electronic format. The compilation generally involved recasting the State financial records into the classification categories used for reporting by the Census Bureau.

The initial local government data collection phase used two methods to obtain data: mail canvass and central collection from State sources. In about 30 States, all or part of the data for local governments were obtained from cooperative arrangements between the Census Bureau and a State government agency. These usually involved a data collection effort carried out to meet the needs of both agencies--the State agency for purposes of audit, oversight, or information, and the Census Bureau for statistical purposes. Data for the balance of local governments in the annual surveys were obtained via mail questionnaires sent directly to county, municipal, township, special district, and school district governments.

The mail canvass involved the use of detailed Census Bureau schedules with related reporting instructions. Census Bureau examiners reviewed the mail reports and used extensive correspondence to supplement and verify incomplete and questionable information.

As with mail canvass questionnaires, centrally collected financial data sometimes needed supplementation for such items as debt, assets, or particular functional expenditures or revenue items. Census Bureau staff obtained these supplementary data from special tabulations in other State offices, printed reports, secondary sources, or from mail requests directly to the county, municipal, or township governments.

Through these efforts, expenditure information was obtained for the Federal Government, all State governments, and all large county and city governments.

Annual Public Employment Survey

Federal Government civilian employment data were obtained from records maintained by the U.S. Office of Personnel Management. These records did not provide the information necessary to compute Federal full-time equivalent employment.

State government data were collected through a mail survey of all State departments, agencies, and institutions. In approximately half of the States employment data are collected centrally for the State government. In some cases additional mail supplementation is necessary. As with the Finance Survey these States change from year to year. A sample of local governments also was surveyed by mail questionnaire. State agencies and local governments that did not respond by the close of the request period received followup requests. Second request mail consisted of post card reminders. Third request mail was a second mailing of the original request with a survey form. Mail returned to the Census Bureau because of address problems was re-addressed and remailed. In addition, large governments that had not responded for several years were contacted by telephone to identify the appropriate office or individual to receive and complete forms.

After extensive nonresponse followup, useable replies were received from more than 70% of the sample canvassed for the 1993 Survey of Public Employment, and similar response levels were achieved in other years.

Data review and adjustments

Once the data are collected, intensive computer editing of the data at various stages of processing minimizes errors that may be introduced during processing in the annual finance and employment survey programs. For the mail portion of the surveys, figures reported by government officials are generally accepted as being substantially correct. In some cases varying interpretations of the instructions or deficiencies in the responding governments' records may make it difficult for officials to render complete and accurate reports for their governments.

These difficulties are handled by: careful definition of terms and detailed instructions in difficult cases; supplemental correspondence and telephone followup to officials; and intense examination of data collected through verification of internal consistency and comparison with previous reports and other sources of data.

The data extracted from the regular Census Bureau programs for the CJEE Extracts received additional examination. After compilation for the general finance survey a special reviewer examined in detail the expenditure data for State governments and large local governments, and investigated special data compilation problems in order to adjust the data as needed. The local government expenditure and employment estimates were reviewed, potential problems investigated, and data were revised, where necessary. Data for each of the States and large counties and cities displayed individually in the CJEE Extracts tables and spreadsheets were scrutinized and compared to prior years' data. A separate computer edit was then performed. Where possible, both expenditure and employment data were adjusted to correct errors, reclassify activities, and narrow differences with the CJEE Surveys. Specific procedures included referring to alternate sources of data, estimating missing data, and refining data through proration (for example, sheriff offices, where some employees perform police functions, others perform judicial functions (bailiffs), and others perform corrections (jail) functions).

Data limitations

The survey sample for the local government CJEE Extracts justice expenditure and employment estimates was not designed specifically to produce data on these activities. Thus, the sampling variability, or "standard error," for the justice sectors is apt to be larger than for the major categories in the Census Bureau's regular surveys and for the same functions in the CJEE Survey series. The "standard error" is a measurement of variation among the estimates from all possible samples, of which this is one, having the same size and selected using the same sampling design. Estimates derived from the different samples would vary from each other (and also from a complete census using the same data collection procedures). The standard error, therefore, measures the precision with which an estimate from one of these samples approximates the average result of all the possible samples.

Interval estimates with a prescribed confidence level can be calculated for each statistic by using the sample estimate and the standard error as estimated from the sample. For example, a 90% confidence interval can be constructed by adding 1.6 times the estimated standard error to the estimate and subtracting 1.6 times the estimated standard error from the estimate. If intervals were constructed in such a manner for all possible samples of the same design and size, about 90% of them would include the complete enumeration statistic.

In reviewing the sample-based estimates, bear in mind that, because State government figures are not subject to sampling variation, the State-local aggregates shown for individual States are more reliable (on a relative standard error basis) than the local government estimates they include. Conversely, the sampling variability for smaller components, such as type of local government detail, is likely to be greater than that for the State and local total estimates. Because the national estimates of local government expenditure and employment are based on summations of individual State data, they are more reliable than the State-area data.

The data also are subject to possible inaccuracies in classification, response, and processing. Every effort was made to keep such errors to a minimum through care in examining, editing, and tabulating the data submitted by government officials. Followup procedures were used extensively to clarify inadequate and inconsistent survey returns.

Readers should be generally cautious in comparing governments because differences among States and local governments in functional responsibilities, governmental structure, degree of urbanization, and population density can affect the comparability of expenditure and employment data. For example, some State governments directly administer certain activities that elsewhere are undertaken by local governments, with or without fiscal aid, and the same variation in the division of responsibilities exists for counties and cities.

Data differing from other publications

The CJEE Extracts data differ in some cases from the Census Bureau's annual finance and employment survey data because of the more extensive review procedures used for this special compilation, the refinements of the data involved, and certain definitional differences. The CJEE Extracts trend data for 1985, 1988, and 1990 also differ from those published by BJS in its CJEE Survey series. Those CJEE Survey data should be used in trend analyses with other CJEE Survey data for 1971-79. The 1985, 1988, and 1990 CJEE Extracts data should be used in trend analyses only with other CJEE Extracts data.

Definitions of terms and concepts

Following is a glossary of terms and concepts used in the CJEE Extracts program and comments regarding their limitations. These definitions are based largely on those used in the Census Bureau's governmental finances and employment statistics program.
Federal Government--the term Federal encompasses all activities of the United States Government other than employment of the Armed Forces. District of Columbia data are excluded from this category and included with data for municipalities.
State governments--this category refers to the governments of the 50 States that constitute the United States.
Local governments--the Census Bureau classifies local governments by five major types: county, municipality, township, independent school district, and special district.
Population--the "resident population" data used are for July 1 of each year from the U.S. Census Bureau, Current Population Reports. They are consistent with the 1980 and 1990 decennial enumerations and they do not include adjustments for census coverage errors. They are the most current estimates available when the tables were assembled. The data in the trend tables may differ from population data used in single year tables earlier in this series and in other sources that used estimates available at the time they were prepared.

Governmental expenditure

Expenditure--all amounts of money paid out (net of recoveries and any correcting transactions) other than for retirement of debt (including interest), investment in securities, extensions of loans, or agency transactions. It includes only external cash payments and excludes any intragovernmental transfers and noncash transactions, such as the provision of meals or housing of employees. It also includes any payments financed from borrowing, fund balances, intergovernmental revenue, and other current revenue. In several instances, two or more governments share the expense of maintaining a court or a justice agency. In these cases, the allowable direct expenditure amount is reported for each government in the appropriate category.

When a government pays pensions directly to retired employees from appropriated funds, such payments are included as expenditure of the government concerned. However, State and local government contributions to retirement systems they operate are not included in expenditure data because many governments make lump-sum contributions to plans covering all government employees and cannot report separately for justice employees. Neither in governments' basic accounting records (from which criminal justice expenditure figures are drawn) nor in the records of their general-coverage employee benefit systems is there usually any breakdown of amounts contributed in terms of the various agencies or functions involved. Nor has an adequate procedure for calculating the proportion of such contributions allocable to justice employees been developed because of the wide variation in the coverage of various plans, employee status requirements, benefit rates, and so forth. Expenditure is divided into major categories by character and object as follows:

Direct expenditure--is all expenditure except that classified as intergovernmental and is further divided into two categories:
   Direct current--includes salaries, wages, fees, commissions, and the purchase of supplies, materials, and contractual services.
   Capital outlay--includes expenditure for the three object categories of construction, equipment, and purchase of land and existing structures.

Data are presented separately in the CJEE Extracts program for State construction of correctional institutions; the "other" category in those tables includes equipment and the purchase of land and existing structures.

Construction--production of fixed works and structures as well as additions, replacements, and major alterations thereto undertaken either on a contract basis by private contractors or through force account construction by the employees of the government. Included are the planning and designing of specific projects; grading, landscaping, and other site improvement; and providing equipment and facilities that are integral parts of the structure.

Expenditure for interest on general debt, assistance and subsidies, and insurance benefits are not applied to specific functions because they are not ordinarily available on a functional basis from government financial reports. In instances where bonded or mortgaged general indebtedness is identified for specific purposes, the interest payments are aggregated with other interest expenditures, which makes reliable and consistent breakouts of such data over a long period of time impossible.

Intergovernmental expenditure--comprises payments from one government to another, including grants-in-aid, shared revenues, fiscal assistance, and amounts for services performed by one government for another on a reimbursable or cost-sharing basis (for example, payments by one government to another for boarding prisoners). It excludes amounts paid to other governments for purchase of commodities, property, or utility services; any tax imposed and paid as such; and employer contributions for social insurance (for example, contributions to the Federal Government for old-age, survivors', disability, and health insurance and local government payments to State-operated retirement systems on behalf of their employees).
Total expenditure--is direct and intergovernmental expenditure of a government or type of government. In the expenditure tables, certain totals have been adjusted to exclude duplicative intergovernmental expenditure amounts. For example, money paid by a State government to a county government within that State is reported by the State government as an intergovernmental expenditure and by the county government as a direct expenditure when the money is spent (for salaries, wages, equipment, and so forth). Therefore, to arrive at a combined State-local government total that does not duplicate these transactions, intergovernmental expenditure amounts are deducted from the State-local total because those amounts also are reflected in the direct expenditure of the recipient government. The same treatment is used for intergovernmental payments between counties and municipalities within the same State when

computing local totals. Totals reported for "all governments" also are adjusted to exclude duplicative intergovernmental expenditure involving the Federal Government.

Governmental employment

Employment and employees refer to all persons gainfully employed by and performing services for a government. Employees include all persons paid for personal services performed, including persons paid from federally funded programs, paid elected officials, persons in a paid-leave status, and persons paid on a "per meeting," annual, semiannual, or quarterly basis. Unpaid officials, pensioners, persons whose work is performed on a fee basis, and contractors and their employees are excluded from the count of employees.

This definition includes two classes:

Full-time employees--include those persons whose hours of work represent full-time employment in their employer government during the pay period including October 12 for 1980-95. Generally, it includes full-time temporary or seasonal workers employed during that pay period. Beginning in 1997, the reference month changed from October to March.

Part-time employees--are those persons who work less than the standard number of hours for full-time work in their employer government and persons paid by more than one government.

Full-time equivalent employment--is a statistical measure that estimates the total workforce accounting for the less than full-time employment of part-time employees. Prior to 1986, the formula for computing full-time equivalent (FTE) employment was payroll-based; specifically, it was calculated by dividing the total payroll amount (full-time plus part-time) by the full-time payroll amount and multiplying the resulting quotient by the number of full-time employees. Beginning in 1986, it is computed by dividing the part-time hours paid by the standard number of hours for full-time employees in the particular government and then adding the resulting quotient to the number of full-time employees. In both formulae, the calculation is performed separately at the individual function type for each respondent government. Consequently, summaries by State, type of government, and function are aggregates of individual calculations.

The formula was changed because the previously used payroll-based formula necessarily assumed that there is little or no difference between average wage rates for full-time and part-time workers--however, this is seldom the case. Part-time pay scales are generally below those for full-time workers, thus resulting in an understatement of full-time equivalent employment. The understatement was estimated at between 2.8% and 3.8% at the national level. The previously used payroll-based methodology may also produce a "trend bias" if the rate of change in part-time employment is different from that in full-time employment. Users should keep in mind the expected understatement of FTE in years prior to 1986 when making trend comparisons.

October/March payrolls--represent gross payrolls for the 1-month period of October or March and comprise the gross payroll before deductions. It includes all salaries, wages, fees, or commissions paid to employees during the pay period including October 12 for 1980-95. Beginning in 1997, the reference month changed from October to March. Payroll amounts reported for a period other than 1 month were converted to represent 1-month amounts.

Governmental functions

General government functions include all activities other than those classed as public utilities (water supply, electric power, gas supply, and transit systems), liquor stores (dispensaries operated by 17 State governments and by local governments of 6 States, as of 1992), and insurance trust systems (no employment data are associated with insurance trusts). All government functions include the latter.

Justice--is the combined functions of police protection, judicial and legal services, and corrections as defined below. As noted below, it consistently includes civil justice functions as well as criminal justice functions where criminal functions cannot be segregated in available source documents.

Police protection--is the function of enforcing the law, preserving order and traffic safety, and apprehending those who violate the law, whether these activities are performed by a police department, a sheriffs' department, or a special police force maintained by an agency whose primary responsibility is outside the justice system but that has a police force to perform these activities in its specialized area (geographic or functional). This category includes: regular police services; police patrols and communications; crime prevention activities; temporary lockups and "holding tanks"; traffic safety and engineering (but not highway planning and engineering); vehicular inspection and licensing; buildings used exclusively for police purposes; the maintenance of buildings used for police purposes; medical examiners and coroners; law enforcement activities of sheriffs' offices; and unsworn school crossing guards, parking meter readers, and animal wardens, if employed by a police agency.

Private security police are outside the scope of the survey.

The special police forces included in the data are only those that are part of a general purpose government. Special police forces that are part of independent school districts or special districts are not included in the data because these districts are not general purpose governments.

Police protection employment data are further divided between sworn employees, which represent persons with the power of arrest, and nonsworn employees, which are all others.

In most States, sheriffs' departments are multifunctional agencies providing police protection, judicial, and/or correctional services. In order to allocate expenditure and employment data to the proper activity, the data for sheriffs' departments are prorated, resulting in differences from other police reporting programs such as BJS's Law Enforcement Management and Administrative Statistics program and the FBI's Uniform Crime Reporting program, which report the numbers of employees in law enforcement agencies regardless of functions performed.

Short-term custody and detention are considered part of the police protection function. Data for lockups or "tanks" holding prisoners less than 48 hours are included in the police protection category. Data for institutions with authority to hold prisoners 48 hours or more are included in the corrections category.

Judicial and legal services--covers all civil and criminal activities associated with courts, including prosecution and public defense.

The "judicial and legal services" category in the CJEE Extracts series includes the following court functions covered as a separate category in the periodic CJEE Survey: civil and criminal functions of courts at all levels of legal jurisdiction--appellate (last resort and intermediate), general jurisdiction, and limited jurisdiction; activities associated with courts, such as law libraries, grand juries, petit juries, and medical and social service activities (except probation, which is classified as corrections where separately identifiable); court reporters, judicial councils, bailiffs, "register of wills," and similar probate functions; and court ("civil") activities of sheriffs' offices in some jurisdictions.

Also included in the "judicial and legal" category are all civil and criminal justice activities of prosecution and legal service agencies. It includes the following prosecution and legal service activities covered as a separate category in the periodic CJEE Survey: attorneys general, district attorneys, State's attorneys, and their variously named equivalents; corporation counsels, solicitors, and legal departments with various names including those providing legal advice to the chief executives and subordinate departmental officers, representation of the government in law suits and the prosecution of accused violators of criminal law; and various investigative agencies having full arrest powers and attached to offices of attorneys general, district attorneys, or their variously named equivalents.

These activities are included whether performed by one office or several because in some jurisdictions a single office provides all legal services, whereas in others a prosecutor's office handles only criminal matters and a separate attorney's office performs all civil legal services.

Also included in the "judicial and legal" category are the civil and criminal justice activities of public defenders, other agencies that provide legal counsel and representation in either criminal or civil proceedings, and other government programs that pay the fees of court-appointed counsel. It includes the following public defense activities covered as a separate category in the periodic CJEE Survey: court-paid fees to individually retained counsel; fees paid by the court to court-appointed counsel; government contributions to private legal aid societies and bar association-sponsored programs; and activities of an established public defender office or program.

This category excludes monetary judgments and claims or other payments of a government as a defendant in judicial or administrative proceedings, and legal units of noncriminal justice agencies, whose functions may be performed by a legal service department in other jurisdictions (such as a county counsel).

Corrections--is that function of government involving the confinement and rehabilitation of adults and juveniles convicted of offenses against the law and the confinement of persons suspected of a crime and awaiting adjudication.

Corrections direct expenditure for State governments is further divided into two subcategories: correctional institutions and other corrections.

Correctional institutions are any facilities for the confinement and correction of convicted adults or juveniles adjudicated delinquent or in need of supervision and for the detention of those adults and juveniles accused of a crime and awaiting trial or hearing. (Data for lockups or "tanks" holding prisoners less than 48 hours are included in the police protection category.)

Correctional institutions include: prisons and penitentiaries; reformatories; jails; houses of correction; other variously named correctional institutions, such as correctional farms, workhouses, industrial schools, and training schools; institutions and facilities exclusively for the confinement of the criminally insane; institutions and facilities for the examination, evaluation, classification, and assignment of inmates; and facilities for the confinement, treatment, and rehabilitation of drug addicts and alcoholics, if the institution is administered by a correctional agency.

When an institution maintains a prison industry or agricultural program, data on the cost of production or the value of prison labor used by agencies of the same government, if identifiable, are excluded (and classified as expenditure for the function using the product or services). Expenditure for the manufacture, production, sale, and distribution of goods produced for sale or use outside the government is included under this heading. It excludes the costs of maintaining prisoners in institutions of other governments, which are classified as an intergovernmental expenditure for which the "institutions" vs. "other corrections" distinctions are not applied.

Other corrections consists of all noninstitutional correctional activities including: parole boards and programs; pardon boards; nonresidential resettlement or halfway houses for those not in need of institutionalization; probation activities and programs, even if administered by a court; and correctional administration not directly connectable to institutions. Payments to another government for boarding prisoners are classified as "intergovernmental expenditure" for which the "institutions" and "other corrections" distinctions discussed above are not applied. In practice, intergovernmental payments of this type are difficult to detect for insignificant amounts between local government and for miscellaneous items that cannot be directly related to institutional care.

Appendix 2

The Municipal Year Book 2004 Definitions of terms and survey response rates

Note: This information was excerpted from International City/County Management Association, *The Municipal Year Book 2004* (Washington, DC: International City/County Management Association, 2004), pp. xi-xiii, 79, 102, 123; and information provided by the International City/County Management Association. Non-substantive editorial adaptations have been made.

Regions

Northeast--the New England and Mid-Atlantic Divisions;
North Central--the East and West North Central Divisions;
South--the South Atlantic, and the East and West South Central Divisions;
West--the Mountain and Pacific Coast Divisions.

Geographic divisions

New England--Connecticut, Maine, Massachusetts, New Hampshire, Rhode Island, and Vermont;
Mid-Atlantic--New Jersey, New York, and Pennsylvania;
East North Central--Illinois, Indiana, Michigan, Ohio, and Wisconsin;
West North Central--Iowa, Kansas, Minnesota, Missouri, Nebraska, North Dakota, and South Dakota;
South Atlantic--Delaware, Florida, Georgia, Maryland, North Carolina, South Carolina, Virginia, West Virginia, and the District of Columbia;
East South Central--Alabama, Kentucky, Mississippi, and Tennessee;
West South Central--Arkansas, Louisiana, Oklahoma, and Texas;
Mountain--Arizona, Colorado, Idaho, Montana, Nevada, New Mexico, Utah, and Wyoming;
Pacific Coast--Alaska, California, Hawaii, Oregon, and Washington.

Metro status

To be classified by the U.S. Office of Management and Budget (OMB) as a Metropolitan Statistical Area (MSA), an area must include either at least one city with a population of 50,000 or more or a U.S. Census Bureau-defined urbanized area of at least 50,000 and a total metropolitan population of at least 100,000 (75,000 in New England).

The OMB further groups metropolitan areas of 1,000,000 or more population into consolidated metropolitan statistical areas (CMSAs) and primary metropolitan statistical areas (PMSAs).

Central cities--The core cities of an MSA having a population of at least 25,000 and meeting two commuting requirements: at least 50% of the employed residents of the city must work within the city and there must be at least 75 jobs for each 100 residents who are employed. Cities between 15,000 and 25,000 population may also be considered central cities if they are at least one-third the size of the MSA's largest city and meet the two commuting requirements.
Suburban cities--The other cities, towns, and incorporated places in an MSA.
Independent cities--The incorporated places not located within an MSA.

County types

Metro--Counties located within an MSA.
Nonmetro--Counties located outside the boundaries of an MSA.

Forms of government

Mayor-council--An elected council or board serves as the legislative body. The head of government is the chief elected official, who is generally elected separately from the council and has significant administrative authority.

Many cities with a mayor-council form of government have a city administrator who is appointed by the elected representatives (council) and/or the chief elected official, and who is responsible to the elected officials. Appointed city administrators in mayor-council governments have limited administrative authority--they often do not directly appoint department heads or other key city personnel and their responsibility for budget preparation and administration, although significant, is subordinate to that of the elected officials.

Council-manager--An elected council or board and chief elected official (e.g., the mayor) are responsible for making policy. A professional administrator appointed by the council or board has full responsibility for the day-to-day operations of the government.
Commission--An elected commission performs both legislative and executive functions, generally with departmental administration divided among the commissioners.
Town meeting--All qualified voters of a municipality meet to set policy and elect officials to carry out the policies they have established.
Representative town meeting--Voters select a large number of citizens to represent them at the town meeting(s). All citizens may attend and participate in the meeting(s), but only representatives may vote.

Appendices 569

For counties, forms of government shown in table 1.71 relate to the structural organizations of the legislative and executive branches of counties. There are three basic forms of county government:

Commission--A governing board that shares the administrative and, to an extent, legislative responsibilities with several independently elected functional officials.

Council-manager/administrator--An administrator is appointed by, and responsible to, the elected council to carry out directives.

Council-elected executive--Two branches of government: the executive and the legislative. The independently elected executive is considered the formal head of the county.

Survey format

This is the third year the International City/County Management Association (ICMA) has offered an online version of the annual local governments surveys. In July 2003, paper surveys were mailed to all municipal and county governments with populations of 2,500 or more and to those under 2,500 that are recognized by ICMA as having a council-manager form of government or as providing for an appointed general management (chief administrative officer) position. The mail survey gave the Web site address for the online version and provided a unique identification number for each local government. After allowing time for local governments to respond, ICMA mailed a second paper survey to those that had not responded to the first mailing or had not submitted the online version.

Table. Survey response rates for 2003

	Police and fire			Municipal officials			County officials		
	Number of cities surveyed	Responses Number	Responses Percent	Number of cities surveyed	Responses Number	Responses Percent	Number of counties surveyed	Responses Number	Responses Percent
Total, all cities	3,215	1,645	51%	8,050	4,172	52%	3,040	1,116	37%
Population group									
Over 1,000,000	9	6	67	9	5	56	28	14	50
500,000 to 1,000,000	22	11	50	22	12	55	63	32	51
250,000 to 499,999	36	21	58	37	17	46	110	51	46
100,000 to 249,999	178	105	59	178	105	59	276	126	46
50,000 to 99,999	403	216	54	403	253	63	383	150	39
25,000 to 49,999	775	396	51	779	470	60	638	226	35
10,000 to 24,999	1,792	890	50	1,815	1,031	57	869	278	32
5,000 to 9,999	NA	NA	NA	1,864	967	52	386	136	35
2,500 to 4,999	NA	NA	NA	1,951	867	44	173	63	36
Under 2,500	NA	NA	NA	992	445	45	114	40	35
Region									
Northeast	877	304	35	2,129	860	40	190	53	28
North Central	897	473	53	2,404	1,358	57	1,054	452	43
South	825	481	58	2,316	1,262	55	1,372	422	31
West	616	387	63	1,201	692	58	424	189	45
Geographic division									
New England	353	115	33	838	388	46	46	8	17
Mid-Atlantic	524	189	36	1,291	472	37	144	45	31
East North Central	650	321	49	1,536	821	54	437	172	39
West North Central	247	152	62	867	537	62	617	280	45
South Atlantic	380	242	64	1,032	648	63	545	251	46
East South Central	164	64	39	487	210	43	360	53	15
West South Central	281	175	62	798	404	51	467	118	25
Mountain	158	102	65	450	243	54	276	125	45
Pacific Coast	458	285	62	751	449	60	148	64	43
Metro status									
Central	540	288	53	541	333	62	458	211	46
Suburban	2,057	1,021	50	4,720	2,436	52	341	123	36
Independent	618	336	54	2,789	1,403	50	2,241	782	35

Appendix 3

Crime in the United States Definitions of terms

Note: The following information has been excerpted from U.S. Department of Justice, Federal Bureau of Investigation, *Crime in the United States, 2002* (Washington, DC: USGPO, 2003), pp. 442-444, 448, 454-457. Non-substantive editorial adaptations have been made. See U.S. Department of Justice, Federal Bureau of Investigation, *Uniform Crime Reporting Handbook* (Washington, DC: USGPO, 1984) for further definitions and information on classification and counting rules.

Population definitions

For purposes of statistical presentation, the cities and counties in the United States are divided into groups based on population size. The population group classifications used by the Uniform Crime Reporting (UCR) Program are shown in Table 1.

Table 1. Population group, political label, and population coverage

Population group	Political label	Population coverage
I	City	250,000 and over
II	City	100,000 to 249,999
III	City	50,000 to 99,999
IV	City	25,000 to 49,999
V	City	10,000 to 24,999
VI	City[a]	Less than 10,000
VIII (Rural county)	County[b]	NA
IX (Suburban county)	County[b]	NA

[a]Includes universities and colleges to which no population is attributed.
[b]Includes State police to which no population is attributed.

Metropolitan Statistical Area (MSA)--This includes a central city of at least 50,000 people or an urbanized area of at least 50,000. The county containing the central city and other contiguous counties having strong economic and social ties to the central city and county also are included. Counties in an MSA are designated "suburban" for UCR purposes. An MSA may cross State lines. Due to changes in the geographic composition of MSAs, no year-to-year comparisons of data for those areas should be attempted. New England MSAs are comprised of cities and towns instead of counties. For purposes of tabular presentation, the UCR Program assigns New England cities and towns to the proper MSAs. Some counties, however, have both suburban and rural portions. Data for State police and sheriffs in those jurisdictions are included in statistics for the rural areas. MSAs made up approximately 80% of the total U.S. population in 2002.

Rural counties--Rural counties are those outside MSAs and are comprised of mostly unincorporated areas. Law enforcement agencies in rural counties cover areas that are not under the jurisdiction of city police departments. Rural county law enforcement agencies served 12% of the national population in 2002.

Suburban areas--These areas consist of cities with populations of less than 50,000 as well as unincorporated areas within an MSA, and exclude central cities. Suburban areas can, therefore, be divided into suburban cities and suburban counties.

Other cities--Other cities are urban places outside MSAs; most of these areas are incorporated. These cities comprised 8% of the 2002 national population.

As a general rule, sheriffs, county police, and State police report on crimes committed within the limits of counties, but outside cities; local police report on crimes committed within city limits.

The major source of UCR data is the individual law enforcement agency. The number of agencies included in each population group will vary slightly from year to year due to population growth, geopolitical consolidation, municipal incorporation, etc. Each year, population figures for individual jurisdictions are estimated by the UCR Program. For the 2002 edition of *Crime in the United States*, the UCR Program obtained current population estimates from the U.S. Census Bureau to estimate 2002 population counts for all contributing law enforcement agencies. The Census Bureau provided revised 2001 State and national population estimates and provisional 2002 State and national population estimates. Using these census data, the national UCR Program updated the 2001 Census Bureau city and county estimates and calculated the 2002 State growth rates. The UCR Program updated population figures for individual jurisdictions by applying the 2002 State growth rates to the updated 2001 Census Bureau data.

Table 2. Population group and number of contributing agencies

Population group	Number of agencies
I	71
II	171
III	423
IV	803
V	1,867
VI	8,735[a]
VIII (Rural county)	3,437[b]
IX (Suburban county)	1,817[b]
Total	17,324

[a]Includes universities and colleges to which no population is attributed.
[b]Includes State police to which no population is attributed.

Regions and divisions

The United States is divided into four regions; these regions are further divided into nine divisions. The following is a list of States within divisions and regions.

Northeast:
New England--Connecticut, Maine, Massachusetts, New Hampshire, Rhode Island, Vermont.
Middle Atlantic--New Jersey, New York, Pennsylvania.

Midwest:
East North Central--Illinois, Indiana, Michigan, Ohio, Wisconsin.
West North Central--Iowa, Kansas, Minnesota, Missouri, Nebraska, North Dakota, South Dakota.

South:
South Atlantic--Delaware, District of Columbia, Florida, Georgia, Maryland, North Carolina, South Carolina, Virginia, West Virginia.
East South Central--Alabama, Kentucky, Mississippi, Tennessee.
West South Central--Arkansas, Louisiana, Oklahoma, Texas.

West:
Mountain--Arizona, Colorado, Idaho, Montana, Nevada, New Mexico, Utah, Wyoming.
Pacific--Alaska, California, Hawaii, Oregon, Washington.

The Crime Index, Part I, and Part II offenses

The Crime Index

The following offenses and attempts to commit these offenses are used in compiling the Crime Index: (1) murder and nonnegligent manslaughter, (2) forcible rape, (3) robbery, (4) aggravated assault, (5) burglary,

(6) larceny-theft, (7) motor vehicle theft, and (8) arson. Arson was added as the eighth index offense in October 1978. (Manslaughter by negligence and simple or minor assaults are not included in the Crime Index.) Offenses in the UCR Program are divided into two groups, Part I and Part II. Information on the volume of Part I offenses known to law enforcement, those cleared by arrest or exceptional means, and the number of persons arrested is reported monthly. Only arrest data are reported for Part II offenses.

Part I offenses

Criminal homicide--a. Murder and nonnegligent manslaughter: the willful (nonnegligent) killing of one human being by another. Deaths caused by negligence, attempts to kill, assaults to kill, suicides, accidental deaths, and justifiable homicides are excluded. Justifiable homicides are limited to: (1) the killing of a felon by a law enforcement officer in the line of duty and (2) the killing of a felon, during commission of a felony, by a private citizen. **b.** Manslaughter by negligence: the killing of another person through gross negligence. Traffic fatalities are excluded. While manslaughter by negligence is a Part I crime, it is not included in the Crime Index.

Forcible rape--The carnal knowledge of a female forcibly and against her will. Included are rapes by force and attempts or assaults to rape. Statutory offenses (no force used--victim under age of consent) are excluded.

Robbery--The taking or attempting to take anything of value from the care, custody, or control of a person or persons by force or threat of force or violence and/or by putting the victim in fear.

Aggravated assault--An unlawful attack by one person upon another for the purpose of inflicting severe or aggravated bodily injury. This type of assault usually is accompanied by the use of a weapon or by means likely to produce death or great bodily harm. Simple assaults are excluded.

Burglary--breaking or entering--The unlawful entry of a structure to commit a felony or a theft. Attempted forcible entry is included.

Larceny-theft (except motor vehicle theft)--The unlawful taking, carrying, leading, or riding away of property from the possession or constructive possession of another. Examples are thefts of bicycles or automobile accessories, shoplifting, pocket-picking, or the stealing of any property or article that is not taken by force and violence or by fraud. Attempted larcenies are included. Embezzlement, "con" games, forgery, worthless checks, etc., are excluded.

Motor vehicle theft--The theft or attempted theft of a motor vehicle. A motor vehicle is self-propelled and runs on the surface and not on rails. Specifically excluded from this category are motorboats, construction equipment, airplanes, and farming equipment.

Arson--Any willful or malicious burning or attempt to burn, with or without intent to defraud, a dwelling house, public building, motor vehicle or aircraft, personal property of another, etc.

Part II offenses

Other assaults (simple)--Assaults and attempted assaults where no weapon is used and that do not result in serious or aggravated injury to the victim.

Forgery and counterfeiting--Making, altering, uttering, or possessing, with intent to defraud, anything false in the semblance of that which is true. Attempts are included.

Fraud--Fraudulent conversion and obtaining money or property by false pretenses. Included are confidence games and bad checks, except forgeries and counterfeiting.

Embezzlement--Misappropriation or misapplication of money or property entrusted to one's care, custody, or control.

Stolen property; buying, receiving, possessing--Buying, receiving, and possessing stolen property, including attempts.

Vandalism--Willful or malicious destruction, injury, disfigurement, or defacement of any public or private property, real or personal, without consent of the owner or persons having custody or control. Attempts are included.

Weapons; carrying, possessing, etc.--All violations of regulations or statutes controlling the carrying, using, possessing, furnishing, and manufacturing of deadly weapons or silencers. Attempts are included.

Prostitution and commercialized vice--Sex offenses of a commercialized nature, such as prostitution, keeping a bawdy house, and procuring or transporting women for immoral purposes. Attempts are included.

Sex offenses (except forcible rape, prostitution, and commercialized vice)--Statutory rape and offenses against chastity, common decency, morals, and the like. Attempts are included.

Drug abuse violations--State and local offenses relating to the unlawful possession, sale, use, growing, and manufacturing of narcotic drugs. The following drug categories are specified: opium or cocaine and their derivatives (morphine, heroin, codeine); marijuana; synthetic narcotics--manufactured narcotics that can cause addiction (demerol, methadone); and dangerous non-narcotic drugs (barbiturates, benzedrine).

Gambling--Promoting, permitting, or engaging in illegal gambling.

Offenses against the family and children--Nonsupport, neglect, desertion, or abuse of family and children. Attempts are included.

Driving under the influence--Driving or operating any vehicle or common carrier while drunk or under the influence of liquor or narcotics.

Liquor laws--State or local liquor law violations, except "drunkenness" and "driving under the influence." Federal violations are excluded.

Drunkenness--Offenses relating to drunkenness or intoxication. Excluded is "driving under the influence."

Disorderly conduct--Breach of the peace.

Vagrancy--Begging, loitering, etc. Includes prosecutions under the charge of suspicious person.

All other offenses--All violations of State or local laws, except those listed above and traffic offenses.

Suspicion--No specific offense; suspect released without formal charges being placed.

Curfew and loitering laws (persons under age 18)--Offenses relating to violations of local curfew or loitering ordinances where such laws exist.

Runaways (persons under age 18)--Limited to juveniles taken into protective custody under provisions of local statutes.

Offense estimation

Not all law enforcement agencies provide data for complete reporting periods. The UCR Program generates estimated crime counts for agencies with incomplete reporting. These estimated counts are used to generate offense totals for Metropolitan Statistical Areas (MSAs), cities outside MSAs, and rural counties. Using the known crime experiences of similar areas within a State, the national UCR Program computes estimates by assigning the same proportional crime volumes to nonreporting agencies. The size of agency; type of jurisdiction, e.g., police department versus sheriff's office; and geographic location are considered in the estimation process.

Various circumstances require the national Program to estimate certain State offense totals. For example, some States do not provide forcible rape figures in accordance with UCR guidelines; reporting problems at the State level have, at times, resulted in little or no usable data; and the conversion of summary reporting to National Incident-Based Reporting System (NIBRS) has contributed to the need for unique estimation procedures.

The Illinois (1985 to 2002), Michigan (1993), and Minnesota (1993) State UCR Programs were unable to provide forcible rape figures in accordance with UCR guidelines. The rape totals were estimated using national rates per 100,000 inhabitants within the eight population groups and assigning the forcible rape volumes proportionally to each State. The Delaware State UCR program was unable to provide 1998 forcible rape figures in accordance with UCR guidelines; the 1998 forcible rape total was estimated by reducing the number of reported offenses by the proportion of male forcible rape victims statewide.

In recent years, a number of States have been involved in the NIBRS conversion process. During the conversion process, little or no data were available from law enforcement agencies in these States. The following is a summary of States providing either incomplete data or no data for certain years, either due to NIBRS conversion or due to other reporting problems:

1988:	Florida, Kentucky
1991:	Iowa
1993:	Illinois, Kansas
1994:	Illinois, Kansas, Montana
1995:	Illinois, Kansas, Montana
1996:	Florida, Illinois, Kansas, Kentucky, Montana
1997:	Illinois, Kansas, Kentucky, Montana, New Hampshire, Vermont
1998:	Illinois, Kansas, Kentucky, Montana, New Hampshire, Wisconsin
1999:	Illinois, Kansas, Kentucky, Maine, Montana, New Hampshire
2000:	Illinois, Kansas, Kentucky, Montana
2001:	Illinois, Kentucky
2002:	Illinois, Kentucky

State totals were estimated using procedures based on data availability specific to each State, and the population group and geographic division to which the State belongs.

Table 3. Total U.S. population, 1960-2002[a]

Year	Population
1960	179,323,175
1961	182,992,000
1962	185,771,000
1963	188,483,000
1964	191,141,000
1965	193,526,000
1966	195,576,000
1967	197,457,000
1968	199,399,000
1969	201,385,000
1970	203,235,298
1971	206,212,000
1972	208,230,000
1973	209,851,000
1974	211,392,000
1975	213,124,000
1976	214,659,000
1977	216,332,000
1978	218,059,000
1979	220,099,000
1980	225,349,264
1981	229,146,000
1982	231,534,000
1983	233,981,000
1984	236,158,000
1985	238,740,000
1986	241,077,000
1987	243,400,000
1988	245,807,000
1989	248,239,000
1990	248,709,873
1991	252,177,000
1992	255,082,000
1993	257,908,000
1994	260,341,000
1995	262,755,000
1996	265,284,000
1997	267,637,000
1998	270,296,000
1999	272,691,000
2000	281,421,906
2001	284,796,887
2002	288,368,698

[a] Population figures are U.S. Census Bureau provisional estimates as of July 1 for each year except 1960, 1970, 1980, 1990, and 2000, which are the decennial census counts.

Appendix 4

Census of Jails, Annual Survey of Jails, and Survey of Inmates in Local Jails
Methodology and survey sampling procedures

Note: The following information was excerpted from U.S. Department of Justice, Bureau of Justice Statistics, *Prison and Jail Inmates at Midyear 2003*, Bulletin NCJ 203947 (Washington, DC: U.S. Department of Justice, May 2004), pp. 11, 12; *Census of Jails, 1999*, NCJ 186633 (Washington, DC: U.S. Department of Justice, 2001), p. 11; *Profile of Jail Inmates, 2002*, Special Report NCJ 201932 (Washington, DC: U.S. Department of Justice, July 2004), pp. 11, 12; *Jails and Jail Inmates 1993-94*, Bulletin NCJ-151651 (Washington, DC: U.S. Department of Justice, April 1995), pp. 14-16; and information provided by the U.S. Department of Justice, Bureau of Justice Statistics. Non-substantive editorial adaptations have been made.

Methodology

Census of Jails

The Census of Jails, previously known as the National Jail Census, is taken every 5 to 6 years and is conducted for the U.S. Department of Justice, Bureau of Justice Statistics (BJS) by the U.S. Census Bureau. Data are presented for censuses conducted in 1983, 1988, 1993, and 1999. Questionnaires were mailed to all locally administered jails in the Nation. The number of jails included in the three previous censuses and the response rates are: 1983, 3,358 jails with 99% responding; 1988, 3,316 jails with 100% responding; and 1993, 3,304 jails with 90% responding.

The most recent census, conducted in 1999, included all locally administered confinement facilities that hold inmates beyond arraignment (usually more than 72 hours) and are staffed by municipal or county employees. The census also included 47 jails that were privately operated under contract to local governments, 42 regional jails, and 11 facilities maintained by the Federal Bureau of Prisons and functioning as jails.

Excluded from the census were physically separate temporary holding facilities, such as drunk tanks and police lockups, that do not hold persons after being formally charged in court (usually within 72 hours of arrest). Also excluded were State-operated facilities in Alaska, Connecticut, Delaware, Hawaii, Rhode Island, and Vermont, which have combined jail-prison systems. However, 15 independently operated jails in Alaska were included.

The mailout used for the census was derived from a facility list maintained by the U.S. Census Bureau for BJS, correctional association directories, and other secondary sources. Census questionnaires were mailed to 3,160 jail jurisdictions on June 25, 1999. In addition to a paper form, BJS offered respondents in large jurisdictions an electronic version via the Internet, which allowed them to complete and submit their questionnaire online. Six jurisdictions were added to the initial mailout, and 82 were deleted, resulting in a total of 3,084 jail jurisdictions.

Extensive followup, in the form of mail and fax reminders and repeated telephone contacts, resulted in a nearly 100% response rate for the following critical data items: sex of inmates held; number of inmates on June 30, 1999; male and female inmates under age 18; male and female inmates age 18 and older; jail rated capacity; number of jail deaths during the preceding 12 months; and total number of staff.

Of the 3,084 jurisdictions in the final universe, 251 provided information on critical data items only. Data from six jurisdictions that did not respond to any items on the questionnaire were imputed based on previous survey and census reports.

Estimation procedures

Because there was nonresponse and incomplete data on census items other than the seven critical items, national totals had to be estimated. The following procedures were used to estimate totals when data were incomplete:

1. Each item was assessed for coverage and internal consistency. To estimate totals, extreme values were examined and verified by checking other census information and originally submitted forms. Detailed categories also were checked to determine if they summed to the reported totals.

2. To provide national and State total estimates of staff, item values were summed and then multiplied by a nonresponse adjustment factor (NAF). The NAF was a ratio of the total number of inmates in all jails to the number of inmates in jails that reported valid staff data.

3. All estimates were rounded to the nearest 100.

4. All rates, ratios, and percentage distributions were based on reported data only.

Annual Survey of Jails

In each of the years between the full censuses, a sample survey of jails is conducted to estimate baseline characteristics of the Nation's jails and inmates housed in the jails. Data from the Annual Survey of Jails are presented for 1984-87, 1989-92, 1994-98, and 2000-2003. The reference date for each of these surveys was June 30, except 1990 and 2001 when the reference date was June 29, and 1991 and 1996 when it was June 28. All surveys prior to the 1994 survey were based on all jails in jurisdictions with 100 or more jail inmates and a stratified random sample of jurisdictions with an average daily population of less than 100 inmates. For 1984, 1,164 jails in 893 jurisdictions were included; in 1985, 1,142 jails in 874 jurisdictions were included; in 1986, 1,137 jails in 868 jurisdictions were included; in 1987, 1,135 jails in 866 jurisdictions were included; in 1989, 1,128 jails in 809 jurisdictions were included; in 1990, 1,135 jails in 804 jurisdictions were included; in 1991, 1,124 jails in 799 jurisdictions were included; and in 1992, 1,113 jails in 795 jurisdictions were included.

A new sample of jail jurisdictions was selected for the 1994-98 surveys using information from the 1993 Census of Jails. A new sample was again selected and used for the 2000-2003 surveys based on information from the 1999 Census of Jails. A jurisdiction is a county (parish in Louisiana) or municipal government that administers one or more local jails. The sample included all 940 jail facilities in 878 jurisdictions. All 55 multijurisdiction jails (jails operated jointly by two or more jurisdictions) were selected with certainty.

Jails in 356 other jurisdictions were automatically included in the sample if the jail held juveniles and had an average daily population of 250 or more inmates on June 30, 1999 or if they held only adults and had an average daily population of 500 or more.

The remaining jurisdictions were stratified into two groups: jurisdictions with jails holding at least one juvenile on June 30, 1999, and jurisdictions with jails holding adults only. Using stratified probability sampling, 467 jurisdictions were then selected from 10 strata based on the average daily population in the 1999 jail census.

Data were obtained by mailed and web-based survey questionnaires. After followup phone calls, the response rate for the 2003 survey was 100% for critical items such as rated capacity, average daily population, and number of inmates confined.

Sampling error

Survey estimates have an associated sampling error because jurisdictions with smaller average daily populations were sampled for the survey. Estimates based on the sample survey may differ from the results of conducting a complete census. Different samples could yield somewhat different results. Standard error is a measure of the variation among the estimates from all possible samples, stating the precision with which an estimate from a particular sample approximates the average of all possible samples. The estimated relative sampling error for the total number of persons held in the custody of jail authorities of 691,301, was 0.51%. Readers interested in standard error estimates should consult the Source (Source, *Prison and Jail Inmates at Midyear 2003*, p. 14).

Measures of population

Two measures of jail inmate population are used: the average daily population for the year ending June 30 and the inmate count on June 30 of each year. The average daily population balances out any extraordinary events that may render atypical the inmate count on June 30. The June 30 count provides data on characteristics of inmates, such as race, Hispanic origin, and age, that may not be available on an annual basis.

In 1995 the Annual Survey of Jails obtained, for the first time, separate counts of the total number of offenders under jail jurisdiction, those held in jail facilities, and those supervised outside of jail facilities. Previous surveys and censuses included a small but unknown number of offenders under community supervision. To estimate the percent change from 1994 to 1995 in the jail population, the 1995 survey included a count of inmates held at midyear 1994.

In the 1996 survey the number of persons supervised outside a jail facility included for the first time persons under drug, alcohol, mental health, or other medical treatment. Comparison with 1995 estimates should exclude these persons.

Juveniles

In annual jail surveys beginning in 1994 and in the 1999 jail census, jail authorities were asked to report the number of inmates under age 18. Of the 9,458 persons under age 18 being held in jail on June 30, 1999, 91% were identified as juveniles tried or scheduled to be tried as adults.

Most, but not all, States defined a juvenile as a person under age 18 who is subject to juvenile court jurisdiction. Exceptions usually depend on offense severity or an offender's adjudication history.

Statutes and judicial practices sometimes allow youths to be held in adult jails. Often juveniles accused of acts that are crimes for adults may be held in jails or police lockups, given certain conditions: separation by sight and sound from the general population and detention for a limited time (typically less than 6 hours).

Survey of Inmates in Local Jails

The 2002 Survey of Inmates in Local Jails was conducted for BJS by the U.S. Census Bureau. Similar surveys of jail inmates were conducted in 1972, 1978, 1983, 1989, and 1996. Interviews for the 2002 survey were conducted from January through April 2002.

Sample design

The sample for the 2002 survey was selected from a universe of 3,365 jails that were enumerated in the 1999 Census of Jails. The sample design was a stratified two-stage selection where jails were selected in the first stage and inmates to be interviewed were selected in the second stage. In the first stage, six separate strata were formed based on the size of the male, female, and juvenile populations. In two strata all jails were selected--those jails housing only females and those with more than 1,000 males or more than 50 females or both. In the remaining four strata a systematic sample of jails was selected. Each jail within a stratum had an equal probability of selection. Overall, 465 jails were selected. Interviews were conducted in 417; 39 jails refused or were excluded for administrative reasons, and 9 were closed or had no inmates to survey.

In the second sampling stage, interviewers from the U.S. Census Bureau visited each selected facility and systematically selected a sample of male and female inmates using predetermined procedures. A total of 6,982 inmates were interviewed, and 768 refused to participate, for a second stage nonresponse of 9.9%.

Interviews were about 1 hour long and used computer-assisted personal interviewing (CAPI). With CAPI, computers provide the interviewer questions, including followup questions tailored to preceding answers. Before the interview, inmates were told verbally and in writing that participation was voluntary and that all information provided would be held in confidence.

Based on the completed interviews, estimates for the entire jail population were developed using weighting factors derived from the original probability of selection in the sample. These factors were adjusted for variable rates of nonresponse across strata and inmate characteristics. Further adjustments were made to conform the survey estimates to counts of jail inmates obtained from the 1999 Census of Jails and the 2001 Annual Survey of Jails.

Accuracy of the survey estimates

The accuracy of the estimates from the 2002 Survey of Inmates in Local Jails depends on two types of error: sampling and measurement. Sampling error is variation that occurs by chance because a sample rather than a complete enumeration of the population was conducted. Sampling error is measured by estimated standard error and varies by the size of the estimate and the size of the base population. Measurement error can be attributed to many sources, such as nonresponse, differences in the interpretation of questions among inmates, recall difficulties, and data processing errors. In any survey the full extent of the measurement error is never known.

Appendix 5

Public opinion survey sampling procedures

Note: The sampling procedures of six public opinion surveys or survey organizations are presented in this appendix: The Gallup Poll, the Phi Delta Kappa/Gallup Education Poll, the Harris Poll, the National Opinion Research Center, The Pew Research Center for the People & the Press, and the Youth Risk Behavior Surveillance System.

GALLUP POLL

Information on The Gallup Organization's survey sampling procedures was excerpted from The Gallup Organization, Inc. [Online]. Available: http://www.gallup.com [Dec. 1, 2004]. Non-substantive editorial adaptations have been made.

The Gallup Organization's public opinion polling methods are based on the fundamental sampling principle of equal probability of selection. This principle states that if every member of a population has an equal probability of being selected into a sample, the sample will be representative of the population.

Gallup polls prior to the mid-1980s were based on in-person interviewing among a national probability sample of interviewing areas throughout the United States. Readers interested in a discussion of the survey methodology and sampling for the in-person interviews should consult previous editions of SOURCEBOOK. By 1986, a sufficient proportion of American households had at least one telephone, making telephone interviewing a viable and substantially less expensive alternative to the in-person method.

For most Gallup polls (with the exception of specialized polls), the target population is referred to as "national adults." Specifically, the target population is the civilian, non-institutionalized population, age 18 and older, living in households with telephones within the continental United States. College students living on campus, armed forces personnel living on military bases, prisoners, hospital patients, and others living in group institutions are not represented in Gallup's sampling frame.

The sampling methodology involves random generation of phone numbers derived from a listing of all household telephone numbers in the continental United States. This process starts with a computerized list of all telephone exchanges in the U.S. and estimates of the number of residential households for each exchange. The random digit dialing (RDD) procedure creates computer-generated phone numbers for each exchange and generates samples of telephone numbers from those lists. In essence, this procedure creates a list of all possible household phone numbers in the U.S. and then selects a subset of numbers from that list for inclusion in the sample. The RDD procedure is utilized to avoid bias from exclusion of unlisted residential phone numbers.

The typical sample size for Gallup polls designed to represent the national adult population is 1,000 respondents. There is some gain in sampling accuracy resulting from increasing sample sizes. However, once the survey sample reaches a certain threshold (i.e., 600-700), there are fewer and fewer accuracy gains derived from increasing the sample size. Gallup polls and other major polling organizations use sample sizes between 1,000 and 1,500 because they provide a solid balance of accuracy against the increased economic cost of larger samples. With a sample size of 1,000 national adults, (derived using careful random selection procedures), the results are estimated to be accurate within a margin of error of plus or minus 3 percentage points.

Systematic procedures are in place to maintain the integrity of the sample. If there is no answer or the line is busy, the number is stored in the computer and redialed a few hours later or on subsequent nights of the survey period. Procedures are utilized to assure that the within-household selection process is random in households that include more than one adult. One method involves asking for the adult with the latest birthday; if that adult is not home the number is stored for a call back. These procedures are standard methods for reducing the sample bias that would otherwise result from under-representation of persons who are difficult to find at home.

Most interviews are conducted by telephone from regional interviewing centers around the country. Trained interviewers use computer assisted telephone interviewing (CATI) technology, which displays the survey questions on a computer monitor and allows questionnaires to be tailored to specific responses given by the individual being interviewed. In most polls, once interviewing has been completed, the data are carefully checked and weighted before analysis begins. The weighting process is a statistical procedure by which the sample is checked against known population parameters to correct for any possible sampling biases on the basis of demographic variables such as age, gender, race, education, or region of the country.

For certain survey items, Gallup uses a split sample technique to measure the impact of different question wordings. One-half (approximately 500 respondents) of a given sample is randomly selected and is administered one wording of a question, while the other half is administered another wording. This allows Gallup to compare the impact of differences in question wording.

The four regions of the country as reported in Gallup public opinion survey results are:

East--Maine, New Hampshire, Vermont, Massachusetts, Rhode Island, Connecticut, New York, New Jersey, Pennsylvania, Maryland, Delaware, West Virginia, District of Columbia;

Midwest--Ohio, Michigan, Indiana, Illinois, Wisconsin, Minnesota, Iowa, Missouri, North Dakota, South Dakota, Nebraska, Kansas;

South--Virginia, North Carolina, South Carolina, Georgia, Florida, Kentucky, Tennessee, Alabama, Mississippi, Arkansas, Louisiana, Oklahoma, Texas; and

West--Montana, Arizona, Colorado, Idaho, Wyoming, Utah, Nevada, New Mexico, California, Oregon, Washington, Hawaii, Alaska.

Urbanization--Central cities have populations of 50,000 and above. Suburbs constitute the fringe and include populations of 2,500 to 49,999. Rural areas are those that have populations of under 2,500.

Race, ethnicity--Nonwhite is comprised of individuals who report themselves as any combination of the following classifications: Hispanic, American Indian, other Indian, Asian, and black. Black and Hispanic are subcategories of nonwhite. However, due to variation in respondent reporting, the category white may also include some Hispanics.

Sampling error

All sample surveys are subject to sampling error, that is, the extent to which the results may differ from those that would be obtained if the entire population surveyed had been interviewed. The size of sampling errors depends largely on the number of interviews.

The following table may be used in estimating sampling error. The computed allowances have taken into account the effect of the sample design upon sampling error. They may be interpreted as indicating the range (plus or minus the figure shown) within which the results of repeated samplings in the same time period could be expected to vary, 95% of the time, assuming the same sampling procedure, the same interviewers, and the same questionnaire.

Recommended allowance for sampling error (plus or minus) at 95% confidence level

Percent-ages near	Sample size					
	1,000	750	600	400	200	100
10	2	3	3	4	5	7
20	3	4	4	5	7	9
30	4	4	4	6	8	10
40	4	4	5	6	8	11
50	4	4	5	6	8	11
60	4	4	5	6	8	11
70	4	4	4	6	8	10
80	3	4	4	5	7	9
90	2	3	3	4	5	7

The table would be used in the following manner: Assume a reported percentage is 33 for a group that includes 1,000 respondents. Proceed to row "Percentages near 30" in the table and then to the column headed, "1,000." The figure in this cell is four, which means that at the 95% confidence level, the 33% result obtained in the sample is subject to a sampling error of plus or minus four points.

PHI DELTA KAPPA/GALLUP POLL

Information on the Phi Delta Kappa/Gallup Poll was excerpted from George Gallup, Jr., *The Gallup Report*, Report No. 276, p. 41; and Report No. 288, p. 41 (Princeton, NJ: The Gallup Poll); Stanley M. Elam, "The 22nd Annual Gallup Poll of the Public's Attitudes Toward the Public Schools," *Phi Delta Kappan* (September 1990), p. 54; Stanley M. Elam, Lowell C. Rose, and Alec M. Gallup, "The 23rd Annual Gallup Poll of the Public's Attitudes Toward the Public Schools," *Phi Delta Kappan* (September 1991), p. 56; "The 24th Annual Gallup/Phi Delta Kappa Poll of the Public's Attitudes Toward the Public Schools," *Phi Delta Kappan* (September 1992), p. 52; "The 25th Annual Phi Delta Kappa/Gallup Poll of the Public's Attitudes Toward the Public Schools," *Phi Delta Kappan* (October 1993), p. 152; "The 26th Annual Phi Delta Kappa/Gallup Poll of the Public's Attitudes Toward the Public Schools," *Phi Delta Kappan* (September 1994), p. 56; Stanley M. Elam and Lowell C. Rose, "The 27th Annual Phi Delta Kappa/Gallup Poll of the Public's Attitudes Toward the Public Schools," *Phi Delta Kappan* (September 1995), p. 56; Stanley M. Elam, Lowell C. Rose, and Alec M. Gallup, "The 28th Annual Phi Delta Kappa/Gallup Poll of the Public's Attitudes Toward the Public Schools," *Phi Delta Kappan* (September 1996), p. 58; Lowell C. Rose, Alec M. Gallup, and Stanley M. Elam, "The 29th Annual Phi Delta Kappa/Gallup Poll of the Public's Attitudes Toward the Public Schools," Phi Delta Kappa [Online]. Available: http://www.pdkintl.org/kappan/kpoll97.htm [Dec. 31, 1997]; Lowell C. Rose and Alec M. Gallup, "The 30th Annual Phi Delta Kappa/Gallup Poll of the Public's Attitudes Toward the Public Schools," Phi Delta Kappa [Online]. Available: http://www.pdkintl.org/kappan/kp9809-a.htm [Jan. 5, 1999]; Lowell C. Rose and Alec M. Gallup, "The 31st Annual Phi Delta Kappa/Gallup Poll of the Public's Attitudes Toward the Public Schools," *Phi Delta Kappan* (September 1999), pp. 55, 56; "The 32nd Annual Phi Delta Kappa/Gallup Poll of the Public's Attitudes Toward the Public Schools," *Phi Delta Kappan* (September 2000), pp. 57, 58; "The 33rd Annual Phi Delta Kappa/Gallup Poll of the Public's Attitudes Toward the Public Schools," *Phi Delta Kappan* (September 2001), pp. 57, 58; "The 34th Annual Phi Delta Kappa/Gallup Poll of the Public's Attitudes Toward the Public Schools," *Phi Delta Kappan* (September 2002), pp. 56, 57; and "The 35th Annual Phi Delta Kappa/Gallup Poll of the Public's Attitudes Toward the Public Schools," *Phi Delta Kappan* (September 2003), p. 52.

The Phi Delta Kappa/Gallup polls are modified probability samples of adults, 18 years of age and older, living in the United States.

Sample sizes and survey dates for Phi Delta Kappa/Gallup polls

	Sample size	Survey dates
1988	NA	Apr. 8-10
1989	NA	May 5-7; June 9-11
1990	1,594	Apr. 6-18; May 4-22
1991	1,500	May 3-17
1992	1,306	Apr. 23-May 14
1993	1,306	May 21-June 9
1994	1,326	May 10-June 8
1995	1,311	May 25-June 15
1996	1,329	May 2-22
1997	1,517	June 3-22
1998	1,151	June 5-23
1999	1,103	May 18-June 11
2000	1,093	June 5-29
2001	1,108	May 23-June 6
2002	1,000	June 5-26
2003	1,011	May 28-June 18

Prior to the 1993 survey, data collection was done through personal, in-home interviewing of the civilian population (excluding persons in institutions such as prisons and hospitals). Beginning with the 1993 survey, the data collection design utilized the Gallup Organization's standard national telephone sample, i.e., an unclustered, directory-assisted, random-digit telephone sample, based on a proportionate stratified sampling design. Random-digit samples are used to avoid listing bias. Numerous studies have shown that households with unlisted telephone numbers are different in important ways from listed households. "Unlistedness" is due to household mobility or to customer requests to prevent publication of the telephone number. To avoid this source of bias, a random-digit procedure designed to provide representation of both listed and unlisted (including not-yet-listed) numbers was used.

Telephone numbers for the continental United States were stratified into four regions of the country and, within each region, further stratified into three size-of-community strata. Only working banks of telephone numbers were selected. Eliminating nonworking banks from the sample increased the likelihood that any sample telephone number would be associated with a residence. This method generates a sample of telephone numbers that is representative of all telephone households within the continental United States.

Within each contacted household, an interview was sought with the household member who had the most recent birthday. This method of respondent selection provides an excellent approximation of statistical randomness in that it gives all members of the household an opportunity to be selected.

Up to three calls were made to each selected telephone number to complete an interview. The time of day and the day of the week for callbacks were varied so as to maximize the chances of finding a respondent at home. All interviews were conducted on weekends or weekday evenings in order to contact potential respondents among the working population.

The final sample was weighted so that the distribution of the sample matched current estimates from the U.S. Census Bureau's Current Population Survey for the adult population living in telephone households in the continental United States.

For further information on the survey sampling procedures see Lowell C. Rose and Alec M. Gallup, "The 35th Annual Phi Delta Kappa/Gallup Poll of the Public's Attitudes Toward the Public Schools," *Phi Delta Kappan* (September 2003), p. 52.

HARRIS POLL

Information on the Harris Poll survey sampling procedures was provided to SOURCEBOOK staff by Harris Interactive, Inc., formerly Louis Harris and Associates, Inc.; similar procedures used in earlier surveys are described in Louis Harris and Associates, Inc., *The Harris Yearbook of Public Opinion 1970: A Compendium of Current American Attitudes* (New York: Louis Harris and Associates, Inc., 1971), pp. 511-514.

Harris Poll surveys are based on a national sample of the civilian population of the continental United States. Alaska and Hawaii are not represented in the sample, nor are persons in prisons, hospitals, or religious and educational institutions. The sample is based on census information on the population of each State in the country, and on the population living in standard metropolitan areas and in the rest of the country. These population figures are updated by intercensal estimates produced annually by the U.S. Census Bureau, and sample locations are selected biennially to reflect changes in the country's demographic profile.

National samples are stratified in two dimensions--geographic region and metropolitan (and non-metropolitan) residence. Stratification insures that the samples will reflect, within 1%, the actual proportions of those living in the country in different regions and metropolitan (and non-metropolitan) areas. Within each stratum the selection of the ultimate sampling unit is achieved through a series of steps, a process that is technically called multi-stage unclustered sampling. Each sampling unit yields one interview. First States, then counties, and then minor civil divisions (cities, towns, townships) are selected with probability proportional to census estimates of their respective household populations.

The Harris Poll survey has four of these national samples, and they are used in rotation from study to study. The specific sample locations in one study generally are adjacent to those used in the next study. For most surveys covering the entire country, more than one national sample may be employed. Harris Poll surveys of nationwide samples usually include approximately 1,250 respondents.

All interviews prior to 1978 were conducted in person, in the homes of respondents. At each household the respondent was chosen by means of a random selection pattern, geared to the number of adults of each sex who live in the household. Interviews lasted approximately 1 hour. Almost all interviews conducted as of 1978 have been telephone interviews. Respondents are selected on the basis of random digit dialing. When the completed interviews are received in New York, a subsample of the respondents are recontacted to verify that the data have been accurately recorded. Questionnaires are edited and coded in the New York office. The Harris sampling procedure is designed to produce a national cross-section that accurately reflects the actual population of the country 18 years of age and older living in private households. This means that the results of a survey among a national sample can be projected as representative of the country's civilian population 18 years of age and older.

Harris Poll survey national results are reported for the East, Midwest, South, and West regions of the country, defined as follows:

East--Maine, New Hampshire, Vermont, New York, Massachusetts, Rhode Island, Connecticut, Pennsylvania, Maryland, New Jersey, Delaware, West Virginia;
Midwest--North Dakota, South Dakota, Nebraska, Kansas, Minnesota, Iowa, Missouri, Wisconsin, Illinois, Michigan, Indiana, Ohio;
South--Kentucky, Virginia, Tennessee, North Carolina, South Carolina, Georgia, Alabama, Mississippi, Florida, Louisiana, Arkansas, Oklahoma, Texas; and
West--Washington, Oregon, California, Idaho, Nevada, Utah, Arizona, Montana, Wyoming, Colorado, New Mexico.

Sampling error

The results of the surveys are subject to sampling error, i.e., the difference between the results obtained from the sample and those that would be obtained by surveying the entire population. The size of a possible sampling error varies to some extent with the size of the sample and with the percentage giving a particular answer. The following table sets forth the range of error in samples of different sizes and at different percentages of response.

For example, if the response for a sample size of 1,200 is 30%, in 95 cases out of 100 the response in the population will be between 27% and 33%. This error accounts only for sampling error. Survey research also is susceptible to other errors, such as data handling and interview recording.

Recommended allowance for sampling error (plus or minus) at 95% confidence level:

Response percent	1,600	1,200	900	500	250	100
10(90)	2	2	2	3	5	7
20(80)	2	3	3	4	6	10
30(70)	3	3	4	5	7	11
40(60)	3	3	4	5	7	12
50	3	3	4	5	8	12

NATIONAL OPINION RESEARCH CENTER

Information on the survey procedures employed by the National Opinion Research Center was excerpted from the National Opinion Research Center, **General Social Surveys, 1972-2002: Cumulative Codebook** (Chicago: National Opinion Research Center, University of Chicago, 2003), pp. v, vi, 61, 1288, 1289, 1299, 1525, 1526.

The National Opinion Research Center (NORC) maintains a national probability sample. The General Social Surveys (GSS) are interviews administered to the NORC national samples using a standard questionnaire. They have been conducted during February, March, and April from 1972 to 1978, 1980, 1982 to 1991, 1993, 1994, 1996, 1998, 2000, and 2002.

Completed interviews for General Social Surveys, 1972-2002

	Completed interviews
Total	43,698
1972	1,613
1973	1,504
1974	1,484
1975	1,490
1976	1,499
1977	1,530
1978	1,532
1980	1,468
1982	1,860
1983	1,599
1984	1,473
1985	1,534
1986	1,470
1987	1,819
1988	1,481
1989	1,537
1990	1,372
1991	1,517
1993	1,606
1994	2,992
1996	2,904
1998	2,832
2000	2,817
2002	2,765

Note: The figure for 1982 includes an oversample of 354 black respondents; the figure for 1987 includes an oversample of 353 black respondents.

Sampling frames are based on 1970 census information for surveys conducted in 1972-78, 1980, and 1982. For all interviews conducted from 1984-91, the national sampling frame was based on 1980 census information. A split sample transition design was used in the 1983 survey; one-half of the sample was drawn from the 1970 frame and one-half from the 1980 frame. Again in 1993, a split sample transition design was employed for the 1993 survey to measure the effect of switching from the 1980 sample frame to the 1990 sample frame. Half the sample was drawn from each frame. Beginning in 1994, the 1990 sample frame has been used. Since 1973, the median length of the interview has been about one and a half hours. This study employed standard field procedures for national surveys, including interviewer hiring and training by area supervisors in interviewing locations when necessary.

Each survey is an independently drawn sample of English-speaking persons 18 years of age and older, living in non-institutional arrangements within the United States. Alaska and Hawaii are not included in samples drawn from the 1970 sampling frame, but are represented in one-half of the 1983 surveys and all those conducted from

1984-2002. Block quota sampling was used in the 1972, 1973, and 1974 surveys and for half of the 1975 and 1976 surveys. Full probability sampling was employed in half of the 1975 and 1976 surveys and in all of the surveys conducted subsequent to 1976.

The sample is a multi-stage area probability sample to the block or segment level. At the block level, quota sampling is used with quotas based on sex, age, and employment status. The cost of the quota samples is substantially less than the cost of a full probability sample of the same size, but there is, of course, the chance of sample biases mainly due to not-at-homes, which are not controlled by the quotas. However, in order to reduce this bias, the interviewers are given instructions to canvass and interview only after 3:00 p.m. on weekdays or during the weekend or holidays. The first stage of sample selection includes selection of the Primary Sampling Units (PSUs). The PSUs employed are Standard Metropolitan Statistical Areas (SMSAs) or nonmetropolitan counties selected in NORC's Master Sample. These SMSAs and counties were stratified by region, age, and race before selection. The units of selection of the second stage were block groups (BGs) and enumeration districts (EDs). These BGs and EDs were stratified according to race and income of the residents. The third stage of selection was that of blocks, which were selected with probabilities proportional to size. In places without block statistics, measures of size for the blocks were obtained by field counting. The average cluster size is five respondents per cluster.

The quotas call for approximately equal numbers of males and females with the exact proportion in each segment determined by the 1970 census tract data. For women, the additional requirement is imposed that there be the proper proportion of employed and unemployed females in the location. Again, these quotas are based on the 1970 census tract data. For males, the added requirement is that there be the proper proportion of males over and under age 35 in the location. Past experience suggests that, for most purposes, this quota sample of 1,500 could be considered as having about the same efficiency as a simple random sample of 1,000 cases.

The 1975 and 1976 studies were conducted with a traditional sample design, one-half full probability and one-half block quota. The sample was divided into two parts for several reasons: (1) to provide data for possibly interesting methodological comparisons; and (2) on the chance that there are some differences over time, that it would be possible to assign these differences to either shifts in sample designs, or changes in response patterns. Having allowed for the appearance of all items in the transitional sample design, the GSS then switched to a full probability sample beginning with the 1977 survey.

Rotation

Since its inception, the GSS has employed a *rotation design* under which most of its items appeared on two out of every three surveys. While this design proved to be useful for both monitoring change and augmenting the content of the GSS, it had the disadvantage of irregularly spacing the data and allowing gaps in the time series. This problem was particularly acute during 1978-82 because of the lack of funding for surveys in 1979 and 1981. At that juncture 4-year gaps regularly appeared in the data and 6-year lapses existed for bivariate correlations between items from different rotations. Even with annual surveys 2-year gaps and 3-year intervals for bivariate correlations occur. To reduce this imbalance in the time series and reduce the length of intervals, in 1988 the rotation, across-time design previously used was changed to a *split-ballot design*. Under this design rotations 1, 2, and 3 occur across random sub-samples within each survey rather than across surveys (and years). Each sub-sample (known as ballots) consists of 1/3 of the sample. Permanent items are not affected by this switch. They continue to appear for all cases on all surveys. Rotating items now appear on all surveys and are asked of two-thirds of respondents on each survey. Over a 3-year cycle the same number of respondents are asked the "rotating" items as before (3,000), but instead of coming in two segments of 1,500 each from two surveys, they appear in three segments of 1,000 each from three surveys.

The 1993 GSS was the last survey conducted according to this design. In 1994 two major innovations were introduced to the GSS.

First, the traditional core was substantially reduced to allow for the creation of mini-modules (i.e., blocks of about 15 minutes devoted to some combination of small- to medium-sized supplements). The mini-modules space provides greater flexibility to incorporate innovations and to include important items proposed by the social science community.

Second, a new biennial, split-sample design was used. The sample consists of two parallel sub-samples of approximately 1,500 cases each. The two sub-samples both contain the identical core. The A sample also contains a standard, topical module, the mini-modules, and an International Social Survey Program (ISSP) module (on women, work, and the family). The B sample has a second topical module, mini-modules, and an ISSP module (on the environment). In effect, one can think of the A sample as representing a traditional GSS for 1994 and the B sample representing a traditional GSS for 1995. Rather than being fielded separately in two different years they are fielded together.

Beginning in 1996, and in subsequent even-numbered years, the same design described for 1994 was repeated. In addition, in 1994 only, a transitional design was utilized to calibrate any impact of deletions from the core.

Beginning in 2002, the GSS underwent a change in survey mode. In the past, the GSS was administered using a paper and pencil format. Starting in 2002, the GSS was conducted by computer-assisted personal interviewing (CAPI). In addition, the measurement of race was revised by the GSS in 2002. In the past, the GSS relied on interviewer perception to report the race of the respondent. Beginning in 2002, race is determined solely through self-report by the respondent.

Survey results are reported for four regional categories, with the States classified in the following way:

Northeast--Connecticut, Maine, Massachusetts, New Hampshire, New Jersey, New York, Pennsylvania, Rhode Island, Vermont;

North Central--Illinois, Indiana, Iowa, Kansas, Michigan, Minnesota, Missouri, Nebraska, North Dakota, Ohio, South Dakota, Wisconsin;

South--Alabama, Arkansas, Delaware, District of Columbia, Florida, Georgia, Kentucky, Louisiana, Maryland, Mississippi, North Carolina, Oklahoma, South Carolina, Tennessee, Texas, Virginia, West Virginia;

West--Alaska, Arizona, California, Colorado, Hawaii, Idaho, Montana, Nevada, New Mexico, Oregon, Utah, Washington, Wyoming.

THE PEW RESEARCH CENTER FOR THE PEOPLE & THE PRESS

Information on The Pew Center's 2003 Values Survey was excerpted from The Pew Research Center for the People & the Press, ***The 2004 Political Landscape: Evenly Divided and Increasingly Polarized*** (Washington, DC: The Pew Research Center for the People & the Press, 2003), p. 77.

Results are based on telephone interviews conducted under the direction of Princeton Survey Research Associates with a nationwide sample of 2,528 adults, 18 years of age and older, from July 14 to Aug. 5, 2003. Based on the total sample, one can say with 95% confidence that the error attributable to sampling and other random effects is plus or minus 2 percentage points.

Respondents who indicated they would prefer to complete the interview in Spanish, and

Spanish-speaking households in which no eligible English-speaking adult was available, were contacted by a Spanish-speaking interviewer.

The sample is a random digit sample of telephone numbers selected from telephone exchanges in the continental United States. The random digit aspect of the sample is used to avoid "listing" bias and provides representation of both listed and unlisted numbers (including not-yet-listed). The design of the sample ensures this representation by random generation of the last two digits of telephone numbers selected on the basis of area code, telephone exchange, and bank number.

The telephone exchanges were selected with probabilities proportional to their size. The first eight digits of the sampled telephone numbers (area code, telephone exchange, bank number) were selected to be proportionally stratified by county and by telephone exchange within county. That is, the number of telephone numbers randomly sampled from within a given county is proportional to that county's share of telephone numbers in the United States. Only working banks of telephone numbers are selected. A working bank is defined as 100 contiguous telephone numbers containing one or more residential listings.

At least 10 attempts were made to complete an interview at every sampled telephone number. The calls were staggered over times of the day and days of the week to maximize the chances of making a contact with a potential respondent. All interview breakoffs and refusals were recontacted at least once in order to attempt to convert them to completed interviews. In each contacted household, interviewers asked to speak with the "youngest male 18 or older who is at home." If there is no eligible male at home, interviewers asked to speak with "the oldest woman 18 or older who is at home." This systematic respondent selection technique has been shown empirically to produce samples that closely mirror the population in terms of age and gender.

Nonresponse in telephone interview surveys produces some known biases in survey-derived estimates because participation tends to vary for different subgroups of the population, and these subgroups are likely to vary also on questions of substantive interest. In order to compensate for these known biases, the sample data are weighted in analysis.

The demographic weighting parameters are derived from analysis of the most recently available U.S. Census Bureau's Current Population Survey (March 2002). This analysis produced population parameters for the demographic characteristics of households with adults age 18 and older, which are then compared with the sample characteristics to construct sample weights. The analysis included only households in the continental United States that contain a telephone.

YOUTH RISK BEHAVIOR SURVEILLANCE SYSTEM

Information on the Youth Risk Behavior Surveillance System was excerpted from Jo Anne Grunbaum et al., "Youth Risk Behavior Surveillance--United States, 2003," CDC Surveillance Summaries, *Morbidity and Mortality Weekly Report* 53 SS-2 (Washington, DC: USGPO, May 21, 2004), pp. 1-3.

The Youth Risk Behavior Surveillance System (YRBSS) is conducted biennially by the U.S. Department of Health and Human Services, Centers for Disease Control and Prevention and monitors priority health risk behaviors among youth and young adults. The 2003 national school-based survey, a component of the YRBSS, employed a three-stage cluster sample design to produce a nationally representative sample of students in grades 9 through 12. The first-stage sampling frame contained 1,262 primary sampling units (PSUs), consisting of large counties, subareas of large counties, or groups of smaller, adjacent counties. From the 1,262 PSUs, 57 were selected from 16 strata formed on the basis of the degree of urbanization and the percentage of black (non-Hispanic) and Hispanic students in the PSU. The PSUs were selected with probability proportional to school enrollment size. At the second sampling stage, 195 schools were selected with probability proportional to school enrollment size. To enable separate analysis of black and Hispanic students, schools with substantial numbers of black (non-Hispanic) and Hispanic students were sampled at higher rates than all other schools. The third stage of sampling consisted of randomly selecting one or two intact classes of a required subject (e.g., English or social studies) or a required period (e.g., second period) from grades 9 through 12 at each chosen school. All students in the selected classes were eligible to participate in the study.

The school response rate was 81% and the student response rate was 83%, for an overall response rate of 67%. A total of 15,240 questionnaires were completed in 158 schools. Of these, 26 questionnaires failed quality control and were excluded from the analysis resulting in 15,214 usable questionnaires.

Survey procedures were designed to protect students' privacy by allowing for anonymous and voluntary participation. Students completed the self-administered questionnaire during one class period and recorded their responses directly on a computer-scannable booklet or answer sheet.

A weighting factor was applied to each student record to adjust for nonresponse and for the varying probabilities of selection, including those resulting from the oversampling of black (non-Hispanic) and Hispanic students. Numbers of students in racial/ethnic groups other than white (non-Hispanic), black (non-Hispanic), and Hispanic were too low for meaningful analysis. The weights were scaled so that the weighted count of students was equal to the total sample size and so that the weighted proportions of students in each grade matched national population proportions. The data are representative of students in grades 9 through 12 in public and private schools in the 50 States and the District of Columbia.

Appendix 6

Monitoring the Future Survey methodology and definitions of terms

Note: The following information was excerpted from Jerald G. Bachman, Lloyd D. Johnston, and Patrick M. O'Malley, ***Monitoring the Future 2000*** (Ann Arbor, MI: Institute for Social Research, University of Michigan, 2001), pp. 2-11, 13, 14; Lloyd D. Johnston et al., ***Monitoring the Future National Survey Results on Drug Use, 1975-2003***, Volumes I and II (Bethesda, MD: U.S. Department of Health and Human Services, 2004); and information provided by the Monitoring the Future Project. Non-substantive editorial adaptations have been made.

Survey methodology

The research design involves annual data collections from high school seniors during the spring of each year, beginning with the class of 1975. Each data collection takes place in approximately 120 to 146 public and private high schools selected to provide an accurate cross-section of high school seniors throughout the coterminous United States.

Since 1986, the results of a followup survey of those young adults 1 to 10 years beyond high school have been presented. These results should accurately characterize approximately 85% of the young adults in the class cohorts 1 to 10 years beyond high school who are high school graduates. The high school dropout segment, missing from the senior year surveys, also is missing from the followup segments.

Also, since 1980, the results of followup surveys of those high school students who have continued on to college have been presented. The college sample is limited to the most typical one for college attendance: 1 to 4 years past high school, which corresponds to the modal ages of 19 to 22 years old. This age category should encompass approximately 70% to 75% of all students enrolled in college full-time.

Sampling procedures

The procedure for securing a nationwide sample of high school seniors is a multistage one. Stage 1 is the selection of particular geographic areas, Stage 2 is the selection of one or more high schools in each area, and Stage 3 is the selection of seniors within each high school.

Stage 1: Geographic areas. The geographic areas used in this study are the primary sampling units (PSUs) developed by the Sampling Section of the Survey Research Center (SRC) for use in the Center's nationwide interview studies. These consist of 74 primary areas throughout the coterminous United States--including the 12 largest metropolitan areas, which contain about 30% of the Nation's population. Of the 62 other primary areas, 10 are in the Northeast, 18 in the North Central area, 24 in the South, and 10 in the West. Because these same PSUs are used for personal interview studies by the SRC, local field representatives can be assigned to administer the data collections in practically all schools.

Stage 2: Schools. In the major metropolitan areas more than one high school is often included in the sampling design; in most other sampling areas a single high school is sampled. In all cases, the selections of high schools are made such that the probability of drawing a school is proportionate to the size of its senior class. The larger the senior class (according to recent records), the higher the selection probability assigned to the high school. When a sampled school is unwilling to participate, a replacement school as similar to it as possible is selected from the same geographic area.

Stage 3: Students. Within each selected school, up to 350 seniors may be included in the data collection. In schools with fewer than 350 seniors, the usual procedure is to include all of them in the data collection. In larger schools, a subset of seniors is selected either by randomly sampling classrooms or by some other random method that is convenient for the school and judged to be unbiased. Sample weights are assigned to each respondent so as to take account of variations in the sizes of samples from one school to another, as well as the (smaller) variations in selection probabilities occurring at the earlier stages of sampling.

The three-stage sampling procedure described above yielded the number of participating schools and students indicated in Table 1.

One limitation in the design is that it does not include in the target population those young men and women who drop out of high school before graduation (or before the last few months of the senior year, to be more precise). This excludes a relatively small proportion of each age cohort--between 15% and 20% of each age cohort nationally, according to the U.S. Census Bureau. This is not an unimportant segment, since certain behaviors such as illicit drug use and delinquency tend to be higher than average in this group. However, the addition of a representative sample of dropouts would increase the cost of the present research enormously, because of their dispersion and generally higher level of resistance to being located and interviewed.

For the purposes of estimating characteristics of the entire age group, the omission of high school dropouts does introduce certain biases; however, their small proportion sets outer limits on the bias. For the purposes of estimating changes from one cohort of high school seniors to another, the omission of dropouts represents a problem only if different cohorts have considerably different proportions who drop out. The Source has no reason to expect dramatic changes in those rates for the foreseeable future, and recently published Census Bureau statistics indicate a great deal of stability in dropout rates since 1970.

Some may use the high school data to draw conclusions about changes for the entire age group. The Source does not encourage such extrapolation but suspects that the conclusions reached often would be valid, since over 80% of the age group is in the surveyed segment of the population and the Source expects that changes among those not in school are very likely to parallel the changes among those who are.

One other important feature of the base-year sampling procedures should be noted. All schools (except for half of the initial 1975 sample) are asked to participate in two data collections, thereby permitting replacement of half of the total sample of schools each year. One motivation for requesting that schools participate for 2 years is administrative efficiency; it is a costly and time-consuming procedure to secure the cooperation of schools, and a 2-year period of participation cuts down that effort substantially. Another important advantage is that whenever an appreciable shift in scores from one graduating class to the next is observed, it is possible to compare whether the shift might be attributable to some differences in the newly sampled schools. This is done simply by repeating the analysis using only the 60 or so schools that participated both years. Thus far, the half-sample approach has worked well; and examination of drug prevalence data from the "matched half-samples" shows that the half samples of repeat schools yielded drug prevalence trends that were virtually identical to trends based on all schools.

Questionnaire administration

Questionnaire administration in each school is carried out by the local SRC representatives and their assistants, following standardized procedures detailed in a project instruction manual. The questionnaires are administered in classrooms during normal class periods whenever possible, although circumstances in some schools require the use of larger group administrations. Teachers are not asked to do anything more than introduce the SRC staff members and (in most cases) remain in the classroom to help guarantee an orderly atmosphere for the survey. Teachers are urged to avoid walking around the room, so that students may feel free to write their answers without fear of being observed.

The actual process of completing the questionnaires is straightforward. Respondents are given sharpened pencils and asked to use them because the questionnaires are designed for automatic scanning. Most respondents can finish within a 45-minute class period; for those who cannot, an effort is made to provide a few minutes of additional time.

Content areas and questionnaire design

Drug use and related attitudes are the topics that receive the most extensive coverage in the Monitoring the Future Project; but the questionnaires also deal with a wide range of other subject areas, including attitudes about government, social institutions, race relations, changing roles for women, educational aspirations, occupational aims, and marital and family plans, as well as a variety of background and demographic factors. The list below provides an outline of the 20 general subject areas into which all items are categorized. Given this breadth of content, the study is not presented to respondents as a "drug use study," nor do they tend to view it as such.

Measurement content areas

A. Drugs. Drug use and related attitudes and beliefs, drug availability and exposure, surrounding conditions and social meanings of drug use. Views of significant others regarding drugs.

B. Education. Educational lifestyle, values, experiences, and environments.

C. Work and leisure. Vocational values, meaning of work and leisure, work and leisure activities, preferences regarding occupational characteristics and type of work setting.

D. Sex roles and family. Values, attitudes, and expectations about marriage, family structure, sex roles, and sex discrimination.

E. Population concerns. Values and attitudes about overpopulation and birth control.

F. Conservation, materialism, equity, etc. Values, attitudes, and expectations related to conservation, pollution, materialism, equity, and the sharing of resources. Preferences regarding type of dwelling and urbanicity.

G. Religion. Religious affiliation, practices, and views.

H. Politics. Political affiliation, activities, and views.

I. Social change. Values, attitudes, and expectations about social change.

J. Social problems. Concern with various social problems facing the Nation and the world.

K. Major social institutions. Confidence in and commitment to various major social institutions (business, unions, branches of government, press, organized religion, military, etc.).

L. Military. Views about the armed services and the use of military force. Personal plans for military service.

M. Interpersonal relationships. Qualitative and quantitative characteristics of cross-age and peer relationships. Interpersonal conflict.

N. Race relations. Attitudes toward and experiences with other racial groups.

O. Concern for others. Concern for others; voluntary and charitable activities.

P. Happiness. Happiness and life satisfaction, overall and in specific life domains.

Q. Other personality variables. Attitudes about self (including self-esteem), locus of control, loneliness, risk-taking, trust in others, importance placed on various life goals, counter-culture orientation, hostility.

R. Background. Demographic and family background characteristics, living arrangements.

S. Deviant behavior and victimization. Delinquent behaviors, driving violations and accidents (including those under the influence of drugs), victimization experiences.

T. Health. Health habits, somatic symptoms, medical treatments.

Because many questions are needed to cover all of these topic areas, much of the questionnaire content was divided into five different questionnaire forms in 1976-88 and six different questionnaire forms for 1989 and beyond, which are distributed to participants in an ordered sequence that produces virtually identical subsamples. About one-third of each questionnaire form consists of key or "core" variables that are common to all forms. All demographic variables and some measures of drug use are included in this "core" set of measures. This use of the full sample for drug and demographic measures provides a more accurate estimation on these dimensions and also makes it possible to link them statistically to all of the other measures that are included in a single form only.

Representativeness and validity

The samples for this study are intended to be representative of high school seniors throughout the 48 coterminous States. As previously mentioned, this definition of the sample excludes one important portion of the age cohort: those who have dropped out of high school before nearing the end of the senior year. But given the aim of representing high school seniors, it is useful to consider the extent to which the obtained samples of schools and students are likely to be representative of all seniors and the degree to which the data obtained are likely to be valid.

There are at least four ways in which survey data of this sort might fall short of being fully accurate. First, some sampled schools refuse to participate, which could introduce some bias. Second, the failure to obtain questionnaire data from 100% of the students sampled in participating schools also could introduce bias. Third, the answers provided by participating students are open to both conscious and unconscious distortions, which could reduce validity. Finally, limitations in sample size and/or design could place limits on the accuracy of estimates.

School participation

As noted in the description of the sampling design, schools are invited to participate in the study for a 2-year period. With very few exceptions, each school that has participated for one data collection has agreed to participate for a second. Thus far, approximately 65% of the schools initially invited to participate have agreed to do so each year; for each school refusal, a similar school (in terms of size, geographic area, urbanicity, etc.) was recruited as a replacement. However, because securing high school cooperation has become more difficult in recent years, payment of schools as a means of increasing their incentive to participate was implemented in the 2003 survey.

The selection of replacement schools almost entirely removes problems of bias in region, urbanicity, and the like that might result from certain schools refusing to participate. Other potential biases are more subtle, however. For example, if it turned out that most schools with "drug problems" refused to participate, that could seriously bias the drug estimates derived from the sample. And if any other single factor was dominant in most refusals, that also might suggest a source of serious bias. In fact, however, the reasons for schools refusing to participate are varied and largely a function of happenstance events of the particular year. Thus, there is a fair amount of confidence that school refusals have not seriously biased the surveys.

Student participation

Completed questionnaires are obtained from approximately 80 to 85% of all students sampled. The single most important reason that students are missed is that they are absent from class at the time of data collection, and in most cases it is not workable to schedule a special followup data collection for them.

Students with high rates of absenteeism also report above-average drug use. Therefore there is some degree of bias introduced by missing the absentees. That bias could be largely corrected through the use of special weighting; however, this course was not chosen because the bias in estimates (for drug use, where the potential effect was hypothesized to be the largest) was determined to be quite small and because the necessary weighting procedures would have introduced undesirable complications.

In addition to absenteeism, student nonparticipation occurs because of schedule conflicts with school trips and other activities that tend to be more frequent than usual during the final months of the senior year. Of course, some students refuse to complete or turn in a questionnaire. However, the proportion of explicit refusals amounts to less than 1.5% of the target sample for each grade.

Research design for the surveys of lower grades

Beginning in 1991 the study was expanded to include nationally representative samples of eighth and tenth grade students. In general, the procedures used for the annual surveys of eighth and tenth grade students closely parallel those used for high school seniors, including the procedures for selecting schools and students, questionnaire administrations, and questionnaire formats. A major exception is that only two different questionnaire forms were used in 1991-96 and four forms were used beginning in 1997, rather than the six forms used with seniors. Identical forms are used for both eighth and tenth grades, and, for the most part, questionnaire content is drawn from the twelfth grade questionnaires. Thus, key demographic variables and measures of drug use and related attitudes and beliefs are generally identical for all three grades. Fewer questions about lifestyles and values are included in these forms than in the twelfth grade forms, in part because it is believed that many of these attitudes are more likely to be formed by twelfth grade, and therefore are best monitored there. For the national survey of eighth graders, approximately 150 schools are sampled, and approximately 16,000 to 19,000 students are surveyed. For the tenth graders, approximately 130 schools are sampled, and approximately 14,000 to 17,000 students are surveyed. (See Table 2.)

Research design for the followup surveys after high school

Beginning with the graduating class of 1976, a sample of each class is followed and surveyed by mail after high school graduation. From the approximately 15,000 to 17,000 seniors originally participating in a given class, a representative sample of 2,400 individuals was chosen for followup. In order to ensure sufficient numbers of drug users in the followup surveys, those fitting certain criteria of current drug use (that is, those reporting 20 or more uses of marijuana or use of any of the other illicit drugs in the previous 30 days) were selected with higher probability (by a factor of 3.0) than the remaining seniors. Differential weighting is used in all followup analyses to compensate for the differential sampling probabilities.

The 2,400 selected respondents from each class were randomly assigned to one of two matching groups of 1,200 each; one group was surveyed on even-numbered calendar years, and the other group was surveyed on odd-numbered years. This biennial procedure is intended to reduce respondent burden.

Until 2002, each respondent was followed for up to seven times; at the seventh followup, which would occur either 13 or 14 years after graduation, the respondents had reached the modal ages of 31 or 32. Beginning in 2002, the seventh followup was discontinued, and each respondent was followed for up to six times, corresponding to the modal ages of 29 or 30. Additional followups occur at modal ages 35, 40, and 45.

Followup procedures

Using information provided by respondents at the time of the senior survey (name, address, phone number, and the name and address of someone who would always know how to reach them), students selected for the panels are contacted by mail. Newsletters are sent each year, and name and address corrections are requested. Questionnaires are sent by certified mail in the spring of each year. A check for $5.00 made out to the respondent is attached to the front. Beginning with the class of 1992, the followup checks have been raised to $10.00 to compensate for the effects of inflation over the life of the study. Reminder letters and post cards are sent at fixed intervals thereafter and finally, those not responding receive a prompting phone call from the Survey Research Center's phone interviewing facility in Ann Arbor, MI. If requested, a second copy of the questionnaire is sent.

Panel retention rates

Retention rates in the biennial followups of all panel members ages 19 to 30 (corresponding to the first six followups) decline with the length of the followup interval. For the 5-year period from 1999 to 2003, the response rate in the first followup (corresponding to 1 to 2 years past high school) averaged 60%; for the second through the sixth followups (corresponding to 3 to 12 years past high school) response rates averaged 54%. Among the very long-term respondents--the 35- and 40-year-olds--the retention rates remain good. Among the 35-year-old respondents surveyed from 1999 to 2003 (corresponding to 17 years past high school), the average response rate was 52%. Among the 40-year-old respondents surveyed from 1999 (the first survey of this age group) to 2003, corresponding to a 22-year followup interval, the average retention rate was 59%. Among 45-year-olds surveyed in 2003, the retention rate was 59%.

Since attrition is to a modest degree associated with drug use, corrections to the prevalence estimates are presented for the followup panels. These raise the prevalence estimates from what they would be uncorrected, but only slightly. It is believed that the resulting estimates are the most accurate obtainable, but still low for the age group as a whole due to the omission of dropouts and absentees from the population covered by the original panels.

Validity of self-report data

Survey measures of delinquency and drug use depend upon respondents reporting what are, in many cases, illegal acts. Thus, a critical question is whether such self-reports are likely to be valid. Like most studies dealing with these areas, there is no direct, objective validation of the present measures; however, the considerable amount of inferential evidence that exists strongly suggests that the self-report questions produce largely valid data. A number of factors suggest a reasonable amount of confidence about the validity of the responses to what are presumably among the most sensitive questions in the study: a low nonresponse on the drug questions, a large proportion admitting to some illicit drug use, the consistency of findings across several years of the present study, strong evidence of construct validity (based on relationships observed between variables), a close match between these data and the findings from other studies using other methods, and the findings from several methodological studies that have used objective validation methods.

Accuracy of the sample

A sample survey never can provide the same level of accuracy as would be obtained if the entire target population were to participate in the survey--in the case of the present study, about 2.5 to 3.0 million seniors per year. But perfect accuracy of this sort would be extremely expensive and certainly not worthwhile considering that a high level of accuracy can be obtained by a carefully designed probability sample. The accuracy of the sample in this study is affected both by the size of the student sample and by the number of schools in which they are clustered. Virtually all estimates based on the total sample have confidence intervals of plus or minus 1.5 percentage points or smaller--sometimes considerably smaller.

Interpreting racial differences

Data are given for the two largest racial subgroups in the population--those who identify themselves as white or Caucasian and those who identify themselves as black or African-American. Data are not given for the other ethnic categories (American Indians, Asian Americans, Mexican Americans, Puerto Ricans, or other Latin Americans) since each of these groups comprises a small percentage of the sample in any given year, which means that their small Ns (in combination with their clustered groupings in a limited number of schools) would yield estimates that would be too unreliable. In fact, even black respondents--who constitute approximately 12% of each year's sample--are represented by only 269 to 425 respondents per year on any single questionnaire form. Further, because the sample is a stratified clustered sample, it yields less accuracy than would be yielded by a pure random sample of equal size. Therefore, because of the limited number of cases, the margin of sampling error around any statistic describing black respondents is larger than for most other subgroups described in this survey. There are factors in addition to unreliability, however, that could be misleading in the interpretation of racial differences. Given the importance that has been placed on various racial differences reported in the social science literature, the reader is cautioned to consider the various factors that could account for differences. These factors fall into three categories: differential representation in the sample, differential response tendencies, and the confounding of race with a number of other background and demographic characteristics.

Differential representation--A smaller segment of the black population than of the white population of high school age is represented by the data contained here. Insofar as any characteristic is associated with being a school dropout or absentee, it is likely to be somewhat disproportionately underrepresented among blacks in the sample.

Differential response tendencies--In examining the full range of variables, certain racial differences in response tendencies were noted. First, the tendency to state agreement in response to agree-disagree questions is generally somewhat greater among blacks than among whites.

There also is a somewhat greater than average tendency for black respondents to select extreme answer categories on attitudinal scales. For example, even if the same proportion of blacks as whites felt positively (or negatively) about some subject, fewer whites are likely to say they feel very positively (or very negatively). In the process of interpreting racial differences, the reader should be aware that differences in responses to particular questions may be related to these more general tendencies.

A somewhat separate issue in response tendency is a respondent's willingness to answer particular questions. An exaggerated missing data rate for black males on the set of questions dealing with the respondent's own use of illicit drugs has been observed. Clearly, a respondent's willingness to be candid on such questions depends on his or her trust of the research process and of the researchers themselves. The reader is advised to consult the Source for exceptional levels of missing data when making comparisons on any variable in which candor is likely to be reduced by lower system trust. One bit of additional evidence related to trust in the research process is that higher proportions of blacks than whites indicated that if they had used marijuana or heroin they would not have been willing to report it in the survey.

Covariance with other factors--Some characteristics such as race are highly correlated with other variables--variables that may in fact explain some observed racial differences. Put another way, at the aggregate level one might observe a considerable racial difference on some characteristic, but once one controls for certain background characteristics such as socio-economic level or region of the country--that is, comparing the black respondents with whites who come from similar backgrounds--there may be no racial difference at all.

Definitions of terms

Drug types--Definitions or identifiers used in survey forms include:
Marijuana--pot, grass or hashish;
Other psychedelics--mescaline, peyote, psilocybin, PCP. In 2001, the question text was changed from "other psychedelics" to "other hallucinogens" and "shrooms" was added to the list of examples;
Amphetamines--uppers, pep pills, bennies, speed;
Quaaludes--quads, methaqualone;
Barbiturates--downers, goofballs, reds, yellows;
Heroin--smack, horse;
Other narcotics--methadone, opium, codeine, paregoric. In 2002, the list of examples of narcotics other than heroin was updated by replacing Talwin, laudanum, and paregoric with Vicodin, OxyContin, and Percocet.
Inhalants--glue, aerosols, laughing gas;
Tranquilizers--Librium, Valium, Miltown. In 2001, Miltown was replaced with Xanax.

Beginning with the 1979 survey, amyl and butyl nitrites were considered "other inhalants" for questions on one alternate survey form (N is one-fifth of total sample size in 1979-88 and N is one-sixth of total sample size in 1989-2003). This change was made because not all users of this subclass of inhalants were reporting themselves as inhalant users. Hallucinogen use had been similarly underestimated because some users of the hallucinogenic drug PCP do not report themselves as users of hallucinogens--even though PCP was included as an example of a hallucinogenic drug in earlier surveys and on other questions. The alternate questionnaire form contained a special set of questions about PCP that provided other street names for it (e.g., angel dust). As a result of these definition changes, since 1979 data for drug use in these two drug classes have been adjusted for underreporting. For more information, see the Source.

Four-year college plans--Percentage distributions are given separately for (1) respondents who indicate that they "definitely will" or "probably will" graduate from a 4-year college program and (2) those who say that they "definitely won't" or "probably won't" graduate from a 4-year college program. Respondents not responding are omitted from both columns. A number of those who do not expect to complete a 4-year college program do expect to get some postsecondary education.

Illicit drug use: Lifetime--Percentage distributions are given separately for five mutually exclusive subgroups differentiated by their degree of involvement with illicit drugs. Eligibility for each category is defined below.

None--Includes respondents who indicated that they had not used marijuana at any time and did not report use of any of the following illicit drugs in their lifetime: LSD, other psychedelics, cocaine, amphetamines, tranquilizers, methaqualone, barbiturates, heroin, or other narcotics.

Marijuana only--Includes other respondents who indicated that they had used marijuana (or hashish) but had never used any of the other illicit drugs listed above.

Few pills--Includes respondents who indicated having used one or more of the above listed drugs (other than marijuana) but who had not used any one class of them on three or more occasions and who had not used heroin at all.

More pills--Includes respondents who had used any of the above listed drugs (other than marijuana) on three or more occasions but who had never used heroin.

Any heroin--Includes respondents who indicated having used heroin on one or more occasions in their lifetime.

Race--Percentage distributions are given separately for those describing themselves as "white or Caucasian" and "black or African-American." Comparable data for the other racial or ethnic groups (Mexican Americans, Asian Americans, American Indians, etc.) are not shown because of the low number of cases in each group. For tables in section 3 presenting use of alcohol and illicit drugs, the category Hispanic is added, which includes respondents who in 1975-1990 describe themselves as Mexican American or Chicano, or Puerto Rican or other Latin American. After 1990, this group includes respondents who describe themselves as Mexican American or Chicano, Cuban American, Puerto Rican American, or other Latin American. After 1994, the term Puerto Rican American was shortened to Puerto Rican.

Region--Percentage distributions are given separately for respondents living in each of four mutually exclusive regions of the country. The regional classifications are based on U.S. Census Bureau categories and are defined as follows:

Northeast--Census classifications of New England and Middle Atlantic States; includes Maine, New Hampshire, Vermont, Massachusetts, Rhode Island, Connecticut, New York, New Jersey, and Pennsylvania.

North Central--Census classifications of East North Central and West North Central States; includes Ohio, Indiana, Illinois, Michigan, Wisconsin, Minnesota, Iowa, Missouri, North Dakota, South Dakota, Nebraska, and Kansas.

South--Census classifications of South Atlantic, East South Central, and West South Central States; includes Delaware, Maryland, District of Columbia, Virginia, West Virginia, North Carolina, South Carolina, Georgia, Florida, Kentucky, Tennessee, Alabama, Mississippi, Arkansas, Louisiana, Oklahoma, and Texas.

West--Census classifications of Mountain and Pacific States; includes Montana, Idaho, Wyoming, Colorado, New Mexico, Arizona, Utah, Nevada, Washington, Oregon, and California.

Sex--Percentage distributions are given separately for males and females. Respondents with missing data on the question asking the respondent's sex are omitted from both groupings.

Weighted number of cases (N)--The number of cases is stated in terms of the weighted number of respondents rather than the actual number, since all percentages have been calculated using weighted cases. The actual number of respondents is about 15% higher than the weighted number for data collected in 1975, 1976, and 1977. For data collected in 1978 or later, the actual number of respondents is roughly equal to the weighted number. Weighting is used to improve the accuracy of estimates by correcting for unequal probabilities of selection that arise in the multi-stage sampling procedures. Table 3 presents the number of weighted cases for each subgroup of the high school seniors samples.

Table 1. Sample sizes and student response rates for high school seniors

	1990	1991	1992	1993	1994	1995	1996	1997	1998	1999	2000	2001	2002	2003
Total number of schools	137	136	138	139	139	144	139	146	144	143	134	134	120	122
Public schools	114	117	120	121	119	120	118	125	124	124	116	117	102	103
Private schools	23	19	18	18	20	24	21	21	20	19	18	17	18	19
Total number of participating students[a]	15,676	15,483	16,251	16,763	15,929	15,876	14,824	15,963	15,780	14,056	13,286	13,304	13,544	15,200
Student response rate (percent)[b]	86	83	84	84	84	84	83	83	82	83	83	82	83	83

[a] Sample weights are assigned to each respondent to correct for unequal probabilities of selection that arise in the multi-stage sampling procedure.

[b] The student response rate is derived by dividing the attained sample by the target sample (both based on weighted numbers of cases). The target sample is based on listings provided by schools. Because such listings may fail to take account of recent student attrition, the actual response rate may be slightly underestimated.

Table 2. Sample sizes and student response rates for eighth and tenth grades

	1991	1992	1993	1994	1995	1996	1997	1998	1999	2000	2001	2002	2003
Tenth grade													
Total number of schools	121	125	128	130	139	133	131	129	140	145	137	133	129
Public schools	107	106	111	116	117	113	113	110	117	121	117	113	109
Private schools	14	19	17	14	22	20	18	19	23	24	20	20	20
Total number of participating students[a]	14,996	14,997	15,516	16,080	17,285	15,873	15,778	15,419	13,885	14,576	14,286	14,683	16,244
Student response rate (percent)[b]	87	88	86	88	87	87	86	87	85	86	88	85	88
Eighth grade													
Total number of schools	162	159	156	150	152	152	152	149	150	156	153	141	141
Public schools	131	133	126	116	118	122	125	122	120	125	125	115	117
Private schools	31	26	30	34	34	30	27	27	30	31	28	26	24
Total number of participating students[a]	17,844	19,015	18,820	17,708	17,929	18,368	19,066	18,667	17,287	17,311	16,756	15,489	17,023
Student response rate (percent)[b]	90	90	90	89	89	91	89	88	87	89	90	91	89

[a] Sample weights are assigned to each respondent to correct for unequal probabilities of selection that arise in the multi-stage sampling procedure.

[b] The student response rate is derived by dividing the attained sample by the target sample (both based on weighted numbers of cases). The target sample is based on listings provided by schools. Because such listings may fail to take account of recent student attrition, the actual response rate may be slightly underestimated.

Table 3. Weighted sample sizes in subgroups for high school seniors

	Class of 1990	Class of 1991	Class of 1992	Class of 1993	Class of 1994	Class of 1995	Class of 1996	Class of 1997	Class of 1998	Class of 1999	Class of 2000	Class of 2001	Class of 2002	Class of 2003
Total sample	15,676	15,483	16,251	16,251	15,389	15,876	14,824	15,963	15,780	14,056	13,286	13,304	13,544	15,200
Sex														
Male	7,862	7,617	7,582	7,582	6,918	7,293	6,806	7,269	7,286	6,485	5,991	5,962	5,992	6,736
Female	7,241	7,277	8,053	8,053	7,957	7,891	7,261	7,793	7,618	6,804	6,492	6,543	6,679	7,554
Race														
White	11,410	10,754	11,029	11,029	10,656	11,012	9,890	10,210	10,280	9,499	8,447	8,187	8,396	9,722
Black	1,614	1,757	2,244	2,244	1,671	1,693	1,719	2,001	1,885	1,692	1,707	1,567	1,443	1,739
Region														
Northeast	3,358	2,862	2,887	2,887	2,695	2,881	3,122	3,405	2,952	2,572	2,616	2,591	2,641	3,210
North Central	4,284	4,089	4,529	4,529	4,031	4,380	3,878	4,249	3,948	3,668	3,252	3,753	3,407	3,687
South	5,262	5,330	5,787	5,787	5,636	5,593	5,345	5,469	5,928	5,108	4,687	4,300	4,534	5,212
West	2,773	3,202	3,048	3,048	3,027	3,022	2,479	2,839	2,952	2,708	2,732	2,659	2,961	3,092
College plans														
Complete 4 years	10,245	10,402	11,339	11,339	11,064	11,396	10,954	11,226	11,260	10,344	9,471	9,678	9,908	11,229
None or under 4 years	4,332	4,089	3,813	3,813	3,424	3,351	2,746	3,342	3,157	2,848	2,654	2,563	2,492	2,856

Note: Data for 1990-2003 are based on six questionnaire forms; Ns for one-form questions are approximately one-sixth of the total sample N.

Appendix 7

National Survey on Drug Use and Health
Survey methodology

Note: The following information was excerpted from U.S. Department of Health and Human Services, Substance Abuse and Mental Health Services Administration, *Results from the 2003 National Survey on Drug Use and Health: Main Findings* (Rockville, MD: U.S. Department of Health and Human Services, 2004), pp. 7, 87-95. Non-substantive editorial adaptations have been made.

Survey methodology

The National Survey on Drug Use and Health (NSDUH) is an annual survey of the civilian, noninstitutionalized population of the United States age 12 and older and is sponsored by the U.S. Department of Health and Human Services, Substance Abuse and Mental Health Services Administration. Prior to 2002, the survey was called the National Household Survey on Drug Abuse (NHSDA). Because of improvements to the survey in 2002, the 2002 data constitute a new baseline for tracking trends in substance use and other measures. Therefore, estimates from the 2002 and 2003 NSDUHs should not be compared with estimates from the 2001 and earlier NHSDAs to assess changes in substance use over time.

NSDUH collects information from residents of households, noninstitutional group quarters (e.g., shelters, rooming/boarding houses, college dormitories, migratory worker camps), and civilians living on military bases. Persons excluded from the survey include homeless persons who do not use shelters, military personnel on active duty, and residents of institutional group quarters, such as jails, prisons, hospitals, and nursing homes. Since 1999, the NSDUH interview has been carried out using computer-assisted interviewing (CAI). Most of the questions are administered with audio computer-assisted self-interviewing (ACASI). ACASI is designed to provide the respondent with a highly private and confidential means of responding to questions to increase the level of honest reporting of illicit drug use and other sensitive behaviors. Less sensitive items are administered by interviewers using computer-assisted personal interviewing (CAPI).

Nationally, 130,605 addresses were screened for the 2003 survey, and 67,784 completed interviews were obtained. The survey was conducted from January through December 2003. Weighted response rates for household screening and for interviewing were 90.72% and 77.39%, respectively.

Although the design of the 2002 and 2003 NSDUHs is similar to the design of the 1999 through 2001 surveys, there are methodological differences that affect comparability of 2002 and 2003 estimates with estimates from prior surveys. In addition to the name change, each NSDUH respondent is now given an incentive payment of $30. These changes, implemented as of the 2002 survey, resulted in substantial improvement in survey response rates. The changes also affected respondents' reporting of many critical items that are the basis of prevalence measures reported by the survey each year. Comparability also could be affected by improved data collection quality control procedures that were introduced beginning in 2001, and by incorporating new population data from the 2000 decennial census into NSDUH sample weighting procedures. Analyses of the effects of each of these factors on NSDUH estimates have shown that 2002 and 2003 data should not be compared with earlier NHSDA survey data.

The 2002 and 2003 surveys were part of a coordinated 5-year 50-State sample design with an independent, multistage area probability sample for each of the 50 States and the District of Columbia to facilitate State-level estimation. For the 5-year 50-State design, 8 States were designated as large sample States (California, Florida, Illinois, Michigan, New York, Ohio, Pennsylvania, and Texas) with samples large enough to support direct State estimates. For the 2003 survey, sample sizes in these States ranged from 3,541 to 3,711. For the remaining 42 States and the District of Columbia, smaller, but adequate, samples were selected to support State estimates using small area estimation (SAE) techniques. Sample sizes in these States ranged from 856 to 964 in 2003.

States were first stratified into a total of 900 field interviewer (FI) regions (48 regions in each large sample State and 12 regions in each small sample State). These regions were contiguous geographic areas designed to yield the same number of interviews on average. Within FI regions, adjacent census blocks were combined to form the first-stage sampling units, called area segments. A total of 96 segments per FI region were selected with probability proportional to population size. Eight sample segments per FI region were fielded during the 2003 survey year.

These sampled segments were allocated equally into four separate samples, one for each 3-month period during the year, so that the survey is essentially continuous in the field. In each of these area segments, a listing of all addresses was made, from which a sample of 170,762 addresses was selected. Of the selected addresses, 143,485 were determined to be eligible sample units. In these sample units (which can be either households or units within group quarters), sample persons were randomly selected using an automated screening procedure programmed in a handheld computer carried by the interviewers. The number of sample units completing the screening was 130,605. Youths age 12 to 17 and young adults age 18 to 25 were oversampled at this stage so that each State's sample was approximately equally distributed among three major age groups. Because of the larger sample size, there was no need to oversample racial/ethnic groups, as was done for NHSDAs prior to 1999. A total of 81,631 persons were selected nationwide. The final sample of 67,784 persons was representative of the U.S. general population age 12 and older.

The data collection method involves in-person interviews, incorporating procedures that would be likely to increase respondents' cooperation and willingness to report honestly about their illicit drug use behavior. Confidentiality is stressed in all written and oral communications with potential respondents. Respondents' names are not collected with the data and computer-assisted interviewing (CAI) methods, including audio computer-assisted self-interviewing (ACASI), are used to provide a private and confidential setting to complete the interview.

Introductory letters are sent to sampled addresses, followed by an interviewer visit. A 5-minute screening procedure conducted using a handheld computer involves listing all household members along with their basic demographic data. The computer uses the demographic data in a preprogrammed selection formula to select zero to two sample person(s), depending on the composition of the household. This selection process is designed to provide the necessary sample sizes for the specified population age groupings.

The interviewer requests the selected respondent to identify a private area in the home to conduct the interview away from other household members. The interview averages about 1 hour and includes a combination of CAPI and ACASI. The interview begins in CAPI mode with the FI reading the questions from the computer screen and entering the respondent's replies into the computer. The interview then transitions to the ACASI mode for the sensitive questions. In this mode, the respondent can read the questions silently on the computer screen and/or listen to the questions read through headphones and enter his or her responses directly into the computer. At the conclusion of the ACASI section, the interview returns to the CAPI mode with the interviewer completing the questionnaire. All respondents who complete a full interview are given a $30 cash payment.

Even though editing and consistency checks are done by the CAI program during the interview, additional, more complex, edits and consistency checks also are conducted. Cases are retained only if respondents provided data on lifetime use of cigarettes and at least nine other substances. An important aspect of subsequent editing routines involves assignment of codes when respondents legitimately were skipped out of questions that definitely did not apply to them (e.g., if respondents never used a drug of interest). For key drug use measures, the editing procedures identify inconsistencies between related variables. Inconsistencies in variables pertaining to the most recent period that respondents used a drug are edited by assigning an "indefinite" period of use (e.g., use at some point in the lifetime, which could mean use in the past 30 days or past 12 months). Inconsistencies in other key drug use variables are edited by assigning missing data codes. These inconsistencies then are resolved through statistical imputation procedures discussed below.

For some key variables that still have missing or ambiguous values after editing, statistical imputation is used to replace these values with appropriate response codes. For example, the response is ambiguous if the editing procedures assigned a respondent's most recent use of a drug to "use at some point in the lifetime," with no definite period within the lifetime. In this case, the imputation procedures assign a definite value for when the respondent last used the drug (e.g., in the past 30 days, more than 30 days ago but within the past 12 months, more than 12 months ago). Similarly, if the response is completely missing, the imputation procedures replace missing values with nonmissing ones.

In most cases, missing or ambiguous values are imputed using a methodology called predictive mean neighborhoods (PMN), which was developed specifically for the 1999 survey and used in all subsequent survey years. PMN is a combination of a model-assisted imputation methodology and a random nearest neighbor hot-deck procedure. Whenever feasible, the imputation of variables using PMN is multivariate, in which imputation is accomplished on several response variables at once. In general, hot-deck imputation replaces a missing or ambiguous value taken from a "similar" respondent who has complete data. For random nearest neighbor hot-deck imputation, the missing or ambiguous value is replaced by a responding value from a donor randomly selected from a set of potential donors. Potential donors are those defined to be "close" to the unit with the missing or ambiguous value, according to a predefined function, called a distance metric. In the hot-deck stage of PMN, the set of candidate donors (the "neighborhood") consists of respondents with complete data who have a predicted mean close to that of the item nonrespondent. In particular, the neighborhood consists of either the set of the closest 30 respondents or the set of respondents with a predicted mean (or means) within 5% of the predicted mean(s) of the item nonrespondent, whichever set is smaller. If no respondents are available who have a predicted mean (or means) within 5% of the item nonrespondent, the respondent with the predicted mean(s) closest to that of the item nonrespondent is selected as the donor.

Although statistical imputation could not proceed separately within each State due to insufficient pools of donors, information about each respondent's State of residence was incorporated in the modeling and hot-deck steps. For most drugs, respondents were separated into three "State usage" categories as follows: respondents from States with high usage of a given drug were placed in one category, respondents from States with medium usage into another, and the remainder into a third category. This categorical "State rank" variable was used as one set of covariates in the imputation models. In addition, eligible donors for each item nonrespondent were restricted to be of the same State usage category (i.e., the same "State rank") as the nonrespondent.

The general approach to developing and calibrating analysis weights involved developing design-based weights, as the inverse of the selection probabilities of the households and persons. Adjustment factors, then were applied to the design-based weights to adjust for nonresponse, to poststratify to known population control totals, and to control for extreme weights when necessary. In view of the importance of State-level estimates with the 50-State design, it was necessary to control for a much larger number of known population totals. Several other modifications to the general weight adjustment strategy that had been used in past surveys also were implemented for the first time beginning with the 1999 CAI sample.

This general approach was used at several stages of the weight adjustment process, including (1) adjustment of household weights for nonresponse at the screener level, (2) poststratification of household weights to meet population controls for various demographic groups by State, (3) adjustment of household weights for extremes, (4) poststratification of selected person weights, (5) adjustment of personweights for nonresponse at the questionnaire level, (6) poststratification of person weights, and (7) adjustment of person weights for extremes.

An important limitation of the NSDUH estimates of drug use prevalence is that they are designed to describe only the target population of the survey, i.e., the civilian noninstitutionalized population age 12 and older. Although this population includes almost 98% of the total U.S. population age 12 and older, it does exclude some important and unique subpopulations who may have very different drug-using patterns. The survey excludes active military personnel, who have been shown to have significantly lower rates of illicit drug use. Persons living in institutional group quarters, such as prisons and residential drug treatment centers, are not included in the NSDUH and have been shown in other surveys to have higher rates of illicit drug use. Also excluded are homeless persons not living in a shelter on the survey date, another population shown to have higher than average rates of illicit drug use.

Table 1. NSDUH sample sizes by demographic characteristics

	2002	2003
Total	68,126	67,784
Sex		
Male	32,767	32,611
Female	35,359	35,173
Age group		
12 to 17 years	23,645	22,665
18 to 25 years	23,066	22,738
26 years and older	21,415	22,381
Race, ethnicity		
White, non-Hispanic	46,548	45,870
Black, non-Hispanic	8,278	8,153
American Indian or Alaska Native	921	845
Native Hawaiian or other Pacific Islander	273	252
Asian	1,890	2,048
More than one race	1,405	1,543
Hispanic	8,811	9,073

Note: These sample size figures are the unweighted number of completed interviews in the 2002 and 2003 National Surveys on Drug Use and Health.

Appendix 8

National Crime Victimization Survey
Survey methodology and definitions of terms

Note: This information was excerpted from U.S. Department of Justice, Bureau of Justice Statistics, *Criminal Victimization in the United States, 2002 Statistical Tables*, NCJ 200561 [Online]. Available: http://www.ojp.usdoj.gov/bjs/pub/pdf/cvus02.pdf [Mar. 3, 2004]; *Criminal Victimization, 2003*, NCJ 205455 (Washington, DC: U.S. Department of Justice, September 2004), pp. 11, 12; and information provided by the U.S. Department of Justice, Bureau of Justice Statistics. Non-substantive editorial adaptations have been made.

Survey methodology

The National Crime Victimization Survey (NCVS) collects data from residents living throughout the United States, including persons living in group quarters, such as dormitories, rooming houses, and religious group dwellings. Crew members of merchant vessels, Armed Forces personnel living in military barracks, and institutionalized persons, such as correctional facility inmates, were not included in the survey. Similarly, U.S. citizens residing abroad and foreign visitors to this country were excluded. With these exceptions, individuals age 12 and older living in units selected for the sample were eligible to be interviewed.

Data collection

Each housing unit selected for the NCVS remains in the sample for 3 years, with each of seven interviews taking place at 6-month intervals. An NCVS interviewer's first contact with a housing unit selected for the survey is in person. The interviewer may then conduct subsequent interviews by telephone.

To elicit more accurate reporting of incidents, the NCVS uses the self-respondent method, which calls for the direct interviewing of each person 12 years and older in the household. An exception is made to use proxy interviewing instead of direct interviewing for the following three cases: 12- and 13-year-old persons when a knowledgeable household member insists they not be interviewed directly, incapacitated persons, and individuals absent from the household during the entire field-interviewing period. In the case of temporarily absent household members and persons who are physically or mentally incapable of granting interviews, interviewers may accept other household members as proxy respondents, and in certain situations non-household members may provide information for incapacitated persons.

Some interviews were assigned to Computer-Assisted Telephone Interviewing (CATI), a data collection method that involves interviewing from centralized facilities and using a computerized instrument. In the CATI-eligible part of the sample, all interviews are done by telephone whenever possible, except for the first interview, which is primarily conducted in person. The telephone interviews are conducted by CATI facilities in Hagerstown, MD and Tucson, AZ.

Sample design and size

Survey estimates are derived from a stratified, multi-stage cluster sample. The primary sampling units (PSUs) comprising the first stage of the sample were counties, groups of counties, or large metropolitan areas. Large PSUs were included in the sample automatically and are considered to be self-representing (SR) since all of them were selected. The remaining PSUs, called non-self-representing (NSR) because only a subset of them was selected, were combined into strata by grouping PSUs with similar geographic and demographic characteristics, as determined by the 1990 census.

The initial 1990 design consisted of 93 SR PSUs and 152 NSR strata, with one PSU per stratum selected with probability proportionate to population size. A sample reduction was done in October 1996, reducing the number of NSR PSUs by 42 to 110. Therefore, the current NCVS sample consists of 93 SR and 110 NSR PSUs. The NCVS sample design continued use of both 1980- and 1990-based samples through 1997. Beginning in 1998 only the 1990-based sample remains.

In the second stage of sampling, each selected stratification PSU is divided into four nonoverlapping frames (unit, area, permit, and group quarters) from which the NCVS independently selects its sample. From each selected stratification PSU, clusters of approximately four housing units or housing unit equivalents are selected from each frame. For the unit and group quarter frames, addresses come from the 1990 census files. For the permit frame, addresses come from building permit data obtained from building permit offices. This ensures that units built after the 1990 census are included in the sample. For the area frame, sample blocks come from the 1990 census files. Then, addresses are listed and sampled in the field. A new sample, based on addresses drawn from the 2000 census, will be phased in beginning in 2005.

In order to conduct field interviews, the sample is divided into six groups, or rotations, and each group of households is interviewed once every 6 months over a period of 3 years. The initial interview is used to bound the interviews (bounding establishes a timeframe to avoid duplication of crimes on subsequent interviews), but is not used to compute the annual estimates. Each rotation group is further divided into six panels. A different panel of households, corresponding to one-sixth of each rotation group, is interviewed each month during the 6-month period. Because the survey is continuous, newly constructed housing units are selected as described, and assigned to rotation groups and panels for subsequent incorporation into the sample. A new rotation group enters the sample every 6 months, replacing a group phased out after being in the sample for 3 years.

For the 2002 survey, approximately 42,000 households and 76,050 persons age 12 and older were interviewed. The response rates were 92% of eligible households and 87% of eligible individuals. For the 2003 survey, approximately 83,660 households and 149,040 persons age 12 and older were interviewed. The response rates were 92% of eligible households and 86% of eligible individuals.

Race and ethnicity categories

In 1997 the Office of Management and Budget introduced new guidelines for the collection and reporting of race and ethnicity data in government surveys. These methodological changes were implemented for all demographic surveys as of Jan. 1, 2003. Individuals are now allowed to choose more than one racial category. In prior years they were asked to select a single primary race.

Beginning with the 2003 NCVS data, racial categories consist of the following: white only, black only, other race only (American Indian, Alaska Native, Asian, Pacific Islander if only one of these races is given), and two or more races (all persons of any race indicating two or more races). About 0.9% of persons in the NCVS sample and about 2.6% of victims of crimes of violence identified two or more races. Also, individuals are now asked whether they are of Hispanic ethnicity before being asked about their race, and are now asked directly if they are Spanish, Hispanic, or Latino.

Collection year estimates

Beginning with data for 1996 (and 1995 data printed in selected reports), all NCVS estimates are now based on interviews conducted during the calendar year being estimated. This procedure is referred to as "collection year" reporting. Previously, estimates were based on victimizations occurring during a given calendar year. This procedure is referred to as "data year" reporting. This change in the reporting procedure was undertaken in an effort to expedite publication of NCVS data. NCVS respondents are interviewed every 6 months and asked to recall any crime incidents that have occurred in the 6 months since the previous interview. For this reason, 6 months of data collection beyond the end of the calendar year were needed to gather information on all incidents occurring during a calendar year. Under the collection year procedure estimates for any given year will include some incidents that actually took place during the previous calendar year, and will exclude some incidents that would have been reported in interviews conducted in the following calendar year.

Data year estimates differ slightly from calendar year estimates. The differences will be greater during periods of changing crime rates and less during periods of stable rates.

Series victimizations

A series victimization is defined as six or more similar but separate crimes that the victim is unable to recall individually or describe in detail to an interviewer. These series crimes have been excluded from the tables because victims were unable to provide details for each separate event.

Estimation procedure

Annual collection year estimates of the levels and rates of victimization are derived by accumulating four quarterly estimates. The estimation procedure involves the application of a base weight to the data for each individual interviewed. Readers interested in detailed information on the estimation procedure should consult the original source.

Accuracy of estimates

The accuracy of an estimate is a measure of its total error, that is, the sum of all the errors affecting the estimate: sampling error as well as nonsampling error.

The sample used for the NCVS is one of a large number of possible samples of equal size that could have been obtained by using the same sample design and selection procedures. Estimates derived from different samples would differ from one another due to sampling variability, or sampling error.

The standard error of a survey estimate is a measure of the variation among the estimates from all possible samples. Therefore, it is a measure of the precision (reliability) with which a particular estimate approximates the average result of all possible samples. The estimate and its associated standard error may be used to construct a confidence interval. A confidence interval is a range of numbers that has a specified probability that the average of all possible samples, which is the true unknown value of interest in an unbiased design, is contained within the interval. About 68% of the time, the survey estimate will differ from the true average by less than one standard error. Only 10% of the time will the difference be more than 1.6 standard errors, and just 1 time in 100 will it be greater than 2.5 standard errors. A 95% confidence interval is the survey estimate plus or minus twice the standard error. Thus there is a 95% chance that a result based on a complete census would fall within the confidence interval.

In addition to sampling error, the estimates are subject to nonsampling error. While substantial care is taken in the NCVS to reduce the sources of nonsampling error throughout all the survey operations, by means of a quality assurance program, quality controls, operational controls, and error-correcting procedures, an unquantified amount of nonsampling error remains.

A major source of nonsampling error is related to the inability of respondents to recall in detail the crimes that occurred during the 6 months prior to the interview. Research based on interviews of victims obtained from police files indicates that assault is recalled with the least accuracy of any crime measured by the NCVS. This may be related to the tendency of victims to avoid reporting crimes committed by offenders who are not strangers, especially if they are relatives. In addition, among certain groups, crimes that contain elements of assault could be a part of everyday life, and are therefore forgotten or not considered important enough to mention to a survey interviewer. These recall problems may result in an understatement of the actual rate of assault.

Another source of nonsampling error is the inability of some respondents to recall the exact month a crime occurred, even though it was placed in the correct reference period. This error source is partially offset by interviewing monthly and using the estimation procedure mentioned earlier. Telescoping is another problem in which incidents that occurred before the reference period are placed within the period. The effect of telescoping is minimized by using the bounding procedure previously described. The interviewer is provided with a summary of the incidents reported in the preceding interview and, if a similar incident is reported, it can be determined whether or not it is a new one by discussing it with the victim. Events that occurred after the reference period are set aside for inclusion with the data from the following interview.

Other sources of nonsampling error can result from other types of response mistakes, including errors in reporting incidents as crimes, misclassification of crimes, systematic data errors introduced by the interviewer, and errors made in coding and processing the data. Quality control and editing procedures were used to minimize the number of errors made by the respondents and the interviewers.

Since field representatives conducting the interviews usually reside in the area in which they interview, the race and ethnicity of the field representatives generally match that of the local population. Special efforts are made to further match field representatives and the people they interview in areas where English is not commonly spoken. About 90% of all NCVS field representatives are female.

Standard errors measure only those nonsampling errors arising from transient factors affecting individual responses completely at random (simple response variance); they do not reveal any systematic biases in the data. As calculated in the NCVS, the standard errors would partially measure nonsampling error arising from some of the above sources, such as transient memory errors, or accidental errors in recording or coding answers, for example.

Definitions of terms

Age--The appropriate age category is determined by the respondent's age on the last day of the month before the interview.

Aggravated assault--Attack or attempted attack with a weapon, regardless of whether an injury occurred, and attack without a weapon when serious injury results.

With injury--An attack without a weapon when serious injury results, or an attack with a weapon involving any injury. Serious injury includes broken bones, lost teeth, internal injuries, loss of consciousness, and any unspecified injury requiring 2 or more days of hospitalization.

Threatened with a weapon--Threat or attempted attack by an offender armed with a gun, knife, or other object used as a weapon, not resulting in victim injury.

Annual household income--The total income of the household head and all members of the household for the 12 months preceding the interview. Includes wages, salaries, net income from businesses or farms, pensions, interest, dividends, rent, and any other form of monetary income.

Assault--An unlawful physical attack or threat of attack. Assaults may be classified as aggravated or simple. Rape, attempted rape, and sexual assaults are excluded from this category, as well as robbery and attempted robbery. The severity of assaults ranges from minor threats to incidents that are nearly fatal.

Ethnicity--A classification based on Hispanic culture and origin, regardless of race.

Head of household--A classification that defines one and only one person in each housing unit as the head. Head of household implies that the person rents or owns (or is in the process of buying) the household unit. The head of household must be at least 18, unless all members of the household are under 18, or the head is married to someone 18 or older.

Hispanic--Persons who describe themselves as Mexican-American, Chicano, Mexican, Mexicano, Puerto Rican, Cuban, Central American, South American, or from some other Spanish culture or origin, regardless of race.

Household--A person or group of people meeting either of the following criteria: (1) people whose usual place of residence is the same housing unit, even if they are temporarily absent; (2) people staying in a housing unit who have no usual place of residence elsewhere.

Household burglary--Unlawful or forcible entry or attempted entry of a residence. This crime usually, but not always, involves theft. The illegal entry may be by force, such as breaking a window or slashing a screen, or may be without force by entering through an unlocked door or an open window. If the person entering has no legal right to be present in the structure a burglary has occurred. The structure need not be the house itself for a burglary to take place; illegal entry of a garage, shed, or any other structure on the premises also constitutes household burglary. If breaking and entering occurs in a hotel or vacation residence, it is still classified as a burglary for the household whose member or members were staying there at the time the entry occurred.

Completed burglary--To successfully gain entry to a residence by a person who has no legal right to be present in the structure, by use of force, or without force.

Forcible entry--A form of completed burglary in which force is used to gain entry to a residence. Examples include breaking a window or slashing a screen.

Unlawful entry without force--A form of completed burglary committed by someone having no legal right to be on the premises, even though no force is used.

Attempted forcible entry--A form of burglary in which force is used in an attempt to gain entry.

Incident--A specific criminal act involving one or more victims and offenders. For example, if two people are robbed at the same time and place, this is classified as two robbery victimizations but only one robbery incident.

Marital status--Every person is assigned to one of the following classifications: (1) married, which includes persons in common-law unions and those who are currently living apart for reasons other than marital discord (employment, military service, etc.); (2) separated or divorced, which includes married persons who are legally separated and those who are not living together because of marital discord; (3) widowed; and (4) never married, which includes persons whose marriages have been annulled and those who are living together and not in a common-law union.

Metropolitan Statistical Area (MSA)--Office of Management and Budget defines this as a population nucleus of 50,000 or more, generally consisting of a city and its immediate suburbs, along with adjacent communities having a high degree of economic and social integration with the nucleus. MSAs are designated by counties, the smallest geographic units for which a wide range of statistical data can be obtained. However, in New England, MSAs are designated by cities and towns since these subcounty units are of great local significance and considerable data are available for them. Currently, an area is defined as an MSA if it meets one of two standards: (1) a city has a population of at least 50,000; (2) the Census Bureau defines an urbanized area of at least 50,000 people with a total metropolitan population of at least 100,000 (or 75,000 in New England). The Census Bureau's definition of urbanized areas, data on commuting to work, and the strength of the economic and social ties between the surrounding counties and the central city determine which counties not containing a main city are included in an MSA. For New England, MSAs are determined by a core area and related cities and towns, not counties. A metropolitan statistical area may contain more than one city of 50,000 and may cross State lines. Within this general classification unit, there are three subclassifications: urban, suburban, and rural. They are defined as follows:

Urban areas--The largest city or grouping of cities in a metropolitan statistical area.

Suburban areas--A county or group of counties containing a central city, plus any contiguous counties that are linked socially and economically to the central city. Suburban areas are categorized as those portions of metropolitan areas situated "outside central cities."

Rural areas--A place not located inside a metropolitan statistical area. This category includes a variety of localities ranging from sparsely populated rural areas to cities with populations less than 50,000.

Motor vehicle--An automobile, truck, motorcycle, or any other motorized vehicle legally allowed on public roads and highways.

Motor vehicle theft--Stealing or unauthorized taking of a motor vehicle, including attempted thefts.

Completed motor vehicle theft--The successful taking of a vehicle by an unauthorized person.

Attempted motor vehicle theft--The unsuccessful attempt by an unauthorized person to take a vehicle.

Non-Hispanic--Persons who report their culture or origin as something other than "Hispanic" as defined above. This distinction is made regardless of race.

Nonstranger--A classification of a crime victim's relationship to the offender. An offender who is either related to, well known to, or casually acquainted with the victim is a nonstranger. For crimes with more than one offender, if any of the offenders are non-strangers, then the group of offenders as a whole is classified as nonstranger. This category only applies to crimes that involve contact between the victim and the offender; the distinction is not made for crimes of theft since victims of this offense rarely see the offenders.

Offender--The perpetrator of a crime; this term usually applies to crimes involving contact between the victim and the offender.

Offense--A crime. When referring to personal crimes, the term can be used to refer to both victimizations and incidents.

Personal crimes--Rape, sexual assault, personal robbery, assault, purse snatching and pocket picking. Includes both attempted and completed crimes.

Personal crimes of violence--Rape, sexual assault, robbery, or assault. Includes both attempted and completed crimes; does not include purse snatching and pocket picking. Murder is not measured by the NCVS because of the inability to question the victim.

Completed violence--The sum of all completed rapes, sexual assaults, robberies, and assaults.

Attempted/threatened violence--The unsuccessful attempt of rape, sexual assault, robbery, or assault. Includes attempted attacks or sexual assaults by means of verbal threats.

Property crimes--Burglary, motor vehicle theft, or theft. Includes both attempted and completed crimes.

Purse snatching/pocket picking--Theft or attempted theft of property or cash directly from the victim by stealth, without force or threat of force.

Race--Racial categories for the 2002 survey (and earlier years) are white, black, and other. The category "other" is composed mainly of Asians, Pacific Islanders, American Indians, Aleuts, and Eskimos. The race of the head of household is used in determining the race of the household for computing household crime demographics. See discussion above for changes to the racial categories beginning in 2003.

Rape--Forced sexual intercourse including both psychological coercion as well as physical force. Forced sexual intercourse means vaginal, anal, or oral penetration by the offender(s). This category also includes incidents involving penetration using a foreign object such as a bottle. Includes attempted rapes, male as well as female victims, and both heterosexual and homosexual rape. Attempted rape includes verbal threats of rape.

Rate of victimization--See "Victimization rate."

Robbery--Completed or attempted theft, directly from a person, of property or cash by force or threat of force, with or without a weapon, and with or without injury.

Completed/property taken--The successful taking of property from a person by force or threat of force, with or without a weapon, and with or without injury.

Completed with injury--The successful taking of property from a person, accompanied by an attack, either with or without a weapon, resulting in injury.

Completed without injury--The successful taking of property from a person by force or the threat of force, either with or without a weapon, but not resulting in injury.

Attempted to take property--The attempt to take property from a person by force or threat of force without success, with or without a weapon, and with or without injury.

Attempted without injury--The attempt to take property from a person by force or threat of force without success, with or without a weapon, but not resulting in injury.

Attempted with injury--The attempt to take property from a person without success, accompanied by an attack, either with or without a weapon, resulting in injury.

Sexual assault--A wide range of victimizations, separate from rape or attempted rape. Includes attacks or attempted attacks generally involving unwanted sexual contact between victim and offender. Sexual assaults may or may not involve force and include such things as grabbing or fondling. Sexual assault also includes verbal threats.

Simple assault--Attack without a weapon resulting either in no injury, minor injury (for example, bruises, black eyes, cuts, scratches, or swelling), or in undetermined injury requiring less than 2 days of hospitalization. Also includes attempted assault without a weapon.

With minor injury--An attack without a weapon resulting in such injuries as bruises, black eyes, cuts, or in undetermined injury requiring less than 2 days of hospitalization.

Without injury--An attempted assault without a weapon not resulting in injury.

Stranger--A classification of the victim's relationship to the offender for crimes involving direct contact between the two. Incidents are classified as involving strangers if the victim identifies the offender as a stranger, did not see or recognize the offender, or knew the offender only by sight. Crimes involving multiple offenders are classified as involving nonstrangers if any of the offenders was a nonstranger. Since victims of theft without contact rarely see the offender, no distinction is made between strangers and nonstrangers for this crime.

Tenure--The NCVS recognizes two forms of household tenancy: (1) owned, which includes dwellings that are mortgaged, and (2) rented, which includes rent-free quarters belonging to a party other than the occupants and situations where rental payments are in kind or in services.

Theft--Completed or attempted theft of property or cash without personal contact. Incidents involving theft of property from within the sample household would classify as theft if the offender has a legal right to be in the house (such as a maid, delivery person, or guest). If the offender has no legal right to be in the house, the incident would classify as a burglary.

Completed--To successfully take without permission property or cash without personal contact between the victim and offender.

Attempted--To unsuccessfully attempt to take property or cash without personal contact.

Victim--The recipient of a criminal act, usually used in relation to personal crimes, but also applicable to households.

Victimization--A crime as it affects one individual person or household. For personal crimes, the number of victimizations is equal to the number of victims involved. The number of victimizations may be greater than the number of incidents because more than one person may be victimized during an incident. Each crime against a household is assumed to involve a single victim, the affected household.

Victimization rate--A measure of the occurrence of victimizations among a specified population group. For personal crimes, this is based on the number of victimizations per 1,000 residents age 12 and older. For household crimes, the victimization rates are calculated using the number of incidents per 1,000 households.

Victimize--To commit a crime against a person or household.

Appendix 9

Drug Abuse Warning Network
Methodology, estimation procedures, and data limitations

This information was excerpted from U.S. Department of Health and Human Services, Substance Abuse and Mental Health Services Administration, *Emergency Department Trends from the Drug Abuse Warning Network, Final Estimates 1995-2002*, Drug Abuse Warning Network Series: D-24 (Rockville, MD: U.S. Department of Health and Human Services, 2003), pp. 34, 35, 117-125, 129-134, T-3, T-5; and information provided by the U.S. Department of Health and Human Services, Substance Abuse and Mental Health Services Administration. Nonsubstantive editorial adaptations have been made.

Methodology

These data were collected by the Substance Abuse and Mental Health Services Administration through the Drug Abuse Warning Network (DAWN). The data are weighted estimates representing all drug abuse-related emergency department episodes in the 48 contiguous States, the District of Columbia, and 21 metropolitan areas. For 2002, the sample consisted of 549 eligible hospitals; 437 sample hospitals provided data to DAWN. The table below details hospital participation in DAWN and the estimates of total drug-related episodes and drug mentions for 1994-2002.

	Hospitals Number providing data	Response rate	Drug-related episodes	Drug mentions
1994	488	76%	518,880	899,600
1995	489	77	513,429	899,977
1996	452	74	513,841	906,078
1997	465	77	526,671	941,627
1998	471	79	542,250	981,286
1999	488	82	554,570	1,013,688
2000	466	81	601,392	1,098,915
2001	458	81	638,345	1,165,148
2002	437	80	670,307	1,209,938

Hospitals eligible for DAWN are non-Federal, short-stay general surgical and medical hospitals in the coterminous United States that have a 24-hour emergency department. The American Hospital Association's (AHA) 1984 and 1985 Annual Surveys of Hospitals were used to obtain a sampling frame. Hospitals in the sampling frame were stratified according to several characteristics.

First, the sampling frame was divided into the 21 DAWN metropolitan areas and the remainder of the country (called the National Panel). Hospitals having 80,000 or more annual emergency department visits were assigned to a single stratum for selection with certainty. Then, the remaining hospitals in the 21 metropolitan areas were classified by location--inside or outside the central city, and by whether the hospital had an organized outpatient department and/or a chemical/alcohol inpatient unit--whether they had zero, one, or both types of units. Similarly, hospitals in the National Panel were classified by the presence/absence of such units. Total eligible hospitals in the original sample numbered 685.

The number of eligible sample facilities has not remained at the original 685 because some hospitals have closed or become ineligible since the sample was selected. To preserve the integrity of the sample, a sample maintenance procedure is employed to randomly select "newly eligible" hospitals from the AHA survey each year using the same selection probabilities. This procedure allows the sample to be kept up-to-date and representative of DAWN-eligible hospitals in the coterminous United States.

The national response rate was 80% in 2002; this rate is based on the number of eligible hospitals in the sample and the number actually responding. Data from the 21 oversampled metropolitan areas were pooled with data from the National Panel to produce the national estimates.

For the purpose of reporting to the DAWN system, drug abuse is defined as the nonmedical use of a substance for psychic effect, dependence, or suicide attempt/gesture. Nonmedical use includes: the use of prescription drugs in a manner inconsistent with accepted medical practice; the use of over-the-counter drugs contrary to approved labeling; or the use of any other substance (heroin, cocaine, marijuana/hashish, glue, aerosols, etc.) for psychic effect, dependence, or suicide.

Within each facility participating in the DAWN system, a designated DAWN reporter, usually a member of the emergency department or medical records staff, is responsible for reviewing medical charts to identify drug abuse episodes, and recording and submitting data on each case. An episode report is submitted for each drug abuse patient who visits a DAWN emergency department and meets the following criteria: (1) the patient was treated in the hospital's emergency department; (2) the patient's presenting problem(s) was induced by or related to drug use, regardless of when the drug use occurred; (3) the case involved the use of an illegal drug or the use of a legal drug or other chemical substance for nonmedical purposes; and (4) the patient's reason for using the substance(s) included one of the following: dependence, suicide attempt or gesture, or psychic effects. Each report of a drug abuse episode includes demographic information about the patient and information about the circumstances of the episode. In addition to drug overdoses, reportable emergency department episodes may result from the chronic effects of habitual drug use or from unexpected reactions. Unexpected reactions include cases where the drug's effect was different than anticipated (e.g., caused hallucinations). DAWN cases do not include accidental ingestion or inhalation of a substance with no intent of abuse, or adverse reactions to prescription or over-the-counter medications taken as prescribed. Up to four different substances, in addition to alcohol-in-combination, can be specified for each episode. It should be noted that alcohol is reported to DAWN only when used in combination with a reportable substance. It also should be noted that episodes involving children under 6 years of age are not reported to DAWN.

A drug episode is defined as an emergency department visit that was induced by or related to the use of an illegal drug, or the nonmedical use of a legal drug or substance for persons age 6 and older. The number of emergency department episodes reported in DAWN is not equivalent to the number of individuals involved. One person may make repeated visits to an emergency department or to several emergency departments, thus producing a number of episodes. No patient identifiers are collected, therefore it is impossible to determine the number of individuals involved in the reported episodes.

A drug mention refers to a substance that was mentioned (recorded) during a drug-related emergency department episode. In addition to alcohol-in-combination, up to four substances may be reported for each drug-related episode; thus, the total number of mentions exceeds the total number of episodes. It should be noted that a particular drug mentioned may or may not be the sole or confirmed "cause" of the episode. Even when only one substance is reported for an episode, allowance still should be made for reportable drugs not mentioned or for other contributory factors.

Estimation procedures

The national estimates of total emergency department drug episodes and drug mentions are obtained by adding the estimates from the 21 metropolitan areas and the estimate from the National Panel for each estimation category. The weights are calculated each quarter for each hospital in the sample and are the product of a three-component model that considers (1) the base sampling weight calculated as the reciprocal of the sampling probability; (2) an adjustment for nonresponse, based either on complete nonparticipation or failure to provide data for all the reporting days in a given time period; and (3) a correction factor, applied within metropolitan areas, that adjusts the total number of emergency department visits among participating sample hospitals to the total for the population of hospitals as determined from the sampling frame.

Revised estimates

DAWN estimates for 1994-2000 have been revised as a result of improvements in the coding and classification of drugs mentioned in emergency department visits. Revisions to estimates published previously are the result of a major change in the underlying method by which drugs are coded and classified in DAWN. DAWN relies on a detailed "drug vocabulary" to categorize the thousands of substances that are reported each year. The drug vocabulary is the language--the codes and terminology--that DAWN uses to record and classify drugs and other substances collected from emergency departments. It was necessary to implement substantial changes to the existing vocabulary to ensure that reported substances are accurately and consistently classified.

In 1999, an internal DAWN workgroup composed of DAWN staff and representatives from two DAWN contractors convened to evaluate the old DAWN drug vocabulary. The workgroup concluded that an externally maintained code set--one designed and maintained by subject matter experts apart from DAWN--would serve DAWN's needs better than a system developed and maintained in-house.

The drug terminology produced by Multum Information Services Inc., a private sector firm, provided a framework into which components that are unique to substance abuse and DAWN could be added. These include street names for illicit substances, metabolites commonly reported in DAWN mortality data, household products and other non-medicinal substances, and substances classified based on their route of administration as "inhalants."

In 2000, DAWN adopted the Multum Lexicon, a drug vocabulary and classification tool developed and maintained by Multum Information Services, Inc. Multum distributes the Lexicon (a complete database in Microsoft Access format) and regular updates through its website. DAWN uses only a fraction of the Multum Lexicon because DAWN case reports typically lack the most precise drug product information. For example, DAWN case reports supply drug names, but not strength or dosage, so it is not feasible to code drugs at the level of detail supported by the Multum Lexicon. On the other hand, the specificity of drug information reported to DAWN varies depending on the detail available in the source documents, that is, emergency department medical records or death investigation files. The Multum Leixcon not only accommodates such variability but it provides a consistent method for aggregating very detailed information (such as brands) into consistent generic drug categories.

To accommodate DAWN data on substances that are not part of the Multum Leixcon, DAWN staff adopted the Multum Lexicon structure and designed a drug database that incorporates Multum Lexicon content for generic names, brand or trade names, and 3-level nested categories, and adds other DAWN reportable substances in a compatible structure.

The result of this combination of the Multum Lexicon and DAWN-specific substances is referred to as the DAWN Drug Reference Vocabulary. All drug entries in DAWN were translated into the new vocabulary. When possible, automated procedures were used to make this translation. When necessary, drug entries were assigned manually. All assignments were subjected to multiple, iterative layers of quality control. New DAWN data files, beginning with the 1994 data, were developed and revised estimates were produced. The revised estimates for total emergency department episodes deviate only slightly (no more than 0.08% in any year) from previously published estimates.

Preliminary versus final estimates

Final estimates are produced once a year when all hospitals participating in DAWN have submitted their data for that year and when additional ancillary data used in estimation become available. The differences between preliminary and final estimates are due to several factors:

(1) Final estimates include data from a small number of late-reporting hospitals. Data from some late-reporting facilities are received for each time period. Therefore, later files will usually include more complete data (i.e., have a higher response rate).

(2) Additional hospitals are added to the sample and incorporated into the final estimates for a given year (not the preliminary estimates for that same year). Most of these hospitals are "newly eligible" because they became DAWN eligible sometime after the original sample was selected. The final DAWN estimates are produced after the most current AHA's Annual Survey of Hospitals file is received. This file was used initially to establish a sampling frame for DAWN. Subsequently, the most current AHA file is used once a year to maintain the representativeness of the sample. Between the releases of the preliminary and final estimates, the use of the newer AHA survey can result in hospitals being added to the sample and incorporated into the final estimates.

(3) Data from the most current AHA file are used to produce the final weights.

Data limitations

When producing estimates from any sample survey, two types of errors are possible--sampling and nonsampling errors. The sampling error of an estimate is the error caused by the selection of a sample instead of utilizing a census of hospitals. Sampling error is reduced by selecting a large sample or by using efficient sample design and estimation strategies such as stratification, optimal allocation, and ratio estimation. Nonsampling errors occur from nonresponse, difficulties in the interpretation of the collection form, coding errors, computer-processing errors, errors in the sampling frame, and reporting errors. Many procedures are in place to minimize nonsampling errors such as data auditing and periodic retraining of data collectors. Further, nonrespondent hospitals are identified for additional recruitment. Late reporters are assigned for priority data collection and respondents with changes in reporting are designated for followup.

It also is important to recognize that DAWN does not provide a complete picture of medical problems associated with drug use, but rather focuses on the impact that these problems have on hospital emergency departments in the United States. If a person is admitted to another part of the hospital for treatment, treated in a physician's office, or treated at a drug treatment center, the episode is not included in DAWN.

Appendix 10

Arrestee Drug Abuse Monitoring
Methodology and survey sampling information

Note: The following information was excerpted from U.S. Department of Justice, National Institute of Justice, *2000 Arrestee Drug Abuse Monitoring: Annual Report*, NCJ 193013, pp. 3, 4, 9-15; *Preliminary Data on Drug Use and Related Matters Among Adult Arrestees and Juvenile Detainees, 2002*, p. 1 and Table 1; *Drug and Alcohol Use and Related Matters Among Arrestees 2003*, p. 3 and Table 1 (Washington, DC: U.S. Department of Justice); and information provided by the U.S. Department of Justice, National Institute of Justice. Non-substantive editorial adaptations have been made.

Methodology

The Arrestee Drug Abuse Monitoring (ADAM) program measures the extent of drug and alcohol use and drug involvement among persons arrested and booked as adults in selected city and county detention facilities operated by local police and sheriffs' departments. The data are collected in booking facilities in participating city/county areas. The participating counties, i.e., ADAM sites, are selected according to a standard protocol involving numerous site requirements. For example, each ADAM site must provide access to all booking facilities in the jurisdiction so that every booked arrestee has some probability of being included in the sample. In addition, the site must provide case flow information for each booking facility so that a sampling plan can be established. Sites also must provide access to interview rooms that ensure confidentiality.

Data collection occurs at each ADAM site by trained civilian interview teams who are not law enforcement officials or booking facility staff. Arrestees are approached usually on the same day but always within 48 hours of their arrest and asked to participate in the study. The interviewers conduct personal interviews that are approximately 30 minutes in length. After the interview, each arrestee is asked to provide a urine sample, which is analyzed to detect drug use. The interviews and the urine specimens are kept anonymous and confidential, and all participation is voluntary. At most sites, more than 80% of the individuals approached agree to participate and, of those, more than 80% agree to provide urine specimens.

Data collection takes place four times a year at each site, once each calendar quarter. Data collection periods are generally two consecutive weeks each quarter. Data are collected from adult male and adult female arrestees. In the context of the ADAM study, "adult" refers to the facilities where the data are collected, not necessarily the age of the arrestee. Some arrestees who are less than 18 years of age are booked as adults because of the type of offense involved. Male and female arrestees may be booked in the same or in separate facilities, depending on the local jurisdiction. The adult male arrestees were selected through probability-based sampling and the data are weighted according to methods discussed below. However, female arrestees were selected through purposive sampling and the data are self-weighted. As a result, adult male and female data are not fully comparable within sites. Also, because the number of females arrested is much lower than the number of males, some ADAM sites do not interview female arrestees. Therefore, data for female arrestees are not shown in SOURCEBOOK.

Beginning with the 2000 data collection, a redesign of the ADAM program was fully implemented. A probability-based study design was adopted, catchment areas were redefined to make them uniform among the sites, and county-level and facility-level sampling plans were implemented to ensure that all arrestees have some probability of being included in the study.

ADAM sites typically are named for the largest city in the area. However, the catchment area has been broadened to encompass the entire county at all sites.

A sample of booking facilities is drawn at each site. The method varies depending on the number of booking facilities in a county. For counties having only one facility, all cases are drawn. Sites with two to five facilities are stratified by size and cases are sampled proportionate to the size of the facility. For sites having more than five, facilities are clustered by size and those in each cluster are sampled proportionate to size.

The method for selecting arrestees is uniform for all facilities. There is a target number of interviews to be completed each quarter at each site. A portion of arrestees are selected at the time of day when the volume of arrestees is high, others are randomly selected from arrests occurring during the rest of the 24-hour period, and arrestees who cannot be interviewed because they were released early are represented through statistical imputation.

To ensure accurate weighting of cases to represent the entire arrestee population, data were collected on all arrests processed at each booking facility during the two-week interview period. The probability-based sampling of male arrestees and the application of weights result in statistically reliable estimates for the male arrestee population of the target counties.

The ADAM program uses EMIT (Enzyme Multiplied Immunoassay Testing) to screen for the presence of drugs in urine. EMIT tests have been shown to be one of the most consistently accurate drug testing methods, with greater than 95% accuracy and specificity for most drugs. Most urine specimens are collected the day of arrest but all are collected within 48 hours of arrest. Specimens are removed daily from the ADAM site facilities. The urine testing for ADAM focuses on the "NIDA-5" drugs, which are cocaine, marijuana, methamphetamine, opiates, and phencyclidine (PCP). These five substances comprise the panel of commonly used illegal drugs identified by the National Institute on Drug Abuse.

Table. ADAM sample sizes, male arrestee interviews, 2003

Primary city	County catchment/ study area	Total interviews	Weighted number
Total		22,666	180,455
Albany, NY	Capital area	450	2,799
Albuquerque, NM	Bernalillo County	535	3,265
Anchorage, AK	Anchorage Borough	322	943
Atlanta, GA	Fulton and DeKalb Counties	869	8,169
Birmingham, AL	Jefferson County	530	1,749
Boston, MA	Suffolk County	111	452
Charlotte, NC	Charlotte-Metro	599	3,754
Chicago, IL	Cook County	930	28,672
Cleveland, OH	Cuyahoga County	736	2,915
Dallas, TX	Dallas County	1,497	8,960
Denver, CO	Denver County	580	2,573
Des Moines, IA	Polk County	430	914
Honolulu, HI	Oahu	370	1,502
Houston, TX	Harris County	87	1,894
Indianapolis, IN	Marion County	498	6,842
Las Vegas, NV	Clark County	981	5,347
Los Angeles, CA	Los Angeles	349	957
Miami, FL	Miami-Dade County	294	3,244
Minneapolis, MN	Hennepin County	677	3,437
New Orleans, LA	Orleans Parish	522	7,505
New York, NY	Manhattan	730	10,529
Oklahoma City, OK	Oklahoma County	582	2,926
Omaha, NE	Douglas County	537	4,928
Philadelphia, PA	County of Philadelphia	684	1,919
Phoenix, AZ	Maricopa County	1,347	11,645
Portland, OR	Multnomah County	564	2,703
Rio Arriba, NM	Rio Arriba County	133	200
Sacramento, CA	Sacramento County	540	5,223
Salt Lake City, UT	Salt Lake County	631	2,844
San Antonio, TX	Bexar County	611	8,778
San Diego, CA	San Diego County	730	7,523
San Jose, CA	Santa Clara County	715	4,599
Seattle, WA	King County	731	4,758
Spokane, WA	Spokane County	372	2,006
Tampa, FL	Hillsborough and Pinellas Counties	801	6,310
Tucson, AZ	Pima County	447	2,657
Tulsa, OK	Tulsa County	695	3,664
Washington, DC	Washington, DC	358	1,148
Woodbury, IA	Woodbury County	91	202

Note: The number of sites participating in the ADAM program varies from year to year.

Appendix 11

Federal Justice Statistics Program Methodology and definitions of terms

Note: The following was excerpted from U.S. Department of Justice, Bureau of Justice Statistics, *Compendium of Federal Justice Statistics, 2001*, NCJ 201627 (Washington, DC: U.S. Department of Justice, 2003), pp. 109-123. Non-substantive editorial adaptations have been made.

Methodology

The data are from the Bureau of Justice Statistics' (BJS) Federal Justice Statistics Program database. The database is constructed from source files provided by the Executive Office for U.S. Attorneys, the Administrative Office of the United States Courts (AO), the United States Sentencing Commission, the U.S. Marshals Service, the Drug Enforcement Administration, and the Federal Bureau of Prisons. The AO also maintains data collected by the Federal Pretrial Services Agency, the U.S. Courts of Appeals, and the Federal probation and supervision service.

Some records in the Federal Justice Statistics database are matched according to a statistically weighted combination of names, other personal identifiers, dates of court appearances, types of offenses, and other relevant information contained in the files. Using the matched data files, it is possible to combine information about two or more stages of the processing of a criminal matter or case, from the prosecutor's decision of whether to file a criminal case, through adjudication, and, if the defendant is convicted, through prison and/or supervised release. Unless otherwise noted, cases have been selected according to some event that occurred during the 2001 Federal fiscal year (Oct. 1, 2000 through Sept. 30, 2001).

The unit of analysis is a combination of a person (or corporation) and a matter or case. For example, if a single person is involved in three different criminal cases during the time period specified in the table, he or she is counted three times in the tabulation. Similarly, if a single criminal case involves a corporate defendant and four individual defendants, it is counted five times in the tabulation.

The unit of analysis for incarceration, probation, parole, or other supervised release is a person entering custody or supervision, or a person leaving custody or supervision. For example, a person convicted in two concurrent cases and committed once to the custody of the Federal Bureau of Prisons in the indicated time period is counted as one admission to a term of incarceration. A person who terminates probation twice in the indicated time period, such as with a violation and again after reinstatement, is counted as two terminations of probation.

Generally, the tables include both individual and organizational defendants. Organizational defendants are not included in tables describing defendants under pretrial release and detention, defendants sentenced to incarceration, and offenders under post-conviction supervision. Juvenile offenders are included in the reported statistics.

The offense classifications in the tables are based on the classification system used by the AO. Specific offenses in the AO classification are combined to form the BJS categories in the tables. These categories are designed to be as consistent as possible with BJS publications on State criminal justice systems. Offense categories for tables focusing on prisoners are based on combinations of offense designations used by the Bureau of Prisons. They are similar to the BJS categories used in the other tables but may not be directly comparable.

Where more than one offense is charged or adjudicated, the most serious offense, the one that may or did result in the most severe sentence, is used to classify the offense. In tables focusing on prisoners, the data are classified according to the conviction offense having the longest sentence imposed, or if equal sentences were imposed or there was no imprisonment, to the offense carrying the highest AO offense severity code. The offense description may change as a case goes through the criminal justice process. Tables indicate whether charged or adjudicated offenses are used.

The availability of particular items of information is affected by the data source. Data on prosecutors' decisions prior to court filing are provided for cases investigated by U.S. attorneys, but not for those handled by other litigating divisions of the U.S. Department of Justice. Criminal Division cases enter the database once they are filed in U.S. District Court, however. Many items of social and demographic information come from presentence investigation records, supervision records, or sentencing records, and are available only for arrested defendants who were convicted and/or began serving a sentence involving supervised release. This particularly affects sex, race, ethnicity, and prior record information.

Time served in prison is the number of months from a prisoner's arrival into jurisdiction of the Bureau of Prisons until first release from prison, plus any jail time served and credited. The calculation is the same as that currently used by the Bureau of Prisons. Because other publications may include different groups of prisoners, calculate time served differently, or use a different offense classification, these data may differ from estimates of time served in previous publications by the Bureau of Prisons or in publications based on other data sources.

These data are designed to permit the user to make valid comparisons within each table and to compare percentages (but not raw totals) across tables. The total number of subjects/defendants that is based on records linked between two files is generally less than the total number of records in either source file. Accordingly, comparisons of absolute numbers across two or more tables, or between these data and other data sources, are not necessarily valid.

In addition, readers should note that offender characteristics, classifications of lengths of prior sentences of incarceration, and time served differ from the 1993 and prior years' Federal justice compendia. Therefore, comparisons of these elements with the 1993 compendium or compendia prior to 1993 should not be attempted.

Definitions of terms

Agriculture--Violation of Federal statutes on agriculture and conservation, for example, violations of the Agricultural Acts, Insecticide Act, and Packers and Stockyards Act; also violation of laws concerning plant quarantine and the handling of animals pertaining to research.

Antitrust--Violation of Federal antitrust statutes, which aim to protect trade and commerce from unlawful restraints, price fixing, monopolies, and discrimination in pricing or in furnishing services or facilities.

Arson--Willfully or maliciously setting, or attempting to set, fire to any property within the special maritime and territorial jurisdiction of the United States.

Assault--Intentionally inflicting, attempting, or threatening to inflict bodily injury to another person; applies to anyone within the special maritime and territorial jurisdiction of the United States or to any Government official, foreign official, official guest, internationally protected person, or any officer or employee of the United States designated in 18 U.S.C. 1114; also certain violations of the Fair Housing Act of 1968.

Bail--The sum of money promised as a condition of release, to be paid if a released defendant defaults.

Bribery--Offering or promising anything of value with intent to unlawfully influence a public official, bank employee, officer or employee of the Government, witness, or any common carrier as well as soliciting or accepting such an offer. Soliciting or receiving anything of value in consideration of aiding a person to obtain employment in the U.S. Government. Receiving or soliciting any remuneration, directly or indirectly, in cash or in kind in return for purchasing, ordering, leasing, or recommending to purchase any good, service, or facility.

Burglary--Breaking and entering into another's property with intent to steal within the special maritime and territorial jurisdiction of the United States; includes breaking and entering into any official bank, credit union, savings and loan institution, post office, vessel or steamboat assigned to the use of mail service, or personal property of the United States, or breaking the seal or lock of any carrier facility containing interstate or foreign shipments of freight or express.

Civil rights--Violations of civil liberties such as the personal, natural rights guaranteed and protected by the U.S. Constitution. Includes the Civil Rights Acts, such as those enacted after the Civil War, and more recently in 1957 and 1964.

Collateral bond--An agreement made by a defendant as a condition of pretrial release that requires the defendant to post property valued at the full bail amount as an assurance of his or her intention to appear at trial.

Communication--Violations covering areas of communication such as the Communications Act of 1934 (including wiretapping and wire interception). A communication is ordinarily considered to be a deliberate interchange of thoughts or opinions between two or more persons.

Conditional release--Release from detention contingent on any combination of restrictions that are deemed necessary to guarantee a defendant's appearance at trial or the safety of the community.

Conspiracy--An agreement by two or more persons to commit or to effect the commission of an unlawful act or to use unlawful means to accomplish an act that is not in itself unlawful; also any overt act in furtherance of the agreement. A person charged with conspiracy is classified under the substantive offense alleged.

Counterfeiting--Falsely making, forging, or altering any obligation or security of the United States, foreign obligation or security, coin or bar stamped at any mint in the United States, money order issued by the U.S. Postal Service, domestic or foreign stamp, or seal of any department or agency of the United States. Passing, selling, attempting to pass or sell, or bringing into the United States any of the above falsely made articles. Making, selling, or possessing any plates or stones used for printing counterfeit obligations or securities of the United States, foreign obligations or securities, Government transportation requests, or postal stamps; or knowingly and intentionally trafficking in falsified labels affixed to phonorecords, motion pictures, or audio visual works.

Customs laws--Violations regarding taxes that are payable upon goods and merchandise imported or exported. Includes the duty, toll, tribute, or tariff payable upon merchandise exported or imported.

Deposit bond--An agreement made by a defendant as a condition of release that requires the defendant to post a fraction of the bail before he or she is released.

Detention--The legally authorized confinement of persons after arrest, whether before or during prosecution. Only those persons held 2 or more days are classified as detained.

Drug offenses--Manufacture, import, export, distribution, or dispensing of a controlled substance (or counterfeit substance), or the possession of a controlled substance (or counterfeit substance) with intent to manufacture, import, export, distribute, or dispense. Also using any communication facility that causes or facilitates a felony under title 21. Also furnishing of fraudulent or false information concerning prescriptions as well as any other unspecified drug-related offense.

Embezzlement--Fraudulently appropriating property by a person to whom such property has been lawfully entrusted. Includes offenses committed by bank officers or employees; officers or employees of the U.S. Postal Service; officers of lending, credit, or insurance institutions; any officer or employee of a corporation or association engaged in commerce as a common carrier; court officers of the U.S. courts; or officers or employees of the United States. Stealing from employment and training funds, programs receiving Federal funds, and Indian tribal organizations; or selling, conveying, or disposing of any money, property, records, or thing of value to the United States or any department thereof without authority.

Escape--Departing or attempting to depart from the custody of a correctional institution; a judicial, correctional, or law enforcement officer; or a hospital where one is committed for drug abuse and drug dependency problems. Knowingly advising, aiding, assisting, or procuring the escape or attempted escape of any person from a correctional facility, an officer, or the above-mentioned hospital as well as concealing an escapee. Providing or attempting to provide to an inmate in prison a prohibited object or making, possessing, obtaining, or attempting to make or obtain a prohibited object. Instigating, assisting, attempting to cause, or causing any mutiny or riot at any Federal penal, detention, or correctional facility or conveying into any of these institutions any dangerous instrumentalities.

Explosives--Violations of Federal law involving importation, manufacture, distribution, and storage of explosive material. Includes unlawful receipt, possession, or transportation of explosives without a license, where prohibited by law, or using explosives during commission of a felony. Also includes violations relating to dealing in stolen explosives, using mail or other forms of communication to threaten an individual with explosives, and possessing explosive materials at an airport.

Failure to appear--Willful absence from any court appointment.

Felony--A criminal offense punishable by death or imprisonment for a term exceeding 1 year.

Financial conditions--Monetary conditions upon which release of a defendant before trial is contingent. Includes deposit bond, surety bond, and collateral bond (see individual definitions).

Food and drug--Violations of the Federal Food, Drug, and Cosmetic Act, such as regulations for clean and sanitary movement of animals, adulteration or misbranding of any food or drug, failure to transmit information about prescription drugs, and intent to defraud and distribute adulterated material.

Forgery--Falsely and with intent to defraud, making or materially altering, or possessing with intent to pass off as genuine any U.S. Postal Service money order; postmarking stamp or impression; obligation or security of the United States; foreign obligation, security, or bank note; contractor's bond, bid, or public record; seal of a court or any department or agency of the Government; the signature of a judge or court officer; ships' papers; documents on entry of vessels; deed; power of attorney; customs matters; coin or bar; and so forth. Also making, possessing, selling, or printing plates or stones for counterfeiting obligations or securities.

Fraud--Unlawfully depriving a person of his or her property or legal rights through intentional misrepresentation of fact or deceit other than forgery or counterfeiting. Includes violations of statutes pertaining to lending and credit institutions, the U.S. Postal Service, interstate wire, radio, television, computer, credit card, veterans benefits, allotments, bankruptcy, marketing agreements, commodity credit, the Securities and Exchange Commission, railroad retirement, unemployment, Social Security, food stamps, false personation, citizenship, passports, conspiracy, and claims and statements, excluding tax fraud. Excludes fraud involving tax violations that are shown in a separate category under "public-order, other offenses."

Gambling--Transporting, manufacturing, selling, possessing, or using any gambling device in the District of Columbia or any possession of the United States or within Indian country or the special maritime and territorial jurisdiction of the United States. Also transporting gambling devices in the jurisdiction of the United States, (except under authority of the Federal Trade

Commission or any State that has a law providing for their exemption from these provisions), transmitting wagering information in interstate or foreign commerce, interstate transporting of wagering paraphernalia, importing or transporting lottery tickets, or mailing lottery tickets or related matter.

Hispanic--Ethnic category based on classification by reporting agency. Hispanic persons may be of any race.

Immigration--Offenses involving illegal entrance into the United States, illegally reentering after being deported, willfully failing to deport when so ordered, willfully remaining beyond days allowed on conditional permit, or falsely representing oneself as a citizen of the United States. Includes violations relating to agricultural workers and to limitations on immigrant status. Also bringing in or harboring any aliens not duly admitted by an immigration officer.

Incarceration--Any sentence of confinement, including prison, jail, and other residential placements.

Kidnaping--Unlawfully seizing any person, for ransom or reward, except in the case of a minor by a parent. Includes receiving, possessing, or disposing of any money or other property that has been delivered as ransom or reward in connection with a kidnaping as well as conspiring to kidnap. Includes kidnaping or attempting to kidnap any Government official, the President of the United States, the President-elect, the Vice President, any foreign official, any official guest, or any internationally protected person.

Larceny--Taking and carrying away with intent to steal any personal property of another. Stealing, possessing, converting to one's own use, or illegally selling or disposing of anything of value to the United States or any of its departments or agencies. Stealing anything of value from a bank, the U.S. Postal Service, or any interstate or foreign shipments by carrier. Receiving or possessing stolen property or pirate property. Stealing or obtaining by fraud any funds, assets, or property that belongs to or is entrusted to the custody of an Indian tribal organization. Excludes the transportation of stolen property.

Liquor--Violations of Internal Revenue Service laws on liquor as well as violations of liquor laws not cited under these laws, such as dispensing or unlawfully possessing intoxicants in Indian country; transporting intoxicating liquors into any State, territory, district, or possession where sale is prohibited; shipping packages containing unmarked and unlabeled intoxicants; shipping liquor by C.O.D.; knowingly delivering a liquor shipment to someone other than to whom it has been consigned; and violating in any way the Federal Alcohol Administration Act.

Mailing or transportation of obscene materials--Knowingly using the mail for mailing obscene or crime-inciting matter. Also transporting for sale or distribution, importing, or transporting any obscene matter in interstate or foreign commerce.

Migratory birds--Taking, killing, or possessing migratory birds, or any part, nest, or egg thereof, in violation of Federal regulations or the transportation laws of the State, territory, or district from which the bird was taken. Misuse or nonuse of a migratory-bird hunting and conservation stamp.

Misdemeanor--A criminal offense punishable by a jail term not exceeding 1 year and any offenses specifically defined as a misdemeanor by the Administrative Office of the United States Courts for the purposes of data collection. (Includes offenses previously called minor offenses that were reclassified under the Federal Magistrates Act of 1979.)

Mixed sentence--A sentence requiring the convicted offender to serve a term of incarceration, followed by a term of probation. Unless otherwise noted, offenders receiving mixed sentences are included in both incarceration and probation categories.

Most serious offense--The offense with the greatest potential sentence. For Federal prisoners, the offense with the longest term of incarceration actually imposed.

Motor vehicle theft--Interstate or foreign transporting, receiving, concealing, storing, bartering, selling, or disposing of any stolen motor vehicle or aircraft.

Murder--The unlawful killing of a human being with malice aforethought, either expressed or implied. Nonnegligent manslaughter is the unlawful killing of a human being without malice; includes committing or attempting to commit murder (first or second degree) or voluntary manslaughter within the special maritime and territorial jurisdiction of the United States. Killing or attempting to kill any Government official, the President of the United States, the President-elect, the Vice President, any officers and employees of the United States, any foreign officials, any official guests, or any internationally protected persons. As applied to the owner or charterer of any steamboat or vessel, knowingly and willfully causing or allowing fraud, neglect, misconduct, or violation of any law resulting in loss of life.

National defense--Violations of the national defense laws of the Military Selective Service Act, the Defense Production Act of 1950, the Economic Stabilization Act of 1970 (which includes prices, rents, and wages), the Subversive Activities Control Act, alien registration, treason (including espionage, sabotage, sedition, and the Smith Act of 1940), also violations relating to energy facilities, curfew and restricted areas, exportation of war materials, trading with an enemy, illegal use of uniform, and any other violations of the Federal statutes concerning national defense.

Negligent manslaughter--Causing the death of another, within the special maritime and territorial jurisdiction of the United States by wanton or reckless disregard for human life. Also negligent manslaughter of any Government official, the President of the United States, the President-elect, the Vice President, any officers and employees of the United States, any foreign officials, any official guests, or any internationally protected persons. Also includes misconduct, negligence, or inattention to duties by ship officers on a steamboat or vessel resulting in death to any person.

Nolo contendere--Defendant's plea in a criminal case indicating that he or she will not contest charges, but not admitting or denying guilt.

Nonviolent sex offenses--Transporting, coercing, or enticing any individual (including minors) to go from one place to another in interstate or foreign commerce, in the District of Columbia, or in any territory or possession of the United States with the intent and purpose to engage in prostitution, or any sexual activity for which any person can be charged with a criminal offense.

Offense--Violation of U.S. criminal law. Where more than one offense is charged, the offense with the greatest potential sentence is reported.

Other property offenses--Offenses that involve the destruction of property moving in interstate or foreign commerce in the possession of a common or contract carrier. The malicious destruction of Government property, or injury to U.S. postal property such as mailboxes or mailbags. Trespassing on timber and Government lands also is included.

Other public-order offenses--Violations of laws pertaining to bigamy; disorderly conduct on the U.S. Capitol grounds; civil disorder; and travel to incite riot. Included in "public-order, non-regulatory offenses."

Perjury--Making any false material declarations under oath in any proceeding before or ancillary to any court or grand jury of the United States. Includes knowingly or willfully giving false evidence or swearing to false statements under oath, or by any means procuring or instigating any person to commit perjury. Also includes any officers and employees of the Government listed under 13 U.S.C. 21-25 who willfully or knowingly furnish or cause to be furnished any false information or statement.

Personal recognizance--Pretrial release condition in which the defendant promises to appear at trial and no financial conditions are required to be met

Pretrial release--The release of a defendant from custody, for all or part of the time, before or during prosecution. The defendant may be released either on personal recognizance, unsecured bond, or on financial conditions. Includes defendants released within 2 days after arrest and defendants who were initially detained but subsequently released after raising bail or having release conditions changed at a subsequent hearing.

Property offenses, fraudulent--Property offenses involving the elements of deceit or intentional misrepresentation. Specifically includes embezzlement, fraud (excluding tax fraud), forgery, and counterfeiting.

Property offenses, non-fraudulent--Offenses against property: burglary, larceny, motor vehicle theft, arson, transportation of stolen property, and other property offenses (destruction of property and trespassing). These offenses are termed "non-fraudulent" only for the purpose of distinguishing them from the category "property offenses, fraudulent," above.

Public-order, non-regulatory offenses--Offenses concerning weapons; immigration; tax law violations (tax fraud); bribery; perjury; national defense; escape; racketeering and extortion; gambling; liquor; mailing or transporting of obscene materials; traffic; migratory birds; conspiracy, aiding and abetting, and jurisdictional offenses; and "other public-order offenses." These offenses are termed "non-regulatory" only for the purpose of distinguishing them from the category "public-order, regulatory offenses," below.

Public-order, regulatory offenses--Violations of regulatory laws and regulations in agriculture, antitrust, labor, food and drug, motor carrier, and other regulatory offenses that are not specifically listed in the category "public-order, non-regulatory offenses" above.

Racketeering and extortion--Racketeering is demanding, soliciting, or receiving anything of value from the owner, proprietor, or other person having a financial interest in a business, by means of a threat or promise, either expressed or implied. Extortion is the obtaining of money or property from another, without his or her consent, induced by the wrongful use of force or fear. Includes using interstate or foreign commerce or any facility in interstate or foreign commerce to aid racketeering enterprises such as arson, bribery, gambling, liquor, narcotics, prostitution, and extortionate credit transactions; obtaining property or money from another, with his or her consent induced by actual or threatened force; violence, blackmail, or committing unlawful interference with employment or business; transmitting by interstate commerce or through the mail any threat to injure the property, the person, or the reputation of the addressee or of another; or kidnaping any person with intent to extort.

Robbery--Taking anything of value from the person or presence of another by force or intimidation, within the special maritime and territorial jurisdiction of the United States. Includes robbery of bank property, U.S. postal property, or personal property of the United States. Assaulting or putting the life of any person in jeopardy by the use of a dangerous weapon while committing or attempting to commit such robbery.

Sexual abuse--Rape, assault with intent to commit rape, and carnal knowledge of a female under 16 who is not one's wife, within the territorial and special maritime jurisdiction of the United States. Also includes cases of sexual abuse, including abuse of a minor and abuse in Federal prisons.

Supervised release--Under the Sentencing Reform Act of 1984, a form of post-imprisonment supervision to be imposed by the court as a part of the sentence of imprisonment at the time of initial sentencing. Unlike parole, a term of supervised release does not replace a portion of the sentence of imprisonment, but rather is an order of supervision in addition to any term of imprisonment imposed by the court.

Surety bond--An agreement by the defendant as a condition of release that requires a third party (usually a bail bondsman) to promise to pay the full bail amount in the event that the defendant fails to appear.

Tax law violations--Tax fraud offenses such as income tax evasion and fraud; counterfeiting any stamps with intent to defraud the collection or payment of tax; willfully failing to collect or pay tax; failure to obey summons to produce any papers concerning taxes; failing to furnish receipts for employees of tax withheld; failing to furnish information relating to certain trusts, annuity, and bond purchase plans; putting fraudulent or false statements on tax returns; and not obtaining a license for a business that makes a profit from foreign items. Also included are violations of excise and wagering tax laws and other laws from the Internal Revenue Service code.

Technical violation--Failure to comply with conditions of pretrial release, probation, or parole, excluding alleged new criminal activity. May result in revocation of release status. Examples of conditions that may be imposed and then violated include remaining within a specified jurisdiction, or appearing at specified intervals for drug tests.

Threats against the President--Knowingly and willfully depositing in the mail, at any post office, or by any letter carrier a letter, paper, writing, print, missive, or document containing any threat to take the life of or to inflict bodily harm upon the President, Vice President, or any other officer in order of succession to the Presidency. Knowingly and willfully making such threats in any way to the above-named people.

Traffic offenses--Driving while intoxicated or any moving or parking violation on Federal lands.

Trafficking--Knowingly and intentionally importing or exporting any controlled substance in schedules I-V (as defined by 21 U.S.C. 812). Manufacturing, distributing, dispensing, selling, or possessing with intent to manufacture, distribute, or sell a controlled substance or a counterfeit substance. Exporting any controlled substance in schedules I-V. Manufacturing or distributing a controlled substance in schedule I or II for purposes of unlawful importation. Making or distributing any punch, die, plate, stone, or any other thing designed to reproduce the label on any drug or container or removing or obliterating the label or symbol of any drug or container. Knowingly opening, maintaining, or managing any place for the purpose of manufacturing, distributing, or using any controlled substance.

Transportation--Violations of Federal statutes relating to the Motor Carrier Act, which regulate (routes, rates) motor carriers of freight and passengers in interstate commerce.

Transportation of stolen property--Transporting, selling, or receiving stolen goods, stolen securities, stolen moneys, stolen cattle, fraudulent State tax stamps, or articles used in counterfeiting if the above articles or goods involve or constitute interstate or foreign commerce.

Unsecured bond--An agreement by the defendant as a condition of release in which the defendant agrees to pay full bond amount in the event of nonappearance at trial, but is not required to post security as a condition of release.

Violation (of pretrial release, probation, or parole)--Allegation of either a new crime or a technical violation while on pretrial release, probation, or parole.

Violent offenses--Threatening, attempting, or actually using physical force against a person. Includes murder and non-negligent manslaughter, negligent manslaughter, assault, robbery, sexual abuse, kidnaping, and threats against the President. (See specific offenses.)

Weapons--Violations of any of the provisions of 18 U.S.C. 922, 923 concerning the manufacturing, importing, possessing, receiving, and licensing of firearms and ammunition. Manufacturing, selling, possessing, or transporting (within any territory or possession of the United States, within Indian country, or within the special maritime and territorial jurisdiction of the United States) any switchblade knife; or making, receiving, possessing, or transporting a firearm not registered in the National Firearms Registration Transfer Record. Engaging in importing, manufacturing, or dealing in firearms if not registered with the secretary in the Internal Revenue Service District in which the business is conducted, or not having paid a special occupational tax. This code covers cases where in a crime-of-violence- or drug-trafficking-enhanced punishment is handed down when committed with a deadly weapon.

Appendix 12

National Judicial Reporting Program
Survey sampling procedures and definitions of terms

Note: The following information has been excerpted from U.S. Department of Justice, Bureau of Justice Statistics, *Felony Sentences in State Courts, 1998*, Bulletin NCJ 190103, pp. 12, 13; *2000*, Bulletin NCJ 198821, pp. 11, 12 (Washington, DC: U.S. Department of Justice). Non-substantive editorial adaptations have been made.

Survey sampling procedures

A sample of 300 counties was drawn for the 1988 National Judicial Reporting Program (NJRP) survey. With little exception, these same 300 counties were the source of NJRP data for 3 subsequent NJRP surveys (1990, 1992, 1994). For the 1996 NJRP survey a new sample was drawn, consisting of 344 counties. The 344 counties included 98 that had been in the NJRP sample in the 4 previous surveys (1988, 1990, 1992, 1994) and 246 that had never been part of an NJRP sample. The 98 consisted of 80 counties selected by chance alone; plus 18 of the Nation's largest counties selected not by chance but (given their large 1995 population size) with certainty. The same 344 counties were used for the 1998 and 2000 NJRP surveys.

The 2000 survey used a two-stage, stratified cluster sampling design. In the first stage the Nation's 3,195 counties or county equivalents were divided into 14 strata. Each county was assigned to one stratum by meeting the conditions for that stratum.

The stratum to which a county was assigned depended on three criteria:
1. Whether the county was among the Nation's 75 largest according to 1995 resident population,
2. Ease of data collection (in a State where data collection is generally not costly; one where data collection is generally moderately costly; one where data collection is generally very costly),
3. The size of the county's 1995 resident population.

The largest 75 counties in the United States (as defined by 1995 resident population) were separated from the Nation's 3,195 counties or county equivalents. Each State was then assigned a "cost-factor" that reflected the overall ease or method of collecting their data. Next, counties in each "cost-factor" group were separated into categories based on the size of their 1995 population. This resulted in 13 strata from which a sample of 325 counties was drawn. The 14th stratum consisted of the 19 counties with the largest populations in 1995; every county in this stratum was selected.

The final sample included 344 counties: 45 out of the 75 largest counties and 299 out of the remaining 3,120 counties. Because the 75 largest counties account for a disproportionately large amount of serious crime in the Nation, they were given a greater chance of being selected than the remaining counties. None of the counties refused to participate.

At the second stage of sampling, a systematic sample of felons sentenced for murder or nonnegligent manslaughter, sexual assault (including rape), robbery, aggravated assault, burglary, felony larceny/motor vehicle theft, fraud/forgery/embezzlement, drug trafficking, drug possession, weapons offenses, and other offenses was selected from each county's official records. The total sample numbered 429,471 cases. Of these, 272,889 cases were in the 75 largest counties.

Rates at which cases were sampled varied by how the data were submitted, by stratum, and by crime type. Among counties in States that submitted electronic data, all cases were typically included regardless of the offense type. Among counties in States that either submitted electronic data that required manual processing time or had data from jurisdictions that were collected manually (on-site), a sample of the cases was taken.

The survey targeted and recorded initial sentences imposed in 2000. If a sentence was imposed on one date and then modified at a later date, the revision was ignored. The survey recorded sentences that were actually executed and excluded suspended sentences. If a prison sentence was initially imposed but immediately suspended in its entirety, the case was coded as probation because that was the actual sentence.

Because the year of conviction was not a defining characteristic, some cases in the sample involved persons convicted before 2000, but not sentenced until 2000.

In 34 counties it was impractical to target sentences imposed in 2000. Cases sampled from these counties were all sentenced in 1999.

The 2000 conviction data that were submitted by four Illinois counties were very different from prior years' NJRP data files as well as other court data sources. Consequently, the conviction data submitted by these counties for the 1998 NJRP survey were used in place of the 2000 data.

In 2000, Missouri was unable to provide data for seven counties in the sample. These counties were replaced with seven others in the same respective strata.

The second stage weights for two sampled counties from Florida were adjusted to account for less than a full year of reporting.

Based on these sampling methods, an estimated total of 924,700 persons were convicted of a felony in State courts in 2000.

Sources of data

For 61% of the 344 counties sampled for the 2000 survey, NJRP data were obtained directly from the State courts. Sources of data from other counties included sentencing commissions, statistical agencies, departments of public safety, probation departments, State police departments, and departments of corrections. Individual-level NJRP records were obtained either electronically (83% of the counties) or manually (17% of the counties). Electronic methods of data submission included: diskettes, magnetic tape, and Internet transmission. Manual methods included photocopies of official documents, survey questionnaires completed by court officials, and on-site collections. All data were collected by the U.S. Census Bureau.

Sampling error

NJRP data were obtained from a sample and not from a complete enumeration. Consequently, they are subject to sampling error. A standard error, which is a measure of sampling error, is associated with each number reported. In general, if the difference between two numbers is at least twice the standard error of that difference, there is at least 95% confidence that the two numbers do in fact differ; that is, the apparent difference is not simply the result of surveying a sample rather than the entire population.

National estimates of the number of convictions for individual crime categories and for the aggregate total had a coefficient of variation of 3.6%. Standard errors did not take into account missing data, which are substantial for certain tables.

Crime definitions

Before the sample was drawn, each felon sentenced in the sampled counties in 2000 was placed into 1 of the 11 offense categories identified above. If the felon was convicted of more than one felony offense, the offense category was the most serious offense. The hierarchy from most to least serious offense was murder, sexual assault, robbery, aggravated assault, burglary, drug trafficking, weapons, forgery/fraud/embezzlement, larceny/motor vehicle theft, drug possession, and all other felonies. The hierarchy was determined from an analysis of two factors that reflect how seriously the justice system treats different offenses: the sentence length imposed and the time actually served in prison before release. In general, the higher the offense is in the hierarchy, the more serious it is in terms of the two factors. Sample selection procedures gave each sentenced felon a single chance to be in the sample. However, felons who appeared in court on more than 1 day for different offenses and received a sentence at each reappearance had more than a single chance.

At the data analysis stage, cases were aggregated according to their offense designation at time of sampling, with the single exception of "other violent." "Other violent" is a category shown in the tables, but it was not a category at sampling. The "other violent" category was formed from the sampling category "other felonies." That is, after sampling, sampled cases designated "other felonies" were coded either "violent," "nonviolent," or "not ascertained," based on data available. Cases coded "not ascertained" were rare. For data analysis purposes, cases coded "other violent" were removed from the "other felonies" category and shown separately in the tables. The offense categories shown in the tables are defined as follows:

Murder and nonnegligent manslaughter--Murder is (1) intentionally causing the death of another person without extreme provocation or legal justification or (2) causing the death of another while committing or attempting to commit another crime. Nonnegligent (or voluntary) manslaughter is intentionally and without legal justification causing the death of another when acting under extreme provocation. The combined category of murder and nonnegligent manslaughter excludes involuntary or negligent manslaughter, conspiracies to commit murder, solicitation of murder, and attempted murder.

Rape and sexual assault--Rape includes forcible intercourse (vaginal, anal, or oral) with a female or male. Includes forcible sodomy or penetration with a foreign object (sometimes called "deviate sexual assault"); excludes statutory rape or any other nonforcible sexual acts with a minor or with someone unable to give legal or factual consent. Includes attempts. Other sexual assault includes (1) forcible or violent sexual acts not involving intercourse with an adult or minor, (2) nonforcible sexual acts with a minor (such as statutory rape or incest with a minor), and (3) nonforcible sexual acts with someone unable to give legal or factual consent because of mental or physical defect or intoxication. Includes attempts.

Robbery--The unlawful taking of property that is in the immediate possession of another, by force or the threat of force. Includes forcible purse snatching but excludes nonforcible purse snatching, which is classified as larceny/theft. Includes attempts.

Aggravated assault--(1) Intentionally and without legal justification causing serious bodily injury, with or without a deadly weapon or (2) using a deadly or dangerous weapon to threaten, attempt, or cause bodily injury, regardless of the degree of injury, if any. Includes attempted murder, aggravated battery, felonious assault, and assault with a deadly weapon.

Other violent--Violent offenses excluding murder and nonnegligent manslaughter, rape and sexual assault, robbery, and aggravated assault. Includes offenses such as kidnaping, extortion, and negligent manslaughter. Includes attempts.

Burglary--The unlawful entry of a fixed structure used for regular residence, industry, or business, with or without the use of force, to commit a felony or theft. Includes attempts.

Larceny--The unlawful taking of property other than a motor vehicle from the possession of another, by stealth, without force or deceit. Includes pocket picking, nonforcible purse snatching, shoplifting, and thefts from motor vehicles. Excludes receiving and/or reselling stolen property (fencing) and thefts through fraud or deceit. Includes attempts.

Motor vehicle theft--The unlawful taking of a self-propelled road vehicle owned by another. Includes the theft of automobiles, trucks, and motorcycles but excludes the theft of boats, aircraft, or farm equipment (which is classified as larceny/theft). Also includes receiving, possessing, stripping, transporting, and reselling stolen vehicles and unauthorized use of a vehicle (joyriding). Includes attempts.

Fraud, forgery, and embezzlement--Using deceit or intentional misrepresentation to unlawfully deprive a person of his or her property or legal rights. Includes offenses such as check fraud, confidence games, counterfeiting, and credit card fraud. Includes attempts.

Drug possession--Includes possession of an illegal drug, but excludes possession with intent to sell. Includes attempts.

Drug trafficking--Includes manufacturing, distributing, selling, smuggling, and possession with intent to sell. Includes attempts.

Weapons offenses--The unlawful sale, distribution, manufacture, alteration, transportation, possession, or use of a deadly or dangerous weapon or accessory.

Other offenses--All felony offenses not listed above. Includes receiving stolen property, driving while intoxicated or other traffic offenses, bribery, obstructing justice, escaping from custody, family offenses (such as child neglect, contributing to the delinquency of a minor, nonpayment of child support), and nonviolent sexual offenses (such as pornography offenses, pimping, prostitution). Includes attempts.

Appendix 13

State Court Processing Statistics
Methodology, definitions of terms, and crimes within offense categories

Note: The following information has been excerpted from U.S. Department of Justice, Bureau of Justice Statistics, *Felony Defendants in Large Urban Counties, 2000*, NCJ 202021 (Washington, DC: U.S. Department of Justice, 2003), pp. 1, 37, 38. Non-substantive editorial adaptations have been made.

Methodology

Since 1988, the Bureau of Justice Statistics has sponsored a biennial data collection on the processing of felony defendants in the State courts of the Nation's 75 most populous counties. Previously known as the National Pretrial Reporting Program, this data collection series was renamed the State Court Processing Statistics (SCPS) program in 1994 to better reflect the wide range of data elements collected. The SCPS program collects data on the demographic characteristics, criminal history, pretrial processing, adjudication, and sentencing of felony defendants. The SCPS data do not include Federal defendants.

In 2000, the 75 largest counties accounted for about 37% of the Nation's population, 49% of all reported serious violent crimes, and 39% of all reported serious property crimes.

The sample was designed and selected by the U.S. Census Bureau. It is a two-stage stratified sample with 40 of the 75 most populous counties selected at the first stage, and a systematic sample of State court felony filings (defendants) within each county selected at the second stage.

The 40 counties were divided into 4 first-stage strata based on court filing information. Ten counties were included in the sample with certainty because of their large number of court filings. The remaining counties were allocated to the three noncertainty strata based on the variance of felony court dispositions.

The second-stage sampling was designed to represent all defendants who had felony cases filed with the court during the month of May 2000. The participating jurisdictions provided data for every felony case filed on selected days during that month. The number of days selected depended on the stage-one stratum in which the county had been placed. Each jurisdiction provided 5, 10, or 20 randomly selected business days' filings for May 2000. Data from jurisdictions that were not required to provide a full month of filings were weighted to represent the full month.

Data on 14,877 sample felony cases were collected from the 40 sampled jurisdictions. These cases represented the estimated 54,590 cases filed during the month of May 2000 in the 75 most populous counties. A small number of cases (162 weighted) were omitted from analysis as they could not be classified into one of the four major crime categories (violent, property, drug, public-order).

Data were collected from the following counties: Alabama (Jefferson); Arizona (Maricopa, Pima); California (Alameda, Contra Costa, Los Angeles, Orange, Riverside, San Bernardino, San Diego, San Mateo, Santa Clara); Connecticut (New Haven); Florida (Broward, Miami-Dade, Palm Beach, Pinellas); Georgia (Fulton); Hawaii (Honolulu); Illinois (Cook); Indiana (Marion); Maryland (Baltimore, Montgomery); Michigan (Macomb, Wayne); New Jersey (Essex); New York (Bronx, Kings, Nassau, Westchester); Ohio (Franklin); Pennsylvania (Philadelphia); Tennessee (Shelby); Texas (Dallas, El Paso, Harris, Tarrant, Travis); Utah (Salt Lake City); and Virginia (Fairfax).

Definitions of terms

Terms relating to pretrial release

Released defendant--Any defendant who was released from custody prior to the disposition of his or her case by the court. Includes defendants who were detained for some period of time before being released and defendants who were returned to custody after being released because of a violation of the conditions of pretrial release.

Detained defendant--Any defendant who remained in custody from the time of arrest until the disposition of his or her case by the court.

Failure to appear--A court issues a bench warrant for a defendant's arrest because he or she has missed a scheduled court appearance.

Types of financial release

Full cash bond--The defendant posts the full bail amount in cash with the court. If the defendant makes all court appearances, the cash is returned. If the defendant fails to appear in court, the bond is forfeited.

Deposit bond--The defendant deposits a percentage (usually 10%) of the full bail amount with the court. This percentage of the bail is returned after the disposition of the case, but the court often retains a small portion for administrative costs. If the defendant fails to appear in court, he or she is liable to the court for the full amount of the bail.

Surety bond--A bail bond company signs a promissory note to the court for the full bail amount and charges the defendant a fee for the service (usually 10% of the full bail amount). If the defendant fails to appear, the bond company is liable to the court for the full bail amount. Frequently the bond company requires the defendant to post collateral in addition to the fee.

Property bond--Also known as collateral bond, involves an agreement made by a defendant as a condition of pretrial release requiring that property valued at the full bail amount be posted as an assurance of his or her appearance in court. If the defendant fails to appear in court, the property is forfeited.

Types of nonfinancial release

Unsecured bond--The defendant pays no money to the court but is liable for the full amount of bail should he or she fail to appear in court.

Release on recognizance--The court releases the defendant on a signed agreement that he or she will appear in court as required. This category also includes citation releases in which arrestees are released pending their first court appearance on a written order issued by law enforcement or jail personnel.

Conditional release--Defendants are released under specified conditions. If monitoring or supervision is required, this usually is done by a pretrial services agency. In some cases, such as those involving a third-party custodian or drug monitoring and treatment, another agency may be involved in the supervision of the defendant. Conditional release sometimes includes an unsecured bond.

Other type of release

Emergency release--Defendants are released in response to a court order placing limits on a jail's population.

Offense categories

Felony offenses were classified into 16 categories. These were further divided into the four major crime categories of violent, property, drug, and public-order offenses. The following offense categories contain a representative summary of most of the crimes contained in each category; however, these lists are not meant to be exhaustive. All offenses, except murder, include attempts and conspiracies to commit.

Violent offenses

Murder--Includes homicide, nonnegligent manslaughter, and voluntary homicide. Does not include attempted murder (which is classified as felony assault), negligent homicide, involuntary homicide, or vehicular manslaughter (which are classified as "other violent offenses").

Rape--Includes forcible intercourse, sodomy, or penetration with a foreign object. Does not include statutory rape or nonforcible acts with a minor or someone unable to give legal consent, nonviolent sexual offenses, or commercialized sex offenses.

Robbery--Includes the unlawful taking of anything of value by force or threat of force. This classification includes armed, unarmed, and aggravated robbery, carjacking, armed burglary, and armed mugging.

Assault--Includes aggravated assault, aggravated battery, attempted murder, assault with a deadly weapon, felony assault or battery on a law enforcement officer, and other felony assaults. Does not include extortion, coercion, or intimidation.

Other violent offenses--Includes vehicular manslaughter, involuntary manslaughter, negligent or reckless homicide, nonviolent or nonforcible sexual assault, kidnaping, unlawful imprisonment, child or spouse abuse, cruelty to a child, reckless endangerment, hit and run with bodily injury, intimidation, and extortion.

Property offenses

Burglary--Includes any type of entry into a residence, industry, or business with or without the use of force with the intent to commit a felony or theft. Does not include possession of burglary tools, trespassing, or unlawful entry where the intent is not known.

Larceny/theft--Includes grand theft, grand larceny, and any other felony theft, including burglary from an automobile, theft of rental property, and mail theft. Does not include motor vehicle theft, receiving or buying stolen property, fraud, forgery, or deceit.

Motor vehicle theft--Includes auto theft, conversion of an automobile, receiving and transferring an automobile, unauthorized use of a vehicle, possession of a stolen vehicle, larceny or taking of an automobile.

Forgery--Includes forging a driver's license, forging official seals, notes, money orders, credit or access cards or names of such cards or any other documents with fraudulent intent, uttering a forged instrument, counterfeiting, and forgery.

Fraud--Includes possession and passing of worthless checks or money orders, possession of false documents or identification, embezzlement, obtaining money by false pretenses, credit card fraud, welfare fraud, Medicare fraud, insurance claim fraud, fraud, swindling, stealing a thing of value by deceit, larceny by check.

Other property offenses--Includes receiving or buying stolen property, arson, reckless burning, damage to property, criminal mischief, vandalism, criminal trespassing, possession of burglary tools, and unlawful entry.

Drug offenses

Drug trafficking--Includes trafficking, sales, distribution, possession with intent to distribute or sell, manufacturing, and smuggling of controlled substances. Does not include possession of controlled substances.

Other drug offenses--Includes possession of controlled substances, prescription violations, possession of drug paraphernalia, and other drug law violations.

Public-order offenses

Weapons--Includes the unlawful sale, distribution, manufacture, alteration, transportation, possession, or use of a deadly weapon or accessory.

Driving-related--Includes driving under the influence of drugs or alcohol, driving with a suspended or revoked license, or any other felony in the motor vehicle code.

Other public-order offenses--Includes flight/escape, parole or probation violations, prison contraband, habitual offender, obstruction of justice, rioting, libel, slander, treason, perjury, prostitution, pandering, bribery, and tax law violations.

Appendix 14

Juvenile Court Statistics Methodology, definitions of terms, and offenses within categories

This information was excerpted from A. Stahl, T. Finnegan, and W. Kang, "Easy Access to Juvenile Court Statistics: 1985-2000" [Online]. Washington, DC: U.S. Department of Justice, Office of Juvenile Justice and Delinquency Prevention, 2002. Available: http://ojjdp.ncjrs.org/ojstatbb/ezajcs/ [Apr. 15, 2003]; and Charles Puzzanchera et al., *Juvenile Court Statistics 1998*, NCJ 193696 (Washington, DC: U.S. Department of Justice, 2003), pp. 59, 60. Non-substantive editorial adaptations have been made.

Methodology

These data are national estimates of juvenile delinquency cases handled in 2000 by U.S. courts with juvenile jurisdiction. The estimates are derived from data provided to the National Center for Juvenile Justice's National Juvenile Court Data Archive by State and county agencies responsible for collecting and/or disseminating information on the processing of youth in juvenile courts.

Courts with juvenile jurisdiction also may handle other matters, including status offenses, i.e., behaviors that are considered an offense only when committed by a juvenile (e.g., running away from home), traffic violations, child support, adoption, and child abuse and neglect. However, the data presented in this edition of SOURCEBOOK focus on the courts' handling of juveniles charged with criminal law violations. These data are not the result of a uniform data collection effort. They are not derived from a complete census of juvenile courts or obtained from a probability sample of courts. These national estimates are developed using compatible information from courts that are able to provide data to the Archive. Data collection is an ongoing process and estimates for previous years are updated as more detailed case-level data are provided to the Archive.

The Archive collects data in two forms: court-level aggregate statistics and detailed case-level data. Court-level aggregate statistics are either abstracted from the annual reports of State and local courts or are contributed directly to the Archive. These data typically are counts of the delinquency and status offense cases handled by courts in a defined time period (calendar or fiscal year). Case-level data are usually generated by the automated client-tracking systems or case-reporting systems managed by juvenile courts or other juvenile justice agencies. These systems provide detailed data on the characteristics of each delinquency and status offense case handled by courts.

The structure and content of each data set is examined in order to design an automated restructuring procedure that will transform each jurisdiction's data into a common case-level format. The aggregation of these standardized case-level data files constitutes the national case-level database. The compiled data from jurisdictions that contribute only court-level statistics constitute the national court-level database. Together, these two multi-jurisdiction databases are used to generate national estimates of delinquency and status offense cases. Although juvenile courts with jurisdiction over more than 98% of the U.S. juvenile population contribute either case-level data or court-level aggregate statistics to the Archive, not all of this information can be used to generate the national estimates. To be used, the data must be in a compatible unit of count (i.e., case disposed), the data source must demonstrate a pattern of consistent reporting over time (at least 2 years), and the data file contributed must represent a complete count of cases disposed in a jurisdiction during a given year.

The national estimate of 1,657,533 total delinquency cases processed in 2000 was generated by data received from the following two sources:

(1) Detailed case-level data describing 969,757 delinquency cases that met the criteria for inclusion in the development of national estimates.

(2) Compatible court-level aggregate statistics on an additional 108,245 delinquency cases reported from jurisdictions that were unable to provide detailed case-level data.

In all, compatible case-level data and court-level statistics on delinquency cases were received from 1,991 jurisdictions containing 71% of the Nation's youth population at risk in 2000.

A multivariate weighting procedure is employed that adjusts for a number of factors related to juvenile court caseloads, e.g., the court's jurisdictional responsibilities (upper age); the size and demographic composition of the community; the age, sex, and race profile of the youth involved in juvenile court cases; and the offenses charged against the youth. The basic assumption underlying the estimation procedure is that similar legal and demographic factors shape the volume and characteristics of cases in reporting and nonreporting counties of comparable size and features.

The unit of count is a case disposed by a court with juvenile jurisdiction. A case represents a youth processed by a juvenile court on a new referral regardless of the number of charges contained in that referral. A youth charged with four burglaries in a single referral represents a single case, whereas a youth referred to court for three burglaries and referred again the following week on another burglary charge represents two cases, even if the court eventually merges the two referrals for efficient processing.

The offense coded was the most serious offense for which the youth was referred to court. Attempts to commit an offense were included under that offense category except attempted murder, which was included in the aggravated assault category.

The term disposed means that a definite action has been taken or that a plan of treatment has been selected or initiated. It does not necessarily mean that the case is closed or terminated in the sense that all contact between the court and the youth has ceased.

Definitions of terms

Adjudicated--Judicially determined (judged) to be a delinquent.

Delinquent act/offense--An act committed by a juvenile for which an adult could be prosecuted in a criminal court, but when committed by a juvenile is within the jurisdiction of the juvenile court.

Detention--The placement of a youth in a restrictive facility between referral to court intake and case disposition.

Dismissed--Cases dismissed (including those warned, counseled, and released) with no further action anticipated. Among cases handled informally, some cases may be dismissed by the juvenile court because the matter is being handled in another court.

Juvenile--Youth at or below the upper age of juvenile court jurisdiction. See Upper age of jurisdiction and Youth population at risk.

Nonpetitioned cases--Informally handled cases that duly authorized court personnel screen for adjustment without the filing of a formal petition. Such personnel include judges, referees, probation officers, other officers of the court, and/or an agency statutorily designated to conduct petition screening for the juvenile court.

Petitioned cases--Formally handled cases that appear on the official court calendar in response to the filing of a petition or other legal instrument requesting the court to adjudicate the youth delinquent or to waive (transfer) the youth to criminal court for processing as an adult.

Placement out-of-home--Cases in which youth were placed in a residential facility for delinquents, or were otherwise removed from their homes and placed elsewhere.

Probation--Cases in which youth were placed on informal/voluntary or formal/court-ordered probation or supervision.

Race--The race of the youth referred as determined by the youth or by court personnel.

White--A person having origins in any of the original peoples of Europe, North Africa, or the Middle East. (Nearly all Hispanics were included in the white racial category.)

Black--A person having origins in any of the black racial groups of Africa.

Other--A person having origins in any of the original peoples of North America, the Far East, Southeast Asia, the Indian Subcontinent, or the Pacific Islands.

Transfer/waiver--Cases that were waived or transferred to criminal court as the result of a waiver or transfer hearing in juvenile court. Cases are included in this category only if the transfer resulted from judicial actions alone. Some cases can be transferred to criminal court through the actions of prosecutors. However, these data report judicial waivers only. Excluded are cases that were transferred to criminal court under concurrent jurisdiction provisions.

Upper age of jurisdiction--The oldest age at which a juvenile court has original jurisdiction over an individual for law-violating behavior. For the time period covered by these data in 3 States (Connecticut, New York, and North Carolina) the upper age of jurisdiction was 15, in 10 States (Georgia, Illinois, Louisiana, Massachusetts, Michigan, Missouri, New Hampshire, South Carolina, Texas, and Wisconsin) the upper age of jurisdiction was 16, and in the remaining 37 States and the District of Columbia the upper age of jurisdiction was 17. It must be noted that in most States there are exceptions to the age criteria that place or permit youth at or below the State's upper age of jurisdiction to be under the original jurisdiction of the adult criminal court. For example, in most States if a youth of a certain age is charged with one of a defined list of what are commonly labeled "excluded offenses," the case must originate in the adult criminal court. In addition, in a number of States, the district attorney is given the discretion of filing certain cases either in the juvenile or in the criminal court. Therefore, while the upper age of jurisdiction is commonly recognized in all States, there are numerous exceptions to this age criterion.

Youth population at risk--For delinquency and status offense matters, this is the number of children from age 10 through the upper age of jurisdiction. In all States the upper age of jurisdiction is defined by statute. In most States individuals are considered adults when they reach their 18th birthday. Therefore, for these States, the delinquency and status offense youth population at risk would equal the number of children who are 10 through 17 years of age living within the geographical area serviced by the court.

Offenses within categories

Crimes against persons--This category includes criminal homicide, forcible rape, robbery, aggravated assault, simple assault, and other person offenses defined below.

Criminal homicide--Causing the death of another person without legal justification or excuse. Criminal homicide is a summary category, not a single codified offense. The term, in law, embraces all homicides where the perpetrator intentionally killed someone without legal justification, or accidentally killed someone as a consequence of reckless or grossly negligent conduct. It includes all conduct encompassed by the terms murder, nonnegligent (voluntary) manslaughter, negligent (involuntary) manslaughter, and vehicular manslaughter. The term is broader than the Crime Index category used in the Federal Bureau of Investigation's Uniform Crime Reports (UCR) in which murder and nonnegligent manslaughter does not include negligent manslaughter or vehicular manslaughter.

Forcible rape--Sexual intercourse or attempted sexual intercourse with a female against her will by force or threat of force. The term is used in the same sense as in the UCR Crime Index. (Some States have enacted gender-neutral rape or sexual assault statutes that prohibit forced sexual penetration of either sex. Data reported by these States do not distinguish between forcible rape of females as defined above and other sexual assaults.) Other violent sex offenses are included in the "other offenses against persons" category.

Robbery--Unlawful taking or attempted taking of property that is in the immediate possession of another by force or the threat of force. The term is used in the same sense as in the UCR Crime Index and includes forcible purse snatching.

Assault--Unlawful intentional inflicting, or attempted or threatened inflicting, of injury upon the person of another.

Aggravated assault--Unlawful intentional inflicting of serious bodily injury, or unlawful threat or attempt to inflict bodily injury or death, by means of a deadly or dangerous weapon with or without actual infliction of any injury. The term is used in the same sense as in the UCR Crime Index. It includes conduct included under the statutory names aggravated assault and battery, aggravated battery, assault with intent to kill, assault with intent to commit murder or manslaughter, atrocious assault, attempted murder, felonious assault, and assault with a deadly weapon.

Simple assault--Unlawful intentional inflicting, or attempted or threatened inflicting, of less than serious bodily injury without a deadly or dangerous weapon. The term is used in the same sense as in UCR reporting. Simple assault is often not distinctly named in statutes since it consists of all assaults not explicitly named and defined as serious. Unspecified assaults are included in the "other offenses against persons" category.

Other offenses against persons--This category includes kidnaping, violent sex acts other than forcible rape (e.g., incest, sodomy), custody interference, unlawful restraint, false imprisonment, reckless endangerment, harassment, and attempts to commit any such acts.

Crimes against property--This category includes burglary, larceny, motor vehicle theft, arson, vandalism, stolen property offenses, trespassing, and other property offenses defined below.

Burglary--Unlawful entry or attempted entry of any fixed structure, vehicle, or vessel used for regular residence, industry, or business, with or without force, with intent to commit a felony or larceny. The term is used in the same sense as in the UCR Crime Index.

Larceny--Unlawful taking or attempted taking of property (other than a motor vehicle) from the possession of another, by stealth, without force and without deceit, with intent to permanently deprive the owner of the property. This term is used in the same sense as in the UCR Crime Index. It includes shoplifting and purse snatching without force.

Motor vehicle theft--Unlawful taking, or attempted taking, of a self-propelled road vehicle owned by another, with the intent to deprive the owner of it permanently or temporarily. The term is used in the same sense as in the UCR Crime Index. It includes joyriding or unauthorized use of a motor vehicle as well as grand theft auto.

Arson--Intentional damaging or destruction by means of fire or explosion of the property of another without the owner's consent, or of any property with intent to defraud, or attempting the above acts. This term is used in the same sense as in the UCR Crime Index.

Vandalism--Destroying or damaging, or attempting to destroy or damage, the property of another without the owner's consent, or public property, except by burning.

Stolen property offenses--Unlawful and knowing receipt, purchase, or possession of stolen property, or attempting any of the above. The term is used in the same sense as the UCR category stolen property; buying, receiving, possessing.

Trespassing--Unlawful entry or attempted entry of the property of another with the intent to commit a misdemeanor, other than larceny, or without intent to commit a crime.

Other property offenses--This category includes extortion and all fraud offenses, such as forgery, counterfeiting, embezzlement, check or credit card fraud, and attempts to commit any such offenses.

Drug law violations--Unlawful sale, purchase, distribution, manufacture, cultivation, transport, possession, or use of a controlled or prohibited substance or drug, or drug paraphernalia, or attempts to commit these acts. Sniffing of glue, paint, gasoline, and other inhalants also are included; therefore, the term is broader than the UCR category drug abuse violations.

Offenses against public order--This category includes weapons offenses, nonviolent sex offenses, nonstatus liquor law violations, disorderly conduct, obstruction of justice, and other offenses against public order as defined below.

Weapons offenses--Unlawful sale, distribution, manufacture, alteration, transportation, possession, or use of a deadly or dangerous weapon, or accessory, or attempt to commit any of these acts. The term is used in the same sense as the UCR category weapons; carrying, possessing, etc.

Sex offenses--All offenses having a sexual element, not involving violence. The term combines the meaning of the UCR categories prostitution and commercialized vice and sex offenses. It includes offenses such as statutory rape, indecent exposure, prostitution, solicitation, pimping, lewdness, fornication, and adultery.

Liquor law violations, not status--Being in a public place while intoxicated through consumption of alcohol, or intake of a controlled substance or drug. It includes public intoxication, drunkenness, and other liquor law violations. It does not include driving under the influence. The term is used in the same sense as the UCR category of the same name. (Some States treat public drunkenness of juveniles as a status offense, rather than delinquency and therefore would not be included in the data presented. Where a person who is publicly intoxicated performs acts that cause a disturbance, he or she may be charged with disorderly conduct.)

Disorderly conduct--Unlawful interruption of the peace, quiet, or order of a community, including offenses such as disturbing the peace, vagrancy, loitering, unlawful assembly, and riot.

Obstruction of justice--This category includes intentionally obstructing court or law enforcement efforts in the administration of justice, acting in a way calculated to lessen the authority or dignity of the court, failing to obey the lawful order of a court, and violations of probation or parole other than technical violations, which do not consist of the commission of a crime or are not prosecuted as such. It includes contempt, perjury, obstructing justice, bribing witnesses, failure to report a crime, and nonviolent resisting arrest.

Other offenses against public order--This category includes other offenses against government administration or regulation, e.g., escape from confinement, bribery, gambling, fish and game violations, hitchhiking, health violations, false fire alarms, and immigration violations.

Appendix 15

Correctional Populations in the United States Survey methodology, definitions of terms, and jurisdictional explanatory notes

Note: The following information has been excerpted from U.S. Department of Justice, Bureau of Justice Statistics, *Correctional Populations in the United States, 1997*, NCJ 177613 (Washington, DC: U.S. Department of Justice, 2000); *Prisoners in 2003*, Bulletin NCJ 205335 (Washington, DC: U.S. Department of Justice, November 2004), pp. 10-12; and *Probation and Parole in the United States, 2003*, Bulletin NCJ 205336 (Washington, DC: U.S. Department of Justice, July 2004), pp. 7, 8. Non-substantive editorial adaptations have been made.

Survey methodology for prisoner data

The Bureau of Justice Statistics (BJS), with the U.S. Census Bureau as collection agent, obtains yearend and midyear counts of prisoners from departments of correction in the 50 States and the Federal Bureau of Prisons through the National Prisoner Statistics (NPS) program. In an effort to collect comparable data from all jurisdictions, NPS distinguishes prisoners in custody from those under jurisdiction. To have custody of a prisoner, a State must hold that person in one of its facilities. To have jurisdiction means that a State has legal authority over the prisoner. Prisoners under a State's jurisdiction may be in the custody of a local jail, another State's prison, or other correctional facility. Some States are unable to provide both custody and jurisdiction counts.

Excluded from NPS counts are persons confined in locally administered confinement facilities who are under the jurisdiction of local authorities. NPS counts include all prisoners in State-operated facilities in Alaska, Connecticut, Delaware, Hawaii, Rhode Island, and Vermont, which have combined jail-prison systems.

As of Dec. 31, 2001, the transfer of responsibility for sentenced felons from the District of Columbia to the Federal Bureau of Prisons was completed. The District of Columbia no longer operates a prison system and has been excluded from NPS.

In each jurisdiction, the questionnaire was completed by a central agency reporting for institutions within the correctional system. This procedure was also used by the Federal Bureau of Prisons in supplying data on Federal institutions. Because the information was derived from a complete enumeration rather than a survey, the statistical data are not affected by sampling error. Response errors were held to a minimum by means of a systematic telephone followup and, where necessary, other control procedures. Thus, the yearend counts are generally considered reliable. Because of the absence of standardized administrative and record keeping practices from State to State, the data for admissions and releases are not always entirely comparable across jurisdictions.

Many States revise the yearend number reported for the previous year. Those revisions are made in the total, not the detail. For example, the number of blacks, whites, and members of other races for 1996 were not changed by a State in 1997 to equal its revised 1996 total.

National Prisoner Statistics category definitions

Jurisdiction population--Includes all prisoners under jurisdiction of State correctional authorities on December 31 regardless of location. Does not include other jurisdictions' prisoners (for example, prisoners from other States, pretrial detainees) merely housed in prisons.

Custody population--Includes all prisoners in the State's custody, that is, housed in State correctional facilities on December 31. Does not include State prisoners housed outside State prison facilities; does include other jurisdictions' prisoners (for example, prisoners from other States, the courts, local jails) housed in the State's facilities.

Admissions

New court commitments--Includes all prisoners who were admitted with new sentences, that is, these prisoners were not readmitted for any sentences for which they had already served some prison time. This category includes probation violators entering prison for the first time on the probated offenses. Does not include parole violators with new sentences.

Parole violators with new sentences--Includes all parolees returned with new sentences.

Other conditional release violators with new sentences--Includes all individuals on conditional release (other than parole) who are returned with new sentences, for example, returns from supervised mandatory release, from shock probation, etc.

Parole violators only, no new sentences--Includes all parolees returned only for formal revocations of parole that were not accompanied by new sentences. If the parole was not formally revoked, that is, the parolee was held only temporarily pending a hearing, no admission occurred for NPS purposes.

Other conditional release violators only, no new sentences--Same as above, substituting conditional release violator for parole violator.

Transfers from other jurisdictions--Includes all prisoners transferred from another jurisdiction to a State's jurisdiction to continue sentences already in force. Does not include admissions if State does not acquire jurisdiction. Does not include movements from prison to prison within State.

Absent without leave (AWOL) returns, with or without new sentences--Includes all returns from AWOL, that is, failures to return from authorized temporary absences such as work furlough, study release, mercy furlough, or other authorized temporary absence.

Escapee returns, with or without new sentences--Includes all returns from escape, that is, unlawful departures from a State correctional facility or from the custody of State correctional personnel.

Returns from appeal/bond--Includes all prisoners reinstated to correctional jurisdiction from long-term jurisdictional absences on appeal or bond. Does not include returns from short-term movements (less than 30 days) to court (that is, where the State retains jurisdiction).

Other admissions--Includes all other admissions not covered by the above categories.

Releases

Unconditional--An unconditional release occurs only if the released prisoner cannot be imprisoned for any sentence for which he/she was in prison.

Expirations of sentence--Includes all prisoners whose maximum court sentences minus credits have been served.

Commutation--Includes all prisoners whose maximum sentences have been changed (lowered) to time served to allow immediate unconditional release.

Other unconditional release--Includes all other unconditional releases not covered by the above categories.

Conditional--A conditional release occurs if the released prisoner, upon violating the conditions of release, can be imprisoned again for any of the sentences for which he/she was in prison.

Probation--Includes all prisoners who have been placed under probation supervision and conditionally released; includes all shock probation (split sentence) releases.

Supervised mandatory release--Includes all prisoners who must, by law, be conditionally released. This type of release may also be called mandatory conditional release.

Parole--Includes all prisoners conditionally released to parole.

Other conditional release--Includes all other conditional releases not covered by the above categories.

Death:

Execution--Self-explanatory.

Acquired immune deficiency syndrome (AIDS)--The immediate cause of death in AIDS mortalities may be Pneumocystis Carinii Pneumonia, Kaposi's Sarcoma, or other diseases related to HIV infection.

Illness/natural causes--Self-explanatory. AIDS-related deaths not included in this category.

Suicide--Self-explanatory.

Accidental injury to self--Includes all prisoners who accidentally cause their own deaths (for example, a fall from a ladder, mishandling electrical equipment).

Caused by another--Includes all prisoners whose deaths were caused accidentally or intentionally by another prisoner or prison personnel.

Other deaths--Includes all other deaths not covered by the above categories.

Race

Classification by race often depends on the reporting program and the State. A few States reported two categories: white and nonwhite. A few others categorized Hispanic offenders as belonging to "other race." The number of persons with certain racial backgrounds were sometimes estimated.

White--Persons having origin in any of the original peoples of Europe, North Africa, or the Middle East.

Black--Persons having origin in any of the black racial groups of Africa.

American Indian or Alaska Native--Persons having origin in any of the original peoples of North America, who maintain cultural identification through tribal affiliation or community recognition.

Asian or Pacific Islander--Persons having origin in any of the original peoples of the Far East, Southeast Asia, the Indian Subcontinent, or the Pacific Islands. This area includes, for example, China, India, Japan, Korea, the Philippine Islands, and Samoa.

Other--Any other race not covered by the above categories.

Not known--Any prisoner whose racial origin is unknown by the reporting jurisdiction.

Ethnic origin

A person of Hispanic origin may be of any race; however, a few States treat the ethnic category as a racial one. Reporting officials usually rely on self-definition, but some States classify according to surname.

Hispanic--Persons of Mexican, Puerto Rican, Cuban, Central or South American, or other Spanish culture or origin, regardless of race.

Not Hispanic--Persons not covered by the above category.

Not known--Any prisoner whose ethnic origin is unknown by the reporting jurisdiction.

Explanatory notes for 2003 prisoner data

Alaska--Prisons and jails form one integrated system. All NPS data include jail and prison populations. Counts exclude individuals in electronic and special monitoring programs.

Arizona--Population counts are based on custody data. Counts exclude 174 sentenced prisoners housed in contracted local jails who were awaiting transfer to the Department of Corrections.

California--Population counts include felons and civil addicts who are temporarily absent, such as in court, jail, or hospital.

Colorado--Population counts include 247 male and 8 female prisoners in the Youthful Offender System.

Connecticut--Prisons and jails form one integrated system. All NPS data include jail and prison populations.

Delaware--Prisons and jails form one integrated system. All NPS data include jail and prison populations. Jurisdiction counts exclude prisoners housed in other State's facilities.

District of Columbia--The District of Columbia is no longer counted as a prison system because the 1997 Revitalization Act transferred responsibility for housing sentenced felons to the Federal Bureau of Prisons. For comparisons with previous years, jurisdiction and custody counts in the District of Columbia were 2,692 on Dec. 31, 2001 and 3,241 on Dec. 31, 2002.

Federal--Custody counts include prisoners housed in privately operated secure facilities under contract with the Federal Bureau of Prisons or with a State or local government that has an intergovernmental agreement. Custody counts exclude offenders housed under home confinement.

Florida--Population counts for Dec. 31, 2002 are based on custody data, including prisoners in privately operated facilities and are not comparable to 2003 data.

Georgia--Population counts are based on custody data, including prisoners in privately operated facilities.

Hawaii--Prisons and jails form one integrated system. All NPS data include jail and prison populations.

Illinois--Population counts are based on jurisdiction data. Counts of prisoners with a sentence of more than 1 year include an undetermined number with a sentence of 1 year.

Iowa--Population counts are based on custody data. Counts of prisoners with a sentence of more than 1 year include an undetermined number with a sentence of 1 year or less.

Kansas--Population counts of prisoners with a sentence of more than 1 year include an undetermined number with a sentence of 1 year or less.

Louisiana--Counts are as of Dec. 29, 2003. Population counts include 15,173 males and 1,376 females housed in local jails as a result of a partnership with the Louisiana Sheriffs' Association and local authorities.

Massachusetts--By law, offenders may be sentenced to terms of up to 2 1/2 years in locally operated jails. Such offenders are included in counts and rates for local jails. About 6,200 prisoners with sentences of more than 1 year were held in local jails in 2003.

Michigan--Jurisdiction counts exclude 42 prisoners held in local jails.

Montana--Counts include 263 prisoners under intensive supervision in the community.

Nevada--Population counts are as of Jan. 1, 2004.

New Jersey--Population counts of prisoners with a sentence of more than 1 year include an undetermined number with a sentence of 1 year.

Ohio--Population counts of prisoners with a sentence of more than 1 year include an undetermined number with a sentence of 1 year or less.

Oklahoma--Population counts of prisoners with a sentence of more than 1 year include an undetermined number with a sentence of 1 year. The female count dropped significantly because the Department of Corrections bought a private prison.

Oregon--Prisoners with less than a 1 year maximum sentence remain under the control of local counties.

Rhode Island--Prisons and jails form one integrated system. All NPS data include jail and prison populations.

South Carolina--Population counts include 66 prisoners either unsentenced or under other confinement status.

Tennessee--Population counts of prisoners with a sentence of more than 1 year include an undetermined number with a sentence of 1 year.

Texas--Jurisdiction counts include prisoners serving time in a pre-parole transfer or intermediary sanctions facility, substance abuse felony punishment facility, temporary releases to counties, and paper-ready prisoners in local jails.

Vermont--Prisons and jails form one integrated system. All NPS data include jail and prison populations.

Washington--A recently revised law allows increasing numbers of prisoners with sentences of less than 1 year to be housed in prison.

Capital punishment explanatory notes

The data reported for capital punishment may differ from data collected by other organizations. The differences occur for the following reasons:

(1) Prisoners under sentence of death are initially added to the National Prisoner Statistics (NPS) counts when they enter correctional facilities rather than when judges pronounce sentence.

(2) Following the year when prisoners are first counted, their admissions or releases as a result of court order are attributed to the year for the sentence or court order. For example, a prisoner sentenced in November 1995 entering prison custody in January 1996 would be counted as an admission in the 1996 report; the 1997 report would count him or her as being under sentence of death at yearend 1995. Similarly, a prisoner whose sentence is overturned in 1994 but who remains in the count until 1996 when the court's decision is reported would be subtracted from the 1994 and 1995 counts.

(3) NPS counts of persons under sentence of death are always for the last day of a calendar year and will differ from more recent counts.

Survey methodology for probation and parole data

These data are based on yearend counts of persons on probation and parole and entries and exits occurring during the calendar year. The data were collected by the U.S. Department of Justice, Bureau of Justice Statistics through standard questionnaires mailed to the Nation's probation and parole agencies.

Counts of probationers include only adults who have been placed under the supervision of a probation agency as part of a court order, regardless of whether convicted. Both active and inactive supervision cases are included. The data exclude juveniles and persons on bench, court, or summary probation who have not been placed under the supervision of a probation agency.

Counts of parolees include only adults who have been conditionally released to parole supervision, whether by a parole board decision or by mandatory conditional release. Both active and inactive supervision cases are included. Parolees sentenced to incarceration regardless of sentence length are included. The data excluded juveniles. For both probation and parole counts the following provisions apply:

(1) For interstate compacts, counts include a State's probationers and parolees sent to another State for supervision, but exclude probationers and parolees supervised for another State.

(2) For entries, individuals entering into the probation or parole system more than once during the year are counted as multiple entries.

(3) For exits, individuals exiting from the probation or parole system more than once during the year are counted as multiple exits.

2003 probation and parole data

The 2003 Probation and Parole Surveys provide a count of the total persons supervised in the community on Jan. 1 and Dec. 31, 2003, and a count of the number entering and leaving supervision during the year. These surveys cover all 50 States, the District of Columbia, and the Federal system.

Data for the Federal system are from the Administrative Office of the United States Courts as provided to the BJS Federal Justice Statistics Program.

Because many States update their population counts, the Jan. 1, 2003 numbers may differ from those previously published for Dec. 31, 2002.

The 2003 Annual Probation Survey was sent to 469 respondents--34 central State reporters, the District of Columbia, the Federal system, and 433 separate State, county, or court agencies. States with multiple reporters were Alabama (3), Arizona (2), Colorado (9), Florida (43), Georgia (5), Idaho (2), Kentucky (3), Michigan (128), Missouri (2), Montana (4), New Mexico (2), Ohio (187), Oklahoma (3), Tennessee (3), Washington (35), and West Virginia (2). One local agency in Ohio did not provide data. For this agency, the Dec. 31, 2002 population count was used as the Jan. 1, 2003 and Dec. 31, 2003 counts.

Since 1997, the probation survey coverage has been expanded to include 186 additional agencies previously excluded from the survey. At yearend 2003, 193,607 probationers were under the supervision of these agencies. For year-to-year comparisons, use total counts based on the same reporting agencies--3,266,837 in 1997 to compare with the final 1996 counts; 3,417,613 in 1998 to compare with final 1997; and 3,772,773 in 1999 to compare with final 1998.

Entries to probation supervision were estimated by the Source for nonreporting agencies in recent years. Reported entries for 2003 were 1,918,470.

The 2003 Annual Parole Survey was sent to 54 respondents--52 central reporters, the California Youth Authority, and 1 municipal agency. States with multiple reporters were Alabama (2) and California (2).

Federal parole as defined here includes supervised release, parole, military parole, special parole, and mandatory release.

Total correctional population

To estimate the total correctional population in tables 6.1 and 6.2, the four correctional populations are assumed to contain individuals with only one status at a time. This assumption may not be valid. Multiple correctional statuses may occur because (1) probation and parole agencies are not always notified of new arrests, jail entries, or prison admissions; (2) absconders on agency caseloads in one jurisdiction may actually be incarcerated in another jurisdiction; and (3) individuals may be admitted to jail or prison before formal revocation hearings by a probation or parole agency.

By adding the number of persons on probation, on parole, in jail, and in prison, some persons may be counted more than once; consequently, the sum will be a slight overestimate of the total number of persons under correctional supervision at any one time.

Military corrections data

In 1994 the U.S. Department of Defense Corrections Council established an annual military confinement report. The council, comprised of representatives from each branch of military service, adopted a standardized questionnaire with a common set of definitions. BJS obtains yearend counts of persons in the custody of U.S. military authorities from these reports. The annual confinement report provides yearend counts of persons held in U.S. military confinement facilities inside and outside the continental United States, by branch of service, sex, race, and Hispanic origin, conviction status and sentence length, and offense. The confinement report also includes the number of facilities and their design and rated capacities.

List of index reference terms

Abortion
AIDS
Air piracy
Alcohol
Aliens
Amphetamines
Antitrust
Appeals
Arrests
Arson
Assault
Attitudes
Attorney general
Auto theft
Bail
Barbiturates
Bombings
Bribery
Budget
Burglary
Capital punishment
Cigarettes
Clearance rates
Clemency
Cocaine
Commutations
Compensation
Controlled substances
Corrections
Counsel
Counterfeiting
Courts
Courts-martial
Crime
Curfew and loitering laws
Death penalty
Deaths
Defendants
Delinquency
Detention, pretrial
Disorderly conduct
Disposition of defendants
Driving while intoxicated
Drug abuse violations
Drug Enforcement Administration
Drugs
Embezzlement
Employment
Executions
Expenditures
Explosives
Extortion
Family and children
Felonies
Firearms
Fires
Forgery and counterfeiting
Fraud
Gambling
Grand jury
Guilty pleas

Guns
Handguns
Hashish
Heroin
Homicide
Households experiencing crime
Immigration
Immunity
Internal Revenue Service
Jails
Judges
Juries
Juvenile corrections
Juvenile courts
Juvenile delinquency
Juvenile institutions
Kidnaping
Larceny-theft
Law enforcement
Lawyers
Liquor laws
Loansharking
Magistrates
Marijuana
Misdemeanors
Motor vehicle theft
Murder and nonnegligent manslaughter
Narcotic drug laws
National Crime Victimization Survey
Obscenity
Offenders
Offenses known to police
Opinion polls
Pardons
Parole
Payroll
Penitentiary
Personnel
Petit jury
Pocket-picking
Police
Pornography
Prisoners
Prisons
Probation
Property crime
Prosecution
Prostitution and commercialized vice
Public defense
Public officials
Public opinion
Purse-snatching
Racketeering
Rape, forcible
Rehabilitation programs
Revocation
Robbery
Runaways
Seizures
Self-reported criminal activity
Sentences
Sex offenses
Shoplifting
Status offenders
Stolen property
Suicide
Suspicion
Tax law violations

Terrorism
Traffic violations
Trials
Uniform Crime Reports
U.S. Air Force
U.S. Army
U.S. Attorneys
U.S. Coast Guard
U.S. Courts of Appeal
U.S. Customs Service
U.S. District Courts
U.S. Marine Corps
U.S. Marshals Service
U.S. Navy
U.S. Pardon Attorney
U.S. Postal Inspection Service
U.S. Secret Service
U.S. Supreme Court
Vagrancy
Vandalism
Vehicle theft
Victimization
Violent crime
Weapons
Wiretaps
Writ of certiorari

Index

ABORTION
    Public opinion, 2.2, 2.91, 2.100, 2.101
        As important problem, 2.2
        College freshmen, 2.91
        Legality, 2.100, 2.101
AIDS
    Among State and Federal prisoners, 6.74-6.78
        Deaths, 6.76-6.78
        Sex, 6.75
        Total cases, 6.74, 6.75
AIR PIRACY
    See Terrorism
ALCOHOL
    Arrestees reporting use, 4.32
    Arrests for alcohol-related offenses, 4.1, 4.3, 4.6-4.16, 4.27, 4.28
        Age, 4.6, 4.7, 4.9, 4.10, 4.12, 4.14, 4.16
        Cities, 4.3, 4.11, 4.12
        Race, 4.10, 4.12, 4.14, 4.16
        Rates, 4.3
        Rural counties, 4.3, 4.15, 4.16
        Sex, 4.8, 4.9, 4.11, 4.13, 4.15
        Size of place, 4.3
        State, 4.28
        Suburban areas, 4.3, 4.13, 4.14
    College students, 3.77-3.83, 3.85
    Court cases, Federal, 5.10, 5.24, 5.25
        Number of defendants
            Disposed, 5.24
            Sentenced, 5.25
    Driving after drinking, 3.55, 3.56, 3.102
    Driving while intoxicated
        Characteristics of statutes, 1.112, 1.113
            Blood alcohol tests, 1.112, 1.113
        Fatal accidents, 3.103, 3.104
        Federal parks, 3.116
        Jail inmates, current offense, 6.19, 6.20
    Involvement in automobile crashes, 3.103-3.105
        Fatalities, 3.103-3.105
    Military personnel, use, 3.91
    Problems or criminal behavior related to use, 3.85, 3.99, 3.100
    Public opinion, 2.3, 2.77, 2.78, 2.80-2.82, 2.84-2.86
        As important problem, 2.3
        Availability, 2.84
        Disapproval of use, 2.85, 2.86
        Harmfulness, 2.77, 2.80-2.82
        Students, 2.80, 2.84, 2.86
        Teenagers' perceptions of those who use, 2.78
    Treatment facilities, 6.62

ALCOHOL (continued)
    Use
        Among arrestees, 4.32
        Among college students, 3.77-3.83, 3.85
        Among drivers in fatal accidents, 3.104
        Among jail inmates prior to offense, 6.22
        Among military personnel, 3.91
        Among students, 3.55-3.57, 3.62, 3.63, 3.68-3.72
            At school, 3.55, 3.57
            Driving after use, 3.55, 3.56
            Frequency, 3.63
        As source of family trouble, 3.99, 3.100
        At school, 3.55, 3.57
        Binge drinking, 3.77-3.81, 3.83, 3.98
        Driving after drinking, 3.102
        Problems or criminal behavior related to use, 3.80, 3.82, 3.85, 3.99, 3.100
        Self-reported, 3.49-3.51, 3.53, 3.55-3.57, 3.62-3.64, 3.68-3.72, 3.74-3.81, 3.83, 3.85-3.88, 3.95-3.100, 3.102
            Binge drinking, 3.77-3.81, 3.83, 3.98
            College students, 3.71, 3.72, 3.77-3.81, 3.83, 3.85
            Driving after drinking, 3.102
            High school seniors, 3.49-3.51, 3.53, 3.63, 3.64, 3.68, 3.69
                Driving under the influence, 3.49-3.51, 3.53
            High school students, 3.55-3.57, 3.62, 3.63, 3.70
            National households, 3.86-3.88
            Problems or criminal behavior related to use, 3.99, 3.100
            Young adults, 3.74-3.76, 3.86-3.88
    See also:
        Arrests
        Drugs
        Public opinion
ALIENS
    See Immigration
AMPHETAMINES
    See Drugs
    See Narcotic drug laws
ANTITRUST
    Community supervision, Federal offenders, 6.4
    Court cases, Federal, 5.10, 5.13, 5.17, 5.19, 5.26-5.29, 5.31-5.37, 5.41
        Cases filed, 5.10, 5.41
        Citizens and non-citizens, 5.35
        Convictions, 5.17
        Dispositions, 5.17

ARSON, Court cases, Federal (continued)
        Defendant characteristics, 5.26, 5.27
        Method of conviction, 5.17, 5.34
        Organizations sentenced, 5.33
        Pretrial action, 5.13
        Sentences, 5.29, 5.31-5.33
        Sentencing guideline cases, 5.26-5.29, 5.31-5.36
    Parole and supervised release, 6.4, 6.70
    Probation, 6.4, 6.8
    Sentences, 5.19, 5.26, 5.27, 5.29, 5.31-5.34, 5.36
        Organizations, 5.33
APPEALS
    Federal
        Civil
            Commenced in U.S. Courts of Appeals, 5.66
            Filed in U.S. Courts of Appeals, 5.67
            Writ of certiorari to U.S. Supreme Court, 5.70
        Criminal
            Filed in U.S. Courts of Appeals, 5.67
            Writ of certiorari to U.S. Supreme Court, 5.70
        Prisoner petitions
            Filed in U.S. Courts of Appeals, 5.67
            Filed in U.S. District Courts, 5.65
ARRESTS
    Age, 4.4-4.7, 4.9, 4.10, 4.12, 4.14, 4.16, 4.22-4.24
    Alcohol-related, 4.1, 4.3, 4.6-4.16, 4.27, 4.28
    Alcohol use among arrestees, 4.32
    At airports, 3.177
    Cities, 4.3, 4.11, 4.12, 4.19, 4.21
    Clearance of offenses by arrest, 4.19, 4.20, 4.22-4.24
    Drug Enforcement Administration, 4.40, 4.41
    Drug-related, 4.1, 4.3, 4.6-4.16, 4.29, 4.38, 4.40, 4.41
        Region, 4.29
        State, 4.38
    Drug treatment, arrestees, 4.31
    Drug use among arrestees, 4.30
    Federal, 4.33-4.35, 4.41
    Juveniles, 4.25, 4.26
        Taken into police custody, 4.25, 4.26
    Number of, 4.1, 4.3, 4.5-4.16, 4.24, 4.35, 4.38
    Offense charged, 4.1, 4.3, 4.5-4.16, 4.19, 4.22, 4.24, 4.33-4.35
    Percent of population arrested, 4.4
    Property offenses, 4.5, 4.16, 4.20, 4.21, 4.35
    Race, 4.10, 4.12, 4.14, 4.16
    Rates, 4.3, 4.17, 4.18
    Region, 4.17, 4.18

ARRESTS (continued)
    Resulting from wiretap, 5.5
    Rural counties, 4.15, 4.16, 4.19, 4.21, 4.22
    Sex, 4.8, 4.9, 4.11, 4.13, 4.15
    Size of place, 4.3, 4.19, 4.21, 4.22
    State, 4.5
    Suburban areas, 4.13, 4.14, 4.19, 4.21, 4.22
    Time to sentencing, State courts, 5.50
    U.S. Postal Inspection Service, 5.74
    Violent offenses, 4.5, 4.17, 4.20, 4.21, 4.35
    See also:
        Specific offenses (e.g., Assault, Motor vehicle theft)

ARSON
    Arrests, 4.1-4.3, 4.5-4.16, 4.18, 4.24, 4.33
        Age, 4.5-4.7, 4.9, 4.10, 4.12, 4.14, 4.16, 4.24
        Cities, 4.3, 4.11, 4.12
        Clearance by arrest, 4.24
        Federal, 4.33
        Race, 4.10, 4.12, 4.14, 4.16
        Rates, 4.2, 4.3, 4.18
        Region, 4.18
        Rural counties, 4.15, 4.16
        Sex, 4.8, 4.9, 4.11, 4.13, 4.15
        Size of place, 4.3
        State, 4.5
        Suburban areas, 4.13, 4.14
        Type of target, 4.24
    Community supervision, Federal offenders, 6.4
    Court cases, Federal, 5.17, 5.26-5.29, 5.31, 5.32, 5.34-5.36
        Citizens and non-citizens, 5.35
        Convictions, 5.17
        Defendant characteristics, 5.26, 5.27
        Dispositions, 5.17
        Method of conviction, 5.17, 5.34
        Sentences, 5.26, 5.27, 5.29, 5.31, 5.32
        Sentencing guideline cases, 5.26-5.29, 5.31, 5.32, 5.34-5.36
    Deaths, civilian, 3.166, 3.167
    Hate crimes, 3.112
    Jail inmates
        Current offense, 6.19, 6.20
    Juveniles in custody, 6.10
    Offenses known to police, 3.110, 3.112, 3.115, 3.116, 3.166-3.169, 4.24
        Cities, 3.110
        Civilian deaths, 3.166, 3.167
        Federal parks, 3.115, 3.116
        Hate crimes, 3.112
        Property loss and damage, 3.166
        Type of target and structure, 3.168, 3.169, 4.24
        Vehicle fires, 3.167, 4.24
    Parole and supervised release, 6.4, 6.70, 6.71
    Prisoners
        Current offense, 6.56
        Recidivism, 6.50

ARSON (continued)
    Probation, 6.4, 6.8
    Self-reported, 3.43-3.45
        High school seniors, 3.43-3.45
    Sentences, 5.19, 5.29, 5.31, 5.32
    Suspicious structure fires, 3.166, 3.167
        Civilian deaths, 3.166, 3.167
        Property loss and damage, 3.166
        Vehicle fires, 3.167

ASSAULT
    Arrests, 4.1-4.3, 4.5-4.17, 4.19, 4.22, 4.33, 5.50
        Age, 4.5-4.7, 4.9, 4.10, 4.14, 4.16, 4.22
        Cities, 4.3, 4.11, 4.12, 4.19, 4.22
        Clearance by arrest, 4.19, 4.22
        Federal, 4.33
        Race, 4.10, 4.12, 4.14, 4.16
        Rates, 4.2, 4.3, 4.17
        Region, 4.17
        Rural counties, 4.3, 4.15, 4.16, 4.19, 4.21
        Sex, 4.8, 4.9, 4.11, 4.13, 4.15
        Size of place, 4.3, 4.19, 4.22
        State, 4.5
        Suburban areas, 4.3, 4.13, 4.14, 4.19, 4.22
        Time to sentencing, State courts, 5.50
    Basis for wiretaps, 5.3
    Community supervision, Federal offenders, 6.4
    Convictions
        Federal courts, 5.17
        Method of conviction, 5.17, 5.46, 5.50
        Number of, 5.44, 5.46
        Offender characteristics, 5.45
    Court cases, Federal, 5.10, 5.13, 5.17, 5.19, 5.24-5.29, 5.31, 5.32, 5.34-5.36, 5.67
        Appeals, 5.67
        Citizens and non-citizens, 5.35
        Convictions, 5.17
        Defendant characteristics, 5.26, 5.27
        Dispositions, 5.17, 5.24
        Method of conviction, 5.17, 5.34
        Sentences, 5.25, 5.29
        Sentencing guideline cases, 5.26-5.29, 5.31, 5.32, 5.34-5.36
    Court cases, State, 5.44-5.50
        Convictions, 5.44-5.46, 5.50
            Method of conviction, 5.46, 5.50
            Number of, 5.44
            Offender characteristics, 5.45
        Sentences, 5.47-5.50
            Length of sentence, 5.48
            Method of conviction, 5.50
            Time from arrest, 5.50
            Type of additional penalty, 5.49
    Court cases, urban counties, 5.51-5.60
        Arrests, 5.51
        Convictions, 5.57, 5.58
        Defendant characteristics, 5.52

ASSAULT, Court cases, urban counties (continued)
        Pretrial release, 5.54-5.56
        Prior convictions, 5.53
        Sentences, 5.59, 5.60
    Hate crimes, 3.112
    Jail inmates
        Current offense, 6.19, 6.20
    Juveniles in custody, 6.10
    Offenses known to police, 3.106-3.110, 3.112, 3.115, 3.116, 3.143, 3.144, 4.19
        Cities, 3.110, 4.19
        Federal parks, 3.115, 3.116
        Hate crimes, 3.112
        Rates, 3.106-3.108
        Region, 3.144
        Size of place, 3.107-3.109
        Type of weapon, 3.143, 3.144
    On law enforcement officers, 3.152, 3.153, 3.163-3.165
        Circumstances, 3.163, 3.164
        Type of weapon, 3.153, 3.163
        With injury, 3.153, 3.165
    Parole and supervised release, 6.4, 6.70, 6.71
    Prisoners
        Firearms possession during offense, 6.37
        Recidivism, 6.50, 6.51
        Time served, 6.44
    Probationers
        Number, 6.4
        Outcomes, 6.8
    Self-protective measures taken, 3.18, 3.20
    Self-reported, 3.43-3.45
        High school students, 3.43-3.45
    Sentences, 5.19, 5.25, 5.29, 5.31, 5.32, 5.47-5.50, 5.59, 5.60, 6.44, 6.58
        Federal courts, 5.19, 5.25, 5.29
        Length of sentence, 5.19, 5.48, 5.60, 6.44
        Method of conviction, 5.50
        Time from arrest, 5.50
        Time served, 6.44
        Type of collateral penalty, 5.49
        Type of sentence, 5.19, 5.47, 5.59
    Victimizations, 3.1-3.18, 3.20, 3.27-3.36, 3.42
        Age of victim, 3.4, 3.6, 3.7, 3.11
        Households experiencing, 3.27
        Lone-offender incidents, 3.28, 3.29
        Multiple-offender incidents, 3.30, 3.31
        Number, 3.1, 3.2, 3.5, 3.7-3.10
            Characteristics of victims, 3.5, 3.8, 3.9
        Place of occurrence, 3.32
        Race and ethnicity of victim, 3.4, 3.8-3.11
        Rates, 3.1-3.13
            Age of victim, 3.4, 3.6, 3.7, 3.11
            Family income of victim, 3.4, 3.12
            Locality of residence, 3.4, 3.13

Index 613

ASSAULT, Victimizations, Rates (continued)
    Race and ethnicity of victim, 3.4, 3.8-3.11
    Sex of victim, 3.4, 3.5, 3.7, 3.10
    Reporting to police, 3.33-3.36
        Reasons for not reporting, 3.35
        Reasons for reporting, 3.34
        Victim characteristics, 3.36
    Self-protective measures taken, 3.18, 3.20
    Sex of victim, 3.4, 3.5, 3.7, 3.10
    Victim-offender relationship, 3.14-3.18
        Type of weapon, 3.17
        Victim use of self-protection, 3.18
        Weapon use, 3.17
  See also:
    Violent crime

ATTITUDES
  See Public opinion

ATTORNEY GENERAL
  See Courts
  See Trials

AUTO THEFT
  See Motor vehicle theft

BAIL
  County court defendants, 5.55
  Federal defendants, 5.13, 5.15

BARBITURATES
  See Drugs
  See Narcotic drug laws

BOMBINGS
  Incidents known to police, 3.170-3.172
    Injuries and deaths, 3.170
    Property damage, 3.170
    State, 3.172
    Target, 3.171

BRIBERY
  Arrests, Federal, 4.33
  Basis for wiretap, 5.3
  Community supervision, Federal offenders, 6.4
  Court cases, Federal, 5.17, 5.24-5.29, 5.31-5.36
    Citizens and non-citizens, 5.35
    Convictions, 5.17
    Defendant characteristics, 5.26, 5.27
    Dispositions, 5.17
    Method of conviction, 5.17, 5.34
    Number of defendants
        Disposed, 5.24
        Sentenced, 5.25, 5.29
    Organizations sentenced, 5.33
    Sentences, 5.25, 5.29, 5.31-5.33, 6.58
    Sentencing guideline cases, 5.26-5.29, 5.31-5.36
  Parole and supervised release, 6.4, 6.70, 6.71
  Probation, 6.4
  Prisoners, Federal, 6.56
  Sentences, 5.25, 5.29, 5.31-5.33, 6.58
    Organizations, 5.33
    Time served, 6.58

BUDGET
  See Expenditures

BURGLARY
  Arrests, 4.1-4.3, 4.5-4.16, 4.18, 4.19, 4.22, 4.23, 4.33, 5.50
    Age, 4.5-4.7, 4.9, 4.10, 4.12, 4.14, 4.16, 4.22, 4.23
    Cities, 4.3, 4.11, 4.12, 4.19, 4.22
    Clearance by arrest, 4.19, 4.22
    Federal, 4.33
    Race, 4.10, 4.12, 4.14, 4.16
    Rates, 4.2, 4.3, 4.18
    Region, 4.18
    Rural counties, 4.3, 4.15, 4.16, 4.19, 4.22
    Sex, 4.8, 4.9, 4.11, 4.13, 4.15
    Size of place, 4.3, 4.19, 4.22
    State, 4.5
    Suburban areas, 4.3, 4.13, 4.14, 4.19, 4.22
    Time to sentencing, State courts, 5.50
  Basis for wiretap, 5.3
  Community supervision, Federal offenders, 6.4
  Convictions
    Federal courts, 5.17
    Method of conviction, 5.17, 5.46
    Number of, 5.17, 5.44, 5.46
    Offender characteristics, 5.45
  Court cases, Federal, 5.10, 5.13, 5.17, 5.19, 5.24-5.29, 5.31, 5.32, 5.34-5.36, 5.67
    Appeals, 5.67
    Citizens and non-citizens, 5.35
    Convictions, 5.17
    Defendant characteristics, 5.26, 5.27
    Dispositions, 5.17, 5.24
    Method of conviction, 5.17, 5.34
    Pretrial action, 5.13
    Sentences, 5.19, 5.25, 5.29, 5.31, 5.32
    Sentencing guideline cases, 5.26-5.29, 5.31, 5.32, 5.34-5.36
  Court cases, State, 5.44-5.50
    Convictions, 5.44-5.46, 5.50
        Method of conviction, 5.46, 5.50
        Number of, 5.44
        Offender characteristics, 5.45
    Sentences, 5.47-5.50
        Length of sentence, 5.48
        Method of conviction, 5.50
        Time from arrest, 5.50
        Type of additional penalty, 5.49
  Court cases, urban counties, 5.51-5.60
    Arrests, 5.51
    Convictions, 5.57, 5.58
    Defendant characteristics, 5.52
    Pretrial release, 5.54-5.56
    Prior convictions, 5.53
    Sentences, 5.59, 5.60
  Federal Bank Robbery and Incidental Crimes Statute, 3.149-3.151
    Deaths, injuries, and hostages, 3.151

BURGLARY (continued)
  Hate crimes, 3.112
  Jail inmates
    Current offense, 6.19, 6.20
  Juveniles in custody, 6.10
  Offenses known to police, 3.106-3.112, 3.115, 3.116, 3.145, 4.19
    Average loss, 3.111
    Cities, 3.110, 4.19
    Federal parks, 3.115, 3.116
    Hate crimes, 3.112
    Place and time of occurrence, 3.145
    Rates, 3.106-3.108
    Size of place, 3.107-3.109, 4.19
  Parole and supervised release, 6.4, 6.70, 6.71
  Prisoners
    Federal, time served, 6.58
    Recidivism, 6.50, 6.51
    Time served, 6.44
  Probationers
    Number, 6.4
    Outcomes, 6.8
  Sentences, 5.19, 5.25, 5.29, 5.31, 5.32, 5.47-5.50, 5.59, 5.60, 6.44, 6.58
    Federal courts, 5.19, 5.25, 6.58
    Fines, 5.32
    Incarceration, 5.29
    Length of sentence, 5.19, 5.31, 5.48, 5.60, 6.44
    Method of conviction, 5.50
    Probation, 5.29
    Restitution, 5.32
    Time served, 6.44, 6.58
    Type of collateral penalty, 5.49
    Type of sentence, 5.19, 5.47, 5.59
  Victimizations, 3.1-3.3, 3.21-3.27, 3.33-3.35
    Households experiencing, 3.27
    Locality of residence, 3.21, 3.25, 3.26
    Number, 3.1, 3.2, 3.22, 3.23
    Race and ethnicity of head of household, 3.22, 3.23, 3.26
    Rates, 3.1-3.3, 3.21-3.26
        Family income, 3.21, 3.24
        Locality of residence, 3.21, 3.25, 3.26
        Race and ethnicity of head of household, 3.22, 3.23, 3.26
    Reporting to police, 3.33-3.35
        Reasons for not reporting, 3.35
        Reasons for reporting, 3.34

CAPITAL PUNISHMENT
  Executions, 6.79, 6.82, 6.84-6.86
    Murder and death penalty trend, 6.79
    Offense, 6.86
    Race, 6.86
    Region, 6.82, 6.85
    State, 6.82, 6.84, 6.85
  Method of execution authorized, 6.87
  Movement of prisoners under sentence of death, 6.84
    Removed from death row, 6.84

CAPITAL PUNISHMENT (continued)
   Number of prisoners under sentence of death, 6.79-6.83
      Age, 6.81
      Murder and death penalty trend, 6.79
      Race and ethnicity, 6.80, 6.81, 6.83
      Region, 6.82
      Sex, 6.81, 6.83
      State, 6.80, 6.82
   Public opinion, 2.49-2.58, 2.93
      College freshmen, 2.93
      Deterrent effect, 2.57, 2.58
      Fairness of application, 2.54
      For murder, 2.49-2.53
      Reasons for favoring, 2.55
      Reasons for opposing, 2.56
      Selected groups, 2.53
      Versus life without parole, 2.49
CIGARETTES
   Public opinion
      Disapproval of use, 2.85
      Harmfulness, 2.79, 2.81
      Teenagers' perceptions of those who use, 2.78
   Use
      Among students, 3.55, 3.57, 3.62
      At school, 3.55, 3.57
CLEARANCE RATES
   See Arrests
   See Offenses known to police
   See Specific offenses (e.g., Assault, Motor vehicle theft, etc.)
CLEMENCY
   Federal applications, 5.72
COCAINE
   See Drugs
   See Narcotic drug laws
COMMUTATIONS
   Federal applications granted, 5.72
   See also:
      Clemency
COMPENSATION
   See Employment
CONTROLLED SUBSTANCES
   See Drug Enforcement Administration
   See Drugs
   See Narcotic drug laws
CORRECTIONS
   Correctional officers, Federal, 1.104, 1.108
   Correctional population, total, 6.1, 6.2
   Education programs, 1.109, 6.45, 6.46
      Educational attainment, 6.45
      Programs and participation, 1.109, 6.46
   Employment and payroll, 1.17, 1.19, 1.21-1.24
      Federal, 1.17, 1.21
      Local, 1.17, 1.19, 1.21, 1.22
      State, 1.17, 1.19, 1.21-1.24
   Expenditures, 1.2-1.4, 1.6-1.11
      Federal, 1.2-1.4
      Local, 1.2-1.4, 1.6
      State, 1.2-1.4, 1.6, 1.8, 1.10, 1.11

CORRECTIONS (continued)
   Federal budget authorities and outlays, 1.12
   Federal institutions
      AIDS and HIV cases, 6.74-6.77
         Deaths, 6.76, 6.77
      Capacity, 1.102, 1.106
      Characteristics of correctional personnel, 1.104, 1.106-1.108
         Correctional officers, 1.104, 1.108
         Staff, 1.104, 1.106, 1.107
      Characteristics of facilities, 1.102, 1.103, 1.106
      Characteristics of prisoners, 6.31, 6.34, 6.53-6.56
         Type of offense, 6.56
      Education programs, 1.109, 6.45, 6.46
         Educational attainment, 6.45
         Programs and participation, 1.109, 6.46
      Number of prisoners, 6.13, 6.28, 6.30, 6.31, 6.34, 6.53, 6.54
         Sex, 6.53, 6.54
      Number of prisons, 1.102, 1.103
      Population, 1.106, 6.31, 6.34
      Rate of imprisonment, 6.28, 6.29
      Security level, 1.102, 1.106, 6.55
      Type of facility, 1.102, 1.103, 1.106
   Jails
      AIDS and HIV cases, 6.26, 6.27
      Average daily population, 6.14
      Capacity, 1.98, 6.14
      Education programs, 1.109, 6.45, 6.46
         Educational attainment, 6.45
         Programs and participation, 1.109, 6.46
      Employees, 1.99-1.101, 1.105
      Inmate to employee ratio, 1.98
      Inmates, 1.105, 6.13-6.16, 6.18-6.24
         Alcohol use, 6.22
         Conviction status, 6.18, 6.19
         Current offense, 6.19, 6.20
         Drug use, 6.21
         Family background, 6.23
         Number, 6.1, 6.13-6.16, 6.18
         Race and ethnicity, 6.18, 6.20
         Sex, 6.18, 6.20
      Number of jails, 1.98
      Privately operated jails, 1.105
   Military confinement facilities, 6.64
   Population, 6.1
   Private correctional facilities, 1.102-1.104, 6.31
   State institutions
      AIDS and HIV cases, 6.74-6.78
         Deaths, 6.76-6.78
      Capacity, 1.102
      Characteristics of correctional personnel, 1.104
         Correctional officers, 1.104
         Staff, 1.104

CORRECTIONS, State institutions (continued)
      Characteristics of facilities, 1.102, 1.103
      Characteristics of prisoners, 6.31, 6.34, 6.40
         Prisoners under age 18, 6.40
      Education programs, 1.109, 6.45, 6.46
         Educational attainment, 6.45
         Programs and participation, 1.109, 6.46
      Expenditures, 1.9-1.11
      Mental health treatment, 6.72, 6.73
      Movement of prisoners, 6.66
      Number of prisoners, 6.1, 6.13, 6.28, 6.30, 6.31, 6.34
      Number of prisons, 1.102, 1.103
      Population, 6.31, 6.34
      Rate of imprisonment, 6.28, 6.29
      Security level, 1.102
      Type of facility, 1.102, 1.103
   See also:
      Jails
      Juvenile corrections
      Parole
      Prisoners
      Prisons
      Probation
      Public opinion
COUNSEL
   See Prosecution
   See Public defense
COUNTERFEITING
   See Forgery and counterfeiting
   See U.S. Secret Service
COURTS
   Employment and payroll, 1.17, 1.19, 1.21-1.24, 1.80, 1.90
      Federal, 1.17, 1.21, 1.80
      Local, 1.17, 1.19, 1.21, 1.22
      State, 1.17, 1.19, 1.21-1.24
   Expenditures, 1.2-1.4, 1.6-1.8, 1.12, 1.96
      Federal, 1.2-1.4, 1.12, 1.96
      Local, 1.2-1.4, 1.6
      State, 1.2-1.4, 1.6, 1.8, 1.96
   Federal
      Abuse of public office cases, 5.79
      Budget authorities and outlays, 1.12
      Defendants
         Characteristics, 5.14, 5.15, 5.18, 5.20, 5.21, 5.26, 5.27
         Citizens and non-citizens, 5.35
         Convicted, 5.18
         Drug cases, 5.32, 5.34
         Method of conviction, 5.34
         Offense type, 5.13, 5.16, 5.18-5.21, 6.8
         Pretrial, 5.13-5.16
            Detained, 5.13-5.15
            Hearings, 5.14
            Outcome, 5.16
            Released, 5.13, 5.15

Index 615

COURTS, Federal, Defendants (continued)
  Sentences, 5.19-5.21, 5.23, 5.25, 5.29-5.33
    Organizations, 5.33
    To prison, 5.19, 5.23, 5.25, 5.29
    To probation, 5.23, 5.25
  Sentencing guideline cases, 5.26-5.36, 5.39
  Immigration and nationality laws, 5.75, 5.76
    Convictions, 5.76
    Prosecutions, 5.75
  Judicial salaries, 1.80
  Jury fees, 1.96
  Pretrial action, 5.13-5.16
  Sentences, 5.19-5.21, 5.23, 5.25, 5.29-5.33
    Fines, 5.32, 5.33
    Length of sentence, 5.21, 5.23, 5.30, 5.31
    Organizations, 5.33
    Prison, 5.19, 5.23, 5.25, 5.29
    Probation, 5.23, 5.25, 5.29
    Restitution, 5.32, 5.33
  U.S. attorneys' offices
    Abuse of public office cases, 5.79
  U.S. Courts of Appeal
    Appeals commenced, terminated, and pending, 5.66
    Appeals filed, 5.67
    Characteristics of appointees, 1.81
    Judgeships authorized, 5.66
  U.S. District Courts
    Antitrust cases filed, 5.41
    Appeals from, 5.67
    Characteristics of appointees, 1.82
    Criminal cases filed, 1.83, 5.7, 5.8, 5.10, 5.43
      Amount of time to disposition, 5.43
      Per judgeship, 5.8
      Type of offense, 5.10
    Criminal cases pending, 5.8, 5.9, 5.11
    Criminal cases terminated, 5.7-5.9, 5.11
    Defendants
      Characteristics, 5.14, 5.15, 5.18, 5.20, 5.21
      Charged with drug law violations, 5.37
      Convicted, 5.18, 5.22
      Disposed, 5.12, 5.22, 5.24, 5.38, 5.43
        Amount of time to disposition, 5.43
        Type of disposition, 5.22, 5.24
        Type of offense, 5.24
      Drug cases, 5.37, 5.38

COURTS, Federal, U.S. District Courts, Defendants (continued)
        Offense, 5.7, 5.13, 5.16, 5.18-5.21, 6.8, 6.70
        Organizations, 5.33
        Pretrial action, 5.13-5.16
        Sentences, 5.19, 5.20, 5.23, 5.25, 5.29-5.31, 5.33, 5.38
          Length of sentence, 5.23, 5.25, 5.30, 5.31, 5.38
          Organizations, 5.33
          Type of offense, 5.25, 5.29
    Judgeships authorized, 5.8
    Juror utilization, 1.94, 1.95
    Length of trials, 5.42
    Magistrate duties, 1.84
    Number of detainees, 5.12
    Prisoner petitions filed, 5.65
    Sentencing guideline cases, 5.26-5.36
  U.S. Pardon Attorney
    Clemency applications, 5.72
  U.S. Sentencing Commission guideline cases, 5.26-5.32, 5.34-5.36, 5.39
  U.S. Supreme Court Activities, 5.68
    Cases argued and decided on merits, 5.71
    Cases filed, disposed of, and pending, 5.69
    Petitions on writ of certiorari, 5.70
    Public opinion, 2.9, 2.10, 2.14, 2.15, 2.72, 2.74
  Judges, 1.90-1.93
    Salaries, 1.90
    Selection and retention, 1.91-1.93
  Juveniles, 5.61, 5.63, 5.64
    Characteristics, 5.61, 5.63, 5.64
    Juvenile court case outcomes, 5.63, 5.64
    Offense type, 5.61, 5.63, 5.64
  Military, 5.80-5.83
  Public opinion, 2.9, 2.10, 2.14, 2.15, 2.47, 2.72, 2.74, 2.75
    Severity, 2.47
    U.S. Supreme Court, 2.9, 2.10, 2.14, 2.15, 2.72, 2.74
  State
    Abuse of public office cases, 5.79
    Dispositions, 5.44-5.50
      Convictions, 5.44-5.46, 5.49
        Method of conviction, 5.46, 5.50
        Number of, 5.44, 5.46
        Offender characteristics, 5.45
      Sentences, 5.47-5.50
        Method of conviction, 5.50
        Type of collateral penalty, 5.49
        Type of sentence, 5.47

COURTS (continued)
  Urban counties, 5.51-5.60
    Arrests, 5.51
    Convictions, 5.57, 5.58
    Defendant characteristics, 5.52
    Pretrial release, 5.54-5.56
    Prior convictions, 5.53
    Sentences, 5.59, 5.60
  See also:
    Courts-martial
    Defendants
    Guilty pleas
    Judges
    Prosecution
    Public defense
    Public opinion
COURTS-MARTIAL
  U.S. Air Force, 5.82
  U.S. Army, 5.80
  U.S. Coast Guard, 5.83
  U.S. Marine Corps, 5.81
  U.S. Navy, 5.81
CRIME
  See Offenses known to police
  See Public officials
  See Public opinion
  See Specific offenses (e.g., Rape, Robbery)
  See Victimization
CURFEW AND LOITERING LAWS
  Arrests, 4.1, 4.3, 4.6-4.16
    Age, 4.6, 4.7, 4.9, 4.10, 4.12, 4.14, 4.16
    Cities, 4.3, 4.11, 4.12
    Race, 4.10, 4.12, 4.14, 4.16
    Rates, 4.3
    Rural counties, 4.15, 4.16
    Sex, 4.8, 4.9, 4.11, 4.13, 4.15
    Size of place, 4.3
    Suburban areas, 4.13, 4.14
DEATH PENALTY
  See Capital punishment
  See Prisoners
  See Public opinion
DEATHS
  In jails, 6.27
  In prisons, 6.76-6.78
  Of law enforcement officers, 3.154-3.157, 3.159-3.161
  Resulting from bank crime, 3.146
  Suicide, 3.136-3.139
  Terrorist incidents, 3.159, 3.175
  See also:
    Capital punishment
    Murder and nonnegligent manslaughter
    Prisoners
DEFENDANTS
  Federal courts
    Abuse of public office, 5.79
    Characteristics, 5.14, 5.15, 5.18, 5.20, 5.26, 5.27
    Citizens and non-citizens, 5.35
    Convicted, 5.7, 5.18
    Disposed of, 5.7
    Immigration and nationality laws, 5.75, 5.76

DEFENDANTS, Federal courts (continued)
    Method of conviction, 5.34
    Offense, 5.13, 5.16, 5.18-5.21, 6.8
    Organizations, 5.33
    Pretrial action, 5.13-5.16
        Detained, 5.13-5.15
        Hearings, 5.14
        Outcome, 5.16
        Released, 5.13, 5.15, 5.16
    Sentences, 5.19-5.21, 5.23,
        5.25-5.34, 5.36, 5.39
        Fines, 5.32
        Length of sentence, 5.23,
            5.25, 5.30, 5.31
        Organizations, 5.33
        Prison, 5.23, 5.25, 5.29-5.31
        Probation, 5.23, 5.25, 5.29
        Restitution, 5.32, 5.33
    Sentencing guideline cases,
        5.26-5.36, 5.39
    U.S. attorneys' offices, 5.7, 5.79
    U.S. Courts of Appeal, 5.66, 5.67
    U.S. District Courts
        Antitrust cases filed, 5.41
        Citizens and non-citizens,
            5.35
        Convictions, 5.7
        Criminal cases, 5.7, 5.8, 5.11,
            5.43
            Amount of time to
                disposition, 5.43
        Number of defendants, 5.7,
            5.22-5.25, 5.37
        Number of detainees, 5.12
        Organizations, 5.33
        Prisoner petitions filed, 5.65
        Sentences, 5.23, 5.25,
            5.29-5.33
        Sentencing guideline cases,
            5.26-5.36
    U.S. Pardon Attorney, 5.72
    U.S. Supreme Court, 5.68-5.71
    State courts
        Abuse of public office, 5.79
        Dispositions, 5.44-5.50
        Convictions, 5.44-5.50
        Sentences, 5.47, 5.48
    Urban county courts, 5.51-5.60
        Arrests, 5.51
        Convictions, 5.57, 5.58
        Defendant characteristics, 5.52
        Pretrial release, 5.54-5.56
        Prior convictions, 5.53
        Sentences, 5.59, 5.60
    See also:
        Courts
        Courts-martial
        Guilty pleas
        Public defense
        Public officials
DELINQUENCY
    See Juvenile corrections
    See Juvenile delinquency
    See Self-reported criminal activity
DETENTION, PRETRIAL
    See Bail
    See Courts
    See Defendants

DISORDERLY CONDUCT
    Arrests, 4.1, 4.3, 4.6-4.16, 4.28
        Age, 4.6, 4.7, 4.9, 4.10, 4.12, 4.14
        Cities, 4.3, 4.11, 4.12
        Race, 4.10, 4.12, 4.14, 4.16
        Rates, 4.3
        Rural counties, 4.15, 4.16
        Sex, 4.8, 4.9, 4.11, 4.13, 4.15
        Size of place, 4.3
        State, 4.28
        Suburban areas, 4.13, 4.14
    In Federal parks, 3.116
DISPOSITION OF DEFENDANTS
    See Courts
    See Defendants
DRIVING WHILE INTOXICATED
    See Alcohol
    See Public opinion
    See Traffic violations
DRUG ABUSE VIOLATIONS
    See Defendants
    See Drugs
    See Narcotic drug laws
DRUG ENFORCEMENT ADMINISTRATION
    Arrests, 4.40, 4.41
    Budget, 1.76
    Convictions, 5.40
    Federal budget authority, 1.15
    Number of officers, 1.72
    Seizures and removals, 4.36-4.39, 4.42
        Asset seizure, 4.38, 4.42
        Drug laboratories, 4.39
        Drug seizure, 4.36-4.38
        Plots, 4.38
        Type of drug, 4.36, 4.37, 4.39
    Staff, 1.76
    See also:
        Drugs
DRUGS
    Arrestees reporting use, testing
        positive, 4.30
    Arrests for drug-related offenses, 4.1,
        4.3, 4.6-4.16, 4.29, 4.33-4.35, 4.40,
        4.41, 5.50
        Age, 4.6, 4.7, 4.9, 4.10, 4.12, 4.14,
            4.16
        Cities, 4.3, 4.11, 4.12
        Federal, 4.33-4.35, 4.41
        Race, 4.10, 4.12, 4.14, 4.16
        Rates, 4.3
        Rural counties, 4.15, 4.16
        Sex, 4.8, 4.9, 4.11, 4.13, 4.15
        Size of place, 4.3
        Suburban areas, 4.13, 4.14
        Time to sentencing, State courts,
            5.50
        Type of drug, 4.29, 4.40, 4.41
    Asset seizure, 4.38, 4.42
    Basis for wiretap, 5.3
    College students, 3.71-3.73, 3.84
    Community supervision, Federal
        offenders, 6.4
    Convictions, 5.17, 5.44-5.46, 5.50
    Court cases, Federal, 5.13, 5.16-5.21,
        5.24-5.40, 5.67, 6.58, 6.59
        Appeals, 5.67
        Citizens and non-citizens, 5.35
        Convictions, 5.17, 5.20, 5.40

DRUGS, Court cases, Federal (continued)
        Defendant characteristics, 5.26,
            5.27
        Dispositions, 5.17, 5.22, 5.24, 5.37
        Method of conviction, 5.17, 5.34,
            5.39
        Offender characteristics, 5.18,
            5.20, 5.21, 5.39
        Organizations sentenced, 5.33
        Pretrial action, 5.13, 5.16
        Sentences, 5.19-5.21, 5.25, 5.29,
            5.31-5.33, 5.38, 6.58, 6.59
            Time served, 6.58, 6.59
        Sentencing guideline cases,
            5.26-5.36, 5.39
    Court cases, State, 5.44-5.50
        Convictions, 5.44-5.46, 5.50
            Method of conviction, 5.46,
                5.50
            Number of, 5.44
            Offender characteristics, 5.45
        Juveniles, 5.61-5.64
            Case outcomes, 5.63, 5.64
            Characteristics, 5.61-5.64
        Sentences, 5.47-5.50
            Length of sentence, 5.48
            Type of additional penalty,
                5.49
    Court cases, urban counties, 5.51-5.60
        Arrests, 5.51
        Convictions, 5.57, 5.58
        Defendant characteristics, 5.52
        Pretrial release, 5.54-5.56
        Prior convictions, 5.53
        Sentences, 5.59, 5.60
    Driving after drug use, 3.102
    Drug Enforcement Administration, 1.76,
        4.36, 4.37, 4.39, 4.40, 4.42, 5.40
        Arrests, 4.40
        Asset seizures, 4.42
        Budget, 1.76
        Convictions, 5.40
        Drug seizures, 4.36, 4.37, 4.39
        Staff, 1.76
    Drug treatment, arrestees, 4.31
    Emergency department episodes,
        3.92-3.94
        Patient characteristics, 3.92-3.94
        Type of drug, 3.93, 3.94
    Expenditures, 1.14, 1.15
        Federal drug control spending,
            1.14, 1.15
    In Federal parks, 3.116
    Jail inmates
        Current offense, 6.19, 6.20
        Drug use, 6.21
    Juvenile court cases, 5.61-5.64
        Case outcomes, 5.63, 5.64
        Demographic characteristics,
            5.61-5.64
    Juveniles in custody, 6.10
    Military personnel, use, 3.89, 3.90
    Parole and supervised release, 6.4,
        6.70, 6.71
    Prisoners
        Current offense, 6.56
        Federal, 6.57

DRUGS, Prisoners (continued)
    Firearms possession during
        offense, 6.37, 6.38
    Recidivism, 6.50-6.52
    Time served, 6.44
Probationers
    Number, 6.4
    Outcomes, 6.8
Problems or criminal behavior related
    to use, 3.85
Public opinion
    As important problem, 2.1-2.3
    Availability, 2.83, 2.84
    Disapproval of use, 2.85, 2.86
    Drug testing in schools, 2.7, 2.8
    Harmfulness, 2.76, 2.77, 2.79-2.82
    High school seniors, 2.70, 2.79,
        2.83, 2.85, 2.87-2.89
    Importance of drug problem, 2.1,
        2.4
        In schools, 2.4
    Legalization, 2.68, 2.69, 2.88-2.90
    Level of spending, 2.41, 2.43
    Locker searches in schools, 2.7,
        2.8
    Marijuana, 2.69, 2.77
        Medical use, 2.69
    Progress coping with drug
        problem, 2.44
    Students, 2.76, 2.80, 2.84, 2.86
    Teenagers' perceptions of those
        who use, 2.78
    Testing for use, 2.7, 2.8
    Young adults' views, 2.81
Seizures, 4.36-4.39, 4.42, 4.43
    Drug Enforcement Administration,
        4.36-4.39, 4.42
    U.S. Customs Service, 4.43
Sentences, 5.19-5.21, 5.25, 5.29-5.33,
    5.47-5.50, 5.59, 5.60, 5.63, 5.64,
    6.44, 6.58, 6.59
    Federal courts, 5.19-5.21
    Fines, 5.32
    Incarceration, 5.25, 5.29
    Juveniles, 5.63, 5.64
    Length of sentence, 5.19-5.21,
        5.25, 5.31, 5.60, 6.44
    Method of conviction, 5.50
    Organizations, 5.33
    Probation, 5.25, 5.29
    Restitution, 5.32
    Time served, 6.44, 6.58, 6.59
    Type of collateral penalty, 5.49
    Type of sentence, 5.19, 5.59
Testing of arrestees, 4.30
Treatment facilities, 6.62
U.S. Sentencing Commission guideline
    cases, 5.26-5.36, 5.39
Use
    Among arrestees, 4.30
    Among jail inmates prior to
        offense, 6.21
    Among military personnel, 3.89,
        3.90
    Among students, 3.55, 3.57, 3.62,
        3.63, 3.65-3.73, 3.84, 3.85
        At school, 3.55, 3.57

DRUGS, Use, Among students (continued)
        College students, 3.71-3.73,
            3.84, 3.85
        High school seniors, 3.63,
            3.65-3.70
        High school students, 3.55,
            3.57, 3.62, 3.63, 3.65-3.67,
            3.70
    As source of family problems,
        3.101
    At school, 3.55, 3.57
    Driving after use, 3.102
    Problems or criminal behavior
        related to use, 3.85, 3.101
    Self-reported, 3.49-3.51, 3.53,
        3.55, 3.57, 3.62, 3.63, 3.65-3.76,
        3.84-3.88, 3.102
        Driving after use, 3.102
        Driving under the influence,
            3.49, 3.51, 3.53
        National households,
            3.86-3.88
        Students, 3.55, 3.57, 3.62,
            3.63, 3.65-3.73, 3.84, 3.85
            At school, 3.55, 3.57
            College students,
                3.71-3.73, 3.84, 3.85
            High school seniors,
                3.63, 3.65-3.70
            High school students,
                3.55, 3.57, 3.62, 3.63,
                3.65-3.67, 3.70
        Type of drug, 3.62, 3.71,
            3.72, 3.74-3.76
        Young adults, 3.74-3.76,
            3.86-3.88
    See also:
        Arrests
        Drug Enforcement Administration
        Narcotic drug laws
        U.S. Customs Service
EMBEZZLEMENT
    Arrests, 4.1, 4.3, 4.6-4.16, 4.33
        Age, 4.6, 4.7, 4.9, 4.10, 4.12, 4.14,
            4.16
        Cities, 4.3, 4.11, 4.12
        Federal, 4.33
        Race, 4.10, 4.12, 4.14, 4.16
        Rates, 4.3
        Rural counties, 4.15, 4.16
        Sex, 4.8, 4.9, 4.11, 4.13, 4.15
        Size of place, 4.3
        Suburban areas, 4.13, 4.14
    Community supervision, Federal
        offenders, 6.4
    Convictions, 5.17
    Court cases, Federal, 5.10, 5.13, 5.17,
        5.19, 5.25-5.29, 5.31-5.36, 5.44,
        5.67, 6.58
        Appeals, 5.67
        Citizens and non-citizens, 5.35
        Convictions, 5.17
        Defendant characteristics, 5.26,
            5.27
        Dispositions, 5.17, 5.44
        Method of conviction, 5.17, 5.34
        Organizations sentenced, 5.33

EMBEZZLEMENT, Court cases, Federal
(continued)
        Pretrial action, 5.13
        Sentences, 5.19, 5.25-5.27, 5.29,
            5.31-5.34, 5.36
        Sentencing guideline cases,
            5.26-5.29, 5.31-5.36
        Time served, 6.58
    Court cases, State, 5.44-5.50
        Convictions, 5.44-5.46, 5.50
            Method of conviction, 5.46,
                5.50
            Number of, 5.44
            Offender characteristics, 5.45
        Sentences, 5.47-5.50
            Length of sentence, 5.48
            Method of conviction, 5.50
            Time from arrest, 5.50
            Type of additional penalty,
                5.49
    In Federal parks, 3.116
    Parole and supervised release, 6.4,
        6.70, 6.71
    Probation, 6.4, 6.8
    Sentences, 5.19, 5.29, 5.31-5.33, 6.58
        Federal courts, 5.19
        Fines, 5.32
        Length of sentence, 5.19, 5.31
        Organizations, 5.33
        Prison, 5.25, 5.29
        Probation, 5.25, 5.29
        Restitution, 5.32
        Time served, 6.58
        Type, 5.19
    U.S. Postal Inspection Service, 5.74
EMPLOYMENT
    Corrections, 1.17, 1.21-1.24,
        1.99-1.101, 1.105-1.108
        Federal, 1.17, 1.21, 1.106-1.108
            Characteristics of personnel,
                1.107, 1.108
        Jails, 1.99-1.101, 1.105
        Local, 1.17, 1.21-1.24
        State, 1.17, 1.21-1.24
    Courts, 1.17, 1.21-1.24
        Federal, 1.17, 1.21
        Local, 1.17, 1.21
        State, 1.17, 1.21-1.24
    Judicial and legal services, 1.17,
        1.21-1.24, 1.85, 1.87, 1.89
        Federal, 1.17, 1.21
        Local, 1.17, 1.21, 1.22
        Prosecutors' offices, 1.85, 1.87,
            1.89
        State, 1.17, 1.21-1.24, 1.85, 1.87,
            1.89
            Prosecutors' offices, 1.85,
                1.87, 1.89
    Justice system, 1.17-1.26, 1.79
        Federal, 1.17, 1.18, 1.20, 1.21,
            1.79
        Local, 1.17-1.22, 1.25, 1.26
        State, 1.17-1.22, 1.25, 1.26
    Federal agencies, 1.72-1.75
        Characteristics of officers, 1.75
        Inspectors general, 1.73
        Number of officers, 1.72-1.74

EMPLOYMENT (continued)
    Payroll and salaries, 1.17-1.19, 1.26,
        1.61, 1.65, 1.69-1.71, 1.80, 1.90
        Cities, 1.69, 1.70
        Corrections, 1.17, 1.19
        Counties, 1.71
        Courts, 1.80, 1.90
        Judicial and legal services, 1.17,
            1.19
        Justice system, 1.17-1.19
        Police, 1.17, 1.19, 1.26, 1.61,
            1.65, 1.69-1.71
            Cities, 1.69, 1.70
            Counties, 1.71
            State police, 1.61
    Police, 1.17, 1.21-1.50, 1.55-1.60,
        1.63-1.68
        Cities, 1.55-1.58, 1.66-1.68
        Counties, 1.66-1.68
        Federal, 1.17, 1.21
        Female police officers, 1.56, 1.58,
            1.60
        Full-time sworn personnel,
            1.23-1.36, 1.55-1.59
        Local, 1.17, 1.21, 1.22, 1.25, 1.27,
            1.29, 1.33, 1.35, 1.37, 1.39,
            1.41, 1.43, 1.45, 1.47, 1.49
        Minority police officers, 1.56, 1.58,
            1.60
        Number of employees, 1.27-1.34,
            1.57, 1.59
        Officer characteristics, 1.37, 1.38,
            1.60
        Region, 1.64, 1.66-1.68
        Sheriffs, 1.27, 1.30, 1.34, 1.36,
            1.38, 1.40, 1.42, 1.44, 1.46,
            1.48, 1.50
        Special jurisdiction departments,
            1.27, 1.32
        State police, 1.17, 1.21-1.27, 1.31,
            1.59, 1.60
        Suburban, 1.66-1.68
        Tribal police, 1.63
    See also:
        Expenditures
        Specific area (e.g., Corrections,
            Courts)
EXECUTIONS
    See Capital punishment
    See Prisoners
EXPENDITURES
    Corrections, 1.2-1.4, 1.6-1.11, 1.17,
        1.19
        Federal, 1.2-1.4, 1.17
        Local, 1.2-1.4, 1.6, 1.17, 1.19
        Per capita, 1.8
        State, 1.2-1.4, 1.6, 1.8, 1.10, 1.11,
            1.17, 1.19
    Courts, 1.2-1.4, 1.6-1.8, 1.12, 1.17,
        1.19, 1.96
        Federal, 1.2-1.4, 1.12, 1.96
        Juries, 1.96
        Local, 1.2-1.4, 1.6
        Per capita, 1.8
        State, 1.2-1.4, 1.6, 1.8, 1.96
    Drug control, 1.14, 1.15
        Federal budget, 1.14, 1.15

EXPENDITURES (continued)
    Edward Byrne law enforcement funds,
        1.16
    Judicial and legal services, 1.2-1.4,
        1.6-1.8, 1.12, 1.17-1.19, 1.86
        Federal, 1.2-1.4, 1.12, 1.17
        Local, 1.2-1.4, 1.6, 1.17, 1.19
        Per capita, 1.8
        State, 1.2-1.4, 1.6, 1.8, 1.17, 1.19,
            1.86
            Per capita, 1.8
            Prosecutors' offices, 1.86
    Justice system, 1.1-1.7, 1.12, 1.13,
        1.17-1.19
        Federal, 1.1-1.5, 1.12, 1.13, 1.17
        Local, 1.1-1.6, 1.17, 1.19
        State, 1.1-1.6, 1.17, 1.19
    Office of Justice Programs, 1.13
    Payroll and salaries, 1.17-1.19, 1.26,
        1.61, 1.69-1.71, 1.80, 1.87, 1.90
        Cities, 1.69, 1.70
        Corrections, 1.17, 1.19
        Counties, 1.71
        Courts, 1.80, 1.90
        Judicial and legal services, 1.17,
            1.19, 1.87
            Prosecutors' offices, 1.87
        Justice system, 1.17-1.19
        Police, 1.17, 1.19, 1.26, 1.61,
            1.69-1.71
            Cities, 1.69, 1.70
            Counties, 1.71
            State police, 1.61
    Police, 1.2-1.4, 1.6-1.8, 1.12, 1.17,
        1.19, 1.26, 1.61, 1.62
        Federal, 1.2-1.4, 1.12, 1.17
        Local, 1.2-1.4, 1.6, 1.17, 1.19
        Per capita, 1.8, 1.62
        State, 1.2-1.4, 1.6, 1.8, 1.17, 1.19,
            1.61, 1.62
            Operating expenditures, 1.62
            Salaries, 1.61
    See also:
        Employment
        Specific area (e.g., Law
            Enforcement, Courts)
EXPLOSIVES
    See Bombings
EXTORTION
    Arrests, Federal, 4.33
    Basis for wiretap, 5.3
    Community supervision, Federal
        offenders, 6.4
    Court cases, Federal, 5.13, 5.17, 5.19,
        5.24-5.29, 5.31, 5.32, 5.34-5.36,
        5.67, 6.58
        Appeals, 5.67
        Citizens and non-citizens, 5.35
        Convictions, 5.17
        Dispositions, 5.17, 5.24
        Method of conviction, 5.17
        Pretrial action, 5.13
        Sentences, 5.19, 5.25, 5.29
        Sentencing guideline cases,
            5.26-5.29, 5.31, 5.32, 5.34-5.36
        Time served, 6.58

EXTORTION (continued)
    Federal Bank Robbery and Incidental
        Crimes Statute, 3.149-3.151
    Parole and supervised release, 6.4,
        6.70, 6.71
    Prisoners, Federal, 6.56, 6.58
        Time served, 6.58
    Probation, 6.4, 6.8
FAMILY AND CHILDREN
    Alcohol, problems resulting from use,
        3.99, 3.100
    Offenses against
        Arrests, 4.1, 4.3, 4.6-4.16
            Age, 4.6, 4.7, 4.9, 4.12, 4.14,
                4.16
            Cities, 4.3, 4.11, 4.12
            Race, 4.10, 4.12, 4.14, 4.16
            Rates, 4.3
            Rural counties, 4.15, 4.16
            Sex, 4.8, 4.9, 4.11, 4.13, 4.15
            Size of place, 4.3
            Suburban areas, 4.13, 4.14
FELONIES
    See Offenses known to police
    See Specific offenses (e.g., Robbery,
        Arson)
FIREARMS
    See Guns
    See Public opinion
FIRES
    Number of fires, civilian deaths, and
        property loss, 3.166, 3.167
    Vehicle fires, 3.167
    See also:
        Arson
FORGERY AND COUNTERFEITING
    Arrests, 4.1, 4.3, 4.6-4.16, 4.33
        Age, 4.6, 4.7, 4.9, 4.10, 4.12, 4.14,
            4.16
        Cities, 4.3, 4.11, 4.12
        Federal, 4.33
        Race, 4.10, 4.12, 4.14, 4.16
        Rates, 4.3
        Rural counties, 4.15, 4.16
        Sex, 4.8, 4.9, 4.11, 4.13, 4.15
        Size of place, 4.3
        Suburban areas, 4.13, 4.14
    Community supervision, Federal
        offenders, 6.4
    Court cases, Federal, 5.10, 5.13, 5.17,
        5.19, 5.24-5.29, 5.31, 5.32, 5.34-5.36,
        5.67
        Appeals, 5.67
        Citizens and non-citizens, 5.35
        Convictions, 5.17
        Defendant characteristics, 5.26,
            5.27
        Dispositions, 5.17, 5.24
        Method of conviction, 5.17, 5.34
        Pretrial action, 5.13
        Sentences, 5.19, 5.25, 5.29, 5.31,
            5.32, 5.36
        Sentencing guideline cases,
            5.26-5.29, 5.31-5.36

FORGERY AND COUNTERFEITING (continued)
- Court cases, State, 5.44-5.50
  - Convictions, 5.44-5.46, 5.50
    - Method of conviction, 5.46, 5.50
    - Number of, 5.44
    - Offender characteristics, 5.45
  - Sentences, 5.47-5.50
    - Length of sentence, 5.48
    - Method of conviction, 5.50
    - Time from arrest, 5.50
    - Type of additional penalty, 5.49
- In Federal parks, 3.116
- Parole and supervised release, 6.4, 6.70, 6.71
- Probation, 6.4, 6.8
- Sentences, 5.19, 5.25, 5.29, 5.31, 5.32, 6.58
  - Federal courts, 5.19
  - Fines, 5.32
  - Length, 5.19, 5.31
  - Prison, 5.25, 5.29
  - Probation, 5.25, 5.29
  - Restitution, 5.32
  - Time served, 6.58
  - Type, 5.19
- U.S. Postal Inspection Service, 5.74

FRAUD
- Arrests, 4.1, 4.3, 4.6-4.16, 4.33
  - Age, 4.6, 4.7, 4.9, 4.10, 4.12, 4.14, 4.16
  - Cities, 4.3, 4.11, 4.12
  - Federal, 4.33
  - Race, 4.10, 4.12, 4.14, 4.16
  - Rates, 4.3
  - Rural counties, 4.15, 4.16
  - Sex, 4.8, 4.9, 4.11, 4.13, 4.15
  - Size of place, 4.3
  - Suburban areas, 4.13, 4.14
- Banking investigations, 3.148
- Community supervision, Federal offenders, 6.4
- Court cases, Federal, 5.10, 5.13, 5.17, 5.19, 5.24-5.29, 5.31-5.36, 5.67, 5.71, 5.76, 6.58
  - Appeals, 5.67
  - Citizens and non-citizens, 5.35
  - Convictions, 5.17
  - Defendant characteristics, 5.26, 5.27
  - Dispositions, 5.17, 5.24
  - Immigration and nationality laws, 5.76
  - Method of conviction, 5.17, 5.34
  - Organizations sentenced, 5.33
  - Sentences, 5.25-5.27, 5.29, 5.31-5.33, 6.58
  - Time served, 6.58
  - Sentencing guideline cases, 5.26-5.29, 5.31-5.36
- Court cases, State, 5.44-5.50
  - Convictions, 5.44-5.46, 5.50
    - Method of conviction, 5.46, 5.50
    - Number of, 5.44
    - Offender characteristics, 5.45

FRAUD, Court cases, State (continued)
- Sentences, 5.47-5.50
  - Length of sentence, 5.48
  - Method of conviction, 5.50
  - Time from arrest, 5.50
  - Type of additional penalty, 5.49
- Financial institution fraud, 3.148
- In Federal parks, 3.116
- Jail inmates
  - Current offense, 6.19, 6.20
- Parole and supervised release, 6.4, 6.70, 6.71
- Prisoners
  - Current offense, 6.56
  - Recidivism, 6.50, 6.51
  - Time served, 6.44, 6.58
- Probationers
  - Number, 6.4
  - Outcomes, 6.8
- Sentences, 5.19, 5.25, 5.29, 5.31-5.33, 6.44, 6.58
  - Federal courts, 5.19
  - Fines, 5.32
  - Incarceration, 5.19, 5.25, 5.29
  - Length of sentence, 5.19, 5.31, 6.44
  - Organizations, 5.33
  - Probation, 5.19, 5.25, 5.29
  - Restitution, 5.32
  - Time served, 6.44, 6.58

GAMBLING
- Arrests, 4.1, 4.3, 4.6-4.16, 4.33
  - Age, 4.6, 4.7, 4.9, 4.10, 4.12, 4.14, 4.16
  - Cities, 4.3, 4.11, 4.12
  - Federal, 4.33
  - Race, 4.10, 4.12, 4.14, 4.16
  - Rates, 4.3
  - Rural counties, 4.3, 4.15, 4.16
  - Sex, 4.8, 4.9, 4.11, 4.13, 4.15
  - Size of place, 4.3
  - Suburban areas, 4.3, 4.13, 4.14
- Basis for wiretap, 5.3
- Community supervision, Federal offenders, 6.4
- Court cases, Federal, 5.17, 5.24-5.29, 5.31-5.36
  - Citizens and non-citizens, 5.35
  - Convictions, 5.17
  - Defendant characteristics, 5.26, 5.27
  - Dispositions, 5.17, 5.24
  - Method of conviction, 5.17, 5.34
  - Organizations sentenced, 5.33
  - Sentences, 5.25, 5.29, 5.31-5.33
  - Sentencing guideline cases, 5.26-5.29, 5.31-5.36
- In Federal parks, 3.116
- Parole and supervised release, 6.4
- Probation, 6.4
- Sentences, 5.25, 5.29, 5.31-5.33, 6.58
  - Organizations, 5.33
  - Time served, 6.58

GRAND JURY
- See Juries

GUILTY PLEAS
- Court cases, Federal, 5.22, 5.24, 5.34, 5.37, 5.43
  - Drug law violations, 5.37
- Court cases, State, 5.46, 5.50
  - Processing time, 5.50
  - Type of offense, 5.46, 5.50

GUNS
- At school, 3.55-3.58
- Arrests for weapon-related offenses, 4.1, 4.3, 4.6-4.16, 4.33
  - Age, 4.6, 4.7, 4.9, 4.10, 4.12, 4.14, 4.16
  - Cities, 4.3, 4.11, 4.12
  - Federal, 4.33
  - Race, 4.10, 4.12, 4.14, 4.16
  - Rates, 4.3
  - Rural counties, 4.3, 4.15, 4.16
  - Sex, 4.8, 4.9, 4.11, 4.13, 4.15
  - Size of place, 4.3
  - Suburban areas, 4.3, 4.13, 4.14
- Background checks for purchase, 1.110, 1.111
  - Number, 1.110
  - Rejections, 1.110, 1.111
- Community supervision, Federal offenders, 6.4
- Court cases, Federal, 5.10, 5.13, 5.17, 5.19, 5.24-5.29, 5.31, 5.32, 5.34-5.36, 5.67, 6.58
  - Appeals, 5.67
  - Citizens and non-citizens, 5.35
  - Convictions, 5.17
  - Defendant characteristics, 5.26, 5.27
  - Dispositions, 5.17, 5.24
  - Method of conviction, 5.17, 5.34
  - Pretrial action, 5.13
  - Sentences, 5.19, 5.25, 5.29, 5.31, 5.32
  - Sentencing guideline cases, 5.26-5.29, 5.31, 5.32, 5.34-5.36
  - Time served, 6.58
- Court cases, State, 5.44-5.50
  - Convictions, 5.44-5.46, 5.50
    - Method of conviction, 5.46, 5.50
    - Number of, 5.44
    - Offender characteristics, 5.45
  - Sentences, 5.47-5.50
    - Length of sentence, 5.48
    - Method of conviction, 5.50
    - Time from arrest, 5.50
    - Type of additional penalty, 5.49
- Court cases, urban counties, 5.51-5.60
  - Arrests, 5.51
  - Convictions, 5.57, 5.58
  - Defendant characteristics, 5.52
  - Pretrial release, 5.54-5.56
  - Prior convictions, 5.53
  - Sentences, 5.59, 5.60
- Detected at airports, 3.177
- Jail inmates
  - Current offense, 6.19, 6.20
- Juveniles in custody, 6.10

GUNS (continued)
    Ownership, 2.59, 2.60, 2.62, 2.66
        Firearm in home, 2.59, 2.60
        Public opinion, 2.66
    Parole and supervised release, 6.4, 6.70, 6.71
    Possession, at school, 3.58
    Prisoners
        Current offense, 6.56
        Possession during offense, 6.35-6.38
        Recidivism, 6.50
    Probationers
        Number, 6.4
        Outcomes, 6.8
    Public opinion, 2.2, 2.63-2.66, 2.95
        As an important problem, 2.2
        Laws covering sale, 2.63, 2.64
        Public policies, 2.64-2.66, 2.95
    Self-reported carrying, 3.43-3.45, 3.55-3.57
        At school, 3.55-3.57
    Sentences, 5.19, 5.25, 5.29, 5.31, 5.32, 5.59, 5.60, 6.58
        Federal courts, 5.19
        Fines, 5.32
        Incarceration, 5.19, 5.25, 5.29
        Length, 5.19, 5.31, 5.60
        Probation, 5.19, 5.25, 5.29
        Restitution, 5.32
        Time served, 6.58
        Type, 5.59
    U.S. Postal Inspection Service, unlawful mailings, 5.74
    See also:
        Public opinion
        Specific offenses (e.g., Murder, Robbery)
HANDGUNS
    See Guns
HASHISH
    See Drug Enforcement Administration
HEROIN
    See Courts
    See Drugs
    See Narcotic drug laws
    See Self-reported criminal activity
HOMICIDE
    See Murder and nonnegligent manslaughter
HOUSEHOLDS EXPERIENCING CRIME
    See Specific offenses (e.g., Rape, Burglary)
    See Victimization
IMMIGRATION
    Aliens located, 4.46
    Arrests, Federal, 4.33
    Community supervision, Federal offenders, 6.4
    Court cases, Federal, 5.10, 5.13, 5.17, 5.24-5.29, 5.31-5.36, 5.67, 5.75-5.77, 6.58
        Appeals, 5.67
        Citizens and non-citizens, 5.35
        Convictions, 5.17, 5.75, 5.76
            Type of offense, 5.76
        Defendant characteristics, 5.26, 5.27

IMMIGRATION, Court cases, Federal (continued)
        Dispositions, 5.17, 5.24, 5.76
        Filings, 5.10
        Immigration offenders processed, 5.77
        Method of conviction, 5.17, 5.34
        Organizations sentenced, 5.33
        Pretrial action, 5.13
        Prosecutions, 5.75
        Sentences, 5.25, 5.29, 5.31-5.33, 6.58
            Time served, 6.58
        Sentencing guideline cases, 5.26-5.29, 5.31-5.36
    Deportations, 4.46, 4.47
        Aliens located, 4.46
        Reason deported, 4.47
    Detainees, 6.61
    Jail inmates
        Current offense, 6.19, 6.20
    Matters referred to U.S. attorneys, 5.78
    Parole and supervised release, 6.4, 6.70, 6.71
    Prisoners, Federal, 6.56, 6.60
    Probation, 6.4, 6.8
    Sentences, 5.19, 5.25, 5.29, 5.31-5.33, 6.58
        Federal courts, 5.19
        Fine, 5.32
        Length, 5.19, 5.31
        Organizations, 5.33
        Prison, 5.25, 5.29
        Probation, 5.25, 5.29
        Restitution, 5.32
        Time served, 6.58
IMMUNITY
    See Clemency
    See Courts
    See U.S. Pardon Attorney
INTERNAL REVENUE SERVICE
    See Tax law violations
JAILS
    AIDS and HIV cases, 6.26, 6.27
    Capacity, 1.98, 6.14
    Education programs, 1.109, 6.45, 6.46
        Educational attainment, 6.45
        Programs and participation, 1.109, 6.46
    Employees, 1.99, 1.100, 1.101, 1.105
        Occupational category, 1.99
        Privately operated jails, 1.105
        Race and ethnicity, 1.101
        Sex, 1.100
    Indian jails, 6.25
    Inmates, 1.98, 1.105, 6.1, 6.14-6.27
        AIDS and HIV cases, 6.26, 6.27
        Alcohol use, 6.22
        Conviction status, 6.18, 6.19
        Current offense, 6.19, 6.20
        Deaths, 6.27
        Drug use, 6.21
        Family background, 6.23
        Indian jails, 6.25
        Inmate to employee ratio, 1.98
        Juvenile inmates, 6.14
        Number, 1.105, 6.14, 6.16, 6.18, 6.24

JAILS, Inmates (continued)
        Privately operated jails, 1.105
        Race and ethnicity, 6.17, 6.18, 6.20, 6.24
        Sex, 6.17, 6.18, 6.20, 6.24
        Type of supervision, 6.15, 6.16
    Number of jails, 1.98
    See also:
        Corrections
        Juvenile corrections
        Prisons
JUDGES
    Federal, 1.80-1.84, 5.8, 5.66
        Characteristics of appointees, 1.81, 1.82
        Criminal cases filed per judgeship, 1.83
        Duties performed by magistrates, 1.84
        Number, 5.8, 5.66
        Salaries, 1.80
    State, 1.90-1.93
        Salaries, 1.90
        Selection and retention, 1.91-1.93
    See also:
        Employment
JURIES
    Federal grand juries, 1.94
    Federal petit juries, 1.95
    Jury fees, 1.96
JUVENILE CORRECTIONS
    Juveniles in detention facilities, 6.9-6.12
        Characteristics, 6.11
        Number, 6.9, 6.10, 6.12
        Type of facility, 6.12
    Juveniles in local jails, 6.14
    Juveniles taken into custody, 4.25, 4.26
JUVENILE COURTS
    Cases processed, 5.61-5.64
        Demographic characteristics, 5.61-5.64
        Dispositions, 5.63, 5.64
        Offense type, 5.62-5.64
JUVENILE DELINQUENCY
    At school, 3.58
    Juvenile court cases, 5.61-5.64
    Juveniles in detention facilities, 6.9-6.12
        Characteristics, 6.11
        Number, 6.9, 6.10, 6.12
        Type of facility, 6.12
    Juveniles taken into custody, 4.25, 4.26
    Public opinion, 2.48
        Treatment of violent juveniles, 2.48
    Self-reported, 3.43-3.45, 3.54, 3.58
        At school, 3.58
        High school students, 3.43-3.45
        Students, 3.54, 3.58
    See also:
        Alcohol
        Drugs
        Juvenile corrections
        Traffic violations
JUVENILE INSTITUTIONS
    See Juvenile corrections

KIDNAPING
- Arrests, Federal, 4.33
- Basis for wiretap, 5.3
- Community supervision, Federal offenders, 6.4
- Court cases, Federal, 5.10, 5.13, 5.17, 5.19, 5.24-5.29, 5.31, 5.32, 5.34-5.36
  - Citizens and non-citizens, 5.35
  - Convictions, 5.17
  - Defendant characteristics, 5.26, 5.27
  - Dispositions, 5.17, 5.24
  - Method of conviction, 5.17, 5.34
  - Pretrial action, 5.13
  - Sentences, 5.19, 5.25, 5.29, 5.31, 5.32
  - Sentencing guideline cases, 5.26-5.29, 5.31, 5.32, 5.34-5.36
- Jail inmates
  - Current offense, 6.19, 6.20
- Juveniles in custody, 6.10
- Parole and supervised release, 6.4, 6.70, 6.71
- Prisoners
  - Recidivism, 6.50
  - Time served, 6.58
- Probation, 6.4, 6.8
- Sentences, 5.19, 5.25, 5.29, 5.31, 5.32, 6.58
  - Federal courts, 5.19
  - Fines, 5.32
  - Length, 5.19, 5.31
  - Prison, 5.25, 5.29
  - Probation, 5.25, 5.29
  - Restitution, 5.32
  - Time served, 6.58
  - Type, 5.19

LARCENY-THEFT
- Arrests, 4.1-4.3, 4.5-4.16, 4.18, 4.19, 4.22, 4.33, 5.50
  - Age, 4.5-4.7, 4.9, 4.10, 4.12, 4.14, 4.16, 4.22
  - Cities, 4.3, 4.11, 4.12, 4.19, 4.22
  - Clearance by arrests, 4.19, 4.22
  - Federal, 4.33
  - Race, 4.10, 4.12, 4.14, 4.16
  - Rates, 4.2, 4.3, 4.18
  - Region, 4.18
  - Rural counties, 4.3, 4.15, 4.16, 4.19, 4.22
  - Sex, 4.8, 4.9, 4.11, 4.13, 4.15
  - Size of place, 4.3, 4.19, 4.22
  - State, 4.5
  - Suburban areas, 4.3, 4.13, 4.14, 4.19, 4.22
  - Time to sentencing, State courts, 5.50
- At school, 3.61
- Basis for wiretap, 5.3
- Community supervision, Federal offenders, 6.4
- Convictions
  - Federal courts, 5.17
  - Method of conviction, 5.17, 5.34, 5.46, 5.50
  - Number of, 5.17, 5.44, 5.46
  - Offender characteristics, 5.45

LARCENY-THEFT (continued)
- Court cases, Federal, 5.10, 5.13, 5.17, 5.19, 5.24-5.29, 5.31-5.36, 5.67, 6.58
  - Appeals, 5.67
  - Citizens and non-citizens, 5.35
  - Convictions, 5.17
  - Defendant characteristics, 5.26, 5.27
  - Dispositions, 5.17, 5.24
  - Method of conviction, 5.17, 5.34
  - Organizations sentenced, 5.33
  - Pretrial action, 5.13
  - Sentences, 5.19, 5.25, 5.29, 5.31-5.33
  - Sentencing guideline cases, 5.26-5.29, 5.31-5.36
  - Time served, 6.58
- Court cases, State, 5.44-5.50
  - Convictions, 5.44-5.46, 5.50
    - Method of conviction, 5.46, 5.50
    - Number of, 5.44
    - Offender characteristics, 5.45
  - Sentences, 5.47-5.50
    - Length of sentence, 5.48
    - Method of conviction, 5.50
    - Time from arrest, 5.50
    - Type of additional penalty, 5.49
- Court cases, urban counties, 5.51-5.60
  - Arrests, 5.51
  - Convictions, 5.57, 5.58
  - Defendant characteristics, 5.52
  - Pretrial release, 5.54-5.56
  - Prior convictions, 5.53
  - Sentences, 5.59, 5.60
- Federal Bank Robbery and Incidental Crimes Statute, 3.149-3.151
  - Deaths, injuries, and hostages taken, 3.151
- Hate crimes, 3.112
- Jail inmates
  - Current offense, 6.19, 6.20
- Juveniles in custody, 6.10
- Offenses known to police, 3.106-3.112, 3.115, 3.116, 3.146, 3.160, 4.19
  - Average loss, 3.111
  - Cities, 3.110, 4.19
  - Federal parks, 3.115, 3.116
  - Hate crimes, 3.112
  - Rates, 3.106-3.108
  - Size of place, 3.107-3.109, 4.19
  - Type of target, 3.146
- Parole and supervised release, 6.4, 6.70, 6.71
- Prisoners
  - Federal, 6.58
  - Recidivism, 6.50, 6.51
  - Time served, 6.44, 6.58
- Probationers
  - Number, 6.4
  - Outcomes, 6.8
- Self-reported, 3.43-3.45
  - High school seniors, 3.43-3.45
- Sentences, 5.19, 5.25, 5.29, 5.31-5.33, 5.48, 5.49, 5.59, 5.60, 6.44, 6.58
  - Federal courts, 5.19, 5.25, 5.29

LARCENY-THEFT, Sentences (continued)
- Length of sentence, 5.19, 5.25, 5.48, 5.60, 6.44
- Organizations, 5.33
- Time served, 6.44, 6.58
- Type of collateral penalty, 5.49
- Type, 5.19, 5.25, 5.29, 5.59
- U.S. Postal Inspection Service, 5.74
- Victimizations, 3.1-3.3, 3.21-3.27, 3.32-3.42, 3.61
  - At school, 3.40-3.42, 3.61
  - High school seniors, 3.37-3.42
  - Households experiencing, 3.27
  - Locality of residence, 3.21, 3.25, 3.26
  - Number, 3.1, 3.2, 3.22, 3.23
    - Race and ethnicity of head of household, 3.22, 3.23
  - Place of occurrence, 3.32
  - Race and ethnicity of head of household, 3.22, 3.23
  - Rates, 3.1-3.3, 3.21-3.26
    - Family income, 3.21, 3.24
    - Locality of residence, 3.21, 3.25, 3.26
    - Race and ethnicity of head of household, 3.22, 3.23, 3.26
  - Reporting to police, 3.33-3.35
    - Reasons for not reporting, 3.35
    - Reasons for reporting, 3.34
- See also:
  - Property crime

LAW ENFORCEMENT
- Bureau of Alcohol, Tobacco and Firearms
  - Number and characteristics of officers, 1.72, 1.75
- Drug Enforcement Administration
  - Budget, 1.76
  - Number of officers, 1.72, 1.76
  - Seizures and removals, 4.37-4.39
  - Staff, 1.76
- Edward Byrne law enforcement funds, 1.16
- Employment and payroll, 1.17, 1.19, 1.21-1.38, 1.45, 1.46, 1.55-1.61, 1.63, 1.64, 1.66-1.75
  - Cities, 1.55-1.58, 1.64, 1.66-1.70
  - Federal, 1.17, 1.21, 1.72-1.75
  - Female police officers, 1.56, 1.58, 1.60
  - Full-time sworn personnel, 1.23-1.36, 1.55-1.59
  - Inspectors general, 1.73
  - Local, 1.17, 1.19, 1.21, 1.22, 1.27, 1.29, 1.33, 1.35, 1.45
  - Minority police officers, 1.56, 1.58, 1.60
  - Number of employees, 1.27-1.34, 1.57
  - Officer characteristics, 1.37, 1.38, 1.60
  - Region, 1.64, 1.66-1.68
  - Sheriffs, 1.27, 1.30, 1.34, 1.36, 1.46
  - Special jurisdiction departments, 1.27, 1.32

LAW ENFORCEMENT, Employment and payroll (continued)
  State, 1.19, 1.21-1.24, 1.26-1.32
    State police, 1.27, 1.31, 1.59-1.61
      Salaries, 1.61
    Suburban, 1.66-1.68
    Tribal police, 1.63
  Expenditures, 1.2-1.4, 1.6-1.8, 1.12, 1.17, 1.62, 1.65
    Federal, 1.2-1.4, 1.12
    State, 1.2-1.4, 1.6, 1.8
    State police, 1.62
  Federal budget authorities and outlays, 1.12
  Federal Bureau of Investigation
    Number and characteristics of officers, 1.72, 1.75
  Federal Bureau of Prisons
    Number and characteristics of officers, 1.72, 1.75, 1.108
  Immigration and Naturalization Service
    Deportations, 4.47
    Detainees, 6.61
    Number and characteristics of officers, 1.72, 1.75
  Internal Revenue Service
    Number and characteristics of officers, 1.72, 1.75
  Local police departments, 1.27, 1.29, 1.33, 1.35, 1.37, 1.39, 1.41, 1.43, 1.45, 1.47, 1.49, 1.51, 1.53
    Budgets, 1.43
    Community policing, 1.51, 1.53
    Education requirements, 1.39
    Full-time sworn personnel, 1.27, 1.29, 1.33, 1.35
    Number of departments, 1.27, 1.29, 1.33
    Number of employees, 1.27, 1.29, 1.33
    Officer characteristics, 1.37
    Salaries, 1.45
    School resource officers, 1.53
    Training requirements, 1.41
    Weapons authorized, 1.47, 1.49
  National Park Service
    Number and characteristics of officers, 1.72, 1.75
  Officers killed and assaulted, 3.152-3.165
    Accidentally killed, 3.154, 3.162
    Characteristics of offenders, 3.160, 3.161
    Characteristics of officers, 3.158, 3.159
    Circumstances, 3.155-3.157, 3.162-3.164
    Extent of injury, 3.153, 3.165
    Federal officers, 3.152, 3.153
    Number, 3.153-3.155, 3.159
    Terrorist incidents, 3.159
    Trend, 3.153-3.155
    Type of weapon, 3.153, 3.163, 3.165
  Police departments, number of, 1.27-1.34

LAW ENFORCEMENT (continued)
  Public opinion, 2.12, 2.13, 2.17, 2.20-2.27, 2.72, 2.73, 2.83
    Confidence in, 2.12, 2.13
    High school seniors, 2.73
    Honesty and ethics, 2.17, 2.20, 2.21
    Increased powers, 2.27
    Performance, 2.22
    Racial profiling, 2.26
    Use of force, 2.23-2.25
  Racial profiling, 2.26
  Sheriffs' offices, 1.27, 1.30, 1.34, 1.36, 1.38, 1.40, 1.42, 1.44, 1.46, 1.48, 1.50, 1.52, 1.54
    Budgets, 1.44
    Community policing, 1.52, 1.54
    Education requirements, 1.40
    Full-time sworn personnel, 1.27, 1.30, 1.34, 1.36
    Number of departments, 1.27, 1.30
    Number of employees, 1.27, 1.30, 1.34
    Officer characteristics, 1.38
    Salaries, 1.46
    School resource officers, 1.54
    Training requirements, 1.42
    Weapons authorized, 1.48, 1.50
  Special jurisdiction departments, 1.27, 1.32
  State police departments, 1.27, 1.31, 1.59-1.62
    Full-time sworn personnel, 1.27, 1.31, 1.59
    Minority police officers, 1.60
    Number of employees, 1.27, 1.31, 1.59
    Officer characteristics, 1.60
    Operating expenditures, 1.62
    Salaries, 1.61
  Tribal police, 1.63
  U.S. Capitol Police
    Number and characteristics of officers, 1.72, 1.75
  U.S. Customs Service
    Number and characteristics of officers, 1.72, 1.75
    Seizures, 4.43, 4.44
  U.S. Marshals Service
    Budget, 1.78
    Number and characteristics of officers, 1.72, 1.75
    Staff, 1.78
    Workload, 1.77
  U.S. Postal Inspection Service
    Arrests and convictions, 5.73, 5.74
    Mail fraud cases, 5.73, 5.74
    Number and characteristics of officers, 1.72, 1.75
  U.S. Secret Service
    Number and characteristics of officers, 1.72, 1.75
  See also:
    Offenses known to police

LAWYERS
  See Prosecution
  See Public defense
  See Public opinion
LIQUOR LAWS
  See Alcohol
  See Public opinion
  See Traffic violations
LOANSHARKING
  Basis for wiretap, 5.3
MAGISTRATES
  See Courts
  See Judges
MARIJUANA
  Arrestees testing positive, 4.30
  Court cases, Federal, 5.10, 5.24, 5.25, 5.39
    Dispositions, 5.24
    Sentences, 5.25
    Sentencing guideline cases, 5.39
  Drug Enforcement Administration
    Cannabis Eradication Program, 4.38
    Seizures, 4.36-4.38
  Emergency department episodes, 3.93, 3.94
  Military personnel, use, 3.90
  Public opinion
    Availability, 2.83, 2.84
      High school seniors, 2.83
    Disapproval of use, 2.85, 2.86
      High school seniors, 2.85
    Harmfulness, 2.76, 2.77, 2.79-2.82
      High school seniors, 2.79
      Young adults, 2.81
    Legalization, 2.67-2.69, 2.87-2.90
      College freshmen, 2.90
      High school seniors, 2.88, 2.89
      Medical use, 2.69
    Students, 2.76, 2.80, 2.84, 2.86
  Seizures, Drug Enforcement Administration, 4.36-4.38
  Sentences, 5.29, 5.31, 5.32, 5.39
    Fines, 5.32
    Length of sentence, 5.31
    Prison, 5.29
    Probation, 5.29
    Restitution, 5.32
  Testing of arrestees, 4.30
  Use
    Among arrestees, 4.30
    Among jail inmates prior to offense, 6.21
    Among military personnel, 3.90
    Among students, 3.55, 3.57, 3.62, 3.63
      At school, 3.55, 3.57
    At school, 3.55, 3.57
    Self-reported, 3.49-3.53, 3.55, 3.57, 3.62, 3.63, 3.65, 3.68-3.76, 3.86-3.88
      College students, 3.71, 3.72

Index 623

MARIJUANA, Use, Self-reported (continued)
    High school seniors,
      3.49-3.51, 3.53, 3.63, 3.65,
      3.68, 3.69
        Driving under the
          influence, 3.49-3.51,
          3.53
    High school students, 3.55,
      3.57, 3.62, 3.63, 3.70
    National households,
      3.86-3.88
    Young adults, 3.74-3.76,
      3.86-3.88
  See also:
    Defendants
    Drugs
    Narcotic drug laws
MISDEMEANORS
  See Offenses known to police
  See Specific offenses (e.g., Assault, Larceny-theft)
MOTOR VEHICLE THEFT
  Arrests, 4.1-4.3, 4.5-4.16, 4.18-4.20,
    4.22, 4.33
    Age, 4.5-4.7, 4.9, 4.10, 4.12,
      4.14, 4.16, 4.22
    Cities, 4.3, 4.11, 4.12, 4.19, 4.22
    Clearance by arrest, 4.19, 4.22
    Federal, 4.33
    Race, 4.10, 4.12, 4.14, 4.16
    Rates, 4.2, 4.3, 4.18
    Region, 4.18
    Rural counties, 4.3, 4.15, 4.16,
      4.19, 4.22
    Sex, 4.8, 4.9, 4.11, 4.13, 4.15
    Size of place, 4.3, 4.19, 4.22
    State, 4.5
    Suburban areas, 4.3, 4.13, 4.14,
      4.19, 4.22
  Community supervision, Federal
    offenders, 6.4
  Convictions, 5.17
  Court cases, Federal, 5.10, 5.13, 5.17,
    5.19, 5.24-5.29, 5.31, 5.32, 5.34-5.36,
    5.67, 6.58
    Appeals, 5.67
    Citizens and non-citizens, 5.35
    Convictions, 5.17
    Defendant characteristics, 5.26,
      5.27
    Dispositions, 5.17, 5.24
    Method of conviction, 5.17, 5.34
    Pretrial action, 5.13
    Sentences, 5.19, 5.25, 5.29, 5.31,
      5.32
    Sentencing guidelines, 5.26-5.29,
      5.31, 5.32, 5.34-5.36
    Time served, 6.58
  Court cases, State, 5.44-5.50
    Convictions, 5.44-5.46, 5.50
      Method of conviction, 5.46,
        5.50
      Number of, 5.44
      Offender characteristics, 5.45
    Sentences, 5.47-5.50
      Length of sentence, 5.48
      Method of conviction, 5.50

MOTOR VEHICLE THEFT, Court cases,
State, Sentences (continued)
      Time from arrest, 5.50
      Type of additional penalty,
        5.49
  Hate crimes, 3.112
  Jail inmates
    Current offense, 6.19, 6.20
  Juveniles in custody, 6.10
  Offenses known to police, 3.106-3.112,
    3.115, 3.116, 4.19
    Average loss, 3.111
    Cities, 3.110, 4.19
    Federal parks, 3.115, 3.116
    Hate crimes, 3.112
    Rates, 3.106-3.108
    Size of place, 3.107-3.109, 4.19
  Parole and supervised release, 6.4,
    6.70, 6.71
  Prisoners
    Recidivism, 6.50, 6.51
    Time served, 6.44, 6.58
  Probationers
    Number, 6.4
    Outcomes, 6.8
  Self-reported, 3.43-3.45
    High school seniors, 3.43-3.45
  Sentences, 5.19, 5.25, 5.29, 5.31, 5.32,
    5.47, 5.48, 6.44, 6.58
    Federal courts, 5.19, 5.25, 5.29
    Fines, 5.32
    Length of sentence, 5.19, 6.44
    Prison, 5.25, 5.29
    Probation, 5.19, 5.25, 5.29
    Restitution, 5.32
    Time served, 6.44, 6.58
    Type of sentence, 5.19
  Victimizations, 3.1-3.3, 3.21-3.27,
    3.32-3.35
    Households experiencing, 3.27
    Locality of residence, 3.21, 3.25,
      3.26
    Number, 3.1, 3.2, 3.22, 3.23, 3.26
      Race of head of household,
        3.22, 3.23
    Place of occurrence, 3.32
    Rates, 3.1-3.3, 3.21-3.26
      Family income, 3.21, 3.24
      Locality of residence, 3.21,
        3.25, 3.26
      Race and ethnicity of head of
        household, 3.22, 3.23, 3.26
    Reporting to police, 3.33-3.35
      Reasons for not reporting,
        3.35
      Reasons for reporting, 3.34
  See also:
    Property crime
MURDER AND NONNEGLIGENT
MANSLAUGHTER
  Arrests, 4.1-4.3, 4.5-4.17, 4.19, 4.20,
    4.22, 4.33, 5.50
    Age, 4.5-4.7, 4.9, 4.10, 4.12, 4.14,
      4.16, 4.22
    Cities, 4.3, 4.11, 4.12, 4.19, 4.22
    Clearance by arrest, 4.19, 4.22
    Federal, 4.33

MURDER AND NONNEGLIGENT
MANSLAUGHTER, Arrests (continued)
    Race, 4.10, 4.12, 4.14, 4.16
    Rates, 4.2, 4.3, 4.17
    Region, 4.17
    Rural counties, 4.3, 4.15, 4.16,
      4.19, 4.22
    Sex, 4.8, 4.9, 4.11, 4.13, 4.15
    Size of place, 4.3, 4.19, 4.22
    State, 4.5
    Suburban areas, 4.3, 4.13, 4.14,
      4.19, 4.22
    Time to sentencing, State courts,
      5.50
  Basis for wiretap, 5.3
  Clearance by arrest, 4.19, 4.22
  Community supervision, Federal
    offenders, 6.4
  Convictions
    Federal courts, 5.17
    Method of conviction, 5.17, 5.46,
      5.50
    Number of, 5.17, 5.44, 5.46
    Offender characteristics, 5.45
  Court cases, Federal, 5.13, 5.17, 5.19,
    5.24-5.29, 5.31, 5.32, 5.34-5.36,
    5.67, 6.58
    Appeals, 5.67
    Citizens and non-citizens, 5.35
    Convictions, 5.17
    Defendant characteristics, 5.26,
      5.27
    Dispositions, 5.17, 5.24
    Method of conviction, 5.17, 5.34
    Pretrial action, 5.13
    Sentencing guideline cases,
      5.26-5.29, 5.31, 5.32, 5.34-5.36
  Court cases, State, 5.44-5.50
    Convictions, 5.44-5.46, 5.50
      Method of conviction, 5.46,
        5.50
      Number of, 5.44
      Offender characteristics, 5.45
    Sentences, 5.47-5.50
      Length of sentence, 5.48
      Method of conviction, 5.50
      Time from arrest, 5.50
      Type of additional penalty,
        5.49
  Court cases, urban counties, 5.51-5.60
    Arrests, 5.51
    Convictions, 5.57, 5.58
    Defendant characteristics, 5.52
    Pretrial release, 5.54-5.56
    Prior convictions, 5.53
    Sentences, 5.59, 5.60
  Hate crimes, 3.112
  Jail inmates
    Current offense, 6.19, 6.20
  Juveniles in custody, 6.10
  Offenses known to police, 3.106-3.112,
    3.115-3.131, 3.134, 4.19, 4.22, 6.79
    Age of victim, 3.119, 3.121,
      3.124-3.126, 3.130
    Average loss, 3.111
    Circumstances, 3.120
    Cities, 3.110, 4.22

MURDER AND NONNEGLIGENT MANSLAUGHTER, Offenses known to police (continued)
  Federal parks, 3.115, 3.116
  Hate crimes, 3.112
  Involving intimates, 3.131
  Murder and death penalty trend, 6.79
  Offender characteristics, 3.127-3.130
  Race of victim, 3.123-3.126, 3.129-3.131
  Rates, 3.106-3.108, 3.126-3.128
  Region, 3.118
  Sex of victim, 3.122, 3.124-3.126, 3.129-3.131
  Size of place, 3.107, 3.109, 4.19
  Sniper attacks, 3.134
  Type of weapon, 3.117-3.119
  Victim-offender relationship, 3.120
Parole and supervised release, 6.4, 6.70, 6.71
Pretrial release and detention, 5.13
Prisoners
  Current offense, 6.56
  Federal, 6.58
  Firearms possession during offense, 6.37
  Recidivism, 6.50, 6.51
  Time served, 6.44, 6.58
Probationers
  Number, 6.4
  Outcomes, 6.8
Sentences, 5.19, 5.25, 5.29, 5.31, 5.32, 5.48, 5.49, 5.59, 5.60, 6.44, 6.58
  Federal courts, 5.19
  Fines, 5.32
  Incarceration, 5.19, 5.25, 5.29
  Length of sentence, 5.19, 5.31, 5.48, 5.60, 6.44
  Method of conviction, 5.50
  Probation, 5.19, 5.25, 5.29
  Restitution, 5.32
  Time served, 6.44, 6.58
  Type of collateral penalty, 5.49
  Type of sentence, 5.25, 5.59
Victimizations, 3.125, 3.126, 3.130, 3.131, 3.133-3.135
  In the workplace, 3.135
  Involving intimates, 3.131
  Rates, 3.125, 3.126
  September 11 terrorist attacks, 3.133
  Sniper attacks, 3.134
  Victim characteristics, 3.125, 3.126, 3.130, 3.131
Workplace homicides, 3.135
See also:
  Capital punishment
  Deaths
  Violent crime

NARCOTIC DRUG LAWS
Drug abuse violations, arrests, 4.1, 4.3, 4.6-4.16, 4.29, 4.38
Drug Prevention and Control Act
  Defendants disposed, 5.24
  Defendants sentenced, 5.25

NARCOTIC DRUG LAWS (continued)
Narcotic Addict Rehabilitation Act
  Defendants disposed, 5.22
U.S. Postal Inspection Service, 5.74
See also:
  Drugs
  Prisoners
  Public opinion

NATIONAL CRIME VICTIMIZATION SURVEY
See Assault
See Burglary
See Larceny-theft
See Motor vehicle theft
See Property crime
See Rape, Forcible
See Robbery
See Victimization
See Violent crime

OBSCENITY
See Pornography

OFFENDERS
See Arrests
See Courts
See Defendants
See Juvenile delinquency
See Offenses known to police
See Prisoners
See Public officials
See Specific offenses (e.g., Murder, Robbery)
See Victimization

OFFENSES KNOWN TO POLICE
Arson, 3.110, 3.112, 3.115, 3.116, 3.166-3.169, 4.24
  Cities, 3.110
  Federal parks, 3.115, 3.116
  Hate crimes, 3.112
  Type of target and structure, 3.168, 3.169, 4.24
Assault, 3.106-3.112, 3.115, 3.116, 3.143, 3.144, 3.152, 3.153, 3.164, 3.165, 4.19, 4.22
  Cities, 3.110
  Federal parks, 3.115, 3.116
  Hate crimes, 3.112
  On law enforcement officers, 3.152, 3.153, 3.164, 3.165
  Rates, 3.106-3.108
  Size of place, 3.107-3.109, 4.19
  Type of weapon, 3.143, 3.144
Bombings, 3.170-3.172
  Injuries and deaths, 3.170
  Property damage, 3.170
  State, 3.172
  Target, 3.171
Burglary, 3.106-3.109, 3.111, 3.112, 3.115, 3.116, 3.145, 4.19, 4.22
  Average loss, 3.111
  Cities, 3.110, 4.19
  Federal parks, 3.115, 3.116
  Hate crimes, 3.112
  Place and time of occurrence, 3.145
  Rates, 3.106-3.108
  Size of place, 3.107-3.109, 4.19
Hate crimes, 3.112-3.114

OFFENSES KNOWN TO POLICE (continued)
In Federal parks, 3.115, 3.116
Larceny-theft, 3.106-3.112, 3.115, 3.116, 3.146, 4.19, 4.22
  Average loss, 3.111
  Cities, 3.110, 4.19
  Federal parks, 3.115, 3.116
  Hate crimes, 3.112
  Rates, 3.106-3.108
  Size of place, 3.107-3.109
  Type of target, 3.146
Law enforcement officers killed and assaulted, 3.152-3.158, 3.160, 3.161, 3.163-3.165
  Characteristics of offenders, 3.160, 3.161
  Characteristics of officers, 3.158
  Circumstances, 3.156, 3.157, 3.163, 3.164
  Extent of injury, 3.153, 3.165
  Federal officers, 3.152, 3.153
  Type of weapon, 3.153, 3.163, 3.165
Motor vehicle theft, 3.106-3.112, 3.115, 3.116, 3.147, 4.19, 4.22
  Average loss, 3.111
  Cities, 3.110, 4.19
  Federal parks, 3.115, 3.116
  Hate crimes, 3.112
  Rates, 3.106-3.108
  Size of place, 3.107-3.109
Murder and nonnegligent manslaughter, 3.106-3.112, 3.115-3.129, 3.134, 3.158, 4.19, 4.22
  Age of victim, 3.119, 3.121, 3.124-3.126
  Average loss, 3.111
  Circumstances, 3.120
  Cities, 3.110, 4.19
  Federal parks, 3.115, 3.116
  Hate crimes, 3.112
  Offender characteristics, 3.127, 3.128
  Race of victim, 3.123-3.126, 3.129
  Rates, 3.106-3.108, 3.126-3.128
  Sex of victim, 3.122, 3.124-3.126, 3.158
  Size of place, 3.107-3.109, 4.19
  Sniper attacks, 3.134
  Type of weapon, 3.117, 3.119
  Victim-offender relationship, 3.120
Property crime, 3.106-3.109, 4.19-4.22
  Clearance by arrest, 4.20-4.22
  Rates, 3.106-3.109
  Size of place, 3.107-3.109, 4.19
Rape, forcible, 3.106-3.112, 3.115, 3.116, 4.19, 4.22
  Average loss, 3.111
  Cities, 3.109, 4.19
  Federal parks, 3.115, 3.116
  Hate crimes, 3.112
  Rates, 3.106-3.108
  Size of place, 3.107-3.109, 4.19
Robbery, 3.106-3.112, 3.115, 3.116, 3.140-3.142, 4.19, 4.22
  Average loss, 3.111

Index 625

OFFENSES KNOWN TO POLICE,
Robbery (continued)
    Cities, 3.110, 4.19
    Federal parks, 3.115, 3.116
    Hate crimes, 3.112
    Place of occurrence, 3.142
    Rates, 3.106-3.109
    Region, 3.141
    Size of place, 3.107-3.109, 4.19
    Type of weapon, 3.140, 3.141
Violent crime, 3.106-3.109, 4.19-4.21
    Rates, 3.106-3.108
    Size of place, 3.107-3.109, 4.19
See also:
    Arrests
    Self-reported criminal activity
    Specific offenses (e.g., Assault, Arson)
    Victimization

OPINION POLLS
See Public opinion

PARDONS
See Clemency
See U.S. Pardon Attorney

PAROLE
Federal offenders, 6.4, 6.70, 6.71
Jail inmates, violations, 6.19, 6.20
Parolees, 6.1, 6.4, 6.65-6.67, 6.70, 6.71
    Federal, 6.4, 6.66, 6.70, 6.71
        Outcomes, 6.70, 6.71
    Movement, 6.66
    Number, 6.1, 6.4, 6.66
    Offense, 6.70, 6.71
    Outcome, 6.67, 6.70
    Rate, 6.65, 6.66
    State, 6.66, 6.67
    Trends, 6.1, 6.65, 6.67
See also:
    Corrections

PAYROLL
See Employment

PENITENTIARY
See Corrections
See Prisons

PERSONNEL
See Employment

PETIT JURY
See Juries

POCKET-PICKING
See Larceny-theft
See Victimization

POLICE
See Employment
See Expenditures
See Law enforcement
See Public opinion

PORNOGRAPHY
Court cases, Federal, 5.26-5.29, 5.31, 5.32, 5.34-5.36
    Citizens and non-citizens, 5.35
    Defendant characteristics, 5.26, 5.27
    Method of conviction, 5.34
    Sentences, 5.29, 5.31, 5.32
    Sentencing guidelines, 5.26-5.29, 5.31, 5.32, 5.34-5.36
Public opinion, 2.97

PORNOGRAPHY (continued)
Sentences, 5.29, 5.31, 5.32, 5.34
U.S. Postal Inspection Service
    Arrests and convictions, 5.74

PRISONERS
Correctional population incarcerated, 6.1, 6.2
Federal
    Age, 6.53, 6.54
    AIDS and HIV cases, 6.74, 6.76-6.78
    Capital punishment, 6.80-6.86
        Executions, 6.82-6.86
        Number under sentence of death, 6.80-6.83
    Deaths, 6.76-6.78
    Drug offenses, 6.56, 6.57
    Education programs, 1.109, 6.45, 6.46
        Educational attainment, 6.45
        Programs and participation, 1.109, 6.46
    Female prisoners, 6.41
    Firearms possession during offense, 6.35-6.37
    Immigration detainees, 6.61
    Immigration offenders, 5.77, 6.60
    Noncitizens in custody, 6.42
    Number of, 6.13, 6.30-6.32, 6.53, 6.54
    Offenders returning to prison, 6.68, 6.69
    Population, 6.13, 6.28-6.32, 6.34, 6.41, 6.53, 6.54
        Housed in other facilities, 6.32
        Race and ethnicity, 6.34
        Rate, 6.28, 6.29
        Sex, 6.28, 6.31, 6.41
        Trends, 6.13, 6.53
    Race and ethnicity, 6.34, 6.53-6.56, 6.80, 6.81
        Death penalty prisoners, 6.80, 6.81
    Rate, 6.28, 6.29, 6.41
        Sex, 6.28, 6.41
    Recidivism, 6.68, 6.69
    Region, 6.34, 6.53, 6.54
    Releases, 6.58, 6.59
    Security level, 6.55
    Sex, 6.28, 6.31, 6.41, 6.53, 6.54, 6.81
        Death penalty prisoners, 6.81
        Rate, 6.28
    Time served, 6.58, 6.59
    Type of facility, 6.31
    Type of offense, 6.56
Jail inmates
    AIDS and HIV cases, 6.26, 6.27
    Alcohol use, 6.22
    Conviction status, 6.18, 6.19
    Current offense, 6.19, 6.20
    Deaths, 6.27
    Drug use, 6.21

PRISONERS, Jail inmates (continued)
    Education programs, 1.109, 6.45, 6.46
        Educational attainment, 6.45
        Programs and participation, 1.109, 6.46
    Family background, 6.23
    Indian jails, 6.25
    Inmate to employee ratio, 1.98
    Juvenile inmates, 6.14
    Number, 6.1, 6.13, 6.14, 6.16, 6.18, 6.24, 6.25
    Privately operated jails, 1.105
    Race and ethnicity, 6.17, 6.18, 6.20, 6.24
    Sex, 6.14, 6.17, 6.18, 6.20, 6.24
    Trends, 6.1, 6.14
    Type of supervision, 6.15, 6.16
Petitions filed, 5.65, 5.67
Private correctional facilities, 6.31, 6.34, 6.40
State
    Age, 6.39, 6.40
        Under age 18, 6.39, 6.40
    AIDS and HIV cases, 6.74-6.78
    Capital punishment, 6.79-6.86
        Executions, 6.79, 6.82, 6.84-6.86
        Number under sentence of death, 6.79-6.83
    Deaths, 6.76-6.78
    Education programs, 1.109, 6.45, 6.46
        Educational attainment, 6.45
        Programs and participation, 1.109, 6.46
    Female prisoners, 6.41
    Firearms possession during offense, 6.35-6.38
    Mental health treatment, 6.72, 6.73
    Noncitizens in custody, 6.42
    Population, 6.13, 6.28-6.34, 6.41
        Housed in jails or other facilities, 6.32
        Race and ethnicity, 6.33, 6.34
        Region, 6.29, 6.30
        Sex, 6.28, 6.31, 6.33, 6.41
        State, 6.29, 6.30
        Trends, 6.13
    Race and ethnicity, 6.33, 6.34, 6.80, 6.81
        Death penalty prisoners, 6.80, 6.81
    Rate, 6.28, 6.29, 6.33, 6.41
        Sex, 6.28, 6.41
    Recidivism, 6.47-6.52
        Offense, 6.50-6.52
        Prisoner characteristics, 6.47, 6.49
        Time to recidivism, 6.48
    Region, 6.29, 6.30, 6.34
    Sex, 6.28, 6.31, 6.33, 6.41, 6.80, 6.81
        Death penalty prisoners, 6.81
        Rate, 6.28, 6.33, 6.41

PRISONERS, State (continued)
    Time served, 6.43, 6.44
    Type of facility, 6.31
  U.S. Air Force, 6.64
  U.S. Army, 6.64
  U.S. Coast Guard, 6.64
  U.S. Marine Corps, 6.64
  U.S. Navy, 6.64
  See also:
    Capital punishment
    Clemency
    Corrections
    Juvenile corrections
    Parole
    Probation
    Sentences

PRISONS
  Federal, 1.102-1.104, 1.106-1.108
    Capacity, 1.102
    Characteristics of correctional personnel, 1.104, 1.107, 1.108
    Characteristics of facilities, 1.102, 1.103, 1.106
    Number of prisons, 1.102, 1.103
    Security level, 1.102
    Type of facility, 1.102, 1.103
  Offenses committed in Federal prisons, 5.26, 5.27, 5.29, 5.31, 5.32, 5.34-5.36
  Private correctional facilities, 1.102-1.104
  Staffing, 1.104, 1.107
  State, 1.102-1.104, 6.72, 6.73
    Capacity, 1.102
    Characteristics of correctional personnel, 1.104
    Characteristics of facilities, 1.102, 1.103, 1.106
    Mental health treatment, 6.72, 6.73
    Number of prisons, 1.102, 1.103
    Security level, 1.102
    Type of facility, 1.102, 1.103
  See also:
    Corrections
    Jails

PROBATION
  Federal offenders, 5.19, 6.4, 6.8
  Investigative reports by Federal officers, 1.97
  Jail inmates, violations, 6.19, 6.20
  Officers, Federal, 6.7
  Probationers
    Education programs, 1.109, 6.45, 6.46
      Educational attainment, 6.45
      Programs and participation, 1.109, 6.46
    Federal, 6.3-6.8
    Movement, 6.3, 6.6
    Number, 6.1, 6.3, 6.4, 6.6
    Rate, 6.3
    Region, 6.3
    State, 6.3
  Sentences, 5.19, 5.25, 5.29, 5.47, 5.48, 6.8
    Average length, 5.25, 5.48

PROPERTY CRIME
  Arrests, 4.1-4.3, 4.5-4.16, 4.18-4.23, 4.33-4.35
    Age, 4.5-4.7, 4.9, 4.10, 4.12, 4.14, 4.16, 4.22, 4.23
    Cities, 4.11, 4.12, 4.19, 4.21, 4.22
    Clearance by arrest, 4.19-4.23
    Federal, 4.33-4.35
    Race, 4.10, 4.12, 4.14, 4.16
    Rates, 4.2, 4.3, 4.18
    Region, 4.18
    Rural counties, 4.3, 4.15, 4.16, 4.19, 4.21, 4.22
    Sex, 4.8, 4.9, 4.11, 4.13, 4.15
    Size of place, 4.19, 4.21, 4.22
    State, 4.5
    Suburban areas, 4.3, 4.13, 4.14, 4.19, 4.21, 4.22
  Community supervision, Federal offenders, 6.4
  Convictions, 5.17
  Court cases, Federal, 5.13, 5.16-5.21, 6.58, 6.59
    Convictions, 5.17, 5.18
    Dispositions, 5.17
    Method of conviction, 5.17
    Offender characteristics, 5.18, 5.20, 5.21
    Pretrial action, 5.13, 5.16
    Sentences, 5.19-5.21
    Time served, 6.58, 6.59
  Court cases, State, 5.44-5.50
    Convictions, 5.44-5.46, 5.50
      Method of conviction, 5.46, 5.50
      Number of, 5.44
      Offender characteristics, 5.45
    Sentences, 5.47-5.50
      Length of sentence, 5.48
      Method of conviction, 5.50
      Time from arrest, 5.50
      Type of additional penalty, 5.49
  Court cases, urban counties, 5.51-5.60
    Arrests, 5.51
    Convictions, 5.57, 5.58
    Defendant characteristics, 5.52
    Pretrial release, 5.54-5.56
    Prior convictions, 5.53
    Sentences, 5.59, 5.60
  Jail inmates
    Current offense, 6.19, 6.20
  Juvenile court cases, 5.61-5.64
    Case outcomes, 5.63, 5.64
    Demographic characteristics, 5.61-5.64
    Offense type, 5.63, 5.64
  Juveniles in custody, 6.10
  Offenses known to police, 3.106-3.109, 4.19
    Rates, 3.106-3.108
    Size of place, 3.107-3.109, 4.19
  Parole and supervised release, 6.4, 6.70, 6.71
  Pretrial release and detention, 5.13

PROPERTY CRIME (continued)
  Prisoners
    Current offense, 6.56, 6.58
    Firearms possession during offense, 6.37, 6.38
    Recidivism, 6.50-6.52
    Time served, 6.44, 6.58
  Probationers
    Number, 6.4
    Outcomes, 6.8
  Sentences, 5.19-5.21, 5.47-5.49, 5.59, 5.60, 6.44, 6.58, 6.59
    Federal courts, 5.19-5.21
    Incarceration, 5.19
    Length of sentence, 5.19-5.21, 5.60, 6.44
    State courts, 5.47-5.49
    Time served, 6.44, 6.58, 6.59
    Type of sentence, 5.19, 5.59
  Victimizations, crimes of theft, 3.1-3.3, 3.21-3.27, 3.32-3.35
    Households experiencing, 3.27
    Locality of residence, 3.21
    Number, 3.1, 3.2, 3.22, 3.23, 3.26
      Race and ethnicity of victim, 3.22, 3.23, 3.26
    Place of occurrence, 3.32
    Race and ethnicity of head of household, 3.21
    Rates, 3.1-3.3, 3.21-3.26
      Family income of victim, 3.21, 3.24
      Locality of residence, 3.21, 3.25, 3.26
      Race and ethnicity of victim, 3.22, 3.23, 3.26
    Reporting to police, 3.33-3.35
      Reasons for not reporting, 3.35
      Reasons for reporting, 3.34
  See also:
    Specific offenses (e.g., Burglary, Larceny-theft)

PROSECUTION
  Federal budget authorities and outlays, 1.12
  Judicial and legal services
    Employment and payroll, 1.17, 1.19, 1.21-1.24
    Expenditures, 1.2-1.4, 1.6-1.8, 1.12
    Prosecutors' offices, 1.85-1.89
      Budget, 1.86, 1.89
      DNA evidence, 1.88
      Personnel, 1.85, 1.89
      Salaries, 1.87, 1.89
  See also:
    Courts
    Defendants
    Sentences

PROSTITUTION AND COMMERCIALIZED VICE
  Arrests, 4.1, 4.3, 4.6-4.16, 4.33
    Age, 4.6, 4.7, 4.9, 4.10, 4.12, 4.14, 4.16
    Cities, 4.3, 4.11, 4.12

Index 627

PROSTITUTION AND COMMERCIALIZED
VICE, Arrests (continued)
    Federal, 4.33
    Race, 4.10, 4.12, 4.14, 4.16
    Rate, 4.3
    Rural counties, 4.15, 4.16
    Sex, 4.8, 4.9, 4.11, 4.13, 4.15
    Size of place, 4.3
    Suburban, 4.13, 4.14
  Court cases, Federal, 5.26-5.29, 5.31, 5.32, 5.34-5.36
    Citizens and non-citizens, 5.35
    Defendant characteristics, 5.26, 5.27
    Method of conviction, 5.34
    Sentences, 5.29, 5.31, 5.32
    Sentencing guideline cases, 5.26-5.29, 5.31, 5.32, 5.34-5.36
  In Federal parks, 3.116
PUBLIC DEFENSE
  See Employment
  See Expenditures
PUBLIC OFFICIALS
  Abuse of public office cases, 5.79
  Judges, 1.80, 1.90-1.93
    Salaries, 1.80, 1.90
    Selection and retention, 1.91-1.93
  Public opinion
    Justice system, 2.72, 2.75
    Lawyers, 2.17-2.19
    Occupations and institutions, 2.9, 2.10, 2.14, 2.15, 2.17-2.21, 2.75
    Police, 2.20, 2.21, 2.23-2.25
      Use of force, 2.23-2.25
    U.S. Supreme Court, 2.9, 2.10, 2.14, 2.15, 2.72, 2.74
PUBLIC OPINION
  Abortion, 2.2, 2.91, 2.100, 2.101
    College freshmen, 2.91
    Legality, 2.100, 2.101
  Alcohol, 2.3, 2.77-2.82, 2.84-2.86
    As important problem, 2.3
    Availability, 2.84
    Disapproval of use, 2.85, 2.86
      High school seniors, 2.85
    Harmfulness, 2.77, 2.79-2.82
      High school seniors, 2.79
      Young adults, 2.81
    Teenagers' perceptions of those who use, 2.78
  Capital punishment, 2.49-2.58, 2.93
    College freshmen, 2.93
    Deterrent effect, 2.57, 2.58
    Fairness of application, 2.54
    For murder, 2.49-2.53
    Reasons for favoring, 2.55
    Reasons for opposing, 2.56
    Selected groups, 2.53
    Versus life without parole, 2.49
  Cigarettes, 2.3, 2.78-2.81, 2.85
    Disapproval of use, 2.85
    Harmfulness, 2.81, 2.82
    Teenagers' perceptions of those who use, 2.78
  College freshmen, 2.90-2.95

PUBLIC OPINION (continued)
  Courts, 2.9, 2.10, 2.14, 2.15, 2.47, 2.72, 2.74, 2.75, 2.92
    College freshmen, 2.92
    Severity, 2.47
    U.S. Supreme Court, 2.9, 2.10, 2.14, 2.15, 2.72, 2.74
      High school seniors, 2.72, 2.74
  Crime, 2.1, 2.2, 2.4, 2.6, 2.28, 2.33-2.42, 2.70, 2.71, 2.88, 2.89, 3.58
    Approaches to lowering crime rate, 2.28
    As important problem, 2.1, 2.2
    Changes in level of crime, 2.33-2.36
    Fear, 2.6, 2.37, 2.39, 2.40, 3.58
      At school, 2.6, 3.58
      High school seniors, 2.70, 2.71, 2.88, 2.89
    In schools, 2.4
    Level of spending, 2.41, 2.42
    Own neighborhood, 2.35, 2.36
  Criminal justice system, 2.11, 2.45
    Confidence in, 2.11
    Fairness of, 2.45
  Doctor-assisted suicide, 2.96
  Drugs
    As important problem, 2.1-2.4
      In schools, 2.4
    Availability, 2.83, 2.84
      High school seniors, 2.83
    Disapproval of use, 2.85, 2.86
      High school seniors, 2.85
    Drug testing in schools, 2.7, 2.8
    Harmfulness, 2.76, 2.77, 2.79-2.82
      High school seniors, 2.79
      Young adults, 2.81
    High school seniors, 2.70, 2.79, 2.83, 2.85, 2.87-2.89
      Availability, 2.83
      Disapproval of use, 2.85
      Harmfulness, 2.79
      Legalization, 2.87-2.89
    Legalization, 2.67-2.69, 2.87-2.90
      College freshmen, 2.90
      High school seniors, 2.87-2.89
      Marijuana, medical use, 2.69
    Level of spending, 2.41, 2.43
    Locker searches in schools, 2.7, 2.8
    Progress coping with drug problem, 2.44
    Teenagers' perceptions of those who use, 2.78
    Testing for use, 2.7, 2.8
  Environment, stricter laws, 2.102
  Fear of victimization, 2.5, 2.6, 2.29, 2.37, 2.39, 2.40, 3.58
    At school, 2.5, 2.6, 3.58
    Terrorism, 2.29
  Guns, firearms, 2.2, 2.59-2.66, 2.95
    As important problem, 2.2
    Laws covering sale, 2.63, 2.64

PUBLIC OPINION, Guns, firearms (continued)
    Ownership, 2.59-2.62
      Firearm in home, 2.59-2.61
      Type of firearm, 2.62
    Public policies, 2.64-2.66, 2.95
      Police permit prior to purchase, 2.66
      Registration, licensing, manufacture, 2.64
  Homosexual relations, legality, 2.98, 2.99
  Justice system, 2.72, 2.75
    High school seniors, 2.72, 2.75
  Juveniles, treatment of, 2.48
  Lawyers, 2.17-2.19
  Marijuana, 2.67-2.69, 2.76, 2.77, 2.79-2.90
    Availability, 2.83, 2.84
      High school seniors, 2.83
    Disapproval of use, 2.85, 2.86
      High school seniors, 2.85
    Harmfulness, 2.76, 2.77, 2.79-2.82
      High school seniors, 2.79
      Young adults, 2.81
    Legalization, 2.67-2.69, 2.87-2.90
      College freshmen, 2.90
      High school seniors, 2.87-2.89
    Medical use, 2.69
  Occupations and institutions, 2.9, 2.10, 2.13-2.15, 2.17-2.25, 2.45, 2.72-2.75
    Courts and justice system, 2.45, 2.72, 2.75
    Lawyers, 2.17-2.19
    Police, 2.13, 2.17, 2.20-2.25, 2.72, 2.73
      High school seniors, 2.72, 2.73
      Use of force, 2.23-2.25
    Selected occupations and institutions, 2.9, 2.10, 2.14, 2.72
      High school seniors, 2.72
    U.S. Supreme Court, 2.9, 2.10, 2.14, 2.15, 2.72, 2.74
      High school seniors, 2.72
  Police, 2.12, 2.13, 2.17, 2.20-2.27, 2.72, 2.73
    Confidence in, 2.12, 2.13
    Honesty and ethics, 2.17, 2.20, 2.21
    Increased powers, 2.27
    Performance, 2.22, 2.72, 2.73
    Racial profiling, 2.26
    Use of force, 2.23-2.25
  Pornography, 2.97
  Problems in country and community, 2.41, 2.70
    High school seniors, 2.70
    Level of spending, 2.41
  Problems in schools, 2.4, 2.5
  Rehabilitation of criminals, 2.46
  Terrorism, 2.16, 2.29-2.32
    Civil liberties, 2.31
    Confidence in government, 2.16

PUBLIC OPINION, Terrorism (continued)
  Fear of attack, victimization, 2.29, 2.30
  National ID card, 2.32
  U.S. Supreme Court, 2.9, 2.10, 2.14, 2.15, 2.72, 2.74
    Confidence in, 2.9, 2.10, 2.14, 2.15
    High school seniors, 2.72, 2.74

PURSE-SNATCHING
  See Larceny-theft
  See Victimization

RACKETEERING
  Arrests, Federal, 4.33
  Basis for wiretap, 5.3
  Community supervision, Federal offenders, 6.4
  Court cases, Federal, 5.13, 5.17, 5.19, 5.25-5.29, 5.31, 5.32, 5.34-5.36, 6.58
    Citizens and non-citizens, 5.35
    Convictions, 5.17
    Defendant characteristics, 5.26, 5.27
    Dispositions, 5.17
    Method of conviction, 5.17, 5.34
    Pretrial action, 5.13
    Sentences, 5.19, 5.25, 5.29, 5.31, 5.32
    Sentencing guideline cases, 5.26-5.29, 5.31, 5.32, 5.34-5.36
    Time served, 6.58
  Dispositions, 5.24
  Parole and supervised release, 6.4, 6.70, 6.71
  Pretrial release and detention, 5.13
  Prisoners, time served, 6.58
  Probation, 6.4
  Sentences, 5.19, 5.25, 5.29, 5.31, 5.32, 6.58
    Fines, 5.25, 5.32
    Length, 5.19, 5.25, 5.31
    Prison, 5.19, 5.25, 5.29
    Probation, 5.19, 5.25, 5.29
    Restitution, 5.32
    Time served, 6.58

RAPE, FORCIBLE
  Arrests, 4.1-4.3, 4.5-4.19, 4.22, 4.33, 5.50
    Age, 4.4-4.7, 4.9, 4.10, 4.12, 4.14, 4.16, 4.22
    Cities, 4.3, 4.11, 4.12, 4.19, 4.22
    Clearance by arrest, 4.19, 4.22
    Federal, 4.33
    Race, 4.10, 4.12, 4.14, 4.16
    Rates, 4.2, 4.3, 4.17
    Region, 4.17
    Rural counties, 4.3, 4.15, 4.16, 4.19, 4.22
    Sex, 4.8, 4.9, 4.11, 4.13, 4.15
    Size of place, 4.3, 4.19, 4.22
    State, 4.5
    Suburban areas, 4.3, 4.13, 4.14, 4.19, 4.22
    Time to sentencing, State courts, 5.50
  Basis for wiretap, 5.3
  Clearance by arrest, 4.19, 4.22

RAPE, FORCIBLE (continued)
  Community supervision, Federal offenders, 6.4
  Convictions
    Federal courts, 5.17
    Method of conviction, 5.17, 5.46, 5.50
    Number of, 5.17, 5.44, 5.46
    Offender characteristics, 5.45
  Court cases, Federal, 5.13, 5.17, 5.19, 5.24, 5.25, 6.58
    Convictions, 5.17
    Dispositions, 5.17, 5.24
    Method of conviction, 5.17
    Pretrial action, 5.13
    Sentences, 5.19, 5.25
    Time served, 6.58
  Court cases, State, 5.44-5.50
    Convictions, 5.44-5.46, 5.50
      Method of conviction, 5.46, 5.50
      Number of, 5.44
      Offender characteristics, 5.45
    Sentences, 5.47-5.50
      Length of sentence, 5.48
      Method of conviction, 5.50
      Time from arrest, 5.50
      Type of additional penalty, 5.49
  Court cases, urban counties, 5.51-5.60
    Arrests, 5.51
    Convictions, 5.57, 5.58
    Defendant characteristics, 5.52
    Pretrial release, 5.54-5.56
    Prior convictions, 5.53
    Sentences, 5.59, 5.60
  Hate crimes, 3.112
  Jail inmates
    Current offense, 6.19, 6.20
  Number, large cities, 3.110
  Offenses known to police, 3.106-3.112, 3.115, 3.116, 4.19
    Average loss, 3.111
    Cities, 3.110, 4.19
    Federal parks, 3.115, 3.116
    Hate crimes, 3.112
    Rates, 3.106-3.108
    Size of place, 3.107-3.109, 4.19
  Parole and supervised release, 6.4
  Pretrial release and detention, 5.13
  Prisoners
    Recidivism, 6.50, 6.51
    Time served, 6.44
  Probation, 6.4, 6.8
  Sentences, 5.19, 5.47-5.49, 5.59, 5.60, 6.44
    Federal courts, 5.19
    Length of sentence, 5.19, 5.48, 5.60, 6.44
    Time served, 6.44
    Type of collateral penalty, 5.49
    Type of sentence, 5.47, 5.59
  Victimizations, 3.1-3.18, 3.20, 3.27-3.33, 3.36
    Age of victim, 3.4, 3.6, 3.7, 3.11
    Households experiencing, 3.27
    Lone-offender incidents, 3.28, 3.29

RAPE, FORCIBLE, Victimizations (continued)
  Multiple-offender incidents, 3.30, 3.31
  Number, 3.1, 3.2, 3.5, 3.8-3.10
    Characteristics of victim, 3.5, 3.8, 3.9
  Place of occurrence, 3.32
  Race and ethnicity of victim, 3.4, 3.8-3.11
  Rates, 3.1-3.13
    Age of victim, 3.4, 3.6, 3.7, 3.11
    Family income of victim, 3.4, 3.12
    Locality of residence, 3.4, 3.13
    Race and ethnicity of victim, 3.4, 3.8-3.11
    Sex of victim, 3.4, 3.5, 3.7, 3.10
  Reporting to police, 3.33, 3.36
  Self-protective measures taken, 3.18, 3.20
  Sex of victim, 3.4, 3.5, 3.7, 3.10
  Victim-offender relationship, 3.14-3.18
    Type of weapon, 3.17
  Weapon use, 3.17
  See also:
    Violent crime

REHABILITATION PROGRAMS
  Public opinion, 2.46
  See Corrections

REVOCATION
  See Parole
  See Probation

ROBBERY
  Arrests, 4.1-4.3, 4.5-4.17, 4.19, 4.22, 4.33, 5.50
    Age, 4.5-4.7, 4.9, 4.10, 4.12, 4.14, 4.16
    Cities, 4.3, 4.11, 4.12, 4.19, 4.22
    Clearance by arrest, 4.19, 4.22
    Federal, 4.33
    Race, 4.10, 4.12, 4.14, 4.16
    Rates, 4.2, 4.3, 4.17
    Region, 4.17
    Rural counties, 4.3, 4.15, 4.16, 4.19, 4.22
    Sex, 4.8, 4.9, 4.11, 4.13, 4.15
    Size of place, 4.3, 4.19, 4.22
    State, 4.5
    Suburban areas, 4.3, 4.13, 4.14, 4.19, 4.22
    Time to sentencing, State courts, 5.50
  Community supervision, Federal offenders, 6.4
  Convictions
    Federal courts, 5.17
    Method of conviction, 5.17, 5.46, 5.50
    Number of, 5.17, 5.26, 5.46
    Offender characteristics, 5.45

ROBBERY (continued)
    Court cases, Federal, 5.10, 5.13, 5.17, 5.19, 5.24-5.29, 5.31, 5.32, 5.34-5.36, 5.67, 6.58
        Appeals, 5.67
        Citizens and non-citizens, 5.35
        Convictions, 5.17
        Defendant characteristics, 5.26, 5.27
        Dispositions, 5.17, 5.24
        Method of conviction, 5.17, 5.34
        Pretrial action, 5.13
        Sentences, 5.19, 5.25, 5.29, 5.31, 5.32
        Sentencing guideline cases, 5.26-5.29, 5.31, 5.32, 5.34-5.36
        Time served, 6.58
    Court cases, State, 5.44-5.50
        Convictions, 5.44-5.46, 5.50
            Method of conviction, 5.46
            Number of, 5.44
            Offender characteristics, 5.45
        Sentences, 5.47-5.50
            Length of sentence, 5.48
            Time from arrest, 5.50
            Type of additional penalty, 5.49
    Court cases, urban counties, 5.51-5.60
        Arrests, 5.51
        Convictions, 5.57, 5.58
        Defendant characteristics, 5.52
        Pretrial release, 5.54-5.56
        Prior convictions, 5.53
        Sentences, 5.59, 5.60
    Federal Bank Robbery and Incidental Crimes Statute, 3.149-3.151
        Deaths, injuries, and hostages taken, 3.151
    Hate crimes, 3.112
    Jail inmates
        Current offense, 6.19, 6.20
    Juveniles in custody, 6.10
    Offenses known to police, 3.106-3.112, 3.115, 3.116, 3.140-3.142, 4.19
        Average loss, 3.111
        Cities, 3.110, 4.19
        Federal parks, 3.115, 3.116
        Hate crimes, 3.112
        Place of occurrence, 3.142
        Rates, 3.106-3.108
        Region, 3.141
        Size of place, 3.107-3.109, 4.19
        Type of weapon, 3.140, 3.141
    Parole and supervised release, 6.4, 6.70, 6.71
    Prisoners
        Current offense, 6.56
        Firearms possession during offense, 6.37
        Recidivism, 6.50, 6.51
        Time served, 6.44, 6.58
    Probationers
        Number, 6.4
        Outcomes, 6.8
    Self-reported, 3.43-3.45

ROBBERY (continued)
    Sentences, 5.19, 5.25, 5.29, 5.31, 5.32, 5.48, 5.49, 5.59, 5.60, 6.44, 6.58
        Federal courts, 5.19
        Fines, 5.32
        Incarceration, 5.19, 5.25, 5.29
        Length of sentence, 5.19, 5.25, 5.31, 5.48, 5.60, 6.44
        Probation, 5.19, 5.25, 5.29
        Restitution, 5.32
        Time served, 6.44, 6.58
        Type of collateral penalty, 5.49
        Type of sentence, 5.25, 5.29, 5.59
    Victimizations, 3.1-3.18, 3.20, 3.27-3.36
        Age of victim, 3.4, 3.6, 3.7, 3.11
        Households experiencing, 3.27
        Lone-offender incidents, 3.28, 3.29
        Multiple-offender incidents, 3.30, 3.31
        Number, 3.1, 3.2, 3.5, 3.8-3.10
            Characteristics of victims, 3.5, 3.8, 3.9
        Place of occurrence, 3.32
        Race and ethnicity of victim, 3.4, 3.8-3.11
        Rates, 3.1-3.13
            Age of victim, 3.4, 3.6, 3.7, 3.11
            Family income of victim, 3.4, 3.12
            Locality of residence, 3.4, 3.13
            Race and ethnicity of victim, 3.4, 3.8-3.11
            Sex of victim, 3.4, 3.5, 3.7, 3.10
        Reporting to police, 3.33-3.36
            Reasons for not reporting, 3.35
            Reasons for reporting, 3.34
            Victim characteristics, 3.36
        Self-protective measures taken, 3.18, 3.20
        Sex of victim, 3.4, 3.5, 3.7, 3.10
        Victim-offender relationship, 3.14-3.18
            Type of weapon, 3.17
            Victim use of self-protection, 3.18
        Weapon use, 3.17
    See also:
        Violent crime
RUNAWAYS
    Arrests, 4.1, 4.3, 4.6-4.16
        Age, 4.6, 4.7, 4.9, 4.12, 4.14, 4.16
        Cities, 4.3, 4.11, 4.12
        Race and ethnicity, 4.10, 4.12, 4.14, 4.16
        Rates, 4.3
        Rural counties, 4.15, 4.16
        Sex, 4.8, 4.9, 4.11, 4.13, 4.15
        Size of place, 4.3
        Suburban areas, 4.13, 4.14
SEIZURES
    See Drug Enforcement Administration
    See U.S. Coast Guard
    See U.S. Customs Service
    See U.S. Marshals Service

SELF-REPORTED CRIMINAL ACTIVITY
    Alcohol use, 3.63, 3.98, 3.102
        Among students, 3.63
        Driving after drinking, 3.102
    At school, 3.58
    Delinquency, 3.43-3.45, 3.54, 3.58
        Among students, 3.43-3.45, 3.54, 3.58
        At school, 3.58
        Gang activity, 3.54
        Weapon carrying, 3.58
    Drug use, 3.55, 3.57, 3.62, 3.63, 3.65-3.69, 3.71-3.76, 3.102
        Driving after use, 3.102
        Students, 3.55, 3.57, 3.62, 3.63, 3.65-3.73, 3.84, 3.85
            At school, 3.55, 3.57
            College students, 3.71-3.73, 3.84, 3.85
            High school seniors, 3.63, 3.65-3.70
            High school students, 3.55, 3.57, 3.62, 3.63, 3.65-3.70
        Type of drug, 3.72, 3.74-3.76
        Young adults, 3.74-3.76
    See also:
        Alcohol
        Arrests
        Drugs
        Traffic violations
SENTENCES
    Federal offenders, 5.19-5.21, 5.23, 5.25-5.34, 5.36, 5.38, 5.39, 6.58, 6.59
        Characteristics, 5.26, 5.27
        Drug crimes, 5.39
        Fines, 5.19, 5.25, 5.32
        Incarceration, 5.19-5.21, 5.25, 5.29-5.31, 5.38, 6.58, 6.59
            Length of sentence, 5.19, 5.21, 5.23, 5.25, 5.30, 5.31, 5.38
            Number of, 5.19, 5.20
            Offense, 5.19-5.21
            Time served, 6.58, 6.59
        Offense, 5.19-5.21
        Organizations sentenced, 5.33
        Probation, 5.19, 5.29
        Restitution, 5.32
        Sentencing guideline cases, 5.26-5.36, 5.39
        Split sentence, 5.19
        Type and length of sentence, 5.19, 5.23, 5.25, 5.29-5.33
    Public opinion, 2.50-2.52
        Capital punishment, 2.50-2.52
    State offenders, 5.47-5.50, 6.43, 6.44
        Incarcerated, 5.48
        Jail, 5.48
        Length of sentence, 5.48, 6.43, 6.44
        Offense type, 5.49, 5.50, 6.44
        Prison, 5.47, 5.48
        Probation, 5.48
        Processing time, 5.50
        Type of collateral penalty, 5.49

SENTENCES (continued)
　Urban county courts, 5.59, 5.60
　　Incarceration, 5.59, 5.60
　　　Length of sentence, 5.60
　　Jail, 5.59
　　Offense type, 5.59, 5.60
　　Prison, 5.59
　U.S. Sentencing Commission guideline cases, 5.26-5.36, 5.39
　See also:
　　Courts
　　Corrections
　　Defendants
　　Parole
　　Prisoners
　　Probation
　　Public opinion
SEX OFFENSES (except forcible rape and prostitution)
　Arrests, 4.1, 4.3, 4.6-4.16, 4.33
　　Age, 4.5, 4.7, 4.9, 4.10, 4.12, 4.14, 4.16
　　Cities, 4.3, 4.11, 4.12
　　Federal, 4.33
　　Race, 4.10, 4.12, 4.14, 4.16
　　Rates, 4.3
　　Rural counties, 4.15, 4.16
　　Sex, 4.8, 4.9, 4.11, 4.13, 4.15
　　Size of place, 4.3
　　Suburban areas, 4.13, 4.14
　Community supervision, Federal offenders, 6.4
　Convictions, 5.17
　Court cases, Federal, 5.13, 5.17, 5.19, 5.24-5.29, 5.31, 5.32, 5.34-5.36, 6.58
　　Citizens and non-citizens, 5.35
　　Convictions, 5.17
　　Defendant characteristics, 5.26, 5.27
　　Dispositions, 5.17, 5.24
　　Method of conviction, 5.17, 5.34
　　Pretrial action, 5.13
　　Sentences, 5.19, 5.25, 5.29, 5.31, 5.32
　　Sentencing guideline cases, 5.26-5.29, 5.31, 5.32, 5.34-5.36
　　Time served, 6.58
　Court cases, State, 5.44-5.50
　　Convictions, 5.44-5.46, 5.50
　　　Method of conviction, 5.46
　　　Number of, 5.44
　　　Offender characteristics, 5.45
　　Sentences, 5.47-5.50
　　　Length of sentence, 5.48
　　　Time from arrest, 5.50
　　　Type of additional penalty, 5.49
　In Federal parks, 3.116
　Jail inmates
　　Current offense, 6.19, 6.20
　Juveniles in custody, 6.10
　Parole and supervised release, 6.4, 6.70, 6.71
　Prisoners
　　Current offense, 6.56
　　Firearms possession during offense, 6.37

SEX OFFENSES (except forcible rape and prostitution), Prisoners (continued)
　　Recidivism, 6.50
　　Time served, 6.44, 6.58
　Probationers
　　Number, 6.4
　　Outcomes, 6.8
　Sentences, 5.19, 5.25, 5.29, 5.31, 5.32, 6.44, 6.58
　　Federal courts, 5.19
　　Fines, 5.25, 5.32
　　Length of sentence, 5.19, 5.31, 6.44
　　Prison, 5.19, 5.25, 5.29
　　Probation, 5.19, 5.25, 5.29
　　Restitution, 5.32
　　Time served, 6.44, 6.58
　　Type of sentence, 5.19, 5.25, 5.29
　Sex offender registries, 6.63
　Victimizations, 3.1, 3.2, 3.4-3.6, 3.8, 3.9, 3.12, 3.14, 3.27, 3.33, 3.36, 3.85
　　Age of victim, 3.4, 3.6
　　During consumption of alcohol or drugs, 3.85
　　Households experiencing, 3.27
　　Locality of residence, 3.4
　　Number, 3.1, 3.2, 3.5, 3.8, 3.9
　　Race and ethnicity of victim, 3.4, 3.8, 3.9
　　Rates, 3.1, 3.2, 3.4-3.6, 3.8, 3.9, 3.12
　　　Age of victim, 3.4, 3.5
　　　Family income of victim, 3.4, 3.12
　　　Race and ethnicity of victim, 3.4, 3.8, 3.9
　　　Sex of victim, 3.4, 3.5
　　Reporting to police, 3.33, 3.36
　　Sex of victim, 3.4, 3.5
　　Victim-offender relationship, 3.14
SHOPLIFTING
　See Larceny-theft
STATUS OFFENDERS
　See Juvenile corrections
　See Juvenile delinquency
　See Self-reported criminal activity
STOLEN PROPERTY (buying, receiving, possessing)
　Arrests, 4.1, 4.3, 4.6-4.16, 4.33
　　Age, 4.6, 4.7, 4.9, 4.10, 4.12, 4.14, 4.16
　　Cities, 4.3, 4.11, 4.12
　　Federal, 4.33
　　Race, 4.10, 4.12, 4.14, 4.16
　　Rates, 4.3
　　Rural counties, 4.15, 4.16
　　Sex, 4.8, 4.9, 4.11, 4.13, 4.15
　　Size of place, 4.3
　　Suburban areas, 4.13, 4.14
　Court cases, Federal, 5.13, 5.17, 5.24, 5.25, 6.58
　　Dispositions, 5.17, 5.24
　　Pretrial action, 5.13
　　Sentences, 5.25
　　Time served, 6.58
　In Federal parks, 3.116
　Jail inmates
　　Current offense, 6.19, 6.20

STOLEN PROPERTY (buying, receiving, possessing) (continued)
　Prisoners
　　Recidivism, 6.50
　　Time served, 6.58
　Probationers
　　Number, 6.4
　　Outcomes, 6.8
　Sentences, 5.25, 6.58
　　Time served, 6.58
　See also:
　　Burglary
　　Larceny-theft
　　U.S. Customs Service
SUICIDE
　Emergency department episodes, 3.92, 3.93
　Rates, 3.136-3.139
　Students, 3.54-3.56
SUSPICION
　Arrests, 4.1, 4.3, 4.6-4.16
　　Age, 4.6, 4.7, 4.9, 4.10, 4.12, 4.14, 4.16
　　Cities, 4.3, 4.11, 4.12
　　Race, 4.10, 4.12, 4.14, 4.16
　　Rate, 4.3
　　Rural counties, 4.15, 4.16
　　Sex, 4.8, 4.9, 4.11, 4.13, 4.15
　　Size of place, 4.3
　　Suburban areas, 4.13, 4.14
TAX LAW VIOLATIONS
　Arrests, Federal, 4.33
　Court cases, Federal, 5.13, 5.19, 5.24-5.29, 5.31-5.36, 5.67, 6.58
　　Appeals, 5.67
　　Citizens and non-citizens, 5.35
　　Defendant characteristics, 5.26, 5.27
　　Dispositions, 5.24
　　Method of conviction, 5.34
　　Organizations sentenced, 5.33
　　Pretrial action, 5.13
　　Sentences, 5.19, 5.25, 5.29, 5.31-5.33
　　Sentencing guideline cases, 5.26-5.29, 5.31-5.36
　　Time served, 6.58
　Parole and supervised release, 6.4, 6.70, 6.71
　Pretrial release and detention, 5.13
　Prisoners
　　Federal, time served, 6.58
　Probation outcomes, 6.8
　Sentences, 5.19, 5.25, 5.29, 5.31-5.33, 6.58
　　Federal courts, 5.19
　　Fines, 5.25, 5.32
　　Length, 5.19, 5.31
　　Organizations, 5.33
　　Prison, 5.25, 5.29
　　Probation, 5.25, 5.29
　　Restitution, 5.32
　　Time served, 6.58
TERRORISM
　Public opinion, 2.16, 2.29-2.32
　　Civil liberties, 2.31
　　Confidence in government, 2.16

Index 631

TERRORISM, Public opinion (continued)
    Fear of attack, victimization, 2.29, 2.30
    National ID card, 2.32
  U.S. citizens or property, 3.173-3.176
    Casualties, 3.175
    Incidents, 3.174, 3.176
    Targets, 3.174
  Victims of September 11 attacks, 3.133
  See also:
    Arson
    Bombings
    Deaths
TRAFFIC VIOLATIONS
  Alcohol involvement, 3.103-3.105
  Arrests, Federal, 4.33
  Jail inmates
    Current offense, 6.19, 6.20
  Self-reported, 3.46-3.53
    High school seniors, 3.46-3.53
      Driving under the influence, 3.49-3.51
  See also:
    Alcohol
    Public opinion
TRIALS
  State courts
    Convictions by trial, 5.46, 5.50
      Offense type, 5.46, 5.50
      Processing time, 5.50
  U.S. District Courts
    Length, 5.42
  See also:
    Courts
    Defendants
    Juries
    Sentences
UNIFORM CRIME REPORTS
  See Arrests
  See Offenses known to police
U.S. AIR FORCE
  Alcohol use among personnel, 3.91
  Courts-martial, 5.82
  Drug use among personnel, 3.89, 3.90
  Prisoners, 6.64
U.S. ARMY
  Alcohol use among personnel, 3.91
  Courts-martial, 5.80
  Drug use among personnel, 3.89, 3.90
  Prisoners, 6.64
U.S. ATTORNEYS
  Asset forfeiture recoveries, 4.45
  Cases filed, 5.6, 5.7
  Grand jury proceedings, 5.6
  Immigration matters referred, 5.78
  Personnel and work hours, 1.79
  Requests for immunity, 5.1
U.S. COAST GUARD
  Courts-martial, 5.83
  Prisoners, 6.64
U.S. COURTS OF APPEAL
  Appeals commenced, terminated, and pending, 5.66
    Per judgeship, 5.66
  Appeals filed, 5.67
  Characteristics of appointees, 1.81
  Judgeships authorized, 5.66

U.S. COURTS OF APPEAL (continued)
  See also:
    Courts
    Defendants
    Sentences
U.S. CUSTOMS SERVICE
  Number and characteristics of officers, 1.72, 1.75
  Seizures, 4.43, 4.44
    Drugs, 4.43
    Property, 4.44
U.S. DISTRICT COURTS
  Antitrust cases filed, 5.41
  Appeals from, 5.67
  Criminal cases filed, 1.83, 5.6, 5.7, 5.9-5.11, 5.43
    Amount of time to disposition, 5.43
    Per judgeship, 1.83
  Characteristics of appointees, 1.82
  Criminal cases pending, 5.9, 5.11
  Criminal cases terminated, 5.7-5.9, 5.11
  Defendants, 5.7, 5.12-5.16, 5.18-5.39
    Charged with drug law violations, 5.37
    Convicted, 5.18
    Dispositions, 5.7, 5.22, 5.24
    Organizations sentenced, 5.33
    Pretrial action, 5.13-5.15
    Sentenced, 5.19-5.21, 5.23, 5.25, 5.29-5.33
      Length of sentence, 5.21, 5.23, 5.25, 5.30, 5.31
      Organizations, 5.33
      Type of offense, 5.23
    Terminated, 5.7
    Time held in custody, 5.12
  Immigration offenders processed, 5.77
  Juror utilization, 1.95
  Length of trials, 5.42
  Magistrate duties, 1.84
  Number of detainees, 5.12
  Prisoner petitions filed, 5.65
  See also:
    Courts
    Defendants
    Sentences
U.S. MARINE CORPS
  Alcohol use among personnel, 3.91
  Courts-martial, 5.81
  Drug use among personnel, 3.89, 3.90
  Prisoners, 6.64
U.S. MARSHALS SERVICE
  Budget, 1.78
  Number and characteristics of officers, 1.72, 1.75
  Staff, 1.78
  Workload, 1.77
U.S. NAVY
  Alcohol use among personnel, 3.91
  Courts-martial, 5.81
  Drug use among personnel, 3.89, 3.90
  Prisoners, 6.64
U.S. PARDON ATTORNEY
  Clemency applications, 5.72

U.S. POSTAL INSPECTION SERVICE
  Arrests and convictions, 5.73, 5.74
  Mail fraud, 5.73
  Number and characteristics of officers, 1.72, 1.75
U.S. SECRET SERVICE
  Number and characteristics of officers, 1.72, 1.75
U.S. SUPREME COURT
  Activities, 5.68
  Cases argued and decided on merits, 5.71
  Cases filed, 5.69
  Petitions on writ of certiorari, 5.70
  Public opinion, 2.9, 2.10, 2.14, 2.15, 2.72, 2.74
    Confidence in, 2.9, 2.10, 2.14, 2.15
    High school seniors, 2.72, 2.74
VAGRANCY
  Arrests, 4.1, 4.3, 4.6-4.16, 4.28
    Age, 4.6, 4.7, 4.9, 4.10, 4.12, 4.14, 4.16
    Cities, 4.3, 4.11, 4.12
    Race, 4.10, 4.12, 4.14, 4.16
    Rates, 4.3
    Rural counties, 4.15, 4.16
    Sex, 4.8, 4.9, 4.11, 4.13, 4.15
    Size of place, 4.3
    Suburban areas, 4.13, 4.14
VANDALISM
  Arrests, 4.1, 4.3, 4.6-4.16
    Age, 4.6, 4.7, 4.9, 4.10, 4.12, 4.14, 4.16
    Cities, 4.3, 4.11, 4.12
    Race, 4.10, 4.12, 4.14, 4.16
    Rates, 4.3
    Rural counties, 4.15, 4.16
    Sex, 4.8, 4.9, 4.11, 4.13, 4.15
    Size of place, 4.3
    Suburban areas, 4.13, 4.14
  Households experiencing, 3.27
  In Federal parks, 3.116
VEHICLE THEFT
  See Motor vehicle theft
VICTIMIZATION
  Among intimate partners, 3.15, 3.16
  Assault, 3.1-3.18, 3.20, 3.27-3.36
    Age of victim, 3.4, 3.6, 3.7, 3.11
    Households experiencing, 3.27
    Lone-offender incidents, 3.28, 3.29
    Multiple-offender incidents, 3.30, 3.31
    Number, 3.1, 3.2, 3.5, 3.8-3.10
    Place of occurrence, 3.32
    Race and ethnicity of victim, 3.4, 3.8-3.11
    Rates, 3.1-3.13
    Reporting to police, 3.33-3.36
    Self-protective measures taken, 3.18, 3.20
    Sex of victim, 3.4, 3.5, 3.7
    Victim-offender relationship, 3.14-3.18
  At school, 3.55-3.57, 3.59-3.61
  Bullying, 3.61

VICTIMIZATION (continued)

- Burglary, 3.1-3.3, 3.21-3.27, 3.33-3.35
  - Households experiencing, 3.27
  - Locality of residence, 3.21, 3.25, 3.26
  - Number, 3.1, 3.2, 3.22, 3.23
  - Rates, 3.1-3.3, 3.21-3.26
  - Reporting to police, 3.33-3.35
- During consumption of alcohol or drugs, 3.85
- Fear of victimization, 2.6, 2.39, 3.55-3.57, 3.59
  - At school, 2.6, 3.55-3.57, 3.59
- Firearm-related, 3.17, 3.59
- Hate crimes, 3.112-3.114
- Larceny-theft, 3.1-3.3, 3.21-3.27, 3.32-3.35, 3.37-3.42
  - At school, 3.40-3.42
  - High school seniors, 3.37-3.42
  - Households experiencing, 3.27
  - Locality of residence, 3.21, 3.25, 3.26
  - Number, 3.1, 3.2, 3.22, 3.23
  - Place of occurrence, 3.32
  - Rates, 3.1-3.3, 3.21-3.26
  - Reporting to police, 3.33-3.35
- Lone-offender incidents, 3.28, 3.29
  - Perceived age of offender, 3.28
  - Perceived race of offender, 3.29
- Motor vehicle theft, 3.1-3.3, 3.21-3.27, 3.32-3.35
  - Households experiencing, 3.27
  - Locality of residence, 3.21, 3.25, 3.26
  - Number, 3.1, 3.2, 3.22, 3.23
  - Race of head of household, 3.22, 3.23, 3.26
  - Rates, 3.1-3.3, 3.21-3.26
  - Reporting to police, 3.33-3.35
- Multiple-offender incidents, 3.30, 3.31
  - Perceived ages of offenders, 3.30
  - Perceived races of offenders, 3.31
- Murder and nonnegligent manslaughter, 3.125, 3.126, 3.130, 3.131, 3.133, 3.135
  - Characteristics of victims, 3.125, 3.126, 3.130, 3.131
  - Involving intimates, 3.131
  - Rates, 3.125, 3.126
  - September 11 terrorist attacks, 3.133
  - Workplace homicides, 3.135
- Property crimes of theft, 3.1-3.3, 3.21-3.27, 3.32-3.35
  - Households experiencing, 3.27
  - Locality of residence, 3.21, 3.26
  - Number, 3.1, 3.2, 3.22, 3.23
  - Race and ethnicity of head of household, 3.22, 3.23, 3.26
  - Rates, 3.1-3.3, 3.21-3.26
  - Reporting to police, 3.33-3.35
- Rape, 3.1-3.18, 3.20, 3.27-3.33, 3.36
  - Age of victim, 3.4, 3.6, 3.7, 3.11
  - Households experiencing, 3.27
  - Locality of residence, 3.13
  - Lone-offender incidents, 3.28, 3.29

VICTIMIZATION, Rape (continued)

- Multiple-offender incidents, 3.30, 3.31
- Number, 3.1, 3.2, 3.5, 3.8-3.10
- Place of occurrence, 3.32
- Race and ethnicity of victim, 3.4, 3.8-3.11
- Rates, 3.1-3.13
- Reporting to police, 3.33, 3.36
- Self-protective measures taken, 3.18, 3.20
- Sex of victim, 3.4, 3.5, 3.7
- Victim-offender relationship, 3.14-3.18
- Robbery, 3.1-3.18, 3.20, 3.27-3.36
  - Age of victim, 3.4, 3.6, 3.7, 3.11
  - Households experiencing, 3.27
  - Lone-offender incidents, 3.28, 3.29
  - Multiple-offender incidents, 3.30, 3.31
  - Number, 3.1, 3.2, 3.5, 3.8-3.10
  - Place of occurrence, 3.32
  - Race and ethnicity of offender, 3.29, 3.31
  - Race and ethnicity of victim, 3.4, 3.8-3.11
  - Rates, 3.1-3.13
  - Reporting to police, 3.33-3.36
  - Self-protective measures taken, 3.18, 3.20
  - Sex of victim, 3.4, 3.5, 3.7
  - Victim-offender relationship, 3.14-3.18
- Self-protective measures taken, 3.18-3.20
  - Type of measure, 3.19
- Self-reported, 3.37-3.42, 3.58
  - At school, 3.58
  - High school seniors, 3.37-3.42
    - At school, 3.40-3.42
- Violent crime, 3.1-3.20, 3.27-3.36, 3.60, 3.61, 3.125, 3.126
  - Age of victim, 3.4, 3.6, 3.7, 3.11
  - At school, 3.60, 3.61
  - Characteristics of victims, 3.4, 3.125, 3.126
  - Households experiencing, 3.27
  - Lone-offender incidents, 3.28, 3.29
  - Multiple-offender incidents, 3.30, 3.31
  - Number, 3.1, 3.2, 3.5, 3.8-3.10
  - Place of occurrence, 3.32
  - Race and ethnicity of victim, 3.4, 3.8-3.11
  - Rates, 3.1-3.13, 3.125, 3.126
  - Reporting to police, 3.33-3.36
  - Self-protective measures taken, 3.18-3.20
  - Sex of victim, 3.4, 3.5, 3.7
  - Victim-offender relationship, 3.14-3.18
  - Weapon, 3.17
- See also:
  - Specific offenses (e.g., Assault, Arson)

VIOLENT CRIME

- Among intimate partners, 3.15, 3.16, 3.132
- Arrests, 4.1-4.3, 4.5-4.17, 4.19-4.23, 4.33-4.35
  - Age, 4.5-4.7, 4.9, 4.10, 4.12, 4.14, 4.22, 4.23
  - Cities, 4.3, 4.11, 4.12, 4.19, 4.21, 4.22
  - Clearance by arrest, 4.19, 4.21-4.23
  - Federal, 4.33-4.35
  - Race, 4.10, 4.12, 4.14, 4.16
  - Rates, 4.2, 4.3, 4.17
  - Region, 4.17
  - Rural counties, 4.3, 4.15, 4.16, 4.19, 4.21, 4.22
  - Sex, 4.8, 4.9, 4.11, 4.13, 4.15
  - Size of place, 4.3, 4.19, 4.21, 4.22
  - State, 4.5
  - Suburban areas, 4.3, 4.13, 4.14, 4.19, 4.21, 4.23
- At school, 3.60, 3.61
- Community supervision, Federal offenders, 6.4
- Convictions, 5.17
- Court cases, Federal, 5.13, 5.16-5.21, 6.58, 6.59
  - Convictions, 5.17, 5.18
  - Dispositions, 5.17
  - Method of conviction, 5.17
  - Offender characteristics, 5.18, 5.20, 5.21
  - Pretrial action, 5.13, 5.16
  - Sentences, 5.19-5.21
  - Time served, 6.58, 6.59
- Court cases, State, 5.44-5.50
  - Sentences, 5.47-5.50
- Court cases, urban counties, 5.51-5.60
  - Arrests, 5.51
  - Convictions, 5.57, 5.58
  - Defendant characteristics, 5.52
  - Pretrial release, 5.54-5.56
  - Prior convictions, 5.53
  - Sentences, 5.59, 5.60
- Jail inmates
  - Current offense, 6.19, 6.20
- Juvenile court cases, 5.61-5.64
  - Case outcomes, 5.63, 5.64
  - Demographic characteristics, 5.61-5.64
- Juveniles in custody, 6.10
- Law enforcement officers killed and assaulted, 3.152-3.158, 3.160-3.164
- Offenses known to police, 3.106-3.110, 3.125-3.128, 4.19
  - Cities, 3.110
  - Rates, 3.106-3.108, 3.125-3.128
  - Size of place, 3.107-3.109
- Parole and supervised release, 6.4, 6.70, 6.71
- Pretrial release and detention, 5.13
- Prisoners
  - Current offense, 6.53, 6.56
  - Firearms possession during offense, 6.37, 6.38
  - Recidivism, 6.50-6.52
  - Time served, 6.43, 6.44, 6.58

Index 633

VIOLENT CRIME (continued)
    Probationers
        Number, 6.4
        Outcomes, 6.8
    Reporting to police, 3.33-3.35
    Sentences, 5.19-5.21, 5.59, 5.60, 6.43, 6.44, 6.58, 6.59
        Federal courts, 5.19-5.21
        Length of sentence, 5.19, 5.21, 5.60, 6.43, 6.44, 6.58
        Time served, 6.43, 6.44, 6.58, 6.59
        Type of sentence, 5.19, 5.59
    Victimizations, 3.1-3.20, 3.27-3.36, 3.60, 3.61, 3.85, 3.119, 3.125, 3.126, 3.132
        Age of victim, 3.4, 3.6, 3.7, 3.11, 3.119, 3.125, 3.126
        Among intimate partners, 3.15, 3.16, 3.132
        At school, 3.60, 3.61
        During consumption of alcohol or drugs, 3.85
        Firearm-related, 3.17
        Households experiencing, 3.27
        Lone-offender incidents, 3.28, 3.29
            Perceived age of offender, 3.28
            Perceived race of offender, 3.29
        Multiple-offender incidents, 3.30, 3.31
            Perceived ages of offenders, 3.30
            Perceived races of offenders, 3.31
        Number, 3.1, 3.2, 3.5, 3.8-3.10, 3.15, 3.17, 3.20
            Characteristics of victim, 3.5, 3.8, 3.9
        Place of occurrence, 3.32
        Race and ethnicity of victim, 3.4, 3.8-3.11, 3.125, 3.126
        Rates, 3.1-3.13, 3.125, 3.126
            Age of victim, 3.4, 3.6, 3.7, 3.11
            Family income of victim, 3.4, 3.12
            Locality of residence, 3.4, 3.13
            Race and ethnicity of victim, 3.4, 3.8-3.11
            Sex of victim, 3.4, 3.5, 3.7, 3.10
        Reporting to police, 3.33-3.36
            Reasons for not reporting, 3.35
            Reasons for reporting, 3.34
            Victim characteristics, 3.36
        Self-protective measures taken, 3.18-3.20
        Sex of victim, 3.4, 3.5, 3.7, 3.10
        Victim-offender relationship, 3.14-3.18
            Type of weapon, 3.17
        Victim use of self-protection, 3.18
        Weapon, 3.17

VIOLENT CRIME (continued)
    See also:
        Specific offenses (e.g., Rape, Murder)
WEAPONS
    See Guns
    See Public opinion
    See Specific offenses (e.g., Murder, Robbery)
WIRETAPS
    Court-authorized orders, 5.2-5.5
        Arrests, 5.5
        Convictions, 5.5
        Jurisdiction, 5.2, 5.4
        Type of offense, 5.3
WRIT OF CERTIORARI
    See U.S. Supreme Court

EVALUATION FORM

Sourcebook of Criminal Justice Statistics 2003
NCJ 208756

Dear *Sourcebook* reader:

Please help us improve future editions of the **Sourcebook of Criminal Justice Statistics** by answering the following questions. This form is a self-mailing piece; please fold as indicated on the other side, stamp, and mail, or you may fax this form to Rhonda Keith at 202-354-4113. General comments and queries may be sent via e-mail to askbjs@ojp.usdoj.gov. Thank you!

1. For what purpose did you consult the *Sourcebook*? _____

_____

_____

2. Was *Sourcebook* adequate for that purpose?

    ☐ Quite adequate   ☐ Adequate   ☐ Somewhat adequate   ☐ Not adequate   ☐ Quite inadequate

    a. Specifically, what helped or hindered your achieving that purpose? _____

_____

_____

3. On about how many separate occasions have you consulted the *Sourcebook*? _____

4. Can you point out specific table notes that are not clear or additional terms that need to be defined? _____

5. Are there sources of data of strong interest to you included in the *Sourcebook*, but that you were not aware of before consulting the *Sourcebook*? (Please specify sources.) _____

_____

_____

6. To achieve your purpose, was it necessary for you to consult the original sources of the data? For what reason? _____

_____

7. Are there data from other primary sources that you would suggest including in future *Sourcebook*s? _____

_____

_____

8. In addition to this print edition of *Sourcebook*, have you had occasion to use:

    ☐ *Sourcebook* CD-ROM version   ☐ *Sourcebook* Online Web site (http://www.albany.edu/sourcebook/)

9. Would you be willing to pay nominal fees ($15 or less each) for both the printed and CD-ROM versions of *Sourcebook*?

    ☐ Yes   ☐ No, printed version only   ☐ No, CD-ROM version only   ☐ No, I'd rely on *Sourcebook* Online

10. With which type of organization are you associated (or what areas interest you the most)?

☐ Courts	☐ Juvenile services	☐ Religious	☐ Academic (student)
☐ Corrections	☐ Legislative	☐ Justice-related business	☐ Library
☐ Law enforcement	☐ Media	☐ Academic (faculty)	☐ Other (please explain) _____

Sourcebook 2003
NCJ 208756

11. For what purposes do you expect to use the *Sourcebook*?

- ☐ Research
- ☐ Planning
- ☐ Reports
- ☐ Speeches
- ☐ Legislation
- ☐ Classroom instruction
- ☐ Hearings
- ☐ Media stories
- ☐ Policy development
- ☐ Litigation
- ☐ Training
- ☐ Other (please explain) _____
- ☐ Book publication
- ☐ Reference collection

Additional comments

_____
_____
_____
_____
_____

- - - - - - - - - - - - (FOLD HERE) - - - - - - - - - - - -

U.S. DEPARTMENT OF JUSTICE
Office of Justice Programs
Bureau of Justice Statistics
Washington, DC 20531

Place first-class stamp here

Bureau of Justice Statistics
Attention: R. Keith
U.S. Department of Justice
Washington, DC 20531

- - - - - - - - - - - - (FOLD HERE) - - - - - - - - - - - -

OPTIONAL

Name	Telephone ( )
Number and street	
City	State	ZIP code
E-mail address		

Positioning *Sourcebook of Criminal Justice Statistics* for the 21st Century
Executive Summary

Carol A. Hert
Syracuse University
October 28, 2004

Over the last several years, the maturing of Web technologies, Federal mandates for increased efficiency and effectiveness in information dissemination, and the public's changing perceptions of the role of information in their lives have influenced the dissemination activities of Federal agencies. It was in this climate that the current project was developed and undertaken. The project reported here had the goal of providing an integrated look at *Sourcebook of Criminal Justice Statistics* (hereafter referred to as *Sourcebook*): its users, mission, its future in light of current and emergent technologies and the information environment.

The project consisted of three research activities. These were:

- A preliminary assessment of the state of knowledge about users of *Sourcebook* developed using document analysis, site visits, and focus groups (Section two of the report).
- Usability studies to examine user behavior with a range of criminal justice statistical websites (Section three).
- A Delphi study to determine points of consensus on the future mission of *Sourcebook* and on the related requirements for achieving that mission (Section four).

These methodologies, findings, and specific recommendations of the three activities are summarized in separate sections of this report. The rationales for the three activities and their relationships are provided in an introductory section. Finally, a synthesis of findings across the three activities and resultant recommendations appears in the concluding section (Section five).

Key findings and recommendations from each project activity

Each project activity resulted in a set of findings and recommendations. These are summarized here.

The User Assessment Activity

The goal of the user assessment was to provide a baseline picture of what was currently known about users of *Sourcebook* in order to determine what further user studies should be done. Findings are not detailed here (but are in Section two), given their role in supporting further work. The knowledge of existing usage of *Sourcebook* in its current manifestation and the Delphi preliminary results led the researcher to recommend the following user research strategies. Their intent was not to further document existing usage but to look towards how users and usage might change as *Sourcebook* moves into the future. Two views of *Sourcebook* were expressed. The first supports *Sourcebook*'s role as a set of pre-aggregated tables. The second considers *Sourcebook* within the larger information environment.

Sourcebook as set of pre-aggregated tables

Critical to its function as the access point for pre-aggregated tables is assuring that the "right" pre-aggregated tables are available. The current *Sourcebook* has an established rigorous procedure for determining which tables should be included. This procedure, combined with an analysis of usage of the tables in the online version and an exploration of possible redundancy of tables (because they exist in other sources) can indicate which tables are important to provide in pre-aggregated format, as well as how to identify new ones and monitor that list in the future.

The researcher recommends that SUNY Albany continue monthly listings of the top 100 tables accessed online (with titles and section listings) so that the comparisons made in this document can be extended. In addition, a list of pages not accessed during the month should be tabulated.

Sourcebook in the Criminal Justice Statistical Information Landscape

Sourcebook is one component of the system of criminal justice statistical information that includes the creators and users of the information, the information and its presentation containers, the technologies available to create, disseminate and use it, and the surrounding socio-political landscape. To understand users and uses of *Sourcebook*, particularly as they might be changing in the future, therefore involves investigations beyond *Sourcebook*.

One challenge to understanding user behavior in relationship to *Sourcebook*, and criminal justice statistical information more generally, is that users change and adapt as rapidly as the tools they use. Thus, looking at user behavior in association with one tool (such as *Sourcebook*) in one instantiation at a particular moment in time provides limited guidance in developing an understanding of users that can be utilized for a long period of time. A strategy that can mitigate this situation is to shift the focus to understanding user behavior on particular tasks without unduly constraining the information strategies and sources users employ. This approach provides a more generalized picture of those strategies and the desired characteristics of sources enabling a researcher to make recommendations about the types of features and services a source could provide to facilitate user information seeking. This approach provided information that complements that of the Delphi study, by providing future-oriented information grounded in current behaviors. The researcher designed a study to meet the requirements above. The study addressed the following questions: When engaged in specific criminal justice statistical information tasks, how do people use the primary criminal justice statistical sources? What features and services of these sources facilitate or hinder the resolution of those tasks? The study and its results are described in Section three of the report.

The Usability Study

The analysis yielded three types of findings from the usability study:

- Generalized patterns of behavior for each site for each task performed on that site. Findings generalized across all tasks, tools, users.
- Usability problems identified for *Sourcebook* with recommendations for their resolution. The generalized patterns for each site are not reported here but are in Section three.

Generalized findings

The findings generalized across tasks, tools, and users do not indicate that users tailor their behavior to the specific website they are using. They:

- Perform word matching activities.
- Don't modify their search engine behavior to the search engine or collection being used.
- Have difficulty using pdf files.

A fourth general finding is that the mismatch between search engine boundaries and site boundaries caused problems for users. In addition to the findings that reflect general Web behavior, some of the findings are more specifically related to compendia and statistical information. These were:

- Among the study participants, the tasks did not present situations where their domain knowledge was lacking.

- The organization of information by criminal justice system (most noticeable on *Sourcebook*) was rarely used or caused difficulties in some of the tasks.
- Predictability of presentation of criminal justice statistical information was used to facilitate retrieval.
- Searching for information about geographic entities is challenging, as people want to search by the name of the entity rather than type of entity.

These findings incorporated with others from the usability study led to a set of summary recommendations from the usability study and follow the section on specific recommendations related to usability for *Sourcebook*.

Usability problems identified for *Sourcebook* with recommendations for their resolution

Because of this project's focus on *Sourcebook of Criminal Justice Statistics*, the researcher reframed the usability findings specific to *Sourcebook* from the perspective of usability problems and their resolution. The usability problems identified for *Sourcebook Online* were:

- The introductory text isn't helpful in working on the tasks. All the information on content is below the fold.
- Users felt that *Sourcebook* had the feel of "just taking the print version and putting it online."
- There was an unclear organization of contents and tables within sections. People realized both listings weren't alphabetical and couldn't find another structure it represented to help them use the organization.
- The search syntax doesn't map to other search engines and every user of search engine got it wrong at least once (and many, multiple times).
- When you have invalid search syntax, you get a message saying to check link for search rules but it is not linked to that page. A user has to go back to search first and find the rules on that page.
- Some people thought the pdf and excel files for each table actually represented different tables and would look at both.
- No way to get to earlier years (mentioned when someone wanted to use the strategy of looking for the same table in a different year).
- The multiple search options (what component of *Sourcebook* was being searched) didn't seem to be clear to people. People input a search without considering where the search would be executed.
- Options for searching across sections (via search of index or table titles) were not obvious leading people to attempt to navigate by section (which was challenging for the juvenile task).
- All available options for accessing data are not clear on a section's introductory screen (contents and tables listings are below fold, and sometimes the search option is below the fold as well).
- There were comments on the data lag from UCR and BJS.
- URL includes "1995" appeared to some as representing the 1995 data.
- Many tables in pdf versions have footnotes to Appendices which people wanted to be directly linked.
- The indexing doesn't always follow standard practice reducing the indexing's ability to get people to the correct content. For example, using the term "death penalty" leads to three terms that have "see" references rather than "see also" references. Even better indexing practice would be to use an entry such as "death penalty—public opinion" (indicating a subset of the available information on the death penalty) with a link directly to the set of relevant tables.
- Searching the index resulted in very long listings of entries of a different format from search listings in the table section. Search option on index page should be at the top of the screen.
- The pdf files of the full sections were rarely used.

The following recommendations address these problems in two tiers of recommendations with tier one representing problems that are most easily resolved.

Tier One Recommendations

1. Provide navigational options at top or left side of screens. These would include search option, access to index, and section links. Usability testing is suggested to see if users locate links and understand functionality to be found via the links.

2. Information on how to use the search engine should be available on the search page and also when the user gets error messages. A no-click option to get the information would be best.

3. Current text appearing on homepage as introductory information should be relocated - some may be appropriate to add to the existing "about *Sourcebook*" section, other information might go to a "how to use *Sourcebook*" section which provides information on downloading, searching, etc. Usability testing is suggested to determine what content should appear under what link and what the link label should be. Card sorting techniques may be a useful approach for both components of usability testing.

4. Instead of using file names for files (e.g., table346.wk1), provide links that say Table 3.46 pdf file format, Table 3.46 spreadsheet format.

5. Remove "1995" from main *Sourcebook* URL.

6. Provide links to appendices and sources from within a table.

7. Reorganize listings of table titles and section headings.

8. Consider ongoing provision of pdfs of file sections. Monitor their usage.

9. Provide additional years of data online.

10. Conduct usability tests to determine structure of search result entries.

Tier Two Recommendations

These recommendations may require more extensive usability testing/research than Tier One recommendations or might need to be considered in the context of a shift away from pdf formats to HTML or XML markup strategies. In addition, many of the recommendations, while arising from the usability studies, are not recommendations for specific usability changes.

1. Examine indexing practice. Monitor usage of the index and search to determine the extent to which an index is used.

2. Reorganize listings of table titles and section headings.

3. Enhance access to earlier years of data by direct linking from within a table (to its earlier iterations).

4. Enhance access to related information by inclusion of links to related tables from within a given table.

5. Work with BJS and other data providers to address issues of harmonization and currency of data.

Summary recommendations from the usability study

The findings of the usability studies point to the extent to which the Web and the standard approaches to web design currently shape user behavior. The dominant results of the usability study indicate that users don't use criminal justice statistical websites differently then they might use any other website: they perform word recognition tasks and don't tailor their behavior to the specific content or features of a given website. Pdf files represent special problems and equivalent boundaries for content and search engines help. This implies the baseline for any redesign of a website. It is recommended that:

- The extent to which user terminology matches agency/expert terminology be investigated. The extent to which users can find the terms they are looking for in the context of few non-relevant terms, the better they are at finding information.

User terminology should be identified and strategies for mapping it to the more specific expert terminology developed.
- Pdf file usage needs to be further investigated. For those who are printing, pdfs provide a useful printing format. However for activities involving finding information within a document or using a document online, they represent significant challenges.
- Where possible, search engines should be indexing the content of the site they are associated with. Larger sites may benefit from allowing users to choose to search specific components of the site but should not over-partition the contents (as is the case at the moment on *Sourcebook*). In all cases, there should be an explanatory note indicating the contents the engine is searching and the depth of indexing of entities (such as to the table title level or document title level).

In terms of the findings related to the usage of Web-based criminal justice statistical information, it is recommended that:

- The effort involved in organizing content by the criminal justice system should be investigated. If it is not helpful online, it may not be a reasonable use of resources. In any event, access will be enhanced by a topical index.
- The topical index might include names of geographic entities with pointers to appropriate data. If this is too cumbersome, entries could be added for geographic names with a note indicating how to access relevant data (e.g., by topic with subdivision by geographic entity). If possible, the associated search engine should incorporate the names of geographic entities.
- Since predictability of presentation was useful to some study participants, one strategy to consider would be the making of links among the documents for all years of a publication.

The Delphi Study

The final result of the Delphi study was a mission statement for *Sourcebook of Criminal Justice Statistics* and an associated set of requirements considered essential or complementary to attaining that mission. The final mission statement follows:

Final Mission Statement for the *Sourcebook of Criminal Justice Statistics* as Generated by the Delphi

Sourcebook serves, and is marketed, as the definitive source of criminal justice statistical (CJS) information at the Federal, State, and local level for criminal justice practitioners, researchers, policy makers, and statisticians.

Sourcebook is a tool that promotes and champions the statistics and their producers. It provides data in a variety of ways (i.e., tables, chart, graphics) with associated metadata and explanations, and links to source data.

Sourcebook links to relevant criminal justice sites, commentary, and analysis. It also provides access to downloadable data sets. It is able to present both the detailed view of CJS information as well as a big picture of the range and nature of that information (partially by linking to new data sources as they become available). It provides a snapshot of CJS information at a moment in time, as well as remaining current. Its information enables historical and other comparative analyses (i.e., geographic, etc.).

If possible, *Sourcebook* is provided in English and other languages, has online tutorial functions, and provides a suite of data analysis tools.

Sourcebook should not be privatized.

Due to its length, the set of requirements is not presented here but can be found in Table 4.3.5 of the full report.

The findings lead to a set of recommendations concerning the positioning of *Sourcebook of Criminal Justice Statistics* in the coming years. These are:

- *Sourcebook* should continue to provide vetted, quality information. *Sourcebook* is playing a key role in "setting the bar" for quality information in the domain of criminal justice statistics, particularly for information that is produced outside of the Federal statistical agencies. Sophisticated procedures are currently in place at the University at Albany to assure the quality; these should be maintained.
- *Sourcebook* should continue to identify new sources of information and incorporate them when they meet appropriate quality standards. Numerous participants commented on new fields of endeavor that are important to be represented in *Sourcebook*. The field of criminal justice will continue to change, and *Sourcebook* will need to continually reflect those changes. This might mean that the current organization of *Sourcebook* will change to reflect changes in the organization of the field.
- *Sourcebook* should expand its efforts at attaining feedback from users and soliciting their input. If *Sourcebook* is to retain its premier status more attention needs to be given to understanding its users and their needs for criminal justice statistics.
- *Sourcebook* should exploit the technological opportunities of the Web. In the short term, *Sourcebook* should start providing links to source materials, linking technical information directly to appropriate tables, and link to relevant criminal justice sites. It might be appropriate for *Sourcebook* to include a "reference shelf" section that would provide links to sources, commentary, indexes, etc. As a second tier of activities, it should explore the technical options available for transforming statistical presentations (such as tables to graphics) or provide such additional presentations "manually." Having a robust search engine is also a concern. Also at the second tier, it should assess technologies for enabling users direct access to data to perform unique manipulations. This effort would need to occur in the context of *Sourcebook*'s important role as a vetted source of the most important information. In the longer term, ongoing efforts need to be in place to stay abreast of, and incorporate new technological advances.
- Technological advances need to occur with attention to usability and other user concerns. Delphi participants indicated attention to usability, indexing, and terminology issues as critical requirements for attaining the mission of *Sourcebook*.
- *Sourcebook* should develop a mechanism for providing an archive of past *Sourcebook*s and enabling reoccurring tables to be linked from one *Sourcebook* to the next.

Integrated findings and final general recommendations

The final section of the report brings together the findings of the study into an integrated picture and presents recommendations for action. Integration of the findings from the multiple project activities involved 1) identifying agreements in findings among all study activities, 2) assessing the meaning of findings which were the result of one study, and 3) considering conflicting findings. The findings are:
- There is still a recognized need for the functions of a statistical compendium.
    o However, only a small number of tables in online *Sourcebook* receive large usage.
    o There is a desire on the part of users for new features that take advantage of technological advances.
- Usage of compendia in the web environment is impacted by the behavior of web users, general usability issues, and the lag of data from original sources.
- Information media have different "affordances" resulting in a lack of direct

transferability of function, content and form among the media.

Finding: There is still a recognized need for the functions of a statistical compendium.
Recommendations: It is recommended that:

- Strategies be identified to provide a source of vetted criminal justice statistical information that appears coherent and unified to the user and supports the traditional roles of a statistical compendium.
    o The existing *Sourcebook* product should form the launch pad for these efforts.
    o Reallocation of resources from table presentation to efforts to identify and provide a uniform approach to linking to sources should be considered.
    o Establishing a metadata standard that can support identification, transmission, and presentation of information from those linked sources should be explored.

Finding: Usage of compendia in the web environment is impacted by the behavior of web users, general usability issues, and the lag of data from original sources. **Recommendations:** It is recommended that:

- Existing usability problems with *Sourcebook* should be addressed. In section three, these were provided in two tiers of feasibility.
- Efforts to support word recognition tasks should be increased. These include:
    o Enhancement of indexing structures to incorporate user terminology
    o Assessment of web page look and feel to enable more rapid recognition of words on the part of users or as one person suggested one site provided "all the right words without other words." Haas and Hert (2000) provide the details of a strategy to identify and map user terminology to expert terminology. Additional usability studies (including strategies such as card sorting) would be helpful in identifying terminology issues associated with information organization and categorization.
    o Providing a new search engine on *Sourcebook*, the functionality of which is compatible to other search engines.
    o Ongoing monitoring of technological advancements in search engines.
- Strategies to minimize time lag and assure harmonization across multiple sources of the same data need to be considered. These will include:
    o Development of standardized metadata across sources.
    o Development of Web services that could import data in real-time thus assuring that compendium data are identical to source data.

Finding: Information media have different "affordances" resulting in a lack of direct transferability of function, content and form among the media. **Recommendations:** It is recommended that:

- *Sourcebook* and BJS should determine their priority for information dissemination in different media, develop individualized missions for those dissemination media, and do this in the context of the affordances of those media.
    o These priorities need to be assessed in the context of resource, workflow, and marketing ramifications.

The coming years will be exciting and challenging for those charged with disseminating criminal justice statistical information. Users will still need the value provided by the traditional statistical compendium but technologies will continue to shape the ways in which that value can be provided or new value can be added. This project has presented a picture of how *Sourcebook of Criminal Justice Statistics* is currently providing value to users and how it can be enhanced to meet the changing needs of users within the changing technological environment so as to continue to provide the values it has provided for over thirty years.